THE CAMBRIDGE INTERNATIONAL HANDBOOK OF CLASS ACTIONS

Economic activity is more globally integrated than ever before, but so is the scope of corporate misconduct. As more and more people across the world are affected by such malfeasance, the differences in legal redress have become increasingly visible. This transparency has resulted in a growing convergence towards an American model of robust private enforcement of the law, including the class-action lawsuit. This handbook brings together scholars from nearly two dozen countries to describe and assess the class-action procedure (or its equivalent) in their respective countries and, where possible, to offer empirical data on these systems. At the same time, the work presents a variety of multidisciplinary perspectives on class actions, from economics to philosophy, making this handbook an essential resource to academics, lawyers, and policymakers alike.

Brian T. Fitzpatrick is the Milton R. Underwood Chair in Free Enterprise and Professor of Law at Vanderbilt Law School. His research focuses on class action litigation and federal courts. In 2010, he published what is still the most comprehensive empirical study of class action settlements in American federal courts. He is also the author of the provocative book, *The Conservative Case for Class Actions* (2019). Professor Fitzpatrick joined Vanderbilt's law faculty in 2007 after serving as the John M. Olin Fellow at New York University School of Law. He clerked for Judge Diarmuid O'Scannlain on the US Court of Appeals for the Ninth Circuit and Justice Antonin Scalia on the US Supreme Court. Professor Fitzpatrick practiced commercial and appellate litigation for several years at Sidley Austin in Washington, DC, and served as Special Counsel for Supreme Court Nominations to US Senator John Cornyn.

Randall S. Thomas holds the John S. Beasley II Chair in Law and Business, Vanderbilt Law School. He works on issues such as hedge fund shareholder activism, executive compensation, corporate voting, corporate litigation, shareholder voting, and mergers and acquisitions. He joined the Vanderbilt law faculty in 2000 to develop and direct the Law and Business Program, having served previously for ten years on the law faculty of the University of Iowa.

The Cambridge Handbook of Class Actions

An International Survey

Edited by

BRIAN T. FITZPATRICK

Vanderbilt University School of Law

RANDALL S. THOMAS

Vanderbilt University School of Law

CAMBRIDGE
UNIVERSITY PRESS

CAMBRIDGE
UNIVERSITY PRESS

Shaftesbury Road, Cambridge CB2 8EA, United Kingdom

One Liberty Plaza, 20th Floor, New York, NY 10006, USA

477 Williamstown Road, Port Melbourne, VIC 3207, Australia

314–321, 3rd Floor, Plot 3, Splendor Forum, Jasola District Centre, New Delhi – 110025, India

103 Penang Road, #05–06/07, Visioncrest Commercial, Singapore 238467

Cambridge University Press is part of Cambridge University Press & Assessment, a department of the University of Cambridge.

We share the University's mission to contribute to society through the pursuit of education, learning and research at the highest international levels of excellence.

www.cambridge.org
Information on this title: www.cambridge.org/9781009295697

DOI: 10.1017/9781108770927

First published 2021
First paperback edition 2023

A catalogue record for this publication is available from the British Library

Library of Congress Cataloging-in-Publication data
NAMES: FitzPatrick, Brian T., author. | Thomas, Randall S., 1955– author.
TITLE: The Cambridge handbook of class actions : an international survey / edited by Brian T. Fitzpatrick, Vanderbilt University School of Law; Randall S. Thomas, Vanderbilt University School of Law.
DESCRIPTION: Cambridge, United Kingdom ; New York, NY : Cambridge University Press, 2021.
IDENTIFIERS: LCCN 2020029076 (print) | LCCN 2020029077 (ebook) | ISBN 9781108488587 (hardback) | ISBN 9781108770927 (ebook)
SUBJECTS: LCSH: Class actions (Civil procedure)
CLASSIFICATION: LCC K2243 .F58 2021 (print) | LCC K2243 (ebook) | DDC 347/.053–dc23
LC record available at https://lccn.loc.gov/2020029076
LC ebook record available at https://lccn.loc.gov/2020029077

ISBN 978-1-108-48858-7 Hardback
ISBN 978-1-009-29569-7 Paperback

This book is dedicated to Richard Nagareda.

Contents

Contributors

Nina Abbey is a senior associate at Maurice Blackburn Lawyers based in Sydney, Australia. Since graduating with Bachelor degrees in Communications and Laws (First Class Honours) from the University of Technology (Sydney), Nina has worked on a range of class actions, including a number of complex product liability claims. Most recently, Nina was a part of the team to successfully resolve the class actions on behalf of Australian consumers against Volkswagen, Audi and Skoda in relation to the international dieselgate emissions issue.

Neil Andrews is Professor of Civil Justice and Private Law at the University of Cambridge.

Maria José Azar-Baud is Associate Professor at University of Paris-Saclay and lecturer at Universities Panthéon-Sorbonne and Panthéon-Assas, has a double PhD (Panthéon-Sorbonne and Buenos Aires Universities) focusing on Collective Redress in Comparative Law (Dalloz 2013). She is a former lawyer at the Bar of Buenos Aires and the author of more than seventy contributions. Aside from lecturing, Maria José chairs the Observatory of Group Actions, is a counsel and seats at the Executive Board of two European nonprofit organizations acting as plaintiffs in mass tort cases, seeking to grant access to justice on a collective scale.

Robert G. Bone received his BA from Stanford University and JD from Harvard Law School. He started on the USC Law faculty and then spent twenty-three years on the Boston University Law faculty before moving to UT Law School. Professor Bone is a leading scholar in the fields of civil procedure, complex litigation and intellectual property. He is the author of *The Economics of Civil Procedure*, coauthor of *The Law of Class Actions and Other Aggregate Litigation*, and author of numerous articles analyzing the economics of procedure, class actions, case aggregation and other topics. He has been honored for his scholarship and teaching.

Beat Brändli graduated at the University of St Gallen, Switzerland, in 2009 with an MA in Law and Economics. He subsequently completed his doctoral thesis on procedural economics in Swiss law in 2013. In the meantime, he worked as a teaching assistant and at various Swiss courts. He passed his bar exam at the end of 2013. From 2014 to 2016, he worked as an attorney at a renowned Swiss law firm. In 2016, he was appointed assistant professor in St Gallen. In 2017 he was elected as a part-time District Judge in Baden, Switzerland.

Theo Broodryk is an associate professor and manager of the Law Clinic. Professor Broodryk is an admitted attorney of the High Court of South Africa, a Y1 NRF rated researcher and the author of *Eckard's Principles of Civil Procedure in the Magistrates' Court*. He is a senior researcher at the Ius Commune Research School in the program 'Foundations and Principles of Civil Procedure in Europe', a Beaufort (Colenso) Fellow at St John's College, Cambridge, and previously attended Stanford Law School as a visiting scholar. Professor Broodryk is a member of the International Association of Procedural Law.

Eli Bukspan's teaching and research focus on contract and corporate law. His book, The Social Transformation of Business Law, is the first academic law book written on this topic in Israel. Bukspan received an LLB with distinctions from Tel Aviv University and an SJD from Harvard Law School and clerked for the Chief Justice of the Israeli Supreme Court, the Honorary Meir Shamgar. He was a network fellow at the Edmond J. Safra Center for Ethics at Harvard University, a research fellow at the John M. Olin Center for Law, Economics and Business: Program on Corporate Governance at Harvard Law School and a fellow guest researcher at the University of California Berkeley School of Law. Bukspan's public roles include serving as the chair of the Israeli Fund for Class Action Funding (awarded the 2016 Distinguished Class Action honorary recognition for his role in advancing the important cause of Class Actions in Israel), the chair of the Licenses Committee and a member of the Advisory Committee to Banks Issues, Banking Supervision Department, Bank of Israel, and the chair of the Ethics committee of the Maala Index at the Tel Aviv Stock Exchange (a nonprofit CSR standards-setting organization in Israel).

Helena Campos Refosco serves as Judge of Instruction at Brazil's Supreme Court, where she assists Justice Ricardo Lewandowski. She has been a judge since 2006, when, at age twenty-three, she gained recognition as the youngest member of the Bench at the São Paulo State Court of Justice. Helena also holds a PhD, cum laude, from the University of São Paulo Law School. As part of her doctoral studies, she embarked on a six-month Visiting Research Fellowship at Harvard Law School (Fall/Winter, 2015/16), delving into the areas of Law and Development, Human Rights, and Complex Litigation. E-mail: helenarefosco@alumni.usp.br.

Maureen Carroll is an assistant professor of law at the University of Michigan Law School, where she teaches and writes about civil procedure, class actions and civil rights litigation. Professor Carroll received her JD from UCLA School of Law, where she was ranked first in her class. Following law school, Professor Carroll clerked for the Hon. Stephen Reinhardt of the US Court of Appeals for the Ninth Circuit and worked as a staff attorney in impact litigation for Public Counsel in Los Angeles.

Nikki Chamberlain is a lecturer in the Faculty of Law at the University of Auckland in New Zealand. Nikki has a BA/LLB (Hons) degree from the University of Auckland and an LLM degree from Vanderbilt University. Prior to lecturing, Nikki practiced eight years as a commercial litigator at a large commercial law firm in Auckland, Minter Ellison Rudd Watts. She appeared as counsel in the Court of Appeal, High Court, District Court and Family Court. Nikki has expertise in Torts, Privacy and New Zealand and American Civil Procedure. Nikki's research is currently addressing class action reform in New Zealand.

Eunice Chua is the CEO of FIDReC and a research fellow at the SMU School of Law. She is qualified as an advocate and solicitor of the Singapore Supreme Court and an associate mediator of the Singapore Mediation Centre. Prior to her appointment at FIDReC, Eunice was an assistant professor of law at the SMU School of Law where she specialized in alternative dispute resolution, evidence and procedure. Eunice previously served as a Justices' law clerk and an assistant registrar of the Supreme Court of Singapore. She was also the first Deputy Chief Executive Officer of the Singapore International Mediation Centre.

Hans De Wulf is Professor of Company Law at Ghent University, Belgium. He teaches various courses on corporate law, including comparative corporate governance, EU company law and M&A. His research interests include private enforcement issues, the interface between liability (including tort) rules and corporate law, the regulation of shareholder services providers. He was a core member of the drafting committee of Belgium's 2019 Companies Act.

Daisuke Eguchi is an associate of Nishimura & Asahi. He is admitted to practice in Japan (2017). His practice area covers a wide range of general corporate matters. Nowadays, he has been focusing on M&A, Health Care and consumer laws. In particular, with regard to consumer laws, he has been handling consultations with companies concerning requests from consumer groups.

Brian T. Fitzpatrick is the Milton R. Underwood Chair in Free Enterprise and Professor of Law at Vanderbilt Law School. His research focuses on class action litigation and federal courts. In 2010, he published what is still the most comprehensive empirical study of class action settlements in federal court, and, last year, he published his highly anticipated book, *The Conservative Case for Class Actions* (University of Chicago Press). Professor Fitzpatrick joined Vanderbilt's law faculty in 2007 after serving as the John M. Olin Fellow at New York University School of Law. He graduated first in his class from Harvard Law School and went on to clerk for Judge Diarmuid O'Scannlain on the US Court of Appeals for the Ninth Circuit and Justice Antonin Scalia on the US Supreme Court. After his clerkships, Professor Fitzpatrick practiced commercial and appellate litigation for several years at Sidley Austin in Washington, DC, and served as Special Counsel for Supreme Court Nominations to US Senator John Cornyn. Before earning his law degree, Professor Fitzpatrick graduated summa cum laude with a bachelor's of science in chemical engineering from the University of Notre Dame.

Sean Griffith is the T. J. Maloney Chair in Business Law at Fordham Law School in New York City. He is the author, with Tom Baker, of *Ensuring Corporate Misconduct: How Liability Insurance Undermines Shareholder Litigation* (University of Chicago Press, 2010), as well as many journal articles addressing corporate and securities litigation. Professor Griffith received his law degree magna cum laude from the Harvard Law School, where he was an editor of the Harvard Law Review and a John M. Olin Fellow in Law and Economics.

Paolo Giudici is Professor of Business Law at the School of Economics and Management of the University of Bozen-Bolzano. He is an ECGI Research Associate and professorial fellow at Tilburg University. His research started with antitrust, and then he moved to capital markets law and company law, with a key interest in civil liability and private enforcement. Currently he is working on venture capital and blockchain startups. Before starting his academic career he was a practicing business lawyer. In the continental Europe tradition, he continues to serve as legal counsel and advocate in matters concerning his areas of academic expertise.

Axel Halfmeier teaches private law and procedural law at Leuphana University, Lüneburg, Germany. He studied law at University of Hamburg, Germany (Dr. iur. 1999) and at University of Michigan Law School (LLM 1996), then practiced law as an attorney and held several other academic positions in Germany before joining Leuphana. Among other things, he is interested in collective litigation and in the relationship between private law and a sustainable society.

Deborah Hensler is the Judge John W. Ford Professor of Dispute Resolution, Associate Dean for Graduate Studies, Emerita and cofounder of the Law and Public Policy Laboratory at Stanford Law School. With Professor Christopher Hodges of Oxford University, she organized the first international conference on the globalization of class actions, which led to international teaching, research and writing collaborations that endure to this day. Professor Hensler's scholarship on mass tort litigation in the United States stretches back to the 1980s, and she has studied and written about the evolution of mass and class actions within and outside the United States for the past four decades. She inaugurated a seminar on global litigation at Stanford Law School in 2012, at a time when global litigation was not yet widely recognized as a subject for scholarship and education. Professor Hensler is the lead author of *Class Action Dilemmas: Pursuing Public Goals for Private Gain* (Rand, 2000) and coeditor of *Class Actions in Context: How Culture, Economic and Politics Shape Collective Litigation* (Edward Elgar, 2016). Professor Hensler is a fellow of the American Academy of Political and Social Scientists and of the American Academy of Arts and Sciences. From 2011 to 2016, she held a personal chair in empirical studies of mass claims resolution at Tilburg University (the Netherlands). She has taught empirical research methods and class action law at Catolica Universidad, Lisbon (Portugal), the University of Hong Kong, Melbourne University (Australia) and Universite Paris-Dauphine (France). Prof. Hensler received a BA from Hunter College of the City University of New York, a PhD in Political Science from the Massachusetts Institute of Technology and an honorary doctorate in law from Leuphana University (Germany).

Samuel Hickey graduated with a Bachelor of Laws (Hons I) from the University of Queensland before undertaking a Judicial Clerkship at the Federal Court of Australia. Samuel then practiced as a commercial litigator at the Sydney office of an international law firm before reading for a Master of Laws at Harvard Law School. Samuel then commenced practice as a white collar defense lawyer in New York City. Samuel has published in leading English and Australian law journals, and has been cited with approval by the Full Court of the Federal Court of Australia.

Robin Hui Huang is Professor of Law at Chinese University of Hong Kong, Adjunct Professor at University of New South Wales; Li Ka Shing Visiting Professor at McGill University; Honorary Professor at East China University of Political Science and Law. He specializes in corporate law, securities regulation, financial law, commercial dispute resolution and foreign investment, with a focus on Chinese and comparative law issues. He has published in top-rated journals in the US, the UK, Australia, Canada, Germany, Israel, Hong Kong and Mainland China. His research has informed judicial, regulatory and legislative decisions.

Jasminka Kalajdzic, BA (Ottawa), LLB, LLM (Toronto), is an associate professor of law at the University of Windsor's Faculty of Law, where she teaches courses on legal ethics, evidence and class actions. Professor Kalajdzic is widely published, including *Class Actions in Canada: The Promise and Reality of Access to Justice* (2018) and *The Law of Class Actions in Canada*, coauthored with the Honourable Warren Winkler, Justice Paul Perell and Alison Warner (2015). Professor Kalajdzic was the coprincipal researcher and coauthor of the Law Commission of Ontario's *Class Action Report* (2019). She speaks regularly about class actions at scholarly and judicial conferences in Canada, the United States and Europe, and has organized two international conferences, on class actions and on commercial litigation funding. She served two terms as a member of the Law Foundation of Ontario's Class Proceedings Committee, and is the Canadian representative in an International Research Collaborative on Collective Litigation. She coteaches a comparative class action seminar with colleagues at Stanford, Tilburg and Leuphana Universities. In July 2017 she was a visiting senior fellow at the University of Melbourne where she taught a course on class actions with Justice Bernard Murphy and Dr Deborah Hensler. She is the founder and clinic director of the Class Action Clinic, which opened its doors in October 2019. It is the first clinic in the world to focus on the needs and interests of class members.

Robert Klonoff graduated from Yale Law School in 1979 and clerked for US Fifth Circuit Chief Judge John R. Brown. He later served as an assistant to the US Solicitor General and as a partner at Jones Day. Professor Klonoff has argued eight cases before the US Supreme Court, and dozens of cases in other federal and state courts. He has testified as an expert witness in numerous class actions, and has personally represented clients on both the plaintiff and defense side in more than 100 class actions. In 2018, Professor Klonoff received the Albert Nelson Marquis Lifetime Achievement Award in the field of law from *Who's Who in America*.

Shay Lavie is an assistant professor at Tel Aviv University, Faculty of Law, teaching civil procedure, law and economics and class actions. He received an SJD degree from Harvard Law School (2012), where he was the recipient of the Byse Fellowship, teaching the workshop Regulation through Litigation. He holds degrees from Columbia Law School (LLM, 2007, Harlan Fiske Stone Scholar), and the Hebrew University (LLB, 2005, Magna Cum Laude). He served as a law clerk to the then Chief Justice of the Israeli Supreme Court, Aharon Barak, and practiced in class action law firms, in the US and in Israel. His academic work integrates diverse methodologies, including doctrinal analysis, law and economics insights, game theoretical tools and quantitative methods. It was awarded competitive grants (such as the Israeli Science Foundation) and published in a variety of venues.

Michael Legg specializes in complex civil litigation, including regulatory litigation and class actions, and in innovation in the legal profession. He is admitted to practice in Australia (NSW) and the United States (New York) where he gained extensive experience in litigation. Michael has been a member of the Law Council of Australia's Class Actions Committee since 2011. He served as a member of the Expert Panel, Academic for the Australian Law Reform Commission Inquiry into Class Action Proceedings and Third-Party Litigation Funders in 2018. He holds law degrees from UNSW (LLB), the University of California, Berkeley (LLM) and the University of Melbourne (PhD).

Patricia Gil Lemstra is a PhD Candidate at Tilburg University Law School.

Joseph A. McCahery is Professor of International Economic Law at Tilburg University Law School, Researcher at Tilburg Law and Economics Centre and European Corporate Governance Institute (ECGI) and the author of, among other books, the *Corporate Governance of Non-Listed Companies*.

Vince Morabito is a professor in the Department of Business Law and Taxation at Monash University in Melbourne, Australia. His work on class actions and litigation funding has been published in leading law journals in Australia, England, Canada, the United States and New Zealand. He has also been a consultant to various law reform commissions and similar entities in Australia, England and Hong Kong. In 2008, he commenced the first ever empirical study of Australia's class action regimes.

Taeko Morita is a partner of Nishimura & Asahi. She is admitted to practice in Japan (2004) and New York (2011). Her practice area covers a wide range of general corporate matters. Recently, she has been focusing on areas of corporate governance and consumer laws. With respect to consumer laws, she has been handling matters related to consumer lawsuits, the Consumer Contract Act, the Act on Specified Commercial Transactions and the Act against Unjustifiable Premiums and Misleading Representations.

Hai Jin Park is an attorney at law in Korea. She is currently pursuing a JSD degree at Stanford Law School and a PhD minor in Computer Science at Stanford University. Hai Jin earned her LLB at Seoul National University and LLM and JSM at Stanford Law School. Her academic interests lie in torts, class action, insurance and technology. Before coming to Stanford, Hai Jin served as a district court judge and as a litigator at the largest law firm in Korea.

Catherine Piché, LLM (magna cum laude, Ottawa, 1997), LLB (Dalhousie University, 1999), LLM (NYU, 2001), DCL (McGill, 2011) is Full Professor of Law at the Faculty of Law of the Université de Montréal, specializing in civil procedure and evidence law, complex litigation and class actions, comparative law and conflicts of laws. She is also currently acting as Associate Dean, Research and International Affairs (since September 2019). She is the founder and director of the Class Actions Lab, which works on issues related to class actions in Quebec from theoretical, practical and empirical perspectives. At the Lab, she is involved with the Quebec Ministry of Justice working closely on the reform of class actions in Quebec. Professor Piché holds a doctor of laws on class actions from McGill University's Institute of Comparative Law, entitled "Fairness in Class Action Settlements," and published by Carswell. In addition to other several prominent publications in the field of class actions, she also was the coprincipal researcher and coauthor of the Law Commission of Ontario's Class Action Report (2019). Professor Piché publishes and speaks regularly about class actions at judicial seminars and conferences in Europe, Asia, South America and the United States. Recently, she founded with colleagues the first law commission of the province of Quebec, the Institut Québécois de Réforme du Droit et de la Justice, and became its scientific director. Professor Piché is a member of the Quebec and New York bars. For several years, she practiced commercial litigation in large law firms in New York and Montreal, where she defended class actions and acted in complex litigations. She also clerked at the Federal Court of Canada, Appeal Division.

Carlos Portugal Gouvêa is Professor of Commercial Law at the University of São Paulo Law School. He earned his SJD degree from Harvard Law School in 2008, having received a grant from the Fulbright Commission. Mr Gouvêa has a Bachelor of Laws degree from Universidade de São Paulo, Brasil. Mr Gouvêa is the founding partner of PGLaw, a law firm focused on corporate governance issues, applied to mergers and acquisitions, capital markets and commercial litigation. From 2015 to 2018, Mr Gouvêa was a member of the Appeals Counsel of the National Financial System of Brazil. E-mail: carlosgouvea@usp.br.

Hyeok-Joon Rho got his PhD at Seoul National University, Korea. Before he joined the academia in 2003, he had worked as a judge of the Seoul Southern District Court and as a senior associate at Woo & Yoon. He made various academic visits to law schools outside Korea: at Bucerius Law School in Germany as Humboldt research fellow, at Nagoya University School of Law in Japan as visiting professor and at Harvard Law School in the US as visiting scholar. His research projects include corporate governance, securities law and trust law.

Julian Schimmel is a principal lawyer at Maurice Blackburn Lawyers based in Sydney, Australia. As a specialist in class action litigation, he has extensive experience representing plaintiffs and class members in complex group actions in Australian courts. Julian has particular expertise in prosecuting and resolving product liability claims relating to a range of different products including major medical device litigation as well as the Volkswagen diesel emissions issue.

Randall Thomas works on issues such as hedge fund shareholder activism, executive compensation, corporate voting, corporate litigation, shareholder voting and mergers and acquisitions. He joined the Vanderbilt law faculty in 2000 to develop and direct the Law and Business Program, having served previously for ten years on the law faculty of the University of Iowa.

Christoph Van der Elst is Professor of Business Law and Economics at Tilburg University and at Ghent University and held/holds visiting professorships at different universities worldwide. He is an ECGI research associate, an independent director of Aphilion and a member of the Belgian Bar (Cottyn) and the audit committee of the Ghent University Hospital. His current research interests are particularly focusing on shareholder engagement, ESG and distributed ledger technology.

Susan Watson holds joint appointments in the Faculties of Law and Business at the University of Auckland. Her primary research focus is on the characteristics of the modern corporation; how those characteristics emerged and how they contribute to the success of the corporate form. Her monograph for Hart Publishing *The Making of the Modern Company* will be completed in 2020. Susan is currently Acting Dean of Business at the University of Auckland and President of the CLTA, a collective of corporate law academics in the Australasian region.

Wim Weterings is attorney at law (salary partner) at Dirkzwager Legal & Tax, Liability & Insurance department and Associate Professor at Tilburg University Faculty of Law, department of Private and Business Law. His (research) focus is on corporate liabilities – including director's liability – mass damage and insurance. He is a board member of the Dutch Association for Insurance Sciences and a member of the advisory committee on Insurance Law (Dutch Bar Association). He is also an editor of several journals related to tort and insurance law.

Beatrice Zuffi is Associate Professor of Civil Procedure at the Law School of the University of Padua, where she teaches also the classes of Alternative Dispute Resolution Methods and Arbitration Law. She has held several lectures for the postgraduate program SSPL (Specialisation School for Legal Professions) in Padua, Verona and Trento, as well as for the PhD Law Course of the University of Padua and the LLMM International business lawyer in Treviso. Author of two books on English arbitration law (Giappichelli ed., 2008) and – together with Professor Claudio Consolo – on Italian consumer class action (CEDAM, 2012), she has published articles, essays and commentaries especially in the field of ADR and collective litigation.

Foreword

The Global Expansion of Class Actions: Power, Politics and Procedural Evolution

Deborah R. Hensler

There's safety in numbers.[1]
Alone we can do so little, together we can do so much.[2]
El pueblo unido, jamas sera vencido.[3]
Modern society seems increasingly to expose men to such group injuries for which individually they are in a poor position to seek legal re-dress, either because they do not know enough or because such redress is disproportionately expensive. If each is left to assert his rights alone if and when he can, there will at best be a random and fragmentary enforcement, if there is any at all. This result is not only unfortunate in the particular case, but it will operate seriously to impair the deterrent effect of the sanctions which underlie much contemporary law. The problem of fashioning an effective and inclusive group remedy is thus a major one.[4]

Across different time periods, cultures and social contexts, people have understood that collective action may succeed when individual action would fail. Yet legal dispute resolution is usually limited to individual action – one claimant seeking relief for harm attributed to one respondent, without regard to the interests or consequences for similarly situated individuals or society.[5] When a small number of individuals or entities have been permitted to proceed together it is usually because they have individual claims (or defenses) that are so closely related that it makes little sense to require them to proceed separately. In medieval England, as Yeazell has taught us, groups of people seeking remedies for common harm were permitted to bring actions for

1 Harriet Harman, "Women Have Changed the Mood, Now We Need to Change Policy," *The Guardian*, February 21, 2018, analyzing the factors that produced the #metoo movement: "Third, the lesson is that there's safety in numbers. One woman on her own would just have been crushed by Weinstein's powerful legal and PR team and driven out of the industry. But no man can do that when there are a multitude of women's voices." www.theguardian.com /commentisfree/2018/feb/21/women-have-changed-the-mood-now-we-need-to-change-policy.

2 Hellen Keller (attributed). Some interpret this statement as referring to communication; for others, it is a call to group action to achieve common goals. See e.g., Quote Investigator, April 21, 2014, at https://quoteinvestigator.com/2014/04/21/together/; Desert Health, July–August 2014, at https://deserthealthnews.com/stories/alone-can-little-together-can-much/.

3 Sergio Ortega, "El Pueblo Unido," 1973, Union Songs, at https://unionsong.com/u443.html.

4 Harry Kalven and Maurice Rosenfield, "The Contemporary Function of the Class Suit," 8 *U. Chic L Rev* 684, 686 (1941)

5 See, e.g., Roscoe Pound, "Do We Need a Philosophy of Law?" 5 *Columbia L. Rev*. 339, 346(1905). ("Men have changed their views as to the relative importance of the individual and of society; but the common law has not . . . The common law . . . is concerned, not with social righteousness, but with individual rights. It tries questions of the highest social import as mere private controversies between John Doe and Richard Roe. And this compels a narrow and one-sided view . . . ")

damages as well as injunctive relief in courts of equity,[6] and at least since the twentieth century social associations – for example, consumer protection organizations – have been empowered in many civil law jurisdictions to bring legal actions on behalf of their members. However, group actions for collective harm had disappeared from the English courts by the mid-1800s and suits by associations, where permitted, have generally been restricted to declaratory and injunctive relief and provide nothing to group members in the way of restitution.[7]

Since 2000, this picture has changed dramatically: in civil law and common law jurisdictions in the Americas, Asia and Europe and in nations with diverse political systems and traditions, new procedures that allow large numbers of people and entities to band together to obtain remedies for harm, including under some circumstances compensation, have proliferated.[8] To date, at least thirty-five nations, including a majority of the world's most economically powerful nations, have established a modern form of group litigation – often termed a "class action," by reference to the US class action procedure.[9] How these procedures should be designed and in what circumstances they should be permitted have been sources of continuing controversy. The expansion of class actions since 2000 is a story of tension between a desire for an efficient mechanism for resolving mass claims and a fear of enabling collective action against powerful public and private institutions by less powerful members of society: workers, consumers, indigenous peoples, small businesses and others with little access to levers of political power.[10]

6 Stephen Yeazell, *From Medieval Group Litigation to the Modern Class Action*, Yale University Press, 1987. Yeazell's narrative of the rise of class actions, focusing on the importance of groups, relationships within and between groups, group norms and group action in the medieval era replaced an earlier narrative that identified the English "bill of peace," an efficiency measure, as the source of the modern class action. See Deborah Hensler, "Of Groups, Class Actions and Social Change: Reflections on *From Medieval Group Litigation to the Modern Class Action*," *UCLA Law Rev in Discourse*, August 31, 2013, at www.uclalawreview.org/of-groups-class-actions-and-social-change-reflections-on-from-medieval-group-litigation-to-the-modern-class-action/.

7 As Axel Halfmeier describes in this volume with regard to Germany, this older form of group action still plays an important private enforcement role in some jurisdictions. Yet, as the German experience shows, its potential power as a form of collective action is hobbled by the prohibition on obtaining damages and (recently) prohibitions on outside financing. *Id.*, "Collective Litigation in German Civil Procedure," this volume.

8 Only a few jurisdictions adopted representative class action statutes before 2000. The United States adopted its modern class action rule in 1966. Australia adopted a federal class action statute in 1992. Quebec adopted a representative class action in 1978 and Ontario and British Colombia followed suit in the early 1990s. The Canadian federal class action statute was adopted in 2001.

9 Deborah Hensler, "From Sea to Shining Sea: How and Why Class Actions Are Spreading Globally," 65 *Kansas L Rev* 965, 966 (2017). In 2007, when Christopher Hodges and I organized the first global conference on class actions, we were able to identify only eighteen jurisdictions with a procedure resembling a representative class action. See Deborah Hensler, "The Globalization of Class Actions: An Overview," in Deborah Hensler, Christopher Hodges and Magdalena Tulibacka, *The Globalization of Class Actions*, 622 The Annals of the American Academy of Political and Social Science 7, 13 (March 2009).

10 See, e.g., Report From the Commission to the European Parliament, The Council and the European Economic and Social Committee on the implementation of the Commission Recommendation of 11 June 2013 on common principles for injunctive and compensatory collective redress mechanisms in the Member States concerning violations of rights granted under Union law (2013/396/EU), available at https://eur-lex.europa.eu/legal-content/EN/TXT/PDF/?uri=CELEX:52018DC0040&from=EN:

> On the basis of a broader horizontal approach, the Commission adopted a Recommendation on 11 June 2013 on common principles for injunctive and compensatory collective redress mechanisms in the Member States concerning violations of rights granted under Union law ('the Recommendation'). The Recommendation established principles which should be applicable in relation to violations of rights granted under Union law across all policy fields and in relation to both injunctive and compensatory relief. It follows from the Recommendation that all Member States should have collective redress systems at national level that follow the same basic principles throughout the Union, taking into account the legal traditions of the Member States *and safeguarding against potential abuse. At the same time, in view of the risks associated with collective*

Few jurisdictions have formally articulated an "access to justice norm" as the rationale for adopting a class action, Australia[11] and Canada[12] being the leading examples of jurisdictions that have done so.[13] Instead, many jurisdictions have labored hard to devise a procedural mechanism that while formally permitting a representative class action does everything possible to dissuade claimants from making use of the procedure. In Europe particular effort has been devoted to restricting the use of class actions for private enforcement by consistently referring to the new procedures, in formal law and informal practice, as "collective redress" mechanisms. Spurred by international lobbying efforts by the US Chamber of Commerce,[14] European policy-makers who have proposed adopting collective litigation procedures have whenever possible noted that their intent is to avoid "American style class actions."[15] In Europe and Asia, limiting the use of class actions may involve restricting funding for litigation as well as designing procedures that hinder

litigation, the principles set out by the Recommendation also aim to strike an appropriate balance between the goal of ensuring sufficient access to justice and also the need of preventing abuses through appropriate safeguards. Emphasis mine.)

11 See, Edmund Fernandez, "Class Actions in Australia: A Quarter of a Century Later," GenRe, 2018, available at www.genre.com/knowledge/publications/cmint18-1-en.html ("In March 1992, Part IVA of the Federal Court of Australia Act 1976 (Cth) was enacted, enabling class actions to be pursued for the very first time. Access to justice and judicial economy were given as reasons when the bill was introduced in the Australian Parliament by the then Attorney-General.") See also Justice Bernard Murphy, "Access To Justice Under The Part IVa Regime," Keynote Address at seminar "Class Actions – Current Issues after 25 years of Part IVa," University of New South Wales (Australia), March 23, 2017, available at www.fedcourt.gov.au. Justice Murphy is a member of the federal bench of Australia.

12 Borden Ladner Gervais, "Class and Collective Actions in Canada," Lexology, March 1, 2019, available at www.lexology.com/library/detail.aspx?g=df53fca8-7604-4ecb-91b6-bf039a0159fb. See also Jasminka Kalajdzic, *Class Actions In Canada: The Promise And Reality Of Access To Justice*, UBC Press, 2018.

13 Members of the US federal judiciary advisory committee that drafted the 1966 version of Rule 23 have written that committee members sought to facilitate civil rights litigation of the sort exemplified by *Brown* v. *Board of Education* (347 U.S. 483 (1954)) which led to the US Supreme Court overturning the policy of "separate but equal" that had long reigned in the United States with regard to education and other public services. Although *Brown* was ultimately successful, African-Americans' decades-long efforts to obtain remedies for civil rights violations through class litigation were often thwarted by judges' rulings denying class certification on technical bases. The 1966 revision of Rule 23 simplified the structure of federal class actions in order to diminish, if not eliminate, technical barriers to proceeding. See "An Oral History of Rule 23," a transcript of an interview conducted by Samuel Issacharoff with Arthur Miller, who was the assistant to Professor Benjamin Kaplan, the Reporter for the Advisory Committee, 74 *NYU Annual Survey Amer. Law* 105, 109–110 (2018). The 1966 class action reformers seem to have been less committed to the idea of increasing access to the courts for small-value damage claims by providing a mechanism for cost spreading. There was support for facilitating securities and anti-trust class actions but only a few committee members thought enabling claims that individually pursued would be "economically unviable" should be a goal of rule reform. *Id.*, at 111. According to Miller, "when drafted, it [Rule 23] had a modest dimension. There was a sense that in application it would have a limited application. It has proven to have a dimension many times the size of anything conceived of by the people in that room . . . " *Id.*, at 112. As Miller wrote later, the revised rule did facilitate claims that were authorized by the 1970s surge in environmental and consumer protection litigation. Arthur Miller, "Of Frankenstein Monsters and Shining Knights: Myth, Reality, and the "Class Action Problem," 92 *Harv. Law Rev.* 664 (1979): 664–94. By the 1990s, the notion that Rule 23 was being used to enable pursuit of what had come to be called "negative value" claims had become part of mainstream legal discourse on the uses and abuses of class actions. See e.g., Henry Monaghan, "Antisuit Injunctions and Preclusion Against Absent Nonresident Class Members," 98 *Colum. L. Rev.* 1148 (1998). See also Linda Mullenix, "Complex Litigation: Negative Value Suits," 26 *Nat'l L.J.* 11 (March 22, 2004).

14 On the US Chamber of Commerce's lobbying efforts against class actions in Europe and Australia, see Deborah Hensler, "Third-Party Financing of Class Action Litigation in the United States: 1515," 63 *DePaul L. Rev.*, 1101 (2013). As an example of the reach of the US Chamber with regard to class action politics I was once asked to meet with a European civil servant charged with helping shape their country's class action policy outside their office so the Chamber would not be aware they were meeting with me as by this time I had apparently been labeled a supporter of class actions.

15 The European Union has been debating the adoption of a class action procedure since 2009. To my knowledge, every draft of proposed rules and commentary regarding them include language asserting a desire to avoid "American-style" class actions, often using coded terms such as "abusive" litigation. See e.g., Council of the European Union, "Proposal for a Directive of the European Parliament and of the Council on representative actions for the protection of the collective interests of consumers," November 21, 2019, Annex, Paragraph 4: "It is important to ensure the

class members from organizing to pursue litigation. In the United States, corporate counsel, with the strong and consistent support of the US Supreme Court, have pursued a unique strategy for precluding the use of Rule 23: incorporating mandatory arbitration provisions that explicitly forbid collective proceedings within and outside the court in workplace and consumer contracts.[16] Taken together, public and private efforts to provide a mechanism for collective action while tightly restricting its use, have resulted in procedural evolution, rather than revolutionary change.

What explains the proliferation of procedural options for group litigation in so many jurisdictions? Over the past fifty years, economic, political and cultural changes have increased the potential for mass claims for personal and financial injury. Arising out of the same factual circumstances, mass claims arrive at the court's doorsteps within a brief time, challenging even wealthy jurisdictions' courts' ability to deal with them expeditiously. Some attribute the rise of a so-called "compensation culture" to whiney citizens and greedy lawyers seeking lucrative opportunities to litigate.[17] However, the actual explanation is more complicated and implicates economic, social and cultural change. With the expansion of the global economy, there is an increased potential for defective products and fraud and other illegal behavior to affect large numbers of people.[18] The rise of an accountability culture has made the idea of holding

necessary balance between access to justice and procedural safeguards against abusive litigation which could unjustifiably hinder the ability of businesses to operate in the internal market. To prevent the misuse of representative actions, elements such as punitive damages and the absence of limitations as regards the entitlement to bring an action on behalf of the harmed consumers should be avoided and clear rules on certain various procedural aspects, such as the designation and funding of qualified entities the origin of their funds and nature of the information required to support the representative action, should be laid down. This Directive should not affect national rules concerning the allocation of procedural costs." Available at https://data.consilium.europa.eu/doc/document/ST-14210-2019-INIT/en/pdf.

16 See Katherine Stone and Alexander Colvin, "The Arbitration Epidemic," Economic Policy Institute (EPI) Briefing Paper, December 7, 2015, available at www.epi.org/files/2015/arbitration-epidemic.pdf. This admittedly one-sided assessment of the Supreme Court's endorsement of this strategy cites the key court decisions to 2015. More recent decisions have further precluded class proceedings when contracts include mandatory arbitration clauses. See, e.g., *Lamps Plus, Inc.* v. *Varela*, 139 S. Ct. 1407 (2019) (holding that ambiguity in a contract provision regarding collective proceedings cannot be construed in favor of such proceedings). On the relationship between US Supreme Court decisions on civil procedural issues and judges' party affiliation, see Stephen Burbank and Sean Farhang, *Rights And Retrenchment: The Counterrevolution Against Federal Litigation*, Cambridge University Press, 2017 (finding correlations between the party of the president that appointed them and the justices' decisions on access-limiting procedural rules).

17 See, e.g., [U.K.] House of Commons Constitutional Affairs Committee, Compensation Culture, Third Report of Session 2005–2006, Volume 1, available at https://publications.parliament.uk/pa/cm200506/cmselect/cmconst/754/754i.pdf (in inquiry regarding the consequences of legalizing conditional fee agreements (i.e., "no win, no pay") finding evidence of increased concern about risks of litigation within the business community notwithstanding a lack of evidence of a compensation culture incentivizing increased litigation). See also James Hand, "Compensation Culture: Cliché or Cause for Concern?," 37 *J. Law & Soc* 569 (2010). Hand's article begins with the proposition that there is an American (US) compensation culture, and then proceeds to present evidence of the absence of such a culture in the UK. However, American legal analysts have found little evidence of such a culture in the US. See, e.g., Marc Galanter, "The Day After the Litigation Explosion," 46 *Md. L. Rev.* 3 (1986) and William Haltom and Michael McCann, *Distorting The Law: Politics, Media and the Litigation Crisis*, University of Chicago Press, 2004. Most US civil lawsuits are filed in state courts. State court case filings decreased by 16 percent from 2009 to 2015; tort lawsuits account for about 5 percent of all civil lawsuits in most state courts. See tables available at www.courtstatistics.org.

18 The European Union has attributed the need for a new EU-wide consumer protection mechanism in part to this phenomenon. See, e.g., European Commission, "Proposal for a Directive of the European Parliament and of the Council on Representative Actions for the Protection of the Collective Interests of Consumers," November 4, 2018, ("... The Risk of infringements of Union law affecting the collective interests of consumers is increasing due to economic globalisation and digitalisation. Traders that infringe EU law may affect thousands or even millions of consumers with the same misleading advertisement or unfair standard contract terms in a number of different economic sectors. In light of increasing cross-border trade and EU-wide commercial strategies, these infringements increasingly also affect consumers in more than one Member State.")

perceived wrongdoers to account for their actions more popular.[19] Legislatures and courts have created new substantive legal rights, facilitating legal action to achieve accountability. The neoliberal mandate to reduce government regulation and recognition of the potential for regulated entities to suborn the regulators have made the notion of relying exclusively on public agencies to identify and sanction bad behavior less attractive.[20] Social media permit rapid sharing of information (and misinformation) about mass harms and naming of wrongdoers. Although there is little evidence that people generally – wherever they reside – are more disputatious than in the past, there are numerous examples of large numbers of people coming forward when mass harms occur to claim compensation or restitution from perceived wrongdoers.[21]

Policy-makers have established a variety of procedural mechanisms to respond to the challenge of mass legal claims. These procedures – all of which are represented in this volume – include:

"True" class actions in which a representative class member is authorized to file a lawsuit the outcome of which will bind everyone in a class of similarly situated people or entities without regard to whether they have filed legal claims and without them being present in court;[22]

Actions in which an association or special purpose entity (but not a class member) can litigate to obtain declaratory relief for its members or subscribers, allowing others subsequently to pursue claims for monetary relief, relying on the court's decision on liability in the initial case;[23]

Actions in which parties with claims arising out of the same law and facts can "register" (or perhaps be required to register) their claims and then be bound by the decision on liability of a court-selected "model" case when they subsequently pursue individual claims for compensation;[24] and

Settlement vehicles that allow claimants represented by associations or special purpose vehicles and putative defendants to approach the court together to seek approval of a binding settlement, including in instances where defendants have not been formally held liable by a court.[25]

Many of the jurisdictions that have adopted these procedures refer to them formally or colloquially as class actions (albeit intended only for "collective redress") and debates surrounding their

[19] Corporate social responsibility initiatives exemplify this culture, as does management rhetoric urging leaders to build a culture of accountability in the workplace. See, e.g., Zack Dugow, "Three Steps for Building a Culture of Accountability," Forbes, June 27, 2019 at www.forbes.com/sites/forbestechcouncil/2019/06/27/three-steps-for-building-a-culture-of-accountability/#7b30bdb310a0; A. Crane, et al. "The Corporate Social Responsibility Agenda," in *The Oxford Handbook of Corporate Social Responsibility*, Oxford University Press, 2008; Thomas Jones, "Corporate Social Responsibility Revisited, Redefined," 22 *Calif Management Rev* 59 (1980).

[20] For a discussion of regulatory capture in the context of the Volksvagen "clean diesel" scandal, see Thomas Eger and Hans-Bernd Schaefer "Reflections on the Volkswagen Emissions Scandal," (January 25, 2018). Available at SSRN: www.govinfo.gov/content/pkg/GPO-OILCOMMISSION/pdf/GPO-OILCOMMISSION.pdf.

[21] For case studies of mass claims resolved through group actions, see Deborah Hensler, Christopher Hodges, and Ianika Tzankova, *Class Actions in Context: How Culture, Economics and Politics Shape Collective Litigation*, Edward Elgar, 2016.

[22] Exemplified by the Australian, Canadian, Israeli and US class action procedures, and now – albeit with a different structure – the new Netherlands collective action statute effective January 1, 2020.

[23] Exemplified by the Dutch class action statute as adopted in 1995.

[24] Exemplified by the German KapMuG and English Group Litigation Order.

[25] Pioneered by the Dutch WCAM adopted in 2005 and since emulated by other Western European jurisdictions.

adoption frequently reference "American-style class actions," although only a minority incorporate the key ingredients of Fed. R. Civ. P. 23, the US class action rule.

The implementation of class actions or other group procedural mechanisms may differ in myriad ways; procedures that seem on the surface to be the same or very similar may in practice operate differently as they intersect with other aspects of the litigation regime – rules, cultural expectations, political contexts – in which they are inserted. The rich literature on "legal transplants" details the consequences of borrowing a rule, procedure, or institutional design from another jurisdiction.[26] Keeping this in mind, it is still useful to engage in comparative analysis of the structural features of the class action and group procedural mechanisms that have been adopted over the last fifty years. The key differences among class actions are:

Scope: What types of substantive legal claims can be brought forward using the class or group procedure?

Standing: Who (what person or entity) may come forward to represent the class? (Note that this question does not arise for purely aggregative procedures that allow group treatment for some aspects of litigation but only for individually filed claims.)

Opt Out versus Opt In: Is every person or entity that fits the definition of the class automatically included in the litigation unless they proactively remove themselves, or must members of the putative class come forward to sign up to the litigation? (This question also does not arise for procedures that aggregate individually-filed claims, which by definition have "opted in.")

Remedies: Is the sole remedy injunctive or declaratory relief, or can the class obtain damages through the class or group litigation, without subsequent individual litigation?

Binding versus Nonbinding Outcomes: in a true class action every class member who has opted in or declined to exercise their opt-out right is bound by the outcome, including decisions on damages.[27] By contrast, procedures that aggregate individual claimants may produce a decision on the law and facts that is *res judicata* but not determinative of the outcome of subsequent individual claims. And procedures that permit associations to come forward to litigate on behalf of their members may provide redress to their members but not other similarly situated claimants who are not association members.

Financing: not a formal part of most jurisdictions' class action rules, the rules that govern financing of civil litigation (often incorporated in rules of professional responsibility) play a critical role in whether a class action procedure – whatever its form – will be used.

26 The notion of "legal transplants" was introduced by Alan Watson. *Id.*, *Legal Transplants: An Approach to Comparative Law*, University of Georgia Press, 1976. See also Jaako Husa, "Developing Legal System, Legal Transplants, and Path Dependence: Reflections on the Rule of Law," 6 *Chinese J. Comp. Law* 129 (2018) (describing how "path dependence" has affected the adoption of a "rule of law" paradigm in China and Poland). The new Dutch collective action statute might be regarded as an "internal legal transplant," as experience with WCAM as well as knowledge of common law class action regimes encouraged lawmakers to extend class action remedies outside the settlement context to include damages.

27 In a regime in which putative class members must decide whether to be part of the class before the merits are decided they are required to accept the risk that they will not prevail in court on the merits, in which case they will be barred from obtaining compensation. On the face of Rule 23, decisions to opt-out must be made early in the litigation. (Rule 23 (c) (1) (a) instructs the judge presiding over the litigation to decide certification at "an early practicable" time. By inference, notice would then follow.) In practice, however, most damage class actions take the form of "settlement class actions," in which the required notice to putative class members includes information both about the pendency of the action and about the proposed settlement, including compensation amount and lawyers' fees. On settlement class actions as the prevailing mode of damage class actions in the United States, notwithstanding the lack of a rule authorizing same, see Deborah Hensler, "Opioid Negotiation Class May Be Organic Procedure Evolution," Law360, September 30, 2019, available at www.law360.com/articles/1204097/opioid-negotiation-class-may-be-organic-procedure-evolution.

Virtually all of these design features of collective litigation procedures evoke sharp controversy when policy-makers debate adopting them, with corporate lobbies and their allies generally pressing for features that will limit their use, and consumer, worker and environmental advocates pressing for procedural designs that they hope will enable litigation. Wielding a broad brush, one might conclude that trans-substantive procedures that grant standing to class members to represent a class of all similarly situated claimants who do not opt out, provide damages as well as equitable remedies to class members and incentivize lawyers or third-parties to finance the litigation are more likely to be used than procedures that are narrow in scope, incorporate restrictive standing rules and require class members to opt in, limit remedies to injunctive or declaratory relief and restrict funding sources. But in practice collective and group litigation design choices are more complex, as they interact in sometimes unanticipated ways with other features of civil justice regimes and implicate multiple and sometimes competing goals of civil litigation. Moreover, over time collective and group litigation procedures evolve as judges, practitioners and interest groups become more comfortable with the idea and reality of litigating on behalf of mass claimants.

SCOPE

When jurisdictions adopt class action or nonclass group procedures, they often limit the applicability of the procedure to one or a few specific types of substantive claims. Often this is the outcome of intensive lobbying by corporate opponents of class actions. In the face of such controversy, legislators strike a compromise by only authorizing the use of a collective procedure in a single area.[28] Logically, the impact of these procedures will be less than for "trans-substantive" procedures of the type familiar to common law jurisdictions. As a practical matter, if a procedure can only be used in a single area of the law, fewer lawyers – and judges, if there are specialized courts in the jurisdiction – will become familiar with the procedure, which may slow its incorporation into the local legal culture. Despite this, there are examples of jurisdictions that have adopted class action procedures or group litigation procedures for use in one area of substantive law only but later expanded their use to other types of substantive legal claims. In an era of increased demand for accountability, citizens who are aware that procedures exist for facilitating mass claiming in one area may press policy-makers to make these available for an incident that seems to call out for a new procedure. The Netherlands is an example of a jurisdiction that first adopted a collective settlement procedure – WCAM – to enable pharmaceutical manufacturers to resolve mass product defect claims and later accepted the application of the procedure to shareholder and other financial claims.[29] Israel,[30] Brazil[31] and France[32] are other examples of jurisdictions where

28 Germany and France both offer recent examples of these political dynamics. In Germany, as related by Halfmeier in this volume, the Green Party pushed for adoption of a broad collective litigation procedure but the model declaratory action was narrowly drawn to apply to consumer claims brought by a single long-standing consumer organization. In France, as described by Maria José Azar-Baud and Véronique Magnier in this volume, different sector-specific procedures were adopted serially.

29 Ianika Tzankova and Deborah Hensler, "Collective Settlements in the Netherlands: Some Empirical Observations," in Christopher Hodges and Astrid Stadler, *Resolving Mass Disputes: ADR and Settlement and Mass Claims*, Edward Elgar, 2013.

30 Amichai Magen and Peretz Segal, "Israel," in Deborah Hensler, Christopher Hodges and Magdalena Tulibacka, *The Globalization of Class Actions*, 622, Annals of the American Academy of Political and Social Science 244, 245 (March 2009).

31 Carlos Portugal Gouvêa and Helena Campos Refosco, "Class Actions in Brazil: Overview, Current Trends and Case Studies," this volume.

32 Maria José Azar-Baud and Véronique Magnier, "Class Action *à la française*," this volume.

the scope of class actions has been extended over time. As a political matter, the gradual expansion of the procedure to incorporate other substantive legal claims suggests that the "camel's nose under the tent" concern of class action opponents is well-grounded.

Extending authorization for class actions from one substantive law domain to another, however, is not a sure thing. Germany is perhaps the most recent example of a jurisdiction that long resisted extending the use of a group proceeding from the first category of substantive law in which it was authorized – shareholder claims – to a second area, consumer claims. As described by Halfmeier in this volume,[33] the KapMuG is properly described as an aggregative procedure in which a "model case," selected from a register of individual claims arising from the same facts, yields a decision on common facts and law that is *res judicata* for subsequent individual litigation by those whose claims were registered. In contrast, the "model declaratory action" (Musterfeststellungsklage) for consumer claims authorizes a previously established consumer organization to seek declaratory relief on behalf of consumers who, if the organization prevails, are then bound by the court's decision on common facts and law when suing individually for damages. To claim the benefit of the Musterfeststellungsklage procedure in subsequent individual damage actions, individuals must opt in. Consistent with the discussion above on the factors propelling the spread of collective litigation procedures, the German legislature adopted the procedure under pressure from German Volkswagen owners who chafed at the fact that they were precluded from seeking monetary compensation for the company's fraudulent installation of devices to enable the automobiles to violate pollution standards, while under the terms of class action settlements consumers in the United States and Canada were able to secure generous compensation. To date, more than 400,000 German consumers have opted in to the procedure. Although the German legislature adopted this second group litigation procedure, it has resisted to date pressure to extend such procedures to other substantive law domains.[34]

STANDING

Common law jurisdictions that have adopted class action procedures, including Australia, Canada, Israel and the United States, authorize an individual member of the putative class (which may comprise natural persons or entities such as small businesses) to come forward to represent the class.[35] The Canadian, Israeli and US procedures all require a judge to certify a class action; Australia has no such requirement but a defendant against whom an action is brought may challenge its appropriateness for class treatment. An important issue for the judge to decide in the certification process is whether the putative class plaintiff can properly represent the class. In US law, the criteria are "typicality" – are the plaintiff's claims typical of those of the class members? – and "adequacy of representation" – usually interpreted as whether the plaintiff has the resources to pursue the litigation to the benefit of the class, but also potentially teeing up the issue of whether the class members' interests are so heterogenous that no one or even a few class members can represent all.[36] In sum, common law class action procedures prioritize the

33 Halfmeier, "Collective Litigation in German Civil Procedure," this volume. 34 *Id.*

35 As described by Nikki Chamberlain and Susan Watson in this volume, New Zealand's current class action regime has evolved piecemeal from judicial interpretation of the representative action rule inherited from the British. A review of the area with an eye to procedural reform is currently underway. In practice, representative litigation in New Zealand has been brought by class members deemed properly representative of a class of others with common interests.

36 *Amchem Prods.* v. *Windsor* – 521 U.S. 591, 117 S. Ct. 2231 (1997) (vacating certification of a class of future asbestos claimants on these grounds but holding forth the possibility that the problem could be cured by establishing "subclasses," each with its own representative and counsel).

identity of the class representative with class members. The concern of policy-makers and judges is that the interests of class members be well-represented.

In the United States, concerns about "agency costs" – potential conflicts of interest between parties and their representatives – focus on *class counsel* not class representatives.[37] What De Wulf, describing the evolution of collective litigation procedures in Belgium in this volume, terms the "bounty hunter" model of entrepreneurial litigation is understood to apply to the incentives of class counsel to invest in litigation, celebrated by some and reviled by others.[38] To assure that the class representative is not in cahoots with class counsel to advantage the former in relation to other class members, the judge presiding over the case appoints class counsel – including if they wish holding a competition of lawyers seeking the position – and if, and only if, the class prevails, the judge awards lawyer fees and expenses.[39] Moreover, judges are required to review and approve the "fairness, reasonableness and adequacy" of any proposed class action settlement, after a call for objections and a public hearing. In contemporary American practice, proposed attorney fees come in for scrutiny as well and an active objector practice identifies potential conflicts of interest among class members and between class counsel and class members.[40] To minimize incentives for bounty-hunting class members, incentive payments to representatives to cover their time and expenses are strictly limited in American case law.[41]

In Canada, the putative class representative retains class counsel but the judge presiding over the case reviews the retainer agreement, including any third-party financing provisions (discussed further below in Model 2: Third-Party Funding). In Australia federal judges for several years adopted the practice of reviewing financial arrangements among class representatives, class counsel and funders at the conclusion of a case and, invoking a "common fund" doctrine borrowed from the United States, used their discretionary power to assure fairness of allocation of benefits and costs among class members. In December 2019, a divided High Court held that federal judges do not have the power under the federal (and New South Wales) statutory class action regime to issue common fund orders, sending this system into disarray.[42]

37 See, e.g., John Coffee, "Understanding the Plaintiff's Attorney: The Implications of Economic Theory for Private Enforcement of Law through Class and Derivative Actions," 86 Colum. L. Rev. 669 (1986) and Michael Dorf, "The Indictment of the Milberg Weiss Law Firm and America's Love/Hate Relationship with Class Action Litigation," FindLaw, May 22, 2006, available at https://supreme.findlaw.com/legal-commentary/the-indictment-of-the-milberg-weiss-law-firm-and-americas-lovehate-relationship-with-class-action-litigation.html.

38 *Id. See also* Deborah Hensler et al., *Class Action Dilemmas: Pursuing Public Goals for Private Gain*, RAND, 2000.

39 FRCP 23(g) and 23(h). A dramatic example of the failure of strictures against collusion between class counsel and class representatives in federal law occurred when lawyers at Milberg Weiss, which at one time was the largest plaintiff securities class action firm in the United States, put together a roster of individual shareholders to whom they promised kick-backs for agreeing to serve as class representatives. See Harrison Smith, "Obituaries: Melvin I. Weiss, Class Action King Felled By Kickback Scheme Dies at 82," *Washington Post*, February 6, 2018, available at www.washingtonpost.com/local/obituaries/melvyn-i-weiss-class-action-king-felled-by-kickback-scheme-dies-at-82/2018/02/06/8fe2140e-0b4e-11e8-8b0d-891602206fb7_story.html. A founding partner of Milberg, Weiss, Mr Weiss was also noted for playing a leading role in the Holocaust litigation against Swiss banks, in which he served pro bono. Pursued by federal investigators for his role in the kickback scheme, he was indicted for racketeering, served a year in prison and paid millions in fines. Others in the firm and the firm itself were also indicted. To my knowledge, there have been no other reports of such kickback schemes although there is anecdotal evidence of defendants paying off potential class representatives and lawyers in exchange for the latter agreeing not to pursue a class action.

40 FRCP 23 (e). See especially 23 (3) (e) (2), directing the judge's attention to various provisions of a proposed settlement.

41 Federal case law allows "incentive payments" to class representatives, but amounts must be approved by the judge presiding over the litigation and are generally for modest amounts. See Theodore Eisenberg and Geoffrey Miller, "Incentive Awards to Class Action Plaintiffs: An Empirical Study," 53 *UCLA L Rev* 1303 (2005–2006).

42 *BMW Australia Ltd* v. *Brewster & Anor* and *Westpac Banking Corporation & Anor* v. *Lenthall & Ors*, HCA 45 (2019). Vince Morabito, "An Evidence-Based Approach to Class Action Reform in Australia: Common Fund Orders,

In contrast to the common law model, most civil law jurisdictions in Europe and Asia seek to put distance between the class representative and the class by granting standing only to associations or special purpose foundations.[43] In some jurisdictions, these associations must have been authorized by the government to bring collective actions before suing. For example, in Taiwan, a private foundation that is publicly funded and overseen by Taiwan's Securities & Exchange Commission was established in 2003 by the Securities Investors and Fortunes Trade Protection Act to bring damage class actions on behalf of investors.[44] In Japan, standing to file consumer class actions is limited to "qualified consumer organizations" certified by the Prime Minister.[45] In Germany, only one consumer protection organization is authorized currently to bring model declaratory actions on behalf of consumers.[46] In France, where class actions have been authorized using a "sector" by "sector" approach, only preestablished registered associations devoted to pursuing interests regarding the relevant sector – that is, consumer protection, health care delivery – have standing to sue, and judges decide whether the group bringing the action has satisfied the standing requirement during an admissibility process akin to common law jurisdictions' certification process.[47] Under the most recent amendment of the collective litigation regime in Belgium, business interest associations as well as preexisting consumer organizations may bring representative actions.[48] Dutch standing rules are less restrictive: standing is granted not only to preexisting associations – for example, consumer protection associations – but also to "special purpose vehicles" – foundations established especially to pursue the instant collective action or collective settlement.[49] Jurisdictions that adhere to the association model of class actions generally prohibit these associations from benefiting financially from the litigation – for example, by receiving compensation beyond their expenses that they might then plough back into the organization's coffers to subsidize their activities. This creates a necessity for outside funding, that has led to reliance on third-party entrepreneurial funders, as discussed below in Model 2: Third-Party Funding. Ironically, these funders generally are not subject to strict regulation.

Although granting standing to individual class members may create an opportunity for abuse if a class representative colludes with class counsel to design a settlement agreement that benefits both of them at the expense of other class members – an opportunity that judicial oversight is intended to prevent in common law jurisdictions – it is unclear how limiting standing to preexisting or government-authorized organizations much less to special purpose vehicles formed with the intent of winning damages solves the problem of potential conflicts of interest

Funding Fees and Reimbursement Payments" (January 31, 2019), chapter 3, "Common Fund Orders in Federal Class Actions." Available at SSRN: https://ssrn.com/abstract=3326303.

43 There are exceptions to this observation. In Denmark, a court may appoint a class member to represent a class on an opt-in basis, but only the consumer ombudsman, a public official, is authorized to bring an opt-out class action on behalf of consumers. Opt-in class actions may be admitted by the court for any substantive legal claim over which it has jurisdiction, provided other requirements are met. Eric Werlauff, "Class Actions in Denmark," in Deborah Hensler, Christopher Hodges and Magdalena Tulibacka, *The Globalization of Class Actions*, 622 The Annals of the American Academy of Political and Social Science, 201, 204 (Mach 2009).

44 Kuo-Chang Huang, "Using Associations as a Vehicle for Class Actions: The Example of Taiwan," in Deborah Hensler, Christopher Hodges and Ianika Tzankova, *Class Actions In Context: How Culture, Economics And Politics Shape Collective Litigation*, Edward Elgar, 2016, at 81.

45 Taeko Morita and Daisuke Eguchi, "A Review of the Current Status of, and Future Issues Facing Consumer Class Action Systems in Japan," this volume. Actions for injunctive relief may be brought only by a certified qualified consumer organization. Actions for damages may be brought only by specially selected organizations within the list of qualified consumer organizations.

46 Halfmeier, "Collective Litigation in German Civil Procedure," this volume.

47 Maria José Azar-Baud and Véronique Magnier, this volume.

48 De Wulf, this volume.

49 Tzankova and Hensler, *supra* note 30.

among class members, between class members and class representatives and between class members and counsel. Nor does practice support the proposition. In a large-scale high-value consumer litigation against Dexia Bank in the Netherlands, the Dutch consumer protection organization Consumentenbond that took the lead in the litigation found itself facing angry members when it agreed to a settlement that not all of its members found attractive; subsequently, the organization vowed not to take on a prominent role in future class actions.[50] In a more recent WCAM settlement, an eyepopping $1.5 billion settlement of claims against Fortis bank deriving from the global financial crisis, several special purpose foundations, a long-standing investor association (VEB) and a commercial recovery service (Deminor) joined with Fortis' successor (Ageas) in petitioning the Amsterdam Court of Appeals to approve their previously negotiated settlement. The several associations asserted claims on behalf of investors who had signed onto their efforts and agreed to share some of their proceeds from the settlement (termed "success fees") with their chosen association (termed "active claimants") as well as on behalf of other affected investors ("inactive claimants"). The parties initially submitted to the court a settlement agreement that provided substantially different recoveries to the so-called active and non-active claimants, but when the court refused to approve this arrangement, the settlement terms were revised to eliminate this distinction with regard to calculations of recoveries. Settlement provisions with regard to the fees of different claimant organizations were not revised, but the court did object to a 25€ million "success fee" recovered by VEB, apparently on the grounds that a nonprofit membership association should not benefit from litigating on behalf of a broader interest group.[51] Notwithstanding the difference in standing rules between "American-style class actions" and the Dutch associational model, settlement dynamics and allocation of damages and fees between lawyers and shareholders in this litigation seem remarkably similar to what one would observe in an American shareholder class action.[52]

OPT IN VERSUS OPT OUT

Class actions in common law jurisdictions generally permit the litigation to go forward without first identifying all those who will be bound by it; by contrast, most civil law jurisdictions have preferred opt-in regimes. Opt-out regimes are criticized by those opposed to class actions on the grounds that they deny individual autonomy and hence violate constitutional rights. Although putative class members in opt-out regimes have a choice as to whether to remain a part of the class, the not unreasonable argument is that many class members may not be aware that a litigation is going forward on their behalf and hence will not exercise their rights. Stringent notice requirements, including widespread media campaigns, are intended to mitigate this risk but it still seems likely that some will miss this information. In practice, putative class members are most likely to miss out on information about the litigation and fail to exercise their rights when the amounts of potential recovery are small. Requiring an opt-in regime in such situation will either result in no lawsuit at all or substantially limit defendants' potential financial exposure. As a result, the deterrence effect of collective litigation is much reduced. In contrast,

50 Tzankova and Hensler, *supra* note 30.

51 This description of the Fortis settlement relies on Jonathan Richman and Ianika Tzankova, "Fortis Case Confirms Viability of Dutch Settlement Law," Law360, July 27, 2018; Kevin Lacroix, "Dutch Court Declares Largest Ever European Investor Claims Settlement Binding," the D & O Diary, July 2018; and conversations with Prof. Ianika Tzankova. The lawyers acting for the claimants included at least two US law firms, Grant & Eisenhofer and Kessler, Topaz, Metler, Check.

52 Whether the stronger Claim Code adopted in 2011 or the new requirements for claim organizations included in the new collective action statue will change these dynamics remains to be seen.

the consequence of an opt-out regime is to incentivize litigation that yields a remedy that imposes a sanction on defendants for culpable behavior. Moreover, when potential individual recoveries are substantial, experience suggests that media coverage of litigation as well as required notice campaigns will reach a large proportion of class members, some of whom may opt out to pursue what they anticipate will be larger individual recoveries. Notwithstanding normative rhetoric, political support for opt-in regimes is explained by the understanding that such a regime will likely result in fewer actions on behalf of fewer claimants, with the consequence that defendants' financial exposure will be limited.[53]

Political debate about opt-in versus opt-out provisions often ignores the fact that opt-out regimes are very useful to defendants when they are faced with large numbers of viable legal claims for damages. In these circumstances, many defendants would prefer an opt-out regime that offers a binding outcome – "global peace" – for the class members who do not opt out. It is notable in this regard that the Dutch collective settlement statute (WCAM), designed collaboratively by pharmaceutical manufacturers and claimant advocates, established an opt-out resolution scheme. The new collective litigation statute also provides for opt-out classes of Netherlands claimants but requires claimants outside the Netherlands to opt in.[54]

The belief that opt-in classes will necessarily be smaller than opt-out class actions has been challenged recently by experience with the new German model declaratory actions for consumer claims. As described by Halfmeier in this volume,[55] within months of a consumer action being filed against Volkswagen using the new procedure, upwards of 400,000 German consumers had opted in. While the Volkswagen scandal has attracted an unusual level of attention worldwide, in an era of social media we may observe more instances of large-scale opt-in class actions.

REMEDIES

Injunctive and declaratory relief may have enormous significance when rights claims are pursued against institutions – viz. the gay marriage litigation in the United States,[56] California prisoners' successful suit against the state for prison overcrowding that resulted in a dramatic reorganization of the state's criminal sentencing system[57] and the widely known *Brown* v. *Board of Education*[58] case that sounded the death knell for de jure segregation in the United States. Collective litigation for declaratory or injunctive relief may clarify the interpretation and application of law and prevent harmful behavior in the future. However, limiting remedies to injunctive or declaratory relief tends to depress the level of collective claiming. The reasons for this are clear (and well-understood by lobbyists and public policy-makers who enact class action

53 On corporate preference for opt-in regimes, see, e.g., Andrew Austin, "EU Class Actions: The Council Finally Plays Its Hand" (blog post), November 27, 2019, discussing the penultimate draft of the European Union Directive on Representative Actions, noting approvingly the adoption of an opt-in model for class actions arising out of cross-border transactions, available at https://riskandcompliance.freshfields.com/post/102fv6b/eu-class-actions-the-council-finally-plays-its-hand. Austin also notes approvingly additional restrictions on what organizations can bring class actions in the revised draft. The EU Commission has been debating adoption of a procedure for collective litigation of consumer claims since 2009.

54 C. F. Van der Elst and W. C. T. Weterings, "The Solid Dutch Mechanisms for Collective Settlement," this volume. The Danish class action regime is also interesting in this regard. Class actions generally proceed on an opt-in basis. Only the Ombudsman, a public official, is allowed to bring a damages class action on an opt-out basis. In recent years, the ombudsman has shared at public conferences that he yields this as a weapon against corporate defendants who he believes usually would prefer to settle with him than to face such a large-scale action.

55 Halfmeier, "Collective Litigation in German Civil Procedure," this volume.

56 *Obergfell* v. *Hodges*, 135 S.Ct. 1732 (2015). 57 *Brown* v. *Plata*, 563 U.S. 493 (2011). 58 347 U.S. 483 (1954).

statutes):[59] even membership and public interest organizations need to concern themselves with financing their activities. If the representatives of class actions cannot obtain any monetary rewards for their actions and if, as discussed further below in the section on Litigation Financing, options for funding litigation are severely limited, few actions will go forward. In contrast, if remedies include monetary compensation – and perhaps additional damages meant to sanction illegal behavior – more litigation may ensue. Concern about the latter explains the prohibition against punitive damages in the proposed European Union Directive on Representative Actions.[60]

BINDING VERSUS NONBINDING OUTCOMES

By their nature, collective actions for injunctive or declaratory relief will affect all members of a class, whether brought by individual class members, registered preexisting associations or special purpose vehicles. The Board of Education of Topeka must either end the practice of segregating public-school children by race or not; a bank must either revise its offers to account holders or not; Volkswagen must either correct any software intended to distort emissions inspection results or not. The power of damage class actions – and their possible attraction for defendants who have practically conceded (albeit perhaps only internally) that they need to compensate consumers, shareholders or employees – is that whether class members receive any compensation and how much will be determined by the outcome of a collective lawsuit. Where individual claim values are very small – as in most but not all consumer litigation – class members' whose rights to compensation are litigated on a group rather than individual basis lose very little practically speaking by losing control over their claim, which is too small for them to litigate individually. But a damage class may include claimants with claims of varying legal strength and monetary value, hence, policy-makers' concern about imposing a collective structure on the litigation. The response in common law jurisdictions is to incorporate an opt-out provision and to layer the collective proceeding with requirements – notice to class members, hearings on settlement fairness, provisions for objectors, judicial review of settlement terms and (at least in the United States) judicial appointment of class counsel and award of class counsel fees – intended to protect the interests of class members who choose to remain in the class. The more common response in civil law jurisdictions is to require group members to seek damages in individual litigation following upon a successful collective litigation by an association or a judicial decision on a "model case." Interestingly, the legislative designers of the Dutch collective settlement scheme seem not to have considered the sorts of conflict of interest issues that worry common law judges presiding over opt-out damage class actions. Although the special purpose vehicles and defendants pursuing settlement must submit their proposed settlement for review and approval in order to secure a binding agreement, until recently Dutch judges did not inquire very deeply into the details of settlements and gave little consideration to the funding agreements and fees that accompanied proposed settlements.[61] This situation may change under the 2019 claim code and the 2020 Dutch collective action statute.

59 Early in the more than a decade-long pursuit of an EU-wide collective litigation regime, lobbyists were able to limit proposals for collective litigation to injunctive actions. See European Commission, "Proposal for a Directive of the European Parliament and the Council on representative actions for the protection of the collective interests of consumers, and repealing Directive 2009/22/EC," *supra* note 19. Directive 2009/22/EC established the framework for collective actions for injunctions.

60 See EU Council, "Proposal for a Directive of the European Parliament and of the Council on representative actions for the protection of the collective interests of consumers," *supra* note 16.

61 See, e.g., Richman and Tzankova, *supra* note 48.

LITIGATION FINANCING

Litigation requires financial resources. Whether collective litigation will prove feasible and under what circumstances and to what extent depends critically on jurisdictions' rules with regard to legal financing. These rules include how lawyers may be paid – for example on a contingency basis or on an hourly fees and expense basis, perhaps with success fees tacked on – and whether losing parties face adverse costs. In recent years, as third-party funders have emerged seeking to profit by investing in high-value commercial litigation, regulation of funding has become another important aspect of jurisdictions' financing regime. Existing litigation financing rules are rarely reconsidered when collective litigation procedures are adopted, although one assumes that how these rules might facilitate or hinder use of the procedures is on the minds of policy-makers.

To date, three models of class action finance have emerged: a private law firm driven model with limited recourse to third-party funders; a third-party funder driven model with limited reliance on private law firms; and a model in which nonprofit associations such as special purpose foundations partner with third-party funders. The United States and Canada are the two leading examples of the first model, Australia the leading model of the second and the Netherlands the leading example of the third.

Model 1: *Relying on Private Law Firms*

In the United States, in suits for damages, lawyers generally represent plaintiffs on a contingent fee basis. In individual litigation, courts generally do not inquire into the provisions of contingent fee contracts. In class actions, however, as described above, US judges award fees and expenses at the conclusion of litigation if the class prevails, in accord with common law doctrine that has evolved over decades. As a result, most class actions are funded by law firms, meaning that firms invest time and money up-front, with the expectation that if the class prevails at trial or in settlement, the judge will award fees that cover these expenses and reward the lawyers for taking on the risk of losing the amount they invested in the litigation.[62] Banks have played an important role in this regime by providing generous lines of credit to the most successful firms, which in return deposit escrow funds in accounts with these banks. Perhaps because of the availability of entrepreneurial law firms that can afford to invest in litigation and the lack of adverse cost risks, third-party litigation funders have moved slowly into the US market, and with some notable exceptions have stayed away from class litigation.[63]

62 Successful plaintiff class action firms are richly rewarded. But the widely shared view in Europe and Asia that class action lawyers routinely obtain one-third of any settlement is incorrect. Whether judges award fees as a percentage of a common benefit fund or on an hours and expenses "lodestar" basis, generally fee awards decline as a percentage of the common fund as settlement amounts rise. For very large settlements, the average rate is a bit over 10 percent. Theodore Eisenberg and Geoffrey P. Miller, "Attorney Fees in Class Action Settlements: An Empirical Study," 1 *Journal of Empirical Legal Studies* (2004); Brian Fitzpatrick, "An Empirical Study of Class Action Settlements and Their Fee Awards," 7 *Journal of Empirical Legal Studies* 811 (2010). An important feature of civil litigation in the United States is that generally neither side faces an adverse costs order if they lose. Civil rights class actions are often brought by public interest firms or organizations funded by donations; if the actions succeed the organizations will often be awarded fees paid by defendants. See, e.g., KPIX, "Arizona to Pay $300,000 to Lawyers in Same Sex Marriage Case," December 22, 2015, available at www.12news.com/article/news/local/arizona/arizona-to-pay-300000-to-lawyers-in-same-sex-marriage-case/24373150.

63 See Hensler, *supra* note 15. Recent controversy over third-party funding in the United States has focused on whether the existence or terms of funding agreements must be disclosed to the court or opposing parties. For a review of disclosure rules related to third-party financing, see Patrick Tighe, "Survey of Federal and State Disclosure Rules

In Canada, where contingent fee contracts were historically prohibited, some provinces have lifted the prohibition for class actions. Unlike parties in the United States, in most Canadian provinces, class representatives are subject to adverse cost orders. To address this risk, third-party funders have become important actors in high-value class litigation. Under the 1992 Ontario Class Proceedings Act, the terms of the representative plaintiff's contingent fee agreement with class counsel are subject to court approval and judges have extended their review to include provisions regarding third-party funding.[64] Public funds, subsidized and replenished by percentage charges against common benefit funds, play an important role in several Canadian provinces in facilitating class litigation that does not attract private litigation funding.

Model 2: *Third-Party Funding*

Third-party funding for high-value commercial litigation arose first in Australia and has long been regarded there as essential for class litigation. Australian lawyers are forbidden to enter into contingency fee contracts with their clients although they can offer their services on a "no win, no pay" basis. (Australian lawyers may obtain "up charges" on their hourly bills but such charges are strictly limited.) In the early years after the adoption of the federal class action statute, most cases were brought by labor unions, using their own funds. The need to pay up-front and continuing legal fees plus the risk of adverse costs – neither of which would be shared with other class members – deterred potential class representatives from coming forward in other types of cases. Third-party funding emerged as the solution to the financial challenge: in return for a portion of any damages class members obtained, funders would provide at least a portion of up-front and ongoing costs to maintain the litigation,[65] while also assuming the risk of adverse costs. In contrast to the prohibition against lawyers charging contingent fees, there was no regulation of funders' fees.

Australia's experience with third-party funding of class actions offers important lessons about how funding may reshape class action regimes while providing the means of ensuring its efficacy. The need to secure funding changed the de jure opt-out class action regime in Australia into a de facto opt-in regime, as the funders needed to contract with potential class members to guarantee payment and profit. Various modifications of class definition and damage allocation ensued, as judges sought to assure fairness without hindering the ability of claimants to pursue class actions.[66] With rising concerns about how third-party funding was shaping class action practice, in 2017 the Australian Law Reform Commission mandated an inquiry into current practice and recommendations for reform. The final report of the Commission recommended greater court oversight of litigation funding agreements, the introduction of contingency fee agreements between lawyers and class representatives and a prohibition on closed classes – that is classes

Regarding Litigation Funding," Memorandum to Advisory Committee on the Civil Rules, February 7, 2018. See also *Gbarabe* v. *Chevron Corp.*, 2016 U.S. Dist. LEXIS 103594 (ruling by Judge Susan Illston, of N.D. California, requiring plaintiff lawyers to disclose a funding agreement). Subsequently the Northern District passed adopted ground rules specifying when the existence of such agreements must be disclosed. N.D. California, LR 3-15 (a)(1), adopted January 23, 2017. Judge Illston has since denied defendants' disclosure motion in another case. *MLC Intellectual Property LLC* v. *Micron Technology, Inc.*, No. 14-cv-03657, 2019 WL 118595 (N.D.Cal. Jan. 7, 2019).

64 See, e.g., *Houle* v. *St. Jude Medical*, 2017 ONSC 5129.

65 Funders would generally require class counsel to front some of their expenses to assure that the lawyers would have "skin in the game."

66 In December 2019, the High Court of Australia issued a decision holding that judges do not have the authority to issue so-called "common fund" orders under the federal class action statute.

comprising exclusively those parties who have signed funding agreements – among other changes in law and practice.[67]

Model 3: *Partnerships between Nonprofit Organizations and Commercial Funders*

As described above and in contributions to this volume, most civil law jurisdictions that have adopted collective litigation procedures have limited standing to nonprofit organizations, either long standing associations, government certified special purpose associations or special purpose vehicles organized as foundations. In some instances, organizations have been able to use membership dues or special membership contributions to fund litigation. For example, Consumentenbond, the leading Dutch consumer organization, solicited members to make modest contributions to support the class action against Dexia Bank and VEB, the Dutch association of small investors, has used membership funds to support its participation in various shareholder collective settlements.[68] For the most part, however, collective litigation in Europe has been subsidized by third-party funders, including the leading Australian funder, which seeing an opportunity in Europe, expanded its horizon to include the newly authorized collective litigation procedures.[69] As in Australia, regulation of third-party funders has been light and essentially left to the market, as special purpose foundations negotiate contracts with funders to subsidize their litigation and settlement activities. In the Netherlands, the self-regulatory instrument is the "claim code" that imposes certain obligations on the foundation board. Adopted in 2011, the effectiveness of the code was at first in question but in 2016 a Dutch court dismissed a foundation's collective action against Rabobank, for inadequately guarding its members interests in violation of the claim code.[70] The claim code was revised in 2019 to address governance of foundations and third-party funding,[71] and the new collective action statue includes new rules for representative organizations.

****

The proliferation of collective litigation and group litigation procedures around the world offers rich opportunities for exploring the consequences of different substantive and procedural regimes for efficiency, access to justice and regulatory enforcement. Although some of the cases highlighted in this volume might be considered successes or failures of collective litigation, determining what procedural features are more likely to achieve policy-makers' goals requires systematic collection of data, which has to date been lacking. A first step would be collection and publication of each jurisdiction's cases, indicating the nature of the substantive legal claims, the parties bringing the litigation, the defendants against whom they are acting, key stages of the process, outcomes (including for cases yielding compensation, information about distribution plans), costs and financing (distinguishing law firm financing, self-financing by organizations,

67 Australia Law Reform Commission, *Integrity, Fairness and Efficiency—An Inquiry into Class Action Proceedings and Third-Party Litigation Funders* (Report 134, 2018), available at www.alrc.gov.au/wp-content/uploads/2019/08/alrc_report_134_webaccess-1.pdf. I served as a member of the academic experts advisory panel to the Commission.

68 See Ianika Tzankova, "Funding of Mass Disputes: Lessons from the Netherlands," 8 *J. Law, Econ. & Pol.* 549 (2012) and Tzankova and Hensler, *supra* note 30.

69 Burford Capital, the leading global publicly traded funder has mainly eschewed collective litigation and has focused its Asian business on international arbitration rather than litigation.

70 "Dutch Foundation Dismissed for Inadequate Safeguarding of Members' Interests," National Law Review, July 15, 2016, available at www.natlawreview.com/article/dutch-foundation-dismissed-inadequate-safeguarding-members-interests.

71 C. F. Van der Elst and W. C. T. Weterings, "The Solid Dutch Mechanisms for Collective Settlement," this volume.

third-party funding and public funding) and time to disposition. As challenging as it seems to some jurisdictions to collect such information – and as concerning to some to share it publicly – an even more daunting task is to extract data in comparable form from jurisdictions with widely varying legal systems. Ultimately, the best that courts and researchers may be able to do is share their own data along with qualitative explanations of how their procedures work in practice. This volume is an important contribution to that comparative effort.

Acknowledgments

The authors would like to acknowledge financial support for this project from the Program on Law & Business and the Branstetter Litigation & Dispute Resolution Program, both at Vanderbilt Law School.

PART I

The United States

1

The US Class Action from a Utilitarian Perspective

Balancing Social Benefits and Social Costs

Robert G. Bone[*]

1.1 INTRODUCTION

The class action is a powerful tool for adjudicating large aggregations of claims in a single proceeding.[1] While it has roots in the representative suit of the eighteenth and nineteenth centuries, the class action in the United States first assumed its modern form in 1966, with extensive revisions to Rule 23 of the Federal Rules of Civil Procedure. Ever since then, it has been the subject of intense and highly polarized debate.[2] Today the class action is under siege, as critics launch sharp attacks and supporters respond with pointed counterattacks. This chapter's goal is to step back from the fray and reflect on the normative underpinnings of the class action in a more balanced way.

There are at least two features that make the class action so controversial. First, it is based on the principle that a party can represent the litigating interests of other persons and bind the latter as though they were litigating on their own.[3] Critics are quick to point out that this principle is in tension with the litigation system's bedrock commitment to giving each individual her own personal "day in court."[4]

The second feature has to do with the practical effects of class litigation. The class action has the capacity to effect significant redistributions of economic and social power. For example, small-claim class actions make it possible for large groups of injured individuals to hold powerful corporate actors legally accountable in ways that would be impossible without the class device.

* I am grateful to Professor Randall S. Thomas for helpful comments on an early draft.

1 This chapter draws its examples from class action practice in United States federal courts and focuses on the federal class action rule, Rule 23 of the Federal Rules of Civil Procedure. It does not deal specifically with state court class actions, although the normative analysis applies generally to all class actions whether they are filed in federal or in state court. Nor does it address the federal collective action under the Fair Labor Standards Act, which resembles the class action but differs in several important respects, most notably by relying on opt-in rather than opt-out. *See* Fair Labor Standards Act, 29 U.S.C. § 216 (2012); Genesis HealthCare Corp. v. Symczyk, 569 U.S. 66 (2013). Finally, the focus is on plaintiff class actions, not the relatively rare defendant class action.

2 However, there was a period of relative stability in the 1980s. *See* David Marcus, *The History of the Modern Class Action, Part I: Sturm und Drang*, 1953–1980, 90 WASH. U. L. REV. 587, 643–51 (2013). For accounts of the eighteenth and nineteenth century representative suit and the history of the class action device, *see* STEPHEN C. YEAZELL, FROM MEDIEVAL GROUP LITIGATION TO THE MODERN CLASS ACTION (1987); Robert G. Bone, *Personal and Impersonal Litigative Forms: Reconceiving the History of Adjudicative Representation*, 70 B.U. L. REV. 213 (1990).

3 Hansberry v. Lee, 311 U.S. 32, 42–43 (1940).

4 *See* Ortiz v. Fibreboard Corp., 527 U.S. 815, 846–48 (1999); Taylor v. Sturgell, 553 U.S. 880, 892–93 (2008); Robert G. Bone, *The Puzzling Idea of Adjudicative Representation: Lessons for Aggregate Litigation and Class Actions*, 79 GEO. WASH. L. REV. 577, 580–89 (2011).

For another example, the class action can make it easier to challenge systemic wrongdoing perpetrated by government officials and obtain broad injunctive relief that attacks the problems at their source. In both of these examples, the class action empowers individuals who would otherwise have difficulty obtaining redress against those with much greater power – and not surprisingly the more powerful object.

For these reasons, class action proponents often find themselves having to defend the modern class action against sharp criticism. Whether defending or criticizing the class action, it is important to frame one's arguments in normative terms that take account of how well the device serves the purposes of civil adjudication and how well it fits within adjudication's legitimate sphere. This chapter describes one way to do this – through a utilitarian approach that balances social benefits and social costs. From a utilitarian perspective, the main benefits of the class action have to do with avoiding duplicative litigation costs and improving outcome quality, and the main costs have to do with procedural complexity, magnification of litigation stakes, and agency and collective action problems. The question for the utilitarian is whether the social benefits exceed the social costs.

Conducting this evaluation is complicated by two factors: the limited availability of reliable empirical information, and the fact that most class actions end in settlement. Because of limited empirics, predictions of class action effects must rely to a large extent on assumptions about what rational actors are likely to do. And because of the prominence of settlement, the analysis must consider the class action's impact on settlements as well as trial judgments.

It is also important to bear in mind that the class action should be evaluated compared to realistic alternatives. For example, as we shall see, class litigation suffers from agency problems, but so do ordinary lawsuits. Indeed, agency costs can be particularly serious in exactly those types of individual suits that are most suitable for class aggregation. This means that the class action might reduce agency costs compared to the real world of individual suits settled *en masse*.

The following discussion evaluates the class action from a utilitarian perspective. Section 1.2 describes the utilitarian approach in general and distinguishes it from other ways to evaluate procedural rules. Section 1.3 briefly summarizes how United States preclusion law works when suits are brought separately. This furnishes a baseline against which to compare the class action and evaluate its benefits and costs. Section 1.4 summarizes the social benefits of the class action, and Section 1.5 examines the social costs. Section 1.6 pulls the strands together by analyzing three controversial issues that are the subject of current debate: mandatory versus opt-out classes, cy pres distributions, and sampling.

1.2 THE UTILITARIAN APPROACH TO PROCEDURE

The analysis in this chapter focuses on one version of utilitarianism: law-and-economics. Law-and-economics applies modern economic analysis to law. Roughly speaking, the goal is to choose legal rules that minimize social costs, or equivalently, maximize social benefits net of costs. When deciding whether a procedure like the class action should be adopted, one balances the marginal social benefit the procedure confers against the marginal social cost it generates.[5]

A procedure can produce benefits in two ways: by reducing process (or administrative) costs and by reducing the risk of outcome error. Typically a new procedure increases process costs by

[5] The beginning of the law-and-economics approach to civil procedure is usually traced to three articles published in the early 1970s: William M. Landes, *An Economic Analysis of the Courts*, 14 J. L. ECON. 61 (1971); Richard A. Posner, *An Economic Approach to Legal Procedure and Judicial Administration*, 2 J. LEG. STUD. 399 (1973), and John P. Gould, *The Economics of Legal Conflicts*, 2 J. LEG. STUD. 279 (1973).

inviting more motions and requiring more judicial deliberations. But it can also reduce these costs. For example, one argument for the class action is that it reduces the process costs of repeatedly litigating identical issues.

However, the most important benefit of procedure is the reduction in the risk of outcome error that it makes possible and the associated error costs it thereby avoids. "Outcomes" include decisions of legal and factual issues, dispositions of motions, final judgments after trial, and settlements – as well as outcomes of no liability that result from a party's inability to sue. An outcome is "erroneous" when it diverges from what the substantive law mandates on the facts of the case.[6]

Error reduction, however, is not an end in itself; it is a means to the end of reducing the expected costs of error. If individuals know there is some chance of avoiding liability when they should be held liable, they will be less inclined to comply with the substantive law. Noncompliance, in turn, generates social costs by frustrating the substantive law's ability to achieve its goals. Similarly, if individuals know they might be held liable even when they comply, they expect less of a benefit from complying, so their incentives to comply are weaker. And once again, a failure to comply generates social costs.

Thus, both the probability of litigation error and the cost of error matter to a law-and-economics analysis. More precisely, what matters is "expected error cost." Expected error cost is the social cost of error discounted by the probability an error will occur. There are two types of error – false negatives and false positives.[7] Adding a new procedure normally reduces one type and increases the other. For example, the small-claim class action, as we shall see, can reduce the expected cost of false negative error by enabling private enforcement of the substantive law, but it can also increase the expected cost of false positive error by over-deterring socially valuable activity.

Of course, a new procedure adds process costs of its own, including the private and public costs of administering the procedure through motions, deliberations, and decisions. Process costs are particularly salient in the class action context because of the complexity of the device, the intensity of advocacy it engenders, and the difficulty of implementing it properly.

This simple account captures the core of the law-and-economics approach. There are complexities, however, one of which deserves special mention because it is relevant to the discussion later in this chapter. The simple account assumes a functional distinction between substance and procedure: substantive law shapes real world incentives in order to promote policy goals, and procedural law applies the substantive law accurately to ensure that the desired incentives are realized. From a law-and-economics perspective, however, there is no fundamental distinction between substance and procedure: both are tools for shaping incentives. A rational actor choosing whether to comply with the law considers *all* the consequences of noncompliance, and these include not only the likely outcome of a lawsuit if one is filed, but also the process costs of defending the suit. Thus, deterrence can be strengthened directly by increasing process costs without changing outcomes.[8] And courts sometimes look past the substantive rules to the policies those rules aim to promote and adjust procedure to serve those policies more effectively.[9]

6 I do not mean to suggest that there is always a uniquely correct outcome. Even when there are many equally acceptable outcomes, it is still sensible to refer to an outcome as erroneous if it falls outside the acceptable set.

7 Or as statisticians refer to them, Type I and Type II errors. *See generally* Robert G. Bone, Economics of Civil Procedure 128–39 (2003).

8 *See* Louis Kaplow, *Multistage Adjudication*, 126 Harv. L. Rev. 1179, 1195, 1235 (2013).

9 Moreover, the simple account assumes that judges apply preexisting legal rules, but in the United States at least, judges do more than that: they make law through the common law process. It is conceivable that judges do a better job of common-law making with some procedures than with others. For example, a class action might enhance common-law making by facilitating the presentation of different views and arguments. Whether procedure generates benefits of this sort, however, depends on whether there is a link between procedure and common law reasoning.

Law-and-economics – and utilitarianism more generally – is not the only way to evaluate procedure. One might instead adopt a rights-based approach that values outcome accuracy in moral rather than economic terms and focuses on producing outcomes that honor each party's rights.[10] The key difference from utilitarianism lies in the nature of a right. In rights-based theory, a right trumps or constrains reliance on social utility maximization or broad collective goals to justify actions that interfere with what the right guarantees.[11] Because of its focus on individual rights, a rights-based theory has much more trouble justifying the outcome-averaging effects of a class action and counting process-cost reduction in favor of class action treatment.

Some theorists argue for a dignitary theory of procedure.[12] Dignitary theory focuses not on outcome quality, but on the way litigants are treated by the process itself. Dignitary theorists argue that each party has a deontological right to a litigation process that treats her with dignity and respect, and that this general right includes a more specific right to participate personally in the process. The logic of this argument is not self-evident and the existence of a process-oriented participation right is unclear.[13] If such a right exists, however, it poses a challenge to the class action, since the class action deprives absent class members of the opportunity to participate in and control their own lawsuits.[14]

One terminological point before proceeding. At times, the following discussion refers to law-and-economics by name, but more frequently, it refers to utilitarianism. To be clear, whenever I refer to a "utilitarian" approach, theory, framework, and the like, I mean the law-and-economics version of utilitarianism.

1.3 A BRIEF LOOK AT US PRECLUSION LAW

Before the revision of Rule 23 in 1966, neither the class action nor its predecessor, the representative suit, was strictly a preclusion device, although both generated preclusive effects under some circumstances.[15] The modern class action, by contrast, is first and foremost a vehicle for preclusion: a properly certified and managed class action is supposed to have full claim and issue preclusive effects on all members of the class.[16]

The reason class-wide preclusion is so important has to do with the limited scope of United States preclusion law applied to individual suits. Each person has a right to her own personal "day in court," and this right is understood to guarantee personal control over one's own lawsuit. Thus, with very few exceptions – the class action being one – a person who was not a party to the first suit and did not have a chance to control the litigation of that suit is free to litigate the issues anew in her own lawsuit.[17]

10 *See, e.g.*, Ronald Dworkin, *Principle, Policy, Procedure*, in A Matter of Principle 72, 93–94 (1985); Robert G. Bone, *Agreeing to Fair Process: The Problem With Contractarian Theories of Procedural Fairness*, 83 B.U. L. Rev. 485, 511–16 (2003).

11 Ronald Dworkin, *Principle, Policy, Procedure*, in A Matter of Principle 72, 73–74 (1985).

12 *See, e.g.*, Jerry L. Mashaw, Due Process in the Administrative State (1985).

13 *See* Robert G. Bone, *Rethinking the "Day in Court" Ideal and Nonparty Preclusion*, 67 N.Y.U. L. Rev. 193, 264–88 (1992).

14 *See, e.g.*, Martin H. Redish, Wholesale Justice: Constitutional Democracy and the Problem of the Class Action Lawsuit (2009).

15 Robert G. Bone, *Personal and Impersonal Litigative Forms: Reconceiving the History of Adjudicative Representation*, 70 B.U. L. Rev. 213, 264–84, 287–91 (1990).

16 Technically, the class action court cannot predetermine preclusive effects in future suits. 7AA Charles Alan Wright, Arthur R. Miller, & Mary Kay Kane, Federal Practice and Procedure § 1789 (3d ed. 2019). However, the class action was clearly designed to maximize the likelihood that judges in future cases will give preclusive effect to a class judgment.

17 Taylor v. Sturgell, 553 U.S. 880, 892–95 (2008).

To illustrate the consequences, consider the following mass tort hypothetical. Suppose a pharmaceutical company, Drug Inc., markets a new drug, Xyrex, to treat arthritis. Suppose there are roughly 50,000 Xyrex users nationally who have developed heart problems after taking the drug. These 50,000 users all have legal claims against Drug Inc. for damages, and their claims share common issues, such as whether Xyrex is capable of causing heart problems (which is relevant to general causation) and what and when Drug Inc. knew or should have known about the drug's side effects (which is relevant to a duty to warn and breach of that duty).

Without a class action, each of the 50,000 Xyrex users can litigate the same common issues in their own individual suits. As nonparties to earlier suits, plaintiffs in later suits would not be claim or issue precluded. Thus, if the first plaintiff to sue lost on the general causation and duty-related issues, the second plaintiff, as a nonparty to the first suit, could relitigate those same issues – and possibly win. And the same is true for the third plaintiff, the fourth, the fifth, and so on. Moreover, it doesn't matter how vigorously the first plaintiff litigated. In theory at least, the 50,000th plaintiff could relitigate the same issues even if the first 49,999 plaintiffs all fought hard but still lost. The impact on social costs is obvious.

1.4 SOCIAL BENEFITS OF THE CLASS ACTION

The following discussion examines five potential benefits of the class action: (1) promoting judicial economy; (2) avoiding serious externalities; (3) improving outcome accuracy by reducing litigation asymmetries; (4) enhancing remedial efficacy; and (5) enabling private enforcement of the substantive law.[18]

1.4.1 *Promoting Judicial Economy*

One of the most common arguments in favor of the class action is that it promotes judicial economy by saving the costs of repetitive litigation of common issues.[19] As the previous section explained, the class action does this by overcoming the legal obstacles to binding nonparty plaintiffs.

As sensible as this argument might seem, there is a serious problem with it. It assumes that plaintiffs will actually litigate common issues repeatedly if not prevented from doing so by the class action. In truth, this is extremely unlikely. If a string of early cases all result in plaintiff losses, it is highly improbable that later plaintiffs will sue – or more precisely, very unlikely that they will be able to find lawyers willing to take their cases. Alternatively, if the first few lawsuits generate enough pro-plaintiff decisions, the defendant Drug Inc. will settle the rest. Thus, only a few plaintiffs will actually litigate; most will refrain from suing or settle in light of the early results. To be sure, there could still be some relitigation, but this is not necessarily inefficient. A few suits litigating the same common issues can supply useful information about claim values that helps parties reach settlement in later cases.

Given this, it is not clear how much support judicial economy actually lends to the class action. But there are other benefits, and the rest of this section examines them.

[18] The discussion of social benefits and costs in Sections 1.4 and 1.5 draws, in part, on two of my previous publications: Robert G. Bone, Economics of Civil Procedure 259–98 (2003), and Robert G. Bone, *Class Action*, in Procedural Law and Economics 67–84 (C. W. Sanchirico, ed., 2d ed., 2012).

[19] 1 William B. Rubenstein, Newberg on Class Actions § 1:9 (5th ed. 2019). "Judicial economy" focuses on the litigation system and ignores broader efficiency effects. Thus, the class action might improve judicial economy and still be globally inefficient.

1.4.2 *Avoiding Externalities*

Suppose fifty individuals all have identical rights in a limited fund that is too small to satisfy all their claims. If they sue individually, the early filers might exhaust the fund, leaving later filers without any assets to satisfy their claims. The late filers can obtain judgments, of course, but their judgments would be worthless without assets to collect. One way to solve this problem is to force all fifty claimants into a class action and distribute the limited fund proportionately among them.[20] Thus, the class action solves an externalities problem: it prevents early filers from imposing external costs on later filers.[21]

In theory at least, this rationale extends beyond the classic limited fund to mass tort cases in which defendant's total expected liability exceeds its available assets.[22] Suppose that Drug Inc. in our hypothetical faces 50,000 suits and that each plaintiff has a 70% chance of proving liability and expects to recover $5 million if she prevails. Drug Inc.'s total expected liability is: 50,000 × 5 million × 0.7 = $175 billion. Suppose this is more than Drug Inc.'s insurance coverage and corporate assets. Under these circumstances, plaintiffs who file early will obtain full recovery and the rest will receive nothing at all. A class action facilitates a more equal distribution.

A more equal distribution is a benefit from a rights-based perspective, but it is not clear how much of a benefit it is from a law-and-economics perspective.[23] The prospect of paying huge damages should have the same deterrent effect regardless of how the aggregate amount is distributed. It is possible that the ex ante incentives of prospective plaintiffs to take care or purchase insurance would be affected by knowing that there is some probability they might receive nothing. But this is far from clear. In any case, if an equal or proportionate distribution is called for, the class action is a good way to achieve it.

1.4.3 *Improving Outcome Accuracy*

The limited fund rationale applies only in those special situations where a limited fund exists. Other rationales apply more generally. One of these focuses on the way that the class action can improve outcome accuracy by eliminating a structural bias associated with asymmetric litigation investment.[24]

The bias results from economy-of-scale advantages that benefit the defendant in mass litigation. As a repeat player facing multiple plaintiffs with related suits sharing common issues, a defendant can spread the cost of preparing the common issues over all the lawsuits. Because of this, the defendant will invest more than the plaintiff in preparing these issues. Assuming that the

20 One might wonder why a claimant would bring a class action if she expects to receive less than from an individual suit. Compulsory joinder rules can render individual litigation infeasible. Also, the plantiff might wish to share costs, or the attorney might prefer a class action and be able to file one if agency costs are high.

21 *See* 2 William B. Rubenstein, Newberg on Class Actions §§ 4:16–4:17 (5th ed. 2019). This is not the only type of externality that the class action addresses. Individual suits can impose inconsistent obligations on a defendant, and the class action avoids this result by preventing multiple suits. See *id.* §§ 4:5–4:8.

22 During the 1980s and 1990s, federal courts toyed with using the limited fund rationale to certify mass tort class actions under Rule 23(b)(1)(B) of the Federal Rules of Civil Procedure, but the Supreme Court effectively ended this practice in its 1999 *Ortiz v. Fibreboard* decision. Ortiz v. Fibreboard Corp., 527 U.S. 815 (1999); *see* 2 William B. Rubenstein, Newberg on Class Actions § 4:19 (5th ed. 2019) (discussing the availability of the limited fund class action after *Ortiz*).

23 It is easy to see why it is a benefit from a rights-based perspective. If each plaintiff has an identical legal right to compensation, an unequal distribution fails to show the same degree of concern and respect to all rightholders. The class action matches equality of right with equality of recovery.

24 See David Rosenberg & Kathryn E. Spier, *Incentives to Invest in Litigation and the Superiority of the Class Action*, 6 J. Legal Analysis 305, 347–48 (2014).

party who invests more is more likely to win, it follows that the defendant will prevail on common issues more often than plaintiffs – and more often than it should. Moreover, since settlement is negotiated in the shadow of trial, individual settlements will end up skewed in favor of the defendant as well. The class action, by aggregating claims on the plaintiffs' side, gives the class comparable scale economies and thus helps to even out litigation investment incentives across the party line.[25]

To see this point more clearly, let us return to the Drug Inc. hypothetical. Suppose P-1 sues Drug Inc. for damages from Xyrex. Drug Inc. must decide how much to invest in researching the legal issues, investigating the factual issues, hiring experts, and otherwise preparing general causation, breach of duty, and other issues in P-1's suit that will also arise in the other 49,999 suits. In making these investment decisions, Drug Inc. will take account of the fact that it can use the results to defend all 50,000 lawsuits. As a result, the private benefit of any dollar spent in defending the common issues in P-1's suit will be multiplied by 50,000 suits, and therefore Drug Inc. will invest much more than it would if P-1's suit were the only one. For P-1, however, her suit *is* the only one. It follows that Drug Inc. will invest much more in P-1's suit than P-1 will, and the resulting asymmetry biases the outcome in favor of the defendant Drug Inc.[26]

The class action mitigates these adverse effects. It does so by aggregating the claims of the 50,000 plaintiffs into a single lawsuit and giving the class attorney a stake in all of them. Since her fee depends on the size of the total recovery, the class attorney will invest an amount that reflects the total stakes, just as the defendant does. The asymmetry might not be completely eliminated since the class attorney takes only a fraction of the total while the defendant pays it all, but assuming declining marginal returns to litigation investment, it is quite likely that the class attorney's fraction will be large enough to induce investment at a sufficiently high level.[27]

1.4.4 *Enhancing Remedial Efficacy*

A class action can enhance remedial efficacy in cases where the plaintiffs seek complex injunctive relief and also in cases where the socially optimal outcome is a global settlement of damages claims.

[25] It is worth noting that there is another way in which the class action can improve outcome accuracy, especially in large-scale mass tort litigation. Experience teaches that in the absence of a class action, mass tort lawyers will assemble large inventories of clients and settle all the inventory claims *en masse* through an aggregate settlement. Because clients cannot adequately monitor their attorneys and because professional responsibility rules apply only weakly, these aggregate settlements give mass tort lawyers wide latitude to negotiate large fees for themselves and suboptimal recoveries for class members. A class action can improve on this individual-litigation baseline by enlisting the judge to monitor attorney performance and evaluate settlement adequacy. To be sure, judges face significant obstacles to doing this job well, but the result is still likely to be better than no effective supervision at all. On informal aggregation generally and large-scale collective representation outside of the class action setting, see Howard M. Erichson, *Informal Aggregation: Procedural and Ethical Implications of Coordination Among Counsel in Related Lawsuits*, 50 Duke L. J. 381, 386–401 (2000) (discussing the phenomenon of informal aggregation through coordination of multiple cases before a single attorney or coordination among multiple attorneys); Howard M. Erichson, *Beyond the Class Action: Lawyer Loyalty and Client Autonomy in Non-Class Collective Representation*, 2003 U. Chi. Legal F. 519, 524–25 (2003) (describing mass collective representation in litigation outside of the class action).

[26] This assumes that all the plaintiffs hire different lawyers so each lawyer must prepare anew. It also assumes that the various plaintiffs' lawyers do not cooperate to share information and strategies. Neither assumption completely holds true in the real world. *See* Howard M. Erichson, *Informal Aggregation: Procedural and Ethical Implications of Coordination Among Counsel in Related Lawsuits*, 50 Duke L. J. 381, 386–401 (2000).

[27] There are other sources of litigation investment asymmetry that case aggregation through the class action can help mitigate. *See generally* Robert G. Bone, *Preclusion*, in Procedural Law and Economics 350, 359–61 (C. W. Sanchirico. ed. 2012) (explaining how US preclusion rules can create investment asymmetries and skewed outcomes when suits are individually litigated).

1.4.4.1 Complex Injunctive Relief

A complex injunction orders reforms that effect major changes in a defendant's institutional structure. For example, a court might order structural changes to a firm's employment practices in order to root out employment discrimination at its source, or require extensive alterations to state prison conditions to prevent unconstitutional treatment.

The class action facilitates this type of remedy in several ways. It prevents inconsistent decrees, enables broad relief, and helps to avoid mootness problems.[28] If plaintiffs filed multiple suits, different judges might order different injunctions that conflict. Partly to avoid this result, judges sometimes limit – and are even required to limit – the scope of injunctions in individual suits, and this can frustrate the fashioning of effective relief. The class action solves these problems by aggregating all the potential suits into one proceeding, thereby avoiding inconsistent injunctions and making a broad structural remedy possible. The class action also mitigates the risk that changed circumstances will moot an individual suit. It does this by aggregating lots of plaintiffs, some whom are likely to have a live controversy and be willing to take over as class representatives.[29]

In addition, the class action makes it easier for a judge to invite informational input useful for crafting or evaluating, a complex remedy. In a class action, a court can arrange for notice to be sent to members of the class and invite their intervention in order to solicit their views. It is worth noting, however, that this benefit might not be as substantial as it was in the past. Today, Facebook, Twitter, websites, and other Internet media make it much easier to keep interested class members informed and give them opportunities to express their views and interact without having to intervene in the suit.[30]

Admittedly, the obstacles to remedial efficacy in individual suits are largely the law's own making. We could change the rules so that courts adjudicating individual suits can grant broad relief. We could also bar inconsistent decrees, permit continuing litigation despite mootness problems, and make it easy for judges to invite input from nonparties in individual suits. But as long as the law remains as it is – and there are good policy reasons for some of these restrictions[31] – the class action has advantages for crafting and implementing injunctive remedies.

1.4.4.2 Global Resolution of Damages Claims

Global settlements that resolve all present and future claims and fix the defendant's total liability can generate substantial efficiency benefits. These settlements take many different forms, but all involve a settlement fund and some kind of distribution mechanism. In particularly complex cases, the distribution mechanism can involve an administrative-type structure with someone in charge of reviewing proofs of claim and determining individual distributions.

To illustrate the efficiency benefits of a global settlement, consider our Xyrex hypothetical. In the absence of a global settlement binding all Xyrex users, including those who have not yet manifested compensable injury, Drug Inc. must deal with the uncertainty of future litigation.[32] To avoid this uncertainty, the company should be willing pay a "peace premium" for a global

[28] *See* 2 William B. Rubenstein, Newberg on Class Actions § 4:26 (5th ed. 2019).

[29] *See also* 1 William B. Rubenstein, Newberg on Class Actions § 2:17 (5th ed. 2019).

[30] *Cf.* Elizabeth J. Cabraser & Samuel Issacharoff, *The Participatory Class Action*, 92 N.Y.U. L. Rev. 846 (2017) (describing a "participatory class action" made possible, in part, by ease of communication over the Internet).

[31] Among other things, the judge is more likely to focus on the whole problem when everyone affected is involved in the case.

[32] At least until the statute of limitations expires on all the remaining claims.

settlement covering all present and future claims.[33] As a result, plaintiffs receive a larger aggregate recovery; Drug Inc. reduces its costs; and the judicial system avoids the process costs of future litigation.

Of course, global settlements are not always efficient. Designing and implementing such a settlement can add substantial process costs. Moreover, rational parties, who have no reason to consider public interests that are not also private interests, might agree to a settlement that makes them better off but sacrifices social goals.[34] Also, current claimants have incentives to capture most of the settlement for themselves, and in a world of high agency costs, attorneys can manipulate global settlements in ways that maximize their own fees and the payout to current clients at the expense of future claimants.[35]

Still, if a global settlement is efficient, a utilitarian approach favors using the class action to achieve it. Given the requirements of Rule 23 and the United States Supreme Court's interpretation of the Rule, it is not easy these days to use the class action for this purpose, at least in products liability cases like our Xyrex example. But a utilitarian approach supports a broader application than the Court's unduly restrictive rules allow.[36]

1.4.5 *Enabling Substantive Law Enforcement*

The discussion so far has assumed that rational plaintiffs file individual suits. This assumption does not always hold true. Sometimes the expected cost of litigating an individual suit exceeds the expected trial award. This can happen with personal injury claims that require very expensive scientific studies and costly expert testimony. But it is much more common in cases where the defendant's conduct causes small harms to many individuals. In these cases, each person's injury is too small to make an individual suit worthwhile even though the aggregate harm is very large.

To illustrate, suppose a company misrepresents the health benefits of its natural food product and thousands of consumers buy the product in reliance on the misrepresentation. None suffer any physical injury, but all pay more for the product than they should. Each has a state-created consumer fraud claim to recover damages, but no one has enough at stake to justify the sizable cost of hiring an attorney and litigating individually.

In these small claim cases, the class action makes litigation possible.[37] It does so by aggregating all the claims and linking the class attorney's fee to the total class recovery.[38] Indeed, the attorney

[33] *See* Samuel Issacharoff & D. Theodore Rave, *The BP Oil Spill Settlement and the Paradox of Public Litigation*, 74 La. L. Rev. 397, 413–16 (2014) (describing three potential benefits defendants obtain from global settlements, including economy of scale benefits, avoidance of adverse selection risks, and greater certainty about the scope of liability).

[34] For example, parties to a global settlement have no reason to consider all the social benefits from general deterrence since they capture only a small fraction of those benefits for themselves. So they might agree to a settlement that is too low relative to the social optimum for deterrence. For a discussion of the divergence between private interests and public interests in settlement generally, see Steven Shavell, *The Fundamental Divergence Between the Private and the Social Motive to Use the Legal System*, 26 J. Leg. Stud. 575 (1997).

[35] *But see* Elizabeth J. Cabraser & Samuel Issacharoff, *The Participatory Class Action*. 92 N.Y.U. L. Rev. 846, 865-67 (2017) (noting that active involvement of future claimants through the Internet and participation in websites affected the Third Circuit's willingness to approve the settlement class in *NFL Concussion Litigation*).

[36] There are other remedial advantages to a class action. For example, a class action might be necessary for an effective medical monitoring remedy. On (b)(2) class actions for medical monitoring, see Day v. NLO, Inc., 144 F.R.D. 330, 335–36 (S.D. Ohio 1992); 2 William B. Rubenstein, Newberg on Class Actions § 4:45 (5th ed. 2019).

[37] See Jonathan R. Macey & Geoffrey P. Miller, *The Plaintiffs' Attorney's Role in Class Action and Derivative Litigation: Economic Analysis and Recommendations for Reform*, 58 U. Chi. L. Rev. 1, 8-9 (1991).

[38] There is strong empirical support for the proposition that class action fee awards, no matter how they are calculated, increase with settlement amount, though at a declining rate. *See* Theodore Eisenberg, Geoffrey P. Miller, & Roy Germano, *Attorneys' Fees in Class Actions: 2009–2013*, 92 N.Y.U. L. Rev. 937, 946 (2017); Theodore Eisenberg & Geoffrey Miller, *Attorney Fees and Expenses in Class Action Settlements: 1993–2008*, 7

in these cases is functionally (though not legally) the real party in interest; she is the only one with a significant stake in the litigation and the only one with control over the suit as a practical matter.[39] Some cases, such as securities fraud class actions with large institutional investors, have class members with large claims as well as class members with small claims. While the institutional investors are likely to have enough at stake to pursue individual suits, the class action still makes litigation possible for the class members with small claims.

Obviously, these small claim class actions do not reduce litigation costs. They increase costs by making a lawsuit possible where none would otherwise exist. Nor does the class action solve externality problems or improve outcome accuracy compared to individual suits. Without a class action, there would be no individual suits, and thus no externalities and no asymmetric litigating incentives to worry about.

The reason for the class action in these cases is to enable private enforcement of the substantive law – through a trial judgment or, more likely, a class-wide settlement – and private enforcement is valuable from a utilitarian perspective for the enhanced deterrence it creates.[40] Without a class action, actors would be able to violate the substantive law without worrying about legal accountability to their victims, so long as they produced small harms to large numbers of geographically dispersed individuals.[41] To be sure, private enforcement also compensates injured class members, but compensation is not likely to be significant when class members suffer only very minor harms.[42]

Private enforcement is not the only way to achieve deterrence. Public enforcement is available as well. In consumer fraud and antitrust cases, the Federal Trade Commission (FTC) and state agencies can sue for injunctive relief and civil penalties. Moreover, in federal securities fraud cases, the Securities Exchange Commission has the power to sue. However, public enforcement has serious limitations; agencies must deal with budget constraints and are vulnerable to agency capture and political pressure. Thus, supplementing with private enforcement can be desirable.[43]

The optimal mix of public and private enforcement is difficult to determine, but it is not usually the judge's job to make such a determination. Often the legislature decides in advance by authorizing private enforcement alongside public enforcement in the statute that regulates the

J. EMPIRICAL LEG. STUD. 248 (2010); Brian T. Fitzpatrick, *An Empirical Study of Class Action Settlements and Their Fee Awards*, 7 J. EMPIRICAL LEG. STUD. 811 (2010).

39 Jonathan R. Macey & Geoffrey P. Miller, *The Plaintiffs' Attorney's Role in Class Action and Derivative Litigation: Economic Analysis and Recommendations for Reform*, 58 U. CHI. L. REV. 1, 5, 19–25 (1991). For example, suppose a class includes three million consumers of the product. Suppose that on average each consumer spent $100 on the product and suppose that $50 can be recovered in damages. Finally, suppose that the plaintiffs have a 60 percent chance of winning on liability. The expected value of the average claim is $0.6 \times 50 = \$30$. Thus, the aggregate expected value of the class action is 30×3 million = $90 million. Assuming that the class action settles for this expected value, an attorney who receives twenty percent as a fee award would earn $18 million, an amount likely to yield a very substantial profit after deducting expenses.

40 *See* Brian T. Fitzpatrick, *Do Class Action Lawyers Make Too Little?*, 158 U. PA. L. REV. 2043, 2067–69 (2010).

41 Small claims make individual suit impractical, and geographic dispersion creates transaction cost obstacles to groups of claimants organizing on a voluntary basis.

42 *See* Brian T. Fitzpatrick, *Do Class Action Lawyers Make Too Little?*, 158 U. PA. L. REV. 2043, 2067–69 (2010). In those class actions with a mix of large and small claims, such as securities fraud suits with institutional investors, those with large claims are likely to be interested in compensation. Still, it is not clear that even in these cases compensation provides a strong utilitarian reason for class treatment distinct from deterrence.

43 For a discussion of the role of private enforcement in a public regulatory scheme, see J. Maria Glover, *The Structural Role of Private Enforcement Mechanisms in Public Law*, 53 WM. & MARY L. REV. 1137 (2012). Also, it is worth noting that class actions sometimes follow on public enforcement actions. *See, e.g.*, Zachary D. Clopton, *Redundant Public-Private Enforcement*, 69 VAND. L. REV. 285, 296–97 (2016) (noting that "coattail class actions" are not uncommon in the antitrust and securities law fields).

targeted activity.[44] Under these circumstances, the judge must do the best she can to ensure that the legislature's intent is effectuated, and in cases involving small claims, this often calls for use of the class action.

At the same time, there are costs to using the class action for private enforcement, including the cost of over-deterring social desirable conduct. These costs are explored in the following section. Ultimately, the utilitarian case depends on whether the deterrence benefits of enlisting private enforcement as a supplement to public enforcement exceed the costs.

1.5 SOCIAL COSTS OF THE CLASS ACTION

The class action generates substantial costs of its own. This section discusses five of these costs: (1) process costs, (2) costs to individual participation, (3) agency costs, (4) adverse selection costs, and (5) costs associated with an increased risk of frivolous suits. In addition, some critics raise legitimacy objections. They argue that the class action can force courts to act in ways that are inconsistent with the proper exercise of adjudicative power. The following discussion briefly addresses each of these points in turn.

1.5.1 *Process Costs*

The process costs of class litigation are formidable. Parties battle over certification and judges expend substantial resources monitoring the litigation and reviewing settlements. To be sure, virtually all class actions settle; indeed, some even settle before a lawsuit is filed.[45] But class settlements are costly to negotiate, and judges must still engage in the burdensome process of deciding whether to certify the class and approve the settlement.

1.5.2 *Participation Costs*

The class action deprives absent class members of the opportunity to control their own lawsuits. This is a serious problem for someone who values the right to a personal day in court on dignitary grounds, but it is not likely to be a serious problem for someone with a utilitarian bent. To a utilitarian, individual control is valuable instrumentally, for its positive impact on outcome quality. Injured persons have strong incentives to investigate and litigate vigorously, so giving them control over their own lawsuits is likely to produce a more intensive vetting of the issues and therefore a more accurate outcome.

The class action in fact fares reasonably well by this outcome standard. The class attorney has strong incentives to investigate and litigate vigorously when her fee depends on the amount of class recovery. Admittedly, in a world of high agency costs, there is always a risk that the class attorney will collude with the defendant on a settlement that shortchanges the class, but attorneys shortchange their clients in individual litigation as well.

A utilitarian must also count any utility losses resulting from class members being denied the satisfaction of controlling their own suits. Obviously, this is a concern only for those class

44 Or courts might interpret the statute to allow private enforcement in order to effectuate the legislature's intent. It does not matter whether the statutory authorization is express or implied; either way, courts are obliged in future cases to implement the private enforcement option in the way that best serves the statutory purpose.

45 In these so-called "settlement class actions," the defendant and the prospective class attorney negotiate a settlement and then file suit. Upon filing, they move for class certification and judicial approval in order to bind all plaintiffs to the settlement terms.

members with large enough claims to support individual suits. And even in these cases, the magnitude of the utility loss depends on how much litigants care about controlling litigation for its own sake. Given that lawyers usually exercise the control, the answer is probably not much.

To be sure, there is strong empirical evidence showing that individuals are more satisfied with the outcome and the process when they have an opportunity to participate, especially when they have a chance to "tell their story" to the decision-maker.[46] But class members do get a chance to have their common story told through named plaintiffs and the class attorney, and if a class member feels strongly enough about telling her own individual story, she has a right to intervene in the class suit. Moreover, in federal class actions for monetary relief certified under Rule 23(b)(3), each class member has a right to opt out of the class and litigate on her own if she wishes.[47] While opt out does not work perfectly in practice, it still provides an opportunity for many of those who value litigant control to exercise that control. Finally, the Internet offers many opportunities for other kinds of participation.[48]

1.5.3 *Agency Costs*

Principal-agent problems arise when the class attorney conducts the litigation with an eye to promoting her own self-interest rather than the interests of the class. This is a particularly serious problem for class actions because of the large potential fee awards that make attorney self-dealing lucrative, as well as the lack of expertise and free-riding incentives that impede effective monitoring by class members. When self-interested attorneys have unencumbered control, they can collude with defendants on "sweetheart settlements" that minimize the defendant's payout, reward the class attorney with a large fee, and shortchange the class.[49] There are limits to this strategy; a settlement cannot be so deficient that its flaws are obvious to the trial judge. But this still leaves plenty of room for low-value settlements that undermine deterrence.

There are a number of ways to reduce this problem, although all produce costs of their own. For example, federal securities fraud class actions rely, in part, on institutional investors with large stakes to monitor class counsel.[50] For the most part, however, US class action law relies on the trial judge to ensure the adequacy of class counsel and check for attorney opportunism. There are problems with this approach. When a proposed settlement is presented to the court, both the class attorney and the defendant seek approval. Thus, there is no one with an incentive to bring attorney disloyalty to the judge's attention or contest the settlement's adequacy unless a class member intervenes to press objections. Moreover, even when objectors appear, a judge cannot be confident they have the best interests of the class in mind; their purpose might instead be to leverage a side

[46] *See, e.g.*, E. ALLAN LIND & TOM R. TYLER, THE SOCIAL PSYCHOLOGY OF PROCEDURAL JUSTICE (1988); JOHN THIBAUT & LAURENS WALKER, PROCEDURAL JUSTICE: A PSYCHOLOGICAL ANALYSIS (1975).

[47] Fed. R. Civ. P. 23(c)(2). Rule 23, however, does not confer an opt out right on class actions certified under 23(b)(1) and 23(b)(2).

[48] *See* Elizabeth J. Cabraser & Samuel Issacharoff, *The Participatory Class Action*. 92 N.Y.U. L. REV. 846, 856–60 (2017) (arguing that the combination of Internet technology and MDL practice has made the class action a much more participatory device).

[49] In addition, mass tort settlement class actions can involve reverse auction dynamics. *See* 4 WILLIAM B. RUBENSTEIN, NEWBERG ON CLASS ACTIONS § 13:60 (5th ed. 2019). In a reverse auction, the seller accepts the lowest rather than the highest bid, so bidders have incentives to underbid one another. In the mass tort setting, attorneys bid to be chosen by the defendant as the one to negotiate a global settlement on behalf of the class, and the defendant chooses the attorney who is willing to settle for the smallest amount. A good way to structure such a settlement from the attorney's perspective is to include a large fee and relatively little for the class.

[50] The judge solicits applications for the role of lead plaintiff and makes the selection based on a presumption in favor of the applicant who has the largest financial stake in the litigation. Once chosen, the lead plaintiff then selects class counsel. 15 U.S.C. § 77z-1(a)(3)(B) (2006). The hope is that the lead plaintiff will monitor the class counsel it has chosen.

payment. And it is not clear how seriously judges take objections in any event when settlement approval would remove a complex and costly piece of litigation from their dockets.[51]

From a deterrence perspective, sweetheart settlements are a problem when the settlement amount is substantially less than the expected value of the class claims. It does not matter who receives the settlement – the attorney or the class – so long as the defendant pays a sufficiently large amount.[52] The distribution of the settlement affects compensation, of course, but compensation matters from a utilitarian perspective only if it affects ex ante choices about victim precautions, insurance, and the like. These effects might be significant in large claim class actions, but they are not significant in class actions where the individual stakes are small.[53]

In sum, class attorneys have incentives to serve their own self-interest at the expense of the class. This is a problem if it results in suboptimal settlements that sacrifice deterrence or generates inefficient ex ante incentives on the plaintiff's side. There are procedural mechanisms that can help reduce these risks, but they operate imperfectly and add process costs of their own. The total costs – the social costs of agent disloyalty *plus* the costs of measures aimed at preventing disloyalty – must be balanced against the class action's benefits.

One additional point is worth mentioning. Any evaluation of agency costs in the class action setting should be comparative. This is important because the realistic alternatives to the class action also suffer from principal-agent problems. This is certainly true for individual litigation. Although plaintiffs have more potential control over their own attorneys in individual suits, they usually lack the information and expertise to exercise that control effectively.

Professional responsibility rules and malpractice suits impose some discipline, but their efficacy largely depends on client reporting and enforcement, which is limited by the same information and expertise deficiencies that undermine effective monitoring. In theory, the market for legal services might reward attorney loyalty, but the market works only if consumers are well informed about attorney reputations and sufficiently knowledgeable to be able to act on the information they possess.[54]

1.5.4 *Adverse Selection*

Since the defendant cannot distinguish weak from strong claims without discovery and maybe even trial, the class attorney has an incentive to pack the class with weak claims and insist on a larger settlement for the larger class. Although the defendant will anticipate this strategy and reduce its settlement offer accordingly, there is a limit to what the defendant can do given the informational asymmetry. In this way, the class action adversely selects for weak claims.[55]

[51] *See* Howard M. Erichson & Benjamin C. Zipursky, *Consent Versus Closure*, 96 CORNELL L. REV. 265, 291 (2011) (noting judicial incentives to approve mass settlements).

[52] *See* Brian T. Fitzpatrick, *Do Class Action Lawyers Make Too Little?*, 158 U. PA. L. REV. 2043 (2010). The distribution might be important to deterrence if it somehow affected the class attorney's litigation investment or settlement incentives. But it is not clear how this could occur.

[53] A rational risk-neutral individual makes choices ex ante based on expected value, which averages over high and low amounts. Thus, problems arise only when class members are risk-averse and the settlement amount is low relative to the aggregate value of the claims.

[54] Also, at least for mass torts, the agency costs associated with individual litigation can be quite high. This is so because mass tort attorneys denied access to the class action have strong incentives to assemble large inventories of clients and negotiate aggregate settlements that dispose of all their inventory claims *en masse*. These attorneys, free from judicial oversight, are arguably in a better position to negotiate sweetheart settlements.

[55] *See* John C. Coffee, Jr., *The Regulation of Entrepreneurial Litigation: Balancing Fairness and Efficiency in the Large Class Action*, 54 U. CHI. L. REV. 877, 906–07 (1987) (describing the adverse selection problem in large claim class actions).

As a result of this adverse selection, the defendant ends up paying more than it should under the substantive law, which can lead to over-deterrence. Moreover, the presence of weak cases dilutes the amount class members with strong cases receive if, as is typical, the class settlement is distributed on an average basis.[56] This skewed distribution does not affect deterrence, but it might affect ex ante precaution and insurance choices. More importantly, the prospect of receiving a significantly diminished recovery can lead class members who believe they have strong cases to opt out of the class, thereby undermining the utility of the class device.

1.5.5 *Frivolous Suits*

Many US judges and commentators criticize the class action for its potential to pressure settlements in frivolous suits.[57] They worry that a class suit so magnifies the stakes that it makes frivolous litigation attractive, thereby chilling socially desirable conduct.[58] While this is a controversial claim and hard to verify empirically, there are two reasons why it is plausible at least in theory.[59]

One reason is relatively straightforward and applies even when the defendant is risk-neutral. To illustrate, return to our Xyrex hypothetical involving 50,000 injured Xyrex users. Suppose that all 50,000 suits are meritless. Juries still make mistakes, of course, even in objectively meritless suits. So assume a 0.02 risk of jury error, and also assume that a jury awards $500,000 on average whenever it mistakenly finds liability. Under these circumstances, rational plaintiffs who know their suits lack merit will not file individually, at least if the defendant also knows that the suits are meritless.[60] The expected trial award in an individual suit is $10,000 (0.02 × 500,000 = $10,000), which is far less than the cost of litigating a typical mass tort suit.

The class action changes this result dramatically. With a 0.02 risk of jury error, the aggregate expected value of the class claims is: 0.02 × 500,000 × 50,000 = $500 million. With this much at stake, a rational attorney will file suit, anticipating a substantial fee award if the class action settles

56 Since class counsel without the benefit of trial will have difficulty sorting between weak and strong cases, any distribution must average in some way. As class size increases with the addition of weak claims, the amount of the settlement increases, but not necessarily enough to keep the average constant when the defendant anticipates the class attorney's strategy and responds by limiting the amount it is willing to add.

57 *See, e.g.*, In the Matter of Rhone-Poulenc Rorer, Inc., 51 F.3d 1293 (7th Cir. 1995). This complaint has been around almost since the beginning of the modern class action. *See* David Marcus, *The History of the Modern Class Action, Part I: Sturm und Drang, 1953–1980*, 90 WASH. U. L. REV. 587, 611–12 (2013) (describing attacks on the class action in the late 1960s and early 1970s).

58 The class action can chill socially desirable conduct in another way not linked to frivolous suits. Sometimes Congress or state legislatures enlist private parties to enforce a statutory duty by specifying a fixed amount of statutory damages to be awarded automatically without proof of compensable harm. If a class action is brought, the statutory damage amount is multiplied by the number of class members and the resulting liability can bankrupt a small company even when the violation is not very serious and causes no tangible harm. Hence, the pressure to settle for a substantial sum is likely to be intense, which can produce over-deterrence relative to what the legislature intended. *See, e.g.*, Parker v. Time Warner Entertainment Co., 331 F.3d 13 (2d Cir. 2003).

59 For a discussion, see Robert G. Bone & David S. Evans, *Class Certification and the Substantive Merits*, 51 DUKE L. J. 1251, 1296–302 (2002).

60 The assumption of symmetric information is important. For example, if the defendant does not know for sure whether the plaintiff's suit is meritless, the defendant might be willing to settle what is in fact a meritless suit for a substantial amount. *See* Avery Katz, *The Effect of Frivolous Lawsuits on the Settlement of Litigation*, 10 INT'L REV. L. & ECON. 3 (1990). Moreover, even when both sides know that the suit is meritless, there is still a theoretical possibility that plaintiffs will file and obtain nuisance settlements in small amounts. *See* David Rosenberg & Steven Shavell, *A Model in Which Suits Are Brought for Their Nuisance Value*, 5 INT'L REV. L. & ECON. 3 (1985). *But see* Robert G. Bone, *Modeling Frivolous Suits*, 145 U. PA. L. REV. 519, 537–41 (1997) (explaining why nuisance settlements are unlikely in cases with symmetric information about the merits).

or is successfully tried. And faced with a credible threat of suit, even a risk-neutral defendant might be willing to settle and for a substantial sum.[61]

The second way a class action might encourage frivolous suits is a bit more complicated to explain. Simply put, a class action can create a high-stakes gamble that pressures risk-averse defendants (or at least risk-averse employees) to settle rather than put the company at risk of crippling liability.[62] Consider our Xyrex hypothetical. Assuming all 50,000 suits are litigated individually, there are 50,000 possible outcomes. The defendant might win all 50,000 suits and pay nothing in damages, or it might lose one suit and win the other 49,999 and pay $500,000 in damages, or it might lose two suits and win 49,998 for a total payment of $1 million, and so on – all the way up to 50,000 losses and a total payment of $25 billion. The most likely result lies at the mean of the distribution, which is 49,000 wins (98 % of the suits) and 1000 losses (2 % of the suits), with the defendant paying a total of $500 million in damages. Moreover, the defendant can be reasonably confident of actually paying an amount fairly close to this $500 million figure.[63]

The risks increase markedly with a class action. If all 50,000 plaintiffs sue as a class, there are only two possible outcomes: either the defendant wins and pays nothing in damages, or the defendant loses and pays $25 billion dollars. The expected value is the same as it was for individual suits – $500 million – but the chance of actually having to pay the $25 billion or something close to it is much larger. Assuming the worst outcome would bankrupt the company and assuming risk-aversion is in play, the defendant might be willing to settle for a large amount rather than deal with the possibility of crippling liability – and this is so even if the defendant knows full well that all the individual claims are meritless.

Still, the notion that the class action invites frivolous suits is heavily contested. Some argue that settlement pressure is not nearly as severe in practice as it is often portrayed in theory.[64] There are also other procedures that reduce the risk, such as stricter pleading requirements, pre-certification summary judgment, and post-certification settlement review. This is not the place to delve into this debate. It is enough to note that a risk of frivolous suits, even if significant, does not warrant jettisoning the class action completely; given the class action's substantial benefits, it is probably better to reform the device to reduce the risks.

1.5.6 *Legitimacy*

Some critics attack the class action on legitimacy grounds. They argue that class actions are illegitimate when they alter the remedial scheme prescribed by the substantive law or otherwise sacrifice core values of adjudication. Examples include small claim class actions that aim at deterrence without providing meaningful compensation and class actions that produce global settlements without respecting core values of adversarial litigation.[65]

61 The discussion here and in the following two paragraphs simplifies the analysis by assuming that common issues are dispositive so all individual claims can be fully resolved in the class action.

62 *See, e.g.*, In the Matter of Rhone-Poulenc Rorer, Inc., 51 F.3d 1293, 1297–99 (7th Cir. 1995).

63 The variance of this win-loss distribution is 980 (i.e., 50,000 × 0.98 × 0.2), and the standard deviation is 31.3. This means that the defendant can expect to win close to 49,000 suits with a very high probability. In fact, the probability of losing 50,000 suits or any number close to that figure is vanishingly small. Specifically, the probability of the defendant's losing all 50,000 suits is $0.2^{50,000}$, which is virtually zero.

64 *See, e.g.*, Charles Silver, *We're Scared to Death: Class Certification and Blackmail*, 78 N.Y.U. L. Rev. 1357 (2003).

65 *See, e.g.*, Martin H. Redish, Wholesale Justice: Constitutional Democracy and the Problem of the Class Action Lawsuit (2009); Martin H. Redish, Peter Julian, & Samantha Zyontz, *Cy Pres Relief and the Pathologies of the Modern Class Action: A Normative and Empirical Analysis*, 62 Fla. L. Rev. 617, 649–51 (2010).

This critique is best understood as a claim about normative legitimacy.[66] The point is not that the class action *is perceived* as illegitimate, but rather that it *is* illegitimate because it does not fit what courts are supposed to do. As such, the argument needs an account of adjudicative legitimacy, which in turn must be based on a theory of civil adjudication that explains what courts are and are not supposed to do. Many of the critiques presuppose some kind of rights-based theory. This is not the place to explore the contours of such a theory, although it is worth noting that even a rights-based theory can accommodate liberal use of the class action.[67] This chapter focuses on utilitarian theories, and it is not at all clear that there is any legitimacy problem with the class action from a utilitarian perspective.

If a utilitarian theory of adjudication instructed judges to interpret and apply statutes and class action rules flexibly to serve utilitarian ends on a case-by-case basis, then global settlements and small-claim class actions might be justified as legitimate insofar as they maximize social welfare in particular cases, consistent with a liberal interpretation of relevant statutes and class action rules. But this is not the only possibility. A utilitarian theory instead might tightly constrain a judge's resort to utilitarianism even when the judge is confident that the cost-benefit balance justifies certifying a class action on the case-specific facts. Under this stricter view, a judge might have to work within a narrow, textually based reading of relevant statutes and rules and be unable to approve a global class settlement or certify a deterrence-focused small-claim class action unless the statute or rule clearly authorized it. Strict limits of this sort can make sense on utilitarian grounds if the long-term benefits of constraining judicial discretion exceed the short-term costs of denying class actions in cases where the case-specific utilitarian balance clearly justifies them.[68]

However, it is not obvious that strict limits on use of the class action can be justified in this way.[69] Rule-like constraints might make sense if litigation conditions were relatively uniform across cases, but conditions vary in ways that significantly affect the cost-benefit balance. Because of this, case-specific flexibility can reap substantial benefits.

Even so, the critique from legitimacy is a useful reminder that evaluating the class action is not just a matter of balancing case-specific benefits and costs. Even a utilitarian must engage the deeper question, whether the class action in general fits what courts are supposed to do in the broader institutional scheme.

1.6 APPLICATION TO CURRENT CLASS ACTION ISSUES

Over roughly the past two decades, federal courts have cut back on the availability of federal class actions, much to the dismay of class action proponents. Controversy rages over a host of issues. The following discussion briefly examines three of these issues from a utilitarian perspective: (1)

66 Perceived (or sociological) legitimacy focuses on what people believe. On this view, the class action is illegitimate if enough people believe it is illegitimate. But there simply no reason to suppose that broad segments of the general public care enough about the class action to formulate beliefs one way or another about its legitimacy.

67 A rights-based theory must take account of practical litigation impediments to rights enforcement, and the class action – including some uses of the class action that most trouble the critics – can be justified as a means of overcoming those impediments and properly enforcing rights. *See, e.g.*, Robert G. Bone, *In Defense of the Cy-Pres-Only Class Action*, 24 Lewis & Clark L. Rev. 571, 588–93 (2020).

68 This is an application of the familiar distinction between rule utilitarianism and act utilitarianism.

69 One might appeal to traditional practice as a constraint on what judges are allowed to do, but tradition has many dimensions and many interpretations. Moreover, arguments from tradition fail on their own terms without a convincing reason why courts should adhere to tradition when conditions have changed.

the choice between mandatory and opt-out class actions; (2) the availability of cy pres, and (3) the proper use of sampling.[70]

1.6.1 *Mandatory versus Opt-Out Classes*

In a mandatory class action, all class members are locked into the class and none can opt out. In an opt-out class action, all class members have a right to exit the class if they wish.[71] In US federal courts, there are two types of mandatory class actions and one type of opt-out class action.[72] However, some judges, including members of the US Supreme Court, have from time to time suggested that the US Constitution might require an opt-out right in all class actions for monetary relief, even those that qualify for mandatory treatment today.[73]

It is easy to see how an opt-out right might have value in a rights-based theory. If a class member has an opportunity to opt out, her choice to forego that opportunity and remain in the class can support an inference that she consents to the representational nexus, damage averaging, and other aspects of the class action that are otherwise difficult to square with a rights-based approach.[74] But opt out is much more difficult to justify in a utilitarian theory.

For one thing, opt out can scuttle the benefits of a class action. For example, if class members could opt out of a limited-fund class action, many might do so in an effort to get full satisfaction from the limited fund, and the result would reproduce the very problems that the class action was meant to solve. Moreover, if class members could opt out of a class action for complex injunctive relief, they might seek conflicting injunctions and scuttle the remedial benefits the class action was meant to create. Not surprisingly, Rule 23 makes a class action mandatory in both of these cases, a choice that makes abundant sense from a utilitarian point of view.[75]

[70] Others include the requisite degree of class-wide commonality; *see* Robert G. Bone, *The Misguided Search for Class Unity*, 82 GEO. WASH. L. REV. 651 (2014); the necessity of identifying individual class members; *see* Robert G. Bone, *Justifying Class Action Limits: Parsing the Debates over Ascertainability and Cy Pres*, 65 U. KAN. L. REV. 913 (2017); the need for each class member to have independent standing; *see* Theane Evangelis & Bradley J. Hamburger, *Article III Standing and Absent Class Members*, 64 EMORY L. J. 383, 387 (2014); the evidentiary burden for class certification; *see* Comcast Corp. v. Behrend, 569 U.S. 27 (2013); In re Hydrogen Peroxide Antitrust Litig., 552 F.3d 305 (3d Cir. 2008); the availability of settlement class actions; *see* Amchem Prods., Inc. v. Windsor, 521 U.S. 591 (1997); the propriety of issue classes; *see* McReynolds v. Merrill Lynch, Pierce, Fenner & Smith, Inc., 672 F.3d 482 (7th Cir. 2012); the enforceability of class waivers in arbitration; *see* AT&T Mobility LLC v. Concepcion, 563 U.S. 333 (2011); American Express Corp. v. Italian Colors Rest., 570 U.S. 228 (2013) – and more.

[71] A third possibility is an opt-in class. Under the opt-in model, no one benefits or is bound unless she affirmatively chooses to be a class member. The Fair Labor Standards Act uses an opt-in model. *See* Fair Labor Standards Act, 29 U.S.C. § 216 (2012); Genesis HealthCare Corp. v. Symczyk, 569 U.S. 66 (2013). Moreover, a few commentators have argued in favor of opt-in for some class action cases. *See, e.g.*, John Bronsteen, *Class Action Settlements: An Opt-In Proposal*, 2005 U. ILL. L. REV. 903 (proposing opt-in for class actions that settle, but not for class actions that are litigated to final judgment); Scott Dodson, *An Opt-In Option for Class Actions*, 115 MICH. L. REV. 171 (2016) (proposing that the class should be allowed to choose between opt-out and opt-in). I do not analyze opt-in class actions here, but it is worth noting that they are not easy to defend on utilitarian grounds.

[72] Rule 23 defines the different types. The two mandatory class actions are created by 23(b)(1) and 23(b)(2), and the opt-out class is created by 23(b)(3).

[73] *See, e.g.*, Wal-Mart Stores, Inc. v. Dukes, 564 U.S. 338, 363 (2011).

[74] In fact, however, inferring consent from a failure to opt out is more problematic than it might seem. *See* Robert G. Bone, *The Puzzling Idea of Adjudicative Representation: Lessons for Aggregate Litigation and Class Actions*, 79 GEO. WASH. L. REV. 577, 593 (2011).

[75] Fed. R. Civ. P. 23(b)(1) and 23(b)(2).

In addition, opt out fits small-claim damages class actions very poorly.[76] It requires expenditures on notice to inform class members of their opt-out rights without producing meaningful social benefits when class members have too little at stake to bother opting out. The utilitarian case for opt out is somewhat stronger for large-claim class actions and also for class actions with a mix of small and large claims. As long as there are only a few class members who want to opt out, extending an opt-out right preserves much of the benefit of the class action while also satisfying idiosyncratic preferences for individual control. However, the fraction of class members preferring opt out must be quite small or the class action can unravel.[77] Moreover, in class actions with a mix of small and large claims, there is a benefit to keeping the large claim holders in the class to monitor the class attorney.[78]

An opt-out right can produce signaling benefits.[79] When many class members opt out, it signals the judge that there might be problems with the class action. However, this signaling benefit is diluted by the noisiness of the signal. Attorneys sometimes opt their clients out for strategic reasons that have nothing to do with class action problems. The attorney, for example, might be after a larger fee from individual litigation or might perceive an advantage in threatening opt out to leverage a larger share of the class action fee. If genuine opt outs were readily distinguishable from strategic opt outs, the opt-out right could be an effective signaling device. But distinguishing genuine from strategic opt out is bound to be very difficult.

Thus, a utilitarian approach most likely justifies mandatory classes in many more cases than the current law allows.[80] In any event, this brief discussion is enough to raise serious questions about the desirability of opt out in a wide range of class actions.

1.6.2 *Cy Pres*

One of the more controversial issues today is the use of cy pres to distribute class recovery.[81] The cy pres doctrine has been around for decades. It allows a court to distribute all or part of a class settlement or judgment to a charity when it is not practically feasible or desirable to distribute to class members who otherwise would receive it.[82] In some cases, each class

76 The drafters of the 1966 Rule 23 revision did not follow a utilitarian approach when they chose an opt-out right for 23 (b)(3) damages class actions. They were primarily motivated by rights-based concerns about binding class members on the basis of adequate representation alone.

77 An opt-out right endangers one of the most important benefits of the class action – improving outcome accuracy by reducing litigation asymmetry. As more class members opt out, the expected class recovery declines and with it the expected fee award. A class attorney expecting a lower fee will invest less in the class action. To be sure, class members might choose to remain in the class in order to reap the benefits of a more even playing field, but given the averaging effects, those with high-value claims might do better on their own. In that case, the class action is likely to unravel at the high end, reducing the class attorney's incentives to invest.

78 Indeed, the selection of lead plaintiffs in private securities class action litigation aims to enlist institutional investors in the task of monitoring class counsel (*see* Section 1.5.3).

79 To be sure, it also allows class members with high-value claims to escape the averaging effects of the class action, but this is much more important for a rights-based than for a utilitarian theory, especially if opt out risks unraveling the class action.

80 *See* David Rosenberg, *Mandatory-Litigation Class Action: The Only Option for Mass Tort Cases*, 115 Harv. L. Rev. 831, 847–53, 861–66 (2002).

81 The discussion in this section draws on my previously published work on cy pres in class actions: Robert G. Bone, *Justifying Class Action Limits: Parsing the Debates Over Ascertainability and Cy Pres*, 65 U. Kansas L. Rev. 914, 944–47 (2017); and Robert G. Bone, *In Defense of the Cy-Pres-Only Class Action*, 24 Lewis & Clark L. Rev. 571 (2020).

82 *See* Rhonda Wasserman, *Cy Pres in Class Action Settlements*, 88 S. Cal. L. Rev. 97, 114–18 (2014). Cy pres is short for "cy pres comme possible," which means as "as near as possible." *Id.* at 114. The doctrine traces its origin to equity and charitable testamentary trusts.

member's share of the aggregate settlement is too small to cover the administrative costs of distribution.[83] In other cases, few class members bother to claim their small shares, leaving a large portion of the fund undistributed. In both situations, the court faces the same problem: how to dispose of the undistributed funds. The cy pres doctrine gives a simple solution: distribute the funds to a charity engaged in activities that indirectly benefit the class.[84]

Critics raise a number of objections to cy pres that on close inspection are unpersuasive. For example, some worry that cy pres weakens a class attorney's incentives to maximize class recovery.[85] But it is not clear why this would occur. As long as the fee is proportional to class recovery, the attorney's incentives should not be affected by the distribution. A class attorney might shortchange the class, but this risk exists with or without cy pres.

Many critics also worry that cy pres gives too much discretion to judges and attorneys to pick their favorite charities. But if this is a serious problem – which is questionable – the solution is not to bar cy pres.[86] One need only forbid the selection of a charity with which the judge or the attorneys have an existing or past relationship.

Some critics complain that any undistributed funds belong to the class and thus cy pres misappropriates class property.[87] However, a class is not an entity that can own anything, and when a class action settles, class members have property rights only insofar as the settlement agreement provides and therefore must live with a cy pres distribution if the agreement includes one.

Most critics focus on the fact that cy pres compensates third parties who have suffered no injury and have no legal claims at stake. It is not clear exactly why this is so troubling. Insofar as deterrence is concerned, all that matters is how much the defendant pays, not who receives the payment. However, the criticism has greater force if it is understood to be an objection to courts promoting deterrence without providing substantial compensation to rightholders. The idea is that courts must focus on providing compensation when the substantive law gives class members formal legal rights to compensation.

Understood this way, the objection is about the legitimacy of courts promoting substantive policies at the expense of substantive legal rights. But it is not at all clear that this objection is tenable within a utilitarian theory. Suppose a legislature adopts a statute creating an individual right to compensation for harm and does so primarily to promote deterrence through cost internalization. If it is clear from the outset of a lawsuit that individual claims are too small to justify distributing the proceeds of an aggregate settlement or judgment to class members, a judge unable to rely on cy pres might have no choice but to deny certification of a small-claim class action, even when doing so scuttles enforcement of the substantive law and thus frustrates the legislature's deterrence goal.

It is hard to imagine how a utilitarian could accept such a result. More generally, it is difficult to see how aggregate welfare could be improved by limiting courts to such a narrow approach when doing so leaves rightholders without any relief and shortchanges the policies the

83 *See, e.g.*, In Re Google Referrer Header Privacy Litig., 869 F.3d 737 (9th Cir. 2017), *rev'd on other grds.* Frank v. Gaos, 139 S.Ct. 1041 (2019); Lane v. Facebook, Inc., 696 F.3d 811 (9th Cir. 2012), *cert. denied* Marek v. Lane, 571 U.S. 1003 (2013).

84 Rhonda Wasserman, *Cy Pres in Class Action Settlements*, 88 S. CAL. L. REV. 97, 102–05, 117 (2014) (noting that "litigants and courts have enthusiastically latched onto cy pres as a potential solution to the problem of unclaimed class action settlement funds").

85 Robert G. Bone, *Justifying Class Action Limits: Parsing the Debates Over Ascertainability and Cy Pres*, 65 U. KANSAS L. REV. 914, 944–47 (2017).

86 *Id.* at 947–48.

87 *Id.* at 948–51.

substantive law was meant to serve. Although a utilitarian need not accept all uses of cy pres,[88] it is implausible that she would bar a cy pres distribution of leftover settlement funds when the lawsuit involves a statutory claim and the legislature's purpose was to enlist private enforcement to serve deterrence goals.

1.6.3 *Sampling*

One advantage of the class action is that it facilitates the use of statistical methods to adjudicate large-scale aggregations.[89] With all the claims before the court, the judge can select a random sample, try each sampled case, and extrapolate the results to the rest of the class. One straightforward way to do this is to average the sample verdicts and give each class member the sample average.[90] The parties can litigate the reliability of the sampling methodology and the method of extrapolation, but as long as the sampling is statistically sound and the extrapolation is properly done, the average of the sample verdicts binds everyone.[91]

This might seem a radical way to adjudicate class action claims, and some Supreme Court Justices have caricatured it as "Trial by Formula."[92] But a few lower courts have used it even when the class claims implicate significant individual liability and damages issues.[93] Moreover, the Supreme Court itself has allowed sample averaging in a limited way where it furthered the remedial policies underlying the substantive law.[94]

There is reason to worry about sampling from a rights-based perspective since plaintiffs with high-value claims receive only an average recovery and plaintiffs not selected for the sample are denied the opportunity to litigate their own suits. However, as a policy matter, sampling fits rather comfortably within a utilitarian framework. The social benefits can be substantial. Sampling allows a court to adjudicate both common and individual issues together in the class action, rather than leave the individual issues for individual suits after the common questions have been determined. This is especially useful when the amounts at stake are too small to justify litigating individual issues separately[95] or the number of separate suits is unmanageably large.[96] The class action might end in a settlement, obviating the need to actually

[88] The most troubling use is the cy-pres-only distribution, which gives the entire settlement to the cy pres beneficiary and nothing at all to the class. *See, e.g.*, In Re Google Referrer Header Privacy Litig., 869 F.3d 737 (9th Cir. 2017), *rev'd on other grds*. Frank v. Gaos, 139 S.Ct. 1041 (2019); Robert G. Bone, *In Defense of the Cy-Pres-Only Class Action*, 24 Lewis & Clark L. Rev. 571 (2020). However, a utilitarian should have no objection to this device in appropriate circumstances.

[89] For more extensive analyses of the use of statistical methods to adjudicate, see Robert G. Bone, *Statistical Adjudication: Rights, Justice, and Utility in a World of Process Scarcity*, 46 Vand. L. Rev. 561 (1993); Robert G. Bone, A *Normative Evaluation of Actuarial Litigation*, 18 Conn. Ins. L.J. 227 (2011); and Robert G. Bone, Tyson Foods *and the Future of Statistical Adjudication*, 95 N. C. L. Rev. 607 (2017).

[90] This can be done either by assigning the sample average to each class member individually, or by entering a judgment for aggregate class damages calculated by multiplying the sample average by the total number of class members. Ordinarily there is not much difference between these two options. In the end, an award of aggregate class damages must be distributed, and giving each class member the sample average is a sensible way to do it.

[91] If the court worries about bypassing the jury in the non-sampled cases, it can submit the sample data to a jury and leave it to the jury to determine the extrapolated results after hearing evidence and argument. *See* Hilao v. Estate of Marcos, 103 F.3d 767 (9th Cir. 1996).

[92] Wal-Mart Stores, Inc. v. Dukes, 564 U.S. 338, 367 (2011).

[93] *See, e.g.*, Hilao v. Estate of Marcos, 103 F.3d 767, 782–84 (9th Cir. 1996).

[94] *See* Tyson Foods, Inc. v. Bouaphakeo, 136 S. Ct. 1036 (2016); Robert G. Bone, Tyson Foods *and the Future of Statistical Adjudication*, 95 N. C. L. Rev. 607 (2017).

[95] *See, e.g.*, Tyson Foods, Inc. v. Bouaphakeo, 136 S. Ct. 1036 (2016).

[96] *See, e.g.*, Hilao v. Estate of Marcos, 103 F.3d 767 (9th Cir. 1996).

litigate the individual issues, but any settlement will be affected by the feasibility of litigating individual issues separately.

Moreover, as long as the methodology is statistically sound, sampling does not sacrifice deterrence. Deterrence depends on aggregate class damages and aggregate damages calculated using a sample average should be a very good approximation of true damages for the class as a whole.[97] To be sure, class members obtain an average recovery, so high-end plaintiffs receive less than the value of their claims and low-end plaintiffs receive more.[98] But this affects only risk-averse individuals, and they can often manage the risk-bearing costs by purchasing insurance. Moreover, in many cases, the cost of the insurance should roughly equal the average amount awarded by sampling.[99] Thus, assuming a carefully designed sampling protocol, there should be little objection to sampling on utilitarian grounds.[100]

There is one important qualification to this analysis. As was true for cy pres above, the utilitarian case for sampling assumes that it is legitimate for a court to design procedure with an eye to promoting deterrence policies even when doing so produces outcomes that deviate from substantive rights. As we saw above, this is a contestable assumption and defending it requires a theory of adjudication, which is well beyond the scope of this chapter. However, assuming a utilitarian theory permits direct resort to substantive policies under some circumstances – which is very likely – sampling makes sense in many class action scenarios.

1.7 CONCLUSION

This chapter has outlined a framework for evaluating the class action on normative grounds. It argued that the most common defense of the class action, that it saves duplicative litigation costs, is actually quite weak in a system with settlement, but that other benefits are stronger, including mitigating costly externalities, enhancing remedial efficacy, improving outcome accuracy, and enabling private enforcement of the substantive law. The class action also adds costs, including management and litigation costs, agency costs, adverse selection costs, and costs associated with frivolous suits. And for some critics, the device raises serious questions of legitimacy.

Evaluating these benefits and costs, as well as legitimacy concerns, requires a normative theory, and different normative theories have different implications. This chapter focused on one such theory, the law-and-economics version of utilitarianism, and showed that the class action fares quite well under this theory. Indeed, some of the most controversial aspects of the class action today – including the certification of mandatory classes and the use of cy pres and sampling – are fairly easy to defend from a utilitarian perspective.

97 The reason for this has to do with the statistical properties of a sample average compared to the population average. *See* Robert G. Bone, *Statistical Adjudication: Rights, Justice, and Utility in a World of Process Scarcity*, 46 VAND. L. REV. 561, 578–79 (1993).

98 And the difference between the average and the true value of the claim can be reduced even further by using stratified sampling techniques. *See* Robert G. Bone, *Statistical Adjudication: Rights, Justice, and Utility in a World of Process Scarcity*, 46 VAND. L. REV. 561, 583–84 (1993).

99 *See* David Rosenberg, *Class Actions for Mass Torts: Doing Individualized Justice by Collective Means*, 62 IND. L. J. 561, 591–93 (1987). And those who are risk-neutral should not be affected by the distribution, since they make ex ante choices based on expected value and expected value averages over the highs and lows.

100 The design of the sampling protocol can affect litigation investment incentives and settlement. Robert G. Bone, *Statistical Adjudication: Rights, Justice, and Utility in a World of Process Scarcity*, 46 VAND. L. REV. 561, 587–94 (1993); Robert G. Bone, A *Normative Evaluation of Actuarial Litigation*, 18 CONN. INS. L.J. 227 (2011). Design variables include such things as who should pay for the costs of litigating the sample cases – the sample plaintiffs or the entire class – and whether to give sample plaintiffs their actual verdicts or the sample average.

One thing is clear. Whatever normative theory one applies – be it utilitarian, rights-based, or some other approach – it is crucial to evaluate the class action in a rigorous and balanced way. This may seem obvious, but it is all too often forgotten in the midst of the highly polarized and politically charged debates that are commonplace today. The future of the class action depends on it, and so too does a fair and efficient system of civil adjudication.

2

Civil Rights, Access to Counsel, and Injunctive Class Actions in the United States

Maureen Carroll

2.1 INTRODUCTION

According to a familiar story about class actions in the United States, aggregation promotes access to counsel by increasing the amount of money from which counsel fees can be taken.[1] Courts usually award class counsel a percentage of the monetary recovery obtained on behalf of the class,[2] and class treatment can turn a $30 case into a $3 million case. But what about class actions that do not involve monetary relief at all?

Some civil rights plaintiffs seek to stop a violation, rather than to obtain compensation for past harm, and therefore choose to pursue only an injunction or declaratory judgment. Other civil rights plaintiffs have no choice but to pursue only injunctive or declaratory relief, for reasons ranging from statutory constraints to immunity doctrines.[3] Unlike in aggregated-damages cases, class treatment in injunction-only cases does not have a multiplicative effect that makes the litigation more lucrative – and thus more attractive – from a law firm's perspective.[4] Indeed, one might expect that the prospect of class certification would *decrease* access to counsel in such cases, because federally funded legal aid organizations are prohibited from working on class actions.[5]

1 The United States Supreme Court has referred to this access-promoting effect as "[t]he policy at the very core of the class action mechanism." Amchem Prod., Inc. v. Windsor, 521 U.S. 591, 617 (1997) (quoting Mace v. Van Ru Credit Corp., 109 F.3d 338, 344 (7th Cir. 1997)).

2 *See infra* Section 2.3.

3 *See, e.g.*, Harlow v. Fitzgerald, 457 U.S. 800 (1982) (holding that that qualified immunity limits a plaintiff's ability to recover monetary damages from government officials); Edelman v. Jordan, 415 U.S. 651 (1974) (holding that the Eleventh Amendment limits a plaintiff's ability to recover monetary relief from state defendants); Samuel R. Bagenstos, *The Perversity of Limited Civil Rights Remedies: The Case of "Abusive" ADA Litigation*, 54 UCLA L. Rev. 1, 2 (2006) (noting that the public accommodations title of the Americans with Disabilities Act of 1990 does not authorize private plaintiffs to seek damages).

4 Class treatment might increase the remedial cost to the defendant in an injunction-only case, but it might not. *See* Maureen Carroll, *Class Action Myopia*, 65 Duke L.J. 843, 866–68 (2016). In any event, the counsel fee in an injunction-only case will not generally increase in proportion to the defendant's remedial cost. *See infra* Section 2.3.

5 *See* 45 C.F.R. § 1617.3 (prohibiting recipients of federal Legal Services Corporation funding from "initiating or participating in any class action"); *see also* Velazquez v. Legal Servs. Corp., 164 F.3d 757 (2d Cir. 1999), *aff'd*, 531 U.S. 533 (2001) (rejecting statutory and constitutional challenges to this restriction). This restriction applies at the entity level, such that any legal organization that receives LSC funding cannot work on a class action even if it uses non-LSC funds to do so. An LSC-funded organization can coordinate its activities with an affiliate that does work on class actions (or engages in other restricted activities), but only if it maintains legal, physical, and financial separation from any such affiliate. *See* 45 C.F.R. § 1610.7. As a result, "[i]n many states, justice planners have had to set up two, duplicative legal aid systems in order to ensure that state and other funds are not constrained by the non-LSC funds

This chapter will explore the relationship between class treatment and access to counsel in injunction-only civil rights cases. It will demonstrate that class certification does promote access to counsel in such cases, but through a different set of mechanisms than those at play when a plaintiff class seeks monetary relief. Broadly speaking, while aggregated-damages class actions can attract counsel through the prospect of money-making,[6] injunction-only class actions can attract counsel through the prospect of resource-leveraging.[7]

Through its effects on areas ranging from justiciability to remedial scope, the injunctive class action offers a resource-constrained legal organization the prospect of broadening its impact without a commensurate increase in spending. Accordingly, class treatment can both increase the attractiveness of taking on the representation and expand the group of claimants served by the representation that takes place.

2.2 A BRIEF HISTORY OF RULE 23

This section provides an overview of the federal class action rule, from its initial adoption several decades ago to the role it plays in aggregate litigation today. Scholars have traced the roots of the American class action back to medieval times.[8] For a briefer history, the year 1934 provides a useful entry point.

2.2.1 *The Federal Rules of Civil Procedure*

In 1934, Congress gave the United States Supreme Court "the power to prescribe general rules of practice and procedure" for cases heard in the federal court system.[9] The Court, in turn, appointed an Advisory Committee of attorneys and academics responsible for drafting those procedures (and, subsequently, for amending them as needed).[10]

The Advisory Committee's initial work resulted in the adoption, in 1938, of a single set of procedural rules to govern civil lawsuits in federal district courts.[11] The Federal Rules of Civil Procedure remain in place today, though they have been amended multiple times. The Federal Rules do not directly apply to the independent court systems run by each state, but over time, most states have adopted procedural rules modeled after them.[12]

restriction." Rebekah Diller & Emily Savner, *Restoring Legal Aid for the Poor: A Call to End Draconian and Wasteful Restrictions*, 36 FORDHAM URB. L.J. 687, 689 (2009).

6 *See infra* Section 2.3. 7 *See infra* Section 2.4.

8 *See generally* STEPHEN C. YEAZELL, FROM MEDIEVAL GROUP LITIGATION TO THE MODERN CLASS ACTION (1987); Robert G. Bone, *Personal and Impersonal Litigative Forms: Reconceiving the History of Adjudicative Representation*, 70 B.U. L. REV. 213 (1990).

9 *See* 28 U.S.C. § 2072(a) ("The Supreme Court shall have the power to prescribe general rules of practice and procedure and rules of evidence for cases in the United States district courts (including proceedings before magistrate judges thereof) and courts of appeals.").

10 *See* Brooke D. Coleman, *#SoWhiteMale: Federal Civil Rulemaking*, 113 NW. U. L. REV. 407, 411–12 (2018). Currently, "there are more judges and fewer academics on the Committee, flipping the original composition of solely practitioners and professors." *Id.* at 412.

11 *See* Fed. R. Civ. P. 1 (stating that, with limited exceptions, "[t]hese rules govern the procedure in all civil actions and proceedings in the United States district courts").

12 *See* John B. Oakley & Arthur F. Coon, *The Federal Rules in State Courts: A Survey of State Court Systems of Civil Procedure*, 61 WASH. L. REV. 1367, 1369 (1986) (noting "the pervasive influence of the Federal Rules on at least some part of every state's civil procedure"). *But see* John B. Oakley, *A Fresh Look at the Federal Rules in State Courts*, 3 NEV. L.J. 354, 355 (2003) ("Not only has the trend toward state conformity to the federal rules stopped accelerating – it has substantially reversed itself.").

Rule 23 of the Federal Rules of Civil Procedure governs class actions, setting forth conditions under which one or more members of a class can sue or be sued "on behalf of all."[13] In the original version of the rule, class certification required that "the right sought to be enforced for or against the class" must fit into one of three categories.[14] The binding effect of the judgment depended on which of those three categories applied: in "true" and "hybrid" class actions the judgment bound the entire class, while in "spurious" class actions it bound only the named parties (including intervenors).[15]

Courts and litigants struggled to understand the "obscure and uncertain" terminology in the 1938 version of the rule.[16] In addition, some objected to the "one-way" intervention prevalent in spurious class actions, in which courts essentially allowed claimants to wait for a decision on the merits before deciding whether they would join the class.[17] The rule was widely understood to be a failed effort, eventually prompting the Advisory Committee to consider significant reforms.[18]

2.2.2 *The 1966 Amendments*

Rule 23 took on its modern structure through an extensive set of amendments that went into effect in 1966.[19] Under the modern version of the rule, each class action must satisfy a set of four prerequisites: numerosity,[20] commonality,[21] typicality,[22] and adequacy of representation.[23] Each class action must also fall into one of four categories, which are set forth in Rule 23(b).[24]

The modern version of Rule 23 is transsubstantive, meaning that it is "written to apply broadly regardless of the nature of the underlying substantive claim."[25] At the same time, the drafters of the 1966 amendments intended for the rule to facilitate effective remedies in civil rights litigation.[26] That intent found expression in Rule 23(b)(2), which applies when "the party

[13] Fed. R. Civ. P. 23(a).

[14] Specifically, the 1938 version of the rule required the right to be

(1) joint, or common, or secondary in the sense that the owner of a primary right refuses to enforce that right and a member of the class thereby becomes entitled to enforce it;
(2) several, and the object of the action is the adjudication of claims which do or may affect specific property involved in the action; or
(3) several, and there is a common question of law or fact affecting the several rights and common relief is sought.

Fed. R. Civ. P. 23(a) (1938).

[15] Fed. R. Civ. P. 23 – Advisory Committee Note to 1966 Amendments. [16] *Id.*

[17] *See* Benjamin Kaplan, *Continuing Work of the Civil Committee: 1966 Amendments of the Federal Rules of Civil Procedure*, 81 HARV. L. REV. 356, 385 (1967).

[18] *See* David Marcus, *The History of the Modern Class Action, Part I: Sturm Und Drang, 1953–1980*, 90 WASH. U.L. REV. 587, 600–01 (2013).

[19] *See* Maureen Carroll, *Class Action Myopia*, 65 DUKE L.J. 843, 852 (2016); David Marcus, *The History of the Modern Class Action, Part I: Sturm Und Drang, 1953–1980*, 90 WASH. U.L. REV. 587, 588 (2013).

[20] Fed. R. Civ. P. 23(a)(1) ("the class is so numerous that joinder of all members is impracticable").

[21] Fed. R. Civ. P. 23(a)(2) ("there are questions of law or fact common to the class").

[22] Fed. R. Civ. P. 23(a)(3) ("the claims or defenses of the representative parties are typical of the claims or defenses of the class").

[23] Fed. R. Civ. P. 23(a)(4) ("the representative parties will fairly and adequately protect the interests of the class").

[24] Two of these categories are discussed *infra* notes 26–32 and accompanying text. The others, which appear in Rule 23(b)(1)(A) and (B), apply in a much narrower set of situations and are seldom used. *See generally* Robert H. Klonoff, *Class Actions for Monetary Relief Under Rule 23(b)(1)(A) and (b)(1)(B): Does Due Process Require Notice and Opt-Out Rights?*, 82 GEO. WASH. L. REV. 798 (2014) (discussing the history and scope of these provisions).

[25] Robert G. Bone, *Walking the Class Action Maze: Toward A More Functional Rule 23*, 46 U. MICH. J.L. REFORM 1097, 1123 (2013).

[26] *See* David Marcus, *Flawed but Noble: Desegregation Litigation and Its Implications for the Modern Class Action*, 63 FLA. L. REV. 657, 702–08 (2011); *see also infra* Section 2.4.

opposing the class has acted or refused to act on grounds that apply generally to the class, so that final injunctive relief or corresponding declaratory relief is appropriate respecting the class as a whole."[27] In the notes it published alongside the 1966 amendments, the Advisory Committee wrote that "[i]llustrative" of situations falling under Rule 23(b)(2) were "various actions in the civil-rights field where a party is charged with discriminating unlawfully against a class."[28]

Rule 23(b)(2) thus had its genesis in an existing (if recent) type of aggregate litigation. By contrast, Rule 23(b)(3) was "a new category deliberately created," as its principal author described it.[29] Rule 23(b)(3) applies when "questions of law or fact common to class members predominate over any questions affecting only individual members" (the predominance requirement), and "a class action is superior to other available methods for fairly and efficiently adjudicating the controversy" (the superiority requirement).[30] Although the text of Rule 23(b)(3) does not refer to the remedies that class members may seek, its primary purpose and effect is to allow the aggregation of claims for monetary relief.

Regardless of which category of Rule 23(b) applies, the judgment in a certified class action binds every member of the class, regardless of the outcome.[31] Moreover, everyone who falls within the class definition is a member of the class by default; opting in is not required. Members of classes certified under Rule 23(b)(3), however, must be given the chance to opt out.[32]

2.2.3 *Modern Class-Action Practice*

Hundreds of putative class actions are filed in the federal courts each month.[33] Due in part to the financial incentives at play,[34] a large majority of these cases involve aggregated-damages class actions.[35] Indeed, when most people in the United States think of class actions, claims for monetary relief are surely the ones that come to mind.[36]

Injunction-only class actions, however, continue to be certified, and they continue to play an important role in civil rights litigation. For example, federal courts have recently certified injunction-only class actions in cases involving family separation at the border,[37] the education of children with disabilities,[38] the health and safety of children in foster care,[39] medical care for incarcerated persons,[40] and the reproductive rights of immigrant detainees,[41] to name just a few.

27 Fed. R. Civ. P. 23(b)(2). With regard to the phrase "corresponding declaratory relief," the Advisory Committee explained that "[d]eclaratory relief 'corresponds' to injunctive relief when as a practical matter it affords injunctive relief or serves as a basis for later injunctive relief." Fed. R. Civ. P. 23 – Advisory Committee Note to 1966 Amendments.

28 Fed. R. Civ. P. 23 – Advisory Committee Note to 1966 Amendments.

29 Benjamin Kaplan, *Continuing Work of the Civil Committee: 1966 Amendments of the Federal Rules of Civil Procedure*, 81 HARV. L. REV. 356, 399 (1967).

30 Fed. R. Civ. P. 23(b)(3).

31 *See* Fed. R. Civ. P. 23 – Advisory Committee Notes to 1966 Amendments ("all class actions maintained to the end as such will result in judgments including those whom the court finds to be members of the class, whether or not the judgment is favorable to the class").

32 Fed. R. Civ. P. 23(c)(2)(B). The rule does not require courts to afford members of other categories of class actions the chance to opt out. Fed. R. Civ. P. 23(c)(2)(A).

33 *See* Emery G. Lee III & Thomas E. Willging, *The Impact of the Class Action Fairness Act on the Federal Courts: An Empirical Analysis of Filings and Removals*, 156 U. PA. L. REV. 1723, 1751 (2008). Nearly all class actions involve the aggregation of plaintiffs, rather than defendants. Thomas E. Willging, Laural L. Hooper, & Robert J. Niemic, *An Empirical Analysis of Rule 23 to Address the Rulemaking Challenges*, 71 N.Y.U. L. REV. 74, 119–20 (1996).

34 *See infra* Section 2.3.

35 *See* Maureen Carroll, *Class Action Myopia*, 65 DUKE L.J. 843, 849 & n.27 (2016).

36 *Cf. id.* at 870 (characterizing modern debates about class actions).

37 *See* Ms. L. v. U.S Immigration & Customs Enf't, 330 F.R.D. 284 (S.D. Cal. 2019).

38 DL v. D.C., 860 F.3d 713 (D.C. Cir. 2017).

39 B.K. v. Snyder, 922 F.3d 957 (9th Cir. 2019).

40 Braggs v. Dunn, 317 F.R.D. 634 (M.D. Ala. 2016).

41 J.D. v. Azar, 925 F.3d 1291 (D.C. Cir. 2019).

2.3 AGGREGATION AND MONEY-MAKING

This section discusses the relationship between class treatment and counsel profit. In particular, it explains why aggregated-damages class actions can often harness law firms' profit motives in ways that injunction-only class actions cannot.

Two things bear noting at the outset. First, federal courts in the United States follow the American Rule, which creates a default expectation that every litigant will pay for its own counsel fees.[42] Second, a class lacks the capacity to enter into a fee agreement with class counsel. A class is merely a group of persons whose claims share certain characteristics; it has no internal governance or decision-making structure.[43] Accordingly, although individual class members can make binding commitments without judicial involvement or review, the class as a whole cannot. Instead, the court must determine whether and how much class counsel will be paid.[44]

2.3.1 *Common-Fund Awards*

The common-fund doctrine provides that "a litigant or a lawyer who recovers a common fund for the benefit of persons other than himself or his client is entitled to a reasonable attorney's fee from the fund as a whole."[45] As the Supreme Court has explained, this equitable doctrine "rests on the perception that persons who obtain the benefit of a lawsuit without contributing to its cost are unjustly enriched at the successful litigant's expense."[46]

Although the doctrine predates the modern class action, most common-fund cases now involve the compensation of class counsel.[47] The common-fund doctrine translates neatly to the context of class actions for monetary relief; if a court were to permit absent class members to keep the entirety of a fund recovered on their behalf, they would be unjustly enriched at class counsel's expense.[48]

In aggregated-damages class actions, courts usually grant class counsel a percentage of the monetary relief as a common-fund award.[49] In injunction-only class actions, however, there is no monetary recovery from which to take payment – no "fund" from which to take a common-fund award. Because the common-fund doctrine does not apply, it cannot create a financial incentive for a law firm to seek class treatment in an injunction-only case.

2.3.2 *Fee-Shifting Awards*

By congressional design, the enforcement of public law in the United States is heavily dependent on private litigation. For example, individuals file roughly 15,000 employment discrimination lawsuits every year, while the relevant agency files only a few hundred.[50] This reliance on private

42 By contrast, "in most Western legal systems other than the United States, the prevailing norm is the English rule, which provides that the losing party must pay the winner's reasonable fees." Theodore Eisenberg & Geoffrey P. Miller, *The English Versus the American Rule on Attorney Fees: An Empirical Study of Public Company Contracts*, 98 CORNELL L. REV. 327, 329 (2013).

43 *See generally* Samuel Issacharoff, *The Governance Problem in Aggregate Litigation*, 81 FORDHAM L. REV. 3165 (2013).

44 *See* Fed. R. Civ. P. 23(h) (setting forth procedures by which "the court may award reasonable attorney's fees and nontaxable costs that are authorized by law or by the parties' agreement").

45 Boeing Co. v. Van Gemert, 444 U.S. 472, 478 (1980). 46 *Id.*

47 WILLIAM B. RUBENSTEIN, 5 NEWBERG ON CLASS ACTIONS § 15:53 (5th ed. 2019).

48 *See* Charles Silver, *A Restitutionary Theory of Attorneys' Fees in Class Actions*, 76 CORNELL L. REV. 656, 713 (1991).

49 *See* Brian T. Fitzpatrick, *An Empirical Study of Class Action Settlements and Their Fee Awards*, 7 J. EMPIRICAL LEGAL STUD. 811, 832 (2010); Theodore Eisenberg & Geoffrey P. Miller, *Attorney Fees and Expenses in Class Action Settlements: 1993–2008*, 7 J. EMPIRICAL LEGAL STUD. 248, 267–68 (2010).

50 *See* David Freeman Engstrom, *Agencies As Litigation Gatekeepers*, 123 YALE L.J. 616, 689 & n.242 (2013).

litigants, rather than government officials, untethers enforcement activity from the constraints imposed by agency budgets and presidential priorities.[51]

Due to the important role they play in the overall enforcement regime, plaintiffs who sue to enforce civil rights laws are sometimes called "private attorneys general."[52] Many claimants cannot afford to pay their attorneys out of pocket, however, and the contingent percentage fee – like the common-fund doctrine – can facilitate representation only in cases that involve monetary relief.

Claims for injunctive or declaratory relief can thus fall into a gap in the market for legal services, and because many civil rights plaintiffs seek only injunctive or declaratory relief,[53] this market gap has the potential to stymie civil rights enforcement. In an effort to prevent that result, Congress has enacted a set of fee-shifting statutes, which allow a prevailing plaintiff to recover a reasonable attorney's fee from the defendant in specified types of cases.[54]

Even in those specified cases, however, fee-shifting statutes do not create a financial incentive for counsel to bring injunction-only class actions. Consider a case seeking an injunction against a state statute. If the lawsuit causes the state to repeal the statute before a court has enjoined its enforcement, the plaintiffs will usually not be deemed eligible for a court-ordered fee.[55] This type of "strategic capitulation" can deprive counsel of fees in both class and nonclass actions.[56]

Alternatively, consider a case in which the defendant offers to provide all of the injunctive relief requested, but only if the plaintiffs will waive their entitlement to a fee-shifting award.[57] This type of "sacrifice offer" can occur in either a class or a nonclass action,[58] but in a nonclass case, retainer agreements and client choices can blunt its impact or lead to its rejection.[59] In a class action, however, retainer agreements do not bind the class, and class counsel must decide whether to accept or reject a settlement offer on the absent class members' behalf.[60] Class counsel might deem themselves obligated to accept a sacrifice offer, and as a result, they might receive no compensation for their work on the case.[61]

When courts do issue statutory fee-shifting awards, the amounts are structurally under-compensatory in both class and nonclass cases. Fee-shifting awards are not based on the number of individuals whose rights were vindicated.[62] Instead, courts calculate fee-shifting awards using the lodestar method, which multiplies each attorney's reasonable hourly rate by the number of hours the attorney reasonably spent on the litigation.[63] Although courts will order a fee shift only

[51] *See generally* SEAN FARHANG, THE LITIGATION STATE (2010).

[52] *See, e.g.*, Newman v. Piggie Park Enterprises, Inc., 390 U.S. 400, 402 (1968) ("If [a civil rights plaintiff] obtains an injunction, he does so not for himself alone but also as a 'private attorney general,' vindicating a policy that Congress considered of the highest priority.").

[53] *See supra* note 3 and accompanying text.

[54] *See, e.g.*, 42 U.S.C. § 1988 ("In any action or proceeding to enforce a provision of . . . title VI of the Civil Rights Act of 1964 . . . the court, in its discretion, may allow the prevailing party . . . a reasonable attorney's fee as part of the costs").

[55] *See* Buckhannon Bd. & Care Home, Inc. v. W. Va. Dep't of Health & Human Res., 532 U.S. 598 (2001); *see also* Maureen Carroll, *Fee-Shifting Statutes and Compensation for Risk*, 95 INDIANA L.J. 1021, 1030 nn. 54-56 (2020) (discussing caveats and exceptions).

[56] Catherine R. Albiston & Laura Beth Nielsen, *The Procedural Attack on Civil Rights: The Empirical Reality of Buckhannon for the Private Attorney General*, 54 UCLA L. REV. 1087, 1091 (2007).

[57] *See* Evans v. Jeff D., 475 U.S. 717 (1986).

[58] *See* David Luban, Taking Out the Adversary: The Assault on Progressive Public-Interest Lawyers, 91 CAL. L. REV. 209, 241 (2003).

[59] *See* Maureen Carroll, *Fee-Shifting Statutes and Compensation for Risk*, 95 INDIANA L.J. 1021, 1030 (2020).

[60] After class counsel makes this initial decision, the court must review the settlement to ensure that it is "fair, reasonable, and adequate" as to any class members who would be bound by it. *See* Fed. R. Civ. P. 23(e)(2).

[61] This sequence of events occurred in Evans v. Jeff D., 475 U.S. 717 (1986).

[62] *See* Maureen Carroll, *Aggregation for Me, but Not for Thee: The Rise of Common Claims in Non-Class Litigation*, 36 CARDOZO L. REV. 2017, 2073–74 & n.324 (2015).

[63] *See* Hensley v. Eckerhart, 461 U.S. 424 (1983).

if the plaintiff prevails, and the lodestar uses noncontingent hourly rates, courts will not adjust the lodestar amount to reflect the counsel's risk of nonpayment.[64]

Class treatment does not fundamentally alter the under-compensatory effects of denying compensation for risk.[65] On the one hand, seeking class certification will usually require class counsel to do additional work (as compared to a single, nonclass case), which will drive up the hours-worked component of the lodestar. On the other hand, the absence of risk enhancement means that, rather than devoting time to seeking class certification in a fee-shifting case, a profit-motivated attorney would do better to spend that time on a case paid via hourly billing.[66]

2.4 AGGREGATION AND RESOURCE-LEVERAGING

Under the compensation systems discussed above, a law firm will not usually have a profit motive to seek class treatment in an injunction-only case.[67] Moreover, a nonprofit law firm that receives federal legal aid funding *cannot* bring a class action, regardless of the type of relief sought.[68] Why, then, would any law firm bring a class action on behalf of plaintiffs seeking only injunctive relief?

A significant number of law firms in the United States exist to serve their vision of the public interest,[69] rather than to make a profit, and the bulk of these firms do not receive federal legal aid funding.[70] Instead, these public interest law organizations (PILOs) rely on private grants and contributions, among other funding sources.[71] Money is perpetually in short supply, and despite paying dramatically below-market salaries and taking other steps to keep costs down, a PILO generally cannot afford to take on all of the cases that would further its organizational mission.[72] As this section explains, a class action offers this type of firm the potential for preserving and amplifying the effects of the resources it expends on a particular case.

2.4.1 *Effective Remedies*

Class treatment can allow a PILO to make better use of its limited resources by helping to make any resulting injunctive relief more effective. In particular, class certification helps to ensure that

64 *See* City of Burlington v. Dague, 505 U.S. 557 (1992).

65 An important qualification relates to post-decree monitoring fees, for which noncontingent hourly rates are reasonable rather than structurally under- compensatory, because the plaintiffs' fee eligibility has already been established. *See* Maureen Carroll, *Fee-Shifting Statutes and Compensation for Risk*, 95 INDIANA L.J. 1021, 1063 (2020). To the extent that class treatment facilitates post-decree monitoring fees, fee-shifting statutes can provide a firm with a financial incentive to seek class certification in an injunction-only case that it is otherwise inclined to pursue.

66 This choice would be the rational one because the expected value of each hour spent on a fee-shifting case, which must be discounted for the risk of ineligibility for fees, is less than the expected value of a billable hour, which will be billed to the client regardless of the outcome.

67 Presumably, if a deep-pocketed client requested that an injunction-only case be brought as a class action and agreed to pay for the attorneys' work on behalf of the class, a rational, profit-motivated law firm would be inclined to accept. It is unlikely, however, that law firms receive many such requests.

68 *See supra* note 5 and accompanying text.

69 *See* Laura Beth Nielsen & Catherine R. Albiston, *The Organization of Public Interest Practice: 1975–2004*, 84 N. C. L. REV. 1591, 1605–06 (2006) (estimating that "there were a little over 1,000 PILOs [public interest law organizations] operating in the United States in 2000"). Though significant in absolute numbers, the more than 1,000 PILOs represent only a small slice of the U.S. market for legal services, which contains more than 15,000 private law firms that employ five or more lawyers each. *See* George P. Baker & Rachel Parkin, *The Changing Structure of the Legal Services Industry and the Careers of Lawyers*, 84 N.C. L. REV. 1635, 1650 fig. 2a (2006).

70 In a recent study, only 25 percent of a random sample of nonprofit public interest law firms received federal legal aid funding. Catherine R. Albiston & Laura Beth Nielsen, *Funding the Cause: How Public Interest Law Organizations Fund Their Activities and Why It Matters for Social Change*, 39 LAW & SOC. INQUIRY 62, 78 (2014).

71 *Id.* at 76.

72 *See* Deborah L. Rhode, *Public Interest Law: The Movement at Midlife*, 60 STAN. L. REV. 2027, 2053–62 (2008).

the remedy will address not merely the injuries suffered by a few affected individuals, but the underlying violation itself.

2.4.1.1 Curing an Injury versus Curing the Violation

Class treatment has particular value when there is a gap between the remedy needed to cure an individual's injury and the remedy needed to cure the defendant's violation. Consider, for example, the racial segregation of K-12 (i.e., elementary and secondary) public schools. On the one hand, the Supreme Court has held that a formerly segregated school district has "the affirmative duty to take whatever steps might be necessary to convert to a unitary system in which racial discrimination would be eliminated root and branch."[73] As this language makes clear, the remedy for such a violation is a broad one. On the other hand, the Supreme Court has also held that an injunction "must . . . be limited to the inadequacy that produced the injury in fact that the plaintiff has established."[74] In a nonclass case, depending on the specifics of the plaintiff's injury and the evidence presented, the remedy that flows from this principle might be a narrow one.[75]

This gap had consequences for the desegregation litigation of the 1950s and 1960s. After students in nonclass cases proved that their school district engaged in large-scale racial discrimination, some courts would issue an injunction that required only particular school assignments for the particular plaintiff students.[76] That type of remedy would leave the underlying violation essentially intact; certainly, it would fall short of the command to eliminate racial discrimination "root and branch."[77] From the perspective of a public interest law organization making case selection decisions, this potential for an essentially meaningless remedy would make a nonclass desegregation lawsuit a questionable use of its resources.[78]

This possibility – that the injunction available to an individual plaintiff will not address the root cause of that plaintiff's injury – is not specific to desegregation lawsuits. Consider a nonclass case seeking to enjoin the National Security Agency's metadata program, under which the NSA "indiscriminately collect[ed] the telephone call records of millions of Americans."[79] Two plaintiffs successfully challenged the program, obtaining a preliminary injunction against it. That relief, however, required only that the NSA stop collecting the data from those two claimants' telephone accounts; it allowed the data collection to continue for millions of others.[80] A public interest law organization might not be eager to invest a substantial amount of its limited resources in order to obtain such a meager result.

By matching the identity of the plaintiffs to the extent of the defendant's violation, an injunction-only class action can close this gap between individualized and comprehensive remedies. Indeed, the drafters of Rule 23(b)(2) had this gap firmly in mind, and they perceived

73 Green v. Cty. Sch. Bd. of New Kent Cty., Va., 391 U.S. 430, 437–38 (1968).

74 Lewis v. Casey, 518 U.S. 343, 357 (1996); *see also* Califano v. Yamasaki, 442 U.S. 682, 702 (1979) ("[T]he scope of injunctive relief is dictated by the extent of the violation established.").

75 *See* Maureen Carroll, *Class Actions, Indivisibility, and Rule 23(b)(2)*, 99 B.U. L. Rev. 59, 79 (2019).

76 David Marcus, *Flawed but Noble: Desegregation Litigation and Its Implications for the Modern Class Action*, 63 Fla. L. Rev. 657, 680 (2011).

77 *See id.* at 680.

78 *Cf.* Maureen Carroll, *Class Action Myopia*, 65 Duke L.J. 843, 859 (2016) (noting that this remedial approach "could result in integration only after multiple lawsuits and great expense"). From the perspective of the student, this remedy might be unattractive as well. *See* David Marcus, *Flawed but Noble: Desegregation Litigation and Its Implications for the Modern Class Action*, 63 Fla. L. Rev. 657, 680 n.134 (2011) ("[I]f successful, a plaintiff would find him- or herself the sole black student in an all-white school – hardly a pleasant prospect for the student").

79 Klayman v. Obama, 142 F. Supp. 3d 172, 176 (D.D.C. 2015).

80 *Id.* at 198.

a serious need for the class action rule to address it.[81] In recent years, courts have become more comfortable with issuing injunctions that extend beyond the plaintiff in a nonclass case.[82] Courts and scholars have questioned that remedial approach,[83] however, and it can be difficult to predict whether a court will issue a broad injunction in any particular nonclass case.[84] From the perspective of a public interest law organization, a class action can thus offer a better value proposition than a nonclass case – or series of nonclass cases – that might leave the violation unchecked even after the plaintiffs prevail.

2.4.1.2 Providing Net Benefits versus Shifting the Harm

Beyond leaving a violation unchecked, a nonclass case might end up making things worse, at least from other claimants' point of view. As explained below, class treatment can help to assure a public interest law organization that an injunction-only case will produce net benefits, as opposed to merely redistributing the harm among fewer members of the affected group.

The potential absence of a net benefit is of particular concern in litigation against underfunded public institutions or agencies. Consider, for example, a recent lawsuit against the US Department of Veterans Affairs (VA), which provides health care and other benefits for military veterans. The plaintiffs sought an injunction compelling the VA to reduce the lengthy delays that now characterize certain stages of its benefit determinations.[85] If a nonclass claim of this type were to succeed, the most straightforward way to reduce the delay facing the individual claimant would be to move her to the front of the queue. That "line-jumping" relief would speed things up for that individual, but it would slow things down for everyone who had been in line ahead of her.[86] A public interest law organization might not want to put its limited resources toward obtaining that result. By contrast, a class-wide remedy could address the root cause of the delays, benefiting all of the affected veterans at once.[87]

Class treatment facilitates injunctive relief that reduces rather than reallocates harm in other types of litigation as well. Consider, for example, recent litigation seeking to improve mental health services in Alabama prisons.[88] There, the district court determined that it would be "impossible to grant any meaningful relief on this claim without granting it on a class-wide basis."[89] The court reasoned that an order granting relief only to a single prisoner "would rob Peter to pay Paul; the court would be playing a zero-sum game, shifting mental-health care

81 *See* David Marcus, *Flawed but Noble: Desegregation Litigation and Its Implications for the Modern Class Action*, 63 FLA. L. REV. 657, 700–01 (2011).

82 *See* Samuel L. Bray, *Multiple Chancellors: Reforming the National Injunction*, 131 HARV. L. REV. 417, 418 (2017) (discussing this trend). These injunctions may be motivated, at least in part, by the remedial gap discussed in the text. *See, e.g.*, City of Chicago v. Sessions, No. 17 C 5720, 2017 WL 4572208, at *3 (N.D. Ill. Oct. 13, 2017) (refusing to stay the nationwide aspect of a preliminary injunction in a nonclass case because doing so would "allow the Attorney General to impose what this Court has ruled are likely unconstitutional conditions across a number of jurisdictions").

83 *See* Maureen Carroll, *Class Actions, Indivisibility, and Rule 23(b)(2)*, 99 B.U. L. REV. 59, 105 n.263 (2019) (collecting decisions and commentary critical of injunctions that extend beyond the plaintiff).

84 *See* Maureen Carroll, *Aggregation for Me, but Not for Thee: The Rise of Common Claims in Non-Class Litigation*, 36 CARDOZO L. REV. 2017, 2034 (2015) (discussing district courts' de facto discretion over this aspect of remedial scope).

85 Godsey v. Wilkie, No. 17–4361, 2019 WL 2462344 (Vet. App. June 13, 2019). Specifically, veterans face "a multiyear wait before [a VA regional office] even looks at an appealed case to determine whether further development and/or adjudication is warranted before certifying and transferring a case to the Board [of Veteran's Appeals]." *Id.* at *12.

86 *See id.* at *13 (noting the "undesirable consequence of line-jumping associated with individual petitions alleging delay").

87 *Id.* at *10 ("[P]etitions alleging systemic delay are 'best addressed in the class-action context, where the court could consider class-wide relief that would inure to all similarly situated claimants.") (quoting Ebanks v. Shulkin, 877 F.3d 1037, 1039–40 (Fed. Cir. 2017)).

88 Braggs v. Dunn, 317 F.R.D. 634 (M.D. Ala. 2016). 89 *Id.* at 668.

resources from one prisoner to another."[90] By contrast, a class-wide injunction could expand the resources available to the prisoners as a group – for example, by requiring the prison to hire additional psychiatrists.[91] By facilitating systemic relief, class treatment can make this type of case more attractive to a public interest law organization at the outset, and it can expand the group of people served by the litigation when it concludes.

2.4.2 *Merits Decisions*

Sometimes, a public interest law organization will bring a lawsuit for purposes of generating binding legal precedent on a particular issue.[92] Even when that is not the case, a firm operating in the "private attorney general" model will generally not want a case to be dismissed before it can be adjudicated or settled. Unless post-filing events have made clear that any decision on the merits would be unfavorable, such a firm would likely view a non-merits dismissal (and the resulting absence of any resolution or relief) as a waste of the resources it has invested in the litigation.

Class treatment can help to prevent that waste of resources, especially in injunction-only cases. Consider dismissals for lack of justiciability. In order for a federal court to have the power to decide a case, "an actual controversy must be extant at all stages of review, not merely at the time the complaint is filed."[93] In particular, if the plaintiff seeks to enjoin particular conduct by the defendant, she must show that she personally faces the threat of injury from that conduct – not merely that the conduct harmed her in the past, nor even that it continues to harm or threaten harm to others.[94]

Class certification changes the mootness analysis, shifting the focus from the named plaintiff (as an individual) to the plaintiff class (as a group). A named plaintiff must generally have a live claim at the time of certification, but once the class has been certified, the class representative can continue to litigate on behalf of the class even if her personal claim becomes moot.[95] At that point, the plaintiffs can avoid a dismissal for mootness so long other members of the class have live claims for injunctive relief.[96] Consider a plaintiff who files a nonclass case alleging that her employer has an unlawful employment policy. If she leaves her job while the case is still pending, she cannot continue to seek an injunction against the policy.[97] Instead, because her now-former employer's policy no longer threatens to harm her, her claim for injunctive relief will be dismissed as moot.[98] If that same plaintiff obtains class certification, however, she can continue to seek a class-wide injunction against the challenged policy even if she later changes jobs.[99]

90 *Id.* Moreover, the court doubted that a truly individual remedy could be crafted at all: "Although the court could order, for example, that a particular prisoner who currently requires psychiatric care be seen by a psychiatrist, it cannot order that adequate staffing be provided to the extent necessary to address any one particular prisoner's mental-health care needs as they develop in the future." *Id.*

91 *Id.*

92 *Cf.* Pamela S. Karlan, *Disarming the Private Attorney General*, 2003 U. ILL. L. REV. 183, 201 (2003) ("The creation of binding precedents is a beneficial byproduct of litigation A private attorney general whose activities produce precedent is thus in some important ways more effective than a private attorney general whose activities produce only local change.").

93 Preiser v. Newkirk, 422 U.S. 395, 401 (1975).

94 *See* City of Los Angeles v. Lyons, 461 U.S. 95, 101–02, 109 (1983).

95 *See* Sosna v. Iowa, 419 U.S. 393, 402 & n.11 (1975).

96 *Id.* at 402. If the class representative's claim has become moot, the court might revisit the question whether she will adequately represent the class. *See, e.g.*, DL v. D.C., 860 F.3d 713, 726 (D.C. Cir. 2017).

97 *See* Arizonans for Official English v. Arizona, 520 U.S. 43, 72 (1997).

98 *Id.*

99 *Cf. id.* (emphasizing that the plaintiff did not sue on behalf of a class).

Different plaintiffs will react differently to the mooting of their individual claims. For example, someone who brings a case for purely self-interested reasons might not especially care whether others remain subject to a policy that no longer affects her. Presumably, however, a public interest law organization (and any client who made it through the PILO's screening process) would be very concerned about the policy remaining in effect.[100] Class treatment allows the PILO to continue the fight, building on the resources it has already invested instead of having to start over.

Mootness is an omnipresent concern in nonclass cases, but it looms especially large for PILOs that represent certain types of plaintiffs, such as public school students or incarcerated persons.[101] A student might graduate or move to a different school district, or a defendant might release or transfer an incarcerated person to a different facility, before the litigation ends. In these types of cases, using class certification as a bulwark against mootness is not so much desirable as critical.[102]

Class treatment can help a PILO to avoid other barriers to merits decisions as well. For example, the Individuals with Disabilities Education Act (IDEA) requires a claimant to exhaust her administrative remedies before bringing her claim to court.[103] An IDEA claimant's failure to exhaust normally results in dismissal of the case. If the claimant alleges "systemic" violations of the IDEA, however, some courts will allow the litigation to continue in spite of the failure to exhaust.[104] Although some courts have applied this exception in nonclass cases,[105] others have treated it as a "class action exception," applicable to class plaintiffs only.[106]

Consider a PILO that becomes aware of a widespread, systemic IDEA violation. If the exception described above is unavailable, the PILO will be able to seek relief only on behalf of those who have exhausted their administrative remedies with respect to the violation. It might find that none of the potential claimants have done so, or that those who have done so represent a mere fraction of those affected. Moreover, the PILO might lack the resources to shepherd the affected individuals through the administrative process. By contrast, in courts that recognize this exception, class treatment can enable the PILO to represent every member of the affected group, even without undertaking individualized, resource-intensive representation of multiple claimants in administrative proceedings.

100 In the context of standing to seek injunctive relief, the Supreme Court has assumed that a plaintiff categorically lacks a "personal stake in the outcome" if she is no longer subject to the conduct she seeks to enjoin. *See, e.g.*, City of Los Angeles v. Lyons, 461 U.S. 95, 101 (1983). That assumption strikes me as incorrect. Under the doctrine as it currently stands, however, class treatment offers a second-best approach to the "personal stake" problem that *Lyons* and cases like it have addressed.

101 Maureen Carroll, *Aggregation for Me, but Not for Thee: The Rise of Common Claims in Non-Class Litigation*, 36 CARDOZO L. REV. 2017, 2037 (2015).

102 *See id.* at 2037–38. Still, such cases will not uniformly suffer mootness dismissals in the absence of class treatment, especially if brought on behalf of an organizational plaintiff or multiple individuals. *See id.*

103 *See* 20 U.S.C. §§ 1415(i)(2)(A), 1415(l).

104 *See* Doe v. Arizona Dep't of Educ., 111 F.3d 678, 681 (9th Cir. 1997) (collecting cases in which "several courts have recognized that IDEA claims raising 'systemic' or 'structural' allegations may not need to be administratively exhausted"). *But see* Parent/Prof'l Advocacy League v. City of Springfield, Massachusetts, 934 F.3d 13, 27 (1st Cir. 2019) (noting that "[o]ther circuits have defined an exception to the IDEA's exhaustion rule for 'systemic' suits," but declining to decide whether to recognize such an exception); Jamie S. v. Milwaukee Pub. Sch., 668 F.3d 481, 494 (7th Cir. 2012) ("[W]e neither accept nor reject the Ninth Circuit's reasoning in *Doe [v. Arizona Department of Education*, 111 F.3d at 678.]").

105 *See, e.g.*, Heldman v. Sobol, 962 F.2d 148 (2d Cir.1992).

106 J.S. ex rel. N.S. v. Attica Cent. Sch., 386 F.3d 107, 113 (2d Cir. 2004); Jamie S. v. Milwaukee Bd. of Sch. Directors, No. 01-C-928, 2012 WL 3600231, at *4 (E.D. Wis. Aug. 20, 2012).

2.4.3 *Claimant Participation*

In cases involving injunctive relief, the court and the litigants will often have a great deal of work to do even after a finding of liability has been made. After the liability determination comes the remedy stage, where the shaping of an injunction can require choices among different approaches to curing the defendant's violation. Moreover, even after the court has issued an injunction, its enforcement can require ongoing attention to the defendant's conduct.

Over the past few decades, public interest law organizations in the United States have occasionally been criticized on a number of grounds related to the remedy and enforcement stages of injunction-only cases. One such criticism relates to public interest lawyers privileging their own views over those of the people they represent, especially with regard to the content of injunctive relief. In desegregation cases, for example, some firms drew criticism for continuing to prioritize racial integration as a remedy even after African American parents made clear that they would have preferred improvements to their neighborhood schools.[107]

Another criticism relates to PILOs disengaging after obtaining a favorable judicial decision, regardless of the extent to which the decision has actually affected the reality on the ground.[108] Merely assuming that a defendant will obey an injunction, without further verification or monitoring, can render a victory hollow. Indeed, some have argued that resistance to the implementation of judicial relief severely constrains the ability of litigation to bring about meaningful social change.[109]

By facilitating claimant participation in the shaping and enforcement of injunctive relief, class treatment offers the potential for mitigating these concerns. Not only does class certification make it easier for members of the affected group to intervene,[110] but "[l]arge swaths of class action law concern cases in which unnamed class members may monitor the proceedings, oversee class counsel, retain individual counsel, and help mold the ultimate relief in the case."[111] The court has discretion whether to order class-wide certification notice,[112] but absent class members must receive notice of any proposed settlement,[113] and those who disagree with the proposed injunctive relief will have the opportunity to lodge an objection with the court.[114] Perhaps most important, "[a] favorable judgment in a class action embraces absent class members and gives them authority to enforce its terms."[115]

Subjectively, some public interest lawyers might not appreciate all of these participation-promoting aspects of class treatment, but they offer important safeguards against attorney domineering and insensitivity to affected communities. With regard to remedial choices, the airing of intraclass disagreements can produce an injunction more responsive to the views of the claimant group. With regard to remedial implementation, the expansion of enforcement authority can help to ensure that gains made in litigation will translate into changed conditions on the ground. Each of these effects can improve a public interest law organization's (abstract) return on its (concrete) investment in the case.

107 *See* Derrick A. Bell, Jr., *Serving Two Masters: Integration Ideals and Client Interests in School Desegregation Litigation*, 85 YALE L.J. 470 (1976).

108 *See* Scott L. Cummings, *Empirical Studies of Law and Social Change: What Is the Field? What Are the Questions?*, 2013 WIS. L. REV. 171, 199–200 (2013) (discussing this critique).

109 *See, e.g.*, GERALD N. ROSENBERG, THE HOLLOW HOPE (1991).

110 *See* Robert G. Bone, *The Misguided Search for Class Unity*, 82 GEO. WASH. L. REV. 651, 703 n.222 (2014); *see also* Fed. R. Civ. P. 23(d)(1)(B)(iii).

111 Elizabeth J. Cabraser & Samuel Issacharoff, *The Participatory Class Action*, 92 N.Y.U. L. Rev. 846, 849 (2017).

112 Fed. R. Civ. P. 23(c)(2)(A). 113 Fed. R. Civ. P. 23(e)(1)(B). 114 Fed. R. Civ. P. 23(e)(5)(A).

115 Maureen Carroll, *Aggregation for Me, but Not for Thee: The Rise of Common Claims in Non-Class Litigation*, 36 CARDOZO L. REV. 2017, 2038 (2015).

2.5 CONCLUSION

This chapter has explored the ways in which injunction-only class actions promote access to counsel. Courts and other decision-makers would do well to keep these benefits in mind, especially when considering steps that would affect the availability of class certification under Rule 23(b)(2).

The history of the rulemaking process shows some success on that front. In 2001, for example, the Advisory Committee proposed making some type of certification notice mandatory in class actions certified under Rule 23(b)(2).[116] The proposal reflected, in part, the claimant-participation interests discussed above. In response to the proposal, public interest law organizations argued that the costs of notice would reduce their ability to bring class actions, thereby reducing the number of claimants they would be able to serve.[117] The Advisory Committee modified the proposal, and as noted previously, the rule now gives courts discretion whether to require certification notice for a Rule 23(b)(2) class.[118] The Committee noted that this approach was "meant to strike a fair balance between the competing concerns."[119] Whatever the merits of the balance the Committee ultimately struck, it showed a commendable sensitivity to the potential impact on access to counsel.

Congress has not always demonstrated that same sensitivity. In 1996, for example, it adopted a set of restrictions on recipients of federal legal aid funding, including the prohibition on "initiat[ing] or participat[ing] in a class action suit."[120] Lawmakers who supported the prohibition argued that LSC had become focused on promoting a radical liberal agenda rather than serving disadvantaged individuals' legal needs.[121] Even assuming the validity of that critique,[122] however, prohibiting class actions throws the baby out with the bathwater. Because a class action offers an efficient mechanism for serving many disadvantaged individuals' needs at once, the prohibition reduces funded organizations' capacity to serve those individuals.[123] It is past time for

116 Robert H. Klonoff, *Class Actions for Monetary Relief Under Rule 23(b)(1)(A) and (b)(1)(B): Does Due Process Require Notice and Opt-Out Rights?*, 82 Geo. Wash. L. Rev. 798, 828–29 (2014). The change would have applied to class actions certified under Rule 23(b)(1)(A) and (B) as well. *Id.*

117 *Id.* at 829.

118 Fed. R. Civ. P. 23(c)(2)(A). As noted previously, unlike with notice of class certification, courts must order notice of a proposed class settlement. *See* Fed. R. Civ. P. 23(e)(1)(B).

119 Robert H. Klonoff, *Class Actions for Monetary Relief Under Rule 23(b)(1)(A) and (b)(1)(B): Does Due Process Require Notice and Opt-Out Rights?*, 82 Geo. Wash. L. Rev. 798, 829 (2014) (quoting the minutes of an Advisory Committee meeting held in May 2002); *see also* Fed. R. Civ. P. 23 – Advisory Committee Note to 2003 Amendments ("The court may decide not to direct notice after balancing the risk that notice costs may deter the pursuit of class relief against the benefits of notice.").

120 *See* Omnibus Consolidated Rescissions and Appropriations Act of 1996, PL 104–134, April 26, 1996, 110 Stat 1321; *see also supra* note 5 and accompanying text.

121 *See* Mauricio Vivero, *From "Renegade" Agency to Institution of Justice: The Transformation of Legal Services Corporation*, 29 Fordham Urb. L.J. 1323, 1329–33 (2002)(discussing the history of the LSC restrictions); *see also* Alan Houseman & Linda E. Perle, Securing Equal Justice for All: A Brief History of Civil Legal Assistance in the United States 36 (2018) ("[T]he Congressional majority was determined to redefine the role of federally funded legal services by refocusing legal services advocacy away from law reform, lobbying, policy advocacy, and impact litigation and toward basic representation of individual clients.").

122 *But see* Mauricio Vivero, *From "Renegade" Agency to Institution of Justice: The Transformation of Legal Services Corporation*, 29 Fordham Urb. L.J. 1323, 1329 (2002) (explaining that "LSC statistics on annual caseloads contradict this view").

123 *See* David Luban, *Taking Out the Adversary: The Assault on Progressive Public-Interest Lawyers*, 91 Cal. L. Rev. 209, 224 (2003) (noting that "the vast majority of cases that legal-services lawyers turn down will never be brought by anyone," and thus "the [LSC] restrictions ensure that entire subgroups of low-income people will never be heard in the legal system").

this restriction to be removed, so that federally funded legal aid organizations can do their jobs more efficiently and effectively.[124]

As for the Supreme Court, it wrote in 2011 that Rule 23(b)(2) "does not require that class members be given notice and opt-out rights, presumably because it is thought (rightly or wrongly) that notice has no purpose when the class is mandatory, and that depriving people of their right to sue in this manner complies with the Due Process Clause."[125] In light of the access-promoting effects discussed above, it would be unfortunate if the Court continued to flirt with this idea that mandatory Rule 23(b)(2) classes are unconstitutional. Absent class members' due process rights should not be weaponized against them.

This chapter has focused on the plaintiff-side benefits of injunction-only class actions, but of course, such actions also have downsides for claimants and their counsel. Foremost among these is preclusion, because a certified class action constrains further litigation on behalf of absent class members, regardless of whether they win or lose.[126] In addition, because plaintiffs must affirmatively demonstrate that they comply with the requirements of Rule 23(a) and (b), law firms (including public interest law organizations) must devote time and resources to obtaining class certification.[127] For all of the reasons discussed above, however, the benefits of injunction-only class actions will often be worth the costs.

124 *Cf.* Catherine Albiston, Su Li, & Laura Beth Nielsen, *Public Interest Law Organizations and the Two-Tier System of Access to Justice in the United States*, 42 LAW & SOCIAL INQUIRY 990, 1017 (2017) ("[S]ystemic reform and rule change may be a more efficient and cost-effective means of assisting [PILOs'] disadvantaged clients than serial litigation of cases one at a time.").

125 Wal-Mart Stores, Inc. v. Dukes, 564 U.S. 338, 363 (2011).

126 Due in large part to these preclusive effects, one commentator has argued that class treatment in injunction-only cases benefits the defendant and not the plaintiffs, and that attorneys for the plaintiffs should therefore bring such cases solely on a nonclass basis. *See* Timothy Wilton, *The Class Action in Social Reform Litigation: In Whose Interest?*, 63 B.U. L. REV. 597 (1983).

127 *See* Wal-Mart Stores, Inc. v. Dukes, 564 U.S. 338, 350 (2011) ("A party seeking class certification must affirmatively demonstrate his compliance with the Rule – that is, he must be prepared to prove that there are *in fact* sufficiently numerous parties, common questions of law or fact, etc.").

3

Class Action Nuisance Suits

Evidence from Frequent Filer Shareholder Plaintiffs

Sean J. Griffith[*]

3.1 INTRODUCTION

No account of class action litigation in the United States would be complete without reckoning with its dark side – nuisance litigation. A nuisance suit is a claim filed for settlement value in spite of knowledge on both sides that the claim is weak or non-meritorious.[1] Common indicia of nuisance suits include frequent filings, often in the form of ready-made complaints with minor factual variation, repeat-play plaintiffs, and resolutions that yield insubstantial monetary recoveries to the class but that nevertheless entitle plaintiffs' counsel to recover fees from the defendant. On the basis of these characteristics, class action nuisance litigation is perhaps best illustrated by shareholder suits challenging corporate mergers and acquisitions (M&A) transactions.

Claims challenging M&A transactions are filed frequently. Until 2016, they were filed in 85 to 95 percent of all deals over $100 million,[2] and evidence suggests that any downturn since then may have been temporary.[3] These filings make the same allegations with minor factual variations, challenging the fairness of the deal as well as the adequacy of the corporation's disclosures to its shareholders.[4] These claims are often filed repeatedly by the same named plaintiffs, frequently individual investors with a small holding in the subject company. Finally, M&A suits typically settle for no monetary compensation. Instead, the shareholders receive a few lines of supplemental disclosures. In theory, these disclosures benefit the shareholder class by increasing the amount of information at their disposal in the shareholder vote. In fact, however, these disclosures have no observable impact on the shareholder vote.[5] Rather, their principal purpose

* Thanks to Joel Fleming, Claire Hill, Kevin Miller, Anthony Rickey, Scott Rothstein, and Randall Thomas for helpful comments on earlier drafts of this manuscript, and thanks to Amith Arcot, Julian Constain, Dmytro Usyk, and Alex Wang for excellent research assistance. All viewpoints and any errors expressed herein are mine alone.

1 William H. J. Hubbard, "Sinking Costs to Force or Deter Settlement." *Journal of Law, Economics & Organization* 32, 2016: 545–85.

2 Matthew D. Cain and Steven Davidoff Solomon, *Takeover Litigation in 2015*, at 2. Berkeley Center for Law, Business & Economics, Working Paper, 2017. http://ssrn.com/abstract=2715890.

3 Cornerstone Research. "Securities Class Action Filings: 2018 Year in Review." 2019. www.cornerstone.com/Publications/Reports/Securities-Class-Action-Filings-2018-Year-in-Review.pdf.

4 Dan Awrey, Blanaid Clarke & Sean J. Griffith, "Resolving the Crisis in U.S. Merger Regulation: A Transatlantic Alternative to the Perpetual Litigation Machine." *Yale Journal on Regulation* 35, 2018: 1–65.

5 Jill E. Fisch, Sean J. Griffith & Steven Davidoff Solomon. "Confronting the Peppercorn Settlement in Merger Litigation: An Empirical Analysis and a Proposal for Reform." *Texas Law Review* 93, 2015: 557–624.

is to serve as a basis for an award of fees to the plaintiffs' attorney under the "corporate benefit" doctrine, with the result that the only monetary recovery goes to the lawyers, not the plaintiffs.[6]

This chapter examines class action nuisance suits through the lens of M&A litigation. This is an ideal setting not only because M&A claims are so often pursued for nuisance value but also because these suits have evolved in response to several changes in the law aimed at eliminating them. In this evolutionary process, M&A suits have made both substantive and procedural adaptations. Far from going extinct, they have instead continued to proliferate in altered forms.

As evidence, the chapter uses an original hand-collected dataset of litigation filed by seven "frequent filer" shareholder plaintiffs over a five-year period, 2014 through 2018.[7] During this period, these plaintiffs filed a total of 282 shareholder suits. This chapter compiles data on their claims, documenting the substantive allegations, procedural form, and the identity of counsel, as well as the outcomes of claims. It finds that over this period, frequent filer suits transformed from state court challenges to mergers based on fiduciary duty into federal court challenges to merger disclosures based on the federal securities laws. It also finds that the outcomes of these suits transformed from class-wide settlements based on supplemental disclosures ("disclosure settlements") to mootness dismissals based on the defendant's having corrected the alleged disclosure deficiencies ("mootness resolutions").[8] The common denominator between disclosure settlements and mootness resolutions is that both entitle plaintiffs' counsel to collect fees from the corporation while the plaintiff class receives nothing but disclosures.

The evolutionary phases of this litigation are direct responses to legislative and judicial efforts to contain these suits. Claims moved from state to federal court to evade state law precedent that had become hostile to disclosure settlements. Once in federal court, these claims mutated again, transforming from disclosure settlement into mootness resolutions in order to avoid judicial scrutiny and the provisions of the Private Securities Litigation Reform Act of 1995 (the PSLRA). Furthermore, there is evidence of further evolution in these federal disclosure-based claims. Plaintiffs have now begun to file disclosure-based claims against corporations in contexts other than M&A. And plaintiffs have begun to file as individuals rather than as a class, apparently as a further precaution against application of the PSLRA.

The chapter argues that the PSLRA, consistently applied, would address these problems. The PSLRA bars the award of attorneys' fees for nonmonetary recoveries. It also requires plaintiffs to meet a high standard of materiality at pleading, prevents plaintiffs from seeking to represent a class more than five times in three years, and requires a set of sworn undertakings by class action claimants. Consistent application of the PSLRA, however, requires judicial coordination which has so far been lacking among federal district courts but which could be achieved through several mechanisms. Courts should use these mechanisms to coordinate their response to the problem of merger and disclosure-related nuisance suits.

From this introduction, the chapter proceeds as follows. Section 3.2 provides the relevant background, situating concerns over nuisance suits in the unique context of merger litigation.

6 Sean J. Griffith, "Correcting Corporate Benefit: How to Fix Shareholder Litigation by Shifting the Doctrine on Fees" *Boston College Law Review* 56, 2015: 1–59.

7 The phrase "frequent filer" has been used to refer to the lawyers that regularly bring nuisance litigation on behalf of shareholder plaintiffs. See In re Revlon, Inc. Shareholders Litig., 990 A.2d 940, 943 n.1 (Del. Ch. 2010) (coining the phrase "frequent filer" to refer to "repeat players who regularly bring representative actions on behalf of stockholders with small ownership stakes"). Here I use the phrase to refer to the shareholder plaintiffs themselves rather than the lawyers who file claims on their behalf.

8 *See, e.g.*, Rosenfeld v. Time Inc., 2018 WL 4177938, at *2 (S.D.N.Y. Aug. 30, 2018) ("Sometimes these settlements are characterized as 'mootness fees,' in which the corporation moots the lawsuit by making the allegedly withheld disclosures, and pays plaintiffs' counsel a "voluntary" fee in return. Such settlements principally benefit plaintiff's counsel.") (internal citations omitted).

Section 3.3 describes the empirical methodology employed by this chapter. Section 3.4 reports the findings of my study, discussing filing and outcome characteristics and providing insights on the relationship between frequent filer plaintiffs and the disclosure bar. Section 3.5 interprets the findings, arguing that they are evidence of strategic pleading, first to avoid hostile state court precedent and, second, to avoid application of the PSLRA. Section 3.6 offers recommendations on how courts can address the problems uncovered in this chapter. Finally, Section 3.7 concludes with a brief summary.

3.2 NUISANCE SUITS IN THE CONTEXT OF MERGER LITIGATION

Shareholder claims challenging merger litigation surged in 2009. Prior to 2009, shareholder plaintiffs typically challenged a quarter to a third of all deals. Starting in 2009, shareholder plaintiffs began to challenge essentially every deal. Because these claims contained the threat of an injunction that could destroy or at least substantially disrupt the transaction, defendants were motivated to settle. The resulting deal provided no monetary recovery to the class but allowed plaintiffs' counsel to recover their fees from the company on the basis of a few lines of supplemental disclosures. In exchange, defendants got a class-wide release of claims and, most importantly, could go forward with the deal without the risk of injunction.[9]

However, because the release of claims provided in connection with disclosure settlements affected the rights of absent class members, courts had to approve the fairness of the settlement.[10] Although these hearings are intended to constrain the ability of counsel to settle class claims at little or no value to the class, in fact the judges presiding over fairness hearings are rarely informed of the low value of the settlement disclosures. Instead, because both plaintiffs' and defense counsel want the settlement to be approved, the former adversaries work together towards that goal.[11] Given the absence of meaningful adversarial process at settlement and the parties' lack of candor about the settlement's real value, these settlements were routinely approved.[12]

The incentives created by the easy availability of fees for no real litigation effort proved irresistible to a subclass of plaintiffs' lawyers, the "disclosure bar," who built business models around regularly filing and swiftly resolving merger claims.[13] But this wave of merger litigation had deleterious effects in Delaware, the leading jurisdiction of incorporation of large US businesses and therefore the principal forum for corporate law litigation. Merger cases flooded the Delaware Court of Chancery and made a mockery of the ideal of shareholder litigation that court had sought to uphold.[14] After tolerating the situation for several years, the Delaware courts signaled that they had seen enough. In January 2016, the

9 Sean J. Griffith, "Settlement and Fees in Merger Litigation." in *Research Handbook On Mergers & Acquisitions*. Hill & Solomon, eds. Edward Elgar Publishing, 2016.

10 William B. Rubenstein, "The Fairness Hearing: Adversarial and Regulatory Approaches." *UCLA Law Review* 53, 2006: 1435–82.

11 Jonathan R. Macey & Geoffrey P. Miller, "The Plaintiffs' Attorney's Role in Class Action and Derivative Litigation: Economic Analysis and Recommendations for Reform." *University of Chicago Law Review* 58, 1991: 1–118.

12 Sean J. Griffith, "Innovation in Disclosure-Based Shareholder Suits." *Case Western Reserve Law Review* 69, 2019.

13 Joel Edan Friedlander, "How Rural/Metro Exposed the Systemic Problem of Disclosure Settlements." *Delaware Journal of Corporate Law* 40, 2016: 877–919.

14 William B. Chandler & Anthony A. Rickey, "The Trouble with Trulia: Re-Evaluating the Case for Fee-Shifting Bylaws as a Solution to the Overlitigation of Corporate Claims" Unpublished paper, Apr. 4, 2017, available at https://ssrn.com/abstract=2946477.

Court of Chancery in *In re Trulia Stockholder Litigation* left no doubt that disclosure settlements would no longer be welcome in Delaware.[15] The court held:

> [P]ractitioners should expect that disclosure settlements are likely to be met with continued disfavor in the future unless the supplemental disclosures address a plainly material misrepresentation or omission . . . In using the term "plainly material," I mean that it should not be a close call that the supplemental information is material as that term is defined under Delaware law.[16]

But by the time *Trulia* was decided, a cottage industry in disclosure settlements was already well established. What would happen to this industry in the wake of *Trulia*? The next section seeks to shed light on this question by analyzing the litigation patterns of frequent filer plaintiffs.

3.3 EMPIRICAL METHODOLOGY

To collect data on the litigation patterns of frequent filer plaintiffs, I assembled a list of plaintiffs whose names I had frequently encountered in my own research or litigation activities.[17] I then supplemented my list by surveying members of the Delaware bench and bar to identify the names of plaintiffs known to repeatedly file shareholder suits. This produced seven plaintiffs – Robert Berg, Stephen Bushansky, Natalie Gordon, Paul Parshall, Matthew Sciabacucchi, John Solak, and Shiva Stein – each of whom has repeatedly been a named shareholder plaintiff in merger litigation.[18]

Next, I searched court dockets for these plaintiffs' names to assemble a set of cases in which they had been involved. I restricted my search to the five-year period spanning the Court of Chancery's *Trulia* decision in January 2016. I searched from January 2014 through year-end 2018. I ran these searches in Bloomberg Law, an online service that collects docket information from all federal courts as well as prominent state courts, including the Delaware Court of Chancery. Within the Bloomberg Law dockets database, I searched all federal and state trial court filings involving any of my seven named plaintiffs. I then sorted these results by hand, eliminating any suits that did not involve "shareholder litigation," which I defined as litigation filed on the basis of the plaintiff's status as a shareholder, principally including federal securities law claims and state fiduciary duty claims. After throwing out unrelated litigation and rejecting cases where critical docket information, such as the complaint, was missing and otherwise unattainable, I was left with a sample of 282 shareholder suits filed by these plaintiffs over a five-year period.

15 129 A.3d 884, 898 (Del. Ch. 2016). I filed a brief as *amicus curiae* in *Trulia*. See 2015 'WL 6391945 (Del.Ch., Oct. 16, 2015).

16 129 A.3d at 898.

17 I have filed objections to disclosure settlements. See, e.g., In re Riverbed, Inc. Stockholders Litigation, C.A. No. 10484–VCG, 2015 WL 5458041 (Del. Ch. Sept. 17, 2015); Vergiev v. Aguero et al. (Metalico Stockholders' Litigation), UNN-L-2276–15 (Sup. Ct. NJ, Union Cty., June 6, 2016); Sean J. Griffith v. Quality Distribution, Inc., No. 2D17-3160 (Dist. Ct. App., Fla. 2nd Dist., July 13, 2018); Stein v. Goldman Sachs Group, Inc., C.A. No. 2017–0354-SG (Del. Ch., Oct. 23, 2018); In re PMFG Stockholder Litigation, C.A. No. 11223-VCS (Del. Ch., Sept. 1, 2016); Bushansky v. Remy Int'l, Inc., 262 F. Supp. 3d 742, 750 (S.D. Ind. Aug. 16, 2017); In re Pharmacyclics, Inc. Shareholder Litigation, No. 2015–1-CV-278055 (Sup. Ct. Cal., Santa Clara Cty., July 19, 2016). I have also provided expert testimony in merger litigation. See, e.g., Richards, et al., v FX Energy, Inc., A-15–726409-C (Dist. Ct., Clark County, Nev., 2016): Corwin v British Am. Tobacco, 14 CVS 8130 (NC Bus. Court, 2016); In re Compuware S'holder Litig., 14–011437-CB (Cir. Ct., Wayne County, Mich., 2015); Gordon v. Verizon Communications, Inc., No. 653084/13, 2014 WL 7250212 (NY Sup. Ct., 2014).

18 I know nothing about these people other than the fact that their names regularly appear as named plaintiffs in shareholder litigation. I know nothing about their motives, nor am I certain that a single person has in fact filed all of the complaints listed under a single name. It is possible, if highly unlikely, that more than one person sharing the same name has filed some of these suits.

With regard to sample construction, some caveats are in order. First, the list of named plaintiffs for which I searched was informally obtained. I did not attempt to write a code that would identify all repeat shareholder plaintiffs who had filed claims in electronically searchable dockets, although such a search is at least theoretically possible. Instead, I relied on my own experience and the suggestions of those members of the Delaware bench and bar that were willing to respond to my queries. As a result, the sample is not comprehensive. There may be repeat shareholder plaintiffs whose filings I missed. And the sample may not be representative of the litigation activity of all repeat play plaintiffs. In particular, the sample is likely Delaware-biased, suggesting that frequent filers who focus on federal courts or other state jurisdictions may have been missed. Moreover, there may be other repeat claimants who pursue predominantly meritorious claims, but if so, they are not the claimants studied here. I do not claim that my sample is comprehensive or even, necessarily, representative. My only claim is that the litigation activity of these seven plaintiffs sheds light on how some repeat claimants have pursued merger litigation, both before and after *Trulia*.

Second, the Bloomberg Law dockets database does not contain all merger litigation filed in the United States. For the 2014 through 2018 time period, Bloomberg Law offers comprehensive coverage of federal district court dockets and, critically, of the Delaware Court of Chancery docket. However, docket coverage in Bloomberg Law is less exhaustive for other state trial courts.[19] As a result filings in Delaware and in federal district courts may be overrepresented in the sample, and filings in other state courts may be missing. However, Delaware's predominance as the leading state of incorporation and the fact that shareholder suits can only be filed in three places – in the state of incorporation, the headquarters state, or federal district court – suggest that the predominance of Delaware and federal court filings is not entirely coincidental.

3.4 FINDINGS

This section presents data from my frequent filer dataset. Table 3.1 below summarizes the data by category. The subsections following the table discuss what the data reveal about lawsuit characteristics, outcomes, and the relationship between frequent filer plaintiffs and the disclosure bar.

TABLE 3.1 *Summary data*

		Year				
		2018	2017	2016	2015	2014
Type of Filing	Merger	43	97	24	25	24
	Derivative	3	4	4	8	2
	Proxy	13	15	8	0	0
	Traditional Securities	0	0	0	4	1
	Other	1	2	1	1	1
Forum	Federal	52	112	23	12	5
	State	7	6	14	26	23
Outcome	Settlement	2	2	4	13	13
	Dismissal	51	106	25	9	5
	Motion	0	2	3	5	1

19 For details on dockets covered in Bloomberg Law, see Bloomberg Law, All Coverage: Docket Coverage, available at www.bloomberglaw.com/dockets/coverage/detail (last visited June 5, 2019).

3.4.1 *Filing Characteristics*

Two features jump out of the lawsuit filings in the sample. First, the vast majority of filings (76 percent) are merger claims. Second, although the vast majority of these claims were initially filed in state courts, this trend shifted dramatically over the sample period. In 2014, 82 percent of these plaintiffs' claims were brought in state courts. In 2015, the percentage of claims brought in state court fell to 68 percent, then in 2016, fell even more, to 41 percent. By 2017 and 2018, the relationship had reversed entirely, with 96 percent and 87 percent of their claims being brought in federal rather than state court. These relationships are depicted in the figures below.

Figure 3.1 breaks plaintiff filings into types of claims. It categorizes claim types as merger suits, derivative suits, traditional securities class actions, proxy suits, and other. Merger suits include state law merger claims as well as federal court filings challenging merger proxy statements under Rule 14a-9, a Securities and Exchange Commission (SEC) rule applying to misstatements and omissions in the proxy materials of public companies. Because shareholders may bring class action claims to enforce Rule 14a-9, merger claims brought under it mirror the disclosure aspects of state law fiduciary duty claims. Moreover, like state merger claims, federal claims under Rule 14a-9 can be settled for supplemental disclosures.

"Proxy suits" are defined to include claims alleging inadequate proxy statement disclosures under Rule 14a-9 that do *not* relate to M&A transactions. The proxy rules require detailed disclosure of a number of items, including the prior experience and compensation of directors and officers, details of fees paid to the company's independent public accountants, and details concerning stock-based compensation plans. As a result, shareholders could bring claims alleging disclosure violations touching any subject on which shareholders are asked to vote. However, non-merger proxy suits arise most often in compensation-related disclosures. For example, Item 10(a) of Form S-K requires fairly detailed disclosure of stock incentive and other compensation plans, including the number of persons in each class of participants entitled to participate in the plan. Errors or omissions in such disclosures could thus give rise to 14a-9 complaints seeking to enjoin shareholder voting on the plan until corrective disclosure can be made. As Figure 3.1 shows, such claims have become an increasingly common claim pursued by the plaintiffs in my study.[20]

The rest of the categories are fairly obvious. Derivative suits are fiduciary duty claims filed by individual shareholders seeking redress for a harm done to the corporation itself. Traditional securities class actions are claims filed under the sections of the federal securities laws that shareholder plaintiffs have historically used to seek relief – principally Rule 10b-5 promulgated under Section 10 of the Securities Exchange Act of 1934. The plaintiffs in my sample filed only five traditional securities class action filings (three by Stein, one by Sciabacucchi, one by Solak), all of which allege claims under Rule 10b-5. Finally, Figure 3.1 includes a catchall category for "other" shareholder suits, predominantly including books and records actions filed under Section 220 of the Delaware General Corporation Law.

Figure 3.1 demonstrates that merger claims brought by frequent filer claimants did not disappear after *Trulia*. Moreover, the ratio by which merger suits predominate other shareholder claims *increased* slightly in the wake of *Trulia*. Prior to 2016, the sample contains roughly three merger suits for every other type of shareholder claim. After 2016, there are four times as many merger suits as there are other forms of shareholder suits. In 2016, the year in which *Trulia* was decided, there were only twice as many merger suits as there were other types of shareholder filings.

20 Interestingly, however, all but one of the non-merger proxy claims in the sample were filed by a single litigant, Stein, with the sole remaining non-merger proxy claim brought by Bushansky.

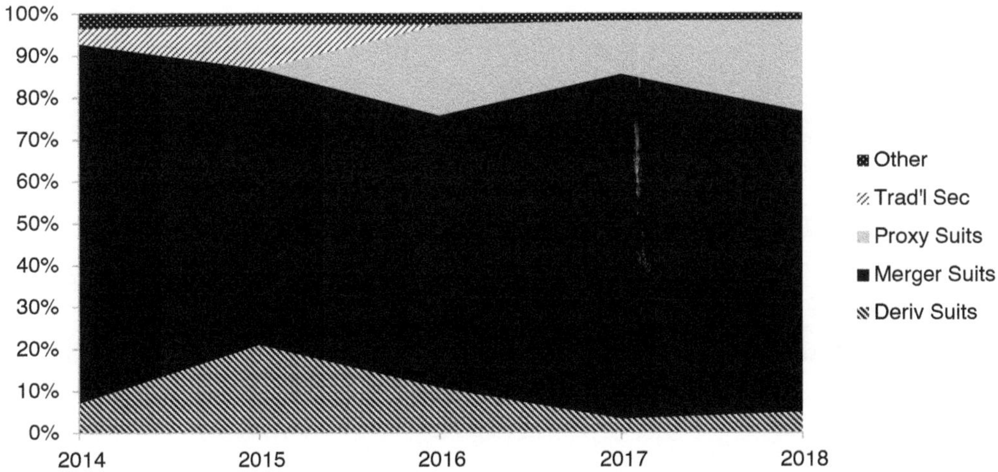

FIGURE 3.1 Lawsuit filings by type of claim

Nevertheless, Figure 3.1 reveals that the type of suit that accounts for most *non*-merger litigation has changed in the wake of *Trulia*. Proxy suits challenging non-merger disclosures have largely taken the place of both derivative suits and traditional securities filings in the sample. These proxy suits were first filed in 2015 but have become increasingly common since *Trulia*. Moreover, they share a critical feature with most merger claims filed in the wake of *Trulia*: they are filed in federal court under Rule 14a-9 of the federal proxy rules.

Figure 3.2 demonstrates what may be the most significant change in litigation activity in the wake of *Trulia*. The vast majority of shareholder suits in the sample are now filed in federal court. As the figure illustrates, this trend began in earnest in the year prior to *Trulia*, a time when Delaware courts began to suggest that they might soon act to restrain merger litigation. Having brought only two federal claims in 2014 and five in 2015, all but one of the frequent filers in my sample started filing federal claims aggressively in 2016.[21] From 2016 through 2018, the remaining six frequent filers brought 148 federal securities lawsuits. This is consistent with other researchers' findings. For example, a Cornerstone study shows that in 2015, the year before *Trulia*, 34 lawsuits were filed in federal courts relating to mergers; in 2017, the year after *Trulia*, there were 198, and in 2018, there were 182.[22]

Combining the insights of Figures 3.1 and 3.2 reveals that frequent filer plaintiffs are now bringing merger claims at an even greater rate than they brought them pre-*Trulia*. However, they are now bringing these claims in federal rather than state court, subject to Rule 14a-9 rather than state corporate law. Moreover, the next most common form of frequent filer suit from 2015 on, non-merger proxy claims, are also filed federal court cases under Rule 14a-9. In sum, frequent filer plaintiffs seem to have responded to *Trulia* by substituting Rule 14a-9 claims for state law merger claims and, having found their way into federal court under the proxy rules, by bringing additional proxy claims wherever they could find them.

[21] The exception is Gordon, most of whose claims were brought before 2016 and all of which were brought under state law.

[22] Cornerstone Research, *supra* note 3, at 14; Matthew D. Cain, Jill E. Fisch, Steven Davidoff Solomon & Randall S. Thomas. "The Shifting Tides of Merger Litigation." *Vanderbilt Law Review* 71, 2018: 631–32.

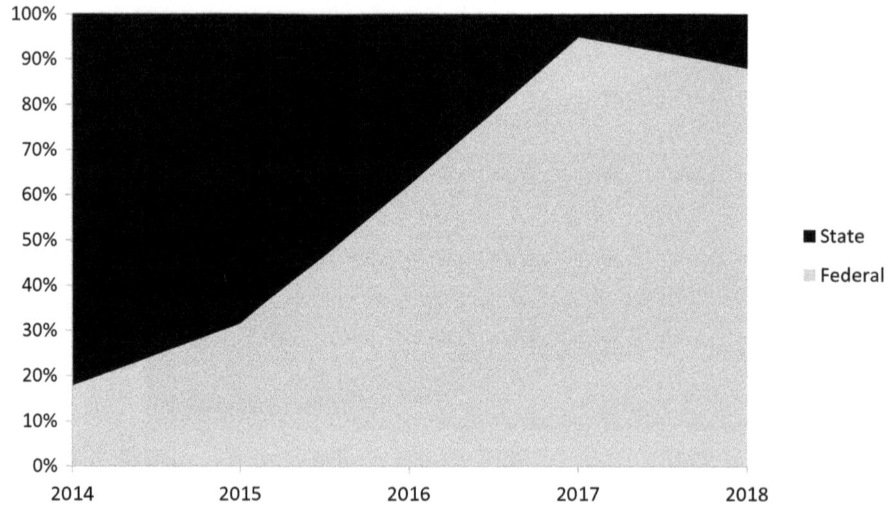

FIGURE 3.2 Lawsuit filings by jurisdiction

3.4.2 *Outcome Characteristics*

Docket analysis also reveals a shift in outcomes. To analyze outcomes, I separated claims that had reached a conclusion into three categories: settlements, dismissals, and successful defendant motions. At the beginning of the sample period, settlements strongly predominated dismissals. In 2014 and 2015, for example, there were two times as many settlements as dismissals and over four times as many settlements as successful defendant motions. But this trend reversed sharply in 2016, as illustrated in Figure 3.3, below.

It is important to note that the dismissals captured in Figure 3.3 are not the result of a motion to dismiss or any other defense-side motion. Such dispositive motions are coded as "Motions." Instead, these dismissals are some form of voluntary dismissal. Most often, these claims are dismissed because the defendant has taken some action that has the effect of "mooting" the plaintiffs' claim, typically by making corrective disclosures to eliminate the alleged deficiencies of the proxy statement. As shown in Figure 3.3, mootness resolutions replaced disclosure settlements, more or less immediately after *Trulia*.

From a tactical perspective, mootness resolutions have the benefit of clearing the way for plaintiffs' attorneys to recover fees without the risk inherent in a fairness hearing. Because the defendant has made corrective disclosures in response to the complaint, the plaintiff's attorney is entitled to recover fees from the defendant under the corporate benefit doctrine.[23] In theory, these fees can be contested by defendants and, if the plaintiff prevails in a hearing, ordered by the court. In practice, however, defendants often elect not to oppose fee requests. Figure 3.3 depicts the transformation of disclosure settlement into mootness resolutions.

Why would defendants willingly pay plaintiffs' fees without receiving the release of claims? Are not defendants who settle for mootness vulnerable to copycat claims filed by other shareholder plaintiffs challenging different aspects of disclosure? Again, the answer is in theory, yes; in practice, no. The corrective disclosures that moot shareholder claims typically issue very shortly before the shareholder vote. Once the shareholder vote occurs, the ability to receive a fee award in exchange for nonpecuniary relief disappears. Plaintiffs may still pursue damages claims, but in such cases the

[23] Griffith, *supra* note 6.

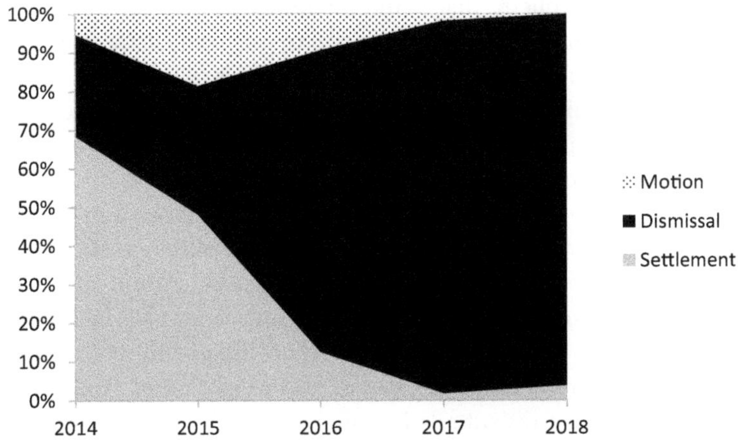

FIGURE 3.3 Lawsuit outcomes

applicable legal standards are no longer favorable to plaintiffs. Both sides thus know that once the vote passes, the holdup value of the plaintiffs' claim returns to near zero. As a result, mootness resolutions offer something for the lawyers on both sides. By waiting until shortly before the vote, defendants minimize the window available to other potential claimants and, in making the disclosures, effectively eliminate the potential for an injunction. At the same time, plaintiffs' lawyers receive fees averaging $265,000 for claims that they need scarcely litigate.[24]

3.4.3 *Frequent Filer Plaintiffs and the Disclosure Bar*

Docket analysis also reveals patterns in the relationship between frequent filer plaintiffs and the law firms that bring their claims. Coding the law firms listed on frequent filer complaints reveals the recurrence of a core set of plaintiffs' law firms. This is no surprise. Prior research on merger litigation has tended to focus on the law firms bringing the most complaints.[25] Many of the same law firms appear in the frequent filer data as well – including, for example, Barrack Roddos, Faruqi & Faruqi, Pomerantz, Rigrodsky & Long, RM Law, WeissLaw, and Wolf Haldenstein. But starting with the plaintiff rather than the law firm allows the lawyer-client relationship to be examined from a different angle, shedding light on the relationship between the plaintiff and the law firm.[26]

What does the data reveal about specific claimants and law firms? Four of the seven claimants in my study regularly file litigation with the same law firm. For example, RM Law was involved in twenty-five of thirty-one of Berg's filings, WeissLaw was involved in forty-two out of forty-three of Bushansky's filings, Faruqi & Faruqi was involved in all of Gordon's filings, and Rigrodsky & Long was involved in fifty-seven out of fifty-nine of Parshall's filings. These patterns may suggest

24 Cain, Fisch, Solomon & Thomas, *supra* note 22; Matthew D. Cain, Jill E. Fisch, Steven Davidoff Solomon & Randall S. Thomas, "Mootness Fees." 72 *Vanderbilt Law Review* 1777, 2019.

25 Adam B. Badawi and David H. Webber. "Does the Quality of the Plaintiffs' Law Firm Matter in Deal Litigation?" *The Journal of Corporation Law* 41, 2015: 359–91; Friedlander, *supra* note 13; Sean J. Griffith, Sean J. and Anthony A. Rickey. "Who Collects the Deal Tax, Where, and What Delaware Can Do About It." in *Handbook On Representative Shareholder Litigation*. Erickson, Griffith, Webber & Winship, eds. Edward Elgar Publishing, 2018; C. N. V. Krishnan, Steven Davidoff Solomon & Randall S. Thomas. "Who Are the Top Law Firms? Assessing the Value of Plaintiffs' Law Firms in Merger Litigation." *American Law and Economics Review* 18, 2016: 122–54; David H. Webber, "Lead Plaintiffs and Lead Counsel in Deal Litigation." in *Research Handbook on Mergers and Acquisitions*. Davidoff Solomon and Hill, eds. Edward Elgar, 2016.

26 Jessica Erickson, "The New Professional Plaintiffs in Shareholder Litigation." *Florida Law Review* 65, 2013: 1089–138.

that it is the lawyer, not the client, that is the interested party behind most of these filings. However, the pattern is also not inconsistent with an engaged plaintiff who has developed a relationship of trust and confidence with a particular lawyer or law firm.

The remaining three claimants, however, reveal different filing patterns. For example, fourteen different firms brought Solak's eighteen cases. Although many law firms recur in these filings – for example, Robbins & Arroyo was involved in six Solak cases, Wolf Haldenstein was involved in four, and Rigrodsky & Long was involved in three – it is difficult to discern a consistent pattern in the Solak cases. Likewise, although Rigrodsky & Long was involved in eleven of twenty-one of Sciabacucchi's lawsuits, various other law firms were involved in the other ten. Similarly, Stein's ninety-six suits were filed by thirty-eight different combinations of law firms. Three of these recur more frequently than the others – Wolf Haldenstein (forty-two), Barrack Rodos & Bacine (thirty-eight), and Pomerantz (eighteen) – but it is difficult to discern a consistent relationship between the plaintiff and a single law firm.

Cross-referencing law firm and claim type, however, reveals further patterns. As already noted, the vast majority of the claims in my sample are merger claims. The only other type of claim regularly filed by these plaintiffs in recent years are proxy suits – that is 14a-9 claims *not* related to M&A. There are thirty-six proxy suits in the sample, and as noted above, thirty-five of them were brought by Stein. Who were the lawyers?

There is greater consistency in the law firms bringing Stein's proxy suits than there is among the firms bringing her litigation as a whole. Of Stein's thirty-five proxy suits, thirty-three of them were brought by either Wolf Haldenstein or Barrack Roddos & Racine. In two such cases, both firms were involved. In contrast, the remainder of Stein's suits, including her forty-five merger suits, were brought by an assortment of firms, from which it is difficult to discern any pattern. This indicates specialization within the plaintiffs' bar. These two firms bring claims that other law firms are not bringing.[27] While it remains unclear whether the plaintiff chooses the lawyer or the lawyer chooses the plaintiff, it appears to be true that the type of case makes a difference in the choice.

Finally, if we consider qualitative factors, it is possible to observe that although the vast majority of these lawsuits end in disclosure settlements and mootness resolutions, a small number of them were litigated seriously enough to result in significant pro-plaintiff judicial decisions. Three of these, both brought by Sciabacucchi, stand out. In the first, *Sciabacucchi v. Liberty Broadband*,[28] plaintiffs produced a meaningful doctrinal development when they successfully argued that a shareholder vote could be coerced when it involves a choice made "in avoidance of a detriment created by the structure of the transaction ... rather than a free choice to accept or reject the proposition voted on."[29] In the second, *Sciabacucchi v. - Salzberg*,[30] plaintiffs succeeded in arguing that forum selection provisions adopted by Delaware corporations are invalid to the extent that they require any claim under the Securities Act of 1933 to be filed only in federal court, a significant and controversial holding both limiting the scope of forum selection provisions and affirming concurrent state and federal jurisdiction over Securities Act claims. A third Sciabacucchi case, *In re: Tangoe*, resulted in a judicial opinion holding the business judgment rule inapplicable to a merger in light of the inadequacy of corporate disclosures prior to the shareholder vote.[31] Interestingly, these three cases were brought by a law firm that filed only five of Sciabacucchi's twenty-two

27 The only proxy suit not involving Stein was brought by Bushansky and involved WeissLaw.
28 C.A. No 11418-VCG, 2017 WL 2352152 (Del. Ch., May 31, 2017). 29 Id., at *2.
30 C.A. No. 2017–0931-JTL, 2018 WL 6719718 (Del. Ch., Dec. 19, 2018).
31 Tangoe, Inc. Stockholders Litig., C.A. No. 2017–0650-JRS, 2018 WL 6074435 (Del. Ch. Nov. 20, 2018) (holding *Corwin* "cleansing" inapplicable in light of inadequate disclosures).

claims: Heyman Enerio.[32] The other two Sciabacucchi claims brought by this firm resulted in significant monetary recoveries at settlement.[33]

The Sciabacucchi cases brought by Heyman Enerio suggest further specialization. The Heyman Enerio firm was not listed on any other cases in the dataset, whether filed by Sciabacucchi or any of the six other plaintiffs, yet the firm succeeded in litigating or settling the five cases into which it was brought. This suggests that at least some frequent filer plaintiffs (or, alternatively, the law firms with the client relationship) differentiate between high value and low value claims, and for their high value claims, partner with law firms not otherwise associated with high-volume, low-value litigation.

3.5 IMPLICATIONS

A basic implication from these findings is that plaintiffs and their lawyers are highly adaptive. The data demonstrates two significant shifts in frequent filer claims during the sample period: first, litigants shifted their claims from state to federal courts at the beginning of 2016. Second, around the same time, litigants began to shift from settlements to mootness resolutions. The first of these shifts likely reflects *Trulia*. The second may partially reflect federal receptivity to *Trulia*, but it likely also reflects the PSLRA.

3.5.1 Evading *Trulia*

As described above, *Trulia* left no doubt that disclosure settlements were no longer welcome in Delaware. Settlements would no longer be certified unless they presented "plainly material" disclosures.[34] The disclosure bar's choice was stark: adapt or die.

The response to *Trulia* was immediate. Merger litigation quickly shifted to federal court under Section 14(a) of the Securities Exchange Act. In 2015, the year before *Trulia*, there were 34 total lawsuits filed in federal courts relating to mergers; in 2017, the year after *Trulia*, there were 198, and in 2018, there were 182.[35] In the years since *Trulia*, federal courts have continued to experience high rates of merger-related filings, with the Third Circuit (which contains Delaware) experiencing the largest individual portion of this increased volume.[36]

Initially, these plaintiffs presented settlements in federal court much as they had in state court prior to *Trulia*. But fairness hearings are required in class settlements, and federal judges soon took the opportunity presented by the fairness hearing to recognize these claims as nuisance suits and deny the settlement. For example, in *In Re: Walgreen Co. Stockholder Litigation*, the Seventh Circuit Court of Appeals referred to disclosure settlements as "no better than a racket" and expressly adopted *Trulia*'s "plainly material" language.[37]

In response, the disclosure bar shifted tactics again, this time converting disclosure settlements to resolutions based on mootness. Mootness fees avoid judicial scrutiny when, as is often the case, defendants agree to the plaintiffs' fee request. Because there is no class settlement and therefore no

[32] The firm changed names during the sample period, from Proctor Heyman Enerio/ to Heyman Enerio Gattuso & Hirzel. For the sake of brevity I refer to the firm by the two names that persisted in each iteration: "Heyman Enerio."

[33] In re Handy & Harman, Ltd. S'holders Litig., C.A. No. 0882-VC (Del. Ch. Dec 08, 2017) (preliminary settlement for $30 million): In re Pilgrim's Pride Corp. Deriv. Litig., C.A. No. 0058-JTL (Del. Ch., Jan. 24., 2018) (preliminary settlement for $42.5 million).

[34] 129 A.3d. at 898. [35] Cornerstone Research, *supra* note 3, at 14. [36] *Id.*

[37] 832 F.3d 718, 724–25 (7th Cir. 2016). The Seventh Circuit has since doubled-down on Walgreen, recognizing the "racket" of non-meritorious class action filings in contexts other than merger litigation. In re Subway Footlong, 2017 WL 3666635 (7th Cir. Aug. 25, 2017). ("A class action that seeks only worthless benefits for the class and yields only fees for class counsel is no better than a racket and should be dismissed out of hand.")

class-wide release of claims, there is no fairness hearing and, often, no further filing other than the notice of dismissal. Mootness resolutions are now common: "Of the in 2018, 92% of completed deal cases were brought in federal court. In that same year, in at least 63% of litigated cases, plaintiffs' attorneys received a mootness fee."[38]

Mootness resolutions have tactical value to the disclosure bar not only because they avoid the judicial scrutiny otherwise associated with settlement. Mootness resolutions are also valuable to the disclosure bar in federal cases because they enable them to evade potential application of the PSLRA.

3.5.2 *Evading the PSLRA*

Congress enacted the PSLRA to contain the perceived spread of non-meritorious securities class actions. Several provisions of the PSLRA are directly relevant to the 14a-9 claims into which most merger litigation has now evolved. First, the PSLRA expressly limits attorney's fees to a fraction of damages recovered.[39] Hence, if no damages are recovered, courts cannot award fees from the company. Second, the PSLRA requires plaintiffs to state with specificity why each alleged misstatement or omission is materially misleading.[40] Third, the PSLRA requires plaintiffs to identify, at the time of filing, other securities claims filed during the prior three years "in which the plaintiff has sought to serve as a representative party on behalf of a class."[41] Fourth, the PSLRA bars any plaintiff from leading more than five securities class actions in any three-year period.[42] Fifth, and finally, the PSLRA requires courts to make Rule 11 findings with regard to any "complaint, responsive pleading, or dispositive motion" filed by plaintiffs' attorneys.[43] These provisions would seem to substantively impede the proliferation of merger-related nuisance claims in federal court. However, each of these requirements has a different trigger – some are triggered upon filing, some upon class certification, others upon final adjudication. This provides plaintiffs with an opportunity to avoid them through strategic pleading.

First, with regard to the provision limiting attorneys' fees to a fraction of damages, the PSLRA states that: "Total attorneys' fees and expenses awarded by the court to counsel for the plaintiff class shall not exceed a reasonable percentage of the amount of any damages and prejudgment interest actually paid to the class."[44] Because no damages or prejudgment interest are paid to the class in a disclosure settlement or a mootness resolution, a straightforward reading of the plain text of this provision, uncontradicted by the legislative history, bars courts from awarding attorneys' fees in such cases.[45] Although some district courts have hesitated to accept this reading of the statutory text,[46] others have adopted it.[47]

38 Cain, Fisch, Solomon & Thomas, *supra* note 24.

39 15 U.S. Code § 78u–4(a)(6).

40 15 U.S. Code § 78u–4(b)(1).

41 15 U.S. Code § 78u–4(a)(2)(A)(v).The certification also requires the plaintiff to commit not to accept any payment in connection with the litigation other than her pro rata share of any recovery, except as approved by the court.

42 15 U.S. Code § 78u–4(a)(3)(B)(vi).

43 15 U.S. Code § 78u–4(c)(1).

44 15 U.S. Code § 78u–4(a)(6).

45 An alternative interpretation – that Congress intended only to limit attorneys' fees to a reasonable percentage of damages when damages are paid, not to ban fee awards for non-pecuniary relief – imports assumed meanings into otherwise unambiguous statutory text and is, in any event, unsupported by legislative history. Courts in other jurisdictions have read parallel statutes to bar non-pecuniary relief in class action settlements. Kazman v. Frontier Oil Corp., 398 S.W.3d 377 (Tex. App., Houston, 2013).

46 See, e.g., Taxman v. Covidien plc, 1:14-cv-12949 (D. Mass., Sept. 21, 2015) TRANSCRIPT at 48 ("[I]t is an awful lot of weight to read on that one sentence, that Congress rewrote the common benefit rule with respect to federal securities litigation in that sort of backhanded way, rather than directly. . . . I don't read the language quite as powerfully as you do.").

47 See Adam Franchi v. Bay Bancorp, Inc., et al., No. 1:17-cv-03699, Memorandum Opinion Denying Motion for Fees (D. Md. Oct. 25, 2018) (holding that because the plaintiff's complaint was filed under the Exchange Act and was mooted by defendant's supplemental disclosures, resulting in "no monetary benefit [to plaintiff] or the putative

On its face, this provision applies only to fees "awarded by the court." This applies most obviously to settlements. As discussed above, fees paid in most mootness resolutions are privately negotiated between plaintiffs and defense counsel. Hence, no court award. However, should a defendant contest a fee request, the only way for plaintiffs' counsel to be paid would be for the fee to be awarded by a court on the basis of the attorneys' efforts on behalf of the class. In this case, the PSLRA would appear to apply. As a result, an attorney petitioning for fees based upon her efforts in a class-based claim is asking for something the PSLRA bars the court from awarding.[48]

Nevertheless, a route around the PSRLA's ban on fees for nonmonetary relief remains. This provision, like many provisions of the PSLRA, depends upon the existence of a class. The provision applies to fees awarded "to counsel for the plaintiff class." Whether settled or resolved for mootness, when claims are filed as class actions and assert a right to recovery on that basis, any fee award derives from the existence of class claim and should therefore be covered under the PSLRA. But individual claims – that is, claims filed by a plaintiff in her individual capacity not claiming to represent a class – would seem to evade this provision. Indeed, the provisions of the PSLRA are generally applicable to "each private action arising under [the federal securities laws] ... brought as a plaintiff class action pursuant to the Federal Rules of Civil Procedure."[49] By negative inference, it is not applicable to individual actions.

Perhaps following this logic, a pattern of filing 14a-9 claims as individual rather than class actions has begun to emerge in my frequent filer data. The first individual (rather than class or derivative) complaint filed by a plaintiff in my dataset appeared in 2015, with the number of such claims steadily increasing each year: seven in 2016, fourteen in 2017, and twenty-two in 2018. Apart from being filed as individual complaints, with no reference to a class, these complaints are otherwise indistinguishable from class actions claims. The only meaningful difference is that as nonclass filings, they are not subject to the PSLRA.

Other provisions of the PSLRA can also be evaded even more easily, either by filing as a class but never seeking certification or, instead, by filing individual actions. For example the provision requiring courts to make Rule 11 findings is triggered by "final adjudication of the action."[50] In the case of mootness resolutions, therefore, Rule 11 findings are not required because courts do not treat voluntary dismissals, with or without prejudice, as "final adjudication."[51] Likewise, the PSLRA's presumptive prohibition against leading more than five class actions in a three-year period may only apply at class certification, when lead plaintiffs are actually appointed. Nevertheless, there is at least an argument that a plaintiff seeks to lead a class action when she files a class complaint and that therefore the presumptive ban should be interpreted to apply at filing, not only at certification.

The PSLRA's pleading and certification requirements, however, are clearly applicable at the time of filing. Plaintiffs therefore cannot avoid the requirement that they plead with specificity by

class ... the Court concludes that [plaintiff] and the putative class are not entitled to an award of attorney's fees"); See also Mostaed v. Crawford, 2012 WL 3947978, at *7 (E.D.Va. Sept. 10, 2012) ("[P]laintiffs must be denied attorneys' fees because the [PSLRA] amended the [Exchange Act] to prevent the award of attorneys' fees except where counsel's efforts have led to monetary relief that is 'actually paid to the class of claimants.'"); In re Microstrategy, Inc., 172 F. Supp.2d 778, 784–85 (E.D.Va 2001) (holding that the PSLRA operates as a "limitation on the fees and expenses awarded by a court").

48 *Franchi*, No. 1:17-cv-03699, *supra* note 47. *See also* Mostaed, 2012 WL 3947978, at *7 (holding "federal law clearly precludes" attorney's fees when plaintiffs have not received a monetary judgment).

49 15 U.S. Code § 78u–4(a)(1).

50 15 U.S. Code § 78u–4(c)(1).

51 Rosenfeld, 2018 WL 4177938, at *6 (S.D.N.Y. Aug. 30, 2018); Blaser v. Bessemer Trust Co., N.A., No. 01cv11599 (DLC), 2002 WL 31359015, at *3 (S.D.N.Y. Oct. 21, 2002); Unite Here v. Cintas Corp., 500 F. Supp. 2d. 332, 336-37 (S.D.N.Y. 2007). See also Manchester Mgmt. Co., LLC v. Echo Therapeutics, Inc., 297 F. Supp. 3d 451, 465-66 (S.D.N.Y. 2018) (collecting cases).

seeking a mootness resolution. Applied strictly, this requirement would force plaintiffs to articulate precisely why specific misstatements or omissions make the proxy materially misleading. Pleading with specificity means not merely claiming, as plaintiffs often do, that disclosure is good and more is better. Rather, it means stating precisely why each claimed omission – such as non-GAAP financial measures left out of the summary of the fairness opinion – makes the proxy statement materially misleading. For example, a federal court recently abrogated a disclosure-based mootness resolution on the basis of the materiality of the disclosures alleged in the complaint.[52] Holding that the proper inquiry was the materiality of the alleged disclosure deficiencies, not the corrective disclosures made by defendant subsequent to the filing of the complaint, the court found that none of the alleged disclosures met the standard of materiality and should therefore have been dismissed "out of hand."[53]

Likewise, the PSLRA's certification requirement applies at filing, irrespective of class certification.[54] Pursuant to this requirement, plaintiffs must certify that they are "willing to serve as a representative party on behalf of a class" and disclose the number of actions "in which the plaintiff has sought to serve as a representative party on behalf of a class" in the last three years.[55] Because a plaintiff seeks to represent a class every time she files a class action, mootness claims filed as class actions therefore cannot evade the certification requirement.

The plaintiff's filing of the undertakings required in the certification creates an opening for further judicial inquiry into the adequacy of the plaintiff and her counsel. For example, if a plaintiff disclosed that she had filed multiple representative actions during that period, the court could ask additional questions, such as:

- What results were obtained by the plaintiff in her representatives actions filed over the past three years?
- Has plaintiffs' counsel filed other representative actions on behalf of other plaintiffs over the same period? If so, what were the results obtained in these actions?

Such questions would reveal whether the plaintiff is a frequent filer and unmask her counsel as a member of the disclosure bar. The court may also inquire into the relationship between the named plaintiff and plaintiffs' counsel. Are their financial or familial relationships that suggest the named plaintiff may be an inadequate monitor of class counsel? Federal courts have authority to enquire into these matters under Rule 23(a)(4), which requires the court to determine whether "the representative parties will fairly and adequately protect the interests of the class." If the court is troubled by what it finds, it might inquire further:

- Is the plaintiff willing to provide the putative class with notice and an opportunity to object to any resolution of the claim?
- Would the parties consent to the judicial appointment of an *amicus* to evaluate the materiality of the allegations in the complaint, with such costs to be taxed to the parties?

The point here is that courts can and should use the certification requirement as an opening to seek further undertakings and commitments from the parties in order to safeguard the interests of the putative class.

52 House v. Akorn, Memorandum Opinion and Order, 1:17-cv-05018, 2019 WL 2576531 (N.D. Ill., June 24, 2019).

53 Id., at *5.

54 15 U.S. Code § 78u–4(a)(2)(A) (applicable to "[e]ach plaintiff seeking to serve as a representative party on behalf of a class").

55 15 U.S. Code § 78u–4(a)(2)(A)(v).

However, like the bar on attorneys' fees for nonpecuniary relief, the certification and pleading requirements can be avoided by filing individual rather than class actions. The PSLRA applies to litigation in which a plaintiff has either been certified as a class representative or files a claim seeking class certification. Individual actions are neither of those things. It would therefore seem that plaintiffs can avoid the PSLRA by filing individual actions and resolving them for mootness. How the law should respond to these tactics is the subject of the next section.

3.6 RECOMMENDATIONS

The PSLRA ought to stop the flood of merger-related nuisance litigation into federal court and reverse the flow back into state courts. Not only does the PSLRA bar the award of attorneys' fees for nonmonetary recoveries, it also requires plaintiffs to meet a high standard of materiality at pleading, prevents plaintiffs from seeking to represent a class more than five times in three years, and requires sworn undertakings by class action claimants. Recognizing their inability to recover fees in federal court, plaintiffs' lawyers would move their cases back to state court, where even if the salad days of disclosure settlements are over, courts remain receptive to awarding attorneys' fees based on mootness resolutions.[56]

Why, then, has this not happened? The obvious answer is that the PSRLA is not applied consistently. Indeed, that 6 plaintiffs brought 148 federal securities lawsuits from 2016 through 2018 when the PSLRA would have limited them to a maximum of 30 suggests that the statute is often not applied at all.[57] But why is that?

This part argues that three parties are to blame for the inconsistent application of the PSLRA: plaintiffs, defendants, and judges. First, plaintiffs thwart the PSLRA by pleading strategically. Second, defendants frustrate the PSLRA because they so frequently acquiesce to paying plaintiffs' attorneys' fees rather than contesting them. Third, judges have been unable (or unwilling) to coalesce around a single interpretation of the PSLRA and a coherent approach to mootness resolutions. In the sections below, I sketch these problems and offer solutions to each, noting the obstacles that remain.

3.6.1 *Prevent Strategic Pleading by Plaintiffs*

Plaintiffs plead strategically to avoid application of the PSLRA. By aiming for mootness resolutions rather than disclosure settlements, they are able to avoid class certification and "final adjudication." Furthermore, by filing individual rather than class actions, they are able to avoid any risk that the PSLRA will be applied to them. Consistent with this account, I found that the plaintiffs in my sample increasingly filed 14a-9 claims as individual rather than class actions. Courts should respond to this trend by refusing to award attorneys' fees to individual claimants based on the value of class-wide relief and instead award fees, if at all, only on the basis of the named plaintiff's proportional share of the benefit. Awarding fees to individual claimants based on class-wide relief is unsupported by doctrine and inconsistent with fundamental norms of equity.

[56] Indeed *Trulia* suggested that mootness was the "preferred scenario" for resolving disclosure-based claims. 129 A.3d at 897. Moreover, subsequent decisions in Delaware have suggested a lower standard of materiality for awarding mootness fees as opposed to disclosure settlements. See In re Xoom Corp. S'holder Litig., 2016 Del. Ch. LEXIS 117, at *10 (Aug. 4, 2016) (awarding a $50,000 mootness fee for "disclosure provid[ing] some benefit to stockholders, whether or not material"). Under the circumstances, plaintiffs seem to have stayed away given Delaware's tendency to award mid-five-figure fees rather than the low six-figure fees now common in federal court.

[57] See *supra* note 21 and accompanying text.

Underlying both the common fund doctrine, under which courts award attorneys' fees for monetary recoveries, and the corporate benefit doctrine, under which courts award fees for nonmonetary recoveries, is a principle of fee-*sharing*.[58] Under both doctrines, the attorney is awarded by the class of beneficiaries on the basis of the benefit they share. This is most apparent when the attorney's fee is taken from the monetary recovery to be shared by the class. But the principle also operates in derivative suits and class actions when attorneys' fees for nonmonetary benefits are assessed against the corporation. In the derivative suit context, the corporation is the legal plaintiff and therefore the attorney's client, thus justifying the assessment of fees against it. In the context of a certified class, assessing fees against the corporation is justified by the fact that, through certification of the class and appointment of lead counsel, the attorney is made the legal representative of all shareholders. Because the corporation is an asset of all shareholders, assessing fees against the corporation ensures that they are shared by the class of beneficiaries represented by the attorney.

There is no equivalent basis for fee-sharing when the plaintiff files an individual suit rather than a class action. When plaintiffs' lawyers bring individual actions, their client is the named plaintiff and no-one else. Just as any monetary recovery from the suit would belong exclusively to the named plaintiff, not the corporation (as in a derivative suit) or all shareholders (as in a class action), the common fund doctrine does not apply and attorneys' fees must be recovered from the named plaintiff. Likewise, in the absence of a derivative suit or a certified class, there is no legal basis for fee-sharing. In an individual action, the attorney does not represent the corporation or all shareholders as a class. Assessing attorneys' fees against the corporation in the context of an individual action therefore amounts to fee-*shifting*, not fee-*sharing*. Fee-shifting is not supported by either the common fund or corporate benefit doctrines.[59]

A logically consistent approach to attorneys' fees for individual actions would limit an attorney's fees in such cases to her client's proportional interest in the class-wide benefit. Outside of the context of derivative suits and certified class actions, courts should not award fees on the basis of class-wide benefits. Instead, the attorney should be awarded a sum based on the value the disclosure achieves for the specific named plaintiff. So if, for example, a shareholder plaintiff has 0.0001 percent of the common stock of a company, the proportionality principle implies that the plaintiffs' attorney should receive a fee no greater than 0.0001 percent of the value of the class-wide benefit. Thus, assuming the total aggregate value of a highly material supplemental disclosure is $500,000, a court should award plaintiffs' counsel no more than $50 in fees.

This does not mean that attorneys cannot be compensated for having achieved class-wide relief. It means only that if they wish to recover fees on that basis, then they must do so under one of the two recognized procedural methods for doing so. They must file either a derivative suit or a class action. The derivative suit is the traditional vehicle for obtaining equitable or injunctive relief – benefits such as the prevention of an unlawfully convened meeting or reversal of an *ultra vires* action – from a corporation, but such benefits may also be achieved through class actions. Indeed, the history of merger litigation pre-*Trulia* typically involved state fiduciary duty suits brought as class actions.[60]

The distinction between class and derivative actions, on the one hand, and individual complaints, on the other, is not a procedural peccadillo. Both the class and derivative suit contain substantive mechanisms to prevent abuse. Foremost among these in the derivative suit

[58] Griffith, *supra* note 6, at 40–42. [59] Griffith, *supra* note 6.

[60] Robert B. Thompson and Randall S. Thomas, "The New Look of Shareholder Litigation: Acquisition-Oriented Class Actions," *Vanderbilt Law Review* 57, 2004: 133.

context is the demand requirement, which prevents individual plaintiffs from bringing representative litigation to which the board of directors objects. The theory here is that shareholders already have representatives (the board), and unless these representatives harbor some conflict of interest, they are the ones to determine whether the lawsuit is in the interests of all shareholders. Likewise, certification provides important protections for class members. Class certification provides a mechanism for shareholders to object to the appointment of lead plaintiff and lead counsel. Class certification also creates mechanisms for class members to opt out of the representation or object to the outcome. Finally, securities class actions trigger the additional protections of the PSLRA reviewed above.

Individual actions provide no such protections. When an individual action is resolved for mootness, there is no opportunity for other shareholders to object to either the benefit or to the fees. As nonparties to the dispute, they have no standing to intervene. Attributing benefits and taxing fees to them thus amounts to an imposition of outcome and a shifting of fees without giving them any choice in the matter. Not only is this contrary to the procedural requirements of Rule 23, more fundamentally it is contrary to basic norms of equity to appoint a de facto shareholder representative in a process that denies shareholders the opportunity to question the appointment, to contest the adequacy of the representative, and to object to the value of the resulting relief. Treating individual actions as the equivalent of representative actions lets a single plaintiff speak for a corporation's entire shareholder base when no one – no court, no corporation, and no shareholder – has evaluated that shareholder's adequacy as a representative or inquired into her motivations.

Another way of seeing this is through the lens of litigation agency costs. Representative actions – class and derivative suits – contain mechanisms for ensuring that the agent (the attorney) remains accountable to the principal (the shareholders). Individual actions, because the attorney is assumed to be directly accountable to her client, do not. Allowing attorneys to recover representative fees for filing individual actions avoids these mechanisms and renders the lawyers wholly unaccountable to the broader interests attributed to them. It would not be surprising if such unconstrained agents represented no one but themselves.

Courts should therefore refuse to award representative fees to attorneys that file individual actions. Awarding class-based attorneys' fees to individual claimants is inconsistent with fundamental principles of fairness and unsupported by the theory underlying both the common fund and corporate benefit doctrines. If courts consistently refused to award representative fees for individual actions, plaintiffs could still file individual claims. And some large institutional investors probably would do so. But most individuals probably would not, simply because they are likely unwilling to pay their lawyers directly and their lawyers, unable to recover fees from the corporation, would likely be unwilling to take the case. Instead, the lawyers would channel such claims back into class or derivative suit filings – a salutary result since class and derivative claims, unlike individual suits, contain mechanisms for ensuring the accountability of the attorney-agent to the interests of the shareholder class.

3.6.2 *Motivate Defendants to Resist*

All of the above focuses on the judicial *award* of fees. However, as already noted, most merger suits today are not resolved with a judicial award of fees, but rather with the corporate defendant acquiescing to pay the plaintiffs' attorneys based on mootness. How then, does clarifying the basis on which fees may and may not be awarded by courts affect a system in which fees are not collected by judicial order? Even if courts could not award class-based fees for individual filings, claimants could still file individual actions and resolve them for mootness fees without involving a court. Alternatively, plaintiffs might not even file a complaint at all but simply send defendants a letter threatening to do so unless they moot their concerns and acquiesce to paying them a fee for their troubles. Considering their willingness to pay rather than fight, defendants appear to be complicit in this arrangement, which explains why the strongest arguments under the PSLRA are so rarely raised. How then does a reform focusing on the judicial award of fees respond to a world in which fees are often paid without ever being awarded by a court?

The answer lies in the notion that all bargaining takes place in the shadow of the law.[61] What parties agree to do privately depends upon what they may be ordered to do publicly. Applied here, this means that the amount that judges can reasonably be expected to award in a contested fee application sets a ceiling on plaintiffs' ability to claim fees from the defendant. As a result, plaintiffs' inability to recover fees in court should reduce or even eliminate defendants' willingness to pay them in private negotiations.

In addition to the legal merits, a second contributing factor to settlement value is the cost of deciding a claim. If the process for determining a claim's value is long and costly, it may have positive settlement value without regard to its underlying legal merit. Thus, even if plaintiffs' attorneys are not entitled to a judicial award of fees, they may nevertheless be able to extract fees from the defendant up to the cost of litigating the claim. Judicial uncertainty contributes to these demands. The more uncertain the outcome in court, the greater the risk of further process. The risk and cost of judicial proceedings encourages defendant acquiescence to fee demands without regard to the merits of the underlying legal entitlement.

Nevertheless, these costs are largely within judges' power to control. Judges could streamline these processes by unambiguously refusing to award class-based fees for individual actions and by consistently applying the provisions of the PSLRA. Were they to do so, the legal value of the plaintiffs' entitlement to legal fees would fall to zero and the cost of litigating them would likewise fall to the cost of filing a one page motion to dismiss simply citing the PSLRA. Unfortunately, as discussed below, federal judges have been neither clear nor consistent in their approach to these issues.

3.6.3 *Coordinate the Judicial Response*

In a prior coauthored article, I argued that the problem of merger-related nuisance suits would be solved by moving this litigation into federal court.[62] My coauthors and I reasoned, consistent with the arguments above, that such claims would not survive an encounter with the PSLRA. Since the publication of that article, however, *Trulia* solved the problem in Delaware, yet merger-related nuisance litigation continues, largely unabated, in federal court.

Our mistake lay in failing to account for differences in the organizational structure of the Delaware judiciary, on the one hand, and the federal judiciary, on the other. These differences give Delaware an advantage over the federal courts in responding to perceived litigation excesses. Most notably, in Delaware a single court, the Court of Chancery, hears all corporate law cases, and although the judges on that court sit individually, the court has only seven (then five) members. Moreover, because the members of the Court of Chancery hear so many related cases and regularly meet to discuss them, it is relatively easy for the court to design a coherent and

61 Robert Cooter, Stephen Marks & Robert Mnookin. "Bargaining in the Shadow of the Law: A Testable Model of Strategic Behavior." *Journal of Legal Studies* 11, 1982: 225–51.

62 Fisch, Griffith & Solomon, *supra* note 5.

consistent approach to recurring issues or, as in the case of disclosure-based merger litigation, systemic problems.

The federal judiciary, by contrast, consists of approximately 650 district court judges scattered across the country. They do not specialize in a particular type of case. Moreover, in spite of the relatively large number of 14a-9 claims filed in federal district courts, individual judges are not especially likely to be assigned one and may rarely encounter securities class actions during their entire career on the bench. Most federal judges do not have a background in corporate or securities law and are therefore unlikely to be familiar with the operation of the PSRLA or the policy issues surrounding it.[63] They do not generally meet to coordinate their approach on issues and are not bound follow other district court rulings even within the same circuit. Although district courts are bound to follow the rulings of their Circuit Court of Appeals, rulings in merger-related nuisance suits are rarely appealed. For this reason, binding appellate precedent is largely absent in this area – the notable exception being the Seventh Circuit[64] – leaving federal district courts largely uncoordinated and unconstrained.

Additionally, federal judges are likely to be operating in an informational vacuum when the 14a-9 claims they have been assigned are resolved for mootness. Judges operating in an adversarial system, as opposed to an inquisitorial system, rely on the parties to inform them of relevant legal issues. However, unless the defendant contests the fee, there is no adversarial process before the judge in a mootness resolution. As a result, neither the requirements of the PSLRA nor any other serious issue, such as the filing of individual as opposed to class actions, is raised to the judge. Only a highly motivated judge thoroughly steeped in corporate and securities law issues is likely to raise concerns *sua sponte*. Moreover, district court judges have a history of disregarding the PSLRA, even when the terms of the statute require them to act – for example, by requiring certified undertakings or making Rule 11 filings.[65] When, as in the case of a mootness resolution, the parties have arranged for the discrete disappearance of their dispute, judges are unlikely to intervene to prevent the removal of a case from their docket.

As a result, it is somewhat naïve to expect individual federal judges to solve the problem of merger-related nuisance suits.[66] Were one federal district court judge to read the PSLRA and apply it as written, there would still be 649 or so that might not.[67] In order for federal courts to solve the nuisance suit problem rather than exacerbating it, there must be a coordination mechanism around which federal district courts can organize a unified approach to 14a-9 filings and application of the PSLRA to them. Fortunately, coordination mechanisms exist.

The Federal Judicial Conference (the Conference) consists of representatives from all levels of the federal judiciary and, through its standing and advisory committees, develops judicial policy for US courts.[68] The Conference could and should consider changes to procedural rules

63 Stephen M. Bainbridge & G. Mitu Gulati. "How Do Judges Maximize? (The Same Way Everybody Else Does – Boundedly): Rules of Thumb in Securities Fraud Opinions." *Emory Law Journal* 51, 2002: 85–86.

64 *See supra* note 37 and accompanying text.

65 Todd Henderson & William H. J. Hubbard. "Judicial Noncompliance with Mandatory Procedural Rules Under the PSLRA." *Journal of Legal Studies* 44, 2015: S87–S105.

66 My former coauthors have doubled down on this approach in a new paper, advocating amendments to FRCP 23 to require mootness awards to be approved by a federal district court judge (Cain, Fisch, Solomon & Thomas, *supra* note 24). However, without some a means of coordinating the judiciary, such an approach essentially creates a lottery in which success depends largely upon the judge one draws, the same basic system that prevailed in disclosure settlements pre-*Trulia* (Marianna Wonder, "The Changing Odds of the Chancery Lottery." *Fordham Law Review* 84, 2016: 2381–412). A simpler and more promising approach, I argue, lies in coordinating the federal judiciary around consistent application of the PSLRA.

67 One is an exaggeration. There are at least three. See *supra* note 47 and accompanying text.

68 28 U.S.C. § 331 (creating the Federal Judicial Conference).

to develop a coherent and coordinated approach to merger and disclosure-related litigation filed in federal courts. Specifically, the Conference should adopt a rule precluding judges from awarding attorneys' fees based on class-wide benefits for filing individual actions. Fees based on class-wide benefits should only be available to attorneys filing class or derivative actions. Furthermore, the Conference could and should require federal district court judges to apply the provisions of the PSLRA to all securities class action filings.

In addition to the Conference, the Federal Judicial Center (the Center) offers educational programming to federal judges on various substantive and procedural matters.[69] The Center could and should design educational programming around the trends in merger-related nuisance suits described in this chapter. It should also design educational programming about the provisions of the PSLRA and their applicability to these suits.

Coordination through the Conference and the Center would enable the federal judiciary to develop a unified approach to what has become a systemic problem. Merger and disclosure-related claims filed under the federal securities laws and the mootness-based resolutions that accompany them are problematic not only because they impose a meaningless tax on corporations and their investors, the easy availability of fee-based resolutions may disincentivize attorneys from investing in cases of legitimate wrongdoing. And taxing fees and costs to corporations without giving the shareholders an opportunity to opt-out or object is fundamentally inequitable and deprives them of statutory rights under Rule 23 and the provisions of the PSLRA.

3.7 CONCLUSION

This chapter has examined the problem of merger-related nuisance suits. It has supplied empirical evidence from a dataset of frequent filer plaintiffs, finding that over a five-year period seven individual plaintiffs filed 282 shareholder suits. Analysis of these filings reveals that they have been designed strategically to avoid hostile state court precedent as well as application of the PSRLA. The most recent innovation along these lines appears to be filing of individual rather than class-based complaints.

Federal courts already have the means, through the PSLRA, to correct these problems. However, doing so requires coordination. Fortunately, coordination mechanisms exist. The Federal Judicial Conference and the Federal Judicial Center should be used to develop a unified approach to stop the flood of merger-related nuisance litigation.

[69] 28 U.S.C. §§ 620 (creating the Federal Judicial Center).

4

How Many Class Actions Are Meritless?

Brian T. Fitzpatrick

One of the most frequent criticisms of class action lawsuits is that they are often meritless.[1] This is an important component of the campaign against class actions. If most class actions are meritless, then many of the virtues of private enforcement become moot: even if private lawyers are more effective than government bureaucrats at enforcing the law, if most of the enforcement efforts are misguided, why would we *want* them to be effective? The profit motive would simply be giving us more of something we don't want. Better to have someone ineffectual than someone effectual when it comes to delivering bad stuff.

We saw this criticism in the last chapter from Sean Griffith for a small corner of the class action world. There is little reason, however, to think most or even many class action lawsuits are meritless. Moreover, businesses have a cheap and effective way to deal with the meritless class actions that are filed – it's called a motion to dismiss. In other words, meritless class actions are not such a big problem that it would justify crippling the entire class action system as corporate America and some conservatives want to do.

As a matter of theory, this should not be particularly surprising: it is one of the virtues of private enforcement that class action lawyers do not make any money unless their lawsuits succeed. How can a lawyer succeed if his or her cases have no merit? Won't the company win every case, leaving the lawyer impoverished? Yes. As the Columbia law professor John Coffee concludes: "the existing theory and empirical evidence do not provide support for the claim that plaintiff's attorneys have strong incentives to bring nonmeritorious actions."[2]

Let me begin by acknowledging that, *of course*, every once in a while a lawyer will file a stupid class action lawsuit. There are one million lawyers in the United States. Occasionally, one of them does something stupid. This is not only true of class action lawsuits, but all kinds of lawsuits: there are stupid lawsuits filed of every stripe. And it is not only true of lawyers: every profession includes in their ranks some individuals who sometimes do stupid things.[3]

But when lawyers do stupid things, defendants have at their disposal a cheap and easy way to get relief: they can file a motion to dismiss. Under current law, if the defendant can show the

[1] See, e.g., Joanna Schwartz's statement that "[t]he Chamber of Commerce has [argued] that class action claims are often meritless." "The Cost of Suing Business," *DePaul Law Review* 65 (2016): 673.

[2] John C. Coffee, "Understanding the Plaintiff's Attorney: The Implications of Economic Theory for Private Enforcement of Law Through Class and Derivative Actions," *Columbia Law Review* 86 (1986): 676–677.

[3] See, e.g., John Schwartz, "If Tech Execs Act Like Spoiled Brats, Should We Spank Them?," *New York Times*, July 14, 2017.

lawsuit has no legal basis or no "plausible" factual basis, then the judge will dismiss the case – no ifs, ands, or buts.[4] These motions are inexpensive to file.

Defendants take advantage of the motion to dismiss all the time. Statisticians at the Federal Judicial Center (FJC) twice examined a large sample of class actions in federal court – once in 1996 and once in 2008 – and both times they found that, in the vast majority of cases, the defendants filed a motion to dismiss the case.[5] How often did courts grant them and dismiss the case? Less than 20 percent of the time. Scholars of securities fraud class actions have found similar dismissal rates, 20–30 percent.[6]

What do these numbers mean? They mean that only a *small minority* of class action cases could possibly be described as meritless. Why? Because the number of meritless cases is surely much *lower* than the number of dismissed cases. After all, not every dismissed case is

4 The US Supreme Court – to much criticism by liberal scholars – has made it easier and easier for judges to dismiss meritless cases on a motion to dismiss. See Ashcroft v. Iqbal, 556 U.S. 662 (2009); Bell Atl. Corp. v. Twombly, 550 U.S. 544 (2007). I am one of few scholars to defend the Court's decisions on this issue. See "*Twombly* and *Iqbal* Reconsidered," *Notre Dame Law Review* 87, no. 4 (2012).

5 Thomas E. Willging, Laural L. Hooper, and Robert J. Niemic find that motions to dismiss are filed in between 31 percent and 63 percent of cases depending on the district. "Empirical Study of Class Actions in Four Federal District Courts: Final Report to the Advisory Committee on Civil Rules," (Federal Judicial Center, 1996), 171, table 24. The same study finds that between 17 percent and 20 percent of cases terminate on the motion to dismiss (ibid., 172, table 27). A later study by Emery G. Lee III and Thomas E. Willging finds that motions to dismiss are filed in a high percentage of cases, though it is unclear exactly how high because the motions tallied may have overlapped with each other. "Impact of the Class Action Fairness Act on the Federal Courts: Preliminary Findings from Phase Two's Pre-CAFA Sample of Diversity Class Actions," (Federal Judicial Center, November 2008), 5, table 4. This study finds that 12 percent of cases are terminated on the motion to dismiss (6, table 6). The second study reports a high rate at which plaintiffs voluntarily dismissed their own cases (38 percent) (2). It is not clear if these were meritless cases that plaintiffs knew they would lose after they saw the defendants' motions to dismiss, if they had merit and the defendants entered into a settlement with the plaintiffs to prevent them from seeking to certify the cases as class actions, or if they had merit and plaintiffs dismissed them in one venue to file them elsewhere. As Lee and Willging write:

> Voluntary dismissals may represent a financial or equitable-relief settlement of the individual claims of the named plaintiffs or a dismissal of such claims without a settlement . . . Dismissal without a settlement can also be divided into two types of cases: those dismissed for all time because of lack of merit or a solvent defendant, and those dismissed with an eye toward litigating the same case in another court. Docket records almost never indicate which of those scenarios is applicable to a given case. In the voluntary dismissals, plaintiffs and defendants may have agreed to file a proposed class settlement in another forum. Or . . . plaintiffs may have plans to pursue the dismissed claims in another, presumably more favorable, federal venue. (10)

However, the study does cast doubt on the possibility that voluntary dismissal was primarily driven by plaintiffs realizing their cases were meritless, as "[d]efendants . . . were less likely to file dispositive motions in these cases than in other types of cases" (10). Another possibility is that the superior litigation resources of the defendants wore down the lawyers who brought these cases. See Hensler's comment that these dismissals may have also been for "lack of resources": the lawyers may have had "less financial wherewithal to persevere against deep pocket corporate defendants." "Can Private Class Actions Enforce Regulations? Do They? Should They?," in *Comparative Law and Regulation* (Northampton, MA: Edward Elgar Publishing, 2016), 258.

6 Choi, Nelson, and Pritchard find that before 1995, securities class actions were dismissed 21.4 percent of the time, but after 1995, such suits were dismissed 30.4 percent of the time. "The Screening Effect of the Private Securities Litigation Reform Act," *Journal of Empirical Legal Studies* 6, no. 1 (2009): 36, table 1D. See also: Cox, Thomas, and Bai, who find 28.6 percent of securities fraud class actions were dismissed between 1993 and 2006, " Do Differences in Pleading Standards Cause Forum Shopping in Securities Class Actions?: Doctrinal and Empirical Analyses," *Wisconsin Law Review* 324 (2009): 421–453; Choi and Pritchard find 35.9 percent of securities fraud class actions were dismissed with prejudice between 2003 and mid-2007, "Supreme Court's Impact on Securities Class Actions: An Empirical Assessment of *Tellabs*," *Journal of Law, Economics, & Organization* 28, no. 4 (2012): 859; Stefan Boettrich and Svetlana Starykh find 27.5 percent of all securities fraud class actions between 2000 and 2017 were dismissed with prejudice, *Recent Trends in Securities Class Action Litigation: 2017 Full-Year Review*, NERA Economic Consulting, January 29, 2018, 19. Although some of these studies and those in the previous note predate the Supreme Court's 2007 adoption of the requirement that lawsuits be at least "plausible" to survive a motion to dismiss, scholars have found that district courts dismissed lawsuits because they doubted their merits long before the Supreme Court gave them the green light to do so. Brian T. Fitzpatrick, "*Twombly* and *Iqbal* Reconsidered," *Notre Dame Law Review* 87, no. 4 (2012): 1631–1632.

meritless.[7] Sometimes the law is unclear and litigants have a good faith disagreement about how it should be interpreted; sometimes courts decide not to interpret the law your way. It is hard to call a lawsuit like that "meritless."

But the more important point is that, whatever the number of meritless class actions, defendants have a cheap and easy way to get rid of them – and they use it all the time.

Nonetheless, some people will tell you that this is not good enough. They say sometimes judges make mistakes on the motion to dismiss and do not dismiss meritless cases. Thus, defendants end up having to fight the lawsuits, and this costs money. They say defendants end up settling these meritless cases to avoid the expense, distraction, and risks of litigation.[8]

It is true that, if it will cost less money to settle a meritless case than to fight it, then it is rational for a defendant to settle it instead.[9] It is also true that it is rational for a defendant to settle a case if there is even a small chance a crazy jury will award a huge sum of money at trial – even if the defendant would win at trial 99 times out of a 100.[10]

But it is rational for a defendant to do these things even when the case is *not* meritless. Defendants are willing to pay extra to settle even *good* cases to avoid litigation expenses[11] and litigation risk.[12] Indeed, I worry enough about these "oversettlements" that I've devoted myself to reforms to mitigate them.[13] But in this chapter the question is, how often does this happen in *meritless* cases? How often do judges let cases unlikely to succeed slip past the motion to dismiss? All the available data points to one answer: not often.

First, if cases are unlikely to succeed, defendants will not be willing to pay much to settle them. After all, litigation expenses to fight the case will only amount to so much. Our best estimate for the most a defendant might be willing to pay in what we call a *nuisance settlement* – a settlement to avoid the nuisance of litigating – is \$1–3 million.[14] Any settlement above these amounts is unlikely to come from a meritless case – and even settlements below that amount do not

7 As Choi, Nelson, and Prichard note, there is no general agreement on how to define a meritless case: "[t]he difficulty of assessing merit . . . makes it impossible to measure precisely the proportion of nuisance settlements to settlements based on the strength of the claims." "The Screening Effect of the Private Securities Litigation Reform Act," 36.

8 As Choi, Nelson, and Pritchard note, "defendants, anxious to avoid the distraction of litigation, high defense attorney fees, negative publicity surrounding a securities lawsuit, and the specter of potentially bankrupting damages, may be willing to pay a 'nuisance' settlement to make the case go away, even when they perceive the likelihood of the plaintiff succeeding at trial as rather low." (Ibid., 36).

9 Steven Shavell describes how it is rational for a defendant to settle a claim for any amount less than or equal to the anticipated defense costs of trial and the expected value of the plaintiff's claim. *Foundations of Economic Analysis of Law* (Cambridge, MA: Harvard University Press, 2009), 401–402. Shavell goes on to say that "[t]he larger are the legal expenses of either party, the greater are the chances of settlement, clearly, since the sum of legal costs will rise, and thus the greater will be the likelihood that the sum of legal costs will exceed any excess of the plaintiff's expectation over the defendant's expectation" (406).

10 This concern reflects the fact that defendants can be risk averse. Shavell explains that

> [w]hen we introduce risk aversion into the basic model [of settlement], we see that [risk aversion] leads to a greater likelihood of settlement. The reason is simply that a trial is a risky venture because its outcome is unknown. To a risk-averse party, settlement is more attractive than it is to a risk-neutral party. Further, as the degree of risk aversion of either party increases, or as the amount at stake increases – the size of the judgment or the size of legal fees – settlement becomes more likely, other things being equal. (Ibid., 406–407).

11 Shavell's model of settlement indicates that the anticipated cost of trial is, for rational actors, a part of every decision to settle (ibid., 401–402). Shavell further explains that settlement for a greater amount than the expected value of the plaintiff's claims is rational because "if the plaintiff's minimum acceptable amount [for a settlement] is less than the defendant's maximum acceptable amount, a mutually beneficial settlement is possible – a settlement equal to any amount in between these two figures would be preferable to a trial for each party" (ibid., 402).

12 For a discussion of how risk aversion can increase settlement, see footnote 10 above.

13 See Brian T. Fitzpatrick, *The Conservative Case for Class Actions* (Chicago, Chicago University Press, 2019) chapter 9.

14 Dain C. Donelson, Justin J. Hopkins, and Christopher G. Yust rely on several studies for this range, noting that settlements are unlikely to be related to the actual loss by shareholders and suggest that the defendants settled the suit

necessarily come from meritless cases; there are some cases with small damages.[15] How often do class actions settle for such small amounts? A fraction of the time. In my empirical study of all class action settlements over a two-year period, I found that the median settlement was *over $5 million*; only 40 percent of settlements were for $3 million or less; one third for $2 million or less; and 20 percent for $1 million or less.[16] And remember: not every settlement below these thresholds is meritless. In other words, no matter how you slice the data, the vast majority of class action settlements are *not* nuisance settlements.

Second, many times defendants settle cases that have not only survived a motion to dismiss but other tests of the merits. For example, in many cases, defendants do not settle until after the judge denies the motion for summary judgment. With this motion, after examining all the evidence, the judge can dismiss the case if no "reasonable" jury could find for the plaintiff. It is even *more difficult* for a case to survive summary judgment than it is to survive a motion to dismiss. Yet, in the FJC studies I mentioned above, most class action settlements followed a judge's decision to deny a motion to dismiss, to deny a motion for summary judgment, or both.[17] Likewise, two scholars who studied settlements in antitrust class actions found that "most of the cases . . . were validated in whole or in part" either by criminal penalties, government recoveries, or by favorable rulings on motions to dismiss, rulings on summary judgment, or even at trial.[18]

Third, the judges who should be *most concerned* by a defendant being "forced" to settle meritless cases do not appear concerned at all. Who are these judges? Conservative judges, of course. If defendants had been forced to settle meritless class action cases, you would think that conservative Republican judges would be saying or doing something about it. Yet, when the antitrust scholars I mentioned above examined class action settlements, they found "a large number of the opinions [by the judges handling the cases] contain[ed] generous and gratuitous praise for the plaintiffs' counsel handling the case," including opinions by Republican judges.[19] I found something similar when I examined the attorneys' fees awarded in my empirical study of every class action settlement in federal court over a two-year period. Judges have a great deal of discretion over the fee awards that class action attorneys receive when they settle their cases. Surely, then, Republican judges would punish the lawyers that brought meritless cases with low fee awards. If so, there must not be many meritless cases that end in settlement: no matter how I ran the data, Republican judges awarded the same fees as Democratic judges.[20] In other words,

solely to avoid continued litigation expenses." "The Role of Directors' and Officers' Insurance in Securities Fraud Class Action Settlements," *Journal of Law and Economics* 58, no. 4 (2015): 751.

15 Stephen J. Choi writes that "[a]lthough settlements under $2 million may include both nuisance and nonnuisance suits, settlements over $2 million are likely meritorious." "Do the Merits Matter Less After the Private Securities Litigation Reform Act?," *Journal of Law, Economics, & Organization* 23, no. 3 (2007): 613.

16 Brian T. Fitzpatrick, "An Empirical Study of Class Action Settlements and Their Fee Awards," *Journal of Empirical Legal Studies* 7, no. 4 (2010): 828, table 5.

17 Willging, Hooper, and Niemic find that between 63 percent and 83 percent of settled cases had survived a ruling on a motion to dismiss or motion for summary judgment. "Empirical Study of Class Actions in Four Federal District Courts: Final Report to the Advisory Committee on Civil Rules," 411, table 58. Lee and Willging state that, based on their own findings, "in the typical class settlement case, the plaintiffs generally have to overcome at least one challenge directed at the merits of the case—a motion to dismiss or for summary judgment." "Impact of the Class Action Fairness Act on the Federal Courts," 10.

18 Joshua P. Davis and Robert H. Lande, "Toward an Empirical and Theoretical Assessment of Private Antitrust Enforcement," *Seattle University Law Review* 36 (2013): 1280–1281.

19 Ibid., 1284.

20 My article on that research states:

> Of the 444 fee awards using the percentage-of-the-settlement approach [the most common method of determining legal fees in class action cases], 52 percent were approved by Republican appointees, 45 percent

if meritless class actions are such a big problem, apparently the judges who hear the cases are unaware of it.

But even more telling than all this data is something else: despite ample opportunity and incentive to do so, critics have never identified very many meritless class actions. There are probably around 700 class action settlements every year in the United States, and those are just the settled cases; there are probably several times that many class action cases filed every year.[21] If meritless class actions were such a big problem, surely the critics would have hundreds and hundreds of examples to share with us, right? Wrong.

I looked and I looked for the list of hundreds of meritless class action cases maintained by the class action critics, but I could not find it. Instead, I found only two things. The first was a famous study from 1991 by Stanford law professor Janet Alexander, where she argues that securities fraud class actions were filed and settled without regard to whether there was any fraud, but rather, only with regard to how far a company's stock price had dropped; all companies with big drops were sued, and, when they were sued, the cases almost invariably settled for 25 percent of the drop.[22] If it were true that securities fraud class actions were all meritless, it would be saying something: there *are* hundreds of securities fraud class actions filed every year; this would go a long way toward proving the critics' claims. But it is not true. Professor Alexander's study relied upon a *very* small sample size and her methodology has been criticized extensively by other scholars.[23] Moreover, there have been countless studies of securities fraud class actions since hers, and they suggest quite the contrary: these class actions are filed and settled with *ample* regard for the merits – especially after Congress made it more difficult to file securities fraud class actions by enacting the Private Securities Litigation Reform Act of 1995.[24]

were approved by Democratic appointees, and 4 percent were approved by non-Article III judges (usually magistrate judges). The mean fee percentage approved by Republican appointees (25.6 percent) was slightly greater than the mean approved by Democratic appointees (24.9 percent). The medians (25 percent) were the same. ("An Empirical Study of Class Action Settlements," 833).

21 Deborah Hensler estimates that 6500 class actions are filed in the United States every year. See Hensler, "Can Private Class Actions Enforce Regulations? Do They? Should They?" 252, table 9.2. That number strikes me as quite high because it implies that only roughly one out of ten class actions ends in a class action settlement, and studies suggest that proportion is too low. See, e.g., ibid., 257, table 9.4.

22 As Professor Alexander summarizes her findings, for the class actions she studied the "link between settlement and the merits appears to have broken." "Do the Merits Matter: A Study of Settlements in Securities Class Actions," *Stanford Law Review* 43 (1991): 505.

23 See, e.g., Leonard B. Simpson and Wiliam S. Dato's response that Professor Alexander's study is "fundamentally flawed" and that "her conclusions are inconsistent with both a replication of her study done with the most obvious flaws corrected, and a broader, more reliable study." "Legislating on a False Foundation: The Erroneous Academic Underpinnings of the Private Securities Litigation Reform Act of 1995," *San Diego Law Review* 33 (1996): 962. See also Joel Seligman's critique of Professor Alexander's data and methodology. "The Merits Do Matter: A Comment on Professor Grunderfest's 'Disimplying Private Rights of Action under the Federal Securities Laws: The Commissioner's Authority'," *Harvard Law Review* 108 (1994): 453. James Bohn and Stephen Choi also critique Professor Alexander's data, and describe her results as "unconvincing." "Fraud in the New-Issues Market: Empirical Evidence on Securities Class Actions," *University of Pennsylvania Law Review* 144 (1996): 923.

24 See, e.g., James D. Cox and Randall S. Thomas's finding that "[w]e therefore see that merits do appear to matter in the settlements reached in class actions." "Mapping the American Shareholder Litigation Experience: A Survey of Empirical Studies of the Enforcement of the U.S. Securities Law," *European Company and Financial Law Review* 6, no. 2 and 3 (2009): 195. See also Donelson, Hopkins, and Yust's conclusion that "[o]ur findings suggest that most securities fraud class action settlements are meritorious". "The Role of Directors' and Officers' Insurance in Securities Fraud Class Action Settlements," 747. Choi writes that "evidence suggests a closer relation between factors related to fraud and securities class actions after the passage of the PSLRA." "Do the Merits Matter Less After the Private Securities Litigation Reform Act?," 630. Similarly, Quinn Curtis and Minor Myers find that "incidence of lawsuits ... was linked to merits-related measures of backdating activity" and "the size of settlement is related to the merits of cases." "Do the Merits Matter? Empirical Evidence on Shareholder Suits from Options Backdating Litigation," *University of Pennsylvania Law Review* 164, no. 2 (2016): 295. However, see James Bohn and Stephen

The second thing I found are lists published by the US Chamber of Commerce of the "ten most ridiculous lawsuits" filed every year.[25] The lists go back many years and I did not examine all of them, but I did examine five recent lists (2013–2017) to see how many class action lawsuits were on there. The answer? Ten.[26] Of the thousands upon thousands of class actions filed over that five-year period, the Chamber has identified only ten "ridiculous" ones. That's not many.

Perhaps there were many other ridiculous class actions that the Chamber wanted to put on these lists, but they got bumped because there were so many *even more* ridiculous *non*class action lawsuits that it had to put on the lists instead. It's impossible to know. But we can at least take a look at the ten that made it to learn what corporate America considers the worst of the worst of our class action system. If these ten aren't that bad, then we might conclude that there probably aren't hundreds and hundreds of *other* meritless ones out there:

- A lawsuit against Subway for false advertising because its "foot long" sandwiches were sometimes only eleven inches long.[27] (In fairness to the Chamber, a number of copycat lawsuits were filed as well, so this entry might be counted as several lawsuits instead of just one.) Subway did not file a motion to dismiss and the case settled.[28]
- A lawsuit against Jimmy John's for consumer fraud because its menus said certain sandwiches included alfalfa sprouts even though they did not.[29] Jimmy John's did not file a motion to dismiss and the case settled.[30]
- Two lawsuits against Starbucks for consumer fraud because it underfilled its drinks: one lawsuit was because it put too much milk in its drinks and the other was because it put in too much ice.[31] Both lawsuits were dismissed.[32]

Choi's contrary result in the context of IPO litigation, where they write that "although the results of these five tests are mixed, on the whole they do provide strong evidence that at least a significant fraction of IPO suits are frivolous." "Fraud in the New-Issues Market," 950. As Sean Griffith showed in the previous chapter, one area of class actions that may be rife with frivolous cases is merger litigation; see also Minor Myers and Charles R. Korsmo's finding that the field seems "driven largely by factors unrelated to legal merit". "The Structure of Stockholder Litigation: When Do the Merits Matter," *Ohio State Law Journal* 75, no. 5 (2014): 829.

25 "ILR Releases Top Ten Most Ridiculous Lawsuits of 2016," U.S. Chamber Institute for Legal Reform, last accessed October 23, 2017, www.instituteforlegalreform.com/resource/ilr-releases-top-ten-most-ridiculous-lawsuits-of-2016; "The Top Ten Most Ridiculous Lawsuits of 2015," U.S. Chamber Institute for Legal Reform, last accessed October 23, 2017, www.instituteforlegalreform.com/resource/us-chamber-releases-most-ridiculous-lawsuits-of-2014; "U.S. Chamber Releases Most Ridiculous Lawsuits of 2013," U.S. Chamber Institute for Legal Reform, last accessed October 23, 2017, www.instituteforlegalreform.com/resource/us-chamber-releases-most-ridiculous-lawsuits-of-2013-.

26 See the sources cited in the previous note.

27 See "Subway Sued Over 'Footlong' Subs," U.S. Chamber Institute for Legal Reform, accessed October 23, 2017, www.facesoflawsuitabuse.org/2013/01/subway-sued-over-footlong-subs/; see also Schwartz, "The Cost of Suing Business," 674. Ted Frank comments that this case represents "a pretty clear-cut example of lawyers abusing the system." Robert Loerzel, "Foot Fight: Subway Sandwich Suit Raises Class Action Questions," *ABA Journal*, February 2017, 17.

28 See *In re* Subway Footlong Sandwich Mktg. & Sales Practices Litig., 316 F.R.D. 240 (E.D. Wis. 2016). This settlement was rejected on appeal by the Seventh Circuit and the Court of Appeals viewed the claims as meritless. See *In re* Subway Footlong Sandwich Mktg. & Sales Practices Litig., 869 F.3d 551, 557 (7th Cir. 2017).

29 See "Jimmy John's Lawsuit 'Sprouts' Hefty Payday for Lawyers – Vouchers for Victims," U.S. Chamber Institute for Legal Reform, accessed October 23, 2017, www.facesoflawsuitabuse.org/2014/10/jimmy-johns-lawsuit-sprouts-hefty-payday-for-lawyers-vouchers-for-victims/.

30 See Notice of Proposed Class Action Settlement in Heather Starks v. Jimmy John's, LLC, et al., Case No. BC501113 (Cal. Sup. Ct.).

31 See "Starbucks Feels the Heat from Two Abusive Lawsuits," U.S. Chamber Institute for Legal Reform, accessed October 23, 2017, www.facesoflawsuitabuse.org/2016/07/too-much-ice-in-iced-coffees-too-much-steamed-milk-in-lattes-starbucks-feeling-the-heat-of-lawsuit-abuse/.

32 See Pincus v. Starbucks Corporation, No. 16-cv-04705 (N.D. Ill. Oct. 14, 2016); Strumlauf v. Starbucks Corp., No. 16-CV-01306-YGR, 2018 WL 306715, at *9 (N.D. Cal. Jan. 5, 2018).

- A lawsuit against a lip balm company, Fresh, Inc., for deceiving consumers because not all of the lip balm in the tube was accessible on account of how the twist-up mechanism in the tube works; this lawsuit was dismissed.[33]
- A lawsuit against the College Board for breach of contract (among other things) because a misprint led some students to get more time than others on a section of the SAT; the College Board ended up throwing out the section for all test takers.[34] This lawsuit was dismissed, too.[35]
- A lawsuit against Mastercard for fraud for continuing to advertise a promotion where a portion of every credit card purchase would go to charity even though the company's donation had hit its maximum for that year;[36] this lawsuit, too, was dismissed.[37]
- A consumer fraud lawsuit against Jelly Belly for listing the primary ingredient on some of its jellybean packages as "evaporated cane juice" instead of "sugar."[38] This lawsuit survived Jelly Belly's motion to dismiss and was ongoing at last inquiry.[39]
- A lawsuit against Starbucks for unpaid wages because Starbucks clocked out their employees before they locked up the store (which takes about four minutes).[40] Starbucks did not file a motion to dismiss, but it did file a motion for summary judgment, and the court granted that motion. The case was on appeal at last inquiry.[41]
- A lawsuit against several Dunkin' Donuts franchises for advertising "butter" on the menu but serving margarine instead.[42] The franchises did not file a motion to dismiss and settled the case.[43]

The first thing to take away from this list is that many of these lawsuits were dismissed at the beginning. Four out of ten (with a fifth dismissed before trial on summary judgment). Isn't this a pretty good indication that our system is working? When people file meritless lawsuits, companies can dismiss them without spending much money.

The second thing to note about this list is that many of these cases are not particularly meritless. I agree with the Chamber that the Subway lawsuit is ridiculous (which makes it all the more baffling that Subway didn't move to dismiss it): Subway uses the same ball of dough for

33 See "Court Tosses Lawsuit over Lip Balm Left in Tube," U.S. Chamber Institute for Legal Reform, accessed October 23, 2017, www.facesoflawsuitabuse.org/2016/04/court-tosses-lawsuit-over-lip-balm-left-in-tube/; Ebner v. Fresh, Inc., 838 F.3d 958 (9th Cir. 2016).

34 See "Mom and Son Sue over Typo that Gave Test Takers Extra Time," U.S. Chamber Institute for Legal Reform, accessed October 23, 2017, www.facesoflawsuitabuse.org/2016/04/mom-and-son-sue-over-sat-typo-that-gave-students-extra-test-time/.

35 See Ellinghaus v. Educational Testing Service et al., No. 2:15-cv-03442 (E.D.N.Y., Sep. 30, 2016).

36 See "Mastercard Blasts 'Baseless' Lawsuit Over its 'Stand Up to Cancer' Fundraising Promotion," U.S. Chamber Institute for Legal Reform, accessed October 23, 2017, www.facesoflawsuitabuse.org/2016/01/mastercard-blasts-baseless-lawsuit-over-its-stand-up-to-cancer-fundraising-promotion/.

37 See Doyle v. Mastercard International Inc., No. 16–04270 (2d Cir. Jul. 6, 2017).

38 "Deceived by Jelly Beans, Woman Files Lawsuit Against Jelly Belly," U.S. Chamber Institute for Legal Reform, accessed February 6, 2017, www.facesoflawsuitabuse.org/2017/08/deceived-by-jelly-beans-woman-files-lawsuit-against-jelly-belly/.

39 See Gomez v. Jelly Belly Candy Co., No. ED-CV-1700575-CJCFFMX, 2017 WL 2598551, at *1 (C.D. Cal. June 8, 2017).

40 "Time Clock Lawsuit Filed Against Starbucks," U.S. Chamber Institute for Legal Reform, www.facesoflawsuitabuse.org/2017/07/time-clock-lawsuit-filed-against-starbucks/.

41 See Troester v. Starbucks Corp., 680 F. App'x 511, 515 (9th Cir. 2016).

42 "Massachusetts Man Files Class Action Lawsuits Over Fake Butter," U.S. Chamber Institute for Legal Reform, www.facesoflawsuitabuse.org/2017/04/massachusetts-man-files-class-action-lawsuit-over-fake-butter/.

43 Daniel Victor, "Butter or Margarine? In Dunkin' Donuts Lawsuit, Man Accepts No Substitute," *New York Times*, April 4, 2017.

every sandwich; some of them just bake a little differently than the others. In other words, consumers get the exact same amount of bread no matter what.[44] I also agree with the Chamber that the lip balm lawsuit is a stretch; as the court dismissing the case pointed out, it is obvious to anyone who uses the lip balm that the twist-up mechanism renders some of the balm inaccessible.[45] I also agree with the Chamber about the Starbucks consumer fraud lawsuits: if you don't like how your barista is making your drink, tell him or her to make it differently.

But the other lawsuits? I am not so sure. Why should Jimmy John's and Dunkin' Donuts be permitted to tell people on their menus that items include certain ingredients when they don't? If, by analogy, a menu says a "hamburger with cheese" and the hamburger does not come with cheese, I think you have every right to be unhappy. I feel much the same way about Jelly Belly: the only reason it uses the words "evaporated cane juice" in the list of ingredients is to try to trick customers who are trying to avoid sugary products. (On the other hand, the nutrition information elsewhere on the package does use the word "sugar," so I am not sure if consumers would ever ultimately get tricked.) The Starbucks unpaid wages lawsuit is also a close call in my mind: four minutes does not seem like much time to complain about, but if you lose four minutes of compensation every day and work five days a week, fifty weeks a year, that's 1000 minutes or almost 17 hours – half a work week. That's real money.

The other lawsuits don't strike me as even remotely ridiculous. The College Board messed up. They tried to make the best of it by throwing out the section of the exam with the misprint, but what if some students thought they did really well on that section? Why should they be punished because the College Board messed up? The SAT is traumatizing enough; why shouldn't the College Board refund some or all of the test-taking fee? And Mastercard? It promotes these charitable campaigns because it wants you to use its cards more often so it can make more money; it shouldn't be allowed to keep promoting the campaign when the campaign is really over. (It is not surprising to me that the reason the court dismissed this case had nothing to do with the merits, but because the plaintiff could not show he was injured.[46])

But you don't have to agree with my conclusions on any of these lawsuits. My point is simply that, if this is the *worst of the worst* of our system, and many of these lawsuits are even *debatable*, then isn't our system in pretty good shape?

Fair enough, you might be thinking, but do I have a list of hundreds and hundreds of *meritorious* class actions? How can I criticize the Chamber for not having a list of all the bad class actions if I don't have a list of all the good ones? As the saying goes, "you can't beat something" – even if the Chamber's something is not very good – "with nothing."

Truth be told, I don't think I need a list. As I demonstrated above, I have something even better on my side: data. Data that says the vast majority of class action cases survive a motion to dismiss, a motion for summary judgment, or both, before they are settled. But, in order to give the data a bit of color, I will share with you some real-life examples of good cases. This is not a best-of-the-best list like the Chamber's worst-of-the-worst list; I have not scoured our entire court system to find the most meritorious class actions. It is simply a list of some of the lawsuits that I happened to be personally involved with as an expert witness over the same years covered by the Chamber's lists. But I think you'll find that these are some pretty worthwhile lawsuits nonetheless:

44 To quote the Seventh Circuit, "all of Subway's raw dough sticks weigh exactly the same, so the rare sandwich roll that fails to bake to a full 12 inches actually contains no less bread than any other." *In re* Subway Footlong Sandwich Mktg. & Sales Practices Litig., 869 F.3d 551, 554 (7th Cir. 2017).

45 See Ebner v. Fresh, Inc., 838 F.3d 958, 965 (9th Cir. 2016).

46 See Doyle v. Mastercard International Inc., No. 16–04270 (2d Cir. Jul. 6, 2017).

- Bank of America and a number of other banks held their customers' debit card transactions for a day or two before processing them so they could change the order in which the transactions were processed from chronological order to an order where the biggest transactions were processed first and the smallest transactions were processed last. Why? Because the big to small order would make customers go into overdraft more quickly and maximize the number of overdraft fee transactions the banks could charge. Customers of each bank brought class action lawsuits on behalf of all the others customers for fraud and breach of contract.[47]
- What happens when you try to send someone money through Western Union and the transaction is not completed for some reason? Western Union didn't tell you and kept your money instead. (At least until the law required it to turn your money over to the government years later; by then, of course, the address they had for you was probably no longer any good.) Several customers brought a class action lawsuit on behalf of all the others for fraud and breach of contract.[48]
- Ten different Asian manufacturers of flat-screen monitors agreed with one another not to compete on the prices they charged. Needless to say, this made devices with flat screens like computers and televisions more expensive. Several customers sued the companies on behalf of other customers for antitrust violations. Even the United States Department of Justice got into this one, investigating the companies for criminal conduct.[49]
- Remember when the quasi-government home-loan company, Fannie Mae, lied to its shareholders about its financial health by engaging in some tricky accounting? When it came to light, heads rolled and Fannie Mae was eventually taken over by the government. When their stock became worthless, several shareholders sued Fannie Mae and its corporate executives on behalf of other shareholders.[50]
- Have you ever heard of a leveraged buyout? It is when private investors decide to borrow a bunch of money to buy a public company and take it private. They then try to improve the company and later take it public again, hoping to sell it for more than they bought it for.[51] There are not many private investors who have the means and wherewithal to do this, so it was easy for the few of them to agree amongst themselves not to bid against each other when one of them wanted to buy a company. That meant companies were bought up for less than they might have been. Several shareholders of the target companies sued on behalf of all the shareholders for antitrust violations.[52]

47 See generally *In re* Checking Account Overdraft Litigation, No. 1:09-md-02036 (S.D. Fla. 2011).

48 See generally Tennille v. W. Union Co., 785 F.3d 422, 426 (10th Cir. 2015).

49 See generally *In re* TFT-LCD (Flat Panel) Antitrust Litigation, Docket No. 3:07-md-01827 (N.D. Cal.)

50 See generally *In re* Fannie Mae Sec Litig., Docket No. 1:04-cv-01639 (D.D.C.).

51 Laura Femino describes the practice as follows:

> A [leveraged buyout] is the acquisition of a target company financed by debt that is secured by the assets of the target company and paid with the target's future cash flows. Put more simply: The acquiring company borrows money from the lending bank to purchase the target company. That loan is secured by the target's assets and future cash flows. The acquirer might also use some of its own capital for the purchase along with the borrowed funds. The acquirer then uses these funds to buy the target from the target's current shareholders, often at a large premium, and the acquirer becomes the new owner. ("Ex Ante Review of Leveraged Buyouts," *Yale Law Journal* 123, no. 6 [2014]: 1834)

52 See generally Kirk Dahl et al. v. Bain Capital Partners LLC et al., No. 1:07-cv-12388 (D. Mass.).

- I am not Jewish, but I understand that many Jews take seriously the sanctity of those who have passed away: bodies are not supposed to be disturbed once they are buried.[53] That's why the Eden Memorial Jewish cemetery in Los Angeles sold burial plots with plenty of room between them. But Eden started to run out room in its cemetery. So what did it do? It decided to try to squeeze in a few more burial plots here and there. After all, how would the dead know if Eden encroached upon the plots they and their loved ones had purchased? Well, they found out the hard way: when Eden dug the new plots with backhoes, it breached the concrete burial chambers in the adjacent plots. Many of those who had bought the plots sued on behalf of the others for breach of contract and fraud.[54]
- The largest oil spill in American history occurred when BP's Deepwater Horizon offshore drilling platform exploded off the coast of Louisiana in 2010. Businesses all along the Gulf were devastated because vacationers did not travel to the Gulf for years. Many of them sued BP for their lost profits on behalf of all the other businesses. Again, even the federal and state governments got in on this one.[55]
- To those of us on the right side of the political spectrum, some of our favorite parts of federal and state constitutions are the so-called takings clauses. They say that the government cannot take your property without paying you compensation. Thank goodness it says so because a public utility in Missouri that had a legal right to run electrical wires across private land decided one day that it wanted to start a telecommunications business. Without telling any of the landowners, the utility started running telecommunications cable across their properties as well. Several landowners sued on behalf of all the others for takings and trespass.[56]
- The federal government is legally obligated to enter into contracts with Native American tribes who want to perform services that the federal government would otherwise provide for their tribe members. Yet, for many years, Congress never appropriated enough money to pay the Native American tribes all the monies they were due on their contracts. Several tribes sued on behalf of all the others for breach of contract.[57]
- The heads of all the major technology companies on the West Coast were tired of competing with one another for talent. So what did they do? They agreed to stop trying to hire each other's employees away from one another. With no one competing over them anymore, that depressed the employees' salaries. Some of the employees sued on behalf of all the others for antitrust violations.[58]
- This one you definitely remember: for nearly a decade, Volkswagen secretly inserted software into some of its diesel engines that turned off the emission controls on the cars unless the cars were being tested for emissions. Some of the cars were spewing forty times the legal limit of various toxins. Many of these cars were marketed to consumers as environmentally friendly. After the cheating was discovered by a private

[53] Rabbi Maurice Lamm provides a description of the principle in his book *The Jewish Way in Death and Mourning* (Middle Village, NY: Jonathan David Publishers, 2000), 64–69. Portions of the book have been republished online, and can be accessed here: www.chabad.org/library/article_cdo/aid/281579/jewish/The-Grave.htm. It is worth noting that this prohibition is not absolute, and there are some limited circumstances in which those who have been buried can be exhumed under Jewish law (ibid). Needless to say, those circumstances were not present in this case.

[54] See generally Robert Scott, et al. v. Service Corporation International, et al., No. BC421528 (Cal. Sup. Ct. L.A.).

[55] See generally *In re* Oil Spill by the Oil Rig "Deepwater Horizon" in the Gulf of Mexico, No. 2:10-md-02179 (E.D. La.)

[56] See generally Barfield et al. v. Sho-Me Power Electric Cooperative et al., No. 2:11-CV-04321 (E.D. Mo.).

[57] See generally Ramah Navajo Chapter, v. Jewell, No. 1:90-CV-957 (D.N.M.).

[58] See generally *In re* High-Tech Employee Antitrust Litig., No. 5:11-CV-02509 (N.D. Cal.).

organization, both the government and several consumers (on behalf of all the others) sued for fraud.[59]

- Here's another well-known one: former football players sued the NFL for hiding the brain-injury dangers associated with playing football. The NFL knew for years that the concussions the players suffered were more dangerous than they let on. Several former players sued on behalf of all the others for physical injuries caused by the NFL's breach of legal duties owed to them.[60]
- Did you know that FedEx charges you more when you send a package to a home versus a business? Well, they do. What happened if you didn't check a box on the part of the delivery slip that said "home or business"? FedEx ran the address through an inaccurate database and picked one for you. If the database couldn't find it, FedEx assumed it was the more expensive option (a home address) – even if the delivery person could see when he or she arrived that it was a business. Several customers sued on behalf of the others for breach of contract.[61]

I think you'd be hard pressed to find many people who think there's a single stinker in this bunch. Not only were these meritorious cases, but they all sought to stop the kinds of things even conservatives think are important to stop: breach of contract, fraud, and horizontal price fixing. Yet, most of these lawsuits would not have been possible but for the class action device; most of us were either unaware that this stuff was going on or we wouldn't have been able to find a lawyer willing to bring the lawsuit for us because, on our own, the case wouldn't have been worth much. It is true that, as I noted, in some of the cases the government got involved, but not in many. Most of the time, it was either a class action or nothing at all.

Indeed, I think the truth of the matter is probably this: far from there being too many class action lawsuits in our country, there are *too few*. As I have told you, there are only around 700 settlements every year in state and federal courts combined. How many companies are there in this country? Hundreds of thousands, if not millions.[62] How often are they stealing small amounts from people every year? 700 times? I don't know about you, but I suspect those hundreds of thousands if not millions of companies are doing things that they shouldn't be doing many, many more than 700 times every year. Consider, for example, how many class actions are filed every year in Israel: if you control for the relative population of the two countries, lawyers there file *six times* the number of class action lawsuits that lawyers here do.[63] Is there more corporate wrongdoing in Israel than there is here? I doubt it. Sophisticated academic studies confirm this point. For example, three economists have estimated that 15 percent of major, publicly traded companies commit securities fraud every year; yet only 4 percent of them face a class action lawsuit.[64]

59 See generally *In re* Volkswagen "Clean Diesel" Mktg., Sales Practices, & Prod. Liab. Litig. No. 3:15-MD-02672 (N.D. Cal.).

60 See generally *In re* Nat'l Football League Players' Concussion Injury Litig., No. 2:12-MD-02323-AB (E.D. Pa.).

61 See generally Gokare P.C. v. Federal Express Corp., Case No. 11-CV-02131 (W.D. Tenn.).

62 The IRS says that, in 2013, roughly 5.9 million active corporations filed taxes. *SOI Tax Stats – Corporation Complete Report Section 1* (Washington, DC: 2013): 1. However, it is likely that not all of these corporations actually function as separate entities, as many companies are organized in networks of subsidiaries.

63 See Hensler, "Can Private Class Actions Enforce Regulations? Do They? Should They?," 252, table 9.2.

64 See Alexander Dyck, Adair Morse, and Luigi Zingales, "How Pervasive is Corporate Fraud?" (working paper, Rotman School of Management, No. 2222608, August 2014), available at http://faculty.chicagobooth.edu/luigi.zingales/papers/research/pervasive.pdf.

With so many good cases still unfiled, why would lawyers waste their time with meritless ones? The simple answer is they don't. Whatever the number of meritless cases, they are not so numerous that we should throw the class action system out with the bathwater.

Nonetheless, if we are still worried about meritless cases, there are easy changes we can make to our system to discourage them even further: require judges to stay class action litigation until they decide a company's motion to dismiss and then allow the company to take an immediate appeal if the judge denies its motion. I discuss these changes in my new book THE CONSERVATIVE CASE FOR CLASS ACTIONS.[65]

[65] See *supra* note 14.

5

The Future of Aggregate Litigation in the United States

Robert Klonoff[*]

In 2013, I explained that, starting in the mid-1990s, federal courts began to erect significant barriers to class certification.[1] I did not pronounce class actions dead, but I did express concern that they had been seriously eroded. Four years later, I wrote that the decline had stabilized somewhat, and noted that the Supreme Court and the federal courts of appeals had issued a surprising number of pro-plaintiff rulings.[2]

Other scholars have also weighed in on the future of class actions. For instance, Professor Myriam Gilles has opined that "it is likely that, with a handful of exceptions, class actions will soon be virtually extinct."[3] Professor Brian Fitzpatrick has expressed fear of "a world without class actions."[4] Professor Arthur Miller is more optimistic, asserting that "reports of aggregate litigation's death are greatly exaggerated."[5]

In this chapter, I build on my prior writings and offer thoughts about the future of aggregate litigation in the United States federal courts. My goal is to predict what the aggregate litigation landscape will look like over the next ten years. Section 5.1 sets the stage with an overview of the two most important aggregation devices (apart from bankruptcy): class actions and federal multidistrict litigation. Section 5.2 offers a number of specific predictions, broken down into three categories: factors that will restrict aggregate litigation; factors that will be largely neutral; and factors that will promote at least some types of aggregate litigation.

5.1 SETTING THE STAGE: AGGREGATE LITIGATION IN THE UNITED STATES

5.1.1 *Class Actions*

The US Supreme Court has authority to promulgate rules of procedure governing federal courts.[6] The current federal class action rule, Federal Rule of Civil Procedure 23 (Rule 23), is a product of this rulemaking process.[7] The current rule, adopted in 1966, is a substantial revision

* My research assistants, Gracey Nagle and Anna Fugate, provided valuable assistance in the preparation of this chapter.

1 Robert H. Klonoff, *The Decline of Class Actions*, 90 WASH. U. L. REV. 729, 733 (2013) [hereinafter *Decline*].

2 Robert H. Klonoff, *Class Actions II: A Respite from the Decline*, 92 N.Y.U. L. REV. 971, 973 (2017) [hereinafter *Respite*].

3 Myriam Gilles, *Opting Out of Liability: The Forthcoming, Near-Total Demise of the Modern Class Action*, 104 MICH. L. REV. 373, 375 (2005).

4 Brian T. Fitzpatrick, *The End of Class Actions?*, 57 ARIZ. L. REV. 161, 199 (2015).

5 Arthur R. Miller, *The Preservation and Rejuvenation of Aggregate Litigation: A Systemic Imperative*, 64 EMORY L.J. 293, 306 (2014).

6 *See* 28 U.S.C. § 2072.

7 Virtually all states also have their own class action rules governing litigation in the state courts. Most state rules resemble federal Rule 23, but a number of states have very different approaches. *See* ROBERT H. KLONOFF, CLASS

of the 1938 version. The rule has been amended periodically since 1966, but the basic structure is largely intact. No precise statistics exist on the number of class actions filed each year, but rough estimates put the figure at about 12,500 class actions per year – about 7500 in federal courts and about 5000 in state courts.[8]

The federal class action rule is "trans-substantive" – that is, it applies without regard to the type of case (e.g., consumer, antitrust, environmental). To be sure, certain subject-specific statutes augment Rule 23, such as the Private Securities Litigation Reform Act (PSLRA).[9] But such statutes are rare; in most cases, Rule 23 is controlling.

5.1.1.1 Requirements for Class Certification

Numerous requirements must be met before a class action can be certified.

Proper Class Definition. A plaintiff must provide an objective class definition (e.g., all current owners of 2012–15 Toyota Tacoma pickup trucks). A few courts also require a feasible administrative process for ascertaining class members (known as "heightened ascertainability").[10] Under such a requirement, plaintiffs must show that class members can be identified "without extensive and individualized fact-finding or 'mini- trials.'"[11] Such a requirement could foreclose, for example, consumer class actions in which the identities of the class members are unknown, and consumers are unlikely to have kept receipts.[12] Most circuits have rejected the doctrine,[13] and even the Third Circuit, which originally adopted the requirement, has partially retreated.[14]

Rule 23(a) Requirements. Rule 23(a) sets forth four explicit requirements that must be met in every class action. First, the class must be "so numerous that joinder of all members is impracticable."[15] Some courts have suggested that there must be at least twenty-five to forty class members.[16]

Although numerosity has traditionally been easy to establish, a number of recent federal court of appeals opinions have imposed strict evidentiary burdens on plaintiffs in establishing

ACTIONS AND OTHER MULTI-PARTY LITIGATION IN A NUTSHELL 264–67 (5th ed. 2017) [hereinafter CLASS ACTION NUTSHELL].

8 Deborah R. Hensler, *The Future of Mass Litigation: Global Class Actions and Third-Party Litigation Funding*, 79 GEO. WASH. L. REV. 306, 308 n.7 (2011) (rough figure of 7500 per year in federal court); Emery G. Lee III & Thomas E. Willging, *The Impact of the Class Action Fairness Act on the Federal Courts: An Empirical Analysis of Filings and Removals*, 156 U. PA. L. REV. 1723, 1741–42 (2008) (roughly 5000 class actions per year in state court).

9 Pub. L. No. 104–67, 109 Stat. 737 (1995) (codified as amended in scattered sections of 15 U.S.C.).

10 *See, e.g.*, Carrera v. Bayer Corp., 727 F.3d 300 (3d Cir. 2013). *But see, e.g.*, Mullins v. Direct Digital, LLC, 795 F.3d 654, 657 (7th Cir. 2015) (refusing to adopt a heightened ascertainability requirement), *cert. denied*, 136 S. Ct. 1161 (2016).

11 Marcus v. BMW of N. Am., LLC, 687 F.3d 583, 593 (3d Cir. 2012).

12 *Carrera*, 727 F.3d at 304–08 (allegations by a putative class that Bayer falsely advertised certain health effects of its One-A-Day WeightSmart; the court found ascertainability problem because class members were unlikely to have receipts for their purchases, and Bayer had no records of such purchasers).

13 *See* Bruce D. Greenberg, *More Appellate Courts Reject the Third Circuit's "Ascertainability" Doctrine*, LITE DEPALMA GREENBERG L. BLOG (July 6, 2017) www.litedepalma.com/more-appellate-courts-reject-the-third-circuitsascertainability-doctrine (noting that a string of federal circuits have rejected ascertainability).

14 *See* City Select Auto Sales v. BMW Bank of N. Am., 867 F.3d 434, 441–42 (3d Cir. 2017) (holding that the district court erred in denying class certification on ascertainability grounds; contrary to prior decisions, the Third Circuit allowed class members to rely on affidavits).

15 FED. R. CIV. P. 23(a)(1).

16 CLASS ACTION NUTSHELL at 52; Stewart v. Abraham, 275 F.3d 220, 226–27 (3d Cir. 2001).

numerosity. For instance, in *Mielo v. Steak 'n Shake Operations, Inc.*[17] the Third Circuit found numerosity lacking in a nationwide class action challenging wheelchair mobility in Steak 'n Shake restaurant parking lots in violation of the Americans With Disabilities Act. Although 417 separate restaurant locations were at issue, the court was not convinced that there were even 40 class members. That was so despite evidence that there were 15–20 million people in the US with mobility disabilities, and despite a statement from a Steak 'n Shake executive that thousands of disabled customers use Steak 'n Shake's parking lots. Similarly, in *Vega v. T-Mobile USA, Inc.*,[18] the Eleventh Circuit found numerosity lacking in a suit claiming that T-Mobile employees in Florida were denied sales commissions. Although plaintiffs' evidence showed that there were thousands of such employees nationwide, the court faulted plaintiffs for not offering evidence on the number of such employees within Florida.[19]

Second, there must be "questions of law or fact common to the class."[20] Even a single question of law or fact will suffice,[21] although the issue must be a substantial one. In *Wal-Mart Stores, Inc. v. Dukes*, the Supreme Court ruled that the "common contention ... must be of such a nature that ... determination of its truth or falsity will resolve an issue that is central to the validity of each one of the claims in one stroke."[22]

Third, "the claims or defenses of the representative parties [must be] typical of the claims or defenses of the class."[23] Here, the focus is on the class representative, who is responsible for representing the unnamed class members. The purpose of typicality is to ensure that there are no troublesome issues involving the representative that could prejudice the class as a whole.[24]

Finally, the rule requires that "the representative parties will fairly and adequately protect the interests of the class."[25] This requirement, which overlaps with typicality, applies to both the class representative and class counsel. Again, the concern is to ensure that those representing the unnamed class members do not have serious conflicts of interest or other flaws that would detract from that task.[26]

Rule 23(b) Categories. In addition to satisfying the three threshold requirements and the four Rule 23(a) requirements, a class action must satisfy one of the four categories of Rule 23(b)(3).

- Rule 23(b)(1)(A) applies when individual actions "would create a risk of ... inconsistent or varying adjudications with respect to individual class members that would establish incompatible standards of conduct for the party opposing the class."[27] It is designed to protect *defendants* from conflicting obligations imposed by different courts.[28]
- Rule 23(b)(1)(B) is designed to protect *class members* from being prejudiced by individual adjudications. A (b)(1)(B) class can be maintained if separate

[17] 897 F.3d 467 (3d Cir. 2018).
[18] 564 F.3d 1256 (11th Cir. 2009).
[19] *See Decline* at 768–71 (also discussing other examples).
[20] Fed. R. Civ. P. 23(a)(2).
[21] Wal-Mart Stores, Inc. v. Dukes, 564 U.S. 338, 359 (2011) (stating that "'even a single [common] question' will do").
[22] *Id.* at 350.
[23] Fed. R. Civ. P. 23(a)(3).
[24] Class Action Nutshell at 51.
[25] Fed. R. Civ. P. 23(a)(4).
[26] Class Action Nutshell at 59–70.
[27] Fed. R. Civ. P. 23(b)(1)(A).
[28] Class Action Nutshell at 76–78.

adjudications would "be dispositive of the interests of the other members not parties to the individual adjudications or would substantially impair or impede their ability to protect their interests."[29] For example, if there is a fund that is not large enough to compensate all class members, a class action would ensure that all class members share in the fund (and that it does not run out before some plaintiffs can litigate their claims).[30]

- Rule 23(b)(2) authorizes a class action when "the party opposing the class has acted or refused to act on grounds that apply generally to the class, so that final injunctive relief or corresponding declaratory relief is appropriate respecting the class as a whole[.]"[31] Rule 23(b)(2) is commonly used in civil rights cases and other cases seeking an injunction or other structural relief. Under *Dukes*, Rule 23(b)(2) certification is not appropriate if monetary relief constitutes a nontrivial part of the claim.[32]
- Rule 23(b)(3) allows certification when "the questions of law or fact predominate over any questions affecting only individual members, and ... a class action is superior to other available methods for fairly and efficiently adjudicating the controversy."[33] Predominance requires a comparison of the common and individual issues.[34] Superiority focuses on whether another alternative, such as nonclass joinder, is a superior option.[35] Rule 23(b)(3) is the usual vehicle for class actions seeking monetary remedies.

Classes under Rule 23(b)(1) and Rule 23(b)(2) are mandatory: they do not allow class members to exclude themselves.[36] Moreover, notice of class certification is not required.[37] By contrast, Rule 23(b)(3) classes permit class members to opt out, and (b)(3) requires notice of class certification.[38]

Defendants have argued that when damages must be calculated on an individualized basis, the predominance requirement cannot be satisfied. In general, these arguments have been unsuccessful. The courts, including the Supreme Court, have recognized that individualized damages, standing alone, do not defeat class certification.[39]

Issue Classes. In addition to the four provisions authorizing class actions, the rule also provides that "[w]hen appropriate, a class may be brought or maintained as a class action with respect to

29 Fed. R. Civ. P 23(b)(1)(B).
30 *See* Class Action Nutshell at 101–06; Ortiz v. Fibreboard Corp., 527 U.S. 815 (1999) (discussing limited fund class actions).
31 Fed. R. Civ. P 23(b)(2).
32 Wal-mart Stores, Inc. v. Dukes, 564 U.S. 338, 360 (2011).
33 Fed. R. Civ. P 23(b)(3).
34 Class Action Nutshell at 130–43.
35 *Id.* at 143–45 (enumerating several alternative methods of resolution that courts should consider when appropriate). *See also* Rule 23(b)(3)(A)–(D) (identifying criteria for assessing superiority).
36 Class Action Nutshell at 92.
37 *Id.*
38 *Id.* In narrow circumstances, certain US statutes provide for opt-in classes. *See, e.g.*, Class Action Nutshell at 403–04 (discussing opt-in classes under the Fair Labor Standards Act, 29 U.S.C. § 216(b)).
39 *See* Robert H. Klonoff, *Class Actions in the Year 2026: A Prognosis*, 65 Emory L.J. 1569, 1618 (2016) [hereinafter *Prognosis*] (citing cases); Tyson Foods, Inc. v. Bouaphakeo, 136 S. Ct. 1036, 1045 (2016) ("When 'one or more of the central issues in the action are common to the class and can be said to predominate, the action may be considered proper under Rule 23(b)(3) even though other important matters will have to be tried separately, *such as damages* or some affirmative defenses peculiar to some individual class members.'") (emphasis added).

particular issues."[40] The court decides only the specific issues, leaving the individualized issues to be resolved at a later time (perhaps in follow-on cases).

The circuits were at one time in conflict on issue classes. The question in dispute was whether an issue class could be certified even in a situation in which the plaintiff could not satisfy the predominance requirement of Rule 23(b)(3). Most courts held that Rule 23(b)(3) predominance did not need to be established for an issue class, but one circuit held that predominance was still a requirement and that an issue class was merely a housekeeping device.[41] There now appears to be universal agreement that the predominance requirement of Rule 23(b)(3) does not apply when certification is only for an issue class.[42] Thus, a court may certify an issue class to resolve common issues, even in a circumstance in which a Rule 23(b)(3) class could not be certified.

Several issue classes have been allowed in recent years. For instance, in *Martin v. Behr Dayton Thermal Prods., LLC*,[43] the Sixth Circuit ruled that a toxic tort case that was problematic under Rule 23(b)(3) was appropriate for an issue class under Rule 23(c)(4). The court thus upheld the district court's designation of seven common issues for resolution. Similarly, in *McReynolds v. Merrill, Lynch, Pierce, Fenner & Smith*,[44] the Seventh Circuit upheld an issue class under Rule 23(c)(4) in an employment case on the issue of whether the defendant engaged in practices having a discriminatory effect (disparate impact).[45]

Constitutional Requirements. In addition to the foregoing, two basic constitutional requirements (discussed herein) must be met: the class representatives must have standing to sue, and their claims must be live (and not moot). Both requirements stem from Article III of the US Constitution, which provides that a federal court may act only when there is a "case or controversy."

Standing. The class representative must have standing to sue, that is, must have suffered injury in fact.[46] Some courts have gone further, requiring that plaintiffs establish standing not only for the class representatives but for unnamed class members as well.[47] Other courts, however, hold that a class action is permissible as long as at least one class representative has standing.[48] The Supreme Court has not yet definitively ruled on the contours of standing in class actions. In *Spokeo v. Robins*,[49] the Supreme Court (in a 6–2 opinion) remanded a case to the Ninth Circuit to reconsider its decision finding that standing had been satisfied. The majority reasoned that the Ninth Circuit erred in its analysis of Article III by focusing solely on particularity and not on concreteness. The opinion did not break new ground. In *Frank v. Gaos*,[50] a case the Supreme Court took to address an issue of remedies (cy pres, discussed below), the Court instead remanded the case to the Ninth Circuit to address standing in light of *Spokeo*. Again, the Court did not break any new ground.

40 Fed. R. Civ. P. 23(c)(4).
41 Castano v. Am. Tobacco Co., 84 F.3d 734, 745 & n.21 (5th Cir. 1996).
42 *See* Patricia Bronte et al., *"Carving at the Joint": The Precise Function of Rule 23(c)(4)*, 62 DePaul L. Rev. 745, 745–46 (2013) (citing post-*Castano* Fifth Circuit authority and concluding that there is no longer a circuit conflict).
43 896 F.3d 405 (6th Cir. 2018), *cert. denied*, 139 S. Ct. 1319 (2019).
44 672 F.3d 482 (7th Cir. 2012) (abrogated on other grounds).
45 *See also, e.g.*, In re Nassau Cty. Strip Search Cases, 461 F.3d 219, 230–31 (2d Cir. 2006) (approving an issue class); Manual For Complex Litigation (Fourth) (2004) § 21.24 (issue class is appropriate if it "materially advances the disposition of the litigation").
46 Spokeo v. Robins, 136 S. Ct. 1540, 1545 (2016).
47 *See, e.g.*, Denney v. Deutsche Bank AG, 443 F.3d 253, 264 (2d Cir. 2006).
48 *See, e.g.*, Neale v. Volvo Cars of N. Am., LLC, 794 F.3d 353, 364 (3d Cir. 2015); Kohen v. Pac. Inv. Mgmt. Co., 571 F.3d 672, 676 (7th Cir. 2009).
49 136 S. Ct. 1540 (2016).
50 139 S. Ct. 1041 (2019).

Live Claims. The class representative must be a member of the class and must have live claims.[51] One strategy that defendants have used in recent years in an attempt to derail class actions is to "pick off" the cases of the class representatives by offering the full amount of their claims. By mooting those plaintiffs' claims, defendants hope to avoid class action lawsuits (since the case of each representative who comes forward to represent the class will be rendered moot). The Supreme Court had the opportunity to endorse this strategy but declined to do so.

In *Campbell-Ewald Co. v. Gomez*,[52] the class representative did not accept a defendant's offer of judgment, but the defendant argued that the unaccepted offer still mooted Gomez's individual claims. In a 6–3 decision, the Supreme Court rejected the defendant's argument that the offer, even if unaccepted, moots the representative's claim. Importantly, however, the Court noted: "We need not, and do not, now decide whether the result would be different if a defendant deposits the full amount of the plaintiff's individual claim in an account payable to the plaintiff, and the court then enters judgment for the plaintiff in that amount."[53] In subsequent cases, lower courts have found that an offer of judgment did not moot the case even though the funds were deposited in the district court's registry.[54] And some courts have held that, even if the defendant could moot the plaintiff's individual claims, the plaintiff would still be entitled to litigate the issue of class certification on behalf of the class members, thereby defeating the whole point of the defendant's attempt to buy off the plaintiff and derail the class action.[55]

5.1.1.2 Important Procedural Issues

In addition to the Rule 23 and constitutional requirements for class certification, a variety of other procedural points must be addressed to complete the discussion of United States class actions.

Burden of Proof. When plaintiffs are seeking class certification, they have the burden to show, by a preponderance of the evidence, that all of the requirements for certification have been established. This frequently means that plaintiffs must support class certification with evidence, not merely allegations.[56]

Relevance of the Merits. At the class certification stage, courts should not undertake to determine which side will win the case.[57] Yet, in some circumstances, district courts must address merits-related issues when those issues overlap with class certification requirements.[58] Courts have rejected certification in numerous cases because of deficient evidentiary showings by plaintiffs.[59] Indeed, this focus on the merits has derailed many class actions.[60] But in *Amgen*

[51] CLASS ACTION NUTSHELL at 43–46.
[52] 136 S. Ct. 663 (2016).
[53] *Id.* at 672.
[54] *See, e.g.*, Geismann, M.D., P.C. v. Zocdoc, Inc., 909 F.3d 534, 543 (2d Cir. 2018), *cert. denied*, 139 S. Ct. 1605.
[55] *See, e.g.*, Chen v. Allstate Ins. Co., 819 F.3d 1136, 1138 (9th Cir. 2016); Bennett v. Office of Fed. Emps. Grp. Life Ins., 683 F. App'x 186, 188 (4th Cir. 2017) (unpublished).
[56] *See* CLASS ACTION NUTSHELL at 174.
[57] *See* Szabo v. Bridgeport Machs, Inc., 249 F.3d 672, 677 (7th Cir. 2001) (explaining that "a court may not say something like let's resolve the merits first and worry about the class [certification] later") (internal quotation marks omitted).
[58] CLASS ACTION NUTSHELL at 168–73.
[59] *See Decline* at 747–55 (discussing cases).
[60] *See, e.g.*, In re Hydrogen Peroxide Antitrust Litig., 552 F.3d 305, 307 (3d Cir. 2008); Tucker v. BP America Prod. Co., 278 F.R.D. 646, 651 (W.D. Okla. 2011).

Inc. v. Connecticut Retirement Plans and Trust Funds,[61] the Supreme Court limited the reach of this case law, making clear that "the office of a Rule 23(b)(3) certification ruling is not to adjudicate the case; rather, it is to select the 'metho[d]' best suited to adjudication of the controversy 'fairly and efficiently.'"[62] The circuits have applied the teachings in *Amgen* and, as a result, have refused to consider various defense arguments against certification that go to the merits.[63]

Appellate Review of Class Certification Rulings. Prior to 1998, it was very difficult to appeal a decision granting or denying class certification, because such a decision is not a final judgment until after a verdict at trial. In 1998, Rule 23 was amended to add a new subdivision (f), which provides that "[a] court of appeals may permit an appeal from an order granting or denying class-action certification" if a request to appeal is filed within fourteen days.[64] As a result of Rule 23(f), the federal appellate courts have issued many opinions on class certification issues.[65]

Federal versus State Court. In 2005, the Class Action Fairness Act (CAFA) became law.[66] Under CAFA, most major class actions can now be removed (transferred) by defendants from state court to federal court.[67]

Cy Pres. A major issue in some class actions, especially in the settlement context, is the permissibility of "cy pres" payments. Cy pres refers to the designation of class members' recovery (in whole or part) to a third party, usually a charitable or public interest organization.[68] The idea underlying cy pres is that funding for a public interest organization or other charity will indirectly benefit the class as a whole (e.g., a contribution to a public interest organization for health research). Cy pres prevents wrongdoers from being unjustly enriched when damages are too small to be distributed to individual class members in a cost-effective way.[69]

Some courts and commentators have expressed concern that, under a cy pres approach, some or all of the recovery is diverted from class members, who nonetheless are barred from relitigating the claims. The concern is most serious when the entire class recovery goes to a third party.[70] That was the case in *Frank v. Gaos*, mentioned above. As noted, the Court ended up resolving the case on standing grounds and did not reach the cy pres issue. Justice Thomas, however, concluded that standing was satisfied and thus addressed cy pres. In his view, when no funds go to class members, but the lawyers recover fees, then the class has not been adequately represented.[71] Also, a settlement where no funds go to the class is not fair, reasonable, and adequate under Rule

61 568 U.S. 455 (2013).
62 *Id.* at 460.
63 *See, e.g., Respite* at 990 (citing numerous examples).
64 FED. R. CIV. P. 23(f).
65 *See generally Decline*, at 741, 832–38 (statistics regarding Rule 23(f) appeals).
66 Class Action Fairness Act of 2005, Pub. L. No. 109–2, 119 Stat. 4 (codified as amended in scattered sections of 28 U.S.C.).
67 *Decline* at 284–89.
68 *See, e.g.*, CLASS ACTION NUTSHELL at 347–51.
69 *See, e.g.*, Rhonda Wasserman, *Cy Pres in Class Action Settlements*, 88 S. CAL. L. REV. 97, 107 n.43 (2014) (cy pres is "'preferable to the unjust enrichment of the defendant'").
70 *See infra* at § 5.2.1.7 (discussing concerns about cy pres as the sole remedy in a class settlement). *See also, e.g.*, In re Google Inc. Cookie Placement Consumer Privacy Litig., 934 F.3d 316, 320–22 (3d Cir. 2019) (settlement approval vacated and remanded because, *inter alia*, defendant agreed to cy pres contributions to third party organizations whose selection was not closely scrutinized by the district court and included organizations to whom the defendant regularly contributed funding).
71 139 S. Ct. at 1047 (dissenting).

23(e).[72] And, according to Justice Thomas, a class action that extinguishes a class member's causes of action without providing a remedy is not a superior method for resolving the controversy.[73] The use of cy pres as recovery is less controversial when a court uses it solely to distribute *unclaimed* damages, rather than as a tool for distributing the damages as a whole. In such circumstances, the primary recovery still goes to the class.[74]

Arbitration. A negative value suit is one in which the "stakes to each class member [are] too slight to repay the cost of suit."[75] For example, no lawyer would take an individual case, on a contingent fee basis, alleging that a $50 set of headphones is defective and prone to catch on fire. The expert evidence required to prove a defect, not to mention the lawyer time involved, would make it a no-win proposition. Indeed, even a case not traditionally thought of as a negative value case – such as an employment discrimination case – might not be brought if the plaintiff must pursue an individual lawsuit instead of a class action. Thus, a key goal of defendants is to force plaintiffs to litigate their cases individually (which virtually no plaintiff will do when the potential upside does not justify the expenditure of substantial attorney time and expenses). One way for defendants to force plaintiffs to litigate their claims individually, if at all, is to require that plaintiffs arbitrate their claims.

The Supreme Court has upheld such arbitration clauses despite vigorous challenges. In *AT&T Mobility LLC v. Concepcion*,[76] the Court (in a 5–4 opinion) held that a federal statute, the Federal Arbitration Act,[77] preempted a state unconscionability defense. Several later cases have made clear – over vigorous dissents – that the Supreme Court will not retreat in this area.[78] Because the Supreme Court has been emphatic regarding the reach of the FAA and the general inapplicability of state law as a defense, the lower courts have been very reluctant to invalidate arbitration clauses, absent egregious circumstances, such as fraud or ambiguity within the agreement itself.[79]

Class Settlements. At one time, virtually all class actions settled (or were dismissed) prior to trial. In recent years, however, numerous class actions have gone to trial.[80] Nonetheless, it is still true that most class actions settle. Under Rule 23(e)(2), a court may approve a classwide settlement only after conducting a hearing and finding that the settlement is "fair, reasonable, and adequate."[81] When a class settlement occurs before a class has been certified, the court must also determine that the case satisfies the various requirements for class certification.[82] In recent

72 *Id.*

73 *Id. See also* Marek v. Lane, 134 S. Ct. 8, 9 (2013) (Roberts, C.J., statement on denial of certiorari) (noting need of the Court to address "fundamental concerns surrounding the use of [cy pres] remedies in class action litigation").

74 *See, e.g.*, Caligiuri v. Symantec Corp., 855 F.3d 860, 863 (8th Cir. 2017); In re Easysaver Rewards Litig., 906 F.3d 747, 760–61 (9th Cir. 2018), *cert. denied*, 139 S. Ct. 2744 (2019).

75 In re Rhone–Poulenc Rorer Inc., 51 F.3d 1293, 1300 (7th Cir. 1995).

76 131 S. Ct. 1740 (2011).

77 9 U.S.C. §§ 1–14.

78 *See, e.g.*, Am. Express Co. v. Italian Colors Rest., 133 S. Ct. 2304 (2013) (enforcing arbitration clause despite argument that such an approach would undermine enforcement of federal antitrust laws); Epic Sys. Corp. v. Lewis, 138 S. Ct. 1612 (2018) (finding arbitration contracts in employment agreements enforceable). *But see* Lamps Plus, Inc. v. Varella, 139 S. Ct. 1407 (2019) (class arbitration barred when there was ambiguity in the agreement); New Prime Inc. v. Oliveira, 139 S. Ct. 532 (2019) (refusing to enforce arbitration clause against truckers because of a specific exception in FAA for employees engaged in interstate or foreign commerce).

79 *See, e.g.*, Jones v. Waffle House, Inc., 866 F.3d 1257 (11th Cir. 2017); Saizhang Guan v. Uber Technologies, Inc., 236 F. Supp. 3d 711 (E.D.N.Y. 2017). *But see, e.g.*, Blair v. Rent-A-Center, Inc., 928 F.3d 819 (9th Cir. 2019).

80 *See Prognosis* at 1643–45.

81 Fed. R. Civ. P. 23(e)(2).

82 *Cf.* Amchem Prods, Inc. v. Windsor, 521 U.S. 591, 620 (1997) (noting that manageability is not a requirement for a settlement class, because there will not be a trial).

years, courts have become increasingly rigorous in ensuring that class settlements are fair and that class members are properly represented.[83]

Attorneys' Fees. An important part of any class settlement (and any award after trial) is attorneys' fees and expenses for class counsel. Rule 23(h) authorizes a court in a class action to "award reasonable attorney fees and nontaxable costs authorized by law or by agreement of the parties."[84] Class members must be notified of a motion for a fee award, and they are entitled to object to the proposed fees.[85] In general, fees can be awarded based on (1) a percentage of the fund recovered by the class; (2) hours invested by attorneys in the case, using reasonable hourly rates and possibly adding an enhancement; (3) a combination of #1 and #2; or (4) criteria set by case law.[86] Under the "American Rule," absent a statutory fee-shifting provision, parties in US litigation generally pay their own attorneys' fees regardless of who wins or loses. In addition, in most class actions, class counsel's fees and costs are contingent on success, and plaintiffs (and unnamed class members) pay nothing if the suit is not successful.[87]

5.1.2 *Federal Multidistrict Litigation*

Although the class action device is not unique to the United States, there is another procedure that *is* unique – federal multidistrict litigation. The multidistrict litigation (MDL) statute, enacted in 1968, provides, inter alia, that "[w]hen civil actions involving one or more common questions of fact are pending in different [federal] districts, such actions may be transferred to any district for coordinated or consolidated pretrial proceedings."[88] Such transfers are made by a special panel, known as the Judicial Panel on Multidistrict Litigation (the MDL Panel). The MDL Panel consists of seven federal circuit and district court judges designated by the Chief Justice of the United States.

In selecting the court where the cases should be transferred for pretrial purposes, the MDL Panel considers a variety of factors, including (among others) the location of the various cases; the locations of the parties, witnesses, and pertinent evidence; and the workload and experience of the various judges being considered.[89] The stated purpose of section 1407 is to achieve judicial efficiency in *pretrial* proceedings; however, most cases are either settled or dismissed in the MDL court without ever being transferred back to their courts of origin.[90]

Since the statute's enactment, the MDL Panel has transferred more than 635,000 cases for coordinated or consolidated pretrial proceedings.[91] Virtually every recent, high-profile aggregate civil case has involved an MDL proceeding – including *BP Deepwater Horizon*, *National*

83 *Prognosis* at 1623–35.

84 Fed. R. Civ. P. 23(h).

85 Fed. R. Civ. P. 23(h)(1), (h)(2).

86 Class Action Nutshell at 352–56. *See* Johnson v. Georgia Highway Express, Inc., 488 F.2d 714, 717–19 (5th Cir. 1974) (listing twelve factors for assessing fees). The case law criteria are usually considered in conjunction with one of the other methods. *See, e.g.*, Keil v. Lopez, 862 F.3d 685, 701 (8th Cir. 2017) (discussing percentage method, lodestar cross-check, and *Johnson* factors).

87 Class Action Nutshell at 355.

88 28 U.S.C. § 1407(a).

89 Manual For Complex Litigation (Fourth) (2004) § 20.131, at 221.

90 Abbe Gluck, *Unorthodox Civil Procedure: Modern Multidistrict Litigation's Place in the Text Understanding of Procedure*, 165 U. Penn. L. Rev. 1670, 1673 (2017) (only 3 percent of MDL cases are remanded to the transferor courts).

91 Margaret S. Williams, *The Effect of Multidistrict Litigation on the Federal Judiciary over the Past 50 Years*, 53 Ga. L. Rev. 1245, 1270 (2019).

Football League Concussion, *Volkswagen Clean Diesel*, and numerous pharmaceutical cases.[92] In 2018, MDL cases constituted 50.9 percent of the entire federal civil docket, excluding Social Security and prisoner cases.[93] As many as 21 percent of newly filed federal civil cases each year are part of MDLs.[94] Most of these cases are mass torts, which are normally not suitable as class actions.[95]

5.2 PREDICTIONS

In this section, I offer predictions regarding the aggregate litigation landscape during the next ten years. I first focus on factors that will undermine aggregation. I then discuss factors that, while heavily litigated in the courts, are unlikely to have a major impact on aggregation going forward. Finally, I discuss factors that will promote certain kinds of aggregate litigation.

5.2.1 *Negative Factors*

5.2.1.1 The Composition of the Federal Bench

Predictions on the future of aggregate litigation are necessarily informed by politics. Federal judges, including US Supreme Court justices, are appointed by the President and serve for life – in many instances, for several decades. In general, liberal judges tend to be open-minded and even expansive regarding aggregate litigation, whereas conservative judges tend to be skeptical and more inclined to support limits on aggregate lawsuits.[96]

In the class action arena, some of the most contentious Supreme Court rulings have been 5–4 decisions.[97] Justice Scalia, a staunch conservative and leading author of opinions disfavoring class actions,[98] died in 2016 and was replaced by another very conservative justice, Neil Gorsuch. In 2018, Justice Kennedy (sometimes a swing vote who joined the liberals) retired and was replaced by Brett Kavanaugh, who is expected to be a more reliable vote for conservatives.[99] Thus, the Court majority is now unambiguously conservative. Moreover, the two oldest justices, Justices Ginsburg (age eighty-seven) and Breyer (age eighty-two), are both liberals, so even if a Democrat is elected

92 Class Action Nutshell at 461. *See generally* Robert H. Klonoff, Federal Multidistrict Litigation in a Nutshell (2019) (hereafter MDL Nutshell).

93 Daniel Fisher, *Multidistrict Litigation Swamps Courts as Rules Struggle to Catch Up; Is Reform on the Way?*, Legal Newsline (Mar. 21, 2019), https://legalnewsline.com/stories/512312998-multidistrict-litigation-swamps-courts-as-rules-struggle-to-catch-up-is-reform-on-the-way.

94 Williams, *supra* note 91 at 1271 (criticizing statistics based on percentage of MDL cases in total civil docket, noting that MDL cases tend to remain pending, on average, for twice as long as non-MDL cases).

95 Amy Saack, *Global Settlements in Non-Class MDL Mass Torts*, 21 Lewis & Clark L. Rev. 847, 852 (2017).

96 Ese Olumhense, *Republicans Introduce Bill to 'Kill' Class Action Lawsuits*, Fox 6 Now (Mar. 9, 2017, 5:04 PM), https://fox6now.com/2017/03/09/republicans-introduce-bill-to-kill-class-action-lawsuits-tmwsp/ ("Class action reform is a common priority for conservatives, who believe these suits are frequently abused."). For an empirical analysis of the strong association between politics and class certification outcomes, *see* Stephen B. Burbank & Sean Farhang, *Politics, Identity, and Class Certification on the U.S. Courts of Appeals*, U Penn. Public Law & Legal Theory Research Paper Series (Aug. 14, 2019).

97 For instance, in *Dukes*, the Court was split 5–4 over the proper test for commonality under Rule 23, with the conservatives prevailing in adopting a defendant-friendly standard. Similarly, in AT&T Mobility LLC v. Concepcion, 563 U.S. 333 (2011), the Court was split 5–4 in an opinion allowing defendants to invoke arbitration clauses to prevent judicial litigation on a classwide basis.

98 *Prognosis* at 1639.

99 Amanda Bronstad, *Kavanaugh's Record on Class Actions Thin, but Leaves Clues He'd Restrain Them*, Law.Com (Jul 16, 2018, 7:38PM), www.law.com/nationallawjournal/2018/07/16/kavanaughs-record-on-class-actions-thin-but-leaves-clues-hed-restrain-them/.

President in 2020, it is most likely (barring unexpected health issues or retirements of younger justices) that the Democratic President's first two appointments would simply replace liberals with other liberals and thus not alter the political composition of the Court. Observers predict that this political reality does not bode well for the future of aggregate litigation.[100]

In addition, most of the crucial law on class actions is made at the federal court of appeals level. Thus, changes in the composition of the federal circuit courts are also highly relevant in predicting the future of aggregate litigation. At the time of submission of this chapter for publication, President Trump had appointed 53 federal circuit judges and 149 other federal judges.[101] He has appointed more federal appellate judges than any other President during the same three-year period.[102] The average age of his circuit court appointments is 49.4 years old.[103] And observers believe that Trump's judicial appointments are more conservative than those of prior Republican Presidents.[104] With this dramatic impact on the federal judiciary at all levels, and with Trump-appointed judges expected to serve for decades, it is reasonable to expect that the federal courts will be skeptical of aggregate lawsuits for many years to come.

5.2.1.2 The Impact of Predominance

In the next decade, the predominance requirement will continue to pose a substantial barrier on certain kinds of class actions. The predominance requirement of Rule 23(b)(3) has served as an impediment to three important kinds of cases.

First, mass tort cases frequently involve individualized causation issues (e.g., was the heart attack caused by the defendant's drug or by the plaintiff's history of smoking?), and courts have repeatedly held that such cases are not suitable for class certification.[105] In a series of cases dating back to the late 1960s (with a temporary retreat in the 1980s), courts ruled that personal injury lawsuits usually failed to satisfy the predominance requirement of Rule 23(b)(3).[106] As noted, unable to pursue class actions in most mass tort cases, plaintiffs have looked to coordination under the MDL statute.[107] I do not see that situation changing in the next decade. Courts are now entrenched in ruling that, in most personal injury cases, individual issues outweigh common issues, thus foreclosing class certification of mass torts.[108]

One countertrend is in the settlement context. A few courts have been willing to certify personal injury class actions for settlement purposes. Examples include *National Football League Concussion* and *Deepwater Horizon*.[109] The class action mechanism is well suited to

100 Daniel Fisher, *Brett Kavanaugh Would Mean a Pro-Business Court for Decades*, CHIEF EXECUTIVE (Sept. 6, 2018), https://chiefexecutive.net/brett-kavanaugh-pro-business-court-decades/.

101 JUDICIAL APPOINTMENT TRACKER, www.heritage.org/judicialtracker.

102 Gary Martin, *VanDyke Nomination for 9th Circuit Court Clears Procedural Vote*, LAS VEGAS REVIEW JOURNAL (Dec. 10, 2019, 5:14 PM), www.reviewjournal.com/news/politics-and-government/vandyke-nomination-for-9th-circuit-court-clears-procedural-vote.

103 *See* Daniel Bush, *Trump's Conservative Picks Will Impact Courts for Decades*, PBS NEWSHOUR (Oct. 25, 2019, 4:32 PM), www.pbs.org/newshour/politics/trumps-conservative-picks-will-impact-courts-for-decades.

104 Li Zhou, *Study: Trump's Judicial Appointees are More Conservative than Those of Past Republican Presidents*, VOX (Jan. 25, 2019, 6:00 AM), www.vox.com/2019/1/25/18188541/trump-judges-mconnell-senate.

105 CLASS ACTION NUTSHELL at 388–91.

106 *See Decline* at 732–35 (noting skepticism regarding mass torts class actions from late 1960s through early 1980s, surge in mid-1980s, and skepticism again thereafter); Arthur R. Miller, *Of Frankenstein Monsters and Shining Knights: Myth, Reality, and the "Class Action Problem,"* 92 HARV. L. REV. 664, 677–82 (1979) (describing that history).

107 *See* MDL NUTSHELL at 392.

108 *See* CLASS ACTION NUTSHELL at 388–90.

109 *See* CLASS ACTION NUTSHELL at 391–92.

achieving prompt resolution in mass tort cases, provided that the defendant's overarching goal is settlement, not expensive and contentious litigation. But apart from the rare cases in which defendants are looking for a global settlement, few personal injury mass torts will be certified as class actions in the coming years.

Second, fraud claims frequently require proof of reliance by the plaintiff, and courts have held that reliance issues render fraud cases inappropriate for Rule 23(b)(3) class actions.[110] This tendency to reject class certification of fraud claims has become essentially a per se rule that courts have applied in a variety of contexts, including state law fraud actions and federal racketeering actions. I do not envision this law changing in the next decade; cases asserting fraud claims and requiring proof of individualized reliance will be difficult, if not impossible, to mount as class actions. The one exception is when the law permits a classwide presumption of reliance. As discussed below, such a presumption exists in securities fraud suits under the federal securities laws.

Third, nationwide or other multistate class actions brought under state law require courts to apply the laws of multiple states. Numerous courts have held that the application of multiple states' laws defeats predominance.[111] As one court has explained, "[i]f more than a few of the laws of the fifty states differ," then "the district judge would face an impossible task of instructing a jury on the relevant law."[112]

5.2.1.3 Application of Numerosity

In my view, the courts will continue to vigorously enforce numerosity. They will eschew common sense approaches and require rigorous proof from plaintiffs. In most cases, this will not be an impediment because plaintiffs can easily show numerosity with evidence. But as the cases discussed above illustrate, there are a variety of circumstances in which plaintiffs will have great difficulty marshaling specific evidence on numerosity. This will be the case, for example, when the plaintiff has evidence of numerosity on the national level but is bringing only a statewide class action, for which precise numbers of class members are not available.

5.2.1.4 Restrictions on Rule 23(b)(2) Classes

In light of the severe limitations that *Dukes* imposes on the ability to bring class actions for money under Rule 23(b)(2), virtually all class action suits for money will be brought under Rule 23(b)(3). As a result, plaintiffs will have to satisfy the very demanding predominance and superiority requirements. Indeed, this has already happened in several cases post *Dukes*.[113]

110 *Decline* at 793–96.

111 *Id.* at 796–99.

112 Pilgrim v. Universal Health Card, LLC, 660 F.3d 943, 948 (6th Cir. 2011) (citation and internal quotation marks omitted). *But see, e.g.*, In re Hyundai & Kia Fuel Econ. Litig., 926 F.3d 539, 561–64 (9th Cir. 2019) (en banc) (in settlement context, variations in state law did not defeat class certification).

113 *See, e.g.*, Ellis v. Costco Wholesale Corp., 657 F.3d 970, 975 (9th Cir. 2011) (vacating the district court's certification under Rule 23(b)(2) and remanding for consideration of whether the class qualifies for certification under Rule 23(b)(3), under which gender discrimination allegations were redressable by both monetary and injunctive relief); Nationwide Life Ins. Co. v. Haddock, 460 Fed.App'x 26, 29 (2d Cir. 2012) (vacating Rule 23(b)(2) certification and remanding for reconsideration of appropriateness of certification under Rule 23(b)(3), where plaintiffs sought declaratory, injunctive and disgorgement relief for alleged ERISA funds mismanagement); July v. Bd. of Sch. Comm'rs, 291 F.R.D. 653, 659 (S.D. Ala. 2013) (denying class certification under Rule 23(b)(2) because plaintiffs sought back pay, and denying class certification under Rule 23(b)(3) because plaintiffs could not satisfy predominance).

Thus, cases that might have been certified under Rule 23(b)(2) in the past will frequently be rejected for class treatment under Rule 23(b)(3).

5.2.1.5 Standing

In the next decade, standing will be a major point of attack by defendants. Although, as noted, the Supreme Court has not issued a seminal ruling on standing in class actions, the defense bar is watching closely for the right case.[114] Two prongs of attack will be pursued. First, the defense will argue that the class representatives cannot satisfy standing merely by showing that a statute authorizes suit and provides a statutory recovery. Rather, the plaintiff must demonstrate actual injury. Second, the defense will argue that standing must be satisfied, as a threshold issue, not just for the class representative but for the entire class.

Certain types of cases will be especially vulnerable to standing challenges. A prime example is data breach cases. A string of data breach class actions have been brought in recent years, alleging that account records were hacked, putting in jeopardy confidential financial information of putative class members. Potentially millions of class members are involved in such cases.[115]

Data breach cases would seem to be strong candidates for class certification because of the critical overarching issues of defendant's action (or lack of action) leading to the breach.[116] A major problem in class action data breach cases, however, is standing. The federal circuits are divided. When plaintiff representatives are unable to show that the seizure of their personal data has led to identity theft, some circuits have concluded that the harm (a threat of identity theft) is not sufficient to confer standing. In the Fourth Circuit, for example, "a mere compromise of personal information, without more, fails to satisfy the injury-in-fact element."[117] By contrast, in the Seventh Circuit, an increased risk of identity theft is sufficient to confer standing.[118]

Antitrust class actions will also face standing challenges in the coming years. Like plaintiffs in data breach cases, plaintiffs who complain of harm caused by violations of antitrust law also generally share common factual allegations of illegal action by defendant. Yet class certification has been denied when a segment of the proposed class is likely uninjured.[119]

114 In Salcedo v. Hanna, 936 F.3d 1162, 1172 (11th Cir. 2019), the Eleventh Circuit held that a single unsolicited text message cannot confer standing under federal consumer protection laws, noting that "[the Ninth Circuit] has reached the opposite conclusion." Such a direct circuit conflict increases the likelihood that the Supreme Court will take up the issue.

115 Soo Youn, *The Capital One Data Breach Is Alarming, but These Are the 5 Worst Corporate Hacks*, ABC News (July 30, 2019, 12:13 PM), https://abcnews.go.com/Technology/marriotts-data-breach-large-largest-worst-corporate-hacks/story?id=59520391.

116 Numerous data breach cases have been certified as class actions after the courts have found the requirement of class certification to be satisfied. *See, e.g.*, In re Home Depot, Inc. Customer Data Sec. Breach Litig., No. 1:14-md-02583-TWT (N.D. Ga. Aug. 23, 2016) (order granting final approval of class action settlement); Hapka v. Carecentrix, Inc., No. 2:16-cv-02372-KGG (D. Kan. Feb. 15, 2018) (order granting final approval of class action settlement).

117 Hutton v. Nat'l Bd. of Examiners in Optometry, Inc., 892 F.3d 613, 621 (4th Cir. 2018).

118 Lewert v. P.F. Chang's China Bistro Inc., 819 F.3d 963 (7th Cir. 2016) (noting that the theft of data by third parties itself was the injury). *See also* Patel v. Facebook, 932 F.3d 1264 (9th Cir. 2019), *cert. denied*, 140 S. Ct. 937 (2020).

119 In re Rail Freight Fuel Surcharge Antitrust Litig., 292 F. Supp. 3d 14, 138 (D.D.C. 2017), *aff'd* 934 F.3d 619 (D.C. Cir. 2019) (plaintiffs' class not certified when their expert's methodology showed up to 12.7 percent of the class was uninjured, because "all or virtually all" defined class members must be injured to satisfy the predominance requirement).

5.2.1.6 Arbitration

I believe that, during the next decade, one of the most dramatic impacts on aggregate litigation will be the Supreme Court's restrictive case law on arbitration clauses. It is that case law that has caused Professors Gilles and Fitzpatrick to conclude (as noted at the outset of this chapter) that class actions will be all but dead in a matter of years.

First, arbitration clauses have been enforced in a wide array of consumer class actions. Those include situations in which plaintiffs and defendants are in a contractual relationship,[120] and even those in which arbitration clauses are added through inserts in product packages.[121] The fact that such clauses might have been subject to attack as contracts of adhesion under state law no longer matters in light of the Supreme Court's jurisprudence.[122]

Because many, if not most, consumer cases are negative value suits, the impact of these arbitration cases is not simply to shift the suits from aggregate cases to individual cases. Realistically, the result is to eliminate such suits altogether, thus giving defendants a green light to engage in misconduct with no legal consequences.

Second, arbitration clauses threaten to eliminate substantial numbers of aggregate employment actions. An employer can easily require employees to sign arbitration clauses as a condition of employment.[123] As a result, courts faced with arbitration clauses have held that suits alleging violation of wage and hour laws, and suits alleging employment discrimination or harassment, cannot be pursued as aggregate cases but must be brought individually in arbitration.[124]

Again, the consequences of this law are dramatic. Many employment cases are simply too expensive and complicated to bring as individual actions. They often require extensive and expensive expert testimony. Thus, as in the consumer context, the arbitration case law means not merely a shift from aggregate litigation to individual suits, but instead a shift to no litigation at all in many instances. This state of affairs has generated extensive criticism by judges and scholars.[125] Yet, absent an amendment to either the Federal Arbitration Act or to the underlying employment statutes,[126] the courts cannot authorize aggregate litigation in light of the Supreme Court's restrictive case law.

120 *See* In re Cox Enterprises, Inc. Set-top Cable Television Box Antitrust Litig., 835 F.3d 1195, 1199 (10th Cir. 2016); Gutierrez v. Wells Fargo Bank, NA, 889 F.3d 1230, 1234 (11th Cir. 2018), *cert. denied*, 139 S. Ct. 941 (2019).

121 *See* Dye v. Tamko Building Prods., Inc., 908 F.3d 675 (11th Cir. 2018) (homeowners were bound by arbitration provision printed on roof shingle packaging); Fitzpatrick, *supra* note 4 at 176–77 ("businesses can bind consumers to contractual language by placing the language on the product's packaging," even though the consumers "could not read the language until after . . . purchas[ing] the product"). *But see* Norcia v. Samsung Telecomm. Am., LLC, 845 F.3d 1279, 1281–82 (9th Cir. 2017) (arbitration clause not enforced when hidden in a 101-page brochure).

122 *See* DIRECTV, Inc. v. Imburgia, 136 S.Ct. 463, 465–66 (2015).

123 *See* Fitzpatrick, *supra* note 4 at 176 ("At the time of hiring – or, indeed, at any time thereafter – businesses can (and often do) ask their employees to sign contractual agreements, including clauses to arbitrate any dispute that might arise.")

124 *See* Epic Sys. Corp. v. Lewis, 138 S. Ct. 1612 (2018); Bekele v. Lyft, Inc., 918 F.3d 181 (1st Cir. 2019); Zoller v. UBS Sec. LLC, No. 16 C 11277, 2019 WL 2371724 at *1 (N.D. Ill. June 5, 2019); Voll v. HCL Technologies Ltd., No. 18-CV -04943-LHK (N.D. Cal. Jan. 9, 2019) (order granting motion to compel arbitration). *See also, e.g.*, Dorman v. Charles Schwab Corp., 934 F.3d 1107 (9th Cir. 2019) (holding that employee claims brought under ERISA may be subject to mandatory arbitration).

125 *See* Gilles, *supra* note 3 at 419; Fitzpatrick, *supra* note 4 at 199. *See also* Erin Mulvaney, *Federal Arbitration Law Poses Barrier to #MeToo State Laws*, Bloomberg L. (Sept. 7, 2019, 6:09 PM), http://biglawbusiness.com/federal-arbitration-law-poses-barrier-to-metoo-era-state-laws (noting that 65.1 percent of companies with 1,000 or more employees have mandatory arbitration procedures).

126 The US House of Representatives passed the Forced Arbitration Injustice Repeal Act or the FAIR Act in September 2019, which would invalidate arbitration agreements imposed on employees and consumers, but the law has yet to be considered by the Republican-controlled Senate. Alexia Fernandez Campbell, *The House Just*

Third, although this has not yet occurred, Professor Fitzpatrick worries that the arbitration case law could extend to the securities context, given that purchasers of stock have essentially a contractual relationship with the companies issuing the stock.[127] If this were to occur, then a huge area of aggregate litigation – securities fraud – would be limited to individual suits in arbitration. In most instances, an individual shareholder would not have enough at stake to litigate the complicated, protracted, expert-intensive issues involved in securities fraud suits.

5.2.1.7 Cy Pres

I believe that a majority of the Supreme Court will eventually adopt Justice Thomas's analysis in *Frank* and disapprove of a cy pres remedy when none of the relief goes to the class. I am much less certain of the outcome in a situation in which the funds going to third parties are merely the excess after reasonable efforts have been made to distribute the bulk of the proceeds directly to class members.[128] Yet, even if the Court strikes down cy pres remedies only in the former situation, it will preclude what in some circumstances is the only feasible approach, since individual recoveries may be too small to distribute individually (i.e., when the cost of distribution exceeds the amount being distributed). Major restrictions on cy pres remedies will dramatically impact consumer class actions, because frequently not enough is at stake to justify distribution to individual class members.

5.2.2 *Neutral Factors*

A number of contentious aggregate litigation issues had the potential to dramatically curtail the scope of class actions. As the case law has played out, however, many such issues have ended up not having the dire impact that many had feared. This section discusses several of those issues.

5.2.2.1 Ascertainability

As discussed above, the heightened ascertainability requirement essentially eliminates class actions in situations in which plaintiffs cannot show, at the outset, a feasible method of identifying class members. This is a potential problem in many consumer cases, especially those in which consumers have no way of proving, short of an affidavit, that they were part of a defined class.

The topic has received significant academic coverage, and defendants have litigated the issue repeatedly across the country. But the requirement, created by the Third Circuit, has not gained traction.

Several circuits have rejected heightened ascertainability in compelling, well-reasoned opinions.[129] And, as noted, the Third Circuit has itself retreated from its own extreme position. There is nothing in the language of Rule 23 or the Advisory Committee Notes accompanying the

Passed a Bill That Would Give Millions of Workers the Right to Sue Their Boss, VOX (Dec. 21, 2019), www.vox.com/identities/2019/9/20/20872195/forced-mandatory-arbitration-bill-fair-act.

127 *See* Fitzpatrick, *supra* note 4 at 177–78 ("[S]hareholders . . . buy their shares subject to the terms and provisions found in the corporation's charter and bylaws . . . . [L]ike employees and customers, shareholders are in something of a contractual relationship with corporations.").

128 *See* PRINCIPLES OF THE LAW OF AGGREGATE LITIGATION § 3.07, at 223–24 (2010) (urging that cy pres be allowed in these circumstances).

129 *See, e.g.*, Briseno v. ConAgra Foods, Inc., 844 F.3d 1121 (9th Cir.), *cert. denied*, 138 S. Ct. 313 (2017); Mullins v. Direct Digital, LLC, 795 F.3d 654 (7th Cir. 2015), *cert. denied*, 133 S. Ct. 338 (2016).

rule to support a separate heightened ascertainability requirement. Because the Supreme Court looks closely at the text in these kinds of situations, I believe it unlikely that the Court will embrace the Third Circuit's approach.

5.2.2.2 Individualized Damages

In *Comcast Corp. v. Behrend*,[130] the Supreme Court ruled that Rule 23(b)(3)'s predominance requirement was not satisfied because "respondents' [damages] model [fell] far short of establishing that damages are capable of measurement on a classwide basis."[131] Although the plaintiffs in that case conceded that class certification would not be proper without a way to prove damages on a classwide basis, defendants began to argue that, even without such a concession, a class action could not be certified if damages were individualized. Such a rule would have eliminated most class actions. It is a rare case in which damages can be established purely by formula – without at least some individualized factual determinations.

Consider, for example, a sex discrimination claim. Even if there are overarching common issues, such as whether the defendant engaged in a pattern and practice of discrimination, individualized issues will exist, including findings regarding lost wages, pain and suffering, and other compensatory damages issues. The recognition that most class actions involved at least some individualized damages determinations led courts (pre-*Comcast*) to conclude, virtually unanimously, that individualized damages did not defeat class certification.[132]

Yet, despite plaintiffs' concession in *Comcast*, the defense bar took *Comcast* as an invitation to argue, in case after case, that individualized damages were fatal to certification. As discussed above, the Supreme Court in *Tyson Foods* stated (in a case that did not raise the issue) that individualized damages did not defeat class certification. Numerous lower courts, post-*Comcast*, have taken that same approach.[133] I do not envision either the Supreme Court or the federal circuits retreating from this position. At most, courts might hold that, in a particular case, individualized damages, *along with myriad other individualized issues*, create predominance problems. In short, as the case law has played out, I do not see the issue of individualized damages as posing a fundamental threat to aggregate litigation.

5.2.2.3 Pick Offs

As noted, defendants in class actions have aggressively made offers of judgment to class representatives in an effort to moot their claims (and, in turn, moot the class actions because of the absence of class representatives in the case). This strategy posed a grave threat to aggregate litigation. Since individual plaintiffs' lawyers presumably have only a small stable of clients with particular claims, buying off a small number of plaintiffs could leave counsel without a viable class representative. And other lawyers, aware of the pick-off strategy, might be deterred from bringing class action lawsuits using their clients as representatives.

In what many viewed as a surprising outcome, the Supreme Court in *Campbell-Ewald* rejected the pick-off strategy. As noted, however, the Court left open the question of whether mootness could be established if the defendant actually deposited the funds in the court's

130 133 S. Ct. 1426 (2013).
131 *Id.* at 1433.
132 *Prognosis* at 1617.
133 *See, e.g.*, Nguyen v. Nissan N. Am., Inc., 932 F.3d 811, 817 (9th Cir. 2019); Roach v. T.L. Cannon Corp., 778 F.3d 401, 402 (2d Cir. 2015).

registry. Thus, there was still a possibility that the strategy could work, as long as defendant took the additional step of depositing the funds in the court's registry. But, as noted above, the circuits, following *Campbell-Ewald*, have generally rejected the pick-off strategy in that context as well. In short, the pick-off strategy does not appear to pose a significant threat to aggregate litigation.

5.2.2.4 Proof on the Merits

As discussed above, prior to *Amgen*, a number of lower courts had denied class certification by essentially making merits determinations. Such an approach had the potential to eliminate most class actions. In many cases, prior to merits discovery, plaintiffs are simply not in a position to offer persuasive and dispositive proof on merits issues. In *Amgen*, however, the Supreme Court made clear that the function of class certification is not to decide the merits but rather to determine if there are *questions* that, if answered favorably for plaintiffs, would be dispositive on a classwide basis. As noted, after *Amgen*, numerous courts have rejected defendants' arguments that class certification should be denied because of plaintiff's failure to prove particular issues on the merits. Thus, while the trend of requiring proof on the merits once posed a serious threat to plaintiffs' ability to certify class actions, that threat appears to have subsided, as the lower courts pay close attention to the teachings of *Amgen*.

5.2.2.5 Commonality

The Supreme Court's strict definition of commonality will likely have little impact on cases under Rule 23(b)(3), since (b)(3) already requires that common issues predominate over individual issues. The primary impact will be in cases under (b)(1) and (b)(2), since those provisions do not have a predominance requirement.[134] Because most class actions (and virtually all class actions for money) are brought under (b)(3), the impact of the commonality definition in *Dukes* going forward will be less substantial than many on the plaintiff side had feared.

Although *Dukes* itself was an employment discrimination case, it does not appear that the commonality test in *Dukes* has materially changed the landscape even in employment cases. As one commentator has noted, courts that were receptive to class action claims before *Dukes* appear to remain receptive after the decision.[135]

Because the commonality test potentially impacts (b)(1) and (b)(2) classes, *Dukes* raised the possibility that public interest lawsuits – such as those by prisoners, juveniles, and immigrants – would be more difficult to certify. Those types of suits are traditionally brought under Rule 23(b)(2). It appears, however, that *Dukes* has not dramatically hindered such suits.

For instance, in *D.G. ex rel. Strickland v. Yarbrough*, the district court refused to decertify – in light of *Dukes* – a class of foster children seeking declaratory and injunctive relief under Rule 23 (b)(2) related to the state's alleged failure to adequately monitor their foster placements.[136] The court confined *Dukes* mainly to the employment discrimination context.[137] Likewise, in *Reid v. Donelan*, the district court certified a class of noncitizens who had been held in Massachusetts immigration detention facilities for more than six months without individualized bond

134 *Decline* at 778–79; *Respite* at 992–93.

135 Michael Selmi & Sylvia Tsakos, *Employment Discrimination Class Actions After* Wal-mart v. Dukes, 48 AKRON L. REV. 803, 804 (2015).

136 278 F.R.D. 635, 636, 646 (N.D. Okla. 2011).

137 *Id.* at 639.

hearings.[138] The defendant had allegedly applied a statute authorizing detention without opportunity for bond identically to each member of the class, and the court therefore found commonality satisfied. It reasoned that, under *Dukes*, "the answer to a single, legal question disposes of the claims of the entire class."[139]

To be sure, *Dukes* has impacted class certification in some structural reform cases. For example, in *Jamie S. v. Milwaukee Public Schools*, the Seventh Circuit decertified a class of special education students alleging violations of the Individuals with Disabilities Education Act and seeking structural reform of the district's special education programs. Citing *Dukes*, the court held that the commonality requirement was not satisfied, because the plaintiffs failed to demonstrate a "question of law or fact that can be answered *all at once* and that the *single answer* to that question will resolve a central issue in all class members' claims."[140] Similarly, in *M.D. ex rel. Stukenberg v. Perry*, the Fifth Circuit overturned the district court's certification of a class of foster children seeking declaratory and injunctive relief under (b)(2), and remanded the case for "a rigorous analysis" of the commonality requirement under 23(a)(2) in light of *Dukes*.[141] But these cases appear to be the minority, and they may have come out the same way even without the new formulation of commonality in *Dukes*. The bottom line, in my view, is that public interest class actions will continue to be frequently certified as class actions.

5.2.2.6 Settlements and Attorneys' Fees

With respect to class settlements, I have two predictions. First, I believe that courts will continue a recent trend of carefully scrutinizing class settlements. Federal appellate courts have become very thorough in scrutinizing class settlements, and have struck down a number of settlements in recent years because of, inter alia, (1) conflicts of interest among plaintiffs' counsel, and (2) deficient recoveries for class members.[142] I believe that this trend will continue. Second, courts will continue to scrutinize attorneys' fees awards with rigor.[143]

Strict review of settlements and attorneys' fees, however, is salutary, and such review poses no real threat to the ability of plaintiff lawyers to bring legitimate class actions. Thus, I do not see this law as deterring meritorious aggregate litigation.

5.2.3 *Favorable Factors*

5.2.3.1 Fraud on the Market for Securities Cases

Despite dire predictions for many types of cases, one area in which aggregation is likely to remain common is in the securities fraud area. Subject to the caveat above (regarding the possibility that companies will use arbitration agreements in connection with the issuance of securities), I believe that securities fraud cases will remain robust in the coming ten years.

138 297 F.R.D. 185, 187 (D. Mass. 2014).
139 *Id.* at 190–91.
140 668 F.3d 481, 497 (7th Cir. 2012) (emphasis in original).
141 675 F.3d 832, 838 (5th Cir. 2012).
142 *See Prognosis* at 1623–35.
143 *See, e.g.*, In re Home Depot Inc., 931 F.3d 1065, 1072 (11th Cir. 2019) (district court abused its discretion in using a multiplier to account for risk in a fee-shifting case); Chieftain Royalty Co. v. Enervest Energy Institutional Fund XIII-A, L.P., 888 F.3d 455, 459 (10th Cir. 2017) (reversing district court's percentage-of-the-fund analysis for awarding attorney fees because governing state law required the lodestar approach), *cert. denied*, 139 S. Ct. 482 (2018).

Notwithstanding the enactment of the PSLRA, which was designed to rein in securities fraud class actions, such actions continued to thrive. The Supreme Court has generally been supportive. For example:

- In *Erica P. John Fund, Inc. v. Halliburton Co.* (*Halliburton I*), the Court unanimously held that a securities fraud plaintiff need not prove that the defendant's misconduct caused the economic loss at issue (a concept known as "loss causation") to certify a class.[144]
- In *Amgen*, the Court held that proof of the materiality of the alleged misrepresentations was not a prerequisite to class certification.[145]
- In *Halliburton v. Erica P. John Fund, Inc.* (*Halliburton II*),[146] the Court addressed the question of whether it should overrule the "fraud on the market" principle of *Basic, Inc. v. Levinson*.[147] That principle presumes that investors rely on public information, including material misrepresentations, when the stock trades on a well-developed market. *Basic* enables plaintiffs in class actions to avoid the argument that individualized reliance issues defeat class certification. The Court rejected several arguments by Halliburton as to why *Basic* was wrongly decided.[148] Thus, while fraud claims are normally not permitted to be brought on a classwide basis, the "fraud on the market" concept ensures that securities fraud cases can continue to be brought as class actions.

Recent statistics confirm that securities suits are still thriving. They are "at or near record levels," with 403 new federal class actions filed in 2018, "nearly double" the average for 1997–2007.[149] Moreover, more than 400 new federal class actions were filed in 2019.[150] I do not expect this trend to subside (unless such cases become stymied by arbitration clauses).[151]

There is a simple reason why securities fraud class actions have not been severely impacted by the overall decline in class actions: They are highly suitable for class certification. With the availability of the *Basic* presumption of reliance, individual reliance issues are relatively rare. In virtually all securities fraud class actions, the common issues will resolve the case for everyone in the class; the classes are usually large and easily identifiable; and in most instances damages can be calculated mathematically based on the number of shares bought or sold during a specific time frame.

5.2.3.2 Issue Classes

As discussed above, issue classes have become more common in recent years, and there no longer exists a circuit conflict on whether predominance must be shown. Issue classes have been

144 131 S. Ct. 2179, 2183 (2011).
145 Amgen Inc. v. Connecticut Retirement Plans & Tr. Funds, 133 S. Ct. 1184, 1191 (2013).
146 134 S. Ct. 2398, 2405 (2014).
147 108 S. Ct. 978 (1988).
148 134 S. Ct. at 2407–13.
149 Alexander "Sasha" Aganin & John Gould, *Securities Class Action Filings – 2018 Year in Review*, Harvard Law School Forum On Corporate Governance And Financial Regulation (Feb. 8, 2019), https://corpgov.law.harvard.edu/2019/02/08/securities-class-action-filings-2018-year-in-review/.
150 *See* Jay B. Kasner, Scott D. Musoff & Susan L. Saltzstein, *In 2020, Securities Class Action Filings Likely to Continue Record Pace* (Skadden, Arps, Slate, Meagher & Flom LLP and Affiliates 2020), available at https://www.skadden.com/insights/publications/2020/01/in-2020-securities-class-action-filings.
151 Antitrust cases also continue to be certified, although not with the consistency of securities fraud cases. *See, e.g.*, In re Namenda Direct Purchaser Antitrust Litig., 331 F. Supp. 3d 152 (S.D.N.Y. 2018); In re Domestic Drywall Antitrust Litig., 322 F.R.D. 188 (E.D. Pa. 2017); In re Qualcomm Antitrust Litig., 328 F.R.D. 280 (N.D. Cal. 2018). *But see, e.g.*, In re Asacol Antitrust Litig., 907 F.3d 42 (1st Cir. 2018); Garnica v. HomeTeam Pest Defense, Inc., 230 F. Supp. 3d 1155 (N.D. Cal. 2017).

used in environmental cases, employment cases, and a variety of other contexts. The *Martin* case discussed above is a perfect example: a complicated environmental case that raised concerns under Rule 23(b)(3) was nonetheless appropriate for a common issues trial under Rule 23(c)(4). I believe that issue classes will remain a powerful device in the next ten years, especially for some cases that cannot qualify for certification under Rule 23(b)(3).

5.2.3.3 Multidistrict Litigation

I believe that MDL will remain vibrant, especially in circumstances (like mass torts) in which aggregation is important but the cases are not suitable for class certification. In 2018, the MDL Panel created twenty-eight new MDLs, including eight product liability MDLs.[152] Although the defense bar has urged some modifications of the MDL process, such as allowing more frequent interlocutory review of important issues,[153] there has been no concerted effort by the defense bar to derail MDLs altogether. Indeed, defendants often agree to centralization under the MDL statute, recognizing the efficiencies of such an approach. I expect that the MDL Panel will continue to utilize the MDL statute in appropriate cases to achieve efficiencies.

Unlike class actions, which are subject to significant and onerous requirements, an MDL can be created on a much less demanding standard of "common question[s] of fact.[154]" Many MDLs have been ordered in situations in which the constituent cases would not be suitable for class certification. And even when class actions are feasible, MDLs that include class actions provide the benefit of avoiding competing class actions with conflicting rulings.[155] Thus, as class actions inevitably decline in some areas, MDL will remain a vibrant device for achieving significant benefits of aggregation, including coordinated discovery and uniform rulings on major legal issues.

5.3 CONCLUSION

As this chapter has shown, certain kinds of class actions, particularly consumer and employment class actions, are in jeopardy. And there is no likelihood that cases previously found ill-suited for class certification (such as mass torts, fraud cases, and cases involving multiple states' laws) will be reexamined in the coming ten years and found to be suitable for class actions. Thus, it can be said that class actions are on the decline. Some types of class actions will remain robust, however, such as securities fraud cases. And I see little indication that MDL will disappear as an alternative mechanism for achieving aggregation.

152 *And Now A Word From The Panel: MDL Year In Review*, LAW360 (Jan. 29, 2019, 2:03 PM) www.law360.com/articles/1123086/and-now-a-word-from-the-panel-mdl-year-in-review.

153 *See* MDL NUTSHELL at 355–59.

154 28 U.S.C. § 1407(a).

155 *See id.* at 30.

PART II

The Americas

6

Mandatory Arbitration of Intra-corporate Disputes in Brazil

A Beacon of Light for Shareholder Litigation?

Patricia Gil Lemstra[1]

Joseph A. McCahery

6.1 INTRODUCTION

Over the last two decades, policymakers and researchers have shown an interest in resolving shareholder disputes through mandatory arbitration and a ban on class actions.[2] Litigation is increasingly seen as problematic due to the increase in nuisance lawsuits and the increase in settlement value, the costs of which are ultimately borne by shareholders.[3] Earlier literature has examined the benefits of mandatory arbitration across several contexts, including Delaware corporate law.[4] While researchers have identified several important benefits of mandatory intra-corporate arbitration, such as reduced cost and delays, relatively little is known about the attitudes and interests of the parties – such as corporations, limited liability companies, small and medium-sized enterprises, their law firms, and institutional investors – regarding intra-corporate conflicts and dispute resolution via mandatory arbitration.

To be sure, policymakers around the world have reacted differently to mandatory arbitration of shareholder claims. In Italy, for example, the enforcement of arbitration agreements of listed companies or companies with diffused shares is prohibited.[5] Similarly, the United States Securities and Exchange Commission (SEC) has again recently opposed the inclusion of an arbitration provision in the corporate documents of listed companies.[6] However, it is worth

1 We thank Carlos Eduardo Stefen Elias, Marcelo Godke Veiga, Selma Maria Ferreira Lemes, Randall Thomas, Walfrido Jorge Warde Junior and seminar participants at the 4th Pan-American Arbitration Congress in Sao Paulo and the International Class Action Conference at Vanderbilt University Law School for helpful comments. Evvi Angelis provided excellent research assistance.

2 Brian T. Fitzpatrick, "The End of Class Actions?" (2015) 57 (1) *Arizona Law Review*; Vanderbilt Public Law Research Paper No. 15–2; Vanderbilt Law and Economics Research Paper No. 15–5 https://papers.ssrn.com/sol3/papers.cfm?abstract_id=2576304.

3 John C. Coffee Jr., "Reforming the Securities Class Action; An Essay on Deterrence and Its Implementation" (2006) *Columbia Law Review* 1534.

4 Paul Weitzel, "The End of Shareholder Litigation? Allowing Shareholders to Customize Enforcement through Arbitration Provisions in Charters and Bylaws" (2013) *Brigham Young University Law Review* 65; Joseph Lee, "Intra-Corporate Dispute Arbitration and Minority Shareholder Protection: A Corporate Governance Perspective" (2017) 83 *Arbitration* 85.

5 *Sentenza Cassazione Civile n 20674 del 13/10/2016 1.*

6 Johnson & Johnson, SEC No-Action Letter 2019 www.sec.gov/divisions/corpfin/cf-noaction/14a-8/2019/dorisbehrjohnsono21119-14a8.pdf (February 11, 2019) accessed December 29, 2019. *See* SEC Chairman Jay Clayton, "Public Statement on Shareholder Proposals Seeking to Require Mandatory Arbitration Bylaw Provisions" www.sec.gov/news/public-statement/clayton-statement-mandatory-arbitration-bylaw-provisions accessed December 29, 2019.

noting that some courts show clear signs of favoring mandatory intra-corporate arbitration.[7] Moreover, some former and current SEC commissioners have expressed favorable views of mandatory arbitration.[8] In certain countries, such as China, arbitration is allowed, and it is encouraged in Chile and Argentina as a way to attract foreign investment.[9] Notably, Brazil has, perhaps, the most open attitude towards arbitration for intra-corporate disputes, mandating it as a prerequisite for registering in specific listing segments.[10]

Two opposing views can be distinguished with respect to arbitration for intra-corporate disputes. The first view holds that shareholders' right to redress through class actions is not a procedural, but a substantive, right. Hence, the choice of arbitration, whenever it includes a class action waiver, would result in shareholders losing their right to a judicial remedy.[11] The second view leads us to expect that mandatory arbitration bylaws and other corporate documents are procedural, as they merely determine the forum for dispute resolution and have no effect on substantive rights.[12] However, there is controversy regarding the nature of the bylaws and corporate charters. On the one hand, proponents who defend the applicability of contractual theory view bylaws and corporate charters as binding contracts between the company and its shareholders,[13] arguing for the validity of the mandatory arbitration provision in the referred corporate documents.[14] On the other hand, critics argue that the fiduciary doctrine should apply as a response to the natural disadvantage of minority shareholders, in terms of both their expertise and their ability to access evidence, endure costs and bargain effectively.[15]

In addition, ample literature examines the preference among companies for arbitration over litigation.[16] However, there is a division in the literature regarding the specific factors influencing the selection of mandatory arbitration.[17] For example, most surveys indicate that costs are

7 The US Supreme Court's and Delaware Court of Chancery's decisions have repeatedly favored arbitration in commercial contracts. *See, e.g., American Express Co.* v. *Italian Colors Restaurant*, 133 S. Ct. 2304 (2013), and *Boilermakers Local 154 Ret. Fund* v. *Chevron Corp.*, 73 A.3d 934 (Del. Ch. 2013).

8 Former SEC Commissioner Michael Piwowar signaled a possible change in the SEC's attitude towards arbitration for intra-corporate dispute resolution. Samuel M. Ward and Michael A. Toomey, "The Problems With Mandatory Arbitration of Securities Claims" (*Law360*, 2017) 6 www.barrack.com/sites/default/files/The%20Problems%20with%20Mandatory%20Arbitration%20of%20Securities%20Claims%20Law360%20Ward.Toomey.pdf accessed July 5, 2019. Current SEC Commissioner Hester Peirce has also shown support to the corporate mandatory arbitration clause. Alison Frankel, "SEC commissioner Peirce signals shareholder arbitration is not dead yet" (*REUTERS*, 2019) www.reuters.com/article/us-otc-arbitration/sec-commissioner-peirce-signals-shareholder-arbitration-is-not-dead-yet-idUSKBN1QP2DY accessed November 11, 2019.

9 International Finance Corporation, "Investing Across Borders 2010: Indicators of foreign direct investment in 87 countries." http://documents.worldbank.org/curated/en/826251468341077303/pdf/643710WP0Inves00Box03615 35B0PUBLIC0.pdf accessed December 29, 2019.

10 *See* John Armour and Caroline Schmidt, "Building Enforcement Capacity for Brazilian Corporate and Securities Law" [2017] European Corporate Governance Institute (ECGI) – Law Working Paper No. 344/2017 https://papers.ssrn.com/sol3/papers.cfm?abstract_id=2901698.

11 Salvatore Graziano and Robert Trisotto, "Keeping Investors out of Court – The Looming Threat of Mandatory Arbitration" (*Harvard Law School Forum on Corporate Governance and Financial Regulation*, 2019) 3 http://blogs.law.harvard.edu/corpgov/%5Cnfiles/1481/corpgov.html accessed November 25, 2019.

12 *See Boilermakers Local 154 Ret. Fund* v. *Chevron Corp.*, 73 A.3d 934 (Del. Ch. 2013).

13 *See CA, Inc.* v. *AFSCME Emps. Pension Plan*, 953 A.2d 227, 239 (Del. 2008).

14 *Del Cnty Emps Ret Fund* v. *Portnoy*, Civil Action No 13–10405-DJC, D Mass [2014] 16.

15 Ann M. Lipton, "Manufactured Consent: The Problem of Arbitration Clauses in Corporate Charters and Bylaws" (2016) 104 *Georgetown Law Journal* 59.

16 Rick Porter, "The Not So Great Debate: Arbitration v. Litigation" (Chubb) www.chubb.com/bm-en/_assets/documents/bermuda_arbitration_vs_litigation_4.9.pdf accessed June 23, 2019.

17 PwC/Queen Mary "2013 International Arbitration Survey" shows *expertise of the decision maker* as the top benefit of arbitration, whereas *enforceability of awards* is the most valuable characteristic of international arbitration according to White & Case/Queen Mary "2018 International Arbitration Survey: The Evolution of International Arbitration."

considered a meaningful concern when parties have a preference for arbitration.[18] Still, few of the extant studies have focused specifically on arbitration as a method of intra-corporate dispute resolution. While it is common knowledge that firms in Brazil – in reaction to an overloaded and slow judiciary – increasingly rely on arbitration to solve intra-corporate disputes,[19] researchers still tend to concentrate mainly on settlement values and the number of arbitration cases.[20] In the absence of data on the mechanisms at the institutional level, we use a survey to understand the variety of practices that law firms, corporations, limited liability companies and small and medium-sized enterprises use to manage and resolve their conflicts. We examine parties' preferred method of intra-corporate dispute resolution, the important factors that play a role in parties' choice for a dispute resolution method and whether there is variance in these preferences depending on the value involved in the dispute, as well as the reasons and impediments for choosing arbitration. In addition, we test existing assumptions about parties' view of the binding force of mandatory arbitration for intra-corporate dispute resolution in Brazil, the importance of law firms' advice in the choice of a dispute resolution method and the most significant expenses with intra-corporate arbitration. To complement the first survey, we obtained data from a second survey of institutional investors.

In this chapter, we focus on the rise of arbitration as a solution for intra-corporate disputes in Brazil and consider the extent to which arbitration is likely to fill the dispute gap. In Section 6.2, we briefly examine the main components of the legal and judicial system and highlight the recent introduction of mandatory intra-corporate arbitration. In Section 6.3, we introduce our survey data and investigate the attitudes of parties regarding the structure and practice of intra-corporate dispute resolution in Brazil. Section 6.4 concludes.

6.2 INTRA-CORPORATE DISPUTE RESOLUTION IN BRAZIL

In this section, we provide a brief review of recent trends in corporate litigation in Brazil. We examine the factors that influence parties in their selection of mandatory arbitration mechanisms for resolving shareholder disputes. We then present the civil procedure process at the state and federal level and the filing of both derivative and class-action lawsuits. Finally, we describe the structure and characteristics of intra-corporate dispute arbitration. This analysis will serve as a foundation for our hypotheses.

6.2.1 *History and Background*

In recent years, the importance of reform of the Brazilian judicial system has grown widely. In this context, there are a number of factors influencing the efficient resolution of intra-corporate disputes. For example, a lengthy delay in issuing a final binding decision for corporate disputes results in significant losses to both the company and the

18 The results of both the PwC/Queen Mary 2013 survey and the White & Case/Queen Mary 2018 survey show that arbitration is the preferred choice of most businesses for international dispute resolution. Some of the disadvantages are delays and cost. *See* Christian Fischer and Miriam Frey, "Solving International Commercial Disputes: A Critical Summary and First Insights from Firm-Level Data" www.etsg.org/ETSG2018/papers/310.pdf accessed December 29, 2019.

19 *See* Gilberto Giusti and Ricardo Tadeu Dalmaso Marques, "Brazil" in *The Dispute Resolution Review* (Jonathan Cotton ed. 7th ed. 2015).

20 *See* Selma Lemes, *"Arbitragem em Números e Valores." Seis Câmaras. 8 Anos* http://selmalemes.adv.br/artigos/An%C3%A1lise-%20Pesquisa-%20Arbitragens%20Ns.%20e%20Valores-%202010%20a%202017%20-final.pdf accessed June 23, 2019.

shareholders.[21] Indeed, research on the speed of dispute resolution by the Brazilian judiciary shows that it takes, on average, three years and nine months for a court of first instance to issue a decision.[22] The relative lack of speed can often create difficulties for shareholders who require the court to issue a faster final decision regarding the challenge of a board decision or a shareholder resolution. Unsurprisingly, shareholder activism appears to be largely ineffective due to legal and other constraints that play a significant role in minimizing institutional investor actions, with very few exceptions, against Brazilian companies.[23,24]

In order to overcome these problems, policymakers have implemented a set of reforms to address the existing weaknesses of the judiciary and to ensure the rapid and efficient settlement of corporate disputes.[25] Given the specific nature of corporate disputes, in an attempt to revive corporate litigation, Brazil has introduced specialized judicial circuits in Sao Paulo for adjudicating business matters. It is reasonable to expect these measures to result in shorter resolution periods.[26] Moreover, Constitutional Amendment n. 45/2005 has instituted a sort of binding precedent in the Brazilian system, the so-called *sumula vinculante*,[27] which are pronouncements issued by the Supreme Courts with its final position on specific issues. Subsequently, the new Code of Civil Procedure (Federal Law n. 13,105/2015), which became effective in 2016, has extended binding power to the Superior Court's decisions in disputes involving constitutionality or for repetitive cases or appeals.[28]

However, the effect of these measures to build a high-quality system for resolving corporate disputes are unclear to date. As indicated already, trust in the judiciary continues to decline.[29] This raises the important question regarding the role of mandatory intra-corporate arbitration as an alternative to the shareholder dispute resolution regime. The effectiveness of this approach has been popular with both local and international investors. Table 6.1 provides preliminary evidence of the popularity of arbitration: new cases increased from 128 in 2010 to 293 in 2018.[30]

21 *See* Luciana Gross Cunha 2017. Relatório ICJBrasil, 1 semestre 2017, http://bibliotecadigital.fgv.br/dspace/bitstream/handle/10438/19034/Relatorio-ICJBrasil_1_sem_2017.pdf?sequence=1&isAllowed=y accessed July 12, 2019.

22 Justiça em Números 2018: ano-base 2017/Conselho Nacional de Justiça – Brasília: CNJ, 2018 www.cnj.jus.br/wp-content/uploads/2011/02/8d9faee7812d35a58cee3d92d2df2f25.pdf accessed July 12, 2019.

23 Paula Guimaraes et al., "Shareholder Activism Impact on Efficiency in Brazil" (2019) 19 *Corporate Governance International* 141 www.emerald.com/insight/content/doi/10.1108/CG-01-2018-0010/full/pdf?title=shareholder-activism-impact-on-efficiency-in-brazil.

24 Petrobras, a major oil and gas company in Brazil, faced different class actions in New York after a money-laundering and corruption scheme was unveiled through the "Car Wash" operation (*see In Re: Petrobras Securities Litigation*, 312 F.R.D. 354 (2016)), resulting in a US$2.95 billion settlement in 2018. *See* SEC "Press Release on Petrobras Reaches Settlement with SEC for Misleading Investors" (September 27, 2018) www.sec.gov/news/press-release/2018-215. This was the most significant settlement involving a foreign issuer.

25 *See* Gov Risk, "UK-Brazil Cooperation: Improving Efficiency and Performance in Brazil's Judiciary," 2016/17. Available at www.cnj.jus.br. *See, also*, Guimaraes et al. (n. 23) 141.

26 *See* Marcelo Guedes et al., "Opinion" (February 13, 2018) www.conjur.com.br/2018-fev-13/opiniao-varas-empresariais-tj-sp-sao-avanco-brasil accessed July 12, 2019.

27 Although the *sumulas vinculantes* have not been particularly useful to solve intra-corporate disputes, they may have an indirect effect in solving the high backlog of cases in the Brazilian Judiciary.

28 Articles 927 and 988.

29 *See* Luciana Gross Cunha, "Relatório ICJBrasil, 1 semestre 2017" http://bibliotecadigital.fgv.br/dspace/bitstream/handle/10438/19034/Relatorio-ICJBrasil_1_sem_2017.pdf?sequence=1&isAllowed=y accessed July 12, 2019.

30 Selma Lemes, "Arbitragem em Números e Valores. Seis Câmaras" 8 *Anos* http://selmalemes.adv.br/artigos/An%C3%A1lise-%20Pesquisa-%20Arbitragens%20Ns.%20e%20Valores-%202010%20a%202017%20-final.pdf accessed June 23, 2019. For 2018, *see* "Câmaras de Arbitragem: Sua Briga é o Nosso Negócio, Revista Exame," Grupo Abril, March 6, 2019, p. 46 https://exame.abril.com.br/revista-exame/sua-briga-e-o-nosso-negocio/ accessed May 20, 2019.

TABLE 6.1 *Cases submitted to arbitration versus value involved: 2010–18 (in billions)*

	2010	2011	2012	2013	2014	2015	2016	2017	2018
Cases	128	129	158	188	218	222	249	275	293
Value (BRL)	2.8	4.2	4.7	4.2	11.7	10.7	24.3	26.3	88.3

Table 6.1 also reports that the value of arbitration increased from BRL 2.8 billion (approximately US$ 700 million) in 2010 to BRL 88.3 billion (approximately US$ 22 billion) in 2018. Finally, another important indication is that corporate disputes represent the majority of cases (42.58 percent) resolved by Center for Arbitration and Mediation of the Chamber of Commerce Brazil-Canada (CAM-CCBC), which is the Arbitration Chamber with the highest number of arbitrated cases in Brazil.

6.2.2 *Judicial System in Brazil*

Our discussion so far has focused on mandatory dispute resolution. In this section, we will provide a brief introduction to the Brazilian judicial system, which is based on the civil law tradition, operating at both the federal and state levels. First, regarding the legal framework, the court system is regulated by the Constitution and a federal statute, Federal Law 13,105/2015, the Civil Procedure Code. Cases involving the national interest, government agencies or federal public companies (Articles 108–09) fall under the jurisdiction of federal courts, while cases involving matters outside the scope of other courts (including labor, electoral and military) are governed by state courts.

Second, with regard to civil procedure, the state-level justice system consists of first instance courts, where judges handle cases and issue judicial verdicts. Second instance state courts, by contrast, consist of panels of judges who adjudicate appeals lodged against decisions by the court of first instance. Similarly, regional federal courts[31] are responsible for adjudicating appeals lodged against decisions of the federal court of first instance.[32] Within the Brazilian system, which is quite complex, there are two higher courts. The Superior Court of Justice, governed by article 105 of the Constitution, may review appeals of treaty or federal law decisions by regional federal courts or second instance courts. The Federal Supreme Court, the highest court in Brazil, has the duty to review decisions of federal and state courts involving constitutional issues and challenges involving article 102 of the Constitution.[33]

Third, the protection of minority shareholders against violations of their rights and irregularities and against fraudulent actions is possible through different types of lawsuits. Arguably, most claims are handled at state level unless a federal entity is one of the parties involved in the dispute, in which case jurisdiction is shifted to the federal level (e.g., cases involving state-controlled companies or cases to which the Securities and Exchange Commission of Brazil (CVM) is a party). On the one hand, shareholders can file derivative or direct claims against directors and officers. However, derivative claims are uncommon in Brazil due to legal obstacles

31 There are also courts to deal specifically with electoral, labor and military disputes.

32 Regional Federal Courts can also issue decisions over original lawsuits in some specific cases.

33 *See* Antonio Gidi, "Class Actions in Brazil – A Model for Civil Law Countries" [2003] *American Journal of Comparative Law* 318 https://papers.ssrn.com/sol3/papers.cfm?abstract_id=903188. *See also* chapter 7, "Class Action in Brazil: Overview, Current Trends and Case Studies," by Carlos Portugal Gouvea and Helena Campos Refosco, for a comprehensive account of the structure and history of the legal system in Brazil.

imposed by Law of Corporations (Lei das S.A.).[34] According to its article 159, companies may bring an action for civil liability against an officer only if approved through a resolution passed in a shareholders' general meeting. Whenever such approval is denied, shareholders representing at least 5 percent of the company's capital may institute proceedings[35] at their own initial costs, whereas recovery of damages must be transferred to the company, and reimbursement of incurred costs is capped at the value of the damages recovered. Finally, class actions, or so-called public civil lawsuits, regulated by Law n. 7,913/1989 and Law n. 7,347/1985 (Law of Public Civil Action), are possible in the case of collective securities claims. In that case, the Public Prosecutor's Office has standing to file lawsuits.[36]

6.2.3 *Solving Brazil's Deadlock*

The foregoing discussion strongly suggests that an alternative shareholder dispute resolution system would have substantial beneficial effects. To be sure, using arbitration procedures to resolve intra-corporate disputes is not new to Brazil, although it has increased in popularity since 2016. Arbitration was introduced in Brazil as early as 1850 through a provision in the Commercial Code that provided for mandatory arbitration of all intra-corporate disputes. Although quite innovative, this provision was soon declared unconstitutional, and arbitration practically disappeared.[37] For the most part, the potential benefits of corporate arbitration were not widely known during the nineteenth and twentieth centuries.[38] Thus, it is easy to understand why local businesses and legal professionals were never able to initiate the reforms needed to reintroduce arbitration agreements. Finally, in 1996, arbitration was reinstated through an Arbitration Act (Law n. 9.307/96),[39] and in 2001, Lei das S.A. was amended to allow companies to incorporate arbitration agreements into their bylaws or articles of association.[40] In 2002, Brazil ratified the New York Convention.[41] Nevertheless, some controversy remained over the need for the consent of all shareholders for arbitration to be binding.[42] Thus, in an attempt to put an end to such

34 *See* Bruno M. Salama and Viviane Muller Prado, "Legal Protection of Minority Shareholders of Listed Corporations in Brazil: Brief History, Legal Structure and Empirical Evidence" (2011) 4 *Journal of Civil Law Studies* 14.

35 Law of Corporations, art. 159, paragraph 4.

36 According to Law n. 9.307/96, article 1, the collective security claims can also be initiated by the Prosecutor's Office in case of a request by CVM. There is a divide in the literature regarding CVM's standing to file collective securities claims, as well as that of associations and the stock exchange. *See* Fernanda Vicentini and Vicente de Paula Marques Filho, "Collective Protection for Investors in the Stock Market and the Warranty of Access to Justice," 18–19, www.publicadireito.com.br/artigos/?cod=d79c6256b9bdac53 accessed January 10, 2020.

37 Christos A. Ravanides, "Arbitration Clauses in Public Company Charters: An Expansion of the ADR Elysian Fields for Descent into Hades" (2008) 18 *American Review of International Arbitration* 437.

38 Arbitration for intra-corporate dispute resolution was relegated to obscurity as of 1867, not only because it became discretionary, but also in view of significant obstacles to its implementation. As of Decree n. 3.900/1867, the arbitration clause included in bylaws and articles of association was no longer enforceable without the execution of an additional agreement between the parties at the time of the dispute, confirming the parties' intention to solve the dispute through arbitration (article 9). In addition, a requirement of arbitral award's ratification by a judge was introduced (article 59). These obstacles were overcome when Arbitration Act (Law n. 9.307/96) was enacted.

39 Law n. 9.307/96 was declared constitutional in 2001 by the Brazilian Supreme Court in leading case Sentença Estrangeira 5.206.

40 According to article 109 § 3, "the corporation's bylaws may establish that any disputes between the shareholders and the corporation, or between the majority and minority shareholders may be resolved by arbitration under the terms specified by it."

41 On June 7, 2002, Brazil ratified the New York Convention, and it became effective on September 5, 2002. Due to a variety of political obstacles, Brazil delayed the approval and ratification of the New York Convention for forty-four years.

42 Although many Brazilian scholars argued that the arbitration clause approved by the majority of shareholders is mandatory, some scholars, such as Modesto Carvalhosa, indicated that the arbitration clause granted a discretionary

discussion, policymakers enacted Law n. 13.129/2015 to amend the Law of Corporations, clarifying in its article 136-A that the arbitration agreement, whenever included in the corporate bylaws after approval by shareholders representing at least one half of the voting shares, is binding on all shareholders.[43] The legislation also recognized the arbitrability of disputes between public administration and private parties in relation to contracts executed with governmental authorities.[44]

Recall that an arbitration procedure can be used only to solve disposable property rights disputes or conflicts of a pecuniary nature. According to prior studies, the number of arbitration procedures involving corporate disputes increased by 80 percent. A survey of arbitrations found that the number of new cases increased from fifty in 2013 to ninety in 2017.[45] It is, however, unfortunate that there are no data available on the exact amount involved in these claims. In 2017, the total amount involved in the 275 new cases – including not only claims involving corporate disputes, but all matters that involve disposable property rights or conflicts of a pecuniary nature – submitted to arbitration was R$ 26.3 billion (approximately US$ 6.5 billion),[46] while the average amount per case was US$ 23.6 million. It is likely that the emergence of the arbitration industry, coupled with growing investors' awareness, will lead to greater efficiencies and an increase in the use of the system. Unsurprisingly, the ICC Commission on Arbitration recently ranked Brazil the third largest user of arbitration as of 2018, after France and the United States.[47]

In sum, as the trust in the Brazilian judiciary continues to decline, arbitration for the resolution of corporate disputes has been experiencing a significant rise as of the enactment of the Arbitration Act in 1996 and the amendment of the Law on Corporations that allowed companies to incorporate arbitration agreements into their bylaws or articles of association.

6.3 DATA DESCRIPTION

In this section, we describe the research design of our survey. We obtain our data for this chapter from two surveys. In the first survey, conducted between September and October 2017 (the 2017 survey), we asked Brazilian law firms, corporations, limited liability companies and small and medium-sized companies about their choice of dispute resolution mechanism. We also conducted an additional survey between January and March 2019 (the 2019 survey) to obtain information on the preferred method of dispute resolution of institutional investors with stakes in Brazilian companies.

6.3.1 *Characterization of Respondents*

To gather information on how parties use arbitration procedures to settle disputes within a company, we designed the 2017 Survey with ten questions in three areas: (1) identifying and filtering the target group; (2) documenting the methods of intra-corporate dispute resolution;

right for shareholders to choose arbitration, so arbitration would be binding only in the case of express consent from any and all shareholders.

43 According to article 136-A of Corporations Law, dissenting shareholders have the right to withdraw from the corporation and be reimbursed for the value of their shares.

44 Law 13,129/2015, article 1, paragraph 1.

45 Data made available by Selma Maria Ferreira Lemes to authors (March 21, 2019) (on file with authors).

46 Ibid. Approximately 33 percent of new cases involved intra-corporate disputes in 2017.

47 https://iccwbo.org/media-wall/news-speeches/icc-arbitration-figures-reveal-new-record-cases-awards-2018/, accessed June 20, 2019.

and (3) mandatory arbitration for intra-corporate dispute resolution. We designed the survey questions to test our hypotheses and phrased the questions to avoid financial jargon, except if the questions addressed specific intra-corporate disputes or procedure-related issues.

We created the 2017 survey in Word and solicited survey responses via email using the snowballing method. Our responses came from contacts with two law firms in Sao Paulo[48] and fifty of the authors' personal contacts who worked at different entities. The 2019 survey was designed in Qualtrics and solicited survey responses via LinkedIn and email. Using data from Anbima, FGV and the Central Bank of Brazil, we identified the largest banks and institutional investors in terms of assets and invited 957 of them to respond to our survey through e-mail in addition to 184 LinkedIn messages. We also distributed the survey to fifty-seven of the authors' personal contacts who worked for different institutional investors. In total, we received 102 responses to our invitations, implying a response rate of 8.5 percent.

Tables 6.2 and 6.3 provide summary statistics on the different respondent types in both the 2017 survey and the 2019 survey. In the 2017 survey, law firms made up around 38.5 percent of the sample; about a third of the respondents were corporations (30 percent), and the remaining 31.5 percent consisted of limited liability companies (10.5 percent), SMEs (10.5 percent) and other (entrepreneurs, scholars, investment managers) (10.5 percent). In the 2019 survey, banks made up around 33.3 percent of the sample; about 20.6 percent of the respondents were funds/asset management companies, and the remaining 44.1 percent consisted of financial consultancy/advisory companies (7.8 percent), private equity funds (6.9 percent), pension funds (5.9 percent), insurance companies (5.9 percent), hedge funds (4.9 percent), mutual funds (2 percent), real estate funds (1 percent) and others.

The respondents to our 2019 survey tended to work in higher management positions, which is beneficial to our analysis of the selection of dispute resolution mechanism. Out of the 102 respondents, half identified themselves as CEOs or Officers, while 30 percent had senior management positions. In sum, this suggests that the bulk of our 2019 survey respondents held senior positions, with some influence on substantive levels of involvement when it came to issues such as intra-corporate arbitration.

6.3.2 *Choice of Dispute Resolution Mechanism*

Having supplied a general description of the characteristics of respondents in our sample, in the next section, we will provide an analysis of their preferences regarding intra-corporate dispute resolution.

TABLE 6.2 *2017 Survey sample characteristics*

Target group	N	%
Law firms	22	38.5%
Corporations	17	30%
Limited liability companies	6	10.5%
SME	6	10.5%
Other (entrepreneurs, scholars, investment managers, etc.)	6	10.5%
Total	57	100%

48 Warde Advogados and Godke Advogados circulated the survey to their clients.

TABLE 6.3 *2019 Survey sample characteristics*

Target group	N	%
Banks	34	33.3%
Fund/asset management companies	21	20.6%
Financial consultancy/advisory companies	8	7.8%
Private equity funds	7	6.9%
Pension funds	6	5.9%
Insurance companies	6	5.9%
Hedge funds	5	4.9%
Mutual funds	2	2%
Real estate fund	1	1%
Other	10	9.8%
Non respondents	2	2%
Total	102	100%

The rise in the number of parties that include arbitration clauses in their contracts, such as corporate bylaws, statutes and articles of association, results partly from the view that mandatory arbitration in the corporate setting is a more efficient dispute resolution mechanism than litigation. This establishes a link between sophisticated parties and the inclusion of arbitration clauses. Much empirical research has documented the frequency with which mandatory arbitration clauses are included in corporate bylaws.[49] Therefore, in our survey, we asked respondents several questions about their preferred method of dispute resolution.

Prior research has looked at the litigation versus arbitration trade-off without explaining the parties' preferences for different alternative dispute resolution mechanisms.[50] Similarly, Dari-Mattiacci shows that the important drivers of choice of method include the uncertainty of the law, the amount at stake and the costs of litigation.[51] We examine whether the amount at stake in a dispute influences respondents' preferred method of dispute resolution.

We report the responses separately for disputes up to US$ 12.5 million and higher than US$ 12.5 million. Table 6.4 confirms that most respondents in our 2017 survey sample preferred arbitration over other forms of dispute resolution, and that preference increased as much as 10.53 percent whenever disputes involve values higher than US$ 12.5 million. These results suggest that Brazil is a sophisticated country with respect to arbitration practice and experience and that arbitration costs play a role in the choice of a method for intra-corporate dispute resolution. To be sure, the PWC/QM survey on choice in arbitration reports that usage of arbitration remains popular in some industries, such as Energy and Construction.[52] Overall, the results provide support for the literature that views arbitration as the preferred method of dispute resolution.

We next turn to how often respondents saw arbitration as the preferred method of dispute resolution. Table 6.4 shows that only 14.04 percent of the respondents believed that arbitration is

49 *See, e.g.*, Peter Molk and Verity Winship, "LLCs and the Private Ordering of Dispute Resolution" (2016) 41 *Journal of Corporation Law* 795; Ravanides (n 37).

50 A number of scholars have pointed to the shortcomings of this approach, *Cf.* Deborah R. Hensler, "Court-Ordered Arbitration: An Alternative View" (1990) *The University of Chicago Law Forum* 399.

51 Giuseppe Dari-Mattiacci, "Arbitration versus Litigation" (2007) 58(6) *Revue Economique* 1291.

52 PWC/QM, (2013) "Corporate Choices in International Arbitration: Industry perspectives" www.arbitration.qmul.ac.uk/media/arbitration/docs/pwc-international-arbitration-study2013.pdf accessed January 10, 2020.

TABLE 6.4 *2017 Survey preferred method and how often is arbitration appropriate*

This table reports the views of respondents to the 2017 Survey on their preferred method of dispute resolution.

Preferred Method (up to US$ 12.5M)	%	Count
Arbitration	57.89%	33
Other (Mediation or Conciliation)	17.54%	10
Court Litigation	15.79%	9
I don't know	7.02%	4
No response to this question	1.75%	1
Preferred Method (higher than US$ 12.5M)	**%**	**Count**
Arbitration	68.42%	39
Court Litigation	14.04%	8
Other (Mediation or Conciliation)	10.53%	6
I don't know	7.02%	4
	100%	57
How often is arbitration appropriate for intra-corporate dispute resolution	**%**	**Count**
Always	21.05%	12
Often	26.32%	15
Sometimes	36.84%	21
Rarely	10.53%	6
Never	3.51%	2
	100%	57

rarely or never appropriate for intra-corporate dispute resolution, while 47.37 percent of the respondents believed that arbitration is always or often appropriate. Overall our respondents' views are consistent with those reported by PWC/QM, which show that most respondents rank arbitration as the preferred method of dispute resolution across industries.

As discussed earlier, the 2019 survey was conducted with institutional investors, and the threshold was lowered to US$ 2.5 million to better understand how preferences vary according to the settlement value involved in the dispute.

Table 6.5 documents that most institutional investors in our sample prefer mediation or conciliation over arbitration for disputes involving up to US$ 2.5 million.[53] However, respondents chose mediation or conciliation and arbitration almost equally for disputes involving values higher than US$ 2.5 million. Overall, our results provide support for the literature that mediation or conciliation are low cost and effective mechanisms to settle a dispute.[54]

These results seem to confirm our hypotheses that the parties' preferences vary according to the dispute value, and that mediation or conciliation is the preferred method of intra-corporate dispute resolution when the values involved are lower than US$ 2.5 million. There was an almost

53 Note that mediation is a dispute resolution mechanism that relies on an independent third-party mediator who attempts to find points of agreement in order to reach a settlement. Similarly, conciliation involves reaching a settlement based on concessions.

54 Thomas Stipanowich and J. Ryan Lamare, "Living with 'ADR': Evolving Perceptions and Use of Mediation, Arbitration and Conflict Management in Fortune 1,000 Corporations" (2014) *Harvard Negotiation Law Review* 1.

TABLE 6.5 *Institutional investors' preferred method*
This table reports the views of respondents to the 2019 Survey on their preferred method of dispute resolution.

Preferred Method (up to US$ 2.5M)	Mean	Variance	Std. deviation	Count
Mediation or Conciliation	2.644	0.395	0.628	87
Arbitration	1.874	0.507	0.712	87
Court Litigation	1.483	0.415	0.645	87
Preferred Method (higher than US$ 2.5M)	Mean	Variance	Std. deviation	Count
Mediation or Conciliation	2.244	1.488	1.220	86
Arbitration	2.198	0.560	0.749	86
Court Litigation	1.558	0.626	0.791	86
Important factors when choosing a DR Method	Mean	Variance	Std. deviation	Count
Quality of the decision	5.500	3.387	1.840	98
Time to resolution	5.092	2.765	1.663	98
Costs	4.010	3.021	1.738	98
Predictability	3.929	3.593	1.895	98
Confidentiality	3.469	2.705	1.645	98
Preserving a good relationship among the parties involved	3.367	4.503	2.122	98
Possibility of challenge to decision	2.633	2.255	1.502	98

equal preference among institutional investors for mediation or conciliation and arbitration to solve intra-corporate disputes involving values higher than US$ 2.5 million.

Furthermore, Table 6.5 shows that most investors in our sample prefer arbitration over court litigation for intra-corporate dispute resolution. These findings are consistent with those reported by Rick Porter, which show that most respondents rank arbitration as the preferred method of dispute resolution across industries when compared to court litigation.[55]

In addition, we also look at the reasons for choosing a dispute resolution method. To further dissect our hypothesis, we asked respondents about the important factors when choosing a dispute resolution method. Table 6.5 shows that quality of the decision and time to resolution are the most important reasons when assessing the selection of dispute resolution methods, and that costs are the third factor in order of importance. Overall, these results show support for the literature on the factors influencing the selection of a dispute resolution method.[56]

6.3.3 *Mandatory Arbitration*

We have established so far that the 2017 Survey's respondents expressed a clear preference for arbitration for intra-corporate dispute resolution and that the preference became stronger as the value under discussion increased. But note that there was no comparable support for arbitration

55 Porter (n 16).
56 White & Case/Queen Mary (2018) "2018 International Arbitration Survey: The Evolution of International Arbitration" www.whitecase.com/sites/whitecase/files/files/download/publications/qmul-international-arbitration-survey-2018-19.pdf. *See also* Porter (n 16).

TABLE 6.6 *2017 Survey responses on mandatory arbitration*
This table reports the respondents' assessment of whether arbitration should be mandatory when it is included in shareholders' agreements about dispute resolution.

Should arbitration be mandatory when included in shareholders' agreements for dispute resolution?	N	%
Yes, and should also be binding on minority shareholders	28	49.12%
Yes, but should not be binding on minority shareholders	10	17.54%
No, should not be mandatory	12	21.05%
Other	6	10.53%
No answer	1	1.75%
Total	57	100%
Top 2 main reasons why arbitration should be mandatory	N	%
Arbitrator's expertise	20	71.43%
Speed	16	47.14%
Neutrality	8	28.57%
Secrecy	1	3.57%
Costs	1	3.57%
Reduces litigation burden	1	3.57%
Whenever included in the statutes	1	3.57%
Solution ends up being negotiated with external mediation	1	3.57%
No answer	1	3.57%
Total	50	
Top 2 main reasons why arbitration should not be mandatory	N	%
High costs	13	59.09%
Lack of trust	7	31.82%
Lack of publicity	2	9.09%
Speed	1	4.55%
No answer	5	22.73%
Total	28	

among the 2019 survey's respondents. First, institutional investors tended to prefer mediation or conciliation to resolve intra-corporate disputes that involved amounts of up to US$ 2.5 million. Second, we see that they equally preferred arbitration and mediation or conciliation in cases involving amounts higher than US$ 2.5 million.

The inclusion of arbitration in corporate documents as a mandatory form of corporate dispute resolution has triggered academic debate about the enforceability of such mandatory provisions. To contribute to this debate, we asked respondents whether arbitration should be mandatory when included in shareholders' agreements.

Table 6.6 indicates that twenty-eight of the respondents believed that mandatory arbitration should be binding when included in shareholders' agreements about dispute resolution (49.12 percent). These twenty-eight respondents were asked to select the top main reasons why arbitration should be mandatory in the particular situation. Out of the fifty valid responses, 71.43 percent of respondents included arbitrator's expertise in their two top reasons that arbitration should be binding, while 47.14 percent chose speed.

Table 6.6 also shows that twenty-two respondents (38.60 percent) believed that mandatory arbitration, even when included in shareholders' agreements, should not be binding either to minority shareholders or to both minority and majority shareholders. The evidence suggests that respondents were divided on whether mandatory arbitration clauses should be included in shareholders' agreements.

When asked why mandatory arbitration should not be binding, the twenty-two respondents (38.59 percent) were given five alternatives: (i) speed; (ii) lack of publicity; (iii) lack of trust; (iv) high costs; and (v) others. There were twenty-eight valid responses. Among the twenty-two respondents who believed that mandatory arbitration should not be binding either to minority shareholders or to both minority and majority shareholders, thirteen chose high costs (59.09 percent) as their top two reasons, whereas seven chose lack of trust (31.82 percent).

Among the five minority shareholders who answered the survey, one respondent indicated that mandatory arbitration, even when included in shareholders' agreements, should not be binding to minority shareholders, and two believed that it should not be binding to either minority or majority shareholders. Only two minority shareholders believed that it should be binding to minority shareholders. Six of the nine majority shareholders who answered the survey believed that mandatory arbitration should always be binding when included in shareholders' agreements, while two believed that it should not be binding to majority and minority shareholders, and one had no opinion.

Table 6.7 indicates that forty-four of the respondents believed that arbitration should be mandatory when included in corporate documents regarding dispute resolution (43.14 percent). The respondents were further asked to select the top reasons for choosing arbitration as a method of intra-corporate dispute resolution. Most investors indicated time to resolution, quality of the decision and selection of arbitrator as the top reasons for choosing arbitration for intra-corporate dispute resolution. Institutional investors' response of time to resolution as the most important factor for choosing arbitration contrasts with prior literature[57], and it probably derives from the lack of trust in the Brazilian judiciary. What other factors are also likely to influence the arbitration decision? Confidentiality and predictability also appear to be important drivers. When asked about the impediments for choosing arbitration as a method of intra-corporate dispute resolution, most investors identified high costs, limited number of arbitrators and lack of expertise of arbitrator. In sum, these results, with the exception of time to resolution, are consistent with the literature's findings about the factors influencing the selection of a dispute resolution mechanism.[58]

Table 6.7 reports that a total of fifty-seven respondents (55.88 percent) indicated that mandatory arbitration, even when included in shareholders' agreements, should not be binding either to minority shareholders or to both minority and majority shareholders. Again, there seems to be evidence of a divide among institutional investors regarding the inclusion of a mandatory arbitration provision in shareholders' agreements.

6.3.4 *Law Firms' Advice and Expenses*

We have established that a majority of institutions are likely to increase their use of arbitration to resolve intra-corporate disputes activity particularly for disputes involving values higher than US

57 PWC/QM (n 52).

58 Porter (n 16). *See also* White & Case/Queen Mary (2018) "2018 International Arbitration Survey: The Evolution of International Arbitration" www.whitecase.com/sites/whitecase/files/files/download/publications/qmul-international-arbitration-survey-2018-19.pdf.

TABLE 6.7 *2019 Survey's responses on mandatory arbitration*
This table reports the respondents' assessment of whether arbitration should be mandatory when included in corporate documents for dispute resolution.

Should arbitration be mandatory when included in corporate documents for dispute resolution?	N	%		
Yes, and it should also be binding on minority shareholders	44	43.14%		
Yes, but it should not be binding on minority shareholders	27	26.47%		
No, it should not be mandatory	30	29.41%		
No response	1	0.98%		
Total	**102**	**100%**		
Top reasons for choosing arbitration as a method of intra-corporate dispute resolution	**Mean**	**Variance**	**Std. deviation**	**Count**
Time to resolution	6.357	2.418	1.555	98
Quality of the decision	6.061	3.419	1.849	98
Selection of arbitrator	5.082	3.065	1.751	98
Confidentiality	4.520	4.438	2.107	98
Predictability	4.337	4.040	2.010	98
Preserving good relationships	3.551	4.497	2.121	98
Lower costs if compared with judicial claims	3.398	5.809	2.410	98
Enabling choice for specific listing segment in Brazil	2.694	2.998	1.732	98
Top impediments to choosing arbitration as a method of intra-corporate dispute resolution	**Mean**	**Variance**	**Std. deviation**	**Count**
High costs	5.224	4.939	2.222	98
Limited number of arbitrators	4.429	3.691	1.921	98
Lack of expertise of arbitrator	4.173	3.382	1.839	98
Lack of neutrality	4.051	3.822	1.955	98
Excessive bureaucracy	3.541	2.808	1.676	98
Lack of transparency	3.449	3.075	1.753	98
Time to resolution	3.133	3.560	1.887	98

$ 2.5 million. The mixed views over the role of lawyers and their impact on the resolution of corporate arbitration disputes[59] has triggered both policy and academic debates about whether investors should increase (or decrease) their reliance on lawyers. To contribute to this debate, we asked questions about whether institutional investors expect advice from law firms to add value or play an important role in arbitration procedures.

Table 6.8 indicates that most institutional investors, when faced with intra-corporate disputes, regard lawyers' advice as extremely or very important for the choice of a dispute resolution method. Prior evidence shows that the most important legal advice tends to involve technical industry knowledge and expertise in the arbitral process.[60] As noted above, there are also good

59 White & Case/QM, "2018 International Arbitration Survey: The Evolution of International Arbitration" 36/37 www.whitecase.com/sites/whitecase/files/files/download/publications/qmul-international-arbitration-survey-2018-19.pdf.

60 PWC/QM (n 52).

TABLE 6.8 *Law firms' advice*
This table reports the respondents' assessment of the importance of law firms' advice in the choice of a dispute resolution method.

Importance of Law Firms' Advice	N	%
Extremely important	34	33.33%
Very important	53	51.96%
Moderately important	9	8.82%
Slightly important	5	4.90%
Not important at all	1	0.98%
Total	102	100%

TABLE 6.9 *Most significant expenses in intra-corporate arbitration*
This table reports the views of institutional investors about the most significant expenses in ICA.

Most Significant Expenses in ICA	Mean	Variance	Std. deviation	Count
Legal counsel fees and expenses	3.022	1.386	1.177	45
Arbitrators' fees	2.667	1	1	45
Institutional costs paid to organizations that administer the arbitration procedure	2.200	1.300	1.140	45
Expert's fees and expenses	2.111	0.874	0.935	45

business reasons that some institutional investors seek to rely on lawyers' advice. For example, literature suggests that the parties benefit from elite law firms assisting parties in large transactions and lowering information asymmetry due to their market knowledge.[61] Conversely, relying more on outside counsel for their expertise and reputation raises the possibility of increased agency costs and conflicts with other parties, such as officers.

As predicted, we report in Table 6.9 that institutional investors find that legal fees and expenses are the most significant expenses in intra-corporate arbitration procedures. Finally, we find that institutional investors apparently do not find that experts' fees and expenses are significant expenses in an arbitral proceeding.

6.4 CONCLUSION

In this chapter, we analyzed new datasets based on two surveys: a 2017 survey with 57 Brazilian respondents – including corporations, limited liability companies, small and medium-sized enterprises, law firms and others – regarding their preferences about various aspects of mandatory intra-corporate dispute resolution; and a 2019 survey representing 102 institutional investors with a stake in Brazilian companies. We chose to use surveys in order to understand both companies' and investors' views about (1) the preferred method of intra-corporate dispute resolution; (2) the

[61] Elisabeth de Fontenay, "Law Firm Selection and the Value of Transactional Lawyering" [2015] 41 *Journal of Corporation Law* 393.

appropriateness of arbitration as a method of dispute resolution for intra-corporate disputes; (3) the factors influencing the choice of a dispute resolution method; (4) the reasons and impediments for choosing arbitration as a method for intra-corporate dispute resolution; (5) whether arbitration should be mandatory when included in shareholders' agreements for dispute resolution; and (6) the significance of legal fees and advice in the arbitration process.

We find that the most significant factors that institutional investors take when choosing a dispute resolution method for solving intra-corporate disputes are quality of the decision, time to resolution and costs.

In line with the literature, we find that a majority of respondents to both surveys preferred arbitration over court litigation as a method of intra-corporate dispute resolution. We also find that corporations are likely to rely more heavily on arbitrators' expertise (71.43 percent) in support of mandatory arbitration, followed by speed (47.14 percent) and neutrality (28.57 percent). While these figures are indicative of perceived support for mandatory arbitration, these respondents also regard high costs (59.09 percent) and lack of trust (31.82 percent) as barriers to the adoption of mandatory arbitration provisions.

Interestingly, less than half of the institutional investors (43.13 percent) thought that arbitration should be mandatory. Similarly, less than half of respondents of the 2017 survey (49.12 percent) supported mandatory arbitration. Our empirical investigation also looked at the features that institutional investors identified as supporting their decision to choose arbitration. Respondents clearly identified time to resolution and quality of the decision as factors likely to influence the intention to choose arbitration, whereas high costs were the main impediment. It is worth noting that the respondents preferred to use mediation or conciliation to resolve their intra-corporate disputes whenever the values involved were up to US$ 2.5 million. But note that they showed equal preference for arbitration and mediation or conciliation whenever the values involved were higher than US$ 2.5 million.

Furthermore, most institutional investors consider legal advice as extremely or very important for the choice of a dispute resolution method, and report that legal fees and expenses are the most significant expenses in intra-corporate arbitration procedures.

To conclude, our analysis sheds light on the importance of the increasing popularity of mandatory intra-corporate arbitration. This paper contributes to the growing literature on arbitration's role in encouraging an effective redress for shareholders and reducing shareholder litigation. Finally, our study recognizes that arbitration is perceived as an effective procedure in Brazil for intra-corporate dispute resolution and offers increased benefits to parties enforcing arbitration provisions.

7

Cold Facts from the Great White North

Empirical Truths, Contemporary Challenges and Class Action Reform

Jasminka Kalajdzic and Catherine Piché

Class actions are a well-entrenched form of litigation in Canada, one that has led to and continues to produce successful outcomes from an access to justice perspective. Justice Robert Sharpe of the Ontario Court of Appeal succinctly explained the importance and impact of class actions this way:

> The most significant modern development in civil justice in Canada has been the emergence of the class action. Class actions respond to the challenges that confront our regime of civil justice, in particular, the need to enhance access to justice and to ensure the efficient and effective use of scarce judicial resources. But class actions are anything but simple. Grouping multiple claims under a single procedural umbrella is a complex and challenging undertaking that has stretched the minds of some of our finest jurists and advocates.[1]

While class actions in Canada are generally similar to those available in the US, there are key procedural and substantive differences between the two countries' collective processes. Moreover, the class action regimes in each Canadian province are not themselves identical. In this chapter we describe the key features of Canadian class action systems. Our discussion then turns to the state of empirical research on class actions in Canada, and an overview of the existing data. We address some of the contemporary challenges in class action litigation, and conclude with remarks on our experience with class action reform in Ontario and Quebec.

7.1 OVERVIEW OF THE CANADIAN CLASS ACTION SYSTEM

7.1.1 *Structure*

In Canada's constitutional structure, civil justice is the jurisdiction of the provinces, which legislate both the procedural and much of the substantive law applicable to class action lawsuits.[2] Canada is a bi-juridical state; Quebec is a mixed civil law/common law jurisdiction while the

[1] Warren K. Winkler, Paul M. Perell, Jasminka Kalajdzic and Alison Warner, *The Law of Class Actions in Canada* (Canada Law Book eds., 2014), "Foreword", at ix. Also cited in Law Commission of Ontario, *Class Actions: Objectives, Experiences, and Reforms – Consultation Report* (March 2018), at 1, online at www.lco-cdo.org/wp-content/uploads/2018/03/Class-Action-Consultation-Paper-FINAL1.pdf.

[2] Division of powers between the federal and provincial governments is complicated, and beyond the scope of a footnote. For our purposes, it suffices to note that the Federal government appoints judges of the Superior Courts (trial level) and Courts of Appeal of each province, but it is the provincial legislatures which enact class actions statutes. Although a Federal Court exists with class action rules of its own, this court has limited subject-matter

remaining provinces and territories belong to the common law tradition. Class actions came to Canada in the late 1970s as part of the province of Quebec's progressive social agenda.[3] In 1993, Ontario was the first English-speaking, common law province to enact class action legislation, followed by British Columbia in 1996. As of the time of writing, all but one province (Prince Edward Island) have class action legislation.[4] It is noteworthy that the three most populous provinces in Canada, Ontario, Quebec and British Columbia, are also the most active class action jurisdictions. All of these class action statutory regimes were inspired by US Federal Rule 23.[5] The three objectives of class actions – access to justice, judicial economy and behavior modification – were originally identified by the Ontario Law Reform Commission in its 1982 Report, and have guided courts in interpreting class action legislation around the country ever since.[6]

In all Canadian jurisdictions, any legal person may initiate a class action. In the common law provinces, the proposed representative plaintiff must have standing to sue; that is, they themselves must have a cause of action against the defendant(s). In Quebec, associations may also sue on behalf of their members.[7] Standing rules are strictest in Ontario, the most active class action jurisdiction, as a result of the so-called *Ragoonanan* rule: for every defendant there must be at least one representative plaintiff with a reasonable cause of action disclosed in the pleadings against that defendant.[8] As a result, in class actions involving multiple defendants filed in Ontario, class counsel must locate and name multiple representative plaintiffs, each with standing to sue at least one defendant. Conversely, the more liberal class standing rule operates in British Columbia,[9] Quebec[10] and other provinces, thereby facilitating litigation against industry participants.

Class actions in Canada are trans-substantive, without limitation to the types of causes of action that can be pleaded or the kind of relief claimed.[11] In light of the economics of class action

jurisdiction not applicable to most class proceedings. Importantly, the Federal Court does not have the ability to coordinate multi-provincial lawsuits, in a manner that would make a US MDL procedure possible.

3 Jasminka Kalajdzic, W.A. Bogart and Ian Matthews, "Class Actions in Canada: Country Report Prepared for the Globalization of Class Actions Conference", 622 *Annals of the American Academy of Political and Social Sciences* 41, 42 (2009); Catherine Piché, "The Cultural Analysis of Class Action Law", 2 *LSU Law Center Journal of Civil Law Studies* 102, 118 (2009).

4 Despite the lack of legislation, class actions are possible in Prince Edward Island pursuant to the court's common law authority: *King & Dawson* v. *Government of PEI*, 2019 PESC 27 (CanLII).

5 For a discussion of the history of Canadian class actions, see Shaun Finn, "In a Class All Its Own: The Advent of the Modern Class Action and Its Changing Legal and Social Mission", 2 *Can Class Action Rev* 333 (2005), and Suzanne Chiodo, *The Class Action Controversy: The Origins and Development of the Ontario Class Proceedings Act* (Irwin Law eds., 2018).

6 Ontario Law Reform Commission, *Report on Class Actions* (1982), 291 [OLRC Report 1982], online at https://digitalcommons.osgoode.yorku.ca/library_olrc/112/; *AIC Limited* v. *Fischer*, [2013] 3 SCR 949 [*Fischer*] and *Hollick* v. *Toronto (City)*, 2001 SCC 68 [*Hollick*].

7 As a result of robust consumer protection legislation and active consumer rights organizations, Quebec consumer protection associations initiate many class proceedings.

8 *Ragoonanan Estate* v. *Imperial Tobacco Canada Ltd.*, 2000 CanLII 22719 (ON SC).

9 *Furlan* v. *Shell Oil*, [2007] 7 W.W.R. 433 (BCCA) ["causation should be considered in the context of the proposed class generally and not the individually named plaintiffs" (at 441)].

10 *Bank of Montreal* v. *Marcotte*, [2014] 2 SCR 725, 2014 SCC 55 (CanLII). For a comparative analysis of standing rules in Ontario, B.C., Australia and the United States, see Vince Morabito, "Standing to Sue and Multiple Defendant Class Actions in Australia, Canada, and the United States", 41–2 *Alberta Law Review* 295 (2003).

11 As mentioned at note 2, above, however, the Federal Court has limited subject-matter jurisdiction. Class actions can only be initiated in the Federal Court if the defendant is a Federal agency or government, or if the matter is under Federal constitutional jurisdiction, most commonly tax law, bankruptcy, banking, patents and trademarks, or immigration.

litigation, however, the vast majority of class actions are damages actions.[12] Indeed, a claim for declaratory or injunctive relief alone may be fatal to certification.[13]

Like class actions under US Federal Rule 23(b)(3), class actions in Canada operate on an opt-out basis. In the majority of provinces, the statutory opt-out right applies to both resident and nonresident class members. In two provinces, nonresident class members must opt in.[14] As a result, in most of Canada, a national or even international class may be certified in an action filed in one province.

Canadian class actions, like their American cousins, are without question entrepreneurial; they are financed by class counsel who universally work on a contingency fee basis, and who often pay for disbursements and provide an indemnity against adverse costs orders in the five provinces that maintain a fee-shifting rule.[15] Over the past decade, commercial litigation funders have made modest inroads, funding less than two dozen class actions across the country.[16] The first third party funding (TPF) agreement was approved for an Ontario class action in 2011.[17] Unlike litigation funding in personal injury claims which function like nonrecourse loans, TPF agreements in class actions resemble investment contracts pursuant to which the funder pays for some or all disbursements and provides a cost indemnity in return for a percentage of the settlement or trial judgment.[18] These agreements are subject to court approval; while most class action statutes do not explicitly address TPF, the courts have assumed jurisdiction to approve or reject funding contracts as part of their supervisory authority to protect the interests of the class.[19] Of greatest concern is ensuring that funders have no control of the litigation and that their return on investment does not approach champertous levels. In the early days, funders received fees of less than 10 percent of the outcome of a class action, net of counsel fees. More recently, an Ontario judge approved an agreement under which the funder pays both class counsel fees and disbursements on a non-recourse basis and provides a costs indemnity, in return for a 22–26 percent fee.[20]

Ontario and Quebec are virtually unique among all class action jurisdictions in that they also offer not-for-profit litigation funding.[21] In Ontario, the legislature created the Class Proceedings

12 For a discussion of the entrepreneurial nature of class actions in Canada and its impact on case selection by class counsel, see Jasminka Kalajdzic, *Class Actions in Canada: The Promise and Reality of Access to Justice* (UBC Press eds., 2018), 70–89 [*Class Actions in Canada*].

13 Most recently, climate change litigation against the federal government was denied authorization (the equivalent terminology for certification in Quebec) on the basis that declaratory relief could be obtained by other means: *Environnement Jeunesse* c. *Procureur général du Canada*, 2019 QCCS 2885 (CanLII).

14 New Brunswick: Class Proceedings Act, RSNB 2011, c. 125, s 18; Newfoundland & Labrador: Class Actions Act, SNL 2001, c. C-18.1, s 17. British Columbia very recently amended its statute to repeal the opt-in requirement for non-resident class members: Class Proceedings Act, RSBC 1996, c.50, s. 16, am. 1 Oct 2018 (BC Reg 129.2018).

15 Ontario, New Brunswick, Nova Scotia, Saskatchewan and Alberta follow the English rule ("loser pays") in class actions, as in all civil litigation. Quebec's rules limit such costs to a modest tariff, and so for all intents and purposes, is considered a no-costs jurisdiction.

16 This figure is based on publicly reported decisions approving litigation funding agreements. It is noteworthy that Quebec has only seen one case funded by commercial third parties since the enactment of its class action legislation.

17 *Dugal* v. *Manulife Financial Corporation*, 2011 ONSC 1785 [*Dugal*].

18 A detailed explanation of the history and nature of TPF in class actions can be found in Jasminka Kalajdzic, Peter Cashman and Alana Longmoore, "Justice for Profit: A Comparative Analysis of Australian, Canadian and U.S. Third Party Litigation Funding", 16 *Am J Comp L* 93 (2013).

19 *Fehr* v. *Sun Life Assurance Company of Canada*, 2012 ONSC 2715. Pursuant to amendments passed in Ontario in July 2020 but not yet proclaimed in force as at the time of writing, third party funding agreements are explicitly addressed and require court approval "as soon as practicable after they are entered into": Class Proceedings Act, 1992, SO 1992, c 6, s. 33.1.

20 *JB & M Walker Ltd/1523428 Ontario Inc* v. *TDL Group*, 2019 ONSC 999.

21 Israel also has a Public Class Action Fund that operates differently, but for largely the same goals: see Eli Bukspan's chapter in this book. India has introduced a public fund for its new securities class action regime but there is little information available about it: see Brian Fitzpatrick's chapter in this book.

Fund (CPF) concurrently with the enactment of the class action statute. The CPF is administered by the Law Foundation of Ontario and aims to provide disbursement assistance only (not legal fees) and a costs indemnity to successful applicants in return for a 10 percent levy on the net recovery of the class. The CPF is considered a "novel initiative to provide 'affirmative action' for representative plaintiffs who might otherwise be deterred from initiating class actions in a fee-shifting regime" and has been lauded as the "signature feature of a progressive class action regime."[22] To date, the CPF has funded approximately 10 percent of all class actions in the province.[23]

By comparison, the Quebec *Fonds d'aide aux actions collectives* financially assists 41 percent of all ongoing class actions in the province (227 out of 560 cases).[24] The Fonds assists with legal fees and disbursements, including the costs of notice, as well as counsel fees and expert reports.[25] It is well capitalized with yearly provincial subsidies and warranties from the provincial government which guarantee payment of capital and interest of any loan or other financial commitment made.[26] Importantly, it also retains a percentage of any recovery made in every class action filed in the province.[27] To meet access to justice objectives, this right of the Fonds to collect a levy applies to every action.[28]

Despite judicial acknowledgment that class actions are inherently entrepreneurial, counsel fees remain a lightning rod of controversy. As explored in Section 7.2 below, there is increasing judicial concern about the quantum of fees sought by class counsel at settlement,[29] and several reform recommendations have been made to improve scrutiny of fee requests.[30] At present, class counsel regularly obtain up to 25 percent of a settlement, or more, and judges have, for the most part, preferred a percentage of settlement approach to calculating fees over the lodestar or multiplier method.[31]

7.1.2 *State of Empirical Information and Projects*

Understanding class actions requires an intimate knowledge about the law "in action," about trends and statistics, and about the practical challenges to this kind of litigation. As one of us has written, there is a "dearth of data on judicial activity in Canada in all sectors of litigation, including class actions."[32] The state of empirical knowledge in Canada is, with the exception of Quebec, uniformly poor; court documents and dockets are not available online, court information systems do not track significant events in the life of a class action, and retrieval

22 *Class Actions in Canada*, *supra* at 134.

23 Law Commission of Ontario, *Class Actions Objectives, Experiences and Reforms* (July 2019) at 84 [*LCO Report*], online at www.lco-cdo.org/en/our-current-projects/class-actions/final-report/.

24 See Fonds d'aide aux actions collectives, *Annual Report* 2018–2019, 26 online at www.faac.justice.gouv.qc.ca/doc/RapportAnnuel2018-2019.pdf.

25 See Act respecting the Fonds d'aide aux actions collectives, Ch. F-3.2.0.1.1, online at http://legisquebec.gouv.qc.ca/en/ShowDoc/cs/F-3.2.0.1.1.

26 For a discussion of the role of Quebec's public fund in class proceedings and an argument in favor of public overseeing entities in class actions, see Catherine Piché, "Public Financiers as Overseers of Class Proceedings", 12 N.Y.U. J.L. & Bus. 779 (2016) [*Public Financiers*].

27 See Regulation respecting the percentage withheld by the Fonds d'aide aux actions collectives, Ch. F-3.2.0.1.1, r. 2 , online at http://legisquebec.gouv.qc.ca/en/ShowDoc/cr/F-3.2.0.1.1,%20r.%202.

28 *Public Financiers*, *supra* at 781.

29 *Brown* v. *Canada (Attorney General)*, 2018 ONSC 3429, at para. 51.

30 *LCO Report*, *supra* at 77.

31 *Class Actions in Canada*, *supra* at 131.

32 For a discussion about the class action as an effective mechanism to compensate class members based on empirical data collected by the Class Actions Lab from cases led in the province of Quebec, see Catherine Piché, "Class Action Value", 19 *Theoretical Inquiries* L. 261, 263 (2019) [*Class Action Value*].

and review of paper court files is expensive, inefficient and ultimately unhelpful.[33] Empirical data to date has been limited to informal data gathered by the provinces' superior court class action judges and occasionally by court registries; voluntary bar association class action registries; reports produced by law firms, usually based on publicly reported judicial decisions; and informal and sometimes impressionistic numbers circulating within the class action bar and among judges.[34] Claims administrators possess much information about settlement outcomes, but they often consider it to be proprietary or confidential, and ultimately, lack the incentives to disclose it.

Things are evolving on the empirical front, however, at least for the two most populated provinces in Canada, Ontario and Quebec. In 2019, the Law Commission of Ontario (LCO) issued a Report on Class Actions that provided important, albeit limited, data regarding class proceedings in Ontario over the past twenty-five years.[35] Similarly, the Class Actions Lab at the University of Montreal published an extensive review about class actions in Quebec over the same time period.[36] With this information at hand, we can now begin to understand how and why class actions have evolved in these two provinces, and what reforms might be necessary.

The LCO project on class actions was initiated in 2017, and considered Ontario's experience with class actions since the *Class Proceedings Act* came into force.[37] The project's mandate was to research class actions in Ontario and to conduct an independent, evidence-based, and practical analysis of class actions from the perspective of their three above-stated objectives: access to justice, judicial economy, and deterrence. The LCO sought to understand class actions' financial, policy and cultural impacts across Canada. A final report published in July 2019 included a significant number of important conclusions regarding empirical data and statistics in Ontario, and recommended the adoption of mandatory reports to the court to improve transparency and empirical data. A year later, the Ontario government passed amendments to the *Class Proceedings Act* that incorporated most of the LCO's recommendations.[38]

The University of Montreal's Class Actions Lab project, which one of us leads, has sought to address member compensation through an assessment of the value and benefit of class litigation, and incidentally, its costs as assumed by the parties and the system.[39] It has identified specific parameters that can be used to empirically value class action costs and benefits, and a significant list of criteria directly associated with higher rates of participation and compensation. The Lab has created an extensive database containing data covering the twenty-five year period, and relative to costs and fees, delays, merits decisions and appeals, interlocutory motions,

33 The LCO's efforts to access court files were described this way: "The physical files which the LCO ordered from the courts were not easy to access and were disorganized, incomplete and very difficult to search through. The LCO also worked with courthouse staff to access information on court files from computer terminals at the Toronto and Windsor courthouse. This was a lengthy, inefficient and unproductive process. The computers accessible to LCO staff were slow, difficult to search through, and contained only incomplete information." *LCO Report*, *supra* at 104–05.

34 *Class Action Value*, *supra* at 264; *LCO Report*, *supra* at 13. See the following studies that afford some empirical and qualitative data and credible analyses regarding class actions in Canada: *Class Actions in Canada*, *supra*; Jon Foreman and Genevieve Meisenheimer, "The Evolution of the Class Action Trial in Ontario", 4:2 *The Western Journal of Legal Studies* 3 (2014), online: http://ir.lib.uwo.ca/uwojls/vol4/iss2/3.

35 *LCO Report*, *supra*.

36 For an empirical study of class actions in the Canadian province of Quebec over a twenty-five year period, and data relative notably to take-up rates, costs and fees, delays, and settlements, see Catherine Piché, *L'action collective: ses succès et ses défis* (Themis eds., 2019) [*Class Action Successes and Challenges*], and Catherine Piché, "Understanding Class Actions through a Historical Overview and Empirical Data from Quebec from the Past Twenty-Five Years", 15:1 *Can. Class Actions Rev.* 203 (2019) [*Understanding Class Actions*].

37 At the invitation of the LCO, we were colead researchers on the project.

38 Bill 161, *Smarter and Stronger Justice Act*, 2020, 1st Sess, 42nd Legislature, Ontario, 2020 [Bill 161].

39 See Class Actions Lab Website, online at www.classactionslab.ca/.

settlements, and compensation and take-up rates, among other topics. The project has concluded that class actions compensate class members, but that this compensation remains imperfect by way of the numbers of members compensated, the extent to which they are compensated, and the exorbitant costs of bringing such actions.[40] A new project involving the Lab is working on legislative reform of the certification process, attorney fees, and the use of technologies in class actions. This project will serve to support a legislative bill expected to be introduced in the Quebec National Assembly in the next year.

These studies contribute to a better understanding of class action practice in Canada. The most salient findings are summarized below.

7.1.3 *Data on Class Actions in Canada*

Since the advent of class action legislation in Canada, the volume of class actions in Ontario and Quebec has steadily increased. Over the past twenty-five years (1993–2018), 1459 cases were filed in Ontario in total, with an average of 54 new cases per year.[41] There has been an overall increase in the number of yearly case filings, with the year 2014 topping at 130 cases, the year 2015 at 110 cases, and the year 2017 at 108 cases.[42] In Quebec, by comparison, 1306 cases were filed for that period, which represents an average of 50 cases per year.[43] Data from the years 2017 and 2018 reveals an average of 67 new cases filed per year.[44] While Quebec sees significantly fewer new cases yearly than Ontario, its case volume remains proportionately high, given that its population is roughly half of Ontario's (eight million versus fourteen million). In both provinces, the steady

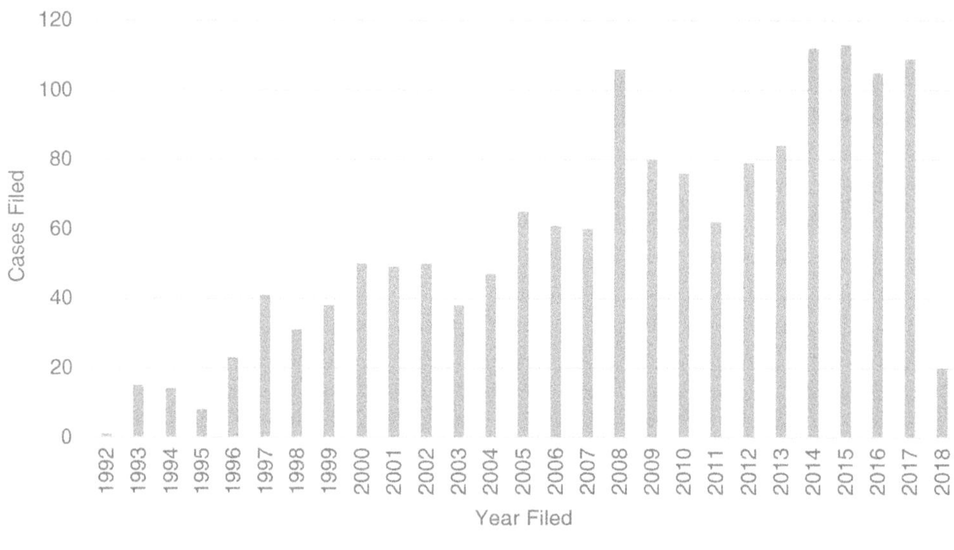

FIGURE 7.1 Ontario class actions filed in the past twenty-five years[45]

40 *Class Action Value, supra* at 263.

41 *LCO Report, supra* at 14. For a point of reference, the population of Ontario stands at approximately 14.7 million: www.ontario.ca/page/ontario-demographic-quarterly-highlights-first-quarter-2020.

42 See prior drafts of the *LCO Report*, on file with authors.

43 *Class Action Successes and Challenges, supra* at 33.

44 *Understanding Class Actions, supra* at 217.

45 Source: *Understanding Class Actions* at 218. Also see chart on Estimated Number of Class Action Matters, *LCO Report* at 14.

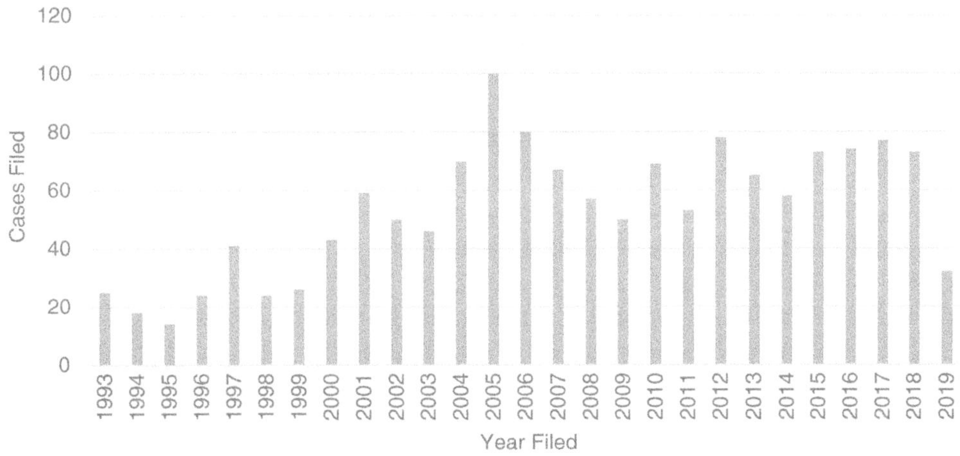

FIGURE 7.2 Quebec class actions filed in the past twenty-five years[46]

increase in class action activity and few peaks noted in recent years appear to coincide with a noteworthy support for class actions as an access to justice tool in the Canadian jurisprudence.[47]

In terms of the substantive areas of the law involved, the most common claims raised in Ontario are those involving securities law (16 percent of cases), followed closely by *Competition Act* (antitrust) claims and product liability claims[48] (each 15 percent of all cases), and consumer protection suits (12 percent).[49] These statistics are consistent with snapshots taken in 2009 and 2014, that concluded antitrust, securities and product liability cases accounted for over 60 percent of all class actions.[50] By comparison, in Quebec, consumer protection cases are most frequent (20.52 percent of all cases), followed by state liability (15.15 percent) and product liability (13.4 percent), including several pharmaceuticals law cases.[51] Environment and nuisance claims are raised in 6.19 percent of cases, and employment and securities law claims are each raised in 5.26 percent of all cases.[52] This data could suggest that the strong consumer protection laws in Quebec serve to compensate small-value claims raised by consumers through the class action device.[53] Importantly, consumer class actions also tend to lead to the highest take-up rates, and thereby benefit Quebecers to a greater extent.[54]

Delay in class actions is a fundamental access to justice issue. Indeed, as time passes, the likelihood of compensation and for a behavior modification or deterrence effect to be felt are reduced.[55] Existing data allows us to understand how delays vary between Ontario and Quebec as between the time of filing of the case and the first stage of certification (called "authorization" in

46 *Id.*, at 217.

47 See e.g., *L'Oratoire Saint-Joseph du Mont-Royal* c. *J.J.*, 2019 CSC 35; *Infineon Technologies AG* v. *Option consommateurs*, 2013 CSC 59; *Vivendi Canada Inc.* v. *Dell'Aniello*, 2014 CSC 1; *Bank of Montreal* v. *Marcotte*, 2014 CSC 55; *Fischer*, *supra*; *Hollick supra*; *Western Canadian Shopping Centres Inc.* v. *Dutton*, 2001 SCC 46, [2001] 2 S.C.R. 534.

48 The LCO included claims involving pharmaceuticals and medical devices, as well as consumer products, in the product liability category. See Appendix C of the LCO *Consultation Paper* (March 2018) 42, online at www.lco-cdo.org/wp-content/uploads/2018/07/Class-Action-Consultation-Paper.pdf.

49 *LCO Report*, *supra* at 15.

50 *Class Actions in Canada*, *supra* at 18.

51 *Class Action Successes and Challenges*, *supra* at 36–42.

52 *Id.*

53 *Id.* at 41.

54 *Id.* at 272.

55 *Id.* at 163–65.

Quebec). Ontario sees cases certified, on average, roughly two years after commencement of litigation.[56] Quebec certifies its class actions after two years and 185 days, on average. Reaching certification is much quicker now in the Montreal District since the Quebec Superior Court restructured its class action division around an exclusive team of ten judges assigned cases for case management up until authorization.[57] Further, settlements do not lead to significantly quicker outcomes, as it takes on average four years and 243 days for a case to be settled in Quebec, much longer to settle an already authorized case,[58] and five years and 290 days, on average, for the Superior Court to issue a final judgment on the merits. A little less than two additional years are needed for the court of appeal to confirm or reverse a trial judgment.[59]

In Ontario, the LCO has estimated that approximately one-third (37 percent) of certification motions have been approved on consent out of the total of 423 certification motions examined.[60] Further, it found that taking into account appeals of certification decisions, approximately 72 percent of contested certification motions are successful, in whole or in part.[61] Quebec statistics are almost identical, with 70.87 percent of cases being granted authorization (including appeals of authorization).[62] It is noteworthy that the Class Actions Lab has concluded that appeals of class action authorization judgments have led to a considerable increase of more than 7 percent in authorization rates (from 63.22 percent to 70.87 percent).[63] In the third largest province, British Columbia, 62.66 percent of contested certification hearings lead to a decision to certify.[64]

7.2 CONTEMPORARY CHALLENGES AND TRENDS

In Canada, class actions have been used widely in many areas of the law, and have led to a great variety of types of relief. As noted above, class actions have been used to pursue claims in areas such as products liability and mass torts (including environmental and nuisance class actions), securities and corporate law, pharmaceuticals law, labor and employment law, contracts and negligence law, civil rights, constitutional law, antitrust law, and patent and trademark law. New areas of the law are being invoked as well, such as privacy, sexual harassment and gender discrimination.[65] It is not uncommon to see multiple actions commenced over the same dispute, within the same province or simultaneously in several jurisdictions. This part will serve to address how these newer forms of collective litigation are challenging on several levels.

56 *Understanding Class Actions*, *supra* at 224.

57 *Class Action Successes and Challenges*, *supra* at 48–49.

58 *Id.* at 51.

59 *Id.*

60 *LCO Report*, *supra* at 14.

61 *Id.* at 16.

62 *Class Action Successes and Challenges*, *supra* at 78–79.

63 *Id.*

64 Ward K. Branch, *Class Actions in Canada*, looseleaf (Canada Law Book Eds., 2008) at para. 22.30 [*Branch Looseleaf*].

65 See e.g., *Les Courageuses* c. *Rozon*, 2018 QCCS 2089 (CanLII) (sexual harassment class action authorized), and *Rozon* c. *Les Courageuses*, 2020 QCCA 5 (CanLII) (appeal confirming authorization decision); *Davidson* v. *The Queen*, 2017 FC 533 and *Merlo, Davidson* v. *The Queen*, 2017 FC 533 (settlement approved of class action based on claims alleging that all female employees of RCMP were subjected to sexual discrimination, bullying, and harassment by male members of the RCMP); *Rivers* v. *Waterloo Regional Police Services Board*, 2019 ONCA 267 (CanLII) (Ontario Court of Appeal confirms that Superior Court of Justice is without jurisdiction to hear a proposed class action on behalf of current and former female officers alleging systemic gender-based discrimination, Charter breaches, and sexual harassment by male members of the Service, over a thirty-year period.); *Lewis* v. *WestJet Airlines Ltd.*, 2017 BCSC 2327.

7.2.1 *Multijurisdictional Class Actions*

Canada has seen more and more parallel or overlapping class proceedings, involving similar or identical causes of action and allegations in proposed class actions in multiple Canadian provinces, often copying existing US class actions. These proceedings addressing wrongs and harms that transcend the borders of a single province raise complex issues to which courts have not yet entirely responded. Courts have struggled with how to manage duplicate national class actions commenced in various jurisdictions covering the same subject matter, and national class actions commenced at the same time as provincial class actions.

Most problematically, parallel class actions in different provinces have led to conflicting decisions. For instance, in two proposed class actions filed by junior hockey players in Ontario and Alberta alleging the unlawful denial of employee status and associated benefits by defendant hockey clubs, courts certified both cases but determined the certification criteria differently, in particular with regards to the causes of action.[66] In another instance, a controversial proposed settlement in a multijurisdictional class action involving aboriginal claims was denied by the Ontario Superior Court of Justice and approved the next day by the Federal Court of Appeal.[67] Because approval was required from both courts for the settlement to be effective, the settlement agreement was revised and the courts eventually agreed to approve it.[68]

Apart from the constitutional, jurisdictional and conflict of laws issues raised by these cases, there are important challenges regarding their management. Carriage and jurisdiction are at issue, as well as settlement implementation, and requests for stays or dismissals. The Supreme Court of Canada ruled in *Endean* v. *British Columbia* that provincial Superior Court judges may hear motions in multijurisdictional class proceedings outside their home provinces.[69] Since then, video-link hookups have served to link courtrooms in multiple provinces, allowing participants to view all courtrooms simultaneously and permitting hearings to be conducted within one day.

As a fundamental, codified principle of civil procedure, the avoidance of a multiplicity of proceedings acknowledges that identical class actions in more than one jurisdiction may cause disruptions and burdensome duplicity of claims.[70] Accordingly, courts have wondered whether it is preferable to determine the class claims in one jurisdiction over the other, in a parallel proposed class action.[71] In the absence of a constitutional framework for class actions involving members residing in more than one province in Canada, national class actions commenced in a single province in fact serve to limit the duplication of costs and efforts, and avoid multiple proceedings.

In 2018, the Canadian Bar Association passed a resolution approving a revised "Canadian Judicial Protocol for the Management of Multijurisdictional Class Actions and the Provision of Class Action Notice," which proposes a framework for a coordinated approach to

66 *Walter* v. *Western Hockey League*, 2017 ABQB 382; *Berg* v. *Canadian Hockey League*, 2017 ONSC 2608.

67 *Brown v. Canada (A.G.)*, 2018 ONSC 3429; *Riddle & al. v. The Queen*, 2018 FC 641.

68 *Brown* v. *Canada (A.G.)*, 2018 ONSC 5426.

69 *Endean* v. *British Columbia*, 2016 SCC 42, [2016] 2 S.C.R. 162.

70 Section 138 of the Courts of Justice Act.

71 See e.g., *Ammazzini* v. *Anglo American PLC*, 2016 SKQB 53 (where court ordered a conditional stay of a putative multi-jurisdictional class action in Saskatchewan found to be essentially duplicative of the proceedings in Ontario). The Court of Appeal upheld the substance of the decision in *Ammazzini* v. *Anglo American PLC*, 2016 SKCA 164. When the matter came again before Justice Currie in the form of a request for a permanent stay, following certification and settlement of the Ontario action, the stay was thought to be inextricably linked with the fairness and reasonableness of the Ontario settlement to the proposed class members in Saskatchewan. The stay was granted in *Ammazzini* v. *Anglo American PLC*, 2019 SKQB 60.

multijurisdictional class actions.[72] While not mandatory or binding, the Protocol provides a framework for a coordinated approach to multijurisdictional class actions, thereby creating a notification mechanism to inform the various courts and parties across Canada of the existence and progress of simultaneous class actions. Parties may agree that their case management judge speak to other judges in other jurisdictions who are case managing overlapping class actions, and may also agree to ask their case management judge to direct that a joint case management hearing be held with a judge in any other action.[73] Even in the absence of such an agreement, the judge may still decide to communicate with judges in other jurisdictions about the case.[74]

In addition, multijurisdictional class proceedings have been addressed through legislation. For instance, the statutes of British Columbia, Alberta, Manitoba, Saskatchewan, Québec, New Brunswick and Newfoundland and Labrador specifically allow the inclusion of nonresident class members, but the latter two provinces require nonresidents to opt in.[75]

Furthermore, Saskatchewan, British Columbia, Alberta and most recently Ontario provide statutory guidance to the courts in adjudicating multijurisdictional proceedings, and addressing problems of parallel class actions, by establishing an opt-out mechanism for out-of-province class members, outlining revised criteria for preferability of jurisdiction that courts may use in a motion for certification of a multijurisdictional class action, and allowing special orders to be made regarding multijurisdictional class actions. Saskatchewan adopted the Class Actions Amendment Act in 2007,[76] while Alberta amended its class action legislation to allow opt-out multijurisdictional class actions, and to require courts to consider "the advantages and disadvantages of litigation being conducted in more than one jurisdiction" in the preferability analysis, as does Ontario's statute amended in July 2020.[77] More recently, British Columbia's Class Proceedings Amendment Act reformed the existing framework from an opt-in mechanism to an opt-out one, and adopted the same multijurisdictional class action provisions contained in Alberta's, Saskatchewan's and Ontario's statutes.[78]

Finally, whether class action settlement approval orders, certification decisions or judgments issued by a superior court of another province are to be recognized is determinable according to well-established principles requiring a "real and substantial connection," adequate representation and procedural fairness.[79] The International Bar Association Task Force on International Procedures and Protocols for Collective Redress has published Guidelines for Recognizing and

[72] See *Canadian Judicial Protocol for the Management of MultiJurisdictional Class Actions and the Provision of Class Action Notice*, available online at www.cba.org/getattachment/Our-Work/Resolutions/Resolutions/2018/Class-Action-Judicial-Protocols-(1)/18-03-A.pdf [*Canadian Judicial Protocol*].

[73] *Id.* at s. 7.

[74] *Id.* at s. 7 *in fine*.

[75] See, e.g., Class Proceedings Act, S.A. 2003, c. C-16-5, s. 9.1(1) (Alberta); Class Proceedings Amendment Act, 2018, SBC 2018, c 16 (British Columbia); The Class Proceedings Act, C.C.S.M. c. C. 130, s. 6(3) and 16 (Manitoba); Class Actions Act, S.N.L. 2001, c. C-18.1, ss. 9(1)(g) (Newfoundland & Labrador); The Class Actions Act, S.S. 2001, c. C-12.01, s. 6.1 (Saskatchewan); Article 577 Code of Civil Procedure (Québec).

[76] The Class Actions Amendment Act, 2007, SS 2007, c 21, http://canlii.ca/t/5385x.

[77] See Class Proceedings Act, 2003, ch. C-16.5, online at www.qp.alberta.ca/documents/Acts/C16P5.pdf, notably ss. 5(8) and 9.1; Bill 161, *supra*, Schedule 4, s. 5(6).

[78] Bill 21 – 2018: *Class Proceedings Amendment Act*, 2018, online at www.leg.bc.ca/parliamentary-business/legislation-debates-proceedings/41st-parliament/3rd-session/bills/first-reading/gov21-1.

[79] See Janet Walker, "Crossborder Class Actions: A View from Across the Border", 2004.3 *Michigan State Law Review* 755–98 (2004); Janet Walker, "Class Proceedings in Canada – Report for the 18th Congress of the International Academy of Comparative Law", All Papers, Paper 41 (2001), available online at http://digitalcommons.osgoode.yorku.ca/all_papers/41.

Enforcing Foreign Judgments for Collective Redress that provide a test focusing on natural justice and due process considerations in enforcement decisions.[80]

7.2.2 *Rise in Privacy Law Class Actions*

The rising use of digital technologies and artificial intelligence has made privacy a serious and pressing issue. Privacy has in fact been recognized by the Supreme Court of Canada as having a "quasi-constitutional status," a specific role in protecting one's physical and moral autonomy.[81] Because organizations and corporations generate and accumulate an increasingly significant volume of personal data of all kinds, in the form of financial statements, medical records or the like, and that is being retained in mobile or cloud-based digital platforms, there may be a loss of privacy following a hacking event,[82] or misuse or improper disposal of information that may be private or sensitive.

Media coverage of corporate errors made by big corporations like Google and Apple renders users of technology more aware of the vulnerabilities. More than ever, our knowledge, communications and identity are a part of this increasingly vast virtual context. Many have called this era one of "digital revolution," a revolution that is reshaping society in many ways that make us vulnerable to identity theft of course, but also to class actions. The data shows, in fact, that privacy class actions have been on the rise for the past decade in Canada. In Quebec alone, twenty-five cases have been brought over a twenty-five year period, and of those, twenty-one in the past six years, and twelve in the years 2018–19.[83] Thus, privacy class actions are addressed here because they are becoming increasingly prevalent and present unique challenges.

In Canada, many statutes govern the management of personal information.[84] These statutes have a distinct form and content, but are founded upon common principles. As such, no one may collect, use or disclose personal information unless relevant and necessary to the stated purpose of record relating to the individual concerned.[85] While consent is essential there are specific exceptions to the requirement. Further, each concerned individual has access to their personal information and may ask to correct the information that might be incorrect, subject to specific and limited exceptions.[86] With the coming into force of Canada's new mandatory breach reporting regime pursuant to the Personal Information Protection and Electronic Documents Act,[87] it is likely that the increased notification will contribute to rising numbers of privacy class action filings.

80 See Report online at https://iclg.com.

81 *Douez* v. *Facebook, Inc.*, 2017 SCC 33, [2017] 1 S.C.R. 751 at para. 59 ("Privacy legislation has been accorded quasi-constitutional status ... This Court has emphasized the importance of privacy – and its role in protecting one's physical and moral autonomy – on multiple occasions").

82 See e.g., *Bennett* v. *Lenovo*, 2017 ONSC 1082 and 2017 ONSC 5853 (where the case was certified and the summary judgment motion dismissed).

83 This number comes from Class Actions Lab Statistics, See *Class Action Successes and Challenges*, at 296–97 and Quebec Class Actions Database (online), on file with authors. Do note that three new privacy cases were filed in 2019 and nine in 2018, according to the database.

84 See Personal Information Protection and Electronic Documents Act, S.C. 2000, c. 5 [PIPEDA]; Act respecting the Protection of Personal Information in the Private Sector, chapter P-39.1, The Personal Health Information Act of 2004 (Ontario) 2004, SO 2004, c. 3, The Personal Information Protection Act (Alberta), SA 2003, Ch. P-6.5; the Personal Information Protection Act (British Columbia), SBC 2003, Ch. 63.

85 See Privacy Act, R.S.C., 1985, c. P-21, s. 4 et seq. and PIPEDA, s. 5 et seq.

86 See Privacy Act, *id.*, s. 12(2); PIPEDA, s. 4.9.5 and 16.

87 Section 10.1 of PIPEDA will require organizations to notify individuals (unless prohibited by law) and report to the Commissioner, all breaches where it is reasonable to believe that the breach creates a "real risk of significant harm to the individual."

Canadian courts initially showed reluctance to certify privacy claims, notably in cases where companies use new technologies that allegedly expose personal information, or where financial institutions fail to properly dispose of computers containing customers' personal information.[88] Courts then stated that the mere demonstration of risk of identity theft or fraud, or fear of falling victim to that occurrence was not a compensable harm if there was no loss.[89] In the past few years, however, the trend has been towards certifying privacy class actions.[90]

The main issue in data or privacy class actions is in determining damages. Moreover, causation and damages often involve individualized questions that defeat commonality or predominance.[91] In the early years of privacy class actions, the Supreme Court of Canada distinguished between compensable damages and ordinary annoyances that are not compensable, stating that "compensable injury . . . must be serious and prolonged and rise above the ordinary annoyances, anxieties and fears that people living in society routinely, of sometimes reluctantly, accept . . . minor and transient upsets do not constitute personal injury, and hence do not amount to damage."[92] Accordingly, to prove damages as a victim of fraud or identity theft, there must be "something more than a mere allegation of stress and of taking routine steps,"[93] such as setting up credit monitoring and security alerts following the breach, or cancelling cards and closing accounts.[94]

No decision on the merits has been issued in privacy class actions in Canada, but many decisions have been issued regarding certification, motions to dismiss and settlement approval. Interestingly, some courts have certified punitive damages as common questions.[95] Recently, federal courts have even certified class actions without requiring evidence of actual damages suffered.[96] Courts have recognized that the traditional common law torts of breach of contract, negligence and breach of fiduciary duty apply in the privacy breach context, but have also developed the new tort of intrusion upon seclusion (invasion of privacy).[97] Overall, it can be said that a broad and liberal approach has been taken by courts with regards to privacy rights.[98]

88 *Cole* v. *Prairie Centre Credit Union Ltd.*, [2007] 1 W.W.R. 115 (Sask. Q.B.) (Court found that claim did not disclose a cause of action, that the plaintiffs failed to plead any facts that would support a negligence claim, and that there was no wilful conduct alleged that would create a breach of privacy claim); *Mazzonna* v. *DaimlerChrysler Financial Services Canada Inc.*, 2012 QCCS 958 (court denied certification because no color of right alleged in relation to damages – standard for mental distress damages not met and potential need for credit monitoring too speculative). Also see *Ladas* v. *Apple Inc.*, 2014 CarswellBC 2882, 2014 BCSC 1821 (court denied certification).

89 *Larose* v. *Banque Nationale du Canada*, 2010 QCCS 5383, *Sofio* c. *Organisme canadien de réglementation du commerce des valeurs mobilières (OCRCVM)*, 2015 QCCA 1820.

90 See *Tocco* v. *Bell Mobility Inc.*, 2019 ONSC 2916 (CanLII); *Tucci* v. *Peoples Trust Company*, 2017 BCSC 1525 (CanLII); *M.M.* v. *Family and Children's Services of Lanark Leeds and Grenville*, 2017 ONSC 7665; *Daniells* v. *McLennan*, 2017 ONSC 3466, 2017 ONSC 6887; *Fortin* v. *Mazda Canada inc.*, 2016 QCCA 31 (leave to appeal to SCC denied, 36898 (August 11, 2016) (Court of Appeal ruled that inconveniences suffered by the owners of vehicles did not exceed the normal inconveniences affecting all of the owners in a particular year); *Canada* v. *John Doe*, 2016 FCA 191 (CanLII); *Union des consommateurs* v. *Bell Canada*, 2012 QCCA 1287 (leave to appeal to SCC denied, 34994 (January 17, 2013)) (case certified on appeal where Bell users' privacy prima facie violated by the use of a certain DPI technology); *Zuckerman* c. *Target Corp.*, 2017 QCCS 110; *Larose*, *id.*; *Rowlands* v. *Durham Region Health*, 2011 ONSC 719.

91 *Kaplan* v. *Casino Rama*, 2019 ONSC 2025 (CanLII) (court dismissed certification due to lack of commonality),

92 *Mustapha* v. *Culligan of Canada Ltd.*, 2008 SCC 27, par. 9. Also see *Sofio*, *supra* at para. 25.

93 *Zuckerman* c. *Target Corp.*, 2017 QCCS 110 at para. 87.

94 *Id.* at para. 73.

95 *Belley* v. *TD Auto Finance Services Inc/Services de financement auto TD inc.*, 2015 QCCS 168 (leave to appeal dismissed, 2015 QCCA 1255).

96 *Canada* v. *John Doe*, 2016 FCA 191 (CanLII); *Condon* v. *Canada*, 2015 FCA 159 (CanLII).

97 See e.g., *Drew* v. *Walmart Canada Inc*, 2017 ONSC 3308, 10 CPC (8th) 182; *AgnewAmericano* v. *Equifax Canada*, 2018 ONSC 275, 288 ACWS (3d) 27 (where the Ontario Superior Court recognized that "the statutory tort of violation of privacy applies to a defendant who 'wilfully permits hackers to access their network to obtain personal information' of its customers."); *Tucci, supra*; *Doe, supra*; *Bennett, supra*.

98 *Tucci, supra*.

Finally, Canada's anti-spam legislation (CASL) protects consumers and businesses from the misuse of digital technology, including spam and other electronic threats.[99] The private right of action in section 47 of CASL has not yet come into force. It will allow affected private persons to seek an order against those they allege have contravened the anti-spam and anti-malware provisions, and have contravened the collection, use or disclosure of personal information under the Personal Information Protection and Electronic Documents Act, while engaging in reviewable conduct under the Competition Act (antitrust) regarding false and misleading representations, the whole without proof of damages. It is to be expected that this section of CASL will serve to found class action filings in the future.

7.2.3 *Grappling with Class Counsel Fees*

A recurring theme in reform discussions is the need to strengthen court oversight, especially at the settlement approval and fee approval stages. The role of the courts is key to protecting class member interests and in turn, to protecting the integrity of the class action system as a whole. How much class counsel should be paid continues to vex judges. While courts have come to accept that class actions are entrepreneurial and that class counsel should be well compensated in successful cases, they are cognizant of the risk of overcompensation and abuse of the class action device. As one judge stated bluntly, "Windfalls should be avoided because class action litigation is not a lottery and the [Class Proceedings Act] was not enacted to make lawyers wealthy."[100] From corporate executives who rail against "esurient plaintiffs' counsel"[101] and decry the "absolute fraud" of lawyers making "outrageous" fees,[102] to the Attorney General of Ontario criticizing "deep-pocketed" class counsel who bring "frivolous lawsuits result[ing] in tens of millions of dollars in legal costs for the taxpayer each year,"[103] the question of fees in class actions remains acutely controversial. From a public policy perspective, disproportionate counsel fees "can generate considerable cynicism and public distrust of class actions, plaintiff counsel and the justice system generally."[104]

In Canadian class actions, fees, like settlements, must be approved by a judge. Both the fee approval and settlement approval processes, however, suffer from a common weakness; the judge is tasked with vetting the proposals in an adversarial void, where neither the defendant nor the average class member contests submissions by class counsel.[105] Judges acknowledge the challenges of the process, and have sparingly appointed *amicus curiae* ("friend of the court") to provide assistance.[106]

[99] An Act to promote the efficiency and adaptability of the Canadian economy by regulating certain activities that discourage reliance on electronic means of carrying out commercial activities, and to amend the Canadian Radio-television and Telecommunications Commission Act, the Competition Act, the Personal Information Protection and Electronic Documents Act and the Telecommunications Act (S.C. 2010, c. 23), available online at https://laws-lois.justice.gc.ca/eng/acts/e-1.6/fulltext.html.

[100] *Brown* v. *Canada (Attorney General)*, 2018 ONSC 3429.

[101] *Class Actions in Canada*, *supra* at 141, quoting Senior VP and General Counsel of Manulife Financial.

[102] *Id.* at 128, quoting the president of Maple Leaf Foods.

[103] Anita Balakrishnan, "MAG says Crown liability changes defend taxpayers from 'deep-pocketed lawyers'" *Law Times* (22 July 2019), online at www.lawtimesnews.com/practice-areas/litigation/mag-says-crown-liability-changes-defend-taxpayers-from-deep-pocketed-lawyers/277302.

[104] *LCO Report*, *supra* at 71.

[105] *Class Actions in Canada* at 136–40 and cases cited. See also doctoral thesis on class action settlements, and their approval, role of the courts and parties, and fairness factors and approach: Catherine Piché, *Fairness in Class Action Settlements* (Carswell eds., 2011).

[106] See e.g., *Bozsik* v. *Livingston*, 2019 ONSC 2268 and *Smith Estate* v. *National Money Mart Company*, 2011 ONCA 233.

While class action legislation requires court approval and that fees be "fair and reasonable," it is judges who have developed criteria to consider. While many factors have been cited regularly by courts as relevant to the determination of a fair and reasonable fee,[107] there appears to be agreement that the two most important considerations are the risks undertaken by class counsel, and the success achieved on behalf of the class. Still, approaches are not uniform. Some judges give considerable deference to the fee agreement signed by the representative plaintiff, treating fee awards like any other contractual arrangement between lawyer and client.[108] Some prioritize predictability of fees and favor a fee of less than 33 percent as presumptively valid.[109] Others, eager to avoid "any practice in class actions that are likely [sic] to give the profession of advocate a profit-seeking or commercial character,"[110] insist upon greater scrutiny of fees sought by counsel, and regularly reduce the fee award sought by counsel.

There is judicial support for class counsel's preferred method of calculating the fee, the percentage of recovery approach, on the basis that it encourages counsel to maximize class compensation and discourages inefficiency.[111] In recent years, however, judges have struggled with awarding a percentage of so-called mega-fund cases (settlements or judgments of over $100 million).[112] Over the objections of some (but not all) class counsel, various courts have confirmed that the greater the amount recovered, the lower the percentage of the recovery to be awarded to counsel, to ensure the fee bears an appropriate relationship to the results achieved.[113] Notably, the LCO specifically recommended the adoption of a sliding scale in its report.[114]

Statistics on how much class action counsel are actually earning are not available given the challenges of empirical study already discussed. Small-scale studies, however, are available and reveal that the average percentage of settlement value is about 22 percent.[115] One author has found that the average multiplier in fee approval decisions decreased from 2.48 in a 2007 study to 1.95 in a 2013 study.[116] These modest numbers are often overwhelmed by publicity around exceptionally large fee awards. A study conducted at the Quebec Class Actions Lab has shown that class counsel fees represent on average 27.45 percent of the total settlement award.[117] There has been little discussion about whether these ratios are appropriate.

The most recent and vexing issue regarding fees arises in the context of settlements of multijurisdictional class actions. Where multiple lawsuits are filed in different provinces against the same defendants, approval must be obtained from the judges in each province, with the attendant risk of duplicative fees. The problem is compounded when the settlement is structured such that defendants agree to pay fees directly to plaintiffs' lawyers, in addition to the sum to be paid to the class. Attorneys increasingly argue that judicial scrutiny is unwarranted in such circumstances, because the fees and class compensation are not linked. In a recent Ontario case,

107 Ten factors, including the importance of the matter to the class and skill demonstrated by counsel, are routinely cited. See e.g., *Welsh* v. *Ontario*, 2018 ONSC, para. 94.

108 See e.g., *Cassano* v. *Toronto Dominion Bank*, [2009] OJ No 2922 (SCJ) and 799376 *Ontario Inc (c.o.b. Lonsdale Printing Services) (trustee of)* v. *Cascades Fine Papers Group Inc.*, [2008] OJ No 5290 (SCJ).

109 *Cannon* v. *Funds for Canada Foundation*, 2013 ONSC 7686 (CanLII).

110 *Guilbert* v. *Sony BMG Music Canada (Inc)*, [2007] QJ No. 775 (Sup Ct) at para. 113.

111 See e.g., *Ramdath* v. *George Brown College*, 2016 ONSC 2662; *Seed* v. *Ontario*, 2017 ONSC 3534.

112 *Brown* v. *Canada (Attorney General)*, 2018 ONSC 3429 at para. 58.

113 *Manuge* v. *Canada*, 2013 FC 341 at para. 50.

114 *LCO Report, supra* at 76.

115 *Branch Looseleaf, supra* at 235–38 (average percentage: 22.6 percent); Benjamin Alarie and Peter Anthony Flynn, "Accumulating Wisdom: An Updated Empirical Examination of Class Counsel's Fees in Ontario Class Actions", 9 (2) *Can Class Action Rev* 355 (2014) [*Accumulating Wisdom*] (22 percent or 1.95 multiplier).

116 Benjamin Alarie, "Rethinking the Approval of Class Counsel's Fees in Ontario Class Actions", 4 *Can Class Action Rev* 15, 29 (2007) (study of twenty-nine cases); *Accumulating Wisdom, supra* at 371 (study of 109 cases).

117 *Understanding Class Actions, supra* at 237.

counsel submitted that their fee could not be reduced as it was a term of the settlement, a settlement that had already been approved by a judge of the Federal Court.[118] While the Ontario judge and several objecting class members heavily criticized the attempt to shield counsel fees from scrutiny in this manner, the lawyers were ultimately successful.[119]

In light of these controversies, the LCO recommended that the Ontario statute be amended to clarify that all counsel fees, regardless of method of calculation or source of payment, must be "fair and reasonable" and subject to judicial approval. Assessment of "risk" in determining the fairness of the fee should be expanded to include more than just the risk of losing on certification or at trial, but also taking into account the impact of parallel litigation and third party investigations on the case. The LCO further recommended that judges hold back some portion of the approved fee pending a report to the court on the outcome of the settlement distribution process.[120] All of these recommendations aim to create more robust oversight of class counsel fees, in order to promote access to justice for class members and the interests of the administration of justice, among others.

These controversies about fees are not merely of academic importance. How lawyers are compensated affects access to justice in both direct and indirect ways. Overcompensation, of course, directly reduces the sum of money available to class members. In addition, however, how lawyers are paid and the incentives created by fee arrangements impacts the kinds of cases lawyers will pursue. Class counsel are, after all, the gatekeepers to this form of litigation; if money is the engine that drives class action litigation, judicial approaches to fees are, quite literally, key.

7.2.4 A *Spectrum of Costs Regimes*

Canada's patchwork of costs rules is perhaps unique among countries with class action regimes. As mentioned above, five provinces maintain the fee-shifting ("loser pays") rule for class actions. Over the past decade, courts in these provinces have become more and more willing to impose very high costs orders against both plaintiffs and defendants, particularly at certification.[121] Three other provinces have a full no-cost rule, absent litigation misconduct. Quebec is ostensibly a loser-pays jurisdiction, but under the Code of Civil Procedure, cost orders only include disbursements, experts' fees and a minimal flat fee based on a Tariff. Reimbursement of legal fees is rarely granted, and only upon proof of bad faith.

Under the five fee-shifting provinces' statutes, it is the representative plaintiff – not other class members – who is liable for adverse costs orders. No rational person would ever agree to adopt such a risk, with no corresponding up side.[122] In reality, however, the representative plaintiff almost never pays such costs orders personally, but rather is indemnified by class counsel, the CPF or a commercial funder. In turn, class counsel either pay the costs order or they trade away appeal rights in exchange for the defendant not enforcing the order.[123] And in the case of funders, the indemnity comes at a cost of at least 10 percent of the settlement of judgment. The practical

118 *Brown* v. *Canada (Attorney General)*, 2018 ONSC 3429.

119 The complicated case history and maneuvering by the lawyers is recounted in *Riddle* v. *Canada*, 2018 FC 900 (CanLII) and *Brown* v. *Canada (AG)*, 2018 ONSC 5486.

120 *LCO Report*, *supra* at 74–77. The Ontario government adopted the latter recommendations in the amendments to the Class Proceedings Act, but did not introduce language requiring court approval of fees "regardless of method of calculation or source of payment".

121 Certification costs orders routinely exceed $300,000 and have been as high as $525,000 against the unsuccessful plaintiff in *Fresco* v. *Canadian Imperial Bank of Commerce*, 2010 ONSC 1036, aff'd 2010 ONSC 4724, rev'd on other grounds 2012 ONCA 444. In the words of one judge: "costs in class proceedings have gotten out of control": *Hughes* v. *Liquor Control Board of Ontario*, 2018 ONSC 4862 at para. 14.

122 The Chief Justice of Ontario agrees in *Dugal*, *supra* at paras 28–30.

123 *LCO Report*, *supra* at 80.

effects of this costs regime on access to justice were identified by the LCO: indemnities decrease the net recovery to the class; using costs as bargaining chips impacts the substantive and procedural rights of class members, and; the risk of costs deters public interest litigants, including legal clinics and nonprofit organizations.[124]

For these reasons, the LCO recommended that Ontario adopt a modified no-costs rule. Under its proposal, there would be no costs payable by the losing party at certification, all appeals of certification and any motions ancillary to certification. Other steps in the class action – most notably summary judgment motions and trial – would remain subject to the normal fee-shifting rule. The LCO recommended a narrower no-cost rule than currently exists in three other provinces[125] and the Federal Court, where no costs may be ordered against any party for any stage after and including certification. It did so on the basis that the imposition of costs at certification has created significant barriers to justice unique to class proceedings and unrelated to the merits of the action. At the same time, the LCO concluded that it was worthwhile to preserve a core purpose of fee-shifting; deterring unmeritorious motions and lawsuits.

This compromise, however, was not adopted by the business-friendly, Conservative government of Ontario. While the move to a modified no-costs regime was viewed as plaintiff-friendly, and indeed was vigorously resisted by defendant stakeholders in the LCO consultation process and in the legislative debates leading to passage of Ontario's statutory amendments, it is worth noting that the unavailability of costs for a successful party at certification probably would have affected class counsel's bottom line more than any other party's. After all, statistically speaking, plaintiffs are more likely to succeed at the certification motion than defendants, and so are the most frequent beneficiaries of costs awards that they then use to help fund the litigation.

The Supreme Court of Canada once described class actions as the "sport of kings."[126] The significant expense associated with Canadian class actions will continue to affect which cases are selected, how they are litigated, when they are settled, and whether they go to trial. The varying costs rules will mean some jurisdiction shopping is inevitable, and the availability of funders will complicate the dynamic. It is not a coincidence that CPF-funded cases represent a disproportionate number of appeals and trials;[127] shifting the risk of costs to a third party frees class counsel to adopt riskier litigation behavior, sometimes with spectacular success. The development of more creative funding arrangements, therefore, is an issue to watch in the next decade in Canada.

7.3 CLASS ACTION REFORM IN CANADA

7.3.1 *State of Reform Efforts*

Like other first and second generation regimes, Canadian jurisdictions are taking stock of how class actions are working, their unintended consequences and the unanticipated developments in their practice.[128] In Canada, class actions operate pursuant to class action statutes in nine

124 *Id.* at 80–81.

125 The three provinces are British Columbia, Manitoba and Newfoundland. Although technically a fee-shifting jurisdiction, Quebec applies a modest tariff that results in very small costs orders and thus do not result in any of the consequences apparent in Ontario.

126 *Kerr* v. *Danier Leather Inc.*, [2007] 3 SCR 331 at para 63.

127 *LCO Report*, *supra* at 80.

128 In recent years, reform by way of the Rules Committee has taken place in the United States, and law reform commissions in Australia, Victoria, and Ontario have recommended significant changes to class actions in these jurisdictions. See 28 U.S.C. §2074 (West through Pub. L. No. 115-223); John Roberts, Chief Justice of the U.S.,

provinces, at common law in the tenth province and pursuant to Rules of Court in the Federal Court. Reform of class actions, therefore, can take place at the legislative level, in the Federal Rules Committee, through the development of practice directions formulated by committees of bench and bar members and by way of case law. By far, the greatest evolution in class action practice and regulation over the past quarter century has taken place at the court level. In the absence of any explicit statutory provisions, judges have had to fashion criteria and procedures for settlement approval, the certification test, cy près distributions, third party funding agreements, national and international class membership, determination of carriage and many ethical issues, including the rights of class members and representative plaintiffs.

Statutory amendments and reform by way of practice directions have been far less frequent than judge-made reforms. Over the past decade, legislative reform has taken place in five provinces. In 2010, Alberta amended its statute to address competing multijurisdictional class actions, adopting the Uniform Law Conference of Canada (ULCC) provisions in this regard.[129] In 2015, the Saskatchewan legislature amended the province's class actions statute to allow for awards of costs.[130] Prior to the amendment, Saskatchewan was a no-costs jurisdiction for class actions. Quebec enacted significant changes in its Code of Civil Procedure in 2016. Among the most important of the amendments was the introduction of an appeal route for defendants from certification and the codification of criteria for determining jurisdiction when an action overlaps with a multijurisdictional class action filed in another province.[131] In 2018, British Columbia amended its statute to adopt the ULCC provisions on multijurisdictional class actions, and an opt-out regime for nonresident class members.[132] And most recently, Ontario introduced numerous amendments to its statute, ranging from modifications of appeal routes to explicit provisions for carriage motions and multijurisdictional class actions.[133]

The theme of managing multijurisdictional class actions repeated itself in Ontario in 2019, but not by way of statutory reform: a practice direction was issued by the Superior Court.[134] The effort was led by a committee of judges and lawyers from both sides of the bar. In Quebec, the court also used its rulemaking authority to introduce new requirements for mandatory reports to the court at the conclusion of a settlement distribution scheme,[135] and to organize through new directives a structured class actions chamber of ten judges in charge of managing class actions up until authorization.[136]

Finally, the LCO report discussed throughout this chapter represents the most extensive effort to effect wide-ranging reforms of any single class action statute in Canada in over twenty-five years. The Attorney-General implemented many of the forty-seven recommendations made by

Proposed Amendments to the Federal Rules of Civil Procedure (Apr. 26, 2018), www.supremecourt.gov/orders/courtorders/frcv18_5924.pdf; Australia Law Reform Commission, "Integrity, Fairness and Efficiency—An Inquiry into Class Action Proceedings and Third-Party Litigation Funders" (December 2018); Victoria Law Reform Commission, "Access to Justice – Litigation Funding and Group Proceedings" (June 2018) *LCO Report*.

129 Class Proceedings Amendment Act, SA 2010, c15.

130 The Class Actions Amendment Act, 2015, SS 2015, c 4.

131 Code of Civil Procedure, CQLR c C-25, art. 578 and 577, respectively.

132 Class Proceedings Amendment Act, 2018, SBC 2018, c 16.

133 Bill 161, *supra*.

134 Consolidated Provincial Practice Direction (effective May 17, 2019), online: www.ontariocourts.ca/scj/practice/practice-directions/provincial/.

135 Regulation of the Superior Court of Québec in civil matters, chapter C-25.01, r. 0.2.1, Rule 59, online: http://legisquebec.gouv.qc.ca/en/ShowDoc/cr/C-25.01,%20r.%200.2.1/.

136 See Directives of the Superior Court of Quebec, District of Montreal (May 2019), online at www.tribunaux.qc.ca/c.superieure/avis/pdf/Directives%20du%20District%20de%20Montr%C3%A9al.pdf?.

the LCO, but sparked considerable controversy by amending the test for certification to include the American superiority and predominance requirements, a move specifically rejected by the LCO and the Class Action Clinic.[137]

Worth noting is the absence of heavy political lobbying in Canada to significantly restrict the availability of class actions. While industry and corporate representatives made lengthy submissions to the LCO Project urging changes to various aspects of the class action statute, none proceeded on the basis that class actions have been harmful on the whole.[138] Ironically, the most radical reform suggestions were made not by Canadian defense lawyers or their clients, but by the US Chamber of Commerce.[139]

7.3.2 *Challenges in Reform Efforts*

As indicated above, we coauthors worked together on the LCO project, and one of us is currently involved in a law reform project with the Quebec Ministry of Justice. In the law reform projects with which we have been involved, we have committed to evidence-based policy-making and law reform aiming to ensure that our system of law meets the justice needs of Canadian society. The exercise has been and continues to be challenging.

Class actions law is fast-evolving in Canada. Because these are well-funded, high stakes lawsuits, prosecuted and defended by experienced litigators, class action motions (and increasingly trials) are frequently brought before the courts. With new actions filed almost daily, several court decisions being issued weekly in the most populated provinces, varied practice directions and broad media coverage of class actions throughout Canada, it is difficult to keep track of the law's status and evolution. Hence, planning the law's reform is challenging. The speed with which judges make new law to keep pace with novel issues is only one obstacle; more pressing are the practical difficulties that academics and policy-makers face in pursuing evidence-based research in a polarized practice area, as discussed below.

7.3.2.1 Difficulty Accessing Information and Court Records

The most significant challenge in law reform efforts has been accessing the required data and records relating to class actions. As briefly discussed earlier in this chapter, the province of Ontario does not have an electronic dockets system, or a system making detailed information about case files available online, like British Columbia and Quebec. In the LCO project, the Ontario Ministry of the Attorney General (MAG) first provided us with several historical lists of data relative to class proceedings taken from the FRANK court database (inaccessible to the public).[140]

137 The Class Action Clinic is housed at the University of Windsor and is focused on providing legal information and advice to class members, as well as advocacy and public policy initiatives. For a summary of the objections to the changes to the certification test, see Jasminka Kalajdzic, "Ontario the Outlier: How Changes to the Class Proceedings Act Might Make Certification More Difficult in Ontario than Anywhere Else" [blog], July 6, 2019, online: https://classactionclinic.com/2020/07/06/ontario-the-outlier-how-changes-to-the-class-proceedings-act-might-make-certification-more-difficult-in-ontario-than-anywhere-else/.

138 See LCO webpage listing submissions online at www.lco-cdo.org/en/our-current-projects/class-actions/submissions-to-the-consultation-paper/.

139 See US Chamber of Commerce submission online at www.lco-cdo.org/wp-content/uploads/2018/06/U.S.-Chamber-Institute-for-Legal-Reform-CA-Submission.pdf. For example, the US Chamber recommended that a merits assessment be added as a criterion for class certification and that defendants be permitted to settle individual class members' claims post-certification. *Id.* at 3.

140 See *LCO Report*, *supra* at 103. However, we must specify that we later found that those lists were incomplete, inconsistent and contained inaccuracies and duplications.

Importantly, MAG data did not include a complete or basic record of important milestones or outcomes within each file or action.[141]

Accordingly, in order to obtain information about class proceedings in the province, we needed to proceed manually with a search within the CanLII, Quicklaw and Westlaw-type databases to identify class action cases filed and resolved within the province. This search allowed us to obtain a set of decisions on files which we could then search to find specific information about individual files.[142] Adding to this already burdensome process, we consulted law firms, client groups, settlement administrators and others, for any and all additional information that they could provide.[143] The court's physical files were disorganized and incomplete, making their review not worth the considerable effort. The search process overall was inefficient and revealed a tremendous lack of transparency of the Ontario system, to our great disappointment.

Most concerning was the lack of information regarding outcomes in class actions in the LCO Project,[144] and the challenges accessing this information in the Class Actions Lab project.[145] At the conclusion of the lengthy LCO Project, other than anecdotal evidence of take-up rates in a small number of cases, we still do not how many class actions settle, the claims rate in settled cases or how well class members are compensated in Ontario. In Quebec, it has taken more than three years of funded research at the Lab to obtain data on compensation in 109 class action cases. While these results are important, they do not present the complete picture of compensation in Quebec class actions. Further, it is only recently that the Quebec Superior Court of Justice has requested parties and lawyers of record to publish a report on administration of distributions through a revised court rule.[146]

7.3.2.2 The Researcher's Place Vis-à-Vis the Stakeholders

The LCO received thirty written submissions. No law firm provided empirical data about their class actions. No firm was willing or able to disclose information about take-up rates, dormant cases, "abusive class actions," or any other statistics about their inventory of cases. This was surprising, in light of the importance of this evidence and the sophistication of the firms in question. It caused us to wonder more than once whether there was a lack of trust between the researchers and the participants, or an unwillingness to share data that might be contrary to participants' self-interest or that of their clients.

Beyond the practical limitations of relying on stakeholders to provide data is the challenge of weighing competing interests and remaining nonpartisan. The LCO organized consultations with members of the public, lawyers and legal organizations, public and private organizations, academics, governments and others who have an interest in class actions. The consultations included over 130 meetings, several dozen conference calls, and roundtables. The researchers

141 *Id.*

142 *Id.*

143 *Id.*

144 We noted this lack of information in the *LCO Report*, *supra* at 104.

145 *Class Action Value*, *supra* at 286, 289.

146 Regulation of the Superior Court of Québec in civil matters, c C-25.01, r. 0.2.1 (Can. Que.), Rule 59:

59. Report on administration. If a judgment orders the collective recovery of the claims made with individual payment of the members' claims, the special clerk or third person designated by the court must file with the court, after the time limit for members to file their claim has expired, a detailed report on its administration and give notice to the parties and the Fonds . . .

The report lists the members who filed a claim, the amount paid to each member, the remaining balance and the amount withheld for the Fonds . . .

Also see *Class Action Value*, *supra* at 268–29.

were sensitive to the possibility that making recommendations that overwhelmingly "helped" one party or another would create the perception of partisanship. The final report made more than forty recommendations to reform the CPA and related policies. The recommendations addressed a wide array of topics including certification, settlement, carriage, costs, fees and reporting in class actions. Those recommendations may be considered controversial, depending on a stakeholder's perspective.[147] Given the wide scope of the consultations, and the goal to produce an independent, evidence-based and comprehensive analysis of key class action issues, it is inevitable that the report will not please all stakeholders, and that these individuals or interest groups will not embrace its recommendations.

Another challenge in law reform work that relies heavily on qualitative data and consultations is the relationship between the expectations of stakeholders and any ultimate recommendations for reform. Consulting with stakeholders raises expectations. Stakeholders often spent a lot of time and energy discussing issues with us. They expect, not unreasonably, that the issues they discussed and the suggestions they made will be adopted. Their opinions and comfort level, as well as acceptance of reform initiatives, are fundamental to success in reform. In an area of practice that is sharply partisan, however, consensus is almost impossible and buy-in is difficult.

7.4 CONCLUSION

Canada's various class action systems share core features that reflect their American roots. Subtle, but important differences – between Canadian and Rule 23 actions and well as between Canadian provincial jurisdictions – are worth noting in a comparative law project like this book. The developments in class action practice over the past twenty-five to thirty years could not have been envisioned by the law reformers and legislators who worked to bring class actions to Canada. The rise in multijurisdictional and overlapping class actions in particular have created unique problems in Canada's constitutional order that lawyers, judges and policy-makers are still trying to work out. In addition, emerging areas of public concern like privacy breaches create challenges for class action practitioners on both substantive and procedural levels. And the ever-increasing cost of this kind of litigation, coupled with Canada's patchwork of costs regimes, are an access to justice problem with which all stakeholders have to grapple.

Law reform has slowly started to take place in Canada, periodically in the form of legislative amendment, but more frequently by way of judicial tinkering. Ontario's law reform commission recently completed a two-year project and issued forty-seven recommendations; somewhat surprisingly, the Attorney-General adopted many of them within a year of the report's release, but responded to lobbying by corporate interests and defence lawyers by not adopting the no-costs recommendation and by instituting a stricter certification test. These legislative amendments may have ripple effects in the reform of class action statutes in the rest of Canada, and most certainly in Quebec where reform efforts are ongoing.

The peculiar but complex class action procedure, with its fast-paced legal practice that is widely covered by the media, and its public policy and access to justice rationales, makes for highly stimulating law reform work involving a wide range of stakeholders. There will always be in the background a tension between our personal goals as academics and law reform that is workable and politically palatable. The practical limitations imposed by under-resourced and archaic court systems complicate law reform efforts, but they cannot be allowed to torpedo them. Small-scale studies, interviews, surveys, doctrinal research, discussion – all have made law reform possible, and contribute to a rich dialogue about this most important civil justice mechanism.

[147] *LCO Report*, *supra* at 1.

8

Class Action in Brazil

Overview, Current Trends and Case Studies

*Carlos Portugal Gouvêa and Helena Campos Refosco**

8.1 INTRODUCTION

The objective of this chapter is the critical analysis of the primary tool for collective rights defense in Brazil: the class action lawsuit that is part of the Brazil's microsystem for collective litigation.[1] The key question is whether the country's class action system has satisfactorily served its purpose of deterring and punishing rights violations by large businesses in Brazil. Our hypothesis is that such tool has proved insufficient as a remedy for infringements of the rights of third parties (consumers, workers, investors and even government organs) by private companies.

For the benefit of an international readership, the chapter will start by briefly outlining the Brazilian judicial system. This will include explanations of the relevant instruments necessary for an understanding of the procedural dynamics of major collective litigation in the country. In order to test our hypothesis, we present two case studies (in the fields of telecommunications and pharmaceuticals).[2]

8.2 THE LEGAL REGIME FOR CLASS ACTIONS IN BRAZIL

Brazil is a federal state in which national and state court systems coexist with specialized bodies (labor, electoral and military courts). Legislation regulating procedural law is incumbent exclusively upon the federal government.[3] As a general rule, cases involving national interests,

* This chapter was translated to English by Bradley Hayes. Many thanks to him, as well as to Calixto Salomão Filho, David Kennedy, Gustavo Sampaio de Abreu Ribeiro, Jean-Paul Veiga da Rocha, Joanna Vieira Noronha and Yasmin Saba Relvas for this article reflects their invaluable contributions. The views expressed here are those of the authors and not the official policy or position of the institutions they belong to.

1 There exist both general and special types of class actions in Brazil. General class actions are the subject of this analysis. They are the ones that most resembles its United States counterpart and that are designed for the reparation of harms caused by large private and public organizations. Types of special class action lawsuits include the Direct Action of Unconstitutionality (*Ação Direta de Inconstitucionalidade* or ADI), Claim of Non-Compliance with a Fundamental Precept (*Arguição de Descumprimento de Preceito Fundamental* or ADPF), Declaratory Action for Constitutionality (*Ação Declaratória de Constitucionalidade*, or ADC), the Direct Action of Unconstitutionality by Omission (*Ação Direta de Inconstitucionalidade por Omissão*), and collective writs of mandamus or injunction (*Mandado de Injunção Coletivo* and *Mandado de Segurança Coletivo*), among others.

2 For a more detailed treatment of the case study on residential telephone service fees, see the doctoral dissertation of Helena Refosco, published in Portuguese under the title Ação Coletiva e Democratização do Acesso à Justiça (2018).

3 Article 22, I of the Federal Constitution.

authorities and state-owned enterprises are adjudicated in federal courts and the rest fall to state courts. Both state and federal courts handle class action lawsuits. The structure of the legal system is the same in all of the branches of the judicial system. Cases go to courts of first instance (the equivalent to trial courts in common law systems) where single judges hand down decisions. Appeals go to courts of second instance (appeal courts) in which panels of judges review the initial decision. After the initial appeal, some cases may go to the Superior Court of Justice (*Superior Tribunal de Justiça*, usually referred to by its acronym STJ), whose primary responsibility is reviewing the legal reasoning, not the facts, of the case to make sure federal legislation has been interpreted correctly. Lastly, the Supreme Court (*Supremo Tribunal Federal*, or STF) serves the dual purposes of court of final review and constitutional court in Brazil. The 1988 Federal Constitution established this structure.[4]

A military dictatorship that severely restricted the exercise of civil and political rights ruled Brazil from 1965 until 1985. A relevant question is whether the transition back to democracy that started in earnest with the promulgation of the 1988 Constitution has been achieved or whether the process that has now lasted three decades continues to unfold slowly.[5] It could be argued, relying on the theory of pact-making among elites elaborated by O'Donnell and Schmitter to illustrate the transitions from authoritarian to democratic regimes,[6] that only the pact involving the military leaders was fully achieved in Brazil, leading to the end of military rule and the transfer of political power from the military to the political class. As a result, the 1988 Constitution represents a partially realized political pact, and there is no economic pact to speak of, for that would require significant reduction in economic inequality since the return to democracy, which has not occurred.

Social demand for participation and democratization at the beginning of the political transition led to the 1985 Law of Public Civil Action (*Lei da Ação Civil Pública*, or LACP).[7] Its purpose was to incorporate into the Brazilian legal system mechanisms for collective rights defense against violations by private actors, mechanisms that were subsequently reinforced by the 1988 Constitution. Before 1985, only the limited mechanisms established by the Law of Popular Action protected collective rights.[8] Ironically, "popular actions" provided only a legal tool to prevent harmful actions committed by government bodies, but not those carried out by private agents. Yet, the Law of Popular Action is still relevant because the current law is interpreted analogically and used to regulate aspects of procedural law for collective litigation in general. From it comes, for example, the five-year statute of limitations for class action lawsuits.[9]

The Brazilian law drew inspiration from the US class action, albeit indirectly, via Italy,[10] and was more limited in scope. That is because the LACP initially designed the instrument to deal

4 Articles 92 and 126.

5 See Carlos Portugal Gouvêa, *Presidential Supremacy and Democracy in Latin America: Introducing the Problem of Social Inequality in Institutional Design*, 28 Revista da Faculdade de Direito do Sul de Minas 27 (2009).

6 We use the term "pact-making among elites" in the sense proposed by Guillermo O'Donnell & Philippe Schmitter, Transitions from Authoritarian Rule: Tentative Conclusions about Uncertain Democracies (1986).

7 "*Lei da Ação Civil Pública*," Federal Law No. 7.347 of July 24, 1985.

8 "*Lei da Ação Popular*," Federal Law No. 4.717 of June 29, 1965.

9 This understanding was forged during an episode of intense, repetitive litigation related to measures implemented by the government to halt hyperinflation in the 1990s. Still, its jurisprudential grounding remains unsettled, for the statute of limitations refers to the pretensions and not to the actual procedures adopted for protection. The Superior Court of Justice has yet to clarify whether the filing of a class action suspends the statute of limitation for individual claims. The question was raised during the wave of litigation mentioned, yet the Court has not provided an unequivocal answer. *See* Helena Campos Refosco, Ação Coletiva e Democratização do Acesso à Justiça 266 (2018).

10 Antonio Gidi, A Class Action como Instrumento de Tutela Coletiva dos Direitos: as Ações Coletivas em uma Perspectiva Comparada 17 (2007).

with collective action in specific areas. The law was gradually amended to cover any diffuse or collective interest, and also more specific issues, such as urban policies, racial, ethnic or religious issues, and the protection of historic and cultural patrimony.

The system for collective rights defense that the LACP created was eventually complemented by the Consumer Defense Code (CDC)[11] that Brazil implemented in 1990. Despite the name's suggestion, this law established regulations related to all collective procedures, not only those related to consumer demands. The code unnecessarily divides collective rights into three categories: diffuse, collective and 'homogenous' individual rights.[12] This division does not derive from the United States class action system and will be thoroughly criticized in the first case study.

The Federal Constitution of 1988, promulgated following the restoration of democracy in Brazil, expanded and placed much importance on the collective protection of rights. It broadened the range of available legal recourse in addition to bestowing constitutional rank on the general class action and some of the special class actions. The Constitution also granted general standing for associations and trade unions to litigate for the rights of their associates and the professions that they represent.

The Constitution also endowed citizens with new rights against government interference, contributing to a rise in litigation. In the 1990s, the Constitution was amended to legalize the privatization of important public utilities (telephone service and electric power, among others). Once privatized, these fell under the purview of new regulatory agencies. The regulated services also led to a significant rise in litigation – a dynamic exemplified in the first case study examining disputes over telecommunication services. These developments contributed to a crisis of legitimacy for the country's judiciary. The ensuing flood of lawsuits, some of which still await resolution, severely aggravated the backlog of unresolved cases in Brazilian courts.

Hence, at the outset of the twenty-first century, influenced by the World Bank's Justice Reform directives,[13] Brazil initiated an ambitious project for judicial reform. Although one of those directives called for an overhaul of the class action system in order to streamline and unify it,[14] ultimately the procedural reforms were limited to improving the system for adjudicating individual claims, primarily by reinforcing the binding nature of precedents. Many still believe that the system for adjudicating collective claims must be improved, but there is no consensus on what exactly should be modified.

Reforming the system for collective rights defense could help reduce the staggering judicial backlog in Brazil. According to official data, in Brazil, a country with 210 million inhabitants,[15] "[the] Judicial Branch ended the year 2017 with 80.1 million cases pending final judgment."[16]

Moreover, Brazil is a country of stark inequality[17] where completely distinct social and economic systems operate for different sectors of the population. By consequence, the systematic exclusion from the enjoyment of basic rights leads to the paradoxical situation in which access to the court system is effectively blocked for much of the population; it nevertheless remains

[11] Law No. 8.078 of September 11, 1990.

[12] Article 81 of the CDC.

[13] *See* REFOSCO, *supra* note 9 at 39–112.

[14] Brazil, *Segundo Pacto Republicano de Estado por um Sistema de Justiça mais Acessível, Ágil e Efetivo* (2009), www.planalto.gov.br/ccivil_03/Outros/IIpacto.htm.See directive 3.2.

[15] Source: Brazilian Institute of Geography and Statistics – IBGE, www.ibge.gov.br/apps/populacao/projecao/index.html (last access June 12, 2019).

[16] Brazil, *Justiça em Números 2018: ano-base 2017* 73 (2018).

[17] According to figures from the World Bank, the Gini coefficient for Brazil in 2017 was 53.3, which places the country among the most unequal countries in the world and the most unequal country with a similar level of industrialization. *See* https://data.worldbank.org/indicator/si.pov.gini (last access June 12, 2019).

flooded to the point of paralysis with litigation.[18] On one side, it is overloaded with lawsuits related to the public, banking and telecommunication sectors. These are indicative of regulatory difficulties[19] and defective institutional design that combine to incentivize individual claims. On the other side, especially in the area of consumer protection, access to the justice system is extremely restricted. Brazil possesses a Public Defender's Office that provides free legal assistance to needy individuals in both state and federal courts, but the provision of legal assistance alone does not render the justice system accessible. The cost of access to the courts goes beyond lawyer's fees and retainers. Even for people whose income is above the threshold for free legal assistance, the cost of transportation, missing work and other expenses are often determinant impediments.[20] The sluggishness of the judiciary is also constantly mentioned as a factor that discourages them from bringing their disputes to court.[21] Taken together, it becomes clear that, despite the judicial backlog, access to the court system is deficient, which should be deeply troubling for any democracy.

The figures suggest that streamlining the system is necessary, especially with regard to class actions. Lawyers in private practice could contribute to a solution, but, unfortunately, the current system does not provide sufficient incentives, particularly in terms of remuneration, for lawyers to take up class action lawsuits.

The virtual lack in the Brazilian legal system of an equivalent to pretrial discovery also complicates the situation. The Public Prosecutor's Office (*Ministério Público*), at both the federal and state level, is the only institution with the capacity to request information before filing lawsuits using a tool called the "public civil inquiry" (*inquérito civil público*). Although this tool has become prominent in the Brazilian class action system,[22] the institutional design that confers it to the Public Prosecutor's Office alone limits the options of other actors with the legal standing to make collective claims, as will be demonstrated in the case studies. For if the Public Prosecutor's Office does not take interest in a particular class action lawsuit, or simply botches the lawsuit, the private agents involved in the defense of their rights are left with few means to impel the judicial process.

Another facet of the Brazilian legal system that does not directly relate to collective rights defense but does have a direct impact on it is the absence of punitive damage awards. Punitive damage awards could be the most efficient means to deter offenders with ample economic power and would furnish the incentive missing for private lawyers and potential plaintiffs to pursue collective claims in court because the chances of obtaining a significant punitive damage award are much greater with a single class action than through multiple individual lawsuits. In Brazil, however, civil responsibility is almost strictly compensatory and is therefore substantially limited to the calculation of actual harm caused.[23]

[18] The research project "Panorama do Acesso à Justiça" (Panorama of Access to Justice) provides a portrait of the exclusion in which the poor and least educated either do not know that courts can help resolve their conflicts or do not seek access to the courts because of factors such as distance, fear, or expense. Brazil. Conselho Nacional de Justiça, *Panorama de Acesso à Justiça no Brasil, 2004 a 2009* 14 (2011), www.cnj.jus.br/images/pesquisas-judiciarias/Publicacoes/relat_panorama_acesso_pnad2009.pdf.

[19] For instance, in the banking área, *see* the doctoral thesis of Jean-Paul Veiga da Rocha, *A Capacidade Normativa de Conjuntura no Direito Econômico: o Déficit Democrático da Regulação Financeira* (2004), www.teses.usp.br/teses/disponiveis/2/2133/tde-12022015-204835/pt-br.php.

[20] *See* Refosco, *supra* note 9 at 129.

[21] Luciana Gross Cunha et al., Relatório ICJ Brasil – 2o e 3o trimestres / 2014 13 (2015).

[22] Sociedade Brasileira de Direito Público – SBDP, Ações Coletivas no Brasil: Temas, Atores e Desafios da Tutela Coletiva (2017).

[23] Articles 927 and 944 of the Civil Code.

From this general overview of the Brazilian system, we will move to the case studies in which other facets of class action lawsuits in Brazil will be examined more deeply. To avoid repetition, more thorough attention will be given to the first case study on residential telephone service fees than on the second case study on abusive pricing by government pharmaceutical suppliers. We selected litigation pertaining to residential telephone service in order to illustrate the obstacles that hinder collective litigation amassing private individual claims, whereas we chose the case of abusive pricing of pharmaceuticals to illustrate the obstacles that are present in collective litigation led by the Public Prosecutor's Office.

8.3 RESIDENTIAL TELEPHONE SERVICE FEES

8.3.1 *The Background behind Lawsuits Challenging Service Fees*

As was mentioned earlier, under the leadership of President Fernando Henrique Cardoso, a wave of privatization swept Brazil in the 1990s, the telecommunications sector included. As a result, it became necessary to create independent regulatory agencies, such as the National Agency of Telecommunications, or Anatel, as it is known in Brazil. Establishing the fee structure for telecommunication services was one of the competences attributed to Anatel.[24] Prices for local phone calls and basic landline service rose dramatically between 1994 and 2004,[25] at a pace approximately double the rate of inflation (according to the data of IPC-10 and IGP-DI gathered by the Getulio Vargas Foundation).[26]

In 2003, President Luiz Inácio Lula da Silva took issue with the contractual provisions for fee adjustments following the IGP-DI,[27] because he considered this index abusive. His Minister of Communications instructed Anatel to freeze the fee at the current rate until a new agreement with the phone companies could be reached, one that would be fair and in line with the public interest and include as a parameter a different consumer price index, the IPCA.[28] The president of the regulatory agency, believing the contract with the suppliers was clear in this regard, ignored the instructions and authorized the fee increase. Because of his action, the issue was no longer merely the reduction or increase in the fee. The move called into question the very legitimacy of the regulatory agency and the stability of telecommunications regulatory policy. The ensuing reaction of the Minister of Communication helped push the dispute into the courts,[29] as his report explicitly criticized the fee structure for impeding universal access to telephone service by permitting excessive manipulation of the subscription fee, "an item that weighs heavily on the monthly budget of low-income clients."[30]

Starting in 2004, the number of lawsuits challenging the subscription fee for a residential telephone service rose exponentially. Thousands of consumers filed lawsuits in the state of São

[24] Article 103 of Law no. 9472/1997.

[25] Kazuo Watanabe et al., Tutela Judicial dos Interesses Metaindividuais: Ações Coletivas (2007).

[26] Luciano dos Santos Danni, *Análise do Efeito das Reformas Regulatórias e Privatização dos Serviços Públicos no Brasil – Eletricidade e Telefonia*, in Regulação de Serviços Públicos e Controle Externo 416 (2008).

[27] This is the General Price Index (*Índice Geral de Preços – Disponibilidade Interna*) calculated by the Getulio Vargas Foundation.

[28] IPCA stands for *Índice Nacional de Preços ao Consumidor Amplo* and is calculated monthly by the Brazilian Institute of Geography and Statistics (IBGE).

[29] Minister Teixeira disagreed with the decision of Anatel and accused the regulator of surrendering to the phone service suppliers. He went on to suggest that unhappy citizens challenge the fee increase in court with the help of civil society organizations. Text available in Portuguese at www1.folha.uol.com.br/fsp/dinheiro/fi0211200420.htm. (last access June 12, 2019).

[30] Watanabe et al., *supra* note 25.

Paulo alone, in addition to twenty-six collective claims.[31] Although some of these cases are still being processed in the court system, the litigation hit its peak between 2004 and 2008.

We selected this cases study because of its relevance in terms of the telling quantity of individual and class action lawsuits adjudicated[32] and the number of practical problems that the contentious litigation reveals.

8.3.2 *Applicable Jurisdictional Factors*

An example of the practical problems faced has to do with the Brazilian federal system and how it complicates court jurisdiction and legal standing of the parties in class action lawsuits. Because individual claims oppose consumers to the telephone companies, there is no perceived need for the regulatory agency to participate as a passive defendant in the lawsuit. In the case of a class action, however, added difficulty results from the transposition from the individual to collective claim context. In this case study, after many years of class action litigation, throughout which the actions and documents were forwarded to federal courts on the understanding that Anatel was a party to the lawsuit, the STJ reversed this understanding, declaring the regulatory agency's inclusion illegitimate, on the grounds that the ruling on the class actions would not directly affect Anatel's interests.

The STJ's ruling disregards the fact that, if the class action challenges the policy for fee structuring that pertains to the technical competence of the regulatory agency, it is important for the agency to participate in the trial. Its participation adds an extra level of expertise to ensure the best legal decision is taken. Its participation also increases the chances of reaching a satisfactory agreement whose terms can be incorporated into policy to improve the norms in the sector.[33] It is worth noting that the STJ, in later cases unrelated to the ones in question here, adopted conflicting positions regarding Anatel's passive participation in class action lawsuits.[34] Up to now, no binding precedent regulates this important matter, nor do the previous decisions on the subject offer a consistent interpretation.

The structuring of the Brazilian federation into twenty-six states and a federal district also compounds the uncertainty regarding collective litigation. There is an ambiguous norm that requires decisions in civil class actions to be *erga omnes*, applicable to all, *within the limits of the territorial competence of the deciding court*, except when the claim is deemed groundless for lack of proof, in which case any legitimate party may undertake another lawsuit with an identical claim after gathering the necessary evidence.[35]

31 *Id.*

32 In the state of São Paulo alone, 95,000 individual claims have been filed since 2005 in addition to twenty-five class action lawsuits. *Id.* at 74.

33 Lawsuits should improve market dynamics by serving an important regulatory function. They can even be useful to the regulatory agency itself, which often confronts limits on its power and competences. In cases where the lawsuit challenges noncompliance with regulations, the regulator should support the collective action since its own capacity to oblige compliance with the regulation is clearly limited by economic and political factors. Moreover, a study of class action lawsuits has revealed that business leaders in the United States rethink and revise their practices when challenged by lawsuits that they believe have merit (see Class Action Dilemmas: Pursuing Public Goals for Private Gain (Deborah R. Hensler et. al.eds., 2000, at 119). The creation of an institutional space for debate over companies' business decisions and regulatory policies issued by governmental agencies should be contemplated, for the lack of such a forum is keenly felt in Brazil and is an indication of its institutional immaturity. Businesses and regulators alike need a legal forum to carry out tests of proportionality and gauge the reasonableness of their actions – especially in terms of motives and effects yet without disregarding the technical aspects of the law.

34 *See, e.g.*, "*Agravo Regimental*" at Special Appeal 1502179/PE, Rapporteur Justice Herman Benjamin, December 19, 2016.

35 Article 16 of the LACP.

The reference to the "limits of territorial competence" was inserted in the law by the federal government to attempt to limit the potential consequences of the litigation for the federal treasury.[36] The norm thus appears to limit the effective scope of the decision in a class action to the territorial jurisdiction of the court that issues it – which if true would generate endless debate over the exact confines of that territorial jurisdiction, given the multiplicity of administrative boundaries in the Brazilian court system. This would deprive Brazilian class action lawsuits of any national efficacy despite the material harm done at the national level and, in fact, the norm is considered null in most of the Brazilian jurisprudence.[37] Unfortunately, in this case the STJ applied the ambiguous norm criticized here, unduly limiting the reach of the class action lawsuits, as will be shown in the following section.

8.3.3 *Dysfunctional Procedural Categorization in Class Action Lawsuits*

In Section 8.2, we mentioned the ontological categorization of collective rights into three types introduced by the CDC. This segmentation, nonexistent in the United States system,[38] compartmentalizes the rights, which makes their comprehension and treatment in the collective process more difficult. The added difficulty it creates for defending homogenous individual rights – rights that the law considers divisible and thus justiciable through individual claims, as in the present example where residential telephone service fees are paid individually – has serious practical repercussions.

Concretely, there was a controversy about the jurisdiction that should adjudicate the class actions at the national level. Initially, the STJ categorically granted the suspension of all the lawsuits pending their urgent resolution in the federal court in Brasília, whose competency it reaffirmed.

At the final ruling, however, the majority opinion, referring to the divisibility of the individual homogenous rights and the preeminence of the individual claims over the collective claims, maintained that the class actions were completely independent from each other and from the individual claims. The opinion refuted both any sort of aggregation of the claims and the suspension of the individual claims unless solicited by the individual plaintiffs themselves. The court also stated the inadequacy of the procedural instrument used to provoke it to decide on the issue.

It is worth clarifying that, unfortunately, there is no certification of the class action in the Brazilian civil procedure. In practice, this means that there is persistent uncertainty about the boundaries of the lawsuit, whether in terms of the classes of people affected by the outcome or the territories in which the beneficiaries are situated. In the present case, an inappropriate device was used to define the scope of collective action precisely because of the lack of an instrument that would allow such delimitation at an appropriate time.

Regarding the merits of the decision, it is important to note that the STJ subsequently ruled that, in the case of repetitive lawsuits related to the anti-inflationary measures that were part of

36 Law No. 9.494 of September 10, 1997 appended the norm in question to the LACP.

37 This is because the law in question was limited to modifying Article 16 of the LACP, not Article 93 of the CDC, which regulates class actions for harms caused at the national level. *See* Daniela Monteiro Gabbay, *Ações Coletivas e Contencioso de Massa: o Caso da Assinatura Básica de Telefonia Fixa* 125, in ESTRATÉGIAS PROCESSUAIS NA ADVOCACIA EMPRESARIAL (Carlos Alberto Carmona & Sidnei Amendoeira Junior eds., 2011).

38 Antonio Gidi explains that the existent categories in American civil procedure law are "eminently pragmatic" and bear no resemblance to the abstract categories contemplated in Brazilian law that employs the concepts of diffuse rights, collective rights, and homogenous individual rights. *See* GIDI, *supra* note 10 at 15.

the government's economic policy, individual claims could be suspended ex officio.[39] This innovation was grounded in the allegation that treating a collective dispute as a "macrodispute" justified suspending, albeit ex officio, individual claims until a collective resolution applicable to the conflict underlying all the claims could be reached. This change, which has not been adopted in all similar circumstances, should be incorporated explicitly into legislation along with the adoption of a general rule for limited suspension of individual claims. The foreseeability provided by the a priori establishment of the one-year term for the suspension of individual claims would be positive and consistent with the term contemplated in Articles 980 and 1037 section 4 of the Brazilian Civil Procedure Code.[40] This period of time during which the individual claims are suspended should also be open to extension in substantiated, exceptional cases. The rule for limited suspension of individual claims balances (1) the public interest in prioritizing the class action because it economizes scarce public resources that are otherwise consumed adjudicating the individual claims with (2) the private interest in obtaining a judgment in individual claims in accordance with the constitutional guarantee of a timely trial.

Returning to the case study, the majority opinion did not only rule against suspending the individual lawsuits while the class actions were processed. It went on to state that, since the protection of homogenous individual rights was at stake, both the nature of the plaintiff[41] and the territorial limits of the court's competence restricted the reach of the class action, such that the decision of each judge would only comprise *res judicata* in their administrative area.

The categorization of collectively actionable rights adopted by Brazilian law has no practical utility and should be eliminated. In addition to the countless practical difficulties it introduces, it requires personal interpretations of the nature of the "homogenous" individual rights in question. This weakens the collective mechanism for rights protection, effectively reducing access to justice. The truth is that, regardless the elegant attempt to separate collectively actionable interests into categories, in practice there is inherent tension between collective and individual interests no matter what the interest is. The perspectives vary in accordance with the values of each individual and even with time, making the attempt to construct a framework for them futile.

Fortunately, with specific regards to the rule limiting the subjective reach of decisions applicable to homogenous individual rights, the STJ took up the matter again in the following years. It ended up modifying the decision just described, ruling the norm ineffective in a binding precedent[42] for all the Brazilian judiciary to follow.[43]

It is hoped that further retrogression in this matter will not occur, because the absence of clear criteria for competence and the scope of *res judicata* has seriously damaged the credibility and the proper operation of the class action system. Legislation establishing clear, broad criteria for competence and *res judicata* would instill collective litigation with greater legal certainty.

39 STJ, Special Appeal No. 1.110.549 – RS, 2nd Panel, Rapporteur Justice Sidnei Beneti, 28 October 2009.

40 Federal Law No. 13.105 of March 16, 2015.

41 A municipal government office, following this reasoning, could not represent anyone who did not live in that municipality.

42 According to the STJ, the former restrictive interpretation voided the practical utility of the class action and blurred dissimilar concepts, for territorial competence limits the exercise of jurisdiction, not the effect or efficacy of a decision, which, as is commonly known, relate to the limits of the dispute and the legal questions decided.

43 The STJ ruled on the question of repetitive litigation in Special Appeal No. 1243887/PR on 19 October 2011. Repetitive appeals are those that reflect a multiplicity of extraordinary or special appeals (appeals that can be lodged after the first or second appeals have been denied) that are based on an identical legal question. While they are considered, all pending trials, individual or collective, that impinge on the legal question in the national territory are suspended. The ruling of the high courts (STJ or STF) then has the force of binding precedent to be applied throughout the Brazilian judiciary (Articles 1036–41 of the Civil Procedure Code).

8.3.4 *Procedural Promptness, Priority and Aggregation in Class Actions*

In terms of trial speed, class actions make their way through the legal system much more slowly than individual claims. Perhaps it is because of the doubts they provoke (notoriously regarding jurisdiction), or perhaps it is because they are given less priority. In 2007, when the STJ handed down the first binding precedents affirming the legality of the basic subscription fee for residential phone service,[44] the class action lawsuits were still in trial courts (courts of first instance).[45]

In the dissenting opinion, STJ Justice Herman Benjamin commented on the impropriety of the judiciary's handling of the lawsuits. He criticized the decision to use an individual claim, filed by a vulnerable consumer, as the basis for the precedent it established, which ran counter to the welfarist spirit of the 1988 Constitution. Even though the Court was aware of class actions on the same question, it inverted the logic of the collective system and, instead of using a class action to determine a claim preclusion *erga omnes*, took up an individual claim out of pragmatic expedience. Justice Benjamin pointedly observed the paradox of using an individual claim – a context that favors extremely powerful defendants accustomed to litigation (the telephone service provider) – as the basis for a ruling that effectively precludes the claims of thousands of other individual and collective lawsuits against the same entity.

Justice Benjamin emphasized the significance of the strategy deployed by the defendant, a repeat player,[46] and the advantages it perceived from the choice of an individual claim. He declared that the favorable ruling had more to do with strategy than merit, complaining that the decision was legal in its form but that it, whether intentionally or not, had the effect of impairing both access to justice and debate over the legal question. Benjamin's opinion demonstrated the defects of the institutional design for the resolution of collective claims in the Brazilian system. Prioritizing class actions could mitigate the problem and would also be appropriate because the decision in a class action lawsuit covers a collective claim, not only a demand by a single individual. Moreover, giving preference to class actions would encourage other potential plaintiffs to wait for the judiciary to rule on the more complex case before deciding whether to file an individual claim. Conceding priority in such circumstances is not unheard of in the Brazilian judicial tradition,[47] and should be clearly determined by the law.

Furthermore, class actions with national applicability should be aggregated and adjudicated together, in order to combine the strengths and arguments of the plaintiffs. Doing so facilitates the defense of collective interests and does not prejudice those of defendants. Divergent or inconsistent decisions in class actions affect more people and thus their effect is potentially more noxious than divergent decisions in individual lawsuits. Plainly, whenever possible, all lawsuits involving collective rights, including those pertaining to the already criticized category of homogenous individual rights, should be combined and considered together.

The same reasoning cannot be applied to individual disputes, however, because of the difficulty it would create for plaintiffs scattered across a country as large as Brazil, that are entitled to facilitated defense of their interests as consumers and vulnerable individuals. Therefore, in order to attend to the interests of parties in lawsuits who lack sufficient means, assigning competence to a local court to try individual claims is justified.

44 STJ, Special Appeal No. 911.802/RS, 1st Panel, Rapporteur Justice José Delgado, 24 October 2007.

45 WATANABE ET AL., *supra* note 25 at 73.

46 For understanding the concept of repeat players and one-shotters, *see* Marc Galanter, *Why the 'Haves' Come out Ahead: Speculations on the Limits of Legal Change*, 9 LAW & SOCIETY REVIEW 95, 121 (1974).

47 Article 1037, Section 4, of the Civil Procedure Code establishes that repetitive extraordinary or special appeals, as well as habeas corpus, have priority over other appeals.

8.3.5 *Notification, Incentives and the Institutional Design of Class Actions*

This case sheds light on the notification requirements and institutional incentives established by Brazilian law to bring class actions.

Class action notice, in Brazil, is primarily confined to official publications that reach a limited public almost entirely comprised of legal professionals.[48] In our case, this restricted publicity of the class actions was insufficient for interested parties to join while the lawsuit was still underway. Information about the class actions was missing even within the primary institutions representing the plaintiffs. The Public Prosecutor's Offices that had filed some of the class actions could not provide accurate or reliable information regarding the number of class actions filed or the subject matter of the litigation.[49] What this case shows is that the institution most involved in the Brazilian class action system – the Public Prosecutor's Office – does not dispose of internal controls for the class actions filed by its officials.

At the time, official registries that potentially interested parties could consult for information about class actions did not exist. Currently there is a provision for the National Registry of Collective Actions contemplated in the Joint Resolution from February 2011 by the National Council of Justice (CNJ) and the National Council of the Public Prosecutor's Office (CNMP). The data that would permit the registry to perform its function, however, has not been entered.[50] Fully implementing the registry is fundamental for not only improving the administration and management of the lawsuits but also so that citizens can follow the lawsuits that interest them, learning about the process and decisions and restraining from filing unnecessary individual lawsuits.

In contrast to the difficulty of finding information about class actions, the possibility of filing individual claims was duly disclosed. The case study reveals that lawyers interested in representing individual plaintiffs broadly publicized the supposedly high chance of success of these lawsuits through several communication media.[51] The disparity between the publicity given to individual and class action lawsuits calls attention to the difference between the financial incentives behind each.

As a rule in Brazil, except in cases where the beneficiary receives free legal assistance, each party bears its own share of the costs and actions as the lawsuit plays out. For example, each party pays the honoraria of the expert witnesses it chooses to call to testify. Whoever loses the case is responsible for the court fees, which correspond to the costs and expenses covered by the winning party as well as the lawyers' fees and are determined by the judge following the criteria

48 Article 94 of the CDC stipulates that once a class action is filed, an announcement must be published in the official outlet so that interested parties can join as co-plaintiffs without the burden of ample disclosure through social media for consumer defense organizations.

49 Watanabe et al., *supra* note 25 at 11. This study indicates that neither the Public Prosecutor's Office nor Brazilian courts dispose of the necessary information for an empirical analysis of the issue: *Id.* at 24. Civil inquiries represent the primary instrument for collecting evidence before a class action is filed. Conduct adjustment agreements are tools placed at the disposal of the Public Prosecutor's Office that allow them to engage and commit the interested parties to adjust their behavior in accordance with legal requirements through the threat of sanction.

50 Instead of fully implementing this registry, the CNJ and CNMP decided to create new one, the National Observatory on Highly Complex Environmental, Economic, and Social Questions of Major Impact (*Observatório Nacional sobre Questões Ambientais, Econômicas e Sociais de Alta Complexidade e Grande Impacto e Repercussão*). It contains information about the class actions arising from two recent dam failures (the Fundão Dam and the Mina do Córrego do Feijão Dam, commonly referred to in the press as Mariana and Brumadinho). *See* http://observatorionacional.cnj.jus.br/observatorionacional/index.php(last access July 9, 2019).

51 Watanabe et al., *supra* note 25 at 76.

established by the Civil Procedure Code.[52] If the case is settled, the parties are free to negotiate the division of the costs, court and lawyer fees according to their will.

For class actions, in contrast, the law waives the plaintiff's responsibility to cover the initial court fees, expert witness honoraria and any other expenses. Nor does the plaintiff have to pay the trial costs if the class action is dismissed – unless the court finds that a civil organization has acted in bad faith.[53] In the case of a successful suit, the law does not discuss the value to be paid to the lawyers representing the class action, nor does it contemplate settlement between the parties, except for conduct adjustment agreements approved by the Public Prosecutor's Office or when damages for acts of ethnic discrimination are assessed.

The lack of a clear rule regulating lawyer fees has meant that these tend to be fixed along the phases of the lawsuit. They are fixed in the first phase to compensate the lawyers for the preparatory phase that ends when the trial judge adjudicates the class action. In the event of the claim being granted, the judge issues a generic ruling that does not stipulate the value of the award for the coplaintiffs nor the form of payment.[54] After this ruling, each of the aggrieved coplaintiffs requests to the court the amount due to them in an specific incident – each of these claims can be contested by the defendant. The value of the lawyer fees is determined for each lawyer depending on the number of plaintiffs and incidents of wrongdoing they represented.

As is plain to see, Brazil's legal system remains bureaucratic and ineffective. This is compounded by the common understanding that it is necessary, even if the court grants the class action, for each aggrieved party to file individual claims specifying the incidents for which they are due because the awards are so general and ineffective. By consequence, much of what is gained by class actions in terms of efficiency and inclusion in the preparatory phase of the lawsuit is lost in the execution of the damage award, especially if the values involved are not significant. In the current system, collective awards are exceptional. They occur only when individual awards have already been handed down (which does not free a coplaintiff from the need to contract a lawyer to obtain their share of the collective award)[55] or if, after a year from the date of judgment, a number of the aggrieved parties compatible with the seriousness of the harm have not received their share. In that case, it may be solicited for the Fund for the Defense of Diffuse Rights (FDD).[56]

[52] As a general rule, Article 85, § 2 of the Civil Procedure Code holds that lawyers' fees will be fixed between a minimum of 10 and a maximum of 20 percent of the value of the award, of the economic profit perceived or, when measuring it is not possible, of the updated value of the claim, keeping in mind (1) the degree of diligence of the professional, (2) the location where the service was provided, (3) the nature and importance of the claim and (4) the work performed by the lawyer and the time required for it.

[53] Article 18 of the LACP contemplates only the hypothesis that civil organizations, and not public bodies, act in bad faith.

[54] Article 95 of the CDC simply states that, in the event of the claim being upheld, the award will be generic, and the defendant will be responsible for the harms caused.

[55] Article 98 of the CDC establishes that the execution of an award can be collective, when requested by the legitimate parties in accordance with the terms of Article 82, including victims whose awards were already determined, regardless other pending awards.

[56] Pursuant to Law No 9.008/1995, and Articles 13 of the LACP and 100 of the CDC, The FDD is the recipient of values derived, among other sources, from condemnations in class actions, and its resources must be applied in defense of diffuse and collective interests. Because it is a public fund, the use of resources depends on their inclusion in the federal budget. In the last seven years, the contingency reached 98.5% of the R $ 2.3 billion destined to the FDD. Recently, the Federal Court granted an injunction ordering the Union to stop contingenting FDD resources and to allocate all the money to the compulsory purposes (Case 5008138-68.2017.4.03.6105 of the 6th Federal Court of Campinas). Unfortunately, in the case of agreements with the Public Prosecution Service, especially in the Conduct Adjustment Terms, the destination for other entities has been understood as legitimate, which may raise doubts about any conflict of interest of those involved – in the same line of criticism that are made to cy pres in US class action settlements (*see, e.g.*, Rhonda Wasserman, *Cy Pres in Class Action Settlements.* S. CAL. L. REV. 88 (2014)).

There are also a large number of subdivisions within the two primary phases of the class action process that, combined with the lack of clarity regarding lawyer fees already described, may explain why judges traditionally assign quite modest remuneration. The amount does not bear any relation to the potential or actual award, which further aggravates the lack of incentives for lawyers to take up collective causes.

8.3.6 *Joining a Class Action*

In Brazil, joining a class action depends on the object of the lawsuit and the category of the collective right involved – diffuse, collective or homogenous individual rights.[57] As a general rule, favorable decisions benefit people who do not actively participate in the lawsuits as coplaintiffs and definitely those who do. People who file individual claims upon learning of a class action, however, must request the suspension of their individual lawsuit in order to take part in the award of the class action.[58]

Because of the difficulty of clearly distinguishing between the three categories of collectively actionable rights, ideally, the artificial and troublesome distinction should be abandoned and the regime for class actions unified. Moreover, a solution should be found for the disincentives that discourage people from taking part in class actions. One such disincentive is the risk that coplaintiffs face if the class action is dismissed. Dismissal means that the judgment comprises *res judicata* for all of the coplaintiffs, but not for people who abstained from joining as coplaintiffs.[59] People who do not join the class action as coplaintiffs thus obtain the benefit if the suit is successful but not the full disadvantage of an unsuccessful class action.[60] This design feature encourages passive free riding over active participation in class actions.

Adopting the opt-out (or automatic inclusion) system would strengthen the class action by extending the reach of the decision to a greater number of people affected by a particular lawsuit. This system deserves serious consideration in Brazil. It serves the public interest (by facilitating compensatory awards for harm caused, creating disincentives for harmful behavior by large bureaucratic organizations and bolstering society's estimation of the legal system's effectiveness) and also the interests of repeat players, in that it offers an efficient path to global peace.

The opt-in system may be considered appropriate when certain conditions are present, for example, when the class size is small and its members easily identified to facilitate the sharing of information. Requiring an active attitude – an opt-in system – in order for members of a class to receive compensation for an illicit offense, however, aggravates a preexisting defect of the Brazilian class action system: its low degree of effectiveness. As Richard Thaler and Cass Sunstein have shown,[61] people tend to adopt the attitudes that involve the fewest obstacles,

57 According to Article 103 of the CDC, *res judicata* will depend on the result of the lawsuit and the nature of the right involved: if the right is diffuse, collective, or individual, *res judicata* will be (1) *erga omnes* unless the claim is dismissed for insufficient evidence, in which case anyone else with legal standing can attempt another lawsuit with the same argument using new evidence, or (2) *ultra partes*, but limited to the group, category or class except when dismissed for insufficient evidence as described in (1), when involving the hypothesis contemplated in clause II of Article 81, or (3) *erga omnes*, only if the lawsuit is granted, to benefit all the victims and their successors, in the hypothesis of clause III of Article 81.

58 Article 104 of the CDC.

59 Article 103, § 2, CDC.

60 Teori Albino Zavascki, Processo Coletivo: Tutela de Direitos Coletivos e Tutela Coletiva de Direitos (2005).

61 Richard H. Thaler & Cass R. Sunstein, Nudge: Improving Decisions about Health, Wealth, and Happiness (2008).

a trait that discourages them from participating in class actions and deprives them from their benefits.

In the US, critics of the opt-out system focus on the coplaintiff's lack of control over the lawyers representing the case and the risk of collusion or disadvantageous settlements to which companies agree in order to minimize their financial exposure, considering that, to a certain degree, the size of the class might actually endanger the solvency of companies.

Some countries have adopted systems that combine opt-out and opt-in class actions, the former being for residual cases in which the amount of damage per person is small.[62] In light of the purpose of this paper, which is to identify mechanisms to improve Brazil's class action system, priority should be given to aggregating the power of potential litigants, stimulating public debate and attaining better results in terms of damage awards. Hence, the opt-out system would remain preferable as a general rule. Future experience could provide valid exceptions to ground opt-in alternatives. But adopting a general opt-in regime would be extremely important to stimulate collective litigation in Brazil.

8.3.7 *Evidence System*

Another Brazilian system's deficiency that affected the outcome of the basic landline phone subscription fees' litigation is the lack of an adequate system for the discovery of facts. This feature enabled the defendant, a repeat player, to argue that a decision in favor of the class action would cause the collapse of the telephone service or make it impossible for the providers to meet their obligations. In summary, since the system is based on the idea that all evidence shall be provided by the plaintiff, the defendant can present groundless claims without substantive proof, only to create a doubt with regards to the original claims of the plaintiff.

While such threats may often influence judges in practice, they are rarely backed-up by proof in lawsuits, especially in individual claims such as those that preceded the class action lawsuits against the increased residential telephone service fees. This is a major issue, since such individual claims may create negative precedents affecting the class actions filed with regards to the same issue. The idea that the full burden of proof lies on the plaintiff is clearly incompatible with the collective litigation system. Since in collective litigation it is clear that the public interest is at stake, and certain proof require very specialized knowledge, in individual cases, the idea that the burden of proof lies with the plaintiff is still very strong in case law. This creates what we will describe as being the "scarecrow strategy," which is to present a groundless argument, based, for example, on unsubstantiated economic allegations. The effect of such "scarecrow strategy" is to lead to a ruling for lack of proof, which may be effective in many cases in which the period of the statute of limitation might have already extinguished, transforming a ruling based on lack of proof on a definitive victory for the defendants.

The Brazilian legal system significantly differs from the United States system in terms of the expected role of the judge. In the US, it is expected that the judge will exert an active role in structural litigation, abandoning a passive judicial posture.[63] In Brazil, conversely, the general expectation is that the judge will take a passive role in the production of evidence, only deciding what proof is admissible or not, considering the documents, expert opinions and testimony provided by the parties in the lawsuit, regardless of the adequacy of representation – which the

62 This is the case in Denmark, Norway, Sweden and Israel. *See* ADA PELLEGRINI GRINOVER ET AL., O PROCESSO COLETIVO NOS PAÍSES DE CIVIL LAW E COMMON LAW: UMA ANÁLISE DE DIREITO COMPARADO 240 (2nd ed., 2008).

63 *See* Owen M. Fiss, *Foreword: The forms of justice*. HARV. L. REV. 93 (1979); Abram Chayes, *The role of the judge in public law litigation*. HARV. L. REV. 89 (1975).

judge is not expected to supervise. The pretrial discovery phase is also much more limited in scope in Brazil, besides being more formalistic, requiring close oversight by the judge.

The Brazilian system is thus prone to error in two important ways. The first involves the insufficient system for collecting evidence itself, and the second is the compounding effect of this defect on complex litigations. This second effect results from the complex play between individual and collective claims. Basically, individual claims with much more limited evidence, usually subject to the "scarecrow strategy" mentioned above, may be ruled first, and, as a result, impact negatively in the rulings applicable to class actions. Such problem becomes particularly clear in claims in which financial and economic considerations are central, such as in the present case of the telephone service fee studied herein. In this particular case, as it will be analyzed in further detail below (Section 8.3.4), an individual claim created the precedent for the decisions in all of the class actions, without taking into consideration the full economic implications of the decision by upholding the legality of the increase in the phone services fees.

8.3.8 *Remedial Phase and Settlements*

We have already expressed our criticism about the generic decisions in Brazilian class actions that require at least one, and, sometimes, more than one legal proceeding to make a class action effective. The multiplication of thousands of claims that ensues the generic rulings overwhelms the court system, slowing other legal proceedings. Moreover, overflowing dockets generally push the judiciary towards more conservative positions, reducing the prospect of driving social change through the courts.[64] The legislator, as the "architect of options,"[65] must consider the incentives that the institutional design (or its flaws) creates in the interest of favoring legal debate in the broadest sense. The impact of the system's pull towards conservativism is especially felt in consumer law, for modern society is increasingly reliant on contracts of adhesion whose bias towards large corporations has been upheld by the courts.

In the US, there is always the promise of a comprehensive agreement that can serve as an incentive for the company to accept settlements that benefit the group. This global agreement does not threaten to unleash a storm of similar lawsuits as often occurs in Brazil when a class action is successful. In Brazil, there are limited possibilities for out-of-court settlements to class actions.

A notable exception occurred in 2017 in the context of the largest repetitive litigation in Brazil's history. Stemming from the unorthodox measures implemented by the government to combat hyperinflation in the 1980s and 90s,[66] the representatives of the plaintiffs and those of the banks (Febraban and Consif) reached and signed an agreement in 2017 through the mediation and with the approval of Brazil's Attorney General and Central Bank. The agreement determined the amount to be paid by the banks to savings account holders due to the deficient inflation adjustments that occurred as a consequence of the "Bresser," "Verão" and "Collor II" economic plans.

64 For this argument, *see* Marc Galanter, *Why the 'Haves' Come out Ahead: Speculations on the Limits of Legal Change*, 9 Law & Society Review 95, 121 (1974); Duncan Kennedy. A Critique of Adjudication [fin de siècle] (2009).

65 *See* Thaler & Sunstein, *supra* note 61.

66 Various drastic economic measures were implemented during the 1980s and 90s to stave off hyperinflation, including the freezing of financial assets and personal bank accounts. According to the plaintiffs and their representatives, the percentage rate used by banks to determine how much money remained in their savings accounts following the measures was lower than it should have been.

The agreement set a five-year statute of limitations for class actions, matching the Superior Court of Justice's decision in the case of the economic plans.[67] This ruling had overturned the previous understanding that the statute of limitations for individual claims and class actions should be the same and should be determined by the quality of the claim and not the type of lawsuit employed to make it.

By approving the agreement in 2018, the STF affirmed the capacity of private entities with legal standing to settle class actions out of court as well as the legitimacy of contingency fees assigned on the value of the settlement amount. Neither practice is contemplated in current law or was even considered legally possible prior to this case.

8.4 ABUSE OF DOMINANT POSITION TO PURCHASE MEDICATIONS

This case study focuses on the abuse of dominant market position in the pharmaceutical industry. Cases involving the purchases of medications by Brazilian public health organizations illustrate the difficulty that the judiciary has in dealing with economic issues and the risks of the lack of expertise of the Public Prosecutor's Office in these matters. Before going into the details, we will examine the institutional problem that stems from the protagonist role played by the Public Prosecutor's Office in the Brazilian class action system. This problem involves the expectation that the Public Prosecutor's Office is the most legitimate institution for the collective defense of rights in the courts.

8.4.1 *The Primacy of the Public Prosecutor's Office in Class Actions*

This primacy has a legal foundation in certain instances and is merely customary in others.[68] In any case, the academic debate over the institutional configuration for the defense of collective interests requires further development. Certain institutional characteristics of the Public Prosecutor's Office suggest that it should not be the only institution – in practice or in theory – that is responsible for public interest litigation in Brazil.[69]

[67] The STJ justified its change of opinion by noting the lack of any statute of limitations for class actions and recommended applying analogically the five-year term contemplated in Article 21 of Law no. 4717/65 (Special Appeal No. 1.070.896/SC, Rapporteur Justice Luis Felipe Salomão, 4 August 2010). For contrary decisions, *see*: Special Appeal 200.827/SP, Rapporteur Justice Carlos Alberto Menezes Direito, 9 December 2002; Special Appeal No. 761.114/RS, Rapporteur Justice Nancy Andrighi, 3 August 2006; Special Appeal No. 331374/SP, Rapporteur Justice Francisco Falcão, 17 June 2003. Because of the STJ's new understanding, the holders of savings accounts who were waiting for a favorable decision in the class action lawsuits filed their individual claims arguing that the statute of limitations for individual claims was suspended when the class actions were accepted. In response to this argument, some judges held that savings account holders who had not filed individual claims within the twenty-year statute of limitations could not benefit from the suspension of the statute of limitations caused by the class action since each has its own distinct statute of limitations (Special Appeal 22.484/RS, Rapporteur Justice Minister Ricardo Villas Bôas Cueva, 5 December 2014) while other judges held that the class action did suspend the statute of limitations for individual claims (Special Appeal 1426620/RS, Rapporteur Justice Marco Aurélio Bellizze, 12 August 2015). The shift in the STJ's position on the statute of limitations indicates the degree of institutional uncertainty that continues to surround the issue. Although it is obvious that the system should have a clear response for both the statute of limitations and tolling, one does not yet exist. A detailed explanation of the litigation regarding the heterodox economic plans case can be seen in: Helena C. Refosco, Access-to-Justice Reforms: A Brazilian Case Study of Bank Litigation Related to Heterodox Economic Plans, GLOBAL JURIST, available at www.degruyter.com/view/journals/gj/ahead-of-print/article-10.1515-gj-2020-0018/article-10.1515-gj-2020-0018.xml?language=en .

[68] ROGÉRIO BASTOS ARANTES, MINISTÉRIO PÚBLICO E POLÍTICA NO BRASIL (2002). NATALIA LANGENEGGER, LEGITIMIDADE ATIVA DE PESSOAS FÍSICAS EM AÇÕES COLETIVAS: INCENTIVOS E DESINCENTIVOS INSTITUCIONAIS 33 (2014).

[69] Among these characteristics, Oscar Vilhena Vieira emphasizes the following: (1) it possesses utter autonomy to choose the cases it litigates; (2) mechanisms for democratic control or pressure from civil society are absent; (3) it

Furthermore, it is not only in Brazil that this primacy has been questioned. In the early stages of creating systems for collective rights protection, many countries chose to assign their protection to government institutions such as the Public Prosecutor's Office. According to Mauro Cappelletti, the decision to do so has been a failure in most places, whether because of the private, albeit collective, nature of many collective rights, or because of the high degree of specialized expertise required, that the Public Prosecutor's Office rarely possesses.[70]

In this scenario, we would recommend beginning by expanding the competence to launch class actions. In the current system, only public offices or specialized private associations that are over a year old can initiate them.[71] This system only confers a secondary role to the affected parties and their lawyers who, as the US experience demonstrates, possess the conditions and motivation to play a protagonist role in this type of litigation. Government institutions, even when displaying specialized units, often lack incentives for the officials to investigate claims deemed less relevant as deeply as they should. Although public institutions should have an efficiency advantage from repeated litigation experience, their staff's training tends to be of a general nature (partly deriving from the type of process and examinations the institutions use to select employees), which implies additional marginal costs if the officials must acquire more specialized knowledge of public and regulatory policies. In this scenario, it is not difficult to imagine that less than optimal investment will be made in acquiring the additional information, since the cost of acquiring complex information will be borne by the individual, while the results of the investment primarily benefit the collective.

There is also a question of scarcity. As the number of public servants and the amount of resources available to them are finite, it would be logical to concentrate them on legal violations where there are not any market incentives for private lawyers to act. In Brazil, resistance to expanding the competence to initiate class action lawsuits stems from the fear that it would be abused, especially by lawyers exempted from paying court fees if the case is dismissed.[72]

To reduce the resistance to expanded standing, the law could attribute to the judge the power to evaluate the financial capacity of the representatives of the class and the seriousness of the claim. Only after confirming the claim's relevance and the litigant's financial need would the judge exempt the representatives of the class and their lawyers from responsibility for court fees. Also, to certify a class, the court verifies that the choices of plaintiff and lawyer to represent the

tends towards bureaucratization; (4) pronounced political partisanship can be seen in certain departments; there is considerable risk of co-optation by middle-class interests. (*Estado de Direito e Advocacia de Interesse Público* 360–61, in ESTADO DE DIREITO E O DESAFIO DO DESENVOLVIMENTO (Oscar Vilhena Vieira & Dimitri Dimoulis eds., 2011)). Antonio Herman Benjamin has also made critical observations, seeing risks for the institution in terms of: (1) indifference towards certain types of lawsuits; (2) exposure to political pressure; (3) institutional capture; (4) limited human and material resources. (*A Insurreição da Aldeia Global Contra o Processo Civil Clássico: Apontamentos sobre a Opressão e a Libertação Judiciais do Meio Ambiente e do Consumidor* 357, in AÇÃO CIVIL PÚBLICA (LEI 7.347/85 – REMINISCÊNCIAS E REFLEXÕES APÓS DEZ ANOS DE APLICAÇÃO) (Édis Milaré ed., 1995)).

70 Mauro Cappelletti, *Access to Justice as a Theoretical Approach to Law and a Practical Programme for Reform*, 109 S. AFRICAN L.J. 22 (1992). For a critique of the technique adopted in Brazil, that restricts the right to speak for collectivities to certain entities, such as the Public Prosecutor's Office, whose officials do not need to demonstrate the necessary knowledge of the concrete situation to sue, whereas groups are alienated from the right to speak for themselves, *see*: Sérgio Cruz Arenhart, *Processos Estruturais no Direito Brasileiro: Reflexões a Partir do Caso da ACP do Carvão*, REVISTA DE PROCESSO COMPARADO (2015).

71 Article 5 of the LACP establishes that the following organizations have the legal standing to file class actions: the Public Prosecutor's Office, the Public Defender's Office, federal, state, and municipal governments, state-owned or mixed-ownership enterprises or foundations, and associations that are over one year old following the terms of the law and whose objectives involve the protection of either public or social patrimony, the environment, consumers, economic order, open competition, the rights of racial, ethnic or religious groups, or artistic, aesthetic, historical, touristic or scenic patrimony.

72 *See* REFOSCO, *supra* note 9 at 105–09.

class are adequate prior to the initiation of proceedings. This mechanism should allow the judge, from the start of the lawsuit and whenever the need is perceived, to scrutinize carefully the technical and economic capacity of those who volunteer to represent the group, and whose duty it therefore is to perform these roles competently, seriously and credibly.

8.4.2 *The Case of Abusive Pricing of Trastuzumab*

In March 2015, the Law and Poverty Research Group (GDP) of the University of São Paulo School of Law (FDUSP) coordinated by Professors Calixto Salomão Filho and Carlos Portugal Gouvêa, presented the results of the group's empirical research entitled "Discrimination in the Access to Breast Cancer Medicine in Brazil" to the Federal Prosecutor's Office. Not long afterwards, Civil Inquiry no. 1.16.000.000699/2015–87 was opened in order to investigate possible irregularities in the sale of Trastuzumab (commercialized under the name of Herceptin®) by the pharmaceutical company Roche to state (as opposed to federal) health departments. The inquiry was to confirm whether the pricing practices were consistent with the sales made directly to the federal Ministry of Health.

On June 1, 2016, based on the results of that Civil Inquiry, the Federal Prosecutor's Office filed a class action in federal court along with a request for injunction for urgent relief against Roche's Brazilian subsidiary (*Produtos Roche Químicos e Farmacêuticos* S.A.), the Federal Union and the National Institute of Intellectual Property (INPI). The lawsuit was assigned to the 6th Civil Branch of the Judicial Section in the Federal District of Brasília.

Trastuzumab (Herceptin®) is used in chemotherapy and radiation therapy for patients with breast cancer. It is distributed in Brazil by the Roche pharmaceutical laboratory, which holds exclusive patent rights for Trastuzumab from the INPI. In 2012, it was placed on the list of medicaments publicly available that are covered by the Integrated Health System (SUS) for initial treatment and locally advanced breast cancer, but not for the treatment of breast cancer that has reached the metastasis phase. The public health system only purchased the medicament for patients with late-stage breast cancer when the patient obtained a court order for it.[73] The Civil Inquiry revealed that Roche charged a much higher price for these irregular court-ordered purchases. Whereas the medicine sold on average for 3423 Brazilian Reals per unit to the Ministry of Health, the state departments of health that purchased it on court order were paying an average of 7192 Brazilian Reals per unit. This represents abusive exercise by Roche of its industrial property rights consistent with illicit discriminatory pricing made possible by the negotiating power of the buyer.[74] In other words, Roche's monopolistic market power in

73 The practice of resorting to the judiciary by individual litigation for access to medicines or treatments not covered by the public health system is widespread throughout Brazil, driving the system to provide expensive treatments, many not listed in the Unified Health System as adopted medicine to be provided freely to the population and many also not event approved by the National Health Agency for commercialization, and having as recipient of such judicial awards individuals who are, to a large degree, members of the middle class with access to private doctors and lawyers. *See* Carlos Portugal Gouvêa, *Social Rights Against the Poor*, 7 VIENNA J. ON INT'L CONST. L. 454 (2013). For a critique on emancipating people as *rights holders*, *see* David W. Kennedy, *The International Human Rights Regime: Still Part of the Problem?*, in EXAMINING CRITICAL PERSPECTIVES ON HUMAN RIGHTS 19 (Rob Dickinson, Elena Katselli, Colin Murray & Ole W. Pedersen eds., 2012).

74 To support its argument regarding price discrepancy, the Federal Prosecutor's Office compared Roche's sales of Trastuzumab to its government sales of Rituximab (commercial name MabThera®), a drug that is similar in use and in logistical considerations. The results of the analyses were consistent (although not sufficiently proven). The analysis confirmed that there was no significant increase in the price of the decentralized sales compared to the price of the drug sold directly to the Ministry of Health. This demonstrates that the differentiation in the price of Trastuzumab was not explained by the logistical complications that Roche had alleged in response to Civil Inquiry that preceded the Public Civil Action in question.

a scenario of weak public institutions enabled arbitrary profit maximization, for the abusive pricing only occurred when a court had ordered the purchase of the medicament. The abuse also violated the rights of all potential beneficiaries of medications covered by the Integrated Health System.

The Federal Prosecutor's Office thus requested, among other motions:

(1) An injunction for urgent relief (and its subsequent confirmation) ordering Roche to sell Trastuzumab to all Brazilian public health outlets for the same price that the Ministry of Health paid;
(2) An order requiring Roche to reimburse the material harms incurred by the state departments of health between 2012 and the date of the order equal to the amount they had paid Roche in excess of the price paid by the Ministry of Health, a sum estimated at approximately 107.1 million Brazilian Reals;
(3) Moral damages for the harm done to the patients who relied on the Integrated Health System equal to twice the value of the material harm described in (2); and
(4) Condemnation of the INPI for conceding a compulsory license to Roche for reasons of public interest and for abusing the economic power of its patent pursuant to Articles 68 and 71 of Federal Law 9.279 of May 14, 1996.

Roche alleged in its response that it had acted in strict conformity with the legislation in force and the resolutions of the Medication Market Regulation Chamber (CMED). It argued that there were legal and market-related circumstances that justified the difference in the price of the Herceptin® sold to state departments of health and to the Ministry of Health. Therefore, Roche had not committed any illicit anticompetitive act.

The justifying circumstances mentioned were, in sum: economies of scale; risk of defaulted payments from the state departments of health; sales logistics; distance between the locations of distribution and delivery of the medicament; and the variance in tax rates and the obligatory minimum discount (CAP) across states. The main argument was that the costs were driven up by the combination of the lower quantity of the sales and the shorter time Roche had to fill them to comply with the court orders, which forced it to modify its supply line. Roche also argued that the compulsory licensing requirements were not met, that only the Ministry of Health could challenge the price difference and that the judiciary did not possess the competence to judge the merit of this administrative matter.

On August 7, 2017, the judge denied the injunction for urgent relief on the grounds that the argument over the differentiation in prices because of logistical complications was disputed and therefore required additional evidence. The judge also declared that there was no proof that the prices charged by Roche were superior to those fixed by the CMED.

When informed of the judge's denial of the injunction for urgent relief and request for further proof, the Federal Prosecutor's Office responded that it had no additional proof to offer other than the evidence already presented in the case file that were the basis of its request. Here the Federal Prosecutor's Office undeniably missed an opportunity to broaden the debate over an extremely important topic. In the first place, it was the first time an allegation of abusive pricing of medication based on dominant market position had been brought to court. In other words, experts in the area should have been brought in to testify, such as nongovernmental organizations devoted to the subject or national and international research groups, not to mention countless other sources of specialized expertise. The wasted opportunity is truly deplorable for, had it the standing to represent the case, a civil society organization with experience in contentious litigation wouldn't have lost it. At the same time, the case displays the already criticized passive role of the judge in conducting the lawsuit, despite the obvious lack of adequacy of representation of the plaintiff.

On August 22, 2018, in accordance with Article 487, I of the Brazilian Civil Procedure Code, the class action was dismissed. The arguments presented by Roche were granted and the charges of abuse of intellectual property rights were deemed unfounded, as was the infraction of economic order based on exorbitant pricing in a monopolistic market. The decision evidenced the difficulties confronted by the judiciary when adjudicating class actions. Precisely because they involve aggregated dispute resolution, they do not fit the traditional structure for disputes that are easy to break down into elements. They often involve evidence that is economic in nature. In this case, refined knowledge of market economics is required to appreciate the evidence of abusive pricing and price discrepancy in analogical conditions, for price, within the economic system, itself aggregates all of the relevant information. Logistical costs, for example, are always secondary and cannot explain the price discrepancy of over 100 percent as in this case. Moreover, only the seller disposes of the information necessary to formulate an adequate explanation of the actual impact of logistical costs on the product's price.

In the case at hand, the trial judge, who failed to understand economic aspects of the case, was convinced by the strategy of Roche. The strategy consisted of, on one hand, abstaining from providing any concrete information about the logistical costs that could justify the difference in price and, on the other side, alleging that the burden of proof lay with the Federal Prosecutor's Office to show that no justification whatsoever for the discrepancy in price existed. That the strategy was successful is surprising to people well-versed in economic reasoning. In this case, the improbable became reality, for the judge followed the argumentation presented by Roche point by point.

On November 14, 2018, the Federal Prosecutor's Office appealed the decision, reiterating the same arguments contained in the statement of claim. After the defendant presented its counter-arguments, on April 4, 2019, the same Federal Prosecutor's Office, through another member (its regional official), delivered its opinion on the case.[75] The opinion covered in detail the lack of proof that led to the initial dismissal of the class action and ratified the arguments of that judgment. In other words, as unbelievable as it may appear, the Federal Prosecutor's Office, after appealing the dismissal of the class action that it had filed, was asked to produce an opinion on the case as if it were an independent consultant. If that in itself is surprising, then the result of the opinion is absolutely shocking, for the Federal Prosecutor's Office, to all effects the lawyer representing the class action, issued an opinion that rejected its own claims. It is difficult to imagine how the behavior of the Federal Prosecutor's Office could be explained to the citizens affected by the case's dismissal or to the civil society organizations that followed it. The Federal Prosecutor's Office's behavior delegitimizes its status as an organ for the prosecution of rights violations in the future. Who would reach out to a law firm in which one of the lawyers was liable to issue an opinion against a case that the firm is representing? Legally speaking, it is simply absurd and, moreover, a wanton allocation of public resources.

In response to the appalling scenario just described, we suggest there should be a mechanism allowing entities that bring cases to the Public Prosecutor's Office, such as the GDP, to take part in any class action that may ensue.[76] When the Public Prosecutor's Office's advocacy is defective,

75 Communication No. 334/2019/GABPRR47-APMS (Opinion).

76 The Civil Procedure Code has a provision (article 138) in the sense that the judge may, considering the relevance of the matter, the specificity of the subject matter of the claim or the social repercussion of the controversy, solicit or admit the participation of a natural or legal person, specialized agency or entity, with adequate representation, to join the lawsuit. The powers of amicus curiae are defined by the judge in the decision requesting or admitting

whether because of lack of resources or technical knowledge of the disputed issue, it should be able to collaborate with civil society organizations. This would serve to improve the technical quality of the Public Prosecutor's Office's arguments and avoid errors such as the failure to offer proof during the discovery phase.

8.5 CONCLUSION

To a certain degree, the incompleteness of Brazil's democratic transition is revealed by the unsatisfying quality of its system for the collective defense of rights. Nonetheless for notable exceptions,[77] the judiciary usually displays a reactionary posture towards class actions. Not surprisingly, the case law related to different legal aspects of class actions, such as statutes of limitations, legal standing and effective jurisdiction, has been restricted in a way that has favored the continuing epidemic of individual claims in Brazil.

The case studies have proven right our hypothesis that the Brazilian class action is insufficient as a remedy for infringements of the rights of third parties by private companies. As a consequence, Brazilian population – specially the poorest – is left without adequate means for the protections of its collective rights against mass violations by private companies. Businesses can calculate with precision the degree of misbehavior they can maintain, for an immense segment of the population does not have access to justice. There exists, therefore, an enormous stimulus for companies to generate negative externalities. The effect of low-level harms caused to consumers can reach tragic proportions. For instance, in less than five years, two huge environmental disasters related to dam failures have taken place, without the affected population being compensated yet. The failure at Mariana in 2015 released a record level of toxins into the surrounding rivers, whereas Brumadinho's dam collapse caused great loss of human and natural life.

Legislative reforms are necessary to roll back the conservative interpretations imposed by the judiciary in many areas, as we have seen throughout this chapter. New laws on their own, however, will not solve the problems, nor will they relieve the judiciary of its responsibility to participate more effectively in shoring up legal certainty. Otherwise, we will be forced to live like eternal prisoners of the same story that repeats itself every time legislative reforms comes up against a conservative justice system.[78]

Legislative reform of the class action system would need to symbolize a change of mentality. In light of the spreading epidemic of individual claims in Brazil, and in order to avoid its perpetuation, the legislation must be altered to give greater legal standing to initiate class actions to private agents and to give judges greater freedom to supervise the procedures. Creating a mechanism of adequate compensation for private lawyers who take up class actions is essential, one that permits the payment of contingency fees, while at the same time incorporating a system for the certification of the class on an opt-out basis.

intervention. Unfortunately, however, the law does not provide incentives for such participation, which for this reason turns out to be unusual.

77 An example of a notable exception was the granting of the collective habeas corpus order filed on behalf of all women prisoners that were pregnant, or mothers of children and disabled persons under her care. (STF, Habeas Corpus No. 143.641 – SP, 2nd Panel, Rapporteur Justice Ricardo Lewandowski, 20 February 2018.

78 This posture of the judiciary we criticize brings to mind the warnings of Hirschl, who observed how the judiciary, reluctant to confront the other branches of government, seeks refuge in the "safe zone" of individual rights, avoiding politically charged disputes involving the principles of federalism and the separation of power. Hirschl gives the example of Russia under the leadership of Boris Yeltsin, who suspended the Constitutional Court by decree. After reinstating it, the Court largely restrained itself to cases involving individual rights, avoiding politically sensitive cases, such as those involving disputes over the separation of powers. *See* Ran Hirschl, *The New Constitutionalism and the Judicialization of Pure Politics Worldwide*, 75 FORDHAM L. REV. 752 (2006).

Another critical feature missing are specialized courts for collective causes, with fast-track capacity and support from other government offices including, for example, regulatory agencies. Class actions are inherently complex and require judges who feel it is their vocation to adjudicate them, which could occur if specialized courts were created. Judging class actions is undeniably more complex than ruling individual claims. By consequence, it would be mistaken to count the adjudication of a class action that affects millions of people the same as an individual claim when measuring a judge's productivity. Specialized courts could correct this and other distortions by incorporating differentiated objectives.

Adopting by judicial interpretation a shorter statute of limitations for class actions jeopardizes the class action system, which should have clear rules regarding statute of limitations and tolling. Similarly, the formalist distinction between diffuse, collective and homogenous individual rights has proven ineffective and troublesome. This distinction should be struck from the legislation.

Reforming legislation is a small but important step towards a better system for the protection of collective rights. However, there is much to be done in the realm of judicial culture as well as in developing critical thought in law schools. Hopefully then class actions will finally be able to perform the function for which they were meant: to expand access to justice, to reduce social inequality and, by consequence, to strengthen democracy.

PART III

Europe

9

English Systems of Multiparty Litigation

Neil Andrews

9.1 INTRODUCTION

In England and Wales there are four types of collective redress or multiparty claim:[1] (1) test case litigation, supported by the staying of related individual actions; (2) consolidation or joinder, that is, procedural adjustment to accommodate multiparty actions; the result is that multiple parties are coupled together in a single case;[2] (3) opt-in claims coordinated as a Group Litigation Order;[3] and (4) representative proceedings.[4] As for (4), there are two manifestations. First there is a general mechanism, not restricted to any particular context, but aggregated damages have not been available and the relief is normally confined to declarations or injunctions.[5] That general mechanism has a long history and originated in the procedure adopted in Equity before the Judicature Acts 1873–5. Secondly, the Consumer Rights Act 2015 introduced opt-out representative proceedings with aggregated damages. But that mechanism is confined to competition law matters.

9.1.1 *Fundamental Points*

There are seven general issues concerning a civil procedural system's possible adoption of arrangements for collective redress, that is, multiparty claims.

(1) *Threshold requirement.* There must be a significant number of persons who are allegedly harmed, or whose interests are threatened, in the same or a similar way.

(2) *Modes of vindication.* In order to protect those interests, there can be either (1) public or (2) private vindication, or a combination. As for (2), legal systems can offer a choice between, or a combination of, opt-in and opt-out systems. England offers a combination.

[1] Neil Andrews, *Multi-Party Litigation: Fundamental Issues*, in V. Harsagi and C. H. van Rhee (eds.), *Multi-Party Redress Mechanisms in Europe: Squeaking Mice?* (Intersentia Publishing, Cambridge, 2014), 111–26.

[2] Neil Andrews, *Multi-Party Proceedings in England: Representative and Group Actions* 11 Duke J. Com. Int. L. 249, 257 (2001); noting Civil Procedure Rules (1998) 3.1(2)(g); Civil Procedure Rules (1998) 19.1; Civil Procedure Rules (1998) 19.2(3); ordinary joinder of co-claimants in *Lubbe* v. *Cape plc* [2000] 1 *Weekly Law Reports* 1545, House of Lords (over 3,000 claimants).

[3] Civil Procedure Rules (1998) 19.10–19.15; Practice Direction (19B).

[4] Civil Procedure Rules (1998) 19.6; Neil Andrews, *Multi-Party Proceedings in England: Representative and Group Actions* 11 Duke J. Com. Int. L. 249, 250–7 (2001).

[5] E. Oteiza (ed.), *Procesos Colectivos – Class Actions* (I International Conference & XXIII Iberoamerican Procedural Law Convention) (Buenos Aires: IIDP – AADP, 2012) (reports submitted to the International Congress, 6–9 June 2012, Argentina).

The technique of class/group civil procedure can be combined with: (1) mediated settlement or (2) judicially ratified settlement (as in the Dutch system).[6] Outside the USA, where adhesion arbitration clauses have been upheld, class arbitration seems a remote prospect because of the need for free consent to arbitration clauses.

(3) *Who is the representative?* Under the opt-out system, there is the central issue: who will be the representative? In Scandinavian countries,[7] various models are to be found: public representatives, consumer association representatives and private representatives. In the USA and England, the main form of representative is a private individual.

(4) *What type of relief is available?* If damages are available, compensatory sums must (1) involve award of the global amount and (2) provide a criterion for allocation of individual shares (not necessarily equal). Awards paid into court which are to be allocated *cy-près* are not attractive. Punitive damages are not favoured in many systems.

(5) *Special judicial selection and training.* The conduct of large claims involving many claimants (or interested represented persons) is a specialist judicial responsibility. In the interest of sound practice and consistency, judges should be chosen for their high ability and flexibility, and they should be specially trained to carry out this type of demanding case-management and eventual adjudication.

(6) *Visibility.* The public needs to have good access to the following information: (1) what are the procedures and how effective are they? (2) Is there a reliable register of such claims? (3) What judgments have been delivered and for how much?

(7) *Funding.* This is a fundamental problem in the field of multiparty litigation. Without practical or economic access to justice, a legal system will be creating merely empty procedural categories, unused train tracks which carry no traffic. However, public funding has fallen away. England and the USA have used contingency funding. Third-party funding is also growing in importance. In English civil litigation in general, 'economic access to justice'[8] is no longer significantly supported by public expenditure on legal aid. For example, in *A.B.* v. *Ministry of Defence* (2012)[9] Lord Phillips noted that the Legal Services Commission had initially funded claims brought by ex-servicemen, but had refused further funding, whereupon the claim proceeded on a conditional fee agreement basis.[10] The experience in that litigation typifies the general shift within English modern civil litigation towards the 'privatised' conditional fee system. This shift has also affected multiparty litigation. Formally, the rules and guidance permit public financial support of unusually deserving group litigation.[11] In fact public funding for group litigation is seldom granted.[12]

6 C. Hodges and A. Stadler (eds.), *Resolving Mass Disputes: ADR and Settlement of Mass Claims* (Edward Elgar, Cheltenham, 2013), chapters 1–9 (by various authors, concerning approaches in the Netherlands, England, Canada, the USA, Australia and China).

7 As reported by Laura Ervo (surveying Sweden, Norway, Finland and Denmark), in V. Harsagi and C. H. van Rhee (eds.), *Multi-Party Redress Mechanisms in Europe: Squeaking Mice?* (Intersentia Publishing, Cambridge, 2014), 243.

8 The distinction between formal and economic or 'effective' access to justice was acknowledged in *Hamilton* v. *Fayed (No. 2)* [2002] 3 *All England Law Reports* 641, CA, at [65], and [81]; for observations in the context of multi-party proceedings, C. Hodges, *The Europeanisation of Civil Justice: Trends and Issues* 26 Civil Justice Quarterly 96, 98 ff (2007).

9 [2012] UKSC9; [2013] 1 *Appeal Cases Reports* 78.

10 Ibid., at [152].

11 See 'The Funding Code', Part B, section D, issued by the Community Legal Services Commission.

12 R. Mulheron, *Reform of Collective Redress in England and Wales* (2008), chapter 11, at 74 www.civiljusticecouncil.gov.uk/files/collective_redress.pdf; see the following comment by C. Hodges at the 2006 Oxford conference on multiparty actions, cited with his permission: 'The previous freedom with which Legal Aid

9.2 THE TEST CASE MECHANISM

Large numbers of related claims might be stayed pending the outcome of a test case to be decided by the High Court, or a test case might proceed in a context where it is clear that there are many potential actions.[13] Test cases can also be used as part of the group litigation order system, on which see Section 9.4 below.

For example, in the bank charges litigation (2009) the English courts were asked to make a declaration on a point of law. In this test case a governmental agency responsible for consumer protection and regulation of trading practices invoked its statutory powers to seek a declaration. That remedy would be the precursor to a vast number of bank customers ultimately obtaining relief in respect of bank charges levied when current accounts become overdrawn without the bank's permission. But the test case failed on substantive grounds. The Supreme Court of the United Kingdom decided that there was no basis for challenging the relevant charges which, in essence, formed part of the price for having a current account.[14]

The test case technique remains available whenever public bodies have legal power disinterestedly to seek legal declarations (or other relief) on behalf of the community or segments of it. An unusual example in the private sphere is the piloted Financial Markets Test Scheme[15] (operative since 1 October 2015 until at least the end of September 2020). That scheme allows declaratory relief to be 'determined'[16] and 'resolved'[17] in a 'test case',[18] where the facts are agreed,[19] on a point of English law[20] which is contested by parties with 'opposing interests'[21] who are, or were, 'actively in business'[22] in the relevant market, even though no 'present cause of action'[23] has arisen between them. Such matters will be commenced 'by mutual agreement'[24] and then, where appropriate, permitted by the court to proceed as a 'qualifying claim'[25] within the Financial List.[26] Such claims must concern issues of 'general importance to the financial markets'[27] and they will be brought in order to procedure 'authoritative English law guidance'.[28] The court can be constituted, in cases of 'particular importance or urgency',[29] to comprise more than one Financial List judge or one such judge and a Lord or Lady Justice of Appeal. 'A relevant

was dispensed has disappeared. Public funding is restricted, made available for cases only on a prioritised basis, and subject to considerable bureaucracy. The Legal Services Commission is now very wary of funding large cases, and prefers to fund test cases. Only one case (Sabril, alleged visual field constriction, made by Sanofi-Aventis) is currently funded by the LSC: the action is proceeding with test cases'.

13 For details see Spencer Bower, *Turner and Handley's Actionable Misrepresentation* (5th ed., Lexis Nexis, London, 2014), 21.07.

14 *Office of Fair Trading* v. *Abbey National plc* [2009] UKSC6; [2010] 1 *Appeal Cases Reports* 696 (noted M. Chen-Wishart 126 Law Quarterly Review 157 (2010), and explained in Neil Andrews, *Contract Law* (2nd ed., Cambridge University Press, 2015), 15.36).

15 Practice Direction (51M).

16 Ibid., at para. 2.2.

17 Ibid., at para. 2.3.

18 Ibid., at para. 2.5(a).

19 Ibid., at para. 2.5(b).

20 Ibid., at paras 2.1 and 2.3.

21 Ibid., at paras 2.3 and 2.5(a).

22 Ibid., at para. 2.3.

23 Ibid., at para. 2.2.

24 Ibid., at para. 2.3.

25 Ibid., at para. 2.5(a) prescribes this need for judicial permission.

26 Ibid., at para. 1.1(b).

27 Ibid., at para. 2.1.

28 Ibid., at para. 2.1.

29 Ibid., at para. 2.5(d).

trade, professional or regulatory body or association'[30] or interested third parties[31] can be represented or joined in such proceedings. No costs order will be made.[32]

The background to this is that, since 1 October 2015, a new court receives very high-value (normally, over £50 million) litigation concerning financial markets.[33] The court is a 'Financial List', drawn from cases in either the Commercial Court or Chancery Court in London.[34] Such matters are defined as follows:[35]

> 'Financial List claim' means any claim which – (a) principally relates to loans, project finance, banking transactions, derivatives and complex financial products, financial benchmark, capital or currency controls, bank guarantees, bonds, debt securities, private equity deals, hedge fund disputes, sovereign debt, or clearing and settlement, and is for more than £50 million or equivalent; (b) requires particular expertise in the financial markets; or (c) raises issues of general importance to the financial markets. (3) 'Financial markets' for these purposes include the fixed income markets (covering repos, bonds, credit derivatives, debt securities and commercial paper generally), the equity markets, the derivatives markets, the loan markets, the foreign currency markets, and the commodities markets.

Local authorities can sometimes use the civil courts to vindicate public interests, as distinct from the facts or issues underpinning individual claimants' prospective causes of action. There has been considerable civil litigation at the suit of local authorities under section 222(1) of the Local Government Act 1972. That provision is concerned with the vindication of *public rights* by municipal authorities. Section 222(1) empowers such authorities to bring proceedings on behalf of the inhabitants of their area. This procedural mechanism can be used to obtain injunctions though the civil courts in support of the substantive criminal law or in respect of public nuisance. This provision states: 'Where a local authority considers it expedient for the promotion or protection of the interests of the inhabitants of their area – (a) they may prosecute or defend or appear in any legal proceedings and, in the case of civil proceedings, may institute them in their own name'.

The case law concerning section 222 of the 1972 Act was reviewed in *Birmingham City Council* v. *Shafi* (2008)[36] (which was considered in *Re L.* (2010),[37] see next paragraph). In the *Birmingham* case (2008)[38] a City Council unsuccessfully attempted to obtain injunctions against named gang members, to prevent them from entering the city centre or other specified areas where they might foment lawlessness. The Court of Appeal held that section 222 was unavailable because it would outstrip parallel local government powers to obtain very similar relief, namely so-called 'ASBOs' (anti-social behaviour orders), punishable with imprisonment if breached.

[30] Ibid., at para. 2.5(a).
[31] Ibid.
[32] Ibid., at para. 2.5(c).
[33] Civil Procedure Rules (1998) 63A; Practice Direction (63AA); *Civil Procedure 2019* (the 'White Book') (Sweet & Maxwell, London, 2019), para. 2FA–2.1, summarising cases so far decided (for a complete list, www.judiciary.gov.uk/court/financial-list; for contested transfers into this list, *Property Alliance Group Ltd.* v. *Royal Bank of Scotland (No. 4)* [2016] EWHC 207 (Ch); [2016] 1 *Weekly Law Reports* 2783, at [40] (Etherton C.); see also *Financial List Guide* www.gov.uk/government/uploads/system/uploads/attachment_data/file/465590/financial-list-guide.pdf; Lord Briggs, *Civil Courts Structure. Review: Interim Report* (2015) (www.judiciary.gov.uk/wp-content/uploads/2016/01/ccsr-interim-report-dec-15-final1.pdf), 3.20.
[34] Civil Procedure Rules (1998) 63A.2(1).
[35] Civil Procedure Rules (1998) 63A.1(2).
[36] [2008] EWCA Civ 1186; [2009] 1 *Weekly Law Reports* 1961.
[37] [2010] EWHC 2675 (Fam); [2011] Fam. 189.
[38] [2008] EWCA Civ 1186; [2009] 1 *Weekly Law Reports* 1961.

A variation on this theme is altruistic or paternalistic legal intervention by a public body to protect the rights of an individual or a collection of individuals who are de facto unable to protect themselves. An example is *Re L.* (2010),[39] where Sir Nicholas Wall, President of the Family Division, upon application by a local authority, upheld the grant 'without notice' of an injunction, to prevent molestation by an adult son of his vulnerable parents. This injunction was justified even though the parent was not mentally incapable. The judge noted that the court's inherent jurisdiction is available to fill gaps in the protection of vulnerable persons. Here the gap was the fact that the vulnerable parents did not lack mental capacity, and yet protection sought in a paternalistic way was required.[40] The Court of Appeal in *A Local Authority* v. *D.L.* (2012)[41] held that the Mental Capacity Act 2005 has not removed the court's inherent jurisdiction to grant relief to support vulnerable adults, and the latter decision was summarised by Parker J. in X.C. C. v. A.A. (2012)[42] in the context of forced marriages.

Cartier International A.G. v. *British Sky Broadcasting Ltd.* (2018)[43] concerned the position of non-party internet service providers (so-called 'intermediaries') when implementing website-blocking orders (that is, blocking orders made to prevent breach by non-parties of the claimants' trademarks or similar infringements of intellectual property rights). Two 'costs issues' were examined: (1) liability for the costs of the present litigation, which had been taken to final appeal, and (2) the expense of implementing the blocking orders. As for (1), the Supreme Court of the United Kingdom held that the defendant 'intermediaries', who had become subject to a *Norwich Pharmacal* order, requiring them to block use of their sites by intellectual property infringers, were liable for the costs of the action because they had vigorously opposed the application and elevated it to the status of a test claim. Normally, a respondent who is subject to a *Norwich Pharmacal* order would be entitled to be indemnified its costs by the applicant, because such an order generally involves a non-party (the *Norwich Pharmacal* respondent) providing information by way of discovery or other assistance in the applicant's litigation.[44] The costs order was here an exception to that general position, the exception being justified, as mentioned, by the fact that the defendant website providers had made the present litigation into a hard-fought test case. As for (2), the expense incurred in implementing these website blocking orders, that would be borne by the intellectual property holders, who were the claimants in the proceedings.

9.3 CONSOLIDATION AND JOINDER

Consolidation is the combination of actions. The parties might be (1) different, or (2) overlap. As for (1), consolidation might be the accession of actions between parties A and B and between C and D. As for (2), the consolidation might comprise a first action between A and B and a second action between A and C.

Joinder (initial or postponed) is the accession to a claim between A and D of additional parties, so as to become A, B and C, et al, against D, or A against D, E, F, et al.

Consolidation and joinder of co-claimants are established means of accommodating multi-party actions. In both instances, the result is an enlarged body of parties. There is no limit on the

39 Ibid.
40 Ibid., at [11] to [14].
41 [2012] EWCA Civ 253; [2012] 3 *All England Law Reports* 1064.
42 [2012] EWHC 2183 (Fam), at [42] and [43].
43 [2018] UKSC 28; [2018] 1 *Weekly Law Reports* 3259.
44 *Andrews on Civil Processes* (2nd ed., Intersentia Publishing, Cambridge, 2019), 11.16 to 11.23, for discussion of *Norwich Pharmacal* orders in general.

number of co-claimants who can use this form of procedure. Nor is there any limit upon the number of co-defendants who can be subject to this type of proceeding. Here we will note three examples of joinder of co-claimants. The first is *Weir* v. *Secretary of State for Transport (No. 1)*,[45] where a group of claimants formed an 'action committee'. This committee brought a single action in which a very large group of co-claimants (nearly 50,000 shareholders in that case) were full parties to the proceedings. These claimants sought monetary redress against a defendant company.

The second example of such a multi-claimant action is *Attrill* v. *Dresdner Kleinwort Ltd.* (2013).[46] The facts were as follows. In August 2008 the defendant investment bank's management promised its high-earning employees working in London a minimum pool for discretionary bonuses of 400 million euros for the January 2009 bonus distribution 'season'. But in late December 2008, under pressure from the new management (a German bank which had acquired the business), the bank broke this promise. The Court of Appeal held that the promise was enforceable and that there were established criteria for allocation of this bonus chest.

A third example is litigation brought in London in which several hundreds of claimants sought compensation for alleged physical maltreatment (the *Iraqi Civilians* litigation, 2014–16).[47]

The author has elsewhere considered the cognate (but more acute) problem of finding a consensual basis for consolidation and joinder in the context of arbitration.[48]

9.4 GROUP LITIGATION ORDERS[49]

A Group Litigation Order is a special form of joinder, by listing of claims on a group register. The Senior Master and the Law Society maintain a list of Group Litigation Orders.[50] Introduced in 2000, the Group Litigation Order system attractively expanded multiparty litigation beyond the 'same interest' constraint of representative proceedings (see Civil Procedure Rules (1998), Rule 19.6, quoted later in this paragraph). Civil Procedure Rules (1998), 19.10 states: 'A Group Litigation Order ("G.L.O.") means an order… to provide for the case management of claims which give rise to common or related issues of fact or law (the "Group Litigation Order issues")'. By contrast, Civil Procedure Rules (1998), Rule 19.6, provides as follows for representative parties with the same interest: '(1) Where more than one person has the same interest in a claim – (a) the claim may be begun; or (b) the court may order that the claim be continued, by or against one or more of the persons who have the same interest as representatives of any other persons who have that interest'.

45 [2005] EWHC 812 (Ch) (Lindsay J.).

46 [2013] EWCA Civ 394; [2013] 3 *All England Law Reports* 807.

47 *Ali Al-Waheed* v. *Ministry of Defence* [2014] EWHC 2714, at [1] (Leggatt J.); *Iraqi Civilians* v. *Ministry of Defence (No. 2)* [2016] UKSC25; [2016] 1 *Weekly Law Reports* 2001; *Mohammed* v. *Ministry of Defence* [2017] UKSC1; [2017] *Appeal Cases Reports* 649; *Mohammed* v. *Ministry of Defence (No 2)* [2017] UKSC2; [2017] *Appeal Cases Reports* 821; *R (Al- Saadoon)* v. *Secretary of State for Defence* [2016] EWCA Civ 811; [2017] *Queen's Bench Reports* 1017 (1,282 public law claims, and 646 private law claims, with 257 settlements; Ibid., at [2] and [3]).

48 Neil Andrews, 'Arbitration and the Expanding Circle of Consenting Parties', in R. Nazzini (ed.), *Transnational Construction Arbitration: Key Themes in the Resolution of Construction Disputes* (Informa Publishing, London, 2018), chapter 5.

49 R. Mulheron, *Some Difficulties with Group Litigation Orders – And Why a Class Action is Superior* 24 Civil Justice Quarterly 40, 45 (2005); R Mulheron, *Reform of Collective Redress in England and Wales* (2008), at 9 ff and 144 ff www.civiljusticecouncil.gov.uk/files/collective_redress.pdf.

50 Practice Direction (19B), para. 11.

Group Litigation Orders were intended to become the mainstay of the English system's treatment of multiparty litigation (an 'opt-in' system).

There are four main features of the Group Litigation Order system, listed in the following paragraphs.[51]

(1) *Judicial approval.* The court must approve a Group Litigation Order. This process of approval involves: (1) an application to a specified judge,[52] or (2) the court can itself make such an order of its own initiative (on the related topic of consolidation);[53] (3) ratification at a very senior level of the judiciary of a provisional approval given at stage (1) or (2). Stage (3) entails the 'making' of the Group Litigation Order.[54]

(2) *Joining the group.* Group litigation involves 'opting in' by each individual claimant, whereupon a group member enjoys both membership of the group and the general status of a fully fledged 'party to civil proceedings'. A person who is dead is not properly joined unless added to the register using the name of his personal representative.[55]

(3) *Collective judicial management and decision-making.* During the progress of the Group Litigation Order, the court will exercise extensive case-management and it will issue directions. The managing court's[56] orders on 'common' issues are binding on, and in favour of, all those who are registered as members of the group. Such a 'common' issue will normally concern questions of liability or the availability of a particular head of loss. A party who is adversely affected by a judgment or order can seek permission to appeal.[57]

(4) *The group must share the bitterness of defeat.* If the group loses the case, each group member is liable to the victorious party both for that member's share of the common costs of the proceedings and for any individual costs specifically incurred with respect to his claim. But if the group is victorious, the defeated party is liable to pay costs attributable both to the 'common costs' and the 'individual costs'.[58]

In *Barr* v. *Biffa Waste Services* (2009)[59] a Group Litigation Order claim for damages worth circa £1 million involved a very much larger measure of potential costs liability. Coulson J. refused to protect the claimants against their potential costs liability, if they lost. The rejected form of protection would have been a cost cap based on the extent of their ATE cover, that is, their 'after-the-event' legal expenses insurance. But Coulson J. did allow costs-capping based on the claimants' revised costs estimate[60] (another major decision on the costs aspects of a Group Litigation Order action is *Motto* v. *Trafigura Ltd.*, which is examined later in this section).[61]

[51] See also the summary by Lord Walker in *Autologic Holdings plc* v. *Commissioners of Inland Revenue* [2005] UKHL 54; [2006] 1 *Appeal Cases Reports* 118, at [86].

[52] Practice Direction (19B), para. 3.3.

[53] Practice Direction (19B), para. 4.

[54] Practice Direction (19B), paras. 3.5–3.9.

[55] *Kimathi* v. *Foreign and Commonwealth Office* [2017] EWHC 3005 (Q.B.); [2017] 1 *Weekly Law Reports* 1081 (Stewart J.).

[56] Practice Direction (19B), para. 8.

[57] Civil Procedure Rules (1998) 19.12(2).

[58] *Sayers* v. *Merck & SmithKline Beecham plc* [2002] 1 *Weekly Law Reports* 2274, CA; noted M. Goldberg (2002) New L. J. 437–8 and M. Mildred (2002) 65 Modern Law Review 597.

[59] [2009] EWHC 2444 (TCC); [2010] 3 Costs L.R. 317.

[60] Ibid., at [53] ff.

[61] [2011] EWCA Civ 1150; [2012] 1 *Weekly Law Reports* 657.

9.4.1 *Managerial Directions*

Lord Woolf in *Taylor* v. *Nugent Care Society* (2004) noted that wide managerial powers under the Group Litigation Order system operate not only to advance justice within the civil courts as a whole, but such management is specifically designed to promote the efficient and expeditious conduct of the group claim itself.[62]

The court's directions can include the following:[63] (1) providing for one or more claims on the group register to proceed as test claims[64] (this occurred on the question of limitation of actions in *A.B.* v. *Ministry of Defence* (2012), where nine slightly different lead cases were selected from a group consisting of 1,011 claimants);[65] (2) appointing the solicitor of one or more parties to be the lead solicitor for the claimants or defendants[66] (appointment to be a lead solicitor can be lucrative); (3) specifying the details to be included in a statement of case (that is, the claimant's pleading) in order to show that the criteria for entry of the claim on the group register have been met;[67] (4) determining the extent of evidence at trial, including whether the hearing of evidence from certain categories of witness would be proportionate in terms of time and cost;[68] (5) fixing a date after which no claim may be added to the group register unless the court gives permission[69] (there is a mechanism[70] for transferring actions which should join the register and which are commenced prior to the cut-off date); and (6) considering applications for 'costs-capping' (discussed in *Barr* v. *Biffa Waste Services*, 2009).[71]

Hildyard J. in *Re RBS Rights Issue Litigation* (2017)[72] analysed the jurisdiction to order disclosure of a litigant's third-party funding. He did so in the context of a defendant's probable application for security for costs in respect of a large Group Litigation Order claim. In the sequel, Hildyard J. ordered security for costs against a third-party funder in respect of a Group Litigation Order action.[73]

But what of latecomers, if they are not admitted to the register, or if the relevant claimant wholly fails to make an application to join the register? The short answer is that they cannot be barred or struck out. Their claim will subsist as a separate piece of litigation but external to the relevant Group Litigation Order. But, even though they subsist as independent claims, these actions might become subject to special managerial orders, namely stays and costs decisions, as explained in *Taylor* v. *Nugent Care Society* (2004).[74] Lord Woolf said that when a set of claims subject to a Group Litigation Order is proceeding in parallel to an individual action (or a range of individual actions), the Group Litigation Order proceedings should take priority. To achieve this, (1) the court can issue a 'stay' of the individual claim, pending the

62 *Taylor* v. *Nugent Care Society* [2004] EWCA Civ 51; [2004] 1 *Weekly Law Reports* 1129, at [9].

63 For greater detail, C. Hodges, *Multi-Party Actions* (Oxford University Press, 2001), 5.06 and 5.07.

64 Civil Procedure Rules (1998) 19.13(b).

65 [2012] UKSC9; [2013] 1 *Appeal Cases Reports* 78.

66 Civil Procedure Rules (1998) 19.13(c).

67 Civil Procedure Rules (1998) 19.13(d); on this question, Lord Woolf in *Boake Allen Ltd.* v. *Revenue and Customs* [2007] UKHL 25, at [33].

68 *Kimathi* v. *Foreign and Commonwealth Office* [2017] EWHC 3004 (Q.B.); [2017] 1067 (Stewart J.), at [52].

69 Civil Procedure Rules (1998) 19.13(e); Practice Direction (19B), para. 13; e.g., *Practice Direction (Coal Mining Hand Arm Vibration Syndrome etc.)* [2003] 4 *All England Law Reports* 318.

70 Practice Direction (19B), para. 9.1.

71 [2009] EWHC 2444 (TCC); [2010] 3 Costs L.R. 317 (Coulson J.).

72 [2017] EWHC 463; [2017] 1 *Weekly Law Reports* 3539 (Hildyard J.).

73 *Re RBS Rights Issue Litigation* [2017] EWHC 1217 (Ch); [2017] 1 *Weekly Law Reports* 4635.

74 [2004] EWCA Civ 51; [2004] 1 *Weekly Law Reports* 1129; M. Mildred, *Personal injury – civil procedure – group actions – group litigation orders* (2004) J.P.I.L. C67, C69.

outcome of the Group Litigation Order; and (2) the court can also make appropriate costs decisions so as to protect the defendant from incurring unnecessary legal costs in fighting the litigation on a plurality of fronts.

This result seems inevitable. It is not the function of the Group Litigation Order system to invalidate claims which are not brought within the cut-off date applicable to the register. Instead the ordinary limitation period will continue to apply to actions commenced beyond that procedural deadline. However, a compromise can be struck: such independent actions are subject to the overall dictates of the Civil Procedure Rules (1998) system. It follows that their orderly conduct will sometimes require the court to place them in suspense, pending the outcome of significant and overlapping issues within the Group Litigation Order cohort of similar cases.

9.4.2 *Costs in the Group Litigation Order Litigation Concerning Contamination of the Ivory Coast*

The Court of Appeal conducted a detailed examination of Senior Costs Judge Peter Hurst's complicated costs decisions arising after settlement of the Group Litigation Order claim in this matter: *Motto* v. *Trafigura Ltd.* (2011).[75] The case concerned a Group Litigation Order in which nearly 30,000 residents of the Ivory Coast claimed damages for personal injury. The defendant had agreed to pay £30 million as compensation, which was to be held on trust by the lead solicitors, Leigh Day and Partners, and distributed amongst the group claimants. The settlement also contained an undertaking to pay the claimants' costs. The Court of Appeal decided that the defendant was liable to pay costs incurred by the claimants to the following extent: (1) the 'vetting costs' when examining each individual claim, and formulating a pleading, and administering the claim until the cessation of the case by acceptance of the settlement;[76] (2) medical reports on individual claimants[77] – the judge was entitled to award the cost of medical reports on individual claimants, again provided these were consistent with the tests of necessity and reasonableness; and (3) the costs incurred in distributing the agreed damages.[78] But costs were not payable in respect of the time and money spent by the claimants' advisors in negotiating a conditional fee agreement and ATE insurance with which to fund the action.[79]

9.4.3 *Versatile System*

The Group Litigation Order system is a versatile and wide-ranging procedure. Any form of civil wrongdoing and dishonest misconduct can form the basis of 'common issues' in a Group Litigation Order

Furthermore, there has been clear judicial comment on the relative speediness of Group Litigation Order actions. The former Senior Master of the Queen's Bench Division has stated: 'in the Group Litigation Orders with which I have been involved we have achieved settlement or decisions in half or a third of the time that normal litigation might have taken'.[80]

75 [2011] EWCA Civ 1150; [2012] 1 *Weekly Law Reports* 657.
76 Ibid., at [54] to [56].
77 Ibid., at [75] and [76].
78 Ibid., at [98] to [103].
79 Ibid., at [104] to [114].
80 Cambridge seminar, 2010.

Mulheron complained that the Group Litigation Order system had yielded only a modest number of proceedings.[81] But in fact there has been a wide range of Group Litigation Orders, including: (1) claims for personal injury arising from pharmaceutical drugs;[82] (2) allegations of assault during a period of unrest within a (then) British colony;[83] (3) recovery of corporation tax;[84] and (4) loss of corporate 'group tax relief';[85] (5) (shareholders') rights issues.[86] There is a register of Group Litigation Orders. That register (consulted in December 2019) lists, and provides brief details of, 108 such orders which have been made since 2000.[87]

The former Senior Master Robert Turner, in a report presented at a Cambridge seminar in 2012, stated that he had dealt with the following Group Litigation Orders: a hotel in Spain to which tour operators sent parties long after they allegedly knew of the serious risk of food poisoning that existed; the Alder Hey hospital organ removal litigation involving hundreds of deceased young children and their grieving families – the (then) Senior Master of the Queen's Bench Division sent this to mediation with huge success (as the author has explained elsewhere);[88] the hot drinks claims against McDonalds, which failed (in England); long-distance flight thrombosis claims;[89] removal of indigenous inhabitants from the Chagos Islands in the Indian Ocean;[90] the unexploded shells cases from the Army's training areas in Kenya; pension cases where long-serving employees were allegedly cheated out of their final salary pension entitlements; and the Buncefield disaster.[91]

On the Buncefield case, former Senior Master Turner commented, in a report presented at a Cambridge seminar in 2012:

> An example which might be of interest to illustrate the ability of a judge in the High Court to use his own initiative concerned a violent explosion at an oil terminal in North London a few days before Christmas in 2006. The damage involved over three thousand potential litigants, who ranged from householders whose homes had been damaged to international oil companies

[81] R. Mulheron, *Reform of Collective Redress in England and Wales* (2008) www.civiljusticecouncil.gov.uk/files/collective_redress.pdf, noted and discussed in *Andrews on Civil Processes* (Intersentia Publishing, Cambridge, 2013), vol. 1, 22.72–22.75.

[82] *Sayers* v. *Merck & SmithKline Beecham plc* [2001] EWCA Civ 2017; [2002] 1 *Weekly Law Reports* 2274, Court of Appeal (England and Wales).

[83] *Kimathi* v. *Foreign and Commonwealth Office* [2017] EWHC 3004 (Q.B.); [2017] 1067 (Stewart J.).

[84] *Test Claimants in the FII Group Litigation* v. *Revenue and Customs Commissioners* [2012] UKSC18; [2012] 2 *Appeal Cases Reports* 337; see also *Boake Allen Ltd.* v. *Revenue and Customs* [2007] UKHL 25; [2007] 1 *Weekly Law Reports* 1386; and see further *Jazztel plc* v. *Revenue and Customs Commissioners* [2017] EWHC 677 (Ch); [2017] 1 *Weekly Law Reports* 3869 (Marcus Smith J.).

[85] *Autologic Holdings plc* v. *Commissioners of Inland Revenue* [2005] UKHL 54; [2006] 1 *Appeal Cases Reports* 118, at [2]: where Lord Nicholls said, 'six groups of companies have been selected as test cases. They represent a large number of claimant companies in proceedings started in the Chancery Division against the Commissioners of Inland Revenue. This litigation is currently being managed under a group litigation order made by the Chief Chancery Master in May 2003'.

[86] *Re RBS Rights Issue Litigation* [2017] EWHC 463; [2017] 1 *Weekly Law Reports* 3539 (Hildyard J.).

[87] www.gov.uk/guidance/group-litigation-orders.

[88] Neil Andrews, *The Modern Civil Process: Judicial and Alternative Forms of Dispute Resolution in England* (Mohr Siebeck, Tübingen, 2008), 10.13: 'An example of mediation's flexibility concerns a group litigation action brought by parents of deceased children against a children's hospital trust (Alder Hey Hospital, Liverpool). The hospital had removed organs from dead children without their parents' permission. The claim for damages proceeded for some time. The procedural judge (Senior Master Robert Turner) then successfully recommended mediation before an outsider. A settlement was agreed, consisting of five elements: a very modest amount of compensation; a grant by the hospital towards relevant research; an undertaking by the Government to issue better guidelines for hospitals; a memorial to the children; a public apology by the doctors concerned'.

[89] *Deep Vein Thrombosis and Air Travel Group Litigation* [2005] UKHL 72; [2006] 1 *Appeal Cases Reports* 495.

[90] G. Scanlan, *The Chagos Islanders' Case – A Question of Limitation?* 26 Civil Justice Quarterly 292 (2007).

[91] [2008] EWHC 1729 (Comm); [2008] 2 C.L.C. 258.

> whose supply of aviation fuel to airlines at Heathrow had been seriously disrupted. I listed that case for management directions six weeks after the event. I also made it known that I would welcome any lawyers who might have clients with potential claims, to attend. Forty barristers including six Q.C.'s and over a hundred solicitors attended.

Senior Master Robert Turner continued:

> Having heard an outline of the whole event, I divided the potential claimants into five groups depending on the nature and size of their claims and invited the three potential defendants to act together for the time being. I outlined the basic directions which I intended to give and invited the lawyers for the defendants to spend the rest of the day with the lawyers for the claimants devising both suitable directions for the trial of the issues and a scheme for the immediate payment of interim damages to the majority of the claimants, especially those who needed to have repairs to make their homes habitable. I rose from the Bench and left the lawyers to address the exercise that I had set them at eleven o'clock and by four o'clock I returned to court to approve five Group Litigation Orders which resulted in the settlement of the majority of the three thousand cases. This is just an example of the use of the initiative which as judges in the High Court we were encouraged to adopt.

9.5 REPRESENTATIVE PROCEEDINGS

9.5.1 *Nature*

The rationale of representative proceedings is to avoid the expense and practical difficulty or inconvenience of joinder by name of a set or class of identically interested prospective claimants ('active' representative proceedings) or prospective defendants ('passive' representative proceedings).[92]

The essence of 'active' representative proceedings is that the representative claimant brings an action on behalf of himself and others (the represented class). He is the only claimant. Members of that represented class are not parties to the action. Nevertheless, those class members will receive the benefits of a *res judicata* decision (or be subject to that decision), for example the benefit of a favourable declaration of legal entitlement (see next but one paragraph for the rule, Civil Procedure Rules (1998), Rule 19.6). This form of proceeding is, therefore, an opt-out system. Representative proceedings have been relatively uncommon in England.

Where the representative mechanism is used against a defendant (usually because the defendant comprises a consortium of individuals, that is, it is an unincorporated association), it has been suggested that it will require exceptional circumstances for the court to withhold permission for the judgment on liability (or indeed the costs order) against the representative defendant from being enforced against the represented members.[93]

The English rule (Civil Procedure Rules (1998), Rule 19.6(1) and (4), provides:

> (1) Where more than one person has the same interest in a claim – (a) the claim may be begun; or (b) the court may order that the claim be continued, by or against any one or more of the persons who have the same interest as representatives of any other persons who have that interest... (4) Unless the court otherwise directs any judgment or order given in a claim in which a party is acting as a representative under this rule – (a) is binding on all persons represented in the claim;

[92] *Chandra* v. *Mayor* [2017] EWHC 2636 (Ch); [2017] 1 *Weekly Law Reports* 929, at [10] (Judge Purle Q.C.).

[93] Ibid., at [9] (Judge Purle Q.C.).

but (b) may only be enforced by or against a person who is not a party to the claim with the permission of the court.

9.5.2 *Represented Persons' Technical Status*

Only the 'representative' is a 'party' in the full sense. By contrast, the represented party occupies a hybrid position. He is not a party (and thus not liable to provide disclosure of documents).[94] However, represented persons, even if technically not a full party, are not mere bystanders uninterested in the fate of the case. Indeed, they are bound by its result (see Civil Procedure Rules (1998), Rule 19.6(4), cited above in Section 9.5.1). Furthermore, *Chandra* v. *Mayor* (2017) [95] decided that the court will permit a costs order to be enforced against represented persons. In the same case, it was also stated[96] that a representative who personally pays the other side's costs will be entitled to a contribution from the represented persons.

Representative proceedings can be commenced without the court's permission (conversely, the court can order that pending non-representative proceedings should be continued in representative form).[97] Representative proceedings can begin without the represented persons' consent.[98] Nor is it necessary for the representative to have been appointed or elected by the relevant group. Nor need they be informed of its progress. In short, the representative can be a self-appointed general. However, 'the court may direct that a person may not act as a - representative'.[99] This allows the court to bar an unsuitable representative.[100] In *Moon* v. *Atherton* (1972) a represented person was treated as a 'party' under the pre–Civil Procedure Rules (1998),[101] but only for the limited purpose of enabling a person to take over the role of representative when the earlier representative discontinued his claim.

The representative claimant or defendant is *dominus litis* (Latin for 'the one who calls the procedural shots') and so it follows that the representative can compromise the claim or defence. The court does not approve settlements of representative proceedings, unless the represented persons are either under a mental disability or they are minors (under the age of eighteen).[102] Perhaps the courts could use their inherent jurisdiction and control this process of settlement in representative proceedings. Lord Denning M.R. acknowledged this problem in *Moon* v. *Atherton* (1972).[103]

Such a settlement will not bind represented persons unless they specifically assent and become parties to it. But a settlement which is constituted as a judgment by consent would appear to bind represented persons in accordance with Civil Procedure Rules (1998), Rule 19.6(4) (quoted in the text in Section 9.5.1 above). However, if a segment of the represented group

94 *Ventouris* v. *Mountain* [1990] 1 *Weekly Law Reports* 1370 (Saville J.).

95 [2017] EWHC 2636 (Ch); [2017] 1 *Weekly Law Reports* 929, at [9] ff (Judge Purle Q.C.); earlier case law was stated to be no longer applicable.

96 Ibid., at [8] and [15].

97 Civil Procedure Rules (1998) 19.6(1)(b).

98 R. Mulheron, *From Representative Rule to Class Action: Steps rather than Leaps'* 24 Civil Justice Quarterly 424, 442–3 (2005), noting *Independiente Ltd.* v. *Music Trading On-Line (H.K.) Ltd.* [2003] EWHC 470 (Ch), at [32], and *Howells* v. *Dominion Insurance Co. Ltd.* [2005] EWHC 552 (Admin), at [26] (Cox J.).

99 Civil Procedure Rules (1998) 19.6(2).

100 Civil Procedure Rules (1998) 19.6(4).

101 [1972] 2 *Queen's Bench Reports* 435, Court of Appeal (England and Wales).

102 Civil Procedure Rules (1998) 21.10(1) (proceedings by or on behalf of a child or patient); on representation of children generally in family or Civil Procedure Rules (1998) proceedings, *Re* W. [2017] EWHC 450 (Fam); [2017] 1 *Weekly Law Reports* 3451 (Cobb J.).

103 [1972] 2 *Queen's Bench Reports* 435, 442, CA (Lord Denning M.R.).

becomes discontent with how proceedings are being conducted by the representative, that dissatisfied segment can secede from the main group and become co-parties.[104]

9.5.3 *Contexts*

Representative proceedings can provide an efficient means of gaining 'closure' of a dispute affecting a host of persons. A good example is *Equitable Life Assurance Society* v. *Hyman* (2002), where a defendant life insurance company sponsored a representative action. Ultimately, the House of Lords issued a declaration in this action.[105] That declaration established the true interpretation of a clause in the defendant company's life assurance policy. Ninety thousand policy-holders were bound by this decision.

The representative mechanism has also been used to try to obtain effective injunctive relief against a disruptive unincorporated association (a 'protest group'). But the Court of Appeal in *Astellas Pharma Ltd.* v. *Stop Huntingdon Animal Cruelty* (2011) held that the lower court had overstretched itself by attempting to render unidentified persons subject to immediate enforcement of the injunction.[106]

Subject to occasional proceedings for declarations or injunctive relief, representative proceedings are uncommon in England, for these two reasons: (1) the fear of incurring irrecoverable costs; and (2) the restricted scope for gaining compensatory damages under Civil Procedure Rules (1998), Rule 19.6. As for point (2), damages can be awarded in the form of proceeding only if (1) the total award is known and (2) the individual shares are also ascertainable at the time of judgment. The first problem (the costs issue) seems now to be solved, at least procedurally (see next paragraph), but the second problem remains, given the narrow compass for the award of compensatory damages. As for (1), the problem of costs incurred by the representative, *Chandra* v. *Mayor* (2017), a first instance decision,[107] recognises a strong presumption that represented persons will become liable to contribute with respect to costs orders made against the representative. Before this decision, the assumption had been that only the representative was liable for costs. On that assumption, the representative would have been most reluctant to assume the risk of incurring costs liability without the prospect of sharing that liability amongst the members of the relevant class. The support for that assumption was that represented persons are not fully fledged 'parties' and so they are not subject *as parties* to liability for costs.[108] It follows that a representative must bear the entire cost of the litigation if the case is lost. He would then be required to pay the defendant's costs. *Chandra* v. *Mayor* (2017) has changed this. The representative is now assured that the represented class can be made to contribute jointly towards the costs

[104] Neil Andrews, *Principles of Civil Procedure* (Sweet & Maxwell, London, 1994), 7–011, considering, notably, *John* v. *Rees* [1970] *Chancery Reports* 345 (Megarry J.).

[105] [2002] 1 *Appeal Cases Reports* 408, House of Lords.

[106] [2011] EWCA Civ 752; Civil Procedure Rules (1998) 19.6(4).

[107] [2017] EWHC 2636 (Ch); [2017] 1 *Weekly Law Reports* 929, at [9] ff (Judge Purle Q.C.); earlier case law was stated to be no longer applicable.

[108] *Howells* v. *Dominion Insurance Co. Ltd.* [2005] EWHC 552 (Admin) (Cox J.); noted J. Seymour (2005) 24 *Civil Justice Quarterly* 309; *Price* v. *Rhondda U.D.C.* [1923] *Weekly Notes* 228; (1923) 130 *Law Times* 156 (Eve J.); *Moon* v. *Atherton* [1972] 2 *Queen's Bench Reports* 435, 441, Court of Appeal (England and Wales) (Lord Denning M.R.); but in *Chandra* v. *Mayor* [2017] EWHC 2636 (Ch); [2017] 1 *Weekly Law Reports* 929, at [11] and [12], the judge relegated these remarks to (unpersuasive) *dicta* and furthermore held that developments in the costs liability of non-parties in general had overtaken this provisional analysis by Lord Denning M.R.; see, also positively, and as noted in the *Chandra* case, suggestions in *Bank of America National Trust and Savings Association* v. *John Taylor* [1992] 1 *Lloyd's Reports* 484, 495 (Waller J.); and see D. Kell, *Casenote* (1994) 13 Civil Justice Quarterly 233 (1994).

liability which arises if the claim fails. (Of course, if the claim is successful, the defendant will pay the representative claimant's costs.)

The second impediment to damages litigation in representative proceedings has been the courts' traditionally narrow interpretation of the statutory phrase 'where more than one person has the same interest in a claim'.[109] Compensatory damages under Civil Procedure Rules (1998), Rule 19.6, are available only if both the total award and individual shares can be ascertained at the time of judgment.

Until recently, the major obstruction to the award of damages in representative proceedings was the Court of Appeal's (majority) analysis in *Markt & Co. Ltd.* v. *Knight Steamship Co. Ltd.* (1910).[110]

In this case a ship had been sunk by the Russian navy. The reason for this attack was that the vessel was believed to be carrying contraband goods. A representative action was brought in respect of the forty-four cargo-owners against the carrier, on the basis that it had been culpable in exposing the ship to this risk of Russian naval intervention. By a majority (Vaughan-Williams and Fletcher-Moulton L.JJ.; Buckley L.J. dissenting), it was held that the case should not proceed on this basis. As suggested by the author,[111] it is arguable that the *ratio* of the case was that joinder of all forty-four cargo-owners was practicable and desirable on the facts of this case, and therefore representative proceedings, even if available, were inappropriate. Joinder in the *Markt* case would have required recommencement of proceedings, by a consolidated claim brought by each of the forty-four cargo-owners. The court thought that this was practicable (all forty-four could be contacted). Furthermore, it would be desirable, because the court considered that it might facilitate more effective discovery.

On this basis, the court's discussion of representative proceedings and damages was not strictly necessary for its decision and might have been regarded as mere *dicta*.

Despite the manifest procedural unattractiveness of the decision (and even the possibility that claims might have become statute-barred), the court suggested that it is not enough that the suggested class of claimants is suing in respect of the same cause of action (for example, in contract or in the tort of negligence); nor that their claims raise strikingly similar factual issues, perhaps arising from the same incident. The presence, or even the possible presence, of different defences (for example, individual contractual clauses imposing limitations upon liability or, in the case of negligence claims in tort, the possible presence of different degrees of contributory negligence), would preclude a representative claim.[112] It is now apparent that the Civil Procedure Rules (1998) have been held to have removed the long shadow first cast in

109 Civil Procedure Rules (1998) 19.6(1).

110 [1910] 2 K.B. 1021, 1030, 1035, 1040, Court of Appeal (England and Wales).

111 Neil Andrews, *Principles of Civil Procedure* (Sweet & Maxwell, London, 1994), 7-005.

112 In *Markt & Co. Ltd.* v. *Knight SS Co. Ltd.* [1910] 2 K.B. 1021, 1030, Court of Appeal (England and Wales), Vaughan-Williams L.J. emphasised the possibly heterogeneous nature of the set of (contractual) bills of lading applicable between the cargo-owners and the carrier. Fletcher-Moulton L.J., at 1035, took the severe view that an individual claim for damages (whether or not founded on breach of contract) is by definition not a claim for common relief, and therefore incompatible with the spirit of representative proceedings, as earlier expressed by Lord Macnaghten in *Duke of Bedford* v. *Ellis* [1901] *Appeal Cases Reports* 1, 8, House of Lords, who said: 'Given a common interest and a common grievance, a representative suit was in order if the relief sought was in its nature beneficial to all whom the plaintiff proposed to represent'. The dissentient on the representative action point in the *Markt* case, Buckley L.J., at 1048, considered that a representative action could proceed on the basis of a declaration of liability for breach of contract; Buckley L.J.'s suggestion foreshadowed Vinelott J.'s decision in *Prudential Assurance Co. Ltd.* v. *Newman Industries Ltd. (No. 1)* [1981] *Chancery Reports* 229.

1910 by the *dicta* of the *Markt* case. Mulheron[113] and Sorabji[114] have critically examined the *Markt* line of cases, which antedated the Civil Procedure Rules (1998).

However, even before the Civil Procedure Rules (1998), there were a couple of instances where damages had been awarded under the representative rubric: *Monarch Steamship Co. Ltd.* v. *Greystoke Castle (Cargo Owners)* (1947)[115] and *EMI Records Ltd.* v. *Riley* (1981).[116] But the contexts were exceptional. Another pre–Civil Procedure Rules (1998) development was Vinelott J.'s attempt in *Prudential Assurance Co. Ltd.* v. *Newman Industries Ltd. (No. 1)* (1981) to reinvigorate representative claims for compensation by adopting a two-stage process: (1) a representative action establishing the defendant's liability towards members of the represented class, with (2) follow-on individual claims by members of that class to quantify their recoverable loss.[117]

Stage (1) involved the representative obtaining a 'declaratory' common basis of liability. At stage (2) this would be invoked by others similarly harmed by the defendant. Vinelott J., having held that that all relevant conditions had been satisfied,[118] identified various issues on which a declaration could be properly made.[119]

The slow recognition of damages as a feature of representative actions in England is to be contrasted with the class action in the USA.[120] The unified process in the USA class action

113 R. Mulheron, *From Representative Rule to Class Action: Steps rather than Leaps* 24 Civil Justice Quarterly 424, 426–31, 433–5, 437, especially 428–30 (2005); R. Mulheron, *Emerald Supplies Ltd. v. British Airways plc: a Century Later, the Ghost of Markt Lives On* 24 Comp. L. 159 (2009).

114 J. Sorabji, *The Hidden Class Action in English Civil Procedure* 28 Civil Justice Quarterly 498 (2009).

115 As in the claim for economic loss resulting from a maritime collision (the claimants' total loss, already incurred, was ascertained at the time of the litigation): *Monarch Steamship Co. Ltd.* v. *Greystoke Castle (Cargo Owners)* [1947] *Appeal Cases Reports* 265, House of Lords.

116 [1981] 1 *Weekly Law Reports* 923, 926 (Dillon J.).

117 [1981] *Chancery Reports* 229 (Vinelott J.) (not disturbed on this point on appeal [1982] 1 *Chancery Reports* 204, 222– 4, Court of Appeal (England and Wales)).

118 [1981] *Chancery Reports* 229, 254–5 (Vinelott J.).

119 Ibid., at 256.

120 American Law Institute, *Principles of the Law of Aggregate Litigation* (Philadelphia, 2010): main reporter Samuel Issacharoff (N.Y.U.); J. Bronsteen and O. Fiss, *The Class Action Rule* 78 Notre Dame L.R. 1419 (2006); S. B. Burbank, *The Class Action in American Securities Regulation'* 4 Zeitschrift für Zivilprozess International 321 (1999) (especially at 322–6, 332–6, on the history and prospects of federal class actions in the USA); O. Chase, H. Hershkoff, L. Silberman, V. Varano, Y. Taniguchi and A. A. S. Zuckerman, *Civil Procedure in Comparative Context* (Thomson West, St Paul, USA, 2007), 390 ff.; the Duke Law School symposium (coordinated by T. Rowe): *Debates Over Group Litigation in Comparative Perspective* (Duke/Geneva symposium, 2000) 11 Duke Jo. of Int. and Comp. Law 157–421 (2001): J. B. Weinstein, D. H. Hensler, E. H. Cooper and H. Erichson, *Doing Good, Doing Well* (2004) 57 Vand. L.R. 2087 (2004); B. Hay and D. Rosenberg, *"Sweetheart" and "Blackmail" Settlement in Class Actions: Reality and Remedy* 75 Notre Dame L.R. 1377 (2000); E. D. Hensler, *The New Social Policy Torts: Litigation as a Legislative Strategy* 51 DePaul L.R. 493 (2001); R. L. Marcus *Reassessing the Magnetic Pull of Megacases on Procedure* 51 DePaul L.R. 457 (2001) (considering complex commercial, public law and mass tort litigation); A. Miller, *Of Frankenstein Monsters and Shining Knights: Myth, Reality and the 'Class Action Problem'* 92 Harv. L.R. 664 (1979); Symposium on Class Actions and Mass Torts, University of Pennsylvania: E. H. Cooper, *Aggregation and Settlement of Mass Torts* 148 U. of Pennsylvania L.R. 1943 (2000); E. R. Becker and J. M. Marcus, *Penn Law School Mass Torts Symposium: A Response to Professor Cooper* 148 U. of Pennsylvania L.R. 2001 (2000); R. L. Marcus, *Benign Neglect Reconsidered* 148 U. of Pennsylvania L.R. 2009 (2000); D. L. Shapiro, *Class Actions: The Class as Party and Client* 73 Notre Dame L.R. 913 (1998) (considered by L. Silberman, see this note below, at 210–12); J. Resnik, *From Cases to Litigation* 54 Law & Contemp. Prob. 5 (1991); R. Phillips, *Class Action & Joinder in Mississippi* 71 Miss L.J. 447 (2001); P. Schuck, *Agent Orange on Trial: Mass Toxic Disasters in Courts* (Harvard University Press, 1986); E. Sherman, *Consumer Class Actions: Who Are the Real Winners?* 56 Me. L.R. 223 (2004); L Silberman, *The Vicissitudes of the American Class Action – With a Comparative Eye* 7 Tulane Jo. of Int. and Comp. Law 201 (1999); C. Silver, *Class Actions*, in B. Bouckaert and G. De Geest (eds.), *Encyclopaedia of Law and Economics* (Edward Elgar Publishing, 2000), vol. V, 194 ff; S. C. Yeazell, *From Mediaeval Group Litigation to the Modern Class Action* (Yale University Press, New Haven, 1987) (historical survey of representative proceedings in England and the USA).

compresses the *Prudential* case's two-stage procedure into a single procedure, in which a substantial award of damages can be made.

As Sorabji notes,[121] 'Rule 23(a) [of the Federal Courts Rules of Procedure] sets out four conditions which have to be satisfied in order to certify an action as a class action: (i) numerosity... (ii) commonality... (iii) typicality... (iv) the representative party [will] fairly and adequately protect the interests of the class'.

Thus the USA federal rule prescribes the following conditions for a class action: (1) the parties should be so numerous that joinder is impracticable; (2) common issues of fact or law should predominate within the class; (3) the representative should have a claim or defence typical of the class; and (4) he should adequately represent the interests of the class.[122] The rule goes on to distinguish three situations (known familiarly as '(b)(1)', '(b)(2)' and '(b)(3)' categories): (1) where joinder is simply impracticable because of the group's size; (2) where injunctive relief is sought and a class action is 'appropriate'; and (3) where other relief is sought, notably damages, for which the class action is 'superior to other available methods for the fair and efficient administration of the controversy'.

9.5.4 *Pecuniary Relief in Representative Proceedings under the Civil Procedure Rules (1998)*

The decision in *Millharbour Management Ltd.* v. *Weston Homes* (2011)[123] is a positive step forward. The *Millharbour* case made clear that a representative action can be used, in appropriate circumstances, where the representative is seeking compensation on behalf of a relevant class. In this case Akenhead J. confirmed that collective compensatory damages can be awarded in representative proceedings if the following two elements are already ascertainable: (1) the total amount of damages to be awarded to the class (how big is the cake?) and (2) each member's share (how big should each slice be?).

The facts of the *Millharbour* case were as follows. Purchasers of flats, and sub-purchasers of flats, each of whom had bought leasehold interests in these dwellings, complained that the defendant builder had failed to construct satisfactory accommodation. Because of these defects, expensive repair work would be required. At first the cost of this work would be incurred by the management company responsible for maintaining the accommodation on behalf of the leaseholders. That cost would then be passed on to individual tenants as increased 'service charges' in accordance with the contracts between the management company and the leaseholders. The representative action would operate to enable the representatives of these different cohorts of leaseholders to obtain compensation. That compensation would be the amount of the extra service charges payable by the leaseholders to the management company as a result of the repair costs.

In the *Millharbour* case, Akenhead J. concluded his review of the case law on representative proceedings by identifying the following points:[124]

> the following general principles can be derived from the wording of the Civil Procedure Rules (1998), Rule 19.6, and the authorities:

121 J. Sorabji, *The Hidden Class Action in English Civil Procedure* 28 Civil Justice Quarterly 498, 511 (2009).

122 Fed. R. Civ. P., 23, on which L. Silberman, *The Vicissitudes of the American Class Action – With a Comparative Eye* 7 Tulane Jo. of Int. and Comp. Law 201, 204 (1999); for the text, C. Hodges, *Multi-Party Litigation* (Oxford University Press, 2001), 219 ff.

123 [2011] EWHC 661 (TCC); [2011] 3 *All England Law Reports* 1027 (Akenhead J.).

124 Ibid., at [22] (Akenhead J.).

(1) To enable a party to claim, or be claimed against, in a representative capacity for other parties, that party must have the same interest in the claim in question as those who are to be represented. That is a threshold point which must be established by reference to the facts so far as it is possible to ascertain the facts at the time when the court considers the representative capacity of any party. It is legitimate to proceed by reference to the proposed or actual pleadings to ascertain at least what the facts are assumed to be.
(2) It must be possible at any stage during the proceedings to ascertain whether any given person qualifies for membership of the represented class of persons as having the same interest as the party which seeks to represent them.
(3) The question of whether and the extent to which parties have the same interest can only be answered by reference to the facts of the particular case…
(4) … It will be inappropriate, before the final judgment on the issues resolved in relation to the represented parties, for the Court to decide the issues or, indeed, to indicate in some obiter way what the answer may well be. That is simply because the Court will not have heard full argument and will only have unchallenged written evidence before it at that stage.
(5) Once it is clear that there is the same interest, the Court has a discretion whether to allow the relevant party to act or to continue to act in a representative capacity. Indeed, the Court retains a discretion even at and after the judgment to direct that a judgment is not binding or is not to be enforced. Thus, it is conceivable that, if in the judgment findings of fact or other law are such that it emerges that one or more of the represented persons does not have the same interest, the judge could well direct that the judgment is not to be enforced against them.
(6) The overriding objective [in Civil Procedure Rules (1998), Part 1] must always play an important part in the exercise of the discretion. Thus the saving of cost and time to the parties, and indeed to the court, must be factors in appropriate cases to take into account.
(7) Limitation defences could be a factor to take into account depending obviously on when the representative character is sought to be imposed. In general, however, it would be open to a defendant to run a limitation defence in relation to represented parties who were not actual parties to the litigation. If such a defence was established against certain persons, it would be a wholly exceptional case in which the judge allowed the judgment to be enforced by a person who had not been a party to the claim and against whom the limitation defence had been established.

The economic background in the *Millharbour* case is similar to the *Monarch Steamship* case (1947): (1) damages, even though not already known (unlike in the *Monarch SS* case, where the loss was already known), can already be estimated, and in due course will be confirmed (the final amount of the repair costs charged to the leaseholders by the management company): and so the global damages liability will be the cost – consistent with the duty to mitigate – of rectifying the defective building work; (2) there is a pre-existing formula or criterion for allocating that compensation amongst the class members (in the *Millharbour* case it would be the formula used to invoice the tenants for the repair work, under the terms of the tenancy; and in the *Monarch Steamship* case the criterion was the rules for allocating liability for general average amongst cargo-owners).

Furthermore, the facts of the *Millharbour* case are similar to those in *Moon* v. *Atherton* (1972).[125] Both cases concerned the need to repair property occupied by a class of leaseholders

[125] *Moon* v. *Atherton* [1972] 2 *Queen's Bench Reports* 435, Court of Appeal (England and Wales).

or tenants. In the *Moon* case, a dozen leaseholders had already suffered loss. They had bought leases in property constructed in the 1960s. The defendant architect had allegedly failed to inspect building work. And so the roof to the block of flats was defective. The claim was that the defendant should compensate for the repair work. The work had already been carried out. The cost had been shared equally by the dozen leaseholders.

On these facts, the Court of Appeal in *Moon* v. *Atherton* raised no objection to the representative action proceeding. Lord Denning M.R. accepted the defendant's concession that where damages are calculable at the commencement of proceedings, and so have become an ascertainable sum, there is no objection to representative proceedings for recovery of the ascertainable or specific sum.[126] The main point in this decision, however, was that the court can permit another of the victims of this alleged wrong to step into the shoes of the representative if she wishes to discontinue.

In addition to the *Millharbour* case, examined above, a liberal approach to using representative proceedings was adumbrated in a 2003 case, decided four years after the Civil Procedure Rules (1998) had taken effect, *Independiente Ltd.* v. *Music Trading On-Line (H.K.) Ltd.* (2003). In this case Morritt V.-C. said:[127]

> provisions of the civil procedure rules . . . emphasise the need to interpret the phrase 'the same interest' and to apply the provisions of Civil Procedure Rules (1998), Rule 19.6, both flexibly and in conformity with the overriding objective [in Civil Procedure Rules (1998), Part 1]. Accordingly, there are three questions: do the [suggested class members] have (1) a common interest, (2) a common grievance and (3) is the relief sought by the claimants in its nature beneficial to the [class members]?

The claim in the *Independiente* case was for both an injunction and pecuniary relief in respect of breach of class members' copyright. The defendant operated a website through which it sold compact discs which had been released for sale outside of the European Economic Area, with the full permission of the copyright owners. The representative claimants contended that importation of those discs into the UK amounted to infringing acts in respect of those artists which it represented. The claimant maintained that it had a mandate to act on behalf of all the individual copyright-holding members of the British Phonographic Industry Ltd. (BPI) and Phonographic Performance Ltd. (PPL). Sir Andrew Morritt C. agreed. He said:

> (1) 'there was here a common interest: the question whether the supply of CD's via the website . . . was an infringement of the U.K. copyright in the relevant sound recording was a matter common to all members since the same method was used for all the supplies made';
> (2) 'the relevant relief is injunctive or pecuniary. As far as pecuniary relief is concerned it is in its nature equally beneficial to Relevant Members as to the individual claimants. What they do with any money recovered in the action is a matter for them, not the defendants . . . If the Relevant Members are content that the money should go to BPI that is a matter for them. Their wishes in that regard do not prevent the pecuniary relief being in its nature equally beneficial to all.'

The *Independiente* case is similar to *EMI* v. *Riley* (1981)[128] because in both these actions the 'victims' of intellectual property violations had been content that any compensation should go into a special account which would be used as a fighting fund to deter and restrain future intellectual property violations. In effect, individual victims had sacrificed their personal right to

126 Ibid., at 442.
127 [2003] EWHC 470 (Ch), at [23] (Morritt V.-C.).
128 [1981] 1 *Weekly Law Reports* 923, 926 (Dillon J.).

compensation for the sake of the longer-term and collectively co-ordinated protection of their intellectual property rights. By contrast, most represented members in other contexts will have a personal interest in pocketing any payment of compensation for their civil or commercial loss.

Another example of representative proceedings being brought in respect of a damages claim is *Law Debenture Trust Corpn plc* v. *Elektrim* S.A. (2009).[129] In this case a damages action was brought on behalf of bondholders by a representative.

9.5.5 *The* Emerald *Case (2010)*

There has been one setback. The judge at first instance in *Emerald Supplies Ltd.* v. *British Airways plc* (2010)[130] decided that a proposed representative action was procedurally irregular because a stable list of class members could not be drawn up *in limine*,[131] and the Court of Appeal agreed.[132]

9.5.6 *Rejection in 2009 of a Generic Opt-Out Mechanism*

The Government in July 2009 opposed introduction of a generic opt-out class action in England for compensatory claims.[133] Instead the Government proposed that possible reform should proceed on a 'sector by sector' basis, and that an opt-out class action device should be introduced only if, in the relevant context, such a litigation tool would be justified as cost-effective and proportionate, and superior to regulatory powers.[134]

The Financial Services Bill 2009 contained such an opt-out instrument in favour of shareholders who had suffered loss from dealings in the financial services market.[135] But these proposals were excised from the final legislation.[136]

Mulheron remained unimpressed by these governmental decisions.[137] But as we shall now see, vigour has been injected in the context of competition law infringements.

9.6 UK CLASS LITIGATION IN COMPETITION LAW

Schedule 8 to the Consumer Rights Act 2015 has introduced both an opt-in and an opt-out judicial mechanism (and associated settlement mechanisms) for dealing with claims for damages arising in the competition law context.[138] The claims can be for

[129] [2009] EWHC 1801 (Ch), at [1], Sales J., (affirmed [2010] EWCA Civ 1142).
[130] [2010] EWCA Civ 1284; [2011] *Chancery Reports* 345.
[131] [2009] EWHC 741 (Ch); [2009] C.P. Rep. 32, at [38] (Morritt C.).
[132] [2010] EWCA Civ 1284; [2011] *Chancery Reports* 345, at [63] and [64] (Mummery L.J.).
[133] Ministry of Justice, *The Government's Response to the Civil Justice Council's Report Improving Access to Justice Through Collective Actions* (July 2009).
[134] Ibid., at [11].
[135] Financial Services Bill, House of Lords' Bill 26 (2009/10), clauses 18–25.
[136] Financial Services Act 2010.
[137] R. Mulheron, *Recent milestones in class actions reform in England: a critique and a proposal* 127 Law Quarterly Review 288 (2011); see also J. Sorabji, 'Collective Action Reform in England and Wales', in D. Fairgrieve and E. Lein (eds.), *Extraterritoriality and Collective Redress* (Oxford University Press, 2012), chapter 3.
[138] A. Higgins, *Driving with the Handbrake On: Compensation Class Actions under the Consumer Rights Act 2015* 79 Modern Law Review 442 (2016); A. Higgins and A. A. S. Zuckerman, *Class Actions come to England – More Access to Justice and More of a Compensation Culture, but they are Superior to the Alternatives* 35 Civil Justice Quarterly 1 (2016); R. Mulheron, *A Spotlight on the Settlement Criteria under the U.K.'s New Competition Class Action* 35 Civil Justice Quarterly 14; (2016) A. M. Mozetic, *Collective Redress: A Case for Opt-out Class Actions in England and Wales'*35 Civil Justice Quarterly 29 (2016).

injunctions[139] and/or damages (or other pecuniary awards).[140] Exemplary or punitive damages are unavailable.[141]

Such collective proceedings can be commenced by a representative,[142] but that person must obtain from the Competition Appeal Tribunal a 'collective proceedings order'.[143]

The three effects of such an order are (1) to authorise the representative party to proceed,[144] (2) to delineate the relevant class of person whose claims are eligible for inclusion in the proceedings,[145] and (3) to specify whether the proceedings will be opt-in or opt-out.[146] The representative might or might not be a person who is a co-victim within the relevant class.[147] Damages-based agreements are unenforceable in opt-out proceedings.[148]

The collective proceedings do not affect the right to 'bring any other proceedings in respect of the claim'.[149] Limitation periods are suspended during the currency of such collective proceedings, subject to specified termination points.[150]

Opt-in and opt-out proceedings in this context are defined as follows.[151] Opt-in collective proceedings are: 'collective proceedings which are brought on behalf of each class member who opts in by notifying the representative, in a manner and by a time specified, that the claim should be included in the collective proceedings'. Opt-out collective proceedings are:

> collective proceedings which are brought on behalf of each class member except – (a) any class member who opts out by notifying the representative, in a manner and by a time specified, that the claim should not be included in the collective proceedings, and (b) any class member who – (i) is not domiciled in the United Kingdom at a time specified, and (ii) does not, in a manner and by a time specified, opt in by notifying the representative that the claim should be included in the collective proceedings.

In both opt-out and opt-in proceedings before the Tribunal, compensatory damages (or other pecuniary awards)[152] can be awarded by the Tribunal 'without undertaking an assessment of the amount of damages recoverable in respect of the claim of each represented person'.[153]

In opt-out proceedings, the damages will normally be paid to the representative party for distribution amongst the class.[154] There is a high risk that such damages might remain unallocated to class members after a specified date. If so, unallocated damages will either be paid to a nominated charity,[155] or the Tribunal might order that they be paid to the representative in

139 Section 47D, Competition Act 1998, substituted by Schedule 8 to the Consumer Rights Act 2015.

140 Section 47C(9)(d), Competition Act 1998.

141 Ibid., section 47C(1).

142 Ibid., section 47B(2).

143 Ibid., section 47B(4)–(9); on the certification criteria, A. Higgins, *Driving with the Handbrake On: Compensation Class Actions under the Consumer Rights Act 2015* 79 Modern Law Review 442, 454–8 (2016).

144 Ibid., section 47B(7)(a).

145 Ibid., section 47B(7)(b).

146 Ibid., section 47B(7)(c).

147 Ibid., section 47B(8).

148 Ibid., section 47C(8), adopting, at section 47C(9)(c), the definition of Damages Based Agreements in section 58AA (3), Courts and Legal Services Act 1990.

149 Ibid., section 47B(13).

150 Ibid., section 47D(4)–(7).

151 Ibid., section 47B(11).

152 Ibid., section 47C(9)(d).

153 Ibid., section 47C(2).

154 Ibid., section 47C(3).

155 Ibid., section 47C(5); the nominated charity is the Access to Justice Foundation (Explanatory Notes to section 81, Consumer Rights 2015, at para. 438).

respect of the costs incurred in connection with the proceedings.[156] Injunctions can be awarded in opt-out or opt-in competition law collective proceedings.[157]

Judicial decisions (whether judgments or orders) made under these collective regimes are binding on all represented persons.[158] Appeals (which can be brought only by the representative)[159] are possible on points of law or concerning money awards or the grant of an injunction.[160]

In the case of opt-out proceedings, the Tribunal can approve a collective settlement,[161] but 'only if satisfied that its terms are just and reasonable'.[162] Such a settlement will then be binding on all represented persons domiciled in the UK or those who positively opted in to the collective proceedings.[163]

There is also a (detailed) mechanism for gaining the Tribunal's approval of a collective settlement even where no substantive collective proceedings have already begun. But this requires the Tribunal to make a collective settlement order.[164]

It should be noted that in 2013 the European Union had issued recommendations concerning an opt-out 'collective redress mechanisms'.[165] The European Union's Directive on anti-trust damages actions (2014)[166] did not require Member States to adopt such mechanisms in order to facilitate claims for competition law damages. The UK has marched ahead of the European Union, therefore, in this respect.

In a decision which has now been reversed, the Competition Appeal Tribunal in *Merricks* v. *Mastercard Inc.* (2017)[167] had refused to grant authorisation (a collective proceedings order, or CPO) for an opt-out claim under the regime just summarised. The Tribunal was not satisfied that such proceedings would be 'suitable' for the purpose of section 47B of the Competition Act 1998 (as amended).[168] The claims related to a competition infringement in the charges made by a well-known credit card operator. This was a follow-on claim, the infringement having been established in separate proceedings.[169] The class was suggested to be over forty million people who had used this card to purchase goods or services in the UK during the period May 1992 to June 2008

156 Ibid., section 47C(6). For criticism of section 47C(6), A. Higgins, *Driving with the Handbrake On: Compensation Class Actions under the Consumer Rights Act 2015* 79 Modern Law Review 442, 458–67 (2016) (the provision covers the risk that there is a shortfall in the recovery of costs by the victorious representative from the defendant; but this point is omitted by Higgins).

157 Section 47D, Competition Act 1998, substituted by Schedule 8 to the Consumer Rights Act 2015.

158 Ibid., section 47B(12).

159 Ibid., section 49(2A).

160 Ibid., section 49(1A)–(1D).

161 Ibid., section 49A.

162 Ibid., section 49A(5); R. Mulheron, *A Spotlight on the Settlement Criteria under the U.K.'s New Competition Class Action* 35 Civil Justice Quarterly 14 (2016).

163 Ibid., section 49A(8) and (9).

164 Ibid., section 49B.

165 European Commission Recommendation of 1 June, 2013 on common principles for injunctive and compensatory collective redress mechanisms in the Member States concerning violation of rights granted under Union law [2013] O.J. L.201/60; E.U. Commission's Communication on Collective Redress of 11 June 2013, C.O.M. (2013) 401 final.

166 Preamble (13) to the Directive of the European Parliament and of the Council on certain rules governing actions for damages under national law for infringements of the competition law provisions of the Member States and of the European Union (2013/0185 (C.O.D.)), 24 October 2014 http://ec.europa.eu/competition/antitrust/actionsdamages/damages_directive_final_en.pdf.

167 [2017] CAT 16.

168 Section 47B, Competition Act 1998, substituted by Schedule 8 to the Consumer Rights Act 2015.

169 [2017] CAT 16, at [1].

(provided they were sixteen years or over and had been resident in the UK for a continuous period of at least three months).[170] An aggregated damages claim of £16 billion was made.[171] But this refusal to grant certification of the proposed opt-out claim was reversed by the Court of Appeal.[172] In this appeal, it was held that the Competition Appeal Tribunal had applied the wrong test to determine whether certification of the proposed class should be made. The Court of Appeal remitted the certification issue to the tribunal, which would now be expected to revisit its decision, applying the following guidance:[173]

> Once it is accepted that aggregate damages can be awarded and therefore assessed by reference to the loss suffered by the represented class as a whole, it becomes difficult to justify a reversion to an individual calculation of loss for the purposes of distribution. Claimants in this class will know that they stand to be compensated (if at all) on a per capita basis and can choose (if they wish) not to be included in the action. But once the assessment of the aggregate award is complete then . . . Mastercard has . . . no right to object if the class members who have suffered loss by the then proven infringement stand to be compensated in a way which does not exactly or perhaps even approximately replicate the individual losses which have been suffered. The vindication of the rights of individual claimants is achieved by the aggregate award itself.

9.7 CONCLUSION

The secession of the UK from the European Union (in 2020, following the 'Brexit' referendum decision in June 2016) might place the question of effective opt-out representative proceedings back in the limelight. As noted, British adoption of opt-out representative damages claims in the competition law field is a singular break with the general position within the European Union. It is too early to assess whether that type of class action (for compensation following competition law infringement) will become significant in the UK. A more general issue is whether such an opt-out damages-yielding process will become broader in its substantive scope, and no longer be confined to the 'sector' of competition law.

As for this larger issue, caution is advised because there are three dangers in adopting an 'opt-out' system.

(1) *Abuse and possible overkill.* A generic opt-out class action for damages would involve claimants' rights being championed by the joint enterprise of law firms (including foreign firms fishing in England for work) and commercial funders (or syndicates of funders) interested in profiting from others' litigation. This might involve potentially aggressive collective litigation and very large gains being made by law firms (compare the astronomic size, £16 billion, of the claim in the *Mastercard* action, which is now proceedings, as noted above).

(2) *Defensive behaviour.* There is a fear that class action litigation will expose commercial and public entities to expensive and protracted litigation. The fear reflects the reality: it is the essence of such claims that they involve substantial bodies of 'victims' and procedural complexity.

170 Ibid., at [2].
171 Ibid., at [3].
172 [2019] EWCA Civ 674; [2019] 5 *Common Market Law Reports* 4.
173 Ibid., at [61], Patten L.J., giving the court's judgment.

(3) *Increase in the amount of insurance cover.* Even the *prospect* of such claims will be enough to increase the cost of potential defendants' defensive measures. In particular, consumers and businesses will pay more for insurance cover.

But there is little doubt that the combined forces of entrepreneurial law firms, barristers and some academic commentators will continue to press for expansion of the opt-out representative device.

10

Class Actions in Switzerland

Beat Brändli

10.1 INTRODUCTION

Swiss Law as well as the law of its neighboring, continental European countries originally didn't know the procedural instrument of class actions. The reason for this absence compared to former Commonwealth states is twofold. First, Swiss doctrine has always placed the right to be individually heard and the protection of individual interests at the forefront. On the other hand, the procedural economic advantages of class actions were neglected. Second, the Swiss legislature, as many European Parliaments, was afraid of the disadvantages that class action lawsuits allegedly bring for the national economy and the legal system.[1] Regarding the economy, the legislature feared the instrument could cripple even reliable businesses. Concerning the legal system, they were afraid to boost the number of lawsuits, in particular such cases where lawyers could smell the big money.

Nonetheless, the Swiss Civil Procedure Code (CPC) that replaced all the former cantonal civil procedure rules[2] and took effect in 1 January 2011[3] knows various instruments for collective redress, such as the Voluntary Joinder of Parties or the Joinder of Actions and also General and Special Group Actions. Even though these options of legal protection are based primarily on individual procedures they create a collective effect. Within Section 10.2 of this chapter the rationale of collective redress from a Law and Economics perspective shall be shortly explained, taking the Swiss design of civil procedure into consideration. In Section 10.3 we will then focus on the Swiss instruments of collective redress *de lege lata* in detail.[4]

Furthermore, the times and mindsets in Switzerland with regard to class actions are changing. In particular, the well-known case of Volkswagen emissions scandal (also dubbed Dieselgate or Emissionsgate) brought to light that the current civil procedural instruments might not be

[1] See Swiss Federal Council, Dispatch for the Swiss Civil Procedure Code (CPC) of 28 June 2006, 7289; SCHWEIZERISCHE ZIVILPROZESSORDNUNG, Article 89 CPC rec. 5d (Paul Oberhammer, Tanja Domej & Ulrich Haas, eds., 2014); Martin Bernet & Philipp Groz, *Sammelklagen in Europa?*, SZZP 75 et seqq. (1/2008); Laura Jaquemoud-Rossari, *Les parties et les actes des parties, in* LE PROJET DE CODE DE PROCÉDURE CIVILE FÉDÉRALE 112 et seq. (Suzana Lukic, ed. 2008); Lorenz Droese, *Die Sammelklage in den USA und in Europa und die Auswirkungen auf die Rechtslage in der Schweiz, in* HAFTPFLICHTPROZESS, 121 et seqq. (Walter Fellmann & Stephan Weber, eds., 2010).

[2] Until this moment civil procedure was regulated by the twenty-six Swiss cantons autonomously, just like in US states.

[3] Swiss Civil Procedure Code (CPC) of 19 December 2008, Classified (Swiss) Compilation (CC) 272, in force since 1 January 2011. All Swiss Federal Acts and Ordinances can be found on www.admin.ch/gov/en/start/federal-law.html.

[4] "*De lege lata*" is a Latin term meaning "the law as it is (current law)". The expression is opposed to the term "*de lege ferenda*" that stands for the "the law as it will be (future law)" according to existing legislative proposals not yet adopted as law.

sufficient to deal adequately with big scattered damages. With regard to this particular case, the Swiss courts did not hear the Special Group Action filed by the foundation for consumer protection ("Stiftung für Konsumentenschutz" in September 2017 for want of legitimate interest in bringing proceedings,[5] and a Joinder of Actions regarding damages that was submitted in parallel was dismissed due to lack of capacity to act and litigate (decision of the Swiss Federal Court of 16 July 2020, 4A_43/2020). The consumer protection organization "Fédération romande des consommateurs" from the French part of Switzerland advised Swiss injured parties in this context to join the class action lawsuit organized by the German organization "myRights" in Germany. Meanwhile, Volkswagen reached an agreement with authorities and injured parties in the USA within one year of the manipulations becoming known. The damage payments there amount to over 25 billion US Dollars. Because of this and other cases the Swiss Federal Council proposed an amendment of the CPC to the Swiss Parliament, to create better remedial measures for collective redress, including, among other things, a class action for damages (so called Reparatory Class Action). Section 10.4 of this chapter will highlight the amendments planned for the CPC *de lege ferenda*.

Switzerland does not keep statistics of civil procedural data, that is, the number of different legal procedures or actions that took place within a certain timeframe. Furthermore, only very few courts (e.g., the Swiss Federal Court[6]) publish the number of cases filed, taken and completed. However, even in such few publications no differentiation is made according to type of action. Due to this precondition, the author started a short survey of civil courts of the first instance in Switzerland. They were asked the number of cases by the type of instruments for collective legal protection (see Section 10.3) for the past year (2018) as well as since the CPC took effect (2011). The numbers received and its preliminary conclusions regarding the Law and Economics of collective legal protection in Switzerland will be presented in Section 10.5.

In Section 10.6 the chapter is closed by a conclusion of the Law and Economics of class actions in Switzerland. Moreover, the author proposes a few modifications to the ongoing amendment of the CPC to even further improve collective legal protection in Switzerland.

10.2 THE LAW AND ECONOMICS RATIONALE FOR COLLECTIVE REDRESS

"Scattered damage" occurs when many people suffer a minor damage. Unfortunately, due to the costs of proceedings in Switzerland, there is a rational apathy for an individual concerned to assert its minor damage individually. From a Law and Economics perspective this can be illustrated with the following Figure 10.1 showing the decision tree of an individual claimant confronted with a scattered damage of 1,000 Swiss Francs (CHF, this is about 1,000 USD). In order to calculate the expected value of an individual lawsuit, it is necessary to calculate from right to left within the below depicted decision tree (i.e., from the last to the first step of the necessary proceeding).

The expected value of the lawsuit for this individual claimant is the probability of winning multiplied by the monetary outcome of winning plus the probability of losing multiplied by the monetary outcome of losing minus the costs for suing. In Swiss terms, this leads roughly to the following calculation if we assume that the probability of winning and losing the case is both 50 percent: $(0.5 \times 3{,}000) + (0.5 \times -1{,}000) - 2{,}500 = -1{,}500$ CHF. The result shows that the expected value of the individual lawsuit is negative. This is mainly because of the costs of filing the claim (−2,500 CHF) that encompass court (−1,000 CHF) as well as lawyer's fees (−1,500 CHF). In case

5 Decision of the Commercial Court of Zurich of 12 July 2018, HG170181-O, consideration 3; confirming this judgement of the lower court: Decision of the Swiss Federal Court of 8 February 2019, 4A_483/2018.

6 The Swiss Federal Court rules as the court of last instance in Switzerland. In penal and civil cases it can usually be called after the cantonal instances that consist normally of a district court and a (cantonal) court of appeal.

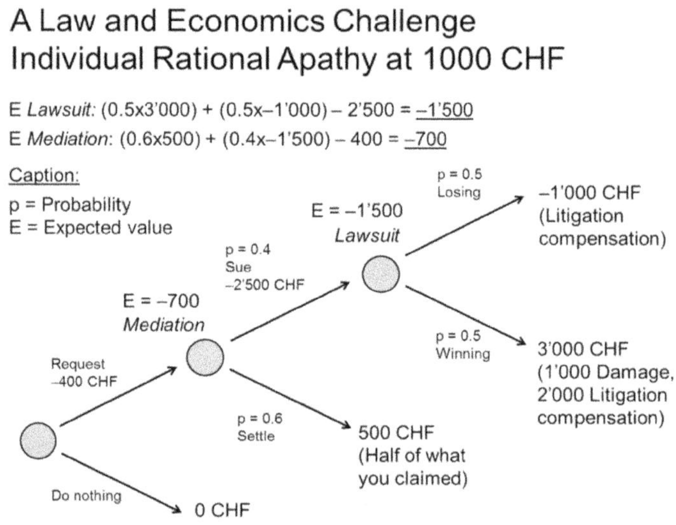

FIGURE 10.1 Individual rational apathy (own representation)

of winning the court fees have to be fully compensated by the defendant, lawyer's fee have to be compensated only to a certain degree according to cantonal statutory law (1,000 CHF).

The expected value of doing mediation, which is a mandatory procedural step that generally must be passed through before a lawsuit in Switzerland, can be calculated based on the above outcome as follows assuming a chance of 60 percent that the case can be settled[7]: (0.6 x 500) + (0.4 x −1,500) − 400 = −700 CHF. The request for mediation costs are about 400 CHF. The outcome if the mediation fails is the expected value of the lawsuit that has already been calculated (−1,500 CHF). The outcome if the mediation succeeds is usually a settlement about the half of the claim (i.e., 500 CHF). The calculated result for the expected value of the mediation is negative as well.

As a consequence of these calculated expected values the rational individual claimant will neither file a request for mediation nor start a lawsuit, as both expected values for these procedural steps are negative. In this case it is simply more favorable to do nothing (outcome 0 CHF).

The presented Swiss civil procedural setup suffers from a law enforcement deficit if this challenge of individual rational apathy cannot be overcome. Especially in the case of scattered damage, compensation would be particularly desirable from an economic point of view, since otherwise the unconsidered economic costs are particularly high. These non-compensated costs represent so-called externalities in economic terms. They can be most easily mitigated by those responsible for the damage (i.e., the injuring party). Only when these causers of the damage have to compensate for it, they will include it in their economic calculation (internalize it). The civil procedural setup should therefore ensure that scattered damages are also sued for. Alternatively to a civil law solution, the state could also punish the corresponding tortfeasors and compensate the injured parties. However, Switzerland prefers as little state intervention as possible and thus a civil procedural solution seems preferable.[8]

One way to overcome this problem of individual rational apathy in civil procedure is the instrument of collective redress. Figure 10.2 below shows the rationale to sue collectively

7 The success rate for (state or private) mediation in Switzerland is about 60–70 percent over all types of cases.

8 *See also* BRIAN T. FITZPATRICK, THE CONSERVATIVE CASE FOR CLASS ACTIONS (2019).

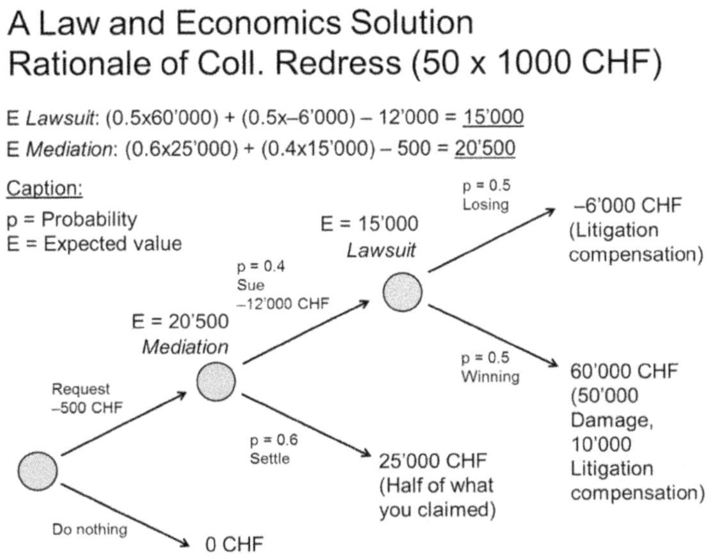

FIGURE 10.2 Rationale of collective redress (own representation)

for scattered damage. In this example, we assume that fifty injured persons assert their respective suffered scattered damage of 1,000 CHF each in a joint proceeding. Without thinking about how this joint action can be brought, the following logic emerges from a Law and Economics perspective. The expected value for the lawsuit by collective redress can be calculated as follows: (0.5 x 60,000) + (0.5 x −6,000) – 12,000 = 15,000 CHF. Note that the probabilities of winning and losing didn't change. Only the costs to file the claim, that is, sue (−12,000 CHF), increased in proportion to the amount in dispute (50 x 1,000 CHF = 50,000 CHF). These costs encompass again court (−4,000 CHF) as well as lawyer's fees (−8,000 CHF). In case of winning the court fees have again to be fully compensated by the defendant, lawyer's fee have to be compensated only to a certain degree according to cantonal statutory law (6,000 CHF). Note that court fees as well as the compensation for lawyer's fees in Switzerland are generally proportionate to the amount in dispute and laid down in (cantonal) statutory laws.

The expected value for the mandatory mediation is now as follows: (0.6 x 25,000) + (0.4 x 15,000) − 500 = 20,500 CHF. Note that the costs for the (state) mediation do differ only slightly compared to the above case (−500 CHF).

In this example of collective redress where fifty concerned people claim their compensation for damage in a single proceeding the expected value of the lawsuit (15,000 CHF) as well as of the mediation (20,500 CHF) are positive and a much better option than to do nothing (0 CHF). As a consequence the concerned persons will be willing to enforce their claims and will definitely request mediation. Likewise, if they don't find a settlement they will also be willing to sue and start a lawsuit.

However, it is essential to consider the various instruments of collective redress individually in order to be able to make a statement as to whether they seem adequate and suitable to overcome the identified problem of individual rational apathy. There are various technical pitfalls why theoretically available instruments do not appear sufficiently efficient for collective redress in practice.

10.3 INSTRUMENTS OF COLLECTIVE LEGAL PROTECTION *DE LEGE LATA*

10.3.1 *Voluntary Joinder of Parties*

The voluntary joinder of parties, also known as a simple cooperative dispute or a subjective accumulation of claims, combines several claims by numerous plaintiffs or defendants in one lawsuit. The several claims are legally independent of each other but factually or legally related. The law explains it as follows:

Article 71 CPC Voluntary joinder

1 Two or more persons whose rights and duties result from similar circumstances or legal grounds may jointly appear as plaintiffs or be sued as joint defendants.
2 Voluntary joinder is excluded if the individual cases are subject to different types of procedure.
3 Each of the joint parties may proceed independently from the others.

The voluntary joinder is, as the name already unveils, voluntary, this at least from the point of view of the plaintiff, and takes place for reasons of expediency. It aims to promote procedural economy and harmony in decision-making.[9] It is always a matter of independent legal petitions in which the process requirements and the asserted claims are to be examined and decided independently. A decision by the court always only has effect between the procedural parties (i.e., between plaintiff and defendant), but not in the relationship between the parties of the joinder.

Each party of the joinder always acts independently of the other comrades-in-arms and can dispose of the subject matter of the dispute without a procedural action obliging the others in any way.[10]

According to Article 71 CPC the voluntary joinder has three requirements: first, the claims asserted must be based on similar facts or legal grounds. In other words, there must be a sufficient factual connection between the claims (also called "connexity").

Second, the claims to be joined must be subject to the same type of procedure. There exist three basic types of procedures in Switzerland: the ordinary proceedings (according to Article 219 et seqq. CPC), the simplified proceedings (according to Article 243 et seqq. CPC) and the summary proceedings (according to Article 248 et seqq. CPC). Besides those basic forms, the Swiss civil procedure knows special proceedings in family law (according to Article 271 et seqq. CPC). The difference that separates the ordinary from the simplified proceeding is in most cases the individual value in dispute, because the simplified proceeding applies only in financial disputes with an individual value in dispute not exceeding 30,000 Swiss Francs. Hence a party that claims for example 50,000 Swiss Francs cannot file a voluntary joinder with a party that claims 20,000 Swiss Francs, as the first is subject to an ordinary and the latter subject to a simplified proceeding.

9 *Cf.* Kurzkommentar Zivilprozessordnung, Article 71 rec. 1 (Paul Oberhammer, ed., 2010); Lucy Gordon-Vrba, Vielparteienprozesse. Kollektive Durchsetzung gleichartiger individueller Kompensationsansprüche unter dem Aspekt der prozessualen Effizienz und Fairness 170 (2007); also already Max Guldener, Schweizerisches Zivilprozessrecht, 3rd Edition, 301 ff. (1979).

10 Swiss Federal Council, *Kollektiver Rechtsschutz in der Schweiz – Bestandesaufnahme und Handlungsmöglichkeiten. Bericht des Bundesrates*, 15 (2013); *CPC commenté*, Article 71 rec. 10 et seqq. (François Bohnet, Jaques Haldy, Nicolas Jeandin, Philippe Schweizer & Denis Tappy, eds., 2011); Oberhammer, *supra* note 10, Article 71 N 8 ff.; Basler Kommentar zur Schweizerischen Zivilprozessordnung, Article 71 rec. 30 et seqq. (Karl Spühler, Luca Tenchio & Dominik Infanger, eds., 2010).

Third, the voluntary joinder requires the same territorial and material jurisdiction[11] for the joint claims, even though the law doesn't mention that explicitly.[12] In practice, the territorial jurisdiction is mostly not an issue, because Article 15 paragraph 1 CPC says that if a claim is directed against two or more defendants, the court that has jurisdiction with regard to one defendant has jurisdiction with regard to all defendants unless jurisdiction is based solely on an agreement on jurisdiction. Due to the fact that territorial jurisdiction often refers to the (real or legal) domicile of the defendant (cf. Article 10 CPC) the same territorial jurisdiction is generally no barrier for claimants that want to join voluntarily. By contrast, the same material jurisdiction could be a problem. For example, if a registered company wants to join forces with natural persons to sue another company from Zurich it can't do so in front of the district court, as the canton of Zurich has a commercial court for disputes between registered companies. However, the natural persons could join the company in front of the commercial court, as they are entitled to choose between the district and the commercial court.

According to Article 72 CPC, the joint parties may appoint a joint representative, failing which service is made to each party individually.

With regard to cost bearing, the court determines generally each party's share of the costs. However, it may hold the parties jointly as well as severally liable for all the costs if it considers such allocation appropriate.[13] As a result, several plaintiffs who are unaware of their mutual solvency take a certain cost risk. The higher the number of claimants, the more the total cost risk for the individual claimant increases. This risk weighs particularly heavily when asserting claims for scattered damage, where there are many injured parties that individually have only a small amount to gain.

Nevertheless, the voluntary joinder of parties is thought to be the most used Swiss legal instrument for collective legal protection. The evaluation of data in Section 10.5 will show if this general assumption can be confirmed and whether it is still used for scattered damages.

10.3.2 *Joinder of Actions*

A joinder of actions or combination of actions, also dubbed an objective accumulation of actions in Swiss legal doctrine, involves a single plaintiff bringing several separate and independent procedural claims against the same defendant in a single action. This results in an accumulation of several matters in dispute in one procedure.[14] The joinder of actions is ruled by Article 90 CPC which reads as follows:

> Article 90 CPC Combination of actions
> The plaintiff may combine two or more claims against the same party in one action, if:

[11] "Same territorial jurisdiction" means territorially, the same district court must have jurisdiction. In general, territorial jurisdiction arises at the domicile or location of the registered office of the defendant (Art. 10 CPC). "Same material jurisdiction" means as regard content of the dispute, the same court must have jurisdiction to handle the matter. E.g., there exist special commercial courts to handle disputes between companies (cf. Art. 6 CPC), i.e., they have exclusive material jurisdiction to deal with disputes between companies but not between natural persons and companies. A joinder of actions between claimants consisting of natural persons and companies might therefore be complicated in a canton (state) with a commercial court.

[12] See Swiss Federal Council, *supra* note 11, 15.

[13] See Art. 106 para. 4 CPC.

[14] In general, the plaintiff is entitled according to the principle of *non ultra petita* (also called the maxim of disposition) to determine the scope of the subject matter of the dispute. The principle is laid down in Art. 58 para. 1 CPC.

a. they are within the material jurisdiction of the same court; and
b. they are subject to the same type of procedure.

Requirements for the combination of actions is on one hand the same material and also territorial jurisdiction of the court. The latter is tacitly assumed by the law. On the other hand, the different actions to be joined must be subject to the same type of procedure.

Article 15 paragraph 2 CPC says that if two or more actions that are factually connected are raised against one and the same defendant, each court that has territorial jurisdiction over any one of the actions has jurisdiction over all of them. This means that a combination of actions is always possible, if they are subject to the same type of procedure and are factually connected.

However, to reach a collective effect in terms of claims of various individuals against one or more defendants, the various individual claims must first be transferred to a single plaintiff who then uses the instrument of joinder of actions. The assignment of claims can regularly be done by Article 164 CO[15] et seqq. Article 165 CO requires the assignment to be done in writing. The whole legal claim must be ceded. It is not possible according to Swiss Law to transfer willingly only the status of litigation, that is, the right to act as a party in a proceeding (in German so-called "gewillkürte Prozessstandschaft"), without ceding also the underlying legal claim.

This assignment of claims results in a single plaintiff that carries the whole litigation cost risk (bear in mind that according to Swiss Law the loser pays all procedural costs, consisting also of the compensation of the other party's costs). The rates for court and party compensation fees are at least declining with higher values at dispute. Moreover, the original claimants may organize themselves contractually to handle such issues. Nonetheless, the cession of claims and the later joinder of actions need some additional organizational (in particular for the coordination) and juridical effort that results in extra time and costs. This might be the reason why, in contrast to Austria, no such practice is yet established in Switzerland on a regular basis.

10.3.3 *General Group Action*

A General Group Action according to Swiss law is an action brought by an association or a similar organization. The association constitutes as the plaintiff to protect the collective interests of a group of persons whose interests it represents due to its bylaws. The association files a claim against a defendant independently from the members of this group. Notwithstanding, the outcome of the General Group Action can be connected with certain effects for the members of the group of persons. The General Group Action is regulated in Article 89 CPC:

Article 89 CPC Group action

1 Associations and other organisations of national or regional importance that are authorised by their articles of association to protect the interests of a certain group of individuals may bring an action in their own name for a violation of the personality of the members of such group.

2 They may request the court:
   a. to prohibit an imminent violation;
   b. to put an end to an ongoing violation;
   c. to establish the unlawful character of a violation if the latter continues to have a disturbing effect.

3 Special legal provisions on group actions are reserved.

15 Federal Act on the Amendment of the Swiss Civil Code (Part Five: The Code of Obligations, CO) of 30 March 1911, CC 220, in force since 1 January 1912.

Article 89 CPC is basically a codification of previous Swiss Federal Court case law, which said since 1947 that associations and other organizations can sue someone in their own name if the dispute concerns violations of personality and they are authorized according to their bylaws to protect economic interests of certain groups of persons.[16] In addition, the Swiss Federal Court required that the members of this group themselves would be entitled to bring an action.[17] However, this latter prerequisite is not mentioned in Article 89 CPC, which now controls the General Group Action. On the other hand, Article 89 CPC requires in addition to the (above cited) former case law the associations also to be of nationwide or at least regional significance.

From a procedural standpoint, this case law that became hard law with the enactment of the CPC grants a special active legitimation to certain associations and organizations. However, according to Article 89 paragraph 2 CPC, a General Group Action may only be brought for injunctive relief, removal or declaration of unlawfulness. This excludes in particular any reparatory (performance) actions, that is, actions for damages, satisfaction or profit distribution. This provision also corresponds to former case law.[18]

Special provisions are reserved pursuant to Article 89 paragraph 3 CPC. The paragraph thus refers to the Special Group Actions that exist in the Federal Equality Act, in the Federal Cooperation Act, the Federal Trademark Protection Act and the Federal Fair Trading Act (see below Section 10.3.4 for Special Group Actions).

A Group Action has no material legal effect for and against the individual members of the group of persons. A possible judgment can only have a reflexive factual effect on all members, in which, for example, everyone benefits from a cease and desist order or a declaratory decision. However, the individual members of the group always remain legitimized to an independent lawsuit.

For example, an association for free physical culture could sue for an injunction and a declaration that the publication and distribution of naked pictures of its members is illegal by a media company. On the other hand, any claims for damages or compensation for personal suffering must always be brought by the individuals concerned themselves.[19]

Since a Group Action cannot be used to sue for damages, in practice there are few incentives for litigation financiers to finance such actions. Besides, in contrast to other countries, as for example Germany, there is no state support in Switzerland for the financing of such lawsuits. In my opinion, this is one of the reasons why the General Group Action (as well as the Special Group Action explained hereinafter) has remained mainly dead letter[20] in practice.

10.3.4 *Special Group Actions*

In addition to the General Group Action due to Article 89 CPC, the following special rules for group actions exist, which may be either more restrictive or more generous than the general provisions. They all create so-called Special Group Actions and take precedence over the general provisions of Article CPC.

[16] For the case law see leading decisions of the Swiss Federal Court (DSFC, in German BGE) 73 II 65 of 20 May 1947, 72; BGE 86 II 18 of 19 January 1960, E. 2; BGE 114 II 345 of 8 November 1988, E. 3b; BGE 121 III 168 of 27 April 1995 E. 4b; analogous justification for antitrust law in BGE 103 II 299 of 27 September 1977, E. 2–5; furthermore, cf. Spühler, Tenchio & Infanger, *supra* note 11, Article 89 rec 10; Oberhammer, *supra* note 10, Article 89 rec. 6 et seq.

[17] See the first case (BGE 73 II 65 of 20 May 1947, 72) where these requirements were developed by drawing an analogy to Art. 2 para. 3 of the former Federal Act on Unfair Competition (today called in the same manner but being totally revised in 1986, see CC 241).

[18] This was mentioned the first time in BGE 86 II 18 of 19 January 1960, E. 2.; see also the later decisions of the Swiss Federal Court in FN 16.

[19] Also making this example Swiss Federal Council, *supra* note 11.

[20] Regarding empirical findings see Section 10.5.

10.3.4.1 According to the Federal Act on Gender Equality

Pursuant to Article 7 paragraph 1 of the Federal Act on Gender Equality[21], organizations which, in accordance with their bylaws, promote equality between women and men or safeguard the interests of workers and have existed for at least two years may, in their own name and independently of the workers concerned, bring an action for a declaratory judgment of discrimination.

As a requirement it is necessary that the outcome of the proceedings is likely to affect a larger number of employment relationships. This Special Group Action is restricted to employee and equality organizations and can only lead to a finding of (gender) discrimination. The lawsuit benefits from special procedural facilitations for the claimant.[22]

10.3.4.2 According to the Federal Act on Unfair Competition

According to Article 10 paragraph 2 of the Federal Act on Unfair Competition,[23] professional and trade associations as well as consumer protection organizations may bring actions pursuant to Article 9 paragraph 1 and 2 of the Act. They may bring an action for an injunction, elimination or determination of unfair conduct.[24] While a consumer protection organization, as an association, files an action to establish the unfair nature of unfair conduct, individual consumers file their individual financial claims.

The instrument works best in connection with individual claims for damages. While, for example, a consumer protection organization suing for a finding that unfair conduct is illegal, individual consumers can refer to that finding and as a consequence sue for their individual financial claims. Nevertheless, the individual plaintiffs must prove the causality of this unlawfulness for their damages as well as their extent of damages in order to be awarded correspondingly.

10.3.4.3 According to the Federal Act on the Protection of Trade Marks

Pursuant to Article 56 paragraph 1 in conjunction with Articles 52 and 55 of the Federal Act on the Protection of Trade Marks and Indications of Source[25] professional and trade associations as well as consumer protection organizations may bring an action for declaration, removal, injunction or disclosure of information concerning indications of source, guarantee marks and collective marks.

10.3.4.4 According to the Federal Participation Act

Under Article 15 paragraph 2 of the Federal Participation Act[26], employees' and employers' associations may bring an action for a declaration of violations of the provisions of the Federal Participation Act.

The Federal Participation Act applies to all companies with fifty or more workers in Switzerland. It entitles the employees to appoint a representative who is to be informed by the

[21] Federal Act on Gender Equality (Gender Equality Act, GEA) of 24 March 1995, CC 151.1, in force since 1 July 1996.

[22] Such as the principle of investigation (the court must officially establish the facts of the case), a facilitation of evidence (the measure of evidence is reduced to prima facie evidence, *cf.* Art. 6 GEA), furthermore, the lawsuit is free of charge.

[23] Federal Act on Unfair Competition of 19 December 1986, CC 241, in force since 1 March 1988.

[24] *See* SHK BUNDESGESETZ GEGEN DEN UNLAUTEREN WETTBEWERB (UWG), Art. 10 rec. 20 ff. (Peter Jung & Philippe Spitz, eds., 2010).

[25] Federal Act on the Protection of Trade Marks and Indications of Source (Trade Mark Protection Act, TmPA) of 28 August 1992, CC 232.11, in force since 1 April 1993.

[26] Federal Act on the Information and Codetermination of Employees in Enterprises (Federal Participation Act) of 17 December 1993, CC 822.14, in force since 1 May 1994.

management about all developments affecting the workforce in good time as well as about the course of business once a year. The representation has participation rights in a number of matters, including occupational safety and health, the sale of a business, collective dismissals and occupational pensions. However, there are no rights of codetermination concerning (certain) corporate governance issues such as in Germany and Austria through a so-called works council (in German "Betriebsrat").

10.3.4.5 According to Article 357b of the Code of Obligations

Article 357b of the Code of Obligations[27] provides for the possibility by the contracting parties to a collective employment agreement, that is, employer associations and unions, to file a declaratory action for conclusion, content and termination of the collective employment agreement against their respective members (employees and employers). The prerequisite is that the employer association and the union agree to it within their collective employment agreement. The employees and employers that form members of these contracting parties are bound by law to the arrangements made within the collective employment agreement.[28]

10.3.4.6 According to the Federal Disability Discrimination Act

Article 9 of the Federal Disability Discrimination Act[29] gives organizations for persons with disabilities operating throughout Switzerland that have been established for at least ten years the right to bring a declaratory action for discrimination or to appeal such a decision. Process requirement is that the discrimination affects a substantial number of persons with disabilities, that is, several people.

10.3.5 *Model Lawsuits*

In a model or test lawsuit (sometimes also called pilot action), a collective interest is safeguarded by first conducting a single typical "model" procedure ("model case") between two parties on a particular issue. Then the court decision or prior settlement between these two parties on certain factual and/or legal issues has an effect as a procedural example for similar subsequent proceedings between other parties, so that in these proceedings it is no longer necessary to litigate on the identical issue in question.

Conceptually, a model lawsuit is always an individual action of the model plaintiff whose further objective is to bring about a material legal effect on a large number of cases of the factual or legal issues decided in the model proceedings. As there is no legal basis in Swiss law for such an external legal effect all the parties involved need to sign a corresponding agreement. As a consequence, an extension of the legal effect to similar cases that are not known yet is usually not possible.[30]

Article 126 CPC provides that further proceedings may be suspended for the duration of a model lawsuit. In particular, a model procedural contract may contain a joint request for suspension of a number of proceedings in favor of a particular pilot action.[31]

27 See *supra* note 16.
28 Art. 357 Code of Obligations.
29 Federal Act on the Elimination of Discrimination against People with Disabilities (Federal Disability Discrimination Act, DDA) of 13 December 2002, CC 151.3, in force since 1 January 2004.
30 *Cf.* Samuel P. Baumgartner, *Class Actions and Group Litigation in Switzerland*, 27 NORTH-WESTERN JOURNAL OF INTERNATIONAL LAW & BUSINESS 301, 342 et seqq. (2007).
31 *Cf.* Spühler, Tenchio & Infanger, *supra* note 11, Article 89 rec. 4 et seqq.

10.4 INSTRUMENTS OF COLLECTIVE LEGAL PROTECTION *DE LEGE FERENDA*

On March 2, 2018 the Swiss Federal Council sent to public consultation[32] a preliminary draft (PD CPC)[33] to amend the CPC. In addition, an explanatory report was published for the suggested amendment.[34] Public consultation ended in June 2018. A dispatch for the amendment together with a draft was published on February 26, 2020 and handed over to the Swiss parliament. However, due to the strong criticism in the consultation process, the Federal Council decided to remove the following instruments of collective legal protection from the ongoing amendment and not yet recommend their implementation to parliament. Instead, it intends to present them separately to parliament at a later date.

The Swiss Federal Council suggests in its preliminary draft three amendments that concern collective redress. First, it proposes a modification of the existing General Group Action (see Section 10.3.3 above). Second, it wants to introduce a real class action for damages (so called Reparatory Class Action); and third, it recommends adopting the instrument of Group Settlement. These three instruments, of which the latter two are completely new to Swiss law, will be presented in the subsequent parts.

10.4.1 *Modification of the General Group Action*

The group action under the suggested Article 89 PD CPC is in principle based on the existing norm but broadened in its possibility of application. The amended Article 89 CPC shall be admissible for all threatened or existing violations of the rights of members of a certain group of persons and is no longer to be limited to actions for declaratory judgement, injunctions and for the elimination of personal injury. The possibility of bringing an action would thus be extended to all substantive claims. This explicitly includes the assertion of damages according to Article 89a PD CPC (new norm for class actions, see Section 10.4.2 below), for which, however, additional requirements must be met.

The previous requirement of an organization of "national or regional importance" will be replaced by the requirement of "a lack of profit orientation". The reason for this is the practical ambiguity of the term "national or regional meaning", which is intended to protect against abusive collective actions. In addition, a new requirement for the filing of a suit has been established: the association or organization must be "suitable for safeguarding the collective interests claimed". According to the explanatory report,[35] this presupposes that the complaining association or organization must have "the technical knowledge as well as the organizational and financial capabilities and resources" to handle such a case.

From a procedural point of view, the modified General Group Action differs only in a few aspects from the applicable law. If an association or organization is entitled to bring an action according to Article 89 PD CPC, it still asserts its own claims in its own

[32] This means that a legislative proposal is made public (nowadays especially always via the Internet) and all interested persons are invited to comment on it within a certain period.

[33] Preliminary Draft for the modification of the CPC, found (in German, French and Italian only) at www.bj.admin.ch/bj/de/home/staat/gesetzgebung/aenderung-zpo.html.

[34] Swiss Federal Council, *Erläuternder Bericht zur Änderung der Zivilprozessordnung (Verbesserung der Praxistauglichkeit und der Rechtsdurchsetzung)* [engl. Explanatory report on the amendment of the Code of Civil Procedure (improvement of practicability and law enforcement)], 2 March 2018, found *supra* note 34.

[35] See note 35.

name, independent of the individual claims of the respective group members. Consequently, it is still not an actual class action.

10.4.2 *Reparatory Class Action*

Article 89a PD CPC proposes a class action for damages. It reads as follows:[36]

Art. 89a PD CPC Reparatory Class Action

1 Any organisation entitled to bring an action under Article 89 may, in its own name, bring a claim for damages or for the return of a profit in accordance with the provisions governing management without authority, subject to the following conditions:

a. Members of the group of persons shall be entitled to such compensation on account of the infringement.
b. Any gains from the lawsuit will predominantly be made by this group of persons or will be used exclusively in their interest.
c. The members of the group of persons concerned have authorised the organisation concerned to conduct the case in writing or in another form which permits proof by text.
d. The organisations are suitable for asserting claims for compensation, in particular because they:

1. are active throughout Switzerland or of national importance,
2. have several years' experience in the legal field concerned or have been authorised by a majority of the persons concerned to litigate.

2 They shall provide all members of the group of persons known to them and the public with adequate information about the action and its content at the latest when filing their complaint, unless they have been authorised by all members of the group of persons affected by the infringement to conduct the proceedings.

3 Insofar as members of the group of persons have already filed a lawsuit to enforce their claims for damages, they may declare their withdrawal in these proceedings following the association lawsuit.

Systematically, Article 89a PD CPC can be seen as *lex specialis* to Article 89 PD CPC which allows but is also limited to the assertion of monetary claims for performance. This usually encompasses compensation for damages. Compensation for personal suffering is excluded by the formulation.[37]

Doctrinally, however, Article 89a PD CPC must be clearly separated from the General Group Action, as it allows suing in its own name for the claims of the affected group members.

In addition to the requirements under Article 89 PD CPC for the General Group Action (cf. Article 89a paragraph 1 PD CPC), Article 89a paragraph 1(a–c) creates a so-called opt-in system. Under this system, an organization is authorized, on the basis of individual authorization by the group members concerned (opting in), to take their case to court, subject to the obligation to pass on any procedural gains predominantly to these persons concerned or to use them exclusively in their interest.

As a further requirement, the organization filing a complaint under Article 89a PD CPC must be suitable for asserting the claims for damages. A suitability in this respect (that is not regarded the same as the suitability under Article 89 PD CPC) may be assumed by name if the

[36] Own translation from the German original preliminary draft.
[37] Swiss Federal Council, *Erläuternder Bericht*, *supra* note 35, 43.

organization is active throughout Switzerland or is of nationwide significance and has several years of experience in the legal field concerned. The required experience is to be assumed if the plaintiff organization has actually been authorized to conduct legal proceedings by a majority of the known members of the group of persons concerned.[38]

In contrast to the already existing instruments of collective legal protection, the application of the Reparatory Class Action is intended to contribute to the avoidance of a large number of parallel or step-by-step proceedings. It is a building block that Swiss civil litigation has lacked thus far from a Law and Economics perspective.

If the court takes such a Reparatory Class Action brought by an organization, a subsequent substantive judgment has material legal effect with regard to the asserted claims of all affected group members that opted-in.

For affected group members who have not granted authorization to bring an action before a court, the judgment has no legal effect. However, the factual and legal issues assessed in the judgment are likely to set a significant precedent. Corresponding group members are still entitled to conduct individual processes.

As with the current Group Action, there is no state aid to finance Reparatory Class Actions. The plaintiff association or organization is responsible for the financing. However, Article 115a PD CPC proposes that associations or organizations do not have to provide an advance on court costs or security if the General Group Action (according to Article 89 CPC) or the Reparatory Class Action (according to Article 89a CPC) seems more appropriate than individual actions. The preliminary draft therefore leaves to the Court whether an advance on court costs and a security should be required. This can make the filing of corresponding processes much easier. Moreover, the possibility to sue for damages creates an incentive for litigation financiers to assume the costs of the litigation in return for a share of the profits.

In this context, it should be noted that it is prohibited for lawyers in Switzerland to agree a pure contingency fee (Latin "pactum de quota litis").[39] However, a contingency fee as a component of the attorney fees (Latin "pactum de palmario") is permissible, at least to the extent that this part is less than the compensation part that is owed regardless of the outcome of the proceedings.[40] These rules may not be circumvented by a lawyer by participating in a litigation financier.

10.4.3 *Group Settlement*

The Group Settlement procedure is based on a procedure introduced in the Netherlands in 2005 and the instrument of out-of-court settlement. The purpose of the Group Settlement is to enable organizations to reach a settlement with the alleged injuring party(s) in the interest of the injured party(s) they represent. According to the preliminary draft it shall be regulated in Article 352 et seq. CPC.

The Group Settlement can then be submitted to the competent court for examination, which can declare it generally binding. This means, it acquires material legal effect for all similar cases, as described in the settlement. Members of the affected group of persons who do not benefit from the settlement or do not wish to be bound by it may opt out and assert their claims individually within a period set by the court. In contrast to the Reparatory Class Action, the Group Settlement was therefore designed on an opt-out system (and not opt-in system).

38 Cf. *id.*, 45 et seq.
39 According to Art. 12 lit. e Lawyers Act (CC 935.61).
40 *Cf.* BGE 143 II 600 of 13 June 2017, E. 2.7.5.

The Group Settlement has high requirements due to the possible declaration of general binding character by the court. First, the right to make a Group Settlement in accordance with Article 352 et seqq. PD CPC is only to be granted to organizations which are also legitimated to bring a General Group Action according to Article 89 PD CPC. Furthermore, the provisions of the Group Settlement procedure contain various requirements for the form and content of any Group Settlement (Article 352b PD CPC) before it can be submitted to the competent court for examination at the joint request of the contracting parties. For the examination of the settlement, the court must orient itself on Article 352f paragraph 1 PD CPC that reads as follows:[41]

Article 352f paragraph 1 PD CPC Approval

1 The Court shall approve a group settlement and make it binding on the parties and all persons affected by the infringement if:

a. the conditions laid down in Articles 352b and 352c are fulfilled [this concerns a formally correct group settlement and joint request of the parties; in particular, the settlement must contain «a description as precise as possible of the group of persons concerned and their number, subdivided where appropriate according to the nature and gravity of the infringement or the damage suffered» (Article 352b paragraph 2 letter b)];
b. compensation for the infringement, the nature and seriousness of the damage suffered and the procedure for claiming, fixing, securing and paying compensation are appropriate;
c. an independent body is appointed to assess the compensation for the persons concerned if the amount and nature of the compensation are not determined by group settlement;
d. the group of persons concerned is sufficiently large so that the declaration of general binding character appears justified for all persons;
e. the organisation concerned can adequately represent the group of persons concerned; and
f. the interests of the persons affected by the group settlement appear to be adequately safeguarded overall.

Due to the deliberate vagueness of a large number of terms, the court has considerable discretion in this respect.

After receipt of the joint request, the Court of First Instance shall examine the conditions for approval of the Group Settlement and shall invite the parties to a public hearing for that purpose. Prior to this, the parties to the settlement are instructed to adequately inform all persons concerned known to them and the public about the content of the Group Settlement as well as the place and date of the court hearing. In order to safeguard their right to be heard and their other procedural rights during the hearing, the parties concerned must be given the opportunity to express their views on the application for authorization and to participate in the proceedings in general.

During the judicial examination of the Group Settlement, other pending proceedings based on the same infringement shall be suspended until the competent court has ruled against the approval of the Group Settlement or the individual plaintiff has declared his withdrawal from the Group Settlement.

If, in the opinion of the competent court, the Group Settlement meets the requirements of Article 352f paragraph 1 PD CPC, it declares it approved. The consequence of this is that it acquires the legal effect of a judicial decision for all persons described in the settlement (i.e., the whole class). If a class member does not exercise its right of withdrawal (opting out) within the

[41] Own translation from the German original preliminary draft.

period set by the court (of at least three months from approval or immediately upon later notice of such approval), the court then again instructs the parties to inform the persons concerned known to them and the public about the court's decision and its general binding character. For this reason, in my view, the Group Settlement should better be called Class Settlement to distinguish it clearly from the Group Action that legally has no binding effect on all cases concerned but only on the parties of the proceeding.

After approval by the court, the representative organization is obliged to implement the settlement agreement. In order to benefit from the amount of compensation agreed in the settlement, the persons concerned must demand performance for themselves. This right expires after three years.

If the court does not approve the settlement, the parties shall inform the known persons concerned and the public thereof. In this case, the effect of the settlement shall extend only to the parties and the persons expressly represented by them. Thus, the explicitly represented persons remain bound by the settlement, unless they have given their consent with the reservation that the group settlement will later become generally binding. Furthermore, the contracting parties themselves are permitted to agree on a right of revocation in the event that a certain percentage of affected, injured persons exercise their right of withdrawal and thus the general binding character of the settlement is de facto no longer guaranteed. The right of revocation expires thirty days after the expiry of the withdrawal period (that set by the court) and depends on the achievement of the agreed quota or percentage. The revoking party must then immediately inform the known persons concerned.[42]

Finally, it is stipulated that no appeal may be lodged against the decision approving the Group Settlement. However, a negative decision could be appealed to the Federal Supreme Court.[43]

10.5 EMPIRICAL FINDINGS

For the purpose of a short empirical survey, 41 Swiss civil courts of first instance were contacted out of 110 existing Swiss civil courts of first instance.[44] These forty-one courts could be contacted by email for general inquiries. The remaining sixty-nine Swiss courts could not be addressed for such purposes by email and were therefore unsuitable for the study for reasons of time and cost.

Only eleven of the requested courts (this amounts to 10 percent of the existing Swiss civil courts) participated in the survey by contributing data.[45] This is mainly due to the fact that the relevant data is not collected statistically, and that the responsible presidents or clerks of the courts had to collect it from their files. Since the evaluation of past cases in particular takes a great deal of time, the courts were also given the opportunity to work with estimates where the evaluation would be disproportionate. Five of eleven of the participating courts have used this

42 *See* Article 352h PD CPC.

43 *See* Article 352i PD CPC.

44 For the different courts of Switzerland as well as the respective numbers cf. Bieri Peter, *Die Gerichte der Schweiz – eine Übersicht*, Justice – Justiz -Giustizia, No. 2 (2014).

45 The Civil Courts that participated by contributing numbers to all five instruments were: Bezirksgericht Küsnacht; Kantonsgericht Zug; Kantonsgericht Glarus; Bezirksgericht See, Murten (FR); Bezirksgericht Schwyz; Bezirksgericht Gersau; Bezirksgericht Arbon; Landegericht Ursern; Regionalgericht Bern-Mitteland (not all departments). The Zivilkreisgericht Basel-Landschaft Ost and the Bezirksgericht Frauenfeld could only deliver numbers to the last three respectively last two of the asked instruments. Many thanks at this point to all participating courts, especially the presidents and court clerks, who sacrificed their time to provide figures for this survey.

opportunity for the figures since 2011. Despite the fact that these figures have been given as estimates, they should also be very precise as they have all been estimated to the single digit.

The participating courts were asked for the number of collective redress actions received (1) in the past year (2018) and (2) since the CPC came into force (2011). They were further asked to differentiate them according to the existing five possibilities for collective actions presented in Section 10.3.

The consolidated results are as follows.

If these numbers are extrapolated to the 110 existing civil courts of first instance, you get the following hypothetical numbers.

In reality, the numbers are likely to be somewhat higher than in Table 10.2, as the larger civil courts in particular did not take part in the survey. The reason for the reluctance of the larger civil courts to participate in the survey is the great fragmentation of procedural responsibility. As a rule, there are several leading judges working there, who only have very limited agreements with each other. This makes consolidated data collection more difficult.

Although the data set obtained is very limited, some important conclusions can be drawn from it. General Group Actions seem to be virtually nonexistent. Special Group Actions as well as Model Lawsuits are very scarcely used.

By far the most commonly used are Voluntary Joinder of Parties. For a large number of plaintiffs, however, this form of action seems unsuitable. On one hand, this is because the effort of coordinating a great number of claimants and there submissions becomes disproportionately high. This holds true in particular, where there is no common legal representative. On the other hand, the (albeit small) risk to be jointly and severally liable for the costs of the whole proceeding becomes unbearable if the number of plaintiffs is more than about ten persons and the potential individual gain is little.

Especially for scattered damage, the Voluntary Joinder of Parties therefore appears to be unsuitable as a procedural instrument. In such cases thus, the Joinder of Actions with prior assignment of claims seems to be the preferred choice so far. This conclusion is also confirmed by the Volkswagen emission scandal case in which a joinder of actions was used to claim for damages.[46]

10.6 FINAL CONCLUSIONS

The current possibilities for bringing actions in the field of collective redress in Switzerland, which are Voluntary Joinder of Parties, Joinder of Actions (with prior assignment of claims), General Group Actions, Special Group Actions and Model Lawsuits (see Section 10.3), appear to be inadequate. This is also the conclusion reached by the Swiss Federal Council. For this reason, it recommends an adaptation of the Swiss Code of Civil Procedure (CPC). The limited empirical results in the survey undertaken confirm this view (see Section 10.5).

In particular, no efficient procedural instrument appears to be available for asserting scattered damage and therefore to tackle the problem of individual rational apathy as explained in Section 10.2 of this chapter. In such cases, there are too many people affected too little to constitute a Voluntary Joinder of Parties. Furthermore, for the joined Parties there is the risk to be held jointly as well as severally liable for the costs of the whole case. The Joinder of Actions seems in the case of scattered damages the best choice so far but seems too great an administrative effort. For both injured parties and potential agents, the incentive to conduct such a lawsuit seems generally too low.

Group Actions as a possible remedy have unfortunately no legal effect on individually injured parties. They are therefore used very rarely, the General Group Action as good as not at all and

46 However, the outcome of the case is still pending at the Commercial Court of Zurich.

TABLE 10.1 *Number of collective redress actions due to the survey (own representation)*

	Voluntary Joinder of Parties	Joinder of Actions	General Group Action	Special Group Action	Model Lawsuits
2018	82	1	0	0	0
since CPC is in force (2011)	699	4	0	1	1

TABLE 10.2 *Hypothetical number of collective redress actions in Switzerland (own representation)*

	Voluntary Joinder of Parties	Joinder of Actions	General Group Action	Special Group Action	Model Lawsuits
2018	820	10	0	0	0
since CPC is in force (2011)	6990	40	0	10	10

the Special Group Action sporadically by groups, which probably complain above all for ideological and not economic reasons.

The modifications and new instruments of collective redress proposed within the framework of the planned amendment of the CPC are therefore to be very welcomed. These are a modified General Group Action, a Reparatory Class Action and a Group Settlement (see Section 10.4). However, the proposed amendment should be adjusted to some extent.

The procedural prerequisites for the (modified) General Group Action as well as the Reparatory Class Action appear to be generally too vague. On the one hand, this refers to the concept of "suitability" of the suing organization, which applies to both General Group Actions and Reparatory Class Actions. In the case of the reparatory collective action", the terms "nation-wide activity" or "significance" as well as "several years of experience" appear too vague. The criteria for admissibility must be defined more clearly as procedural barriers to entry and should be left to the discretion of the court to a lesser extent. Instead of the equally vague "suitability", an authorization by the majority or at least a minimum number of the known members of the group of persons concerned could be demanded ("numerosity"). In addition, it could be demanded that it be made credible that similar factual and legal questions arise among the persons concerned ("commonality").

The jurisdiction of Group Settlements and Reparatory Class Actions should be uniformly structured as alternatives to one another. For example, the actual goal of a comprehensive settlement in the case of mass damage – at least for Switzerland – can currently as well as proposed *de lege ferenda* only be achieved if the presumed mass infringer agrees to it on his own initiative. In my opinion, the proposed amendment of the CPC does therefore not yet contain sufficient incentives for a comprehensive settlement of such cases. It requires a sword of Damocles on both sides in order to lead parties to an economically efficient settlement. Thus, court judgments should also be able to become generally binding in the case of the proposed Reparatory Class Action. This means, analogous to the proposed Group Settlement, an implied opting in should apply to all affected parties and there should only be the possibility of conducting a separate individual process retrospectively by express opting out.

On the one hand, this should provide the organization with the necessary bargaining power for the settlement negotiations, and on the other hand – in the interests of procedural economy – it should not potentially mean that different courts have to familiarize themselves with the same major process. Furthermore, I recommend not to create any special competence, but to leave the general courts the Group Settlements and Reparatory Class Actions. In cantons with commercial courts, the professional competence of these courts could nevertheless be used if the organization decides to take legal action in this way. Moreover, courts of first instance have more practical experience than higher courts in the examination of factual questions, which will be more extensive here.

Contrary to the preliminary draft for the amendment of the CPC, in my opinion, no cost facilitations such as the waiver of advance payment of court costs should be envisaged for Group and Reparatory Class Actions. Only the provision to provide security for the compensation of the parties could be waived in the case of Group and Reparatory Class Actions so that the amount in dispute does not become an excessive obstacle to litigation. The financing of the proceeding and thus also the advance payment of court costs, however, should be available on the market in promising cases. There exist a sufficient number of litigation financiers in Switzerland and there even might be insurance solutions to finance Group and Reparatory Class Actions. The reason why this third-party financing has not worked so far in case of group actions was not the amount of costs or a necessary advance on costs, but the fact that the current Group Action cannot be used to claim damages. As a consequence, there is as yet no monetary incentive to finance such a lawsuit.

11

Class Actions in Belgium

Hans De Wulf

11.1 INTRODUCTION

After years of debate and several failed attempts by various political parties,[1] Belgium enacted its first general Class Action Act on March 24, 2014 (hereafter BCAA).[2] The Act reflects views commonly held by European policymakers on the desirability of class actions.[3] Its scope is limited to the enforcement of an exhaustively listed number of specific statutory provisions, mainly dealing with consumer protection. Actions can only be brought by certain representative organizations, recognized as such by the government, not by ad hoc lead plaintiffs. Only traditional consumer protection groups have been recognized, while Deminor, the most important plaintiff in collective shareholder litigation, has been excluded. The presiding judge has to decide whether the class action will proceed on an opt-in or opt-out basis. In 2018, the law was amended to sometimes allow small and medium sized firms to be class members (in addition to consumers) and de facto initiate proceedings.

This chapter will briefly describe the evolution of the collective litigation landscape in Belgium before zooming in on the 2014 Act, its 2018 amendment and the first cases brought under the Act. It will criticize the limited scope of the law, which excludes securities fraud litigation and most litigation against banks or other defendants from the financial sector. We briefly describe the practice of the FSMA (Financial Services and Markets Authority), a government agency, to enter into settlement

[1] For an overview, see e.g., Stefaan Voet, *Een Belgische vertegenwoordigende collectieve rechtsvordering*, Antwerp: Intersentia, 2012, 62 ff. This book, a PhD thesis from Ghent University, is the most comprehensive discussion of class actions in the Belgian literature from the era before the adoption of the BCAA. It contains references to all relevant prior literature. Two other important relatively early contributions within the Belgian literature were Emilie De Baere, "Procederen inzake massaschade: naar een class action in het Belgisch recht ?", *Tijdschrift voor Prtivaatrecht* 2007, 7–72 and Andrée Puttemans "L'introduction d'une forme d'action collective en droit belge" in *L'action collective ou action de groupe* (A. Puttemans ed.), Brussels: Larcier, 2010, 117.

[2] Act of March 28, 2014, *Belgisch Staatsblad* (BS) 29 April 2014 and incorporated in articles XVII.35 through XVII.70 of the "Wetboek Economisch Recht" (WER, Code of Economic Law), The "Belgisch Staatsblad" (BS) is Belgium's official gazette in which legislation needs to be published in order to become effective, see www.staatsblad.be. The most important commentaries on the BCAA include Emilie De Baere, *De Belgische class action*, Mechelen: Wolters Kluwer, 2017, 176; Joëlle Rozie, Stefan Rutten and Aloïs Van Oevelen (eds.), *Class Actions*, Antwerp: Intersentia, 2015, 155; Jacques Englebert and Jean-Luc Fagnart (eds.), *L'action en réparation collective*, Limal: Anthemis, 2015, 464; Florence Danis, Elodie Falla and Françoise Lefevre, "Introduction aux principes de la Loi relative à l'action en réparation collective et premiers commentaires critiques," *Revue de droit commercial* 2014, 560–590. For an overview in English, see Stefaan Voet, "Consumer Collective Redress in Belgium: Class Actions to the Rescue?," *European Business Organization Law Review* 2015, 121–143 and Stefaan Voet, "Belgium's new consumer class action" in V. Harsagi and C. H. van Rhee (eds.), *Multi-Party Redress in Europe: Squeaking Mice?* Antwerp: Intersentia, 2014, 106.

[3] For an overview of some common themes in the European approach to class actions, see Stefaan Voet, "European Collective Redress: a *Status Quaestionis*," *International Journal of Procedural Law*, Volume 4 (2014), 97–128.

agreements with financial institutions that include an obligation for the financial institution to compensate clients. This could turn into an alternative for class actions in the financial sector. We will conclude with a brief discussion of how Belgian investors who are the victims of securities fraud, can try to use the Dutch collective settlement system, rather than Belgian courts, to pursue compensation. This was illustrated by the Fortis case. However, we have some doubts concerning the legitimacy of the Dutch courts claiming jurisdiction for collective settlements mainly involving non-Dutch investors in non-Dutch companies. Our conclusion will be that Belgium should drop the approach that consists in only allowing class actions by a limited number of organizations co-opted by the government and based on the violation of a limited number of consumer protection laws. It is, however, unlikely that Belgian policymakers will heed our call in the near future.

11.2 SOME HISTORY: THE EVOLUTION OF THE CLASS ACTION DEBATE IN BELGIUM LEADING TO THE 2014 ACT AND ITS 2018 AMENDMENT

11.2.1 *A Slow Start*

The evolution of the Belgian class action landscape broadly follows European trends. When class actions were first discussed in Belgian academic and policymaker circles in the 1980s, it was only to express horror at them. They were perceived at the time as an illustration of the undesirable litigiousness of the US as a society and it was feared that their introduction would ruin whole industries through tort or product liability claims and would lead to a liability insurance crisis. Also, they were perceived to be inextricably linked to what many considered to be a despicable "bounty hunter" or "ambulance chaser" model of entrepreneurial litigation, whereas Belgian lawyers saw themselves not as entrepreneurs, but as Ciceronian professionals far removed from vulgar considerations of lucre. The now (2019) partly abolished prohibition for lawyers to advertise their services and the still existing prohibition on contingency fees[4] were regularly invoked to argue that the US model was in any case impossible to imitate in Belgium.

Until the end of the 1990s, much the same opinions as during the 1980s prevailed, especially among business interest lobbies, including organizations like VBO/FEB (Vereniging van Belgische Ondernemingen/Fédération des enterprises belges), an organization representing the interests of large Belgium firms[5]. But many members of the bar held similar opinions[6].

4 See art. 446*ter* Ger. W. (Belgian Code of Civil Procedure). The ban on contingency fees can largely be avoided through the use of success fees which consist of a (potentially small) fixed fee plus a part of the fee that depends on the outcome of the case, see e.g., Carolien Kaufmann, "Een model voor een Belgische class action? De advocatuur neemt het voortouw", *Rechtskundig Weekblad* 2009–2010, 700, nr. 10. Also, the ban on contingency fees only applies to attorneys. This has enabled consumer protection or shareholder interest organizations to work on the basis of a contingency fee in their relationship with their clients (a large number of consumers or shareholders), whereas the organization itself hires a lawyer that works on a traditional fee basis.

5 For a representative example of a lobbying text used by the VBO (The "Association of Belgian Enterprise," in reality representing the interests of large firms, akin to the American Business Roundtable) against class actions, referring to the costs they would inflict on firms and railing against the perceived excesses of the American system, see the "VBO memorandum for the attention of the future government submitted on the occasion of the federal elections of 13 June 2010": "Class actions: neen aan de geschillenmaatchappij!" ("class actions: no to a society full of fighting and litigation!"), on file with the author. For another typical example of industry resistance against the introduction of class actions, with many of the recurring arguments, see Joëlle Simon, "L'action de groupe: l'illusion tragique" in Institut des jurists d'entreprise (ed.), *Le droit des affaires en évolution- la sanction dans la vie des affaires*, Antwerp: Kluwer, 2007, 90–117. Mrs Simon was then the head of legal affairs of MEDEF, the French counterpart of Belgian VBO.

6 See for instance several attorneys cited as "furious opponents" of the introduction of class actions in Belgium that was then being debated in Hans Brockmans, "Collectieve schaderegelingen," *Trends* (Belgian business weekly) March 1, 2007, 65–68.

Firms' resistance to the introduction of class action techniques was of course self-interested, but initially many others, too, seemed to be wary of class actions because of some widespread misconceptions about the US system.[7] For instance, it was widely assumed or at least argued that in the US and "therefore" in any class action system, the class members did not need a personal interest in the case whereas in reality, class members will have a personal interest in the case and the main question is whether there is enough commonality in their interests to justify them being part of the same class. It was also argued that class actions were incompatible with fundamental rules of due process,[8] in that especially the US opt-out model effectively robbed potential plaintiffs of the right to choose their own attorney, or to develop their own trial strategy (since they are bound by the result of the proceedings, and the strategy developed by class counsel; unless they opt out of course, but many in Belgium believed and still believe that it is next to impossible to design a system that notifies class members in an effective way about their opt-out possibilities).

Collective litigation first received substantial attention in Belgium from the 1970s onwards, when environmental awareness had slowly begun to rise. This led to attempts by groups of people to organize collective litigation to enforce environmental regulation, or to protect pieces of nature against industrial development. Strictly speaking these were not class actions, but a form of collective proceedings in which people set up ad hoc nonprofit legal persons, associations or foundations, to pursue the protection of the (local) environment and/or to aggregate their claims.[9] The Court of Cassation, Belgium's highest regular court, repeatedly ruled that these associations had no standing to sue, because under Belgian law the "*actio popularis*" is outlawed, in other words, the Belgian Code on Civil Procedure requires a personal interest from those who bring suit, and these nonprofit organizations were not deemed to pursue their own interests, but the general interest, which can only be protected by the state through the actions of public prosecutors or government agencies.[10] More specifically, it did not suffice, in the view of our

7 One of the best summaries of standard European misconceptions about the American class action system, and a polite corrective to of each of these, is to be found in an article written by an American-German attorney and scholar, André Fiebig, "The Reality of U.S. Class Actions", *GRUR int.* 2016, 313–325.

8 For a discussion of due process worries from a Belgian perspective, see e.g., Jacques Van Compernolle, "L'introduction d'une *class action* en droit belge: compatibilité ou incompatibilité avec les principes fondamentaux du droit processual?" in *Vers une class action en droit belge?* Bruges: die Keure, 2008, 165–176 with references to the older literature. A more limited number of authors has expressed worries that the introduction of class actions would ride roughshod over well-established rules for calculating damages and establishing causation, see mainly Pierre van Ommeslaghe, "Une class action en droit belge? Et le droit des obligations?" in *Liber amicorum François Glansdorff et Pierre Legros*, Brussels: Bruylant, 2013, 415–441 but also L. Frankignoul, "L'action en réparation collective ou un mécanisme procédural permettant de prendre le droit au sérieux", *Revue général de droit civil* 2012, 194–207.

9 Among the large literature about this phenomenon, see e.g., Hubert Bocken (ed.), *Vorderingsbevoegdheid van milieuverenigingen*, Brussels: Story-Scientia, 1988 or Paul Lemmens, "Het optreden van verenigingen in rechte ter verdediging van collectieve belangen", *Rechtskundig Weekblad* 1983–1984, 2005 ff.

10 The leading case is "Eikendael," Cass. November 19 1982, *Pasicrisie* 1983, I, 338 in which the Court stated: "unless [a specific] statute provides otherwise, an action initiated by a natural or legal person is inadmissible if the plaintiff does not have a personal and direct interest, this is an own private interest; a general [i.e. collective] interest is not a personal and direct interest" and, "the personal and direct interest of a legal person is only that which affects its existence or material or moral goods, especially its assets, honour and good name. The fact that a natural or legal person pursues a goal, even when this is included in its articles of incorporation, does not imply that it has a personal and direct interest." Similar holdings in Cass October 25, 1985, *Pasicrisie* 1986, I, 219 and Cass October 16, 1991, *Pasicrisie* 1992, I, 129 and September 19, 1996, *Pasicrisie* 1996, I, 830. The fact that the Court of Cassation had to issue several such rulings illustrates that its views were contested and organizations and their lawyers tried to test the limits of its doctrine. For a discussion of the difference between sufficient individual interest and collective interest as applied by the Court of cassation, see G. Closset-Marchal, "L'action d'intérêt collectif au regard de la jurisprudence de la cour de cassation" in J. Van Compernolle (ed.), *Les actions collectives devant les différentes jurisdictions*, Liège: Formation permanente CUP, 2005, 5–28.

highest court, to include for example "protection of the environment in Flanders" in the objects clause of the articles of association, to turn this kind of environmental protection into a personal interest of the association for which it had standing to sue.

The more or less uniform anti-class action front began to crumble from the late 1990s onwards. In my subjective appreciation, this resulted from four developments. First, a small group of events – frauds and disasters – led to increased calls for class actions. To begin with, the bursting of the dotcom bubble in the wake of Enron (2000–2001), when massive securities frauds came to light in many European countries[11] and Belgium experienced its own homegrown scandal, Lernout&Hauspie (L&H). In the L&H fraud, a quick settlement was reached in the US,[12] while to the irritation of many the Belgian court case could not even start because it had to wait for the result of an everlasting because of over-careful criminal investigation – let alone that a Belgian class action was possible even though thousands had allegedly been defrauded. This was followed by the 2007–2008 financial crisis when many investors felt (rightly or not is not what matters here) they had been defrauded or had at least suffered unjustifiable losses when their bank stock (Fortis, Dexia, KBC, . . .) collapsed in value. Between the 2001 and 2008 financial markets events, several people had been killed and dozens seriously injured as the result of a major train accident and the explosion of a gas pipeline, which led to calls for a swifter resolution of the victims' damage claims, and a more equal treatment by courts throughout the country than had hitherto been offered by the Belgian legal system.[13] Second, these scandals and disasters reinforced the convictions of a newer generation of academics who contrary to their senior colleagues believed that something could be said in favor of US style class actions[14], although many of their sympathizers in the wider legal community had reservations about the opt-out approach and favored an opt-in system. Probably more important than the new wind in academia was that the aforementioned frauds stimulated the business model of a very small group of lawyers (like Mischäel Modrikamen) or consultancies (like Deminor) who had first come to the fore as defenders of small investors in the wake of the first blossoming of European capital markets and securities regulation in the 1990s. This was still a far cry from a full-blown plaintiff bar, but nevertheless this type of lawyer, not afraid to take on the "financial establishment" and its law firms, had been virtually nonexistent before 1990, just like European hostile takeover bids, contested squeeze-outs (freeze-out mergers) or integrated securities markets had been almost completely absent before that date. These new players on the legal market advocated novel private enforcement techniques.

Third, from the late 1990s onwards EU initiatives proliferated to promote alternative dispute resolution and novel consumer protection techniques.[15] This would culminate in the 2009

[11] Examples include Ahold, WorldCom, Lernout&Hauspie, Balsam, the complete collapse of the German Neuer Markt.

[12] A search of "Lernout" at http://securities.stanford.edu/filings.html will turn up most relevant US court decisions and documents. See esp. *in re Lernout &Hauspie Sec. Litig.* 138 F. Supp. 2d 39 (D. Mass. 2001); *in re Lernout &Hauspie Sec. Litig.* 208 F. Supp. 2d 74 (D. Mass. 2002) and *Warlop* v. *Lernout*, 437 F. Supp. 2d 260 (D. Mass. 2007).

[13] Doubts are justified whether these two disasters were good examples of mass torts that should be dealt with through a class action mechanism: the number of victims ran into the dozens, which is a lot but not a number that cannot be managed by different courts. Consolidation of related cases could have ensured that the same principles were applied to all victims. At the same time, the bodily damage suffered by the victims of these accidents was probably too different between the victims to make a convincing case that a common damage award was warranted/that a class action would have been superior in view of sufficient commonality among the victims. In spite of this, it's undeniable that these two events contributed greatly to the call for a class action mechanism in Belgium, in the public debates in the press, in the political arena and even among academic lawyers.

[14] Among others Stefaan Voet in Ghent, Andrée Puttemans at the ULB (Brussels), myself from the angle of securities class actions.

[15] The earliest noteworthy product of the EU Commission's interest in the topic was the study (commissioned by the Commission) by Jules Stuyck and coauthors, *An Analysis and Evaluation of Alternative Means of Consumer Redress*

Directive on injunctive relief in consumer affairs[16] and the 2013 Directive on out of court settlement of consumer disputes.[17] These EU initiatives did not introduce class actions proper into the EU but strongly encouraged member states to consider new avenues, including collective solutions, in the private enforcement of consumer protection. In this respect it is no coincidence that the Belgian Class Action Act was adopted almost at the same time as the Belgian Act on "Alternative Dispute Resolution for Consumer Disputes"[18] which implemented the 2013 EU Directive: in the eyes of Belgian policymakers, the two Acts were complementary prongs in the struggle to improve consumer protection. The inspiring example of EU antitrust law must also be mentioned. There, the new mantra had become, around the start of the new millennium, that public enforcement needed to be complemented by private enforcement,[19] an idea which then also infected other areas like consumer protection outside antitrust. But as we'll explain in more detail in Section 11.4, retail investors in listed companies were until very recently not perceived as consumers worthy of protection, but rather as people who had voluntarily chosen to put money at risk in the "casino" of financial markets and who therefore were not deserving of special help when they made a loss on their investments ("bets"). This cultural attitude towards investing goes a long way in explaining, I believe, why few of the European countries that have introduced class actions for consumers have created a viable system of securities class actions. In fact, none has done so, although the Dutch mass settlement procedure, developed for other purposes, was successfully "hijacked" for application in securities cases.

The 4th factor that explains that Belgium finally got its class action legislation was that socialist politicians got into the key positions in a series of Belgian coalition governments with a heavyweight socialist politician occupying the ministry of consumer affairs and a socialist prime minister at the time the BCAA was finally adopted on March 28, 2014. This was preceded by three failed attempts at introducing class action legislation in 2008–2009,[20] the first a government bill with two tracks, a settlement track inspired by the Dutch "WCAM" ("Act on Collective settlements"), and an opt-out litigation track inspired by the class action system used in Quebec, Canada.[21] Next, the opposition

other than Redress through Ordinary Judicial Proceedings' 15 December 2006, http://ec.europa.eu/consumers/redress/report_studies/comparative report_en.pdf.

16 Directive 2009/22/EC of the European Parliament and of the Council of 23 April 2009 on injunctions for the protection of consumers' interests, OJ EU 2009 L 110/30. This Directive forced EU member states to allow "qualified entities" (in practice, certain nonprofit consumer protection organizations) to sue for injunctive relief (but not damages) against business (C2B) that had harmed consumers' interests. It replaced an earlier (2002) EU Directive with a similar purpose.

17 Directive 2013/11 of 21 May 2013, OJ L 165/63 (EU).

18 Belgian Act of 4 April 2014 "regarding the out of court resolution of consumer disputes," *BS* 12 May 2014, implementing Directive 2013/11 of 21 May 2013, OJ L 165/63 (EU).

19 The snowball started rolling when the European Court of Justice ruled that the principle of effectiveness of European Union law implied that the victims of anticompetitive behavior should be provided with remedies enabling them to claim damages before the national courts, see the initial cases Courage and Manfredi: Case C-453/99 *Courage Ltd v. Bernard Crehan* [2001], ECR I-06297 ("Courage"), paras 26–28; Joined cases C-295/04 – C-298/04 *Manfredi* [2006], ECR I-06619 ("Manfredi"), paras 60, 89–91. The evolution would culminate in the EU Antitrust Damages Directive. It seems futile to select examples from the vast ocean of literature on the topic, but see e.g., Roger van den Bergh, "Private enforcement of European Competition Law and the Persisting Collective Action Problem," *Maastricht Journal of European and Comparative Law* Vol. 20 (2013), 12–34 and on the Antitrust damages Directive, Barry J. Rodger, Miguel Sousa Ferro and Francisca Marcos, "A panacea for competition law damages actions in the EU? A comparative view of the implementation of the EU Antitrust Damages Directive in sixteen Member States," *Maastricht Journal of European and Comparative Law* Vol. 26 (2019), 480–504.

20 For an overview of these proposals, see e.g., Piet Taelman and Stefaan Voet, "Belgium and Collective Redress: the Last of the European Mohicans" in E. Dirix and Y.-H. Leleu (eds.), *The Belgian Reports at the Congress of Washington of the International Academy of Comparative Law*, Brussels: Bruylant, 2010, 305–346.

21 This no doubt under the influence of the French speaking class action scholars at the ULB, first and foremost Andrée Puttemans and her "pupil" Elodie Falla. On Quebec as a model for Belgium, see explicitly C. Botman, "De la

Green Party came with its own proposal based on an opt-in system. The third proposal was launched by the Flemish Bar Association and envisaged a system whereby an already existing special tribunal[22] which is used to assign cases when there are disagreements among courts about territorial jurisdiction, would decide on admissibility in the sense of certification of the class action and would then refer the case, if certified, to the relevant court of first instance.

11.2.2 *The 2014 Act and its 2018 Amendment*

The BCAA reflects "average" European attitudes towards class actions, as they had evolved by then, as reflected in the 2013 E.U Recommendation on Collective Redress.[23] The Act's scope is limited to the enforcement of an exhaustively listed number of specific statutory provisions, many of them finding their origin in EU Directives, mainly dealing with consumer protection. Actions can only be brought by certain permanent representative organizations, recognized as such by a government department, not by ad hoc lead plaintiffs, be they individuals or organizations. This reflects the lingering aversion in Europe towards the "bounty hunter" model and what is perceived to be excessively entrepreneurial attitudes towards litigation in the US. Only traditional consumer protection groups have been recognized as potential plaintiffs. Deminor, the most important plaintiff in collective shareholder litigation, has been excluded from the possibility of launching a class action. The judge presiding over the proceedings – and only the Brussels court have jurisdiction, for the whole of Belgium – has to decide whether the class action will proceed on an opt-in or opt-out basis.

An Act of March 30, 2018[24] expanded the scope of the original class action act, in that it allowed small and medium sized firms to be class members,[25] whereas under the original 2014 Act only consumers could be class members, and firms as a rule cannot be regarded as consumers for purposes of Belgian law. In addition the 2018 act also allowed "interprofessional organizations" representing the interests of SMEs to act as lead plaintiff, provided they are a member of the "High Council of Self-employed Entrepreneurs and Small and Medium Sized Enterprises," one of the many organizations that proliferated in Belgium from the 1970s onwards and that are interest groups/lobby organizations that have been recognized as semiofficial interlocutors of the Belgian government and its agencies in its contacts with certain interest groups. This 2018 Act beautifully illustrates how neither academic considerations nor disinterested policymaking has governed the development of Belgian law in this area. Rather, a haphazard approach has prevailed, but with as a defining feature a corporatist approach, in which the government limits access to the class action mechanism to "trusted" organizations that for the most part have been the traditional, "co-opted" representatives of certain "civil society" interest groups. The 2018 Act was enacted as a reaction to the so-called "Fibronil crisis": in July 2017 it came to light that some chickens' eggs could have been contaminated with Fibronil, a pesticide-like product used to combat disease in poultry. As a result, massive amounts of eggs but also all kinds of products made on the basis of eggs (like cakes and pastries

réparation du dommage dans l'hypothèse de l'introduction d'une action collective de type opt-out: importation du modèle Québécois?," *Revue Générale des assurances et de la responsabilité* 2013, item 14934, 1–15.

22 The so-called "Arrondissementsrechtbank," which translates as "district Court," but to Americans this may be a misleading translation. One could say that this tribunal decides in complex cases which judicial district is territorially competent to be the litigation venue.

23 Recommendation 2013/396 of the European Commission of 11 June 2013 on common principles for injunctive and compensatory collective redress mechanisms in the Member States concerning violations of rights granted under Union Law, OJ L 206/60 EU.

24 *BS* 22 May 2018. For a (very) brief description of the Act, see Gregory Renier, "L'action en réparation collective pour les consommateurs élargie aux PME" *DCCR* 2018, 141–143.

25 Provided they are SMEs as defined in Recommendation 2003/361/EC of the European Commission of 6 May 2003.

and chocolate mousse) had to be destroyed. Small and medium sized firms, including many local "artisan" bakers, complained that as a result they had suffered great economic losses, and part of the political reaction was to allow these important constituencies to claim damages from the large "agro industry" firms deemed responsible for the potential (!) Fibronil pollution. High Street versus Wall Street in the food sector, as it were.

We will now briefly describe the technical rules concerning class actions in Belgium and add brief evaluations here and there, before concluding with some remarks about alternative enforcement mechanisms in the financial sector, where regular class actions are largely unavailable, and the pitiful reality is that victims of securities fraud perpetrated by Belgian companies probably have a better chance of being compensated by a Dutch court than by a Belgian one.

11.3 MAIN TECHNICAL RULES IN THE CLASS ACTION ACT

Only consumers – which are by definition natural persons – and SMEs as defined in the 2003 EU Recommendation can be class members of a class action in Belgium,[26] and the defendant must be a firm as defined in article 1 of the Belgian Code of Economic Law ("WER" to use the official Belgian acronym).[27] As explained in Section 11.3.2 below, only certain legal persons, namely government-recognized organizations that aim to protect the interests of consumers or of SMEs, can act as lead plaintiff on behalf of the class.[28]

11.3.1 *Causes of Action*

The Belgian Act reflects policymakers' (initial) desire to limit class actions to consumer to business cases, largely geared towards consumer protection through the enforcement of rules on so-called unfair trading practices, but also for example energy markets regulation that protects individual nonbusiness energy consumers. The cause of action must be found in one of thirty-three EU or Belgian consumer protection instruments (laws, regulations . . .) exhaustively enumerated in the Act *or* in an alleged breach of contract by the defendant.[29] This is an attempt to limit class actions mainly to consumer affairs, and a very conscious decision to exclude mass tort cases and securities litigation. A merely technical drawback of this approach is that the list with references to thirty-three specific pieces of legislation is already out of date: some pieces of legislation have been abolished, or replaced by other legislation with a similar but still somewhat different contents, which could give rise to debates about to which extent the references have to be taken extremely literally.

11.3.2 *Who Can Act As Class Representative, That Is, Lead Plaintiff?*

Only representative consumer organizations, "interprofessional organizations" representing SMEs or the Federal Consumer Ombudsperson can initiate proceedings, but the latter cannot go to trial but may only use the class actions procedure to try and reach a settlement.[30] To date, the Belgian consumer ombudsperson has not tried to use this possibility.

The definition of representative consumer organization entails that shareholder associations or organizations for the defense of shareholder interests have no standing to sue. Technically, this

[26] See art. XVII.38 WER.
[27] Art. XVII.36,1° WER.
[28] Art. XVII.39 WER.
[29] See art. XVII.36, 1° WER, referring to art. XVII.37 for the list of thirty-three actionable pieces of legislation.
[30] Art. XVII.39, 3° WER.

is because only members of the "National Council for Consumer Affairs" have standing, as well as legal persons recognized by the minister of consumer affairs whose goal as a legal person is directly connected to the collective damage suffered by the class. Such legal persons must have existed for at least three years before commencing the class action, making it virtually impossible for ad hoc groups to act as lead plaintiffs. Even more important, by law the minister may only recognize organizations that have no "economic purpose"[31] and it is hard to dispute that the best known shareholder interest group in Belgium, Deminor,[32] has economic goals, in that it is a private firm that wants to make a profit for its partners. As indicated, the Belgian legislator very consciously wanted to exclude the possibility of bringing securities class actions under the new Act.

This is especially galling for Deminor, which together with Test-Aankoop[33] has probably always been the most vocal nonacademic organization in favor of class actions in Belgium. Deminor has organized collective litigation in several high profile corporate and securities fraud cases, such as Lernout&Hauspie and recently the Fortis case and its life would have been made much easier had it been eligible as a representative consumer organization.

It is striking that several member organizations of the aforementioned National Council for Consumer Affairs have little or nothing to do with consumer protection – one thinks, for instance, of the Catholic Women's Association. The membership of this Council mainly reflects who was regarded as an organization representative of civil society between the 1950s and early 1990s, with a preponderance of Christian-Democrat, Liberal[34] and Socialist (Social- Democrat) organisations. It has largely failed to evolve. Predictably, all class actions in Belgium to date have been brought by the only member organization whose core business it clearly is to watch over consumers' interests, namely Test-Aankoop/Test-Achat, a private nonprofit organization with no party political affiliations (but well-connected politically). Of course Test-Aankoop can decide to rely on a limited number of specialist law firms to represents its interests in class actions, and it does so, but the fact that the "ideological plaintiffs" that are consumer organizations will act as lead plaintiff and will select a law firm, will make the development of a true plaintiff bar on the US model difficult or at least less likely, and to avoid this was indeed no doubt a policy goal of the Belgian government but also, more openly, of policymakers at the level of the EU. Natural persons cannot act as lead plaintiff "because otherwise some would turn filing class actions into a full-blown, lucrative business" and would launch "illegitimate or reckless procedures."[35]

The limitation of who can act as lead plaintiff was attacked before Belgium's Constitutional Court as being a violation of the constitutional principle of equality, but the appeal to have the Act vacated was judged largely unfounded by the Constitutional Court in its March 17, 2016 opinion. The Court ruled that these limitations were proportionate to the aim of the legislation to "ensure the quality and efficiency of the new procedure" and "to avoid lucrative or reckless procedures" or the pursuit of "seemingly excessive damage awards."[36] The Court did find a violation of EU law insofar as the Act

[31] Art. XVII.39, 2°, first sentence.

[32] Derived from "*défense des minorités*," defense of minority (shareholders).

[33] Or Test-Achat with its French name. This is the most prominent nonprofit consumer organization in Belgium. It has standing to bring consumer cases under the BCAA. In the past, it has not been very active in investor cases; its focus is more on unfair trade practices (like overcharging customers for certain services; or general conditions in sales or utilities contracts that are detrimental to consumers).

[34] In the continental European party-political sense.

[35] Government's Explanatory Memorandum to the Class Action Act, *Parl. St. Kamer* 53 3300/001, p. 25, accessible at www.dekamer.be (search for 53 3300/001).

[36] Belgian Constitutional Court 17 March 2016, nr. 41/2016, at B.26.2, available at www.const-court.be/.

limited the possibility to act as lead plaintiff to *Belgian* representative organizations recognized as such by the competent Belgian minister.[37] This was deemed incompatible with the freedom to offer cross-border services as protected by the EU Treaty. Therefore, the Court ruled that organizations from other EU member states should be enabled to act as lead plaintiff, even if they have not been recognized by the competent Belgian minister like Belgian organizations must, provided they are organizations that are allowed to bring class actions in consumer-related cases in their member state of origin.[38]

11.3.3 *Exclusive Jurisdiction of the Brussels Courts*

The Brussels courts, namely the civil and commercial courts of first instance, and the Court of Appeal, have exclusive jurisdiction for the whole of Belgium for class actions.[39] The aim was not only to avoid unnecessary disputes about territorial jurisdiction but mainly to ensure that one specialist court builds up experience with class actions and assures uniform interpretation of the law throughout Belgium. Over the past twenty-five years, the Belgian legislators have repeatedly chosen to give exclusive competence to a section of the Brussels Court of Appeal, since 2018 called the “Markets Division,” in “specialist” business law matters like antitrust, IP, public takeover bids or energy regulation. For class actions, the Brussels courts of first instance also have jurisdiction. However, because of the general rules of Belgian civil procedure, this first instance court will rarely take a decision beyond certification in class actions.[40] This is because when a decision is appealed, the Court of Appeal becomes competent to decide the whole case, even those aspects of the case that have not yet been dealt with in the intermediate judgment by the court of first instance[41]. If the Brussels court of first instance certifies a class action, this decision will almost always be appealed because of the high stakes in mass litigation, meaning the Court of Appeal will take the final decision on any compensation awards in first and last instance (except that an appeal on points of law is possible to the Court of Cassation). The parties will thus de facto lose the right of appeal which they usually have in Belgian civil procedure.

11.3.4 *The Procedure: Admissibility, Mandatory Attempt at Settlement and Trial*

Proceedings can be divided into two phases, the admissibility stage in which the court decides to certify the case or not, and the substantive phase, which can be subdivided in a settlement phase and a merits phase (trial). The court-approved settlement or judgment will then be executed under the control of a claims settler, working closely with a court registrar.

First, a court will need to certify the action and it can only do so if it finds that a class action is superior to other ways of redress.[42] The first cases have made it abundantly clear that the judge will not and indeed may not decide simply based on the allegations in the initial complaint,[43] but

37 At B.34.4–7.

38 This is now reflected in the amended text of art. XVII.39, 4° WER.

39 Art. XVII.35 WER. An appeal on points of law to the Court of Cassation is possible.

40 See Stefaan Voet, “Belgium’s new consumer class action” in V. Harsagi and C. H. van Rhee (eds.), *Multi-Party Redress in Europe: Squeaking Mice?* Antwerp: Intersentia, 2014, 106.

41 See article 1068 Belgian Code of Civil Procedure.

42 Art. XVII.36 3° WER.

43 As some authors (e.g., Ernst Balate, *L’action en réparation collective*, Mechelen: Wolters Kluwer, 2015, 179) had argued immediately after the enactment of the Act, before any cases had been brought. Interestingly, in the “Dieselgate” (Volkswagen) case, lead plaintiff Test-Aankoop initially refused to submit briefs to the court about the admissibility of the class action it had launched, arguing (as such correctly) that statute does not provide for a debate between parties about admissibility/certification. Apparently Test-Aankoop wanted the court to take

will and must allow plaintiff and defendant to exchange briefs and submit these to the court after which the court will hear the parties in oral pleadings.[44] The judge will first try to ascertain whether there is enough commonality between class members, both in their factual situation and as regards their legal situation (e.g., some may be excluded from the class because their behavior can be deemed to entail that they have waived their right to bring certain claims against the defendant). Next, the judge will judge the "effectiveness" of proceeding through a class action instead of "regular" individual proceedings. Potential class size can be a factor here; in the first cases judges have ruled that, irrespective of whether the case is an opt-out or opt-in case, the number of potential class members the lead plaintiff has been able to recruit at the beginning of the proceedings, is irrelevant when they have to judge whether a class action is more effective than regular proceedings.[45] The judge will also take into account the suitability of the class representative (lead plaintiff organization). Indeed, the official Explanatory Memorandum explicitly states that it's not sufficient for a lead plaintiff to be one of the organizations listed in the Act as being eligible.[46] The available case law does not yet offer guidance on how judges will judge this suitability since all class actions so far have been initiated by Test-Aankoop and few would dare to doubt that Belgium's leading consumer affairs organization is suitable in consumer law cases. It should be noted that the Act does not (explicitly) allow courts to judge the suitability of counsel for lead plaintiff, only the suitability of the lead plaintiff.

The judge will decide on a case by case basis whether the action will proceed under an opt-in or under an opt-out system,[47] but for people or legal persons not residing in Belgium the opt-in rule will always apply, as well as when the case revolves around claims for damages for bodily or mental harm.[48] This means the class could consist of all Belgians who have not opted out, but only those nonresidents[49] who have opted in. In line with received opinion about the impossibility of assembling a decent class for small damages claims, the law also encourages the judge to decide in favor of an opt-out system in case of small individual damages affecting a large number of consumers. Whereas the EU Recommendation had suggested an opt-in system as the default system, without completely excluding the superiority of an opt-out approach in certain cases,[50] there is no such default in Belgian legislation. The judge decides on a case by case basis.

Consumers/potential class members must make the opt-in or opt-out decision after notification of the certification stage.[51] Their decision is irrevocable and they do not get an opportunity to change their mind after the settlement (if any) has been approved by the court. This was a conscious decision by the Belgian government which deemed it undesirable that people

a decision about certification without having a debate between parties. But the court ruled that doing so would be incompatible with fundamental due process principles of civil procedure. See Hakkim Boularbah and Maria-Clara Van den Bossche, "De rechtsvordering tot collectief herstel: *law in Action*" in *Het Economisch recht in beweging*, Brussels: Larcier, 2017, 53.

44 See the intermediate judgment of October 10, 2016 in the Dieselgate case cited by Hakkim Boularbah and Maria-Clara van den Bossche, "De rechtsvordering tot collectief herstel: *law in Action*" in *Het Economisch recht in beweging*, Brussels: Larcier, 2017, 53, as well as the admissibility decision in the Proximus case, Brussels Court of First Instance, April 4, 2017.

45 See esp. one of the intermediate judgments in the "Dieselgate" litigation as discussed by Boularbah and Van den Bossche, *supra* note 43, at 63–64.

46 *Parl.St.* Kamer, nr. 53K3300/001, MvT, 26.

47 XVII.43 § 2, 3° WER.

48 XVII.38 WER.

49 Persons residing outside Belgium. Nationality is not relevant.

50 See art. 21 of the 2013 Recommendation, *supra* note 23.

51 Art. XVII.38 WER.

would base their decision on the results of the settlement and thought it should be clear what the exact size of the class would be at (the end of) the certification stage.[52]

If certification is granted, parties *have* to try and reach a settlement, to be approved by the court, within a timeframe set by the judge.[53] When deciding whether to approve the settlement – a decision which the judge must make within two months – the judge will pay attention not only to the substantive content of the settlement, but also to the reasonableness of the fees of the attorneys and other advisers involved. If no settlement can be reached, the judge will decide the case on its merits. This assumes that no settlement had been reached prior to the initiation of proceedings. But the Act explicitly provides for the hypothesis that parties have reached a settlement before the start of proceedings. In that case they have to jointly submit it to the court, accompanied by evidence in their petition that the certification criteria are met.[54] The Act gives examples of situations where approval of the settlement (whether reached prior or after certification) must be refused.[55] A striking example where the Act imposes such a refusal is the situation where the amount the defendants will pay to the lead plaintiff (class representative) to compensate it for its costs, exceeds the actual costs the representative has incurred. Other reasons for refusal are that the agreed form of redress is manifestly unreasonable or the time provided for in the settlement agreement for class members to actually claim pay-out of their compensation is unreasonably short. The settlement or judgment will be performed under the control of a court-appointed claims settler. In keeping with Belgian traditions, only persons included in a preestablished list which is drawn up by the general assembly of judges of the court of first instance or court of appeal can be appointed as claims settlers, and only attorneys (members of the bar) as well as certain civil servants and people included in a list of court trustees can be included in the list of possible settlors.[56] Of course, attorneys will often be part of a law firm, but firms as such, let alone specialist settlement firms who have others than attorneys as partners or employees, cannot as such be included in the list. Establishing who will actually receive any compensation as a legitimate claimant is not at all left exclusively in the hands of the settler: an important role is also assigned to the court registrar, and both will have to work together.

At various stages of the proceedings,[57] the Act also provides for the possibility of a switch, if the parties so wish, to mediation and they can also use a court-appointed mediator during the mandatory settlement discussion phase. A resolution of the conflict through mediation is clearly and somewhat overoptimistically encouraged by the Act.

11.3.5 *The First Cases*[58]

In view of the fact that so few actions have been brought so far, it may be useful to give an idea about what they were about:[59]

52 *Parl.St.* Kamer, nr. 53K3300/001, 23 and 31.

53 Art. XVII.45 WER.

54 Art. XVII.42 § 2 WER.

55 Art. XVII.49 § 2 WER.

56 Art. XVII.57 WER. See arts. XVII.58 through 62 about the claims settlement process and the collaboration between settler and court registrar.

57 E.g., in the merits phase of court proceedings, see art. XVII.56 WER.

58 See also Hakkim Boularbah and Maria-Clara van den Bossche, "De rechtsvordering tot collectief herstel: *law in Action*" in *Het Economisch recht in beweging*, Brussels: Larcier, 2017, 47–92 and Jacques Laffineur and Grégory Renier, "L'action en réparation collective: un premier état des lieux deux ans après son introduction en droit belge", *DCCR* 2016, issue 112, 3–20.

59 All judgments that declare a class action admissible (= certification) should in principle be listed on the website of the Belgian federal Ministry of Economic Affairs (https://economie.fgov.be/nl/themas/consumentenbescherming/rechtsvordering-tot-collectief/). As of March 9 2019, the last time this website was updated, it listed only three actions.

- Thomas Cook, a now defunct tour operator, was sued because it did not spontaneously offer customers compensation for cancelled flights.[60] In addition to this case which was brought under the BCAA, it is by now common for airline companies and tour operators who refuse to compensate customers for flight delays or cancelled flights to be sued collectively, by groups of consumers who join forces through one and the same law firm, either with Test-Aankoop as an intermediary or not. In this area, there's something of a budding "plaintiff bar": several law firms have devised a system whereby airline customers that register in advance with them, are automatically contacted through email, text or a similar system when the law firm's algorithm has established that their fight is delayed for reasons that could entitle them to compensation. With a few clicks on their smartphone they can then join the collective litigation. However, most of these cases are not brought under the BCAA, but "simply" through power of attorney given by dozens, sometimes hundreds of disgruntled customers to one and the same law firm that charges low rates because the cost can be spread over a moderately large group of plaintiffs. The cases often end in a settlement (settlement being far less common, in general, in Belgium than in the US), but I have been unable to find precise figures about the number of such cases or the settlement rate.
- Similarly, Belgium's national (state-owned) railway company NMBS was sued for forty euros per customer holding an annual subscription because of strikes in 2014–2015[61] and recently a much publicized case was launched against Ryanair, also because of strikes in 2018.[62]
- In the wake of US and German procedures, a class action was launched in Belgium against Volkswagen and D'ieteren NV (the latter being the official importer of Volkswagen in Belgium, and issuer of "certificates of conformity," stating that the vehicles comply with Belgian legislation) as a result of the "dieselgate" emissions scandal, in which Volkswagen installed software in its cars, allegedly to help its vehicles illegitimately improve their performance on environmental tests.[63]
- Proximus, a telecoms company, was sued for the damage it inflicted, according to the plaintiff, on customers by convincing them through allegedly misleading publicity to choose a specific rental formula for TV decoders which, according to the plaintiff, was a worse deal for customers than the pricing plan many already had.[64]

Not counting cases brought for flight delays, I have knowledge of eight cases that were litigated, but some did indeed not get beyond the certification stage (i.e., were ruled inadmissible) and others are still pending. Test-Aankoop also announced a class action against Samsung because customers did not get back cash they were promised as part of a commercial action, but Samsung then compensated customers and the case never reached court.

60 Case reported in *BS* 28 June 2016, also available at http://economie.fgov.be/nl/consument/rechtsvordering_collectief_herstel/test-aankoop_Thomas-Cook/#.WZ6fPP4Ul9A.

61 The case was settled.

62 See www.test-aankoop.be/collectieve-acties/ryanair.

63 The case is still pending, the action was declared admissible by the Brussels Commercial Court in its judgment of December 17, 2017, reported in *BS* May 8, 2018 and also available at https://economie.fgov.be/nl/themas/consumentenbescherming/rechtsvordering-tot-collectief/beslissingen/zaak-test-aankoop-tegen-vw.

64 In its judgment of January 30, 2019, the Brussels Court of Appeal, which had previously ruled that the complaint was admissible, found, after the parties had failed to reach a settlement, that the complaint was unfounded, see the publication of the judgment in Belgium's "Official Gazette," *Belgisch Staatsblad*, February 20, 2019, also accessible through https://economie.fgov.be/nl/themas/consumentenbescherming/rechtsvordering-tot-collectief/beslissingen/zaak-test-aankoop-tegen.

- Eight websites were sued for allegedly illegally selling on tickets for pop concerts at excessively high markups (touting).[65]
- Groupon was sued for allegedly illegally promoting a commercial action of a firm selling a sort of subscription for the continuous delivery of baby diapers to families with babies; the baby diapers producer then failed to deliver the nappies to customers who had signed on.[66]
- In October 2018, Facebook was sued by Test-Aankoop because it allegedly illegally shared data of Belgian users with Cambridge Analytica.[67]

Based on anecdotes in the press and on consumer organization websites, there seem to be quite a few cases of collective litigation or at least pressure that is being brought by groups of disgruntled consumers that do not take the form of a class action. It's difficult to get a systematic overview of the number of such cases. A recent example concerns the costs that banks charge to customers who want to transfer their securities accounts to another bank or financial intermediary. Test-Aankoop assembled the signatures of 14,000 people on a petition against these costs which Test-Aankoop deems excessive and filed a complaint with the FSMA,[68] which could perhaps – it's too early to tell – result in a collective settlement between FSMA and the banks involved, entailing a promise of the banks to compensate customers, of the kind that will be discussed below in Section 11.4.2. In the tour operator (Thomas Cook) and Proximus cases, the Brussels courts ruled that, when deciding whether to choose an opt-in or opt-out system, a major consideration should be whether it's easy for consumers to be aware of the fact that they have suffered damage, and whether they can easily understand what their rights and their legal position are.[69] If this is the case, an opt-in approach is preferable, according to the court. Another consideration is the number of victims: if it is relatively low, an opt-in is preferable. The courts therefore imposed an opt-in in the tour operator case, which only affected the customers of a few cancelled flights, who could easily understand that they had suffered. The courts do not seem to have taken into consideration that the damage of the victims – in any case hard to quantify – was probably very limited in monetary terms, which could have been an argument in favor of an opt-out approach. The high number of potential victims of mis-selling a subscription formula by a telecoms company, who may not have been aware that they had potentially overpaid for services, was cited by the Brussels Court of First Instance as an argument in favor of an opt-out approach. On appeal this was, however, reversed and the Court of Appeal imposed an opt-in system based on its view that the legal situation of potential victims of the alleged mis-selling practices differed considerably between potential class members.[70]

65 In 2018, a settlement was reached between Test-Aankoop and one of the eight websites/companies. I can find no information on the rest of the case, except an announcement by Test-Aankoop on its website that it continues to litigate the case against the other seven.

66 The case was settled out of court, see www.test-aankoop.be/collectieve-acties/groepsvordering-groupon-compensatie.

67 www.test-aankoop.be/collectieve-acties/facebook.The case was pleaded before the Brussels Commercial Court on November 4, 2019. At the time of writing I have no knowledge of a judgment in the case.

68 See www.test-aankoop.be/geld/betalen/nieuws/transferkosten-effecten.

69 See also the discussion in Boularbah and Vandenbossche, *supra* note 43, 83–86.

70 Court of Appeal Brussels, January 30, 2019, §§ 38 through 48 (including reference to the first instance decision). The Court referred to different contractual clauses in different contracts, potentially different amounts of damages due and different assessment of the causal link between mis-selling and damages.

11.4 SECURITIES CLASS ACTIONS AND CONSUMER PROTECTION IN THE FINANCIAL SECTOR: STILL MISSING

Professor Coffee has called the securities class action the 800 pound gorilla in the American class action landscape[71]. The same cannot be said of the situation in Belgium, where the possibility to bring securities class actions was excluded from the BCAA. There is no explicit provision in the Act stating that securities fraud or cases based on securities laws are excluded, but it follows from several provisions in the Act (see Section 11.4.1).

This exclusion is somewhat puzzling since the call for class actions in Belgium grew louder after the fraud cases that came to light as the 2001 dotcom bubble burst, and the cases involving thousands of investors that felt defrauded (rightly or wrongly) as a result of the collapse of two of Belgium's biggest banks, Fortis and Dexia, in the 2007–2008 financial crisis. In an article that I wrote in 2010, before the Belgian Class Action Act had been adopted, I pleaded in favor of introducing class actions in Belgium but with the exclusion of securities class actions because, I argued, these are plagued by an intense form of the well-known "circularity problem."[72] In the meantime I have changed my mind and would argue that in spite of circularity, securities class actions are necessary as a complement of public enforcement of securities laws, which in Belgium is certainly not overzealous. But the point here is that the fear of the circularity issue may have played a role among policymakers in their decision to exclude securities class actions. Probably more important was the widespread feeling among the bar and judges that securities class actions are typically driven by the desire for profit of investors who are happy to cash in profits when things are going well and therefore – that's the sentiment – should accept their losses when things turn sour. Of course this sentiment is unjustified, since in a securities fraud case we are talking about investors that have been defrauded and for whom there is a causal link between their losses and the fraud. But while this sentiment may be unjustified, it's hard to avoid the impression that it played a major role in excluding securities class actions from the Belgian Act. As indicated, this feeling also seems widespread among members of the bar specializing in corporate and securities law, in other words, Belgium has no real plaintiff bar for securities law cases, even though a handful of lawyers have established a reputation as repeat defenders of the interests of "minority shareholders."[73]

11.4.1 *The Difficulties of Bringing Class Actions to Protect Consumers in the Financial Sector*

All this has not stopped practitioners from wondering whether it is really impossible to bring class actions against the financial sector (banks, securities traders, investment companies, insurance companies, ...). A detailed analysis of this very technical question would be out of place in a general overview intended for a non-Belgian audience,[74] so we will limit ourselves to some general remarks. It is beyond doubt that financial firms of all kinds (banks, investment firms, mutual funds) are "eligible" as defendants in a Belgian class action, since they answer to the

[71] John C. Coffee, "Reforming the securities class action: an essay on deterrence and its implementation," 106 *Columbia Law Review* (2006), 1534, at 1539.

[72] Hans De Wulf, "Aandeelhoudersvorderingen met het oog op schadevergoeding- of waarom elke aandeelhouder vergoeding van reflexschade kan vorderen, België class actions moet invoeren en de minderheidsvordering moet hervormen" in *10 jaar Wetboek vennootschappen in werking*, Brussels: Wolters Kluwer, 2011, 476–524.

[73] Especially Mischaël Modrikamen, Laurent Arnauts and Geert Lenssens (the first two initially being partners of one and the same law firm, before Arnauts started his own successful outfit).

[74] A first attempt at tackling this issue in the literature is Grégory Renier and Béatrice Toussaint, "L'action en reparation collective appliquée aux produits bancaires, financiers et d'assurances," *Rev. droit bancaire et financier*, 2015, 169–186.

relevant definition of "firm" (only "firms" as defined in the Belgian Code of Economic Law can be defendants under the BCAA). But only consumers and, since 2018, certain SMEs are eligible as (plaintiff) class members. Shareholders in corporations are not consumers when they want to enforce their individual shareholder rights as enshrined in the Companies Act. But a natural person who directly, without intermediaries, invests in a firm could, if he's not acting in a professional capacity but in the normal administration of his affairs, be regarded as a consumer. The problems is though that the vast majority of retail investors do not invest in commercial firms directly, but through intermediaries such as mutual or index funds. In that case the retail investor is a consumer in its relationship with the fund; but has no direct link or claims against for example a listed company that committed securities fraud or whose directors committed such fraud. The investor/shareholder is the investment fund, but it is not a consumer, since it clearly acts in a professional capacity. So the investment fund cannot become a class member, let alone act as lead plaintiff (the latter impossibility follows from the fact that, as mentioned, only certain recognized consumer organizations or ad hoc recognized nonprofit organizations can act as lead plaintiff). Perhaps more importantly, in Belgium class actions cannot be based on the traditional grounds for bringing a securities class action: violations of disclosure rules as contained in securities regulation or corporate law are not part of the exhaustive list of actionable statutes or European law in the BCAA, nor is the general principle of fraud as based (in Belgium) on tort law (article 1382 Civil Code, the general tort norm, more or less equivalent to the tort of negligence in common law jurisdictions). Nor can mis-selling of financial products usually be prosecuted through a class action, since most mis-selling provisions in Belgian law are based on the European MiFID Regulation,[75] and neither MiFID nor its European or Belgian implementing measures are part of the aforementioned exhaustive list of actionable grounds. Based on the inclusion in this list of parts of a Belgian Act of August 2, 2002,[76] it would be possible, however, to bring a class action against a financial institution caught by the 2002 Act (most financial intermediaries are covered by it) that had offered financial products without being licensed to offer that type of product (e.g., an investment firm offering, without the relevant permit, complex, so-called "branch 23" insurance products which are substantively investment securities wrapped in an insurance product and therefore benefiting from lower taxation of the income they generate). One very general set of norms that is included in the exhaustive list of thirty-three actionable pieces of legislation are the provisions of Book VI of the WER. This Book deals with unfair trading practices and general consumer protection, and is applicable, since May 31, 2014, to financial services and investment products and their providers or traders. It contains some very open, broad norms like a list of unfair contractual clauses, and a ban on "market practices that are unloyal because of their misleading nature" (article VI.94 juncto 97 through 100 of the WER). Some have argued that these provisions could serve as a gateway/loophole to initiate class actions for damage incurred by investors who have bought securities.[77] They argue that the fact that a prospectus has been approved by the competent supervisor and the fact that the prospectus does not itself contain misleading information or omissions, cannot stop a judge from ruling that the concrete way in which the securities were marketed and sold to the public was misleading or violated one of the general rules on publicity from Book VI. This point of view has not been tested in court yet. The fact that this train of thought cannot be dismissed out of hand is due to the not very consistent position taken in

75 See generally www.esma.europa.eu/policy-rules/mifid-ii-and-mifir.

76 "Act on the Supervision of Financial Institutions and Financial Services," as often amended.

77 See esp. Grégory Renier and Béatrice Toussaint, "L'action en *réparation* collective appliquée aux produits bancaires, financiers et d'assurances," *Rev. droit bancaire et financier*, 2015, 169, at 173–175.

Belgian legislation: on the one hand, as repeatedly indicated, it was a very conscious decision of Belgian policymakers to exclude securities class actions and actions based on MiFID rules from the list of actionable offenses under the BCAA. On the other hand, in 2014 the Belgian Parliament, fully aware of what it was doing but not thinking about the potential implications for class actions, extended the application of large parts of general consumer law to the provision of financial services and the offering of financial instruments, from which it had been explicitly excluded by statute from the early 1990s onwards.

In any case, assuming in future plaintiffs succeed in convincing a Belgian court that the aforementioned consumer protection rules are actionable in the context of securities fraud, this would not mean they would have won the day. That is because a workable securities class action system also depends on the acceptance of some form of the fraud on the market theory, and this has always been rejected in Belgium, except for a few narrowly circumscribed cases in securities regulation where statute itself explicitly reverses the burden of proof concerning causality between the fraud and the alleged damages.[78] As long as acceptance of a fraud on the market doctrine is lacking, it will be difficult for potential class members in securities fraud cases to prove enough commonality and/or the superiority of the class action route compared to individual or "regular" aggregated litigation.

11.4.2 *Government Agencies As Damages Collectors on Behalf of Retail Investors?*

In the meantime, a practice of "collective settlements" developed by the Belgian financial supervisor (FSMA,[79] the equivalent, more or less, of the US Securities and Exchange Commission) offers a glimmer of hope for groups of people that feel they are victims of malpractice in the financial sector.

Article 71 § 3 of the Act of August 2, 2002 has granted the FSMA the possibility to enter into settlements with financial institutions that fall under its supervision, instead of using more traditional sanctions like fines, bans from certain activities, appointment of "embedded" special auditors and the like. Initially, the FSMA mainly used this settlement possibility to strike deals with individuals in cases of alleged insider dealing or market manipulation, and without claiming damages, let alone distributing monetary awards among defrauded investors. In recent years, however, the FSMA has begun to use its settlement powers in a way that is somewhat reminiscent of what the American SEC does under its fair funds doctrine (which has a clear statutory basis).[80]

An illustration is the "Bermudan swaps" settlement.[81] In this case regulators in the UK, the Netherlands but also Belgium had found that several banks in each of their jurisdictions had offered rather sophisticated or "complicated" interest rate swaps to unsophisticated SME clients. These swap agreements all contained a clause allowing the bank to unilaterally terminate the agreement under certain conditions which resulted in these contracts being rather favorable to the banks in giving them the possibility to shift risks to their counterparties and to avoid losses on the swaps. The supervisory authorities found that the banks had insufficiently informed their clients about the risks for the clients of entering into these swap agreements and about the rights

78 See on the situation in Europe and Belgium compared to the U.S. Elke Vandendriessche, *Investor Losses*, Antwerp: Intersentia, 2015, esp. 380 ff.

79 Financial Services and Markets Authority.

80 About "fair funds" in the US, see e.g., Urska Velikonja, "Public compensation for private harm: evidence from the SEC's fair Fund distributions," 67 *Stan. L. Rev.* (2015), 2–63, with references to the extensive literature.

81 For the FSMA report on this settlement-the text of the settlement is not publicly available – Google "FSMA Bermudan swaps." The report is available (in Dutch and French only) on www.fsma.be.

banks and clients had under the agreements; that they had performed insufficient suitability tests on their clients before offering them these swap products; and that some banks were not able to sufficiently document their counselling process and had unprofessional archiving practices concerning the agreements. The Belgian supervisory authority FSMA reached a settlement with four Belgian banks in which the banks agreed to the following: to offer clients who had entered into Bermudan swaps to switch to a "plain vanilla" interest rate swap agreement with the bank while, however, maintaining the very low interest rate clients had been allowed to pay under the Bermudan swaps, at no cost to the client; to pay back to clients any costs the bank had already made them pay as part of the Bermudan swaps; and to compensate the clients for any losses they might have already incurred as part of the Bermudan swap deals.

These settlements, which were accepted by the four banks instead of other potential sanctions, are controversial. At the time of the facts and of the settlement, there were no specific statutory sanctions of the MiFID rules on suitability etc. that the FSMA had found the banks to be in violation of. Hence, any sanction would have to follow from general civil law principles. Under these general civil law rules, neither the bank's clients nor the FSMA as a supervisor would have had a viable claim to have the contracts annulled. The clients could perhaps have brought a claim for damages, but judging such a contractual damages claim falls within the exclusive jurisdiction of regular courts, applying regular civil law rules on causation and calculation of damages, whereas here it was not a court but the so-called "internal prosecutor" (effectively, the enforcement division) of the FSMA which struck a deal with the banks in which these promised to compensate investors for their losses. Also, it's the FSMA that will determine (apparently in a discretionary fashion) whether the amounts paid to the banks' clients are sufficient to compensate investors.

In a handful of other cases, too, the FSMA has forced banks, through settlements, to pay damages or at least compensate investors. The "Greek government bonds" settlement with Fortis Bank is an example.[82] In this case, Fortis Bank acting as an investment manager had added Greek government bonds to the investment portfolio of a number of clients that had been classified as more or less risk averse, and this at a time when Fortis bank knew or at least should have been aware that the Greek government was likely to default on those bonds. The FSMA imposed a fine of 700,000 euros on Fortis but, more interestingly, reached a settlement in which Fortis agreed to compensate its customers for all the losses they had incurred on the Greek government bonds that were part of their portfolio.

From a policy perspective a case can be made that it is efficient to allow the competent supervisory authority to reach settlements (collective or not – Belgian law does not explicitly provide for the possibility of "global" collective settlements of the type reached in the Bermudan swaps affair) with firms under its authority, and that it should be allowed, as part of the settlement, to have the financial institutions involved pay compensation to the victims of the institution's misbehavior. In other words, some form of "fair funds" system is arguably desirable in Belgium as well. But as long as there is no clear legal basis for it in statute, it is debatable whether current FSMA practices are compatible with Belgian legislation. Article 71 of the August 2 2002 Act explicitly states that any sums paid as part of the settlement, must be paid to the Belgian Treasury. This seems difficult to square with the practice whereby the FSMA does not even receive those payments itself, but has banks pay them directly to victims. In practice, one often hears the argument that since banks agree to this type of settlement, there must obviously be something in it for them as well ("closure"), so that, according to the proponents of this view, policymakers or lawyers should not make such settlements more difficult to enact than they already are. But from a rule of law perspective this approach seems suboptimal, and

82 Also available on www.fsma.be.

the argument neglects the pressure the FSMA, as the repeat supervisor of financial institutions, can bring to bear on the firms under its authority.

11.4.3 *The Fortis Route: Belgian Investors That Want to Use a Class Action to Be Compensated for Securities Fraud Must Turn to the Dutch Courts*

There is at least one Belgian court decision that explicitly recognizes a US class action settlement in Belgium,[83] and there have been countless cases in which Belgian citizens were part of a class in an American class action, without this being contested. But since the *Morrison* decision of the US supreme Court,[84] it has become almost impossible for Belgian investors in a Belgian listed company to start a class action against that company in the US, unless they had traded in stock of that company in the US. Such a "foreign cubed" action happened, pre-Morrison, in the Lernout&Hauspie (L&H) case, where a settlement was reached between the class and the auditors of L&H in which the auditors partly compensated investors,[85] years before the criminal case against L&H and its auditors was brought to court in Belgium, and even longer before the civil (damages claims) L&H case was allowed to proceed in Belgium, after the criminal case had ended.[86] The civil case is still pending!

11.4.3.1 Non-class Action Techniques Used for Collective Securities Litigation in Belgium

Since Belgium does not allow securities class actions and the (always difficult) American route has been cut off by *Morrison*, Belgian investors that want to start collective securities litigation must rely on the Dutch route, or, if they want to sue in Belgium, rely on traditional nonclass action litigation techniques.[87] In Belgium the latter usually means that either Deminor – a shareholder defense organization – or one of the three law firms that seem to have a quasi-monopoly on these cases are contacted. Several cases have been brought where thousands of investors give power of attorney to Deminor's attorneys or the aforementioned lawyers, sometimes after, as an intermediate step, setting up a legal person (nonprofit association) to which they transfer their claims. They usually also elect domicile at the office of these law firms. The attorneys work on a success fee basis, and individual investors only have to pay a small fee to join the litigation. Joining the action usually requires little more, at least initially, than filling out a brief online form and paying the small fee. The approach is an imitation of an opt-in class

83 As reported in *Rechtskundig Weekblad* 2017, 1442.

84 *Morrison v. National Australia Bank*, 561 U.S. 247 (2010).

85 *Supra* note 12.

86 Some commentators, like my former Ghent colleague Stefaan Voet, optimistically interpret the possibility of retail investors to rely on evidence assembled by public prosecutors in criminal cases, by joining the criminal case as a so-called "civil party" claiming damages, as a beneficial form of "piggybacking." I think this view is too rosy. By law, investors have to wait until the DA's office has finished its criminal investigation and until the end of the criminal trial if one ensues before they can claim any damages (*"le criminal tient le civil en état"* – a rule which was recently (2019) somewhat relaxed). In view of the fact that these cases take many years to prepare because, at least until recently, there was no statutory possibility let alone a culture of settling them (in criminal matters), this meant years of delay for retail investors, and the possibility that the failure of the public prosecutor to have the defendants convicted on criminal charges, for which of course a very high burden of proof prevails, would have a negative influence on the same court's readiness to award civil damages. The L&H case is a good illustration of all this. About that case (but viewing its implications in a different light), see Stefaan Voet, ""The L&H Case: Belgium's Internet Bubble Story" in D. Hensler, C. Hodges and I. Tzankova (eds.), *Class Actions in Context: How Economics, Politics and Culture Shape Collective Litigation*, Cheltenham: Edward Elgar (2016), 299–319.

87 For an overview of these techniques see Piet Taelman and Philippe Thion, "Bundeling van vorderingen," *Tijdschrift voor Privaatrecht* 2003, 1489–1547 or, much briefer but in English Taelman and Voet, *supra* note 20.

action, and it works: several cases have been brought in which a sizeable percentage of potential class members joined this style of collective litigation.[88] Scholars may be correct in arguing that opt-in systems are not *efficient* in organizing cases with lots of victims who claim relatively small amounts of money, too small to justify individual litigation, but those who argue that the opt-in approach is not *viable* in such cases, have been empirically proven wrong by the Belgian experience. The system is nevertheless less efficient than a class action system. The bureaucracy of joining a case, and of identifying all the parties on all procedural pieces is tiresome, but all-in-all not very problematic. A bigger problem is that while showing sufficient commonality between class members in a regular class action system does not require the proof that their situation is substantially identical in all relevant respects, endless argumentation about the differences in situation between investors, for example depending on the time when they invested, is clearly possible and does occur under a system of collective litigation based on awarding power of attorney and where traditional civil law principles apply. The procedural difficulties that can arise under such a system were nicely illustrated in a Belgian case[89] where hundreds of allegedly defrauded Fortis investors had "elected domicile" at the address of the law firm representing them. This implied that all court and procedural documents like summons could be served to that address, instead of to the individual addresses of all the 2200 joined plaintiffs. After the plaintiff law firm had obtained a favorable judgment in first instance, it seems to have advised its clients to revoke this election of domicile, which the clients did. As a result, when the Belgian government (sued because of its bailout of Fortis) appealed the first instance decision, it had to serve the "act of appeal" to more than 2000 different addresses (and apparently initially made the mistake of serving it only to the plaintiff law firm, apparently unaware that its clients had revoked their election of domicile).

11.4.3.2 Fortis As An Illustration of Dutch Claims to Near Universal Jurisdiction

The Fortis case[90] involved Belgium's largest bank. It collapsed and had to be bailed out by the Belgian and Luxembourg (and initially also Dutch) government during the 2008 financial crisis. The collapse of Fortis' share price led to heavy losses for many small retail investors who had sometimes invested a substantial percentage of their savings in additional shares issued in a capital increase by Fortis about a year before its collapse. Belgian investors, who initially sued Fortis successor firm Ageas, some of its directors and executives, and the Belgian government in regular proceedings before Belgian courts, mostly[91] dropped these cases and joined the efforts in The Netherlands to obtain compensation under the Dutch class action system[92]. This system will be discussed in the Dutch report to this volume. Suffice it to say here that the Dutch "WCAM" Act allows victims of securities fraud (or of other actionable facts) to apply to the Amsterdam Court of Appeal to approve a settlement that the plaintiff class has reached with the defendant. The plaintiff

88 For instance, in the L&H litigation, Deminor and Test Aankoop, who joined forces, succeeded in assembling about 13,000 of a total of slightly more than 15,000 plaintiffs (about 86 percent), meaning these shareholders gave power of attorney to those two organizations to represent them. The case remains unreported and concerned one of many cases launched (but often dropped after a while) by shareholders against the government after the bail-out of Fortis bank. But the facts described in the main text were widely reported in the press, see e.g., "Modrikamen treitert regering" ("Modrikamen bullies the government") *De Morgen* (Belgian daily), December 16, 2008.

89 All documents pertaining to the part of the case that was settled can be consulted at www.forsettlement.com/.

90 All documents pertaining to the part of the case that was settled can be consulted at www.forsettlement.com/.

91 The most prominent exception was the investment vehicle of a Belgian billionaire family which did not join the Dutch WCAM case but pursued its own damages claim before the Belgian courts. Apparently they had incurred a loss of more than 100 million euros on their investment in Fortis.

92 All relevant documents concerning this settlement can be found at www.forsettlement.com/.

class is represented by a foundation set up by the law firm or organization that represents the interests of the plaintiff class. Parties cannot go to trial, their only possibility is to first, prior to the start of court proceedings, bring about a settlement between "their" foundation and the defendant(s) and then have this settlement approved by the Amsterdam court. The Dutch system is the only properly functioning securities class action system in Europe. As far as I'm aware, only nine settlements have been submitted to the Court under the WCAM Act, but seven of those dealt with securities class actions and all of them were substantial cases. In the Fortis case, The Amsterdam Court of appeal declared the April 13, 2018 settlement binding in its July 13, 2018 judgment.[93]

The Amsterdam Court of Appeal seems very eager to accept jurisdiction in cases where most class members have no links with the Netherlands or even where the defendant corporation is not Dutch.[94] In the Fortis case there were clear links with the Netherlands, as the Fortis group was a binational Belgian-Dutch group, although very much dominated by the Belgian activities and a Belgian management team. At least the group also contained Dutch subsidiaries and many shareholders were Dutch. A somewhat similar situation arose in the Shell case, Shell being Anglo-Dutch. In that case, the Amsterdam court essentially accepted jurisdiction for all claims for which US courts had declared to have no jurisdiction and the Amsterdam Court clearly indicated it did so because it thought all claimants should have a chance to participate in a "global settlement" of the case. Things were different in the Converium case.[95] Converium was a Swiss multinational company whose shares were not traded on any Dutch exchanges. Only about 200 of about 12,000 class members in the securities fraud case that was settled under WCAM were Dutch, but still the Amsterdam Court of Appeal accepted jurisdiction for the whole class. In a newsletter, the leading Dutch law firm De Brauw wrote that to meet the requirement that at least one of the petitioners is Dutch, it's sufficient for the foundation that "represents" the plaintiff's class interest to have been set up in accordance with Dutch law[96] and this does seem indeed to be borne out by the case law.

The leading cases are Shell[97] and Converium.[98] It would burst the bounds of this contribution to offer a detailed technical analysis of the jurisdictional issues and the arguments surrounding them in cross-border cases that were brought before the Dutch courts.[99] One central argument in both Shell and Converium that the Amsterdam court used to underpin its territorial jurisdiction for persons having their domicile in an EU member state but outside the Netherlands was based on article 6(1) of the Brussels I Regulation,[100] an EU piece of legislation which determines

93 The initial settlement between Fortis and investors involved in the case dates to March 2016, but it was amended several times during the court proceedings to get it approved.

94 See also e.g., Hélène Van Lith, "Internationale bevoegdheid Nederlandse rechter WCAM-zaak", *Ondernemingsrecht* 2011, 117, at 121.

95 For an overview of the case, see www.converiumsettlements.com/EN/case.php,where an English translation of the January 12, 2012 judgment of the Amsterdam Court of appeal is available. This judgment gave binding effect to the settlement between Converium and its investors.

96 See De Brauw Blackstone Westbroek N.V., Ruud Hermans and Jan de Bie Leuveling Tjeenk, "International Class Action Settlements in the Netherlands since *Converium*" in *The ICLG to Class & Group Actions 2012*, 8, at nr. 39.

97 Amsterdam Court of Appeal, May 29, 2009, JOR 2009, 197.

98 Court of Appeal Amsterdam November 12, 2010, JOR 2011, 46. A good (critical) discussion of Converium in English is Benoît Allemeersch, "Transnational class settlements: lessons from Converium," in S. Wrbka, S. van Uytsel and M. Siems (eds.), *Collective Actions: Enhancing Access to Justice and Reconciling Multilayer Interests*, Cambridge: Cambridge University Press, 2012, 364–384.

99 An excellent and extensive treatment of conflicts of laws (private international law) issues surrounding the WCAM is Hélène Van Lith, *The Dutch Collective Settlements act and Private International Law*. Antwerp: Maklu, 2012, 185, also available at ec.europa.eu/competition/consultations/2011_collective_redress/saw_annex_en.pdf.

100 We'll refer to the version of Brussels I that was in force at the time of the cases discussed (originally, Council Regulation (EC) No 44/2001 of 22 December 2000 on jurisdiction and the recognition and enforcement of judgments in civil and commercial matters, OJ 2001, L12, p. 1.). The Regulation has since been replaced by the

jurisdiction in the EU in cross-border cases. According to article 6(1) of Brussels I, in case there are multiple defendants, the court that has jurisdiction over one defendant can claim jurisdiction over all other codefendants if the claims against the defendants are so closely connected that it is "expedient to hear and determine them together to avoid the risk of irreconcilable judgments resulting from separate proceedings." To bring about the desired effect, the Amsterdam Court assumed that all parties involved in the class action settlement submitted to it could be regarded as codefendants. We'll limit ourselves to pointing out that it is odd to assume that the members of the "plaintiff class," namely the allegedly defrauded investors, are "codefendants" in the case. But the Court clearly thinks such a legal nicety should be overruled by the consideration that all parties involved clearly have an interest to avoid conflicting judgments, in several jurisdictions, about one and the same case of alleged securities fraud, and therefore generously offers to claim exclusive jurisdiction. In Converium the Court also based its jurisdiction (over class members based in the EU) on article 5(1) of Brussels I. This provided at the time of proceedings that in matters pertaining to the performance of contracts, the court of the jurisdiction where a contractual obligation needs to be performed, have jurisdiction for claims pertaining to this performance. Since the settlement foundation is set up in accordance with Dutch law and is domiciled in the Netherlands, and it will pay out the damages it receives as part of the settlement to investors in a Dutch bank account, the performance of the obligations from the settlement, being a contract, takes place in the Netherlands, hence the Court's jurisdiction (at least, that's what the Court itself argued). Finally, in both cases (Shell and Converium), the Court also based its jurisdiction over *all* class members from *outside* the EU on the fact that it did have jurisdiction, based on the Dutch Code of Civil Procedure, over *some* defendants domiciled in the Netherlands. Some class members from outside the EU (i.e., whose main residence was often outside the EU and who were citizens of non-EU countries) did indeed have *a* domicile in the Netherlands (allegedly only five in the Shell case).

Irrespective of whether these arguments are convincing from a technical perspective – something which I leave largely undiscussed here – one may wonder whether it is desirable that the Amsterdam court is prepared to act as a venue for large parts of Europe and even the world.

From a technical perspective, the train of thought of the European Court of Justice in "Roche Netherlands" may be relevant here.[101] The European Court there held that when different claims are subject to different substantive law (i.e., material rules from two or more different states), they can never be held to be sufficiently linked in the sense of article 6(1) of the Brussels I Regulation to justify one court having territorial jurisdiction to deal with all these claims. Could it be that this Opinion was inspired by the same sentiment I have, namely that if one accepts universal jurisdiction of the courts of country X, this has an impact on the substantive law that is de facto applied to the case, and that it may be undesirable to undercut the policy decisions reflected in the legal system of one country (e.g., "in Germany we German courts rule that fraud on the market is an unacceptable doctrine") by allowing to settle the case under the law of another jurisdiction that claims universal jurisdiction ?

Of course, one can try to argue – and it is argued by some – that all these legal niceties are largely irrelevant since apparently there is a clear need for global settlements, need which is met

Brussels I*bis* Regulation (Regulation (EU) No 1215/2012 of the European Parliament and of the Council of 12 December 2012 on jurisdiction and the recognition and enforcement of judgments in civil and commercial matters, OJ 2012 L 351 p. 1.). For a brief but authoritative general introduction to the relevance of Brussels I for class actions, see Burkhard Hess, "Cross-border Collective Litigation and the Regulation Brussels I," *IPrax* 2010, 116–121.

101 ECJ, 13 July 2006, case C-539/03, *Roche Nederland/Frederick Primus*.

by the Dutch system: why should anyone object if investors and a defendant corporation voluntarily agree to reach a settlement and give this preclusive effect by having it approved by the Amsterdam Court ? That was clearly the thinking of Converium and its investors, and of Fortis and Deminor and other organizations that represented Fortis investors. They wanted quick and global "closure" so that they could get on with business.

In spite of this, I think the Dutch power grab should be an incentive for other European states to develop their own viable securities class action systems. This would not only be good in that it would avoid non-Dutch citizens having to go through a foreign (namely Dutch) legal system, it would also mean that these states would keep more control over certain policy options, such as what burden of proof it is desirable to impose on plaintiffs in the certification stage of securities class actions.

At the same time, in the Fortis case, the Amsterdam Court of appeal did much, in my view, to bolster its legitimacy in "multinational" class actions. In "Converium," that same court had clearly assumed that its decision to approve the settlement would be automatically recognized in all other EU member states, without any recognition (or exequatur) procedure, just like "judgments" are automatically recognized under the Brussels I Regulation (article 34 of the Brussels I Regulation at the time). This "automatic recognition" also means preclusive effect for the decision in all those member states, at least for those class members who do not opt out of the settlement. But it was, and technically still is, contestable whether a court decision approving a settlement is a "judgment" in the sense of Brussels I, and whether opt-out settlements are brought about in a sufficiently adversarial way, with respect for due process, to deserve automatic recognition.[102] Some argue that "judgment" in Brussels I only refers to court decisions that result from a procedure where the parties that want to have had the possibility to intervene in an adversarial debate about the merits or/and admissibility of claims.[103] In the WCAM procedure, the "battle" between the parties takes place completely out-of-court and only when the settlement agreement is ready can it be submitted to the court. Perhaps more important, in the cases preceding Fortis, one did not have the impression that the Amsterdam court engaged in any thorough evaluation of the content of the settlement. In Fortis it did: it forced parties to offer additional written and oral argument about mainly two issues: whether the distinction the settlement made between Fortis shareholders depending on the moment in time when they had joined the effort to claim damages from Fortis was legitimate; and whether the fees that the organizations representing shareholders demanded from these shareholders and which would be paid out of the settlement amount, were acceptable. By closely looking into these matters and organizing a vigorous debate about them[104] – I think the Court could make a better case than in the past that its ruling to approve the settlement should indeed be regarded as a judgment in the sense of Brussels I, since the ruling is based on an adversarial debate.

102 On this issue, see Van Lith, *supra* note 99, 98 ff., Hess, *supra* note 100 at 120 and also Allemeersch, *supra* note 98, text accompanying his footnotes 28 and 29.

103 Support for this can be found in the "Denilauer" opinion of the ECJ, see case 125/79, *Bernard Denilauer* v. *SNC Couchet Frères*, 1980 ECR I-1553, at § 13.

104 Although the court arguably only did so after one claims organization called "Consumentenclaims" filed formal opposition to the initial settlement with the Amsterdam court, on behalf of a large number of investors, because it disagreed with the fees to be awarded to some other claims organizations such as VEB and Deminor and with the differentiation between class members based on the moment when they had joined the case.

11.5 CONCLUSION

After a long period of resistance, Belgium introduced class actions in 2014. But their application has been restricted, essentially, to cases based on consumer protection legislation while at the same time individual consumers cannot act as lead plaintiffs, since policymakers only trusted certain "representative organizations" as plaintiffs. This restrictive approach is regrettable, since it excludes securities class actions and most class litigation against defendants from the financial sector. The exclusion of securities class actions is especially puzzling since corporate scandals that in a jurisdiction like the US would have given rise to securities class actions contributed heavily to the calls for a class action mechanism in Belgium. The Belgian approach can be explained by the fact that in the final analysis Belgium probably only introduced class actions at all because the European Union put pressure on member states to do this, but limited to consumer cases and with non-entrepreneurial lead plaintiffs. It's unlikely that the near future will see a change in Belgian policymakers' attitudes. In the meantime the Belgian Class Action Act seems to function reasonably well within the limits that are intrinsic to it, even though only a limited number of cases have been brought, like in most other European countries that have introduced class actions over the past ten years or so.

12

The New Italian Regulation on Class Actions

Paolo Giudici and Beatrice Zuffi

12.1 HISTORY

The process that has led collective litigation to have a place in Italian law has been very slow and it is not fully completed at the time we are writing. In this section we analyze this process, which has brought about a major reform of the Italian Code of Civil Procedure in 2019, which is not in force yet at the time of this contribution.

12.1.1 *The Starting Point*

For a very long time the idea that collective and diffuse interests can be vindicated in civil courts had been alien to the civil law tradition.[1] In the Italian legal system, the predominant point of view was that public interests should be protected by the State, so that, in principle exclusively the governmental attorney general ("*pubblico ministero*") could have standing as a representative of collective interests, and in a few instances only.[2] For example, pursuant to the Italian Civil Code the governmental attorney general can challenge in court an illegal decision of an association[3] or can demand for a Court intervention against the directors of a public corporation.[4] However, the governmental attorney general has never been considered an efficient enforcer of associates' or shareholders' interests – a public enforcer of private interests has limited resources, limited access to information and limited incentives to be efficient.[5] As to private attorney generals,[6] originally the Civil Code envisaged a case in which a private party

[1] Mauro Cappelletti, *Vindicating the public interest through the courts: A comparativist's contribution* 25 Buff L. Rev. 643 (1975).

[2] Under Article 2907 Civil Code, rights are protected by civil courts on demand of interested private parties or the Governmental Attorney General under specific provisions. See also article 69 of the Civil Procedure Code, where it is stressed that the "pubblico ministero" can commence civil proceedings in the cases provided for by law.

[3] Article 23 Civil Code.

[4] Article 2409 Civil Code.

[5] Paolo Giudici, *La responsabilità civile nel diritto dei mercati finanziari* (Giuffrè, 2008) 97 ff; *See also* Brian T. Fitzpatrick, *The Conservative Case for Class Actions* (2019).

[6] The use of terms comes from Judge Jerome Frank in Associated Industries v. Ickes, 134 F.2d 694, 704 (2d Cir. 1943): "for then, in like manner, there is an actual controversy, and there is nothing constitutionally prohibiting Congress from empowering any person, official or not, to institute a proceeding involving such a controversy, even if the sole purpose is to vindicate the public interest. Such persons, so authorized, are, so to speak, private Attorney Generals."

could enforce a public interest, when it stated that everyone has standing to claim that a contract or a resolution is null and void.[7] However, courts have interpreted this private power in a restrictive way, holding that a party must have a private interest in the action in order to have standing. Accordingly, the relevant Civil Code's provisions have not been able to create the conditions for a true private attorney general with regard to null and void contracts or resolutions.[8] Some scattered provisions for collective redress, mainly aimed at obtaining declaratory or injunctive relief on the initiative of various kinds of entities, have been foreseen in the Civil Code or had been implemented afterwards mainly through some labor law provisions and the transposition of Directive no. 93/13/EEC on unfair contract terms, but their impact on the enforcement of collective claims has not been particularly significant.[9]

There is an area, however, where traditionally collective interests have been seamlessly protected in civil courts by a private party that is considered a public officer. In bankruptcy law, indeed, the insolvency trustee appointed by the court has standing on behalf of the creditors of the insolvent firm with regard to actions in damages against the directors or the statutory auditors of the corporation or in claw back actions. The trustee's standing concerns, in the language of Italian bankruptcy law, the "*azioni della massa*", that is, the actions of the creditors as a class. Accordingly, the bankruptcy trustee is a representative of a class in a civil court, and this has been for decades the closer equivalent to a class action representative in the Italian law experience.

In all the other fields representative litigation had remained confined to the academic debate in the course of the last century. Taking the US experience as a reference point, scholars were discussing whether the principle of defense provided for in article 24 of our Constitution, in combination with the doctrine of the claim,[10] was a constitutional obstacle to civil proceedings that took part without the direct participation of the interested party.[11] Needless to say, big

7 Giudici, *La responsabilità civile nel diritto dei mercati finanziari* (nt. 5), 96 *ff.*

8 *Id.*, 143.

9 The remedies referred to in the text are those still established by article 2601 of civil code (which entitles trade associations to commence litigation for the prevention of competition unfair conducts); by article 28 of the Workers' Statute (Law no. 300 of 20 May 1970, enabling labor unions to obtain from Courts the cessation of anti-union behaviors); by the Consumer Code (Legislative Decree no. 206 of 6 September 2005, whose articles 37 and 139 give consumers' associations standing to sue professionals and firms for stopping the use of unfair general contract conditions or terms); by article 37 of the Code of equal opportunities between men and women (Legislative Decree no. 198 of 11 April 2006) and by the various provisions aiming at prohibiting discrimination based on religious, sexual, disability, or age grounds (according to which the regional councilors appointed by the Ministry of Labor can promote lawsuits in case of collective discriminations).

In relation to environmental harms, the lousy outcomes of the Law no. 349 of 8 July 1986, which permitted agreed associations or local public bodies to sue against the wrongdoer for the violation of the common interest of nature preservation and for its compensation, brought about their repealing with the entry into force of the new environmental code, enacted by the Legislative Decree no. 152 of 2006 also for implementing Directive no. 2004/35/CE. According to the new rules, as amended in 2009 and in 2013, exclusively the Ministry of Environment has thus become entitled to bring an action for damages caused by pollution or other disasters. Anyway no such initiative has ever been undertaken.

10 Based on article 2907 of civil code and articles 81–99 of the Civil Procedure Code.

11 *See*, for a restatement of this interpretation, Pietro Rescigno, *Sulla compatibilità tra il modello processuale della* "class action" *ed i principi fondamentali dell'ordinamento giuridico italiano*, Giur. it. 2226 (2000); Giulio Cataldi, *Il problematico inserimento delle* class actions *nell'ordinamento italiano*, Quest. giust. 811 (2005); Giorgio Resta, *Azioni popolari, azioni nell'interesse collettivo, class actions: modelli e prospettive di riforma in una recente riflessione*, Riv. crit. dir. priv. 332 (2007). Several influential authors objected this position, stressing the benefit of the US class actions mechanisms: Salvatore Patti, *L'esperienza delle* class actions *in due libri recenti*, Riv. trim. dir. proc. civ. 1559 (1979); Claudio Consolo, Class actions *fuori dagli USA? (Un'indagine preliminare sul versante della tutela dei crediti di massa: funzione sostanziale e struttura processuale minima)*, Riv. dir. civ. 615 (1993); Andrea Giussani, *Studi sulle* class actions (1996).

business was intensively lobbying against class actions, with the usual narrative concerning the US cases of abusive or frivolous litigation.

12.1.2 *The 1998 Reform on Capital Markets and the Derivative Action*

The first notable change occurred at the end of the century. When capital markets law was radically reformed in 1998 through Legislative Decree no. 58 (Consolidated Financial Services Act – CFSA) the growing Law and Finance literature[12] influenced the legislature and brought an important change. This literature, with all its debatable assumptions and conclusions, put a strong emphasis on the protection of minority shareholders and investors, and on the central role that the private enforcement of law can play in developing financial markets. This lesson was heard in Italy by the officials who were preparing the new law, led by Mario Draghi, an economist who later became the President of the Bank of Italy and then of the European Central Bank. These officials were facing an old issue that was preventing institutional investors from investing in Italy. Italian listed companies are mainly controlled by families or firm coalitions. Directors are often the dominant shareholders, and, when not, are appointed by dominant shareholders and, de facto, follow their interests. At that time the Civil Code stated that only the corporation could sue the directors for damages suffered by the company's estate and only with the blessing by a prior decision of its shareholder meeting. Since the shareholder meeting is controlled by the dominant shareholder, actions against directors were virtually unheard out of the bankruptcy context, in which – as mentioned – it is the bankruptcy trustee who acts on behalf of the legal person and its creditors. Accordingly, directors were virtually undeterred as long as the company remained solvent, and related-party transactions aimed at expropriating minority shareholders were widely perceived to be endemic in the Italian business experience. The idea that directors had to be deterred in a more effective way through something similar to US derivative actions started to gain momentum, and in 1998 Article 129 CFSA finally introduced the derivative suit into the fabric of Italian listed companies' law. In the following reform of the general law of Italian corporations the derivative suit was extended to all public and private companies, even though its use is virtually inexistent in public companies because of procedural hurdles that create huge disincentives on minority shareholders who would like to launch an action.[13] In any event, it is not by chance that the first step towards the introduction of a class action started from the derivative action. Indeed this action can be considered the simplest model of class litigation. The class is made by the shareholders. The shareholders hold fungible interests and their fractional interest in the company marks their stake in the outcome of the litigation. The relief is indivisible as it goes to the company, which is the organized group that unifies the class. Accordingly, there is no better class representative than the shareholder.[14] This probably

[12] Rafael La Porta and others, *Legal Determinants of External Finance*, 52 J. Fin. 1131 (1997); Rafael La Porta and others, *Law and Finance*, 106 J. Pol. Econ. 1113 (1998); Rafael La Porta, Florencio Lopez de Silanes and Andrei Shleifer, *Corporate Ownership Around the World*, 54 J. Fin. 471 (1999); Rafael La Porta and others, *Investor Protection and Corporate Governance*, 58 J. Fin. Econ. 3 (2000); Rafael La Porta, Florencio Lopez de Silanes and Andrei Shleifer, *What Works in Securities Laws?* 61 J. Fin. 1 (2006); Rafael La Porta, Florencio Lopez-de-Silanes and Andrei Shleifer, *The Economic Consequences of Legal Origins*, 46 J. Econ. Lit. 285 (2008).

[13] Paolo Giudici, *Representative Litigation in Italian Capital Markets: Italian Derivative Suits and (if ever) Securities Class Actions*, 2–3 E.C.F.R. 246 (2009); Luca Enriques and Federico Maria Mucciarelli, *L'azione sociale da parte delle minoranze*, in Pietro Abbadessa and G. B. Portale (eds), *Il nuovo diritto delle società Liber Amicorum Gian Franco Campobasso*, vol 2 (2006) 861.

[14] Richard A. Epstein, *Class Actions. Aggregation, Amplification and Distortion*, U. Chi. Legal F. 475 (2003).

explains why the first experiment in representative litigation in Italy, out of the insolvency context, started with the derivative action. Then the Parmalat scandal arrived.

12.1.3 *The Parmalat Scandal and the Introduction of Consumer Class Actions*

The Parmalat crash, which occurred in 2003, was the biggest fraudulent bankruptcy and market rigging scandal perpetrated by a private company in Europe.[15] The scandal produced a shock wave, and some authors argued that one of the problems of Italian law enforcement was the virtual absence of significant private enforcement and, more specifically, the absence of securities class actions and discovery mechanisms.[16] After the scam the Parliament took legislative measures aimed at reassuring both retail and professional investors, as well as consumers. With regard to class actions, many bills were presented and failed to be approved. Finally, a first hybrid version of mass redress for damages (that mixed elements of a Brazilian-like collective action with features of the US class actions) was provided for by Law no. 244 of 2007 and introduced into the Consumer Code as Article 140-bis. However, the entry into force of that law was repeatedly postponed, and then Article 140-bis was reformulated by Law no. 99 of 2009, which tried to envisage a more genuine version of class action, even though it was circumscribed by an opt-in system.[17] The new formulation required the "identity" of the claims belonging to the class, and

[15] Andrea Melis, *Corporate Governance Failures: to what extent is Parmalat a particularly Italian Case?*, 13 Corporate Governance: An International Review 478 (2005); Guido Ferrarini and Paolo Giudici, *Financial Scandals and the Role of Private Enforcement: The Parmalat Case*, in John Armour and Joseph A. McCahery (eds), *After Enron* (2006).

[16] Ferrarini and Giudici, *Financial Scandals* (nt. 15).

[17] The Italian literature on article 140-bis of consumer code is plentiful: the following list is by no means exhaustive. Claudio Consolo, Marco Bona & Paolo Buzzelli, *Obiettivo* Class Action (2008); Remo Caponi, *Azioni collettive: interessi protetti e modelli processuali di tutela*, Riv. dir. proc. 1205 (2008); Claudio Consolo, *Tutela giurisdizionale per «adesione» ossia senza domanda giudiziale dei singoli consumatori*, Resp. Civ. 1701 (2008); Giorgio Costantino, *La tutela collettiva risarcitoria. Note a prima lettura dell'art.* 140-bis *cod. cons.*, Foro it. V 17 (2008); Giuseppe Chiné & Giuseppe Miccolis (ed.), Class action *e tutela collettiva dei consumatori* (2008); Romolo Donzelli, *La tutela giurisdizionale degli interessi collettivi* (2008); Alessandro Giorgetti & Valerio Vallefuoco, *Il contenzioso di massa in Italia, in Europa e nel mondo. Profili di comparazione in tema di azioni di classe ed azioni di gruppo* (2008); Andrea Giussani, *Azioni collettive risarcitorie nel processo civile* (2008); Andrea Giussani, *L'azione collettiva risarcitoria nell'art.* 140-bis *cod. cons.*, Riv. dir. proc. 1227 (2008); Sergio Menchini, *La nuova azione collettiva risarcitoria e restitutoria*, Giusto proc. civ. 49 (2008); Elena Poddighe, *I* mass torts *nel sistema della responsabilità civile* (2008); Remo Caponi, *Il nuovo volto della* class action, Foro it. V 383 (2009); Claudio Consolo, *Come cambia, rivelando ormai a tutti e in pieno il suo volto, l'art.* 140-bis *e la* class action *consumeristica*, Corr. Giur. 1297 (2009); Giorgio Costantino, *La tutela collettiva risarcitoria: la tela di Penelope*, Foro it. V 388 (2009); Nicolò Trocker, Class actions *negli USA. E in Europa?*, Contr. Impr. Eur. 178 (2009); Vincenzo Vigoriti & Giuseppe Conte (a cura di), *Futuro Giustizia Azione collettiva Mediazione* (2010); Marco De Cristofaro, *L'azione collettiva risarcitoria "di classe": profili sistematici e processuali*, Resp. Civ. 1932 (2010); Giuseppe Chiné & Giuseppe Miccolis (ed.), *La nuova* class action *e la tutela collettiva dei consumatori* (2010); Paolo Giovanni Demarchi (ed.), *I diritti del consumatore e la nuova* class action (2010); Andrea Giussani, *Il nuovo art.* 140-bis *Codice del consumo*, Riv. Dir. Proc. 595 (2010); Sergio Menchini & Alessandro Motto, *L'azione di classe dell'art.* 140-bis *Codice del consumo*, Nuove leggi civ. comm. 1415 (2010); Ilaria Pagni, *L'azione di classe nel nuovo art.* 140-bis: *le situazioni soggettive tutelate, l'introduzione del giudizio e l'ammissibilità della domanda*, Riv. dir. civ. II 349 (2010); Paolo Porreca, *Ambito soggettivo e oggettivo dell'azione di classe*, Eur. Dir. Priv. 541 (2010); Stefania Bariatti, *Le azioni collettive dell'art.* 140-bis *del codice del consumo: aspetti di diritto internazionale privato e processuale*, Riv. dir. int. Prov. Proc. 19 (2011); Mauro Bove, *La trattazione nel processo di classe*, www.judicium.it; Camilla Beria di Argentine (ed.), *Class action: il nuovo volto della tutela collettiva in Italia* (2011); Giuseppe Conte, *I "diritti individuali omogenei" nella disciplina dell'azione di classe*, Riv. dir. civ. I 609 (2011); Romolo Donzelli, *L'azione di classe a tutela dei consumatori* (2011); Edoardo Ferrante, *La nuova "azione di classe" in Italia*, Cont. Impr. Eur. 1 (2011); Andrea Giussani, *Azione di classe, conciliazione e mediazione*, Riv. Trim. Dir. Proc. Civ. 159 (2011); Andrea Giussani, *Azione di classe e tutela* antitrust: *profili processuali*, Banca Borsa Tit. 371 (2011); Claudio Scognamiglio, *Risarcimento del danno, restituzione e rimedi nell'azione di classe*, Resp. Civ. 501 (2011); Michele Taruffo, *La tutela collettiva nell'ordinamento italiano: lineamenti generali*, Riv. trim. dir. proc. civ. 103 (2011); Ernesto Cesaro & Fernando Bocchini (ed.), *La nuova* class action *a tutela dei consumatori degli utenti. Commentario*

courts interpreted this requirement very narrowly, dismissing the first attempts of using the new instrument by consumer associations. Accordingly, the rule was slightly amended by the Law no. 27 of 2012, with the substitution of the "homogeneity" test for the original "identity" one.[18] Nevertheless, the Consumer Class action continued to be a largely unsatisfactory remedy. Among the roughly forty class actions brought since 2010,[19] fifteen have been declared ineligible,[20] eleven have obtained the order of admissibility[21] and only four cases have been

all'art. 140-bis *cod. cons.*, *sub* art. 49, c. 4, l. 23 luglio 2009 n. 99 (2012); Claudio Consolo & Beatrice Zuffi, *L'azione di classe* ex *art.* 140-bis *cod. cons. Lineamenti processuali* (2012); Amalia Chiara Di Landro, *Interessi dei consumatori e azione di classe* (2012); Tommaso Febbrajo, *L'azione di classe a tutela dei consumatori: profili sostanziali* (2012); Edoardo Ferrante, *L'azione di classe nel diritto italiano* (2012); Edoardo Ferrante, Opt-out *ed incentivi d'oltreoceano: idee per una vera* class action *in Italia e in Europa*, Cont. Imp. Eur. 483 (2012); Andrea Giussani, *L'azione di classe: un primo bilancio*, Riv. Dir. Proc. 1177 (2012); Lorenzo Pelle, *Lo* status *processuale di aderente nell'azione di classe* ex *art.* 140 bis *cod. cons.*, Riv. dir. proc. 955 (2012); Angelo Danilo De Santis, *La tutela giurisdizionale collettiva: contributo allo studio della legittimazione ad agire e delle tecniche inibitorie e risarcitorie* (2013); Beatrice Zuffi, *La responsabilità civile da illeciti di massa e l'azione di classe*, in Maurizio Bianchini, Alessandro Calegari & Gina Gioia (ed.), *Dialogo tra corti e nuove frontiere della responsabilità*, 825 (2016); Giulia Bertolino, *L'* "opt-out" *nell'azione risarcitoria collettiva. Una contrarietà davvero giustificata? Analisi del dibattito e prospettive di riforma*, Riv. trim. dir. proc. civ. 475 (2016); Beatrice Zuffi, *La giurisdizione in materia di servizi pubblici nel quadro dei rapporti tra azione di classe e ricorso per l'efficienza della P.A.*, Giur. it. 867 (2016); Edoardo Ferrante, *La via italiana alla class action fra interesse di classe e regole ostruzionistiche per le adesioni*, Giur. it. 66 (2017); Beatrice Zuffi, *Arriva la prima maxi condanna di classe, anche se i diritti di molti aderenti risultano prescritti... ma davvero la citazione notificata ex art. 140 bis c. cons. non ha effetto interruttivo istantaneo "collettivo"?*, Corr. giur. 247 (2018). For a more comprehensive bibliography *see* Beatrice Zuffi, in Vincenzo Cuffaro (ed.), *Codice del Consumo, sub art. 140-bis*, 950 (2019).

18 Claudio Consolo & Beatrice Zuffi, *L'azione di classe ex art. 140-bis cod. cons.*, 50 ff. (2012).

19 The numbers listed above are drawn from articles, essays, or decisions published on newspapers and academic journals: they might be therefore not totally precise or complete. Shortly after the entry into force of article 140-bis of Consumer Code the Ministry for the Economic Growth created a sort of register for the class action proceedings commenced according to this provision, but the website page has not been held up-dated.

20 Trib. Torino, 4 June 2010 (*R., Codacons* v. *Imi San Paolo*), Corr. giur. 985 (2010), confirmed by C. App. Torino, 27 October 2010, Foro it. I, 3530 (2010); Trib. Roma, 25 March 2011 no. 2784 e 2794 (*R., G., Codacons* v. *Unicredit; R., Codacons* v. *Unicredit*), Foro it. I 1189 (2011); Trib. Torino, 7 April 2011 (*D. F., Codacons* v. *Banca popolare di Novara*), Giur. mer. 372 (2012); Trib. Roma, 11 April 2011 (*M., B., V., Codacons* v. *B.A.T. Italia S.p.A.*), Foro it., I, 3234 (2011), confirmed by C. App. Roma, 27 January 2012, in Claudio Consolo & Beatrice Zuffi, *L'azione di classe* ex *art.* 140-bis *c. cons. Lineamenti processuali*, 501 (2012) and then by Cass. 1 February 2017, no. 2610, Guida dir. 10 32; Trib. Torino, 27th April 2011 (*D. F., Codacons* v. *Banca popolare di Novara*), Nuovo not. giur. 109 (2011); Trib. Firenze, 30 May 2011 (*De Z.* v. *Quadrifoglio S.p.A.*), www.neldiritto.it, confirmed by C. App. Roma, 28 November 2012, in www.classactionromanettuno.org; Trib. Torino, 31 October 2011 (*I., C., ADOC* v. *Gruppo Torinese Trasporti S.p.A.*), confirmed by C. App. Torino, 26 January 2012, both in Claudio Consolo & Beatrice Zuffi, *L'azione di classe* ex *art.* 140-bis *c.cons.*, 467 and 484 (2012); Trib. Milano, 8 November 2011 (*D., ADUC* v. *Microsoft S.r.l.*), in Claudio Consolo & Beatrice Zuffi, *L'azione di classe* ex *art.* 140-bis *c.cons.*, 475 (2012); Trib. Roma, 27th April 2012 (*R., Codacons* v. *Policlinico univ. Agostino Gemelli*), www.sviluppoeconomico.gov.it, confirmed by C. App. Roma, 1 December 2015 and by Cass., 23 October 2018, no. 26725, Diritto & Giustizia (24 October 2018); Trib. Roma, 25 June 2012 (*Ass. Federcons. Campania* v. *Ina Assitalia S.p.A.*); Trib. Milano, 8 November 2013 (*Ass. Altroconsumo representing 16 users* v. *Trenord s.r.l.*), Giur. it. 603 (2014); Trib. Milano, 9 December 2013 (*Codacons* v. *M.R. S.p.A.*), *Foro it.*, I, 590 (2014); Trib. Genova, 13 June 2014, www.osservatorioantitrust.eu (*Comitato "Tutela del risparmio – Banca CARIGE"* v. *Banca CARIGE S.p.A.*); Trib. Venezia, 12 January 2016 (*Altroconsumo* v. *Volkswagen AG & Volkswagen Group Italia*), Foro it. I 1017 (2016).

21 Trib. Milano, 20 December 2010 (*Codacons.* v. *Voden Medical Instrument*), Foro it. 2011 I 1167 (2011), confirmed by C. App. Milano, 3 May 2011, Foro it. I 1243 (2011); Trib. Napoli, 9 December 2011 (*C., C., Asso-Consum. Onlus* v. *Banca della Campania S.p.A.*), www.ilcaso.it, confirmed by C. App. Napoli, 29 June 2012; C. App. Torino, 23 September 2011 (*G., L., S., Altroconsumo* v. *Intesa Sanpaolo*), Foro it. I 3422 (2011), reversing the ruling of Trib. Torino, 28 April 2011, Corr. giur. 1109 (2011): the appellate decision was then confirmed by Cass. 21 November 2016, no. 23631, Foro it. I 600 (2017); Trib. Roma, 2 May 2013 (*C., D.Z.* v. *Municipality of Petacciato*) and Trib. Roma, 2 May 2013 (*C., D.P.* v. *Municipality of Montenero di Bisaccia*), in www.sviluppoeconomico.gov.it; C. App. Milano, 3 March 2014 (*Ass. Codici Onlus* v. *Trenord*), confirmed by Cass. 23 March 2018, no. 7244; C. App. Torino, 17 November 2015 (*Altroconsumo* v. *FCA Italy S.p.A., Fiat Chrysler Automobiles Italy S.p.A.*), Foro it. I 1017, 2016, reversing Trib. Torino, 3 July 2015; C. App. Venezia, 17 June 2016 (*Altroconsumo* v. *Volkswagen Aktiengesellschaft,*

decided on the merits, two of which are still awaiting the final judgment.[22] In relation to a dozen of proceedings pending, no judgment or order has been issued yet. Furthermore, in the first five years, even the class actions that have survived the motion to dismiss have not been very successful because so few class members opted in (at most a few dozen, more frequently less than ten).[23] The causes of this failure are probably several, but at least three groups of them can be mentioned here.

First, the law was poorly drafted. It was too narrow in its scope. Indeed, the remedy was available only to compensate consumers or users harmed by the same violation of contractual rights or the same unfair commercial practice or the same infringement of competition rules.[24] Actions in tort were not covered by the consumer class action. Accordingly, securities class actions were not possible, since liability for misstatements to the market has been traditionally considered a form of liability in tort.[25] Moreover, the opt-in mechanism discourages the aggregation of the class, and therefore the launch of consumer class actions. Article 140-bis was also mute with regard to costs and lawyers' fees, discovery, tolling effect in relation to statute of limitation periods, and collective enforcement of the decision. Lack of clarity on these issues make it too risky for consumers to launch a class action against firms or providers of public services.

Second, plaintiffs and especially consumer associations (which have been de facto the only promoters of these proceedings) seem to have too often handled the remedy in a careless manner. For some actions they have failed to weigh the real soundness of the claims asserted or have been not so accurate in the necessary prior checks relating to the homogeneity and commonality of the consumers' rights allegedly infringed by the defendant's conduct.[26] In other

Volkswagen Group Italia S.p.A.), overturning Trib. Venezia, 12 January 2016, Foro it. I 1024 (2016); Trib. Milano, 10 November 2016 (*Altroconsumo* v. *Samsung Electronics Italia S.p.A.*), as integrated by the order issued on 10 April 2017, www.altroconsumo.it/info/ordinanza-tribunale-milano-samsung; Trib. Cagliari, 10 February 2017 (*Adiconsum* v. *Abbanoa S.p.A*), www.giustiziacivile.com (11 April 2018); Trib. Venezia, 25 May 2017 (*Altroconsumo* v. *Volkswagen Aktiengesellschaft, Volkswagen Group Italia S.p.A.*), Foro it. I 2439 (2017), confirmed by C. App. Venezia, 3 November 2017, Diritto & Giustizia (10 November 2017).

22 Trib. Napoli, 18 February 2013 (*Unione Nazionale consumatori* v. *Wecantour*) entailed the compensation of four tourists with the sum of € 1,300 per person; C. app. Milano, 26th August 2013 (Z., *Codacons* c. *Voden Medical Instruments*), Foro it. I, 3326 (2013), confirmed by Cass. 31 January 2018, no. 2320, sentenced the defendant company to reimburse the plaintiff € 1,450, while the claim of the only other adhering consumer was dismissed; Trib. Torino 10 April 2014 (*G.F., L.E., S.F., Altroconsumo* v. *Intesa San Paolo*), Foro it. I 2618 (2014), confirmed by C. App. 30 June 2016, ruled the restoration for the three plaintiffs and only three of 104 class members who opted-in: the decision was set aside and referred to the 2nd degree Judge for reconsideration by Cass. 15 May 2019, no. 12997; C. App. Milano 25 August 2017 (*Altroconsumo* v. *Trenord*), Corr. giur. 243 (2018) ordered the compensation of more than 3,000 travelers, but also this judgment was annulled: *see* Cass. 31 May 2019, no. 14886.

23 The Italian class action regime works indeed on an opt-in basis. The res judicata effect of judgments issued by the Court in these proceedings does not encompass automatically all the people damaged by the conduct or act on which the collective claim is grounded: every affected person has to file a formal declaration of subscription or adhesion ("*adesione*") to the class action in order to enable the Court to pronounce on her rights. The word "opt-in election" will be used to refer to this act in the following.

24 *See* Beatrice Zuffi, *La responsabilità civile da illeciti di massa e l'azione di classe*, in Maurizio Bianchini, Alessandro Calegari and Gina Gioia (ed.), *Dialogo tra Corti e Nuove frontiere della responsabilità*, 832 (2016); Beatrice Zuffi, *L'azione di classe dal punto di vista degli attori. Parte I – Le azioni di classe nella prospettiva dei proponenti in generale*, in Gian Antonio Benacchio and Michele Carpagnano (ed.), *L'applicazione delle regole di concorrenza in Italia e nell'Unione europea*, 396 (2014).

25 Paolo Giudici, *L'azione di classe e la responsabilità civile nel diritto dei mercati finanziari*, in Centro nazionale di prevenzione e difesa sociale (ed.), *Class action: il nuovo volto della tutela collettiva in Italia* (2011).

26 E.g., in the case *Codacons* v. *Imi San Paolo*, the class action aimed to obtain the compensation due to several current account holders for the illicit application of overdrawn account commissions was rejected because the consumer acting as plaintiff did not hold a bank account with an exposure credit line (which was a hallmark of the class claim).

proceedings the collection of opt-in elections or evidence has not been conducted thoughtfully.[27]

Third, courts have not always shown the pragmatism necessary to deal with this complex form of litigation and too often have applied the rules in an extremely formal way, without taking into the proper consideration the peculiarities and the finality of the class action mechanism. Some decisions found, for instance, that the commonality test was not satisfied in class actions against some transportation companies for the systematic delays and other inconveniences suffered by customers because of the different kind of contracts entered into by the putative class members (single ticket, return ticket, monthly subscription).[28] In other proceedings, the courts observed that the actions were brought by plaintiffs giving a mandate to consumer associations without complying with the prescriptions of article 77 of the Civil Procedure Code. They indeed interpreted article 140-bis of consumer code as if it required the agent (i.e., the association) to be assigned both with substantial and procedural powers, despite that the provision does not refer to article 77 of Civil Procedure Code nor is it clear what kind of mandate is considered here. As a result, the consumer associations were ousted from the proceedings and then the consumers acting as plaintiffs were found unable to adequately represent the class (and to burden the inherent costs).[29] In a class action litigation against a bank for the application of overdrawn account commissions, only three of the over one hundred opt-in elections filed have been deemed valid[30].

Notwithstanding these problems, in recent years there were positive signs of improvement. The orders of admissibility[31] have increased and some class actions have collected several thousands of subscriptions. This has happened especially for the collective lawsuits launched against some carmakers for alleged commercial malpractices on gas consumptions. For instance, in the *FCA* lawsuit 21,031 consumers opted in, while for the *Volkswagen* class action, 76,000 elections have been filed at the Venice Tribunal's registry. In the *Trenord* case more than 6,000 travelers joined the collective proceedings seeking damages suffered due to an extended disruption of rail services. According to the association's website, the class action litigation commenced

27 E.g., in the litigation commenced against *Voden Medical Instrument* for the unfair commercial practice consisting of misleading marketing about an anti-flu remedy, the defendant company demonstrated the lack of standing to sue by the class representative as the medical device resulted bought after the serving of writ of summons and thus the quality of consumer had been considered not genuine, but artificially created.

28 The first degree decisions of ineligibility issued on the quoted cases involving *Trenord* company found that the claims were not sufficiently homogeneous, because of the different kind of travel tickets owned by the class members. These rulings, strongly criticized by the commentators, have been then reversed by the Court of Appeal.

29 According to article 140-bis of consumer code the class action can be brought by one of the consumers or users affected, "also by means of an association, to whom he gives a mandate, or a committee, which he participates." Contrary to the interpretation given by the quoted decisions and by many other authors, Professor Consolo stressed that the role played by the "mandated" association in the context of class litigation is significantly different from that one of an agent representing the party in ordinary civil proceedings and therefore there is no need to abide by article 77 of the Civil Procedure Code. The association involved in a class action is assigned by the plaintiff to give its technical support and aid (i.e., in advertising, in organizing the gathering of adhesions, etc.), rather than acting in his name and on his behalf. Thus Professor Consolo proposed to consider the mandate mentioned in article 140-bis of the consumer code as something other than the agency envisaged by article 77 of the Civil Procedure Code (see Claudio Consolo & Beatrice Zuffi, *L'azione di classe ex art. 140-bis cod. cons., cit.*, 110). Finally, the Court of Appeal of Turin (with the decision of 23 September 2011, in the case *G., L., S., Altroconsumo* v. *Intesa Sanpaolo*) accepted this idea, reversing the first decree order and permitting the class action brought before it to be maintained.

30 This happened before the first and second degree judges in *Altroconsumo* v. *Intesa San Paolo*, but the Cassation recently set aside the ruling and held that the law doesn't establish any formal requirement for the adhesions.

31 According to article 140-bis, par. 6, of the consumer code the class action can be decided on the merits only if at an early stage of the proceedings the Court issues an eligibility order, after having checked that: the claims are not manifestly unfounded; the claims are homogeneous; there are no conflicts of interest; the plaintiff is able to adequately protect the interests of the class.

in the Spring of 2019 for the misuse of users' data by *Facebook* will deal with the compensatory claims of over 100,000 people.

One of the cases just mentioned (*Trenord*)[32] at first appeared to be the first real success attained by consumers through article 140-bis of the Consumer Code. In 2018, the Court of Appeal of Milan ordered the defendant (a railway company) to compensate over 3,000 users for the repeated delays and cancellations caused by a malfunction of the operating system used for scheduling trains and work shifts.[33] But then the Supreme Court of Cassation set aside the judgment and referred the dispute again to a merit court for a new consideration. Thus far, there have been only two favorable judgments on the merits, restoring only a small amount of money to consumers.

In short, in terms of private enforcement the Consumer Class Action has been a failure. Accordingly, the Parliament began again to discuss the introduction of a bill apt to usher in a new season for the remedy.[34] The law approved in the Spring of 2019,[35] which will come into force in 2020,[36] has thus repealed the articles of the consumer code relating to the collective redress and has adopted a broader version both of the compensatory class action and the collective injunctive device, into the Code of Civil Procedure.[37]

The new statute has removed the scope boundaries provided for in the consumer code, but the new class action still works on an opt-in basis. Nevertheless, the lawmakers tried to boost the mechanism through the addition of: a discovery tool,[38] collective distribution[39] and enforcement[40] stages, incentivizing rules for costs and fees,[41] and more detailed chances for settlements.[42]

12.1.4 *The 2019 New Class Action*

The 2019 statute has made important changes to the Italian regulation of class actions, even though some old features have been kept. The law provides for a broader remedy. The new class action is now part of the Code of Civil Procedure. It is a general instrument, available to any

32 *Supra*, note 23.

33 For a commentary on this decision see Beatrice Zuffi, *Arriva la prima maxi condanna di classe, anche se i diritti di molti aderenti risultano prescritti . . . ma davvero la citazione notificata ex art. 140 bis c. cons. non ha effetto interruttivo istantaneo "collettivo"?*, Corr. giur. 247 (2018).

34 *See* Beatrice Zuffi, *La giurisdizione in materia di servizi pubblici tra azione di classe e ricorso per l'efficienza della P.A.*, Giur. it. 875, footnotes 37–38 (2016).

35 Law no. 31 of 12th April 2019. For a first overview *see* Giuseppe Finocchiaro, *"Nuova" class action: dal 19 aprile 2020 operativo il trasloco dal codice del consumo al Cpc*, Guida al diritto 10, 23–25 May (2019); Domenico Dalfino, Paolo & Roberto Pardolesi, Remo Caponi, Romolo Donzelli, Angelo Danilo De Santis, Davide Amadei, *Le nuove forme di tutela collettiva*, in 322 (2019) *Foro it.*; Bruno Sassani (ed.), *Class action. Commento sistematico alla legge 12 aprile 2019, n. 31*, in *Quaderni di Judicium*, 6 (2019); Claudio Consolo, sub articles 840-*bis*-840-*sexiesdecies*c.p.c., in *C.p.c. Commentario, La nuova azione di classe e la nuova inibitoria* (2019); Marco De Cristofaro, *Diritti individuali omogenei e azione di classe. L'azione collettiva risarcitoria di classe*, in Alberto Trabucchi (Giuseppe Trabucchi ed.), *Istituzioni di diritto civile*, 77 (2019).

36 The new rules originally should have become applicable on 18 April 2020, but as the Ministry of Justice has yet to set the necessary changes to the filing information system in order to make all the expected activities electronically feasible, article 8 of Decree-Law no. 162 of 31 December 2019, converted with amendments into Law no. 8 of 28 February 2020, delayed their entry into force for seven months, on 19 November 2020. The new rules will cover exclusively acts and conducts carried out after that date, while previous ones will be governed by the old consumer class action mechanism.

37 *See* articles from 840-bis to 840-*quinquiesdecies* for the compensatory class action; article 840-*sexiesdecies* for the injunctive collective expedient.

38 Article 840-*quinquies*, par. 5–13, c.p.c.

39 Article 840-*octies* c.p.c.

40 Article 840-*terdecies* c.p.c.

41 *See* article 840-*octies*, par. 6 and article 840-*nonies* c.p.c.

42 *See* article 840-*bis*, par. 6 and 840-*quaterdecies* c.p.c.

person and not only to consumers. Accordingly, the action can be launched by any person (who is part of the putative class) or by an organization/association enrolled in a public registry. The competent court is the specialized commercial litigation court in the district of the defendant's headquarters.

The type of claims for which the action can be used are not limited any more. Thanks to the new remedy private companies and providers of public services could be required to refund or compensate the damages caused to a group or a mass of persons in connection to any "illicit act or behavior implemented in the performance of their activities."[43] This means, for example, that actions in tort and securities class actions will find a place in the Italian litigation landscape, and this really sounds like a revolution.

The only ongoing limitation concerns defendants. Exclusively firms and providers of public services can be sued in class actions. Accordingly, it will be subject to discussion on a case-by-case analysis whether associations or foundations are to be considered business firms and might be sued.

The revolutionary modifications that we have mentioned have been counterbalanced with the conservation of the admissibility stage, which warrants a judicial check on the four eligibility criteria imposed for class actions: (1) the manifest soundness of the cause of action; (2) the homogeneity of claims; (3) the lead plaintiff's suitability; (4) the absence of conflicts of interests. If one or more of these requirements are not met, the case is dismissed and cannot reach a decision on the merits.[44]

12.2 THE PROCEEDINGS

The new class litigation, which is conducted according to the special provisions dictated for simplified proceedings (article 702-bis ff. of Civil Procedure Code), can be divided into several stages.

12.2.1 *The Introductory Phase and the Eligibility Stage*

The plaintiff's recourse and the judicial decree for the assignment of the first hearing are to be noticed in the specific page of the Ministry of Justice's website. The firm or provider of public services sued has to present its defenses ten days before the scheduled hearing. Within thirty days from it, the Tribunal shall pronounce upon the admissibility criteria. The order issued can be challenged before the Court of Appeal. If the claim is maintained, a first deadline to file the opt-in elections of other class members is established. Indeed, the new law maintains the opt-in mechanism, even though the time for opt-in elections has been doubled – it will be possible to file them not only after the eligibility order,[45] but also following the judgment declaring the defendant's liability.[46]

In the event that many class proceedings are commenced against the same party for the same facts, the Court shall order the joinder of cases, if the subsequent actions have been filed within sixty days from the publication on the website of the first lawsuit; the cases commenced after this

43 *See* article 840-*bis*, par. 2 and 3, c.p.c.

44 *See* article 840-*ter* c.p.c.

45 Article 840-*quinquies*, par. 1, c.p.c.

46 Article 840-*sexies*, par. 1, c.p.c.

time-limit are instead removed from the Court's register.[47] The law favors the first plaintiff and apparently there is no selection of the lead plaintiff.

12.2.2 *Adjudication and Evidence*

If the class action is declared eligible, the stage relating to the adjudication of defendant's liability takes place. The Tribunal can manage the case in the manner it considers the most appropriate, avoiding worthless formalities and adopting the relevant evidentiary orders. The defendant responsibility can be ascertained on the basis of statistical data or presumptions. Reference to statistical data is another important milestone in the history of Italian law.[48]

Another step forward is the access to discovery.[49] The class action plaintiff can ask the Court to order the disclosure of evidence in the hand of the defendant. In order to obtain the court's order, the plaintiff has to show that there are "facts and evidences" that are reasonably in the hands of the defendant and that are sufficient to "make the claim look plausible." If the defendant does not comply or refuses to discover the evidence or destroys it, a penalty (between € 10,000 and € 100,000) may be imposed; furthermore the court may take this fact as one of the circumstances on which it can ground its decision.[50] There is no space for an explorative search of documents, and discovery orders cannot be issued against a third party. Needless to say, these rules are not a functional equivalent of lawyers' managed discovery as known in the US law system or the UK one, but up to now access to discovery has been very restricted in Italian litigation, at least outside the area of industrial property claims. Accordingly, there is room for some potential improvement, but it will depend very much on how courts interpret the requirement concerning the indication by the plaintiff of the evidence required. If the court will raise barriers by demanding very high standards of specificity, discovery will not be an instrument able to assist plaintiffs' claims in class actions.

If the claim is accepted, the judgment will order the company to compensate the plaintiff (when he is an individual) and will define the elements characterizing the class member's rights, establishing a second (and last) deadline for the filing of opt in elections. In the same decision the Tribunal will appoint a delegated judge and a class representative for the distribution proceedings.

Within 120 days from when the second time lapse for the adhesions has expired, the defendant may lodge a statement of written observations. He may take a position or raise objections in relation to the facts alleged as grounds of the individual claims: the circumstances not specifically contested are indeed to be considered as true by the Court.[51]

47 Unless the subsequent lawsuits involve rights that could not be actionable in the first case. It is reasonably expected that these lawsuits may be resumed if the first class action doesn't attain a decision on the merits.

48 Civil courts have started to discuss in mass tort cases whether statistical data can be used, and how they should be used. The new class action law explicitly recognizes the evidentiary value that courts can attribute to statistical data.

49 The Italian lawmaker has almost entirely replicated in article 840-*quinquies* the rules provided for by Legislative Decree no. 3 of 2017 in relation to the claims for damages caused by infringements of competition law, with some differences. In antitrust lawsuits a claimant who argues that reasonably the counterparty holds available facts and evidence sufficient to support the plausibility of its claim for damages may ask the court to order the defendant or a third party to disclose relevant evidence which lies in their control. If the defendant or the third party fails to comply, penalties (between €15,000 and € 150,000) shall be imposed and the judge may consider the fact (which could be demonstrated by the evidence, if disclosed) as proved. In the ordinary disputes before the civil courts, instead, a party may only request the exhibition of one or more specific documents and there is little or no consequence for noncompliance: the judge may infer evidence against the reluctant party, but he cannot ground a decision on this sole argument (see article 210 ff. of Civil Procedure Code).

50 The wording of this rule could be interpreted as significantly different from that one provided for the noncompliance of exhibition orders issued according to article 210 of Civil Procedure Code. We will see whether the courts will give the right emphasis to this element.

51 Article 840-*octies*, par. 1, c.p.c.

12.2.3 *Distribution and Enforcement*

After the assessment of defendant's liability, the proceedings mutate into a sort of a bankruptcy proceeding.[52] There are, indeed, several hints of this similarity: the activities are directed by the judge appointed by the tribunal; the class representative has to draft a plan for all the credits asserted by class members (as the insolvency trustee has to do for the assessment of liabilities); the delegated judge's decision takes the form of a decree, which also carries a payment order for the class representative's reward and the class counsel's fees.[53] Naturally there is no room here for the allocation of the insolvency estate and the issues relating to the priority order of credits, except for the sums owed to the class representative and the class counsel, who are preferred creditors.[54] A distribution plan shall then be presented by the class representative in order to enable the delegated judge to award (or not) the sums due to every class member.[55] The payments have to be made into a bank or postal account opened for the proceedings.[56] If this payment order is not fulfilled (i.e., should the defendant company fail to pay in time or the whole sum due),[57] the class representative may promote collective enforcement proceedings. These proceedings, which must be commenced according to the ordinary civil procedural rules on enforcement, will end when all the class members have obtained relief or it turns out that no reasonable recovery of their credits is possible, considering also the costs.[58]

12.2.4 *Some Insights on Opt-In Elections, Costs, and Settlements*

To understand better how the procedural machinery just outlined can work in practice, it is worth dwelling at least on three elements.

(1) The elections. The individuals who opt in to the class do not become parties of the proceedings, in the sense that they are not entitled to take any step in the trial, even if they have to be given notice and may access the case file.[59] However, the elections have some of the effects associated with a claim, in the sense that they are able to interrupt the statute of limitation periods[60] and, above all, they allow the Court to pronounce upon the rights invoked by the people who filed the elections. The res judicata effect does not extend to the entire class: judgments adopted during the proceedings bind only the opters-in.[61] According to the new rules it is clear that through the elections the individual empowers the class representative to act on his/her behalf during the proceedings and that a revocation of this special mandate is required in case the class

[52] For a more thorough analyses of this similarity (which is indeed limited to a certain stage and is more a procedural resemblance than a real functional likeness) see Beatrice Zuffi, *La tutela giurisdizionale degli aderenti nella nuova disciplina dell "esecuzione collettiva" di classe*, in *Scritti in memoria di Cipriani*, 1497, (2020).

[53] Article 840-*octies*.

[54] *See* article 840-*terdecies*, par. 3.

[55] Article 840-*octies*, par. 2–5, c.p.c.

[56] Article 840-*duodecies*.

[57] The defendant company can spontaneously fulfil in the way described in article 840-*duodecies* c.p.c.

[58] Article 840-*quinquiesdecies*.

[59] *See* article 840-*quinquies*, par. 1, c.p.c.

[60] Article 840-*septies*, par. 6., c.p.c.

[61] As can be inferred from articles 840-*quinquies*, par. 1, 840-*undecies*, last par. and 840-*decies*, par. 2, c.p.c.

member wants to quit.[62] Thus, a sort of take-or-leave choice is imposed to the opters-in. Should they find the distribution plan drafted by the representative (or the settlement outline submitted by the representative and the defendant) not satisfactory, they can make some observations or raise some objections, but if the delegated judge does not accept them, they have to leave the class, otherwise the decision (or the approved settlement agreement) will be binding for them. If the class members decide to quit (i.e., to revoke the elections), costs inherent to pursuing their claims in separate proceedings must be considered.

(2) Costs. In the Italian system the basic rule on cost and fee allocation is set by article 91 of the Civil Procedure Code, according to which, at the end of the proceedings the court will order the losing party to reimburse his/her opponent's expenses,[63] including lawyers' fees.[64] Among the new rules introduced by law no. 31 of 2019, several provisions deal with the financing issues of class actions.[65] First, the judgment ascertaining the defendant's liability may also establish the sum that every class member has to pay, when filing the adhesion, as expense fund.[66] Second, in the following stage, if the claims of the opted-in class members are accepted, the delegated judge awards not only the sums due to class members for compensation, but also two further amounts,

62 *See* article 840-*septies*, par. 2, g).

63 The constitutional rationale being that the successful party should be put in the same situation as he/she would have been if the other party had not brought or defended the claim. The court can nonetheless deviate from the cost-shifting rule in some situations provided for by law. First, the reimbursement may be excluded if the costs are excessive or unnecessary (*see* article 92, par. 1, c.p.c.). Second, the Court may order a party to reimburse the other party any expense incurred as a result of her/his unfairness, irrespective of who was the winner. Furthermore, the court may decide that each party bears his/her own costs (in whole or in part) if no party is totally successful or in case of overruling or lack of any relevant precedent (*see* article 92, par. 2, c.p.c.). Finally, if a victorious party fails to obtain a judgment more advantageous than the conciliation proposal that was refused by her/him without any good reason, she/he shall bear all the fees and costs incurred after the proposal was made (*see* article 91, par. 2, c.p.c.).

64 Court costs are regulated by the Presidential Decree no. 115 of 30 May 2002 (*Testo unico delle spese di giustizia*). The main cost item consists of the so called *contributo unificato*, a single payment that has to be made by the party who enters the case on the Courts' register, usually the plaintiff. The measure of this contribution is set with reference to the amount in controversy, apart from a few specific types of claims (for which it is a fixed sum). There are also some exemptions (for instance, in cases concerning child maintenance payments or in individual labor disputes no contribution is due). Other fees are charged for specific activities such as the service of documents, but these are not substantial. There is also a fee for the registration of judgments: according to the subject matter, it may be a fixed amount (at present € 168) or a percentage of the value of the claim, ranging from 1 percent to 8 percent. As far as the lawyers' fees are concerned, they are determined according to the parameters provided for by the Ministerial Decree 10 March 2014, no. 55. The criteria set in this regulation for litigation are the amount in controversy and the level of court seized (while for out-of-court work, the value of the dispute only matters). As regards litigation before civil courts, lawyers are entitled to ask two kinds of fees: the so-called "*diritti*," which are predetermined by the above mentioned decree with respect to the single procedural step undertaken (e.g., service of an act, hearing attendance), and the so-called "*onorari*," that are the most important heading pertaining the services performed by lawyers (e.g., study of the controversy, preparation of the claim or the defense). For these last fees only minimum and maximum amounts are set by the Ministry of Justice. It is possible to go beyond the maximum ceilings, but the minimum thresholds are binding.

65 Until the entry into force of the new regime, the fees due to the lawyers are determined according to the value of the individual claim of the party represented (i.e., the consumer acting as plaintiff), pursuant to the ordinary rules summarized in the previous footnote, except for the possibility of a triplication of the fees, as set out by article 4, par. 4 of Ministerial Decree no. 140 of 20 July 2012 in relation to class proceedings commenced according to article 140-*bis* of consumer code. This special provision was meant to encourage plaintiffs and lawyers to bring class actions, but its impact is controversial, because the fees may be triplicated regardless of the outcome of the dispute. The plaintiffs may therefore be exposed to the risk of greater disbursements (compared to those incurred in the ordinary disputes) in case of loss.

66 *See* article 840-sexies, par. 1, h).

determined according to percentages inversely proportional to the number of adhesions gathered: one of these remunerations is for the class representative; the other goes to the plaintiff's lawyer (who should also obtain the ordinary fees from the defendant).[67] The solution found by the Italian lawmaker seems therefore in favor of sharing anticipation of the proceedings' costs between the class members (for a smaller part) and the class counsel (for the larger part). Accordingly, a counsel has incentives to take the lead and become class counsel in order to get the extra fees calculated on a rate basis of the total collective claims' value. Third party funding is not forbidden, but has not been much practiced until now in Italy.[68]

(3) The settlement proposals and agreements. Until the case is heard before the Tribunal, the court may notify the opt-ins of a settlement proposal. If an agreement is reached, it has to be communicated to the class members so that they can enter into it by inserting, within a deadline, an acceptance declaration into the case file.[69] After the judgment on the defendant's liability and the continuation of the proceedings under the delegated judge's supervision, the class representative may draw up, together with the defendant, an outline of settlement agreement, which is served to the class members for possible objections. The delegated judge shall then check this draft and, if the results are suitable for the interests of the class, may approve it. Only the class members who have contested the proposal in due time can revoke the mandate to the representative as far as the settlement subscription is concerned.[70] Confirming what we already said, the adhesion implies a kind of forced choice between the suboptimal deal concluded by the class representative and the burden to take an individual initiative aimed at obtaining the expected relief, with the inherent risks in terms of costs and outcome.

67 *See* article 840-*novies* c.p.c. The delegated judge shall order the defendant to pay directly to the class representative an amount established in consideration of the number of adhesions gathered. This sum must be determined applying on the total value of the class claims percentages which progressively decrease according to the following brackets.

Number of opters-in	Max. percentage for class representative's fee
from 1 to 500	9 %
from 501 to 1,000	6 %
from 1,001 to 10,000	3 %
from 10,001 to 100,000	2.5 %
from 100,001 to 500,000	1.5 %
from 500,001 to 1,000,000	1 %
over 1,000,000	0.5 %

The defendant has also to refund the expenses incurred by the class representative. The delegated judge may increase or decrease the amount of the fee determined according to the indicated brackets to an extent not exceeding 50 percent on the basis of the following criteria: (1) complexity of the case; (2) need for the class representative to be assisted by experts of its choice; (3) quality of the class representative's work; (4) rapid implementation of the activities carried out; (5) number of adhesions filed. The ordinary provisions relating to costs of justice apply.

The delegated judge orders the respondent to pay directly a fee also to the lawyer who defended the claimant up to the delivery of the judgment. This fee has to be calculated in accordance with the same percentages provided for the class representative and may be reduced to a maximum of 50 percent, based on the criteria abovementioned.

68 Read Elena D'Alessandro (ed.), *Perspectives on third party funding in Italy*, in http://hdl.handle.net/2318/1702091.

69 Article 840-*quaterdecies*, par. 1.

70 Article 840-*quaterdecies*, par. 2-9.

12.3 ITALIAN CLASS ACTIONS IN THE INTERNATIONAL AND EUROPEAN CONTEXT

From the comparative perspective the new Italian class action is a strange mixture of pioneering and traditional elements. The innovating hallmarks are the following.

- The operational scope and standing: the remedy represents a cutting-edge model at least as far as these two points of view are concerned. Most European systems[71] offer collective redress only with regard to some type of claims and mainly at the initiative of organizations, associations, or foundations, not also of the individuals damaged. From this perspective, the Italian system follows somewhat the US example.
- The distribution stage: even if some foreign legislation sets rules for the collective enforcement of payment orders issued in favor of a group or class, the solution adopted by law no. 31 of 2019 is pretty original in so far as it introduces a special phase for the recovery of class members' credits, with a strong resemblance to insolvency proceedings. The role played by the class representative is also quite significant and gets the remedy closer to the US class action legislation than to many European equivalents.
- According to the long-established principles about defense right and claim doctrine, which guarantee every person the right to a day in court and prevent forms of representation without consent, the opt-in model has been kept[72] and in this respect a common path has apparently been undertaken by Italy and France, although in the French legislation the adhesion's implications seem to be more accurately regulated.[73]

These concluding remarks cannot neglect the Proposal for a Directive, which was presented before the European Parliament in the Spring of 2018.[74] This bill has been resubmitted in the current legislature and amended both by the Commission[75] and the Council.[76] In the framework of policies launching "A New Deal for Consumers," the objective pursued is to enable qualified entities, which represent the collective interest of consumers, to bring representative actions for the purpose of both injunctive and compensatory measures against traders infringing provisions of Union law. Should the bill be approved, the Member States would enable

[71] *I.e.*, Spain, Portugal, Netherlands, Denmark, Finland, and France.

[72] Unlike what happened in the English, Danish, and Dutch systems, which have cautiously opened to opt-out mechanisms. For an overview on the European context see: *Collective Redress Litigation – A New Challenge for Courts in Europe*, in: Bruns, Kern, Münch, Piekenbrock, Stadler and Tsikrikas (eds.), *Festschrift für Rolf Stürner zum 70. Geburtstag*, 1801 (2013); Eva Lein, Duncan Fairgrieve, Marta Otero & Vincent Smith (eds.), *Collective Redress in Europe – Why and How* (BIICL London, 2015); Christopher Hodges and Stefaan Voet, *Delivering Collective Redress* (2018).

[73] See Beatrice Zuffi, *La bonne nouvelle de l'action de groupe. La Francia si dota finalmente di una tutela collettiva risarcitoria-riparatoria a fronte di pregiudizi materiali di massa svincolata dal previo conferimento di formali mandati da parte dei consumatori lesi*, Int'l. Lis. 3 138 (2014).

[74] Proposal for a Directive of the European Parliament and of the Council on representative actions for the protection of the collective interests of consumers, and repealing Directive 2009/22/EC, COM(2018) 184 final. *See* also the Study *Collective redress in the Member States of the European Union*, commissioned by the European Parliament's Policy Department for Citizens' Rights and Constitutional Affairs at the request of the Committee on Legal Affairs, published in October 2018: www.europarl.europa.eu/RegData/etudes/STUD/2018/608829/IPOL_STU(2018)608829_EN.pdf. A position paper of the *Bureau Européen des Unions Consommateurs* on this Proposal is available at www.beuc.eu/publications/beuc-x-2018-094_representative_actions_beuc_position_paper.pdf.

[75] The Commission's amendments can be downloaded from www.europarl.europa.eu/doceo/document/TA-8-2019-0222_EN.html.

[76] The Council's amendments can be read in https://data.consilium.europa.eu/doc/document/ST-14600-2019-INIT/en/pdf.

representative entities to ask to stop or prohibit an infringement and to seek redress, such as compensation, repair, or price reduction as appropriate and available under Union and national laws.

The text of this Proposal, as resulting after the latest adjustments adopted on November 28, 2019, is aimed at a minimum harmonization, in the sense that, if approved, it will not replace existing national collective redress mechanisms.[77] The Member States would decide whether to design the representative action set out as a part of an existing or future collective redress mechanism or as a separate mechanism, insofar as at least one national representative action mechanism complies with the bill. The impact of the new Italian regulation on class actions therefore could be therefore very light, with the exception, discussed below, of the provisions relating to adjudication of the defendant's liability and the rules concerning discovery.

As far as adjudication is concerned, according to Recital 33 and article 10 of the Draft, a final decision of a court or an administrative authority of any Member State establishing an infringement harming collective interests of consumers can be used as evidence of the existence of that infringement for the purposes of any other actions seeking redress before their national courts or administrative authorities against the same trader for the same infringement, in accordance with national law on evaluation of evidence. The text of this provision is controversial, but despite the failure to discuss the effectiveness *erga omnes* of the collective judgment favorable to the class, the practical result of the European Directive Proposal seems not far from the solution adopted by the Brazilian consumer code.[78] If this directive will be approved persons allegedly damaged in the same country for the same facts, who did not file their elections, would benefit from an adjudication of the trader liability. More precisely, they could rely on the finding of the malpractices or misconducts committed by the defendant, even if they did not participate in any way to the collective litigation which led to that ruling, because in the individual actions subsequently brought for the same facts against the same professionals and firms, the burden of proof would be reversed. It should be for the trader to demonstrate he is not liable, providing contrary evidence.[79]

[77] *See* Recital 4a and article 1, par. 2 of the latest draft as amended by the Council.

[78] In the original text of the Proposal, dated 18 April 2018, the solution was much clearer: a final decision issued by an administrative authority or a court in respect of a collective representative action should have been deemed as irrefutably establishing the existence of that infringement for the purposes of any other actions seeking redress before their national courts against the same trader for the same facts (while in another Member State that decision should have been considered a rebuttable presumption). According to this first version, the European collective *res judicata* rule would have thus worked *eventum litis*: only in the case of acceptance of a collective action the binding effect would have extended to all the class members, while a rejection would have only affected the proceedings' participants. The defendant professionals or firms who had won the collective action could have not asserted issue or collateral estoppel and thus prevented other consumers from seeking compensation in separate lawsuits for the same facts or conducts. Read Beatrice Zuffi, *Le prospettive di riforma dell'azione di classe italiana: una nuova rotta da tracciare fra l'attrazione per l'esperienza statunitense e la via "brasiliana" suggerita dal legislatore europeo*, in Adrian Simons, Aluisio Gonçalves de Castro Mendes, Alvaro Pérez Ragone and Paulo Henrique dos Santos Lucon (eds.), *Estudos em homenagem a Ada Pellegrini Grinover e José Carlos Barbosa Moreira*, 251 (2019).

[79] Article 10 of the Proposal of Directive is mute about the value of the finding that no infringement was committed by the defendant. Obviously, a decision favorable to the trader would bar the claims that were actually litigated, i.e., those of the opters-in, but the consumers who did not take part to the collective litigation, would be entitled to bring individual actions for the same facts and against the same professionals or firms. Recital 33 and article 10 of the Draft do not say that also a decision establishing that no infringement harming collective interests of consumers has occurred could be used as evidence by the defendants.

As far as discovery is concerned, article 13 of the Directive Draft could impose on Member States the obligation to order third parties to disclose further evidence which could support the collective action if it lies in their control.

By the time this book is published, the approval process for the Proposal on representative actions will probably move on and probably the current text will be revised again.[80] However, national laws will not need to be concerned with the provisions of this Directive until at least 2021. Furthermore, it is also possible that the new Italian rules introduced by law no. 31 of 2019 will be amended in some relevant aspects if the Ministry of Justice decides to adopt the adjustments recommended by many scholars and experts.

80 See, for instance, the document no. 9223/20 published on 30th June 2020.

13

Collective Litigation in German Civil Procedure

*Axel Halfmeier**

13.1 INTRODUCTION

Germany does not have class actions in the American sense. On the contrary, there has been a long tradition of opposition to the class action model at least since the 1980s, both in academic discourse and in the political arena. This opposition can be divided into three groups of arguments: first and most traditional, there are arguments based on alleged or perceived violations of constitutional law, in the sense that a class or group litigation would be incompatible with fundamental principles of the individual's right to be heard in court.[1] More recently, a sociocultural argument was elaborated that claimed a difference between US style "regulation through litigation" and a continental European tradition of preventive and supposedly more effective government regulation.[2] Finally, there is the constant lobbying by industry representatives which has been very effective in Germany in painting a picture of the US class action as typically abusive and a waste of economic resources.[3]

It would be beyond the scope of this chapter to thoroughly discuss these arguments and their validity, but let it suffice to say that all three of them are very disputed. The constitutional law argument is particularly weak with regard to opt-in class actions, where participation is based on an explicit and voluntary decision by the class member, and indeed the German legislator has

* Professor of Private Law, Comparative and Procedural Law, Leuphana University Lüneburg, Germany. E-mail: halfmeier@leuphana.de

1 *See, e.g.*, Burkhard Hess, *Cross-Border Collective Litigation and the Regulation Brussels I*, 30 PRAXIS DES INTERNATIONALEN PRIVAT- UND VERFAHRENSRECHTS (IPRAX) 116, 120 (2010): Opt-out-mechanisms "not in accordance with European procedural law"; SONJA LANGE, DAS BEGRENZTE GRUPPENVERFAHREN (2012) at 168: Opt-out procedures regarding larger claims are regarded as unconstitutional.

2 Rolf Stürner, *Das Zivilrecht der Moderne und die Bedeutung der Rechtsdogmatik*, 67 JURISTENZEITUNG 10, 19 (2012) (arguing that trust in regulation through litigation was a "systemic error" that contributed to the financial crisis); Alexander Bruns, *Instrumentalisierung des Zivilprozesses im Kollektivinteresse durch Gruppenklagen*, 71 NEUE JURISTISCHE WOCHENSCHRIFT (NJW) 2753, 2757 (2018) who argues that the class action is a market-oriented form of social regulation that does not fit with German and continental European traditions.

3 It is an interesting paradox that the *Bundesverband der Deutschen Industrie* (BDI), the most important industry lobbying organization in Germany, regularly warns of and argues against the rise of a "litigation industry," *see, e.g.*, the BDI's statement regarding the introduction of the model declaratory action in 2018: BDI, *Stellungnahme zum Gesetzentwurf der Bundesregierung zur Einführung einer zivilprozessualen Musterfeststellungsklage*, 7 June 2018. From the BDI's perspective, the "litigation industry" is not welcome in Germany, in contrast to established industries like the car industry, the weapons industry or the chemical industry.

just last year introduced a special form of opt-in representative action, the *Musterfeststellungsklage* (see below at Section 13.4). With regard to opt-out class actions, the right to be heard certainly requires adequate forms of notification, but this issue is nothing new in the discussion about class actions and has been solved in the US by requiring the best form of notice possible under the circumstances.[4] German and European law is not fundamentally different in this respect and accepts in many other situations that affected persons are not informed individually if this is not possible or feasible under the specific circumstances.[5]

The sociocultural argument that tries to highlight alleged differences between US and European regulatory styles may overlook that there is government regulation in the US as well as private litigation, and also has to address the "regulatory capture" problem which has been very obvious in the recent treatment of the Volkswagen emissions scandal by German authorities.[6]

Finally, the "abuse" paradigm typically fails to indicate what "abuse" is, why the enforcement of possibly existing claims should be labeled as "abuse" and does not even make an effort to survey the empirical literature with regard to class actions in the US, Canada and Australia.

However, the ongoing discussion in Germany about the legitimacy and utility of class actions does not mean that there are no collective litigation instruments in the German law of civil procedure. This chapter will describe and evaluate the three main types: the oldest and most firmly established type is the *Verbandsklage*, a special cause of action for injunctions by certain associations in the fields of competition law and consumer protection (see below at Section 13.2). Since 2005, there is also the *Kapitalanleger-Musterverfahrensgesetz*, which is abbreviated to *KapMuG* and can be translated as the Capital Market Investors Model Proceedings Act (below at Section 13.3). Finally, the youngest member of this family will be discussed, the *Musterfeststellungsklage* (Model Declaratory Action) which was introduced in 2018 as a direct consequence of the Volkswagen emissions scandal (below at Section 13.4) and it will be discussed how plaintiffs and their attorneys work around existing limitations by creatively using the general rules (below at Section 13.5).

To better enable comparative analysis, the description of these three instruments will cover five important characteristics of collective litigation instruments: Standing, the substantive area of application, types of relief available, any requirements and methods to obtain consent from affected class members, costs and financing. Furthermore, some empirical observations will be added to assess the practical relevance of these instruments.

13.2 THE ASSOCIATIONS' ACTIONS: *VERBANDSKLAGE*

The German tradition of associations' actions goes back until 1896, when trade associations were given the right to bring an action against companies that infringed certain provisions of the Act

4 Rule 23 (c) (2) FRCP; Philips Petroleum Co. v. Shutts, 472 U.S. 797, 811 (1985). In view of the similarity of requirements between US and German constitutional law, it is therefore correct to recognize the results of a US class action in Germany if such adequate efforts for notification were made, *see* Astrid Stadler, in Musielak (ed.) ZPO, § 328 margin no. 27 (16th ed. 2019); Axel Halfmeier & Philip Wimalasena, *Rechtsstaatliche Anforderungen an Opt-out-Sammelverfahren: Anerkennung ausländischer Titel und rechtspolitischer Gestaltungsspielraum*, 67 Juristenzeitung 649, 658 (2012).

5 For a discussion of the Dutch law on opt-out collective settlements and the applicable standards of EU law see Axel Halfmeier, *Recognition of a WCAM Settlement in Germany*, 2012 Nederlands Internationaal Privaatrecht (NIPR) 179.

6 Thomas Eger & Hans-Bernd Schäfer, Reflections on the Volkswagen Emissions Scandal (2018) at fn. 67: "Here we have a nice application of *capture theory* . . .," available at SSRN: https://ssrn.com/abstract=3109538.

against Unfair Competition (UWG), in particular by misleading advertising. This cause of action was seen as an early form of private enforcement.

The experiences with it were rather positive, and when the concept of consumer protection was developed in the 1960s, standing was also given to consumer associations. This was first enacted as part of a revision of the Act against Unfair Competition in 1965; the associations' action model was then later extended to further areas of private law. It also plays a significant role in public law, in particular with regard to the enforcement of environmental laws, but this public law aspect cannot not be elaborated here.

13.2.1 *Standing*

The standing requirements for associations' actions in private law are today regulated mainly in the *Unterlassungsklagengesetz* (literally: law on injunctions). Standing is given to certain trade associations, and – most important in practice – to so-called "qualified entities." This term derives from EU law[7] and is used to designate a legal entity that can bring actions against businesses for certain violations. These entities are registered in national registers which are then communicated to the European Commission so that the registered entities also have standing in other EU member states.

In § 4 *Unterlassungsklagengesetz* (UKlaG), certain requirements are laid out which serve to limit the number of qualified entities. For example, a consumer association must have at least seventy-five members, must have been established for more than a year and must have a certain minimum staff and organization so that it can serve the consumer interest not only by bringing actions, but also by counseling and other services. However, the government-funded *Verbraucherzentralen* ("consumer centers") which exist in all German states and also on the Federal level, are always regarded as meeting these requirements, by way of a statutory presumption.

13.2.2 *Substantive Area of Application*

There are mainly three areas of private law in which an association's action can be brought: first, and historically oldest, there is the area of unfair competition, for example misleading advertising and other unfair commercial practices. In this area, the association's action is not limited to the protection of consumer interests, and is frequently brought also by certain trade associations that aim to protect fair competition.

Secondly, the association's action can be brought against unfair contract terms in standard form contracts. When the law against unfair contract terms was created in 1977, an association's action was included as a more market-oriented alternative to government oversight. Today, the substantive provisions against unfair contract terms are integrated into the German Civil Code and the rules for associations' actions in this area can be found in § 1 UKlaG.

Furthermore, § 2 UKlaG now extends the association's action to violations against other consumer protection laws. Examples of these are listed in that provision but it is an open provision that includes also other consumer protection laws that are not explicitly listed. In recent years, data protection laws have been added to this list, so this is another area in which an association's action is possible. However, since the new EU General Data Protection Regulation

7 See Article 3 of Directive 2009/22/EC of the European Parliament and of the Council of 23 April 2009 on injunctions for the protection of consumers' interests, Official Journal EU 2009 L 110/30.

entered into force in May, 2018, there is some uncertainty in the case law whether this Regulation still allows national association's actions to enforce it or whether enforcement is limited to those powers that are explicitly listed in the Regulation.[8]

13.2.3 *Types of Relief*

The association's action cannot be brought for damages, but only for an injunction. Traditionally, the injunction had the form of a cease-and-desist order which prohibited future violations, for example the future use of an unfair – and thus illegal – contract clause. The consumer associations have always criticized this limitation of the association's action, because although it prohibits the illegal behavior for the future, it does not compensate or help the consumers who have already been harmed by the defendant company.[9]

In some cases, the consumer associations have now been successful in extending the concept of an injunction to mandatory orders against the defendant. In particular, the German Federal Court has accepted that where an insurance company has used an illegal contract clause, the injunction can go beyond a mere prohibition of the use of this clause and the court may also order the insurance company to inform all affected customers that the clause was illegal and that they therefore may have a claim for damages or restitution against the company.[10] A further step would be an explicit order to repay illegally gained amounts to the affected customers, and this step was indeed taken by the Court of Appeals in Dresden in a recent case where the amounts and the identities of the affected customers were clearly established.[11] However, this decision is disputed in the literature because it moves the association's action more into the direction of a damages action,[12] and there is no Federal Court decision on this question yet.

In the area of unfair competition, the rules on association's actions also contain a "skimming-off" provision (§ 10 UWG), which enables associations to sue companies for profits gained through illegal activities. However, these profits, if the action is successful, are neither distributed to the affected customers from which they were gained, nor to the suing entity, but must be given in total to the Federal government. This rule results in a certain lack of incentive to engage in such an action, and it has been used only sparingly, in particular because of new restrictions on the financing of such actions (see below at Section 13.2.5).

[8] For a very restrictive view on associations' actions under the new GDPR see Ansgar Ohly, *UWG- Rechtsschutz bei Verstößen gegen die Datenschutz-Grundverordnung?* 121 Gewerblicher Rechtsschutz und Urheberrecht (GRUR) 686 (2019). However, it seems not very intuitive that EU law would want to prohibit its own enforcement. For the data protection directive, the GDPR's predecessor, the European Court of Justice has decided that national rules on associations' actions remain possible, because such an action against the infringement of EU data protection law "in no way undermines the objectives of that protection and, in fact, contributes to the realisation of those objectives." Fashion ID v. Verbraucherzentrale NRW, Judgment of the European Court of Justice of 29 July 2019, case no. C-40/17, margin no. 51.

[9] For a study in this regard see Peter Rott & Axel Halfmeier, *Reform of the Injunctions Directive and Compensation for Consumers* (2018), Study commissioned by BEUC (Bureau Européen des Unions Consommateurs), available at www.beuc.eu/publications/beuc-x-2018-022_reform_of_the_injunctions_directive_and_compensation_for_consumers.pdf.

[10] Bundesgerichtshof (BGH), decision of 14 December 2017, case no. I ZR 184/15, GRUR 2018, 423.

[11] Oberlandesgericht (OLG) Dresden, decision of 10 April 2018, case no. 14 U 82/16, GRUR-RR 2018, 428.

[12] *See, e.g.*, against an action for repayment to consumers: Joachim Bornkamm, In Gesetz gegen den Unlauteren Wettbewerb (UWG), § 8 margin no. 1.108 (Köhler, Bornkamm & Feddersen 37th ed. 2019); in favor of such an action Caroline Meller-Hannich, *Anmerkung zu BGH 14.12.2017*, 2018 Juristenzeitung 629, 632.

13.2.4 *Consent by Class Members*

The association's actions are not based on individual causes of action, but give the association an additional and original cause of action. It is therefore not connected to any individual's claims and does not require any consent by individuals. Neither the successful nor the unsuccessful association's action has any legal consequences for individual claims. The only (theoretical) exception here is found in § 11 UKlaG which states that if a clause in a standard form contract is found to be invalid as a result of an association's action, an affected consumer can rely on this decision in his individual case. However, this provision is not used much in practice.

13.2.5 *Financing*

As the association's action can be brought only for an injunction, the association has no monetary incentive to bring such an action. On the contrary, the German legislator explicitly forbids monetary incentives to bring such an action and labels actions that are brought for profit – for example by bringing multiple actions only to generate more lawyers' fees for the plaintiff's lawyers – as "abusive" and thus inadmissible. The associations that have standing may thus only bring "altruistic" actions. Financially, they carry significant cost risks due to the German "loser pays" system in the area of court fees and attorney's fees. These cost risks are somewhat mitigated by statutory provisions on the basis of which the court may reduce the "value in controversy" and thus the statutory court fees and attorney's fees which are calculated on this basis. For example, if a clause in a standard form contract is attacked, the courts routinely assess the value in controversy as being € 2,500 for each clause, regardless of the actual economic relevance of this clause.[13] This leads to attorney's fees for the plaintiff attorney of about € 500 (plus taxes) in the court of first instance. This shows the drawback of this artificial reduction: although the plaintiff association has only a small cost risk, it is hard to find a qualified attorney who will work on a complicated case for this rather modest fee.

In the area of § 10 UWG – the skimming-off provision mentioned above – some consumer associations had developed a cooperation with third party financing companies: the financing companies carried all of the cost risks in exchange for a share of the skimmed-off profits. As these belong to the Federal government, the government had to agree to this deal, but frequently did so, probably in view of the fact that 70 percent of something is better than 100 percent of nothing: without the third-party financing, these actions would not have been brought at all. However, in two recent decisions, the German Federal Court put an end to such arrangements by declaring such actions abusive and thus inadmissible.[14] According to the court, no financial motives are allowed for an association's suit, not even the financial motives of a third party who finances the case.[15]

In this context, note that German law generally prohibits contingency fees for attorneys – with certain narrow exceptions of which not much use is made. This means that plaintiffs who wish to avoid the considerable cost risks associated with litigation in Germany need to resort to either preventive legal expenses insurance (typically available for private households, but not for businesses) or to third party litigation financing.

[13] BGH, decision of 10 April 2018, case no. VIII ZR 247/17, NJW 2018, 1880 at margin no. 38.

[14] BGH, decision of 13 September 2018, case no. I ZR 26/17, NJW 2018, 3581; BGH, decision of 9 May 2019, case no. I ZR 205/17, GRUR 2019, 850.

[15] *Id.* (decision of 9 May 2019) at margin no. 29.

13.2.6 *Empirical Observations*

The German practice of association's actions is firmly established now for more than fifty years and must be regarded as a successful instrument. It has led to many changes in business behavior, in particular in the area of standard form contracts, where consumer associations have been quite successful in eliminating many unfair clauses, in particular in the financial industry. Insofar as empirical studies are available, they all come to a positive result with regard to the effects of the association's actions.[16] The German type of association's actions has also inspired EU legislation which today forces all member states to provide such or similar instruments.[17]

Nevertheless, the association's action also has an important disadvantage in that it does not provide for damage actions. Not only does this mean that compensation for affected consumers depends on their individual activities, but it also severely limits any deterrence impact that such actions may have: even if a company loses against a consumer association, for example with regard to certain illegal contract clauses, this only means that the company must change its policies for the future and pay a modest amount of court and lawyers' fees – typically in the area of a few thousand Euros. Therefore, reform discussions focus on making the association's action more effective with regard to compensation and possibly linking it with individual claims.[18]

13.3 THE CAPITAL MARKET INVESTORS MODEL PROCEDURE: *KAPMUG*

In 2005, the *Kapitalanleger-Musterverfahrensgesetz* (*KapMuG*) was enacted, which is a completely different model of collective litigation that can only be explained by specific historical circumstances. In 2003, a prospectus liability case against Deutsche Telekom AG led to a flood of several thousands of individual actions which de facto paralyzed the court in Frankfurt, so that the legislator had to come to the rescue and create the *KapMuG*.[19]

The *KapMuG* procedure is not a form of collective litigation in the sense that it would replace individual actions. On the contrary, an ordinary individual action is required to participate in the *KapMuG*. From the mass of individual actions, the court of first instance distills common questions and these are then solved in a model procedure before the higher court. After the decision in the model procedure, all individual cases are taken up again by the lower court and are then decided, using the model decision as *res iudicata* insofar as it is relevant.[20]

[16] Friedrich Bultmann, 30 *Jahre Praxis der AGB-Verbandsklage* (2008), study commissioned by Verbraucherzentrale Bundesverband (VZBV), available at www.vzbv.de/mediapics/gutachten_30_jahre_verbandsklage_vzbv_2008.pdf; Caroline Meller-Hannich & Armin Höland, *Gutachten Evaluierung der Effektivität kollektiver Rechtsschutzinstrumente*, study commissioned by the Federal Ministry for Nutrition, Agriculture and Consumer Protection (2011), available at www.bmel.de/SharedDocs/Downloads/Service/AnWis/Heft523.html; Axel Halfmeier, 50 *Jahre Verbraucherverbandsklage* (2015), study commissioned by Verbraucherzentrale Bundesverband (VZBV), available at www.vzbv.de/sites/default/. . ./Gutachten-50_Jahre_Verbandsklage-vzbv-2015.pdf

[17] EU Directive 2009/22/EC of the European Parliament and of the Council of 23 April 2009 on injunctions for the protection of consumers' interests, Official Journal EU 2009 L 110/30.

[18] See below at Section 13.6.

[19] For a detailed description of the Telekom case and the creation of the *KapMuG see* Axel Halfmeier, *Litigation without end? The Deutsche Telekom case and the German approach to private enforcement of securities law.* In Class Actions in Context (Hensler, Hodges & Tzankova eds., 2016) 279–98.

[20] For a description of the *KapMuG* procedure see also Astrid Stadler, *Developments in Collective Redress: What's new in the new German KapMuG*, 24 European Business Law Review (EBLR) 731 (2013).

13.3.1 *Standing*

As the *KapMuG* is based on ordinary individual actions, there are no special requirements with regard to standing. In the model procedure, however, a "model plaintiff" is selected by the court according to criteria such as the size of the claim and adequacy of representation.[21] The model plaintiff will run the model procedure on the plaintiff side, but all other plaintiffs are also participants to the model procedure and may take part in hearings and submit briefs to the court or bring forward evidence.

13.3.2 *Substantive Area of Application*

When the German legislator created the *KapMuG*, it was seen as an ad hoc solution to the problem of mass securities cases. Therefore, the area of application is limited to damage claims in capital market cases, which in practice mainly means prospectus liability cases as well as ad hoc information cases in which the violation of capital market information obligations is alleged.

13.3.3 *Types of Relief*

The model procedure under the *KapMuG* does not lead to any relief, but only to a decision on questions of law or fact which will then be used to decide the affected individual cases. In these individual actions, the plaintiffs usually seek damages with regard to losses they have suffered on the capital market.

13.3.4 *Consent by Class Members*

The model procedure under the *KapMuG* is neither opt-out nor opt-in, but is a mandatory procedure once it has been initiated. Both a plaintiff and the defendant may apply for a model procedure if there are ten or more individual actions pending that are sufficiently similar and based on the same set of facts. The lower court will then issue the "reference decision" in which it defines the common questions that are referred to the higher court for the model procedure. The reference decision also means that all cases that deal with the same facts and depend on the issues described in the reference decision must be suspended for the duration of the model procedure, and the affected parties automatically become participants in the model procedure.

The parties thus cannot avoid participation in the model procedure. The reason for this very strict approach is that due to its history, the *KapMuG* aims mainly at judicial efficiency. The legislator tried to achieve such efficiency by forcing all actions into one mandatory model procedure with a model decision for all affected individual actions.

It needs to be pointed out that this mandatory effect of the *KapMuG* procedure applies only to those claimants who have in fact brought an individual court action. Other potential claimants that have not filed a suit are not affected by the results of the model decision. The only way for them to benefit from the *KapMuG* procedure is to file an individual action which will then be suspended in view of the model procedure.

In addition, there is the possibility for nonplaintiffs to "register" their claim in a certain time window during the *KapMuG* procedure, which is less costly than filing a regular action. However, this "registration" under the *KapMuG* serves only to stop the limitation period from

[21] On this selection process see Axel Halfmeier, *Auswahl und Funktion des Musterklägers im Kapitalanleger-Musterverfahren*, 37 ZIP Zeitschrift für Wirtschaftsrecht 1705 (2016).

running out, so that the registered investors can later decide whether to file their own suit or not. If they file their suit after the judgment in the model procedure, this judgment will not have any legal *res iudicata* effect on such actions, but may be used only as a de facto example or a form of persuasive authority.

13.3.5 *Financing*

There are very few special cost rules with regard to the *KapMuG*. The model procedure in itself does not create any special costs, but is seen as a part of the individual actions for cost purposes. Only the model plaintiff's attorney earns an extra statutory fee which depends on the value of the case, but cannot exceed about € 27,000. This is therefore rather symbolic and law firms compete for the model plaintiff position not because of extra fees but rather because of the extra prestige and publicity that may be associated with this role.

There is no prohibition on third party financing in capital market cases, so this is regularly used in practice, in particular where larger damage claims by institutional investors are at stake.

13.3.6 *Empirical Observations*

The *KapMuG* procedure has been used in several dozens of cases, but has typically not led to speedy resolutions. The conclusion of settlements is theoretically possible, but only very few are reported. The first *KapMuG* proceedings against Deutsche Telekom AG have gone up and down through the court system in several appellate proceedings and are still not finished today, fifteen years after their start.

In the Volkswagen Dieselgate context, the *KapMuG* has again become very relevant with large investor actions being brought both against Volkswagen AG and also against its mother company Porsche SE. These actions have highlighted new unsolved issues under the *KapMuG* and will – as no settlement is in sight – probably last for many years to come. The *KapMuG* was enacted with a "sunset clause" until November 1, 2020, but the German legislator plans to extend it for another three years in order to avoid that the pending model procedures become worthless.

13.4 THE MODEL DECLARATORY ACTION: *MUSTERFESTSTELLUNGSKLAGE*

The *Musterfeststellungsklage* is the latest development in German law of collective litigation. Just like the *KapMuG*, it can be explained only through specific historic circumstances and political considerations. In the fall of 2015, the Volkswagen emissions scandal was uncovered in the US and quickly thereafter also in Europe. Volkswagen, Germany's largest carmaker, had committed a large-scale fraud against the authorities, against the environment and against its customers. In the US, several class actions were quickly started by plaintiffs' lawyers, and most of these actions were settled before Judge Breyer in San Francisco in late 2016, about a year after the scandal was uncovered. This quick settlement and the rather generous payouts to US Volkswagen customers made a certain impact on the German public discussion, and people started to wonder why German customers affected by comparable fraud did not get anything and also had no procedural instrument to enforce their claims collectively.

In the context of this political discussion, the Federal Ministry of Justice and Consumer Protection created a proposal for a "model declaratory action," in which it mixed elements of the existing association's actions with the idea of a model procedure that was taken from the

KapMuG. After some political negotiations within the ruling coalition of parties, the German parliament enacted the *Musterfeststellungsklage* in 2018 as a new chapter (§§ 606 to 614) within the German Code of Civil Procedure (ZPO).

13.4.1 *Standing*

The standing provisions were among the most disputed aspects in the creation of the *Musterfeststellungsklage*. From the start, it was clear for the parliamentary majority that individual consumers should not be able to bring such an action. Such a proposal in the form of an opt-in group action that could be started by associations or groups of individuals had been proposed earlier by the Green party (a smaller faction in the German parliament) but had been rejected by the majority in parliament.[22] The underlying fear was that with broad standing rules, profit-driven actions could be brought, backed by lawyers and third-party financing companies. This was labeled as a potential for "abuse" by many politicians, although it is hard to see why the enforcement of existing claims should be disparaged in this way and why the financial interest of a company like Volkswagen that clearly was in violation of the law should be less "abusive" in comparison to possible financial interests of plaintiff lawyers and litigation financiers.

Nevertheless, the "abuse" ideology dominated the discussion, so standing was limited to certain qualified entities, as in the area of traditional association's actions. The car industry lobby even succeeded in drawing the standing provisions – found in § 606 par. 1 ZPO – even more narrow than for injunctive actions: Instead of 75 members, 350 members are now required, the association must be registered in the list of qualified entities for four years before bringing an action, and the association may not receive more than 5 percent of its financial means from industry donations. These additional requirements were mainly designed to deny standing to the "Deutsche Umwelthilfe," a private environmental association that had been very successful in enforcing environmental laws before the administrative courts and which is in clear opposition to the German car industry.

Because of these very restrictive standing rules, the model declaratory action is available mainly for the government-financed *Verbraucherzentralen*. In particular the Federal umbrella organization that represents consumer interests, the *Verbraucherzentrale Bundesverband*, received extra subsidies from the government to build up its practice in this area. This means that although the model declaratory action is an instrument of private law and brought by private institutions, the government nevertheless plays an important role by financing the most relevant institutions.

13.4.2 *Substantive Area of Application*

The model declaratory action is not trans-substantive, but can be brought only in consumer law cases. Only consumers may profit from a declaratory judgment in this procedure. In the Volkswagen context, this means that a private (consumer) buyer of one of the affected cars may participate, but a professional buyer (e.g., the owner of a small business) of the exact same car may not. Again, this substantive limitation of the model declaratory action can only be explained politically, as the whole instrument was politically framed as an instrument of "consumer protection." In addition, the decision to give standing only to a limited number of

[22] See the Green party's proposal for a group action, in Drucksachen des Deutschen Bundestags (BT-Drs.) 19/243 of December 12, 2017. It should be disclosed that the author of this chapter assisted the Green party in the drafting of this proposal.

associations contributed to this limitation, because the consumer associations would probably be uncomfortable with representing "business" interests, and private business associations are traditionally hesitant to sue on behalf of some of their members against others.

However, the decision to limit the model declaratory action to consumer cases certainly does impair its functional value and is also at odds with placing it into the general Code of Civil Procedure which normally applies to all private law claims. The opposition proposal for a group action[23] did not have this limitation but would have created a trans-substantive instrument.

13.4.3 *Types of Relief*

As the name indicates, an association that brings the model declaratory action cannot ask for damages, neither for itself nor on behalf of affected consumers. Instead, the association must indicate certain questions of law and/or fact on which the court will then rule in a declaratory judgment. This judgment is not enforceable in itself, but will be used as *res iudicata* with regard to any future individual actions by affected consumers insofar as the questions are relevant in those individual cases.

This means that the model declaratory action is designed as a two-step procedure: the first part is started by the association and ends with the declaratory judgment. In the second part, the association does not participate, but it is up to the individual consumers whether they want to sue the defendant or not, possibly with the help of the declaratory judgment. This two-step arrangement has been criticized in the literature and at a large convention of German lawyers,[24] because it may lead to very long procedures and also relies on the initiative of the individual consumers which may be nonexistent in small-value cases.

13.4.4 *Consent by Class Members*

Although the model declaratory action has its roots in the association's actions and in the *KapMuG*, there is an important difference to the *KapMuG* in that the model declaratory action is not mandatory for all affected consumers. Instead, it uses an opt-in mechanism: once the association has filed the action, the relevant details are published on an official website,[25] and the affected consumers have the chance to opt-in ("register") until the first day of oral arguments. The *res iudicata* effect of the declaratory judgment will then apply only to those consumers who have registered their claims in this way. All others are free to pursue their own actions without any legal effect of the model declaratory action.

Note the difference to the *KapMuG*: there, the "registration" only serves to stop the limitation period, but here, in the model declaratory action, it also makes the results of the declaratory procedure legally binding for the registered consumer. The registration can only be withdrawn until midnight of the first day of oral hearings so that in fact there is not much time for a thorough assessment of the case and how it is run by the association. From the day after the first day of oral hearings, the consumer is bound to the positive or negative results of the model declaratory action, without having any influence on the procedure. The consumer does not even have access

23 See previous footnote.

24 See, with further references, Caroline Meller-Hannich, *Neue Instrumente des kollektiven Rechtsschutzes im Zivilprozess, Gutachten A zum* 72. Deutschen Juristentag (2018), at A 54. As proposed in this study, this traditional convention of German lawyers at its 72nd meeting in Leipzig 2018 criticized the model declaratory action as insufficient.

25 www.bundesjustizamt.de/DE/Themen/Buergerdienste/Klageregister/Allgemeines_node.html.

to the court documents in the model declaratory procedure, which are not public under general German procedural rules.

This binding effect on the registered consumers without any influence on the proceedings is seen by some authors as problematic in view of the constitutional right to be heard.[26] On the other hand, it is the consumers' free choice to register or not. In contrast to the *KapMuG*, they retain their right to bring an ordinary individual action over which they have full control, so that the offer of an additional instrument probably does not infringe any constitutional rights.

13.4.5 *Financing*

In fear of alleged possibilities for "abuse," the model declaratory action is designed to provide no financial incentives for the plaintiff associations. As only declaratory relief is possible, even after a successful action there will not be any money available that could be used for contingency fees or third-party financing. The plaintiff association must therefore carry the cost risks associated with the general loser-pays rule. As it is the practice in the association's actions for injunctions, the legislator has reduced these risks by implementing a ceiling on the value in controversy: even if many millions may be at stake for the defendant, as it is the case in the Volkswagen scandal, the statutory value in controversy is fixed at a ceiling of € 250,000. This leads to attorney's fees on the plaintiff side of about € 6,000 for the procedure in first instance. It will be virtually impossible to prepare and run a complicated case on this budget. For the plaintiff attorney, the model declaratory action therefore has mainly a public relations and prestige value. In mass cases such as the Volkswagen scandal, the plaintiff attorney may also try to attract a large number of individual cases after a successful model declaratory action.

13.4.6 *Empirical Observations*

The model declaratory action was introduced in November 2018, and only a handful of actions have been started since then. The most relevant was certainly the action against Volkswagen AG which was brought by the "Verbraucherzentrale Bundesverband" on the very first day when the law entered into force. This action seeked a declaration that Volkswagen owes its affected consumer customers a damage payment in principle, leaving open the determination of *quantum* of damages for the individual actions. Whether such a declaration is possible under the model declaratory action is disputed, but was not decided by the court as the case resulted in a settlement. The first oral hearings in this case took place in September and November of 2019.[27] Settlement negotiations started in January, 2020 and resulted in a settlement in March, 2020. According to this settlement, payments were made to about 230,000 Volkswagen customers.

In theory, one may think that an opt-in action such as the German model declaratory action is of limited effect because of the initiative needed on the side of the possible claimants. However, the Volkswagen action surprised most experts with the high number of registrations: According to press releases, there were more than 400,000 registrations as of June 2019. Not all of them may have been valid, and it is also disputed whether affected consumers from outside Germany, for

[26] Caroline Meller-Hannich, *Neue Instrumente des kollektiven Rechtsschutzes im Zivilprozess, Gutachten A zum* 72. DEUTSCHEN JURISTENTAG (2018), at A 51; Astrid Stadler, *Kollektiver Rechtsschutz quo vadis?* 2018 Juristenzeitung 793, 798.

[27] Verbraucherzentrale Bundesverband v. Volkswagen AG, OLG Braunschweig, file no. 4 MK 1/18.

example from Austria or other EU member states, may register for this action.[28] Foreign buyers were explicitly excluded from the Volkswagen settlement.

Aside from the Volkswagen action, there are a handful of other model declaratory actions currently pending: for example, there is a capital market case alleging damages for consumer investors,[29] one is brought by a tenants' association against certain rent increases in Munich[30] and two have been brought by a local consumer association against local banks for alleged wrong calculation of interest on savings.[31] One further action was brought against the Mercedes Benz Bank AG with regard to car loans but was rejected by the court for lack of standing, as the plaintiff institution did not fulfill the strict standing requirements outlined above.[32]

With only a handful of actions pending, it is to be expected that there will be very few model declaratory actions in the future. There are only a few associations that have standing and their resources are limited. There are almost no financial incentives for the plaintiffs or for their lawyers to bring such actions. This means that the impact of these actions will be limited to very few cases. The model declaratory action was therefore criticized as symbolic or "placebo" legislation.[33] Nevertheless, the large number of participants and payments in the Volkswagen case show that there can be substantial results in large-scale cases. Even more important, the introduction of the model declaratory action marks a certain turnaround in the German discussion about collective litigation: in the past, the necessity of such instruments was typically denied by politicians and lobbyists and class or group actions were quickly labeled as prone to "abuse." With the model declaratory action, at least a very small step was made towards a more nuanced discussion and towards the acceptance of collective litigation instruments as worthwhile tools in the interest of better compensation and less illegal behavior by companies.

13.5 INNOVATIVE USE OF GENERAL RULES

From a practical point of view, it needs to be noted that in the absence of a general class action rule in Germany, plaintiffs and their attorneys have nevertheless found ways to work with traditional instruments in order to achieve efficiency and the de facto collective enforcement of claims. In particular, they use joinder of individual claims and the assignment of claims to special plaintiff vehicles, often together with third party financing arrangements. Such strategies have been developed mainly in the area of competition (antitrust) damages cases,[34] but have now been extended to the Volkswagen scandal and other mass consumer claims.

In the specific Volkswagen context, this means that there were three possible avenues for affected customers: one is the traditional individual action, and this is used in probably more

[28] See, from an Austrian perspective Thomas Klicka & Petra Leupold, *Deutsche Musterfeststellungsklage und grenzüberschreitende Rechtsdurchsetzung*, 2018 ZEITSCHRIFT FÜR VERBRAUCHERRECHT (VbR, Austria) 208.

[29] Schutzgemeinschaft für Bankkunden e. V. v. Bisnode Deutschland GmbH, OLG Frankfurt/Main, file no. 24 MK 1/18; first oral hearing scheduled for 28 February 2020.

[30] DMB Mieterverein München v. Max-Emanuel Immobilien GmbH, OLG München file no. MK 1/19, the plaintiffs won at the OLG München, decision of 15 October 2019, an appeal is pending at the Federal Court (Bundesgerichtshof), case no. VIII ZR 305/19.

[31] Verbraucherzentrale Sachsen e. V. v. Stadt- und Kreissparkasse Leipzig, OLG Dresden file no. 5 MK 1/19; and Verbraucherzentrale Sachsen e. V. v. Erzgebirgssparkasse, OLG Dresden, file no. 5 MK 2/19, no hearings scheduled yet.

[32] Schutzgemeinschaft für Bankkunden e. V. v. Mercedes Benz Bank AG, OLG Stuttgart file no. 6 MK 1/18, decision of 20 March 2019.

[33] Astrid Stadler, interviewed in Handelsblatt of 9 May 2018.

[34] *See, e.g.*, CDC Hydrogen Peroxide SA v. Akzo Nobel et al., European Court of Justice, judgment of 21 May 2015, case no. C-352/13.

than 60,000 individual cases, many of them financed by traditional legal expenses insurance. The second alternative has been developed mainly by the US law firm of Hausfeld, which represents a German company called "MyRight." This company has – according to its own press releases – collected about 40,000 individual claims by way of transfer of claim to a plaintiff vehicle. For these customers, "MyRight" finances the litigation and carries all financial risks in exchange for a share in the possible future profits. It is disputed by Volkswagen that this business model is legal,[35] but a decision of the German Federal Court in a comparable case seems to imply that such business is legal.[36] Finally, there was the model declaratory action described above where more than 400,000 consumers have registered. This complex situation and the sheer mass of cases has contributed to a public discussion whether the current mechanisms of collective litigation in Germany could be improved and made more efficient. Often this discussion is connected to possible developments in "legal tech" where it is expected that certain mass cases may be solved more efficiently with the help of technology.[37]

For the legal profession, the landscape of collective litigation in Germany has created a somewhat divided field on the plaintiff side: in the *KapMuG* securities actions and also in mass cases that are organized through special claims vehicles, third party financing is possible and widely used, so that the financial incentives on the plaintiff side become quite high. This leads to the involvement of big law firms not only on the defendant side, but also on the plaintiff side. On the other hand, not much money can be made in the area of traditional associations' actions and the new model declaratory action. This is still the area of small firms or even individual lawyers on the plaintiff side that engage in a "David versus Goliath" battle with large commercial law firms that are typically used by the corporate defendants.

13.6 SUMMARY AND OUTLOOK

Although there are the described developments, collective litigation in Germany remains very limited until today. The only instrument with a long and established practice is the association's action for an injunction. Although successful in many areas, the empirical impact of this tool remains limited because of the lack of connection to individual damage claims. The two younger instruments – the *KapMuG* and the model declaratory action – are very cumbersome and have not yet proven to be very effective. Nevertheless, they show that legal change in this area is possible and that even in Germany there is a certain tendency to discuss and implement instruments of collective litigation.

This discussion will certainly gain new momentum the European Union finalizes its new directive on "representative actions." The EU Commission had made a proposal for a fundamental revision of the relevant EU Directive as part of its "New Deal for Consumers" that was announced in 2018.[38] The EU Parliament approved these plans with some changes in

35 Against the legality of the "MyRight" business model: Martin Henssler, *Prozessfinanzierende Inkassodienstleister – Befreit von den Schranken des anwaltlichen Berufsrechts?* 72 Neue Juristische Wochenschrift (NJW) 545 (2019); but see in favor of this model Klaus Tolksdorf, *"Sammelklagen" von registrierten Inkassodienstleistern – eine unzulässige Erscheinungsform des kollektiven Rechtsschutzes?* 41 ZIP Zeitschrift für Wirtschaftsrecht 1401 (2019).

36 BGH, case no. VIII ZR 285/18, decision of 27 November 2019 (on the legality of a commercial service that enforces claims by tenants against landlords for overpaid rent in return for share of the proceeds).

37 Alexandre Biard & Xandra Kramer, *The EU Directive on Representative Actions for Consumers: a Milestone or Another Missed Opportunity?* 27 Zeitschrift für Europäisches Privatrecht (ZEuP) 249, 255 (2019).

38 European Commission, Proposal for a Directive of the European Parliament and the Council on representative actions for the protection of the collective interest of consumers, and repealing Directive 2009/22/EC, document no. COM(2018) 184 final of 11 April 1018.

March 2019,[39] and the "trilogue" negotiations finally resulted in a political agreement in June, 2020.[40]

Once this new EU Directive is formally adopted, it will force the member states to check and possibly change their internal laws and could therefore serve as a basis for a new discussion in Germany. It is interesting to note that the proposed changes on the EU level have many features in common with the German discussion, in particular the exclusive standing for "qualified entities" instead of individuals or groups of plaintiffs, and the insight that such association's actions need to be tied to damages or restitutionary powers in order to make them more effective.[41]

39 European Parliament, Legislative Resolution of 26 March 2019, document no. P8_TA_PROV(2019)0222.

40 Council of the European Union, document no. 9592/20 of 16 July 2020.

41 For a discussion of the EU plans *see* Alexandre Biard & Xandra Kramer, *The EU Directive on Representative Actions for Consumers: a Milestone or Another Missed Opportunity?* 27 ZEITSCHRIFT FÜR EUROPÄISCHES PRIVATRECHT (ZEUP) 249, 255 (2019); Axel Halfmeier & Peter Rott, *Verbandsklage mit Zähnen? – Zum Vorschlag einer Richtlinie über Verbandsklagen zum Schutz der Kollektivinteressen der Verbraucher*, 33 VERBRAUCHER UND RECHT 243 (2018).

14

Class Action à la française

Maria José Azar-Baud and Véronique Magnier

14.1 INTRODUCTION

The introduction of a group action within the French legal system has confirmed the widespread myth of the "French exception." Indeed the legal features of the system, and the method used to enact them are very different from any other existing collective action in comparative law. After decades of debates, France only enshrined a first group action regulation in 2014. The rules passed before this regulation authorized only associations to sue professionals in courts for damages, and it was only in the collective interest of the groups that these actions could be brought. The 2014 French group action and the ones that followed, by contrast, allow individuals to get damages. However, the French model of group action remains very restricted in scope and specific in procedure. One main reason for these limitations is due to the need to enshrine a "virtuous" model that can protect the system from the purported "vices" of the American class actions. By being very cautious, the regulator seems to have not gone far enough though; recent empirical data shows that very few actions have been brought since the enactment of the 2014 act, and none of them have been successful thus far. In order to have a better understanding of the state of the law and empirical results, it is needed to refer to the French historical background. Recommendations are also to be proposed. Hence, this chapter starts with a presentation of the historical background (Section 14.2), followed with key procedural rules and empirical data (Section 14.3), and ends with challenges and recommendations (Section 14.4).

14.2 HISTORICAL BACKGROUND: A THREE-DECADE DEBATE

The unique character of class action *à la française* stems from a balance of the rights at stake, mainly the so-called "adversarial principle," "contradictory principle" and "right of the defense." These are a specificity in French procedural law and jurisprudence. The French courts, acting under the supervision of the European Court of Human rights, have sought to establish the best balance between interests at stake, including both the plaintiffs' and the defendants'. This balance is enshrined in traditional principles and rules that set forth civil and administrative trials. These special features are also to be linked to the historical dichotomy between private and public law, whose procedural rules differ dramatically. It also explains that theories and debates regarding class action in France are traditionally very dynamic, much more than the regulation itself, which is recent and still undeveloped. And once the rules are developed and promoted, one must make sure that it is not only operating "on the shelves," but is also efficient in practice. In this context, it is to be observed that French class action has not fulfilled its promise.

14.2.1 *Traditional Procedural Rules in France*

French civil procedure must comply with several principles. First and foremost, and like American procedure, the French proceeding is accusatorial and not inquisitorial, meaning that parties to a lawsuit are the main actors of the procedure (except in criminal cases where trials are presided over by interrogating judges). Parties commence, develop or stop the proceeding and they produce evidence at their convenience to judges whose task is only to make the ruling at the end. Second, complying with article 6 paragraph 1 of the ECHR,[1] parties to a lawsuit benefit from "Defense rights." Article 6 paragraph 1 states: "in the determination of his civil rights and obligations, everyone is entitled to a fair and public trial," meaning that every party in a proceeding should have a reasonable opportunity to present her case to the court, under such conditions that do not place her at a substantial disadvantage vis-à-vis her opponent.[2] Therefore, parties should be able to present their arguments, challenge the validity of adversarial opinions and none of them should enjoy a position which is more advantageous than that of other parties. In respect of this balance, judges avoid anything that causes asymmetry between parties in court. The so-called "contestation dispute over a right" rule that ensures each party to a lawsuit to physically appear in court and be heard is a consequence of this balance rule. On the opposite, plaintiffs who do not appear in court and have not been heard by judges to present their own arguments in defense violate the dispute over a right rule, and the defendant can legitimately argue that she cannot properly develop her defense in front of victims, specifically when they are unknown or not identified.

Additionally, the historical dichotomy between private and public law has an impact on the class action. The main application of this dichotomy results in a separate set of courts where judges interpreting civil law are totally independent from those interpreting constitutional and public law. Many other procedural differences occur resulting from this dichotomy, and they are also visible in group action procedure.[3]

14.2.2 *Theoretical Dynamism versus Regulators' Status Quo*

The class action issues were subject to decades of debates prior to enshrining group action rules in the legislation. These debates highlight how the academic population has been stimulating and active on class action topics, working tirelessly to come up with solutions that are acceptable to professional organizations and fit with the procedural unique rules. Many conferences were dedicated to the topic, beginning especially in the 1980s. Two well-known taskforces were led under the supervision of the best known specialist in consumer law, Professor Calais Auloy.[4] The proposals that came out of these taskforces in the late 1980s aimed at introducing the class action in French procedure. One specific proposal intended to introduce a group litigation for

[1] The ECHR stands for the European Court of Human rights, a regional human rights judicial body. The Court has jurisdiction to decide complaints ("applications") submitted by individuals and States concerning violations of the Convention for the Protection of Human Rights and Fundamental Freedoms (commonly referred to as the "European Convention on Human Rights"), which principally concerns civil and political rights.

[2] Decision July 16, 1968. Adde ECHR, Oct. 27, 1993; *Dombo Beheer* c. *Netherlands*, Application n°14448/88.

[3] See *infra*, Section 14.3.1.3.

[4] Proposal for a Consumer Code. Report of the commission to codify Consumer law to the Prime Minister, by Pr. Jean Calais-Auloy, La documentation française, 1990, p. 111.

consumers, based on an opt-out system. The proposed reform was found quite innovative, as it was inspired by the American class action model. In particular, a two-step procedure was recommended whereby judges were first to rule on whether a professional could be held liable for the damages suffered, and then, after the decision of liability was made public, to enforce the sentence, once all the parties injured manifested themselves. The proposal looked very similar to an opt-out class action system. However, due to the hostility of the lobbying of professional organizations (MEDEF), the proposal was never acted upon. Later, another taskforce, cochaired by two government representatives, one of the department of Finance and the other of the department of Justice, sat from 2005 to 2006 and submitted a report to their ministers. Its main recommendation was to allow any consumer who suffered "material harm" to sue for damages, personally or collectively, for breach of a contractual obligation by a single professional in the selling of merchandises or services. However, the proposal was never discussed by the French Parliament and was then dismissed. For many there was no change due to the pressure of professional organizations.

14.2.3 *Rules 'on the Shelves' versus Effectiveness and Efficient Practice*

In 2014, a sectoral approach was adopted, moving step by step from the consumer field to health, environmental, discrimination and data protection both before the judiciary and administrative courts. Before that date, though, a series of old rules were implemented with very little success. The French Group Action came up amid an array of "traditional" legal tools that have been in place for several decades.[5] First and foremost, the well-established "ligues de défense" jurisprudence,[6] a case law built up by the *Court de cassation* (the highest instance in the judicial system) since the beginning of the twentieth century, permitted associations to represent the individual interests of their members for compensatory purposes if their articles of incorporation included this possibility.

Furthermore, France has substantial experience in the creation of ad hoc-compensation funds aimed at a *particular damage*, namely those suffered by the victims of terrorism[7] or medically related incidents[8]. These ad hoc structures are often public organizations created by a law and regulated by a decree, financed by the State and the social security system; they function as part of a scheme whereby compensation can be proposed to victims in an out-of-court context.[9]

On top, the Consumer Code provides for four kinds of collective actions[10] addressing the cessation of *unfair practices*, the elimination of *unfair terms* in consumer contracts,[11] *joint*

5 V. Magnier and R. Alleweldt, "Country report" in: Evaluation of the effectiveness and efficiency of collective redress mechanisms in the European Union, www.civic-consulting.de/reports/collective%20redress_study.pdf.

6 See Cass. 1re civ., 27 mai 1975, Dalloz 1976, 318, note G. Viney; L. Boré, *La défense des intérêts collectifs par les associations devant les juridictions administratives et judiciaires*, LGDJ, 1997 ; L. Cadiet and E. Jeuland, *Droit judiciaire privé*, 10th ed. 2017, n° 382 ; M. J. Azar-Baud, *Les Actions collectives en droit de la consommation. Etude du droit français et argentin à la lumière du droit comparé. Nouvelle bibliothèque de thèses*, Dalloz, 2013, n°224.

7 Compensation Fund for Terrorist Acts (Fonds de garantie des victimes d'actes de terrorisme et d'autres infractions, FGTI).

8 Such as the Compensation Fund for Blood Transfusion Patients and Haemophilia (Fonds d'indemnisation des transfusés et des hémophiles FITH), Asbestos victims Compensation Fund (Fonds d'indemnisation des victimes de l'amiante (FIVA) or, more generally, the National Office for the Compensation of Medical Accidents, Iatrogeneous and Nosocomial Infections (Office National d'Indemnisation des Accidents Médicaux, des Affections Iatrogènes et des Infections Nosocomiales, ONIAM).

9 Namely the Public Health Code, art. L. 1142–1 s., R. 1142–42 s. and D. 1142–1 s.; Insurance Code, art. L. 422–1 and R. 422–1; French Code of Criminal Procedure, art. 706–3; Law n° 2000–1257 du 23 déc. 2000, art. 53.

10 M. J. Azar-Baud, *supra* note 6.

11 Art. L. 621–7 to L. 621–11 of the French Consumer Code.

representative actions (*action en représentation conjointe*)[12] and the action for the *compensation of damages* caused to the "collective interest of consumers."[13] The latter has been further extended to *collective interest of the environment*,[14] *users of the health system*,[15] *investors*,[16] the collective rights and liberties of *victims of psychological or physical threats*,[17] *public patrimony*,[18] and other interests covered by the Code of Criminal Procedure.[19] The joint representative action (*action en représentation conjointe*) has also been expanded to plead in the name of victims of damages pertaining to environmental concerns[20] and securities.[21]

All these proceedings have objectives that are *different* from the compensatory collective redress pursued by Group Actions, except for the joint representative action (*action en représentation conjointe*). The latter, in theory, also addresses the compensation of similar injuries sustained by several persons, placed in the same or similar circumstances. However, the conditions subsequently set by the lawmaker in 1992, namely the need of a mandate (to name the association who acts as a proxy) and prohibition of advertising to obtain them, rendered the *action en représentation conjointe* completely useless.[22] This proved that the need of a group action (without mandates) had become even more crucial, and was advocated as such at a national and European level.

14.3 KEY PROCEDURAL RULES VERSUS EMPIRICAL DATA

14.3.1 *Scope of Collective Redress*

The earliest group actions – adopted in 2014 – to the latest – enshrined in 2018 – all share commonalities. Indeed, all of them aim to protect rights that are homogenous, yet separable by nature; that belong to natural persons – namely consumers, users of the French health care system, victims of discrimination or of infringements of their personal data rights – and rarely to legal persons – for example, only environmental-related group actions. Moreover, group actions find their source in the breach *of legal obligations and/or contractual provisions* by a *professional* in a "business to consumer" relation, the *hospital*, *the doctor or the laboratory* in health care, the *controller or the processor* of personal data and the *private or public entity* in the environmental ones.

12 Art. L. 622–1 of the French Consumer Code.
13 Art. L. 621–1 of the French Consumer Code.
14 Art. L. 142–1 of the French Environmental Code.
15 Art. L.1114–2 of the French Code of Public Health, even if the article does not mention the expression "collectif interest."
16 Art. L.452–1 of the French Monetary and Financial Code.
17 Art. 2–17 of the French Code of Criminal Procedure.
18 Art. 2–21 of the French Code of Criminal Procedure.
19 Namely victims of discrimination, sexual offenses, children (art. 2–1 et seq. Code of Criminal Procedure). In this sense, A. Biard and R. Amaro, "Resolving mass claims in France: toolbox & experience," RILE-BACT, n°2016/5, p. 13.
20 Art. L. 142–3 of the French Environmental Code.
21 Arts L. 452–2 et seq. of the French Monetary and Financial Code.
22 See the contribution of the Head of the legal department of the Association by the time of the proceedings in the "mobile phone cartel" affair. G. Patetta, "Une illustration flagrante des limites du système français," Revue Lamy Droit civil, 2010, No 70, p. 59. In that case, UFC-Que Choisir engaged an action for the reimbursement of the 1.2 million euros of overcharges paid by twenty subscribers of the million companies having taken part to the cartel (Orange, SFR and Bouygues). The association had brought an action "dans l'intérêt collectif" and it was characterized as a joint representative action. Thus, the advertising made by the association through its website was considered as illegal under the joint representation rules (at that time art. L. 422–1 Consumer Code). It's noteworthy that of the 200,000 consumers registered on the website, only 12,521 actually joined the proceedings. M. J. Azar-Baud, *supra* note 6, n°231.

The infringements need to be "based on common grounds" and should have caused identical or similar individual damages.

All the above-mentioned common features would have justified a uniform legislative treatment. Nonetheless, the lawmakers adopted a sectoral approach and thus built a taxonomy based on specifics according to the rights at stake, which in our opinion jeopardizes the system as a whole.

14.3.1.1 The Pioneering But Limited Consumer Law Class Action

The first group action lawsuits, enacted within the rules of the Consumer code, were limited to *specific victims* (consumers,[23] thus excluding legal persons even when acting as final consumers, e.g., small and medium sized companies), to *defined infringements* (legal and/or contractual breaches, such as misleading information or lack of conformity) for a *particular purpose* (compensation can only be sought regarding material damages, such as consumers' assets, leaving aside *physical, psychological* and *moral injuries*), and committed in a *limited scope* (consumer disputes related to a *sales* or a *service agreement* and certain consequences of anti-competitive practices).[24] Then, the lawmakers added the field of *real state rental contracts.*[25]

The competition group actions constitute "follow-on group actions," as it was determined that they can only be engaged when the decision of competition authorities (national or European) or the court has identified antitrust violations; the decision has to be final, that is, no longer subject to appeal or to any other review.

The breach of competition law being already established, the court within the group action proceedings would only decide on the amount of the loss and the criteria for group membership (causation), before ordering the publication of the decision.

Follow-on competition group actions have to be initiated within a period of five years from the date of the administrative decision or the court judgment has become final.

14.3.1.2 The Following Socioeconomic Sectorial Actions

HEALTH CARE GROUP ACTION Driven by health scandals generating serial damages, group actions in the field of public health[26] now guarantee the effectiveness of the right to compensation for personal bodily injuries.[27] Although the rule seems to leave aside the *material injury*, it does encompass the impairment of *physical integrity*, *psychological integrity* and even the *harm of anxiety*.

Users of the public health system can compose the group, and the breach consists of a violation of a *legal or a contractual obligation*, therefore overcoming the distinction between "fault-based liability" and "objective liability."[28] Any victim having sustained

[23] See the definition in the preliminary article of the Consumer Code ("a natural person . . .").

[24] Art. L. 623–1 of the French Consumer Code.

[25] Law ELAN n° 2018–1021 (Nov. 23, 2018) on the development of housing, planning and digital (*Loi portant évolution du logement, de l'aménagement et du numérique*).

[26] Referred to in arts L.1143–1 et seq. of the French Code of Public Health.

[27] Art. L. 1143–2 of the French Code of Public Health.

[28] G. Viney, *Le déclin de la responsabilité individuelle*, préf. Tunc A., LGDJ, 1965; *Id.* Introduction à la responsabilité, LGDJ, 3e éd., 2008; *Archives de philosophie du droit, La Responsabilité*, n° 22, Sirey, 1977; F. Chabas, "Cent ans de responsabilité civile", Gaz. Pal. 2000, 2, doct., p. 2 ; Ph. Brun, "La responsabilité civile à l'aube du XXIe siècle, Bilan prospectif", Resp. civ. et assur. 2001, Hors-série, no 6 bis; Y. Lambert-Faivre, "L'évolution de la responsabilité civile

bodily injures, resulting from a defective product, should be eligible to a health-related group action.[29]

Some specifics are noteworthy. First and foremost, only harms caused by products contained in a list within the rules of the French Public Health Code[30] can legitimately be used for a group action lawsuit.[31] The remedy can only be compensatory (not an injunction),[32] which is unfortunate, as it would be more efficient to *remove the defective products* and *enjoin the illegal practice* as well. Last but not least, a prior formal notice is not required[33] in health related group actions[34] and out-of-court settlements are particularly promoted throughout a specific phase during the trial. Interestingly, health-related group actions can even be initiated for the compensation of damages caused before the law came into force (September 28, 2016).[35]

DISCRIMINATION GROUP ACTION The discrimination-related group action[36] aims at guaranteeing the effectiveness of the right to non-discrimination, which is ensured by the Law n °2008–496 of May 27, 2008[37] and supported by the Labour Code[38] and by the Code of Administrative Justice.[39]

Any discrimination within the scope of a working relationship or of the public service employment qualifies as long as the *event* that constitutes a breach has taken place *after November 18, 2016*.[40]

d'une dette de responsabilité à une créance d'indemnisation", RTD civ. 1987, p. 1. P. Jourdain, *Les principes de la responsabilité civile*, Dalloz, Connaissance du droit, 9e éd., 2014, p. 29. Le Tourneau Ph. (dir.), *Droit de la responsabilité et des contrats*, Dalloz Sirey, 11e éd., 2018–2019, no 24 ; L. Cadiet, "Sur les faits et les méfaits de l'idéologie de la réparation", *in* Mélanges P. Drai, Dalloz, 2000, p. 495; M. T. Calais-Auloy, "La libération du droit de la responsabilité par l'abandon de la notion de faute," D. 1998, A.J. n° 14, dernière actualité, p. 1 et seq.; Ph. Brun, "Responsabilité du fait personnel," Rép. de droit civil Dalloz, 2015, actualisé, déc. 2017, n° 5 ; L. Malaurie, L. Aynes and Ph. Stoffel-Munck, *Les obligations*, 9e éd., Defrénois, LGDJ, 2017, n° 49; A. Guegan-Lecuyer, *Dommages de masse et responsabilité civile*, LGDJ, 2006.

29 See, for instance, the point of Professor Bacache who expresses doubts as to the compatibility of the defective products system with consumer group actions. She concludes that the decision of whether to sue on the basis of consumer group action or health group action would mainly depend on the nature of the product in question. Indeed, health group action targets the "producer" such as pharmaceutical companies, the "supplier" such as pharmacies and the wholesalers or the provider promoting the use of a product such as health facilities and doctors, all of whom may face liability. Moreover, although questionable, the group action lawsuit may be directly filed against the liable insurer, which enables the victims to join the direct action and the group action. M. Bacache, "Responsabilité du fait des produits défectueux – Action de groupe et responsabilité du fait des produits défectueux", *Responsabilité civile et assurances* n° 1, Janv. 2016, dossier 16, n°9.

30 Art. L.5311–1 of the Code of Public Health. For some commentators, it is a limitative list (J. Peigne, "Qu'est-ce qu'un produit de santé ?", *Argus n° 7325, 30 août 2013*), whilst for others, it is not (M. Bacache, "Les spécificités de l'action de groupe en droit de la santé", Dalloz 2016 p.64).

31 The article stipulates twenty different products, namely those having health or cosmetic purposes, being designed for human beings, and be under the monitoring of the French National Agency for Health and Safety, such as medicine, medical devices, blood-derived products, cells, human or animal organs and tissues.

32 Art. L1143, 3e par. of the French Code of Public Health.

33 Art. L1143-2 of the French Code of Public Health, last paragraph. Nevertheless, the Law n° 2019–222, of 23 March 2019, "de programmation 2018–2022 et de réforme pour la justice" reforming Law n° 2016–1547 (18 November 2016) "de modernisation de la justice du XXIe siècle" imposes the parties to try a conciliation procedure or a mediation, before seizing the tribunals (art. 4).

34 Whilst the majority of group actions need to fulfill this requirement, see below, Section 14.3.2.2.

35 The Constitutional Council has confirmed its retroactive application. Cons. const., 21 January 2016, n° 2015–727 DC.

36 Outlined in articles 826–2 1° and 2° of the French Code of Civil Procedure, L.1134–6 of the French Labour Code, L.77–10-1 and L.77–11-1 of the Code of Administrative Justice.

37 Transposing into national law various provisions to fight discrimination and supported by article L.1132–1 of the Labour Code as well as the Code of Administrative Justice.

38 Arts 826–2 1° & 2° of the French Code of Civil Procedure; art. L1132-1 & L1134-6 of the Labour Code.

39 L77-10–1 & L77-11–1 of the French Code of Administrative Justice.

40 When the Law of Modernisation of Justice for the XXIst century (n° 2016–1547) came into force, art. 92.

Both direct and indirect forms of discrimination are targeted.[41] Direct discrimination relates to the acts endured by a person treated less favourably than another, in a comparable situation, on the grounds of ethnic origin, gender, marital status, pregnancy, physical appearance, disadvantages resulting from an economic situation, family name, residency, state of health, disability, customs, sexual orientation, age, political opinion, trade union activities and/or race and religion. Thus, the initiation of group action proceedings is justified when the conduct *aims at or leads to* the violation of someone's dignity or to create an intimidating, hostile, degrading, humiliating or offensive environment. Indirect discrimination refers to any seemingly neutral provision, criterion or practice which, for any of the abovementioned reasons, may be of particular disadvantage to persons in relation to others, unless objectively justified by a legitimate aim and the means to achieve that end are necessary and appropriate.[42] Intersectional discrimination,[43] whereby the victims are targeted on more than one ground – that is, from origin and disadvantages resulting from an economic situation – could also justify a group action.[44]

The group can be composed of any person having suffered discrimination, such as employees, applicants for an internship or for a corporate training course, both in the field of labour law or public service.

Finally, the compensation to be claimed in the group action is limited to damages arising *after the receipt of the required out-of-court request* for cessation of the collective violation.[45] Should the request be focused on an indirect discrimination and aim at the termination of the breach, no damages can be ordered.

ENVIRONMENTAL GROUP ACTION To ensure compensation of victims in the aftermath of ecological damage,[46] group actions were introduced in the area of the environment.[47]

The French Civil Code defines the ecological damage as a "non-negligible damage to the elements or functions of ecosystems, or to the collective benefits arising out of the environment that human beings enjoy."[48] Likewise, damage to nature or the improvement of quality of life, water, air, land, landscape, urbanism and maritime fishing can lead to the harm of traditional subjective rights, regardless of whether the victims are few in number – such as some companies whose image has been tarnished or whose products have been contaminated by pollution, or thousands or even millions of residents in the event of a polluted river.[49]

A group action lawsuit covers exclusively the category of massive individual damages, that is to say material, bodily and personally harms, suffered by persons, who are in a similar situation and result from a specific field (water, land, etc.).[50] Thus, it may include the consequences of

41 Art. L. 1134–10 of the Labour Code; art. L77-11–2 Code of Administrative justice.

42 Art. L. 1134–10 of the Labour Code; art. L77-11–2 Code of Administrative justice.

43 Discrimination that takes place on the basis of several personal grounds or characteristics/identities, which operate and interact with each other at the same time in such a way as to be inseparable. https://eige.europa.eu/thesaurus/terms/1262

44 *Contra* S. Amarani-Mekki, "L'action de groupe du 21 siècle Un modèle réduit et réducteur?", *JCP G* n°45, Dec. 2, p. 1196.

45 Art. L1134-8 et seq. of the Labour Code; art. L77-11-3 et seq. Code of Administrative justice.

46 M. J. Azar-Baud, "L'action de groupe, une valeur ajoutée pour l'environnement?", *Vertigo*, revue électronique en sciences de l'environnement, hors-série sept. 22, 2015.

47 Outlined in the articles L.142-3-1 of the French Environmental Code.

48 Art. 1246 of the French Civil Code.

49 A. Guégan-Lecuyer, "La place de la responsabilité civile après la Law du 1er août 2008", *Environnement n*° 6, Juin 2009, dossier 3.

50 Art. L. 142-3-1 of the French Environmental Code.

pollution, violation of nuclear safety and radiation protection, unfair commercial practices, including environmental indications that are misleading or likely to be misleading.

Both individuals and legal persons can be part of the environmental-related group action.[51] The defendant may also be either any natural or legal person belonging to the private or to the public sector[52] and, akin to original scheme of the health-related group actions,[53] the framework provides for the possibility of bringing a "direct group action lawsuit" against the insurer of the allegedly liable person,[54] as a means to increase the compensation chances of the victims, especially in cases of insolvency or bankruptcy proceedings.

The procedural claim may seek the cessation of the breach, the reparation of damages resulting from the damage caused to the environment, or both. The event that gives rise to the liability or the breach must have occurred after the entry into force of the Law of Modernisation of Justice for the twenty-first century,[55] that is November 18, 2016.

PERSONAL DATA GROUP ACTIONS Recent scandals have triggered the debate on the need to protect personal data and unveiled privacy concerns. Hence, the French data protection group action aims at the enforcement of rights contained on the French Act n°78–17 of January 6, 1978 on information technology, data files and civil liberties – namely the right to information, opposition, access, rectification and communication of personal information, contained in digital files and the possibility to exert those rights electronically.

The remedy to be sought was, initially, limited to the cessation of infringements but the reforms in the General Data Protection Regulation[56] enlarged the scope to the compensation of material and moral injuries. Thus, a group action lawsuit may lead to the cessation of acts depriving access to information concerning the purposes of data treatment and/or processing, the categories of processed personal data and the recipients or categories of recipients to whom the data are disclosed, provided the facts take place after the May 24, 2018.

According to the type of personal data violation, the group shall be limited to identified or identifiable natural persons or their heirs. And even if – exceptionally – there is a category of legal persons – groups and political parties – who may be granted a right of access, the group action lawsuit does not benefit them. People within the group must be in a similar situation and the cause of the damage must come from a breach of the provisions of the French Data Protection Act[57] by a data controller or a processor.

The "controller" is defined as the natural or legal person, public authority, agency or other body who, alone or together with others, determines the purposes and means of processing personal data. The concept is "functional" as it aims to hold liable persons who exert de facto influence, that is, it is based on factual rather than formal analysis. The "processor" is defined as the natural or legal person, public authority, agency or other body who processes personal data on behalf of the controller. Its existence depends on a decision made by the controller to delegate

51 Art. L. 142-3-1, II of the French Environmental Code.

52 Art. L. 77-10-3 of the French Code of Administrative Justice.

53 Art. L. 1143-21 of the French Code of Public Health, version of 2016, article repealed by Law for the Modernisation of Justice for the XXIst Century (Law n° 2016-1547, of Nov. 18, 2016).

54 Art. 83 of the Law n° 2016-1547.

55 Law n° 2016-1547 (Nov. 18, 2016).

56 Law n° 2018-493 (June, 20 2018) regarding the personal data protection and transposing "Regulation (EU) 2016/679 of the European Parliament and of the Council of 27 April 2016 on the protection of natural persons with regard to the processing of personal data and on the free movement of such data, and repealing Directive 95/46/EC (General Data Protection Regulation)."

57 Law n° 78-17 (January 6, 1978) on Information Technology, databases and Civil Liberties.

all or part of processing activities to an external organization to process the personal data on behalf of the former.

14.3.1.3 Collective Actions before the Administrative Jurisdictions

Taking into account the specifics of the French system (double degree of jurisdictions: judicial and administrative), the Law of Modernisation of Justice for the twenty-first century[58] enacted two collective actions that have then been enshrined within the rules of the Code of Administrative Justice.

The "group action" before the administrative courts is brought against the State or a public service concession holder, in the field of environment and health. The "action for the recognition of rights" can only be declaratory and in favour of an unidentified group of persons having the same interest. It aims at recognising the individual rights resulting from the application of a law or regulation. Consequently, the compensation of damages cannot be sought. Both actions share common traits with the group action lawsuits and the structure of the proceedings is also comparable. Hence, the duplication of these tools could have been avoided. Notwithstanding, several provisions within the Code of Administrative Justice are noteworthy as they seem much more efficient when it comes to regulating the flow of litigation[59] and will be discussed in the following part of this chapter.

14.3.1.4 Empirical Data

The previous comparative study may suggest French group actions are a powerful procedural tool, able to strengthen the effectiveness of a wide range of substantive rights. To the contrary: they have remained "locked" to those rights that have been awarded with the privilege of a group action.

This sectoral approach ignores the fact that, beyond each particular field, the rights protected by group actions share the same typology: they are individual and divisible; they belong to potential members of a group that will be formed by those who will join over course of the proceedings or those who will accept an amicable (out-of-court) settlement; and they are homogeneous because of the similar or identical factual or legal situation that they share. In this situation, group litigation is not only justified but also needed.

On top of that, despite the existence of a common procedural framework, several rules of the Law of Modernisation of Justice for the twenty-first century[60] are reiterated in the special procedural frameworks (within the substantive rules, e.g., Environmental Code, Public Health Code, etc.). The outcome is an overcomplicated system, which does not completely fit mass litigation. Indeed, whilst a collective trial should focus both on the termination and on the compensation of a damage that can a result thereof, we saw that health-related group actions only seek compensatory relief. Going further, damages to be compensated should include the moral ones, when they can be standardized, like in the data-related group action as well as in the collective redress systems to be found in Quebec or the Latin American model.[61]

58 Law n° 2016-1547 (Nov. 18, 2016).
59 See *infra*, Section 14.3.2.3.
60 Law n° 2016-1547 (Nov. 18, 2016), Title V.
61 See in M. J. Azar-Baud, *supra* note 6, p. 693 et seq.

In total, less than twenty group actions have reportedly been brought before the court,[62] most of them in the field of consumer law, regarding housing law,[63] banking and finance[64] or services.[65] Three of them resulted in an out-of-court settlement.[66] Judgments from the High Court of First Instance (TGI) and decisions after appeal are, for the most part, unfavorable to the plaintiffs and, consequently, to the groups.[67] To date, the Court of Cassation has issued two decisions. One of them delimits the powers of the Pre-Trial Judge (*juge de la mise en état*),[68] the other one interprets restrictively the scope of group actions.[69]

Moreover, two group actions proceedings pertaining to the health care field[70] and four to that of discriminations[71] are pending.

From this compendium that constitutes the Law of Modernisation of Justice for the twenty-first century and its decree, with the legislative and regulatory provisions of the substantial codes, a canvas of the proceedings can now be drawn.

14.3.2 *Procedural Initial Requests*

In the first stage, the judge scrutinizes both the admissibility of the action and the merits of the case. The admissibility (*recevabilité*) is related to the following requirements:[72] the right to sue (standing of the plaintiff); the fact of having a personal interest (which should be analyzed for the group and not on the plaintiff who acts on the grounds of a legal standing); the case is not precluded by the statute of limitations or res judicata. Moreover, the parties having standing to sue must have addressed a prior formal notice to the person allegedly liable and a period of time needs is to have been observed by law if no answer from the latter. Administrative law contains some specificity.

62 M. J. Azar-Baud, "French group actions: between tradition and modernity", European Journal of Consumer Law, 2020/2, pp. 233; "En attendant un registre d'actions de groupe et autres actions collectives – Une revue de presse", *JCP E* 2018, n° 1637.

63 "Confédération Nationale du Logement (CNL) versus société immobilière 3F: TGI de Paris, 27 January 2016, n° RG: 15/00835, Cass., civ., 1st June 19, 2019"; "UFC-Que choisir versus Foncia": TGI de Nanterre, 14 May 2018, n° RG 14/11846; "Syndicat du logement et de la consommation/Confédération syndicale des familles versus Paris Habitat-OPH".

64 "Consommation, Logement et Cadre de Vie (CLCV) *versus* AXA-AGIPI": TGI Nanterre, 2 Dec. 2016, n° RG 15/08610, CA Versailles, 3 Nov. 2017, n° 16/00463, Cass, 1st civ, 27 June 2018, n° 17-10.891; "UFC-Que Choisir *versus* BNP" Paribas, TGI de Paris, 20 Dec. 2017, n ° RG 16/13225; "Consommation, Logement et Cadre de vie (CLCV) *versus* BNP PARIBAS Personal Finance (BNP PPF) ", TGI of Paris, 8 Nov. 2017, n° 17/01643; "UFC-Que choisir *versus* Banque Populaire".

65 "Familles rurales *versus* SFR" (closed): TGI of Paris, 15 April 2016, n° 15/07353, CA of Paris, Pole 2, ch 2, 20 April 2017, n° 16/09997, TGI Paris, 3 Oct. 2018, n° 15/07353; "UFC-Que Choisir *versus* Free mobile (I)"; "UFC-Que Choisir *versus* Free mobile (II)" (settled); "Consommation, Logement et Cadre de vie (CLCV) *versus* BMW Motorrad France": TJ Versailles, 4 June 2020, n° 15/10221.

66 "Syndicat du logement et de la consommation/Confédération syndicale des familles versus Paris Habitat-OPH"; "Familles rurales *versus* Manot of Ker An Poul"; "UFC-Que Choisir *versus* Free mobile (I)".

67 TGI de Paris, 27 janv. 2016; TGI de Nanterre, 14 mai 2018.

68 Cass, 1st civ, June 27, 2018, n°17-10.891.

69 Cass, 1st civ, June 19, 2019, n°18-10.424 : A. Danon, "Logement: avant ELAN, l'action de groupe était impossible", Dalloz, July 5, 2019.

70 "Association of Parents of children suffering from the Syndrome of Anti-Convulsive Depakine (APESAC) versus Sanofi-Aventis France"; "Réseau d'Entraide, Soutien et Informations sur la Stérilisation Tubaire (Network of Support, Support and Information on Tubal Sterilization- (RESIST) versus Bayer".

71 "CGT Union versus SAFRAN AIRCRAFT ENGIEN SAS"; "CGT and UGICT CGT Union versus the city of Lyon"; "Sud Rail versus SNCF"; "CGT Union versus Ile-de-France Savings Bank (BPCE)".

72 M. J. Azar-Baud, *supra* note 6, n° 288 et seq., 336 et seq., 415 et seq., 517 et seq.

14.3.2.1 Standing to Sue: Exclusivity to Registered Association

Standing to sue is granted to "registered associations" (*associations agréées*) in each particular field having been endowed with a group action (for instance consumer, health or environmental associations). In the "common framework," associations that have been duly declared for at least five years, whose statutory purpose includes defending the interests that are at stake in the procedure, namely to act against discrimination or disability, or the protection of private life and personal data, are entitled to engage in a group action.[73]

Specific provisions complete, broaden or restrict this rule with respect to health, discrimination, environment and personal data group actions.

Completing the rule, the French Public Health Code allows standing to registered health associations (*associations agréées*) both at national or regional level (around 500 in total), as long as they do not market health products.[74]

Broadening the rule, trade unions also have standing to sue in discrimination-related group action, if the discrimination took place within the scope of a working relationship or the public service.[75] In the environment-related group actions, standing is not only recognized for "environmental-registered associations" (*associations agréées*) but also, under certain circumstances,[76] for associations defending victims of collective accidents and for associations of victims of physical injuries or economic interests acting "for the defense of their members" can obtain a register (*agrément*) to sue. In data-protection group actions, in order to have standing, the statutory purpose of the associations has to relate to the protection of privacy and personal data; registered consumer associations and representative trade union organizations may act if the beneficiaries of the action are consumers, employees or civil servants.

Restricting the rule, consumer group actions are only granted for the registered associations with a nationwide membership.[77]

Akin to the French Consumer Code, the Code of Civil Procedure caters to the situation of the failure of a party in the course of the procedure. It is provided that another association being in a position to sue in the same lawsuit may request that the judge replace the former through an incidental action. This suggests that the standing to sue is given on the basis of a presumption *iuris tantum* of representativeness.[78]

In sum, only non profit organizations – who are representative because of their "register" (a sort of approval granted by the administrative authority) or by their age – are entitled to bring an action.

73 Art. 63 of the Law n° 2016-1547 (Nov. 18, 2016), and art. L. 77-10-4 of the Code of Administrative Justice.

74 Art. L.1143-2 Code of Public Health. This is how APESAC – a French association of people affected by an epilepsy drug that caused birth defects – filed the very first health-related group action lawsuit before the High Court of First Instance on May 12, 2017, seeking to hold liable a pharmaceutical group for the case of birth defects or developmental delays of children exposed *in utero* to valproate.

75 The group action lawsuit announced by the French General Workers Conféderation (CGT) *versus* Safran company, falls within this context. www.lesechos.fr/economie-france/social/0301292799787-discrimination-syndicale-la-premiere-action-de-groupe-en-passe-darriver-en-justice-2154771.php. A. Boulanger and D. Jonin, "La phase précontentieuse dans l'action de groupe en matière de discrimination en droit du travail", Semaine sociale Lamy n° 1786, p. 5; O. Levannier-Goüel, Y. Tarasewicz, G. Roche, S. Ben Achour, "La première action de groupe est lancée", Semaine sociale Lamy, n° 1741, p. 2.

76 When a public action has been filed by the public prosecutor's office or the victims.

77 Except for some overseas departments where local associations are able to engage a group action (Art. L. 652-1 of the Consumer Code).

78 M. J. Azar-Baud, *supra* note 6, n° 374 and 416.

14.3.2.2 First Step Proceeding: Prior Formal Notice and Legal Delays

Before engaging a group action in the fields of discrimination, data protection and environment (thus except in the scope of consumer, competition and health-related group actions), the person having standing to sue must send an out-of-court prior formal notice, requesting that the defendant cease the illegal practice and/or compensate the group for damages. In the discrimination group action lawsuit, the lawmakers have replaced the "formal notice" by a "request" to be addressed to the employer, who should initiate specific proceedings.[79]

Then, a waiting period – four months in general and six months for the discrimination lawsuit in employment relations[80] – needs to be observed.[81] Only after the end of that length of time, or after the reception of a negative answer from the recipient, can the group action be lodged before the judges.

14.3.2.3 Special Administrative Rules

Whereas before the judicial system, the only rules pertaining to the regulation of the flow of litigation are to be found in *res judicata* and the statute of limitations, the administrative system enshrines rules regarding the relationship between the "administrative collective actions" (including both group action and the action for the recognition of rights lawsuits before administrative courts) and individual lawsuits.[82] It is provided, in the event that a claimant of an individual application is likely to benefit from a group action lawsuit already filed, the president of the tribunal must issue a formal notice to *inform the claimant of the existence of the group action* lawsuit, of *his right to take part in the action*, in particular to join the group, and *of the need to confirm his or her intention to continue* with the individual proceedings.[83] In the absence of such confirmation, within the time limit set by the judge that cannot be less than one month, the person is *deemed to have automatically withdrawn his individual proceedings*. Moreover, even if the claimant maintains his claim, the court may decide *to handle the case* or *to submit it to the president* who assigns the case to a specific court. Likewise, the court may suspend proceedings over the application's findings until the decision made on the group action lawsuit be irrevocable, unless it is contrary to the *claimants'* or the *public interest*.[84] For the sake of coherence, we believe the lawmaker should have considered adding a provision to

79 Art. L77-11-4 & R. 77-11-2 of the Code of Administrative Justice; art. L. 1134-9 of the French Labour Code.

80 In this case, the employer must give notice to the Unions and social economic Comities in the firm of the demand and engage a discussion in order to put an end to the alleged discrimination (Art. L1134-9 of the French Labour Code).

81 Requirement prior to the legal action: formal notice and the expiration of a term. The group litigation does not escape the extrajudicial settlement trend. The *common procedural framework* requires that the person against whom the action is considered, be put on notice in order to cease the breach or to compensate the damage suffered. A time limit of four months must pass before the submission of a claim, so that the defendant may take the appropriate measures. In case of a breach of that time limit, the sanction will be the inadmissibility of the request. This sanction contrasts with article 56 of the French Code of Civil Procedure, which remains applicable to consumption and health related group action lawsuits, where no formal notice is required.

In the discrimination group action lawsuit, instead of a formal notice, a "request" must be addressed to the employer who should initiate specific proceedings and a time limit of six months must run, as of the date of the request to terminate the discrimination or the notice by the employer of the refusal of the application.

In the event that the defendant did not stop the breach nor compensate the damage at an earlier stage, the defendant's liability will be clarified in the course of the proceedings.

82 See M. J. Azar-Baud, "Le cadre judiciaire et administratif des actions de groupe : quelles différences ? quelles conséquences ?", JCP E, n°28, July 13, 2017.

83 Art. R. 77-10-3 & R. 77-12-3 of the Code of Administrative Justice.

84 Arts R. 77-10-3 & R. 77-12-3 of the Code of Administrative Justice.

automatically add the individual applicant to the group in case of withdrawal of the individual application.[85] In the current scenario, the claimant may find himself "considered as having withdrawn" and, if he does not join the group action within the timeframe stipulated by the judge, he won't be able to benefit from the group action decision nor from his individual action.

There are also special rules affecting the limitation periods of individual claims and on debarment (*caducité*) in administrative courts. These special rules mean outcomes can differ depending on whether an action is before the judicial or administrative courts.

STATUTE OF LIMITATIONS As before ordinary courts, group action lawsuits filed before administrative courts *suspend the statute of limitation* of individual actions but also their debarment. In order to understand the difference between the two jurisdictions, let us recall that procedural time limits are shorter before administrative courts than before ordinary ones. In the former, an appeal can be addressed against a decision within two months of publication.[86] Therefore, if a group action lawsuit had been filed, a public official could file an individual action on the same grounds to overturn a decision taken by the Administration (dismissal, sanction, transfer) that he considers illegal, even if the limitation period of four years or the disbarment period of two months had passed. Both in group action lawsuits before the judiciary and in collective actions before the administrative courts, the time limit in a collective action before the administrative jurisdictions starts again for the rest of the period, and not less than six months.

Regarding the action of recognition of rights, the lawmaker has enacted the interruption of limitation periods and debarment; the new time limit "starts to run from the moment of the publicizing of the decision ruling on the collective action." Yet, it is difficult to understand the meaning of this provision because, at first sight, new actions in recognitions of rights are inadmissible due to the *res judicata* effect of the first one.

RES JUDICATA Rules on *res judicata* are also not the same in actions before the judiciary and administrative courts. In the former, they bind members of the group who have been *compensated*, a sort of *res judicata secundum eventum litis*,[87] and any other association having standing to sue, no matter if the association was compensated or not, *a sort of two way preclusion.*

Rules on *res judicata* in the Code of Administrative Justice are more ambitious. It is provided that the president of the tribunal may dismiss a group action and/or an action for the recognition of rights and individual actions when the applicants were eligible for the rejected group action lawsuit, insofar as the *grounds raised are identical* to those decided by the rejection ruling or if the *new grounds are manifestly unfounded.* This possibility given to the judges is a novelty in group actions law and constitutes a sort of "negative" authority resulting from a rejection judgement made by administration. Such measures may be efficient in preventing "frivolous litigation."

14.3.3 *Liability Judgment and Aftermaths*

Only if the defendant is held liable, the judgment will be enforced throughout a new stage for the *publicity* of the sentence (at the cost of the defendant) and the *opening of an opt-in stage*. The enforcement of the decision can be spontaneous (the defendant compensates the victims having opted in). If not, a new phase will be needed in the proceedings for the liquidation and execution purposes.

85 M. J. Azar-Baud, "Le cadre judiciaire," *supra* note 82.

86 Unless the lawmaker has made an explicit exception and in the case of "recours de plein contententieux."

87 M. J. Azar-Baud, "Nuevas acciones de grupo en el derecho francés", La Ley, Feb. 17, 2017, p. 1.

14.3.3.1 Types of Relief

Depending on the field of the action, the purpose of the request may be to obtain compensation[88] or compensation and cessation. The request should be accompanied with model cases,[89] on the basis of which the decision will be granted.

In a decision dealing both with admissibility (certification) and the merits, the judge may order the *cessation* of the practice at stake and to take appropriate measures to achieve this goal. A fine can be imposed in case of delay to perform[90].

The judge can also *hold the defendant liable* towards the group. Consequently, the decision defines:[91]

- the connecting factors to the group and the damages concerned, so that the victims are able to *identify themselves with it and therefore opt-in;*
- the period for the publicizing of the decision by the defendant or by the plaintiff, if the former has failed to publicize and the *minimum* content of information to be produced[92]. This topic is very differently regulated by the administrative jurisdictions (see Section 14.3.2.3);[93]
- the cut-off period within which the members shall opt-in to obtain a compensation;
- the type of compensation procedure, namely compensation on an *individual basis* or collective *liquidation procedure of the damages.*

In case of an appeal, the proceedings are suspended[94] until the decision of the Court of Appeal is handed down.

Through the regulation of the so-called "simplified group action" in the Consumer Code the lawmaker catered to the situation whereby the identity and number of injured consumers are known, and where the group of consumers have suffered harms that are alike (in terms of the sum to be sought through compensation, or in reference to the period or duration of the damages). It is provided that the court, after deciding on the merchant's liability, may order him to compensate the victims directly and individually, within a cutoff period and in accordance with the conditions set in the decision. In this particular case, no opt-in is needed.

For the rest of the group actions, the proceedings continue through the "opt-in" step.

14.3.3.2 Opt-In

Victims belonging to the group, and meeting the requirements described by the judge, should join in the group through *an application form* and *within the time limit* established by the judge,

88 Only compensation can be sought in consumer and in health-related group action lawsuits.

89 As the lawmaker did not specify a number of individual cases to be brought with the summons, the plaintiffs have acted differently and introduced evidence pertaining to a low number of individuals in the first group actions (four, seven and sixteen) and around 200 in the last group action engaged by UFC-Que choisir *versus* Google.

90 Art. 66 of the Law n° 2016-1547; Art. L. 77-10-6 of the Code of Administrative Justice; Art. L. 623-4 of the Consumer Code.

91 Arts 66 to 68 of the Law n° 2016-1547; Art. L. 77-10-7 to L. 77-10-9 of the Code of Administrative Justice (CJA); Art. 826-14 to 826-16 of the Code of Civil Procedure (CPC).

92 CPC, art. 826-16; CJA, art. R. 77-10-15.

93 Ongoing group action lawsuits and actions for the recognition of rights before the administrative court along with the judicial decisions are disclosed on the website of the State Council, which also publishes a summary of the request thus creating a sort of register of collective proceedings. None of this is provided for pertaining to judicial group actions.

In practice, the website of the Council of State (www.conseil-etat.fr/) publishes the list of group actions and actions in recognition of rights engaged in administrative matters, before the administrative jurisdiction.

94 Art. L. 77-10-25 of the Code of Administrative Justice.

that varies according to the field of the group action (i.e., two to six months in consumer-related group actions, six months to five years in health care)[95].

The accession to the group constitutes a mandate,[96] so that the claimant must specify the identity of persons on whose behalf they file the group claim, in every claim of compensation for damages and in the enforcement of the decision, according to the French legal adage "no one shall plead by proxy."[97]

With the approval of the judge, the plaintiff can be assisted by a person belonging to a regulated judicial profession (namely a lawyer or a bailiff), both at this stage and at the compensation phase.

The application to opt-in can take any form enabling the acknowledgment of its receipt and it is addressed to the plaintiff when the judge settled the collective *liquidation procedure of the damages*. If the *individual compensation procedure* needs to be observed, the victim can choose whether to address it to the plaintiff or to the defendant.[98]

Then, the defendant proceeds onto individual compensation.[99] Should the defendant fail to do so, members whose application have not been acknowledged, might refer the matter directly to the judge who ruled on liability, or to the association if they had addressed the application to the organization in the first place.

It's noteworthy that no contract terms may deprive the victims from the right to join a group action. If this happened, the term would be considered as void, or "not written." Then, members of the group are invited to opt-in if compensation is granted to them: this provision prevents them from an early joining that would not lead to an advantage.

14.3.3.3 Negotiation versus Enforcement

Only if the defendant has failed to compensate the members of the group, a third stage of the proceedings is engaged for the enforcement of the decision, which will continue according to the compensation procedure settled in the liability decision, that is to say either a collective procedure of liquidation of damages or an individual procedure of compensation.

When the "collective procedure of liquidation of damages"[100] is ordered, a *negotiation process* is launched, wherein the parties must agree on an *amount* to compensate each member of the group. It's a particular negotiation process, referred to as "curious procedure."[101] It is by no means mediation, as the parties' cooperation is not necessary: the judge decides the collective procedure of liquidation of damages, provided that some conditions are met. The plaintiff negotiates

95 Art. L. 1143-4 of the Code of Public Health.

96 Art. 826-22 of the Code of Civil Procedure.

97 Contra H. Croze, "Un droit commun de l'action de groupe ?", *Procédures* n°2, fév. 2017, étude 4, n°18.

98 Art. 826-16 (4) of the Code of Civil Procedure.

99 Art. L. 623-14 of the Consumer Code; Art. 826-20 CPC and art. R. 77-10-19 CJA.

From a practical point of view, to mobilize the potential members of the groups, it would be appropriate that they were aware of exactly what they are entitled to.

If there is no total agreement, the plaintiff must refer to the judge so that he proceeds to the liquidation of subsisting damages within the limits set by the decision. This is where the expression "collective liquidation procedure" is fully justified. If the plaintiff does not refer to the court within a year from the day the decision ordering the collective liquidation procedure is legally binding, members of the group may file compensation claims to the person found liable thereby triggering the compensation procedure on an individual basis.

For the management of the funds received as part of the group members' compensation, the claimant must refer to the *Caisse de depot et des consignations* to open an account proper to the group which he manages, flows and closure (art .L. 623-10 of the Consumer Code).

100 Art. L. 77-10-9 of the Code of Administrative Justice.

101 H. Croze, *supra* note 97, n°17.

the amount of compensation within the framework set by the decision.[102] The purpose is to agree on an amount to compensate each member of the group, but the negotiation is not freely conducted. The judge determines the elements enabling the assessment of damage likely to be compensated for each category of persons forming the group, along with the time limits and terms in which the negotiation will be undertaken. Being an obligation ordered by the judge, he may even impose a civil penalty up to a maximum of 50,000 euros to whoever uses delay or improper tactics to prevent the conclusion of a settlement.[103]

In the aftermath of the opening of this negotiation stage, individuals wishing to join the group must opt-in, within the time limit set in the liability decision. To show up, they must address a form exclusively to the plaintiff, which is considered as a mandate.

The agreement is subject to the judge's approval, so that he verifies that the parties' interests and group members are sufficiently protected, in accordance with the terms of the framework imposed by the decision.[104]

If the defendant has not compensated the agreed amount, the enforcement of the decision is needed. As the plaintiff also *represents* the members of the group, he triggers the individual procedure for compensation.[105]

The individual procedure of compensation is also followed, being mandatory, in the discrimination and health-related group action lawsuits. The members willing to join the group must address the application to the plaintiff or to the defendant who then proceeds onto individual compensation, according to the extent of their individual damages. Therefore, the judge will have to deal with a multitude of persons.

The abovementioned common frameworks briefly summarized leave room for many exceptions hailing from the range of special provisions.[106]

14.4 CHALLENGES AND RECOMMENDATIONS

In only a few years after its adoption in French civil and administrative procedures, the mechanism of the class action unveils its shortcomings. In this section, we highlight the challenges, perspectives and the avenues for improvement that can be identified under French law.

14.4.1 *Challenges*

14.4.1.1 Sectorial versus Transversal Approaches

As seen above, a sectoral approach has been adopted by French law, moving step by step from the consumer field to health, environmental, discrimination and data protection both before the judiciary and administrative courts. Without a doubt, by modeling group actions in this way, the French legislator has been cautious. However, some suggestions for improvement can be made. In this chapter, we recommend the lawmaker to adopt a more transversal approach.

102 After a year since the decision ordering the collective liquidation proceedings has been handed down and is no longer subject to appeal and if the defendant has not compensated the victim.

103 Art. 73 of the Law n° 2016-1547.

104 The judge can also decide to re-open the period of negotiation if he considers that the interest of the members of the group have not been properly addressed. (art. 73 of the Law n° 2016-1547).

105 Art. 72 *in fine* of the Law n° 2016-1547.

106 For details regarding standing to sue and rules specific to each group action-proceedings, see M. J. Azar-Baud, "Variations autour du régime de l'action de groupe", JCP E, n°27, July, 6 2017.

Whilst it took quite a long time to reach the milestone of the first group actions in the field of consumer law (*Loi Hamon*, 2014), they quickly spread to the field of health (2015), environment, personal data and discrimination (2016).[107] They have also been enshrined in the Code of Civil Procedure and the Code of Administrative Justice,[108] constituting a "common framework." Nevertheless, despite its "given name," the common framework does not apply to all group actions. On the one hand, the consumer and competition group actions are explicitly excluded from it. On the other hand, each specific regime (within the Code of Environment, the Code of Public-Health, the Labor Code or the Act for data protection) introduces restrictions or broadens the system.

The sectoral method is problematic in many respects. First, it provokes an inflation of norms. Second, because of the existence of different regimes, group actions seem difficult to handle.[109] Third, there are unjustified inconsistencies in the treatment of disputes,[110] all to the detriment of intelligibility and simplification of the law.

As a result, further group actions are still needed in other areas, such as the portion of labor law excluded from the current regime,[111] public interest litigation and the protection of victims of violations of economic, social and cultural rights,[112] which are common in comparative law.[113] And even in the fields whereby a group action was adopted, there are still segments that remained outside the scheme such as certain practices in competition law. In a same vein securities class actions do not exist in France, leading French plaintiffs to join a foreign procedural system, such as the US.[114]

Moreover, a group action should be available for the effectiveness of fundamental rights, a solution that would be in accordance with Article 47 of the Charter of Fundamental Rights.

In addition, the remedies to be sought are not the same in the different group actions. Consumer and health-related group actions can only pursue the compensation of damages, whilst the others can also seek the cessation of unlawful acts – and thus allow the accumulation of claims relating to the same dispute in a single instance.[115] Avoiding the duplication of litigation[116] and reinforcing the deterrent and preventive aims of collective litigation should be taken into account.

The same reasoning applies to compensable damages throughout the different group actions. Some of them allow for only one specific type of damage. Such is the case in the consumer group action wherein only the compensation of *material damage* can be sought, or in the health-related group action so as to the compensation of *physical injuries*. Other group actions concern more than one type of harm. Such is the case in the environmental-related group action, wherein compensation can be of *physical and material damages* and, in the personal data-related group

[107] K. Rodriguez, "Zoom sur le droit positif *in* Dossier Action de Groupe", Juris associations 2019, n°591, p. 18.

[108] CPC, art. 826-2 et seq.; CJA, art. L. 77-10-1 et seq. and art. R. 77-10-1 et seq.

[109] M. J. Azar-Baud, *supra* note 106.

[110] M. J. Azar-Baud, *supra* note 82.

[111] For instance affair Goodyear concerning more than 800 employees.

[112] M. C. Ucín, "Litigios de interés público", *Eunomia, Revista en Cultura de la legalidad*, 2017.

[113] For instance in Quebec (see the collective action on behalf of the victims of sexual offences) or Argentina whereby collective actions have been used to challenge the constitutionality of laws violating the freedom of religion, or to have access to medicines and public services.

[114] *In re Vivendi Universal S.A. Securities Litigation*, 2011 WL 590915 (SDNY Feb. 17 2011).

[115] N. Dupont and M. J. Azar-Baud, "Actions de groupe et actions collectives classiques: concurrence ou complémentarité ? Étude à partir du droit de la consommation", *CCC* n° 11, nov. 2018, étude 15.

[116] Civ. 3e, 6 juill. 2017, n° 16-12.599; Paris, 9 nov. 2017, préc., infirmant TGI Paris, 27 janv. 2016, n° 15/00835, *D*. 2016. 1690, note B. Javaux.

action, *material and moral damage* can be pursued. To improve the system, compensation should be granted for all the damages that can be standardized.

Moreover, the differences in the regulation of group actions before the judicial and administrative courts are not justified, in particular the rules on publicity and on the relationship between group actions and individual actions.[117] Harmonization of the judicial mechanism onto the administrative model, which we prefer, would render the system seamless.

In order to simplify, enlarge and harmonize the system, the abovementioned measures tend to ensure the balance between the rights of the parties. Yet, rules on judicial management should be reconsidered on the basis of new means and new powers.

14.4.1.2 Restrictive Rules of Procedure

Confronted with the dilemma between a guarantee of *access to justice for groups* and ensuring the *rights of the defense and avoiding abusive litigation and procedural blackmail*, lawmakers adopted a rigid structure for the "group trial," subject to many conditions.

In the first stage the judge scrutinizes both the admissibility of the action and the merits of the case. The admissibility (*recevabilité*) is related to four requirements[118]: the right to sue (standing); the fact of having a personal interest (which should be analyzed for the group and not on the plaintiff who acts on the grounds of a legal standing); the case is not precluded either because of the statute of limitations or because of res judicata.

In order to ensure that group action cannot constitute an instrument of blackmail,[119] the French legislature has enacted rules on advertising,[120] allowing it only if the defendant's liability is handed down. In the same sense, members of the group are only invited to opt-in if compensation is granted to them: this rule prevents them from joining early and ending up with no gain.

The standing to sue is also a restraint. Only nonprofit organizations – who are representative because of their "register" (a sort of approval granted by the administrative authority) or by their age – are entitled to bring an action. Without a doubt, by modeling group actions in this way, the French legislator has been very cautious.

14.4.1.3 Prohibitive Costs

There is no specific rule to fund a group action in France. First and foremost, no specific fund has been set up following the 2014 group action regulation. Additionally, the traditional rule regarding the way to finance an action is that lawyers are paid on either a fixed amount, or a percentage of an hourly rate. But contingency fees, that is, fees calculated on a percentage of the damages or sum recovered, are illegal in France. They are nonetheless the traditional way to fund class action abroad, mainly in the US.

As for risks of the proceedings, the losers in French trials take the risk of having to pay a big part or the totality of their opponents' costs, according to article 700 of the Code of Civil Procedure, and the decision is decided on a case by case basis by the judge.

117 M. J. Azar-Baud, *supra* note 82.

118 M. J. Azar-Baud, *supra* note 6, 517 et seq.

119 R. Miller, "Of Frankenstein monsters and shining knights: myth, reality, and the 'class action problem'", Harvard law review, vol. 92, 1979, p. 664 to 694; W. Simonn, "Class Actions – Useful Tool or Engine of Destruction", 1973, 55 *F.R. D.* 375; I. Veillard and B. Volders, "La consécration des actions de groupe en Europe, la traversée de l'Atlantique aura-t-elle adouci le 'Monstre à la Frankenstein'?", 2008, n° 2, p. 67 et seq.; C. Piché, "L'emprise des cinq doigts de Frankenstein", (2016) 2 RIDC 291.

120 French Consumer Code, art. L. 623-7 ; L. n° 2016-1547 du 18 nov. 2016, *JO* du 19, art. 67.

To reduce the risk to bear the cost of the trial, contracts between the parties can specify which of them will have to bear this risk in case of lawsuit. But these contracts are often illegal and, notably, not applicable either in consumer contracts (which are not open to negotiation) or, by definition, to civil liabilities towards third parties.

For all these reasons, a group action is costly and risky, explaining why associations scarcely take the risk of the lawsuit.

14.4.1.4 Cross-Border Issues

In a context of increasing cross-border damages, the possibility of the introduction of a group action by a foreign association should be envisioned. As group actions fall within the proceeding rules, the solution would depend on the law of the forum. Admittedly though, even if French legislation does not expressly give them standing, the Constitutional Council's case law[121] admits they should be recognized to enhance the right to a fair trial and to an effective remedy[122] along with the nondiscrimination principle.[123]

14.4.2 *Alternatives*

14.4.2.1 Alternative Dispute Resolution

Alternative dispute resolution (ADR) is becoming an interesting path, either before or within the collective compensatory redress proceedings, being less time consuming and expensive but also for its procedures.

In practice and following the trends in consumer law,[124] ADR has become, gradually, a necessary step before the initiation of the lawsuit. According to a recent law (Loi de programmation 2018–2022 et de réforme pour la justice)[125] which reformed the fourth article of the "Law of Mediation,"[126] an attempt of mediation, of conciliation or of a "participatory procedure agreement"[127] is now mandatory before going to court for claims seeking payment of an amount not exceeding a certain sum to be fixed by a decree.[128] Collective compensatory redress is not mentioned within the exceptions to the compulsory step, which prohibit an action without the

[121] Cons. const., déc. n° 2014-424 QPC, 7 nov. 2014. – Cass. crim., 1er déc. 2015, n° 14-80.394, P+B : JurisData n° 2015-026867 ; L. Usunier, Droit d'agir en justice et actions de groupe transnationales, in Mél. Audit, *Lextenso* 2014, p. 683. CEDH, art. 6 and art. 13. Charter of fundamental rights, art. 47.

[122] Arts 6 and 13 of the European Convention on Human Rights.

[123] Arts 18 and 19 of the Treaty on the Functioning on the European Union.

[124] Directive 2013/11/EU of 21 May 2013 on alternative dispute resolution for consumer disputes and amending Regulation (EC) No 2006/2004 and Diretive 2009/22/EC ; Ordonnance no. 2015-1033 of 20 August 2015 on out-of-court resolution of consumer litigation ("Ordonnance n° 2015-1033 du 20 août 2015 relative au règlement extra-judiciaire des litiges de consommation").

[125] Law n° 2019-222 (Marc 23, 2019).

[126] Law n° 95-125 (February, 8 1995) on the organisation of Jurisdictions and of the civil, criminal and administrative proceedings.

[127] The "Participatory Procedure Convention" is defined as the agreement by which the parties to a dispute undertake to work jointly and in good faith towards the amicable resolution of their dispute or the preparation of their dispute".

[128] "Where the claim seeks payment of an amount not exceeding a certain amount . . . to seize the High Court of first Instance (TGI) the plaintiff must be preceded, at the parties' convenience, by an attempt of conciliation by a judicial conciliator, an attempt of mediation, as defined in article 21 of Act No. 95-125 of 8 February 1995 on the organization of courts and civil, criminal and administrative procedure, or an attempt of a "participatory procedure," except: "1° If at least one of the parties seeks the approval of an agreement"; "(2) Where a prior appeal is required vis-à-vis the author of the decision"; "(3) If the absence of recourse to one of the alternative dispute resolution methods mentioned in the first paragraph is justified by a legitimate reason, in particular the unavailability of conciliators

prior attempt to settle.[129] However, the "collective claim" will likely exceed the amount of the decree, so compensatory collective redress may avoid it in the end.

Furthermore, at any stage during the procedure, the judge may suggest a judicial mediation[130] to the parties, who may choose a conventional mediation instead. Mediation is now possible before the administrative law judge as well.[131]

Particularities exist when it comes to health related group action lawsuits[132] since, in this case, the judge chooses a mediator from a list, who can be assisted by a special commission.[133] The judge settles a legal framework for the mediation-negotiation period, determining time limits and content.[134] To reach this special out-of-court settlement, the association and at least one of the defendants must conclude it. Then, to approve it, the judge will scrutinize the agreement to ensure that it complies with the interests of the group members.[135]

Interestingly, before the adoption of a group action, the Paris Mediation and Arbitration Center (CMAP)[136] developed a set of rules to enable the collective settlement of mass claims[137] within a period of six months. They were inspired by a mediation process between associations and a bank (Crédit Foncier) regarding misleading information on variable rates for housing loans that lead to the first collective agreement.

14.4.2.2 Electronic Platform Practice

Recently, several Internet platforms[138] have flourished to assemble individuals into the more classic joint actions. From an entrepreneurial point of view, they appear to be a success story.[139] Likewise, interest groups are developing marketing tools to raise awareness, which have led to new ways of acting collectively. In 2018, four NGOs launched a campaign called the "Century's Affair" to obtain signatures for a petition to force the government to act against climate change. After collecting more than two million signatures, in March 14, 2019, they introduced a request, before the administrative courts, to declare the State's inaction during the last forty years illegal.

These new developments nevertheless raise issues, specifically when the platforms are conducted by law firms. In France, lawyers are not allowed to canvass clients and were not

of justice within a reasonable time"; "4° If the judge or administrative authority must, pursuant to a specific provision, make a preliminary attempt to conciliate the parties."

129 M. J. Azar-Baud, "Transacciones sobre derechos colectivos indisponibles. Contradicciones de un sistema en pleno desarrollo", La Ley, 18 January 2016, I, AR/DOC/4463/2015.

130 Arts 75 and 76 of the Law n° 2016-1547 (Nov. 18, 2016, see above); Arts L.1143-6 and L.1143-7 of the Code of Public Health.

131 Art. L. 77-10-16 of the Code of Administrative Justice.

132 Art. L. 1143-8 of the Code of Public Health.

133 The decision is not subject to appeal, art. R1143-3 of the Code of Public Health.

134 Art. L1143-8 of the Code of Public Health.

135 In the same line, the Consumer Code (Article L623-22 and L623-23) provides for that the association having standing to sue can participate in mediation. If an agreement is found, the parties must obtain the approval of the judge who will scrutinize it to verify it complies with the interest of the parties.

136 Centre de Mediation et d'Arbitrage de Paris. www.cmap.fr/.

137 See Règlement de médiation collective en matière de consommation, www.cmap.fr/le-cmap/reglement-de-mediation-collective-en-matiere-de-consommation/?lang=en; L. Ascenci and S. Bernheim-Desvaux, "La médiation collective, solution amiable pour résoudre les litiges de masse", *Contrats, concurrences, consommation*, August 2012, n° 8–9, étude 9.

138 Demanderjustice.com, Litige.fr, Saisirprudhommes.com. Mysmartcab.fr, Vpourverdict.com & Ejustice.fr. There are at least three crowdfunding platforms: Weclaim.com, Citizencase.org, Wejustice.com

139 Hereinafter the number of cases the different Platforms declare having engaged: Demander justice.com: more than 900,000; Litige.fr: more than 360,000; Vpourverdict.com: more than 700.

allowed to publicize their practice before case law accepted some form of advertising. Then, the transposal of a Directive from the European Union[140] enlarged the scope of possibilities in 2014 under strict rules arising out of case law and legislation related namely to data protection and privacy as well as according to the rules of ethics. Prior the 2014 Consumer group action law, some law firms websites were ordered to withdraw all advertising, offers of services and solicitations aimed at providing legal advice, drafting legal documents and legal assistance contracts,[141] showing that group actions are still difficult to conduct in France via electronic platforms.

14.4.3 *Recommendations*

14.4.3.1 Adopt a Transversal Approach

Considering the limits of the sectorial approach described above, we defend a more transversal approach. The advantages of such an approach would be twofold.

It is the homogeneity of rights that justifies grouping and not their typology as in the current system. This is why a first avenue for improvement would be to grant group actions for the defense of homogeneous individual interests or mass conflicts, regardless of the typology of rights. Furthermore, the standing to bring group actions is only conferred to certain legal entities, this being nonprofit organizations who are representative because of their "register" (a sort of approval granted by the administrative authority) or by their age (five years of existence). To broaden the exercise of group actions, standing should be granted to ad hoc associations, such as is the case for the environmental-related group action, to public bodies and bodies designated in advance by other Member States of the European Union and included in an official list (as is the case regarding actions for the cessation of unlawful practices in the French Consumer Code). This would promote the pooling of actions with other bodies, including within the European Union, in particular for the management of cross-border disputes, such as Dieselgate.

Second, and as for the victims, only *natural persons* can join in the group, except for the environmental-related group action including legal persons as well.[142] To smooth the judicial management of the groups and to enhance its deterrent effect, the group should include both natural and legal persons, including public legal persons, provided that they fit the description set forth by the judge. Thus, more victims would find in the group action a mechanism for the protection of rights, and the group action would constitute for the defendant an effective way to end disputes in a comprehensive manner, avoiding the risk of subsequent individual claims. The act of adjudicating and the enforcement of judgments would become smoother if there was no need to systematically exclude certain victims from the group. For example, in a dispute concerning the reimbursement of sums unduly received, the defendant would be required to return them to all its customers – whatsoever their nature, natural or legal persons, private or public – and not only to those who are "consumers" (physical persons acting for personal or domestic purposes). A major hindrance would be removed to the exercise of follow-on actions under competition law.

140 Law n° 2014-344, 17 March 2014 transposing Directive 2006/123/EC, Services directive, 12 December 2006.

141 TGI Lille, June 14th, 2005, summary order against Class Action. fr. *Adde*. TGI Paris, Dec. 6, 2005. In this case, the prohibition to advertise the beginning of a group action was accompanied with a €15,000 fine for any offence observed. The offer was judged erroneous, unfair and illegal.

142 French Environmental Code, art. L. 142-3-1, II.

14.4.3.2 Empower Judicial Management

The specific nature of the rights and claims at stake suggests that the judge should be able to adapt the procedural rules that were not envisioned for the collective litigation, at any time during the proceedings. For this purpose, the National School of the Judiciary (ENM) could provide guides and training.

First, at the admissibility stage, the judge should be enabled to verify the applicant's adequate representativeness, on the basis of a list of criteria relating namely to experience, reputation and financial capacity.[143] Some may benefit from an irrefutable presumption of representativeness towards the group, others from a rebuttable presumption.[144] In addition, the legislature should empower the judge for monitoring the agreements related to third-party funding in order to protect the interests of the group's members, following the lines of the European Commission's Proposal (April 2018),[145] adopted (first reading) by the European Parliament and the Council.[146]

Because of the complexity of assessing per capita losses for liquidation and distribution purposes, magistrates could be given the necessary means to manage it.[147] First, when the individualization of damages is difficult, judges should be able to hand down declaratory judgments[148] and, where appropriate, to set up procedures for individual liquidation of damages, such as those currently provided for "discrimination" and "health" group actions, without however being limited to these areas.

Then, when precise assessment is impossible or very difficult, judges should be able to make an "estimation" of the damage or even order a lump-sum for compensation.[149]

Finally, where the amounts awarded by way of compensation are small and/or the cost of distributing compensation disproportionate with respect to the amounts to be awarded, a global and indirect form of compensation, following the fluid recovery system, should be set forth.[150] In this case, the judge should determine who should be given to the funds, if possible relating it to the conflict of the group action proceedings, that is, educational campaigns, or they could feed a fund, as in the Quebec system, to finance future group actions.[151]

The proposed rules on compensation require measures to avoid proceedings on the same subject matter.

143 Model Code of Collective Proceedings for Ibero-America, art. 2, translated into French from Spanish *in* M. J. Azar-Baud, *supra* note 6, annexes.

144 M. J. Azar-Baud, *supra* note 6, préc., n°s 393 et seq.

145 COM (2018) 184: Proposal for a Directive of the European Parliament and of the Council on representative actions for the protection of the collective interests of consumers, and repealing Directive 2009/22/EC, April 11, 2018.

146 European Parliament legislative Resolution of 26 March 2019 on the Proposal for a directive of the European Parliament and of the Council on representative actions for the protection of the collective interests of consumers, and repealing Directive 2009/22/EC (COM(2018)0184 – C8-0149/2018 – 2018/0089(COD)); Council of the European Union, 28 November, 2019.

147 M. J. Azar-Baud, "L'office du juge à l'épreuve des procès collectifs", in 40 ans du Centre de droit de la consommation et du marché – Actes du colloque du 17 avril 2015, Faculté de droit et science politique de Montpellier, coll. "Dynamiques du droit", Oct. 2017.

148 Proposal for a Directive of the European Parliament and of the Council on representative actions for the protection of the collective interests of consumers . . ., art. 6, 2.

149 The legal construct arises out of the Directive 2014/104/UE, but it was not transposed in French Law (Ord. n° 2017-303 et décr. n° 2017-305 du 9 mars 2017, *JO* du 10). S. Carval, "Les actions en dommages-intérêts des victimes de pratiques anticoncurrentielles. À propos de l'ordonnance et du décret du 9 mars 2017", *JCP* 2017, n° 298.

150 Proposal for a Directive of the European Parliament and of the Council on representative actions for the protection of the collective interests of consumers . . ., art. 6, 3.

151 See C. Piché, Class actions in Québec: first empirical report of the *Class actions Lab*, May 2018, Univerité de Montreal, Faculty of law; P.-C. Lafond, *Le recours collectif comme voie d'accès à la justice pour les consommateurs*, Ed Thémis, 1996, p. 456 et seq.

14.4.3.3 Distinguish Collective Litigations from One to Another: Lessons from a Comparative Perspective

In the current system, the decision only binds members who opted in and were compensated through the group action. Those who were not compensated can bring individual lawsuits. Therefore, limiting the scope to decisions in favor of the plaintiff (*res judicata secundum eventum litis*) makes it possible to preserve the right to act individually, whilst challenging the risk of agency (connivance) and incompetence.

Notwithstanding, to avoid successive proceedings, group actions should put an end to the whole dispute. Thus, the *res judicata* authority of a decision in favor of the plaintiff resulting from a group trial should allow the dismissal of future group actions and subsequent individual actions[152] relating to the same contentious matter.

The solution is not the same when it comes to new group actions, as lawmakers provided for a rule according to which new group actions on the same subject matter are not admissible because of the *res judicata* principle.

However, if the same plaintiff (or another organization having standing to sue) obtained new evidence, capable of changing the result of a proceeding, the French system would be upgraded if it followed the *res judicata secundum eventum probationis* rule, as adopted in the CMPCI,[153] the Argentinean and the Brazilian[154] legal systems (*rebus sic stantibus*).

In order to prevent actions from taking place in parallel on the same conflicts, with the legal uncertainty and inefficiency that this entails, it would also be necessary to coordinate disputes and regulate the competition of two or more group actions, and of a group action with individual lawsuits. To this end, the Model Code of Collective Proceedings for the Ibero-American countries[155] (MCCPI) has envisioned four interesting solutions.

First, according to the general French provision pertaining to *lis pendens*, only if the *same dispute* is pending before two courts (of the same level of jurisdiction), the second court must decline jurisdiction in favor of the other if one of the parties so requests. The judge may do so *ex office*.[156] That being said, *lis pendens* will never meet the said requirements in collective redress' practice when the plaintiff is not the same, that is another association bringing the same claim, or whereby the petition is different, that is, an action claiming for an injunction and compensation whereas the other lawsuit pursued only the former purpose. Therefore, *lis pendens*, as actually provided for, does not function as a way to avoid duplicative litigation, since it requires that the plaintiff, defendant and the petition be the same. As provided for in the Model Code of Collective Proceedings for the Ibero-American countries,[157] *lis pendens* should work for all the cases related to the same collective dispute, no matter if the plaintiffs or the petition are different. In other words, a review of the provisions relating to *lis pendens* would lead to confronting the group – and not the plaintiff – with the analysis of subjective identity.

Second, the current system does not provide for *lis pendens* to regulate the relationship between a collective action and individual actions. Conversely, the MCCPI specifies that the

[152] Art. R. 77-10-3 and R. 77-12-3 of the French Code of Administrative Justice.

[153] Art. 33 of the Model Code.

[154] Art. 103, I & II of the Consumer Protection Code. See A. Pellegrini Grinover, The defence of the transindividual interests: Brazil and Ibero-America, http://globalclassactions.stanford.edu/sites/default/files/documents/Brazil_National_Report.pdf.

[155] Iberian-American Institute of Procedural Law, 2004.

[156] Art. 100 of the French Code of Civil Procedure.

[157] Art. 30.

effects of collective res judicata (article 33) shall not benefit the plaintiffs in individual proceedings, if the suspension of the individual proceedings is not required within a period of thirty days from the effective acknowledgment of the collective proceedings. In that system, the defendant shall inform in the collective proceedings the existence of an individual action. Should it fail to do so, the individual plaintiff will benefit from the collective res judicata even if the individual claim is rejected.

The French provisions regarding group actions and recognition before administrative judges[158] are worth following for the judicial group actions as well. According to the former, the judge must inform the plaintiff in an individual lawsuit of the existence of a collective action whereby he could be part of the group. The individual must decide whether to maintain his individual lawsuit or not. Should he fail to do so, there is a presumption that he does not want to continue with his own claim. But for the sake of coherence, together with the said presumption of suspension of the individual proceeding, presumptions of his will to be a member of the group proceedings seems to be needed (in order to avoid being out of both proceedings).

Third the MCCPI provides for the conversion of individual actions into a collective action. Following article 32, if the judge acknowledges the existence of several individual proceedings, brought against the same defendant on the same basis, he shall notify the Public Prosecutor's Office and, if possible, other appropriate representatives, so that if they so wish, they propose a collective action. This possibility does not prevent the defendant from his right to exert his individual claim (without the benefits of the collective action, see above).

Finally, connection (*connexité*) between collective actions is also addressed by the MCCPI in a pioneering way, if compared to the French classic and current solution. Pursuant to article 101 of the French Code of Civil Procedure, if there is such a connection between cases brought before two separate courts and that it is in the interest of smooth justice to have them heard and judged together, one of these courts may be asked to *decline jurisdiction* and to *transfer the case* to the other court. Despite the interest of the said rule, the solution of the Model Code of Collective Proceedings for the Ibero-American countries[159] seems better. According to the latter, the consolidation of all the proceedings solution should be mandatory and work even when the parties are not the same. It is provided for that the judge who heard the first trial prevails.

The system proposed by the MCCPI seems the offer a better and more efficient solution for the whole group and for the defendant. Moreover, it is more efficient since it avoids the cost of the opt-in. Thus, with the said solutions neither opt-in nor opt-out would be necessary, as any member of the group would benefit directly or indirectly from the judgment. Additionally, the defendant would see the case resolved throughout a single decision.

To be efficient, all the advanced measures to regulate the flow of litigation need the creation of a Register of collective actions, such as the one existing in Quebec.[160] The publicity provided for in the Code of Administrative Justice[161] should apply to the judicial group actions as well. This Register of Collective Actions could serve as a link with the expected European Register.[162]

[158] Art. R. 77-10-3 and R. 77-12-3 of the French Code of Administrative Justice.
[159] Art. 31 MCCPI.
[160] www.registredesactionscollectives.quebec. See C. Piche, *supra* note 152.
[161] Art. R. 77-10-10 and R. 77-12-11 of the French Code of Administrative Justice.
[162] Resolution March 2019, art. 5 (a).

14.5 CONCLUSION: PROSPECT FOR THE FUTURE

The number of group actions brought to date in France may seem very low[163] and their outcome discouraging. However, history in this field and contemporary experiences reveal that this is not an isolated phenomenon. In medieval England, the first representative action was not a success until after 200 years.[164] In the United States[165] and Canada, particularly in Quebec,[166] several reforms were necessary before the system was understood and practiced regularly.

Nowadays, when we compare France with Belgium, who adopted collective actions in 2014 as well, we can see that the number of actions is very similar in both countries.

Furthermore, the evolution of collective actions in Europe is a work in progress. The Proposal Directive on representative actions for the protection of the collective interests of consumers, and repealing Directive 2009/22/EC adopted by the Council on June 30, 2020 should be formally adopted in the upcoming months[167]; the Member States will then transpose it within 24 months and apply it within the following 6 ones. The broad - but still sectoral - approach of the European Proposal (see its Annex) will force Member States who are not endowed with collective actions to adopt them, and those having embraced collective actions in some fields to enlarge the scope to the one of the European text. But the European legislator has not gone as far as it was expected; thus, the maturation of the European model is far from been accomplished. This is remarkable not only in terms of the scope of representative actions (which namely does not encompass discrimination or competition) but also because in terms of the double regime *a minima* set out (for the domestic representative actions, each Member State will decide whether to adopt the opt-in or the opt-out regime but, seemingly, the choice of the opt-in will prevail; for cross-border representative actions the opt-in is imposed for non-residents).

Group actions represent a new opportunity for victims, a new tool for associations, a new practice for lawyers and judges, a new way of living in society and of undertaking with ethics. This mechanism seems to be in progress and needs time. Nevertheless, avenues for improvement have been put forward, which are only meaningful if they are taken as a whole.

Far from encouraging a contentious society, we have proposed ways of improving the system as a means of deterring the professional from violating the law, of encouraging him to comply with it, as well as ways to develop alternative methods of solving mass disputes. Ultimately, making group actions an effective and efficient judicial mechanism would lead to greater use.

[163] See M. J. Azar-Baud, "French group action lawsuits: between tradition and modernity", *supra* note 62and the statistics of the Observatory of Group Actions and other Forms of Collective Redress in www .observatoireactiondegroupe.fr.

[164] P.-C. Lafond, *supra* note 152.

[165] See the evolution of class actions *in* A. R. Miller, M. K. Kane, *Federal Practice and Procedure*, Civil, vol. 7A, 2e éd., St. Paul, Minn., West Publishing, 1986, § 1751 et s eq.

[166] P.-C. Lafond, *supra* note 152, p. 6.

[167] See the Interinstitutional File: 2018/0089(COD) *in* http://data.consilium.europa.eu/doc/document/ST-9223-2020-INIT/en/pdf.

15

The Dutch Mechanisms for Collective Redress: Solid, and Excellent within Reach

C. F. Van der Elst and W. C. T. Weterings

15.1 INTRODUCTION

Class-wide settlements of claims can be considered as one of the effective solutions for solving collective action problems in litigation on the one hand and maintaining court effectiveness for managing a large number of similar individual claims on the other hand. Since the late twentieth century, the Dutch legal system offers three collective redress mechanisms that can be attractive for resolving (international) mass claims disputes. Those procedures provide in exceptions of the general rule that no one has an action without an individual interest.[1] First, Dutch courts started to acknowledge the interests of voluntary pooling of individual claims in and by a foundation or association which resulted in the 1994 Act on Collective Actions. A claim organization can start a collective action when it represents the common and similar interests of a group of individuals. Those collective actions provide in economies of scale and improve the accessibility of the civil courts for claimants. It is generally acknowledged that it is in the interest of all parties involved – the injured parties, the defendants, the judiciary and society – that not every (similar) individual claim is brought to court separately[2]. However, this Dutch collective action is subject to an important restriction. Only a declaratory judgment establishing, for example, the unlawfulness of a defendant's conduct, or an injunction can be the result. The representative organization is not entitled to claim monetary damages in the collective action.

Second, partly because of this prohibition on claiming damages, the Act on Collective Settlement of Mass Damage Act (*Wet Collectieve Afwikkeling Massaschade* (WCAM)) was introduced in 2005. With the WCAM, the Netherlands became the frontrunner in the business of "class settlements" in Europe. Organizations representing victims of mass damages were provided with the necessary tools for negotiating and concluding a collective settlement with the party/parties allegedly liable. The Dutch law empowers the Amsterdam Court of Appeal to evaluate this collective settlement and to declare the settlement universally binding.

Since the enactment of the WCAM, a number of high-profile cases, like Shell, DES, Converium, Dexia and recently Fortis/Ageas have been settled and submitted to the Amsterdam Court. It resulted in binding declaratory judgments showing both the effectiveness of the system as well as a number of shortcomings. Mitigating the shortcoming of the WCAM, the Dutch Parliament modernized the WCAM in 2013. The WCAM's field of application was

[1] *See* article 3:303 Dutch Civil Code.

[2] For an analysis *see* M. Olson, *The Logic of Collective Action*, Cambridge, Harvard University Press, 1965.

expanded to include bankruptcy cases, while the key changes lie in providing the Court a pivotal role in the elaboration of a collective settlement and in safeguarding the quality of the claiming entities by adding a representativeness test.

This major modification of the collective settlement procedure did not stop the discussion for the enhancement of the process of optimizing the mechanisms for handling mass claims in the Netherlands. In 2019 the Act on Redress of Mass Damages in a Collective Action (*Wet Afwikkeling Massaschade in Collectieve actie* (WAMCA)) has been adopted and entered into force in 2020. The WAMCA introduced US-style class actions in the Netherlands. WAMCA removed the limitation that a claim organization is not entitled to claim monetary damages in a collective action.

In this chapter, we first give a brief overview of the characteristics and limitations of the collective action in Section 15.2. In Section 15.3, we study the important features of the Dutch collective settlement procedure and analyze the major results the WCAM has reached since 2005. We also provide in a short overview of all WCAM cases. Next, the WCAM's limits and shortcomings is addressed in Section 15.4. Following that, we discuss a number of technical legal problems that can be relatively easily overcome, as well as some other issues that remain more difficult to resolve. Those concerns relate to the voluntarism in the negotiations prior to the settlement, the free-rider behavior of individual victims and the lack of control during the distribution process. Section 15.5 explores how the WAMCA changed collective actions and how this affects the handling of mass damage claims in the Netherlands. Finally, Section 15.6 concludes this chapter.

15.2 COLLECTIVE ACTION

15.2.1 *The First Collective Redress Mechanism in the Netherlands*

While European jurisdictions were slow in adopting class actions and settlements, the Netherlands took the lead in 1994 with the introduction of the right for an association or foundation representing a group of persons having a similar interest to submit a collective claim.

The collective action procedure is laid down in article 3:305 (a) of the Dutch Civil Code (DCC). Aligned with the European Commission's philosophy that any procedure should aim for a fair, equitable, timely and affordable collective redress,[3] only nonprofit organizations are authorized to take part and only declaratory or injunctive relief is available.

15.2.2 *Eligibility Requirements*

Nonprofit organizations can easily fulfil the conditions for becoming a claimant in a Dutch collective action. The court will investigate whether the claimant is a foundation or an association with full legal capacity. Next, it will also study if the articles of association explicitly enable the legal person to initiate collective actions for the collective protection of similarly situated (legal) persons whose interests are infringed.[4]

[3] Commission Recommendation of 11 June 2013 on common principles for injunctive and compensatory collective redress mechanisms in the Member States concerning violations of rights granted under Union Law, OJ L 26 July 2013, nr. 201, 60–65.

[4] Art. 3:305 (a) § 1 DCC. In practice, such collective actions are frequently initiated both by longstanding organizations having a more general purpose, such as the *Consumentenbond* (Dutch Consumers Association) or *Vereniging voor Effectenbezitters* (VEB, Dutch Association for Retail Shareholders), and by special purpose vehicles that have been set up to deal with a specific mass claim. For an overview of the initiating organizations, see infra table 15.1.

The Dutch law requires in article 3:305 (a) § 2 DCC that the claiming entity makes a reasonable attempt to settle the case out-of-court before filing a collective action. Also this requirement can easily be complied with. Article 3:305 (a) § 2 DCC provides that a letter of the claim organization that gives the prospective defendant two weeks to respond will suffice.[5]

To address concerns for potential abuse by claim foundations with merely profit motives, article 3:305 (a) § 2 DCC requires since 2013 also that the interests of the persons on behalf of who the action is set, are sufficiently guaranteed. This provision was not new. In article 7:907 § 3 (e) DCC the court will reject the petition for declaration of the settlement in the WCAM process if the interests of the persons on whose behalf the agreement was concluded are not adequately safeguarded. The introduction of this requirement in article 3:305 (a) DCC in 2013 for class actions provides the court an instrument for a critical judgement of the admissibility of the claim foundation in a collective action. The law remains silent as to how it can be shown that those interests are sufficiently guaranteed and therefore an individual case by case approach is required. This assessment should be based on the benefit of the stakeholders if the claim is assigned, the qualities of the claim foundation and whether 'entrepreneurial lawyering' for personal benefits is prevented.[6]

15.2.3 *Damages in Collective Actions*

The foundation or association can bring to court any legal claim that intends to protect similar interests of other persons.[7] According to Dutch scholars the law requires that interests can be bundled.[8] Any kind of interest of many individuals that a tortfeasor has violated can be protected through this collective claim. The collective action can be initiated for seeking a declaratory judgment holding that a defendant has acted wrongfully, seeking an injunctive relief holding a defendant to perform or abstain from acting, seeking performance of a contractual duty that a defendant has against multiple interested parties, etc.[9]

However, collective claims for monetary compensation were explicitly barred.[10] In 1994, the Dutch legislator was not (yet) prepared to open for such a new system of class actions. It was argued in the parliamentary discussion that questions like the amount of the damages suffered by each particular person, causation and contributory negligence are not appropriate for collective treatment because they involve numerous individualized issues that require unmanageable individualized adjudication.[11] One could not yet see how these individualized matters can be resolved in a collective action. The Dutch supreme court, the Hoge Raad followed this thought

5 *See* art. 3:305 (a) § 2 DCC.

6 B. W. G. van der Velden, "Juridische afwikkeling van massaschade nu (bijna) perfect", *Tijdschrift voor de Ondernemingsrechtpraktijk* 2011, 244.

7 *See* art. 3:305 (a) § 1 DCC.

8 M. J. Kroes, "Soortgelijke belangen, representativiteit en het bemoeizuchtgevaar", *Nederlands Tijdschrift voor Burgerlijk Recht* 2010, 361; M. J. Kroeze, "Collectieve acties en gelijksoortige belangen", *Ondernemingsrecht* 2004, 497.

9 For those and other examples *see* W. van Boom, "Collective Settlements of Mass Claims in the Netherlands," in *Auf dem Weg zu einer europäischen Sammelklage*, M. Casper, A. Janssen, P. Pohlmann and R. Schulze (eds.), Munich, Sellier, 2009, 176.

10 Art. 3:305 (a) §3 DCC. Relief like restitution of undue payments, fulfilment of contractual obligations and injunctive relief may however be claimed.

11 *See Kamerstukken Tweede Kamer*, 1993–1994, 22 486, no. 3 30, (where it is stated that in 1994, the legislator was not willing to tackle the legal issues involved by collective damages claims). A number or arguments were provided to reject collective actions for damages like the difficulties for quantifying the damages and the distribution among the group of persons entitled to compensation. As the extent of the compensation due would differ from person to person, and there would be questions of 'own fault', it would make a collective claim inappropriate.

of reasoning. In the *World Online* case, the Court decided that the individual rights of compensation were too dependent on individual circumstances to allow a claiming entity in a collective action to obtain a declaratory judgment on liability on sustained damages.[12] The court barred the road of having an individual right to compensation for the individual whose interests were at stake.[13]

Notwithstanding the absence of the right to obtain compensatory damages, this type of collective action has been used in a variety of cases since its introduction. Since 1994, more than one hundred collective actions have been initiated.[14] This procedural tool is in particular useful for shareholder actions. As an example, we refer to the shareholders' attempt to seek an injunction to prevent a bank from selling its US branch[15] in an attempt to protect the bank against a hostile takeover bid and, as well, the famous *Vie d'Or* and *Dexia* cases that both resulted in a WCAM collective settlement.[16]

While the collective action cannot be used for compelling the tortfeasor to compensate nor for monetary compensation, a successful action is accommodating as an instrument for obtaining individual compensation in a sequential procedure.[17] When the claim has resulted in a declaratory judgement that the defendant(s) has committed a tort against the persons in whose interest the action was brought, it paves the road for starting up a negotiation round between the incumbent parties, or even a voluntary mass settlement or an individual procedure. However, this road has often been seen as cumbersome for both the defendant(s) and the injured individuals. Issues as proving damage and causation and the uncertain benefits and significant costs of this second round of proceedings for compensation have refrained many parties for starting up another action. Also the claiming entities that started a collective action did the action in their own name, and consequently only the association or foundation and the tortfeasor(s) are bound by the judgment and not the individuals whose interests are at stake but were not directly part of this action.[18] The interested individuals can also dissociate from the outcome of the collective action. One of the reasons the WCAM has been introduced is to mitigate this shortcoming.

15.3 THE 2005 DUTCH COLLECTIVE SETTLEMENT (WCAM)

15.3.1 *The The Second Collective Redress Mechanism in the Netherlands*

The 1994 collective action lacked some very important tools. Not only was the collective action missing a legal enforcement mechanism for ensuring that the tortfeasor would compensate the

12 Hoge Raad November 27, 2009, *LJN*: BH2162, r.o. 4.8.1.

13 Hoge Raad, November 27, 2009, *LJN*: BH2162, r.o. 4.8.1. *See* in this sense also the *Vie d'Or* case: Hoge Raad, October 13, 2006, *NJ* 2008, 527.

14 *See* I. N. Tzankova, "Funding of Mass Disputes: Lessons from the Netherlands," *George Mason University School of Law Working Paper*, 2012/3, 558.

15 *See* Hoge Raad, July 13, 2007, *LJN*: BA 7970 (where a claiming entity representing shareholders seek an injunction to prevent the Dutch bank, ABN AMRO from selling its US branch).

16 Hof Amsterdam January 25, 2007, *JOR* 2007/71 (*Dexia*), Hof Amsterdam, April 29, 2009, *NJ* 2009, 448, LJN BI2717 (*Vie d'Or*).

17 *See* I. N. Tzankova and C. J. M. van Doorn, "Effectieve en efficiënte afwikkeling van massaschade: terug naar de kern van het collectieve actierecht," in F. M. A. 't Hart, *Collectieve acties in de financiële sector*, Amsterdam, NIBE-SVV, 2009, 114.

18 *See* J. Cornegoor, "Collective acties en belangenorganisaties in hun verschijningsvormen," in F. M. A. 't Hart (red.), *Collectieve acties in de financiële sector*, Amsterdam, NIBE-SVV, 2009, 16–17 and H .J. Snijders, C. J. M. Klaassens, G. J. Meijer, *Nederlands burgerlijk procesrecht*, Deventer, Kluwer, 2007, no. 69.

involved interested parties, also the action was deprived of an instrument to make any kind of settlement binding for the involved individuals. The WCAM overcomes both shortcomings: an amicable settlement agreement for the payment of compensation between an allegedly liable party and a foundation or association in the common interest of the involved individuals is entered into and the Amsterdam Court of Appeals makes the settlement binding upon all persons to whom damage was caused. All persons to whom damage was caused, are given the opportunity to opt out of the settlement.[19] At the moment of writing the Amsterdam Court of Appeal has approved nine collective settlements: *DES I and II*,[20] *Dexia*,[21] *Vie d'Or*,[22] *Shell*,[23] *Vedior*,[24] *Converium*,[25] *DSB*[26] and *Fortis*.[27]

These settlements and the WCAM are seen as an excellent Dutch answer while avoiding the contingency fee-driven US-style class action.[28] While a court-approved collective settlement is certainly not new as both Canada and the United States are familiar with this technique,[29] the Dutch WCAM also provides in a "settlement only class" mechanism. The Netherlands seems to be the only country that has a class settlement, but not a class action.[30] The arguments put forward for introducing a collective action were the traditional ones: to enable people with individually non-recoverable claims to bring actions, to enhance access to justice and, to some extent, prevention.[31] The WCAM, however, has a very different background, which might explain why it had the support of the corporations, the potential future tortfeasors.

The direct cause for the WCAM was the *DES* case. The WCAM was initially drafted for this pharmaceutical product liability case. DES (diethylstilbestrol) was marketed by many manufacturers in the Netherlands between 1947 and 1976. Several thousands of woman were prescribed the DES hormone during their pregnancy, preventing premature birth and miscarriage. However, the product allegedly caused severe health problems to the daughters born from woman that were treated with the hormone. These health problems went from abnormalities of the cervix, to cervical cancer and premature births/miscarriages. In 1986 six daughters of woman that were prescribed the DES hormone launched proceedings against thirteen DES manufacturers. After a process that took several years the Dutch supreme court held all manufacturers liable for the injuries and negotiations for a collective compensation scheme.[32]

19 *See* art. 7: 908 § 2 DCC.

20 Amsterdam Court of Appeals, June 1, 2006, *LJN*: AX6440; Amsterdam Court of Appeals, June 24, 2014, *ECLI:NL:GHAMS:2014:2371*.

21 Amsterdam Court of Appeals, January 25, 2007, *LJN*: AZ7033.

22 Amsterdam Court of Appeals, April 29, 2009, *LJN*: BI2717.

23 Amsterdam Court of Appeals, May 29, 2009, *LJN*: BI5744.

24 Amsterdam Court of Appeals, July 15, 2009, *LJN*: BJ2691.

25 Amsterdam Court of Appeals, January 17, 2012, *LJN*: BV1026.

26 Amsterdam Court of Appeal, May 13, 2014, JOR 2015/9.

27 Amsterdam Court of Appeal, July 13, 2018, ECLI:NL:GHAMS:2018:2422.

28 NRC Handelsblad, April 12, 2007, under the heading "Shell wijst de weg in Europese massaclaims" ("Shell points the way forward in European mass claims").

29 *See*, e.g., in the USA and Canada where class actions may also be certified for settlement purposes only. *See Amchem Prods., Inc.* v. *Windsor*, 521 U.S. 591, 618 (1997) ("Among current applications of Rule 23(b)(3), the 'settlement only' class has become a stock device").

30 *See* I. N. Tzankova, "Enkele overpeinzingen naar aanleiding van de Dexia-(be)schikking," *Ondernemingsrecht* 2007, 88 where the author gives a detailed answer to the question "so you have class action, but no class action. How is it possible? Can you explain this?".

31 *Kamerstukken Tweede Kamer*, 22 486, nr. 3, 2.

32 Hoge Raad, October 29, 1992, *NJ* 1994/535: the Supreme Court decision rendering all manufacturers jointly and severally liable for the injuries.

An important question that was addressed, was that an "alternative causation" could be applied in the litigated period.[33]

The pharmaceutical industry wanted to settle the case but was confronted with the absence of any regulatory framework that could result in an overall one-stop solution and a final settlement. Simultaneously, the victims started to unify – a process that in the pre–social media era was relatively complicated – and within weeks many thousands of interested individuals registered in the DES register center. While the industry and the insurers of the pharmaceutical companies could ultimately reach an agreement in 1999 and establish the DES fund, the industry put forward the condition that any kind of settlement is final for all Dutch victims. Thereto, the legislator was addressed for providing in a mechanism that can provide in a binding decision for all individuals of the voluntary settlement, a "tool of legally forcing victims into settling mass claims with some degree of finality."[34] It resulted in the 2005 Collective Settlement of Mass Damage Act (WCAM) that is at the crossroads of tort law, contract law and civil procedure.[35]

Different from the US approach, the Dutch Parliament did not allow the collective action for damages, a mechanism similar to the US class action for damages, as it took into account the fear of the pharmaceutical industry that it could increase the pressure on the business to settle unmeritorious claims. The Dutch Law reflects the request of the businesses "which wanted a means of settling damages collectively but did not want to be forced to settle if it was not what they ultimately desired."[36]

15.3.2 *The Procedure*

The WCAM offers solutions for a number of the shortcomings of collective actions in the 1994 procedure.

The WCAM can only take off when a settlement agreement has been concluded between one or more foundations or associations representing a group – or "class" – of affected persons to whom damage was allegedly caused and one or more allegedly liable parties. As the starting point of the law is an agreement, but obviously there is a long process of negotiations before the court is petitioned by the parties. At the moment that the court is petitioned, it is common practice, although not legally required, that for the execution of the settlement a specific administrator is established. This administrator will be a feature that is part of the negotiated settlement and it is explicitly referred to in the law.[37]

Since July 1, 2013 there is the possibility to start a pretrial appearance pursuant to article 1018a Dutch Code of Civil Procedure (DCCP) to increase the willingness of the incumbent parties to support a collective settlement agreement. This appearance may be requested by a representative foundation or association that in case of a mass claim stands up for the interests of the injured parties.

33 The rule on alternative causation holds that in the case of multiple activities, where each one of them alone would be sufficient to cause damage, but it remains uncertain as to which one in fact caused it, each activity is regarded as a cause. The victim is allowed to claim the whole amount of damages from any of one of the tortfeasors.

34 W. van Boom, "Collective Settlements of Mass Claims in the Netherlands," in *Auf dem Weg zu einer europäischen Sammelklage*, M. Casper, A. Janssen, P. Pohlmann and R. Schulze (eds.), Munich, Sellier, 2009, 178.

35 W. van Boom, "Collective Settlements of Mass Claims in the Netherlands," in *Auf dem Weg zu einer europäischen Sammelklage*, M. Casper, A. Janssen, P. Pohlmann and R. Schulze (eds.), Munich, Sellier, 2009, 178.

36 I. N. Tzankova, "Funding of Mass Disputes: Lessons from the Netherlands," *George Mason University School of Law Working Paper* 2012/3, 561.

37 If there is an administrator appointed in the settlement, it is the "legal entity" referred to in art. 7:907 (3) (h) DCC and it therefore needs to be party to the settlement for the Amsterdam Court to declare the settlement binding upon the injured individuals.

This legal provision offers the parties to make use of the court for facilitating the establishment of a collective settlement. Contrary to what can be expected, the court that must deal with the pretrial meeting is the court that would have been competent in case the law would not have made the Court of Amsterdam competent for collective settlement. The reasoning behind is that the independence of the Amsterdam Court of Appeal must be safeguarded as it will later have to decide to approve (or not) a settlement which could be the result of the pretrial meeting.[38] It is rather surprising as for regular trials a similar reason does not apply. Only an association which is sufficiently representative of the interests of the injured persons intended to benefit from the settlement and which would have also standing in the framework of article 7:907 DCC can introduce a pretrial WCAM-petition. Further, the alleged tortfeasor can also be the petitioner of such request or it can be introduced jointly by both parties. If the Court is open to such a pretrial meeting, both parties must appear or face the sanction of having to pay the other parties' costs.[39] The hearing can be helpful for the mutual understanding of the claiming entities vis-à-vis a reluctant tortfeasor as well as of the tortfeasor being confronted with a number of allegedly representative associations or foundations.[40]

A joint petition of the alleged tortfeasor and the foundation or association acting in the aligned common interest of the injured individuals to the Amsterdam Court of Appeal that is exclusively competent, initiates the WCAM-process.[41] All the beneficiaries for which the settlement agreement has been concluded are given ordinary notice of the hearing that the court organizes. The court can decide to give notice, making use of another kind instrument.[42] The notice must also be published in one or more newspapers the court decides appropriate. In the notice, the beneficiaries will be informed of the date and time of the court hearing, as well as a short description of the content of the settlement agreement, their right to appear at the hearing and the right to file an objection against the petition. The ordinary letter should also contain information of the right for inspection and the right to copy of the settlement agreement at the chancellery of the court as well as the right to submit a statement of defense. The Amsterdam Court hears all arguments of all interested parties. After the hearing, the court can rule in favor of the settlement and declare the settlement binding upon all persons to whom damage was caused. Second, it can rule that the settlement needs to be amended by the parties. Third, the court can reject the petition of the parties. In the last case, the joint petitioners can appeal in cassation.[43]

It is important to note that the WCAM-procedure does not require that the alleged tortfeasor is to be considered liable in tort either inside or outside any preliminary court procedure.[44] The

38 *See Kamerstukken Tweede Kamer* 2011–2012, 33 126, no. 3, 27.

39 *See Kamerstukken Tweede Kamer* 2011–2012, 33 126, no. 3, 26.

40 *See Kamerstukken Tweede Kamer* 2011–2012, 33 126, no. 3, 14; *see* also, I. N. Tzankova, "Funding of Mass Disputes: Lessons from the Netherlands", *George Mason University School of Law Working Paper* 2012/3, 565 where the author explains that the phenomenon of "competing organizations" "seems to be an obstacle for defendants whose litigation strategies require exploration of out-of-court settlement options with the group of claimants. The phenomenon also makes it difficult for claimants to assess which organization to join"; an example of multiple claiming entities competing for the same "clients" can be found in the *DSB* and *Fortis* cases, where several special purpose vehicles were established.

41 *See* art. 7:907 DCC juncto art. 1013 (3) DCCP for the exclusive competence of the Amsterdam Court of Appeal in WCAM cases.

42 It allows the court to make use of more modern communication tools.

43 The latter meaning that the appeal will only address procedural elements but not assess the facts. Previously, cassation was possible when petitioners jointly decided to do so. The law has changed in 2013 and only allows an appeal in cassation if the request is rejected (see art. 1018 DCCP).

44 As stated before, the collective action and the collective settlement may well be invoked in combination. But, this is not a mandatory requirement under the WCAM. In the same sense, one or more individual suits on liability may sometimes serve as a rainmaker and lead to a collective settlement. The *DES* litigation provides an illustration.

WCAM allows entering the settlement precisely because the alleged tortfeasor does not have to concede liability. Obviously, the parties can enter into an agreement within which the liability of the alleged tortfeasor is acknowledged.[45]

The Amsterdam Court must balance many interests when taking the decision on the petition, and in particular take into account substantive and procedural fairness[46]. When its declaration makes the settlement binding, communication is key. All interested individuals must be informed of the binding settlement and they must be provided with the right to opt out of the settlement.[47] Thereto, an individual notice must be sent to the interested parties, raising in cross-border claims significant costs. A significant number of collective actions involve involved many non-Dutch claimants, like it was and is the case in *Shell*,[48] *Vedior*,[49] *Converium*[50] and *Fortis*.[51]

15.3.3 *Dutch-Style Features*

While some of the features of the WCAM procedure resemble the US class action system, there remain a significant Dutch specific aspects. The next sections give a brief overview of the most important specificities of the Dutch collective action: the eligibility of the claimant, the opt-out system, the content of the settlement contract and the settlement fund.

15.3.3.1 Eligibility

The 1994 Law on Collective Actions contains specific requirement for the organization that starts the action in name and behalf of the allegedly injured parties. Similarly, the eligibility criteria for starting mass claim actions resemble those necessary to file a collective action. The claiming entity must either take the legal form of an association or a foundation with full legal competence and provided the foundation or association has the representation of the interests of the allegedly injured parties in its articles of association.[52] The law also contains the condition that the association or the foundation is sufficiently representative of the interests of the potential beneficiaries of the settlement and is representing a sufficiently large number of potential beneficiaries.[53] The Court of Amsterdam must evaluate these specific requirements. However, there are no other specific qualifications nor does the organization need any kind of license and some academics argued additional requirements should be introduced.[54] Since the law has been enacted, there is an increased interests in establishing associations and foundations by class action lawyers.[55] Many of the existing claims are taking care of by

45 Defendants are not necessarily held liable, since they can settle the case before any civil liability procedure is pending. This is one of the reasons why this collective action in principle does not fully compensate all damages; the principle of proportionality. In practice, most allegedly tortfeasors do not acknowledge liability.

46 For a more detailed discussion, *see* Section 15.3.3.4.

47 *See* Section 15.3.2.2.

48 The *Shell* settlement provides compensation for investors residing in over 100 jurisdictions. Investors residing in the USA were however excluded from the Shell settlement.

49 The *Vedior* settlement included both Dutch and foreign investors including US residents.

50 In the *Converium* settlement less than 2 percent of the 12,000 known class members were domiciled in the Netherlands, over 70 percent in Switzerland, and around 13 percent in the UK.

51 Many shareholders of Fortis were Belgian residents.

52 *See* art. 7:907 (1) DCC.

53 *See* art. 7:907 §§ 3(e)–(f) DCC.

54 I. N. Tzankova and J. Kortmann, "Remedies for Consumers of Financial Services: Collective Redress and Improvement of Class Representation," *European Journal of Consumer Law* 2010, 120. A recent new legislation WAMCA takes into account these considerations from academia (see Section 15.5).

55 *See* Table 15.1 for a number of examples of those special purpose vehicles.

those special purpose vehicles,[56] next to some long-standing organizations having a general purpose, such as the *Consumentenbond* (Dutch Consumers Association) and the *Vereniging voor Effectenbezitters* (Dutch Association for Retail Shareholders, the VEB).

15.3.3.2 Opt Out

The WCAM offers the injured persons to opt out the mass settlement after the Court of Amsterdam has declared the settlement binding. The court's declaration makes the settlement automatically binding for all injured individuals. Therefore, the Court of Amsterdam must specify a timeframe during which the injured beneficiaries are entitled to withdrawn from the settlement and make use of the right to opt out. This timeframe should be at least three months during which the beneficiary has to inform the association or foundation in writing she wants to make use of her opt-out right. The law has also specified that for a person that is unfamiliar with the loss being caused and could not have known this loss, the binding settlement has no consequences than after that person becomes familiarized with the damage. From that moment onwards the beneficiary is entitled to a period of at least six months to make use of the opt-out right. While this structure of the process offers protection for the injured parties, it provides difficulties for the tortfeasor as she is unfamiliar with the number of injured parties that will make use of the opt-out right and it extends the settlement period significantly.

There remains one general exit route: the parties can jointly cancel the settlement for lack of a substantial numbers of participants.[57] This option has not yet been used in any of the settlements.

15.3.3.3 The Settlement Contract

The Dutch legislator was familiar with the many difficulties in the American practice of class actions, which appear after the certification stage resulting in many hearings and conflicts.[58] Thereto, the Dutch legislator stressed the autonomy of the contracting parties in entering in the settlement agreement on the one side. The autonomy of the WCAM results in the absence of the acknowledgment of liability by the alleged tortfeasor, generally resulting in a partial compensation of all damages. On the other side, the WCAM prescribed a number of features that the settlement contract must provide, avoiding many discussions that take place at individual or class level in the USA.[59] The settlement must provide in a description of the group or groups for which the settlement has concluded. The size of the group of the beneficiaries must be estimated as

[56] *See*, e.g., the *Shell* case, where a Dutch foundation, the Shell Reserves Compensation Foundation, was created which had as its sole purpose to represent the interests of all non-US shareholders affected by the misrepresentations by Shell and to distribute settlement amounts to those entitled to it under the terms of the court-approved settlement agreement. Another example is the Stichting Converium Securities Compensation Foundation, which was especially set up to represent shareholders in the *Converium* case who allegedly suffered losses resulting of alleged misstatements and omissions concerning the company's financial condition. In the *Vie d'Or* case, a special purpose vehicle had also to be established to collectively protect the interests of the policy holders; in the DSB case three special purpose vehicles were established (Foundation SSP, Foundation PAL and Foundation SBRD), in the Fortis case two (Foundation Investor Claims Against Fortis and Foundation Fortiseffect).

[57] *See* art. 7:908 (4) DCC.

[58] *See Kamerstukken Tweede Kamer* 2003–2004, 29 414, no. 3, 4–6, and *Kamerstukken Tweede Kamer* 2003–2004, 29 414, no. 7, 15–18.

[59] *See* I. N. Tzankova, *Toegang tot het recht bij massaschade* (diss. Tilburg), Deventer, Kluwer, 2007, 154–155. Tzankova states that comparative studies show that even if a collective action is made possible, such procedures appear so problematic and unpredictable that the majority of them end in a settlement.

accurate as possible. The settlement must provide in the compensation that the beneficiaries will receive, the procedure to determine this compensation and the conditions the beneficiaries must comply with for receiving the compensation. Further, the settlement should indicate the name and residence of the association or foundation that will keep the ledger of the opt outs.

The contracting parties are left with considerable room to negotiate the compensation as well as the most appropriate method of distribution of proceeds to injured individuals and other distribution features (like the method of payment, etc.).[60] The Court of Amsterdam must control the settlement, the conditions and the reasonableness of the compensation.[61]

15.3.3.4 Role of the Amsterdam Court of Appeal

Aforementioned, we highlight the Dutch equilibrium of the freedom of the parties to structure the settlement contract and the basic settlement conditions. The WCAM instructed the Amsterdam Court of Appeal to evaluate the substantive and procedural reasonableness of this settlement.[62] Reasonableness of the settlement refers not only to the amount of compensation but also to the method for distributing the compensation to the beneficiaries.[63] The role of the Court is considered key and the court must reject the settlement in any of the following cases:

- The settlement does not contain the information as sketched in Section 15.3.3.3;
- The amount of the compensation is not considered reasonable taking into account the damage caused, the easiness of the distribution process and the possible causes of the damage;
- If there is insecurity for the payment of the claims;
- If the settlement is insufficiently clear in determining the compensation;
- If the interests of the beneficiaries are inadequately safeguarded;
- If the association or foundation is insufficiently representative of the interests of the persons on whose behalf the settlement was concluded;
- If the association or foundation is insufficiently representing the group of interested persons;
- If the settlement does not offer the option of independent reconcilement of disputes following the execution of the settlement;
- If the entity, which will provide in the compensation following the settlement, is not a party of the agreement.

So far, in all the WCAM-cases ruled to date, the Amsterdam Court of Appeal declared the settlement agreements binding, however sometime after the Court of Amsterdam provided the parties the opportunity to elaborate the contract further. Finally, the Court found the settlements reasonable and considered that most of the claiming entities were adequately representing the beneficiaries. This finding still raises the question how the Court should execute the reasonableness test: should the court perform a marginal test or study in considerable detail all elements of the settlement? This question is debated in the Dutch doctrine.[64]

60 *See* art. 7:907, 2 (e) DCC. Next to the mandatory clauses required by the WCAM, its contractual nature allows parties to include specific clauses in the settlement.

61 *See* next Section 15.3.3.4.

62 *See* art. 7:907 § 3 DCC.

63 *See* art. 7:907 § 3 (b) DCC which provides that the Court must reject the binding declaration if the compensation awarded in the settlement agreement is not reasonable, having regard to, inter alia, the extent of the damage, the ease and speed with which the compensation can be obtained, and the possible causes of the damage.

64 In favour of a marginal test, *see* e.g.: N. Frenk, "Massaschade: de Nederlandse benadering," *AV&S* 2007, 33, 221–222; Against, *see* e.g.: A. R. J. Croiset van Uchelen, "Van corporate litigation naar corporate settlement: Het wetsontwerp

From the aforementioned, it becomes clear that the position of the Amsterdam Court is pivotal for the "credibility of the WCAM as an instrument for the efficient and fair settlement of mass damage claims."[65]

15.3.3.5 The Settlement Fund

The WCAM allows and requests the parties to provide in the distribution scheme which is considered appropriate for the specific case. Current practice shows that parties set aside funds in order to attain finality of the arrangement and appoint a separate administrator with the task of distributing the settlement fund among the injured individuals. The settlement agreement contains a plan of allocation of the proceeds of the settlement. Appointing a separate administrator is not a legal requirement and there are cases which have been taken care of by the liquidator or the alleged tortfeasor.

The WCAM only provides in very limited monitoring duties and the claim administrator has no duties to report to the Court about the most important developments after the settlement has been declared binding. There is no reporting of the number of opt-out declarations, of the processing time, of the number of individual payments (take-up rates), of the average level of the individual compensation payment, of the administration costs, and so on.[66] Consequently, once a collective settlement is approved the case disappears from the courts dockets.[67] Recently it has been argued that the law must be amended providing in a monitoring mechanism of the process of distribution.[68]

Current practice shows that in a number of cases the administrator voluntarily discloses the progress of the distribution process. In the next section, we summarize the most important findings of the execution of the settlement contract.[69]

The creation of a settlement fund has a number of advantages for both the defendant and the injured individuals. The fund ensures that the defendant has certainty and finality in terms of its liability to all injured individuals. Next, for the injured individuals, the fund assures that they will each receive "fair compensation predicated on the totality of harm caused both by the defendant *per se* and to each claimant on an individual basis."[70] The fund serves thus "to ensure that claimants are properly compensated and that defendants are not left in possession of any financial benefit derived from their unjust conduct."[71]

collectieve afwikkeling massaschade," in G. van Solinge et al., *Geschrifte vanwege de Vereniging Corporate Litigation 2003–2004*, Deventer, Kluwer, 2004, 142; J. H. A. Verweij, "Hof Amsterdam gaat verder dan Duisenberg-regeling," *V&O* 2007, 3, 44; L. M. van Bochove, C. J. M. van Doorn, "Eerste WCAM-beschikking: DES-zaak nu ten einde? Annotatie bij Hof Amsterdam 1 juni 2006, NJ 2006, 461," *TvC* 2007, 1, 21–22; C. J. M. van Doorn, "De tweede WCAM-beschikking is een feit: tijd voor een terugblik en een blik vooruit," *Aansprakelijkheid Verzekering & Schade* 2007, 108–110, 114.

65 W. van Boom, "Collective Settlements of Mass Claims in the Netherlands," in *Auf dem Weg zu einer europäischen Sammelklage*, M. Casper, A. Janssen, P. Pohlmann and R. Schulze (eds.), Munich, Sellier, 2009, 182.

66 *See*, for an analysis of the shortcomings in and opportunities regarding the disclosure of information in the distribution phase D. Ozmis and I. N. Tzankova, "De evaluatie van de WCAM: de kernthema's uitgelicht," *Tijdschrift voor Civiele Rechtspleging* 2012/2, 42 and D. Eijsermans, *De uitkering van masaschadeclaims. Professionalisering van het distributieproces bij WCAM-schikkingen*, diss., 2020, unpublished manuscript.

67 *See*, however, the *Vie d'Or* case where the representative entity without being obliged to act so and on its own initiative, gave the Court information about the processing time of the settlement.

68 D. Eijsermans, *De uitkering van masaschadeclaims*, diss., 2020, unpublished manuscript.

69 *See* Section 15.3.4.

70 Civil Justice Council, *Improving access to justice through collective actions, (Developing a More Efficient and Effective Procedure for Collective Actions. Final Report), a series of recommendations to the Lord Chancellor*, November 2008, 167.

71 Civil Justice Council, *Improving access to justice through collective actions, (Developing a More Efficient and Effective Procedure for Collective Actions. Final Report)*, a series of recommendations to the Lord Chancellor, November 2008,

Nevertheless, the parties must overcome a significant number of difficult issues. The distribution process can encounter situations where "there are too many opt-outs, too few claims, too many claims, too little money or too much money."[72] The settlement amount has been established in the settlement agreement whilst it was not possible to accurately approximate the number of beneficiaries who will decide not to participate in the settlement by opting out and/or the number and value of losses eventually claimed by those eligible beneficiaries. For a number of these problems, the WCAM has foreseen several solutions.

First, WCAM addresses the situation of too many claims. If the fund is insufficiently financed for the compensation of all individuals – for instance, because it was not possible to precisely calculate in advance the number of eligible injured individuals – article 7:909 (5) DCC provides for a pro rata reduction of the outstanding claims. This method of redistribution has been considered by a Dutch commentator as "particularly unfair if the number of claims thus reduced is outnumbered by far by the claims that were compensated without reduction."[73] Therefore, this Dutch commentator insists on the importance that both the contracting parties and the Amsterdam Court "assess as accurately as possible the number and identity of those affected by the settlement and the rationing process."[74]

Second, if there are too limited number of claimants – which is similar to the situation when many beneficiaries have opted out – and there remains some settlement sum in the fund,[75] the WCAM allows parties to adopt a clause in the settlement authorizing the administrator to redistribute the remainder of the fund among the known beneficiaries. Further, article 7:910 (2) DCC solves the situation when the fund shows a positive result after all the beneficiaries have been paid. The foundation or association can request the Amsterdam Court of Appeal to order the administrator to pay the remaining sum back to the alleged tortfeasor(s). It must be shown to the Court's satisfaction that all persons entitled to compensation have been paid.[76] Practice shows that parties have taken care of this situation ex ante and include clauses on the use of the unclaimed fund in their settlement agreement.[77] In the *Dexia* settlement, for example, a significant part of the proceeds was left in the settlement fund. In accordance

167 (where it is also explained that the fund "through its primarily compensatory basis serves to assist and complement public regulatory action").

[72] *See* F. E. McGovern, "Distribution of Funds in Class Actions-Claims Administration," 35 *J. Corp. L.* 2009, 123 which is one of the few publications addressing the issues of claim distribution.

[73] W. van Boom, "Collective Settlements of Mass Claims in the Netherlands," in *Auf dem Weg zu einer europäischen Sammelklage*, M. Casper, A. Janssen, P. Pohlmann and R. Schulze (eds.), Munich, Sellier, 2009, at 188.

[74] W. van Boom, "Collective Settlements of Mass Claims in the Netherlands," in *Auf dem Weg zu einer europäischen Sammelklage*, M. Casper, A. Janssen, P. Pohlmann and R. Schulze (eds.), Munich, Sellier, 2009, at 188.

[75] In the *DES* case, for instance, an initial amount of € 38 million was paid into a fund in 2006. Years later, it was reported that there is still an amount € 27 million left in this fund; *See Kamerstukken Tweede Kamer*, 2012–2013, 33 126, no. 9, 3.

[76] *See* art. 7:910 (2) DCC and *Kamerstukken Tweede Kamer*, 2012–2013, 33126, nr. 9 (tweede nota van wijziging).

[77] *See* e.g.: art. 3.3. of the settlement agreement in the *Vedior* case: "The remaining Settlement Amount will be applied in the following order:

(a) to pay the costs incurred by SUVS to the extent that the Amount of Financing is insufficient or likely to be insufficient to cover those costs;
(b) to pay to Randstad an amount of EUR 1.41. for each Share of which it has been established that it was sold on 30 November 2007 between 9 a.m. and 11:34 a.m. by an Entitled Party that has indicated that it does not want to be bound to this Agreement;
(c) and to pay a one-off contribution to VEB of which the maximum amount will be EUR 100,000 to be spent on investors' education;
(d) to make a refund to Randstad."

with what was provided in the settlement agreement,[78] "a new foundation was established promoting research and education with regard to collective actions and the resolution of mass disputes."[79]

Finally, there remains the situation where there are unknown beneficiaries – for instance, individuals who cannot be identified or found. Article 7:907 (6) DCC provides that the settlement may provide that the right to compensation shall lapse if the beneficiary has failed to claim compensation within one year starting from the moment the individual became aware – or could have been aware – of her right. It might nevertheless be that the injured individuals are not aware of their right to demand payment of compensation, meaning that the distribution of the fund can be blocked. For the latter situation the WCAM does not offer any kind of solution.[80]

Article 7:909 (1) DCC provides that the administrator is entitled to take *binding decisions* on the right to compensation under the settlement. According to this article, the nature of such a binding decision is that, in principle, recourse to judicial review of the decision is not possible, unless the decision has not been taken with reasonableness and fairness. In the latter case, the court can substitute the decision. The consequence of this legal provision is that an individual who has not opted out of the settlement and is then denied compensation will encounter a hard time to receive any kind of compensation. It has been argued that this may be contrary to the fundamental right to access to justice.[81]

15.3.4 *Experiences with the Dutch* WCAM

At the end of 2019, nine collective settlement agreements (in eight cases) have been successfully declared binding since the WCAM entered into force in July 2005. In the next sections, we briefly discuss the various WCAM cases. Its shows that the WCAM was initially inspired by events causing mass personal injury. However, in practice the WCAM is mainly applied in securities litigation (financial mass claims) and is increasingly used to resolve mass claims disputes internationally.

15.3.4.1 The *DES* Case

The direct cause for the WCAM was the *DES* case. The WCAM was initially drafted for this pharmaceutical product liability case. As already discussed, DES (diethylstilbestrol) was prescribed on a large scale to pregnant women to prevent premature birth and miscarriage. However, the product allegedly caused physical damage to the daughters born from these pregnancies. The collective settlement agreement of EUR 38 million between the DES Centre, which is the organization representing the interests of the DES daughters and the

78 The settlement agreement stated that the remaining proceeds should be used to fund subsequent collective actions.

79 I. N. Tzankova, "Funding of Mass Disputes: Lessons from the Netherlands," *George Mason University School of Law Working Paper* 2012/3, 579.

80 D. M. J. van Abeelen, "Het sluitstuk van de afwikkeling van massaschade: waar blijven de Himalayabeklimmers?," *Tijdschrift voor vennootschaps- en rechtspersonenrecht* 2012, 95–104.

81 A. R. J. Croiset van Uchelen, "Van corporate litigation naar corporate settlement: Het wetsontwerp collectieve afwikkeling massaschade," in G. van Solinge et al., *Geschrifte vanwege de Vereniging Corporate Litigation 2003–2004*, Deventer, Kluwer, 2004, at 138–139. Moreover, as the settlement is a *contract* it is also subject to the rules on unfair general contract terms. Therefore, the question even arises as to whether a settlement clause referring to an independent claims resolution committee is an unfair contract term. According to art. 6:236 (n) Civil Code general contract terms in consumer contracts shall not restrict access to the competent civil court (unless by means of an *arbitration* clause).

pharmaceutical companies that had marketed DES, was declared binding by the Amsterdam Court on June 1, 2006.[82]

A second collective settlement has been reached in this *DES* case. Following the conclusion of the DES I agreement in 2005 with regard to the personal injury of the "DES-daughters," the parties involved also agreed on compensation for the children of these DES-daughters who were born prematurely and also suffered damage, due to the earlier exposure of their mothers. A remainder of the earlier *DES* settlement – an amount of EUR 20.5 million – would be paid as compensation. The Amsterdam Court of Appeal declared this second collective settlement (*DES II*) declared binding on June 24, 2014.[83]

15.3.4.2 The *Dexia* Case

The second case settled under WCAM was the *Dexia* case.[84] Customers of Dexia suffered financial damage allegedly caused by a failure of Dexia to warn sufficiently about the risks of certain equity lease agreements. Several collective actions were started after which, a collective settlement of EUR 1 billion was successfully concluded in 2004 between the Dexia Bank on the one hand and the Lease Loss Foundation, the Eegalease Foundation, the Dutch Consumers' Association and the Dutch Equity Holders' Association on the other hand, grouping together approximately 300,000 claims. The Amsterdam Court was requested to declare this agreement to be binding, which the court granted on January 25, 2007.

15.3.4.3 The *Vie D'Or* Case

In the third WCAM case 11,000 policy holders of the life insurance company Vie D'Or claimed to have suffered financial damage due to the company's bankruptcy. They held the auditors of the company and the public supervisory authorities liable. A collective settlement of EUR 45 million was declared binding by the Amsterdam Court on April 29, 2009.[85]

15.3.4.4 The *Shell* Case

In 2009, a collective settlement brought before the Amsterdam Court of Appeal concerned financial damages of shareholders allegedly caused by Shell's failure to properly disclose information about its oil and gas reserves. The restatement of the oil and gas reserves led to a considerable fall in the price of Shell shares. Shell concluded a collective settlement of $ 448 million with the Dutch Equity Holders' Association, the Shell Reserves Compensation Foundation and two Dutch pension funds which were considered not representative by the Amsterdam Court for the benefit of 500,000 non-US worldwide Shell shareholders. On May 29, 2009, the Court declared this settlement agreement binding.[86]

This was the first time that a collective settlement was declared binding on a majority of injured parties that were residing outside the Netherlands. The collective settlement had a direct influence in many other jurisdictions. The agreement provided compensation for all non-US shareholders who purchased their shares on any stock exchange other than the New York Stock

[82] Court of Appeal Amsterdam, June 1, 2006, *NJ* 2006, 461 (*DES I*).
[83] Court of Appeal Amsterdam, June 24, 2014, ECLI:NL:GHAMS:2014:2371 (*DES II*).
[84] Court of Appeal Amsterdam, January 25, 2007, *NJ* 2007, 427 (*Dexia*).
[85] Court of Appeal Amsterdam, April 29, 2009, *NJ* 2009, 448 (*Vie d'Or*).
[86] Court of Appeal Amsterdam, May 29, 2009, *NJ* 2009, 506 (*Shell*).

Exchange. One of the defending Shell entities was vested in the Netherlands (and listed on the Amsterdam Stock Exchange) and the other Shell entity was British.

15.3.4.5 The *Vedior* Case

In 2009, the Court of Amsterdam declared another, smaller WCAM case binding. This case related to financial damages allegedly suffered by shareholders of Vedior because of a failure of timely disclosing information about an acquisition. Insider trading taking place before the public announcement of the transaction would have caused a decrease of the share price. On July 15, 2009, the Court declared the Vedior settlement agreement of EUR 4.25 million binding.[87] This collective settlement between Vedior and the VEB (the Dutch Shareholders Association) concerned 2,000 claims, including claims of foreign parties, amongst others, a number of US residents.

15.3.4.6 The *Converium* Case

The sixth WCAM case concerned financial loss allegedly suffered by the shareholders as a consequence of misleading statements by reinsurance company Converium. The shares in Converium were listed on the Swiss stock market and its American Depositary Shares on the New York Stock Exchange (NYSE). Securities fraud class actions were filed in a number American courts, which cases were later consolidated before the District Court for the Southern District of New York. This resulted in two settlements for the US shareholders. However, the District Court declared itself incompetent to hear the claims of investors who bought shares in Converium on the Swiss stock market or another securities market outside the USA and who were resident or based outside the USA at the time of the purchase.[88]

For the non-US shareholders, Dutch representative organizations reached another two collective settlements with Converium. These worldwide settlements of USD 58.4 million involved 12,000 shareholders. Only 3 percent of these shareholders holds the Dutch nationality. A petition was filed to the Amsterdam Court of Appeal. On November 12, 2010 the Court of Appeal passed an interim order on its jurisdiction with the provisional finding that the Court of Appeal was competent to hear the request that this "international collective settlement" be declared binding. The Court of Appeal considered in particular relevant the fact that neither Europe nor the United States provides another forum for non-US shareholders to have their settlement declared binding. In its final decision of January 17, 2012, the Court of Appeal upheld its preliminary jurisdiction ruling. With this decision, the Court of Appeal made the WCAM an attractive venue for settling international mass claims on a class-wide basis.

15.3.4.7 The *DSB* Case

The first bankruptcy case that resulted in a WCAM settlement was the bankruptcy of the Dutch DSB Bank in 2009. Consumers suffered financial damages caused by an alleged breach of DSB's duty of care. DSB allegedly sold misleading and nontransparent financial products to its customers. The collective settlement between DSB and three special interest groups was

[87] Court of Appeal Amsterdam, July 15, 2009, *JOR* 2009, 325 (*Vedior*).

[88] The US Supreme Court had limited the extraterritoriality of the federal securities legislation earlier in the case *Morrison versus National Australia Bank*, 561 US, (2010).

declared binding on November 4, 2014.[89] The settlement binds approximately 500,000 potential claimants and the compensation amount is between EUR 300 to EUR 500 million.

15.3.4.8 The *Ageas/Fortis* Case

The most recent WCAM case relates to financial damages of shareholders allegedly caused by miscommunication and mismanagement by Fortis, a Dutch-Belgian banking and insurance group. These shareholders claims led to the largest collective settlement ever in Europe of USD 1.5 billion/EUR 1.3 billion. On July 13, 2018, the Amsterdam Court of Appeal approved the settlement agreement between Ageas, the successor company of Fortis, and several organizations representing the shareholders.[90]

15.3.4.9 Summary

Table 15.1 summarizes the nine binding settlements and identifies the alleged tortfeasors, the representing foundations and associations, the estimated injured parties, the funding of the settlement, the administrator and the kind of wrongdoing resulting in the collective settlement. The summary shows that it is not uncommon that several foundations and associations separately stand up for the rights of allegedly injured persons. Further, the Court of Amsterdam diligently takes care of the representative nature of the foundation or association and regularly rejects an association or foundation as the representative of the allegedly injured parties. Further, the total number of potential beneficiaries is significantly larger than the number of injured parties that filed a claim after the settlement has been declared binding. Unfortunately, due to the limited disclosure requirements, there is no information on how often claimants make use of the opt-out right and start separate procedures. Finally, the Dutch collective settlement is predominantly used for financial products. After the first *DES* case for which the WCAM was originally established, all cases are related to losses for financial products or shares.

15.4 THE LIMITS AND SHORTCOMINGS OF THE WCAM

15.4.1 *The Weaknesses and Limitations of the* WCAM

The general conclusion seems to be, in view of the above, that the Dutch legislator has developed an interesting system with the WCAM to settle mass damage claims in an efficient and effective manner. At the same time, this collective redress mechanism complies with the procedural principle that individual claimants must have a good opportunity to present their case before a court. In addition, practice shows that the role of the Amsterdam Court of Appeal in the WCAM procedure meets the needs of the parties involved to (be able to) achieve collective settlements relatively expeditiously.[91] There are, however, several issues that are currently underexposed or not even possible, but that can have a major impact on successful collective settlement of mass damage claims: (1) funding of claim organizations, (2) non-individually recoverable claims, (3) the voluntary basis of the WCAM mechanism and (4) the limited

89 Amsterdam Court of Appeal, November 4, 2014, ECLI:GHAMS:2014:4560 (*DSB Bank*).

90 Amsterdam Court of Appeal, July 13, 2018, ECLI:NL:GHAMS:2018:2422 (*Ageas*).

91 In the *DES* case and the *Dexia* case, for example, the collective settlements were approved and declared generally binding within 1 to 1.5 years after the petition was filed.

TABLE 15.1 *Overview of the WCAM cases*

Case	Alleged tortfeasor	Representing foundation/association	Number of allegedly injured persons	Amount of settlement	Type of damage/ liability	Administrator
DES I (2006)	pharmaceutical companies and their insurers	Foundation DES Centrum	approx. 200.000 persons have been prescribed treatment; around 6000 claims awarded	€ 38 million (including DES II)	Pharmaceutical product liability	Foundation Beheer Deelnemersgelden
DES II (2014)	pharmaceutical companies and their insurers	Foundation DES Centrum	see DES I (uncertain number of claims); around 50 claims awarded	€ 27.5 million	Pharmaceutical product liability	Foundation Beheer Deelnemersgelden
Dexia (2007)	Dexia	Foundation Leaseverlies, Foundation Eegalease, VEB (Dutch association of securities holders), Consumentenbond (association)	395.000 injured persons, 300,000 interested persons (713,5400 contracts of Dexia with 395,000 clients) (95000 others of which 68,000 amicale settlements)	€ 1 billion	Violation of the duty of care regarding financial products	Dexia
Vie d'Or (2009)	Dutch National Bank, external auditor, actuary and Association of Insurers	Foundation Vie d' Or	11.000 injured persons	€ 45 million	Violation of the duty of care regarding financial products	Foundation Compensation Fund policy holders Vie d'Or

Shell (2009)	Shell Petroleum N.V., The Shell Transport and Trading Company Limited	Shell Reserves Compensation Foundation, VEB (association), Foundation Pension fund ABP (declined), Foundation Pension fund Zorg en Welzijn (declined)	500.000 injured persons	\$ 448 million	Loss of share value	Shell Reserves Compensation Foundation
Vedior (2009)	Vedior (and its successor Randstad)	VEB (association)	2.000 injured persons	€ 4.25 million	Loss of share value	Foundation Uitvoering Vedior Schikking
Converium (2012)	Converium (and its successor Zürich Financial Services Ltd)	VEB (association)	12.000 injured persons	\$ 58.4 million	Loss of share value	Converium Securities Compensation Foundation
DSB (2014)	Liquidators DSB and insurance companies	Foundation SSP, Foundation PAL and Foundation SBRD	345.000 injured persons (56,000 claims)	€ 500 million (max.)	Violation of the duty of care regarding financial products	Liquidators DSB
Fortis (2018)	Fortis (and its successor Ageas)	VEB (association) (declined), Foundation Investor Claims Against Fortis, Foundation Fortiseffect, DRS Belgium	119.000 injured persons	€ 1,308 billion	Loss of share value	Foundation Forsettlemen

information requirements in the distribution process. These issues are discussed in the next sections.

15.4.2 *Funding*

Claim organizations represent the interests of the injured parties in proceedings based on the WCAM (or on article 3:305a BW). However, injured persons do not need to become "members" of a representative organization in order to benefit from the collective settlement negotiated by such an organization. Consequently, a free-rider problem may occur. Injured persons have an incentive to choose a passive strategy and avoid the cost of joining a representative organization seeking a collective settlement. They might as well free ride on the activities of other (active) interested persons who have joined the claim organization and benefit passively. The result may be that financing of mass damage cases becomes a problem.[92] Free rider behavior and rational apathy created by the WCAM may, to some extent, result in claim organizations having insufficient resources to enforce the rights of individual injured parties ("access to justice") and to protect their interests against defendants, who are often wealthy and sophisticated repeat players. In addition, the claim organization derives its representativeness from its group of participants.[93] The more active participants, the more incentives on (allegedly) liable parties to enter into negotiations with the claim organization and the more the claim organization can test its actions (including a negotiated settlement proposal) for support. If too many (large) injured persons see no added value of being an active participant, the WCAM procedure will not function adequately.[94]

A solution for the free rider problem is third-party funding. Commercial parties from abroad regularly finance mass claims in the Netherlands.[95] They provide funding to the organizations that represent the interests of the injured parties.[96] The funding covers the claim organization's legal fees and expenses incurred in the WCAM procedure. If a collective settlement is reached, the costs of the claim organization will be reimbursed from the settlement fund and all beneficiaries (claimants) share in these costs. The collective settlement (fund) usually contains a separate provision for the costs of the claim organization and the compensation for claims organizations often plays an important role in the settlement negotiations.[97] Third-party funders often operate on a no cure no pay basis.[98] Contingency fee arrangements between lawyers and

[92] See I. N. Tzankova, "Hoe globaliseringsproof is het Nederlandse collectieve actierecht?," in: M.G. Faure et al., *Collectieve acties (Preadviezen Nederlandse Vereniging voor Burgerlijk Recht)*, Zutphen, Uitgeverij Paris, 2015, 87, W. M. Schonewille, "De financiering van collectieve acties," *Ondernemingsrecht* 2010/137, par. 2.3, and J. M. K. P. Cornegoor, "Collectieve acties en belangenorganisaties in hun verschijningsvormen," in: F. M. A. 't Hart (ed.), *Collectieve acties in de financiële sector*, Amsterdam, NIBE-SVV, 2009, 25.

[93] M. L. A. Rijndorp and I. Tillema, "Over meelifters, gelukzoekers en rechters die problemen maken als partijen die niet hebben," *Maandblad voor Ondernemingsrecht* 2018–5/6, 123.

[94] I. N. Tzankova, "Wetsvoorstel collectieve schadevergoedingsactie: een oplossing voor welk probleem ook alweer?," *Tijdschrift voor Vergoeding Personenschade* 2017–4, 116.

[95] I. Tillema, "Commerciële actoren in massaschadezaken: pionieren tussen toegang tot het recht en claimcultuur," *Ars Aequi* 2019, 508, I. Tillema, "Commerciële motieven in privaatrechtelijke collectieve acties: olie op het vuur van de claimcultuur?," *Ars Aequi* 2016, 337–346, E. Bauw and T. van der Linden, "Claimorganisaties tussen wildgroei en regulering", *Tijdschrift voor de Ondernemingsrechtpraktijk* 2016–7 and I. N. Tzankova, "Funding of Mass Disputes: Lessons from the Netherlands," *Journal of Law, Economics & Policy* 2012–8, 549–592.

[96] I. N. Tzankova, "Financiering en kosten van massaclaims: Legal realism. Ofwel wat we kunnen leren van de Engelsen (en van andere common law landen)?," in: N. E. van den Berg, R. R. A. Henkemans and A. S. H. Timmer (eds.), *Massaclaims, class actions op z'n Nederlands*, Nijmegen, Ars Aequi Libri, 2007, 171 ff. and I. N. Tzankova, *Toegang tot het recht bij massaschade*, Deventer, Kluwer, 2007, 163–166.

[97] I. Tillema, "Naar een goed geolied mechanisme voor de collectieve afwikkeling van massaschade," *Aansprakelijkheid, Verzekering & Schade* 2019–2, 8–9.

[98] W. H. van Boom and J. L. Luiten, "Procesfinanciering door derden," *RM Themis* 2015–5, 188–199.

their clients are prohibited in the Netherlands.[99] However, third-party funders are not subject to the regulations for lawyers. Such parties, that are regularly linked to private equity, hedge funds and reinsurance companies, consider claim financing as a great opportunity to diversify their investment portfolio. Not only foreign parties but also Dutch parties, for example the Dutch Association of Stockholders (VEB), act as financiers of mass damage claims in the Netherlands.

The involvement of large (foreign) financiers is in principle a positive development. Third-party funding increases effective access to justice for injured parties in mass damage cases, which also was the main reason for introduction of the WCAM procedure. This is also socially desirable as it increases the preventive effect of liability law and gives incentives to companies and their directors to act carefully.[100] These third-party funders will also use their expertise and ensure that their investments do not end up in the wrong claim organizations, and thus have a certain control function. There is, however, a constant fear in the Netherlands that this type of funding leads to so-called "sweetheart settlements" that are not optimal for the injured persons. The financial interests of the claim organization(s) and the third-party funders may deviate from, or conflict with, the interests of the represented injured persons.[101]Therefore, concern has been expressed that third-party funders will focus more (and too much) on generating profit through a WCAM procedure than on obtaining optimal compensation for injured persons.[102] The use of third-party funding is unrestricted and the existing mechanisms in the WCAM does not seem sufficient to prevent possible negligent behavior or even abuse. A first safeguard in the WCAM is the right of interested parties to file objections to the settlement agreement.[103] Another measure is the requirement that the representative claiming entity must operate on a not-for-profit basis. This nonprofit organizations model has advantages. However, under Dutch company law, a claim entity (foundation or association) can be easily established, there is a high degree of freedom and flexibility with regard to the structure of the organization, and there are few transparency obligations.[104] This opens the risk that a claim entity will be set up and used in such a way that private benefits are generated. The representativeness requirement in article 7:907 of the Dutch Civil Code does not provide a sufficient counterweight.

The lack of transparency with regard to, among other things, the financing of and decision-making within the claim organization and the information symmetry between the representative entity and the injured persons requires further measures.[105] On the other hand, the requirements

[99] The Code of Conduct of the Dutch Bar Association (Rule 25, Clause 3) provides that "a lawyer may not agree to charge a proportionate part of the value of the result obtained."

[100] I. N. Tzankova, "Funding of Mass Disputes: Lessons from the Netherlands," *Journal of Law, Economics & Policy* 2012–8, 549–591.

[101] I. N. Tzankova and J. Kortmann, "Remedies for Consumers of Financial Services: Collective Redress and Improvement of Class Representation," *European Journal of Consumer Law* 2010–1, 123.

[102] E. Bauw and T. van der Linden, "Claimorganisaties tussen wildgroei en regulering", *Tijdschrift voor de Ondernemingsrechtpraktijk* 2016–7, 11, I. Tillema, "Commerciele motieven in privaatrechtelijke collectieve acties: olie op het vuur van de claimcultuur?", *Ars Aequi* 2016, 337; M. L. M. N. Heltzel, "Checks and balances bij belangenorganisaties," *Tijdschrift voor Financieel Recht* 2012–5, 153, C. J. M. van Doorn, "De afwikkeling van massaschade; een optimale belangenbehartiging door belangenorganisaties?," *Weekblad voor Privaatrecht, Notariaat en Registratie*, 2013, 6982, § 5.1 and J. M. K. P. Cornegoor, "Collectieve acties en belangenorganisaties in hun verschijningsvormen," in: F. 't Hart (ed.), *Collectieve acties in de financiële sector*, Amsterdam, NIBE-SVV, 2009, 26.

[103] Art. 1014 DCCP.

[104] M. Koelemeijer, "Kenmerken van de stichting", in: J. J. A. Hamers, C. A. Schwarz and D. F. M. M. Zaman, *Handboek Stichting en Vereniging*, Zutphen, Uitgeverij Paris, 2015, 61–66 and D. F. Lunsingh Scheurleer, "Groepsacties en rechtspersoonlijkheid: waarborg of lege huls?," in G van Solinge et al. (ed.), *Relativering van rechtspersoonlijkheid*, Deventer, Kluwer, 2012.

[105] I. Tzankova and J. Kortmann, "Remedies for Consumers of Financial Services: Collective Redress and Improvement of Class Representation," *European Journal of Consumer Law* 2010–1, 124.

for claim organizations and/or third-party funders should not be increased too much. It must be prevented that third-party funders no longer invest in collective redress and that it becomes too difficult for claim organizations to present a mass damage claim.

15.4.3 *Inappropriate Mechanism for Small and/or Scattered Losses*

Although the WCAM applies to all types of mass damage claims, practice demonstrates that the possibility of a collective settlement is of particular importance for the resolution of mass securities claims.[106] The WCAM was initially inspired by personal injury mass tort cases. However, the existing collective settlements are mainly related to security disputes and/or involve financial products and services. Only in the *DES* case were personal injury claims involved.

The nine WCAM cases have in common that the individual injured parties suffered extensive damage. The question arises whether the WCAM can also be an appropriate mechanism for mass damage claims that are not or difficult to recover on the individual level.[107] A collective settlement based on the WCAM requires the cooperation of the allegedly liable party. Until recently, there were no strong alternatives to the settlement negotiations and it was not possible for the injured parties to put serious pressure on a defendant who was unwilling to settle.[108] The alternative to a negotiated collective settlement was to advance with all individual claims in individual court cases.[109] In case of trifling damages, however, there is no underlying threat that the individual injured persons will start legal proceedings and therefore the tortfeasor cannot be incentivized to negotiate. Political pressure and reputational risks could nevertheless bring a tortfeasor to the negotiating table. But, to date, these factors have not been sufficient to reach a collective settlement in the context of widespread scattered losses. The new Act on Redress of Mass Damages in a Collective Action (more about this in Section 15.5) will give injured persons with "non-individually recoverable" mass claims a (more) serious alternative to a negotiated collective agreement.[110] (The threat of) the option to commence a collective action for damages may stimulate the tortfeasor to seriously consider a collective settlement in case of very small damages.[111]

15.4.4 *Voluntary Basis of the WCAM*

Although there have been no successful WCAM cases involving widespread scattered losses, this does not mean at the same time that individual claims of a substantial size will be a sufficient incentive to bring tortfeasors to the negotiation table. The nine WCAM-cases demonstrate that

106 T. Arons and W. H. Van Boom, "Beyond Tulips and Cheese: Exporting Mass Securities Claim Settlements from The Netherlands," *European Business Law Review* 2010, 866.

107 See detailed about small and widespread damages: I. N. Tzankova, *Strooischade. Een verkennend onderzoek naar een nieuw rechtsfenomeen*, Den Haag, SDU, 2005.

108 C. Pavillon, "Leent het materiële privaatrecht zich voor de afwikkeling van massaschade?," *Rechtsgeleerd Magazijn THEMIS* 2019–4, 163.

109 *See* W. H. van Boom, "WCA → WCAM → WAMCA," *Tijdschrift voor Consumentenrecht* 2019–4, 154 and I. Tillema, "Commerciële actoren in massaschadezaken: pionieren tussen toegang tot het recht en claimcultuur," *Ars Aequi* 2019, 507.

110 Kamerstukken II, 2010–2011, 27 879, nr. 34. See also T. Hartlief, "Massaschade en de regelende rechter," *Nederlands Juristenblad* 2017–40, 2935.

111 *See* W. H. van Boom, "WCA → WCAM → WAMCA", *Tijdschrift voor Consumentenrecht* 2019–4, 155 and M. G. Faure and L. T. Visscher, "Een rechtseconomische visie op collectieve actie," in: *Collectieve Acties (Preadviezen Nederlandse Vereniging voor Burgerlijk Recht)*, Zutphen, Uitgeverij Paris, 2015, 7 ff, 46 ff and 64.

the willingness to settle may depend on the tortfeasors' assessment of other factors, such as the number of claims, the likelihood of success of such claims, the legal cost and the (total) expected losses involved.[112] In addition, it seems that other factors, such as political pressure and reputational risks, may also be relevant. If the assessment of the allegedly liable party of these factors is rather negative, the voluntary nature of a WCAM settlement stands in the way of a collective agreement. Here too, the WAMCA may increase the willingness to settle.[113] In any case, the injured persons have the option of another dispute resolution system if an allegedly liable party does not voluntarily negotiate a collective settlement. This may prevent tortfeasor's behavior that negatively impacts social welfare.

15.4.5 *The Distribution Process As Black Box*

Finally, we point to a lack of information (obligations) regarding the execution of WCAM settlements.[114] Strangely enough, little to nothing is known about the distribution process that starts after the Amsterdam Court of Appeal has declared the collective settlement generally binding. Information about this distribution process and what is going on during this process is often not public and there is no reporting obligation for the party that distributes the settlement amounts. Recent developments concerning the execution of the *Fortis/Ageas* settlement show that there are many challenges in the payment of claims.[115] The processing of the Fortis claims has been considerably delayed since many more investors (injured persons) applied than expected. These investors are also likely to receive a lower amount of compensation than was assumed at the conclusion of the settlement.

With the introduction of reporting obligations on the distribution of the settlement amount, relevant data would become public, such as the number of opt-out declarations, the processing time, the number of individual payments (the take-up rate), the average level of the individual compensation, processing of any remaining amount, the supervision of the distribution process, the administration costs, the unknown claims, etc. This could promote the transparency of the WCAM mechanism and provide more insight into the various activities in the distribution process and how these activities are handled. These statistics on collective settlements could also improve the quality of WCAM settlements.[116] If this information (for example the average processing time and the average claiming rate) becomes public, injured persons can make a better-informed choice as to whether or not they want to make use of the opt-out option. Furthermore, it is recommended that the Amsterdam Court of Appeal be given a supervisory role in the distribution phase.[117] The

112 R. M. Hermans, "De oorzaken van het niet tot stand komen van collectieve schikkingen in massaschadezaken," in: M. Holtzer, A. F. J. A. Leijten and D. J. Oranje (eds.), *Geschriften vanwege de Vereniging Corporate Litigation 2014–2015*, Deventer, Wolters Kluwer, 2015, 361–387.

113 M. G. Faure and L. T. Visscher, "Een rechtseconomische visie op collectieve actie," in: *Collectieve Acties (Preadviezen Nederlandse Vereniging voor Burgerlijk Recht)*, Zutphen, Uitgevrij Paris, 2015, 46 ff. Cfr. C. J. M. Klaassen, "De Wet afwikkeling massaschade in collectieve actie: eindelijk werkelijkheid, nu nog gaan werken . . .," *Tijdschrift voor Civiele Rechtspleging* 2019–4, 145.

114 See detailed about this D. M. J. Eijsermans-Van Abeelen, *De uitkering van massaschadclaims. Professionalisering van het distributieproces bij WCAM-schikkingen*, dissertation 2020.

115 S. Jonker & E. van Rein, "Uitkering Fortis-claim vertraagd door massale aanvraag," *Het Financieele Dagblad*, June 18, 2019.

116 Cf. C. J. M. van Doorn and M. de Bruijn, "Collectieve afwikkeling van massaschade: verdeelsleutels voor vergoedingen aan individuele benadeelden," *Nederlands Juristenblad* 2013, 2405.

117 D. M. J. Eijsermans-Van Abeelen, *De uitkering van massaschadclaims. Professionalisering van het distributieproces bij WCAM-schikkingen*, dissertation 2020, chapter 6.

Court of Appeal already assesses the distribution plan, as part of the settlement agreement, but currently has no further involvement in the distribution process.

15.5 RECENT DEVELOPMENT: MASS DAMAGES IN A COLLECTIVE ACTION

15.5.1 *Enabling Collective Claims for Damages*

The Dutch legal system offers collective redress mechanism (collective action and WCAM) that are attractive for resolving (international) mass claims disputes, and that can even be used for events that mainly take place in foreign jurisdictions as illustrated in the *Converium* case. Although Dutch courts are renowned for their thorough assessment of international jurisdiction, which safeguards defendants, they also generally apply a flexible approach regarding their international jurisdiction when a Dutch defendant is involved. The Netherlands therefore occupies an exceptional position in Europe and can provide an attractive alternative for resolving mass damage disputes that cannot be resolved in the United States (like F-cubed claims), or anywhere else in the world.[118] Until recently, a key limitation in Dutch law was that it only allowed collective actions for the purposes of seeking a declaratory judgment.

However, the WAMCA removed this latter limitation. This act entered into force as of January 1, 2020 and broadens the scope of article 3:305a DCC.[119] It introduces US-style class actions in the Netherlands. The WAMCA enables claim organizations to seek monetary damages on behalf of and in favor of a group of injured persons (legal or natural) in a collective action. The competent court can then determine in one collective proceeding whether a defendant is liable to a group of injured persons and what is an appropriate compensation. The WAMCA also contains other provisions that affect the collective action (procedure) and the parties involved.

Transitional law applies, which means that the act will apply to collective actions brought on or after January 1, 2010 for events that took place on or after November 15, 2016.[120] The former regime applies to collective actions that relate to events that took place before November 15, 2016.[121]

15.5.2 *More Checks and Balances*

15.5.2.1 Introduction

The WAMCA contains some important provisions. Those provisions introduce new checks and balances in order to prevent abuse of the Dutch collective action system. Before, a claim vehicle

118 Cf. J. Kortmann and M. Bredenoord-Spoek, "The Netherlands: 'a hotspot for class actions'?," *Global Competition Litigation Review* 2011–1, 13–17 and B. Krans, "The Dutch Class Action (Financial Settlement) Act in international context: the Shell case and the Converium case," *Civil Justice Quarterly* 2012–2, 141–150.

119 The Act on Redress of Mass Damages in a Collective Action (WAMCA) was adopted on March 19, 2019 and published on April 1, 2019 (Dutch Official Gazette 2019, 130). The Decree of December 4, 2019 (Dutch Official Gazette 2019, 447) stipulates that this act enters into force as of January 1, 2020.

120 November 15, 2016 is the date the draft legislative proposal was submitted to the Dutch parliament.

121 This deviates from the main rule of transition law. See C. J. M. Klaassen, "De Wet afwikkeling massaschade in collectieve actie: eindelijk werkelijkheid, nu nog gaan werken…," *Tijdschrift voor Civiele Rechtspleging* 2019–4, 152, C. J. M Klaassen, "Enkele opmerkingen bij het wetsvoorstel afwikkeling massaschade in collectieve actie vanuit procesrechtelijke optiek," in: T. M. C. Arons et al. (eds.), *Collectief schadeverhaal*, Deventer, Wolters Kluwer, 2018, 60–62 and J. S. Kortmann, "Wetsvoorstel afwikkeling massaschade in collectieve actie (34608)," *Nederlands Juristenblad* 2018–8, 558–560.

could be set up relatively easily in the Netherlands and could be used for personal gain instead of looking after the interests of injured parties, although up till now and fortunately the number of cases of improper use seems to be limited in practice. Injured parties, especially consumers, are hardly informed to whom they entrust their interests. They have no means to distinguish the quality of the various claims organizations and neither are they informed of the internal governance of the association or foundation.

The new requirements regarding the governance, representativeness, transparency and funding of representative organizations have been tightened up, and consequently both the risk of misuse of a claim organization as well as a further proliferation of claim organizations is lower. This is also in the interest of allegedly tortfeasors, because they are less likely to be confronted with frivolous and unmeritorious claims. They are also more likely to sit (down) at the negotiation table – or be involved in a collective action – with serious, experienced and knowledgeable parties acting for a sufficient large group of injured persons, which facilitates the resolution of the dispute and/or the course of the collective action.

These provisions are not entirely new act as they have, to some extent, already been laid down in a code of conduct for claim organizations: the Claim Code 2019 – the successor to the Claim Code 2011.[122] Certainly in the early years, the claim code did not seem to have sufficient effect mainly because it is not mandatory to follow the guidelines of the Claim Code. Although in recent years the courts have certainly given increasing weight to this soft law instrument, a much wider scope of application is being established with a mandatory set of rules.

We support the new enhanced threshold requirements for claim organizations. However, some requirements – in particular the requirement with regard to the financial resources of the representative organization and the control over the claim[123] – may have been set too high and may deter the start of collective actions, especially in case of trifling damages.[124]

15.5.2.2 Admissibility Requirements

The WAMCA contains stricter requirements for the admissibility of interest organizations (article 3:305a DCC). From 2020 onwards, a representative organization is only admissible in its claim if:

(1) the claim organization meets all the standing requirements;
(2) the claim organization has sufficiently demonstrated that bringing a collective action is more efficient and effective than bringing individual claims;
(3) the defectiveness of the collective action was not summarily apparent when the writ was submitted.

122 The Claim Code was drafted by an ad hoc Commission and presented in 2011 to the Dutch Ministry of Justice. See B. J. de Jong, "Een claimcode voor stichtingen die collectieve acties initiëren," *Ondernemingsrecht* 2010, 239–242 and J. H. Lemstra and R. W. Okhuijsen, "Consultatiedocument 'Zelfregulering claimstichtingen'," *Financieel Recht* 2010–6, 158–163.

123 Article 3:305 paragraph 2 sub c DCC.

124 W. H. van Boom, "WCA → WCAM → WAMCA," *Tijdschrift voor Consumentenrecht* 2019–4, 159. See also I. N. Tzankova, "Wetsvoorstel collectieve schadevergoedingsactie: een oplossing voor welk probleem ook alweer?," *Tijdschrift voor vergoeding Personenschade* 2017–4, T. M. C. Arons and G. F. E. Koster, "Op weg naar collectief schadeverhaal in het Nederlands recht. Perikelen bij het Wetsvoorstel collectieve schadevergoedingsactie," *Ondernemingsrecht* 2017–10/11, E. Bauw and S. Voet, "Van stok achter de deur tot keurslijf? Een eerste verkenning van het wetsvoorstel tot invoering van een collectieve schadevergoedingsactie," *Nederlands Juristenblad* 2017, 244 ff and M. de Vries, "Voortmodderen met massaclaims," *Advocatenblad* 2017–8, 50–53.

A claim organization only has standing in a class action if it meets certain criteria. As already indicated above, the claiming entity must be not-for-profit (a Dutch foundation or association with full legal capacity) and there must be no financial interest involved of the organization itself in the collective action, such as a financial benefit. Furthermore, the claim organization must be sufficiently representative and demonstrate that it brings a collective action for a sufficient number of persons (given all allegedly injured persons) and claims.

In addition, the WAMCA introduces new governance requirements for the representative claim organization and more precisely the law requires:

- a supervisory board that supervises the management (board) of the organization or a one-tier board structure (a board consisting of executive directors and non-executive/supervisory directors);
- an appropriate and effective mechanism for the participation of the represented persons in the decision-making process of the interest organization;
- sufficient financial resources to bear the costs of the collective action, in which case the representative organization must have sufficient control over the legal action;[125]
- sufficient experience and expertise to bring the collective action;
- a publicly accessible internet page on which specified information is available, such as the objectives and working methods of the organization, the management structure of the organization, annual reports, management reports, remuneration of directors (and members of the supervisory board), contributions claimed from represented persons (if any), and insight into how the possible financial contribution person is calculated.

After the submission of the writ/statement of claim by the representative organization, the court reviews whether the claim organization meets the abovementioned criteria (article 1018c, DCCP). If not, the case will be dismissed. The court also reviews whether the case is fit to be dealt with through collective action proceedings. The questions of law and fact to be answered (regarding the various claims of the various persons involved) must be sufficiently similar. In addition, the group of represented persons must be sufficiently large. If the claim is (also) brought to obtain collective compensation, the persons represented individually and jointly must have a sufficiently large financial interest. If the court considers the number of persons represented to be too low or the financial interest to be too limited, the court can decide that the collective action is not admissible and that individual proceedings are more appropriate in this case.

The court will also briefly examine whether the collective claim has merits when the writ is served.

15.5.2.3 Sufficiently Close Connection with the Netherlands

In addition, a claim organization can only bring a collective action if the legal claim has a sufficiently close relationship with the Netherlands (article 3:305a, paragraph 3 sub b, DCC). This connection will generally be deemed to be present if one of the following three conditions is met:

[125] This requirement could have a negative impact on the possibilities for financing mass damage claims (by third parties).

(1) the majority of the persons on behalf of whom the class action is initiated are Dutch residents,
(2) the defendant resides in the Netherlands and additional circumstances suggest a sufficient relationship with the Netherlands, or
(3) the event(s) on which the class action is based occurred in the Netherlands.

With this more strict scope rule the WAMCA aims to prevent foreign claimants initiating disputes in Dutch proceedings that are not or are only vaguely related to the Netherlands. If the claim is not sufficiently related, the claim organization has no standing. However, these requirements are not entirely new and surprising, since Dutch courts already had taken these requirements in consideration. This scope rule is also, in our opinion, very understandable. Defendants domiciled in the Netherlands (Dutch companies) could otherwise be exposed to collective (damages) actions for the benefit of injured persons anywhere in the world.[126] This would disadvantage Dutch companies compared to their foreign counterparts domiciled elsewhere and would adversely affect the business climate.[127] The Dutch Law on collective actions would also deviate too much internationally. At the same time, this scope rule still leads fairly quickly to the jurisdiction of the Dutch court in a collective action if there is a connection with the Netherlands. This makes the Dutch collective action still an attractive collective redress mechanism for handling of international mass damage claims.

15.5.3 *More Efficient and Effective Proceedings*

The WAMCA also contains provisions that intend to promote the efficiency and effectiveness of the proceedings (Article 1018c et seq., DCCP). The first procedural requirement is that the claim organization has to register its collective action in the central register with the *Raad voor de Rechtspraak* (the Judiciary Council).[128] The registration must be done within two (business) days after submission of the writ and a brief summary of the statement of claim must be provided. After the registration of the collective action, a three-month waiting period will start, during which other (competing) representative organizations can file alternative collective actions related to the same event(s).[129] In case several representative organizations initiate a collective action during this period, these collective actions will be consolidated.[130]

If the court grants standing to multiple representative organizations, it will appoint the most suitable organization as an "Exclusive Representative."[131] This lead claimant organization will

[126] C. J. M. Klaassen, "De Wet afwikkeling massaschade in collectieve actie: eindelijk werkelijkheid, nu nog gaan werken..." *Tijdschrift voor Civiele Rechtspleging* 2019–4, 148.

[127] J. S. Kortmann, "Wetsvoorstel afwikkeling massaschade in collectieve actie (34608)," *Nederlands Juristenblad* 2018–8, 556–557 and U. B. Verboom, "Wetsvoorstel afwikkeling van massaschade in collectieve actie vanuit het perspectief van een tegenstander", in: *Geschriften vanwege de Vereniging Corporate Litigation* 2017–2018, Deventer, Wolters Kluwer 2018, 441–442.

[128] The Decree of 4 December 2019 (Dutch Official Gazette 2019, 446) appoints the Raad voor de Rechtspraak (the Judiciary Council) as the authority that keeps a central register for collective actions. The register is publicly accessible through the website www.rechtspraak.nl. Public court rulings and bankruptcies are also published here.

[129] Alternative collective actions must be commenced before the same court as the first collective action.

[130] In case of collective settlements (WCAM) only the Amsterdam Court of Appeal has jurisdiction but collective actions (for damages) can be brought before any district court in the Netherlands. The normal rules on local jurisdiction of the court apply. This will usually mean that the district court in the place of the defendant's domicile has jurisdiction. See C. J. M. Klaassen, "De Wet afwikkeling massaschade in collectieve actie: eindelijk werkelijkheid, nu nog gaan werken...," *Tijdschrift voor Civiele Rechtspleging* 2019–4, 150 and J. S. Kortmann, "Wetsvoorstel afwikkeling massaschade in collectieve actie (34608)," *Nederlands Juristenblad* 2018–8, 557. This may be different in specific consumer cases. The court first seized is, in principle, competent.

[131] This lead representative organization needs to be able to demonstrate expertise, have a sufficient number of claimants supporting them, and be sufficiently capitalized.

litigate the collective action on behalf of all interested persons.[132] The court also decides on the scope of action and determines for which persons the exclusive representative will act. Persons who are considered not to be part of this so-called "precisely specified group" ("class") are excluded from the collective action. The other claim organizations remain party to the proceedings to prevent them from losing their claim rights.[133]

An opt-out system applies to injured parties residing in the Netherlands. After the appointment of the lead representative organization and the decision of the court on the scope of the action and the definition of the "class," notice will be given to all members of the "class." These notified persons can withdraw from collective representation by the lead organization by making use of the possibility to opt out.[134] The court determines the opt-out period, which is at least one month.[135] The persons who opt out cannot start another collective action with regard to the same event. Individual proceedings between these persons and the alleged liable party (or parties) are possible.[136] However, these proceedings may be postponed at the request of one of the parties (and resumed after at least one year).

Following the appointment of an exclusive representative, the court will set a period for parties to try to negotiate a settlement agreement. If a collective settlement agreement is reached, more or less the same rules as in the WCAM apply.[137] If the court approves the settlement, it will declare this collective settlement binding and there will be a second opportunity for class members to opt out. The opt-out period here is also at least one month.

In case no agreement is reached or the court rejects the settlement, the proceedings will continue. The court may dismiss the claim or award damages to "the precisely specified group." In the context of determining the amount of collective damages the court may adopt a compensation scheme with different amounts of damages per category of injured parties. If the court opts for damage scheduling, it can order the parties to submit a proposal, on the basis of which the court can determine compensation.[138] The court will have to ensure that the amount of compensation awarded is reasonable and that the interests of the persons the collective action aims to protect are sufficiently safeguarded.

The final judgment of the court in the collective action proceeding is binding on all persons who have not made use of the opt-out option(s) and whose interests therefore have been represented in the collective action.[139] An appeal can be lodged against the judgment (and possibly after that cassation; an appeal to the Supreme Court).

An opt-in system applies to injured persons living abroad. Foreign persons have the option of voluntarily joining the Dutch collective action and be represented in the proceeding (by the

[132] The court has the authority to appoint more than one exclusive representative if there is reason to do so due the nature of the collective action or the plaintiffs, or the interests of the persons.

[133] This could lead to discussions regarding the process strategy. See I. Tillema, "Exclusieve en concurrende belangenbehartigers: balanceren op glad ijs?," *Ars Aequi* 2018–6, 476–481, M. F. J. N. van Osch, "De rol van de rechter in het wetsvoorstel massaschade in collectieve actie," *Tijdschrift voor Praktisch Procederen* 2018–4, 110–111 and A. Hammerstein, "Collectief procederen vanuit de visie van een rechter," *Maandblad voor Ondernemingsrecht* 2016–4, 82.

[134] After opting out of the collective action, the injured person cannot benefit from any future collective action regarding the same event(s).

[135] If too many persons opt out, the court may decide that the claim cannot be brought.

[136] W. H. van Boom, "WCA → WCAM → WAMCA," *Tijdschrift voor Consumentenrecht* 2019–4, 155.

[137] C. J. M. Klaassen, "De Wet afwikkeling massaschade in collectieve actie: eindelijk werkelijkheid, nu nog gaan werken…," *Tijdschrift voor Civiele Rechtspleging* 2019–4, 150.

[138] C. Pavillon, "Leent het materiële privaatrecht zich voor de afwikkeling van massaschade?," *Rechtsgeleerd Magazijn THEMIS* 2019–4, 165–167.

[139] W. H. van Boom, "WCA → WCAM → WAMCA," *Tijdschrift voor Consumentenrecht* 2019–4, 155 and E. Bauw and S. Voet, "Van stok achter de deur tot keurslijf? Een eerste verkenning van het wetsvoorstel tot invoering van een collectieve schadevergoedingsactie," *Nederlands Juristenblad* 2017–4, 244.

exclusive representative).[140] The Dutch legislator thus aligns with the Belgian regulation of the "*rechtsvordering tot collectief herstel*" (the "legal action for collective recovery") of 2014 and the English Consumer Rights Act 2015.[141]

However, the court has the authority, by way of exception, to order that the opt-out system also applies to non-Dutch class members that are relatively easily to identify (a precisely specified group of persons). It remains to be seen how the Dutch courts will use this option, given that the legislator has chosen for an opt-in system for foreign people to be in line with the European draft directive on representative actions for the protection of the collective interests of consumers.[142] The expectation is that the Dutch courts will apply that exception only in cases in which the vast majority of the represented injured persons resides in the Netherlands.

15.5.4 *Litigation Costs and Lawyers' Fees*

Under Dutch law, the general rule is that the loser pays all litigation costs (article 237, DCCP). However, this is a (very) limited "loser pays" rule. Usually the winning party can only reimburse the court registry fee, the costs of witnesses and experts and a limited fixed amount for lawyers' fees. The WAMCA (article 1018 l, DCCP) allows the court to deviate in a collective action from this general rule and to award a much higher amount for costs to the winning party.

If the court finds that the defectiveness of the claim is summarily apparent, it can order the claim organization to pay a higher amount of lawyers' fees, up to a maximum of five times the fixed amount, unless fairness dictates otherwise.[143] If the proceedings result in a collective claim settlement ordered by the court, the court may order, if so requested, that the defendant pays reasonable and proportionate court costs and other costs that the claim organization has incurred, unless fairness dictates otherwise. Conversely, the (lead) representative organization may be liable for any (reasonable) adverse costs if it loses the action.

15.5.5 *WCAM (Collective Settlement) versus WAMCA (Damages in a Collective Action)*

Both through the WCAM route and the collective action route (WAMCA), it is possible to reach a collective settlement with regard to mass damages and to have this settlement declared universally binding by the court. The big difference is that the WCAM relates to a *voluntary* out-of-court collective settlement, that can subsequently be declared generally binding by the Amsterdam Court of Appeal (if certain requirements are met and the settlement is approved). In order to (be able to) reach a collective settlement, the allegedly liable party must be willing to settle.

The WAMCA takes collective redress to a "next level" and introduces a procedure for *compulsory* mass damages compensation. If a collective action is commenced and the claim is (also) brought to obtain collective compensation, there is an obligation for the parties to try to

140 W. H. van Boom, "WCA → WCAM → WAMCA", *Tijdschrift voor Consumentenrecht* 2019–4, 159 and C. J. M. Klaassen, "De Wet afwikkeling massaschade in collectieve actie: eindelijk werkelijkheid, nu nog gaan werken. . ., " *Tijdschrift voor Civiele Rechtspleging* 2019–4, 149.

141 J. S. Kortmann, "Wetsvoorstel afwikkeling massaschade in collectieve actie (34608)," *Nederlands Juristenblad* 2018–8, 558.

142 Proposal for a Directive of the European Parliament and of the Council on representative actions for the protection of the collective interests of consumers, and repealing Directive 2009/22/EC, 11 April 2018, COM (2018) 184 final. At the moment of writing the proposal is being discussed by the European Council.

143 W. H. van Boom, "WCA → WCAM → WAMCA," *Tijdschrift voor Consumentenrecht* 2019–4, 159–160.

negotiate a collective settlement agreement after an exclusive representative has been appointed. If no settlement is reached, the court will determine the collective compensation.

Does this mean that the WCAM route will no longer be used? According to our estimation, the WCAM route may be used less but will still remain important. Allegedly liable parties, claim organizations and injured persons will regularly want to (try to) avoid a collective action lawsuit because of the risks, costs, duration and negative reputation effects thereof. The possibility of a collective action with possibly a claim for collective compensation will certainly be a big stick to stimulate the alleged wrongdoer to seriously consider and approach an out-of-court settlement.[144] The collective action is "the best alternative to a negotiated agreement."[145]

Until recently, a collective action could only be used to seek a declaratory judgement that the alleged wrongdoer is liable. In practice, the collective action was regularly a stepping stone towards a collective settlement. The judgment of the court in the collective action was employed as a means of pressure to reach an out-of-court settlement regarding collective compensation of damages. However, it has not been necessary in all WCAM cases to first have established liability in a collective action. There have been nine court approved settlements based on the WCAM to date and only four collective settlements have been preceded by a collective action under Article 3:305 of the Dutch Civil Code. We therefore are of the opinion that after the entry into force of the WAMCA, there will still be voluntarily negotiated collective settlements that will subsequently be declared generally binding through a WCAM procedure.

These out-of-court settlement negotiations will now even more take place against the backdrop of a judicial decision. The parties involved know that if no settlement is reached, the court will (possibly) be asked in a collective action to award damages. In that case they will also sit at the negotiation table (mandatory) and/or they will probably have to make proposals for a damage schedule (which the parties will also prepare during serious settlement negotiations).[146] It is therefore attractive for them to (first) try to resolve the dispute themselves.

This will certainly play a role in low-value scattered damage cases (many injured parties who each suffered minor damage). At the moment, legal proceedings (collective action or individual proceedings) are often not really a "best alternative to a negotiated agreement." With the possibility of collective compensation, the shadow of the law will be more present during (voluntary) out-of-court settlement negotiations.

Although we expect that the WCAM will continue to play an important role, we believe that the upcoming possibility of claiming collective compensation in a collective action will generally boost (international) mass claims in the Netherlands and that the number of collective actions will increase. The draft European directive on representative actions for the protection of the collective interests of consumers will probably also contribute to a growing interest in collective actions. This proposed directive will – if adopted – probably not substantially change Dutch legislation, but will at the same time provide a national legal basis for collective redress in Europe.

144 M. G. Faure and L. T. Visscher, "Een rechtseconomische visie op collectieve actie," in: *Collectieve Acties (Preadviezen Nederlandse Vereniging voor Burgerlijk Recht)*, Zutphen, Uitgevrij Paris, 2015, 46 ff.

145 R. Fisher and W. Ury, *Getting to YES: Negotiating Agreement Without Giving In*, New York, Penguin Books, 2011, chapter 6. See also W. H. van Boom, "WCA → WCAM → WAMCA", *Tijdschrift voor Consumentenrecht* 2019–4, 155.

146 *See* C. Pavillon, "Leent het materiële privaatrecht zich voor de afwikkeling van massaschade?," *Rechtsgeleerd Magazijn THEMIS* 2019–4, 173 and J. de Bie Leuveling Tjeenk and J. B. van de Velden, "Collectief schadeverhaal vanuit de optiek van de aangesproken partij," in: T. M. C. Arons et al. (eds.), *Collectief schadeverhaal*, Deventer, Wolters Kluwer, 2018, 95.

15.6 CONCLUSION

Since 1994, the Netherlands developed different collective action procedures. In particular, the WCAM was the start of a number of high profile cases with considerable attention in the press. Those cases illustrate both the effectiveness of the collective settlement for helping to recover the damages of persons whose interests are infringed on the one side and a number of shortcomings in the process of the settlement contract and the distribution of the fund. With the WAMCA a procedure for compulsory mass damages compensation is introduced which can be helpful in resolving a number of the problems of the voluntary collective settlement of 2005.

Not all problems can be resolved and recent analysis shows that in particular for the mass actions outside financial products or shares, the consequences of WAMCA remain modest. The government is already working on a new legal framework for addressing the earthquakes in the province of Groningen, which are a result of gas extraction and causing massive mining damage to many Dutch residents.[147]

[147] T. Hartlief, "Massaschaderecht in ontwikkeling," *Tijdschrift voor Privaatrecht* 2019, 451–476.

PART IV

Asia and the South Pacific

16

The Emergence and Reform of the New Zealand Class Action

*Nikki Chamberlain and Susan Watson**

16.1 INTRODUCTION

The civil procedure framework that governs the management of class action litigation in New Zealand is ripe for reform. Although parties can commence class-wide litigation in New Zealand in a number of ways, the most commonly utilised, and non-issue specific way, is by the 'representative rule' derived from the United Kingdom and contained in High Court Rule 4.24 (HCR 4.24). Unfortunately, HCR 4.24 contains no further procedural guidance on the management of class-wide litigation than merely providing that a representative plaintiff can sue on behalf of persons with the same interest in the subject matter of a proceeding, either by consent of all plaintiffs represented, or by leave of the court. This failure to provide procedural guidance has put the New Zealand judiciary in a problematic position. On the one hand, there are clear advantages in allowing class-wide litigation. On the other hand, the judiciary has to rely on a rule that was never intended to bear the burden of managing class actions. Courts are in essence forced to allow opt-in class actions while simultaneously developing class action procedure through their inherent powers on a case by case basis. Consequentially, all class action stakeholders are disadvantaged. The management of class actions is uneconomic, inefficient and uncertain.

The issue is becoming acute. Empirical evidence suggests that class-wide actions have increased over the last four decades. Litigation funders, which are currently unregulated, have now entered the New Zealand market. The need for reform is pressing. When considering reform options, New Zealand can look to overseas models. The United States, Canada and Australia have all adopted comprehensive statutory based class action civil procedure rules. The United Kingdom has gone down a different path by instead allowing for Group Litigation Orders. As New Zealand sits at a crossroad, what is the best option for reform?

This chapter addresses both the development of the opt-in class action in New Zealand from its emergence in the 'representative rule' and the problems stakeholders face under the current civil procedure regime. It also evaluates the options for reform measured against the purposes and aims of class action litigation. Specifically, Section 16.2 contains an overview of the legal system and the civil procedure framework in New Zealand. Section 16.3 addresses the history of the 'representative rule' which is used to allow opt-in class actions. Section 16.4 discusses the current state of opt-in class actions in New Zealand, including empirical data on the types of class

* We would like to thank our research assistant, Eilish Buckley, for her research and referencing assistance.

actions, the plaintiff class sizes and financing mechanisms utilised. Section 16.5 concludes with an overview of the issues likely to arise in the future and sets out reform recommendations.

16.2 NEW ZEALAND'S LEGAL SYSTEM

16.2.1 *Overview of New Zealand's Legal System*

Māori are the indigenous people of New Zealand. The legal tradition of Māori can be classified as being part of the chthonic tradition. Prior to colonisation, Māori used their own oral-based law called 'Tikanga Māori' to regulate society. However, in 1840, New Zealand was colonised by the English, who brought with them their English common law traditions. As a result, the English common law tradition became the dominant legal system in New Zealand. In this respect, New Zealand has 'maintained the fundamentals of its common law ancestry: an unwritten constitution; a hierarchy of courts; the application of the doctrine of precedent; and the adversarial litigation system'.[1]

In contemporary New Zealand, there are two primary sources of law: statutes enacted by the New Zealand Parliament, and case law from the New Zealand judiciary in accordance with the common law tradition. The judiciary follows the doctrine of precedent meaning that judicial decisions from superior courts bind those courts below them in the hierarchy. The court structure allows for appeals from judgments of lower courts to higher courts.

The New Zealand courts can be categorised into two broad categories: courts with general jurisdiction, and courts with specialist or specific jurisdiction. The courts with general jurisdiction can hear an array of legal issues and comprise of the District Court[2], the High Court, the Court of Appeal and the Supreme Court. The court of first instance for civil matter claims under NZ$350,000 is the District Court, and for claims over NZ$350,000 is the High Court.[3] The High Court can grant leave to hear civil claims under NZ$350,000.[4] Appeals from the High Court are heard in the Court of Appeal. The Supreme Court, established in 2003, is the final appeal court from the Court of Appeal.[5] The courts with specialist or specific jurisdiction are the Employment Court, the Environment Court and the Māori Land Court. The District Court also has specialist divisions, being the Family Court, the Youth Court and the Disputes Tribunal.

All courts have jurisdiction conferred by statute. However, the High Court is the only court in New Zealand, which has inherent common law jurisdiction meaning it has non-statutory substantive jurisdiction to do whatever 'may be necessary to administer the laws of New Zealand'.[6] As stated on the New Zealand Courts' website, 'the existence of such inherent jurisdiction means there is never a vacuum in obtaining vindication of right according to law'.[7] Civil trials in the High Court are normally heard and determined on judge-alone basis.[8] However, jury trials are common in defamation proceedings.[9]

1 Stephen Penk and Mary-Rose Russell, *New Zealand Law: Foundations and Method* 19 (2nd ed., 2018).
2 The District Court has limits on the types of legal claims it can hear. For example, the District Court cannot hear claims relating to trusts, wills or interests in land: District Court Act 2016, s. 78.
3 District Court Act 2016, s. 74.
4 District Court Act 2016, s. 89.
5 Prior to 2003, the Privy Council in England heard final appeals.
6 Senior Courts Act 2016, s. 12.
7 Courts of New Zealand, 'The Courts – High Court – History and Role' www.courtsofnz.govt.nz.
8 Senior Courts Act 2016, s. 15.
9 See Senior Courts Act s. 16, also Defamation Act 1992, s. 36.

Class-wide actions are most commonly initiated in the High Court although class-wide actions have also been initiated in the Employment Court, the Environment Court and the Māori Land Court. No class-wide actions have been filed in the District Court, despite there being provision to do so under District Court Rule 4.24. As it is the Court most commonly utilised, the focus of this chapter is on class-wide actions commenced in the High Court. We will also briefly address class-wide actions filed in the Employment Court.

16.2.2 *New Zealand's Civil Procedure Framework*

The rules of civil procedure that govern the management of litigation derive mostly from statute. For example, the Senior Courts Act 2016,[10] adopts the High Court Rules that were previously contained in Schedule 2 of the Judicature Act 1908. The High Court Rules 2016 contains the rules of civil procedure for the High Court. Each court has its own set of Rules.[11] In the event those rules are insufficient to manage litigation, the relevant rules also confer inherent power on the courts to regulate their own procedure.

New Zealand does not have specific statutory-based procedural rules to manage class-wide litigation. Plaintiffs most commonly rely upon HCR 4.24 – Rule 4.24 of the High Court Rules – to commence class-wide actions. HCR 4.24 states in its entirety:

> **4.24 Persons having same interest**
> One or more persons may sue or be sued on behalf of, or for the benefit of, all persons with the same interest in the subject matter of a proceeding–
>
> (a) with the consent of the other persons who have the same interest; or
> (b) as directed by the court on an application made by a party or intending party to the proceeding.

In practice, the High Court uses HCR 4.24 to allow class-wide actions and then relies on its inherent powers to develop civil procedure for managing those actions on a case-by-case basis.

Traditionally, actions commenced under HCR 4.24 were referred to as 'representative actions' although this terminology is not expressly used in HCR 4.24 itself, which is entitled 'Persons having same interest'. More recently, various stakeholders have used the term 'class action' to describe proceedings under HCR 4.24. Certain members of the judiciary have suggested that the terms 'representative action' and 'class action' can be used interchangeably.[12] Others use the word 'class' to describe plaintiffs in proceedings filed under HCR 4.24[13] or refer to litigation

10 Previously the Judicature Act 1908.

11 For example, there are the District Court Rules 2014, the Court of Appeal (Civil) Rules 2005, the Supreme Court Rules 2004, the Family Court Rules 2002 and the Employment Court Regulations 2000.

12 In the Supreme Court case, *Paki* v. *Attorney-General* [2014] NZSC 118, [2015] 1 NZLR 67, [216], William Young J stated: 'The appellants are running what in essence is a class action'.

13 Instances of this include *Southern Response Earthquake Services Ltd* v. *Southern Response Unresolved Claims Group* [2017] NZCA 489, [2018] 2 NZLR 312, [34], [59], [78], [81], [91], [119]–[121] and [139]; *Cridge* v. *Studorp Ltd* [2016] NZHC 2451, (2016) 23 PRNZ 281, [7], [26], [31]–[33], [81] and [86]; *Strathboss Kiwifruit Ltd* v. *Attorney-General* [2015] NZHC 1596, (2015) 23 PRNZ 69, [3], [4], [10], [51] and [58]; *LDC Finance (in rec and in liq)* v. *Miller* [2013] NZHC 2993, [8], [17]–[26], [41], [50] and [52]–[54]; *Blue Star Taxis (Christchurch) Society Ltd* v. *Gold Band Taxis (Christchurch) Society Ltd* HC Christchurch CIV-2009-409-2921, 19 November 2010, [22], [62], [67], [70], [71] and [74]; *Houghton* v. *Saunders* (2008) 19 PRNZ 173 (HC), [23], [100], [101], [115], [141], [143], [144], [147], [162], [219] and [223]; *Saunders* v. *Houghton* [2012] NZCA 545, [2013] 2 NZLR 652, [15], [31], [32], [36], [58], [65], [74], [94] and [95]; *Credit Suisse Private Equity LLC* v. *Houghton* [2014] NZSC 37, [2014] 1 NZLR 514, [10], [57], [71], [77], [79], [81], [127], [162], [163], [165]–[167], [170] and [171]; *Saxmere Co Ltd* v. *Wool Board Disestablishment Co Ltd* HC Wellington CIV-2003-485-2724, 6 December 2005, [126], [139], [180], [182]–[185], [195] and [197]; *Stickland* v. *Drummond* HC Auckland CIV-2006-404-3078, 13 May 2008, [10], [14], [15], [17], [18], [31], [38], [39], [42], [44], [46], [51], [53], [54]–

commenced under HCR 4.24 as being a 'class action'.[14] Some law firms and commentators also refer to litigation commenced under HCR 4.24 as 'class actions'.[15]

The putative title of the New Zealand Law Commission's review of the area, due for completion in 2021, is 'Review of Class Actions and Litigation Funding'. The putative title suggests that class actions are part of the New Zealand legal landscape. Different terms are, however, used to describe proceedings under HCR 4.24, creating potential confusion as to whether New Zealand does in fact allow class actions.[16]

A representative action as originally intended by HCR 4.24 is different from how the judiciary currently uses HCR 4.24 to allow opt-in class actions in substance. As a result, the historical terminology used to describe an action under HCR 4.24, being a representative action, is largely irrelevant. The modern use and extended application by the judiciary of HCR 4.24 means that an opt-in class action is already permitted in substance if not explicitly in New Zealand.

As Justin Scott Emerson explains:

> It has often been mistakenly asserted that class actions and representative actions are different devices. New Zealand and England have rules known as 'representative', whereas the United States rules are known as 'class'. Although different in form, these rules are of identical nature, and are merely specialised developments of the more general class action concept. Thus although the New Zealand rule has special characteristics which appear to distinguish it from the American 'class' description, essentially it remains a class action device.[17]

A brief history of the rule follows.

16.3 THE HISTORICAL DEVELOPMENT OF CLASS ACTIONS IN NEW ZEALAND[18]

16.3.1 *Origin of HCR 4.24 and the Representative Action*

HCR 4.24 has its origins in the Court of Chancery in England where it developed in the late seventeenth and early eighteenth centuries as a mechanism to allow persons with the same interests in a proceeding to be represented by a single party.[19] In 1873, the United Kingdom introduced Rule 10 in the Schedule of the Supreme Court of Judicature Act 1873[20] which allowed representative proceedings in the High Court of the United Kingdom.[21]

[57], [63], [64] and [69]; and *Registered Securities Ltd (in liq)* v. *Westpac Banking Corp* (2000) 14 PRNZ 348 (HC), [10], [18] and [28].

14 In 2003, Miller J was the first member of the High Court to refer to an action under HCR 4.24 as a 'class action' in the case of *Saxmere Co Ltd* v. *Wool Board Disestablishment Co Ltd* HC Wellington CIV-2003-485-2724, 6 December 2005, [184].

15 Nicholas Wood and Edward Scorgie, 'Dispute resolution in New Zealand – trends and insights' (17 June 2015) Chapman Tripp www.chapmantripp.com; Liesle Theron 'Class actions in New Zealand' (2016) Global Class Actions Exchange http://globalclassactions.stanford.edu; and 'When does the clock stop for class action plaintiffs? – CoverToCover Issue 8' (4 June 2016) Minter Ellison Rudd Watts www.minterellison.co.nz.

16 Asher J in *Commerce Commission* v. *Carter Holt Harvey Ltd* [2008] 1 NZLR 387 (HC), [39] stated (without providing his reasoning) that r. 78 of the then High Court Rules 'governs representative actions, and if it applied, would exclude class actions'.

17 Justin Scott Emerson, *Class Actions*, 19 VUWLR 183, 184 (1989).

18 The majority of Section 16.3 has been taken from Nikki Chamberlain, *Class Actions in New Zealand: An Empirical Study*, 24 NZBLQ 132 (2018).

19 See generally *Western Canadian Shopping Centres Inc* v. *Dutton* 2001 SCC 46, [2001] 2 SCR 534, [19].

20 Supreme Court of Judicature Act 1873 (UK) 36 & 37 Vict c. 66.

21 Tom Hallett-Hook, Class Actions under New Zealand's Representative Rule: Ingenious Solution or Inadequate to the Task? (LLM Thesis, University of Toronto, 2015), 6.

Rule 10 'representative proceedings' were proceedings where the same interest requirement was strictly applied, meaning that the plaintiff class members had to show that all issues of fact and law were identical between them. The strict interpretation of the same interest requirement, which necessitated that class members have the same causes of action, defences and measure of damages,[22] meant that few cases proceeded as representative proceedings.

However, in 1981 in *Prudential Assurance Co Ltd* v. *Newman Industries Ltd*, Vinelott J interpreted Rule 10 more liberally, holding that there must only be some 'common ingredient' in the cause of action for each class member or some 'common element' to the claims of all class members.[23] He found that if there was a 'common element', then any member of the class 'would be able to rely on the judgment as *res judicata*, and prove the remainder of the elements of the cause of action in separate proceedings', although he did hold that damages would not normally be recoverable.[24]

Mulheron has argued that Vinelott J's judgment moves the representative action closer to the class action, which requires a 'common interest of fact or law' not reflected by the actual wording of Rule 10.[25] For the most part, United Kingdom Courts have been reluctant to adopt Vinelott J's wider interpretation of 'common interest' which, as Mulheron states, 'has undercut most of the utility of the representative action in England'.[26]

16.3.2 *New Zealand's Divergence from the United Kingdom's Representative Action*

In contrast, courts in New Zealand have preferred Vinelott J's reasoning when interpreting HCR 4.24, even though HCR 4.24 is in substance identical to its predecessors and is derived from Rule 10 in the United Kingdom.[27] This divergence began in the 1986 case *RJ Flowers Ltd* v. *Burns*,[28] where McGechan J prefaced his views by recognising that the representative action had not been used much in the preceding twenty-year period, making it difficult to gauge the views of Judges.[29] He stated:

> ... the approach to this application should be liberal. Such was the underlying approach to former Code R 79, even towards the end in the controversial area of claims for damages. It is also the approach implicit in R 4 of the High Court Rules requiring all rules be interpreted so as to secure the 'just, speedy, and inexpensive determination of a proceeding'. Hence, if injustice can be avoided, the rule can and should be applied to serve the interests of expedition and economy, both indeed the underlying reason for its existence. ... The traditional concern to ensure that representative actions are not to be allowed to work injustice must be kept constantly in mind. Subject to those restraints however the rule should be applied and developed to meet modern requirements. It is, as has been said, in *John v Rees* [1970] Ch 345, 370 'not a rigid matter of principle but a flexible tool of convenience in the administration of justice'.[30]

22 Rachael Mulheron, *The Class Action in Common Law Legal Systems: A Comparative Perspective* 80 (2004).

23 *Prudential Assurance Co Ltd* v. *Newman Industries Ltd* [1981] Ch 229 (Ch), 255, 256. See Rachel Mulheron, *The Class Action in Common Law Legal Systems: A Comparative Perspective* 83 (2004).

24 Rachel Mulheron, *The Class Action in Common Law Legal Systems: A Comparative Perspective* 83 (2004), referring to *Prudential Assurance Co Ltd* v. *Newman Industries Ltd* [1981] Ch 229 (Ch), 255.

25 Rachel Mulheron, *The Class Action in Common Law Legal Systems: A Comparative Perspective* 84 (2004).

26 Rachel Mulheron, *The Class Action in Common Law Legal Systems: A Comparative Perspective* 84 (2004).

27 A comprehensive summary of the history of the rule in New Zealand can be found in *RJ Flowers Ltd* v. *Burns* [1987] 1 NZLR 260 (HC), 266. New Zealand first adopted R. 10 from the United Kingdom in r. 79 of the Code of Civil Procedure under sch. 2 of the Supreme Court Act 1882. This was later moved to r. 79 of the Code of Civil Procedure under sch. 2 of the Judicature Act 1908. Then from the period of 1 January 1986 to 31 January 2009, r. 78 of the High Court Rules under sch. 2 of the Judicature Act was used. From 1 February 2009, that rule has been moved to HCR 4.24. From 1 March 2017, the High Court Rules have been contained under s. 154 of the Senior Courts Act 2016.

28 *RJ Flowers Ltd* v. *Burns* [1987] 1 NZLR 260 (HC).

29 *RJ Flowers Ltd* v. *Burns* [1987] 1 NZLR 260 (HC), 267.

30 *RJ Flowers Ltd* v. *Burns* [1987] 1 NZLR 260 (HC), 271.

In 2005, in *Saxmere Co Ltd* v. *Wool Board Disestablishment Co Ltd*, Miller J relied on Canadian jurisprudence where the representative rule had been extended to allow class actions to extend the application of HCR 4.24 in New Zealand.[31] Miller J considered any suggestion in *Flowers* that the New Zealand approach was more restrictive than the Canadian approach needed to be explained given the common equitable source.[32] Miller J opined that there was no good reason to require a separation between liability and damages trials since such a requirement imposed 'a severe procedural constraint on a rule that was designed to ensure a large group of litigants could come at justice'.[33]

In the same way Miller J did not think class actions with different claims or defences should be precluded so long as there was a common issue, identifiable class and the Court did not cause injustice by permitting the action. Where the issues were not common, proof of individual claims or defences would be required:[34] 'This approach accords with the flexible approach taken in *Western Canadian Shopping Centres v Verchere*, which I respectfully consider better reflects the purpose of the Rule and the need to maintain flexibility in its application'. In *Saxmere*, Miller J relied on *Western Canadian*'s definition of a class action, which requires four conditions:

> First, the class must be capable of clear definition, to define those who are entitled to notice or relief and who are to be bound by the judgment. Second, there must be issues of fact or law common to all members. Third, with regard to the common issues, success for one must mean success for all. Fourth, the representative must adequately represent the class.[35]

All conditions were present in that proceeding.[36]

New Zealand's divergence in the application of HCR 4.24 to require 'commonality' as opposed to identical interest and to allow segregation of proceedings to determine damages separately means that a proceeding under HCR 4.24 is more analogous in substance to the American,[37] Australian[38] and Canadian[39] class action than to the United Kingdom's representative action. In proposing the following widely cited[40] definition for a class action, Mulheron suggests '[s]uch judicial interpretations may stretch the boundaries of the representative rule's language, but reflect the more fully developed and sanctioned features of a class action regime'[41]:

> A class action is a legal procedure which enables the claims (or part of the claims) of a number of persons against the same defendant to be determined in the one suit. In a class action, one or more persons ('representative plaintiff') may sue on his or her own behalf and on behalf of a number of other persons ('the class') who have a claim to a remedy for the same or a similar alleged wrong to that alleged by the representative plaintiff ('common issues'). Only the representative plaintiff is a party to the action. The class members are not usually identified as individual parties but merely described. The class members are bound by the outcome of the

31 *Saxmere Co Ltd* v. *Wool Board Disestablishment Co Ltd* HC Wellington CIV-2003-485-2724, 6 December 2005, [182].
32 *Saxmere Co Ltd* v. *Wool Board Disestablishment Co Ltd* HC Wellington CIV-2003-485-2724, 6 December 2005, [179].
33 *Saxmere Co Ltd* v. *Wool Board Disestablishment Co Ltd* HC Wellington CIV-2003-485-2724, 6 December 2005, [182].
34 *Saxmere Co Ltd* v. *Wool Board Disestablishment Co Ltd* HC Wellington CIV-2003-485-2724, 6 December 2005, [182].
35 *Saxmere Co Ltd* v. *Wool Board Disestablishment Co Ltd* HC Wellington CIV-2003-485-2724, 6 December 2005, [176], referring to *Western Canadian Shopping Centres Inc* v. *Dutton* 2001 SCC 46, [2001] 2 SCR 534.
36 *Saxmere Co Ltd* v. *Wool Board Disestablishment Co Ltd* HC Wellington CIV-2003-485-2724, 6 December 2005, [184].
37 Federal Rules of Civil Procedure (US), r. 23; and Class Action Fairness Act 28 USC.
38 Federal Court of Australia Act 1976 (Cth), pt IVA Division 2.
39 Class Proceedings Act SOO 1992 c. 6.
40 This definition has been cited in: Gary Meggitt, *Class Actions in Hong Kong: Yes, No, Maybe*, 43 HKLJ 217, 219 (2013); Michael Legg and Jason Harris, *How the American Dream Became a Global Nightmare: An Analysis of the Causes of the Global Financial Crisis*, 32 UNSWLJ 350, 386 (2009); and Catherine Piche, *The Cultural Analysis of Class Action Law*, 2 Journal of Civil Law Studies 101, 114 (2009).
41 Rachael Mulheron, *The Class Action in Common Law Legal Systems: A Comparative Perspective* 78 (2004).

litigation on the common issues, whether favourable or adverse to the class, although they do not for the most part, take any active part in that litigation.[42]

Regardless of the definition of a class action adopted, it is clear that proceedings filed in New Zealand under HCR 4.24 meet the markers of a class action in substance. Specifically:

(1) HCR 4.24 provides a legal procedure (albeit scant) which enables claims (or part of claims) to be determined in one proceeding.
(2) It appears that the New Zealand judiciary has allowed proceedings where the representative plaintiff is the only party named and other class members are not identified by name under HCR 4.24.[43]
(3) The representative plaintiff brings the action on behalf of one or more class members.
(4) The judiciary has relaxed the traditional interpretation of the common interest requirement to now require a common issue of fact or law of significance for each member of the class represented.[44]
(5) The judiciary accepts that class members will be bound by the outcome of the litigation on common issues whether or not they take an active part in the litigation.[45]

In support, a number of interlocutory judgments from proceedings filed under HCR 4.24 deal with issues that are commonly provided for in statutory-based class action procedure rules in other jurisdictions. These judgments include determinations on whether leave is granted for the representative plaintiff to bring a claim on behalf of the class,[46] whether a proceeding is opt-in or opt-out,[47] what the notice requirements are to notify potential class members of the litigation,[48] discovery issues with a plaintiff class,[49] the ordering of a split trial on common issues and damages,[50] the terms of litigation funding agreements[51] and security for costs.[52]

42 Rachael Mulheron, *The Class Action in Common Law Legal Systems: A Comparative Perspective* 3 (2004).

43 For instance, in *Talley's Fisheries Ltd* v. *Minister of Immigration* (1994) 7 PRNZ 469 (HC); *Purdue* v. *Boyd Knight* (1998) 8 NZCLC 261,720 (HC); *Registered Securities Ltd (in liq)* v. *Westpac Banking Corp* (2000) 14 PRNZ 348 (HC); *Houghton* v. *Saunders* (2008) 19 PRNZ 173 (HC); and *Cooper* v. *ANZ Bank New Zealand Ltd* [2013] NZHC 2827. All of these cases included over 1,000 people in the representative action, and none of the judgments contain any indication that there was a list of names attached to court documentation.

44 *Credit Suisse Private Equity LLC* v. *Houghton* [2014] NZSC 37, [2014] 1 NZLR 514, [53] and [129].

45 *Saunders* v. *Houghton* [2012] NZCA 545, [2013] 2 NZLR 652.

46 *Southern Response Earthquake Services Ltd* v. *Southern Response Unresolved Claims Group* [2017] NZCA 489, [2018] 2 NZLR 312 (leave also in issue in three prior High Court judgments of this case); *Strathboss Kiwifruit Ltd* v. *Attorney-General* [2015] NZHC 1596, (2015) 23 PRNZ 69; *Cooper* v. *ANZ Bank New Zealand Ltd* [2013] NZHC 2827; *LDC Finance (in rec and in liq)* v. *Miller* [2013] NZHC 2993; *Harding* v. *LDC Finance Ltd (in rec)* HC Christchurch CIV-2008-409-1140, 19 November 2009; *Hedley* v. *Kiwi Co-Operative Dairies Ltd* (2000) 15 PRNZ 210 (HC); *Ankers* v. *Attorney-General (No 2)* [1995] NZAR 418 (HC); *Talley's Fisheries Ltd* v. *Minister of Immigration* (1994) 7 PRNZ 469 (HC); *Healthcare Providers New Zealand Inc* v. *Northland District Health Board* HC Wellington CIV-2007-485-1814, 7 December 2007; *Jones* v. *Attorney-General* HC Wellington CP175/02, 8 July 2003; *Registered Securities Ltd (in liq)* v. *Westpac Banking Corp* (2000) 14 PRNZ 348 (HC); *Overseas Containers Ltd* v. *Geo H Scales Ltd* HC Wellington CP395/86, 22 September 1986; and *Hill* v. *Wellington Co-operative Taxi Owner-Drivers' Society Ltd* HC Wellington A4/75, 3 February 1988.

47 *LDC Finance (in rec and in liq)* v. *Miller* [2013] NZHC 2993, [43]–[49]; and *Houghton* v. *Saunders* (2008) 19 PRNZ 173 (HC).

48 *Cridge* v. *Studorp Ltd* [2016] NZHC 2451, (2016) 23 PRNZ 281; and *Houghton* v. *Saunders* (2008) 19 PRNZ 173 (HC).

49 *Southern Response Earthquake Services Ltd* v. *Southern Response Unresolved Claims Group* [2017] NZCA 489, [2018] 2 NZLR 312; *Devcich* v. *Cowley Stanich & Co* (1997) 11 PRNZ 47 (HC); *RJ Flowers Ltd* v. *Burns* [1987] 1 NZLR 260 (HC); and *Purdue* v. *Boyd Knight* [1987] 1 NZLR 260 (HC).

50 *White* v. *James Hardie New Zealand* [2018] NZHC 1627.

51 A summary of the procedural history relating to the terms of the litigation funding is contained in *Credit Suisse Private Equity LLC* v. *Houghton* [2014] NZSC 37, [2014] 1 NZLR 514, [16]–[20] and [95]–[104].

52 *Southern Response Unresolved Claims Group* v. *Southern Response Earthquake Services Ltd* [2016] NZHC 3105 at [75]; and *Houghton* v. *Saunders* (2011) 20 PRNZ 509 (HC), [231].

Furthermore, the language of 'opt-in' and 'opt-out', used in class action litigation, has been used to describe who can join proceedings under HCR 4.24. An opt-in class action is one where a potential class member must affirmatively opt-in to the proceeding to be bound by the judgment or settlement as a 'prerequisite to receiving any benefit for the action'.[53] An opt-out class action is where:[54] '... persons are bound as members of the class unless they take an affirmative step to indicate that they wish to be excluded from the action and the effect of judgment or settlement'. In *Houghton* v. *Saunders* (2008), French J resisted 'opt-out' proceedings under HCR 4.24, stating: '... in my view, an opt out procedure represents too radical a departure from the existing Rules. In the absence of legislative change, the Court must work within the existing Rules which only contemplate "opt in"'.[55] Interestingly, in contrast, the majority of the Supreme Court assumed that "opt-out" class actions were available in that case on appeal.[56] Further, in the landmark decision *Ross v Southern Response Earthquake Services Ltd*, the Court of Appeal expressly allowed an opt-out class action for the first time.[57] The Supreme Court has granted *Southern Response* leave to appeal the decision.[58] At the time of writing, the final appeal has not yet been determined.

Regardless, it is clear the judiciary, at a minimum, is allowing opt-in class actions. Unlike other jurisdictions, however, the law in New Zealand has not evolved to the point where there are specific statutory-based class action civil procedure rules. This is problematic. The judiciary has to use its discretion to determine simple procedural issues, which is inefficient, uneconomic and can create uncertainty for parties. Indeed, French J in *Houghton* v. *Saunders* referred to proceedings under HCR 4.24 as a 'class action' and stated that '[t]he absence of class action rules is creating difficulties for the parties in this case'.[59] The Court of Appeal later observed that when draft class action legislation is available it will 'likely ... provide a framework that will be useful to the judiciary'.[60] In April 2014, the Supreme Court stated that French J 'was justified in the remark'.[61]

With opt-in class actions now permitted in substance under HCR 4.24, we will examine judicial trends and the empirical data on class actions permitted under HCR 4.24 to determine how prevalent class actions have become in New Zealand.

16.4 THE CURRENT STATE OF CLASS ACTIONS IN NEW ZEALAND

16.4.1 *Initiating Class Action Proceedings*

Class actions are most commonly filed in the High Court in New Zealand. Plaintiffs can initiate class-wide proceedings in the High Court under HCR 4.24 or 4.27(g). The District Court has rules identical to HCR 4.24 and 4.27(g), namely DCR 4.24 and 4.27(g). HCR 4.27(g) and DCR 4.27(g) are rarely used. Further, and unsurprisingly, class actions are rarely filed in the District Court. The District Court only has jurisdiction to hear civil claims for damages under NZ $350,000 whereas the High Court hears civil claims for damages over NZ$350,000.[62] The High Court and the District Court can hear proceedings relating to any area of law as the court of first

53 Rachael Mulheron, *The Class Action in Common Law Legal Systems: A Comparative Perspective* 29 (2004).
54 Rachael Mulheron, *The Class Action in Common Law Legal Systems: A Comparative Perspective* 34 (2004).
55 *Houghton* v. *Saunders* (2008) 19 PRNZ 173 (HC), [165].
56 *Credit Suisse Private Equity LLC* v. *Houghton* [2014] NZSC 37, [2014] 1 NZLR 514, [163]–[168].
57 *Ross* v. *Southern Response Earthquake Services Ltd* [2019] NZCA 431.
58 *Southern Response Earthquake Services Ltd* v. *Ross* [2009] NZSC 140.
59 *Houghton* v. *Saunders* [2012] NZHC 1828, [2012] NZCCLR 31, [38],[45].
60 *Saunders* v. *Houghton (No 1)* [2009] NZCA 610, [2010] 3 NZLR 331, [15].
61 *Credit Suisse Private Equity LLC* v. *Houghton* [2014] NZSC 37, [2014] 1 NZLR 514, [49], referring to the remark about class actions in *Houghton* v. *Saunders* [2012] NZHC 1828, [2012] NZCCLR 31, [38], [45].
62 See footnotes 3 and 4 of this chapter.

instance unless there is a specialist court with jurisdiction. For example, the Employment Court hears class actions relating to employment law. The Employment Court Regulations 2000 adopts HCR 4.24 to allow class actions to be initiated in the Employment Court.[63]

16.4.2 *Types of Class Action Proceedings*

Plaintiffs can initiate a class action relating to any substantive area of law provided it is filed in a court with jurisdiction to hear the matter. However, certain statutes specifically allow certain types of class actions. For example, the Human Rights Act 1993 allows the Human Rights Commissioner to commence civil proceedings on behalf of a class of persons who are affected by alleged discriminatory practices in certain circumstances.[64] The Health and Disability Commissioner Act 1994 allows a director of proceedings to commence proceedings on behalf of a class for breach of the Code of Health and Disability Services Consumers' Rights.[65] The Fair Trading Act 1986 authorises a variation to a class action if all members of the class can be identified.[66] The Companies Act 1993 allows the court to appoint a shareholder to represent other shareholders who have the same interest, or substantially the same interest, in relation to the subject matter of the proceedings against the company or a director of the company.[67] These statutes do not, however, provide any procedural guidance on the management of class action litigation. The judiciary instead must rely on HCR 4.24 and their inherent powers to regulate procedure.

16.4.3 *Class Action Remedies*

The relief available in class action proceedings varies depending on the nature of the claim and whether there are any specific statutory prohibitions or entitlements to relief. For example, a person who suffers personal injury by accident and is covered by the Accident Compensation Act 2001 is statutorily barred from suing the relevant tortfeasor for compensatory damages.[68]

Where there is no statutory bar, as a general observation, the remedies available reflect those permitted in other common law jurisdictions, such as damages, declarations and injunctions.[69] The 'basket of remedies' approach is commonly deployed, whereby the court awards the remedy which best redresses the wrong despite the common law or equitable origin of that remedy.[70]

It is common for class action proceedings to be heard on a split trial basis, meaning that plaintiffs seek declarations pertaining to liability on common issues and then damages are determined either on a subclass or individual basis.[71] In relation to damages, unlike the United States, New Zealand is fairly conservative in awarding exemplary or punitive damages.[72]

63 Employment Court Regulation 6(2)(ii).
64 Section 92B(2).
65 Section 50(3).
66 Parts 1 and 5.
67 Section 173.
68 Section 317, Accident Compensation Act 2001.
69 Paul Karlsgodt, *World Class Actions: A Guide to Group and Representative Actions Around the Globe* 454 (2012).
70 This approach was adopted in New Zealand in *Aquaculture Corporation* v. *New Zealand Green Mussel Co Ltd* [1990] 3 NZLR 229, and has since been endorsed in *Crump* v. *Wala* [1994] 2 NZLR 331 and *Chirnside* v. *Fay (No 2)* [2005] 3 NZLR 689.
71 See the split trial application that was approved in *Houghton* v. *Saunders* [2012] NZHC 1828, [2012] NZCCLR 31. A split trial was also ordered in *Cridge* v. *Sturdop* [2016] NZHC 2451 and *White* v. *James Hardie New Zealand* [2018] NZHC 2812.
72 Stephen Todd and others, *Todd on Torts* 1347 (2018).

To date, there have been no exemplary damages awards in class action proceedings. The highest award for exemplary damages awarded in a non-class context is NZ$85,000.[73]

Unlike the United States, New Zealand has a 'loser pays' solicitor-client costs system.[74] The successful parties in a class action proceeding can claim solicitor-client costs on a scaled basis in accordance with Schedules Two and Three of the High Court Rules.[75] A successful party can also apply for increased or indemnity solicitor-client costs.[76]

16.4.4 *Judicial Trends under HCR 4.24*

Most of the cases identified in the empirical study that follows contain one or more interlocutory judgments on procedural matters relating to the management of the relevant class action. We identify some of the judicial trends in interpreting HCR 4.24 and the exercise of judicial discretion below.

16.4.4.1 Leave Requirements

In *Saunders* v. *Houghton*,[77] the Court of Appeal identified general principles to guide a court in determining whether to exercise its discretion to grant leave for a class action under HCR 4.24. In summary, the Court considered a 'generous'[78] approach should be taken and commented:

> The principles now established are that a representative action can be brought where each member of the class is alleged to have a separate cause of action, provided:
>
> (a) the order may not confer a right of action on the member of the class represented who could not have asserted such a right in separate proceedings, nor may it bar a defence which might have been available to the defendant in such separate proceedings;
> (b) there must be an interest shared in common by all members of the group; and
> (c) it must be for the benefit of other members of the class that the plaintiff be permitted to sue in a representative capacity.[79]

The 'same interest' requirement has a relatively low threshold to ensure a 'just, speedy, and inexpensive determination' of the proceeding.[80] The 'same interest' in the proceeding does not necessarily require that the plaintiffs claim the same cause of action, the same facts or the same relief.[81] Rather, it requires the plaintiffs have a 'significant common interest in the resolution of any question of law or fact arising in the proceeding'.[82] Access to justice is an important consideration in deciding whether to grant leave.[83] However, the court may be stricter in applying the 'same interest' requirement if a third-party funder finances the class action.[84] A

73 G v. G [1997] NZLFR 49.
74 New Zealand uses High Court Rules, r. 14.2(1)(a). The United States has the 'American Rule', contained in the Federal Rules of Civil Procedure, rule 54, whereby each party bears responsibility to pay the solicitor-client costs they incur regardless of the outcome of the proceeding.
75 High Court Rules 2016, schs 2 and 3.
76 High Court Rules 2016, r. 14.6.
77 *Saunders* v. *Houghton (No 1)* [2009] NZCA 610, [2010] 3 NZLR 331.
78 *Saunders* v. *Houghton (No 1)* [2009] NZCA 610, [2010] 3 NZLR 331, [10]–[15].
79 *Saunders* v. *Houghton (No 1)* [2009] NZCA 610, [2010] 3 NZLR 331, [13].
80 High Court Rules 2016, r. 1.2.
81 *Saunders* v. *Houghton (No 1)* [2009] NZCA 610, [2010] 3 NZLR 331.
82 *Cridge* v. *Studorp Ltd* [2017] NZCA 376, (2017) 23 PRNZ 582, [11].
83 *Cridge* v. *Studorp Ltd* [2017] NZCA 376, (2017) 23 PRNZ 582, [11].
84 *Saunders* v. *Houghton (No 1)* [2009] NZCA 610, [2010] 3 NZLR 331.

court may grant leave for a class action to proceed solely on the issue of liability while leaving damages to be determined through subclasses or individually.[85]

Where a representative order is granted (by consent or by leave), the Judge must make a continuous appraisal as to whether the representative order should be sustained, varied or rescinded.[86] In the absence of specific statutory-based class action procedure rules, the court must exercise close control of the proceedings and, specifically, ensure there are safeguards in place so that defendants are not disadvantaged.[87]

16.4.4.2 Opt-In and Opt-Out Proceedings

As stated in Section 16.3 of this chapter, historically, the courts have usually only allowed opt-in class action proceedings in New Zealand.[88] Certain members of the judiciary are of the opinion that opt-out proceedings should only be permitted if the legislature enacts statutory authority specifically authorising them.[89]

However, there are a number of class actions identified in the empirical study, which may in fact have operated as opt-out class actions. Specifically, there are three class actions where there are more than 4,001 class members[90] and a further ten class actions where the class size is not specified although it is likely that those class sizes are large given the nature of the class action at issue.[91] In *Credit Suisse Privacy Equity LLC* v. *Houghton*,[92] the Supreme Court assumed that opt-out class actions are allowed under HCR 4.24.

In 2019, the Court of Appeal issued a landmark judgment expressly permitting an opt-out class action under HCR 4.24 and noting that applications for opt-out actions in future cases will turn on the facts of each individual case.[93] The final determination on whether HCR 4.24 provides jurisdiction to allow opt-out class actions is pending at the time of writing with the Supreme Court due to hear an appeal on the issue in 2020.[94]

16.4.4.3 Consent Mechanisms and Notice Requirements

In the absence of statutory-based class action rules, the court's aim is to ensure that there is responsible communication with class members, that there are adequate arrangements to inform and consult all class members on steps in the proceeding, and that no misleading information is provided to encourage new participants in the litigation.[95] In *Smith* v. *Claims Resolution Services Ltd*, the Court stated that is appropriate to approve and direct the form of notice to potential class members

85 *Saunders* v. *Houghton (No 1)* [2009] NZCA 610, [2010] 3 NZLR 331.

86 *Saunders* v. *Houghton (No 1)* [2009] NZCA 610, [2010] 3 NZLR 331, [38]–[40].

87 *Saunders* v. *Houghton (No 1)* [2009] NZCA 610, [2010] 3 NZLR 331, [63].

88 See Section 16.3.2 of this chapter.

89 See the comments by France J at footnote 231 of this chapter.

90 See footnote 190 of this chapter.

91 See Section 16.5.3 of this chapter. Cases where the plaintiff class size is not mentioned are: *Nireaha Tamaki* v. *Baker* (1902) 22 NZLR 97 (SC); *Overseas Containers Ltd* v. *Geo H Scales Ltd* HC Wellington CP395/86, 22 September 1986; *New Zealand Meat Industry Assoc* v. *Accident Compensation Corporation* HC Wellington CP275/87, 19 October 1987; *Howick Engineering Ltd* v. *Manukau City Council* HC Auckland CP2021/91, 11 August 1992; *Wanganui District Council* v. *Tangaroa* [1995] 2 NZLR 706 (HC); *Paki* v. *Attorney-General* [2009] 1 NZLR 72 (HC); *Healthcare Providers New Zealand Inc* v. *Northland District Health Board* HC Wellington CIV-2007-485-1814, 7 December 2007; *Strathboss Kiwifruit Ltd* v. *Attorney-General* [2015] NZHC 1596, (2015) 23 PRNZ 69; *Lin* v. *Registrar of Companies* [2016] NZHC 395; and *Smith* v. *Claims Resolution Service Ltd* [2019] NZHC 127.

92 *Credit Suisse Private Equity LLC* v. *Houghton* [2014] NZSC 37.

93 *Ross* v. *Southern Response Earthquake Services Ltd* [2019] NZCA 431, [11].

94 Leave to appeal has been granted in *Southern Response Earthquake Services Ltd* v. *Ross* [2009] NZSC 140, [1].

95 *Saunders* v. *Houghton* [2009] NZCA 610, [2010] 3 NZLR 331, [63].

and that 'appropriately worded content that is readily comprehensible to a non-lawyer audience is required'.[96]

Usually, the plaintiffs will provide a draft notice to the court, which can be challenged by the defendants and amended as the court sees fit.[97] Judges tend to take an interventionist approach to ensure that the content is accurate. In *Saunders* v. *Houghton*, the Court of Appeal noted that a Judge must bring 'a critical and creative mind to bear on all aspects and implications of the representative order'[98] which includes notice and consent requirements. However, in *Cooper* v. *ANZ Bank New Zealand Ltd*, the Court caveated its urgent approval of a notice to potential class members in relation to litigation funding details:

> ... it is not for the Court to check the content of the notice for accuracy as to matters such as the funding arrangements between a participant and a litigation funder ... [i]t is for the Plaintiff's legal advisers to ensure that the notice contains a fair summary of the position insofar as it relates to that type of issue.[99]

Indeed, the court may not be privy to the details of the litigation funding agreement.[100]

The communication of the notice to potential class members will vary from case to case and can include communicating by way of advertisement in newspapers, via the plaintiff's solicitor's website or directly mailing a copy of the notice to potential class members.[101]

16.4.4.4 Discovery and Interrogatory Orders

The court is concerned to ensure that granting leave for a class action proceeding does not disadvantage a defendant, particularly in relation to discovery.[102] It is common for a court to make orders requiring all plaintiffs and all represented class members to complete discovery. In *Registered Securities Ltd (in liq)* v. *Westpac Banking Corporation*, the defendant argued that the court should not allow the claim to proceed as a class action because the plaintiff class contained over 8,000 'faceless plaintiffs without any obligation to furnish discovery, particulars or answer interrogatories ...'.[103] In response, the Court stated:

> Any plaintiff is obliged to discover all relevant documents in the possession, custody or power of those represented and answer interrogatories which are relevant to that claim: *Sharpe v Small* (1975) 49 ALJR 130 at p 132. I cannot see how a representative action will materially alter what has to be disclosed and available in any event. I am not satisfied that the defendant will be procedurally disadvantaged by joining those other investors in a representative capacity.[104]

For example, in *Devcich* v. *Cowley Stanich & Co*, the Court ordered that all plaintiffs and all class members discover all relevant documents within that individual's control.[105] In *Hedley* v. *Kiwi Co-operative Dairies Ltd*, the Court stated that it could direct the plaintiffs or any member of the plaintiff class to answer interrogatories.[106]

96 *Smith* v. *Claims Resolution Service Ltd* [2019] NZHC 1013, [13].
97 For instance, in *Houghton* v. *Saunders* HC Christchurch CIV-2008-409-348, 26 May 2010.
98 *Saunders* v. *Houghton* [2009] NZCA 610, [38].
99 *Cooper* v. *ANZ Bank New Zealand Ltd* [2013] NZHC 3116, [16].
100 For instance, see *Smith* v. *Claims Resolution Service Ltd* [2019] NZHC 1013, [25]–[26].
101 *Smith* v. *Claims Resolution Service Ltd* [2019] NZHC 1013, [19].
102 *RJ Flowers Ltd* v. *Burns* [1987] 1 NZLR 260 (HC).
103 *Registered Securities Ltd (in liq)* v. *Westpac Banking Corp* (2000) 14 PRNZ 348 (HC), [44].
104 *Registered Securities Ltd (in liq)* v. *Westpac Banking Corp* (2000) 14 PRNZ 348 (HC), [45].
105 *Devcich* v. *Cowley Stanich & Co* (1997) 11 PRNZ 47 (HC), 51.
106 *Hedley* v. *Kiwi Co-Operative Dairies Ltd* (2000) 15 PRNZ (HC), [61] and [65].

Where discovery is sought against a defendant to disclose and/or notify potential class members of the claim, courts will not grant the order if confidentiality issues arise.[107] A court may instead require public advertising to notify potential class members of the claim.[108]

A court may also grant a defendant's application for security for costs for discovery and, in particular, 'generous security' will be appropriate where a third-party litigation funder is involved.[109] The amount to be granted is a matter of impression.[110] In *Paine* v. *Carter Holt Harvey Ltd*, the Court ordered the litigation funder pay NZ$614,000 by way of security for costs to the defendant.[111] However the Court did not stay this proceeding in the interim, as there was 'no reason to believe' the litigation funder could not pay the security.[112]

16.4.4.5 Litigation Funding

Historically, in New Zealand, a third party could not fund litigation due to the torts of champerty and maintenance.[113] A number of common law jurisdictions have abolished these torts.[114] New Zealand still has champerty and maintenance available in a limited form, which permits litigation funding in certain circumstances.[115] The empirical study in this chapter identifies six class actions that involve litigation funders.[116]

In *Saunders* v. *Houghton*, the Court of Appeal accepted that litigation funding of a class action might be permitted where there is an arguable case for rights that warrant vindication, where there is no abuse of process and where the funding arrangement is approved by the court.[117] However, given litigation funding is currently unregulated in New Zealand, courts have needed to make determinations regarding a funder's involvement in litigation creating some disagreement between certain members of the judiciary.

In particular, judges disagree about whether the funding agreement itself must be disclosed to the court without an application or orders. In *Waterhouse* v. *Contractors Bonding Ltd*, Glazebrook J stated that a plaintiff must disclose the identity and location of a funder and its amenability to the jurisdiction of the court.[118] Nevertheless, without further application and orders, the terms of the funding agreement did not need to be disclosed.[119] Her Honour commented that it is not the role of the court to act as general regulators of funding agreements – nor is it the role of the court to assess the merits or fairness of bargains between third-party funders and plaintiffs.[120] She noted the court's role is

107 *Devcich* v. *Cowley Stanich & Co* (1997) 11 PRNZ 47 (HC), 51.

108 *Southern Response Unresolved Claims Group* v. *Southern Response Earthquake Services Ltd* [2016] NZHC 3105, [98]–[99].

109 *Paine* v. *Carter Holt Harvey Ltd* [2019] NZHC 478, [71].

110 *Paine* v. *Carter Holt Harvey Ltd* [2019] NZHC 478, [77].

111 *Paine* v. *Carter Holt Harvey Ltd* [2019] NZHC 478, [79].

112 *Paine* v. *Carter Holt Harvey Ltd* [2019] NZHC 478, [79].

113 Maintenance occurs where a third party assists a party in a civil proceeding to bring or defend that proceeding without lawful justification and damage is thereby caused to the opposing party in the proceeding. Champerty is a form of maintenance where the third party who gives the assistance does so on the basis that he or she receives a share of the damages awarded. See Stephen Todd and others, *Todd on Torts* 1061 (2018).

114 England and certain states in Australia such as Victoria, South Australia and New South Wales have abolished the torts of champerty and maintenance. See Stephen Todd and others, *Todd on Torts* 1067 (2018).

115 Stephen Todd and others, *Todd on Torts* 1063–4 (2018).

116 See footnotes 232–233 of this chapter.

117 *Saunders* v. *Houghton (No 1)* [2009] NZCA 610, [2010] 3 NZLR 331.

118 *Waterhouse* v. *Contractors Bonding Ltd* [2013] NZSC 89, [2014] 1 NZLR 91, [8] and [76], confirming this approach as set down previously by the Court of Appeal in *Contractors Bonding Ltd* v. *Waterhouse* [2012] NZCA 399, [2012] 3 NZLR 826.

119 *Waterhouse* v. *Contractors Bonding Ltd* [2013] NZSC 89, [2014] 1 NZLR 91, [73]–[74].

120 *Waterhouse* v. *Contractors Bonding Ltd* [2013] NZSC 89, [2014] 1 NZLR 91, [76].

merely to adjudicate on any application brought before it in a proceeding (which may in certain situations involve issues around the funding agreement).[121]

In support, the Court of Appeal in *Southern Response Earthquake Services Ltd* v. *Southern Response Unresolved Claims Group* stated that it is not the role of the court to 'approve' the litigation funding agreements and the granting of leave should not be taken as endorsing the funding agreements.[122] However, the court will ensure that it is not allowing an abuse of process by granting leave for a class action where a litigation funder is involved.[123]

In contrast, in *PricewaterhouseCoopers* v. *Walker*, Elias CJ issued a dissenting opinion containing her concern that the majority's opinion would be seen as cementing the approach taken by Glazebrook J in *Waterhouse* v. *Contractors Bonding Ltd* without full argument.[124] Her Honour reiterated that champerty and maintenance are still part of New Zealand law and she intimated that, without statutory regulation, there is risk of oppression. For that reason, the court needs to scrutinise the terms of a funding arrangement closely in order to prevent civil claims from being treated as negotiable investments.[125]

It is clear that the lack of regulation is problematic. The judiciary is hesitant to interfere with private contractual agreements made by third-party funders and class members, while also acknowledging that safeguards need to be in place to ensure that funders do not take advantage of class members.

16.4.5 *Empirical Study Findings on Class Actions in New Zealand*

One of the authors carried out the first empirical study of class actions in New Zealand in 2018 ('the first empirical study').[126] The article focussed on class actions filed under HCR 4.24 in the New Zealand High Court and the Employment Court up to 31 March 2018. Adopting the methodology contained in her article, we have updated the empirical data in this chapter to include all class actions filed up to 1 July 2019. The updated data in this chapter confirms that a number of important trends have continued including that the number of class actions filed in the New Zealand High Court has increased every decade for three decades from 1980 to 2010 and records that trend is highly likely to continue in the period from 2010 to the end of 2020.

16.4.5.1 Date and Number of Class Actions in the New Zealand High Court

Schedule One of the first empirical study contains a detailed breakdown of class actions filed under HCR 4.24 in the New Zealand High Court. Continuing the methodology used in the first empirical

121 *Waterhouse* v. *Contractors Bonding Ltd* [2013] NZSC 89, [2014] 1 NZLR 91, [48].

122 *Southern Response Earthquake Services Ltd* v. *Southern Response Unresolved Claims Group* [2017] NZCA 489, [2018] 2 NZLR 312, [76].

123 For example, where the proceeding is based on clearly misleading funding arrangements or the proceeding is champertous: *Southern Response Earthquake Services Ltd* v. *Southern Response Unresolved Claims Group* [2017] NZCA 489, [2018] 2 NZLR 312, [76].

124 *PricewaterhouseCoopers* v. *Walker* [2017] NZSC 151, [2018] 1 NZLR 735.

125 *PricewaterhouseCoopers* v. *Walker* [2017] NZSC 151, [2018] 1 NZLR 735, [119]–[121]. As noted in Nick Butcher, *Litigation funding and class actions* (2019) 929 LawTalk 66: 'Interestingly, the LPF Group (a litigation funder), filed an official complaint against the Chief Justice with the Judicial Complaints Commissioner over what it claimed were "unfair and unjustified opinions" which create "uncertainty over the validity of legal funding in New Zealand" LPF subsequently dropped their complaint'. See also New Zealand Law Society 'Litigation funder lodges complaint with Judicial Complaints Commissioner' (14 November 2017) www.lawsociety.org.nz.

126 Nikki Chamberlain, *Class Actions in New Zealand: An Empirical Study*, 24 NZBLQ 132 (2018).

study, the authors found an additional four class actions filed in the last decade from 1 January 2010 to 1 July 2019.[127]

A summary of the number of class actions in the High Court for each decade (unless stated otherwise) to 1 July 2019 is contained in Table 16.1.[128]

A total of forty class actions were filed in the High Court up until 1 July 2019. The data shows that the number of class actions filed increased in each decade from the 1980s until 1 January 2010. In particular, there were four class actions in the 1980s, eight class actions in the 1990s and thirteen class actions in the 2000s representing an increase of four to five class actions every decade.

TABLE 16.1 *Number of class actions in the New Zealand High Court*

Years (decade intervals unless stated otherwise)	Number of Class Actions
Pre-1 January 1980	3[129]
1980s	4[130]
1990s	8[131]
2000s	13[132]
1 January 2010 – 1 July 2019	12[133] (with an additional two noting it as a possibility)[134]
TOTAL	40

127 *Smith* v. *Claims Resolution Service Ltd* [2019] NZHC 127; *Minister of Education* v. *James Hardie Ltd* [2018] NZHC 1481; *Ross* v. *Southern Response Earthquake Services Ltd* [2018] NZHC 3288; and *Paine* v. *Carter Holt Harvey Ltd* [2019] NZHC 478. The authors note an additional six months of data is yet to come to complete the data set for the last decade.

128 As some of the cases do not state the date the representative order was made, but rather just mention that it was made, and the relevant interlocutory decision is not available using the search methodologies employed in this study. The data for the date has been collected from the date the relevant proceeding was filed (as opposed to the date a representative order was made).

129 *Nireaha Tamaki* v. *Baker* (1902) 22 NZLR 97 (SC); *Mundy* v. *Cunningham* [1973] 1 NZLR 555 (SC); and *Hill* v. *Wellington Co-operative Taxi Owner-Drivers' Society Ltd* HC Wellington A4/75, 3 February 1988.

130 *RJ Flowers Ltd* v. *Burns* [1987] 1 NZLR 260 (HC); *Overseas Containers Ltd* v. *Geo H Scales Ltd* HC Wellington CP395/86, 22 September 1986; *New Zealand Meat Industry Assoc* v. *Accident Compensation Corporation* HC Wellington CP275/87, 19 October 1987; and *Taspac Oysters Ltd* v. *James Hardie & Co Pty Ltd* [1990] 1 NZLR 442 (HC).

131 *Howick Engineering Ltd* v. *Manukau City Council* HC Auckland CP2021/91, 11 August 1992; *Talley's Fisheries Ltd* v. *Minister of Immigration* (1994) 7 PRNZ 469 (HC); *Purdue* v. *Boyd Knight* [1987] 1 NZLR 260 (HC); *Ankers* v. *Attorney-General (No 2)* [1995] NZAR 418 (HC); *Wanganui District Council* v. *Tangaroa* [1995] 2 NZLR 706 (HC); *Devcich* v. *Cowley Stanich & Co* (1997) 11 PRNZ 47 (HC); *Registered Securities Ltd (in liq)* v. *Westpac Banking Corp* (2000) 14 PRNZ 348 (HC); and *Hedley* v. *Kiwi Co-Operative Dairies Ltd* (2000) 15 PRNZ 210 (HC).

132 *'Akau'Ola* v. *President of the Conference of the Methodist Church of New Zealand* HC Auckland CP183/SW01, 5 December 2001; *Jones* v. *Attorney-General* HC Wellington CP175/02, 8 July 2003; *Erris Promotions Ltd* v. *Commissioner of Inland Revenue* [2004] 1 NZLR 811 (HC); *Saxmere Co Ltd* v. *Wool Board Disestablishment Co Ltd* HC Wellington CIV-2003-485-2724, 6 December 2005; *Paki* v. *Attorney-General* [2009] 1 NZLR 72 (HC); *Stickland* v. *Drummond* HC Auckland CIV-2006-404-3078, 13 May 2008; *Maranatha Ltd* v. *Tourism Transport Ltd* HC Auckland CIV-2006-404-6431, 3 April 2007; *Healthcare Providers New Zealand Inc* v. *Northland District Health Board* HC Wellington CIV-2007-485-1814, 7 December 2007; *Houghton* v. *Saunders* (2008) 19 PRNZ 173 (HC); *Harding* v. *LDC Finance Ltd (in rec)* HC Christchurch CIV-2008-409-1140, 19 November 2009; *Accent Management Ltd* v. *Commissioner of Inland Revenue* (2010) 24 NZTC 24,126 (HC); *Blue Star Taxis (Christchurch) Society Ltd* v. *Gold Band Taxis (Christchurch) Society Ltd* HC Christchurch CIV-2009-409-2921, 19 November 2010; and *Wu* v. *Body Corporate 366611* [2011] 2 NZLR 837 (HC).

133 *Cadman* v. *Visini* (2011) 3 NZTR 21-011 (HC); *LDC Finance (in rec and in liq)* v. *Miller*, [2013] NZHC 2993; *Cooper* v. *ANZ Bank New Zealand Ltd* [2013] NZHC 2827; *Strathboss Kiwifruit Ltd* v. *Attorney-General* [2015] NZHC 1596, (2015) 23 PRNZ 69; *Cridge* v. *Studorp Ltd* [2016] NZHC 2451, (2016) 23 PRNZ 281; *Southern Response Unresolved Claims Group* v. *Southern Response Earthquake Services Ltd* [2016] NZHC 3105; *Lin* v. *Registrar of Companies* [2016] NZHC 395; and *Vlaar* v. *van der Lubbe* [2016] NZHC 2398, (2016) 4 NZTR 26-022; *Smith* v. *Claims Resolution Service Ltd* [2019] NZHC 127; *Minister of Education* v. *James Hardie Ltd* [2018] NZHC 1481; *Ross* v. *Southern Response Earthquake Services Ltd* [2018] NZHC 3288; and *Paine* v. *Carter Holt Harvey Ltd* [2019] NZHC 478.

134 *Proprietors of Wakatū* v. *Attorney-General* [2017] NZSC 17, [2017] 1 NZLR 423; and *Ngāti Te Ata* v. *Minister for Treaty of Waitangi Negotiations* [2017] NZHC 2058.

There were twelve class actions in the period from 1 January 2010 to 1 July 2019, with approximately six months left from the date of writing this chapter until 1 January 2020. For the trend to continue, there would need to be an additional five to six class actions in the remaining six-month period. We note that there are two judgments from 2017 that contain obiter dicta to the effect that the relevant proceeding, while it was not a class action, could have proceeded as one had the application been made (although not currently a class action or reflected in the data as one).[135]

16.4.5.2 'Types' of Class Actions in the New Zealand High Court

A summary of the number of the 'types' of class actions in the High Court to 1 July 2019 is contained in Table 16.2. A pie chart of the data is contained in Figure 16.1.

TABLE 16.2 *Types of class actions in the New Zealand High Court*

Type of Class Action	Number of Class Actions	Years Filed	Trends
Government (Māori)[136]	3	1894[137] 1995[138] 2004[139] (2017 – two possibilities as mentioned in obiter dicta)[140]	Averaging one class action a decade in the 1990s and 2000s in the High Court.
Government (Social Security)	2	1995[141] 2002[142]	Other government actions were brought in last four decades, with an increase in the 2000s. It is too early to state whether this trend will continue in the 2010s.
Government (Tax)	2	2002[143] 2008[144]	
Government (Employment)	3	1987[145] 1993[146] 2007[147]	

135 In *Proprietors of Wakatū* v. *Attorney-General* [2017] NZSC 17, [2017] 1 NZLR 423, [649]–[662] the Supreme Court stated that the claimants would have been granted a representation order if one had been sought.

136 Note this only includes proceedings filed in the High Court. There may be more cases in other courts such as the Māori Land Court or the Environment Court. In this respect, a representative action occurred in the Environment Court in *Norton* v. *Marlborough District Council* EnvC Christchurch C017/09, 30 March 2009; and a representative action proceeded to settlement in the Māori Land Court in *Mansell – Haparangi A4* (2005) 288 Rotorua MB 9 (288 ROT 9). The latter case *Eaton & Anor v. LDC Finance Ltd & Ors* [2013] NZHC 728 are the only cases found where a court has issued a judgment on the mechanics of settlement to a class. Note *Eaton & Anor v. LDC Finance Ltd & Ors* [2013] NZHC 728 is the final judgment with a new lead plaintiff from HC Christchurch CIV-2008-409-1140, 19 November 2009.

137 *Nireaha Tamaki* v. *Baker* (1902) 22 NZLR 97 (SC).

138 *Wanganui District Council* v. *Tangaroa* [1995] 2 NZLR 706 (HC).

139 *Paki* v. *Attorney-General* [2009] 1 NZLR 72 (HC).

140 *Proprietors of Wakatū* v. *Attorney-General* [2017] NZSC 17, [2017] 1 NZLR 423; and *Ngāti Te Ata* v. *Minister for Treaty of Waitangi Negotiations* [2017] NZHC 2058.

141 *Ankers* v. *Attorney-General (No 2)* [1995] NZAR 418 (HC)

142 *Jones* v. *Attorney-General* HC Wellington CP175/02, 8 July 2003.

143 *Erris Promotions Ltd* v. *Commissioner of Inland Revenue* [2004] 1 NZLR 811 (HC).

144 *Accent Management Ltd* v. *Commissioner of Inland Revenue* (2010) 24 NZTC 24,126 (HC).

145 *New Zealand Meat Industry Assoc* v. *Accident Compensation Corporation* HC Wellington CP275/87, 19 October 1987.

146 *Talley's Fisheries Ltd* v. *Minister of Immigration* (1994) 7 PRNZ 469 (HC).

147 *Healthcare Providers New Zealand Inc* v. *Northland District Health Board* HC Wellington CIV-2007-485-1814, 7 December 2007.

TABLE 16.2 *(continued)*

Type of Class Action	Number of Class Actions	Years Filed	Trends
Government (Other)	2	1991[148] 2015[149]	
Investor	6	1993[150] 1997[151] 1997[152] 2006[153] 2008[154] 2013 – this is also a shareholder action.[155]	High percentage of investor actions against auditors for failed companies. Averaging two to three class actions each decade from the 1990s. It is too early to state whether this trend will continue in the 2010s.
Shareholder	3	1999[156] 2008[157] 2013 – This is also an investor action.[158]	Shareholder class actions evenly spread over last three decades.
General Commercial	9	1986 – Contract, Tort.[159] 1986 – Equity.[160] 1988 – Contract.[161] 2003 – Tort, Restitution, Statutory.[162] 2006 – Contract.[163] 2009 – Equity, Statutory.[164] 2009 – Tort.[165] 2016 – Statutory.[166] 2018 – Equity.[167]	Miscellaneous general commercial class actions were filed in the 1980s and 2000s, with a small increase in the 2000s. Interestingly, there were none filed in the 1990s. Two have been filed in the 2010s.

148 *Howick Engineering Ltd* v. *Manukau City Council* HC Auckland CP2021/91, 11 August 1992.
149 *Strathboss Kiwifruit Ltd* v. *Attorney-General* [2015] NZHC 1596, (2015) 23 PRNZ 69.
150 *Purdue* v. *Boyd Knight* [1987] 1 NZLR 260 (HC).
151 *Devcich* v. *Cowley Stanich & Co* (1997) 11 PRNZ 47 (HC).
152 *Registered Securities Ltd (in liq)* v. *Westpac Banking Corp* (2000) 14 PRNZ 348 (HC).
153 *Stickland* v. *Drummond* HC Auckland CIV-2006-404-3078, 13 May 2008.
154 *Harding* v. *LDC Finance Ltd (in rec)* HC Christchurch CIV-2008-409-1140, 19 November 2009.
155 *LDC Finance (in rec and in liq)* v. *Miller* [2013] NZHC 2993.
156 *Hedley* v. *Kiwi Co-Operative Dairies Ltd* (2000) 15 PRNZ 210 (HC).
157 *Houghton* v. *Saunders* (2008) 19 PRNZ 173 (HC).
158 *LDC Finance (in rec and in liq)* v. *Miller* [2013] NZHC 2993.
159 *RJ Flowers Ltd* v. *Burns* [1987] 1 NZLR 260 (HC).
160 *Overseas Containers Ltd* v. *Geo H Scales Ltd* HC Wellington CP395/86, 22 September 1986.
161 *Taspac Oysters Ltd* v. *James Hardie & Co Pty Ltd* [1990] 1 NZLR 442 (HC).
162 *Saxmere Co Ltd* v. *Wool Board Disestablishment Co Ltd.* HC Wellington CIV-2003-485-2724, 6 December 2005.
163 *Maranatha Ltd* v. *Tourism Transport Ltd* HC Auckland CIV-2006-404-6431, 3 April 2007.
164 *Blue Star Taxis (Christchurch) Society Ltd* v. *Gold Band Taxis (Christchurch) Society Ltd* HC Christchurch CIV-2009-409-2921, 19 November 2010.
165 *Wu* v. *Body Corporate 366611* [2011] 2 NZLR 837 (HC).
166 *Lin* v. *Registrar of Companies* [2016] NZHC 395.
167 *Smith* v. *Claims Resolution Service Ltd* [2019] NZHC 127.

TABLE 16.2 *(continued)*

Type of Class Action	Number of Class Actions	Years Filed	Trends
Consumer	6	2013 – Bank Fees.[168] 2013 – Product Liability.[169] 2015 – Product Liability.[170] 2015 – Insurance.[171] 2018 – Insurance.[172] 2018 – Product Liability.[173]	All six class actions by consumers were filed in the last decade since 2010. This shows a new type of class action entering the New Zealand legal landscape.
Trusts and Estates	4	1975[174] 2001[175] 2011[176] 2016[177]	Half of the class actions in relation to trusts and estates were commenced in the 2010s.
Environmental[178]	1	1972[179]	No recent environmental class actions in the High Court.

The data on the 'types' of class actions filed in the High Court is interesting. As a general observation, the total percentage of all class actions filed by a class against the government is 29 per cent, as opposed to those against a commercial party at 71 per cent.

The 'type' of class actions with the highest percentage filed in the High Court is general commercial class actions at 22 per cent, followed by class actions brought by investors (generally against auditors of insolvent companies) and class actions brought by consumers at 15 per cent each. This is followed by class actions brought in relation to trusts and estates at 10 per cent, and class actions brought by shareholders, Māori against the government, and employment disputes against the government at seven per cent each. Various other types of class actions against the government and environmental class actions range between two and five per cent of the total class actions filed in the High Court.

168 *Cooper* v. *ANZ Bank New Zealand Ltd* [2013] NZHC 2827.

169 *Minister of Education* v. *James Hardie Ltd* [2018] NZHC 1481.

170 *Cridge* v. *Studorp Ltd* [2016] NZHC 2451, (2016) 23 PRNZ 281.

171 *Southern Response Unresolved Claims Group* v. *Southern Response Earthquake Services Ltd* [2016] NZHC 3105.

172 *Ross* v. *Southern Response Earthquake Services Ltd* [2018] NZHC 3288.

173 *Paine* v. *Carter Holt Harvey Ltd* [2019] NZHC 478.

174 *Hill* v. *Wellington Co-operative Taxi Owner-Drivers' Society Ltd* HC Wellington A4/75, 3 February 1988.

175 *'Akau'Ola* v. *President of the Conference of the Methodist Church of New Zealand* HC Auckland CP183/SW01, 5 December 2001; and *Jones* v. *Attorney-General* HC Wellington CP175/02, 8 July 2003.

176 *Cadman* v. *Visini* (2011) 3 NZTR 21-011 (HC).

177 *Vlaar* v. *van der Lubbe* [2016] NZHC 2398, (2016) 4 NZTR 26-022.

178 Note that the data reflected in this empirical study only reflects class action proceedings filed in the High Court. There may be additional cases in other courts such as the Environment Court.

179 *Mundy* v. *Cunningham* [1973] 1 NZLR 555 (SC).

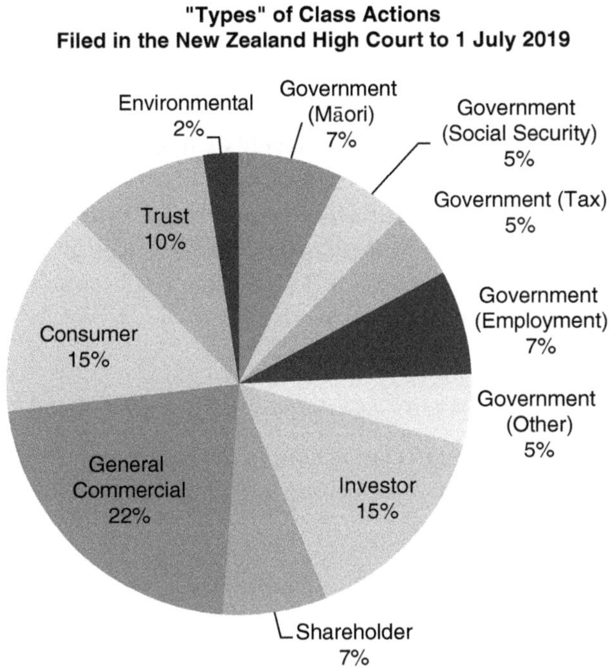

FIGURE 16.1 Pie chart of types of class actions in the New Zealand High Court

The data about the 'types' of class actions that were filed reflect the following trends:

(1) Class actions by Māori against the government appear steadily once every decade in the 1990s and 2000s.[180] Class actions by plaintiffs against the government relating to areas such as social security, tax, employment or other miscellaneous actions have been filed over the last three decades, with the most filed in the 2000s.
(2) Several class actions by investors were filed over the last three decades, averaging two to three filed in the 1990s and 2000s. One has been filed in the 2010s.
(3) Class actions by shareholders occurred steadily over the last three decades, with one filed every decade.
(4) Class actions categorised as 'general commercial' (including actions against commercial parties outside the other categories) show that three class actions were filed in the 1980s, four in the 2000s, two in the 2010s and, interestingly, none in the 1990s.
(5) Class actions filed by consumers (whether that be product liability, insurance or bank litigation) have all commenced in the last decade since 2010 (amounting to a total of six class actions).
(6) Class actions filed in relation to trusts and estates have mostly been filed in the last two decades, with a slight increase in filings in the 2010s.
(7) There are no new environmental class actions, with the only case identified filed in 1972.[181]

[180] This number does not include cases that have been commenced in the Māori Land Court.
[181] This number does not include cases that have been commenced in the Environment Court.

The data indicate that, in general, class actions against the government have been consistent and, in fact, increased in the 2000s. Shareholder and miscellaneous general commercial class actions (mostly containing tortious cause of actions) appear relatively steady over the last three decades, with an increase in these actions in the 2000s. It is too early to state whether these trends will continue in the 2010s, as there are approximately six months left of the decade from 1 July 2019.

The most interesting trend is that class actions commenced by consumers and class actions relating to trusts and estates significantly increased in the 2010s (with all six class actions brought by consumers filed in the decade since 2010). This evidence reflects a new type of class action entering the New Zealand legal landscape.

16.4.5.3 Plaintiff Class Size in Class Actions in the New Zealand High Court

A summary of the plaintiff class size in class actions in the High Court to 1 July 2019 is contained in Table 16.3. A pie chart of the data is contained in Figure 16.2.

TABLE 16.3 *Plaintiff class sizes in class actions in the New Zealand High Court*

Number of Plaintiffs	Number of Proceedings
1–10	6[182]
11–50	7[183]
51–100	2[184]
101–200	3[185]
201–500	3[186]

182 *Hill* v. *Wellington Co-operative Taxi Owner-Drivers' Society Ltd* HC Wellington A4/75, 3 February 1988 (four members); *Ankers* v. *Attorney-General (No 2)* [1995] NZAR 418 (HC) (four members); *Accent Management Ltd* v. *Commissioner of Inland Revenue* (2010) 24 NZTC 24,126 (HC) (seven members); *Wu* v. *Body Corporate 366611* [2011] 2 NZLR 837 (HC) 234 (nine members); *Cadman* v. *Visini* (2011) 3 NZTR 21-011 (HC) (three members); and *Vlaar* v. *van der Lubbe* [2016] NZHC 2398, (2016) 4 NZTR 26-022 (five members).

183 *Taspac Oysters Ltd* v. *James Hardie & Co Pty Ltd* [1990] 1 NZLR 442 (HC) (eight members, later increased to eleven in *Taspac Oysters Ltd* v. *James Hardie & Co Pty Ltd* HC Auckland CL104/88, 23 May 1990); *RJ Flowers Ltd* v. *Burns* [1987] 1 NZLR 260 (HC) (22 members); *'Akau'Ola* v. *President of the Conference of the Methodist Church of New Zealand* HC Auckland CP183/SW01, 5 December 2001 (seventeen members); *Jones* v. *Attorney-General* HC Wellington CP175/02, 8 July 2003 (seventeen members); *Stickland* v. *Drummond* HC Auckland CIV-2006-404-3078, 13 May 2008 (forty members); *Maranatha Ltd* v. *Tourism Transport Ltd* HC Auckland CIV-2006-404-6431, 3 April 2007 (twenty-three members); *Southern Response Unresolved Claims Group* v. *Southern Response Earthquake Services Ltd* [2016] NZHC 3105 (forty-seven members); and *Cridge* v. *Studorp Ltd* [2016] NZHC 2451, (2016) 23 PRNZ 281 (eighteen members).

184 *Devcich* v. *Cowley Stanich & Co* (1997) 11 PRNZ 47 (HC) (seventy-three members); and *Saxmere Co Ltd* v. *Wool Board Disestablishment Co Ltd* HC Wellington CIV-2003-485-2724, 6 December 2005 (fifty-seven members).

185 *Mundy* v. *Cunningham* [1973] 1 NZLR 555 (SC) (119 members); *Harding* v. *LDC Finance Ltd (in rec)* HC Christchurch CIV-2008-409-1140, 19 November 2009(181 members); *Blue Star Taxis (Christchurch) Society Ltd* v. *Gold Band Taxis (Christchurch) Society Ltd* HC Christchurch CIV-2009-409-2921, 19 November 2010 (defendant class had 155 members); *Paine* v. *Carter Holt Harvey Ltd* [2019] NZHC 478 (127 members).

186 *Hedley* v. *Kiwi Co-Operative Dairies Ltd* (2000) 15 PRNZ 210 (HC) (258 members); *Erris Promotions Ltd* v. *Commissioner of Inland Revenue* [2004] 1 NZLR 811 (HC) (200-plus members); and *Blue Star Taxis (Christchurch) Society Ltd* v. *Gold Band Taxis (Christchurch) Society Ltd* HC Christchurch CIV-2009-409-2921, 19 November 2010 (plaintiff class had 225 members).

TABLE 16.3 *(continued)*

Number of Plaintiffs	Number of Proceedings
501–1,000	2[187]
1,001–2,000	1[188]
2,001–4,000	2[189]
Greater than 4,001	3[190]
TOTAL	29

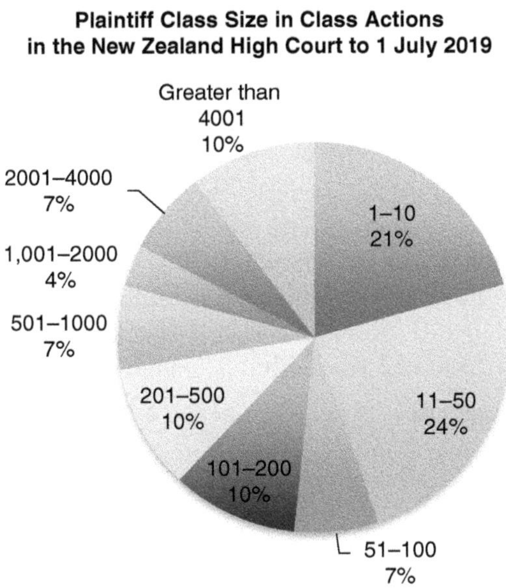

FIGURE 16.2 Pie chart of plaintiff class sizes in class actions in the New Zealand High Court

There is a total of forty class actions in the High Court over the last four decades. The plaintiff class sizes (or approximate class sizes)[191] are mentioned in twenty-nine out of the forty class action judgments available. Of these twenty-nine cases, the data indicates that the most common plaintiff class size ranges between eleven and fifty plaintiffs at 24 per cent, followed by class sizes between one and ten plaintiffs at 21 per cent. Interestingly, the third most common plaintiff class sizes, with a tie at 10 per cent, are class sizes between 101 and 200 plaintiffs, class sizes between 201 and 500 plaintiffs and class sizes with greater than 4,001 plaintiffs. Plaintiff class sizes between 51 and 100 plaintiffs, 501 and 1000 plaintiffs and 2001 and 4000 plaintiffs held seven per cent each of

[187] *LDC Finance (in rec and in liq)* v. *Miller* [2013] NZHC 2993 (800 members); and *Minister of Education* v. *James Hardie Ltd* [2018] NZHC 1481(833 members).

[188] *Purdue* v. *Boyd Knight* [1987] 1 NZLR 260 (HC) (approximately 1,715 members).

[189] *Credit Suisse Private Equity LLC* v. *Houghton* [2014] NZSC 37, [2014] 1 NZLR 514 (2,852 shareholders); and *Ross* v. *Southern Response Earthquake Services Ltd* [2018] NZHC 3288 (up to 3,000 insured).

[190] *Talley's Fisheries Ltd* v. *Minister of Immigration* (1994) 7 PRNZ 469 (HC) (4,500 members); *Registered Securities Ltd (in liq)* v. *Westpac Banking Corp* (2000) 14 PRNZ 348 (HC) (8,203 investors); and *Cooper* v. *ANZ Bank New Zealand Ltd* [2013] NZHC 2827 (13,500 members).

[191] The class sizes include where judgments state approximate numbers and 'up to' numbers. Where there are multiple plaintiff classes, then the largest plaintiff size is contained in the data reflected in this section of the empirical study.

the total twenty-nine cases analysed. The class sizes containing between 1,001 and 2000 plaintiffs totalled four per cent.

There are eleven class actions identified from the High Court judgments that do not state the plaintiff class size, including eight class actions against the government (such as those brought by Māori, social security plaintiffs and employees). These plaintiff class sizes are likely to be large, given the nature of the class actions at issue. There are also three general commercial class actions that do not state the plaintiff class size.

16.4.5.4 Number, Date and 'Type' of Class Actions Funded by Litigation Funders in the New Zealand High Court

A summary of the number, date and 'type' of class actions funded in the High Court is contained in Table 16.4.[192]

Litigation funders have funded a total of six out of forty class actions identified in this study. All six of the class actions funded by a litigation funder have occurred in the last two decades since the year 2000, with five of these six in the decade since 2010. The increase in the prevalence of cases involving a litigation funder in the last decade indicates that litigation funding is on the rise in New Zealand. Five litigation funders are currently actively involved in funding class actions in New Zealand. Joint Action Funding Ltd is funding a shareholder and investor class action. LPF Litigation Funding Ltd is funding a class action against the government. Litigation Lending Services (NZ) Ltd is funding two consumer class actions (bank litigation and insurance litigation). Harbour Funding III Limited Partnership is funding a consumer class action (product

TABLE 16.4 *Number, date and type of class actions funded by litigation finders in the New Zealand High Court*

Year	Number of Class Actions Funded by Litigation Funder	Type of Class Action Funded	Name of Litigation Funder
2008	1[193]	Shareholder and Investor	Joint Action Funding Ltd
2013	1[194]	LLS – Consumer (Bank Litigation)	Litigation Lending Services (NZ) Ltd
2015	2[195]	LPF – Government (General) LLS – Consumer (Insurance)	LPF Litigation Funding Ltd Litigation Lending Services (NZ) Ltd
2018	2[196]	Consumer (Product Liability) Consumer (Insurance)	Harbour Fund III Limited Partnership Claims Funding Australia

[192] See Section 16.4.4.5 in this chapter for the judicial trends on litigation funding agreements.

[193] *Credit Suisse Private Equity LLC* v. *Houghton* [2014] NZSC 37, [2014] 1 NZLR 514.

[194] *Cooper* v. *ANZ Bank New Zealand Ltd* [2013] NZHC 2827.

[195] *Strathboss Kiwifruit Ltd* v. *Attorney-General* [2015] NZHC 1596, (2015) 23 PRNZ 69 (LPF); and *Southern Response Unresolved Claims Group* v. *Southern Response Earthquake Services Ltd* [2016] NZHC 3105 (LLS).

[196] *Strathboss Kiwifruit Ltd* v. *Attorney-General* [2015] NZHC 1596, (2015) 23 PRNZ 69 (LPF); *Southern Response Unresolved Claims Group* v. *Southern Response Earthquake Services Ltd* [2016] NZHC 3105 (LLS); *Paine* v. *Carter Holt Harvey Ltd* [2019] NZHC 478 (Harbour Fund III Limited Partnership); and *Ross* v. *Southern Response Earthquake Services Ltd* [2018] NZHC 3288 (Claims Funding Australia).

TABLE 16.5 *Number of class actions in the New Zealand Employment Court*

Years (decade intervals unless stated otherwise)	Number of class actions in Employment Court
Pre-1980s	0
1980s	0
1990s	7[197]
2000s	1[198]
2010 – 1 July 2019	0 (1 case noting class action mechanism still allowed in Employment Court)[199]
TOTAL	8

liability litigation). Claims Funding Australia is funding a consumer class action (insurance litigation).

16.4.5.5 Date and Number of Class Actions in the New Zealand Employment Court

A summary of the number of class actions in the Employment Court for each decade (unless stated otherwise) to 1 July 2019 is contained in Table 16.5.

A total of eight class actions were filed in the Employment Court under HCR 4.24. Seven out of the eight class actions were filed in the 1990s. One out of the eight class actions was filed in the 2000s. The data discloses that there have been no class actions in the Employment Court since 2010. The data indicates that, unlike in the High Court, the number of class actions being filed in the Employment Court under HCR 4.24 is declining.[200]

16.4.5.6 Plaintiff Class Size in Class Actions in the New Zealand Employment Court

A summary of the plaintiff class size in class actions in the Employment Court to 1 July 2019 is contained in Table 16.6.

We identify a total of eight class actions in the Employment Court over the last four decades. The plaintiff class sizes are contained in three out of the eight class action judgments available. The data indicate that class sizes vary significantly.

The empirical research shows that class actions in the New Zealand High Court between the decades of 1980 and 2010 have increased, whereas class actions in the New Zealand Employment Court have decreased. As previously stated, the focus of this chapter is on class actions in the High Court. As a result, we will not address the reasons for the trends in the Employment Court

197 *Chapman* v. *Waitemata Stevedoring Services Ltd (No 2)* [1992] 3 ERNZ 756 (EmpC); *Fire Service Commission* v. *Duncan* EmpC Wellington WEC14/94, 21 April 1994; *Amlehn* v. *Sanford Ltd* EmpC Christchurch CEC11/97, 9 April 1997; *Kelly* v. *Tranz Rail Ltd* [1997] ERNZ 476 (EmpC); *Whitaker* v. *Vela Fishing Ltd* EmpC Christchurch CC39/98, 11 November 1998; *New Zealand Public Service Assoc Inc* v. *Attorney-General* [1998] 3 ERNZ 1307 (EmpC); and *Andersen* v. *Capital Coast Health* [2000] 1 ERNZ 256 (EmpC).

198 *Air New Zealand Ltd* v. *Flight Attendants and Related Services (New Zealand) Assoc Inc* [2002] 2 ERNZ 770 (EmpC).

199 *Riyanto* v. *Dong Nam Co Ltd* [2015] NZEmpC 67, [2015] ERNZ 691.

200 See footnote 204 in this chapter.

TABLE 16.6 *Plaintiff class size in class actions in the New Zealand Employment Court*

Number of Plaintiffs	Number of Proceedings
1–10	0
11–50	1[201]
51–100	0
101–200	1[202]
201–500	0
501–1,000	0
1,001–2,000	1[203]
2,001–4,000	0
Greater than 4,001	0
TOTAL	3

other than to identify those trends.[204] We will, however, address the possible reasons for the increase in the number of class actions filed in the High Court.

16.4.6 *Reasons for the Increase of Class Actions in the New Zealand High Court*[205]

The use of the class action mechanism was historically slow to develop in New Zealand for a number of reasons. First, there is no statutory framework that specifically governs the management of class actions. The judiciary has utilised the procedural framework available to it in HCR 4.24 to allow class actions, while using its inherent jurisdiction to supplement decision-making on procedural issues. Unsurprisingly, the willingness of the judiciary to allow HCR 4.24 to be used to create class actions is one explanation for the increase in class actions brought by the affected classes.

Second, a significant proportion of class action litigation overseas is for personal injury cases.[206] New Zealand has the Accident Compensation Scheme, which bars most forms of personal injury litigation for compensatory damages,[207] meaning that personal injury class actions are not part of New Zealand's legal landscape. Third, New Zealand courts are relatively conservative with their damages awards in comparison to their American counterparts.[208] As a result, the damages at issue need to be of an amount that makes the pursuit of a class action

201 *Whitaker* v. *Vela Fishing Ltd* EmpC Christchurch CC39/98, 11 November 1998.
202 *Andersen* v. *Capital Coast Health* [2000] 1 ERNZ 256 (EmpC).
203 *Kelly* v. *Tranz Rail Ltd* [1997] ERNZ 476 (EmpC).
204 For example, one of the potential reasons for the decrease of class actions under HCR 4.24 in the Employment Court is because parties decided to run test cases for a select group of plaintiffs as opposed to running an entire class action. Furthermore, it is likely that class actions are proceeding through the courts under a section other than HCR 4.24, for instance under the Employment Contracts Act 1991. However, we will not enquire into this issue further for the purpose of this article.
205 The writing in this section is predominantly quoted from one of the author's articles, being: Nikki Chamberlain, *Class Actions in New Zealand: An Empirical Study*, 24 NZBLQ 132 (2018).
206 Rachel Dunning, *All for one and one for all: Class Action Litigation and Arbitration in New Zealand*, 3 PILJNZ 68, 70 (2016).
207 Accident Compensation Act 2001.
208 Rachel Dunning, *All for one and one for all: Class Action Litigation and Arbitration in New Zealand*, 3 PILJNZ 68, 70 (2016).

economically viable. Fourth, as a general comment, New Zealand's population size[209] and economic environment[210] means that there are fewer class actions than other jurisdictions.

Finally, until recently, litigation funding was not permitted in New Zealand due to the torts of champerty and maintenance. The torts of champerty and maintenance are still permitted in New Zealand, albeit in a limited form. Litigation funding is allowed where there is an arguable case for rights that warrant vindication, where there is no abuse of process, and where the funding arrangement is approved by the court.[211] In this respect, a low-stake class action claim[212] was often not economically feasible, given that plaintiff class members were unlikely to have the equity to fund the litigation without the backing of funders. In addition, unlike the United States, in New Zealand the party that loses the litigation is usually liable to make a contribution towards the costs of the winning party,[213] meaning that the litigation risk and exposure is greater in New Zealand than in the United States. As a result, it is not surprising that the use of class actions is increasing with the entrance of litigation funders into the New Zealand market. In particular, the data in this study show that there has been a rise of consumer class actions as a consequence of litigation funders entering the New Zealand market. Litigation funders are, however, currently unregulated in New Zealand. Both class action civil procedure and litigation funding regulation needs reform, as discussed in Section 16.5 below.

16.5 THE FUTURE OF CLASS ACTIONS IN NEW ZEALAND[214]

16.5.1 *Civil Procedure: Purpose and Process Values in New Zealand*

As there has undeniably been an increase in the number of class actions in New Zealand over time, the question then becomes whether the current civil procedure framework contained in HCR 4.24 is adequate in managing class action litigation. In order to assess this, the purpose of civil procedure needs to be examined in order to assess if its aims are currently being met.

Civil procedure provides the mechanism by which legal disputes are heard and determined. It regulates 'the operation of the legal system in the interest of justice'.[215] In other words, it provides the framework through which rights are vindicated. Civil procedure is less concerned 'about the *what* than about the *how*'.[216] Civil procedure can be determined in a number of ways, including through party agreement, legislation and/or regulation or judicial discretion.

For third-party decision makers like the judiciary, there is no uniform way to determine disputes without civil procedure rules. In this respect, the rule of law, which states that 'the law – and its meaning – must be fixed and publicly known in advance of application',[217] would be

209 The population of New Zealand is just under five million people, based on data from the 2018 census: Stats NZ 'Population' www.stats.govt.nz.

210 New Zealand has a relatively small economy and Gross Domestic Product was calculated as $269 billion in March 2019. See Stats NZ 'Economy' and 'Gross Domestic Product' www.stats.govt.nz.

211 *Saunders* v. *Houghton* [2009] NZCA 610, [2010] 3 NZLR 331, [21]–[34].

212 Low-stake claims are claims where the damages award for each individual class member is small but, when aggregated, makes a claim economically viable for parties that have the appetite to fund the litigation and bear the costs consequences of the litigation.

213 The costs are usually awarded on a scaled basis in accordance with the High Court Rules, although a party can apply for increased or indemnity costs.

214 The writing in this section is predominantly quoted from one of the author's articles, being: Nikki Chamberlain, *Class Actions in New Zealand: An Empirical Study*, 24 NZBLQ 132 (2018).

215 Howard M. Erichson, *Civil Procedure and the Legal Profession*, 79 Fordham L. Rev. 1827, 1827 (2011).

216 Howard M. Erichson, *Civil Procedure and the Legal Profession*, 79 Fordham L. Rev. 1827, 1827 (2011).

217 Richard H. Fallon Jr, *'The Rule of Law' as a Concept in Constitutional Discourse*, 97 Colum L. Rev. 1, 3 (1997).

eroded without civil procedure rules that are binding on all parties who cannot agree their own procedure. Indeed, a basic principle of the rule of law is that laws, including procedural laws, are clear, publicised, stable, just and evenly applied in society.[218]

Civil procedure legal theory, in part, analyses how a society's process values shapes the adoption of process or procedural rules. Andrew Barker QC identifies a number of process values that underpin and align with procedural rules.[219] Process values can include prioritising substantive justice, process legitimacy, procedural fairness, participatory governance, respect for the individual and his or her autonomy, timeliness, efficiency and/or finality.[220]

The process values which underpin New Zealand's civil procedure are expressly stated in rule 1.2 of the High Court Rules (HCR 1.2), titled 'Objective'. HCR 1.2 states: 'The objective of these rules is to secure the just, speedy, and inexpensive determination of any proceeding or interlocutory application'. In our view, the current procedure provided in HCR 4.24 for governing class action litigation does not accord or align with the process values identified in HCR 1.2. We assess below some of the advantages and disadvantages of HCR 4.24 in light of the process values in HCR 1.2.

16.5.2 *Advantages and Disadvantages of HCR 4.24*

The first and most obvious advantage of HCR 4.24 in managing class action litigation is that it allows judicial flexibility. The judiciary can tailor class action procedure to the particular litigation at issue. Judicial flexibility is, however, a double-edged sword.

The brevity of HCR 4.24, combined with judicial flexibility can create problems. First, as previously discussed, HCR 4.24 was never intended to govern class action procedure. As a result, the lack of specific and mandatory procedural rules means that class action litigation is not efficient or economical to run. Simple procedural issues are appealed through the court system at the expense of the class action parties. Admittedly, specific statutory-based class-wide rules would be tested in the courts initially. However, it is likely that the frequency of these cases would diminish as precedent is established on the interpretation of the rules. In addition, judicial flexibility can mean that there is a lack of certainty. For example, there are no rules about judicial review of settlement amounts, cy pres issues (what will happen with settlement funds that are not claimed by class members), or the ability and/or requirements to challenge the appointment of the class representative. Currently there limited no case law to provide guidance to counsel on these issues, creating uncertainty for new parties before the court.

Some would argue another advantage of HCR 4.24 is that it does not overtly promote the class action device and, as a result, the floodgates have not been opened to class action litigation. Insurers are likely to agree with this position. Some may consider that formalising class action procedure rules will equate to an increased number of class action proceedings and, consequently, an increased pressure on defendants to enter into global class-wide settlements.[221] Rightly or wrongly, class actions are perceived to have high 'transaction costs' meaning proceeding to trial is simply unaffordable for defendants.[222]

In response, the reality, as shown in this empirical study, is that class action litigation is already occurring and in fact increasing in New Zealand. Parties who are currently part of a class action

218 World Justice Project 'What is the Rule of Law?' https://worldjusticeproject.org.
219 Andrew Barker, *Ideas on the Purpose of Civil Procedure*, NZ. L. Rev. 437 (2002).
220 Andrew Barker, *Ideas on the Purpose of Civil Procedure*, NZ. L. Rev. 437, 448 (2002).
221 Justin Scott Emerson, *Class Actions*, 19 VUWLR 183, 189 (1989).
222 Justin Scott Emerson, *Class Actions*, 19 VUWLR 183, 187 (1989).

are disadvantaged by the lack of procedural rules. Further, the criticisms of the class action device need to be weighed against the generally accepted advantages of class actions. Class actions have a social utility value as they create access to justice to parties where it would be uneconomical for a party to pursue individual litigation.[223] Class action litigation allows for judicial economy through an efficient use of resources by the court hearing common issues together on a class-wide basis as opposed to individual proceedings for each class member.[224] Class action litigation can deter corporate and government wrongdoing and can encourage compliance with the rule of law.[225] It can provide a mechanism to remedy unjust enrichment. It can also be a tool for social change.[226]

A third advantage of HCR 4.24 is that it does not expressly promote litigation funding and, therefore, arguably, some may say the floodgates have not been opened in New Zealand for third parties to fund litigation. In response, as this empirical study shows, litigation funding is already occurring in New Zealand without regulation. The problem with failing to regulate third-party funders primarily concerns control of the litigation. Litigation funders have different goals than class members and, as a result, they may have different views on decisions such as whether a case should proceed to trial or be settled. There are also issues around whether all class plaintiffs will be required to pay the third-party funders if some refuse to sign up to the litigation funding agreement, leading to the question of whether New Zealand should adopt rules around common fund orders. Regulation would assist in ensuring that the interests of all stakeholders are adequately balanced, and that safeguards are in place for class action parties. Specifically, regulation can dictate the boundaries of funding agreements as well as indicate who is responsible for ensuring compliance with, and enforcement of, the regulations.

Fourthly, some may argue that HCR 4.24 preserves principles of natural justice, as some judges currently interpret HCR 4.24 as only allowing 'opt-in' class actions as opposed to 'opt-out' class actions. The argument is that people should not be bound by the results of litigation that they may not be aware of or take active steps to be part of. To counter this, most common law countries that allow class actions provide procedural rules on notifying potential class members of an opt-out class action. In addition, formal rules allowing for opt-out class actions could enhance judicial economy and, in certain situations, be advantageous to defendants who can save on costs by defending fewer claims because most affected parties will be bound by a final judgment under res judicata, provided that they do not opt-out of the class action proceeding.

Lastly, some may contend that the lack of statutory-based procedural rules is not impeding class action stakeholders. In response, most common law jurisdictions that allow class actions have statutory-based civil procedure rules on class certification, whether a class action can be opt-in or opt-out, notice requirements to potential class members, administration of class action trials, class action judicial settlement approval requirements, damage allocation requirements, cy pres issues and whether class actions can be contracted out of by the use of arbitration agreements. In contrast, New Zealand has no specific statutory-based civil procedure rules on any of these important procedural issues. In the end, New Zealand's lack of procedural rules has a negative impact on the vindication of a class action party's substantive rights.

223 Justin Scott Emerson, *Class Actions*, 19 VUWLR 183, 187 (1989).
224 Justin Scott Emerson, *Class Actions*, 19 VUWLR 183, 187 (1989).
225 Justin Scott Emerson, *Class Actions*, 19 VUWLR 183, 188 (1989).
226 Justin Scott Emerson, *Class Actions*, 19 VUWLR 183, 189 (1989).

16.5.3 *Recommendations for Reform*

The Law Commission is presently reviewing the law relating to class actions and litigation funding, this being the second time reform has been tabled in this area. The New Zealand Rules Committee drafted a Class Actions Bill in 2008. Regrettably, the Bill, based loosely on Australia's class action statutory regime, was never introduced to Parliament.[227] The Law Commission is likely to again address the question of whether reform is required and, if so determined, to evaluate reform options. Clearly, by virtue of the Commission's mandate, the government is acknowledging that reform may be needed. We agree. For the reasons addressed in this chapter, HCR 4.24 is clearly no longer working. The empirical data confirms that the number of class actions in the High Court is increasing. Regulation is required to overcome the deficiencies of HCR 4.24.

In brief, there are three primary methods for class action reform. The first is through regulatory enforcement for class-wide wrongs (such as through a body like the Commerce Commission or the Financial Markets Authority). The second is through private enforcement for class-wide wrongs – in other words, leaving rectification of class-wide wrongs to the market. The third is a combination of the first two options. In evaluating the options, in our view, it should be recognised that regulatory authorities have a finite budget, meaning not all wrongs will be pursued.

In relation to civil procedure options for the private enforcement of class-wide wrongs, there are three main avenues to consider. First, the government could make no change to current procedure. For the reasons considered above, we do not support this option. Second, the government could promote and encourage mass alternative dispute resolution processes (i.e., class arbitration or specialist resolution services for certain types of claims) as opposed to class litigation through the High Court. Thirdly, the government could enact legislation that incorporates specific class action civil procedure rules, as has happened in other jurisdictions such as Australia and the United States. Under the third option, the government could build on the work already done by the Rules Committee in drafting the Class Actions Bill 2008. The Bill covers a number of areas on the procedural management of class action litigation in addition to dealing with limitation periods,[228] litigation funding,[229] and preventing the torts of champerty and maintenance from applying to class actions.[230] This Bill could be updated and amended where appropriate. Alternatively, the government could require the Rules Committee to draft entirely new rules to be enacted. Admittedly, it is logical for the government to build upon the extensive work already completed on the Bill if it decides to leave redress for class-wide wrongs to private actors in the market (whether wholly or in part).

We are proponents of the third option. First, statutory intervention will take the burden off of individual judges and the case management system by reducing the procedural decisions required by the judiciary. A flow on effect will be that class action litigation will be more efficient and cost-effective for the judiciary and class action parties. Second, the legislature is in a better

[227] Noted in Nikki Chamberlain, *Contracting-Out of Class Action Litigation: Lessons from the United States*, NZ L. Rev. 371, 374, footnote 16 (2018): 'The Rules Committee submitted the draft Bill to the New Zealand government in 2009. The draft Bill has only been posted online in its draft form. The Class Actions Bill 2008 and High Court Amendment (Class Actions) Rules 2008 can be viewed at www.globalclassactions.stanford.edu. Originally, the Bill was not released as the Ministry of Justice claimed legal privilege and stated that the documents were likely to be changed by the government. Rules Committee *Note on Class Actions* (30 July 2009). See also Chris Patterson, *Class actions in New Zealand: The necessity for introducing a class action regime*, 5 J. Civ. L. P. 20, 21 (2016).

[228] Draft Class Actions Bill 2008, cl. 14.

[229] Cl. 23 (in a later version of the draft Bill not available publicly).

[230] Cl. 22 (in a later version of the draft Bill not available publicly).

position to balance the needs of class action plaintiffs and defendants after consultation with all relevant stakeholders.[231] Lastly, statutory intervention will provide consistency and certainty on the procedure for class action litigation for the benefit of all stakeholders.[232]

16.6 CONCLUSION

It is plain that class action litigation is increasing in the New Zealand High Court. HCR 4.24, coupled with judicial discretion, is no longer sufficient in managing class actions and litigation funding. Various reform options are available. Regardless of the avenue chosen, reform is clearly needed for the qualitative and quantitative reasons identified in this chapter. The focus should now shift to the best option for reform in New Zealand.

[231] Anthony Wicks, *Class Actions in New Zealand: Is Legislation Still Necessary?*, NZ L. Rev. 73, 107 (2015).

[232] The ideas in this paragraph are taken from Nikki Chamberlain, *Contracting-Out of Class Action Litigation: Lessons from the United States*, NZ L. Rev. 371, 397 (2018) and Nikki Chamberlain, Class Actions in New Zealand: An Empirical Study, 24 NZBLQ 132 (2018).

17

Representative Proceedings in Singapore

Is the Time Ripe for Reform?

*Eunice Chua**

17.1 INTRODUCTION

The only procedure presently available for group litigation in Singapore is the representative proceeding provided for by Order 15 Rule 12 of the Singapore Rules of Court.[1] Although legislation may provide for representative action in specific instances, such as under section 85 of the Building Maintenance and Strata Management Act,[2] which enables a management corporation to bring proceedings on behalf of the subsidiary proprietors of a building or to defend an action on their behalf, this chapter focuses on Order 15 Rule 12 as being widely applicable.

Order 15 rule 12(1) states that "[w]here numerous persons have the same interest in any proceedings . . . the proceedings may be begun, and, unless the Court otherwise orders, continued by or against any one or more of them as representing all or as representing all except one or more of them." Under Order 15 rule 12(3), a judgment or order given in representative proceedings is binding on all the persons being represented whether as plaintiffs or defendants but shall not be enforced against persons that are not party to the proceedings except with the leave of court. In other words, the representative action in Singapore is confined to only known plaintiffs or defendants who have the same identified interests, and the judgments or orders obtained through the representative action are only enforceable against parties to the action unless the court grants leave.

The representative proceeding in Singapore is different from a statutory class action regime in that it does not cater for various uncertainties, which an express class action regime could provide a resolution mechanism for.[3] These include statutory protection to both claimants and

* I would like to thank my supportive family, without whom this piece would not have been written, as well as Mr Dhiraj Chainani for his invaluable research assistance.

1 Supreme Court of Judicature Act (Cap. 322, s. 80) Rules of Court (R5, 2014 Rev. Ed.) O. 15 r. 12.

2 Building Maintenance and Strata Management Act (Cap. 30C, 2008 Rev Ed) s 85. In *Management Corporation Strata Title Plan No 3556 (suing on behalf of itself and all subsidiary proprietors of Northstar @ AMK)* v. *Orion-One Development Pte Ltd (in liquidation) and another* [2019] SGHC 70 at para. 12, the High Court noted the procedural effect of s. 85(1) in allowing a management corporation to bring an action on behalf of a large number of subsidiary proprietors in a development which wish to sue. The court did reiterate however, that a management corporation would be required to identify the specific subsidiary proprietors (being the substantive parties to the action) whom it claims to represent, by naming them individually in an annex to its statement of claim.

3 Rachael Mulheron, "From Representative Rule to Class Action: Steps Rather Than Leaps" [2005] *CJQ* 424 at 436.

defendants, such as compulsory judicial approval of settlement agreements, the aggregate assessment of damages, and cy pres distributions.[4]

Singapore's rule on representative proceedings corresponds to the former Order 15 rule 12 of the English Rules of the Supreme Court. England has since reformed its civil procedure rules to introduce group litigation orders under Part 19(III) of the English Civil Procedure Rules. Hong Kong, which also has identical provisions to Singapore,[5] has had the Law Reform Commission Report on Class Actions published in May 2012, recommending the introduction, under an incremental approach, of a class action regime in Hong Kong.[6] Does Singapore need an alternative to the representative proceeding? Is the time ripe for reform? Can the current procedure stand the test of time? This chapter will critically examine these questions.

17.2 FEATURES OF REPRESENTATIVE PROCEEDINGS IN SINGAPORE

The key ingredients for a representative proceeding to be brought in Singapore under Order 15 rule 12 are, first, numerous persons having the "same interest"; and, second, the court refraining from exercising its discretion to disallow representative proceedings. The Court of Appeal has held that the "same interest" requirement is a jurisdictional threshold requirement.[7] Assuming this requirement is met, the court may then "exercise its discretion to discontinue the proceedings in question as a representative action where the overall circumstances of the case so justify."[8]

The Court of Appeal has further stated that Order 15 rule 12(1) is to be applied in a "broad and flexible" manner to facilitate access to justice.[9] However, the court will also strive to strike a balance between the interests of the claimants and those of the defendants, who may suffer prejudice such as: (1) being unable to obtain discovery against those persons sought to be represented: (2) being unable to cross-examine those persons sought to be represented; and (3) not being entitled to seek costs against those persons sought to be represented in the event of successfully defending the action.[10]

Based on these considerations, the Court of Appeal has laid down the following factors that, if satisfied, will mean that the "same interest" requirement has been met:

(1) The class of represented persons is capable of clear definition in that members of the class of represented persons can be identified by "an objective criterion which bears a rational relationship to the common issues being asserted."[11]
(2) The proposed representatives "adequately represent the interests of the class of represented persons, and must vigorously and capably prosecute the interests of the entire class."[12]
(3) There are "one or more significant issues of fact or law common to all the claimants for determination by the court."[13] Generally, where the "legal and factual inquiry required

4 *Koh Chong Chiah and others* v. *Treasure Resort Pte Ltd* [2013] SGCA 52 at para 37 approvingly quoting Rachael Mulheron, "From Representative Rule to Class Action: Steps Rather Than Leaps" [2005] *CJQ* 424 at 448.
5 See Hong Kong's Rules of the High Court, O. 15 r. 12.
6 Law Reform Commission of Hong Kong, *Report on Class Action* (2012).
7 *Koh Chong Chiah and others* v. *Treasure Resort Pte Ltd* [2013] SGCA 52 at para. 29.
8 *Ibid.* The Court of Appeal cited *Carnie and another* v. *Esanda Finance Corporation Limited* (1995) 182 CLR 398 at 427 with approval.
9 *Koh Chong Chiah and others* v. *Treasure Resort Pte Ltd* [2013] SGCA 52 at paras 32–34.
10 *Ibid.* at paras 36–37.
11 *Ibid.* at para 78.
12 *Ibid.*
13 *Ibid.* at para 57.

for the determination of an issue in a claim in a representative action is also relevant to the determination of the same issue in the other claims in the representative action, . . . it [would be] highly probable that the issue is common to all the claimants."[14] The court will also compare the significance of the common issues between the claimants with the significance of differing issues.[15]

(4) All the claimants must benefit from the relief granted by the court and must have the same interest in the relief granted by the court.[16]

The threshold requirement has been passed in a few cases, including *Abdul Rahim* v. *Ling How Doong & Ors*,[17] where members of a political party were ruled to have the "same interest" because they had a common interest in the election of persons to the Central Executive Committee of the political party,[18] and in *Raffles Town Club Pte Ltd* v. *Tan Chin Seng*,[19] where ten members of a country club brought suit on behalf of 4,885 other members for breach of contract in promising its members a premier club but failing to do so due to admitting too large a number of people, totaling some 19,000.

In *Koh Chong Chiah and others* v. *Treasure Resort Pte Ltd*, 203 members of a country club were found to have the "same interest" in relation to proving the alleged novation of their original membership agreements to the new club owner, the terms of the membership transfer agreement, the repudiation of the respective member agreements between the claimants and the new club owner, and the claim in misrepresentation.[20] However, they did not satisfy the "same interest" requirement in relation to their breach of contract claims because of the different circumstances surrounding the alleged breaches of contract between the various claimants.

The "same interest" test in Singapore appears to be a permissive and practical one and is certainly less strict than that articulated in *Markt & Co Ltd* v. *Knight Steamship Co Ltd*, where the English Court of Appeal, in a departure from the liberal attitude taken in *Duke of Bedford* v. *Ellis*,[21] held that it requires: (1) the same contract between all plaintiff class members and the defendant; (2) the same defence pleaded by the defendant against all the plaintiff class members; and (3) the same relief claimed by the plaintiff class members. The position in Singapore is more like the Hong Kong courts' "common ingredient" test, which allows for separate contracts, separate defences against different class members, and damages to be awarded in representative actions.

However, the Singapore High Court in *Syed Nomani* v. *Chong Yeow Peh*[22] has commented that the broad and flexible approach towards Order 15 rule 12 should not be equally applicable to proceedings against a group of defendants by way of representative proceedings as it is to proceedings by a group of plaintiffs by way of representative proceedings. There, the High Court stated that the potential prejudice caused to represented defendants is likely to be greater as compared to represented plaintiffs, given the liability the represented defendants face if

14 *Ibid.* at para 59.
15 *Ibid.* at para 60.
16 *Ibid.* at para 71.
17 [1994] 2 SLR 668, following *John* v. *Rees* [1970] 1 Ch 345.
18 Jeffrey Pinsler, "Group Litigation in Singapore", ANNALS, AAPSS, 622 (March 2009) at 296–300.
19 [2005] 4 SLR(R) 351.
20 Eunice Chua, "Guidance on Representative Actions: *Koh Chong Chiah and Others v Treasure Resort Pte Ltd* [2013] SGCA 52" *SLW Commentary* (Issue 4/Oct 2013).
21 [1901] AC 1 at 8: "Given a common interest and a common grievance, a representative suit was in order if the relief sought was in its nature beneficial to all whom the plaintiff proposed to represent."
22 [2017] 4 SLR 1064.

judgment is entered against them. It would be unfair to assume that all of them have similar defences in the matter without hearing from them.

In this case, the plaintiff had sued the defendant for over SGD 1 million, which was the sum that the defendant and eleven others were liable to repay the plaintiff under their agreement to share the costs of certain Canadian legal proceedings. The eleven others had not been named in the suit and the court decided that the claim should be prorated to SGD 70,000 given this circumstance. The plaintiff then unsuccessfully applied under Order 15 rule 12(2) to appoint the defendant as a representative of the eleven others. Although the court's decision in this factual context is understandable, it does appear to be too much of a generalisation to hold that representative proceedings against defendants do not deserve a similar broad and flexible approach as with representative proceedings by plaintiffs. Given that the representative action under Order 15 rule 12 is the only general process in Singapore which enables many persons to be directly involved in the litigation, it may be argued that it is important that the rule be interpreted as flexibly as possible to preserve the principle of access to justice.[23]

In relation to the second stage of the inquiry, the court will consider the following factors:[24]

(1) The existence of separate defenses against different claimants;
(2) Whether it is necessary to examine each class member in discovery;
(3) Whether there are important issues raised by some class members but not others;
(4) Whether the proposed class is so small that joinder would be a better solution;[25] and
(5) Costs considerations.

The Court of Appeal has recognized that potentially prejudicial consequences should not be exaggerated. It made clear that the courts would probe claims of prejudice raised at the discretionary stage of the inquiry and not indulge bare or abstract assertions.[26] One commentator has also suggested that it appears from *Koh Chong Chiah and others* v. *Treasure Resort Pte Ltd* that, when in doubt, instead of risking the stifling of a potentially meritorious and workable representative claim, the courts would be willing to allow the representative action to proceed, with the possibility of the trial judge reshaping or discontinuing the proceedings at a later stage should there emerge a real possibility of prejudice.[27]

Ultimately, the court's approach will be to balance the procedural limitations of a representative action against the procedural convenience arising from the use of the procedure.[28]

The court has general case management powers where it is empowered to give administrative directions as it deems fit in the interests of the "just, expeditious and economical disposal of proceedings."[29] There is, in addition, a specific provision for the court to give incidental directions in representative proceedings under Order 15 rule 12(2). Nevertheless, in the case of *Syed Nomani* v. *Chong Yeow Peh*,[30] the court clarified that Order 15 rule 12(2) does not grant the

[23] Jeffrey Pinsler, *Principles of Civil Procedure* (2013) at para. 07.053.
[24] *Koh Chong Chiah and others* v. *Treasure Resort Pte Ltd* [2013] SGCA 52 at paras 67–70, 82–83.
[25] In *Syed Nomani* v. *Chong Yeow Peh* [2017] 4 SLR 1064, the Singapore High Court held that one person seeking to represent eleven others was too small a number.
[26] Monica Chong, "Corridor to Greater Access to Justice: The Representative Action Rule – *Koh Chong Chiah and others v Treasure Resort Pte Ltd* [2013] SGCA 52", *SLW Commentary* (Issue 6/Oct 2013).
[27] *Ibid.*, referencing *Koh Chong Chiah and others* v. *Treasure Resort Pte Ltd* [2013] SGCA 52 at paras 37, 91, 133 and 135.
[28] *Koh Chong Chiah and others* v. *Treasure Resort Pte Ltd* [2013] SGCA 52 at para. 84.
[29] Supreme Court of Judicature Act (Cap. 322, s. 80) Rules of Court (R5, 2014 Rev. Ed.) O. 34A r. 1.
[30] [2017] 4 SLR 1064.

court the power to convert ordinary proceedings to representative proceedings if representative proceedings had not already been brought under Order 15 rule 12(1).

A judgment or order of the court in the course of or at the conclusion of representative proceedings binds the represented persons even though they are not mentioned on the record. Nevertheless, they have the right to dispute their liability pursuant to Order 15 rule 12(5). Another protection for represented persons lies in Order 15 rule 12(3), which provides that a judgment may not be enforced against a represented person unless the court gives its leave.

The issue of remedies in representative proceedings has not yet been commented upon by a Singapore court although it is likely that the courts will consider the proper interpretation of Order 15 rule 12, as well as common law principles, including the developments in other jurisdictions.[31] In *Tan Chin Seng & Others* v. *Raffles Town Club Pte Ltd*, the issue of remedies did not arise as all the members of the group sought the same remedy of rescission and, in the alternative, damages for breach of contract. They failed in the rescission claim and were granted SGD 1,000 each for breach of contract by the High Court, which the Court of Appeal later increased to SGD 3,000.[32] In *Koh Chong Chiah and others* v. *Treasure Resort Pte Ltd*, declaratory relief that did not require an assessment on a personal basis was sought in relation to the repudiation, misrepresentation, and conspiracy claims,[33] which the court permitted to proceed as a representative action.

17.3 LIMITATIONS OF THE PRESENT REGIME

Representative actions have the benefit of allowing the just and efficient disposal of many cases at once without necessarily having to hear every case. They also promote access to justice by allowing plaintiffs to pool resources to seek justice. This is especially pertinent in instances where many persons had been adversely affected by another's conduct and the total amount at issue was significant but each individual's loss insufficient to make it commercially viable for that individual to attempt to vindicate his rights alone.[34] This can be seen in *Tan Chin Seng & Others* v. *Raffles Town Club Pte Ltd*, where many of the members of the group would not have been able to afford independently taking the club to court, and the distribution of potential costs of liability among the nearly 5,000 persons greatly ameliorated the financial burden of litigation.[35] In this instance, the action was initiated by two members of the club who created an internet web page for all members of the club to express their views concerning the circumstances and the possibility of an action against the club.[36]

There is also an argument from judicial efficiency due to the saving of judicial time, avoiding inconsistent findings by different courts, and achieving finality and class-wide resolution for defendants.[37] Also using *Tan Chin Seng & Others* v. *Raffles Town Club Pte Ltd* as an example, although the decision only applied to the nearly 5,000 persons who had bought their membership directly from the club, as a way to avoid the financial crisis it would have been placed in if

31 Jeffrey Pinsler, "Group Litigation in Singapore", *ANNALS, AAPSS*, 622 (March 2009) at 296–300.

32 *Ibid.* at 299.

33 *Koh Chong Chiah and others* v. *Treasure Resort Pte Ltd* [2013] SGCA 52 at para. 110.

34 Lord Woolf, *Access to Justice* (Final Report, 1996) at 223, para. 2; Final Report of the Committee to Develop the Singapore Legal Sector (September 2007) at para. 3.19.

35 Jeffrey Pinsler, "Group Litigation in Singapore", *ANNALS, AAPSS*, 622 (March 2009) at 299–300.

36 Molly Lim SC and Roland Tong, "Class and Public Interest Litigation: The Raffles Town Club Saga" (2006) Paper presented at the 9th General Assembly of the ASEAN Law Association at 18–19.

37 Ontario Law Reform Commission, *Report on Class Actions*, 3 vols (1982), quoted in *Abdool* v. *Anaheim Management Ltd* (1993), 15 OR (3rd) 39; Alberta Law Reform Institute, *Class Actions* (2000), Final Report No 85 at para. 122; Deborah Hensler et al., *Class Action Dilemmas: Pursuing Public Goals for Private Gain* (Santa Monica, RAND Institute for Civil Justice, 2000) at 410 and 402.

the other non-suing members (about 12,000) issued "piggyback" claims, the club proposed a Scheme of Arrangement open to all its founding members such that members who sued and members who did not sue were either given the option of compensation equivalent to the judgment sum of SGD 3,000 in cash, discount in transfer fees on a sale of the membership, or food and beverage coupons.[38] In cases where a limited fund is available to compensate claimants, it also regulates a race among plaintiffs to secure judgment in priority to others.

Empirically, representative actions are rare in the Singapore courts. There have, as at December 2019, only been five reported cases dealing with Order 15 rule 12,[39] and only in three were representative actions successfully brought, and all by plaintiffs.[40] The plaintiffs in all three cases were members of some form of club or association. Unlike in other jurisdictions where class actions may be brought in relation to civil rights cases, mass torts, securities litigation and other financial injury claims, employment cases, antitrust cases, and consumer cases, these have not found their way to the Singapore courts.

This paucity in representative or collective action has been attributed to the following:[41]

(1) The general rule that costs follow the event, that is the loser pays the winner's costs;
(2) The absence of contingency fees;
(3) The absence of awards of extracompensatory damages; and
(4) The notion that a claim should not be prosecuted unless the claimant has consented to the action.

These features of the Singapore civil litigation framework curtail what has been called "the entrepreneurial aspects" that are seen in US class actions.[42] Representative proceedings may not be relied on when seeking compensatory damages because of the risk that the representative must bear the entire cost of litigation if the case is lost. The unavailability of contingency fees and extracompensatory damages further reduce any incentive to pursue such proceedings. In addition, because damages cannot be awarded without identifying the loss suffered by members of the class, and the individual loss must be tabulated precisely, the representative proceeding has been described as "a procedural backwater rather than a flourishing system of multi-party litigation."[43]

There have accordingly been some calls for the introduction of a class action procedure so that these hurdles to bringing representative actions can be addressed, including allowing those who have not opted to participate in the lawsuit to be permitted to harness existing claims.

In September 2007, the Committee to Develop the Singapore Legal Sector issued a report that considered the scope of the existing provisions on representative proceedings too limited and

38 Molly Lim SC and Roland Tong, "Class and Public Interest Litigation: The Raffles Town Club Saga" (2006) Paper presented at the 9th General Assembly of the ASEAN Law Association at 22.

39 These were *Abdul Rahim* v. *Ling How Doong* [1994] 1 SLR(R) 1054; *Management Corp. Strata Title 1279* v. *Khong Guan Realty* [1995] 1 SLR 593; *Raffles Town Club Pte Ltd* v. *Tan Chin Seng and others* [2005] 4 SLR(R) 351; *Koh Chong Chiah and others* v. *Treasure Resort Pte Ltd* [2013] SGCA 52; and *Syed Nomani* v. *Chong Yeow Peh* [2017] 4 SLR 1064.

40 *Abdul Rahim* v. *Ling How Doong* [1994] 1 SLR(R) 1054; *Raffles Town Club Pte Ltd* v. *Tan Chin Seng and others* [2005] 4 SLR(R) 351; and *Koh Chong Chiah and others* v. *Treasure Resort Pte Ltd* [2013] SGCA 52.

41 Molly Lim SC and Roland Tong, "Class and Public Interest Litigation: The Raffles Town Club Saga" (2006) Paper presented at the 9th General Assembly of the ASEAN Law Association at 8–9; Alexander Loke Fay Hoong, "Mounting Hurdles in Securities Litigation: Addressing the Funding and Collective Action Issues" [2010] 22 *SAcLJ* 660.

42 Edward F. Sherman, "Group Litigation Under Foreign Legal Systems: Variations and Alternatives to American Class Actions" (2002) 52 *DePaul L. Rev.* 401 at 424.

43 *Ibid.* at 423, citing Neil Andrews, "Multi-Party Proceedings in England: Representative and Group Actions" (2001) 11 *Duke J. Comp. & Intl L.* 249 at 253.

alluded to class actions being a feature of several common law jurisdictions including Australia, where their availability has been noted to be "of increasing importance in a global economy in which civil wrongs are often committed on a mass scale by large and powerful entities."[44] Although the Committee considered that the class action procedure may be abused if implemented without appropriate limits or controls,[45] it ultimately recommended that "further consideration be given to the issue of whether Singapore should allow class actions and, if so, to consider a suitable model of class actions to be adopted in Singapore," observing that class actions "can be used as a tool to enhance access to justice."[46] These recommendations were accepted in principle by the Singapore Government[47] although there have been no further developments on introducing a class action regime since then.

Perhaps this is in part due to the view that the representative action is a flexible tool, and it is open to the court in a representative action to make the relevant orders to deal with the issues raised by the parties as it deems necessary or just.[48] There may also be resistance, in the same vein as has been observed by English judges, to "a litigious society, where there is an over-excited tendency for citizens and businessmen to 'blame and claim' by bringing actions in the ordinary courts rather than pursuing grievance procedures through political systems of democratic accountability, pressure groups, ombudsmen, arbitration, and conciliation."[49] Singapore's Chief Justice Sundaresh Menon, and indeed the Chief Justices before him,[50] has been committed to developing alternative dispute resolution (ADR) in Singapore. Chief Justice Menon has spoken on more than one occasion about how ADR ought to be understood as "appropriate dispute resolution," which properly situates these various dispute resolution methods within a toolbox that users can select from instead of stigmatizing them as alternatives,[51] as well as described mediation as one of the best ways to increase access to justice.[52]

Nevertheless, it is worthwhile comparing the Singapore position against other alternative models to assess if lessons can be learnt from other jurisdictions.

17.4 ALTERNATIVES TO CONSIDER

Three alternative models are considered in this section. First, the UK model, which essentially supplements representative proceedings by giving the court expanded case management powers

44 Quoting from Bernard Murphy and Camille Cameron, "Access to Justice and the Evolution of Class Action Litigation in Australia" [2006] *MULR* 14.

45 Final Report of the Committee to Develop the Singapore Legal Sector (September 2007) at para. 3.20.

46 Final Report of the Committee to Develop the Singapore Legal Sector (September 2007) at para. 3.28.

47 Press Release issued by the Singapore Ministry of Law, "Government Accepts Key Recommendations of Justice V. K. Rajah's Committee on the Comprehensive Review of Legal Services Sector" (December 7, 2007).

48 *Koh Chong Chiah and others* v. *Treasure Resort Pte Ltd* [2013] SGCA 52 at para. 37 approvingly citing *Carnie and another* v *Esanda Finance Corporation Limited* (1995) 182 CLR 398 at 422.

49 Lord Steyn, Address at the Conference on Debates Over Group Litigation in Comparative Perspectives (July 21–22, 2000). This was cited in Neil Andrews, "Multi-Party Proceedings in England: Representative and Group Actions" (2001) 11 *Duke J. Comp. & Intl L.* 249 at 266.

50 See Yong Pung How, former Chief Justice, "Address at the Official Opening of the Singapore Mediation Centre" (August 16, 1997) where he expressed the hope that mediation would be integrated into the dispute resolution system so that parties could resolve their conflicts fairly, at an affordable cost, and with due despatch; Chan Sek Keong, former Attorney General and Chief Justice, "Speech delivered at the Opening of the Legal Year" (January 6, 1996) who first mooted the idea of introducing mediation for civil disputes in the Singapore High Court.

51 Welcome Address by Chief Justice Sundaresh Menon, Second ACJM Judicial Training, February 23, 2016 at para. 14; Speech by the Honourable Chief Justice Sundaresh Menon at the Global Pound Conference Series 2016 – Singapore "Shaping the Future of Dispute Resolution & Improving Access to Justice,", March 17, 2016, at paras 23–27.

52 Chief Justice Sundaresh Menon, Address at the Joint Launch of the State Courts Centre for Dispute Resolution and "Mediation in Singapore: A Practical Guide" (March 4, 2015) at para. 5.

in group litigation cases. Second, the US model, which provides express prerequisites for all class actions, a process for class certification, supervision over class action settlements, and some other case management powers. Third, the Australian model, which sits between the UK and the US model in that there is no certification procedure but an option to opt out of the class, and other express statutory provisions to deal with supervision over class action settlements and case management powers, including how damages awards may be made and costs dealt with.

17.4.1 *UK Model*

The amendments to the UK Civil Procedure Rules (CPR) in 2000 introduced new provisions in Part 19, Section III of the CPR together with Practice Direction 19B relating to group litigation. These provisions coexist with the existing provisions on representative proceedings.

Under the group litigation provisions, the court may make a Group Litigation Order (GLO) to provide for case management of claims that give rise to common or related issues of fact or law and where "there are or are likely to be a number of claims giving rise to the GLO issues."[53] An application for a GLO may be brought by a plaintiff or defendant and made at any time before or after any claims are issued. The court may also make a GLO on its own initiative.

Practice Direction 19B suggests some pre-action protocols and also provides that the following information be included in the application notice for a GLO or in written evidence filed in support of the application:

(1) A summary of the nature of the litigation;
(2) The number and nature of claims already issued;
(3) The number of parties likely to be involved;
(4) The GLO issues that are likely to arise in the litigation; and
(5) Whether there are any matters that distinguish smaller groups of claims within the wider group.

A GLO will generally contain directions about the establishment of a "group register" on which the claims managed under the GLO will be entered, specify the GLO issues that will identify the claims to be managed as a group under the GLO, and specify the court that will manage the claims on the group register. The group register, once established, becomes the central repository of directions and information on that group litigation.

In terms of case management, Practice Direction 19B provides for a managing judge to be appointed to assume overall responsibility for the management of the claims. The managing judge may make various orders, including:

(1) That one or more of the claims proceed as a test claim;
(2) Appointing a solicitor to be the lead solicitor in the claim;
(3) Requiring plaintiffs to serve Group Particulars of Claim;
(4) Specifying a date after which no claim may be added to the group register unless the court gives permission; and
(5) Directions about how the costs of resolving common issues or the costs of claims proceedings as test claims are to be borne or shared as between the parties on the group register.

[53] CPR. Rr 19.10 and 19.11.

The managing judge will generally hear the GLO issues and plays a key role in deciding whether there are common issues present that can be effectively decided within the class action framework. A Master or District Judge may also be appointed to deal with procedural matters.

In terms of costs that do not normally arise in individual litigation, such as coordinating and communicating among the group and liaising with the media, CPR 48.6 states that unless the court orders otherwise, any order for common costs against group litigants imposes on each group litigant several liability for an equal proportion of the common costs. The general rule is that where a group litigant is the paying party, he will, in addition to any costs he is liable to pay to the receiving party, also be liable for the individual costs of his claim and an equal proportion of his costs, together with all other group litigants. Apart from this, as with Singapore, the usual "costs follow the event" principle, where the costs of an action are awarded to the successful litigant, applies.

The UK model is an incremental step up from the representative proceeding framework. It is in effect a special form of joinder where members of a class may opt in to the litigation, accompanied by extensive case management and issue direction by the courts.[54] Lord Woolf CJ has noted that the impetus for the GLO system was to offer the courts very wide powers to manage proceedings in a more efficient and economic manner to provide expeditious justice.[55] One commentator has observed that there have been claims made by members of the bench that GLOs have achieved settlement or decisions in half or a third of the time that normal litigation would have taken.[56] The GLO framework may further have potentially wider application than a class action framework, for example, where claimants with similar complaints may benefit from collective management by the court, but who are unable to have their cases certified, perhaps because their claims may be more satisfactorily dealt with, at least in part, in separate proceedings.[57] This flexibility of the GLO framework allows for fuller consideration by the court of the common issues and individual divergences in group litigation.[58]

Nevertheless, potential group litigants may still be reluctant to bring group claims under the GLO system due to economic anxiety over potential costs that may be imposed on them, the psychological barrier of a lengthy and difficult litigation, fear of reprisals (for example, by employers), and a misunderstanding of the system of civil compensation.[59] An opt-in approach could mean satellite litigation brought by those who failed to opt in within the designated time frame, and also that one aim of class actions to secure justice for economically and socially disadvantaged class members could be frustrated.[60]

There have also been criticisms about the managing judge ordering one or more of the claims to proceed as test claims. Although efficient, this method of determining cases for the group

54 Neil Andrews, "Fundamentals of Multi-Party or Collective Litigation: Reflections from the Perspective of England" University of Cambridge Faculty of Law Legal Studies Research Paper Series, Paper No. 21/2014 at 12.

55 *Taylor* v. *Nugent Care Society* [2004] 1 WLR 1129 at para. 9.

56 Neil Andrews, "Multi-Party Litigation in England" University of Cambridge Faculty of Law Legal Studies Research Paper Series, Paper No. 39/2013 at 9.

57 Lord Woolf, *Access to Justice* (Final Report, 1996) at para. 16.

58 Neil Andrews, "Multi-Party Proceedings in England" (2001) 11 *Duke J of Comp Int'l Law* 249 at 264; cf. Rachel Mulheron, *The Class Action in Common Law Legal Systems: A Comparative Perspective* (Hart Publishing, 2004) at 70–71, responding to the criticism of the class action procedure as an inflexible device.

59 Neil Andrews, "Multi-Party Litigation in England" University of Cambridge Faculty of Law Legal Studies Research Paper Series, Paper No. 39/2013 at 13.

60 Liz Heffernan, "Comparative Common Law Approaches to Multi-Party Litigation: The American Class Action Procedure" (2003) 25 *Dublin U. L.J.* 102 at 111.

raises questions of whether the chosen plaintiff in the test case will conduct the test case in a way most favorable to himself at the expense of other members of the group, and whether there will be a settlement favorable to the chosen plaintiff but without resolution of the underlying issues giving rise to the litigation in the first place.[61]

17.4.2 *US Model*

In the US, class actions are governed by Federal Rules of Civil Procedure Rule 23. Rule 23(a) provides that:

> One or more members of a class may sue or be sued as representative parties on behalf of all members only if:
>
> (1) the class is so numerous that joinder of all members is impracticable;
> (2) there are questions of law or fact common to the class;
> (3) the claims or defenses of the representative parties are typical of the claims or defenses of the class; and
> (4) the representative parties will fairly and adequately protect the interests of the class.

This rule essentially provides the threshold requirements for a class action.

In addition, at least one further alternative requirement must be shown under rule 23(b), that is:

> (1) that the pursuit of separate actions would risk defendants facing varying adjudications or risk plaintiffs practically having their interest disposed of in other actions;
> (2) injunctive or declaratory relief is appropriate for the class as a whole; or
> (3) the court finds that questions of law or fact common to class members predominate over any questions affecting only individual members, and that a class action is superior to other available methods for fairly and efficiently adjudicating the controversy.

This last requirement is commonly relied on in the USA due to its broad formulation and has in an early empirical study been observed as occurring in roughly 50 percent to 85 percent of the certified classes.[62] It has also been criticized, among other things, as being an enabler of large numbers of trivial lawsuits; an enabler of large product defect lawsuits that lack concrete scientific or technical evidence but aim to force manufacturers to settle; and giving rise to private attorneys identifying potential lawsuits and finding clients for class action suits.[63]

Procedurally, to commence a suit, the parties must move for the court to certify a class. Class certification can be keenly contested and involves many strategic considerations for both plaintiffs and defendants.[64] On certifying the class, the court will direct requirements as to notice being given to the other class members, based largely on the type of relief sought. The court also appoints class counsel under rule 23(c). A class action may only be settled, voluntarily dismissed, or compromised with approval of the court. Notice of any settlement or compromise

[61] The Law Reform Commission of Hong Kong, Class Actions Sub-Committee Consultation Paper on Class Actions (November 2009) at 39, citing Manitoba Law Reform Commission, Class Proceedings Report #100 (1999) at 10–11.

[62] Thomas E. Willging et al., Empirical Study of Class Actions in Four Federal District Courts: Final Report to the Advisory Committee on Civil Rules (Federal Judicial Centre, 1996) at 8.

[63] Deborah R. Hensler, Nicholas M. Pace, Bonita Dombey-Moore, Beth Giddens, Jennifer Gross and Erik K. Moller, "Virtues and Vices" in *Class Action Dilemmas: Pursuing Public Goals for Private Gain* (2000) RAND Corporation at 50.

[64] William Rubenstein et al., *Newberg on Class Actions*, 4th ed. (Westlaw Thomson Reuters), chapter 7.

proposal must be given in a reasonable manner to all class members who would be bound by the proposal. There is also a mechanism for settlements binding on class members to be subject to a court hearing for determination of fairness, reasonableness, and adequacy.[65]

The court also has wide powers to manage class action cases, including determining the course of proceedings to prevent undue repetition or complication in presenting evidence or argument; requiring that members of the class be given opportunity to intervene or present their claims; and requiring the amendment of pleadings to eliminate allegations about representation of absent persons.

The default costs rule in the USA is that each of the parties is responsible for paying their own attorney's fees regardless of win or loss of the lawsuit.

17.4.3 *Australian Model*

The Australian model for class actions may be found in Part IVA of the Federal Court of Australia Act 1976.[66] The intention for the class action procedure in Australia was to enable people to have increased access to legal remedies in court proceedings, rendering substantive law more enforceable and thus encourage a greater degree of compliance with laws that sought to prevent or discourage activities that cause loss or injury to others.[67] In the context of securities regulation, class actions were viewed as contributing to a culture of good corporate governance.[68] The Australian class actions model is accordingly permissive in nature although with safeguards built in.

A class action may be brought in the Federal Court where, under section 33C(1):

(1) at least seven persons have claims against the same person or persons;
(2) the claims arise out of the same, similar or related circumstances; and
(3) the claims of all those persons give rise to at least one substantial common issue of law or fact.

In contrast to the provisions from the USA and UK, this rule provides clarity as to the minimum number of persons that may form part of a class action, and specifically defines the circumstances under which an action may be brought. The provision was drafted to facilitate the commencement of proceedings,[69] and is certainly flexible enough for the court to retain some discretion in deciding whether the claims arise out of "the same, similar or related circumstances" and whether the common issue of law or fact is a "substantial" one.

The relief sought may include equitable relief or may include damages under section 33C(2). Where damages are awarded for group members, subgroup members or individual group members, the court may do so in an aggregate amount without specifying the division in respect of individual group members under section 33Z. Where damages are awarded, the representative applicant can apply to court for reimbursement of the applicant's costs under section 33ZJ(1). Under section 33ZJ(2), the court may, if satisfied that the costs reasonably incurred by the applicant in relation to the class action are likely to exceed the costs recoverable from the respondent, order that an amount equal to the whole or part of the excess be paid to the applicant

65 *Rothstein & Willging* (2005), Managing Class Action Litigation: A Pocket Guide for Judges, Part III.
66 The States of Victoria, New South Wales, and Queensland also have their own class action regimes, but these are largely consistent with the Federal position, which will be the focus of this chapter.
67 Law Reform Commission, Grouped Proceedings in the Federal Court, Report No 46 (1988) at 33.
68 Bernard Murphy and Camille Cameron, "Access to Justice and the Evolution of Class Action Litigation in Australia" (2006) 30 *Melbourne University Law Review* 399 at 404–05.
69 *Wong* v. *Silkfeld Pty Ltd* (1999) 199 CLR 255, 267 at para. 28.

out of the damages awarded. The court also has a broad discretion to make any costs order it thinks just under section 33ZJ(3).

Again, these provisions strike a good balance between certainty and flexibility, as well as manage the risk posed to the representative applicant in terms of costs by allowing recovery out of the damages awarded.

Procedurally, a representative applicant brings the action on behalf of the members of the group as defined in the pleadings (section 33D), and there is no need to name or specify the number of group members in the pleadings. The consent of a person to be a group member is not required under section 33E(1). There is, however, an opt-out procedure for class members to indicate that they do not wish to be part of the proceedings by giving written notice under section 33J.

There is no formal procedure for judicial certification before class action proceedings may be commenced, doing away with a troublesome feature of the US class action model. Rather, the onus is on the respondent to challenge the class action proceeding and to establish that the requisite statutory criteria are not satisfied or to persuade the court that it should exercise its discretion to prevent the class action from continuing. This avenue for discontinuing a class action provides an important safeguard to the abuse of the class action proceeding.

Under section 33N(1), the Federal Court may order that a proceeding should not continue as a class action if:

(1) the costs that would be incurred if the action continues as a class action is likely to exceed the costs if each class member conducted separate proceedings;
(2) the relief sought can be obtained by means of a proceeding other than a class action;
(3) the class action will not provide an efficient or effective means of dealing with the claims or group members; or
(4) it is otherwise inappropriate that the claims be pursued by a class action.

Sections 33M and 33L provide additional grounds for discontinuing the class action, namely, where it appears there are fewer than seven class members, and where the costs incurred by a respondent in identifying and distributing monies pursuant to a judgment award would prove excessive when compared to the likely total of those awards.

Like the US, a class action may not be settled or discontinued without the approval of the court under section 33V. Under section 33ZB, a judgment in a class action must describe or otherwise identify group members who will be affected by it and will bind such persons other than those who have opted out.

Australia does not experience a high volume of class action litigation compared with other jurisdictions, although the class action framework is well utilized, with 563 class actions having been filed in Australian courts as of May 31, 2018.[70] This may be due in part to Australia having common features to the Singapore civil litigation framework that lower economic incentives to bring class actions, including the disallowance of contingency fees and the costs follow the event rule.

Nevertheless, one significant factor that has contributed to the Australian class action framework that cannot yet be replicated in Singapore has been the role of commercial litigation funders.[71] The

[70] Vince Morabito, "An Evidence-Based Approach to Class Action Reform in Australia: Competing Class Actions and Comparative Perspectives on the Volume of Class Action Litigation in Australia" (11 July 2018), available on SSRN at 8, 11.

[71] Vince Morabito, "An Empirical Study of Australia's Class Action Regimes, Fourt Report: Facts and Figures on Twenty-Four Years of Class Actions in Australia" (29 July 2016), available at SSRN: https://ssrn.com/abstract=2815777 at 16.

Federal Court of Australia has made clear that in the event of litigation generating monetary compensation for class action members, the funder supporting the litigation would be able to receive a percentage of the proceeds received by all class members, not just those who had entered into a funding agreement with the funder.[72] This was with a view to encouraging funders to back class actions brought on behalf of all claimants; reduce costs by rendering unnecessary signing up of as many class members as possible, lead to lower funding commissions, and reduce the incidence of competing class actions. Litigation funding is presently permitted in Singapore only in a limited way for international arbitration proceedings, and other arbitration-related court proceedings.[73]

17.4.4 *Status Quo*

Finally, there are also arguments for retaining the status quo. Foremost is that there appears to be little demand for the use of representative proceedings in Singapore in the usual contexts because of the existence of alternative avenues for redress. Put another way, the gaps that the class action procedure were meant to fill in other jurisdictions to support claimants receiving compensation may not exist in Singapore.

The key piece of consumer protection legislation in Singapore is the Consumer Protection (Fair Trading) Act,[74] which was amended in 2009 to cover financial products and services, and then again in 2012 to include a "lemon law" to give consumers additional redress with respect to defective goods. Those with consumer complaints may turn to the Consumer Association of Singapore for assistance at extremely affordable rates and can conveniently lodge their complaints online.[75]

Strong governmental action where vulnerable consumers are concerned has also served to avert mass litigation. In line with cultural norms relating to dispute resolution in Singapore, including the values of Confucianism, a collectivist inclination and the importance of maintaining "face,"[76] the Singapore government has strongly supported the development of alternative dispute resolution avenues to promote a harmonious and less litigious society.[77] For example, after the collapse of Lehman Brothers in 2008, the Monetary Authority of Singapore issued a strong statement urging banks not to be overly legalistic and to do the right thing,[78] resulting in 58 percent of investors receiving compensation as at January 16, 2009.[79] As of May 31, 2009, three banks and one finance company had offered settlements to 67 percent of investors at a value of about SGD 105 million.[80] Over 50 percent of cases had been offered settlements of

[72] *Money Max Int Pty Ltd (Trustee)* v. *QBE INsurance Group Limited* [2016] FCAFC 148, summarized in Vince Morabito, "An Empirical-Based Approach to Class Action Reform in Australia: Common Fund Orders, Funding Fees and Reimbursement Payments" (31 January 2019), available at https://ssrn.com/abstract=3326303 or http://dx.doi.org/10.2139/ssrn.3326303 at 14–15.

[73] Civil Law (Third-Party Funding) Regulations 2017, Regulation 3.

[74] Consumer Protection (Fair Trading) Act (Cap. 52A, 2009 Rev. Ed.).

[75] See Consumer Association of Singapore website www.case.org.sg/complaint_onlinecomplaint.aspx.

[76] Joel Lee and Teh Hwee Hwee (Gen. eds), *An Asian Perspective on Mediation* (Academy Publishing, 2009) at 54.

[77] Ministry of Finance, "Singapore Budget 2008: Expenditure Overview, Ministry of Law" (February 27, 2008); Kevin Y. L. Tan, "Singapore: A Statist Legal Laboratory" in E. Ann Blac and Gary F. Bell, *Law and Legal Institutions of Asia: Traditions, Adaptations and Innovations* (Cambridge University Press, 2011) at 367.

[78] "MAS to Banks: Do the right thing" *The Straits Times* (October 18, 2008).

[79] "58% of investors who complained about Lehman-linked products to be compensated" *Channel News Asia* (January 16, 2009).

[80] Monetary Authority of Singapore Media Release, "MAS Releases Investigation Findings on the Sale and Marketing of Structured Notes Linked to Lehman Brothers" (July 7, 2009), available online: www.mas.gov.sg/news/media-releases/2009/mas-releases-investigation-findings-on-the-sale-and-marketing-of-structured-notes-linked-to-lehman-brothers.

50 percent and above with 26 percent receiving offers of full settlement.[81] 85 percent of these settlement offers were accepted, 3 percent were rejected and the rest had yet to decide.[82] Those who were dissatisfied with the responses from their financial institutions turned to the Financial Industry Disputes Resolution Centre, which in 2015 reported receiving a total of 2,386 credit-linked notes claims arising from the Lehman Brothers collapse.[83] Although the USA saw various large securities class action suits,[84] Singapore saw two reported lawsuits concerning 214 investors in total.[85] Notably, however, some investors in Singapore have tried to bring class actions in the USA,[86] perhaps suggesting that the local representative proceeding framework was not suitable for their purposes.

It should also be observed that while there are numerous benefits associated with a class action framework, there is also a flip side to each of these benefits and the benefits may themselves conflict with one another. For example, the flip side to access to justice for a class of plaintiffs may be unfairness to defendants. In opt-out schemes, where potential plaintiffs are automatically included in the litigation unless they opt out, defendants may face difficulty investigating all claims and preparing its case. In opt-in schemes, it is usually necessary to impose a cutoff date, and this may lead to large numbers of weak or hopeless claims being included together with valid ones. The sheer number of claims may adversely affect a defendant due to unfair publicity and enhance its difficulties in investigating claims. The conflict between the supposed benefits of a class action regime has also been commented on. For example, facilitating access to justice may encourage litigation where none would have been contemplated in the first place, undermining juridical economy.

Further, introducing a class action regime will not necessarily lead to achieving improved access to justice and efficient judicial administration without a change in the litigation climate, particularly relating to costs rules, litigation funding, and the absence of contingency fees. Notably though, the last of these looks set to change after many years of lobbying[87] albeit in the limited context of arbitration cases as well as specified proceedings in the Singapore International Commercial Court and mediation cases connected to them. In August 2019, the Singapore Ministry of Law sought public feedback on proposed legislative amendments to permit conditional fee agreements for these sectors with a view of strengthening Singapore's position as a leading international legal hub. The Ministry described conditional fee agreements

81 *Ibid.*

82 The stockbroking firms had also offered settlements amounting to SGD 2.7 million to 33 percent of investors whose cases had been decided. 70 percent of settlement offers by the stockbroking firms were accepted, 11 percent were rejected and the rest had yet to decide as at May 31, 2009. *Ibid.*

83 Financial Industry Disputes Resolution Centre Ltd Annual Report 2014/2015, available online: www.fidrec.com.sg/website/annualreports/FIDReC%20AR%202014-2015.pdf.

84 See Market News Publishing, "Lehman Brothers Officers and Directors, UBS Sued Over Principal Protection Notes", December 20, 2018; GlobalNewsWire, Law Office of David R. Chase, PA Investigates Claims Involving the Sale of Lehman Brothers' Preferred "Series J" Stock and Structured Products by Securities Broker-Dealers, as well as Claims Involving Losses Resulting from Over-Concentrated Portfolio Positions in the Financial Sector, 27 October 2008.

85 *Soon Kok Tiang* v. *DBS Bank Ltd* [2012] 1 SLR 397; *Teo Wai Cheong* v. *Credit Industriel et Commercial* [2013] 3 SLR 573.

86 Christopher Chen Chao-hung, "Judicial Inactivism in Protecting Financial Consumer against Predatory Sale of Retail Structured Products: A Reflection from Retail Structured Notes Lawsuits in Taiwan" (2014) 27 *Columbia Journal of Asian Law* 165–220 at footnote 5, referencing *In re Lehman Brothers Holdings Inc*, 2011 WL 5103346 (SDNY); *Ka Kin Wong* v. *HSBC USA Inc* 2010 WL 3154976 (SDNY); *Dandong* v. *Pinnacle Performance Ltd* 2011 WL 5170293 (SDNY); *Dandong* v. *Pinnacle Performance Ltd* 2011 WL 6156743 (SDNY).

87 See e.g., Adrian Yeo, "Access to Justice: A Case for Contingency Fees in Singapore" (2004) 16 *SAcLJ* 76; Andy Ho, "Let David Take on Goliath" *The Straits Times* (August 2, 2013); Daniel Chia, "Contingency fees for lawyers can promote dispute resolution" *The Straits Times* (August 17, 2013).

as agreements where a lawyer representing a client in pursuing a claim, receives payment of his legal fees only if the claim is successful; such payment may include an "uplift" or "success" fee, in addition to the lawyer's standard legal fees.[88] At the same time, it also stated that a "separate study" will be done on whether conditional fee agreements "will promote access to justice for categories of proceedings not being considered currently,"[89] suggesting that this may be the first step towards broader use of such conditional fee agreements. It is worth noting that conditional fee agreements are different from contingency fee arrangements, in that the lawyer shares in an agreed percentage of the sum successfully recovered by the client, with no direct correlation to the work done.

In this regard, Singapore has progressed more than Hong Kong. There, despite the Hong Kong Law Reform Commission Report, no concrete steps have been taken beyond establishing a Working Group to study and consider the Report. Nevertheless, it must be acknowledged that as at April 17, 2019, the Working Group has held twenty-five meetings while a subcommittee set up under the Working Group has met thirty times.[90] It has also been reported that although there is not yet a specific timetable for consulting the public, the secretariat of the Working Group has started compiling a draft consultation document that proposes to cover consumer cases, certification criteria, and the design of procedural rules and other ancillary measures.[91]

17.5 CONCLUSION

Calls for reform of representative proceedings in Singapore have been made over the years both generally[92] and in various contexts such as competition law[93] and even as a basis for breach of statutory duty under the Transboundary Haze Pollution Act 2014.[94] Progress has nevertheless been slow on introducing statutory amendments to introduce a class action regime similar to the USA and Australia or a GLO framework as has been done in the UK. Rather, small steps to promote access to justice have been taken, such as providing for low-cost and accessible dispute resolution facilities both within the court system and outside, and, more recently, it appears that conditional fee agreements will likely be permitted in Singapore in limited contexts.

Given the current cultural and legal context of Singapore, it appears that this approach may suffice for the moment and for the immediate future. Nevertheless, it remains an open question that requires further study, as to whether some form of class action regime to supplement the representative proceeding would be required in the longer term. If so, it is suggested that the Australian approach may be a good model for Singapore because it strikes a good balance between providing certainty of process and adequate safeguards on the one hand, and allowing some flexibility where needed and providing a vehicle for numerous claims to be determined with one proceeding. The common English heritage of Singapore and Australia's civil procedure

88 Singapore Ministry of Law, "Public Consultation on Conditional Fee Agreements in Singapore", available online: www.mlaw.gov.sg/news/public-consultations/public-consultation-on-conditional-fee-agreements-in-singapore.

89 K. C. Vijayan, "Feedback sought on conditional fees for lawyers" *The Straits Times* (August 28, 2019).

90 See written reply by Secretary for Justice, Ms Teresa Cheng, SC to a question by Hon Dennis Kwok in the Legislative Council on April 17, 2019, available online: www.info.gov.hk/gia/general/201904/17/P2019041700786.htm.

91 *Ibid.*

92 Final Report of the Committee to Develop the Singapore Legal Sector (September 2007) at para. 3.28.

93 Jeremiah Lau, "A Standalone Action for Singapore's Competition Law Regime: Challenges and Opportunities" (2017) 29 *SAcLJ* 224.

94 Kenneth Lim Chi Shen, "Transboundary Haze Pollution Act 2014: The viability of using representative proceedings to pursue a civil claim under the Act" *SLW Commentary* (Issue 2, October 2015).

rules also means that the changes required to Singapore's existing framework will be minimal. The UK GLO model does not appear to have the benefits that adopting a more progressive class action framework system will bring, especially since Singapore courts already have very broad case management powers. The US model may not be feasible for Singapore to implement given the different cultural and legal contexts of both jurisdictions.

18

Class Action in China

Challenges and Opportunities

Robin Hui Huang[*]

18.1 INTRODUCTION

Since the modern American class action was introduced via the 1966 Amendments to the Federal Rules of Civil Procedure, it has become a very important form of litigation in the USA, where it functions as a key mechanism for private enforcement of law. There has been a long-standing debate on the class action procedure in the USA, but now this debate is no longer confined to American jurists. The class action has crossed borders and has been considered or emulated in many jurisdictions around the globe.

China has followed this international trend but with its uniquely Chinese characteristics. China has long been considering the possibility of transplanting the US-style class action, at least in the area of financial regulation. Currently, China has a civil procedure to aggregate multiple suits arising from the same infringement, which is sometimes dubbed Chinese-style class action, as it bears some resemblance to the class action in the USA, but there are important differences between them.[1]

This chapter will discuss the key elements of the Chinese-style class action, examine the way in which it has been applied in practice, analyse the challenges it faces and finally offer some views on its future direction of development.

18.2 THE LEGAL FRAMEWORK

18.2.1 *Overview*

Under China's Civil Procedural Law,[2] there are three main forms of civil litigation, including individual actions (*dandu susong*), joint actions (*gongtong susong*) and group actions (*qunti susong*). The individual action is the simplest of the three, involving one plaintiff and one defendant. The joint action and the group action are more complicated and will be discussed below in more detail.

* This research project (Project Number: 2019.A4.056.19C) is funded by the Public Policy Research Funding Scheme from the Policy Innovation and Co-ordination Office of The Government of the Hong Kong Special Administrative Region. It also received support from Direct Research Grant at Chinese University of Hong Kong, and China's National Social Science Foundation Project "Legal Enforcement Mechanisms for the Registration-based Reform of Securities Offerings in China". Thanks to Charles Chao Wang for his excellent research assistance.

1 For more details, see infra Section 18.2.2.

2 Zhonghua Renmin Gongheguo Minshi Susongfa [Civil Procedure Law of the People's Republic of China] (passed April 9, 1991, as amended October 28, 2007, August 31, 2012 and June 27, 2017) (Civil Procedural Law).

The Civil Procedural Law in China devotes two provisions to how joint actions operate in China. According to §52, if one or both parties to an individual action consist of two or more persons and the object of action is the same or in the same category, the court can, with the consent of the parties, combine the individual actions into a joint action.[3] Further, §53 provides that where the parties on one side of a joint action are numerous, such parties may recommend a representative or representatives to participate in the action.[4] As the number of litigants is confirmed at the time of filing and a representative is elected in the above joint action, it is also called a "representative action with confirmed plaintiffs at the time of filing." Hence, there are two types of joint action: first, the normal type where the parties are not numerous and thus all of them participate in the litigation, and second, the special type where the parties are numerous and need to elect representatives to litigate.

Group actions are set out under §54 of the Civil Procedural Law, which states:

> Where the subject matter of action for each party is of the same kind, the parties on one side of an action are numerous, but the exact number of such parties is uncertain when the action is instituted, the people's court may publish a notice to describe the case and claims and notify right holders to register with the people's court within a certain period of time.
>
> The right holders which have registered with the people's court may recommend a representative or representatives to participate in the litigation; and if no representative is recommended, the people's court may determine a representative or representatives in consultation with the right holders which have registered with the people's court.

Unlike the joint action with numerous parties as noted above, the number of plaintiffs is not confirmed when the group action is filed, and the court needs to issue a public notice to urge the eligible plaintiffs to register within a certain period of time. After the registration period, the group action will be conducted by representatives elected by registered plaintiffs or appointed by the court. Hence, the group action is also called a "representative action with unconfirmed plaintiffs at the time of filing."

In sum, there are two types of representative actions, one with *confirmed* plaintiffs at the time of filing (the special type of joint action) and the other with *unconfirmed* plaintiffs at the time of filing (group action). In both of them, only some of the litigants will actually litigate the case as representatives of a larger "group" or "class" of litigants, which bears some resemblance to the US-style class action.[5] However, the term "class action" is not legally defined in China, and thus there has been confusion as to what the term means in the Chinese context.[6] In theory, the term "class action" can be used to refer to either the special type of joint action with numerous parties, the group action, or both.

[3] Civil Procedural Law, §52.

[4] Civil Procedural Law, §53.

[5] Indeed, some commentators have argued that the special type of joint action with numerous parties should not be treated as joint action at all, but should instead be group action, because the key feature of group action is to have representatives acting for a "group." See e.g., Wusheng Zhang and Yanyan Yang, "The Law and Practice of China's Group Action" (2007) 2 *Zhongguo Faxue [China Legal Science]* 112, 114.

[6] See e.g., Benjamin L. Liebman, "Class Action Litigation in China" (1998) 111 *Harvard Law Review* 1523 (using the term "class action" to describe suits brought under articles 54 and 55 of the Civil Procedure Law); Guiping Lu, "Private Enforcement of Securities Fraud Law in China: A Critique of the Supreme People's Court 2003 Provisions Concerning Private Securities Litigation" (2003) *Pacific Rim Law and Policy Journal* 795, 799 (stating that "Article 55 of the Civil Procedure Law governs *class actions* where the number of litigants is not fixed") (emphasis added); Wallace Wen-Yeu Wang and Chen Jian-Lin, "Reforming China's Securities Civil Actions: Lessons from PSLRA Reform in the U.S. and Government-Sanctioned Non-Profit Enforcement in Taiwan" (2008) 21(2) *Colum. J. Asian L.* 115, 130 (stating that "[t]his prohibition [over class action] is perplexing, because there were no provisions in China's law allowing such class actions in the first place").

In practice, the form of group action has rarely been used, and several factors may help explain why. First, it is politically unwise for the court to use the group action, as it may run counter to the government's top policy of maintaining social stability. Indeed, asking potential plaintiffs to register via public notice will enlarge the scale and impact of mass disputes, attracting more social attention and running more risk of social unrest. Second, it is technically difficult or costly for the court to conduct the group action. As noted earlier, the court needs to first make a public notice to potential plaintiffs to register and then the registered plaintiffs need to elect representatives. In this process, difficult issues may arise over how to make the public notice, how to decide on the registration period and how to ensure the fairness and efficiency in the election of representatives by a large number of plaintiffs. Clearly, the court will need to devote a lot of resources in terms of manpower and time to solve those pretrial issues.

Third, the case-filing fee charged by the court may play a role in affecting the court's decision on whether to accept a group action. In China, the court charges a case-filing fee, calculated as a percentage of the value of the claim in the case.[7] The rate of the filing fee is progressive on a sliding scale, depending on the value of the claim, as illustrated below:

(1) if the claim is valued below RMB10,000, the fee is fixed at RMB50;
(2) if the claim is between RMB10,000 and RMB 100,000, the rate for this part is 2.5 percent;
(3) for the part between RMB100,000 and RMB200,000, the rate is 2 percent;
(4) for the part between RMB200,000 and RMB 500,000, the rate is 1.5 percent;
(5) for the part between RMB500,000 and RMB 1,000,000, the rate is 1 percent;
(6) for the part between RMB1,000,000 and RMB 2,000,000, the rate is 0.9 percent;
(7) for the part between RMB2,000,000 and RMB 5,000,000, the rate is 0.8 percent;
(8) for the part between RMB5,000,000 and RMB 10,000,000, the rate is 0.7 percent;
(9) for the part between RMB10,000,000 and RMB 20,000,000, the rate is 0.6 percent;
(10) for the part more than RMB 20,000,000, the rate is 0.5 percent.

Hence, the court could charge greater filing fees for multiple cases arising from the same misconduct than hearing all of them as one single case in the form of a group action. For many courts in China, particularly those in economically less developed regions, the filing fee represents an important source of revenue.[8]

Finally, it is undesirable for the court and judges to accept the group action, due to the criteria against which to assess their work performance in China. Compared with individual actions and joint actions, the group action is disadvantaged when the court and judges are assessed against such criteria as the number of cases, the length of case-hearing time and the rate of appeal. Indeed, a group action is counted as one case, but it can be divided into many similar cases when litigated in the form of individual actions or joint actions, which would help the court and the judge to improve their results of work performance assessment and thus get better chances of career advancement and pay increases. Hence, the court and the judge would prefer to accept many cases arising from the same instance of misconduct rather than aggregating them together as one case.

[7] Susong Feiyong Jiaona Banfa [Measures of Charging Litigation Fees] art. 13 (promulgated by the State Council Dec. 29 2006, effective Apr. 1, 2007). The court fee consists of the filing fee (*anjian shouli fei*) and other litigation fees (*qita susong feiyong*), such as the costs of travel, accommodation, living allowances, and expenses paid to expert witnesses, accountants, translators, etc.

[8] Wusheng Zhang and Yanyan Yang, "The Law and Practice of China's Group Action" (2007) 2 *Zhongguo Faxue [China Legal Science]* 112, 118.

As the group action is seldom used in practice, it is practically meaningful to use the term "class action" to refer to the joint action with numerous parties, and to the extent that, as will be discussed in Section 18.2.2 below, it is different from the American class action in some important aspects, it can be more appropriately called the "Chinese-style class action."

18.2.2 *Key Elements*

The key elements of the Chinese-style class action are outlined below and in doing so, a comparison with the US-style class action is conducted, where appropriate, to help generate a better understanding of the Chinese regime. As will be shown, the Chinese-style class action is similar to US-style class action in that there are numerous plaintiffs involved and the judgment of the action applies to members of the plaintiff class who have not participated in the lawsuit. However, there are some important distinctions.

18.2.2.1 Who Can Initiate the Procedure?

Under the Chinese-style class action, the court can, with the consent of the parties, combine the individual actions into a joint action,[9] and where the parties on one side of a joint action are numerous, such parties may recommend a representative or representatives to participate in the action.[10] Hence, the litigants can initiate the procedure by electing a litigation representative or representatives.

18.2.2.2 In What Kinds of Cases Can the Procedure Be Used?

In theory, the Chinese-style class action procedure can be used in any case where there are numerous parties on either side of the litigation. For instance, it has been used in environmental infringement cases,[11] real estate sale cases,[12] and employment dispute cases.[13] In practice, securities misconduct cases are a major type of civil litigation using the Chinese-style class action and thus will be discussed in more detail in this chapter.

On January 9, 2003, the Supreme People's Court (SPC) issued an important judicial interpretation on the bringing and hearing of civil cases against securities misstatements (2003 SPC

[9] Civil Procedural Law, §52.

[10] Civil Procedural Law, §53.

[11] 聂胜等149户辛庄村村民与平顶山天安煤业股份有限公司五矿等水污染责任纠纷案 [*Nie Sheng and Other 148 Villagers of Xinzhuang Village* v. *Fifth Mine Affiliated to Pingdingshan Tian'an Coal Co., Ltd. et al.* for dispute over water pollution liability], Henan Province Pingdingshan City Xinhua District Court, 2014(11) Zuigao Renmin Fayuan Gongbao [Supreme People's Court Gazette];张长建等1721人与福建省（屏南）榕屏化工有限公司环境污染损害赔偿纠纷上诉案 [*Zhang Changjian and other 1720 persons* v. *Fujian (Pingnan) RongPing Chemical Co., Ltd.* (Appeal case over compensation liability for environmental pollution)], Fujian Province High Court, (2005) Min Min Zhong Zi No.349.

[12] 韩某与葫芦岛市中维房地产开发有限公司、葫芦岛市中维置业有限公司商品房销售合同纠纷 [*Mr Han* v. *Huludao City Zhongwei Property Development Co., Ltd., Huludao City Zhongwei Realty Co., Ltd.*, for dispute over realty sale contract], Huludao City Longgang District Court, (2017) Liao 1403 Min Chu Zi No.2714; 余家会、郑佳聪等与中山市正和房地产开发有限公司车位纠纷案 [*Yu Jiaohui and Zheng Jiacong et al* v. *Zhongshan City Zhenghe Property Development Co., Ltd.*, for dispute over car parking space], Guangdong Province Zhongshan City First Intermediate Court, (2018) Yue 2071 Min Chu Zi No.2102.

[13] 雷园园与洛阳庆利宏房地产营销策划有限公司、张欢劳动争议案 [*Lei Yuanyuan* v. *Luoyang City Qinglihong Realty Marketing Co., Ltd. and Zhang Huan*, for dispute over employment], Henan Province Luoyang City Jianxi District Court, (2016) Yu 0305 Min Chu No.1916; 庆阳鑫圆工程有限公司与薛某1、薛某2等劳动争议案 [*Qingyang Xinyuan Construction Co., Ltd.* v. *Xue1 and Xue2 et al*, for dispute over employment], Gansu Province Jingchuan County Court, (2018) Gan 0821 Min Chu No.332.

Circular).[14] Under this instrument, the Chinese-style class action can be used to bring civil cases to seek compensation for securities misstatements,[15] but not other forms of securities misconduct such as insider trading and market manipulation. Over the years, however, the court has gradually relaxed this restriction and extended the procedure to civil cases against insider trading and market manipulation.

18.2.2.3 What Are the Types of Relief?

As a special form of civil proceedings, the class action regime allows the court to grant all types of civil remedies, with the main relief being monetary compensation for the harm suffered by the victims.

18.2.2.4 How to Obtain Consent of the Class Members?

Unlike the "opt-out" rule that applies to US-style class actions, the Chinese-style class actions follow the "opt-in" rule under which the plaintiffs must register with the court at the time the case is filed. The registered plaintiffs elect representatives to litigate the case, and the litigation conduct of such representatives shall bind all the parties represented.[16] It should be noted however that to modify or relinquish any claims, admit any claims of the opposing party or reach a settlement, such representatives must obtain a consent from the parties represented.[17]

18.2.2.5 What Are the Financing Mechanisms?

Chinese lawyers can generally operate under the so-called "risk agency fee" regime (*fengxian daili Shoufei*), a functional equivalent of the contingency fee system in the USA, under which the legal fees are contingent on the case being successfully litigated or settled. Despite some ambiguity over the law in the books, the risk agency fee regime has been used in the context of securities civil actions. A distinctive feature of securities civil suits is "large scale, small claim," that is, overall a large number of investors are injured by the misrepresentation, but individually the injury to each of the investors is small. Owing to this, securities civil suits are called negative-value litigation, because the costs for individual litigants may well exceed the benefits derived from the litigation. With the risk agency fee regime, the risks and costs of litigation are effectively transferred to the lawyers, and usually the lawyers finance the litigation themselves (third-party litigation funding is rare in China). Hence, this provides an incentive for aggrieved investors to participate in securities private litigation.

18.3 CHALLENGES FROM SUBSTITUTE MECHANISMS

18.3.1 *Overview: Problems with Securities Class Action in China*

As noted above, the Chinese-style class action has been mainly used for civil cases against securities misrepresentation. According to a well-cited empirical study, there was a steady

[14] Zuigao Renmin Fayuan Guanyu Shenli Zhengquan Shichang Yin Xujia Chenshu Yinfa De Minshi Peichang Anjian De Ruogan Guiding [Provisions of the Supreme People's Court Concerning the Acceptance and Trial of Civil Compensation Securities Suits Involving Misrepresentation] (effective from 1 February 2003).

[15] SPC Third Circular, art. 12.

[16] Civil Procedural Law, §53.

[17] Ibid. It is not fully clear whether the consent needs to be unanimous or majority-based. According to Professor Weiping Zhang who is the chairman of the China Civil Procedural Law Association, the better view is that the consent can be given by just a majority of the plaintiffs. Telephone Interview, 19 October 2019.

stream of such cases during the first decade after the promulgation of the 2003 SPC Circular (between five and ten cases every year).[18] This is a rather modest number given the high incidence of misrepresentation in China's securities market.

It has been found that the key reason behind this lies in the way the Chinese court handles such action.[19] In practice, the courts have been unsympathetic towards securities civil suits, as evidenced by the difficulty and delays in getting the case accepted and heard and the judgment enforcement problems. To be sure, there are many factors contributing to this, including the problem of local judicial protectionism in handling securities civil cases. Local protectionism means that in dealing with litigation, courts are often biased in favour of parties from their own region. This problem is well-known and deep-rooted in China due to the lack of the courts' independence – the local courts are dependent on the local government in terms of funding, and personnel decisions relating to the local judiciary are also in the hands of the local government. The problem is particularly severe in the area of securities civil cases, because listed companies are usually the mainstay of the local economy and thus the main source of revenue for the local government.

In response to the above issue, the Chinese securities market regulator, namely the China Securities Regulatory Commission (CSRC), has recently tried to use its regulatory power to facilitate settling the compensation issue outside of the courtroom. This has the effect of substituting for, and thus reducing the need for, the class action procedure as a way of producing compensation for the aggrieved investors. In addition, the introduction of public interest group litigation and alternative dispute resolution mechanisms has had similar effects. These substitute mechanisms will be discussed in turn below.

18.3.2 *Advance Compensation Mechanism*

Under the so-called "Advance Compensation Mechanism" (*Xianxing Peifu Jizhi*), the perpetrator of misrepresentation makes advance compensation to aggrieved investors, in return for leniency in terms of administrative or criminal penalty.[20] It represents a win-win situation for both aggrieved investors and the perpetrators: aggrieved investors can easily receive compensation without the need to go through the difficult and costly litigation process; perpetrators can obtain more lenient administrative or criminal penalty as well as a good market reputation.

This mechanism was first used in the 2013 case of *Wanfu Shengke* (Wanfu BioTech, or Wanfu), a company listed on the Shenzhen Stock Exchange which was found to have disclosed false information in its IPO prospectus. The CSRC imposed administrative sanctions on relevant parties, including PingAn Securities (PingAn) for failing to exercise due diligence in performing its role as the sponsor for the IPO of Wanfu. Interestingly, PingAn made a public announcement that it would voluntarily set up a fund to compensate the investors who suffered harm from the case. On May 10, 2013, PingAn set up a compensation fund of RMB0.3 billion. Within only two months thereafter, the compensation scheme paid a total of RMB 0.18 billion, with the participation of 12756 investors, representing 95.01 percent of all eligible claimants and 99.56 percent of all recoverable loss.

18 Robin Hui Huang, "Private Enforcement of Securities Law in China: A Ten-year Retrospective and Empirical Assessment" (2013) 61 *Am. J. Comp. L.* 757.

19 Ibid., 768–70.

20 Robin Hui Huang, Hailong Li, and Gavin Yao Lin, "The Anatomy of Securities Class Action in China: A Functional and Comparative Approach" (2018) 46(4) *Securities Regulation Law Journal* 365.

The Wanfu case was widely considered as a successful innovation, providing an alternative to private securities litigation in compensating aggrieved investors. Indeed, compared to the court litigation, the advance compensation mechanism is a lower-cost, quicker and more convenient way to redress harm suffered by many small and scattered investors. This mechanism has since been used with similar success in two other cases, including the case of Hailianxun Tech (Hailianxun) in 2014 and the case of Xintai Electronic in 2017.

18.3.3 *Public Interest Group Litigation*

As noted before, it has been suggested that local protectionism makes the court unsympathetic towards securities civil suits, and thus a solution to this problem is to make the plaintiff stronger so as to offset the influence of the local protectionism. To this end, the litigation can be brought by a powerful third party on behalf of aggrieved, dispersed investors. One of such mechanisms is the so-called public interest group litigation (*gongyi tuanti susong*).

In 2012, China significantly revised its Civil Procedure Law, introducing the regime of public interest group litigation. The provision governing this regime is couched in very broad terms, stating that an authority or relevant organisation as prescribed by law may instigate a suit against conduct damaging the public interest such as someone who pollutes the environment, or infringes upon the lawful rights and interests of a large number of consumers.[21] In 2017, the Civil Procedure Law was revised again to state that the People's Procuratorate can bring public interest group litigation in relation to the protection of environment and resources, as well as the issue of food and drug safety.[22] In addition, there is a general provision for the so-called "supporting litigation" (*zhengquan zhichi susong*) under which a third party, including a state organ, a social group, an enterprise, or a public institution, may support an entity or an individual which suffers civil infringement in bringing action before a court.[23] Clearly, supporting litigation is broader and more flexible than public interest group litigation, and thus the former can be used when the latter is not available. In a broader sense, however, supporting litigation can be seen as a special form of public interest group litigation.

Although securities fraud is not explicitly mentioned in the provision on public interest group litigation, there is little doubt that as is often the case in practice, securities fraud may harm a large number of investors and thus give rise to public interest concerns. Some commentators have argued that the provision sets out public interest group litigation in principle rather than in detail, listing environment and consumer infringements only as examples, and thus other types of infringements, such as securities misconduct, could potentially fall within the ambit of public interest group litigation.[24] However, due to the ambiguity of the provision and lack of implementing rules, there have been no reported cases of public interest group litigation in relation to securities fraud.

As noted above, the Civil Procedure Law also provides the supporting litigation mechanism, which is more flexible than the public interest group litigation. The supporting litigation mechanism has been used in the context of civil cases against securities misconduct. When a public interest organization (PIO) uses this provision to support securities private litigation,

[21] Zhonghua Renmin Gongheguo Minshi Susongfa [Civil Procedure Law of the People's Republic of China] (passed on April 9, 1991, amended on October 28, 2007, August 31, 2012 and June 27, 2017) (Civil Procedure Law), art. 55 (1).

[22] Ibid., art. 55(2).

[23] Civil Procedure Law, art. 15.

[24] See e.g., Weiping Zhang, "The Institutionalization and Implementation of Civil Public Interest Group Litigation Principles" (2013) 7(4) *Qinghua Faxue* [*Tsinghua Law Journal*] 6, 7.

a mechanism now called "securities supporting litigation," it would achieve a similar function to public interest group litigation in helping aggrieved investors to obtain compensation. The key difference between them is only a matter of formality, being that public interest group litigation is brought in the name of the public interest group for the interest of the victims, while supporting litigation is in the name of the victims with litigation support from public interest groups.

On July 20, 2016, the China Securities Small and Medium-sized Investor Service Centre Limited Liability Company (Investor Service Centre, or ISC), at the request of one shareholder of a company named Pi Tu Pi, filed a suit against the company, its actual controller and other seven senior managerial officers for misrepresentation in the Shanghai First Intermediate People's Court.[25] This marked the first securities supporting litigation in China, which was soon followed by the second one alleging misrepresentations by Kangda Xincai on behalf of eleven investors on August 14, 2016.[26] As of March 2018, the ISC had brought at least eight securities supporting litigations.[27]

In order to understand how the securities supporting litigation works, it is necessary to examine the organizational nature of the ISC. As a public interest organization, the ISC was set up as a limited liability company in Shanghai in December 2014 with approval from the CSRC.[28] Its mission is to serve as an important mechanism to enhance protection of small and medium-sized investors, by holding securities, exercising and protecting rights in the capacity of shareholders, and making claims to government agencies and regulators on behalf of small and medium-sized investors. It is important to note that the ISC is under the direct administration of the CSRC, with its shareholders being China Securities Depository and Clearing Corporation Limited, Shanghai Stock Exchange, Shenzhen Stock Exchange, China Financial Futures Exchange, and Shanghai Futures Exchange.

In practice, the ISC will first select cases to litigate by reference to a list of factors, such as the significance of the case, social influence, the identity of aggrieved investors and the prospect of obtaining compensation. Then, it will try to get in touch with eligible investor plaintiffs and ask them to join the suit. The ISC will assign its lawyers to support the cases free of charge, hence those lawyers are called public interest lawyers. In general, the securities supporting litigation is functionally similar to securities class actions, except that the former is supported and driven by the ISC while the latter is by private lawyers.

In 2015, the Supreme People's Court has made it clear that the acceptance of a public interest group litigation by a people's court does not affect the initiation of an individual action by a victim of the same tort through the traditional litigation route.[29] This means that the public interest group litigation can complement, rather than replace, the class action litigation.

25 Shanghai Yizhongyuan Shouli Quanguo Shouli Zhengquan Zhichi Susong [Shanghai First Intermediate Court Accepts the First Securities Supporting Litigation in China], available at www.chinacourt.org/article/detail/2016/07/id/2043564.shtml.

26 Toufu Zhongxin Zhendui Kangda Xincai Zaojia Shangshi Tiqi Zhichi Susong [Investor Service Centre Brought Securities Supporting Litigation Against the Falsified Listing Documents of Kangda Xincai], available at http://finance.sina.com.cn/stock/t/2016-08-14/doc-ifxuxhas1889281.shtml.

27 Zhengquan Weiquan Xin Tujing, Toufu Zhongxin Litui Zhichi Susong [New Ways for Vindicating Securities Rights; Investor Service Centre Promoting Supporting Litigation], available www.sohu.com/a/225568602_114986.

28 It replaces its short-lived predecessor, China Securities Investor Development Centre Limited Liability Company, which was established in January 2013.

29 Zuigao Renmin Fayuan Guanyu Shiyong "Zhongguo Renmin Gongheguo Minshi Susongfa" de Jieshi [Interpretation of the Supreme People's Court on the Application of the Civil Procedure Law of the People's Republic of China] (issued January 30, 2015, effective February 4, 2015), art. 288.

Nevertheless, as public interest group litigation can in effect achieve a similar effect to the class action, it would reduce the need for class action.

18.3.4 *Alternative Private Enforcement Mechanisms*

In recent years, China has seen the rapid development of alternative dispute resolution forums, including arbitration, mediation, and special dispute resolution mechanisms. In general, they accept a wide range of civil and commercial cases, and, increasingly, are aimed at securities and financial disputes between private parties. Under the taxonomy of law enforcement, they properly belong to the category of private enforcement, and operate as an alternative to securities class action, hence they can be called alternative private enforcement. How will the development of alternative private enforcement impact on traditional court-based private enforcement in the form of securities class action?

With the emergence, strengthening and development of China's market economy after 1978, and the establishment of a relatively complete legal regime for alternative dispute resolution, arbitral tribunals and professionalized mediation services have proliferated. China promulgated its Arbitration Law in 1994, with a view to bringing its arbitration system in line with international standards.[30] There are now a large number of arbitration commissions located throughout China, including the well-known China International Economic and Trade Arbitration Commission (CIETAC) which was founded by a national body called the China Council for the Promotion of International Trade, and more than 200 local arbitration commissions that have been established in most major cities such as Beijing, Shanghai, Guangzhou, and Shenzhen. As early as in 2003, the CIETAC adopted its Financial Dispute Arbitration Rules, which specifically applies to disputes arising from, or in connection with financial transactions.[31] Similarly, many local arbitration commissions have set up specialized financial arbitration divisions in recognition of the growing demand for financial dispute settlement. The first specialized financial arbitration commission was established in Shanghai in December 2007, and many others have soon followed suit, particularly after the global financial crisis of 2008.

In the context of China, it has long been accepted that arbitration enjoys many advantages vis-à-vis litigation in resolving civil and commercial disputes, including organizational independence, efficiency, the relative ease of enforcement, privacy, and the finality of the award.[32] However, such general views regarding preference for arbitration over in-court litigation do not seem to apply to the case of financial and securities-related dispute resolution in China. The main reason is that although arbitration is generally a popular means of dispute resolution for business people in China, it is still quite novel for ordinary people who are involved in financial disputes over matters such as bank deposits, housing loans, securities trading, and insurance contracts. Arbitration jurisdiction requires a prior arbitration clause in the financial services contract, but unlike overseas jurisdictions such as the USA,[33] Chinese financial services providers are not free to unilaterally insert arbitration clauses in financial services contracts. Due to

[30] Zhonghua Renmin Gongheguo Zhongcai Fa [Arbitration Law of the People's Republic of China] (promulgated on August 31, 1994, amended in August 2009 and September 2017).

[31] Sanzhu Zhu, *Securities Dispute Resolution in China* 229 (Ashgate 2007).

[32] Shahla Ali and Robin Hui Huang, "Financial Dispute Resolution in China: Arbitration or Court Litigation?" (2012) 28(1) *Arbitration International* 77, 78–79.

[33] Michael S. Barr, "Mandatory Arbitration in Consumer Finance and Investor Contracts" (2015) 11(4) *NYU J. of Law and Business* 793 (stating that the US consumers are often subject to mandatory pre-dispute arbitration clauses).

the issue of unfamiliarity with arbitration, most financial consumers are reluctant to give their consent to the use of arbitration in the event of disputes.[34]

As to mediation, China has recently promoted the idea of "Grand Mediation" (*Da Tiaojie*) to resolve disputes of all kinds in an effective and harmonious manner.[35] It is against this backdrop that special mediation mechanisms are established for securities disputes. On June 11, 2012, the Securities Association of China (SAC), which is the self-regulatory body of the securities industry in China, issued three important rules on the establishment and operation of a new securities dispute mediation scheme in China, namely the Administrative Measures for the Mediation of Securities Disputes (for trial implementation), Rules for the Mediation of Securities Disputes (for trial implementation), and Administrative Measures for Mediators (for trial implementation). This is the first time that China has set up a specialized and centralized mediation scheme for securities disputes. After about three and a half years of trials, on January 22, 2016, the SAC revised the above three instruments, reorganizing them into two instruments, namely the Administrative Measures for the Mediation of Securities Disputes and Rules for the Mediation of Securities Disputes.[36]

In general, the securities dispute mediation mechanism has been welcomed by the market as a useful mechanism for resolving securities disputes. However, there are still some issues or concerns with respect to it.[37] For instance, legitimate concerns may arise as to whether the SAC can be independent in handling securities disputes. On the one hand, as the SAC is an industry association, there is some possibility that the SAC may sometimes be hijacked by its influential members at the expenses of ordinary investors. On the other hand, there is concern that the SAC may use its powers to coerce its members into reaching a mediation agreement with investors. Securities disputes usually involve a large number of investors, and if not handled properly, they may pose a threat to social stability. The SAC will do everything they can to stop securities disputes from developing into a social stability threat, given that social stability is currently the top priority of the Chinese government.

Apart from the usual types of alternative dispute resolution, efforts have also been made to build special, innovative mechanisms for resolving financial disputes. In September 2013, drawing upon overseas experiences, notably the securities dispute resolution forum operated by the Financial Industry Regulatory Authority (FINRA) in the USA, the Shenzhen Court of International Arbitration (SCIA), together with the CSRC's Shenzhen Bureau, Shenzhen Stock Exchange, Shenzhen Securities Association, Shenzhen Futures Association, and Shenzhen Asset Management Association, etc., established the Shenzhen Securities and Futures Dispute Resolution Centre (SZSFDRC). As the above group of organizers includes regulators, self-regulatory bodies and private providers of dispute resolution services, the SZSFDRC is the first securities dispute resolution institution of its kind in China to adopt a "four in one" mode, which combines professional mediation, commercial arbitration, industry discipline, and administrative regulation in resolving securities-related disputes in China.[38]

34 Shahla Ali and Robin Hui Huang, "Financial Dispute Resolution in China: Arbitration or Court Litigation?" (2012) 28(1) *Arbitration International* 77, 91.

35 Zhonghua Renmin Gongheguo Renmin Tiaojie Fa [People's Mediation Law of the People's Republic of China] (issued on August 28, 2010, effective from January 1, 2011).

36 Zhongguo Zhengquanye Xiehui Zhengquan Jiufen Tiaojie Gongzuo Guanli Banfa [SAC Administrative Measures for the Mediation of Securities Disputes] (issued on January 22, 2016); Zhongguo Zhengquanye Xiehui Zhengquan Jiufen Tiaojie Guize [SAC Rules for the Mediation of Securities Disputes] (issued on January 22, 2016).

37 Robin Hui Huang, "Securities Dispute Mediation in China" (2016) 10(2) *Journal of Comparative Law* 177.

38 See the official website of Shenzhen Court of International Arbitration www.sccietac.org/.

The key innovation of the SZSFDRC is the close integration of arbitration with mediation. After the parties reach a mediation agreement, they can proceed quickly to the next stage of asking the SCIA to issue an arbitral award through a special fast-track, so that the mediation agreement can be legally binding and enforceable. Under this mode, the arbitration fee is applied at a discount of more than 50 percent, depending on the circumstances of each case. If the dispute is between small investors and listed companies or market intermediaries, the mediation service is free of charge. Hence, the SZSFDRC is intended to provide a low-cost, efficient, and effective venue to handle securities-related disputes.

In practice, the SZSFDRC has made good progress in terms of the quantity and quality of cases handled. Its growing popularity in the market can be seen from the rapid increase in the number of inquiries it has received: 140 inquiries in the whole year of 2014 and then 650 in 2015 exclusive of the last month; the ratio of successful mediation was as high as 89 percent; and although it is located in Shenzhen, its influence has become nationwide, with 67 percent of cases involving one or both parties from other provinces and municipalities.[39] Importantly, it has played an important role in handling cases against securities misrepresentation. For instance, as discussed earlier, the Hailianxun case was the second case dealt with through the advance compensation mechanism,[40] but in fact, four victims in this case refused to accept the advance compensation because they were unhappy with the measure of damages. In the end, they reached a settlement agreement with the Hailianxun company separately through the SZSFDRC.

The SZSFDRC is not without its weaknesses, however. With securities regulators and self-regulatory bodies contributing to the establishment of the SZSFDRC, market players, particularly licensed bodies, may have extra incentives to participate in the SZSFDRC's dispute resolution process, as their performance there may be reported to and thus monitored by regulators and industry associations. This suggests by no means that the process becomes mandatory and the parties are forced to reach a settlement agreement. Essentially, as a type of alternative dispute resolution, the SZSFDRC dispute resolution process is consensual. Based on an interview with a staff member of the SZSFDRC, the Intermediate Court of Shenzhen once transferred a securities misrepresentation case to the SZSFDRC. After months of efforts, the disputing parties could not reach a mediation agreement, and finally, the case was returned to the court.[41] Therefore, as a consensus-based dispute resolution forum, the SZSFDRC can usefully complement but not completely replace the court-based securities class action.

18.4 SELF-IMPROVEMENTS AND RECENT REFORMS

As noted earlier, under the Chinese-style class action regime, there can be multiple suits arising from the same instance of infringement. In contrast, under the US-style class action, only one suit is needed to be brought for and on behalf of all eligible plaintiffs. Many commentators have argued that compared to its counterpart in the US, the Chinese-style securities civil actions represents an inefficient use of limited judicial resources because the court needs to deal with multiple suits rather than one single suit as is the case in the USA.[42]

39 Xiaochun Liu, "China's Free Trade Zone and Latest Development of the Resolution Mechanism for Financial Disputes" in Robin Hui Huang and Nicholas Howson (eds), *Enforcement of Corporate and Securities Law: China and the World* (Cambridge University Press, 2017), 211–13.

40 See *supra* Section 18.4.2.

41 Interview, January 8, 2018, Shenzhen.

42 Wallace Wen-Yeu Wang and Chen Jian-Lin, "Reforming China's Securities Civil Actions: Lessons from PSLRA Reform in the U.S. and Government-Sanctioned Non-Profit Enforcement in Taiwan" (2008) 21(2) *Colum. J. Asian L.*

At first blush the above argument possesses considerable intuitive appeal, but a closer examination of how the Chinese regime actually functions in practice suggests that the force of the argument might be exaggerated. To begin with, there are often a small number of suits arising from the same instance of infringement, and thus the form of litigation would have little impact on judicial resources. Further, even when an instance of infringement gives rise to a large number of suits, the consumption of judicial resources may not be significantly more than if the suits were brought as one class action. We will use the case of securities misrepresentation as an example to illustrate the point.

18.4.1 *The Development of the Model Suit Mechanism*

18.4.1.1 The Case-by-Case Experiment before 2019

In the area of securities class action, the Chinese court has been trying to achieve judicial economy by developing, on a case-by-case basis, a procedural innovation called the "model suit," under which the court will choose a representative suit from the multiple suits arising from the same instance of securities misrepresentation to be fully adjudicated, and then apply the judgment to the other suits. This creates efficiencies similar to a class action since all the cases arising from the same misrepresentation involve similar legal issues, for example, presumption of causation and measure of damages, and differ only in the number of shares each plaintiff gets compensated for. Of course, unlike the US-style class action where there is only one suit and thus only one judgment or settlement agreement (for brevity, collectively referred to as judgment in this part), the Chinese court needs to issue multiple judgments, one for each suit arising from the same instance of misrepresentation, rather than one super-judgment covering all plaintiffs. However, the making of multiple judgments involves minimal extra work because the first judgment for the model case can serve as a template for the other judgements upon which modifications can be made for items such as the case number, the plaintiff's name, and the compensation amount. Additionally, this practice dispels the concern over the inconsistency of judgments for a series of cases arising from the same misrepresentation.

The case of *Dongfang Electronics*,[43] the largest securities civil action thus far in terms of the number of plaintiffs (6,989) and cases (2,716), exemplifies the above points. The cases were filed either as individual action or joint action. Faced with the large number of cases arising from the same instance of misconduct, the court chose to hear one exemplary case first on August 24, 2004 and dealt with relevant legal issues such as the presumption of causation, the determination of the relevant dates, the measure of damages, and other relevant issues which apply to all other cases. Thereafter, the court used the exemplary case as a model to hear other cases, and the issues already addressed in the exemplary case did not need to be examined again.

In fact, under the US-style class action which allows one single case to be brought to cover all plaintiffs, the court just determines the total amount of compensation or settlement fund at the stage of litigation, but ultimately it would still need to calculate the damages for each plaintiff

115, 130; G. Li and A. V. Y. Ong, "The Fledging Securities Fraud Litigation in China" (2009) 39 *Hong Kong Law Journal* 697, 710–11; G. Lu, "Private Enforcement of Securities Fraud Law in China: A Critique of the Supreme People's Court 2003 Provisions Concerning Private Securities Litigation" (2003) 12 *Pacific Rim Law and Policy Journal* 795, 800–01.

43 Yixin Song, "Dongfang Dianzi An de Weiquan Gushi [The Story of Rights Defence in the Case of Dongfang Electronics]", *Zhongguo Zhengquan Bao [China Securities News]*, November 27, 2006.

separately. In the USA, a settlement administrator is usually appointed to draw up a distribution plan and carry on the actual distribution work, subject to the approval and monitoring of the court. Hence, the court in China and the USA would have basically the same substantive issues to address and resultant costs, with the main difference being only that the Chinese court deals with those issues in the early stage while the task is deferred to a later stage in the USA.

18.4.1.2 The 2019 Rule of the Shanghai Financial Court

As discussed above, the model suit mechanism has been developed on a case-by-case basis in practice, with some evidence showing that it has helped to improve the workability and cost-effectiveness of the Chinese-style securities class action. This experimentation has received official support from both the regulator and the judiciary. In May 2018, the CSRC held a press conference in Shanghai, listing the "model suit" system as one of the important measures to enhance investor protection in the future.[44]

In January 2019, the Shanghai Financial Court (SFC), which was established in August 2018 as the first and hitherto the only specialist financial court in China, issued a formal rule on the application of the model suit system to securities class action, entitled "Provisions on the Model Suit Mechanism for Securities Disputes (Tentative)" (SFC Rule on Model Suit).[45] This instrument marks the culmination of years of experimentation with the model suit mechanism, providing guidance on how the mechanism is to be applied by the SFC in hearing securities disputes.

According to section 2 of the SFC Rule on Model Suit, the model suit system refers to the mechanism which the SFC uses to deal with the so-called "mass securities disputes" (*quntixing zhengquan jiufen*) by choosing a representative case (also called the model case) from a pool of cases arising from the same instance of securities misconduct, conducting a trial of the representative case and then applying the relevant decisions to the so-called "parallel cases." The term "mass securities disputes" means securities disputes which arise from the same subject matter and there are more than ten persons on the one side of the disputes.[46] The term "parallel cases" refers to other cases that arise from the same subject matter as the model case.

The model case can be selected upon the application of each party to the litigation or by the SFC in accordance with its mandate.[47] There are three main criteria for selecting the model case: first, the model case has factual and legal disputes which are common to the mass securities disputes; second, the factual and legal disputes of the model case are representative; third, the application for selecting the model case is not made for the purpose of delaying the litigation process. If a securities supporting case has been brought by a government agency or a public interest organization (such as the ISC) and meets the criteria for the model case, then it has priority to be selected as a model case.[48]

After the model case has been adjudicated, the court rulings on the factual issues common to the mass securities disputes will apply, by default, to all the parallel cases. As for the rulings on the

44 "The CSRC Held a Conference with Investors in Shanghai," available at the CSRC website: www.csrc.gov.cn/pub/newsite/zjhxwfb/xwdd/201806/t20180601_339011.html

45 Guanyu Zhengquan Jiufeng Shifan Panjue Jizhi de Guiding (Shixing) [Provisions on the Model Suit Mechanism for Securities Disputes (Tentative)], issued by Shanghai Financial Court on January 16, 2019.

46 It is clearly stated that the model suit system applies to mass securities disputes over compensation for misrepresentation, market manipulation, and insider trading within the jurisdiction of the SFC. Other types of mass financial disputes may use the model suit system by analogy. See SFC Rule on Model Suit, §4.

47 SFC Rule on Model Suit, §7.

48 SFC Rule on Model Suit, §6.

legal issues, their application depends on which side of the litigation makes the request: if the plaintiff of the parallel case requests to have direct application, the court should support it, and if the defendant makes the request but the plaintiff objects, the court should have an examination.[49]

To ensure the quality of the hearing of the model case, the model case should be heard in an open court with live broadcasting over Internet, unless the hearing should not be made public for reasons such as privacy or business secrets in accordance with law.[50] After the panel of responsible judges hear the model case, they should submit the case and their preliminary views to the Specialized Committee for Securities Law Cases of the SFC for examination and advice, and if necessary, further to the Adjudication Committee of the SFC for final decision.[51] The judgment of the model case should be made public on Internet within seven days of the date of validity, except for the content which should not be publicly disclosed in accordance with the law.

In May 2019, the SFC heard its first case under the model suit mechanism. This case concerned Fangzheng Keji, a Shanghai-listed company, which was sanctioned for misstatements by the CSRC in May 2017. Thousands of aggrieved investors brought civil suits against Fangzheng Keji for compensation before the SFC, with the total value of claims being RMB169 million. The SFC selected a case as a model case and delivered a judgment in favour of the plaintiffs. The defendant appealed to the Shanghai Municipality High Court, and on August 7, 2019, the appeal was rejected and the SFC judgment reaffirmed.[52]

The SFC's experiment with the model suit mechanism has proved so successful as to attract the attention of the Supreme People's Court. On November 8, 2019, the SPC issued the Minutes of the 9th National Courts' Civil and Commercial Trial Work Conference,[53] which contains official recognition of the model suit mechanism. To start with, §80 of this instrument states that "in terms of the methods of case trial, in addition to the traditional 'docketing each case, separate trial' method, some people's courts have carried out reforms such as consolidating the trial of some cases and entrusted mediation on the basis of *model judgments* and preliminarily realize intensiveness of case trial and economy of litigation," and suggests other courts to use the model suit mechanism when appropriate and needed.[54] Then, §81 and §82 provide guidance on the issues of case docketing and identification. For the important issue of selecting representatives, the SFC's relevant rule is confirmed and almost faithfully reproduced in §83. Hence, the model suit mechanism is no longer limited to the SFC and has now been extended to all courts in China.

49 SFC Rule on Model Suit, §37.

50 SFC Rule on Model Suit, §44.

51 SFC Rule on Model Suit, §45.

52 全国首例证券纠纷示范判决案尘埃落定 方正科技赔偿投资者 [China's First Securities Dispute Was Finally Decided Under the Model Suit Mechanism, and Fangzheng Keji Ordered to Compensate Investors], available at www.360kuai.com/pc/92c3ac05ed10706ed?cota=3&kuai_so=1&sign=360_e39369d1&refer_scene=so_3.

53 第九次全国法院民商事审判工作会议纪要 [Minutes of the 9th National Courts' Civil and Commercial Trial Work Conference] (issued by the Supreme People's Court on November 8, 2019).

54 Ibid., §80 (emphasis added). It should be noted that as a written record of a conference, this document is not law in the strict sense and cannot be cited directly as a basis for adjudication, but it is highly significant to the extent that it represents the SPC's policies and will be followed by all Chinese courts in interpreting relevant legal provisions.

18.4.2 *The 2019 Reform of the Securities Law*

On December 28, 2019, the Chinese Securities Law was significantly revised with effect from March 1, 2020.[55] For the first time, a provision has been added to address the procedural issue of private securities litigation, stating that:[56]

> When an investor files a lawsuit for civil compensation on securities against false statements, among others, the subject matter of the lawsuit is of the same kind, and the parties on one side of a lawsuit are numerous, they may legally elect a representative to participate in legal proceedings.
>
> For a lawsuit filed according to the provisions of the preceding paragraph, if there may be many other investors who have the same claim, the people's court may issue an announcement to state the case facts of the claim, and notify investors to register with the people's court within a certain period. The judgments or rulings rendered by the people's court shall be valid for the registered investors.

In fact, the form of litigation specified in the above provision is the same as §54 of the Civil Procedural Law. Clearly, by mentioning it emphatically in the Securities Law, China wants to encourage the use of this form of litigation, but given the reasons discussed earlier, it is not clear whether it would achieve the purpose.

The third limb of the above provision does introduce a new mechanism, providing that

> An investor protection institution may, as entrusted by 50 or more investors, participate in legal proceedings as a representative, and shall register the obligee confirmed by the securities depository and clearing institution at the people's court in accordance with the provisions of the preceding paragraph, unless the investors have clearly expressed their unwillingness to participate in legal proceedings.

This new mechanism represents an interesting innovation by combining the Chinese-style class action and the US-style class action. On the one hand, as a matter of formality, it conforms to the opt-in requirement of the Chinese-style class action under which all plaintiffs must register with the court; on the other hand, it is functionally equivalent to the opt-out requirement of the US-style class action, to the extent that an investor protection institution is legally empowered to do the registration for all other claimants if the institution has obtained authorization from fifty or more investors. In a sense, the qualification of an investor protection institution, coupled with the authorization of more than fifty investors, serves a similar function to the lead plaintiff requirement under the US class action.

Very recently on 31 July 2020, the Supreme People's Court issued a judicial interpretation on the application of §95 of the 2019 Securities Law, under which the new mechanism is called special representative litigation.[57] Indeed, compared to the ordinary representative litigation, the new mechanism bears more resemblance to the US-style class action in that it adopts a de facto opt-out element by allowing an investor protection institution to register other claimants with the court and bring a representative case on behalf of them. As the new mechanism applies only to the securities cases, it has been widely called Chinese-style Securities Class Action. It has promise as an

[55] Zhonghua Renmin Gongheguo Zhengquanfa (中华人民共和国证券法) [Securities Law of the PRC] (promulgated by the Nat'l People's Cong., Dec. 29, 1998, effective July 1, 1999) (amended 2004, 2005, 2013, 2014, and 2019).

[56] Ibid., §95.

[57] 最高人民法院关于证券纠纷代表人诉讼若干问题的规定（Rules of the Supreme People's Court on Relevant Issues of Securities Dispute Representative Litigation, issued by the Supreme People's Court on 30 July 2020, effective from 31 July 2020.

important form of private securities litigation in China, but given that it has recently been established, it remains to be seen whether it will be as effective and efficient as expected.

18.5 CONCLUSION

The Chinese-style class action has similarities and differences with its US counterpart in some significant aspects, including who can initiate the procedure, in what kinds of cases can the procedure be used, what are the types of relief, how to obtain consent of the class members, and what are the financing mechanisms.

Using securities class action as an example, it seems that the Chinese-style class action faces increasing competition from some mechanisms which have similar functions of generating compensation for aggrieved investors against securities misconduct. This includes the advance compensation mechanism with the support from public regulation, the public interest group litigation, and the nonjudicial proceedings such as arbitration, mediation and recently established special forums for securities dispute resolution. At the same time, the Chinese-style class action has undergone self-improvement through the invention of the model suit system which has been progressively developed on a case-by-case basis for some years, culminating in a formal rule issued by the Shanghai Financial Court in 2019. This will help the Chinese-style class action to continue to operate as an alternative to its US counterpart and play an important role in protecting investors in China. The more recent reform of the Chinese securities law has introduced a new mechanism for private securities litigation, which is more similar to the US-style class action and promises to be a more effective way to protect investors in China.

In sum, the Chinese-style class action is in a state of flux with both challenges and opportunities. The future development of the Chinese-style class action will depend largely on the political economy context in which it operates, particularly how the court is incentivized to use it, and how the Chinese government considers it as an effective way to resolve mass disputes and maintain social stability.

19

Class Actions in Australia

Michael Legg and Samuel J. Hickey

19.1 INTRODUCTION

In drafting the first Australian class actions regime under Part IVA of the Federal Court of Australia Act 1976 (Cth) (FCAA), the Commonwealth legislature had the difficult task of creating a procedure that was appropriate for the Australian jurisdiction, including being in keeping with its litigation culture, while also learning from the procedures already employed in the United States and Canada. After twenty-seven years of federal class actions, it can be said that Australia has fashioned in Part IVA an effective and efficient framework for resolving mass litigation, accompanied by a robust body of jurisprudence. Equally, class action practice in Australia has evolved in ways that would have been beyond the reasonable comprehension of those who initially drafted Part IVA, third-party litigation funding being a key development. This chapter tells the story of Part IVA's creation and maturation, providing an overview of the jurisprudence that has characterised its evolution, as well as an account of contentious issues at the forefront of modern class action practice. Reference is made to the reports authored by Australian law reform commissions on class actions over the years, with particular focus given to the report most recently released by the Australian Law Reform Commission (ALRC) on the intersection of class actions and third-party litigation funding.[1]

This chapter is structured as follows. Section 19.2 details the growth of Australia's federal and state class action regimes. Section 19.3 outlines the frequency with which class actions are filed within each Australian jurisdiction, as well as the types of claims that underscore these actions. Section 19.4 then summarises the procedural framework applicable to class actions in Australia, while Section 19.5 describes several features of the Australian class action landscape that are integral to understanding modern practice. This includes the rise of third-party funding, the introduction of the 'closed class' mechanism to supplement (or circumvent) Australia's 'opt-out' model of class actions, and lastly, Australia's decision not to adopt a certification regime. Finally, Section 19.6 raises topical issues that pose challenges for the future, in particular, the minimisation of lawyer and funder fees, and the management of competing class actions.

[1] Australian Law Reform Commission, Integrity, Fairness and Efficiency—An Inquiry into Class Action Proceedings and Third-Party Litigation Funders (Report No. 134, 2018) (ALRC 2018 Report), 5–6.

19.2 AUSTRALIAN CLASS ACTION REGIMES

Australia's federal class action regime originated from a request made by then Attorney-General Robert Ellicott QC to the ALRC in 1977 that it write a report on the adequacy of, and any changes that should be made to, federal law relating to 'grouped proceedings'.[2] Representative procedures up until that point had existed only in the equitable jurisdiction and court rules of state and territory courts. These procedures had historically received narrow interpretation and fallen into disuse;[3] failing to provide meaningful redress in cases in which the cost of individual proceedings outweighed the value of the claim.[4] The ALRC's final report, titled 'Grouped Proceedings in the Federal Court', was tabled in Parliament in 1988,[5] and recommended the adoption of a federal class actions procedure. The report indicated that doing so would enhance access to justice and improve the efficiency of the court system.[6] The proposed regime was initially controversial. Both the political and business communities harboured fears that it would prove oppressive for businesses and lead to an influx of unwarranted litigation.[7] Parliament nevertheless followed the ALRC's recommendation, and in 1991 amended the FCAA to include a new set of provisions containing Australia's first class actions regime. Those provisions were enshrined under the new Part IVA, under the title 'Representative Proceedings'.[8] Part IVA came into effect on 4 March 1992.

The operation of Part IVA was naturally shaped by the decisions of appellate courts, including judicial affirmation of the meaning of 'a substantial common issue',[9] the legitimacy of third-party funding,[10] but rejection of common fund orders being made at the commencement of proceedings,[11] and the approval of 'closed class' class actions.[12] Equally, much of the development of class action practice has come from innovative approaches from the legal profession, trial judges and the academy.

Part IVA is strengthened by near uniformity with equivalent state legislation in Victoria, New South Wales, Queensland and Tasmania.[13] Australia's remaining states and territories (Western Australia, South Australia, the Northern Territory, and the Australian Capital Territory) do not have legislatively enshrined class actions. It is quite possible that Western Australia will be the first among them to implement such a regime as legislation has been placed before Parliament.[14]

2 Australian Law Reform Commission, Grouped Proceedings in the Federal Court (Report No. 46, 1988) (ALRC 1988 Report), see 'Terms of Reference'.

3 Bernard Murphy and Camille Cameron, 'Access to Justice and the Evolution of Class Action Litigation in Australia' (2006) 30 *Melbourne University Law Review* 399, 401; Miiko Kumar, Michael Legg and Ilija Vickovich, *Civil Procedure in New South Wales* (Thomson Reuters, 3d ed 2016) 448–9.

4 ALRC 1988 Report, pp. 24–5.

5 The substantial time taken to produce the report has been attributed both to resourcing issues, and also the fact that class actions were a divisive topic among members of the commission. See respectively, The Hon. Murray Wilcox AO QC, 'Class Actions in Australia: Recollections of the Early Days' in Damian Grave and Helen Mould (eds), *25 Years of Class Actions in Australia* (Ross Parsons Centre, 2017) p. 6 and Parliamentary Debates, Senate (Cth), 13 November 1991, 3019 (Senator Durack).

6 ALRC 1988 Report, p. 146.

7 See Chief Justice James Allsop, 'Class Actions', Law Council of Australia Forum – Class Actions 2016 Key Topics, Sydney, 13 October 2016.

8 Federal Court of Australia Amendment Bill 1991 (Cth).

9 *Wong* v. *Silkfield Pty Ltd* (1999) 199 CLR 255.

10 *Campbells Cash & Carry Pty Ltd* v. *Fostif Pty Ltd* (2006) 229 CLR 386.

11 *BMW Australia Ltd* v. *Brewster; Westpac Banking Corporation* v. *Lenthall* [2019] HCA 45.

12 *Multiplex Funds Management Limited* v. *P Dawson Nominees Pty Ltd* (2007) 164 FCR 275.

13 Civil Procedure Act 2005 (NSW), Part 10; Civil Proceedings Act 2011 (Qld), Part 13A; Supreme Court Civil Procedure Act 1932 (Tas) Pt VII; Supreme Court Act 1986 (Vic), Part 4A. This Article will focus solely on Part IVA of the FCAA. For a summary of differences see Michael Legg and Ross McInnes, *Australian Annotated Class Actions Legislation* (LexisNexis, 2nd ed., 2018) 26–8.

14 Civil Procedure (Representative Proceedings) Bill 2019 (WA).

Federal and State governments have also recognised the recurrent need to either reform or update the Australian class action regimes.[15] In December 2016 the Victorian Law Reform Commission (VLRC) received a reference to consider access to justice, class actions and litigation funding and in March 2018, the VLRC published its report.[16] The report urged the creation of a more nuanced regulatory framework for litigation funders, the introduction of contingency fees into Victoria, the mandatory disclosure of funding agreements (as is already the position in federal courts), the provision of alternate means of financing class actions, and an increase in the powers of Judges to moderate fees owed to lawyers and funders.[17] The recommendations are yet to be adopted (except for contingency fees which are discussed in Section 19.4), but it is reasonable to anticipate reforms.

In December 2017, then-Attorney General George Brandis QC provided the terms of reference for a second ALRC inquiry into class actions. The report was commissioned for numerous reasons, including fears that lawyers and funders were profiting from the disenfranchisement of class members, and that the advent of litigation funding generally had increased the potential for predatory lending and conflicts of duty and interest in class actions.[18] The terms of reference thus directed the ALRC to identify potential areas of reform at the intersection of class actions and litigation funding. The report, 'Integrity, Fairness and Efficiency – An Inquiry into Class Action Proceedings and Third-Party Litigation Funders', was presented in Parliament in January 2019, and ultimately made twenty-four recommendations for law reform, many of which are geared toward the imposition of burdensome regulations on litigation funders.[19] It is likely that reforms will follow. Many of the significant topics addressed in the report have been canvassed in Sections 19.5 and 19.6 below.

19.3 USE AND TYPES OF CLASS ACTIONS

As of 31 May 2018, 563 class actions had been filed in Australian courts.[20] A considerable majority, 430 (76 per cent), were filed in the Federal Court of Australia.[21] Meanwhile, 88 (15 per cent) were filed in Victoria, 42 (5.7 per cent) in New South Wales and only 3 (0.5 per cent) in Queensland.[22] The average number of Australian class actions filed every 12 months up until May 2018 was 21.4.[23] Jurisdictions such as Israel, Quebec and Ontario consistently see far more class actions filed despite having considerably smaller populations than Australia.[24] There is no real comparison between Australia and the United States when it comes to the sheer number of class actions filed each year, as it was estimated in 2011 that

15 See e.g., VLRC, Civil Justice Review (Report No. 14, 2008); Law Reform Commission of Western Australia, Representative Proceedings (Project No 103, 2015); VLRC, Access to Justice: Litigation Funding and Group Proceedings (Report No. 37, 2018) (VLRC 2018 Report); ALRC 2018 Report.

16 VLRC 2018 Report, 14.

17 VLRC 2018 Report, 13–18.

18 ALRC 2018 Report 5–6.

19 ALRC 2018 Report 9–12. For a summary and critique of the recommendations see Michael Legg, 'Australian Law Reform Commission Class Action and Litigation Funding Report: Empowering Courts, Monitoring Funders, Supporting Contingency Fees for Class Action Lawyers and Proposing Reviews of Shareholder Class Actions and Collective Redress' (2019) 38(4) *Civil Justice Quarterly* 478.

20 Vince Morabito, An Evidence-Based Approach to Class Action Reform in Australia: Competing Class Actions and Comparative Perspectives on the Volume of Class Action Litigation in Australia (July 11, 2018), p. 8.

21 Ibid.

22 Ibid.

23 Ibid.

24 Ibid, pp. 10–11.

TABLE 19.1 *Main types of Australian class actions*

Type of class action	Number filed 1992–2017	Percentage of total filed	Federal	State
Investor (other than shareholder)	99	19.2%	69	30
Shareholder	81	15.7%	66	15
Product liability	70	13.6%	60	10
Employee-employer	56	10.9%	55	1
Mass tort	54	10.5%	15	39
Consumer Protection	47	9.1%	39	8

approximately 12,500 class actions are filed yearly in the United States (7500 in federal courts and 5000 in state courts).[25]

More detail regarding the way in which class actions are utilised in Australia can be gleaned by discussing the top six kinds of claims brought between June 1992 and May 2017.[26]

A steady increase in most of these types of class action can be seen in comparing the first twelve and a half years of class actions in Australia (June 1992 to November 2004) to the following twelve and a half years (December 2004 to May 2017). In the first twelve and a half years there were only fifteen investor, eleven shareholder, fifteen mass tort and fourteen consumer class actions.[27] The next twelve and a half years saw eighty-four investor, seventy shareholder, thirty-nine mass tort and thirty-three consumer class actions.[28] On the other hand, marked declines were apparent when observing the same two time periods and the number of product liability and employee-employer class actions: forty-eight product liability and forty-five employee-employer class actions were filed in the first twelve and a half years of the Australian class action regime being in effect, while only twenty-two and eleven were respectively filed in the next twelve and a half years.[29]

Clearly, the Australian class actions landscape is dominated by investor and shareholder class actions. However, specific focus on the ten-year period between 2007 and 2017 suggests that only shareholder class actions are increasing in number. Forty-two investor class actions were filed between June 2007 and May 2012, and only twenty-nine between June 2012 and May 2017.[30] The steady decrease in investor class actions can be partly explained by claims arising out of the global financial crisis being litigated to conclusion or becoming time-barred.[31] However, the Royal Commission into Misconduct in the Banking, Superannuation and Financial Services Industry which uncovered a range of misconduct may see these numbers increase.[32] Meanwhile, twenty shareholder class actions were filed between June 2007 and May 2012, and forty-three between June 2012 and May 2017.[33] The increase in shareholder class actions appears to be linked to the growth of litigation funding. Since 2013, every single shareholder class action brought in the

25 Deborah L. Hensler, 'The Future of Mass Litigation: Global Class Actions and Third-Party Litigation Funding' (2011) 79 *George Washington Law Review* 306, 308 (footnote 7).

26 Vince Morabito, The First Twenty-Five Years of Class Actions in Australia (Fifth Report; An Empirical Study of Australia's Class Action Regimes; July 2017), p. 27. That report considers other types of class actions, but they are not brought with sufficient frequency so as to warrant mention here.

27 Ibid., p. 28.

28 Ibid.

29 Ibid.

30 Ibid.

31 Ibid.

32 See the Royal Commission's reports here https://financialservices.royalcommission.gov.au/ .

33 Vince Morabito, The First Twenty-Five Years of Class Actions in Australia (Fifth Report; An Empirical Study of Australia's Class Action Regimes; July 2017), p. 28.

federal court has been supported by a third-party funder.[34] The attraction of funders to this type of litigation is unsurprising. The combination of a low threshold for commencing class actions, robust continuous disclosure requirements under the Corporations Act 2001 (Cth), numerous potential claimants (including institutional investors) made these class actions a natural choice for funders.[35] Moreover, there is a lack of jurisprudence as shareholder class actions do not proceed to judgment. The first and only shareholder class action judgment was decided on 24 October 2019. It found a contravention of the law and endorsed market-based causation, but found no loss based on the evidence presented.[36]

19.4 PROCEDURAL FRAMEWORK

Section 33C(1) of the FCAA establishes what is commonly referred to as the 'gateway' or 'threshold' for commencing class actions. It has been described as one of the key reasons why Australia's class actions regime is more 'plaintiff-friendly' than Rule 23 of the Federal Rules of Civil Procedure.[37] It reads as follows:

> 33C Commencement of proceeding
>
> (1) Subject to this Part, where:
>
> (a) 7 or more persons have claims against the same person; and
>
> (b) the claims of all those persons are in respect of, or arise out of, the same, similar or related circumstances; and
>
> (c) the claims of all those persons give rise to a substantial common issue of law or fact;
>
> a proceeding may be commenced by one or more of those persons as representing some or all of them.

The 'seven or more persons' requirement under subsection (1)(a), which is comparable to the American 'numerosity' requirement, is satisfied so long as it is reasonable to assume that there are in fact seven or more persons sharing the same claim.[38] The precondition of there being 'claims' is also undemanding, requiring that only the class representatives advance a 'reasonably arguable cause of action'[39] or 'demand for what is due' against a respondent.[40] It is not necessary that all group members be aware of those claims,[41] that those claims be identical,[42] or that they contemplate completely identical relief.[43]

34 ALRC 2018 Report, 69.

35 Michael Legg, 'Shareholder Class Actions in Australia – The Perfect Storm?' (2008) 31 (3) *University of New South Wales Law Journal* 669.

36 *TPT Patrol Pty Ltd as trustee for Amies Superannuation Fund* v. *Myer Holdings Limited* [2019] FCA 1747.

37 S. Stuart Clark and Christine Harris, 'Multi-Plaintiff Litigation in Australia: A Comparative Perspective' (2001) 11 *Duke Journal of Comparative & International Law* 289, 296–8.

38 *Tropical Shine Holdings Ptd Ltd* v. *Lake Gesture Pty Ltd* [1993] FCA 753; 118 ALR 510, [20] (Wilcox J).

39 *Bray* v. *F Hoffman-La Roche Ltd* [2002] FCA 1405, [32], [42] (Merkel J).

40 *Bray* v. *Hoffmann-La Roche Ltd* (2003) 130 FCR 317, [113] (Carr J). Justice Carr explained that the term 'claim' is to be construed broadly, and explained that the word 'claim' was of broader scope than the phrase 'cause of action', as it also encompasses demands.

41 ACCC v. *Giraffe World Australia* (1998) 84 FCR 512, 523 (Lindgren J).

42 *King* v. *GIO Australia Holdings* (2000) 100 FCR 209, 222–3.

43 FCAA s 33C(2)(iv) and *Smith* v. *University of Ballarat* (2006) 229 ALR 343, [32].

The phrase 'against the same person' in subsection (1)(a) has been the source of jurisprudential divergence in cases with multiple respondents. It was initially construed as imposing a high standard by the Federal Court of Australia, requiring that all representatives *and* class members have claims against all named respondents.[44] Subsequent federal decisions relaxed this standard, finding that while each representative must have a claim against each named respondent, it is not necessary for each individual class member to have a claim against each named respondent.[45]

The requirement under subsection (1)(b) that the claims of the group members be connected through 'same, similar or related circumstances' has also been interpreted liberally, describing 'three sufficient relationships of widening ambit' and only requiring that each claim be based upon the same set of facts.[46] The 'circumstances' described in the subsection may include separate transactions between individual class members and respondents. The word 'related' suggests a lower bar than what a requirement based on 'identity or similarity' would have imposed, and whether claims are sufficiently related necessitates courts to make 'practical judgments' informed by the policy and purpose of Part IVA.[47] The 'substantial common issue of law or fact' requirement under subsection (1)(c), which is similar to the American 'commonality' requirement, only requires that the common issues be 'real or of substance'. There is no requirement for absolute cohesion of the substantive issues.[48] Disparate claims may satisfy section 33C(1)(c) so long as they give rise to commonality in at least one not insubstantial respect.[49] This is to say that there is no equivalent to the 'predominance' requirement under Rule 23(b)(3).

The low threshold for commencement is counter-balanced by procedural mechanisms permitting the discontinuance of class actions. Chiefly, section 33 N permits a court, on its own motion or on application by a respondent, to make a discontinuance order stipulating that a proceeding not continue as a class action provided that making the order would be in the 'interest of justice'. This standard is satisfied when one of four criteria are met: allowing the proceeding to continue as a class action would be more expensive than separate proceedings, the relief sought in the class action could be obtained by means other than a class action, the class action would not provide an efficient and effective means of dealing with the claims of group members, or, finally, it would be 'otherwise inappropriate' that the claims be pursued as a class action.[50] Section 33 N protects against the misuse of the class action procedure, and its function can be compared to the predominance and superiority requirements under Rule 23(b)(3). However, section 33 N applications are rarely successful as the courts prefer to use case management techniques to resolve even a small number of common issues across numerous group members. In *Bright* v. *Femcare Ltd*, a product liability class action dealing with a form of contraception, much of the debate was about the existence of common issues and whether the non-common issues predominated so that determination of the common issues would not advance the resolution of the controversy between the parties. Moreover, the respondents

44 *Philip Morris (Aust) Ltd* v. *Nixon* (2000) 170 ALR 487; [2000] FCA 229.

45 *Bray* v. *F Hoffman-La Roche Ltd* [2003] FCAFC 153, *Cash Converters International Limited* v. *Gray* [2014] FCAFC 111. See John Emmerig and Michael Legg, 'Full Federal Court Relaxes Commencement Requirements for Australian Class Actions' (2014) 3 *Journal of Civil Litigation and Practice* 92.

46 *Zhang* v. *Minister for Immigration, Local Government and Ethnic Affairs* (1993) 45 FCR 384, 404 [38].

47 Ibid., 404 [39].

48 *Wong* v. *Silkfield Pty Ltd* (1999) 199 CLR 255, 267.

49 Justice Michael Lee, 'Certification of class actions: A "solution" in search of a problem?' (Speech delivered at the Commercial Law Association Seminar 'Class Actions – Different Perspectives', 20 October 2017).

50 A court can make a discontinuance order even when the s 33C(1) criteria have been met. See *Bright* v. *Femcare Ltd* (2002) 195 ALR 574, [128]; *Multiplex Funds Management Ltd* v. *P Dawson Nominees Pty Ltd* (2007) 164 FCR 275, [13]–[15], [179]–[192].

contended that the non-common issues would be decided adversely to the applicant and group members so that the resolution of the common issues would be a waste of time and resources.[51] Lindgren J observed:

> let it be assumed that in respect of the resolution of each woman's claim, two-thirds of the time to be spent will have to be devoted to issues unique to that claim and one-third to issues which are common to all claims. Is it still not preferable that the common issues be heard and determined once so as to be binding as between each claimant and the respondents rather than many times?[52]

Similarly Kiefel J (as she was then) stated:

> A consideration as to how many common questions could be seen to arise from the applicant's pleading would not seem to me to be particularly influential in [relation to s33 N], as I have earlier observed. More telling is what their resolution in the representative proceeding might mean for the other claims and how much evidence might be thereby made unnecessary.[53]

The conundrum of the submission put forward by the respondents – they would lose on the common issues but win on the non-common issues resulting in no payment of compensation – was to be dealt with through case management. Lindgren J suggested the use of test cases, subgroups or summary judgment.[54]

Part IVA places no positive duties on the filing party akin to the adequacy and typicality requirements under Rule 23(a)(3)–(4). However, it does seek to root out inadequate representation and the excessive misalignment of representative and class member claims through section 33T. Section 33T permits class members (but not respondents) to make an application to the court to replace a representative with a class member, if the class member who had made the application can show that the incumbent representative party cannot adequately represent the interests of the group. This represents a distinct difference from the US approach under Rule 23 (a)(4), as a class action respondent cannot argue that a named class representative is an inadequate representative. It is indeed arguable that restricting the right of the party possibly most incentivised to challenge inadequate representation, is a poor safeguard against inadequate representation.[55]

Sections 33E and 33J of the FCAA create an 'opt-out' procedure by which claimants are automatically included in the class without having to assent to inclusion and must inform the court if they do not intend to participate in the action. Section 33X(1)(a) further provides that class members must receive notice of their right to opt out, among other things such as the commencement of the class action.[56] Class members who fall within the defined class and do not opt out are bound by the outcome of any judgment per section 33ZB. In combination, these provisions mean that all potential claimants automatically become class members upon the commencement of the class action, that they remain class members unless they opt out of the class action, and that their claims are automatically resolved by the outcome of a class action

51 *Bright* v. *Femcare Ltd* (2002) 195 ALR 574, [19], [77]–[78].

52 Ibid., [77].

53 Ibid., [136].

54 Ibid., [20] and [79].

55 Michael Legg, 'Role of the Judge in the Settlement of Representative Proceedings: Lessons from the United States' Class Action Experience' (2004) 78 *Australian Law Journal* 58, 63–4. The NSW class action legislation added inadequacy of representation as a grounds for discontinuance pursuant to the equivalent of s 33N. See *Hassid* v. *Queensland Bulk Water Supply Authority t/as Seqwater (No 2)* [2017] NSWSC 1064.

56 Note that, per FCAA section 33Y(5), notice not need be delivered personally unless the court determines that it is reasonably practicable and not unduly expensive to do so.

resolved via judgment.[57] Typically, the same can be said for settlement, although complications can arise when a settlement agreement purports to go beyond the scope of claims falling within the scope of section 33C.[58] The right to opt out and to receive notice exists in all class actions, Australia having no equivalent to the 'mandatory class actions' under Rule 23(b)(1)–(2).

As is the case in the United States, Australian class action settlements require court approval. Section 33V states that a class action may not be settled or discontinued without the approval of the court, and that the court has the discretion to make such orders as are just with respect to the distribution of any money paid under a settlement. The case law on section 33V establishes that courts will approve settlement so long as the proposed settlement is fair and reasonable having regard to the claims made on behalf of the class members who will be bound by the settlement, and that the proposed settlement has been undertaken in the interests of class members (as opposed to the interests of the class representative and the respondent only).[59] This high degree of judicial scrutiny is warranted given the active role typically played by third-party funders in the settlement process. The presence of funders complicates the traditional 'friends of the deal' dilemma that arises in unfunded class action settlements by adding another interested party to the mix. It is within the realm of possibility that certain funders might attempt to collude with class counsel to secure the highest return on their investment possible, or at least, hold interests that conflict of those of unnamed class members.[60]

Part IVA also contains a general power at section 33ZF that was provided to allow the courts to address novel issues that may arise in the new class action procedure.[61] The provision provides: 'In any proceeding (including an appeal) conducted under this Part, the Court may, of its own motion or on application by a party or a group member, make any order the Court thinks appropriate or necessary to ensure that justice is done in the proceeding'.

To provide a complete picture of Australian class action procedure, it is necessary to outline the law and practice surrounding the costs of litigation and the payment of counsel's fees. Australia does not permit lawyers to charge on a contingent basis as the United States does.[62] Instead, all Australian jurisdictions operate within the confines of the traditional English method of 'cost-shifting', whereby the loser pays the winner's legal fees (unless the court orders otherwise) pursuant to what is known as an 'adverse costs order'.[63] Shifting the burden of legal costs from winner to loser is done to discourage the filing of cases without merit or that are merely speculative.[64] Accordingly, class representatives, as well as subgroup representatives, are liable for the legal costs borne by a successful respondent in addition to their own legal fees.[65] Class members on the other hand are liable for their own costs only if they elect to appear in the proceeding for the purpose of seeking judicial determination of an issue that would not have otherwise been raised in the class actions.[66] Class members who do not represent the class or

57 *Timbercorp Finance Pty Ltd (in liquidation)* v. *Collins* [2016] HCA 44.

58 Michael Legg and Samuel J Hickey, 'Finality and Fairness in Australian Class Action Settlements' (2019) 41 *Sydney Law Review* 184.

59 *City of Swan* v. *McGraw-Hill Companies Inc* [2016] FCA 343, [32]–[35]; Federal Court of Australia, Class Actions Practice Note (GPN-CA), 20 December 2019, [15.3].

60 Michael Legg, 'Class Action Settlements in Australia – The Need for Greater Scrutiny' (2014) 38(2) *Melbourne University Law Review* 590, 593.

61 Michael Legg and Ross McInnes, *Australian Annotated Class Actions Legislation* (LexisNexis, 2nd ed., 2018) 475.

62 *Bolitho* v. *Banksia Securities Ltd [No 4]* [2014] VSC 582, [50].

63 *Dubbo Refrigerating & Co* v. *Rutherford* (1898) 14 WN (NSW) 180; *Oshlack* v. *Richmond River Council* (1998) 193 CLR 72, [67].

64 VLRC 2018 Report, 116.

65 FCAA s. 33Q.

66 FCAA s. 33R.

a subgroup within the class, or do not agitate individual claims, are not obliged to pay for their own legal costs or their adversary's legal costs should the class action be unsuccessful.[67]

Fee shifting leaves class representatives at a significant disadvantage. Representatives assume the risk of an adverse cost order while class members bear no equivalent risk. It is not unusual for class representatives and class members to stand to benefit only a few hundred dollars from a favourable judgment, whereas legal costs in that same case may run into the tens of millions.[68] The risk of an adverse costs order cannot be borne by class counsel in Australia. Fortunately, and is often the case in funded class actions, a class representative's exposure can be managed by a funder agreeing to provide indemnification against adverse costs orders.[69] Alternatively, a funder can offset the risk of such an order by purchasing 'after-the-event' insurance.[70] After-the-event insurance is obtained once litigation is already afoot, and protects a funder against having to pay an adverse costs order.[71] There are alternative mechanisms for managing risk as well. Law firms can act on a conditional 'no win, no fee' basis, whereby class representatives have no obligation to pay legal fees if their case fails. The 'no win, no fee' model does not protect class representatives from having to pay the opponent's legal fees if an adverse costs order is made. However, after-the-event insurance may be available to minimise the class representatives exposure.[72] It is also standard practice for counsel acting on a no-win, no-fee basis to include an 'up-lift' fee in the legal costs agreement.[73] An up-lift fee is charged out of a favourable judgment or settlement award, and is sought as compensation for class counsel assuming the risk inherent in a speculative case. It is capped by statute at 25 per cent of counsel's fees.[74]

Australia's days of prohibiting lawyers from charging contingency fees in class actions may be coming to an end. The most recent ALRC and VLRC reports recommended lifting the prohibition, stating that lawyers should be able to act in class actions on a contingency basis so long as certain prescriptive conditions are satisfied.[75] In Victoria the legislature has passed legislation to allow a plaintiff to apply to the court for a 'group costs order'. The Court may order that the legal costs payable to the plaintiff's lawyers be a percentage of the amount recovered in the proceedings; and the plaintiff and group members share liability for those legal costs. The amendment also reflects the Australian cost-shifting approach by requiring that lawyer agree to be liable for the costs of the defendant if the case fails, and provide any security for those costs. The court can only make the order if it is satisfied that it is 'appropriate or necessary to ensure justice is done in the proceeding'.[76]

67 FCAA s. 43(1A).

68 VLRC 2018 Report, 117. See also *Camping Warehouse* v. *Downer EDI* [2016] VSC 784. In that case the average payout per class member was expected to be $633.29, whereas the legal fees were $2.85 million.

69 VLRC 2018 Report, 117.

70 Michael Legg, 'Ramifications of the Recognition of a Common Fund in Australian Class Actions: An Early Appraisal' (2017) 91 *Australian Law Journal* 655, 668.

71 *Earglow Pty Ltd* v. *Newcrest Mining Ltd* [2016] FCA 1433, [179]; *Kelly* v. *Willmott Forests Ltd (In liq) [No 5]* [2017] FCA 689, [38]; *Petersen Superannuation Fund Pty Ltd* v. *Bank of Queensland Ltd* [2017] FCA 699, [17].

72 *Wigmans* v. *AMP Ltd* [2019] NSWSC 603, [57].

73 VLRC 2018 Report, 118–19.

74 Ibid.

75 ALRC 2018 Report, 9–12, 185–217; VLRC 2018 Report, 63–8. See also Michael Legg, 'Contingency fees – antidote or poison' (2015) 29 *Australian Bar Review* 244 (recommending a common fund for class action lawyers).

76 Justice Legislation Miscellaneous Amendments Act 2020 (Vic) added a new s. 33ZDA to the Supreme Court Act 1986 (Vic) which took effect from 1 July 2020.

19.5 NOVEL ASPECTS OF AUSTRALIAN CLASS ACTIONS

19.5.1 *Litigation Funding*

Litigation funding has become synonymous with class action litigation in Australia. Of the 513 class actions funded prior to May 2017, 116 (22 per cent) were funded.[77] These statistics underlie a steadily growing class of lenders. As of 2018, there were some twenty-five funders active in Australia[78] Today, the market continues to populate.[79]

In most cases, funding arrangements follow the same structure. The funder will enter into an agreement with the class representative specifying that the funder agrees to pay counsel's fees on the representative's behalf. This agreement will cover additional costs arising over the course of the litigation such as disbursements, project management and claim investigation. The funder will enter into similar agreements with some or all individual class members, stipulating that they agree to give to the funder a set percentage of any favourable judgment award or settlement. The funder will also enter into a separate agreement with class counsel, specifying the exact method of payment. Funding arrangements thus consist of a tripartite contractual relationship involving funder, class counsel and class members, including class representatives.[80] Funding agreements almost invariably contain clauses providing the funder with some level of control over the class action, including in some cases the authority to instruct counsel on a day-to-day basis.[81] Other standard terms include an indemnity for the class representatives for adverse costs orders and an undertaking on behalf of the funder to make any necessary payments of security into court. Additionally, agreements will usually include a funding commission ranging between 25 per cent and 40 per cent, which is deducted from the final settlement or judgment award.[82] Although in competing class actions the rates have declined, as discussed in Section 19.6.2 below. It is unclear whether this decline will spread to all class actions.[83] The agreement may also involve an authorisation of the lawyer to consult the funder as to the terms of proposed settlement.[84] However, the lawyer owes their duties to their clients and group members not to the funder.[85] The involvement of funders in the settlement process can of course be contrasted with the policy of 'non-interference' employed in the United States.[86]

77 Vince Morabito, The First Twenty-Five Years of Class Actions in Australia (Fifth Report; An Empirical Study of Australia's Class Action Regimes; July 2017), p. 33.

78 The Hon Justice S. C. Derrington, 'Litigation Funding: Access and Ethics', Australian Academy of Law Lecture, Brisbane, 4 October 2018, 2.

79 For a sense of litigation funding's continued growth in Australia, see Emily Cadman, 'For the World's Super Rich, Litigation Funding Is the New Black', *Bloomberg Markets* (27 August 2018) available at: www.bloomberg.com/news/articles/2018-08-27/for-the-world-s-super-rich-litigation-funding-is-the-new-black

80 Simone Degeling and Michael Legg, 'Fiduciaries and Funders: Litigation Funders in Australian Class Actions' (2017) 36 *Civil Justice Quarterly* 244, 245–9; Jason Betts, David Taylor and Christine Tan, 'Litigation Funding for Class Actions', in Damian Grave and Helen Mould (eds), *25 Years of Class Actions in Australia* (Ross Parsons Centre, 2017), p. 211.

81 Jason Betts, David Taylor and Christine Tan, Litigation Funding for Class Actions, in Damian Grave and Helen Mould (eds), *25 Years of Class Actions in Australia* (2017), p. 211 citing *Campbells Cash & Carry Pty Ltd* v. *Fostif Pty Ltd* (2006) 229 CLR 386, [277]–[280] per Heyden and Callinan JJ.

82 Ibid., p. 223.

83 *Perera* v. *GetSwift Limited* [2018] FCA 732.

84 Simone Degeling and Michael Legg, 'Fiduciaries and Funders: Litigation Funders in Australian Class Actions' (2017) 36 *Civil Justice Quarterly* 244, 247.

85 Simone Degeling and Michael Legg, 'Fiduciary Obligations of Lawyers in Australian Class Actions: Conflicts between Duties' (2014) 37(3) *University of New South Wales Law Journal* 914.

86 John C. Coffee, Jr., 'Litigation Governance: Taking Accountability Seriously' (2010) 110 *Columbia Law Review* 288, 340–1.

The pivotal moment for this industry came in 2006, when the High Court of Australia stated in the landmark decision, *Campbells Cash & Carry Pty Ltd* v. *Fostif Pty Ltd*, that third-party funding agreements were neither an abuse of process nor contrary to public policy.[87] Although strictly obiter comments this endorsement of litigation funding provided the necessary recognition to legitimise litigation funding in Australian litigation.

The focus then turned to the regulation of litigation funding. The Australian Government has allowed litigation funding to mature in a relatively unregulated market so that it can continue to further access to justice.[88] The first significant instance of regulation occurred in 2009, when the Full Court of the Federal Court of Australia found that funding arrangements met the definition of a 'managed investment scheme' for the purposes of the Corporations Act 2001 (Cth), which in turn required funders to register funding arrangements with corporate regulators and for a 'responsible entity' to provide Product Disclosure Statements to prospective members.[89] This decision was overturned by regulations made pursuant to the Corporations Act.[90]

However, the ALRC's 2018 report suggested a spate of reforms that would drastically change the way in which funders operate. The most notable recommendations are as follows: funding agreements become enforceable only with court approval, courts retain a statutory power to reject, vary or amend the terms of such agreements, funding agreements be governed exclusively by Australian law, and funders be required to implement adequate practices and procedures to manage conflicts of interest and report annually on those procedures to the Australian Securities Investment Commission. Additionally, the report recommends that the Law Council of Australia develop an accreditation system for class action lawyers that provides ongoing education in relation to identifying and managing conflicts of interests, and that the pre-existing ethical regulations applicable to lawyers be amended to prohibit lawyers and law firms from having financial and other interests in funders acting on the same matter as the lawyer or law firm.[91] However, the ALRC, in contrast to its initial discussion paper and the earlier Productivity Commission Inquiry into Access to Justice,[92] did not recommend a licensing regime or a requirement for capital adequacy so as to meet costs orders if a class action was unsuccessful.

The Federal Government, without responding to the ALRC's 2018 report, reversed the earlier regulation so that litigation funding of class actions was once again to be treated as a managed investment scheme and further, the funder would be required to hold an Australian Financial Services Licence from 22 August 2020.[93] However, the regulations may be subject to modifications and exemptions issued by the regulator, the Australian Securities Investment Commission.[94]

Regardless of what regulation might follow, it is likely that litigation funding will remain big business in Australia, and that it will continue to underscore a significant portion of all class actions filed. The only challenge to this position would be if lawyers were prepared to take on the

87 *Campbells Cash & Carry Pty Ltd* v. *Fostif Pty Ltd* (2006) 229 CLR 386.

88 See The Hon Chris Bowen MP, Minister for Financial Services, Superannuation and Corporate Law, 'Government Acts to Ensure Access to Justice for Class Action Member' (speech delivered at IMF (Australia) Ltd Shareholder Class Action Conference, Quay Grand Suites, Sydney, 4 May 2010).

89 *Brookfield Multiplex Limited* v. *International Litigation Funding Partners Pte Ltd* [2009] FCAFC 147; 180 FCR 11.

90 Corporations Amendment Regulation 2012 (No 6) (Cth).

91 ALRC 2018 Report, 9–12.

92 Australian Law Reform Commission, Inquiry into Class Action Proceedings and Third-Party Litigation Funders, (Discussion Paper No 85, June 2018), proposals 3–1, 3–2; Productivity Commission, Access to Justice Arrangements – Inquiry Report No. 72 (September 2014) 632.

93 Corporations Amendment (Litigation Funding) Regulations 2020.

94 See Explanatory Statement to Corporations Amendment (Litigation Funding) Regulations 2020.

risk of financing class actions. The enactment of group litigation orders in the State of Victoria in 2020, referred to in Section 19.4 above, may be the start of such a development.

19.5.2 *Closed Classes*

The black-letter of Part IVA creates an 'opt-out' procedure, meaning that all claimants who fall within the scope of the class definition automatically become class members. Class members are accordingly bound by the resolution of the class action if they do not opt out, and only by opting out can class members preserve claims and defences independent of the class action to pursue them in separate proceedings. Australia adopted the opt out procedure to strengthen both the fairness and efficiency of Part IVA. The opt out procedure was seen as fair because claimants would be included regardless of whether they possessed the sophistication or capability needed to indicate their willingness to be included in proceedings. It was considered efficient because it reduced the scope for competing class actions by ensuring that all claimants would be included in the same class.[95]

The opt out model initially proved irksome for litigation funders. If claimants were automatically class members regardless of whether they had taken affirmative action to join the class or were even aware that their claim existed, then it would be impossible to fund a large class action without assuming the risk that 'free-riders', who had not entered into any funding agreement, benefitting from a favourable judgment or settlement.[96] Once a funder had entered into funding arrangements with enough claimants to justify supporting the class action, other class members would not be incentivised to enter into those same arrangements.

IMF Bentham was the first funder to attempt to overcome this problem by supporting a class action in which the class was narrowly defined so as to include only claimants who had retained a particular law firm. The Federal Court of Australia rejected this approach in 2005 in *Dorajay Pty Ltd* v. *Aristocrat Leisure Ltd*,[97] finding that it constituted an abuse of process and an undue subversion of the purposes of Part IVA.[98] However, the decision in *Dorajay* was not a sign of things to come.[99] Two years later the Full Court of the Federal Court of Australia in *Multiplex Funds Management Ltd* v. *P Dawson Nominees Pty Ltd* found that there was nothing within the wording of Part IVA to prevent counsel from defining a class as including only those claimants who had retained a particular law firm or entered into funding agreements with a particular funder.[100] This textualist reading can of course be contrasted with the US Court of Appeals for the Second Circuit's ruling in *Kern* v. *Siemens Corporation* that by adding the opt out procedure, Congress had specifically intended to prohibit opt in class actions.[101] Nevertheless, the decision in *Multiplex* changed the face of Australian class actions, allowing the filing of 'closed class' proceedings that defined the class in light of whether class members had a relationship with

95 Commonwealth, *Parliamentary Debates*, House of Representatives, 14 November 1991, at 3175 (M. Duffy Attorney-General).

96 Susanna Khouri, Wayne Attrill and Clive Bowman, 'Litigation funding and class actions – idealism, pragmatism and a new paradigm' in Damian Grave and Helen Mould (eds), 25 *Years of Class Actions in Australia* (Ross Parsons Centre, 2017), pp. 237–9.

97 (2005) 147 FCR 394, [125] (Stone J).

98 Ibid. See also *Cadence Asset Management Pty Ltd* v. *Concept Sports Ltd* [2006] FCA 711.

99 Before the Full Court embraced closed classes however, Stone J's judgment in *Dorajay* did receive support in *Rod Investments (Vic) Pty Ltd* v. *Clark* [2005] VSC 449.

100 *Multiplex Funds Management Ltd* v. *P Dawson Nominees Pty Ltd* (2007) 164 FCR 275, [49]. For a critique of the court's reasoning see Michael Legg, 'Funding a Class Action through Limiting the Group: What does Part IVA of the Federal Court of Australia Act 1976 (Cth) permit?' (2010) 33 *Australian Bar Review* 17.

101 393 F 3d 120, 124 (2nd Cir, 2004).

a particular law firm or funder. A closed class is generally understood as 'a class composed of a limited or identified number of persons rather than all those who suffered loss or damage as a result of the conduct of a defendant'.[102] Following the *Multiplex* decision, class actions could thus be brought as either an open class action, permitting all potential claimants to be included in the class, or as a closed class action, including only class members who had retained a particular funder or law firm.[103]

The closed class mechanism operates in conjunction with what are commonly known as 'class closure orders'. Class closure orders are made in anticipation of judgment or settlement and allow the court to close the class prior to the resolution of the class action so that only a limited and ascertainable number of claimants participate in the judgment or settlement.[104] This allows the parties to come to an understanding of the total quantum of class members claims. Class closure orders operate slightly differently depending on whether the action was commenced as a closed or open class action. In the former type of class action, a court will make an order stipulating that class members be given notice that they have the option to either register their interest in the outcome of proceedings with a particular law firm or litigation funder by a specific cut-off date, or to otherwise opt out of the class action and preserve their claims. Class members who register are permitted to enjoy the benefits of judgment or settlement. In addition, some courts made 'barring orders' which had the effect that class members who do not register, but do not opt out either, are bound by the outcome of the class action but unable to reap the benefits of any favourable judgment or settlement.[105] The making of barring orders prior to the approval of a settlement or following a judgment were found to be beyond power by the State of New South Wales Court of Appeal,[106] and has been followed by a Federal Court judge at first instance.[107] If, on the other hand, the proceeding was filed as a closed class action, the court may order that the class be 'reopened' prior to its impending resolution, and once this has occurred then class members are notified of their rights to either register or opt out in the same way as class members in an open class action.[108]

The narrowing of class definitions has sparked heated academic discussion. In support of closed classes, it can be said that they simplify the task of identifying class members and quantifying their claims. Perhaps most favourably, the closed class procedure eliminates the risk of free-riders from seeking an undeserved windfall at the expense of the funder and those class members who enter into funding arrangements.[109] It could also be argued that the procedure increases access to justice simply by facilitating the involvement of litigation funders in class actions by making conditions more favourable to them. However, this point is contentious, as it can equally be said that excluding access to the class for class members who do not retain a particular law firm or funder or who fail to register restricts access to

[102] *Matthews* v. *SPI Elec. (No. 13)* [2013] VSC 17 (Forrest J).

[103] For an overview of the considerations that might inform the decision to commence an open or a closed class action, Michael Legg, 'Ramifications of the Recognition of a Common Fund in Australian Class Actions: An Early Appraisal' (2017) 91 *Australian Law Journal* 655, 659–60.

[104] *Money Max Int Pty Ltd (Trustee)* v. *QBE Insurance Group Limited* [2016] FCAFC 148, [191]; *Muswellbrook Shire Council* v. *The Royal Bank of Scotland NV* [2016] FCA 819 [5–7] (Rares J); *Lam* v. *Rolls Royce PLC (No. 5)* [2016] NSWSC 1322, [15] (Beech-Jones J).

[105] *Matthews* v. *SPI Elec. (No. 13)* [2013] VSC 17, [23] (Forrest J).

[106] *Haselhurst v Toyota Motor Corp Australia Ltd t/as Toyota Australia* [2020] NSWCA 66.

[107] *The Owners - Strata Plan No 87231 v 3A Composites GmbH (No 3)* [2020] FCA 748, [198]-[214].

[108] *Money Max Int Pty Ltd (Trustee)* v. *QBE Insurance Group Limited* [2016] FCAFC 148, [188].

[109] Susanna Khouri, Wayne Attrill and Clive Bowman, 'Litigation funding and class actions – idealism, pragmatism and a new paradigm' in Damian Grave and Helen Mould (eds), 25 *Years of Class Actions in Australia* (Ross Parsons Centre, 2017), p. 245.

justice as well.[110] Indeed, the closed class technique essentially converts Australia's opt out model to an opt in model, which facially undermines the 'access to justice' underpinnings of Part IVA by limiting the number of claimants who might participate in a class actions.[111] There are, of course, other strong responses against the use of closed class proceedings. Perhaps chief among them is the fact that when a closed class action is filed, another law firm may commence a separate class action with the remaining class members who are not part of the closed class.[112] Empirical evidence shows that the *Multiplex* decision increased the number of competing class actions in Australia.[113] Competing class actions are undesirable. They undercut the economies of scale that are one of the key benefits of aggregate litigation, and also create an oppressive environment for respondents fighting litigation on multiple fronts or attempting to settle matters arising from the same transaction with two or more law firms, each with their own funding arrangements and related extrinsic influences.[114]

19.5.3 *Common Fund for Litigation Funding*

The debate surrounding closed classes cooled considerably following the 2016 decision of the Full Court in *Money Max Int Pty Ltd (Trustee)* v. *QBE Insurance Group Limited*.[115] The Court confirmed that it would be permissible for the parties to a class action to seek an order stipulating that a funder be paid from a fund created from the proceeds of a judgment award or settlement. Effectively, this meant that that instead of simply enforcing the funding agreements that had actually been executed between class members and the funder, a court could allow a funder to receive a portion of each class member's recovery, regardless of whether each class member had entered into a funding agreement. Indeed, a court may even elect to impose whatever funding commission had been agreed to in the funding agreement upon the entirety of the class. The decision provided a means by which to eliminate the free-rider problem while diminishing the need to commence proceedings on a closed class basis. The Court itself also intended that the common fund order reduce the number of closed class actions.[116]

Importantly, the Court in *Money Max* stated that in making a common fund order it would retain the discretion to set the commission that each class member would pay out of their received award. This aspect of the Court's decision cannot be overlooked, as it means that funders may still be incentivised to contract with class members individually and support proceedings on a closed class basis in order to avoid the court intervening in the terms of the funding agreement.[117] The decision in *Money Max* is therefore not in any way a death knell for the closed class. However, it is still possible that they might be eliminated from practice through legislative intervention. The most recent ALRC report recommended that closed classes not be permitted as they do not cohere with the broader utilitarian objectives of Part IVA.[118] The closed class mechanism was said to

110 *Multiplex Funds Management Ltd* v. *P Dawson Nominees Pty Ltd* (2007) 164 FCR 275, [137].

111 Michael Legg, 'Reconciling Litigation Funding and the Opt Out Group Definition in Federal Court of Australia Class Actions – The Need for a Legislative Common Fund Approach' (2011) 30 *Civil Justice Quarterly* 52.

112 Ibid.

113 Vicki Waye and Vince Morabito, 'When Pragmatism Leads to Unintended Consequences: A Critique of Australia's Unique Closed Class Regime' (2018) 19 *Theoretical Inquiries in Law* 303, 309. Since Multiplex, the number of competing class actions has increased from one every fourteen months to one every eight months.

114 Michael Legg, 'Reconciling Litigation Funding and the Opt Out Group Definition in Federal Court of Australia Class Actions – The Need for a Legislative Common Fund Approach' (2011) 30 *Civil Justice Quarterly* 52.

115 [2016] FCAFC 148.

116 Ibid., [14], [205].

117 Ibid., [81]–[82].

118 ALRC 2018 Report, 92.

disadvantage vulnerable class members unable to take active steps to register. Moreover, the fact that unregistered class members would be bound by settlement of the class action, but unable to receive settlement proceeds, weighed against the desirability of closed classes.[119]

In December 2019 the High Court of Australia entered the fray in relation to common fund orders with judgment in two proceedings that were heard concurrently: *BMW Australia Ltd* v. *Brewster; Westpac Banking Corporation* v. *Lenthall*.[120] The High Court by a 5:2 majority (Kiefel CJ, Bell, Keane, Nettle, Gordon JJ; Gageler and Edelman JJ dissenting) held that the legislative provision that had been relied on, section 33ZF of the FCAA, did not empower the Federal Court to make a common fund order at the beginning of proceedings. The majority emphasised that the power conferred by section 33ZF is concerned with the question of *how* an action should proceed in order to achieve a just result, and not with the radically different question of whether an action *can* proceed at all. Further, the majority held that the focus of section 33ZF is upon ensuring that justice is done in the proceeding as between the parties to it. As such, the making of an order which defines the relationship between a party to the proceeding (the class member) and a third party (the litigation funder) at the beginning of the proceeding could not be described as necessary or appropriate to ensure that justice is done in the proceeding. Paramount to the majority's position was their view that an application for a common fund order is centrally concerned with determining whether the proceeding is viable at all as a vehicle for the doing of justice between the parties to the proceeding. The question of whether a sufficient incentive was presented to a third-party funder to ensure that proceedings would be pursued is outside the concern to which the text of section 33ZF is addressed.

19.5.4 *No Certification Requirement*

Section 33C(1) embodies Australia's deliberate rejection of a US style certification model.[121] Australia took this path following the ALRC's advice that a mandatory hearing as a precondition for commencement would lead to increased litigation costs as well as expensive and lengthy appeals.[122] The ALRC counselled that there would be 'no need to go to the expense of a special hearing to determine that the requirements have been complied with as long as the respondent has a right to challenge the validity of the procedure at any time'[123] (as noted above in Section 19.4, this right has been enshrined under sections 33L, 33 M and 33 N of the FCAA). Moreover, undeserving filings would be deterred by placing the risk of adverse costs orders on representatives,[124] and class members interests would be better protected by adequate and informative opt-out notices than a certification hearing.[125]

Despite well-laid plans, the Australian Government's decision not to adopt a certification model has created debate. Both sitting Judges and academics have decried the omission of a certification device. The literature has produced two key arguments opposing Australia's current approach.[126] The first being that the lack of certification device has led to excessive

119 Ibid., 95.
120 [2019] HCA 45.
121 ALRC 1988 Report, [146].
122 Ibid., [147].
123 Ibid., [146].
124 Ibid., [148].
125 Ibid., [147].
126 Justice Michael Lee, 'Certification of class actions: A "solution" in search of a problem?' (Speech delivered at the Commercial Law Association Seminar 'Class Actions – Different Perspectives', 20 October 2017).

litigation in the form of interlocutory skirmishes,[127] and the second is that the low threshold permits undeserving cases to be commenced as class actions.[128] Both the perceived prevalence of interlocutory litigation as well as meritless class actions are said to be associated with wasted costs and undue delays. In 2017 Justice Michael Lee of the Federal Court of Australia raised his own counterarguments to these claims. In response to the first claim, his Honour stated that, as the jurisprudence on Part IVA developed, disputation lessened.[129] Any surge of interlocutory litigation that may have once existed can be understood as a necessary teething process of a kind that should be expected to accompany the creation of a new and untested legislative regime. In this respect, many of the arguments alleging unnecessary litigation may simply be dated. In response to the second argument, his Honour said that the underuse of section 33 N indicates that class actions are rarely filed improperly. Justice Lee further added that the 'declassing' approach under section 33 N had three distinctive advantages when it came to dealing with unwarranted filings under Part IVA. First, it is invoked only where there is a perceived problem, avoiding costs being spent in cases where there is no issue. Second, a declassing order can be sought at any stage during the proceeding, not just at commencement, and last, it can also be used as a case management tool, even after trial when the court is dealing with the individual claims of group members, after the common issues have been resolved.[130]

There are, of course, further arguments that cannot be comprehensively considered here. In favour of certification, it can be said that it permits procedural irregularities to be identified and dealt with early on in the litigious process, thus minimising the likelihood of interlocutory challenges and pleading amendments.[131] Certification hearings also provide a useful forum to ventilate concerns surrounding topics such as litigation funding, competing class actions and adequacy of representation.[132]

The debate was considered by the recent ALRC and VLRC reports. The VLRC considered whether Victoria should adopt a certification regime, and came out in the negative.[133] The ALRC similarly rejected the adoption of a certification procedure.[134] However, it did raise the possibility of introducing a 'preliminary hearing process; in some cases to provide a forum to dispose of certain preliminary issues. Namely, competing class actions, litigation funding agreements and potentially contingency fee agreements.[135] The ALRC did maintain, however, that such a hearing should not be viewed as a quasi-certification hearing. If the VLRC and ALRC reports can be taken to reflect the legislative agenda, it can then be said that neither the legislature nor the judiciary appears amenable to the abandonment of Australia's current approach to commencement.

127 *P Dawson Nominees Pty Ltd* v. *Multiplex Ltd* (2007) 242 ALR 111, 116 [18], (Finkelstein J stated that the absence of a certification process had led to offshoot litigation and appeals as well as undue expense and delay); Rachael Mulheron, 'Justice Enhanced: Framing an Opt-Out Class Action for England' (2007) 70 *Modern Law Review* 550.

128 Vince Morabito and Jane Caruana, 'Can Class Action Regimes Operate Satisfactorily without a Certification Device? Empirical Insights from the Federal Court of Australia' (2013) 61 *American Journal of Comparative Law* 579.

129 *Dillon* v. *RBS Group (Australia) Pty Ltd* [2017] FCA 896.

130 Justice Michael Lee, 'Certification of class actions: A "solution" in search of a problem?' (Speech delivered at the Commercial Law Association Seminar 'Class Actions – Different Perspectives', 20 October 2017).

131 VLRC 2018 Report, p. 76.

132 Ibid. See also Michael Legg, 'Competing Class Actions: A Suggested Solution through Certification' (2018) 7(1) *Journal of Civil Litigation and Practice* 38.

133 Ibid., 75–9.

134 ALRC 2018 Report, 102.

135 Ibid, 114–22.

19.6 FUTURE CHALLENGES

19.6.1 *Minimising Lawyer and Funder Fees*

Class actions promote access to justice because they allow for the sharing of costs, economies of scale and can overcome the collective action problem. The ability to aggregate claims and obtain economies of scale is also important because it attracts lawyers and litigation funders who are prepared to provide their labour, knowledge and/or capital in return for a profit. While Australia has class action and funding infrastructure in place to achieve access to justice, the question remains as to what sort of access is being achieved. An important criterion for measuring the success of compensation is that all of those 'who are entitled to compensation . . . actually receive compensation and in the amount to which they are entitled'.[136] Put differently, the effectiveness of a class action regime will be undermined if people have their compensation unnecessarily reduced by transaction costs such as legal fees and funding fees. The Courts have responded with oversight of both legal costs and litigation funding fees.

19.6.1.1 Legal Fees

The Australian courts have inherent power to regulate costs agreements between a solicitor and a client.[137] In the class action context, the power in section 33ZF has been interpreted as allowing for the supervision of costs agreements with lawyers.[138] The reason for court supervision of costs arises because the solicitor seeks costs for themselves for which there is no contradictor.[139]

To assist the Court in determining whether the costs payable to lawyers should be approved, it became common for practitioners to provide an affidavit from an independent costs expert who is able to assess the reasonableness of the costs and disbursements incurred.[140] However, in *Lifeplan Australia Friendly Society Limited* v. *S & P Global Inc*, Lee J noted that this practice was entirely unhelpful.[141] His Honour then suggested that the time may have come for the Court to establish a regular practice of appointing referees to provide a report to the Court on the reasonableness of a solicitor's costs.[142]

Justice Lee did not consider the issue further, although questions concerning the utility of having an expert costs consultant produce evidence on the costs of the lawyer who appointed them have been previously raised, and the bulk of case law and academic literature on this point supports his Honour's view. For instance, it has been argued that the downside is not that a review of legal fees is conducted by a costs expert, but that the costs expert is retained by the lawyers seeking the fee award. The expert may become dependent on the lawyers for repeat work, which is unlikely to continue if legal fees are substantially reduced.[143] Adversarial bias in relation to experts, including selection bias

136 Peter Cane, *Atiyah's Accidents, Compensation and the Law* (Cambridge University Press, 8th ed., 2013) 409.

137 *Woolf* v. *Snipe* (1933) 48 CLR 677, 678.

138 *Johnson Tiles Pty Ltd* v. *Esso Australia Ltd* (1999) 94 FCR 167, [35]–[37].

139 *Modtech Engineering Pty Ltd* v. *GPT Management Holdings Ltd* [2013] FCA 626, [27] drawing on the principles for a taxation of costs set out in *Redfern* v. *Mineral Engineers Pty Ltd* [1987] VR 518, 523.

140 *Courtney* v. *Medtel Pty Ltd (No 5)* (2004) 212 ALR 311, [59].

141 [2018] FCA 379, [40].

142 Ibid., [41]. See Federal Court of Australia, Class Actions Practice Note (GPN-CA), 20 December 2019, [16.2]–[16.3].

143 Michael Legg, 'Class Action Settlements in Australia – The Need for Greater Scrutiny' (2014) 38(2) *Melbourne University Law Review* 590, 601–2.

whereby an expert is chosen because their views will support the party's case, has been of long-standing concern amongst the courts.[144]

The process for assessing legal fees could be improved without any increase in cost if the Court appointed the expert and the expert owed their allegiance solely to the Court.[145] The Supreme Court of Victoria has moved towards this model in relation to settlement distributions by appointing special referees to review costs.[146] At the first case management conference after the approval of the settlement in *Matthews* v. *AusNet Electricity Services Pty Ltd (No 40)*,[147] Forrest J determined that 'an external, high-level costs assessment' was appropriate, and appointed 'an independent costs consultant to conduct a high-level review of the ongoing costs of administration'.[148] The Court drew on the civil procedure rules for special referees and required the costs consultant to address specific questions and to report to the Court.[149] Procedurally this meant that the Court could then adopt or reject the report, but if adopted, the report became the opinion of the Court and part of its judgment on the questions posed.[150]

While an independent, court-appointed costs expert is an improvement, the basis for evaluating the costs is problematic. The traditional test is that the fees are fair and reasonable. Provided the work is needed and carried out by a person at the appropriate level of seniority using rates in the retainer it will not be capable of being challenged. This may be acceptable for non-class action litigation where the client enters a retainer, receives the mandated disclosures and can give instructions, but it is problematic in a class action where there is a need to protect group members.

A review for fairness and reasonableness will not reduce legal fees. As a result proportionality was invoked. However, proportionality has been interpreted by the Courts in a manner that has rendered it ineffective. In *Foley* v. *Gay* Beach J observed:

> I do accept, however, that what is claimed for legal costs should not be disproportionate to the nature of the context, the litigation involved and the expected benefit. The Court should not approve an amount that is disproportionate. But such an assessment cannot be made on the simplistic basis that the costs claimed are high in absolute dollar terms or high as a percentage of the total recovery. In the latter case, spending $0.50 to recover an expected $1.00 may be proportionate if it is necessary to spend the $0.50. In the former case, the absolute dollar amount as a free-standing figure is an irrelevant metric. The question is to compare it with the benefit sought to be gained from the litigation. Moreover, one should be careful not to use hindsight bias. The question is the benefit reasonably expected to be achieved, not the benefit actually achieved. Proportionality looks to the expected realistic return at the time the work being charged for was performed, not the known return at a time remote from when the work was performed; at the later time, circumstances may have changed to alter the calculus, but that

144 See e.g., *Dasreef Pty Ltd* v. *Hawchar* (2011) 243 CLR 58, [57]; NSW Law Reform Commission, *Expert Witnesses – Report 109* (June 2005) [5.5]–[5.13].
145 Michael Legg, 'Class Action Settlements in Australia – The Need for Greater Scrutiny' (2014) 38(2) *Melbourne University Law Review* 590, 608–10.
146 *Rowe* v. *Ausnet Electricity Services Pty Ltd (Ruling No 9)* [2016] VSC 731; *Downie* v. *Spiral Foods Pty Ltd (Ruling No 3)* [2017] VSC 7, [4]. See also Michael Legg, 'Kilmore-East Kinglake Bushfire Class Action Settlement Distribution Scheme: Fairness, Cost and Delay Post-Settlement' (2018) 44(3) *Monash University Law Review* 658.
147 [2015] VSC 131.
148 Ibid., [29]. Osborne J may also have foreseen the need for a determination of whether costs were fair and reasonable: see *Matthews* v. *AusNet Electricity Services Pty Ltd* [2014] VSC 663, [406].
149 Supreme Court (General Civil Procedure) Rules 2015, r. 50.04; *Matthews* v. *AusNet Electricity Services Pty Ltd*, Orders, 5 November 2015; *Matthews* v. *Ausnet (Ruling No. 41)* [2016] VSC 171, [26].
150 See *Rowe* v. *AusNet Electricity Services Pty Ltd (Ruling No. 9)* [2016] VSC 731, [5].

would not deny that the work performed and its cost was proportionate at the time it was performed.[151]

Beach J further explained his approach by reference to the fact that the lawyers are paid on an hourly basis, not through a contingency fee, and are not 'co-venturers' with the applicant. As a result 'the actual outcome is a risk borne by the applicant and group members (and the litigation funder), but not the independent lawyer who is not sharing in the returns of the enterprise'.[152]

This approach creates a number of problems for the effective use of proportionality as a means to monitor costs. Proportionality turns on a clear understanding of the denominator in the equation, that is, what the costs are being compared to. The above approach disparages a comparison with the actual outcome achieved. Rather the correct denominator is said to be to 'the expected realistic return at the time the work being charged for was performed'. However, the actual outcome is clearly identifiable and known. It is the recovery that the proceedings have achieved for the group members. It is the access to justice in quantifiable terms that the lawyers have facilitated. In contrast, the expected return is much more difficult to determine. The expected return from the proceedings is rarely disclosed in a settlement approval hearing, despite recovery compared to loss being a key indicator of the success of a class action seeking compensation.

While the power to review and award legal costs is clear, the procedure and standards are still developing. The Victorian Bill introducing the 'group costs order' for lawyers will undoubtedly also impact the approach to legal fees.[153]

19.6.1.2 Litigation Funding

A number of Federal Court judgments have found that the court has the power to supervise litigation funding charges in class actions. This has arisen in two main ways. The first, as discussed in Section 19.5.3 above, was through the recognition of the common fund approach to funder's fees whereby the funder could be paid a fee from all group members without the need for a funding agreement, but the court was able to review and revise the fee. The second was through the court reviewing the funding fee as part of its statutory obligation pursuant to section 33V to determine if a class action settlement should be approved.

In relation to the first avenue for review the Full Court in *Money Max* saw the scrutiny of the Funder's fee and the likely reduction in that fee from what was proposed under the funding agreement as supporting the making of the common fund orders.[154] The Full Court indicated that it was 'highly likely' that the funding commission of 32.5 per cent or 35 per cent contained in the funding agreement applicable to the QBE shareholder class action would be reduced.[155] This did indeed transpire with the Court approving a payment of 23.208 per cent of the settlement sum of $132.5 million (being $30.75 million) to the funder.[156]

151 *Foley* v. *Gay* [2016] FCA 273 at [24]. See also *Williams* v. *AusNet Electricity Services Pty Ltd* [2017] VSC 474, [109]–[111].
152 *Blairgowrie Trading Ltd* v. *Allco Finance Group Ltd (Receivers & Managers Appointed) (In Liq) (No 3)* [2017] FCA 330, [183].
153 Justice Legislation Miscellaneous Amendments Bill 2019 (Vic).
154 *Money Max Int Pty Ltd* v. *QBE Insurance Group Ltd* [2016] FCAFC 148, [167].
155 Ibid., [85].
156 *Money Max Int Pty Limited (Trustee)* v. *QBE Insurance Group Limited* [2018] FCA 1030.

The first avenue was not thought to create problems in terms of court power as the litigation funder gave an undertaking to be bound by the court's determination of the funding rate as part of receiving the benefit of the common fund order from group members it had not contracted with. However, as explained above in Section 19.5.3, the High Court decision in *BMW Australia Ltd* v. *Brewster; Westpac Banking Corporation* v. *Lenthall* held that the courts lacked power to make a common fund order relying on section 33ZF.

Turning to the second avenue, court power has very much been a live issue. A number of Federal Court judgments have addressed the issue of whether litigation finding fees can be altered by the court, with reliance being placed on FCAA section 33V(2) (if the Court makes an order approving a settlement 'it may make such orders as are just with respect to the distribution of any money paid under a settlement') and section 33ZF ('the Court may, of its own motion or on application by a party or a group member, make any order the Court thinks appropriate or necessary to ensure that justice is done in the proceeding').[157] However, in *Liverpool City Council* v. *McGraw-Hill Financial, Inc (now known as S&P Global Inc)*, Lee J accepted that in an appropriate case the Court may refuse to approve a settlement because a funding commission is excessive or disproportionate.[158] However, after reviewing the heads of power, his Honour doubted that power existed for the Court to interfere and vary funding agreements in the context of a settlement by altering the contractual promises of group members to pay commission.[159]

As discussed in Section 19.5.1I above, the ALRC's 2019 report made a number of recommendations in relation to the regulation of litigation funding. The ALRC was cognisant of the divergence in judicial opinion as to whether the court could unilaterally alter terms of a funding agreement, mainly the fee to be charged. The ALRC addressed this issue through two recommendations: first, that third-party litigation funding agreements with respect to representative proceedings only be enforceable with the approval of the Court; and second, that the Court be given an express statutory power to reject, vary, or amend the terms of such third-party litigation funding agreements.[160] If Parliament adopts these recommendations then the quantum of litigation funding fees will clearly be subject to judicial oversight. However, if Parliament does not legislate then the courts will need to interpret the scope of the key provisions, sections 33V and 33ZF, to determine whether the courts may rewrite contractual bargains to achieve justice.

Assuming that the courts have or receive power to set or vary a litigation funding fee, there remains an issue as to how such a fee should be set. Indeed the High Court in *BMW Australia Ltd* v. *Brewster; Westpac Banking Corporation* v. *Lenthall* observed that there was 'an absence of criteria to guide the exercise of discretion by the court'.[161] However, the Full Court in *Money Max* provided guidance in the context of a common fund order that could be refashioned for use in setting or revising a litigation funder's fee:

> the courts will approve funding commission rates that avoid excessive or disproportionate charges to class members but which recognise the important role of litigation funding in

[157] See *Earglow Pty Ltd* v. *Newcrest Mining Limited* [2016] FCA 1433; *Blairgowrie Trading Ltd* v. *Allco Finance Group Ltd (Receivers & Managers Appointed) (In Liq) (No 3)* [2017] FCA 330, [101]; *Mitic* v. *OZ Minerals Limited (No 2)* [2017] FCA 409, [26]–[32].

[158] *Liverpool City Council* v. *McGraw-Hill Financial, Inc (now known as S&P Global Inc)* [2018] FCA 1289, [22].

[159] Ibid., [47].

[160] ALRC 2018 Report, Recommendation 14.

[161] *BMW Australia Ltd* v. *Brewster; Westpac Banking Corporation* v. *Lenthall* [2019] HCA 45, [59].

providing access to justice, are commercially realistic and properly reflect the costs and risks taken by the funder, and which avoid hindsight bias.[162]

The Full Court set out the following factors as relevant to the determination of the funder's fee:[163]

(a) the funding commission rate agreed by sophisticated class members and the number of such class members who agreed. That can be said to show acceptance of a particular rate by astute class members;
(b) the information provided to class members as to the funding commission. That may be important to understand the extent to which class members were informed when agreeing to the funding commission rate;
(c) a comparison of the funding commission with funding commissions in other Part IVA proceedings and/or what is available or common in the market. It will be relevant to know the broad parameters of the funding commission rates available in the market;
(d) the litigation risks of providing funding in the proceeding. This is a critical factor and the assessment must avoid the risk of hindsight bias and recognise that the funder took on those risks at the commencement of the proceeding;
(e) the quantum of adverse costs exposure that the funder assumed. This is another important factor and the assessment must recognise that the funder assumed that risk at the commencement of the proceeding;
(f) the legal costs expended and to be expended, and the security for costs provided, by the funder;
(g) the amount of any settlement or judgment. This could be of particular significance when a very large or very small settlement or judgment is obtained. The aggregate commission received will be a product of the commission rate and the amount of settlement or judgment. It will be important to ensure that the aggregate commission received is proportionate to the amount sought and recovered in the proceeding and the risks assumed by the funder;
(h) any substantial objections made by class members in relation to any litigation funding charges. This may reveal concerns not otherwise apparent to the Court; and
(i) class members' likely recovery 'in hand' under any pre-existing funding arrangements.

19.6.2 *Competing Class Actions*

Multiple or concurrent group proceedings are undesirable as they increase costs. Put simply, class actions are designed to allow for the sharing of costs and economies of scale. Allowing more than one class action to be brought means that efficiencies are lost and costs are duplicated. Competing class action may also perform an injustice through confusing group members and subjecting defendants to multiple proceedings.[164] The extent of the problem is illustrated by the finding that Australia has had 513 class actions commenced in relation to a total of 335 legal disputes.[165]

162 *Money Max Int Pty Ltd* v. *QBE Insurance Group Ltd* [2016] FCAFC 148, [82].
163 Ibid., [80].
164 *Kirby* v. *Centro Properties Ltd* [2008] FCA 1505, [12]; *Money Max Int Pty Ltd* v. *QBE Insurance Group Ltd* [2016] FCAFC 148, [196].
165 Vince Morabito, An Empirical Study of Australia's Class Action Regimes – Fifth Report (July 2017) 25, 29.

Competing class actions arise because, as identified in *McKay Super Solutions Pty Ltd (Trustee)* v. *Bellamy's Australia Ltd*, '[u]nder Part IVA there is no certification process; representative proceedings can be issued as of right and continue, provided that the conditions in ss 33C and 33H are satisfied and subject to there later being no s 33 N order'.[166]

19.6.2.1 Getswift Limited

To address competing class actions a number of approaches, drawing on traditional civil procedures and the class action regime, have been employed. The Full Court of the Federal Court in the *Getswift* shareholder class action appeal identified five 'realistic options . . . to deal with the potential overlap between competing class proceedings'.[167] First, consolidating competing proceedings into a single class action. Although there were reservations expressed because it would be necessary to resolve not just legal representation but also funding. Second, staying all class actions but one. Third, a joint trial of all proceedings, which the Full Court called the 'wait and see' approach as it effectively involves making no choice. Fourth, altering the group definitions so that there was one open class and all other proceedings use a closed class. As explained above an open class includes all persons who meet the group definition and they do not have to come forward and sign up with a lawyer and/or funder. A closed class is limited to those group members who have signed up with the lawyer/funder running that particular class action. Fifth, is a declassing order under section 33 N which has the effect that one or more class actions cannot continue as a class action. Although the Full Court went on to doubt that a declassing order could be made to address competing class actions.[168]

In the *Getswift* class action the judge at first instance dealt with three competing class classes by determining to stay the Perera and McTaggart Proceedings and allow the Webb Proceeding to go forward. The parties raised a number of arguments to assert why their class action ought to be the one that continued, including the experience of the practitioners and the resources available to them, the state of preparation of each class action, the resources of the funder and their proposals for security for costs, the merits of the cases of the individual applicants, the number of funded group members that had signed funding agreements or retainers, measures for controlling legal costs and expert costs. However, the main factor that determined who would bring the proceeding was the funding model. Justice Lee reasoned that Mr Webb had the most desirable funding model.[169] The Webb funding model was found to be preferable as it had the advantage of producing a direct correlation between the amount ventured and the likely return. The Webb proposal had other novel elements. First, a referee would be appointed to monitor costs on an ongoing basis rather than just review at the end of the litigation, and secondly, the funder was prepared to accept the appointment of a joint expert or a court-appointed expert in relation to loss causation and quantification of loss.[170]

On appeal, the Full Court found that there had been no error by the judge at first instance.[171] The Full went on to observe that 'there is no one right answer to the case management questions

[166] *McKay Super Solutions Pty Ltd (Trustee)* v. *Bellamy's Australia Ltd* [2017] FCA 947, [54].
[167] *Perera* v. *GetSwift Limited* [2018] FCAFC 202, [44].
[168] Ibid.
[169] The funder was to be paid the lesser of: (1) a multiple of the expenses that Therium had paid in the proceeding (being 2.2 times if the parties enter into a settlement agreement on or before 12 April 2019, or 2.8 times if there is a successful resolution after 12 April 2019); or (2) 20 per cent of the net litigation proceeds (e.g., the settlement sum less approved professional fees and disbursements).
[170] *Perera* v. *GetSwift Limited* [2018] FCA 732.
[171] *Perera* v. *GetSwift Limited* [2018] FCAFC 202, [273].

that arise when dealing with competing class actions. There cannot be a 'one size fits all' and different judges will take a different view of some of the incommensurable and conflicting considerations that may arise'.[172] Nonetheless, the Full Court provided some guidelines for courts when dealing with competing class actions, including that where other matters are essentially equal, lower legal costs and funding charges in one class action compared to the others is a 'decisive' factor. Simultaneously, courts need to ensure that lower costs and funding charges are not given undue weight to prevent a 'rush to the bottom' where costs are cut to win the representation, but then a case cannot be properly prepared and prosecuted.[173] Further, courts should take care not to incentivise proceedings being filed in haste as otherwise this will create 'the consequent risks of insufficient due diligence and the commencement of unmeritorious, or at least weak, cases'.[174] The Full Court raised for consideration, particularly in relation to securities class actions, whether it should adopt a process whereby there is an automatic standstill for ninety days after the first proceeding is filed. This would be to allow other solicitors and funders time to properly investigate the claims in the proceeding and not encourage people to institute proceedings in haste.

19.6.2.2 AMP Limited

Five sets of competing open shareholder class actions were commenced against AMP Limited arising from disclosures made before the Financial Services Royal Commission. The first, the *Wigmans* proceeding, was commenced in the Supreme Court of New South Wales. The remaining four were commenced in the Federal Court and transferred to the Supreme Court of NSW by decision of the Full Federal Court.[175] The five proceedings substantially overlapped in the facts alleged, the causes of action pleaded and their group membership. Two of the sets of proceedings were consolidated ('*Komlotex/Fernbrook* proceedings') so that five became four. Otherwise, all parties sought to stay all of the other class actions, except their own.

The judge at first instance drawing on the statements in *Getswift* applied a multifactorial analysis to determine which of the proceedings should progress. Her Honour identified the following relevant factors to be taken into account in the present case:

- the competing funding proposals, costs estimates and net hypothetical return to group members;
- the proposals for security for costs;
- the nature and scope of the causes of action advanced;
- the size of the respective classes;
- the extent of any bookbuild;
- the experience of the legal practitioners and availability of legal resources;
- the state of progress of the proceedings; and
- the conduct of the representative plaintiffs to date.

Her Honour ultimately chose to stay all proceedings except the *Komlotex/Fernbrook* proceedings and placed most weight on the funding proposal that minimised the cost to group members. *Komlotex/Fernbrook* utilised a 'no win, no fee' model that involved group members only being

[172] Ibid., [274].
[173] Ibid., [276].
[174] Ibid., [279].
[175] *Wileypark Pty Ltd* v. *AMP Ltd* [2018] FCAFC 143.

required to pay legal fees upon a successful outcome, and with no litigation funder, so that there was no funding commission.[176]

A five-judge Court of Appeal considered three proposed grounds of appeal brought by Wigmans. As the appeal was in relation to an interlocutory order, leave to appeal was required. Leave was not granted for grounds two (conducting a comparison of returns to group members under the funding proposals was not permitted or, if allowed, was not based on a rational foundation) or three (if a multifactorial approach was allowed, the judge erred in how it was conducted).[177] Ground one addressed what principles are to be applied where one defendant is the subject of multiple 'open' class actions. The test proposed by Wigmans was that if the first class action was regularly commenced, then for it be stayed, it must be shown to be 'clearly inappropriate'. Moreover, subsequently filed class actions are necessarily duplicative and as a result vexatious and oppressive, and ultimately an abuse of process.[178]

President Bell wrote the lead judgment. While the proposed approach did not create a rigid 'first filed' test, it would, in practice, cast an onus that would be very difficult to discharge for later plaintiffs; it was not appropriate. His Honour found that although the order of filing of proceedings is a relevant consideration in any application to stay proceedings, the common law has never favoured a 'first filed' rule as a means of resolving which of the competing proceedings should proceed. Moreover, the case law relied on by Wigmans demonstrated that the resources of the plaintiffs in group proceedings and the availability of funding to such parties have been treated as relevant considerations.[179]

President Bell then turned to section 58 of the Civil Procedure Act 2005 (NSW) which mandates how judges are to determine, inter alia, stay applications, including by mandatory reference to the overriding purpose 'to facilitate the just, quick and cheap resolution of the real issues in the proceedings'. Section 58 provides a broad power and discretion to grant a stay of proceedings. The primary judge exercised the discretion vested in her by the Civil Procedure Act by reference to a range of relevant considerations and in a manner that was open to her and undertaken without error.[180]

His Honour also observed that there is no 'one size fits all' response to competing class actions and approaches, other than a stay may be used. However, it is the strong policy of the law to avoid a multiplicity of proceedings.[181]

Justices of Appeal Meagher and Payne added that in determining how to address competing class actions, 'the persons whose interests must be given primary consideration are the represented group members and the defendants', not the funders and law firms that are competing in the class actions marketplace.[182]

19.6.2.3 ALRC Recommendations

The court's ability to choose multiple approaches to dealing with competing class actions creates uncertainty for court users. Neither applicants, respondents, lawyers or funders can predict with any certainty how a class action will proceed. There is also uncertainty as to the factors that the

176 *Wigmans* v. *AMP Ltd* [2019] NSWSC 603, [350]–[354].
177 *Wigmans* v. *AMP Ltd* [2019] NSWCA 243, [37], [40].
178 Ibid., [44], [71].
179 Ibid., [44], [85]–[87].
180 Ibid., [88]–[93].
181 Ibid., [51], [54].
182 Ibid., [104].

court will weigh if it is going to select one proceeding, although a focus on minimising the costs for group members is clearly of great significance.[183]

The ALRC has proposed amendments that seek to ensure that, wherever possible, there is a single class action in order to litigate a claim, including recommending that the Federal Court be given an express statutory power to resolve competing class actions.[184]

The ALRC also weighed in on how to address competing class actions that are filed in different courts. This was a key concern in relation to AMP Limited. The ALRC put forward two approaches. First was to build on the Protocol for Communication and Cooperation Between Supreme Court of New South Wales and Federal Court of Australia in Class Action Proceedings (November 2018). The protocol was adopted in response to the AMP class action experience. The protocol provides for a joint case management hearing and for the judges from each Court to jointly determine the approach to managing the competing class actions, including selecting which action may proceed. The ALRC recommended that the Supreme Courts of states and territories with class action procedures, should consider becoming parties to the protocol.[185]

The ALRC also argued that the protocol was more effective than the earlier recommendation of the VLRC that a cross-vesting judicial panel for class actions be established. The idea being based on the US Judicial Panel on Multidistrict Litigation. The ALRC expressed concern about the constitutionality of any cross-vesting judicial panel as the exercise of any judicial power is limited to the circumstances where a judge is seized of a matter.[186]

Second, and more controversial, was to recommend that all class actions arising under the Corporations Act 2001 (Cth) and Australian Securities and Investments Commission Act 2001 (Cth) could only be brought in the Federal Court.[187] This would mean that all shareholder, financial product and financial services class action could not be commenced in state courts. The recommendation may need to be acceptable to the states as Australia's corporate law regime operates on the basis that the states have referred their powers over corporations to the Federal Parliament, but such referral is subject to periodic renewal.[188]

19.7 CONCLUSION

'Three decades ago, the only exposure Australians had to class action lawsuits was in Hollywood movies'.[189] However, since then class actions in Australia have attained a high profile with proceedings frequently being reported in the mainstream media. With this fame has come a brighter spotlight and numerous fans and detractors. The truth lies somewhere in between – an important civil procedure that has provided access to justice where previously there may have been none, but at great cost to group members and defendants alike, with significant profits for plaintiff lawyers and litigation funders. Class actions are a necessary mechanism for dealing with mass harm in a developed economy like Australia and a sophisticated jurisprudence has evolved to achieve this objective. However, further refinement is needed to improve efficiency and reduce transaction costs.

183 Michael Legg, 'Judiciary approach to competing class actions fosters cost, delay', *The Australian*, 31 January 2019.
184 ALRC 2018 Report, Recommendation 4.
185 Ibid., Recommendation 6. The Supreme Court of Victoria has now entered into a protocol.
186 Ibid., 125–126.
187 Ibid., Recommendation 7.
188 Michael Legg, 'Australian Law Reform Commission Class Action and Litigation Funding Report: Empowering Courts, Monitoring Funders, Supporting Contingency Fees for Class Action Lawyers and Proposing Reviews of Shareholder Class Actions and Collective Redress' (2019) 38(4) *Civil Justice Quarterly* 478, 487–8.
189 Nick Bonyady, 'Different class: the fight for the future of litigation funding' *The Sydney Morning Herald*, 14 December 2019.

20

Empirical and Practical Perspectives on Twenty-Seven Years of Product Liability Class Actions in Australia

Julian Schimmel, Nina Abbey and Vince Morabito

20.1 INTRODUCTION

In the Second Reading Speech for the 1991 Bill that brought Part IVA of the Federal Court of Australia Act 1976 (Cth) (Part IVA) into law, the Attorney-General articulated the well-known trilogy of benefits that the new class actions regime was expected to bring, which were to enhance access to justice, reduce costs and promote efficiencies in the use of court resources.[1]

It was hoped that Part IVA would achieve these purposes by facilitating claims by people whose individual loss, although significant, was outweighed by the cost or risk of bringing individual legal action. It was also hoped that spreading costs across a group of people would make it possible and economical for these types of claims to be brought, and that efficiencies could be realised by eliminating the need to separately try the same issue. The interests of defendants would be protected by an avoidance of inconsistent verdicts and results and by the resolution of a large number of claims in a single action.[2]

It does not require much imagination to realise that claims arising from the use of faulty products had the potential to give effect to these aims. Indeed, in the seminal 1988 report which provided the foundation and impetus for the introduction of Part IVA, the Australian Law Reform Commission (ALRC)[3] recognised the potential for a class actions regime to be deployed in resolving product liability claims. In discussing the deficiencies of existing court

[1] Commonwealth of Australia, *Parliamentary Debates*, House of Representatives, 14 November 1991, 3174 (Michael Duffy). Conspicuously absent from this list of benefits, expected to be secured from the employment of the Part IVA regime, is behaviour modification/the deterrence of illegal conduct. Conversely, the Supreme Court of Canada has explained that 'class actions serve efficiency and justice by ensuring that actual and potential wrongdoers modify their behaviour to take full account of the harm they are causing': *Hollick* v.*Toronto (City)* 205 DLR (4th) 19, 28–9 (2001).

[2] Australian Law Reform Commission, *Report No 46: Group Proceedings in the Federal Court* (Australian Government Publishing Service, Canberra, 1988), [69].

[3] It is fascinating to note that it took the ALRC approximately eleven years to write this report, prompting one Senator to remark that 'I am unaware of any other report that took such a long time as the one on the subject of class actions. It is quite clear that the [ALRC] was considerably divided on the subject': Commonwealth of Australia, *Parliamentary Debates*, Senate, 13 November 1991, 3019 (Senator Durack).

procedures, the ALRC cited a 1976 article by the Canadian legal scholar, Professor Michael J. Trebilcock, who observed that:

> In a mass-production, mass-marketing, mass consumption society, custom-made, individually tailored law-suits for consumers are often as much an anachronism as the concept that all cars that are put on the market should be handcrafted ... Just as economies of scale dictate mass production for suppliers, so do economies of scale now dictate mass redress procedures for consumers prejudiced by a common legal wrong.[4]

With rapid developments in technology and industry, and with economic growth and the proliferation of international trade during the second half of twentieth century, it was reasonable to expect that product related injuries or loss could occur on a mass scale,[5] and as Justice Finkelstein later remarked (sitting as a member of a panel of the Full Federal Court of Australia),[6] it was thought that mass product liability claims would be especially well suited to the Part IVA regime:

> There is no doubt that a representative proceeding is particularly useful in product liability cases. The reasons are obvious. These cases usually raise common issues relating to matters such as the manufacturing process, the knowledge of any health hazard presented by the use of the manufactured article, whether there has been failure to test the article and whether the manufacturer has any duty to warn about the dangers associated with the use of the article ...

The Bill that contained Part IVA was passed without any amendments and Part IVA came into operation on 4 March 1992. Since then the legislatures of the four Australian states of Victoria, New South Wales (NSW), Queensland and Tasmania have enacted legislative class action regimes for their Supreme Courts which largely replicate Part IVA.[7] A Bill to legislate a class action regime was also recently introduced into the State Parliament of Western Australia.[8]

The purpose of this chapter is to evaluate the operation of the first four regimes, in relation to product liability class actions, during a period of twenty-seven years; this is the period commencing on 4 March 1992 (the day the Part IVA regime commenced) and ending on 3 March 2019 (review period).[9] In undertaking this analysis reliance will be predominantly placed on previously unpublished empirical and practical perspectives. The former perspective will draw on the extensive empirical work conducted by the third-named author over the last twelve years or so whilst the practical insights will stem from the extensive experience of the first and second-named authors in running product liability and other types of class actions including in relation to medical devices as well as the Volkswagen diesel emissions issue.

After first defining what the authors consider to constitute 'product liability class actions', this chapter will set out some of the empirical findings and trends observed in the course of the third-named author's empirical analysis. The differing types of product liability claims brought

4 Australian Law Reform Commission, *Report No 46: Group Proceedings in the Federal Court* (Australian Government Publishing Service, Canberra, 1988), at 58.

5 *Id.*, at 13.

6 *Bright* v. *Femcare Ltd* (2002) 195 ALR 574, 606.

7 The Victorian regime came into operation in January 2000 (see Supreme Court Act 1986 (Vic), Part 4A); the NSW regime in March 2011 (see Civil Procedure Act 2005 (NSW), Part 10); the Queensland regime in March 2017 (see Civil Proceedings Act 2011 (Qld), Part 13A); and the Tasmanian regime in September 2019 (see Supreme Court Civil Procedure Act 1932 (Tas), Part VII).

8 The Civil Procedure (Representative Proceedings) Bill 2019 (WA) was introduced into the Western Australian Parliament on 26 June 2019. As with the four other state analogues of the Part IVA regime, the WA Bill is substantially modelled on Part IVA.

9 The most recent regime, the Tasmanian regime, will not be included as it came into operation *after* the review period.

by Australian consumers will then be analysed, before we then turn to a discussion of some of the practical and procedural challenges faced by consumers attempting to seek redress under Australia's first four class action regimes. Finally, the authors will analyse the outcomes of all product liability class actions with particular emphasis on settlements, before discussing the differing possible approaches to the distribution of settlement funds secured in relation to defective products.

20.2 AUSTRALIA'S PRODUCT LIABILITY CLASS ACTIONS

20.2.1 *What Are Product Liability Class Actions?*

At the outset it is useful to reveal the types of legal claims we regard as falling within the concept of product liability claims and the claims that we do not believe should be treated as product liability class actions. For the purpose of our analysis, we define product liability class actions as any class action which involves allegations of liability flowing from a particular feature or characteristic of a product, but excluding two general categories of claims.

The first excluded category is where liability is only alleged to flow from a representation or statement that was made about a feature or characteristic of the product. These types of claims are better described as consumer claims. This is why we have not included, among product liability class actions, the recent Nurofen federal class action. In this class action, it was alleged that comments, included in the packaging of Nurofen pain relief products, were misleading or deceptive to the extent that they indicated that one or more these products were more effective than others in treating certain types of pain.[10]

The second excluded category is where, although the product's feature or characteristic is implicated in the harm to the claimant, liability allegedly flows from an extraneous event or an unrelated third party's conduct. An example of this type of this class action is provided by *Cameron* v. *Qantas Airways Ltd*, a federal class action where the claimants were Qantas passengers who were involuntarily exposed to the smoking of other passengers.[11] In our view, these types of claims may be better described as mass tort proceedings.

20.2.2 *Volume of Product Liability Class Action Litigation*

We identified the filing of a total of 616 class actions in the country's first four class action jurisdictions/courts during the review period. Seventy-eight or 12.6 per cent of these Australian class actions satisfied the definition of product liability class actions provided above. Sixty-one (78 per cent) of these product liability class actions were filed in the Federal Court while the remaining seventeen were filed in State Supreme Courts: nine in Victoria, seven in NSW and one in Queensland.

The filing of multiple class actions with respect to essentially the same legal disputes – sometimes by the same lawyers ('related class actions') and sometimes by different lawyers ('competing class actions') – means that the total number of legal disputes (406) that have prompted the filing of class action proceedings is substantially less than 616. Similarly, the

[10] See *Hardy* v. *Reckitt Benckiser (Australia) Pty Limited (No 2)* [2017] FCA 785. See also *Williams* v. *FAI Home Security Pty Ltd* [1999] FCA 1177; and NSD492/1997 *Australian Competition and Consumer Commission* v. *Swiss Slimming and Health Institute Pty Limited (In Liq)*, Federal Court of Australia.

[11] *Cameron* v. *Qantas Airways Ltd* (1993) ATPR 41–251.

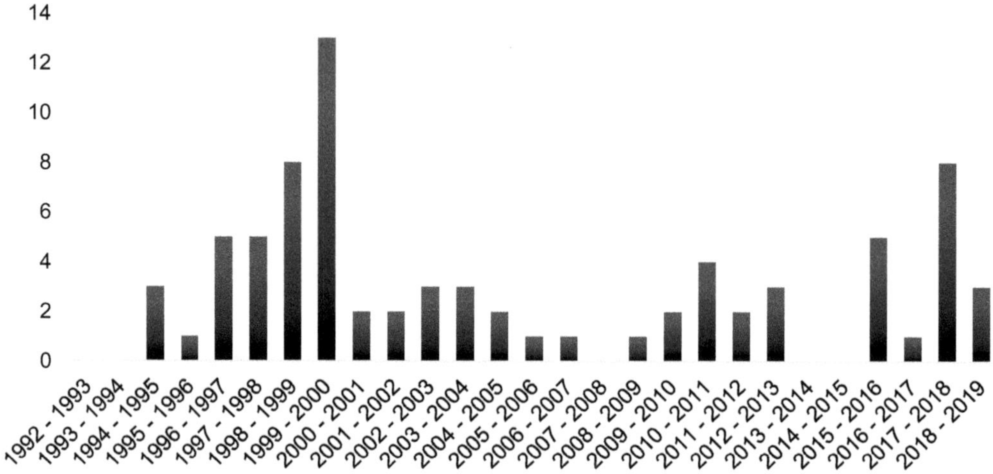

FIGURE 20.1 Annual number of product liability class actions filed between 1992 and 2019. Note: each year commences on 4 March and concludes on 3 March in the following year.

number of legal disputes (forty-nine) which were the subject of product liability class actions is substantially less than seventy-eight. In the case of product liability class actions, the difference (twenty-nine) between the number of class actions and the number of legal disputes is attributable more to the number of related class actions than to the number of competing class actions: the latter will be discussed in more detail below at Section 20.4.2.

As can be seen from the above chart, the end of the 1990s was the most active period for product liability litigation. The five class actions in the March 2015–March 2016 period and the eight product liability proceedings in the March 2017–March 2018 period need to be understood in the context of six of these eight recent class actions being filed by the same firm with respect to dangerous airbags in the 2017–18 period[12] and five proceedings filed in the 2015–16 period were two groups of competing class actions relating to the Volkswagen diesel emissions issue.[13] The total number of legal disputes arising in Australian product liability class actions is set out in Figure 20.2 below.

In analysing the evolution of product liability class actions within Australia's class actions landscape, it is important to consider the number of claims and legal disputes within their broader context. As we discuss in Section 20.4 below, the more modest number of product liability class actions filed in more recent years may be attributable to a combination of positive and negative factors, including the impact of tort reform, the availability of funding structures and the accessibility of alternative avenues of redress for Australian consumers. On the other hand, as we will go on to discuss at Section 20.5 below, despite the apparent decline in the filing of product liability class actions, plaintiffs have achieved significant success, especially in those class actions involving personal injury claims.

20.2.3 *Comparison with Other Common Types of Class Actions*

Shareholder claims were the most common type of class action during the review period, with 117 class actions constituting 18.9 per cent of the total; closely followed by investor class actions with

[12] See *Brewster* v. *BMW Australia Ltd* [2019] NSWCA 35. A total of seven airbags class actions were filed.
[13] See *Cantor* v. *Audi Australia Pty Limited (No 2)* [2017] FCA 1042.

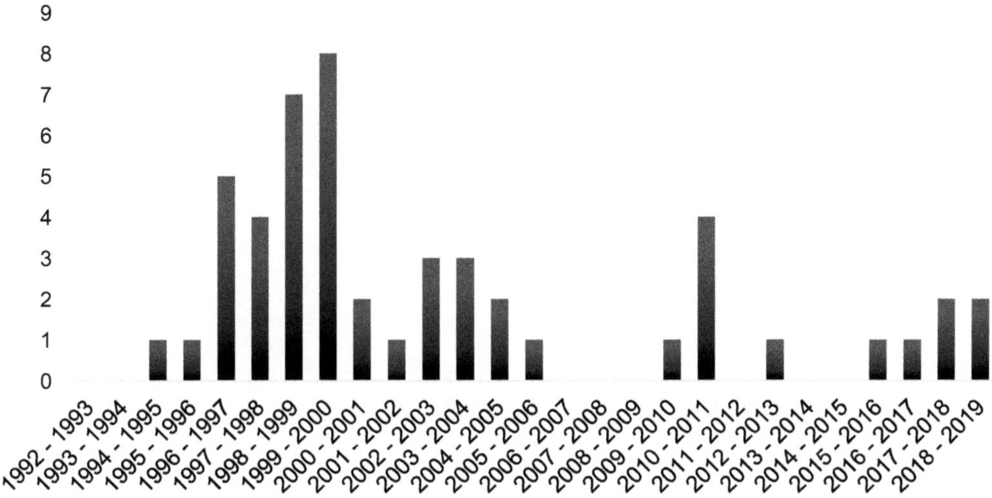

FIGURE 20.2 Annual number of legal disputes resulting in product liability class actions filed between 1992 and 2019. Note: each year commences on 4 March and concludes on 3 March in the following year, and where multiple actions have been filed in relation to the same legal dispute and these multiple actions were filed in different years in our review period, we count the legal dispute as having arisen in the first such year.

111 class actions.[14] Product liability class actions are next (seventy-eight), followed by mass tort class actions (sixty-six) and employment class actions (sixty-five). Even more interesting is the data that emerges after breaking down the first twenty-seven years into two halves and comparing what occurred in each of these periods in terms of the frequency of these five most common types of class actions.

The most striking aspect of these data is that unlike investor, shareholder and mass tort class actions, the volume of product liability litigation has *decreased* in the second half of the period despite the fact that, as already noted, twelve class actions were filed in the second half of the period with respect to identical or substantial claims concerning just two products: airbags and motor vehicles. As noted above at Section 20.2.2 and discussed later in Section 20.4.1, one of the most important causes for this development was undoubtedly the introduction of the so-called tort reform in the mid-2000s. Indeed, commentators have long predicted (including at the time that these reforms were introduced) the impact of tort reform on product liability class actions.[15]

20.2.4 *Legal Basis for Australian Product Liability Class Actions*

The following section provides an overview of the common causes of action frequently relied upon in Australian product liability class action proceedings.

The Part IVA class action regime was part of a suite of reforms that also included the introduction of Part VA of the Trade Practices Act 1974 (Cth) (Trade Practices Act), which was titled 'Liability of manufacturers and importers for defective goods'. These new provisions

[14] The term investor class actions is used to encompass class actions concerning, among other things, management investment schemes and other types of investment schemes, unit trusts, financial advice and financial instruments or products.

[15] For example, see J. Kellam, S. Clark and C. Harris, *Representative actions: A review of 15 years of product liability class action litigation in Australia – Part 2*, 16 TPLJ. 249, 266–7 (2008); S. Clark and C. Harris, *The past, present and future of product liability and other mass tort actions in Australia*, 32 UNSW Law Journal. 1022, 1032–3 (2009).

TABLE 20.1 *Number of class actions filed in the first and second half of the Australian class actions regime, by type*

Category	First 13 and a half years 4 March 1992 to 3 September 2005	Second 13 and a half years 4 September 2005 to 3 March 2019
Claims by shareholders	8 (3.6%)	109 (27.3%)
Claims by investors other than shareholders	20 (9.2%)	91 (22.9%)
Product liability	47 (21.6%)	31 (7.8%)
Mass tort claims	14 (6.4%)	52 (13%)
Claims by employees	45 (20.7%)	20 (5%)
Total number of class actions filed	217	399

came into effect in six months after Part IVA, and they established a series of statutory causes of action for people who suffered injury, loss or damage from their use of defective goods.

Action was able to be taken against the manufacturer of a defective product, and the provisions incorporated a broad definition of 'manufacturer' which encompassed not only the actual manufacturer of goods, but also others in the supply chain such as importers,[16] and in this way the provisions bypassed potential obstacles that might arise from privity of contract.

The key cause of action was in sections 75AC and 75AD, which made a manufacturer strictly liable for injury that was caused by goods whose safety was not such as persons were generally entitled to expect, taking into account a broad range of circumstances including the manner in which and purposes for which the goods were marketed, their packaging, any instructions or warnings and what was expected to be done with the goods.

While these provisions imposed strict liability for defective goods, importantly there was a 'state of the art' defence that could be invoked by a manufacturer if the defect could not have been discovered in light of the state of scientific or technical knowledge at the time that the goods were supplied, and other defences were also available.[17]

Product liability class actions also commonly invoked the provisions in Division 2A of Part V of the Trade Practices Act. Division 2A, which came into effect in 1978, imposed statutory warranties on manufacturers for goods that were not fit for purpose or not of merchantable quality,[18] and manufacturers were likewise defined in a broad way to include importers of goods.[19]

Since 2011, the modern incarnation of the defective goods and statutory warranty provisions is found in the Australian Consumer Law (ACL) which is in Schedule 2 to the Competition and Consumer Act 2010 (Cth) (Competition and Consumer Act):

(1) Part 3–2 of the ACL establishes a series of statutory consumer guarantees that are provided by a supplier to a consumer of goods, including that the goods are of 'acceptable quality'[20] and that they are reasonably fit for a disclosed purpose;[21]

16 Section 74A of the Trade Practices Act, and s. 75AB, which applied s. 74A to claims under Part VA.
17 Section 75AK of the Trade Practices Act.
18 Sections 74B and 74D of the Trade Practices Act; these provisions came into effect in 1978.
19 Section 74A of the Trade Practices Act.
20 Section 54 of the ACL provides that goods are of 'acceptable quality' if (among other things) they are fit for all the purposes for which goods of that kind are ordinarily supplied, free from defects and safe.
21 Section 55 of the ACL. The 'disclosed purpose' is a particular purpose for which goods are acquired and that is made known by the consumer either expressly or implicitly.

(2) Part 3–5 of the ACL contains provisions that are similar to the defective goods provisions in Part VA of the Trade Practices Act, including the 'state of the art' defence and other defences.[22]

Amid the panoply of statutory consumer protection laws, it is these provisions of the Trade Practices Act and the Competition and Consumer Act that have commonly been pleaded in product liability class actions, although they were complemented by other causes of action that have sometimes also been relied upon, including:

(1) Similar causes of action in state or territory consumer legislation such as the Manufacturers Warranties Act 1974 (SA), although since 2011 state consumer protection law has adopted the ACL;
(2) the proscriptions against misleading or deceptive conduct and unconscionable conduct under various consumer protection statutes;
(3) negligence, and it is now generally accepted that the manufacturer of goods owes a duty of care to the user of goods to safeguard them against foreseeable risks of injury when using the goods as intended.[23]

20.3 TYPES OF PRODUCT LIABILITY CLASS ACTIONS

Product liability class actions have been brought in relation to an array of different goods, which can be broadly categorised as follows: (1) medical devices; (2) pharmaceutical products; (3) food and drink; (4) tobacco; (5) motorised transport and related products; (6) agricultural and animal products; and (7) building or industrial products. We will briefly consider class actions within each of these categories.

20.3.1 *Medical Devices*

A total of sixteen class actions have been filed with respect to medical devices.[24]

Three Part IVA proceedings were filed between July and September 1994 with respect to defective silicone breast implants. These three class actions were the first ever product liability class actions filed in Australia. They were also the first Australian class actions where the class of represented persons was limited to only those claimants who had retained the lawyers running (or involved in the running) of the proceeding.[25] This procedural mechanism became known as a 'closed class' and was later embraced by commercial litigation funders, although it has been used by funders less frequently in the last three years or so.[26]

22 See sections 138 to 150 of the ACL. The state of the art defence is in s. 142(c).

23 C. Loveday and A. Morrison, *Australia* in *The International Comparative Legal Guide to Product Liability* 2015 (13th ed., Global Legal Group, 2015) 51.

24 The most recent class action relating to medical devices was filed outside our review period: see S ECI 2019 02916 *Turner* v. *Bayer Australia Ltd* . This class action was filed in the Supreme Court of Victoria in June 2019 against Bayer Australia Ltd and related to allegedly defective contraceptive implants. Because the filing falls outside the review period it is not included in the empirical data reported in this chapter.

25 V. Morabito, *Closed Class Actions, Open Class Actions and Access to Justice* (An Evidence-Based Approach to Class Action Reform in Australia; October 2018) 13.

26 *Id.* at 9–10.

Three class actions have been filed with respect to pacemakers (all settled);[27] two in relation to knee implants (both settled);[28] two with respect to vaginal mesh devices (with a recent and significant post-trial victory in one of them);[29] and one class action with respect to sterilisation clips which was discontinued by the lead plaintiff following numerous procedural challenges.[30] Four class actions have been filed with respect to hip implants which, after consolidation, were reduced to one proceeding that subsequently generated a gross settlement sum of $250 million.[31] This is the largest gross settlement sum ever secured in a Part IVA proceeding and the country's third greatest gross settlement sum in a class action proceeding.

20.3.2 *Pharmaceutical Products*

Ten class proceedings have been filed on behalf of alleged victims of pharmaceutical products. Three class actions were filed on behalf of persons who consumed the non-steroidal anti-inflammatory drug Vioxx, and suffered one or more of specified cardiovascular conditions, thrombotic stroke and vascular disease. At first instance, a victory was secured, with respect to the individual claims of the class representative,[32] but this was reversed by the Full Federal Court[33] and the High Court did not grant the class representative leave to appeal from the Full Federal Court's decision.[34] A settlement sum of less than half a million dollars was subsequently secured.[35]

Settlement proceeds were also secured in class actions filed with respect to the loss and damage caused by: (1) tablets for the treatment of Parkinson's Disease, Restless Leg Syndrome and pituitary gland tumours (Cabaser, Dostinex or Permax);[36] (2) morning sickness pills (Thalidomide);[37] and (3) travel-sickness tablets (Travacalm).[38] The payment by the defendant of $95.5 million, made pursuant to the settlement agreement executed in the two Thalidomide class actions, constitutes the second-largest settlement sum in Australia's product liability class actions.

No favourable outcome was secured in the remaining two class actions filed with respect to allegedly harmful prescribed drugs: a drug for the treatment of acne (Roaccutane); and products

27 See K. Ashley-Griffiths, 'The price of a heartbeat', *Sunday Herald-Sun*, 13 February 2000, 6; 'Pacemaker fault costs PacDun $2.4m', *The Australian*, 20 May 2000, 35; *Darcy* v. *Medtel Pty Ltd (No 3)* [2004] FCA 807; and *Courtney* v. *Medtel Pty Ltd (No 6)* [2004] FCA 1598.

28 See NSD823/2004 *Davies* v. *Smith & Nephew Surgical Pty Ltd* (Application; 20 May 2004), Federal Court of Australia; *Casey* v. *DePuy International Ltd* [2010] FCA 617; and T. Shepherd, 'Patients seek payout on injuries from faulty replacement joints', *The Advertiser*, 14 April 2010, 11.

29 See *Gill* v. *Ethicon Sarl (No 5)* [2019] FCA 1905; and *Philipsen* v. *American Medical Systems LLC (No 2)* [2018] FCA 1580, [1] ([the class representatives] 'claim to have suffered injuries . . . as a result of transvaginal implementation with medical devices . . . for the purpose . . . of treating pelvic organ prolapse and . . . stress urinary incontinence'); R. Jancauskas, *Product Liability Class Actions in Australia*, 129 Precedent. 23, 26 (2015).

30 See B. Murphy and C. Cameron, *Access to Justice and the Evolution of Class Action Litigation in Australia*, 30 Melbourne University Law Review. 399, 413 (2006) ('[t]here were two appeals to the Full Court of the Federal Court and two appeals to the High Court – even before the applicant had received a defence').

31 *Stanford and Another* v. *DePuy International Ltd and Another* [2016] FCA 1452.

32 *Peterson* v. *Merck Sharp & Dohme (Aust) Pty Ltd* [2010] FCA 180.

33 *Merck Sharp & Dohme (Aust) Pty Ltd* v. *Peterson* [2011] FCAFC 128.

34 *Peterson* v. *Merck Sharp & Dohme (Aust) Pty Ltd* [2012] HCATrans 105.

35 *Peterson* v. *Merck Sharp & Dohme (Aust) Pty Ltd (No 7)* [2015] FCA 123.

36 *Collin* v. *Aspen Pharmacare Australia Pty Ltd* [2013] FCA 1336; and *Winterford* v. *Pfizer Australia Pty Ltd* [2015] FCA 426.

37 See V. Morabito and J. Ekstein, *Class actions filed for the benefit of vulnerable persons – an Australian Study*, 35 Civil Justice Quarterly. 61, 79 (2016).

38 *Id.*, at 80.

called Adifax and Ponderax Pacaps intended to assist with weight loss.[39] The former proceeding (filed in the Supreme Court of Victoria) was discontinued by the class representatives twelve months after it was filed, following the realisation by their solicitors that they lacked the resources to run a proceeding of this magnitude whilst the latter proceeding was discontinued under Part IVA and transferred to the Supreme Court of NSW by consent.[40]

20.3.3 *Food and Drink*

This category encompasses the greatest number of product liability class actions, with a total of twenty-one class actions (27 per cent of all product liability class actions). This is despite the fact that only one class action on behalf of victims of harmful food or drink has been filed in the last fifteen years since June 2004 and the remaining twenty food and drinks class actions were therefore all filed in the twelve years between March 1992 and June 2004. It becomes apparent from these data that the dominance of product liability class actions in the first half of class actions in Australia and their declining presence in the second half is largely attributable to the decline in contaminated food and drink class actions. We discuss some of the potential drivers for the decline in food and drink class actions, including the impact of tort reform, in Section 20.4.1 below.

In the course of the review period, food and drink class action proceedings were brought in relation to Kraft peanut butter,[41] pizza,[42] pork rolls at a Vietnamese restaurant,[43] Spanish Mackerel,[44] oysters,[45] food served at a pub in Heidelberg in Melbourne,[46] food provided on a cruise[47] and several others.[48] Some of the contaminated food products were sold or consumed at a single place like a bakery or a restaurant, respectively, whilst others were distributed either nationally or within given States or cities. Many of these class actions claimed compensation for relatively modest food poisoning complaints.

Not surprisingly, the largest settlement produced in a class action concerning contaminated food products was in a class action brought with respect to a product distributed nationally. This was a Victorian class action (filed in September 2010) where it was alleged that Bonsoy milk contained excessive iodine levels, which caused serious thyroid illness. A settlement of $25 million was ultimately achieved.[49] This is the country's third largest gross settlement sum in a product liability class action.

39 *Id.*, at 80–1.
40 *Crandell* v. *Servier Laboratories (Aust) Pty Ltd* [1999] FCA 1461, [1].
41 VID393/1996 *Butler* v. *Kraft Foods and Another*, Federal Court of Australia.
42 VID104/2004 *Hunt* v. *Sofia (Sophia) Pizza House Bistro & Restaurant Pty Ltd*, Federal Court of Australia.
43 No 4335 of 2003 *Nu Ly Tang* v. *Thank Phu Pty Ltd and Another*, Supreme Court of Victoria (salmonella from pork rolls at the Thanh Phu restaurant in Footscray, Victoria).
44 *McLean* v. *Nicholson* [2002] VSC 446.
45 *Ryan* v. *Great Lakes Council* [1999] FCA 177.
46 *Georgiou* v. *Old England Hotel Pty Ltd* [2006] FCA 705.
47 *Neil* v. *P & O Cruises Australia Ltd* [2002] FCA 1325.
48 For additional examples, see The Hon Justice B. Murphy and V. Morabito, 'The First 25 Years: Has the class action regime hit the mark on access to justice?' in D. Grave and H. Mould (eds), *25 Years of Class Actions in Australia: 1992–2017* (Ross Parsons Centre of Commercial, Corporation and Taxation Law, 2017) 13, 23–4.
49 *Downie* v. *Spiral Foods Pty Ltd and Others* [2015] VSC 190.

20.3.4 *Tobacco*

Two Part IVA proceedings were filed against tobacco manufacturers and distributors on behalf of persons who contracted various forms of cancer and/or lung disease (including emphysema) and vascular disease as a consequence of the use of cigarettes over a period of approximately forty years.[50] These proceedings, which were subsequently consolidated, were not allowed to continue as Part IVA proceedings as the Full Federal Court held that the claims in question failed to adhere to the three threshold requirements set out in Part IVA's section 33 C which need to be satisfied in order to employ the Part IVA regime.[51]

A third class action with respect to tobacco was also dismissed. It covered several named health and medical groups and organisations and those who have smoked cigarettes but have not yet experienced symptoms of or been diagnosed with smoking related diseases.[52]

20.3.5 *Motorised Transport and Related Products*

Reference has already been made to five class actions brought with respect to the diesel emission issue and seven proceedings filed with respect to dangerous airbags. The latter set of proceedings is still in progress whilst in the diesel emission class actions a settlement agreement was reached by all the parties to these proceedings in early December 2019. This settlement was approved by the Federal Court in April 2020, with the Court noting that approximately $120 million AUD was estimated to be payable to eligible group members, and that individual settlement payments were estimated to be on average $2,800 within a range from $1,589 to $6,554 depending on factors such as the type and age of the vehicle.[53] The amounts available to be paid to eligible group members are exclusive of legal costs and other payments, and the total amount payable by the respondents was therefore estimated to be approximately $172.7 million plus settlement administration costs and additional legal costs.[54]. Also in progress is a class action in the Federal Court against Ford Motor Company of Australia Limited with respect to allegedly defective automatic transmissions in certain models.[55]

There have also been two class actions with respect to allegedly defective trucks – manufactured by Mack Trucks Australia Pty Ltd[56] and Paccar Australia Ltd[57] – and four class actions in relation to the loss and damage suffered as a consequence of the use of contaminated aviation fuel distributed by Mobil Oil Australia Ltd.[58]

50 *Nixon* v. *Philip Morris (Australia) Ltd* [1999] FCA 1107, [2]–[5].
51 *Philip Morris (Australia) Ltd* v. *Nixon* (2000) 170 ALR 487.
52 See *Tobacco Control Coalition Inc* v. *Philip Morris (Australia) Ltd* [2000] FCA 1004.
53 See *Cantor v Audi Australia Pty Ltd (No 5)* [2020] FCA 637 and the orders made by Foster J on 1 April 2020 in proceedings NSD1459/2015, NSD1472/2015, NSD1472/2015, NSD1307/2015 and NSD1308/2015. The final amount payable by Volkswagen AG is dependent on the number of vehicles in respect of which eligible claims are made by group members. The registration and assessment of claims remains ongoing but is expected to be finalized by the fourth quarter of 2020.
54 *Cantor v Audi Australia Pty Ltd (No 5)* [2020] FCA 637, [170].
55 *Capic* v. *Ford Motor Company of Australia Limited* [2016] FCA 1020. A class action was filed in the Federal Court in July 2019 on behalf of over 250,000 vehicle owners who suffered loss arising from allegedly faulty diesel filters in several Toyota diesel model cars: NSD210/2019 *Williams* v. *Toyota Motor Corporation Australia Limited*, Federal Court of Australia. As this claim falls outside of our review period, it is not included in the empirical data reported in this chapter.
56 *Lowe* v. *Mack Trucks Australia Pty Ltd* [2008] FCA 439, [1]–[7].
57 *Jonsandi Transport* v. *Paccar Australia Ltd* [1999] FCA 1788.
58 It is fascinating to note that one of these four class actions was filed, not on behalf of members of the aviation industry, but instead for owners of motor vehicles who used contaminated aviation fuel for their motor vehicles: VID582/2000 *Haysom* v. *Mobil Oil Australia*, Federal Court of Australia. It was discontinued by the class representative four months after it was filed. With respect to the other three class actions, filed by three different firms, see V. Morabito,

Success, in the form of a settlement, was secured in one of the aviation fuel class actions and in the Paccar class action, although in the latter case the settlement did not include monetary compensation for the claimants.

20.3.6 *Agricultural and Animal Products*

This category encompasses nine class actions: four with respect to various forms of insecticide, pesticide and chemical herbicide;[59] two with respect to cultivator bars and harvesters;[60] one in respect to the allegedly adverse effects of an equine vaccine for the Hendra virus,[61] and finally two class actions in relation to canola seeds[62] and sorghum seeds. The last mentioned product prompted the filing of the first-ever class action filed in the Supreme Court of Queensland, commonly known as the shattercane class action.[63]

Only two of these class actions have been resolved successfully for the benefit of class members: first, a Part IVA proceeding with respect to a harvester resulted in the defendant paying settlement proceeds of over $11 million;[64] second, in the *McMullin* v. *ICI Australia Operations Pty Ltd* Part IVA proceeding, brought with respect to an insecticide developed, manufactured and marketed by the defendants for use in the cotton industry, a favourable post-trial ruling subsequently led to class members receiving compensation of over $100 million.[65]

Another class action was recently filed with respect to the alleged negligent design, manufacture and sale of the Hardi Presidio 2700, a self-propelled spray unit.[66] But it will not be included in the empirical data canvassed in this chapter as it was filed outside the review period.

20.3.7 *Building and Industrial Products*

A Part IVA proceeding was filed in February 2019 on the basis that Alucobond aluminium composite cladding was not safe as it was combustible.[67] It is also noted that a second class action regarding a different aluminium composite cladding product was filed more recently in June 2019;[68] however this claim falls outside of our review period and is therefore not included in the empirical data reported in this chapter. Both of these claims are being conducted by the same law firm, involve the same litigation funder and are being case managed together.

Clashing Classes Down Under – Evaluating Australia's Competing Class Actions through Empirical and Comparative Perspectives, 27 Connecticut Journal of International Law. 245, 302–3 (2012).

59 See *McMullin* v. *ICI Australia Operations Pty Ltd* [1999] FCA 1814; *Symington* v. *Hoechst Schering Agrevo Pty Ltd* [1997] FCA 969; *Schneider* v. *Hoechst Schering Agrevo Pty Ltd* [2001] FCA 102; and NSD851/1996 *Dingle* v. *Ciba-Geiby Australia Ltd*, Federal Court of Australia.

60 See *J F Yandle & Co Pty Ltd* v. *CSN Pty Ltd* [1999] FCA 820; and *Nendy Enterprises Pty Ltd* v. *New Holland Australia Pty Ltd* [2001] FCA 582.

61 *Abbott* v. *Zoetis Australia Pty Ltd (No 2)* [2019] FCA 462.

62 See *Wilkins* v. *Dovuro Pty Ltd* [1999] FCA 1816.

63 No BS4103/17 *Mallonland Pty Ltd and Anor* v. *Advanta Seeds Pty Ltd*, Supreme Court of Queensland. For more details, see www.creeveyrussell.com/au/shattercane-class-action/.

64 The settlement approval judgment may be found at *J F Yandle & Co Pty Ltd* v. *CSN Pty Ltd* [2000] FCA 1823.

65 For an outline of the regime and the fact that it led to $100 million in compensation for class members, see The Hon M. Wilcox AO QC, 'Class actions in Australia: Recollections of the early days' in D. Grave and H. Mould (eds), *25 Years of Class Actions in Australia: 1992–2017* (Ross Parsons Centre of Commercial, Corporation and Taxation Law, 2017) 5, 10.

66 2019/00101980 *Greenshades Pastoral Co Pty Ltd* v. *Hardi Australia*.

67 *The Owners – Strata Plan No 87231* v. *3A Composites GmbH* [2019] FCA 811.

68 NSD940/2019 *The Owners – Strata Plan No 91086* v. *Fairview Architectural Pty Ltd*, Federal Court of Australia.

20.3.8 *Other Consumer Goods*

While the discussion set out above has revealed the filing of class actions with respect to a variety of products, an obvious question is why there have been no class actions with respect to numerous consumer or household goods used by most Australians.

In the authors' view, this is likely to be attributable to particular aspects of Australia's consumer protection laws and the nature of the claims arising from faulty household or consumer goods.

The ACL provides consumers with a variety of legal avenues for redress where they acquired products that are faulty or fail to meet standards or expectations relating to the product.[69] While these statutory rights have previously been asserted in the context of product liability class actions (as discussed above at Section 20.2.4), the most common avenue for redress for consumers in respect of faulty goods involves a consumer exercising their rights[70] to a refund, replacement or repair through the manufacturer, supplier or distributor directly.[71] In other words, rather than instruct lawyers to initiate a class action, a person who purchased a faulty washing machine may be more inclined to approach the retailer or manufacturer in order to seek a refund or a replacement either as a warranty claim or otherwise.

The active role which Australia's consumer regulator plays in the issuing of recalls and warnings in respect of defective consumer goods may also contribute to the lack of class actions brought in respect of consumer and household goods. In 2019 alone, approximately 344 product recalls[72] have (as at 7 July 2019) been issued by the Australian Competition and Consumer Commission in relation to goods as diverse as home and electrical equipment,[73] food and grocery products[74] and clothing.[75] As consumers are warned and products are recalled, the necessity for group redress and access to compensation is understandably reduced as a result of these types of preventative measures.

Where preventative measures fail to prevent the widespread purchase of defective goods or fail to avoid loss or injury associated with the use of defective goods, and consumers are unable to obtain a remedy directly from the manufacturer or supplier, the utility of class action litigation

69 See Section 20.2.4 above.

70 Under s. 272 of the Competition and Consumer Act a consumer may take action for damages against a manufacturer in respect of either a reduction in value of goods which fail to comply with a statutory guarantee, or in relation to any loss or damage suffered which was reasonably foreseeable as a result of the failure to comply with the statutory guarantee. While a consumer may not demand a replacement, repair or refund from a manufacturer directly, such rights commonly arise from voluntary warranties offered by manufacturers. Warranties offered by manufacturers are subject to certain prescribed requirements under the Competition and Consumer Act (see s. 102 of the Competition and Consumer Act).

71 See s. 261 of the Competition and Consumer Act which sets the ways in which a supplier may remedy a failure to comply with a statutory guarantee (for example, by providing a repair, replacement or refund). Where the failure to comply with a guarantee is considered to be a 'major failure' a consumer will be entitled to reject the goods and request either a replacement or refund (see ss. 259(3), 260 to 263). A 'major failure' includes goods which would not have been acquired by a reasonable consumer fully acquainted with the extent of the failure, goods that are unsafe, goods that are unfit for their purpose or depart significantly from their description or model.

72 Australian Competition and Consumer Commission, Product Safety Australia, Browse All Recalls: www.productsafety.gov.au/recalls/browse-all-recalls?f%5B0%5D=accc_solr_date%3A2019. A Recall Actions Database is also operated by the Australian Therapeutic Goods Administration. This database provides information in respect of recall action relating to therapeutic goods sold in Australia: www.tga.gov.au/recall-actions-database.

73 For example, AGS Energy Ltd – Promotional AGS-Branded Wireless Phone Charger: www.productsafety.gov.au/recall/agl-energy-ltd-promotional-agl-branded-wireless-phone-charger.

74 For example, Chapley Group – Hot Cross Buns: www.productsafety.gov.au/recall/chapley-group-hot-cross-buns.

75 For example, BIG W – Ray Ban Brown Tortoiseshell Sunglasses- www.productsafety.gov.au/recall/big-w-ray-ban-brown-tortoiseshell-sunglasses.

must be considered in the context of a number of practical considerations. Class action litigation is typically costly, so in practice the total monetary relief that is sought for class members will need to be sufficient to render the claim economically viable, such that costs are proportionate to the compensation that is sought.

Unlike class actions which involve the use of a defective medical device or pharmaceutical product, consumer goods commonly do not cause incidental losses such as a personal injury or loss of income. In other words, the loss suffered by claimants in relation to consumer goods is therefore usually limited to the cost of replacing or repairing the item itself.[76] Depending on the value of the product and the number of consumers who acquired it, the viability of class actions in relation to consumer goods may be limited by these types of practical considerations.

20.4 ISSUES IN PRACTICE

References have already been made to legislative tort reform having had an impact on the ability to bring product liability class actions. In this section we explore this significant legislative development. We then consider a number of other challenges faced by claimants in product liability class actions.

20.4.1 *Impact of Tort Reform*

In July 2004, legislative changes were introduced by way of a new Part VIB of the Trade Practices Act. Part VIB contained a number of provisions that curtailed damages for personal injury, including:

(1) The introduction of thresholds and caps for general damages whereby a plaintiff receives no compensation for general damages if their injury is assessed as less than 15 per cent of a most extreme case, and the plaintiff receives significantly reduced damages for non-economic loss if the injury is between 15 per cent and 33 per cent of a most extreme case;[77]
(2) the abolition of aggravated damages and exemplary damages;[78]
(3) limits on economic loss claims such that weekly earnings are capped at twice the average weekly earnings, or around $100,000 per year;[79] and
(4) limits on gratuitous care claims by the introduction of thresholds and caps on the weekly number of hours of care that can be claimed and the hourly rate to be applied.[80]

Tort reforms were also introduced in various states and territories, for example the Civil Liability Act 2002 (NSW), and these are relevant to the extent that product liability class actions allege negligence or a cause of action under state or territory legislation.

[76] This is not to suggest that consequential loss or injury never occurs as a result of the use of consumer goods; for example a defective cooking appliance that in some instances caused burns or other physical injuries, or an electrical malfunction in white goods that caused a house fire. However these types of consequential losses are either uncommon or relate to idiosyncratic circumstances that render them unsuitable to the class action procedure.

[77] See ss. 87L-87T of the Trade Practices Act, as in force at the time; these provisions remain in Part VIB of the renamed Competition and Consumer Act.

[78] See s. 87ZB of the Trade Practices Act, as in force at the time; this provision remains in Part VIB of the renamed Competition and Consumer Act.

[79] See s. 87U–87V of the Trade Practices Act, as in force at the time; these provisions remain in Part VIB of the renamed Competition and Consumer Act.

[80] See ss. 87W–87X of the Trade Practices Act, as in force at the time; these provisions remain in Part VIB of the renamed Competition and Consumer Act.

In thinking about the types of cases that might have been deterred by the advent of tort reform, the most obvious examples are food poisoning cases and lower grade injuries caused by medical devices and pharmaceutical products.

Without wanting trivialise the injuries in food poisoning cases, in the majority of cases the losses were reasonably modest, reflecting a relatively transient albeit unpleasant injury that would be unlikely meet the minimum 15 per cent threshold in Part VIB of the Trade Practices Act.[81] As we have seen from Section 20.3.3 above, since this reform, there has been only one class action with respect to claims arising from the consumption of food or drink, the Bonsoy milk proceeding, where it was pleaded that serious thyroid injuries were suffered by the class members. This case may be contrasted to the many previous cases that involved gastrointestinal ailments, the last of which was filed in May 2004, only two months before the federal tort reforms commenced operation.

Although claims arising from adverse effects of pharmaceuticals clearly have the potential to satisfy thresholds for non-economic loss, it is generally recognised that these types of claims present different challenges, particularly in proving causation on the basis of epidemiological evidence, as was the case in the Full Court's decision in the Vioxx litigation in 2011.[82] The evidentiary challenges of product liability claims coupled with limitations introduced by tort reform have undoubtedly impacted on the viability of certain product liability class actions in recent years. Less serious pharmaceutical claims, such as the class action arising from the use of Travacalm,[83] appear to have disappeared in the wake of tort reform, but on the other hand, as noted in Section 20.3.2 above, a settlement of $95.5 million was recently achieved for people who were born with serious birth defects after their mothers had consumed Thalidomide.[84]

While it is impossible to predefine the types of product-related injuries that are likely to satisfy the thresholds for non-economic loss, one area where it is likely are cases involving implantable medical devices. For example, commonly a patient with a failed joint replacement will require invasive corrective surgery to remove and replace the original implant, and this ordinarily requires a substantial period of rehabilitation, often with less optimal results than would have been expected from a successful initial implant, and in many cases there is ongoing permanent disability caused by bone and tissue damage, which sometimes has catastrophic consequences for the patient.

Over the last ten or so years we have seen several implantable device-related class actions being commenced, most recently in relation to hip implants and two different knee implants as well as the two surgical mesh claims. This is one subspecies of product liability class actions that is likely to endure the effects of tort reform and where the class action procedure continues to provide real remedies to individuals who otherwise might not have had access to justice.

81 See however V. Morabito and J. Ekstein, *Class actions filed for the benefit of vulnerable persons – an Australian Study*, 35 Civil Justice Quarterly. 61, 85–6 (2016) where attention is drawn to the fact that 'some of the class members (almost invariably individuals with pre-existing medical problems, children and elderly persons) died or risked death whilst many of the remaining class members required hospitalisation and/or suffered significant health problems'.

82 *Merck Sharp & Dohme (Australia) Pty Ltd* v. *Petersen* [2011] FCFCA 128. For a summary of the challenges that arose in the case, see P. O'Donahoo and D. Kinsey, *The Vioxx Appeal – a bitter pill for pharmaceutical class actions?* 22(6) Australian Product Liability Reporter. 234 (2012).

83 No 5621 of 2003 *Reynolds (An Infant) by her Litigation Guardian Ann Reynolds* v. *Key Pharmaceuticals Pty Ltd*, Supreme Court of Victoria. As explained in V. Morabito and J. Ekstein, *Class actions filed for the benefit of vulnerable persons – an Australian Study*, 35 Civil Justice Quarterly. 61, 80 (2016) the alleged harm included hallucinations, vomiting, delirium, disorientation, spasms, blurred or lost vision, loss of balance and personality changes.

84 No S CI 2011 3527 *Rowe* v. *Grünenthal GmbH and Others*, Supreme Court of Victoria; No S CI 2010 5845 *Robbins* v. *Grünenthal GmbH*, Supreme Court of Victoria.

20.4.2 *Competing Class Actions*

In recent years competing class actions have become one of the most controversial aspects of Australia's class action landscape.[85] The discussion in this section relates to competing class actions and not to related class actions as defined above.

Shareholder class actions have attracted the greatest number of competing class actions;[86] however it is sometimes presumed that this phenomenon of competing class actions is equally pervasive in other areas of class action litigation. In fact, the empirical evidence is that there have only been six instances of class actions filed by different lawyers with respect to the same product liability claims during the review period.

The general perception of the circumstances leading to competing claims is that the claims in question invariably involve claims of significant value. This was the case in three instances of competing product liability class actions: the hip implants,[87] diesel emissions[88] and tobacco litigation[89] and perhaps the litigation concerning the loss and damage caused by contaminated aviation fuel.[90] But the remaining two instances of competing product liability class actions, concerning pork rolls sold at a local bakery[91] and tiramisu and chocolate mousse consumed in a restaurant at the Hilton Hotel in Cairns, Queensland,[92] did not follow the same trend.

Another commonly held belief is that competing class actions involve not only competing solicitors but also competing commercial litigation funders. This scenario has so far not been encountered in product liability class actions, although the diesel emission Part IVA proceedings filed by one of the two law firms in question are financed by a commercial litigation funder; on the other hand, the competing claim (involving different lawyers) does not involve a third-party litigation funder.

Australian courts have sought to resolve the issue of competing class actions through a variety of procedural approaches. Perhaps the most controversial method adopted by the Australian judiciary has been the use of a permanent stay which ensures that only one competing or overlapping proceeding is permitted to continue.[93] Alternative approaches have also included the consolidation of multiple proceedings through judicial encouragement[94] and/or court ordered consolidation.[95]

In five of the six sets of competing product liability class actions filed to date, the 'problem' of competing claims was resolved by the lawyers in question without the need for judicial

85 See V. Morabito, *Competing Class Actions and Comparative Perspectives on the Volume of Class Action Litigation in Australia* (An Evidence-Based Approach to Class Action Reform in Australia, July 2018).

86 *Id.*, at 14.

87 V Morabito, *Clashing Classes Down Under – Evaluating Australia's Competing Class Actions through Empirical and Comparative Perspectives*, 27 Connecticut Journal of International Law. 245, 277–8 (2012).

88 See *Cantor* v. *Audi Australia Pty Limited (No 2)* [2017] FCA 1042.

89 V Morabito, *Clashing Classes Down Under – Evaluating Australia's Competing Class Actions through Empirical and Comparative Perspectives*, 27 Connecticut Journal of International Law. 245, 271–3 (2012).

90 *Id.*, at 302–3.

91 *Id.*, at 259.

92 *Id.*, at 275.

93 See for example *Perera* v. *GetSwift Ltd* [2018] FCAFC 202. See also *Wigmans* v. *AMP Ltd*; *Fernbrook (Aust) Investments Pty Ltd* v. *AMP*; *Wileypark Pty Ltd* v. *AMP Ltd*; *Georgiou* v. *AMP Ltd*; *Komlotex Pty Ltd* v. *AMP Ltd* [2019] NSWSC 603 where the NSW Supreme Court held that only one of five competing proceedings was allowed to proceed. This decision was also subsequently upheld on appeal by the New South Wales Court of Appeal, see *Wigmans* v. *AMP Ltd* [2019] NSWCA 243.

94 See for example *Klemweb Nominees Pty Ltd (as trustee for the Klemweb Superannuation Fund)* v. *BHP Group Limited* [2019] FCAFC 107 where the Full Federal Court ordered that the two plaintiff groups were to confer in an attempt to consolidate the two sets of proceedings.

95 See for example *Southernwood* v. *Brambles Limited* [2019] FCA 1021 where Justice Murphy ordered that two overlapping securities class actions be consolidated into one single proceeding.

intervention. In the diesel emission class actions, the Court held that both sets of proceedings could be heard together. The Court did however indicate its willingness to adopt alternative approaches should a change in circumstances require a different strategy,[96] and it is also noted that, before a settlement was reached between the parties, judgment was reserved in respect of a subsequent application by the defendants in these proceedings.

The willingness of lawyers voluntarily to consolidate competing product liability claims sets these types of proceedings apart from other class actions. In the authors' experience, in personal injury claims one impetus for cooperation and consolidation lies in an attempt to provide class members with autonomy and control in relation to their selected legal representative. For cases involving injuries or traumatic circumstances, the relationship between individual class members and their lawyers can sometimes become highly personal. By consolidating competing claims and attempting to work cooperatively, lawyers can seek to give effect to class members' preferences.[97]

20.4.3 *Settlement Negotiations with Individual Class Members*

Earlier empirical data revealed extremely high opt-out rates in those federal and Victorian class actions where there had been communications between the defendants and the class members regarding the litigation in question.[98]

This phenomenon has also been experienced in several product liability class actions. In *Dingle* v. *Ciba-Geiby Australia Ltd*, one of the pesticide federal class actions, this strategy resulted in the proceeding being discontinued as a result of the two lead plaintiffs and the vast majority of the class members settling their individual claims directly with the defendants.

In one of the four aviation fuel class actions, by the time the proceeding was settled most of the class members had opted out of the litigation following compromises directly made with the defendant.[99] Following direct communications between defendants and class members, over 1,300 class members opted out of *Jonsandi Transport Pty Ltd* v. *Paccar Australia Pty Ltd*, one of the two Part IVA proceedings commenced with respect to allegedly defective trucks.

In one of the three pacemaker class actions, Justice Stone of the Federal Court held that no restrictions should be placed on the ability of the defendants' solicitors to conduct settlement negotiations, over the telephone, with class members.[100] This ruling was made despite the fact that a majority of the surviving class members were elderly (their average age was seventy-nine), frail, infirm, suffered from a range of health problems including cardiac conditions lived alone or with elderly partners and were unlikely to have a sophisticated understanding of their rights or entitlements in the proceeding.[101] The practical effect of this approach was that the defendants

96 *Cantor* v. *Audi Australia Pty Limited (No 2)* [2017] FCA 1042.

97 The ALRC has recommended that the 'stated preferences of group members' be considered as one of the criteria to be considered by courts in attempting to deal with competing claims. See [4.108] of the Final Report regarding Integrity, Fairness and Efficiency – An Inquiry into Class Action Proceedings and Third-Party Litigation Funders, published December 2018.

98 V. Morabito, *Litigation Funders, Competing Class Actions, Opt Out Rates, Victorian Class Actions and Class Representatives* (Second Report; An Empirical Study of Australia's Class Action Regimes; September 2010) 31–2.

99 In B. Murphy and C. Cameron, *Access to Justice and the Evolution of Class Action Litigation in Australia*, 30 Melbourne University Law Review. 399, 430 (2006) attention was also drawn to the fact that 'many of the claims had been settled for less than full value'.

100 *Courtney* v. *Medtel Pty Ltd* (2001) 113 FCR 512.

101 V. Morabito and J. Ekstein, *Class actions filed for the benefit of vulnerable persons – an Australian Study*, 35 Civil Justice Quarterly. 61, 83 (2016).

settled approximately 21 per cent of the class members' claims shortly before the trial.[102] Eleven months later a different approach in the same pacemaker litigation was adopted by Justice Sackville, who held that a defendant was entitled to communicate with unrepresented class members including in order to make settlement offers, but that communications with legally represented class members ought to be conducted through their solicitors.[103]

While the Federal Court's Class Actions Practice Note seeks to give effect to developments in the jurisprudence concerning defendants' direct communications with class members,[104] there may be merit in the courts taking a more interventionist approach in some of these circumstances. It should be presumed that any class action was the catalyst for a defendant's efforts to communicate with and settle the claims of some (unrepresented) class members, but on the other hand this practice has the capacity to affect the practical outcomes for other (represented) class members whose claims continue to be pursued through the class action and it could be argued that the court ought to ensure that the interests of the latter are properly protected.[105]

20.4.4 *Interlocutory Issues*

One area that has generated significant challenges for plaintiffs and their lawyers is the level of interlocutory activity in product liability (and other) class actions, particularly when focussed on the representative character of class actions. Australia's class action regimes do not employ the certification device but judges presiding over class actions have extensive powers to 'declass' class actions; that is, order that they no longer continue as class action proceedings.[106]

Declassing applications in the product liability context have often focussed on the level of individuality in class members' claims and arguments that these individual issues predominate the common issues, and that the class action regime is therefore not an efficient or effective mechanism for the resolution of the group of claims or that separate proceedings by class members would be less costly. One of the best-known examples is *Bright* v. *Femcare Ltd*, where the defendants were successful before the primary judge, but with the plaintiff succeeding on appeal to the Full Federal Court.[107]

There is no doubt that product liability class actions give rise to several significant individual issues,[108] particularly in relation to causation and loss in cases involving personal injury, and it is easy[109] to conjure up a catalogue of legal and factual issues that are incapable of being resolved as common issues.

102 *Id.*

103 *Courtney* v. *Medtel Pty Ltd* [2002] FCA 957.

104 Federal Court of Australia's *Class Actions Practice Note (GPN-CA)* (October 2016), Part 10.

105 See generally V. Morabito, *Judicial Supervision of Individual Settlements with Class Members in Australia, Canada, and the United States*, 38 Texas International Law Journal. 663 (2003).

106 Part IVA's s. 33N(1)(d) (and its State equivalents) provides, among other things, that a declassing order may be made where the Court is satisfied that it is in the interests of justice to do so because 'it is otherwise inappropriate that the claims be pursued by means' of a class action. See generally V. Morabito, *The Federal Court of Australia's Power to Terminate Properly Instituted Class Actions*, 42 Osgoode Hall Law Journal. 473 (2004).

107 *Bright* v. *Femcare Ltd* (2001) 188 ALR 633 (Stone J); *Bright* v. *Femcare Ltd* (2002) 195 ALR 574 (Lindgren, Kiefel and Finkelstein JJ).

108 See, for example, the observation of Jessup J in *Peterson* v. *Merck Sharp & Dohme (Australia) Pty Ltd (No 3)* [2009] FCA 5, [39]: '[i]t is, of course, well within the contemplation of Part IVA that a proceeding properly commenced and prosecuted, thereunder will have non-common questions, or questions which relate to group members as individuals'.

109 For example, see the list of issues in J. Kellam, S. Clark and C. Harris, *Representative actions: A review of 15 years of product liability class action litigation in Australia – Part 2*, 16 TPLJ. 249, 253 (2008).

However, when taken together with the relatively low incidence of declassing applications, the outcome of interlocutory applications in several notable cases[110] and more recently the low success rate for declassing applications[111] suggest that there is now a general acceptance that the class actions regime is capable of resolving a meaningful array of common issues in product liability claims. It could also be said that individual issues can be accommodated within the class action framework through pragmatic case management which draws on among other things the power to create subgroups,[112] or even a declassing order following a favourable post-trial ruling on common issues, and in each scenario the parties and class members would have the benefit of any common findings. In addition, the reality in practice is that the resolution of common issues is likely to provide the catalyst for a settlement that will allow individual issues to be addressed in one way or another pursuant to a judicially approved settlement distribution scheme.[113]

20.4.5 *Funding of Product Liability Class Actions*

The ALRC was conscious of the fact that for its suggested regime to provide access to justice for similarly situated claimants it was important for potential class representatives and their lawyers to have easy access to significant sources of funding, given the higher costs entailed in running a class action and the exposure to greater adverse costs awards in the event of an unsuccessful outcome.[114] As discussed further in this section, product liability class actions have features that have tended against the involvement of litigation funders that have instead become more active in other areas of class action litigation.

The complexity of product liability class actions and the scale of expert evidence has the obvious potential to bring added cost. Common issues within these claims will typically raise numerous scientific, engineering and other technical issues regarding the design, testing, manufacture, safety and performance of the product in question, the state of scientific knowledge at different points in time, and it is common for these issues to be explored through incredibly extensive and complex expert evidence.

It is therefore not surprising that, as outlined in Section 20.5.1 below, on average it has taken three years to settle product liability class actions. Reasons for this include the scale of the evidence and the preparedness of defendants to go to trial and beyond. Another factor may be the level of interlocutory activity particularly in the early period of the operation of class action regimes.

The general willingness of defendants vigorously to defend product liability claims is highlighted by the long trials that were held, not only in the hip implants and Vioxx class actions, but also in the already-mentioned *McMulllin* v. *ICI Australia Operations Pty Ltd* and

110 Most notably in relation to product liability claims, see *Bright* v. *Femcare Ltd* (2002) 195 ALR 574 and *Peterson* v. *Merck Sharp & Dohme (Australia) Pty Ltd (No 3)* [2009] FCA 5. The latter decision was affirmed on appeal in *Merck Sharp & Dohme (Australia) Pty Ltd* v. *Peterson* [2009] FCAFC 26 at [3].

111 V. Morabito and J. Caruana, *Can Class Action Regimes Operate Satisfactorily without a Certification Device? Empirical Insights from the Federal Court of Australia*, 61 American Journal of Comparative Law. 579 (2013).

112 A good example of the way that the Court can creatively case manage this process is *McMullin* v. *ICI Australia Operations Pty Ltd*, as described by The Hon M. Wilcox AO QC, 'Class actions in Australia: Recollections of the early days' in D. Grave and H. Mould (eds), *25 Years of Class Actions in Australia: 1992–2017* (Ross Parsons Centre of Commercial, Corporation and Taxation Law, 2017) 5, 9–10.

113 An example of this is the Tempo pacemaker class action: *Courtney* v. *Medtel Pty Ltd* (2003) 126 FCR 219 (trial at first instance); *Medtel Pty Ltd* v. *Courtney* (2003) 198 ALR 630 (Full Court appeal); *Courtney* v. *Medtel Pty Ltd (No 5)* (2004) 212 ALR 311 and *Courtney* v. *Medtel Pty Ltd (No 6)* [2004] FCA 1598 (settlement approval).

114 Australian Law Reform Commission, *Report No 46: Group Proceedings in the Federal Court* (Australian Government Publishing Service, Canberra, 1988), chapter 8.

in class actions filed with respect to oysters, canola seeds, chemical herbicide and vaginal mesh. Four of those cases (Vioxx, pacemaker, oysters and canola class actions) were also appealed to the Full Federal Court, and special leave to appeal to the High Court was given in two of them (oysters and canola; special leave was refused in the Vioxx and the pacemaker class actions).[115]

The increased cost, complexity and delay in the resolution of product liability claims creates process and liability risks that may reduce the perceived attractiveness of these types of class actions for commercial litigation funders. These risks may be compounded in product liability claims involving personal injury damages, and in this regard it is noted that the most established Australian litigation funder, IMF Bentham Ltd has publicly stated that its investment protocols do not favour class actions for personal injury compensation.[116] This may be contrasted to the funding structures utilised in other types of class actions, particularly shareholder claims, where the main source of funding has come from commercial funders.[117]

But commercial litigation funders did more recently add product liability claims to their portfolios of class actions, starting with two of the diesel emissions class actions, which were filed in October 2015. They were followed by funding of the Ford, shattercane, airbags and cladding products class actions and, most recently, the Toyota class action. Notably, none of these claims involve personal injury damages claims.

Notwithstanding this recent development, plaintiff law firms acting pursuant to conditional/no win no fee agreements was the main source of funding for product liability class actions over the review period. Under these agreements costs are calculated by traditional time based-billings. When we consider the complexity and cost of conducting product liability class actions, many plaintiff firms would have neither the resources nor the fortitude to assume that burden and risk.[118] It is therefore not surprising that forty-one or 52.5 per cent of the seventy-eight product liability class actions saw the involvement of either Maurice Blackburn or Slater & Gordon, the two largest plaintiff class action firms. In none of these forty-one class actions did these two firms have the financial backing of funders.

In its final report regarding class actions and litigation funding published in December 2018, the ALRC recommended that the current ban on the charging of contingency fees (calculated as a percentage of damages)[119] be lifted for solicitors acting on behalf of lead plaintiffs in class action proceedings.[120] In making this recommendation, the ALRC has acknowledged the role that

115 Citations for the Vioxx and pacemaker judgments at first instance and on appeal are in footnotes 31 and 35–9; the judgments in the Wallis Lake oysters class action at first instance, in the Full Court and the High Court are *Ryan* v. *Great Lakes Council* [1999] FCA 177, *Graham Barclay Oysters Pty Ltd* v. *Ryan* [2000] FCA 1099 and *Graham Barclay Oysters Pty Ltd* v. *Ryan* (2002) 211 CLR 540; the judgment of the High Court in the canola seeds class action is *Dovuro Pty Ltd* v. *Wilkins* (2003) 215 CLR 317.

116 J. Walker, S. Khouri and W. Attrill, *Funding Criteria for Class Actions*, 32 UNSW Law Journal. 1036, 1047–9 (2009).

117 V. Morabito, *An Empirical Study of Australia's Class Action Regimes: Fourth Report: Facts and Figures on Twenty-Four Years of Class Actions in Australia* (Australian Research Council, August 2016) 8–9. See generally V. Morabito and V. Waye, *Seeing Past the US Bogey – Lessons from Australia on the Funding of Class Actions*, 36 Civil Justice Quarterly. 21 (2017).

118 For example, as noted above at Section 20.3.2, the class action relating to Roaccutane (medication for the treatment of acne) was discontinued by the class representative on the basis that their solicitors did not have the resources to conduct a large-scale class action proceeding.

119 In the UK this type of fee arrangement is known as a 'damages-based agreement' or DBA. Contingency fees are contrasted with existing conditional fee ('no win no fee') arrangements that are currently permitted in Australia where costs are calculated by traditional time-based billing methods.

120 See Final Report regarding Integrity, Fairness and Efficiency-An Inquiry into Class Action Proceedings and Third-Party Litigation Funders, published December 2018, [7.75].

contingency-based fee arrangements may play in expanding access to justice and reducing the overall costs paid by class members.[121]

The Justice Legislation Miscellaneous Amendment Bill 2019 (Vic), which came into operation in June 2020, will allow plaintiff lawyers running class actions in the Supreme Court of Victoria to receive a percentage, determined by the Court, of any settlement proceeds or damages recovered in the proceedings. Under this new regime, lawyers acting on behalf of the class will be required to indemnify the lead plaintiff for any adverse costs orders and security for costs orders. In the event of a victory, all class members will be required to share liability for the legal costs and disbursements incurred.

It is unclear what impact this type of funding arrangement may have on product liability class actions in Australia. However, given the historical reticence of third-party funders to provide funding for product liability claims, it is certainly possible that contingency fee arrangements may open up further avenues for legal redress, particularly in relation to product liability claims that are considered unsuitable for commercial funding, or in cases where existing conditional fee arrangements are not used because, for example, the spectre of an adverse costs order dissuades potential claimants from assuming the role of lead applicant.[122]

20.5 OUTCOMES OF PRODUCT LIABILITY CLASS ACTIONS

20.5.1 *Resolution and Duration of Product Liability Class Actions*

Table 20.2 reveals the outcomes of those product liability class actions that were resolved at the time of writing.

In Table 20.3 we compare the settlement rates in, and the average duration of settled, product liability class actions with corresponding data for the other most common types of class actions.

As far as length of class actions is concerned, the fact that, on average, it takes three years to secure a settlement in product liability claims is not surprising. Table 20.3 suggests that the settlement rate of product liability class actions compares adequately when considered alongside other types of Australian class actions. In fact, the settlement outcomes of product liability class actions can be said to be *more* successful than other class actions given that all but two of the settled product liability class actions were unfunded and that most of them were filed in the Federal Court. Our empirical data in fact reveals that, to date, all *resolved unfunded federal* class actions have a settlement rate of only 42.8 per cent whilst 72.5 per cent of all resolved funded federal class actions were settled. The settlement rate of 60.6 per cent, with respect to all resolved product liability class actions, also compares favourably with the settlement rate of 53.5 per cent (for all resolved class actions) and the settlement rate of 47.5 per cent for *all resolved unfunded* class actions.

The data in the Table 20.4 is even more illuminating to the extent that it reveals that class actions with respect to pharmaceutical products and medical devices, on average, last longer than the four other most common types of class actions and have higher settlement rates than other types of product liability class actions.

121 *Id.*

122 With limited exceptions, also note that the lead applicant currently bears sole responsibility for adverse costs in a class action, and that class members may not be ordered to pay adverse costs in the event that the class action is unsuccessful: see s. 43(1A) of the Federal Court of Australia Act 1976 (Cth) and equivalent provisions in the state regimes. Last, note that the conventional funding structure used by third party funders includes indemnification of the lead applicant for any adverse costs order.

TABLE 20.2 *Resolution of product liability class actions filed during the review period*

How product liability class actions were ultimately resolved	Number of product liability class actions	Percentage of all resolved product liability class actions
Proceeding settled pursuant to a judicially-approved settlement agreement	37	60.6%
Proceeding discontinued by the class representative	10	16.3%
Proceeding discontinued, as a class action, by the Court	4	6.5%
Proceeding summarily dismissed (for reasons not including want of prosecution or lack of jurisdiction)	3	4.9%
Proceeding discontinued, as a class action, by the class representative	2	3.2%
Post-trial ruling unfavourable to the class representative and the class	2	3.2%
Proceeding transferred to another jurisdiction	2	3.2%
Post-trial ruling favourable to the class representative and the class	1	1.6%

TABLE 20.3 *Average duration and settlement rates of most common class actions filed during the review period*

Category of most common class actions	Settlement rates	Average duration of settled class actions
Claims by investors other than shareholders	71.9%	1,118 days
Mass tort claims	65.3%	1,019 days
Claims by employees	62.9%	224 days
Product liability	60.6%	1,175 days
Claims by shareholders	54.8%	980 days

The extended duration of motorised transport and related products, pharmaceutical and medical device class actions may be explained by a combination of the complexity of issues involved and therefore often the need for extensive expert evidence[123] as well as the relatively high settlement rates of these class actions compared to other categories of product liability class actions. In other words, a defendant may be more willing to test the plaintiff's capacity and resolve in the face of considerable complexity, but once these hurdles have been navigated these cases tend to deliver tangible results for class members.

[123] In contrast, for example, to food poisoning cases involving gastrointestinal complaints; see generally Section 20.3.3.

TABLE 20.4 *Average duration and settlement rates of product liability class actions filed during the review period*

Category of product liability class actions	Settlement rates	Duration of settled class actions
Food and drinks (n = 16)	76%	867 days
Pharmaceutical products (n = 7)	70%	1,167 days
Motorised transport and related products (n = 7)	63.6%	1,410 days
Medical devices (n = 6)	60%	1,230 days
Agricultural and animal products (n = 1)	14%	809 days
Tobacco (n = 0)	0%	-
Building and industrial products (n = 0)	None resolved yet	All ongoing

Another striking feature of the empirical data reported in the above table is that two of the three highest settlement rates relate to categories of product liability class actions that sought compensation for personal injuries. While other categories of product liability class actions (that is, those not involving personal injury claims) have experienced mixed outcomes and success rates, a significant majority (66 per cent) of product liability class actions with personal injury claims were settled for the benefit of class members. In fact, in the era since the introduction of tort reform in 2004, 100 per cent of product liability class actions claiming personal injury compensation have been successfully resolved in favour of class members. These results tend to suggest that plaintiff lawyers have taken a careful and judicious approach to case selection, commencing only those claims with strong liability prospects and, since the early 2000s, the ability to meet the requirements of tort reform discussed in Section 20.4.1 above.

This subspecies of product liability class actions can therefore be counted as one of the most successful among all categories of class actions. This suggests that Australia's class action regimes are operating successfully in providing access to real justice to those who suffer serious physical or mental injuries from their use of defective products. These outcomes also challenge the conventional wisdom that class actions involving personal injury claims attract increased process and liability risks, which as noted above is one of the reasons why litigation funders have shied away from funding these types of claims.

20.5.2 *Compensation Received by Class Members*

In Table 20.5 we present our empirical data with respect to: (1) the settlement proceeds *actually received* by class members; (2) the total number of claimants who have received a share of settlement proceeds and (3) average payments received by individual class members. All this data will be divided into the various categories of product liability class actions where there have been settlements.

This data does not cover all settled product liability class actions given that confidentiality orders[124] prevented the public release of this data with respect to several settlement schemes whilst details with respect to payments made under several process settlement schemes (see Section 20.5.3 below) were not available.

124 For a recent empirical study of the secrecy surrounding a majority of federal class action settlements, see V. Morabito, *Looking into the Fishbowl – Open Justice and Federal Class Action Settlements*, 93 Australian Law Journal. 446 (2019).

TABLE 20.5 *Average compensation paid to class members in product liability class actions filed during the review period*

Category of product liability class actions and total number of recipients	Settlement proceeds received by class members	Average individual compensation to class members
Medical devices (3,225)	$179,007,204	$55,506
Pharmaceutical products (1,868)	$90,100,889	$48,233
Food and drinks (6,246)	$39,546,217	$6,331
Agricultural and animal products (34)	$11,000,000	$323,529
TOTAL (11,373)	$319,654,310	$28,106
Plus *McMullin* (11,755)	$419,654,310	$35,700

The settlement proceeds captured below will be higher still if one takes into account the private settlements reached between defendants and class members or other payments made by defendants for the benefit of class members,[125] although empirical evidence of the quantum of these payments in all product liability class actions is frequently not available. While these types of payments are not included in the data concerning settlements of product liability class actions, it is reasonable to assume that in many instances class members would not have received the benefit of these settlement payments in the absence of a class action.

The average compensation of $28,106 for over 11,370 claimants in settled product liability class actions may be said to represent a positive outcome. An even brighter scenario emerges when one adds the compensation generated directly by the positive post-trial ruling secured in *McMullin*. The data contained in Table 20.5 reveals even better results secured for personal injury claimants in class actions concerning medical devices and pharmaceutical products which also have relatively high settlement rates. With respect to class actions concerning medical devices, the average settlement proceeds will increase once the distribution of the settlement fund in the hip implants class action is completed.[126] And, as already noted, approximately $120 million will be added to the over $400 million set out in the table above, once the settlement of the diesel emission class actions is finalised. The post-trial victory in one of the vaginal mesh class actions will generate compensation for thousands of women unless the appeal recently filed by the defendants is successful.[127]

125 For example, in the hip implant litigation which settled for $250 million plus interest, at the time that the court approved the settlement in June 2016 the defendants had additionally paid approximately $136 million to class members or to third parties on behalf of class members pursuant to a voluntary reimbursement program: see *Stanford and Another* v. *DePuy International Ltd and Another* [2016] FCA 1452, [135]. Typically, these payments consisted of treatment and other related costs associated with class members having revision surgery. The defendants also additionally have responsibility for the payment of certain categories of healthcare liens pursuant to the court approved settlement scheme.

126 The figure for medical devices (contained in the table above) includes payments of $139 million made to 1,561 class members as at June 2020 in the hip implants settlement – the administration of that settlement is ongoing : see affidavit of Julian Schimmel dated 17 June 2020 filed in Federal Court of Australia, NSD 213/2011. Once this settlement administration is completed, it is expected that a total of around $200 million will have been paid to approximately 1,730 class members: see affidavit of Julian Schimmel dated 14 June 2019 filed in Federal Court of Australia, NSD 213/2011.

127 *Gill* v. *Ethicon Sarl (No 5)* [2019] FCA 1905. Damages awarded to the three lead plaintiffs totaled $2,589,040: *Gill* v. *Ethicon Sarl (No 6)* [2020] FCA 279.

In considering the average individual settlement payments of over $300,000 in agricultural and animal products class actions, it must be borne in mind that only one of the class actions in this category was settled and the number of class members was relatively small.

The average settlement proceeds received by class members in food and drink class actions may be contrasted against the average results achieved by claimants in medical device and pharmaceutical claims. The discrepancy in settlement outcomes logically reflects the differing severity of injuries (and associated losses) suffered by the victims in these types of claims, and the more substantial settlement proceeds received by class members in the Bonsoy class action are an outlier in this category, reflecting the more serious thyroid injuries alleged to have been suffered in that case.

Despite the impressive track record of Australian product liability class actions, the settlement of these types of claims involves unique difficulties that do not arise in the settlement of many other types of class actions. Unlike shareholder class actions, where settlement distributions to class members are generally worked out by a mathematical calculation involving the application of a loss assessment formula to class members' share trade data, in product liability class actions the determination of individual entitlements under a settlement scheme is often considerably more complex, particularly in cases involving personal injury claims due to the significant variability in personal injury damages among individual class members.

In Australia two different frameworks or models have typically been used in settlements of product liability class actions, namely, process settlements and global sum settlements. These two approaches are discussed in further detail at Sections 20.5.3 and 20.5.4 below, with a particular focus on the settlement of product liability class actions involving claims of personal injury.

20.5.3 *Process Settlements*

A process settlement typically establishes a facilitative framework for the parties to conduct a negotiation regarding each class member's claim, and with a dispute resolution mechanism that can be engaged if the parties fail to reach agreement.

One of the features of this type of settlement is that it involves, at least to some degree, an adversarial dimension to the assessment of claims, and this distinguishes process settlements from most other types of class action settlements because the defendant retains a participatory role in the resolution of individual class members' entitlements under the settlement scheme.

Other features that are commonly found in process settlements include the following:

(1) a preliminary determination of whether, having regard to agreed criteria and processes, the class member is eligible to receive compensation from the defendant;
(2) a class member is found eligible, their individual entitlements are assessed according to a specified legal framework, subject to modifications that are sometimes incorporated in order to simplify the assessment process, such as the use of predefined categories of non-economic loss;
(3) procedural elements, including timeframes as well as provisions for the exchange of documents and information, that are designed to promote efficiency and reduce costs;
(4) given the adversarial nature of the process, a dispute resolution process that commonly involves referral to an independent barrister or expert;
(5) referral of legal issues to the Court; and
(6) no cap on the respondent's overall financial exposure.

An example of a process settlement is the class action brought on behalf of patients who had been implanted with the LCS Duofix femoral component, which was used in total knee replacement surgery.[128] That case was settled in 2012 on the basis that individual claims would be assessed according to a 'Liability Protocol' and a 'Compensation Protocol' that were agreed between the plaintiff and defendants.

While the benefit of a process settlement is that each class member's compensation payment reflects their unique circumstances in a manner that is reasonably analogous to the way that their entitlements would be assessed by a court, the process can be considerably more expensive than a non-adversarial process where the aim is simply to work out a fair and appropriate distribution. Also, from a defendant's perspective one of the disadvantages of a process settlement is that overall exposure is uncertain, and for this reason in some cases we have seen defendants pressing for global sum settlements that provide certainty and finality.

20.5.4 *Global Sum Settlements*

Unlike process settlements where the overall settlement sum is uncapped, a global sum settlement involves settlement for a fixed sum that is then distributed among class members after the scheme administrator has assessed their claims according to the procedure set out in the settlement distribution scheme. In a global sum settlement the defendant plays little or no part in the assessment of claims and the assessment process is therefore non-adversarial, with the scheme administrator (who is usually but not necessarily the lawyer for the lead plaintiff) ceasing to act for individual class members and instead adopting the role of court-appointed administrator of the scheme whose role it is to oversee the division and distribution of the global sum in a fair and appropriate manner and in light of the non-adversarial process for assessing individual claims pursuant to the settlement distribution scheme.

While global sum settlements might be attractive to defendants because they provide certainty, from the perspective of class members this type of settlement introduces a measure of uncertainty in terms of the adequacy of the settlement sum to fairly compensate all eligible class members. This uncertainty arises from the variability of individual injuries and the fact that in most cases the aggregate value of all class members' claims will not be known at the time that the parties agree to settle.

Negotiation of global sum settlements can be difficult because plaintiff and defendant lawyers will often have wildly divergent perspectives on the value of individual claims and also on the 'profile' of claims within the class as a whole. Plaintiff lawyers try to grapple with this uncertainty and risk by using a variety of strategies to estimate overall quantum, including loss sampling exercises, the distribution of questionnaires and the engagement of actuarial experts to model the loss suffered by the class as a whole. Despite such approaches, injuries claims can be very heterogeneous and therefore a degree of risk might still subsist despite the use of these methods.

The variability of individual injuries and unknown total loss also means that settlement schemes will need to incorporate a mechanism for proportionately adjusting each class member's claim depending on whether the aggregate of all claims is ultimately greater than or less than the sum that is available for distribution. While a degree of adjustment is almost inevitable given the common uncertainty regarding the aggregate claim size, it is also important to note that all class action

[128] *Casey* v. *DePuy International Ltd (No 2)* [2012] FCA 1370.

settlements must be approved by a court as being fair and reasonable and in the interests of class members.[129]

20.5.5 *Alternative Approaches to Settlement Distribution*

In weighing up the alternative approaches to settlement distribution for Australian class actions, commentators have emphasised the need for courts and legal practitioners to strike an appropriate balance between fairness (which includes precision in the assessment of compensation pursuant to the law) and efficiency in the circumstances of each case.[130] This is no easy task. As discussed in Section 20.5.3 above, while process-based settlements may provide a more accurate assessment of individual class members' entitlements, the involvement of a defendant and adversarial nature of the process can ultimately delay the finalisation claims and lead to an increase in legal costs. Conversely, although global sum settlements may present a quicker and more efficient alternative to settlement distribution, there may be less scope for perfection in the assessment of individual class members' entitlements. Global sum settlements also have the added complexity of needing to ensure that the overall quantum of the class is appropriately covered by any agreed settlement sum.

In attempting to balance considerations of efficiency and cost, accuracy and substantive fairness as well as procedural fairness, plaintiff lawyers have started to consider alternative approaches to settlement distributions for product liability class actions. An example of this is the hip implant class action which settled in 2016 for $250 million.[131] In that case, eligible class members were given a choice as to how their compensation entitlements could be determined. On the one hand, class members could elect to undergo a conventional form of individual assessment within the framework of the global sum settlement in which case claims were assessed according to a specified legal framework and the non-adversarial procedures set out in the settlement distribution scheme.

Alternatively, eligible class members were able to take advantage of a novel feature that was introduced into the settlement scheme. Instead of undergoing individual assessment, class members could elect to receive a 'Fast Track Resolution', which was a single, standardised, lump sum payment of $55,000 that covered all heads of damages, although it expressly made no allowance for economic loss. The Fast Track Resolution payments were made available on an expedited basis. Unlike the 'grid settlements' that are commonly used in resolving class actions or MDL claims in US jurisdictions (where a baseline amount is adjusted by a range of factors such as the age of the claimant or the duration of using the product until the onset of the compensable injury) the Fast Track Resolution was simply a uniform standardised amount.[132]

One of the critical features of the Fast Track Resolution is that it is entirely optional. In conventional litigation, an individual plaintiff can of course decide to compromise their claim in whatever way they choose and for whatever reason they choose. Experience suggests that plaintiffs can be motivated to accept a settlement that is less than their legal compensation entitlements in order to minimise delay and/or avoid an invasive or confronting examination of

[129] See for example: s. 33V(1) of the Federal Court of Australia Act 1976 (Cth).

[130] R. Gilsenan and M. Legg, *Australian Class Action Settlement Distribution Scheme Design – Deciding Who Gets What*, 38 University of Queensland Law Journal. 15, 16 and 39 (2019). See also M. Legg, *Class action settlement distribution in Australia: Compensation on the merits or rough justice?* 16 Macquarie Law Journal. 89 (2016).

[131] *Stanford and Another* v. *DePuy International Ltd and Johnson & Johnson Medical Pty Ltd (No 6)* [2016] FCA 1452.

[132] The settlement distribution scheme also contained an adjustment mechanism in which those who elected the Fast Track Resolution were immune from any downward adjustment in the event that the sum of all class members' compensation payments is greater than the total sum available for distribution, while also being entitled to share the benefit of any surplus with class members whose claims were individually assessed.

their personal and health circumstances; in other words, compromise may also be influenced by considerations other than the potential recovery scenarios and clearly identifiable risks of success or failure.

In class actions the court exercises a protective function in order to safeguard the rights and interests of class members who do not have a direct 'voice at the bar table'[133] especially in the decision to settle a class action. In considering an application for approval of a settlement, it stands to reason that the court will generally evaluate the fairness and reasonableness of the proposed settlement in light of (among other things) the legal claims made on behalf of class members and risks associated with their claims. On the other hand, as Justice Mortimer of the Federal Court recognised in the course of approving a settlement, '[f]airness and reasonableness are moderate standards, rather than ones which require absolute certainty or confidence in a particular point of view about legal issues, if there can ever be such certainty in the law in any event'.[134]

As Wigney J recognised in approving the hip implant class action settlement, class members would have an absolute discretion in deciding whether to accept the Fast Track Resolution, which would avoid the need for an assessment process, result in faster payment, and might suit class members who had not suffered significant loss or damage, or who might simply prefer an expedited payment over being involved in what they may regard as a time consuming and invasive assessment.[135]

In this sense, the Fast Track Resolution is empowering because class members can make a choice based on what they feel is in their best interests. Assuming that the Fast Track Resolution is calibrated by reference to the range of damages that might otherwise be considered to be appropriate in light of the spectrum of injuries of those who might be inclined to elect this option,[136] a class member's willingness to accept and receive the specified amount might also be influenced by other, non-monetary factors, such as the desire for finality and closure in respect of a legal claim.

The significantly and unexpectedly high take up rate of the Fast Track Resolution (81 per cent of all eligible class members)[137] tends to suggest that a large proportion of class members preferred prompt payment and/or a less invasive process over the accuracy of their damages assessment and/or maximisation of their monetary benefit from the settlement. Caution may be needed, however, before assuming that class members in other cases would take the same collective approach.

20.6 CONCLUSION

There seems little doubt that over the last twenty-seven years class actions have become an accepted and mainstream legal procedure, and claims arising from the harmful consequences of consumer and other products have been a prominent feature of the landscape.

[133] To borrow a phrase from Jessup J in *Darwalla Milling Co Pty Ltd* v. *F Hoffman-Law Roche Ltd [No 2]* (2006) 236 ALR 322, [66].

[134] *McAlister* v. *New South Wales (No 2)* [2017] FCA 93, [32].

[135] *Stanford and Another* v. *DePuy International Ltd and Johnson & Johnson Medical Pty Ltd (No 6)* [2016] FCA 1452, [110] and [141].

[136] And if necessary also taking into account the relative merits of the claims of different class members.

[137] Affidavit of Julian Schimmel dated 14 June 2019 and filed in Federal Court of Australia, proceeding NSD 213/2011. The election rate of 81 per cent is reported after the claims of more than 86 per cent of the estimated total number of eligible class members had been assessed and paid.

Claimants in product liability class actions have faced a number of challenges including the introduction of tort reform, vigorous interlocutory battles focused on the utility of the class actions regime, the complexity of proceedings and an associated high cost that has largely been funded by plaintiff law firms. While some of these challenges appear to have led to an overall decline in the number of product liability class actions filed in more recent years, the success of Australia's class action regimes in delivering outcomes for those who have suffered injury or loss as a result of their use of faulty products should not be underestimated. Real redress has been achieved for claimants in many and varied cases, and in this regard the categories of product liability class actions involving personal injury claims (generally medical devices, pharmaceutical products and historically also food and drink related claims) have been particularly successful.

There is a broad consensus that product liability claims will continue to feature in class actions practice.[138] In the future we are likely to continue to see a measured and judicious use of the class action regime in attempts to realise justice for people who claim to have been harmed by faulty products.

138 For the defendant lawyer perspective, see S. Clark and C. Harris, *The past, present and future of product liability and other mass tort actions in Australia*, 32 UNSW Law Journal. 1022, 1035 (2009); J. Campbell and R. Drinnan, *Class actions in Australia*, 25(7) Australian Product Liability Reporter. 94, 94 (2014); P. Stevenson, M. Saville, R. Forbes and B. Hackney, *Hips and PIPs – a future for product liability class actions in Australia?* 22(6) Australian Product Liability Reporter. 230 (2012).

21

Securities Class Actions in Korea

Hai Jin Park and Hyeok-Joon Rho

21.1 INTRODUCTION

Between 2015 and 2017, shareholders of one of the three largest shipbuilding companies in Korea and its former auditing firm sued for 210 billion won (approximately 179 million US dollars[1]) in damages over alleged accounting fraud.[2] A total of 1,152 plaintiffs filed more than 70 joint litigation suits instead of bringing a class action suit,[3] without presumably hundreds of thousands of similarly situated victims joining them. After more than ten years since the introduction of class action in securities law, Koreans still seem reluctant to use the mechanism.

Korea is a civil law country that adopted a US-style class action in securities law in 2004. However, since the Securities-Related Class Action Act (SCAA) went into effect in 2005, only ten securities class action lawsuits have been filed.[4] Compared with the seldom-used class action mechanism, nonclass action suits ("securities nonclass action suits") are much more frequently used for seeking compensation for damages arising out of violation of the Financial Investment Services and Capital Markets Act (the Capital Markets Act).[5]

Despite the reluctance of plaintiffs' lawyers to use the tool of class action, public opinion calling for expanding the securities class action regime to include other law areas has been reinforced by a series of scandals that affected multitudes of Korean customers.[6] The

1 According to the exchange rate as of Jul. 5, 2019.

2 Saeha Lee, *GeoRaeJaeGae AbDun DaewooChoSeon … BunShikHoeGye SonBaeSoMan 2100Eok [Daewoo Shipbuilding and Marine Engineering, co., Ltd. ("DSME"), About to Resume Trading … Sued for KRW 210M in Damages for Booking Fraud]*, ETODAY, Oct. 13, 2017, available at www.etoday.co.kr/news/section/newsview.php?idxno=1548581; Eunbi Park, *DaewooChoSeon BunShikHoeGye GongBang – PiHaeJuJu 1152 Myeong, MinSaSoSong JinHaeng Jung [DSME's fraudulent booking dispute—1152 shareholders pursue civil lawsuits]*, ETODAY, Jan. 19, 2017, available at www.etoday.co.kr/news/section/newsview.php?idxno=1444034#csidx7d6dd26c08d964a92d51bc1ba23cee9.

3 Saeha Lee, *id.*

4 *See* Table 21.1.

5 For this chapter, we will use the term "securities nonclass action suits" to describe damage suits of which causes of action are based on the violation of the Capital Markets Act.

6 Yumi Lee, *SoBiJa DanChe "SoBiJa PiHae GuJe WiHae JibDanSoSongJe Dolb HaeYa" [Consumer Organizations "Need to Introduce Class Action to Remedy Harms to Consumers"]*, Yeonhap News, Sep. 17, 2018, available at www.yna.co.kr/view/AKR20180917067400030?input=1195m (reporting that Korean consumer NGOs called for introduction of consumer class actions in the wake of humidifier disinfectant scandal, Volkswagen emissions scandal, major data breach cases, etc.).

current administration prepared a bill transforming the SCAA into a single general class action law.[7] According to the pending bill, class actions can be brought for product liability claims, data breach claims, and various kinds of antitrust claims seeking damages.[8]

The next section will describe how the US-style class action in securities law was introduced in Korea and how it differs from US class action law. The following section will analyze the reason for the reluctance of plaintiffs' lawyers to bring securities class actions in comparison with securities nonclass action suits. Finally, a summary of the pending bill and suggestions for further reforms will be followed by closing remarks.

21.2 AN OVERVIEW OF SECURITIES CLASS ACTION IN KOREA

21.2.1 *History of Adoption*

The motivation to adopt US-style class action in Korea stemmed both from inside and outside the country. The first serious effort to introduce class action in Korea arose in 1990 when the Ministry of Justice created a special committee to draft a class action bill. This bill, however, was never passed because of fears about potential abuse of class actions.[9] The subsequent big push arose from outside the country. In 1997, during the midst of the Asian economic crisis, the International Bank of Reconstruction and Development (IBRD) and the International Monetary Fund (IMF) recommended introducing class action as a condition of a bailout. They believed this would improve and promote transparency in corporate governance systems.[10] Afterward, a class action bill concerning securities law was introduced in the National Assembly in 1998. However, it stalled because of intense opposition from the business community.[11] The Korean Bar Association and a nongovernmental organization (NGO)'s efforts in the early 2000s provided the final momentum that ultimately enabled the bill's passage.[12] The SCAA was enacted in 2004 and went into effect in 2005.

21.2.2 *Features of the Class Action Procedure*

The SCAA introduced an "opt-out" class action[13] in securities law, generally modeled on Rule 23 of the US Federal Rule of Civil Procedures (FRCP). The law also incorporated various measures

7 Heejun Noh, *Park SangGi JangGwan "JibDanSoSong, SilJe JakDongHal Su ItGe DoIbDoeYa" [Minister Park, "We need to introduce class action that can actually work"]*, E-daily, Dec. 13, 2018, available at www.edaily.co.kr/news/read?newsId=03089766619438192&mediaCodeNo=257&OutLnkChk=Y (reporting that the Ministry of Justice submitted a bill expanding class action system through a member of the National Assembly, Jongmin Kim in September).

8 JeungGwonGwanRyeon JibDanSoSongBeob IlBuGaeJeongBeobRyulAn (UiAnBeonHo 2015727) [Bill of Partial Amendment to the Securities-Related Class Action Act (Bill No. 2015727)] ("Bill"), GukHoeUiAnJeongBoSystem [National Assembly Bill Information System], available at http://likms.assembly.go.kr/bill/billDetail.do?billId=PRC_P1L8T0Y9D2Q1A1B5M2Y8S2J8Z0X4G3.

9 Hyuk Jae Kwon, *HanGukESeoUi JipDanSoSongJeDoUi DoIpGwaJeon Mit UnYeongHyeonHwang [The Induction Process and Present Application of Class Action in Korea]*, 28 BEOBHAKNONCHONG 415, 417 (2008).

10 *Id.*

11 *Id.*

12 Jung-Sik Choi, *JeungGwonJipDanSoSongJeDoUi HwalSeongHwaReul WiHan JeAn [Proposal for the Invigoration of Securities Class Action System]*, 53 BUPHAKYEONGU 311, 319 (2014). Korean Bar Association held a conference on the need of enacting a class action law in November 2000 and People's Solidarity prepared a class action bill adopting a US-style class action in October 2000. Kwon, *supra* note 9; Youngjoo Ham, JEUNGGWONGWANRYEONJIPDANSOSONGJEUI HWALSEONGHWA BANGANE DAEHAN YEONGU [A STUDY ON WAYS TO INVIGORATE SECURITIES-RELATED CLASS ACTION], 42 (2013).

13 Article 37 of the SCAA ("A final and conclusive judgment shall be binding on the class members who fail to give an opt-out notice.").

against frivolous lawsuits included in the Private Securities Litigation Reform Act of 1995 and the Securities Litigation Uniform Standards Act of 1998.[14] Responding to the demands of the business circle,[15] the SCAA additionally adopted even more stringent measures than US class action law to thwart frivolous lawsuits.[16]

21.2.2.1 Plaintiffs and Plaintiffs' Attorneys

A securities class action can be filed by any person who is to become the representative plaintiff (Article 7(1)). The representative plaintiff who obtains court permission may conduct litigation on behalf of the class members. The representative plaintiff must be able to represent the interest of the class in a fair and appropriate manner, such as the person who is likely to obtain the most significant economic benefit from the class action suit among the class members (Article 11(1)).

In addition to the requirement for representative plaintiffs, the SCAA imposes so-called size and stake minimums for the class members,[17] requiring at least fifty class members holding as a minimum 1/10,000 of the total number of the outstanding securities of the defendant corporation at the time of conduct on which the claim is based.[18] This provision was included in the bill at the last minute, reflecting the opinions of business communities.[19] There is no such requirement for class members in the United States except that FRCP Rule 23(a)(1) provides that "the class is so numerous that joinder of all members is impracticable."[20]

Furthermore, a representative plaintiff or a plaintiffs' attorney cannot be involved in class actions under the SCAA more than three times in three consecutive years unless the court finds that, considering the circumstances, this plaintiff or attorney can represent the interests of the class fairly and appropriately.[21] This limitation on representative plaintiffs and attorneys was added to prevent the abuse of class actions by professional plaintiffs[22] and by specialized lawyers in class actions.[23] In contrast, the United States does not place a limit on the lawyer and only limits the number of times the lead plaintiff can play the role in a less restrictive manner – up to five times within three consecutive years – in securities class actions.[24]

14 Seok Hoon Han, *JeungGwonJipDanSoSongUi NamSoBangJiDaeChaek [On the Measures to Prevent Abusive Securities Class Actions]*, 12 MinSaBeobYeonGu 89, 91 (2004); Sheron Korpus, *Is Korea's Securities Class Action Law Working?*, 25 Int'l Fin. L. Rev. 53, 53 (2006).

15 Dong Yoon Jeong, *JeungGwonGwanRyun JipDanSoSongJeDoUi GaeYo [Overview of Securities-Related Class Actions]*, 2nd ChungJeong BeobRyul Forum, Oct. 26, 2007, at 3. According to the survey conducted on directors and officers by the Korea Listed Companies Association in January 2005, the biggest worries related to implementing the SCAA concerned frivolous lawsuits (68.8 percent). Hye-Jin Gwon & Nam-Joo Lee, *JeungGwonJipDanSoSongBeobUi SiJangBanEungE DaeHan YeonGu [Research on Market Response of Class-Action Securities Litigation Act of Korea]*, 13 Kor. J. Acc. Res. 79, 84 (2008).

16 Han, *supra* note 14, at 91.

17 *Id.*

18 Article 12 of the SCAA.

19 Ham, *supra* note 12, at 154.

20 Korpus, *supra* note 14, at 54.

21 Article 11 of the SCAA.

22 Deok-Jo Jang & Gi-Ho Kim, *JeungGwonGwanRyeonJipDanSoSongBeobAnUi GeomTo [The Problems in Securities Class Action Bill]*, 24 MinJuBeobHak 369, 376 (2003).

23 Han Jong Kim, *JeungGwonJibDanSoSongUi HwalSeongHwa BangAnE DaeHan YeonGu [A Study on the Revitalization of Securities Class Action]*, 10 HongIkBeobHak 389, 398 (2009).

24 15 U.S.C. §78u–4 (a)(3)(B)(vi).

21.2.2.2 Causes of Action and Remedies

The SCAA allows class actions only for certain types of causes of action to reduce frivolous lawsuits,[25] unlike Rule 23 of the FRCP in the United States, which does not limit causes of action. The enumerated causes of action include the following: (1) false description or representation of a material statement in a registration statement or an investment prospectus (Article 125 of the Capital Markets Act); (2) false description or representation of a material fact in a business report, half-yearly report, quarterly report, or material fact report under Article 159(1) of the Capital Markets Act or a document attached thereto (excluding audit reports prepared by an accounting auditor), or due to an omission of a description or representation of a material fact therein (Article 162 of the Capital Markets Act); (3) insider trading (Article 175 of the Capital Markets Act); (4) market price manipulation (Article 177 of the Capital Markets Act); (5) fraudulent trading (Article 179 of the Capital Markets Act); and (6) auditor's liability (Article 170 of the Capital Markets Act).[26] Article 179 of the Capital Markets Act is comparable to the Securities and Exchange Commission's Rule 10b-5 cause of action in the United States.[27]

Under the SCAA, a class action is allowed only for damage claims. The SCAA defines "securities-related class action" as an action for damages filed by one or more representative parties when any damages are incurred by many persons in the course of the trade or other transactions of securities.[28]

21.2.2.3 Certification Procedure

Anyone who is to serve as a representative plaintiff in the class action should file an application for certification along with a complaint. The following requirements should be met for the case to proceed as a class action: (1) the size and stake minimums must meet what is outlined above; (2) there should be a material legal or factual issue for a claim that is common to all class members; (3) a class action should be appropriate and efficient means to realize the rights of the class members or protect their interests; and (4) no defects on the application or its accompanying documents are permitted.[29]

An "immediate appeal" is allowed for the certification decision both to allow and to deny class action,[30] and the appeal automatically stays the main proceeding until the appeal is finalized, sometimes after reaching the Supreme Court of Korea. The draft bill the Ministry of Justice prepared in 1996 and the 1998 bill of Securities-Related Class Action Act allowed an appeal only to the denial, not the granting, of certification. However, the 2004 final version of the bill allowed an immediate appeal both to the denial and the granting of certification.

Automatically staying the main proceeding until the finalization of the certification decision in effect turns the class action lawsuit into six instances, which includes three instances for the class certification procedure and three instances for the main proceeding.[31] The US federal

25 Kim, *supra* note 23, at 400.

26 Article 3 of the SCAA.

27 Jae-Yeon Lim, JaBonSiJangBeobGwa BulGongJeongGeoRae [Capital Market Act and Unfair Trade] 541 (2014).

28 Article 2(1) of the SCAA. The definition of "class action" remains limited as litigation seeking damages in the pending bill. *See* Bill, *supra* note 8.

29 Article 12(1) of the SCAA.

30 Article 15, 17 of the SCAA.

31 Yeongjoon Jeon, *JeungGwonGwanRyeonJipDanSoSong HeoGaJeolCha GaeSeonBangAn – HeoGaGyeolJeongE DaeHan JeukSiHangGoJeDoUi GaeSeonEul JungSimEuRo [Ways to Improve Certification Procedure in Securities-Related Class Action]*, 5 GyeongJeGaeHyukYeonGu 1, 4 (2016); Article 447 of the KCPA ("an immediate appeal shall suspend the execution of the rulings").

rule[32] allows an appeal to the class certification by leave of the court but does not stay proceedings in the district court.[33]

21.2.2.4 Opt-Out Class Action

A class action allows dispersed victims with relatively small damages to seek remedies without taking on the considerable transaction costs coordination entails.[34] The class action allows for an effective means of joining a large number of plaintiffs, thus achieving the economies of scale[35] while eliminating the free-rider problem.[36] However, it is not the sole tool used to consolidate claims on behalf of similarly situated victims.

In Korea, in addition to class actions, securities nonclass action suits can be brought collectively using two existing avenues: joint litigation (*GongDongSoSong*) and appointed party action (*SeonJeongDangSaJaSoSong*).[37] Both joint litigation and appointed party action require all the plaintiffs or appointers to explicitly join the litigation. The court decision given in such cases only binds those who expressly "opted in" when filing the complaint. In contrast, the Korean version of securities class action is an "opt-out" class action. Class members who do not wish to be subject to the res judicata effect of the decision must file a written opt-out notice to a court within a certain period after certification.[38] All other class members who fail to do so will be subject to the res judicata effect of the court decision, whether or not they actually knew about or actively participated in the litigation.[39]

21.3 UNDERUSE OF SECURITIES CLASS ACTION IN KOREA

In a recent study, Park explored the reason the securities class action is seldom used in Korea, combining interviews with plaintiffs' lawyers and plaintiffs and content analysis of court

32 *Id.*, at 6.

33 FRCP Rule 23 (f) (prescribing that "an appeal does not stay proceedings in the district court unless the district judge or the court of appeals so orders.").

34 John C. Coffee Jr., *Understanding the Plaintiffs' Attorney: The Implications of Economic Theory for Private Enforcement of Law Through Class and Derivative Actions*, 86 COLUM. L. REV. 669, 679 (1987).

35 *See* Arthur R. Miller, *Of Frankenstein Monsters and Shining Knights: Myth, Reality, and the "Class Action Problem,"* 2 Harv. L. Rev. 664, 670–676 (1979) (highlighting the social benefit of enabling small claim adjudication). *See also*, Jonathan R. Macey & Geoffrey P. Miller, *The Plaintiff's Attorney's Role in Class Action and Derivative Litigation: Economic Analysis and Recommendations for Reform*, 58 U. CH. L. REV. 1, 8 (1991). Of course, class action is not without controversy. Although whether social welfare would benefit by promoting greater use of class action is an important question, it is outside the scope of this paper.

36 MANCUR OLSEN, THE LOGIC OF COLLECTIVE ACTION, 1–2 (1965). *See*, Coffee, *supra* note 34, at 679 (noting that litigation is a form of "public good," where a classic free-riding problem would arise, because the result of an action may benefit those who don't have to share the litigation costs).

37 Joint litigation is allowed when the right or obligation at issue in the litigation is shared by many parties or originates from a factually or legally common cause. Article 65 of the Korean Civil Procedure Act ("KCPA"). Each case, however, remains conceived of as separate and independent, and multiple plaintiffs in joint litigation do *not* necessarily share the outcome. Multiple parties whose common interests allow them to bring joint litigation may also choose to bring an appointed party action wherein potential plaintiffs appoint a party ("appointed party") amongst them to represent them. Article 53 of the KCPA. These mechanisms also promote judicial efficiency to a certain extent by consolidating related claims sharing common issues. SI-YOON LEE, NEW CIVIL PROCEDURE ACT, PARKYOUNGSA, 641 (2009).

38 Article 28(1) of the SCAA.

39 Therefore, the number of victims that receive the effect of res judicata will greatly differ for opt-out class actions from opt-in nonclass actions. Especially for dispersed victims with small claims, many would lack economic and psychological incentives to explicitly opt in (in joint litigation or appointed party action) or opt out (in class action). In this case, opt-out class action would result in many more victims benefiting from successful litigation.

decisions on securities class actions and nonclass action suits.[40] This section summarizes the study's results.

21.3.1 *The Landscape of Securities Class Action Suits and Nonclass Action Suits in Korea*

Overall, securities nonclass action suits are more frequently used than are securities class action suits. Since the SCAA went into effect in 2005, as of January 31, 2018, only ten securities class action cases have been filed (see Table 21.1 below).[41] Less than one filing of securities class action

TABLE 21.1 *Overview of class action suits*[42]

No.	Court and Case No.	Date of Filing	Plaintiff	Plaintiffs' law firm	Defendant	Status
1	Suwon District Court (2009 GaHap 8829)	Apr. 13, 2009	Yoon Bae Park, Seoul Investment Club Co., Ltd.	INS	Jinsung TEC Co., Ltd.,	Settled (Apr. 30, 2010)
2-1	Seoul Central District Court (2010 GaHap 1604)	Jan. 7, 2010	Il-Nam Yang, Young-Mi Choi	Hannuri	Royal Bank of Canada	Settled (Feb. 15, 2017)
3	Seoul Southern District Court (2011 GaHap 19387)	Oct. 13, 2011	Jae Hyung Lee et al.	Hannuri	DB Financial Investment Co., Ltd.	Certified (Nov. 29, 2016) and pending (3rd instance)
2-2	Seoul Southern District Court (2011 GaHap 23003)	Nov. 15, 2011	Il-Nam Yang, Young-Mi Choi	Hannuri	Hanwha Securities Co., Ltd.	Transferred[43] and certification denied[44]

[40] Hai Jin Park, *Class Action Scarcity: An Empirical Analysis of the Securities Class Action in Korea*, 21 Eur. Bus. Org. L. Rev. 665 (2020). This is the first empirical research that investigated plaintiffs' lawyers' reluctance to use the class action mechanism and described the landscape of securities class action suits and securities nonclass action suits in Korea.

[41] Initially, thirteen securities class action were filed in court, but three cases among them were consolidated with other cases sharing the same facts, leaving only ten cases. *See* row no. 4, 8, and 9 in Table 21.1. The plaintiffs' lawyers had to file separate lawsuits for multiple defendants and then petition for consolidation of the cases due to the exclusive venue provision in the SCAA, creating an exclusive venue of the case in a district where the defendant resides (Article 4 of the SCAA).

[42] Park, *supra* note 40, Appendix 2.

[43] This case was transferred to Seoul Central District Court for consolidation with Seoul Central District Court 2010 GaHap 1604 and given a new case no. of 2012 GaHap 509676.

[44] The certification procedure of this case (Seoul Central District Court 2012 KaGi 2082) was consolidated with the certification procedure of Seoul Central District Court 2010 GaHap 1604 (Seoul Central District Court 2010 KaGi 9474). However, the plaintiffs did not appeal the decision denying certification on Hanwha Securities Co., Ltd. but only the decision denying certification on the Royal Bank of Canada (Seoul Central District Court Decision No. 2010 KaGi 9474, 2012 KaGi 2082 (Consolidated), rendered on May 1, 2012). The case against the Royal Bank of Canada was certified and finalized on March 28, 2016 (Seoul Central District Court Decision No. 2015 Ma 2056, 2057, rendered on Mar. 28, 2016).

TABLE 21.1 *(continued)*

No.	Court and Case No.	Date of Filing	Plaintiff	Plaintiffs' law firm	Defendant	Status
4	Seoul Central District Court (2012 GaHap 17061)	Mar. 2, 2012	Sun-Deok Kim et al.	Hannuri	Deutsche Bank AG	Judgment for the plaintiff (finalized on Jul. 7, 2017)
5	Seoul Central District Court (2013 GaHap 74313)	Oct. 8, 2013	Tae-Eung Kim et al.	Hannuri	GS Engineering & Construction Corp.	Certified (Jun. 10, 2016) and Pending (1st instance)
6-1	Seoul Southern District Court (2013 GaHap 107585)	Nov. 25, 2013	Ji-Un Kim	Geonjin / Yul	Cheol Jang	Settled (Jan. 21, 2019)
6-2	Seoul Western District Court (2013 GaHap 35856)	Nov. 26, 2013	Ji-Un Kim	Hwan-Bong Byun	Wang-Don Yoo	Transferred and Consolidated[45]
6-3	Suwon District Court (2013 GaHap 26404)	Nov. 26, 2013	Ji-Un Kim	Hwan-Bong Byun	Gene Matrix Co., Ltd.	Transferred and Consolidated[46]
7	Seoul Central District Court (2014 GaHap 30150)	Jun. 10, 2014	Jong-Gu Gang, et al.	Jeongyul	Yuanta Securities Co., Ltd., et al.	Certification denied (finalized, Dec. 27, 2016)
8	Seoul Central District Court (2014 GaHap 31627)	Jun. 13, 2014	Won-Il Seo, et al.	Jeongyul	Yuanta Securities Co., Ltd., Dongyang Co., Ltd., et al.[47]	Pending in certification procedure (3rd instance)
9	Seoul Central District Court (2015 GaHap 9047)	Mar. 27, 2015	Hui-Dong Kim, et al.	Youngjin	STX Offshore & Shipbuilding Co., Ltd., Samjong KPMG Accounting Corp., et al.	Pending in certification procedure (1st instance)
10	Seoul Western District Court (2016 GaHap 30418)	Jan. 19, 2016	Jun-Sik Lee	Hannuri	Samil PwC	Certification denied (finalized, Dec. 4, 2018)

suit per year is a disproportionately small number compared with an average fifty-three securities nonclass action suits per year decided on merits.

45 This case was transferred to Seoul Southern District Court for consolidation with Seoul Southern District Court 2013 GaHap 107585 and given a new case no. of 2014 GaHap 100086.

46 This case was transferred to Seoul Southern District Court for consolidation with Seoul Southern District Court 2013 GaHap 107585 and given a new case no. of 2014 GaHap 100093.

47 Case against defendants except for Dongyang Co., Ltd. has been dismissed in September, 2015.

The research population for securities nonclass action suits in Park's study consisted of district court decisions on merits decided between 2012 and 2016 on cases wherein the cause of action was based on a Capital Markets Act violation. Every decision rendered in every other year – 2012, 2014, and 2016 – was sampled. First, the keyword of "자본시장 (capital market)" was used to search all relevant decisions among district court decisions rendered in 2012, 2014, and 2016 via the court decision search system in the Court Library of Korea. Then the contents of the decisions were manually reviewed to weed out decisions of which cause of action was not based on the violation of the Capital Markets Act. The final set of samples totaled 159, composed of 31 decisions rendered in 2012, 59 decisions rendered in 2014, and 69 decisions rendered in 2016.

Securities nonclass action suits are brought both individually and collectively. Among the 159 sample securities nonclass action cases, although 71 cases (44.7 percent) had only one plaintiff, 41 cases (25.8 percent) involved more than 10 plaintiffs, 13 cases (8.2 percent) involved more than 100 plaintiffs, and one case involved more than 500 plaintiffs. Among 88 cases that joined more than one plaintiff, only two cases were brought as appointed-party litigations and the rest (86 cases) were brought as joint litigations.

Most of the plaintiffs in both types of litigation were individuals, and the participation of institutional investors as plaintiffs was extremely limited in number. No institutional investors have stepped in as representative plaintiffs in securities class actions,[48] and only 8.8 percent (fourteen) of the sample of nonclass action cases had any institutional investors as plaintiffs (see Appendix for additional description for the sample nonclass actions).

21.3.2 *Plaintiffs and Lawyers: How They Find One Another and Decide Which Type of Litigation to File*[49]

Interviews with plaintiffs' lawyers and plaintiffs[50] revealed that a spectrum of ways exist whereby to identify and coordinate the potential plaintiffs for securities litigations. At one end of the spectrum, which is understood as a typical way, are online groups victims have spontaneously formed. When a violation is known to the public, the victims voluntarily organize online groups at leading social networking platforms.[51] The leader(s) of the group then identify potential plaintiffs' lawyers through search engines or recommendations of acquaintances. The online groups generally contact multiple lawyers, and the lawyers compete based on fee amounts and on the quality of the case's legal analysis.

In the middle of the spectrum are NGOs or consumer organizations that sometimes play a role in recruiting victims. For example, these organizations arrange for an information session to be run by plaintiffs' lawyers for the victims. The nonprofit nature and public image of NGOs helps lawyers recruit additional plaintiffs without interfering with professional regulations.[52]

At the other end of the spectrum are a small number of plaintiffs' lawyers who actively search for potential cases and plaintiffs. Some veteran lawyers in securities litigations identify potential

48 National Pension Services (NPS), the largest institutional investor in Korea, participated in GS E&C case not as a representative plaintiff but as a class member by not choosing to opt out.

49 The findings in this subsection were obtained from the same research project as Park, *supra* note 40, but are not included in the paper.

50 For the list of interviewees, *see* Park, *supra* note 40, Appendix 1.

51 This phenomenon has also been observed in massive private information leakage lawsuits. Chang-Wan Son, *JipDanGiHeokSoSongUi BeobJeokMunJe-ByeonHoSaYunRiReul JungShimEuRo-[Legal Issues of Aggregated Planned Litigations-Focusing on Lawyer's Ethics Issues-]*, 54 BFL 6, 11 (2012) (describing the recent trend in Korea, wherein victims who are willing to exercise their rights form a group through the internet and seek compensation collectively).

52 Article 34 of Attorney-At-Law Act prohibits a non-attorney from receiving money or benefits before or after introducing a party to a case to an attorney.

cases by constantly monitoring news reports and then use news media or create online groups to attract potential plaintiffs.[53] Some seasoned lawyers naturally serve as a focal point from which potential plaintiffs seek assistance. Typically, a couple of victims contact the lawyers after a significant or newsworthy scandal breaks, and then the lawyers take the case and inform the media; more victims contact the lawyers after reading the news articles.[54] Maintaining a web page also helps the lawyers receive further information from the victims.

Who initiates the search matters because it affects which type of litigation, class actions or nonclass actions, will be chosen. Often, plaintiffs do not have any prior knowledge about class action suits. Once the plaintiffs are provided relevant information, they will most likely prefer to bring securities nonclass action suits than to become representative plaintiffs in a securities class action suit. The reasons described by the interviewees include possible delays in the class action procedure, the possibility of significant limitation of liability, and uncertainty of enforcement due to insolvency risk. According to some plaintiffs' lawyers, they find it difficult to persuade the victims to bring a class action suit, especially when the victims hold claims of substantial financial value or have formed a group with a large number of victims. The potential plaintiffs who hold large claims or represent a large group of victims usually have too big a stake in the lawsuit such that they do not appreciate the benefit of bringing securities class actions (no need to pay initiation fees or up-front litigation costs, as will be further explicated below in Sections 21.3.4.1 and 21.3.4.2). Therefore, when an online group of victims undertakes the initiative to conduct the search, the lawyers who take the case are more likely to bring securities nonclass actions.[55]

Lawyers determined to bring a class action suit therefore need to find a way to overcome these constraints. Some experienced lawyers describe a small number of plaintiffs who are relatively indifferent to the lawsuit's outcome as the right type of plaintiffs for bringing class action suits. Some lawyers first filed securities nonclass action suits for the initial batch of plaintiffs, and then they brought securities class action suits for the subsequent small group of victims.[56] In this way, the lawyers may accommodate the needs of a large group of plaintiffs who prefer to bring securities nonclass action suits and also bring a securities class action suit using other better suited plaintiffs.

21.3.3 *Who Are the Plaintiffs' Lawyers?*

The number of plaintiffs' lawyers who specialize in securities litigation is small. Among the 90 law firms that represented plaintiffs in 159 sample securities nonclass action suits, most (78, 86.7 percent) only represented one case. Only twelve law firms (13.3 percent) represented

53 Unlike solicitation by visitation or phone call, which is explicitly prohibited by Article 5 (1) of Attorney-At Law Business Advertisement Regulation, creating an online group or blog to recruit plaintiffs is generally interpreted as being allowed in Korea. *See*, Chang-Wan Son, *supra* note 51, at 13.

54 *Id.*

55 The burden of managing securities nonclass action suits involving numerous plaintiffs does not seem to deter experienced lawyers with able tools and staffs from pursuing the option. Lawyers managing a securities nonclass action suit with a multitude of plaintiffs must communicate with the individual plaintiffs and gather consent or information from them. With more experience, lawyers have found ways to successfully minimize the burden of managing multiparty litigation by employing computer programs and experienced staffs. Some experienced lawyers insert special provisions in their fee agreements to simplify the process of obtaining each plaintiff's consent in the course of litigation.

56 The plaintiffs who joined the securities nonclass action suits will be deemed to have opted out in the subsequent securities class action suit. The fact that the plaintiffs' lawyer in a securities class action suit had filed a securities nonclass action suits involving some of the class members and the case was dismissed at an appellate level does not itself make the plaintiffs' lawyer unable to represent the interest of class members fairly and adequately. Seoul High Court 2015 Ra 619 decision, rendered on Jan. 29, 2016.

plaintiffs more than once. The twelve law firms, however, represented 45.3 percent (72) of the sample securities nonclass action suits.

Among the small number of plaintiffs' lawyers repeatedly filing securities litigation, only a handful of law firms have had any experience bringing securities class actions, let alone any successful ones (see Table 21.1). Most of the lawyers who bring securities litigation, therefore, perceive that they are not fully familiar with this type of litigation and are insecure about their ability to carry out securities class actions.

Plaintiffs' lawyers in securities litigation work at small law firms or are de facto solo-practitioners.[57] The dominant player in securities class action, Hannuri, has only eleven lawyers. Those who belong to medium-size law firms (more than fifteen) usually operate under independent accounting, without sharing risks with other partners. Unsteady cash flows predispose the plaintiffs' lawyers to keep their teams small and to minimize their overhead costs.

Plaintiffs' law firms in the United States are also relatively small compared with the defendant firms, but the small size of the firms seems not to interfere with their ability to bring large-scale lawsuits.[58] Often in large-scale litigations, multiple plaintiffs' law firms form an ad hoc law firm to share the work, costs, and fees.[59] This practice has helped plaintiffs' lawyers form a tight-knit community, spreading successful know-how to overcome the size differentials.[60] The practice of sharing experience and costs among plaintiffs' lawyers has not yet developed in Korea. They do not meet regularly or exchange information, conceiving one another as competitors. According to the interviewees, only recently have some plaintiffs' lawyers begun on occasion to coordinate with other plaintiffs' lawyers who happened to be representing the same kind of securities damage lawsuits and to share expert fees.[61]

Moreover, third-party litigation funding[62] is not used in Korea. Third-party funding is generally viewed as unlawful among plaintiffs' lawyers and therefore is not used.[63]

Both the lack of risk diversification measures and the lack of experience in securities class actions condition plaintiffs' lawyers to be less tolerant of risks than plaintiffs' lawyers in the United States. Therefore, they are reluctant to make significant investments up front in a case with a low probability of winning and having the judgment enforced, even when the fees could be significant if successful.

21.3.4 *Costs and Fees*

Generally, in civil nonclass action suits, clients bear most of the risks arising from bringing litigation. In contrast, to bring securities class action suits, substantial up-front investments must

57 Park, *supra* note 40.

58 Coffee, *supra* note 34, at 706–11.

59 *Id.*

60 *Id.*

61 Park, *supra* note 40.

62 Third-party litigation funding refers to an investment in litigation made by a third party with no prior relationship to the plaintiffs, which covers all litigation costs in exchange for a share of the profit if the case is successful, or nothing if the suit is unsuccessful. Marco de Morpurgo, *A Comparative Legal and Economic Approach to Third-Party Litigation Funding*, 19 CARDOZO J. INT'L & COMP. L. 343, 347 (2011). Third-party litigation funding first began to develop in Australia in the beginning of 1990s and spread throughout the world. *Id.*, at 360. *See also*, Jasminka Kalajdzic, Peter Cashman & Alana Longmoore, *Justice for Profit: A Comparative Analysis of Australian, Canadian and U.S. Third Party Litigation Funding*, 61 AM. J. COMP. L. 93 (2013).

63 However, there seems to be no specific provision prohibiting third-party funding in the Attorneys-At-Law Act or other laws. Third-party funding would need to be arranged so as not to violate Article 6 of the Trust Act, which nullifies any trust, the main purpose of which is to have the trustee to proceed with litigation. Jin-Yeong Chung, Sungjean Seo & Dong-Wook Kim, *Class/collective actions in South Korea: overview*, THOMSEN & REUTERS (2017).

TABLE 21.2 *Cost and fee consideration for securities class actions and securities nonclass actions*

	Nonclass action	Class action
Initiation fee	Yes	No
Contingent fee	Yes	Yes
litigation costs and fee-shifting	Plaintiffs	Plaintiffs' lawyers
Average time until district court decision	19.5 months	64 months

be made solely on the plaintiffs' lawyer's part. There is generally no initiation fee to cover filing fees and a portion of the lawyer's time and effort, and the litigation costs tend to be larger under class action suits. Moreover, due to the significant delay in certification procedures under class actions,[64] leading a class action suit is generally thought to require more time and effort on the part of lawyers than is leading a securities damage suit involving multiple plaintiffs (see Table 21.2).

21.3.4.1 Initiation Fee Only for Nonclass Action Suits

In Korea, the attorney fees typically consist of initiation fees and contingent fees, which are freely determined between a client and an attorney.[65] Contingent fees, regarded as a crucial factor enabling class actions in the United States,[66] are allowed and used frequently in civil cases in Korea.[67] Initiation fees generally cover the filing fee and partly compensate for the lawyer's work and are not refundable irrespective of the outcome of the case. Nonetheless, the initiation fees typically included in fee agreement for securities nonclass action suits but not for securities class action suits make the former more attractive for the plaintiffs' lawyers.

In securities class action suits, lawyers generally receive only contingent fees. The contingent fee rate ranged from 12 percent to 30 percent (see Table 21.3 below) among the six cases in which certification procedures were concluded and fee agreements were publicly disclosed. Although the court has discretion to reduce the contingent fee amount upon petition by the representative plaintiff or class members,[68] as of May 31, 2019, the court has found the prearranged rate of contingent fee, ranging from 15 percent to 23 percent, to be appropriate.[69]

Lawyers who bring securities class action suits without receiving any initiation fee must depend solely on contingent fees. As such, if the class action suit should fail, the lawyer would need to accept the entire up-front investment as a loss.

64 For possible reasons for the delay, *see infra* Section 21.3.4.3.

65 Gyooho Lee, *Attorney Fee Arrangements Really Matter in Terms of Access to Justice in Korea*, *in* COST AND FEE ALLOCATION IN CIVIL PROCEDURE: A COMPARATIVE STUDY 204–05 (Mathias Reimann ed., 2011). The contingent fee rate can be freely set between a party and an attorney unless it is unfair. *Id.*, at 205–06.

66 Coffee, *supra* note 34, at 670 note 2.

67 S. Ct., 2015Da200111, July 23, 2015 (S. Kor.); Jae Won Kim, *The Ideal and the Reality of the Korean Legal Profession*, 2 ASIANPACIFIC L. & POL'Y J. 45 (2001). However, a contingent fee arrangement for criminal cases is void for public policy reasons. *Id.*

68 Article 44 (3) of the SCAA.

69 The Court of Korea, Securities Class Action, www.scourt.go.kr/portal/notice/securities/securities.jsp.

TABLE 21.3 *Fee agreement and fee award in securities class action*[70]

		Fee agreement		
No.	Case No.	Initiation fee	Contingent fee	Fee award
1	Suwon Dist. Ct. 2009 GaHap8829	None	20% (1st instance), 25% (2nd instance), 30% (3rd instance)	20% of settlement amount
2	Seoul Central Dist. Ct. 2010GaHap1604	None	15% (1st instance), 20% (2nd instance), 24% (3rd instance)	15% of settlement amount
3	Seoul Southern Dist. Ct. 2011GaHap19387	None	15% (1st instance), 23% (2nd instance), 30% (3rd instance)	
4	Seoul Central Dist. Ct. 2012GaHap17061	None	12% (1st instance), 15% (2nd instance), 18% (3rd instance)	15%[71] of damage award
5	Seoul Central Dist. Ct. 2013GaHap74313	None	20% (1st instance), 25% (2nd instance), 30% (3rd instance)	
6	Seoul Southern Dist. Ct. 2013GaHap107585	None	23% (1st instance), 27% (2nd instance), 30% (3rd instance)	23% of settlement amount

21.3.4.2 Litigation Costs and Fee-Shifting

Typically, litigation costs incurred by filing a civil lawsuit include filing fees, mailing fees, and expert fees. Class actions entail public notice costs, and notifying fees as well.[72] Filing fees in Korea rise in proportion (0.35 percent–0.5 percent) to the claim amount whereas only flat filing fees apply in the United States.[73] In a class action suit in which claim amounts tend to be much larger than in a securities damage suit, the filing fee would be quite large, but a special SCAA provision partly mitigates the burden.[74] Additionally, in a class action suit, plaintiffs' lawyers must make an advance payment of litigation costs[75] within a certain period from the finalization of certification decision, usually 40,000,000–60,000,000 won.[76] Party-appointed expert fees, ranging from 50,000,000 won to 100,000,000 won, are also generally paid by plaintiffs' lawyers in addition to the litigation costs in securities class actions. Another potentially significant cost

70 Park, *supra* note 40.

71 Here, the contingent fee rate in second instance applies because the defendant initially appealed to the first instance decision and then withdrew its appeal at the appellate level.

72 In class action lawsuits, the distribution costs will be additionally incurred at the distribution stage. However, the distribution costs do not necessarily add to the risk of plaintiffs' lawyers because those will be incurred only when the lawsuit is successful and will be paid out of the recovery after deducting the litigation costs and the legal fees.

73 For US filing fees, *see*, Deborah R. Hensler, *The United States of America*, in THE COSTS AND FUNDING OF CIVIL LITIGATION 535, 539 (Christopher Hodges, Stefan Vogenauer & Magdalena Tulibacka eds., 2010). For Korean filing fees, Article 2 of the Act on the Stamps Attached for Civil Litigation, etc.

74 The filing fee under securities class action is half of the usual amount and has an upper limit of 50,000,000 won. Article 7 (2) of the SCAA.

75 Article 16 of the SCAA.

76 *See, e.g.*, Seoul High Court 2015 Ra 656, 657 (consolidated) decision, rendered on Nov. 16, 2015. The remaining amount shall be returned to plaintiffs' lawyer once the litigation is finalized.

arises from identifying the class members. The cost of obtaining class members' financial transaction information from financial companies increases in proportion to the class size and can be quite substantial in a class action suit with large class size.[77]

In addition to the litigation cost, fee-shifting imposes a significant burden on the plaintiffs' lawyers when bringing a class action.[78] The American rule (also known as a rule against fee-shifting), whereby each party undertakes its costs, has been perceived as one of the primary factors allowing plaintiffs' attorneys to take on the role of the private attorney general.[79] In contrast, outside the United States, most countries have adopted a version of the English rule that mandates the losing party to incur all the costs.[80] In Korea, the losing party must bear a portion of the winning party's legal fees (also known as a *partial* fee-shifting rule).[81] The amount of the shifting fees tends to be far higher in class action suits than that arising in securities nonclass action suits because the amount of the shifting fee increases in proportion to the claim amount with a diminishing slope, and the claim amount is much larger in securities class action suits than in securities nonclass action suits.[82]

Generally, in civil lawsuits, plaintiffs bear the litigation costs along with the fee-shifting risk,[83] as is typical for securities nonclass action suits. In securities class action suits, however, the representative plaintiffs are often reluctant to bear the up-front litigation costs and the risk of fee-shifting on behalf of the whole class,[84] considering the benefit of a class action lawsuit would be shared throughout the class. Therefore, lawyers who bring class action lawsuits often assume the burden of litigation costs and the risk of fee-shifting for the representative plaintiffs. In comparison to securities nonclass action suits, the onus of litigation costs and fee-shifting, which can be enormous due to a substantial claim amount and class size, creates a comparative disadvantage for plaintiffs' lawyers in bringing securities class action suits.

To minimize the risk, some lawyers submit a partial claim at the beginning of securities class action suits. For example, the claim amount in one class action was expanded from 101,000,000 won to 8,585,896,483 won after the certification decision was finalized.[85] By filing a nominal claim amount and then expanding it after the class has been certified and the prospectus of the

77 Article 4(1)1. and Article 4-2(1), (4) of the Act on Real Name Financial Transactions and Confidentiality. The court rule requires the petitioner of such order to make an advance payment of the "number of financial companies × number of title holder × 2,000 won." Article 4(1), (2) of GeumYungGeoRaeJeongBo, GwaSeJeongBo JeChulMyeongRyeongE GwanHan YeGyu [The Court Rule on Financial Transaction Information and Tax Information Production Order].

78 Of course, the fee-shifting would relieve part of the burden of litigation costs for the plaintiffs' lawyers in case of winning the case. Nevertheless, compared with securities nonclass action suits, in which plaintiffs, rather than plaintiffs' lawyers, generally bear the burden of litigation costs and fee-shifting risk in the first place, securities class actions expose plaintiffs' lawyers to more risks.

79 Coffee, *supra* note 34, at 670, note 2.

80 John C. Coffee, Jr., *The Globalization of Entrepreneurial Litigation: Law, Culture, and Incentives*, 165 U. Pa. L. Rev. 1895, 1899 (2017).

81 Article 98 of the KCPA. Only a part of the fees paid to lawyers is included in litigation costs as determined by Supreme Court Rules. Article 109 (1) of the KCPA.

82 Annexed Chart 3 following Article 3 of the Rules Regarding Attorney Fees Included in Litigation Costs. Supreme Court Rules No. 2116, amended on November 28, 2007, effective January 1, 2008. According to this rule, the shifting fee would be only 800,000 won in a suit claiming damages of 10 million won, whereas the shifting fee will be 204.8 million won in a suit claiming damages of 20 billion won.

83 Chang-Wan Son, *JipDanGiHeokSoSongUi BeobJeokMunJe-ByeonHoSaYunRiReul JungShimEuRo [Legal issues of Aggregated Planned Litigations-Focusing on Lawyer's Ethics Issues]*, 54 BFL 6, 15(2012).

84 However, one case had more than 1,000 representative plaintiffs who paid certain amounts for filing fees. *See*, row eleven in Table 21.1; Benjamin Joon-Buhm Lee, *Saving the Korean Securities Class Action*, 39 U. Pa. J. Int'l L. 247, 283 (2017).

85 Seoul Central District Court 2012 GaHap 17601 Case. *See*, Court of Korea, *NaUi SaGeonGeomSaek [Search My Case]*, available at www.scourt.go.kr/portal/information/events/search/search.jsp. If the plaintiff submits a partial claim first and later expands it to the full claim amount when the magnitude of damages becomes clear, it will be

TABLE 21.4 *Age of litigation*[86]

Case no.	Certification Proceeding (months)	Main proceeding (months)
Suwon 2009GaHap8829	9	3
Seoul Central 2010GaHap1604	74	11
Seoul Southern 2011GaHap19387	61	(pending)
Seoul Central 2012GaHap17061	50	14
Seoul Central 2013 GaHap74313	32	(pending)
Seoul Southern 2013GaHap107585	58	4
Seoul Central 2014GaHap30150	30	(certification denied)
Seoul Western 2016GaHap30418	35	(certification denied)

lawsuit has become clear, the lawyers can effectively reduce the risk of losing the lawsuit and being responsible for paying the hefty filing fee and the opposing party's large legal fees.

The burden of taking on significant up-front costs constrains the lawyer's decision about which types of cases to bring as class action suits. Some lawyers avoid cases deemed too small or too large cases, preferring cases with the "right size" of the class. Cases that are too small that cannot provide a sufficient amount of contingent fees will be avoided because small contingent fees cannot justify the substantial amount of risk lawyers bear for an extended period.[87] Cases that are too large would incur high litigation costs and render the enforcement uncertain and therefore, will also be avoided.

21.3.4.3 Opportunity Cost: Procedural Delay in Class Action

Another source of costs for the plaintiffs' lawyers is the time and effort that lawyers expend, which could be understood as an opportunity cost. It generally takes more time and effort for the plaintiffs' lawyers to represent securities class action suits than securities nonclass action suits, principally due to the significant delay in the certification procedures. For the eight securities class action suits in which certification procedures have been concluded, the certification procedure took 43.6 months on average (see Table 21.4 below). If we exclude the first case that was certified for settlement only after nine months, it took on average 70 months for the other three cases that reached a settlement or final judgment to be finalized. In the sample securities nonclass action suits, however, it took on average 19.5 months until a district court decision and an additional 11.5 months at the appellate level for the cases reaching the appellate court decision.

One possible explanation for the delay in the certification proceeding would be that the courts are not yet familiar with class action suits in general, and the legal issues in the certification stage have not yet been settled. A more structural cause is that an "immediate appeal" on the decision to certify or to deny automatically stays the main proceeding until the decision is finalized.[88] Among eight securities class action cases in which the certification procedures have been

generally allowed unless it significantly delays the proceeding (e.g., requiring submission and review of new evidences). *See*, Si-yoon Lee, *supra* note 37, 713–17.

86 Park, *supra* note 40.

87 Empirical evidence from the United States also shows that a securities fraud class action is rarely filed against firms offering relatively small potential damage awards for plaintiffs. Stephen Choi, *The Evidence on Securities Class Actions*, 57 VAND. L. REV. 1465, 1508 (2004).

88 *See infra* Section 21.2.2.3.

finalized, five cases had their certification decisions appealed to the Supreme Court, and two cases among these reached the Supreme Court twice.[89]

Plaintiffs' lawyers tend to be less inclined to bring securities class actions that entail the risk of bearing larger litigation costs and the risk of fee-shifting and require more time and effort due to the delay in the certification procedure. Instead, these lawyers rather bring securities nonclass action suits that allow the lawyers to receive initiation fees and to handle the cases in a comfortable way, with no significant attendant risks.

21.3.5 *Uncertainty of Winning and Enforcing the Judgment*

Due to the lack of risk diversification measures and higher up-front litigation costs, lawyers are constrained in the suits they bring and typically file only cases with a higher probability of winning and a greater likelihood of the judgment being enforced as securities class action suits. Because settlements infrequently occur in securities nonclass action suits or securities class action suits, in most cases, the plaintiffs' lawyers must win and have the judgment enforced to recover their contingent fees. When lawyers factor in the higher probability of winning and the likelihood of the judgment being enforced, the pool of potential cases is substantially reduced because lawyers prefer to depend on governmental investigations to prove the violations with ease, and the issuing companies in cases with governmental investigations are often insolvent.

21.3.5.1 Low Settlement Rate

In the United States, most of the securities class action cases that survive the motion stage are settled.[90] In contrast, Korean judges adjudicate the bulk of the securities litigation in Korea.

In securities nonclass action suits, settlement rarely occurs. Most lawyers do not consider the possibility of settlement when bringing a lawsuit, because settlements only occur under special circumstances.[91] Although the exact settlement rate in securities nonclass action suits in district courts is unknown,[92] the high appeal rate for district court decisions and the significantly low settlement rate at the appellate level for the sample securities nonclass action suits demonstrate that the parties generally are not inclined to settle.[93]

89 Park, *supra* note 40.

90 In the USA, from 1997 to 2016, 50 percent of filings of securities class action suits were settled, 43 percent were dismissed, and 6 percent were continuing as of January 12, 2018. Overall, less than 1 percent of the filings reached a trial verdict. Cornerstone Research, *Securities Class Action Filings—2017 year in review*, 15, 44, available at http://securities.stanford.edu/research-reports/1996-2017/Cornerstone-Research-Securities-Class-Action-Filings-2017-YIR.pdf.

91 Settlements were reached under securities nonclass action suits under special circumstances such as when the plaintiff was a very important customer of the defendant or when cases involving the same fact patterns were decided by other courts.

92 The study only analyzed the decision of securities nonclass action suits because the securities nonclass action suits are not categorized separately or tagged at the filing stage.

93 A high portion of the cases (67.3 percent, 107 or 159) decided in district courts were appealed either by the plaintiffs, by the defendants, or by both. Most of these cases did not settle at the appellate level, either (9.5 percent, 10 of 107 settled). The appeal rate for the sample securities nonclass action suits is much higher than the appeal rate of 7.8 percent (261,243) in general civil cases decided in 2012–16 (3,349,516). Moreover, the appeal rate in three-judge panel cases is also much higher in sample securities nonclass action suits (71.1 percent, 91 of 128) than in general civil cases decided in 2012–16 (43.4 percent, 73,845 of 170,260). The settlement rate for the sample securities nonclass action suits is lower than the settlement rate of 21.6 percent (60,140 of 277,837) in general civil cases at the appellate level.

Similarly, securities class action suits are not easily settled. Among the six securities class action cases in which certification decisions have been finalized, only the first case was settled within three years since its filing (see Table 21.4 above). The plaintiffs' lawyer representing the initial case reported that the court had suggested settlement. It was also rumored that the defendant company agreed to it, as it needed to swiftly dispose of the class action lawsuit to continue conducting business with its largest buyer. However, this type of early settlement never occurred since. The second and third case took nearly eighty-five and sixty-one months, respectively, to be settled (see Table 21.4 above) and only happened after a related securities nonclass action suit had been decided on merits.

What causes this disparity in the settlement rate in securities litigations cases between the United States and Korea? Plaintiffs' lawyers suggest various reasons for the low rate of settlement in securities nonclass action suits and securities class action suits: the lack of a discovery system, unsettled legal issues in securities law, the defendants' fear of setting a precedent, accounting firms' reluctance to pay the damage awards, and the possibility of a reduction in awards through the application of the limiting liability doctrine.[94]

Without expecting an early settlement, plaintiffs' lawyers in securities litigation need to actually win the case on its merits and successfully have the judgment enforced to recover their contingent fees. This consideration affects the lawyers' selection of cases, especially for securities class actions, which entail higher stakes because the lawyers do not receive any initiation fees. Plaintiffs' lawyers thus tend to bring only those cases with a high likelihood of success.

21.3.5.2 The Difficulty of Collecting Evidence

In securities litigations generally, it is difficult to collect evidence for the plaintiffs in securities damages suits because the evidence is typically on the defendant's side. Plaintiffs often use alternative evidence-collection methods to gain evidence from defendants or third parties, most importantly, a document production order, as Korean law does not allow pretrial discovery.[95] Document production orders, however, are regarded as ineffective due to the court's reluctance to apply sanctions on noncompliant parties.[96] The only potential sanction on the party who violates a document production order is for the courts to affirm the opposing party's allegation about the document's contents as accurate.[97] This provision though has merely a limited practical effect. The Supreme Court of Korea is of the belief that the court may affirm the opposing party's argument regarding the existence and the content of the

94 The limitation of liability doctrine is recognized based on the principle of fairness to avoid unreasonable outcomes where joint tortfeasors are jointly and severally liable for the entire damages despite their partial contribution. Kwang-Sun Choi, *GaeJeong OeGamBeobSangUi BiRyeChaeklmJeDoE GwanHanGoChal [A Study on the Proportionate Liability in the Newly Amended Act on External Audit of Stock Company]*, 143 JUSTICE 30, 47 (2014). The limitation of liability doctrine can be applied even when the tortious act is intentional or negligence on the plaintiffs' side is not imaginable, whereas comparative negligence cannot be used in those cases. Taeil Han, *BulBeobHaengWi SonHaeBaeSangWonChikUi SuJeongURoSeoUi ChaeklmJeHanGwa BiRyeChaeklmUi BiGyo [A Comparison Between Liability Limitation and Proportionate Liability Based on the Restated Principle of Tort-related Compensation for Damages]*, 29 BEOBHAKNONCHONG 223, 232 (2016). For more detailed explanations for the low rate of settlement in securities litigations in Korea, *see*, Park, *supra* note 40.

95 Article 343 of the KCPA. Document transfer order (Article 352 of the KCPA) or clarification order (Article 294 of the KCPA) are also used.

96 Si-Yoon Lee, *supra* note 37, at 515; Choong-soo Han, *MinSaSoSongJeolChaESeoUi JeongBo Mit JeungGeoGongGaeWa SuJipJeDo – MunSeoMokRokJeChulMyeongRyeongEul JungSimEuRo [Access to Documents and Other Information in Civil Disputes in Korea]*, 12 MINSASOSONG 266, 273 (2008).

97 Articles 349, 350 of the KCPA.

document as true but may not deem the facts that the document were to establish as indeed proven.[98]

Because procuring evidence from defendants by means of civil lawsuit is not easy due to the ineffectiveness of document production orders, lawyers instead depend on governmental investigations–criminal investigation or the FSS investigation[99]–to collect the evidence. More than half of the sample securities nonclass action suits (eighty-seven, 54.7 percent) included related governmental investigations.[100] Notably, most of the cases with causes of actions that are enumerated in the SCAA as causes of action for securities class action (Article 125, 162, 170, 175, 177, 179 of the Capital Markets Act) (78.2 per cent, sixty-eight of eighty-seven) included governmental investigations.

Among the sample securities nonclass action suits, the cases without governmental investigations were more likely to be dismissed (fifty of seventy-two) than were the cases that included governmental investigations (twenty-one of eighty-seven). Moreover, a case with governmental investigations is 35 percent less likely to be dismissed than is a case without governmental investigations – controlling whether a specialized judge panel decided the case, the number of plaintiffs, the experience level of plaintiffs' lawyers, the causes of action. This result is consistent with the lawyers' strategy of choosing cases with governmental investigations as a means of increasing the likelihood of winning.

The difficulty of collecting evidence also persists under securities class action. Although there are several SCAA provisions governing evidence collection,[101] lawyers do not perceive them as helping them collect evidence under class action suits. Among ten class action suits, every case except for one case (nine cases, 90 percent) had included governmental investigations.

To reduce the risk associated with the uncertainty of winning, some lawyers said that they first brought securities damage suits and then filed securities class action suits later when they were more confident in winning the case. This approach, however, is available only for a limited period. Each cause of action enumerated in the SCAA has a statute of limitation, ranging from one to two years from the date of learning about the violation.

21.3.5.3 Uncertainty of the Judgment's Enforcement

The consideration of the likelihood of enforcement effectively reduces the target pool of litigation.

Interestingly, some lawyers argue that in the cases with governmental investigations, the type of cases in which it is easy to prove the violations, the issuing companies are more likely to be insolvent than in the cases without governmental investigations. In the sample securities

98 Supreme Court of Korea 94 Da 395667 judgment, rendered on Mar. 10, 1995; Supreme Court of Korea 2006 Da 9446 judgment, rendered on Sep. 21, 2007.

99 In Korea, the Financial Services Commission (FSC), the policy development agency, regulates all financial services. The Financial Supervisory Services (FSS) functions as an implementation agency under the FSC that mainly handles enforcement. The Securities and Futures Commission (SFC) has the authority to impose administrative sanctions for certain violations under the Capital Markets Act. Young-Cheol Jeong, *Legal Compliance and Korea's Financial Services Market: A Strategic Approach*, 20 Pac. Rim L. & Pol'y J. 483, 490 (2011).

100 Among the eighty-seven cases that had governmental investigations, eighty had criminal proceedings, thirty-four had the FSS sanctions, seven had the FSC sanctions, and eleven had the SFC sanctions preceding the judgment (one case may have multiple types of governmental investigations, and the sum of cases having each type of governmental investigations exceeds the total number of cases having governmental investigations). Park, *supra* note 40.

101 Articles 30–33 of the SCAA.

nonclass action suits, in 52.2 percent (83 of 159) of the cases, the issuing companies were either under bankruptcy proceedings[102] or under rehabilitation proceedings.[103] A considerably higher percentage of cases (70.1 percent, sixty-one of eighty-seven) had their issuing companies under bankruptcy or rehabilitation proceedings when governmental investigations had been undertaken than when they had not been (30.6 percent, twenty-two of seventy-two). This finding affirms the interviewees' description of a link between the defendant's insolvency and the inclusion of governmental investigations.

The phenomenon could be explained in a variety of ways. The deep-pocket defendants might be more compliant with the Capital Markets Act. Perhaps governmental investigations are more often initiated in cases involving companies that are either under bankruptcy or rehabilitation proceedings or about to enter one of the two.

The claim amount in class action suits tends to approximate ten times larger than the claim amount under securities nonclass action suits,[104] causing it to be still more difficult for plaintiffs' lawyers to secure a defendant with sufficient resources to pay the damage awards.

21.3.5.4 Measures against Frivolous Lawsuits in the SCAA

The SCAA's enumerated cause of action (Article 3) seems to decrease the pool of cases that can be brought as class action suits. Only 81 cases (50.9 percent) out of 159 sample securities nonclass action suits contained causes of action that the SCAA enumerates.

Other measures against frivolous lawsuits in the SCAA besides the enumerated causes of action do not seem as problematic as the previous literature had predicted.[105] The courts have interpreted the provisions on the frequency of representation for plaintiffs' lawyers and on size and stake minimums in a manner that reduces plaintiffs' lawyers' burden to meet the requirements. The Seoul High Court ruled that the plaintiffs' lawyer who acted as plaintiffs' lawyer in three securities class action suits in the last three sequential years could become a plaintiffs' counsel if the person could represent the class members' interest fairly and appropriately.[106] The court subsequently allowed Hannuri to represent the fourth case, recognizing the firm's vast experience in securities litigation.[107] In addition, the court ruled that considering the purpose of requiring a stake minimum to prevent class action abuse, the stake minimum must be determined by the number of securities affected by the unfair trading, not by the total number of outstanding securities.[108]

21.4 RECOMMENDATIONS FOR REFORM

Since the enactment of the SCAA, whenever an incident causes damage to a large number of victims outside the SCAA's scope, academics and consumer associations have called for an extension of the class action system to protect the victims in question.[109] Recently, a series of

102 A bankruptcy proceeding in Korea corresponds to Chapter 4 proceeding in the USA.

103 A rehabilitation proceeding in Korea corresponds to Chapter 11 proceeding in the USA.

104 Park, *supra* note 40.

105 For the limit on the frequency of representation for a plaintiffs' attorney, *see*, Korpus, *supra* note 14, at 53–54; Bernard Black, Brian Cheffins & Michael Klausner, *Shareholder Suits and Outside Director Liability: The Case of Korea*, 10 J. Kor. L. 325, 344 (2011). For the size and stake minimums, *see*, *id.*; Coffee, *supra* note 77, at 1915.

106 Seoul High Court decision 2015 Ra 619, rendered on Jan. 29, 2016.

107 *Id.*

108 *Id.*

109 Jung-Ah Hong, *JipDanSoSong YoGeonWanHwa Mit HwakDaeBangAn [Relaxation of Requirement and Enlargement in Class Action]*, in GukMinUi SaengMyeong, SinChe BoHo JeokJeongHwaReul WiHan

incidents that allegedly harmed a large number of consumers[110] reignited the discussion on expanding the scope of class action that later became the ruling and the opposition parties' campaign pledges in the local and presidential election and, eventually, a national political agenda.[111] After consulting with relevant government agencies and departments, the Ministry of Justice prepared an extensive class action bill to be submitted to the General Assembly on September 21, 2018.[112] The bill is an amendment to the SCAA, transforming the law into a single general class action law, to provide the victims of massive accidents with an efficient way to seek compensation for their losses.

The most noticeable change envisioned in the new law is the expanded scope of causes of action that can be brought as class actions, incorporating product liability, cartel activity, resale practice maintenance, unfair labeling and/or advertising, financial consumer protection, data breach, food safety, and financial investment products.[113] Furthermore, the bill aims to mitigate some procedural obstacles, for example, by eliminating an exclusive jurisdiction for defendants, a limitation on the frequency of representing class actions for the plaintiffs' lawyers, and the requirement for the plaintiffs to hold more than 1/10,000 of outstanding shares of the issuing companies (so-called stake minimums).[114]

Nevertheless, even if the pending bill is adopted, fundamental reasons for the underuse of class action mechanisms will likely remain. Notably, one of the significant procedural burdens on plaintiffs and plaintiffs' lawyers unaddressed by the bill is the delay in certification. Even after courts establish precedents and settle legal issues regarding certification procedures over time, the delay due to the automatic stay of the main proceeding triggered by an immediate appeal to the certification decisions would significantly disadvantage the class members compared with the individual plaintiffs who pursue securities nonclass action suits. Delay in compensation might also increase the risk of the defendants becoming insolvent. To address this problem, the SCAA could be amended to allow the main proceeding to go forward despite an appeal to the certification decision, unless the court issues an order to stay the main proceeding under special circumstances that justify such need.

Another substantial burden that would remain after the bill passes is the difficulty of collecting evidence. This burden not only reduces the number of cases but also constrains the type of cases that are brought as securities class actions. The tendency of lawyers to bring cases with preceding governmental investigations as class actions would determine which kind of role class actions play in enforcing the law, along with other tools of public enforcement (criminal and administrative) and private enforcement (nonclass action). The US notion of "private attorney general" complementing public enforcement[115] might not be applicable to plaintiffs' lawyers in Korea

MinSaJeok HaeGyeolBangAnUi GaeSeon Symposium [SYMPOSIUM ON IMPROVING CIVIL APPROACH FOR PROMOTION OF PROPER PROTECTION OF CITIZEN'S LIFE AND BODILY INTEGRITY], Jun. 27, 2016, at 18.

110 Jeongkyu Park, *'ImUiJoJak SuYongBulGa' Volkswagen, BaeSang GeoBuHanChae BeobJeokDaeUngEMan JuMok ['Cannot Admit Defeat Device,' Volkswagen Denies Compensation and Concentrates on Legal Defense]*, NEWSIS, Jul. 13, 2016, available at www.newsis.com/ar_detail/view.html/?ar_id=NISX20160713_0014218067&cID=10401&pID=10400.

111 Bill, *supra* note 8.

112 The bill was submitted by a member of the General Assembly, Jongmin Kim, and is currently pending in the General Assembly.

113 Bill, *supra* note 8.

114 *Id.*

115 There has been a longstanding understanding in the United States that class actions play "a desirable and necessary role of complementing the public enforcement." *See*, James D. Cox & Randall S. Thomas, *Mapping the American Shareholder Litigation Experience: A Survey of Empirical Studies of the Enforcement of the U.S. Securities Law*, 6 EUR. CO. FIN. L. REV. 164, 165 (2009).

who are deprived of effective investigatory tools. One way to make existing tools to gather evidence effective (for example, document production order) would be to strengthen sanctions on disobeying parties.

21.5 CONCLUSION

The Korean example provides several insights for other civil law countries that are considering adopting US-style class actions. The transplanted class action might not be used as frequently or in the identical way if it operates among existing institutions that significantly differ from those of the United States.

In order to design a class action device that best fits the needs of a country, we must determine what role class actions should play, along with other types of enforcement. Although plaintiffs' lawyers in the USA are known to function as "private attorney generals" equipped with a powerful investigatory tool of discovery, many countries outside the United States do not provide plaintiffs a comparably powerful weapon. When plaintiffs' lawyers lack the tools to effectively gather evidence from the defendants' side, they may be forced to piggyback on governmental investigations to prove the wrongdoing of defendants, which may limit not only the number of class action filings but also class action's role of complementing public enforcement.

In addition to tailoring the class action law to fit local needs, enough time should be allowed for legal actors to adapt to the new class action device before hastily judging the success or failure of the transplant. In the United States, a sophisticated plaintiffs' bar has developed over the last five decades by profiting primarily from representing class action suits. Plaintiffs' lawyers outside the United States that have not yet played the role of entrepreneurial lawyers would need enough time and experience to gain expertise and become better connected. Similarly, courts would need to deal with enough cases to develop practices that facilitate the use of the class action procedure.

Moreover, if alternative methods of aggregating claims exist, the incentives for plaintiffs' lawyers to use the new class action device over existing substitutes should be carefully assessed and, if necessary, provided. If the class action device burdens plaintiffs' lawyers with a large up-front investment and causes a significant delay in recovering fees, they would avoid experimenting with the newly introduced class action and would rely instead on the existing substitute of nonclass actions that they are familiar with.

APPENDIX

Number of plaintiffs in sample securities nonclass action suits

Number of plaintiffs	Number of cases	Percentage (%)
500–	1	0.6
400–499	0	0.0
300–399	2	1.3
200–299	2	1.3
100–199	8	5.0
10–99	28	17.6
2–9	47	29.6
1	71	44.7
Total	159	100

Number of defendants in sample securities nonclass action suits

Number of defendants	Number of cases	Percentage (%)
10–19	14	8.8
5–9	19	11.9
2–4	53	33.3
1	73	45.9
Total	159	100

Type of defendants in securities nonclass action suits

Type	Number of cases	Percentage (%)
Issuing company	35	22.0
Financial investment firm	99	62.3
Accounting firm	42	26.4
Republic of Korea or regulatory agencies	23	14.5
Directors or officers of issuing companies	42	26.4

22

A Review of the Current Status of, and Future Issues Facing, Consumer Class Action Systems in Japan

Taeko Morita and Daisuke Eguchi

Japanese law does not permit class action suits that allow a single victim to file a lawsuit on behalf of a larger group of victims, as seen in the United States; however, the law of Japan makes an exception for collective redress by consumers, which can be pursued through the systems described in this chapter. Japan offers two systems for consumer collective redress under special laws that provide for injunctive and compensatory relief. Under these systems, specific consumer groups authorized by the Prime Minister can bring a case to court. Although the injunction-based system was introduced in 2007, and has been used to protect consumers' interests, few cases have been filed under the compensatory system since its introduction in 2016.

This chapter discusses the two Japanese systems of collective redress, and examines some of the issues these systems face in practice.

22.1 INTRODUCTION

Japan's consumer affairs administration contains a number of different groups and organizations. The central entity, called the Consumer Affairs Agency, functions as a control tower for the overall consumer administration. It unifies information, conducts surveys and analyses, and promptly calls attention to consumer issues. The Consumer Commission acts as an independent third-party organization within the Cabinet Office; commission members are appointed by the Prime Minister, with the primary function of monitoring the consumer administration as a whole. In addition to these administrative organizations, certain private consumer organizations that have achieved a certain level of success in dealing with consumer issues also play a fundamental role in the Japanese system of consumer group litigation.

The Japanese collective redress system allows a consumer organization certified by the Prime Minister to file a lawsuit against a business operator on behalf of one or more consumers.

Under basic principles of civil litigation, a consumer victim (i.e., individual plaintiff) sues the business operator (i.e., the defendant) who has perpetrated a wrong against the consumer. However, as an exception to this rule, the Prime Minister may grant private consumer organizations the authority to sue, because: (1) significant differences exist in the quality and quantity of information available to, and the bargaining power of, the consumer and the business operator, (2) litigation requires significant time, money, and labor, which often outstrips the potential recovery of an individual consumer, whose damages are customarily small, and (3) the recovery of damages by an individual consumer is rarely effective at ending or discouraging a business operator's wrongful conduct.[1]

The Japanese system for collective redress consists of two separate systems with distinct but related goals: in one, a "Qualified Consumer Organization" certified by the Prime Minister seeks injunctive relief against unjust acts by a business operator to protect the interests of numerous unspecified consumers (the "Injunction Demand System"); in the other, a "Specified Qualified Consumer Organization" certified from among Qualified Consumer Organizations by the Prime Minister, conducts court proceedings seeking a collective recovery of damages from an unjust business operator on behalf of consumers (the "Redress for Damage System").

The Injunction Demand System was introduced in June 2007 and the Redress for Damage System was introduced in October 2016. Both of these systems: (1) involve the use of Qualified Consumer Organizations or Specified Qualified Consumer Organizations, which are private organizations that play a public role in realization of a fair consumer market while also monitoring the market from the consumer's point of view; (2) contribute to rule formation by eliciting active guidance from the courts with regard to interpretation of the law; (3) together with the actions of the prefectural governments, supplement the functions of the Consumer Affairs Agency, which does not have local branches; and (4) help to eliminate unfair trade practices from the market.[2]

The details of these two collective redress systems, and future issues that may arise with regard to them, are discussed in more detail below.

22.2 THE JAPANESE INJUNCTION DEMAND SYSTEM

The Injunction Demand System was introduced in June 2007, as part of the Consumer Contract Act (*see* Section 22.2.1 below). Under this system, a Qualified Consumer Organization (*see* Section 22.2.2 below) may file a legal action, when business operators engage (or are likely to engage) in wrongful acts (i.e., acts proscribed by certain applicable laws and regulations) against many and unspecified consumers (*see* Section 22.2.3 below), demanding an injunction ordering: (1) the cessation or prevention of the business operator's wrongful acts, (2) the disposal or removal of materials used to carry out the wrongful acts, or (3) other necessary measures to ensure the cessation or prevention of the wrongful acts (*see* Section 22.2.4 below).

22.2.1 *Background and Important Features of the Injunction Demand System*

As of the end of June 2020, lawsuits had been filed against seventy-three business operators under the Injunction Demand System.[3]

[1] www.caa.go.jp/en/policy/consumer_system, last viewed: August 8, 2020 (in English).

[2] *See* Consumer Commission Working Group on Rules Formation in the Consumer Law Field (hereinafter referred to as "Working Group"), *Shōhisha hō bunya ni okeru rūru keisei no arikata tō kentō wākingu gurūpu [Working Group Report on the Formation of Rules in the Consumer Law Field]*, 24.

[3] www.caa.go.jp/policies/policy/consumer_system/collective_litigation_system/about_qualified_consumer_organization/, last viewed: August 8, 2020 (in Japanese only).

According to the *Heisei 30 nen ban shōhisha hakusho [Heisei 30 ed. White Paper on Consumers]*, more than 450 cases involving injunctions had been reported through April 1, 2018, whether or not related lawsuits had been filed. As described later, a Qualified Consumer Organization must first send a written demand to the business operator who will be the defendant in the Injunction Action, in order to encourage early, private settlement, as opposed to engaging directly in litigation, which would involve more time and cost for both the Qualified Consumer Organization and the business operator. It is considered that the significant difference between the number of cases reported (450) and the

The Injunction Demand System was originally introduced in the Consumer Contract Act, which came into force in June 2007; since then, the scope of the system has been expanded to also protect against acts prohibited by other laws. The background, overall structure, and flow of the Injunction Demand System are described in more detail below.

22.2.1.1 Background

The Consumer Contract Act of Japan was enacted in 2000 and went into effect in April 2001, allowing consumers to deny the validity of part or all of contracts that are unjustly solicited or contain unjust clauses. This right of rescission was created due to the structural disparity in the quality and quantity of information and bargaining power between consumers and businesses with regard to commercial transactions and the formation and conclusion of contracts.

Since the enactment and implementation of the Consumer Contract Act, it has been stated that an examination of injunction rights and collective action rights should be conducted in light of trends in judicial reform, in order to make the judicial system, which is the final means of settling disputes, easier for consumers to use to seek redress.[4]

Damage arising from consumer contracts is generally characterized by a large number of similar victims (even though each individual victim's monetary damages may be relatively small). Given the widespread damage these harmful contracts can cause, it is important both to prevent consumer damage from occurring and, should such damage occur, to prevent its spread.[5] Some consumer groups have carried out voluntary activities within Japan, urging business operators to improve their practices and to cease unfair practices; to some extent, these groups have achieved results at deterring unfair business practices. However, there is a limit to the effectiveness of these voluntary activities, as they are not legally supported and some businesses do not always respond sincerely to consumer protection efforts.[6] In light of this, it was considered necessary to grant certain consumer organizations the right to seek injunctions against unfair business practices in order to protect the interests of consumers as a whole.[7]

In addition to the Injunction Demand System, the Redress for Damage System described in Section 22.3 was also considered necessary. However, where the Injunction Demand System focuses on preventing or stopping unfair business practices, the Redress for Damage System provides recourse for individual victims, for example, on the premise that they have the right to claim damages under the Civil Code.[8] Previously, various measures had been taken to allow these claims to be brought effectively through legal proceedings, such as improvement of the Appointed Party System[9] under the Code of Civil Procedure, and it was considered too early to

number actually filed (68) is due to the fact that many issues are resolved through negotiations between the parties before suits are filed with the court.

4 *See* House of Representatives Chamber of Commerce Committee, *Shōhisha keiyaku hō an ni taisuru futai ketsugi [Addendum to the Consumer Contract Bill]* (April 14, 2000), and House of Councilors Committee on Economy and Industry, *Shōhisha keiyaku hō an ni taisuru futai ketsugi [Addendum to the Consumer Contract Bill]* (April 27, 2000).

5 *See* Consumer Group Litigation System Review Committee, Consumer Policy Committee, Quality of Life Council, *Shōhisha dantai soshō seido no arikata ni tsuite [Approaches to the Consumer Group Litigation System]* 2 (June 23, 2005).

6 *Id.* at 3.

7 Quality of Life Council, *supra* note 5.

8 In this regard, the system is very different from the preventative concept, in which a person who had not suffered direct "legal" damage would have not had any legal right to seek an injunction against (or to prevent) unfair acts by a business operator before the Injunction Demand System was introduced.

9 The Appointed Party System is a system in which one or more persons are selected to serve as plaintiffs (or defendants) from among a group of people or entities who share common interests, and the selected persons or entities file lawsuits (or have lawsuits filed against them) as "stand-in parties" for the rest of the group.

introduce a consumer class action system. However, the Redress for Damage System was eventually introduced in October 2016.

22.2.1.2 Important Features of the Injunction Demand System

The Japanese Injunction Demand System has three primary characteristics. First, certain consumer groups which aim to protect the interests of consumers have achieved results by demanding that business operators stop engaging in unfair acts. Consumer groups that have achieved a certain level of results in this manner are granted legal authority for their activities, and given the title of "Qualified Consumer Organization," which includes the Consumers Organization of Japan (COJ) and the Kansai Consumer's Support Organization. These organizations can utilize the Injunction Demand System to demand injunctions, preventing consumer harm before it occurs and protecting the interests of consumers as a whole.

Second, from the viewpoint of protecting the interests of consumers as a whole, the right to demand an injunction applies to and arises from certain types of violations of the consumer laws; specifically, injunctions are available to stop or prevent the types of violations that are likely to harm many consumers through unjust solicitations or unjust contract clauses.

Third, special measures have been taken with regard to court proceedings (which are described in Sections 22.2.4.2 and 22.2.4.3 below), because the parties that exercise the right to demand an injunction (i.e., Qualified Consumer Organizations) are different from the parties to whom the protected interests belong (i.e., consumers).

22.2.2 *Standing: Qualified Consumer Organizations*

Only Qualified Consumer Organizations may file lawsuits seeking injunctions under the Injunction Demand System in Japan. As of June 2020, there were twenty-one Qualified Consumer Organizations in Japan.[10]

In order to become a Qualified Consumer Organization, it is necessary for an entity to obtain certification from the Prime Minister under Article 2, Paragraph 4 of the Consumer Contract Act. The certification requirements are codified in Article 13, Paragraph 3 of the Consumer Contract Act. Certification is valid for six years and may be renewed at the end of each six-year period. (Consumer Contract Act, Article 17, Paragraph 1.)

Table 22.1 outlines the qualification requirements for Qualified Consumer Organizations.

Qualified Consumer Organizations are financed primarily through membership fees and donations from consumers and businesses. More recently, the system was reformed for purposes of more easily permitting Qualified Consumer Organizations to receive third-party funds more widely. In the past, Qualified Consumer Organizations had to record the names, addresses, occupations, and other relevant information about contributors when receiving donations, but observers pointed out that this was a significant obstacle to anonymous donors and to use of donation systems such as crowdfunding.[11] Following the revision of the Ordinance for Enforcement of the Consumer Contract Act in 2017, when a Qualified Consumer Organization receives a donation under a stated threshold amount, and

[10] www.caa.go.jp/policies/policy/consumer_system/collective_litigation_system/about_qualified_consumer_organization/list/, last viewed: August 8, 2020 (in Japanese only).

[11] *See* Japan Federation of Bar Associations, *Shōhisha dantai soshō seido no jikkō teki na unyō ni shisuru shien no arikata ni kansuru kentōkai hōkokusho ni tsuite no ikensho [Written Opinions on the Report of the Study Group on the Modality of Support that Contributes to the Effective Operation of the Consumer Group Litigation System]* 4 (September 16, 2016).

TABLE 22.1 *Key accreditation (qualification) requirements*

Juridical Personality	• NPOs, general incorporated associations, and general incorporated foundations
Results of Activities	• Activities mainly aimed at protecting the interests of many consumers, which have been properly implemented for a considerable period of time.
Organizational Structure & Business Processes	• Applicant has established a system, and operational rules, enabling the applicant to appropriately carry out its business related to injunction demands. • Applicant has established a system whereby activities related to injunction demands are to be examined by consumer counselors, lawyers, and other consumer experts.
Decision-making Method	• Establishment of a board of directors • Board members must not be biased toward any specific company or industry.
Financing Stability	• The applicant has sufficient financial capacity to properly conduct activities related to injunction demands

(Source: Table compiled by the authors based on the figure published on p.142 of ICHIMON ITTŌ SHŌHISHA SAIBAN TETSUZUKI TOKUREI HŌ [Q&A :ACT ON SPECIAL MEASURES FOR CONSUMER COURT PROCEEDINGS], (Legal System Planning Division, Consumer Affairs Agency ed. 2014))

the name of the donor cannot be identified, it is sufficient for the consumer organization to record the date of receipt of the donation, the method by which the donation was raised and the amount of the donation. (Consumer Contract Act, Article 30, and Ordinance for Enforcement of the Consumer Contract Act, Article 21, Item 8.)

22.2.3 *Activities Subject to Injunction Demands*

An injunction demand can be made when a business operator commits or is likely to commit an unjust act against a large number of unspecified consumers, in violation of certain prescribed laws. As of this writing, the "prescribed laws" include Japan's Consumer Contract Act, Act against Unjustifiable Premiums and Misleading Representations, Act on Specified Commercial Transactions, and Food Labeling Act. After its initial creation in the Consumer Contract Act in 2007, the scope of the Injunction Demand System was expanded: (1) in 2009, to include demands for injunctions based on misrepresentations under the Act against Unjustifiable Premiums and Misleading Representations, and acts of unjust solicitation and unjust contract clauses under the Act on Specified Commercial Transactions, and (2) in 2015, to include misrepresentations under the Food Labeling Act.

According to a report published in 2019, the largest number of injunction requests have been based on alleged violations of the Consumer Contract Act.[12] Requests for injunctions based on the Consumer Contract Act are broadly categorized as either unfair solicitation actions or claims regarding unfair clauses; an overwhelmingly large percentage of these claims relate to unfair

[12] *See* Consumer Affairs Agency, *Shōhisha dantai soshō seido sashitome seikyū jirei shū[Collection of Cases of Injunction Demands under the Consumer Group Litigation System]* 12 (March 2019) (www.caa.go.jp/policies/policy/consumer_system/collective_litigation_system/about_system/case_examples_of_injunction/pdf/consumer_system_cms204_190903_01.pdf), last viewed: August 6, 2020 (in Japanese only).

clauses under Articles 8 to 10 of the Consumer Contract Act, with many of them based on cancellation fees per Article 9 and the general provisions of Article 10.[13]

Table 22.2 shows a summary of the legal grounds upon which injunction demands can be brought in Japanese courts (as of July 2019).

TABLE 22.2 *Legal grounds for injunction claims*

Consumer Contract Act	• If, when soliciting a large, non-exclusive group of consumers to enter into consumer contracts, a business operator, an entrusted party, or the agent of a business operator or of an entrusted party (hereinafter, a "business operator, entrusted party, or agent") has engaged or is likely to engage in an action described in Article 4, Paragraphs 1 – 4 of the Consumer Contract Act, a Qualified Consumer Organization may demand that the business operator, entrusted party, or agent cease or refrain from engaging in the relevant action, or remove or dispose of materials used in the relevant act, and may take other necessary measures to stop or prevent the action. • If, when soliciting a large, non-exclusive group of consumers to enter into consumer contracts, an entrusted party or an agent (of either a business operator or an entrusted party) has been engaging, or is likely to engage, in an action described in Article 4, Paragraphs 1 – 4 of the Consumer Contract Act, a Qualified Consumer Organization may demand that the business operator or other person specified in the Consumer Contract Act cease the behavior, instruct them to rectify the behavior or stop them from inducing customers to enter into consumer contracts, and take other necessary measures to stop or prevent the action. • If a business operator or its agent has entered or is likely to enter into consumer contracts that include any unreasonable clause provided in Articles 8 through 10 of the Consumer Contract Act, with a large, non-exclusive group of consumers, a Qualified Consumer Organization may demand that the business operator or its agent cease or prevent the action, or dispose of or remove materials used in the relevant action, and may also take other necessary measures to stop or prevent the action. • If a business operator's agent has entered into or is likely to enter into consumer contracts that include any unreasonable clause provided in Articles 8 through 10 of the Consumer Contract Act with a large, non-exclusive group of consumers, a Qualified Consumer Organization may demand that the business operator or its other agent(s) instruct the relevant agent to rectify the situation or stop the agent from inducing consumers to enter into consumer contracts, and may also take any other necessary measures to stop or prevent the action.

[13] Article 10 of the Consumer Contract Act provides that "A consumer contract clause is void if it deems a consumer's inaction to constitute the manifestation of an intention to be bound by the offer of a consumer contract or by the acceptance of an offer for such a contract, or if it otherwise restricts a consumer's rights or expands a consumer's obligations beyond as when legal or regulatory provisions unrelated to public order are applied, unilaterally prejudicing the interests of the consumer in violation of the fundamental principle provided in Article 1, Paragraph 2 of the Civil Code."

Article 1, Paragraph 2 of the Civil Code codifies and establishes the principle of good faith.

TABLE 22.2 *(continued)*

Act against Unjustifiable Premiums and Misleading Representations	• When a business operator makes or is likely to make any of the following representations to a number of unspecified general consumers, a Qualified Consumer Organization may demand that the business operator stop, or may prevent, those representations, may publicize that the representations fall into category of (i) or (ii) below (representations proscribed by law), or may take other necessary measures to stop or prevent the relevant representations: (i) A representation through which the quality, standard, or other characteristic(s) of goods or services could be misperceived as being much better than they actually are, or significantly better than those of other business operators who supply the same or similar goods or services; or (ii) A representation by which price or any other trade terms relating to goods or services could be misunderstood as being much more favorable to general consumers than the actual terms, or than the terms provided by other business operators who supply the same or similar goods or services.
Act on Specified Commercial Transactions	• When a seller, service provider or other specific business operator has engaged or is likely to engage in any of the prohibited conduct specified by the Act on Specified Commercial Transactions[14] with many and unspecified persons, with regard to Door-to-Door Sales, Mail Order Sales, Telemarketing Sales, Multilevel Marketing Transactions, Provision of Specified Continuous Services, Business Opportunity Sales Transactions, and/or Door-to-Door Purchases, a Qualified Consumer Organization may demand that such seller, service provider or other specific business operator discontinue or prevent the relevant conduct, dispose of or remove any object used in connection with the conduct, or take any other necessary measures to discontinue or prevent the conduct.
Food Labeling Act	• If any Person Engaged in a Food-related Business, as defined in the Food Labeling Act, actually displays or is likely to display information that is significantly contrary to fact with regard to the name, allergens, preservation method, expiration date, ingredients, additives, nutritional or caloric value, or country of origin of any food product(s) to many and unspecified persons, in violation of Food Labeling Standards, a Qualified Consumer Organization may demand that the Person Engaged in a Food-related Business suspend or prevent such action, publicize that the person or entity in question has displayed information that is significantly contrary to fact with regard to the relevant food, or take any other necessary measures to suspend or prevent the action.

[14] Specific violations are codified for each type of transaction, including misrepresentations, intimidation, obstruction of termination, and conclusion of contracts that include unfair clauses.

22.2.4 *Legal Proceedings under the Injunction Demand System*

22.2.4.1 Prerequisites for Filing a Legal Action

When a Qualified Consumer Organization plans to file a lawsuit to demand an injunction (an "Injunction Action"), it must first send a written demand (a "Demand Letter") to the person or entity who will be the defendant in the Injunction Action (the "Opponent"), stating the essence of the claim, the points in dispute, and other relevant facts. The Qualified Consumer Organization may not file the Injunction Action until at least one week has passed from the time when the Opponent received the Demand Letter. (Consumer Contract Act, Article 41, Paragraph 1.) In other words, a Qualified Consumer Organization must first attempt to resolve the issue with the Opponent through a request in writing before resorting to litigation.

This requirement is intended to provide business operators with an opportunity to identify problematical actions and transactions at an early stage and to rectify the situation on their own, as well as to encourage early, private dispute resolution and to encourage appropriate transactions.[15]

Certain other restrictions also apply to the exercise of the right to demand an injunction, in order to ensure the appropriateness of such demands. For example, an Injunction Action may not be brought for purposes of promoting the illicit interests of the Qualified Consumer Organization or any third party, or with the intent of causing damage to the Opponent. (Consumer Contract Act, Article 12–2, Paragraph 1, Item 1.)

22.2.4.2 Procedures in the Event of Multiple Injunction Actions

In principle, the fact that a Qualified Consumer Organization files an Injunction Action does not prevent other Qualified Consumer Organizations from filing actions seeking injunctive relief in the same manner and with respect to the same act by the same business operator. However, in cases where multiple Injunction Actions are brought in the same or similar actions, the court may, after consideration of various issues, including the addresses or locations of the parties, the addresses of witnesses, the similarity of issues or evidence, and other relevant circumstances, transfer part or all of the lawsuit to the court in which the similar actions are pending or another court with jurisdiction over the dispute. (Consumer Contract Act, Article 44.) This transfer may be made either upon a party's petition or *ex officio*, at the court's discretion.

The rationale behind this provision is twofold. First, where a possibility exists that more than one Qualified Consumer Organization may file a lawsuit against the same Opponent(s) regarding the same act(s), it is necessary to centralize the proceedings as much as possible from the perspectives of judicial economy, rationalizing the burden that the defendant would have to bear in responding to the action, preventing conflicting judgments, and other considerations. Second, cases involving similar contract clauses or other prohibited behaviors may have substantial overlap with regard to the legal and factual issues presented; it is also often appropriate for the parties to enjoy the benefits of a common trial.[16]

In principle, when multiple Injunction Actions relating to the same claim against the same business operator, brought by multiple Qualified Consumer Organizations, are pending

[15] *See* Legal System Planning Division of Consumer Affairs Agency (hereinafter referred to as Legal System Planning Division), *Chikujō kaisetsu shōhisha keiyaku hō [Commentary on Consumer Contract Act]* 329 (February 2019 ed., available online).

[16] *Id.* at 337.

simultaneously in the same court of first instance or court of second instance, the oral arguments and judicial decisions shall be made in a consolidated manner. (Consumer Contract Act, Article 45, Paragraph1.) As discussed in more detail in Section 22.2.4.3 below, once an Injunction Action brought by a Qualified Consumer Organization results in a final, binding judgment (or reaches a stage with the same effect as a final and binding judgment), additional Injunction Actions cannot be made against the same Opponent with regard to the same action(s) that formed the basis of the prior suit. (Consumer Contract Act, Article 12–2, Paragraph1, Item 2.) Due to this restriction, it is generally desirable to unify the lawsuits, and the judgment, in such cases whenever possible.[17]

22.2.4.3 Effect of Final Judgments

The Injunction Demand System has no procedure to extend the effect of a judgment, so the principle of relative effect applies, which means the effect of a judgment (*res judicata*) extends only to the parties involved in the lawsuit.

However, when an Injunction Action or other proceeding (including not only litigation, but also procedures for filing a petition for settlement and arbitration/conciliation) brought by a Qualified Consumer Organization reaches final and binding judgment (or a stage that has the same effect as a final and binding judgment, such as judicial settlement, acknowledgment or waiver of claim, conciliation agreement, arbitration award, etc.)[18] in principle, other Qualified Consumer Organizations may not subsequently demand an injunction involving the same Opponent and the same claim. (Consumer Contract Act, Article 12–2, Paragraph 1, Item 2.) Without this restriction on requests for injunctive relief, identical claims could be repeated indefinitely, contradictory judgments could be entered, and adverse effects would arise (e.g., placing an excessive burden on the Opponent, due to the need to respond to multiple identical suits).[19] Unlike the expansion of *res judicata*, this single judgment rule is understood to be a policy-based limitation on the substantive right to bring an Injunction Action, with the aim of eliminating the adverse effects described above.

A final judgment (or its equivalent) under the Injunction Demand System also has the following effects: (1) limiting (preventing) subsequent identical claims from being brought outside litigation; and (2) all concurrent or subsequent litigation involving identical claims is dismissed, as long as the relevant claims have the same content (i.e., basis and relevant facts) and are brought against the same Opponent.

This provision regarding the finality of judgments was a major point of contention during deliberations by the Diet, Japan's legislative body, partly because it was inserted suddenly during the drafting process for the revision bill. This type of provision is not commonly found in the legislation of other countries. However, in many major European countries, (1) only a few qualified consumer protection organizations have received accreditation, or (2) in many cases,

[17] Legal System Planning Division, *supra* note 15, at 338.

[18] However, a final and binding judgment (or the equivalent) should not restrict the exercise of the right to demand an injunction where no substantive ruling on the actual injunction demand has been made (i.e., a final and binding judgment dismissing the action without prejudice, and dismissing an Injunction Demand solely on the grounds that the claim constitutes an abusive claim based on an unjust purpose. Also, a final and binding judgment (or the equivalent) should not restrict the exercise of the right to demand an injunction where a judgment dismisses a claim for confirmation of absence of the right to demand an injunction, or for confirmation of absence of the obligation related to the right to demand because there was no reason to prevent the filing of a lawsuit for an Injunction Demand as a claim for benefit. Certain exceptions, including these (from (*i*) to (*ha*) of Item 2 of Paragraph 1, Article 12–2 of the Consumer Contract Act) are provided in the law.

[19] Legal System Planning Division, *supra* note 15, at 201.

qualified organizations exercise their right to collective action cooperatively. As a result, there are few reported cases outside Japan in which multiple organizations bring the same claim against the same business operator despite an earlier litigation loss.

Within Japan, it has been pointed out that introduction of the provision regarding finality of judgments into the Injunction Demand System is reasonable from the business operators' point of view, because there is no nationwide network of consumer protection organizations, and the level of cooperation between Qualified Consumer Organizations is not high; therefore, it is more likely that multiple consumer organizations will file an action against the same business operators arising from same original claim(s).[20]

Additionally, it should be noted that subsequent demands and actions are not precluded if the grounds for the claim or demand arose *after* the conclusion of oral argument in the Injunction Action where a final and binding judgment (or equivalent) was entered (Consumer Contract Act, Article 12–2, Paragraph 2).

Incidentally, Japanese law currently does not have provisions that permit an individual (consumer or otherwise) to invoke the contents of a judgment in ordinary legal proceedings relating to his or her claim for damages. Based on the purposes of the Injunction Demand System and uncertainties surrounding the functionality of the Japanese version of class action suits (i.e., the Redress for Damage System described in Section 22.3 below), some commentators have suggested that it may be necessary to consider additional measures, including granting consumers the power to invoke the contents of a judgment in ordinary court proceedings relating to his or her claim for damages.[21]

22.3 THE JAPANESE COLLECTIVE REDRESS SYSTEM FOR DAMAGE RECOVERY (THE "REDRESS FOR DAMAGE SYSTEM")

22.3.1 *Background and Important Features of the Redress for Damage System*

In December 2013, the "Act on Special Measures Concerning Civil Court Proceedings for the Collective Redress for Property Damage Incurred by Consumers" (the "Japanese Class Action Act") was established to create a system of collective redress actions for consumers in Japan. The Japanese Class Action Act came into effect in October 2016; its background, overall structure and the flow of class actions under the act ("Damage Recovery Actions") are examined in more detail below.

22.3.1.1 Background and History

According to the Consumer Affairs Agency, the background of the Japanese Class Action Act is as follows. Recent consumer harm in Japan was characterized by: (1) a large number of complaints and inquiries from consumers concerning products and services (approximately 850,000 in fiscal 2012), (2) a high number of transaction-related consultations (over 720,000 in fiscal 2012), and (3) a proliferation of similar consumer and transaction-related damages. Additionally, there are many cases in which consumers who have suffered damage do not consult a lawyer, or take other action,

[20] Kōichi Miki, *Shōhisha dantai soshō seido no gaiyō to hyōka [Overview and Evaluation of the Consumer Group Litigation System]*, *in* MINJI SOSHŌ NI YORU SHŪGO TEKI KENRI HOGO NO RIPPŌ TO RIRON [LEGISLATIONS AND THEORIES OF COLLECTIVE RIGHTS PROTECTION THROUGH CIVIL JUSTICE] 29, 35–36 (Miki ed., 2017).

[21] Yūkyō Hishida, *Shōhisha dantai soshō no kadai [Issues of Consumer Group Litigation]*, 79(1) HŌRITSU JIHŌ 96, 98 (2007).

due to the vast differences in the quality and quantity of available information and the disparate bargaining power between consumers and businesses. Even in the legal system, which provides the ultimate means of recovering damages, bringing an action requires considerable time, labor, and money, but the amount of individual consumer damages is generally small and ordinary consumers often have no knowledge of lawsuits and many may even be unaware that they have been victimized.[22]

In light of the actual situation surrounding consumer harm, it was pointed out that it was necessary to establish a new litigation system, in which individual consumers could bring their claims simply and promptly, in order to ensure the effectiveness and protection of consumer rights. Additionally, national institutions such as the Diet had long requested that the Japanese government consider introduction of a new legal system to provide relief to consumers generally.[23]

These developments led to the enactment of the Redress for Damage System and the creation of the Japanese Class Action Act.

The Redress for Damage System created under the Japanese Class Action Act was designed to improve the relationship between consumers and businesses, encourage vigorous consumer spending, foster the development of sound businesses (and business practices), and promote fair competition. The system was further intended to encourage previously-damaged consumers to resume consumption, thereby stimulating a demand for healthy businesses, which in turn would promote economic growth.

22.3.1.2 Concerns Addressed by the Japanese Class Action System

Many countries around the world have developed, or are developing, class action systems. The designers of these systems often reference the US class action system, either with regard to adopting the system in some form or to highlight the differences between their systems and the US system. This is true in Japan as well. Prior to enactment of the Japanese Class Action Act, discussions on the Japanese version of a class action system were often marked by strong resistance to, and criticism of, class action lawsuits. Specifically, there was concern that class action lawsuits would have a chilling effect on legitimate business activities, and that business owners might be victimized and abused by unjust consumer actions brought in the name of "rights relief."

These concerns were evaluated and addressed as follows. First, the drafters designed the Japanese Redress for Damage System to ensure that proper litigation proceedings could be conducted without inviting inappropriate lawsuits. Specifically, the Redress for Damage System was created with the following features: (1) only Specified Qualified Consumer Organizations certified by the Prime Minister can act as plaintiffs in suits brought under the act, and even those organizations are subject to administrative supervision; (2) the scope of claims is limited to specific claims, basically those involving contracts between a consumer and a business operator, and consolation damages and similar "special damages" are excluded from the scope of permitted damages; and (3) the system is an "opt-in" type, in contrast with the class action system in the United States.[24]

22 *See*, ICHIMON ITTŌ SHŌHISHA SAIBAN TETSUZUKI TOKUREI HŌ [Q&A: ACT ON SPECIAL MEASURES FOR CONSUMER COURT PROCEEDINGS], (Legal System Planning Division ed. 2014).

23 *Id.* For example, the Program for Promotion of Justice System Reform created by the Cabinet in 2002 states that, in response to a small amount and large number of damages, "An introduction of the so-called collective right of action and how to determine the eligible organizations when it is introduced should be examined for each legal field, considering the purpose of an individual substantive law and the rights and interests that the law is intended to protect."

24 Legal System Planning Division, *supra* note 22, at 9.

Second, some scholars pointed out that the adverse litigation effects often seen in US class actions derive from the unique characteristics of the US civil procedure system (i.e., the so-called "Yankee Package"), and not from the mechanism of class actions per se. The peculiar characteristics of the United States legal system, including its civil jury system, the existence of punitive damages, the discovery process, the full success fee system, entrepreneurial lawyer activities, the wide discretion given to judges, the existence of certain courts with extreme prejudices toward plaintiffs, and the American rule[25] regarding attorney fees, contribute to and cause the problems referenced above. Legal scholars specializing in the area of civil procedure have pointed out that similar problems should not arise in Japan, where the legal system lacks these problematic characteristics.[26]

The Brazilian class action system, as in place at the time, provided the basis for the Japanese class action system. (Please *see* Chapter 8 for more information about class action procedures in Brazil.) In Brazil, as in Japan, class actions must involve individual rights that are similar in nature, and the suits take place in two stages. The first stage action involves an appeal for a general benefit judgment, and examines the common issues (*sentença condenatória genérica*). Individual claimants' issues are examined later, in the second stage (*liquidação de sentença*). Civil procedure scholars in Japan consider this type of action highly successful, judging from the number of cases brought.[27]

In addition to the Brazilian class action system, the drafters of the Japanese Class Action Act referred to the then-current legislative thought in Canada and the legislative history of an unenacted bill in France.[28] The Japanese version of a class action system was created based on studies of these systems.

22.3.1.3 Summary of Important Features

The Japanese Redress for Damage System is a two-step litigation system for collective recovery of consumer damages. In particular, the system is designed to address, and provide redress for, the types of consumer damages that occur frequently.

25 Under this rule each party generally bears its own attorney fees, regardless of the outcome of a lawsuit; and although Japan and the United States are the few countries that follow this rule, there are differences in the way the two countries apply the general rule. For example, in Japan attorney fees can be treated as an expense item when calculating damages in tort suits, and the victorious plaintiff can claim reimbursement of attorney fees, while in the United States, tort damages do not generally include attorney fees. *See*, Thomas D. Rowe, Jr. (Kōichi Miki trans.,), *Bengoshi hiyō wa dare ga futan subeki ka [Who Should Pay for Attorney Fees]*, in AMERIKA MINJI SOSHŌ HŌ NO RIRON [THEORY OF THE CODE OF CIVIL PROCEDURE IN AMERICA] 258, 258–260 (Miki trans, 2006) (Masahiko Ōmura & Kōichi Miki, 2006).

26 Miki, *Shūgō teki kenri hogo soshō seido no kōchiku to hikaku hō seido kenkyū no igi [Establishment of a System for Collective Rights Protection and the Significance of Comparative Law System Research]*, in MINJI SOSHŌ NI YORU SHŪGO TEKI KENRI HOGO NO RIPPŌ TO RIRON [LEGISLATIONS AND THEORIES OF COLLECTIVE RIGHTS PROTECTION THROUGH CIVIL JUSTICE], *supra* note 20, at 96, 106–07 (2017).

27 Miki, *Burajiru ni okeru kurasu akushon (shūdan soshō seido) no gaiyō [Overview of Class Actions in Brazil (collective redress system)]*, in MINJI SOSHŌ NI YORU SHŪGO TEKI KENRI HOGO NO RIPPŌ TO RIRON [LEGISLATIONS AND THEORIES OF COLLECTIVE RIGHTS PROTECTION THROUGH CIVIL JUSTICE], *supra* note 20, at 147. Brazil did not publish comprehensive national statistics on the number of class actions, but according to the National Council of Justice of Brazil (*Conselho Nacional de Justica*), 62,210 class actions were brought before the judiciary in Brazil in 2017, of which: (1) 41,686 were public civil actions, (2) 14,119 were administrative misconduct actions, (3) 4,211 were collective civil actions, and (4) 2,194 were popular actions. *See*, www.conjur.com.br/2019-mar-20/opiniao-dados-efetividade-acoes-coletivas-brasil (Portuguese).

28 *Id.* at 153–56. Also, *see* Miki, *Shōhisha shūgō soshō seido no riron to kadai [Theory and Challenges of the Consumer Class Action System]*, in MINJI SOSHŌ NI YORU SHŪGO TEKI KENRI HOGO NO RIPPŌ TO RIRON [LEGISLATIONS AND THEORIES OF COLLECTIVE RIGHTS PROTECTION THROUGH CIVIL JUSTICE], *supra* note 20, at 264, 265; and Miki, *Shōhisha shūgō soshō seido no kōzō to riron [Structure and Theory of the Consumer Class Action System]*, in MINJI SOSHŌ NI YORU SHŪGO TEKI KENRI HOGO NO RIPPŌ TO RIRON [LEGISLATIONS AND THEORIES OF COLLECTIVE RIGHTS PROTECTION THROUGH CIVIL JUSTICE], *supra* note 20, at 293–94.

During the Stage 1 procedure (i.e., Litigation Seeking a Declaratory Judgment on Common Obligations), a Specified Qualified Consumer Organization certified by the Prime Minister acts as a plaintiff, and the court determines whether or not a common obligation exists between a considerable number of consumers and one or more Opponents. If the plaintiff prevails in the Stage 1 procedure, the matter advances to the Stage 2 procedure, in which consumers are given the opportunity to bring individual claims and obtain recovery of damages. Each impacted consumer is given the opportunity to join the Stage 2 procedure (i.e., Proceedings for Determining the Target Claims) wherein a court determines the existence or non-existence and amount of each individual claim through a simple procedure.

Although consumers can participate in Stage 2 procedures (based on the results of Stage 1 procedures conducted by a Specified Qualified Consumer Organization), the actual Stage 2 procedures themselves are also conducted via a delegation of authority to the Specified Qualified Consumer Organization. This reduces the overall time, cost, and labor required to recover damages. Additional benefits include: (1) overcoming the burden of consumers' hesitance to use court proceedings and the ability to recover consumer damages that were previously difficult to recover (either due to consumer hesitance to sue, the small amount of damages at issue, or other factors), (2) the ability to resolve numerous disputes quickly and collectively, and a reduction in the burden business operators face in responding to lawsuits, and (3) more efficient use of court resources.[29]

22.3.2 *Standing: Limited to Specified Qualified Consumer Organizations*

As described above, in a Japanese class action suit under the Redress for Damage System, only a Specified Qualified Consumer Organization (an entity which is specially certified from among Qualified Consumer Organizations) is allowed to conduct procedures. Certifications to pursue an action are granted by the Prime Minister. Rather than charging the court with determining the eligibility (i.e., standing) of the party bringing a proceeding every time a suit was filed, it was decided that the Prime Minister would certify the eligibility of the relevant organization to act as a plaintiff, to reduce the risk of trial delays due to arguments over standing, to reduce the burden on defendant businesses, and to help consumers know to whom they should report information about damages or losses.[30]

As of the end of the June 2020, there were only three Specified Qualified Consumer Organizations in Japan.[31]

Specified Qualified Consumer Organizations are allowed to receive donations from consumers and businesses. For legal improvements to encourage donations, *see* Section 22.2.2, above.[32]

The main requirements for certification of an entity as a Specified Qualified Consumer Organization are as shown in Table 22.3 below (as well as in Table 22.2, above).

29 Legal System Planning Division, *supra* note 22, at 3.

30 Legal System Planning Division, *supra* note 22, at 136.

31 www.caa.go.jp/policies/policy/consumer_system/collective_litigation_system/about_qualified_consumer_organization/list_of_specified/, last viewed: August 8, 2020 (in Japanese only). The three organizations are the COJ, the Kansai Consumer's Support Organization, and Saitama Shōhisha-higai wo Nakusu Kai (Japanese only).

32 If an organization takes an action that is deemed not to be intended to benefit consumers under the instruction or commission of the company (i.e., filing a lawsuit against a company in competition with another company that has made a large amount of donations to the organization) the organization is considered subject to an administrative disposition, such as an order for improvement, as an inappropriate exercise of authority. (Japanese Class Action Act, Article 75, Paragraph 1 and Article 85, Paragraph 2.) *See*, Legal System Planning Division, *supra* note 22, at 151.

TABLE 22.3 *Main additional requirements for certification of Specified Qualified Consumer Organizations*

Results of Activities	• The applicant has been carrying out injunction demands properly for a considerable period of time
Organizational Structure & Processes	• The applicant has established a system and operational rules that enable the applicant to appropriately carry out services related to both injunction demands and collective redress of damages
Decision-Making Methods	• One or more of the directors are lawyers
Financial Stability	• The applicant has a sufficient financial basis to provide stable, continuous services related to collective redress of damages
Remuneration	• In cases where any remuneration or expenses are paid in relation to services related to collective redress of damages, such remuneration or expenses shall not be an unjust amount, from the viewpoint of protecting the interests of consumers
Other	• There is no risk that other services (aside from those related to collective redress of damages) will hinder the proper execution of services related to collective redress of damages

(Source: Compiled by the authors based on the table published on page 142 of ICHIMON ITTŌ SHŌHISHA SAIBAN TETSUZUKI TOKUREI HŌ [Q&A :ACT ON SPECIAL MEASURES FOR CONSUMER COURT PROCEEDINGS], (Legal System Planning Division, Consumer Affairs Agency ed. 2014))

These organizations are engaged in activities designed to protect the interests of consumers, and are required to conduct appropriate business operations in order to ensure the stable implementation of court proceedings and to protect the credibility and integrity of the consumer redress system.

22.3.3 *Scope of Claims and Damages*

Under the Redress for Damage System, claims must conform to the following requirements:

(1) Capable of being quickly and simply resolved by a court during the Simple Determination Proceedings (*dominance*), and

(2) Involve claims that enable the Opponent(s) to understand and roughly estimate the amount of damages suffered by consumers which will be contested in the Proceedings for Determining the Target Claims (*potential to capture disputed earnings*).[33] Additionally, the obligation of business operators to compensate injured consumers for damages suffered is based on the fact that the actual and legal causes of these damages are commonly shared by those injured consumers (*commonality*).

(3) Relate to damages suffered by a substantial number of consumers (*multiplicity*).

22.3.3.1 Eligible Claims

In order to ensure predictability for businesses and consumers, the basic claims concerning consumer contracts are listed in the Japanese Class Action Act.[34] These claims are the ones most commonly asserted with regard to recovery of damages by Japanese consumers.

[33] Legal System Planning Division, *supra* note 22, at 30.
[34] *Id.*, at 26.

Specifically, claims are limited to claims for the payment of money "with respect to consumer contracts" (Japanese Class Action Act, Article 3, Paragraph 1), and take one of the following forms:

(1) a request for performance of obligations under a contract;
(2) a claim for reimbursement based on unjust enrichment;
(3) a claim for damages for breach of contract[35] and;
(4) a claim for damages under the provisions of the Civil Code, based on a tort. (Note that this does not include the right to claim damages under special laws, such as the Financial Instruments and Exchange Act and the Product Liability Act.)

22.3.3.2 Scope of Damages and Defendants

Claims seeking compensation for extended damages, lost profits, personal injuries, and consolation money, are excluded from the scope of permitted damages under the Japanese Class Action Act. (*See* Japanese Class Action Act, Article 3, Paragraph 2.)

Since the claim must relate to "consumer contracts," it is generally assumed that the Opponent will be a counterparty to the relevant contract. However, business operators who perform obligations under a consumer contract and those who solicit, have another person solicit, or encourage solicitation for the conclusion of a consumer contract can also be the defendant for a tort claim referred in Section 22.3.3.1, point (4) above. (*See* Japanese Class Action Act, Article 3, Paragraph 3.) As described in Section 22.3.3.1 above, damages arising from accidents that are not based on consumer contracts are excluded from the permitted claims, as are extended damages, lost profits, personal injury damages, and consolation money. Therefore, Japanese Class Actions currently cannot address situations such as personal injuries resulting from train accidents, or claims for consolation money relating to leaks of personal information on the Internet. Some have pointed out that the kinds of cases referenced above differ based on the facts and circumstances of each case and that they should not be generally excluded from the scope of the Japanese Class Action system, as well as concerns over the fact that consolation payments are excluded from the Redress for Damage System, from the perspective of providing proper relief to victims.[36] However, it is reasonable to exclude these categories of actions from the scope of Japanese Class Actions because these types of actions need individual judgments and therefore are unlikely to satisfy the requirement of dominance (*see* 22.3.3, point (1) above), and the need for individual judgments also makes it difficult for defendants to obtain a general grasp of the potential liability arising from these disputes.

22.3.4 *Flow of Two-Stage Procedure*

22.3.4.1 First Stage Procedures: Trial and Settlement

The first stage of the Redress for Damage System is described in the law as

> an action seeking a declaratory judgment, whereby the Company has an obligation to pay money to these Consumers based on factual and legal causes common to these Consumers, except the

[35] The revised Civil Code, which came into effect on April 1, 2020, classifies the seller's liability for defect warranty as a liability for default.

[36] Miki, *supra* note 28, at 291–92 and 293.

> cases where a claim for a payment of money filed by a Consumer who has no grounds due to circumstances specific to the Consumer, where property damage is incurred by a considerable number of Consumers in connection with Consumer Contracts. (Japanese Class Action Act, Article 2, Item 4)

In plain English, Stage 1 proceedings begin when a Specified Qualified Consumer Organization files a legal action seeking a declaratory judgment to determine that the Opponent(s) have an obligation to pay consumers, (1) based on common factual and legal claims, and (2) based on legally permitted grounds.

Stage 1 proceedings are limited to declaratory judgment actions where the issues involved are common to many rights-holders (i.e., consumers), each of whom has similar rights. With regard to these common issues, the existence or nonexistence of the monetary obligation of the Opponent, and the contents of that obligation, are tried collectively in an action seeking a declaratory judgment. The Stage 1 procedure seeks to examine and determine the common issues, as a prerequisite for the Stage 2 procedure (which is conducted later) that will address the specific claims of each individual rights holder.

The Stage 1 procedure does not examine the existence or nonexistence of individuals' substantive rights to make a claim, per se. Rather, the court is concerned about determining whether the requirements, including dominance, commonality, and multiplicity, have been met to establish the individual rights at issue. For example, in a case involving claims for damages based on a tort, the subject of Stage 1 proceedings would be the Opponent's intentional or negligently wrongful conduct, and the illegality of the Opponent's act(s). The specific amount of damages caused thereby, and the causal relationship between the action and the damages, are considered individual issues, which are then examined during Stage 2 proceedings.[37]

In Stage 1, also known as "Litigation Seeking a Declaratory Judgment on Common Obligations," a Specified Qualified Consumer Organization and an Opponent business operator may also enter into a settlement agreement with regard to the presence or absence of part or all of the obligations upon which the Litigation Seeking a Declaratory Judgment on Common Obligations is brought or based. (Japanese Class Action Act, Article 10.)

However, the sort of settlements which can be reached in first stage proceedings remain controversial. With regard to the content of such settlements, the Japanese Consumer Affairs Agency takes the position that the parties cannot enter into a settlement regarding the disposition of individual consumers' rights under substantive law (for example, a settlement that "the relevant consumers agree not to bring claims in a legal action, in return for receiving a fixed amount of settlement money from the defendant business"). According to the Agency, this is because the Japanese Class Action Act does not grant Specified Qualified Consumer Organizations the authority to dispose of consumers' rights under substantive law.[38]

Some commentators have stated that a judicial settlement (e.g., for a flat rate of 50 percent of the payment amount) that approves a common obligation on a pro rata basis is not acceptable because such a settlement compromises the rights of individual consumers.[39] But some Japanese judges have stated that such a settlement is not considered a prohibited settlement which simply orders payment of a stated amount, regardless of the common obligations, and if the contents of the settlement are found to be in line with the court's beliefs and both parties are convinced, it is

37 *See*, Miki, *supra* note 28, at 294.

38 Legal System Planning Division, *supra* note 22, at 54.

39 *See*, Kazuhiko Yamamoto, Kaisetsu shōhisha saiban tetsuzuki tokurei hō [The Explanation of Act on Special Measures for Consumer Court Proceedings] 191 (2d ed. 2016).

not necessarily unreasonable.[40] Therefore, whether this kind of settlement can be reached should be carefully evaluated.

22.3.4.2 First Stage Procedures: Effect of Judgment

The effect of a final and binding judgment in the first stage procedure extends to, and is binding on, (1) all persons provided for in Article 115 (1)[41] of the Code of Civil Procedure of Japan, (2) Specified Qualified Consumer Organizations which are not parties to the Litigation Seeking a Declaratory Judgment on Common Obligations, and (3) all impacted consumers who opted into the second stage by delegating their claims to the Specified Qualified Consumer Organization. (Japanese Class Action Act, Article 9.) If a Specified Qualified Consumer Organization loses the Stage 1 case, this rule prevents the Opponent, who has presented a thorough and successful defense in the first stage action, from facing another, essentially identical suit from another Specified Qualified Consumer Organization.[42] If a judgment of dismissal is rendered in the first stage, consumers are not affected by the dismissal because no claims have been (and no claims will be) filed in the second stage.

A judgment upholding (i.e., approving) the claims brought in the Stage 1 proceeding has the effect of activating the Stage 2 procedure under the Redress for Damage System via a petition by the plaintiff Specified Qualified Consumer Organization. A judgment dismissing the Specified Qualified Consumer Organization's claim has the opposite effect; if the plaintiffs do not prevail at Stage 1, Stage 2 proceedings will not occur.

The question whether consumers who do not participate in the second stage procedure described below can "incorporate" the content of Stage 1 judgments into separate, individual lawsuits or proceedings remains controversial and undecided.

22.3.4.3 Second Stage Procedures: Trial and Settlement

In the second stage procedure, individual claims against the Opponent(s) are examined based on the judgment or settlement in the first stage proceedings that confirmed the Opponent's common obligations. A form of simplified court proceeding, called "Simple Determination Proceedings" was designed and intended to function as the primary method used in the Stage 2 process. However, since it is also necessary to protect the parties' right to a formal trial (a right guaranteed in Article 32 of the Constitution of Japan), if there is an objection to use of Simple Determination Proceedings, the form of the proceedings shifts, and Stage 2 proceeds as ordinary litigation. (Japanese Class Action Act, Article 52, Paragraph 1.)

Simple Determination Proceedings commence upon the filing of a petition by the same Specified Qualified Consumer Organization that conducted the Stage 1 proceedings. (Japanese Class Action Act, Article 12.) After giving individual notice to all known consumers who hold the

[40] Ken Gotō et al., *Shōhisha saiban tetsuzuki tokurei hō no unyō ni tsuite : kyōtsū gimu kakunin soshō to igi go no soshō ni tsuite [Application of the Act on Special Measures for Consumer Court Proceedings: Litigation for Declaratory Judgment on Common Obligations and Litigation after Objection]*, 1329 HANREI TIMES 5, 26–27.

[41] Article 115, Paragraph 1 provides that a final and binding judgment shall be effective against (1) parties to the litigation, (2) a person (if any) who has become a plaintiff or defendant on behalf of another person, (3) a successor of persons described in (1) or (2) after the conclusion of oral argument, or (4) a person who possesses the subject matter of the claim on behalf of any of (1), (2), or (3).

[42] Legal System Planning Division, *supra* note 22, at 51. If a Specified Qualified Consumer Organization wins the case, the validity of the judgment extends to other Specified Qualified Consumer Organizations, but in such cases, this extension of validity does not have substantial meaning, because only the organization that filed the Stage 1 action is permitted to file a petition to commence the second stage proceedings.

claims at issue ("Target Consumers") and also issuing a public notice,[43] the Specified Qualified Consumer Organization files claims with the court ("Target Claims") for which it has received a delegation of powers from Target Consumers. (Japanese Class Action Act, Article 30. This is considered an "opt-in" system.)

In response to the Stage 2 petition, the Opponent must state its approval or disapproval of the Target Claims within a period specified by the court. In cases where the Opponent fails to state the required approval or disapproval within the designated period, or where the Opponent approves the contents of the Target Claims in its entirety, the contents of the Target Claims are accepted as stated and have the same effect as a final and binding judgment. (Japanese Class Action Act, Article 42.)

If the Opponent contests part or all of the Target Claims, but the Specified Qualified Consumer Organization is satisfied with (i.e., willing to accept) the Opponent's response, no request for a Simple Determination Order is filed and the Target Claims, as modified in accordance with the Opponent's approval or disapproval, become final, with the force of judgment.

However, if the Opponent contests part or all of the Target Claims and the Specified Qualified Consumer Organization does not accept the content of the Opponent's response, the Specified Qualified Consumer Organization must file an application with the court to formally contest the Target Claims. In such cases, the evidence is reviewed and, ultimately, a Simple Determination Order is issued by the court.[44]

The Simple Determination Proceedings usually proceed without oral argument. (Japanese Class Action Act, Article 13.) However, when a Simple Determination Order is made, an interrogation is required (Japanese Class Action Act, Article 44, Paragraph 2), but the examination of evidence is limited to documentary evidence (Japanese Class Action Act, Article 45, Paragraph 1), and examination of witnesses is not allowed.

A Simple Determination Order has the same effect as a final and binding judgment, but any of the plaintiff organization, the Opponent, or any Target Consumer whose claim is filed in the relevant proceeding may file an objection with the court within a stated period of time (Japanese Class Action Act, Article 46.) If such an objection is filed, the action shifts to ordinary litigation and the contents of the relevant claims and objections are determined in accordance with the flow of ordinary civil litigation. In the ensuing action, it is deemed that a lawsuit has been filed with the court that made the Simple Determination Order at the time of the Filing of Proofs of Claims. (Japanese Class Action Act, Article 52.)

43 Known Target Consumers must be notified individually about pending Simple Determination Proceedings by mailing documents or by electronic measures (i.e., e-mail, fax, or handling over magnetic disc) (Japanese Class Action Act, Article 25, Paragraph 1) and the petitioner Specified Qualified Consumer Organization must make a public notice about the proceedings by appropriate means, such as a notice posted on the website of the petitioner organization (Japanese Class Action Act, Article 26, Paragraph 1).

In addition, the Opponent also has certain obligations under the law. Specifically, upon the request of the petitioner organization, the Opponent must disclose certain matters about the proceedings, either via the Internet, by posting the disclosures in a readily visible manner at the defendant's business office or other specified location, or by another similar method. (Japanese Class Action Act, Article 27.) Further, if the Opponent possesses documents containing the name or other information relating to Target Consumers, the Opponent is generally not allowed to refuse a request for disclosure of such information, if made by the Petitioner Organization. (Japanese Class Action Act, Article 28, Paragraph 1.)

44 Miki, *supra* note 28, at 309.

22.3.4.4 Conciliatory Aspects of Second Stage Procedures

In incorporating forms of approval or disapproval and response by both parties into the Japanese class action system, it is believed that policy makers referred to the form exchange procedures used in the second stage of the Canadian class action system (*see* Chapter 7 for a discussion of class actions in Canada) and to bankruptcy proceedings in Japan.[45] In Canadian class actions this procedure is considered a type of ADR based on agreement. As in such cases, in Japanese class actions it also can be considered a procurement procedure like a settlement agreement, since it involves concessions being made for purposes of batch processing (i.e., it incorporates elements of settlement).[46]

22.3.5 *Case Studies*

No lawsuits were filed under the Japanese Class Action Act for some time after it went into effect. The first such lawsuit was filed in December 2018, and as of July 2019, two lawsuits (including the first action) had been filed under the Redress for Damage System. (As of July 2020, four lawsuits had been filed.) In light of this paucity of cases, a joint report on the issue was submitted by the three Specified Qualified Consumer Organizations in July 2019.[47] The report indicates potential issues and makes proposals for improvements to the system. For example, (1) an argument that limited scope of permitted claims makes the system difficult to use, and a proposal to expand its scope, (2) a recommendation that the cost of making the public notice and giving notice to individual victims (*see* Section 22.3.4.3 above) should be borne by the Opponent or, in some cases, an exemption from the obligation to make public notice and give these individual notices should be granted, and (3) a proposal to allow a Specified Qualified Consumer Organization to name the directors or officers of the Opponent as defendants in cases involving malicious acts, where the Opponent is insolvent.[48]

22.3.5.1 Case #1: Discrimination in University Admissions

In December 2018, a nonprofit consumer organization, COJ filed a lawsuit against the Tokyo Medical University seeking a declaratory judgment for confirmation of the University's liability for damages equivalent to the entrance examination fee and other financial damages relating to unfair selection standards for university applicants.[49]

In 2018, a corruption case was reported involving a government official at the Ministry of Education, Culture, Sports, Science and Technology. Subsequent investigations revealed that the University established selection standards for applicants which wrongfully discriminated on

[45] An order of commencement of the proceedings under the Damage Recovery System shares some fundamental characteristics with an order commencing bankruptcy proceedings in Japan. *See* YAMAMOTO, *supra* note 39, at 200. Under Japanese law, when an order of commencement of proceedings is made, a notice (public or private) is given to creditors, calling for them to file proof of claims; thereafter, each creditor (presumably) files a claim. If the bankruptcy trustee approves the claim, the claim is allowed. If the bankruptcy trustee makes an objection, the court makes an assessment order regarding the disputed claim. Thereafter, if there is an objection to the court's decision, an objection lawsuit may be filed.

[46] Miki, *supra* note 28, at 312. In a Japanese Class Action, it is possible to settle during both the first stage procedure and the second stage procedure. (Japanese Class Action Act, Articles 10 and 37.)

[47] www.coj.gr.jp/iken/pdf/topic_190716_01.pdf, last viewed: August 6, 2020 (in Japanese only).

[48] Other issues, and proposals for improvement of the collective redress system in Japan, have also been discussed. *See* Section 22.4 below.

[49] *See* the following website for details, last viewed: August 8, 2020 (in Japanese only): www.coj.gr.jp/trial/topic_20181217_01.html.

the basis of gender and other factors. This led to disadvantageous treatment of women and second-time students in the University's entrance examinations. Since September 2018, the COJ repeatedly asked the University to return an amount equivalent to the examination fee[50] to the candidates who suffered wrongful discrimination.

COJ subsequently filed a Stage 1 lawsuit against the University on the grounds that: (1) the point adjustment made to various University applicants' materials was not disclosed in the application requirements (as a primary claim), and (2) the selection of successful applicants was not carried out in a fair and appropriate manner (as a secondary claim).

In March 2020, the Stage 1 trial in this case concluded. The court confirmed that the University was, in principle, obligated to return an amount equivalent to the examination fee, postage, etc. (but not including transportation expenses or accommodation expenses, because these depended on the circumstances of each candidate). Moreover, in July 2020, the court decided to commence the Stage 2 procedure. It is important to keep an eye on future developments. Additionally, in October 2019, COJ filed a lawsuit against Juntendo University regarding a similar discrimination case.

22.3.5.2 Case #2: Exaggerations in Product Information and Solicitations

In April 2019, COJ filed a Stage 1 lawsuit against *kabushiki kaisha* ONE MESSAGE, as well as an individual who supported ONE MESSAGE's sales and solicitations, seeking a declaratory judgment regarding liability for damages, including an amount equivalent to sales proceeds, on the grounds that ONE MESSAGE made false or extremely exaggerated explanations or solicitations in connection with marketing information and sales of its materials; specifically, these materials allegedly misled people into wrongfully believing that ONE MESSAGE products could help "anyone" make a profit. The suit was filed under the Act on Special Measures for Consumer Court Proceedings, and related to sales and seminars held by ONE MESSAGE in connection with its virtual currency Bible DVD.

Since July 2017, COJ has received a large amount of information regarding damages and products sold by ONE MESSAGE and solicited by the relevant individual. The COJ submitted a request to ONE MESSAGE requesting that full refunds be given to consumers who wished to receive them. Although ONE MESSAGE originally told COJ that it would make the requested refund, on April 18, 2018, ONE MESSAGE made the following statement: "Since there is a case currently pending at the Tokyo District Court, we will respond based on the outcome of the case." Thereafter, the COJ brought the class action lawsuit.[51]

As of July 2019, the trial of the Stage 1 proceeding was ongoing. As with the University admissions case, it will be important to watch this proceeding carefully.

22.4 FUTURE CHALLENGES FACING THE PRIVATE COLLECTIVE REDRESS SYSTEMS IN JAPAN

This section discusses the problems currently facing the class action system in Japan, which are described in the June 2019 publication "Working Group Report on the Formation of Rules in the Consumer Law Field," which was prepared and issued by the Working Group. The report addresses the issues facing the two class action systems in Japan, and its findings are summarized

50 www.coj.gr.jp/zesei/topic_180920_01.html#add_notes04, last viewed: August 6, 2020 (in Japanese only).
51 www.coj.gr.jp/zesei/topic_180315_01.html, last viewed: August 8, 2020 (in Japanese only).

below. In the context of the system for collective redress, the contents of the report are broadly divided into (1) development of systems necessary to enable Qualified Consumer Organizations and Specified Qualified Consumer Organizations to perform their expected functions, and (2) development of the financial base of Qualified Consumer Organizations and Specified Qualified Consumer Organizations.

22.4.1 *Establishment of a System to Make the Most of Available Functions*

It has been pointed out that both the Injunction Demand System and the Redress for Damage System need to make it possible for organizations to respond quickly without being blocked from access to information as information and communication technology spreads. It is also necessary to improve overall business efficiency, to promote the sharing of roles among individual organizations, and to improve the convenience of consumers' access to the system by enabling the various organizations to collaborate with each other on a constant basis.

With regard to the Injunction Demand System, it has been pointed out that: (1) the subject of the right to demand an injunction is limited by comparison with the subject of administrative disposition, (2) it is uncertain, and in need of clarification, whether a certain act is still subject to an injunction if the act has been discontinued prior to issuance of the injunction (e.g., to mount an effective response to situations in which the display of Internet advertisements can change in a short period of time), and (3) there is need for additional measures to address the uneven distribution of evidence on the part of business operators.[52]

With regard to the Redress for Damage System, (1) in light of the current situation, in which extrajudicial activities by the organizations have been successful at encouraging business operators to issue refunds voluntarily, the authority to require business operators to report on the subject and conditions in case their responses to requests for voluntary refunds have been granted to Specified Qualified Consumer Organizations, (2) a measure to address the problem of collectability, as caused by the financial resources of business operators, is required (i.e., introduction of a system that enables a Specified Qualified Consumer Organization to conduct an asset investigation prior to a provisional seizure or seizure), and (3) there is a need for reduction of the burden of expenses required for making notifications to Target Consumers and other public announcements.

22.4.2 *Improvement of the Financial Basis of Consumer Organizations*

Improvement of the financial base of consumer organizations is a major issue in Japan. Currently, these organizations are mainly funded through membership fees and donations from the private sector, such as consumers and businesses. As a result, they do not have sufficient funds. In 2017 a private organization called Consumers Japan established Shōhisha Smile Kikin and began providing financial support to consumer organizations; however, the fund does not have stable financial sponsorship or a strong financial basis.[53] In light of this situation, it has been pointed out that the government needs to provide financial support to ensure the independence of consumer organizations, to develop and establish a basis for consumer groups to receive certification, and to enable each organization to perform its intended function. Although detailed arrangements for public funds have not been discussed in Japan, a few public funds

52 Working Group, *supra* note 2, at 26. Parties to a lawsuit may petition the court to order the other party to submit documents specified by the petitioner, but Japan has no system similar to the discovery process in the United States.

53 www.cao.go.jp/consumer/iinkai/2018/002/doc/181115_shiryou5.pdf, last viewed: August 6, 2020 (in Japanese only).

have been established worldwide. For example, Israel established the Public Fund to Finance Class Action Lawsuits in order to help representative plaintiffs finance the submission and hearing of petitions for approval of class actions that have public and social importance. The number of class action lawsuits in Israel, as well as the frequency of requests for financial support, has increased since establishment of this organization. (Please *see* Chapters 25 and 26 for more details). Although the primary purpose of the Japanese collective redress system is to protect consumer interests, rather than to promote issues of public and social importance, and although it is difficult to build a consensus in Japan for the idea that state organs should support one side of a private dispute, the Israeli system could be a good reference point for examining governmental support for class action lawsuits.

In Japan, it has also been suggested that a system be established to allocate non-distributed funds – meaning money that should have been given back to consumers but which was not returned to individual consumers for various reasons[54] – to the activities of the consumer administration and consumer organizations that contribute to consumer interests.[55]

22.5 SUMMARY AND CONCLUSIONS

As described above, the Japanese consumer class action system contains two parallel systems, both of which face challenges in the future. While both systems have been used to a certain extent, various issues may need to be addressed in the future. The class action systems may also face new challenges as a result of ongoing and future actions and court rulings. Ultimately, however, it is critically important that the realization of a fair market, which is in the best interests of every stakeholder in Japan, become a common goal and understanding, and that the various entities cooperate with one another, and with consumers, toward achieving this critical objective. We believe that it is necessary to continue examining, and moving toward, optimal solutions for the rules and actors in consumer policy, while paying close attention to ongoing trends in the legal systems of other countries.

[54] For example, there are cases in which it is difficult for a business operator to make a voluntary refund because the specific target of the refund is unknown, and cases in which money collected through the Surcharge system under the current Act against Unjustifiable Premiums and Misleading Representations is not supposed to be returned to individual consumers (pursuant to applicable rules for that system).

[55] Working Group, *supra* note 2, at 27.

23

The Indian Securities Fraud Class Action

Is Class Arbitration the Answer?

*Brian T. Fitzpatrick and Randall Thomas**

23.1 INTRODUCTION

In 2013, India enacted one of the most robust private enforcement regimes for securities fraud violations in the world. Unlike in most other countries, Indian shareholders can now initiate securities fraud lawsuits on their own, represent all other defrauded shareholders unless those shareholders affirmatively opt out, and collect money damages for the entire class. The only thing missing is a better financing mechanism: unlike the United States, Canada, and Australia, India does not permit contingency fees, so class action lawyers cannot front the costs of litigation in exchange for collecting a percentage of what they recover. On the other hand, the 2013 law enacted a public financing regime for securities fraud class actions and it is possible third-party financing will be permitted; these mechanisms may make up some of the loss in effectiveness caused by the lack of contingency fees. It is still too early to tell.

All of this is true on paper. Yet, commentators are very pessimistic that the Indian securities fraud class action will do much good. The primary reason is because the Indian court system is notoriously unhurried. We have seen some data that suggests it takes over six years on average to resolve some civil appeals. And that's just the appeal. Who will bother to file a securities fraud lawsuit if it takes a decade to conclude?

The solution to this problem in the 2013 law was to channel the securities fraud class action to a special tribunal. Yet, this solution has been tried before in India, and we understand special tribunals tend to quickly take on the negative characteristics of the general courts. This may be why very few securities fraud lawsuits have been filed since the 2013 law was enacted. As far as we know, there have been very few such lawsuits despite the fact that there are thousands of publicly traded companies in India.

We propose a different solution to the problem of the Indian court system: class arbitration. Professor Vik Khanna suggested arbitration as a solution in an early article after the enactment of the 2013 law, and we pick up that suggestion and run with it here. As we explain, although class arbitration is not perfect, it may better facilitate robust private enforcement than the Indian court system.

In Section 23.2, we describe the new Indian securities fraud class action and explain why commentators are pessimistic that it will live up to its potential. In Section 23.3, we argue that the best way for it to do so is to channel its lawsuits into class arbitration.

* A version of this chapter was previously published at 40 NW. J. INT'L L. & BUS. 203 (2020).

23.2 THE INDIAN SECURITIES FRAUD CLASS ACTION

23.2.1 *Background*

The new Indian securities fraud class action was born of scandal. In 2009, the founder of Satyam Computer Services, a publicly traded Indian information-technology company, confessed to falsifying the financial statements of the company. There were fake customer identities, fake invoices to inflate revenue, forged board resolutions, and loans obtained through illegal means.[1] All told, the fictitious assets and non-existent cash totaled some $1.56 billion.[2] Somehow, all of this evaded the detection of Satyam's auditor, PricewaterhouseCoopers.[3]

This billion-dollar, multi-year fraud started to fall apart when Satyam attempted to acquire two companies without seeking shareholder approval.[4] The target companies were owned in large part by Satyam's founder and his family.[5] When shareholders got wind of it, they objected vociferously, and the acquisition was suspended.[6] But the episode attracted the attention of regulators.[7] Eventually, the founder, members of Satyam's board, and other management personnel went to jail and paid fines,[8] and the company's share price fell from INR 544 to INR 11.50.[9]

What about the shareholders? At the time, Indian law did not permit shareholders to recover any of their losses. Thus, Indian shareholders did not recoup anything from the Satyam fraud. But some shareholders did recoup something: *American* shareholders. Satyam had American Depository Receipts listed on the New York Stock Exchange. Thus, multiple securities fraud class action lawsuits were filed by Satyam's *American* investors in the Southern District of New York.[10] In 2011, Satyam and PricewaterhouseCoopers agreed to settle these lawsuits for over $150 million.[11]

1 *See* Ariya B. Majumdar and Sneha Bhawnani, *Class Action Suits – Genesis, Analysis and Comparison, in* RGNUL Book Series on Corporate Law and Corporate Affairs (Patiala, RGNUL Publications, December 12, 2016). The founder, Mr. Raju, confessed to such fraud through a letter dated January 7, 2009 addressed to its board of directors, copied to Securities and Exchange Board of India (SEBI) and stock exchanges:

> The gap in the Balance Sheet has arisen purely on account of inflated profits over a period of last several years (limited only to Satyam standalone, books of subsidiaries reflecting true performance). What started as a marginal gap between actual operating profit and the one reflected in the books of accounts continued to grow over the years....Every attempt made to eliminate the gap failed. As the promoters held a small percentage of equity, the concern was that poor performance would result in a take-over, thereby exposing the gap. It was like riding a tiger, not knowing how to get off without being eaten...

SEBI order dated July 15, 2014 (WTM/RKA/SRO/64 – 68 /2014).

2 *See* www.newindianexpress.com/states/andhra_pradesh/article55212.ece.

3 Majumdar and Bhawnani, *supra* note 1.

4 *See* Varun Sinha, *Satyam Fraud: Why Ramalinga Raju Was Forced to Confess in 2009*, NDTV Profit (April 9, 2015), http://profit.ndtv.com/news/corporates/articlesatyam-fraud-why-ramalinga-raju-was-forced-to-confess-in-2009–753607.

5 *See* Majumdar and Bhawnani, *supra* note 1.

6 *See supra* note 4.

7 *Id.*

8 *See* Majumdar, Arjya B. and Bhawnani, Sneha, Class Action Suits – Genesis, Analysis and Comparison (December 12, 2016).

9 *See Indian IT scandal boss arrested*, BBC News (January 9, 2001), http://news.bbc.co.uk/2/hi/business/7821087.stm.

10 *See* Kevin LaCroix, *Satyam Agrees to Pay $125 Million to Settle Securities Suit*, The D&O Diary (February18, 2011), www.dandodiary.com/2011/02/articles/securities-litigation/satyam-agrees-topay-125-million-to-settle-securities-suit/.

11 *See Weil Secures Dismissal of Shareholder Class Action Against Satyam's Former Directors*, Weil, Gotshal & Manges LLP (January 4, 2013), www.weil.com/articles/weil-secures-dismissal-of-shareholder-class-actionagainst-satyams-former-directors.

When there is wrongdoing like this that stretches across continents, the difference between the American system of private enforcement and the systems of public enforcement in most other places becomes apparent for all to see. When it does, people in other countries often do not like what they find. That is what happened with the recent scandal where Volkswagen rigged its diesel cars to turn off their pollution controls when they were not being tested for emissions. The 500,000 drivers in America collected billions of dollars in compensation; the ten million drivers in the rest of the world have basically received nothing.[12] The difference was the American class action. Other countries are now beefing up their own consumer class action devices in response.[13]

The same thing happened in India. No one could understand why the Indian shareholders of an Indian company got nothing when they were defrauded, but their American counterparts received millions of dollars. Thus, the Companies Act of 2013 was born to bring American-style private securities fraud enforcement to India. As we explain below in Section 23.2.3, we think the Indian authorities made an admirable attempt in this endeavor.

23.2.2 *The Companies Act of 2013*

Section 245 of the Act and its enabling rules permit either 100 or 5 percent of shareholders – whichever is lesser – to file an application seeking to represent all other shareholders before a special tribunal called the National Company Litigation Tribunal (NCLT) for fraud and other misconduct committed by a company or its officers.[14] Such an application can be filed against any type of company, whether in the public sector or in the private sector, except banking companies.[15] The Act also permits an investor association to file suit on behalf of shareholders.[16]

When considering whether to accept the application, the NCLT considers many of the same criteria American courts consider when they decide whether to certify class actions[17] as well as several additional matters.[18] If the application is accepted, the NCLT is required to consolidate

12 *In re Volkswagen "Clean Diesel" Mktg., Sales Practices, & Prods. Liab. Litig.*, No. 2672 CRB (JSC), 2016 U.S. Dist. LEXIS 148374 (N.D. Cal. Oct. 25, 2016); Patrick McGee, *VW car owners in EU face battle for compensation over scandal*, Financial Times, January 28, 2017, www.ft.com/content/0b9bf1d2-e48611e6-9645-c9357a75844a.

13 In response to the emissions scandal, the German government is pushing a new law that would allow consumer claims to be partially resolved on a collective basis. *See* Andrea Thomas, *Germany Set to Allow Collective Lawsuits Following VW Scandal*, Wall Street Journal, May 9, 2018, www.wsj.com/articles/germany-set-to-allow-collective-lawsuits-followingvw-scandal-1525869967.

14 The Act uses the words "members" and "depositors." *See* Companies Act, No. 18 of 2013, India Code, Sections 2(55), 245(1) & 245(3); Rule 84 of the National Company Law Tribunal Rules, 2016.

15 *See* Companies Act, No. 18 of 2013, India Code, Section 245(9). The Central Government of India has a power to exempt a class or classes of companies from any provisions of the Act for the reason of public interest. *See* Companies Act, No. 18 of 2013, India Code, Section 462.

16 Companies Act, No. 18 of 2013, India Code, Section 245(10).

17 The NCLT is required to consider by rule whether: (1) whether the class has so many members that joining them individually would be impractical making a class action desirable; (2) whether there are questions of law or fact common to the class; (3) whether the claims or defenses of representative parties are typical of the claims or defenses of the class; (4) whether the representative parties will fairly and adequately protect the interests of the class. Rule 85 of the National Company Law Tribunal Rules, 2016.

18 The Act requires the NCLT to consider: (1) whether the application is filed in good faith; (2) any evidence before it as to the involvement of any person other than directors or officers of the company in matters requiring relief; (3) whether the cause of action is one which the member or depositor could pursue in his own right rather than through an action under this section; (4) any evidence before it as to the views of the members or depositors of the company who have no personal interest, direct or indirect, in the matter being proceeded under this section; (5) where the cause of action is an act or omission that is yet to occur, whether the act or omission could be, and in the circumstances would be likely to be authorized by the company before it occurs or ratified by the company after it occurs; (6) where the cause of action is an act or omission that has already occurred, whether the act or omission could

all similar applications from any other jurisdiction and publish notice to the class.[19] Notice is published in newspapers in both English and the language of the state where the registered office of the company is located; additionally, notice is published on the company's website, the websites of the NCLT, the Ministry of Corporate Affairs[20], and the Registrar of Companies[21] and the websites of any stock exchanges the company is listed on.[22] Class members have the right to opt out;[23] if they do not, they have the right to choose which lead applicant the lawsuit should proceed with; if no applicant garners a majority, the NCLT decides.[24]

The Act provides shareholders with what appears to be broad relief. Not only can shareholders win injunctive and declaratory relief[25] – backed up with fines and possible imprisonment if companies and their officers fail to comply[26] – but they can also win American-style compensatory damages from the company, its directors, its auditors, and others.[27] Professor Khanna has worried that the damages provision in the Act does not go far enough. He argues that most of the corporate disputes in India are not shareholder management disputes like in the United States, but disputes between majority shareholders and minority shareholders: that is, majority shareholders try to exploit minority shareholders.[28] He argues that the 2013 Act offers no monetary remedy in these situations because it is unclear whether majority shareholders owe fiduciary duties to minority shareholders, and, even if they do, whether majority shareholders fall under the damages provision in the 2013 Act;[29] this provision covers only the company, directors, auditors and any "expert or advisor or consultant or any other person" for "any fraudulent, unlawful or wrongful act or conduct . . . ."[30] He worries that majority shareholders will not be covered under "other persons" because the "tenor" of the Act is to remedy shareholder-management disputes.[31]

This surprises us. Indian public companies commonly have majority shareholders either because they are state-controlled enterprises or because they were historically family-owned

be, and in the circumstances would be likely to be, ratified by the company. Companies Act, No. 18 of 2013, INDIA CODE, Section 245(4).

19 Rule 87(3) of the National Company Law Tribunal Rules, 2016.

20 The Ministry of Corporate Affairs is an Indian government ministry regulating the functioning of the corporate sector in accordance with law – www.mca.gov.in/MinistryV2/about_mca.html.

21 The Registrar of Companies regulates company-related matters in India, including incorporation, financing, directors, and shareholders – www.mca.gov.in/MinistryV2/registrarofcompanies.html.

22 Rule 87(1) of the National Company Law Tribunal Rules, 2016.

23 Rule 86(3) of the National Company Law Tribunal Rules, 2016

24 Companies Act, No. 18 of 2013, INDIA CODE, Section 245 (5).

25 The Act enables shareholders to obtain orders from the NCLT (1) restraining the company from committing act in breach of the memorandum or articles of the company/ any provisions of the Act or any other law/ any provisions of the resolution passed by members; or (2) declaring a resolution altering the memorandum or articles of the company as void if the resolution was passed by suppression of the material facts or obtained by mis-statement and restraining the company or its directors from acting on such resolution. Companies Act, No. 18 of 2013, INDIA CODE, Section 245(1).

26 Any company which fails to comply with an order passed by the NCLT under is liable for a punishment with a fine of not less than INR 0.5 million which may extend to INR 2.5 million and every officer of the company in default is liable for a punishment with imprisonment for a term which may extend to three years and with fine of not less than INR 25 thousand which may extend to INR 100 thousand. Companies Act, No. 18 of 2013, INDIA CODE, Section 245(7).

27 *Id.*

28 Vikramaditya Khanna, *Enforcement of Corporate and Securities Laws in India: The Arrival of the Class Action? In* ENFORCEMENT OF CORPORATE AND SECURITIES LAW: CHINA AND THE WORLD, 348–51 (Robin Hui Huang & Nicholas Calcina Howson eds., 2017).

29 *Id.* at 351.

30 Companies Act, No. 18 of 2013, INDIA CODE, Section 245, 1(g).

31 Khanna, *supra* note 28, at 354.

businesses.[32] This creates a classic agency cost problem as the actions of the majority shareholder can adversely impact minority shareholders.[33] This fact must have been well known to regulators and the legislature.

Furthermore, the episode that lead to the Act – the Satyam affair – was born of an effort by majority shareholders to take advantage of minority shareholders. It is true that the episode ended with fraud rather than minority exploitation because the acquisition of the target companies was stymied. But do we really think the Indian authorities who enacted the 2013 Act were unconcerned about the events that motivated the episode to begin with? We doubt it. It is a well-established principle to interpret ambiguous language in statutes in light of the purposes behind the legislation.[34] If the Indian authorities wanted to make sure the things that happened in the Satyam episode could not happen again without shareholder compensation, it would be fairly easy to interpret the words "any other person" and "any fraudulent, unlawful, or wrongful act or conduct" to include majority shareholders trying to exploit minority shareholders. Thus, we are not as worried as Professor Khanna about the breadth of the damages provision in the 2013 Act.

23.2.3 *Assessment*

Compared to private enforcement mechanisms available in much of the world, the 2013 Act puts India in the vanguard. Scholars have identified several metrics by which to measure how robust a nation's class actions are,[35] and, on all but one of these metrics, the Indian securities fraud class action fares very well. First, there is who can initiate the action: in some countries, individual shareholders are not permitted to bring class action lawsuits; the lawsuits must be brought by investor associations or the government; this obviously limits their use.[36] The Indian class action does not suffer this limitation. Second, there is who is included in the class action: in most countries, class members must affirmatively opt in to be included; this obviously limits the size and power of class actions.[37] The Indian class action does not suffer this limitation either. Third, there is what relief can be recovered in the class action: in most countries, compensatory damages are not available; this obviously limits the usefulness of class actions.[38] If we are right about how the 2013 Act should be interpreted vis-à-vis minority shareholders, the Indian class action fares better, here, too. On all these metrics, we rate the Indian securities fraud class action as one of the most robust in the world.

The one metric on which the Indian class action may not fare as well as those in nations like the United States, Canada, and Australia is with regard to how the actions are financed. If shareholders do not have access to adequate financing to bring their class actions, then much of the foregoing is for naught. In the United States, Canada, and Australia, class actions are

32 George S. Geis, *Can Independent Blockholding Really Play Much of a Role in Indian Corporate Governance?*, 3 Corporate Governance Review 283, 304–06 (2007) (analyzing share ownership patterns of the fifty largest Indian public companies and finding that 56 percent of them have majority shareholders and 80 percent "have at least 30 percent of their shares owned by insiders or the government.").

33 *Id.* at 308.

34 *See* Antonin Scalia, Reading Law (2012); Subash C. Jain, *Indian Trends in the Interpretative Use of Legislative History*, 24 Stat. L. Review 63–73 (2003).

35 *See* Deborah Hensler, *Can Private Class Actions Enforce Regulations? Do They? Should They? in* Comparative Law and Regulation: Understanding the Global Regulatory Process 244–45 (Francesca Bignami and David Zaring eds., 2016).

36 *Id.*

37 Deborah Hensler, *The Globalization of Class Actions: An Overview*, 622 Annals of the American Academy of Political and Social Science, 15–16 (2009).

38 Hensler, *supra* note 35, at 247.

financed on contingency: either lawyers or third parties invest in the actions and are repaid if successful by collecting a portion of the recovery.[39] This gives shareholders access to capital to fund a large portion of what we call "positive-expected value" actions – actions for which the expected trial judgment exceeds the class's litigation expenses.

It is unclear to us whether contingency-financing like this will be available in India. On the one hand, we understand contingency-financing is forbidden from lawyers.[40] On the other hand, it appears such financing may now be available from third parties;[41] if it takes off, shareholders in India may have all the resources they need. If it does not, securities fraud class actions will have to be financed by the shareholders themselves, with the prospect of recouping their litigation expenses under the loser-pays rule if they succeed.[42] If shareholders are widely dispersed, this makes financing difficult, especially because shareholders are liable for the defendant's litigation expenses if they lose. There is, however, one provision of the 2013 Act that could mitigate the hardship of self-financing, at least to some extent: the Act sets up a public financing mechanism.[43] Although it is too early to tell how much money will be available or what criteria will be used to disperse it, Canada has a fund like this and it has been used with some success.[44] Nonetheless, if we were to make one recommendation to India about how to revise the Act, it would be either to open securities fraud class actions to lawyer contingency-financing (as in the USA and Canada) or to grow third-party contingency-financing (as in Australia). With that caveat, we think the 2013 Act is an impressive attempt at private enforcement of the securities laws.

Nonetheless, the early commentators have been very pessimistic at its chances to do much good, and the pessimism is not confined to our concerns about financing. Perhaps the leading assessment has been the article by Professor Khanna.[45] He argues that the 2013 Act will be of "limited value" because of four shortcomings: "(1) the glacial speed of the Indian courts, (2) lack of contingency fees, (3) the limited availability of monetary remedies . . ., and (4) the interaction between ownership structure in India."[46] We addressed the latter three shortcomings above in this and the previous sections; we agree these could be shortcomings, but we are not as pessimistic that they cannot be overcome. That leaves the most serious shortcoming: the glacial speed of the Indian courts.

A great deal has been written about how slow the Indian court system is. Professor Khanna cited some of this writing and we have read other accounts ourselves.[47] Perhaps our favorite statistic is this one: the average civil appeal in some courts takes over six years to complete![48]

The causes appear to be many. First, there is a lack of judges:

39 *Id.* at 22–25.

40 Umakanth Varottil, *The Evolution of Corporate Law in Post-Colonial India: From Transplant to Autochthony*, 31 AM. U. INT'L L. REV. 253, 320.

41 Bar Council of India v. A.K Balaji, (2018) Civil Appeals No. 7875–7879 (2018) at para. 25. A new start-up company in India is dedicated to litigation financing. *See* www.advok8.in/.

42 Varottil, *supra* note 40, at 320.

43 Companies Act, No. 18 of 2013, INDIA CODE, Section 125, (3)(d).

44 Catherine Piche, *Public Financiers as Overseers of Class Proceedings*, 12 N.Y.U. J.L. & BUS. 779.

45 Khanna, *supra* note 28, at 334–35.

46 *Id.* at 333–58.

47 Hiram E. Chodosh, Stephen A. Mayo, A. M. Ahmadi & Abhishek M. Singhvi, *Indian Civil Justice System Reform: Limitation and Preservation of the Adversarial Process*, 30 N.Y.U. J. INT'L L. & POL. 1 (1998); Barry Bearak, *In India, the Wheels of Justice Hardly Move*, N.Y. TIMES, June 1, 2000; Umakanth Varottil, *India: The Efficacy of India's Legal System as a Tool for Investor Protection* in GLOBAL SECURITIES LITIGATION AND ENFORCEMENT 816, 839 (Pierre-Henri Conac, ed., 2019) ("Cases can on average take 15 years to achieve final outcomes.").

48 *How To Speed Up Judiciary: Let's Make India's Slow Courts World Class*, ECONOMIC TIMES (May16, 2017, 10:45AM), https://economictimes.indiatimes.com/news/politics-and-nation/how-to-speed-upjudiciary-lets-make-indias-slow-courts-world-class/articleshow/58693205.cms.

> India has one of the world's lowest ratios of judges to population in the world, with only 13 judges for every million people, compared with 50 in developed nations. As a result, scores of cases are heard every day, which leads to a large number of adjournments, judges passing cases between them, and increasingly long queues of people waiting outside courtrooms on the off-chance that their case is heard.[49]

One reason there are so few judges is because judges are apparently not paid very well (much less than lawyers); we understand this has led to a steady decline in the number of people who want to become judges.[50]

Second, lawyer compensation. We understand that lawyers charge by "appearance,"[51] which is not unlike charging by the hour. Charging by the hour or by appearance gives lawyers an incentive to drag cases out so they can make more money. One of the virtues of the contingency fee system – besides the one noted above of opening the plaintiff side of litigation to financing – is that it gives lawyers an incentive to wrap things up quickly so they can get paid.

Third, inefficient procedural rules. We understand that the judges in India freely grant lawyers adjournments that would not be tolerated in other countries.[52] Some commentators think these adjournments alone cost India's economy trillions of rupees every year.[53] Similarly, the Code of Civil Procedure does not require litigants to appear in court in person. Instead, litigants can send a "pleader" in their stead.[54] But the pleader cannot accept certain filings; hence, pleaders are often sent as a strategy to delay judgments.[55] Finally, the Code is less flexible than in other countries, and the lack of flexibility can lead risk-averse lawyers to over litigate. For example, litigants are not allowed to amend their original pleadings, which has led to prolific filings that bog down rather than speed up proceedings.[56]

Of course, none of this was lost on the Indian authorities who enacted the 2013 Act. Their solution was to channel all securities fraud class actions to a special tribunal, the NCLT. The NCLT is a new tribunal. Although it was created in 2002,[57] it was under a constitutional cloud until 2015.[58] But it has now been up and running for a few years, at last check with thirteen benches in different regions of India, with the principal bench in New Delhi.[59] Thus, it is too early to tell whether the new tribunal will be affected by the same malaise that affects most other courts in India, but the early signs are not good.[60] Indeed, India has many special courts and they

49 Vidhi Doshi, *India's Long Wait for Justice: 27m Court Cases Trapped In Legal Logjam*, The Guardian (May 5, 2016), www.theguardian.com/world/2016/may/05/indias-long-wait-for-justice-27million-court-cases-trapped-in-a-legal-logjam.

50 Chodosh et. al, *supra* note 47, at 47; Doshi, *supra* note 49.

51 Nick Robinson, *Structure Matters: The Impact of Court Structure on the Indian and U.S. Supreme Courts*, 61 Am. J. Comp. L. Rev. 173, 184 n.50.

52 *Supra* note 49; Daksh, *Access to Justice Survey 2015–16* (August 10, 2016, 6:00 PM) http://dakshindia.org/wp-content/uploads/2016/05/Daksh-access-to-justicesurvey.pdf.

53 Doshi, *supra* note 49.

54 Matthieu Chemin, *Does the Quality of the Judiciary Shape Economic Activity? Evidence from India* (October 11, 2004) http://sticerd.lse.ac.uk/dps/03122004/chemin.pdf.

55 *Id.*

56 *Id.*

57 Afra Afsharipour, *Corporate Governance Convergence: Lessons From The Indian Experience*, Nw. J. Int'l L. & Bus. 335, 360; *see also* Vikramaditya Khanna, *Regulating Squeeze-Outs in India: A Comparative Perspective*, 63 Am. J. Comp. L. 1009, 1018 n. 48.

58 Madras Bar Association v. Union of India (2015), Writ Petition No. 1072 (India).

59 National Company Law Tribunal Benches, www.nclt.gov.in/content/national-company-law-tribunal-benches.

60 www.financialexpress.com/industry/nclt-benches-may-be-doubled-tocope-with-rising-cases/1276014/; www.businessinsider.in/sc-slams-govt-forlack-of-staff-at-nclt/articleshow/68594331.cms.

have not escaped the problems we identified above in this section.[61] For this reason, commentators like Professor Khanna are pessimistic that the NCLT will fare any better.[62] He may be right: as far as we can tell, there have been very few securities fraud class actions filed under the 2013 Act.[63] This is despite the fact that India has thousands of publicly-traded companies.[64] By comparison, in the United States, roughly 2 percent of public-traded companies are sued for securities fraud every year,[65] and the best estimates are that there are three times as many securities fraud violations as there are lawsuits.[66]

If a special tribunal cannot save the Indian securities fraud class action, what can? Professor Khanna suggested arbitration as an answer.[67] As we explain in the next section, we think he is right. Although Professor Khanna did not specify what kind of arbitration he had in mind, the United States has experience with class action arbitration, and we think it could work well in India.

23.3 CLASS ACTION ARBITRATION

23.3.1 *Background*

Arbitration is a well-established private dispute mechanism in the United States. Parties choose whether to send their dispute to one or more arbitrators and whatever result is reached is respected by our court system and entitled to all the same res judicata effect of a court judgment.

The virtues of arbitration are well-known. The parties are allowed to specify their own procedural rules; thus, they can specify rules that streamline litigation and save them money.[68]

61 Marc Galanter & Jayanth K. Krishnan, *Debased Informalism: Lok Adalats and Legal Rights in Modern India, in* Beyond Common Knowledge: Empirical Approaches to the Rule of Law (Erik G. Jensen and Thomas C. Heller, eds., 2003) (discussing the congestion of the Indian courts and unsuccessful attempts to use alternative court systems as a method of avoiding the logjams).

62 Khanna, *supra* note 28, at 354–55.

63 According to the NCLT website as of December 2016, only two actions had been filed: K. N. Pillai v. R Prasanth (Mumbai Bench) and Vijaykumar v. SPM Exports Pvt. Ltd. (Bangaluru Bench). As of November 2018, we found only nine more: Jacob Mathew v. A.V. George and Ors. Mr. Samvid Legal (384/245/PB/2018); Zetatek Technologies Pvt. Ltd v. Gagan Aerospace Ltd & Ors (87/245/PB/2018); Atul Khanna v. Union of India & Ors. (109/245/PB/2018); Shumanto Gupta v. Ablaze Info Solutions Pvt. Ltd & Ors. (408(ND)/2017); Kamlesh Kumar Sen & Ors v. Gee Pee Hi Tech Industies Ltd & Ors (124/245(1)/PB/2018); Abhimanyu Singh & Ors v. Brijnandan Industries Pvt. Ltd. & Ors (129/245/PB/2018); Shiv Sevak Singh v. Ablaze Info Solutions Pvt. Ltd. & Ors (408(ND)/2017); UCO Bank v. Shree Shyam Pulp And Mills Ltd. (129/245/PB/2018); Mr. Sanjay Lalchand Siriah v. M /s White Street Engineering Solutions Pvt Ltd & Ors (212/245/NCLT/MB/MAH/2017).

64 N. Balasubramanian and R.V. Anand, Ownership Trends in Corporate India1–2011 Evidence and Implications, *available at* https://papers.ssrn.com/sol3/papers.cfm?abstract_id=2303684, at 12 (as of 2011, India had 1657 publicly traded companies).

65 Tom Baker & Sean J. Griffith, *The Missing Monitor in Corporate Governance: The Directors' & Officers' Liability Insurer*, 95 Geo. L.J. 1795, 1801 (2007).

66 *See* I. J. Alexander Dyck, Adair Morse & Luigi Zingales, *How Pervasive is Corporate Fraud?* (February 22, 2013). Rotman School of Management Working Paper No.2222608. Available at SSRN: https://ssrn.com/abstract=2222608 or http://dx.doi.org/10.2139/ssrn.2222608.

67 Khanna, *supra* note 28, at 356–67.

68 S. I. Strong, Class, Mass, and Collective Arbitration in National and International Law 297 (2013) ("'Runaway juries' are one reason why US class actions are considered unduly risky and expensive by the corporate community and the elimination of jury trials might well lead to lower awards. Removing the threat of a jury should also have a moderating effect on settlement negotiations, since the parties' discussions will operate within a much more realistic framework."); *see also* Sarah Clasby Engel & Sherry Tropin, *Class Action Arbitration: A Plaintiff's Perspective*, 5 Fiu L. Rev. 145, 150 (2009) ("Rule 21 of the AAA Commercial Arbitration Rules governs the exchange of information between the parties in commercial arbitration under its auspices: at the arbitrator's discretion or at the request of the parties, the arbitrator directs document production and identification of witnesses to be called."); Stephen J. Ware, *The Case For Enforcing Adhesive Arbitration Agreements-with Particular Consideration of Class Actions and Arbitration Fees*, 5 J. Am. Arb. 251, 258 (2006)(discussing how savings from lower "process costs" of arbitration can be passed down to

The cases are handled by professionals selected by the parties; thus, the parties do not have to take their chances before an idiosyncratic judge or jury.[69] The proceedings can remain confidential, thus avoiding negative publicity.[70] Arbitrators have greater flexibility in fashioning remedies and applying procedural rules.[71] Arbitration can overcome jurisdictional hurdles and resolve similar disputes in a single forum.[72] Enforcement of arbitration awards tends to be faster and less costly and many awards are complied with voluntarily.[73]

There are, of course, downsides to arbitration as well. If one party has more bargaining power than the other, they may select procedural rules and a pool of arbitrators that are biased in one party's favor.[74] In addition, because the parties must pay the arbitrators, arbitration can be more expensive than litigation in some respects.[75] Moreover, confidential proceedings undermine the deterrent value of litigation by hiding wrongdoing from the public.[76] Finally, if too many cases go to arbitration, it can retard the evolution of the law in the court system.[77]

consumers and employees); *See* Hal S. Scott & Leslie N. Silverman, *Stockholder Adoption of Mandatory Individual Arbitration for Stockholder Disputes*, 36 HARV. J.L. & PUB. POL'Y 1187, 1210 (2013) ("Wronged stockholders [in individual arbitrations] will receive quicker payment – although the average federal securities class action takes more than four years to settle, studies on arbitration have found it is two to three times faster than similar litigation."); S. I. Strong, *From Class to Collective: The De-Americanization of Class Arbitration*, 26 ARB. INT'L 493, 508 (2010) ("As it turns out, empirical evidence suggests that although U.S. class arbitrations tend to take more time than bilateral arbitrations, class arbitration takes less time than class action litigation. Thus, to the extent that a dispute must be resolved on a collective basis, defendants may be better off in arbitration rather than in court.").

69 STRONG, *supra* note 68, at 299 ("Indeed, many parties prefer arbitration because they can choose experienced panelists with particular expertise in the subject matter at hand. As a result, a properly selected arbitral tribunal may be less likely to make an error that a judge who does not specialize in the issues at bar."); Thomas J. Stipanowich, *Arbitration: The "New Litigation"*, 2010 U. ILL. L. REV. 1, 51 (2010) ("[T]he central and primary value of arbitration is not speed, or economy, or privacy, or neutral expertise, but rather the ability of users to make key process choices to suit their particular needs.").

70 STRONG, *supra* note 68, at 300 ("[P]arties, even to large-scale disputes, may prefer to adopt private and confidential procedures so as to avoid negative publicity that could injure their corporate reputation and goodwill."); Kristen M. Blankley, *Class Actions Behind Closed Doors? How Consumer Claims Can (and Should) Be Resolved by Class-Action Arbitration*, 20 OHIO ST. J. ON DISP. RESOL. 451, 470 (2005) ("Confidentiality is usually heralded as the biggest advantage of choosing an ADR procedure, including arbitration, over litigation.").

71 Blankley, *supra* note 70, at 467 ("Arbitrators are not required to follow the law when making their decisions. One of the 'benefits' of arbitration is that an arbitrator is allowed to consider the equities of a case, even if those equities are contradictory to the law"); Mark C. Weidemaier, *Arbitration and the Individuation Critique*, 49 ARIZ. L. REV. 69, 95–96 (2007) (noting the flexibility arbitrators have in fashioning appropriate remedies and implementing innovative procedures that courts have been hesitant to accept).

72 STRONG, *supra* note 68, at 289, 298 ("Arbitration provides an appealing alternative to problems associated with jurisdiction, since parties to an arbitration agreement grant jurisdiction over the matter to the arbitral tribunal as a matter of consent.").

73 *See* STRONG, *supra* note 68, at 301 (a bigger advantage in international arbitration).

74 Theodore Eisenberg et. al., *Arbitration's Summer Soldiers: An Empirical Study of Arbitration Clauses in Consumer and Nonconsumer Contracts*, 41 U. MICH. J.L. REFORM 871, 872–73 (2008); *See* Hal S. Scott & Leslie N. Silverman, *Stockholder Adoption of Mandatory Individual Arbitration for Stockholder Disputes*, 36 HARV. J.L. & PUB. POL'Y 1187, 1216–17 (2013)("Some critics have cited arbitration and other forms of alternative dispute resolution as having an industry bias . . . ."); Jean R. Sternlight, *Creeping Mandatory Arbitration: Is It Just?*, 57 STAN.L. REV. 1631, 1650 (2005); *see also* Christopher R. Drahozal, *Unfair "Arbitration Clauses"*, 2001 U. ILL. L. REV. 695, 732 (2001) (surveying arbitration clauses in franchisor agreements and specific provisions governing selection of arbitrators). This concern has not appeared to come to fruition in securities arbitration.

75 Mark E. Budnitz, *Arbitration of Disputes Between Consumers and Financial Institutions: A Serious Threat to Consumer Protection*, 10 OHIO ST. J. ON DISP. RESOL. 267, 335.

76 Elizabeth G. Thornburg, *Contracting with Tortfeasors: Mandatory ArbitrationClauses and Personal Injury Claims*, 67 LAW & CONTEMP. PROBS. 253 (2004); Laurie Kratky Dore, *Public Courts Versus Private Justice: It's Time To Let Some Sun Shine In On Alternative Dispute Resolution*, 81 CHI. KENT L. REV. 463.

77 Bruce Hay, Christopher Rendall-Jackson, & David Rosenberg, *Litigating BP's Contribution Claims in Publicly Subsidized Courts: Should Contracting Parties Pay Their Own Way?*, 64 VAND. L. REV. 1919, 1944–46.

Nonetheless, the growing popularity of arbitration in the United States shows that many people see arbitration as, on balance, a net positive. Many consumers, employees, and businesses now enter into contracts that say in the event a dispute arises with the counterparty, the dispute will be sent to arbitration if either party so chooses.

Although most of the disputes that go to arbitration are one-on-one disputes, it is possible to bring class-wide disputes to arbitration, and, for a time, it was done regularly in the United States. It is not done much anymore in the United States because the Supreme Court has ruled that companies are allowed to ban class actions in their arbitration proceedings if they want to, forcing plaintiffs who sue them into one-on-one arbitration.[78] Because one-on-one arbitration is less threatening to companies than class-wide arbitration, companies are now rewriting their arbitration clauses to ban class actions.[79] We have decried this practice because it basically insulates companies from class action liability, neutering the private enforcement of the law.[80] But before the Supreme Court allowed companies to do this, there were many years of experience with class arbitration in the United States. We describe that experience here and explain why it might be the best solution to the concern with sluggish courts in India.

23.3.2 *Class Arbitration in the United States*

Class arbitration is basically a class action that takes place in arbitration rather than court. Like a class action in a court, a class representative seeks to assert claims on her own behalf as well as on the behalf of absent class members.[81] Yet, a neutral arbitrator or panel of arbitrators selected and paid for by the parties typically makes all the decisions that would be entrusted to a judge.[82] Class arbitration first emerged in the United States in the 1980s[83] and received its blessing from the US Supreme Court in 2003.[84]

Although the parties can specify their own rules for class arbitration by contract, the large arbitration organizations like the American Arbitration Association (AAA) have adopted their own default class arbitration rules, and these rules are modeled on the rules that govern in federal court.[85] The following are the three phases of a class arbitration under the AAA's rules:

78 AT&T Mobility LLC v. Concepcion, 563 U.S. 333 (2011).

79 Consumer Financial Protection Bureau, *Arbitration Study: Report to Congress*, March 2015, https://files.consumerfinance.gov/f/201503_cfpb_arbitration-studyreport-to-congress-2015.pdf.

80 Brian Fitzpatrick, *The End of Class Actions?*, 57 ARIZ. L. REV. 161, 199 (2015).

81 *See* STRONG, *supra* note 68, at 150 (quoting another source) ("[A]rbitration is a process by which parties consensually submit a dispute to a non-governmental decision maker, select by and for the parties, to render a binding decision resolving a dispute in accordance with neutral, adjudicatory procedures affording the parties an opportunity to be heard."); *see also* S. I. Strong, *Does Class Arbitration "Change the Nature" of Arbitration? Stolt-Nielsen, at&t, and A Return to First Principles*, 17 HARV. NEGOT. L. REV. 201, 211 (2012) (distinguishing class arbitration from other multiparty proceedings and proving a "working definition" of class arbitration).

82 *See* Mark C. Weidemaier, *Judging-Lite: How Arbitrators Use and Create Precedent*, 90 N.C. L. REV. 1091, 1103 (2012).

83 *See* STRONG, *supra* note 68, at 9; *see also* Gary Born & Claudio Salas, *The United States Supreme Court and Class Arbitration: A Tragedy of Errors*, 2012 J. DISP. RESOL. 21, 21–22 (2012).

84 Green Tree Fin. Corp. v. Bazzle, 539 U.S. 444 (2003) (plurality opinion).

85 AAA, Supplementary Rules for Class Arbitrations (effective Oct. 8, 2003) [hereinafter AAA Rules], *available at* www.adr.org/sites/default/files/Supplementary%20Rules%20for%20Class%20Arbitrations.pdf; JAMS, Class Action Procedures (effective May 1, 2009) [hereinafter JAMS Procedures], *available at* www.jamsadr.com/rulesclass-action-procedures/. The National Arbitration Forum (NAF) once had its own procedures but has since stopped administering class arbitrations. *See* Jean R. Sternlight, *As Mandatory Binding Arbitration Meets the Class Action, Will the Class Action Survive?*, 42 WM. & MARY L. REV. 1, 72 (2000) ("Indeed, one arbitration provider, the National Arbitration Forum (NAF), has marketed its rules to corporations in part with the assurance that its rules do not allow for class actions.").

- **Clause Construction Award.** The arbitrator first determines as a "threshold matter" whether the applicable arbitration clause permits the arbitration to proceed as a class proceeding.[86] After this "award" is rendered, the arbitrator must stay proceedings for at least thirty days to "permit any party to move a court of competent jurisdiction to confirm or to vacate the [award]."[87]
- **Class Determination Award.** The arbitrator then determines whether to certify the proposed class using criteria that parallel Fed. R. Civ. P. 23 for numerosity, commonality of questions of law and fact, typicality, and adequacy of representation.[88] In addition to these criteria, the arbitrator may certify a class only if "each class member has entered into an agreement containing an arbitration clause which is substantially similar to that signed by the class representative(s) and each of the other class members."[89] The arbitrator's class certification determination must be set forth in a "reasoned, partial final award."[90] And again, the rules provide for another thirty day stay of all proceedings to permit any party to seek judicial review of this "award."[91]
- **Final Award.** After notice "given to all members who can be identified through reasonable effort" is given, the arbitration moves to the merits phase.[92] Whether favorable to the class or not, the final award must define the class with specificity, state to whom notice was sent, and identify who (if anyone) elected to exclude herself from the class.[93] The arbitrator must approve any settlement or voluntary dismissal and conduct a fairness hearing.[94] The arbitrator also rules on requests for exclusion from and objections to the settlement.[95] Judicial review of the final award is permitted as well.

The two main costs of class arbitration are filing/administrative fees and arbitrator compensation. The AAA rules provide for a "preliminary filing fee of $3,350" to be paid by the party bringing the class arbitration.[96] If the arbitration proceeds beyond the clause construction phase, that party shall pay a "supplemental fee ... calculated based on the amount claimed in the class arbitration and in accordance with the fee schedule in [commercial cases]."[97] For example, if the amount of the claims in the class arbitration ranges from $1 million to less than $10 million, an additional $8,475 fee is incurred.[98] Arbitrator compensation and hearing room rental fees are not included in these administrative fees.[99] Anecdotal

86 AAA Rules, *supra* note 85, rule 3.
87 *Id.*, rule 3.
88 *Id.*, rule 4. For a detailed discussion comparing the language of the AAA Rules, the JAMS Procedures, and Fed. R. Civ. P. 23, see STRONG, *supra* note 68, at 50.
89 AAA Rules, *supra* note 85, rule 4(a)(6).
90 *Id.*, rule 5; *see also* Alyssa S. King, *Too Much Power and Not Enough: Arbitrators Face the Class Dilemma*, 21 LEWIS & CLARK L. REV. 1031, 1040 (2017) ("The Rules require that class arbitration dockets and decisions be public and set out a series of three decisions that the arbitrator must issue. These decisions are known as awards. The first two are procedural decisions. These awards are known as 'partial awards' rather than 'full' awards, which would decide the merits. If the arbitrator does not plan to revisit a decision, an award is called a 'final award,' so a final procedural decision would be a 'partial final award.'").
91 AAA Rules, *supra* note 85, rule 5(d).
92 *Id.*, rule 6(a).
93 *Id.*, rule 5(d).
94 *Id.*, rule 8(a)(3).
95 *Id.*, rule 8(d).
96 *Id.*, rule 11.
97 *Id.*
98 AAA, Commercial Arbitration Rules and Mediation Procedures: Administrative Fee Schedules (amended and effective May 1, 2018), *available at* www.adr.org/sites/default/files/Commercial_Arbitration_Fee_Schedule_0.pdf.
99 *Id.*

evidence[100] suggests that AAA arbitrators can charge anywhere from $350 to $1,150 per hour.[101] The arbitrator has discretion to shift fees based on the arbitration agreement or applicable law.[102]

The AAA requires at least one arbitrator to be selected from a special roster of arbitrators experienced in class proceedings.[103] AAA arbitrators in general have a minimum of ten years of senior-level business or professional experience or legal practice.[104] Many are former federal and state judges.[105]

The AAA is the largest arbitration association in the United States and it keeps an online docket of all class arbitrations it has administered.[106] As of July 6, 2018, the docket contains 517 total class arbitrations composed of 75 pending and 442 closed arbitrations.[107] The earliest class arbitration is dated December 18, 2002. The most recent is dated May 31, 2018.[108]

Table 23.1 presents detailed summary statistics on the 283 AAA class arbitrations filed from 2003 to sometime in 2009.[109] Table 23.1 shows that in the 135 class arbitration where a clause construction award was rendered, class proceedings were permitted 70 percent of the time. Table 23.1 also shows that of the forty-eight class arbitrations where a class certification award was rendered, roughly half granted class certification.[110] The data also show that, although there were a good number of business-to-business class arbitrations, the most common class arbitrations were consumers suing businesses.

Interestingly, very few of these arbitrations reach the final stage. As of July 6, 2018, there have been only eight "merits awards," with four of them approval of settlements or partial settlements.[111] We do not know what happened to the other arbitrations where class certification was granted; they may still be ongoing.

100 Neither AAA nor JAMS publishes its rosters of arbitrators and their fees.

101 Deborah Rothman, *Trends in Arbitrator Compensation*, DISPUTE RESOLUTION MAGAZINE (Spring 2017), www.americanbar.org/content/dam/aba/publications/dispute_resolution_magazine/spring2017/3_rothman_trends_in_arbitrator.authcheckdam.pdf.

102 AAA Rules, *supra* note 85, rule 11(b) ("Disputes regarding the parties' obligation to pay administrative fees or arbitrator's compensation pursuant to applicable law or the parties' agreement may be determined by the arbitrator. Upon the joint application of the parties, however, an arbitrator other than the arbitrator appointed to decide the merits of the arbitration, shall be appointed by the AAA to render a partial final award solely related to any disputes regarding the parties' obligations to pay administrative fees or arbitrator's compensation.").

103 *Id.*, rule 2(a) (requiring at least one arbitrator to come from the class arbitrator roster).

104 AAA, Qualification Criteria for Admittance to the AAA National Roster of Arbitrators, www.adr.org/sites/default/files/document_repository/Qualification_Criteria_for_Admittance_to_the_AAA_National_Roster_of_ Arbitrators.pdf.

105 AAA, Arbitrators & Mediators, www.adr.org/aaa-panel.

106 AAA, Class Action Case Docket, https://tinyurl.com/yactk68u. Even though the online docket is publicly available, an arbitration-level analysis would be time consuming as each case docket contains PDFs of awards and demands sorting and filtering is allowed by only a few fields (case type, case status, date received, etc.). I am yet to find a study in the literature that has the same type of granular summary statistics on a larger, more up-to-date sample of AAA class arbitration than the 283 the AAA analyzed in its amicus brief.

107 *Id.*; *see also* Gregory A. Litt & Tina Praprotnik, *After* Stolt-Nielsen, *Circuits Split, but AAA Filings Continue*, 27 MEALEY'S INT'L ARB. REP. 1, 1 (2012) (charting AAA class arbitrations filed between 2003 and 2012 on an annual basis).

108 AAA, *supra* note 105.

109 See the notes accompanying Table 23.1 on the uncertainty of the end date of the analysis.

110 *See* Engel & Tropin, *supra* note 68, at 151 ("The AAA's brief filed in *StoltNielson* appears to indicate a greater likelihood of class certification in arbitration than in class action litigation. Once class certification is granted, corporate defendants have a greater incentive to enter into serious settlement negotiations. While class action arbitration may not be the expeditious procedure contemplated when arbitration law was developed, a faster resolution than in litigation may still be likely.").

111 AAA Class Action Case Docket, *supra* note 106 (filtered for award type as "merits awards").

TABLE 23.1 *Summary Statistics of 283 AAA Class Arbitrations Filed from Oct. 8, 2003 to Sometime in 2009**

Criteria	Count	% of Category
(1)	(2)	(3)
Clause Construction Awards		
Permitting Class Proceedings	95	70%
Denying Class Proceedings	7	5%
Stipulation That Agreement Permitted Class Proceedings	33	24%
Total	**135**	
Class Determination Awards		
Granting Class Certification	24	50%
Denying Class Certification	18	38%
Stipulation to Certify A Class	6	13%
Total	**48**	
When Arbitrations Were Settled/Withdrawn/Dismissed		
Pre-Clause Construction Award	97	60%
Post-Clause Construction and Pre-Class Determination	40	25%
Post-Class Determination Award	23	14%
Consolidated into Other Class Arbitration	2	1%
Total	**162**	
Number of Arbitrators		
One Arbitrator	198	83%
Three Arbitrators	38	17%
Total	**228**	
Type of Dispute		
Business to Business		
Franchise	21	26%
Healthcare	20	25%
Financial Services	9	11%
Other	31	38%
Subtotal	**81**	
Business to Individual		
Consumer	106	52%
Employment	96	48%
Subtotal	**202**	
Total	**283**	

Source: Data obtained from Brief of American Arbitration Association as Amicus Curiae in Support of Neither Party, Stolt-Nielsen S.A. v. AnimalFeeds Int'l Corp., 559 U.S. 662 (2010) (No. 8-1198), 2009 WL 2896309.

* The AAA's amicus brief is unclear on the exact start and end date of its analysis: "In the nearly six years that the Class Rules have been in effect, the AAA has administered 283 class arbitrations, 121 of which remain active." The AAA class arbitration rules went into effect on October 8, 2003 and the amicus brief was filed on Sept. 4, 2009.

23.3.3 *Special Concerns with Class Arbitration*

One of the reasons the Supreme Court let companies escape class actions in arbitration is because the Court thought that class arbitration did not reap many of the benefits of individual arbitration.[112] As we noted, although the parties can create their own rules, the AAA's rules largely

112 AT&T Mobility LLC v. Concepcion, 563 U.S. 333, 348 (2011) ("[T]he switch from bilateral to class arbitration sacrifices the principal advantage of arbitration – its informality.").

mirror the class action rules in federal court. It is not clear whether this makes class arbitration any cheaper or quicker. For example, the AAA reported for the cases in Table 23.1:

> [t]he median time from the filing of an arbitration to the Clause Construction Award [was] 281 days and a mean of 313 days. The median time from the Clause Construction Award to the Class Determination Award [was] 416 days and a mean of 501 days. For all 162 closed cases, the median time frame from filing to settlement, withdrawal, or dismissal [was] 583 days with a mean of 630 days.[113]

These durations may not be any quicker than class actions in court, which are settled in less than three years, on average.[114]

Another example is confidentiality. Under the AAA's rules, class arbitration are not entirely confidential proceedings.[115] It is not clear how they could be. After all, class members must be notified of the proceedings in order to have a chance to protect their rights. This makes class arbitration very different from individual arbitration.

A separate concern is that, per a federal statute, judicial review of arbitration decisions is very constrained. Although the AAA rules allow for appeals at three different points, judges can't do much on these appeals. Under the Federal Arbitration Act, judges can overturn arbitration awards only if there has been fraud or other misconduct perpetrated on the arbitrator; mistakes by the arbitrator are not grounds for reversal.[116] This is concerning because one of the most important roles that judges play in class actions is to protect absent class members from exploitation by class counsel and the defendant. Absent class members do not have a role in selecting arbitrators[117] – arbitrators are selected before class certification, and, in any event, absent class members are, well, absent – and some commentators worry the arbitrators will not look out for absent class members like judges do.[118] This concern is magnified if the arbitrators'

113 AAA Brief cited in Table 23.1 at *24.

114 *See* Brian T. Fitzpatrick, *An Empirical Study of Class Action Settlements and their Fee Awards*, 7 J. EMPIRICAL L. STUD. 811 (2010).

115 AAA Supplementary Rules for Class Arbitrations R-9, *available at* www.adr.org/sites/default/files/Supplementary%20Rules%20for%20Class%20Arbitrations.pdf (last visited June 29, 2018); *see also Stolt-Nielsen*, 559 U.S. at 686 (noting that one of the critical differences between class arbitration and bilateral arbitration is the presumption of privacy). *But see* S. I. Strong, *Enforcing Class Arbitration in the International Sphere: Due Process and Public Policy Concerns*, 30 U. PA. J. INT'L L. 1, 46 (2008) (noting that, unlike the AAA, JAMS does not remove the presumption of confidentiality in class arbitrations and does not maintain a public docket of class arbitrations).

116 Sarah Rudolph Cole, *On Babies and Bathwater: The Arbitration Fairness Act and the Supreme Court's Recent Arbitration Jurisprudence*, 48 HOUS. L. REV. 457, 502 (2011) ("The primary criticisms of class arbitration are that it . . . requires courts to use a more deferential standard to review class certification decisions and class arbitration awards than the abuse of discretion standard used to review trial court decisions . . . . "); Peter B. Rutledge & Christopher R. Drahozal, *"Sticky" Arbitration Clauses? The Use of Arbitration Clauses After Concepcion and Amex*, 67 VAND. L. REV. 955, 973 (2014) ("For franchisors, the lack of an appeals process is a very serious cost of using an arbitration clause and an arbitral class waiver."); Neal Troum, *The Problem with Class Arbitration*, 38 VT. L. REV. 419, 436 (2013) ("Arbitration awards are hard to reverse, and intentionally so. Three of the four grounds for vacatur are basic rules of fairness, as much process as Congress has seen fit to impose on arbitration.").

117 Maureen A. Weston, *Universes Colliding: The Constitutional Implications of Arbitral Class Actions*, 47 WM. & MARY L. REV. 1711, 1772–73 (2006).

118 Weston, *supra* note 117, at 1772–73; *see also* Sternlight, *supra* note 85, at 111–12 ("In a nonclass arbitration, the arbitration clause typically will allow plaintiff and defendant jointly to select the arbitrator. Yet, in a class action, presumably the named plaintiff, or more likely the class attorney, will choose an arbitrator or arbitrators on behalf of the absent class plaintiffs.").

compensation comes from the defendant and class counsel.[119] If courts could more meaningfully review the decisions critical for absent class members – certification, settlement, attorneys' fees – commentators would be less concerned. But that review is not possible under American law.

The lack of meaningful judicial review is a concern not just for absent class members but for defendants as well. Class action cases tend to be very high stakes because the size of class-wide damages can threaten companies will substantial liability. If the arbitrators make a million- or billion-dollar mistake, defendants rest more easily if they can get the mistake fixed. But, again, that is not possible. This is one of the facts that led the Supreme Court to deem arbitration as incompatible with class actions.[120] Commentators, too, have been skeptical companies would ever prefer class arbitration to class action litigation in court.[121]

23.4 CLASS ARBITRATION IN INDIA?

Like the United States, Indian law respects arbitration agreements,[122] including agreements to arbitrate fraud claims.[123] Despite the shortcomings listed in the previous section, we think securities fraud class arbitration can solve many of the problems with the Indian court system that have made commentators pessimistic about the new securities fraud class action.

First, consider the inefficient procedural rules in the Indian court system. In arbitration, the parties will be free to devise their own procedural rules, including rules allowing for more flexible pleadings as well as to prohibit plentiful adjournments and delays caused by litigants who fail to appear in person. Although class arbitration may not be any faster than class action litigation in the United States, that is because the rules in arbitration largely mirror those in court. India, by contrast, can use arbitration to avoid its inefficient court rules.

Second, consider the shortage of judges in Indian courts. There will be no shortage of arbitrators because the parties will select as many arbitrators as they need and compensate them for whatever time they need to spend on their cases.

We are less sure that arbitration can significantly change how Indian lawyers are compensated in order to encourage them to speed cases along. We assume it would be unlawful to pay lawyers who arbitrate with contingency fees any more than it would be to pay lawyers who litigate in court. Nonetheless, as we noted above in Section 23.2.3, we think India should rescind its prohibition on contingency fees.

Moreover, we do not believe the concerns with class arbitration in the United States should discourage India from trying it for itself. We have already said that we believe arbitration will be faster than litigation in India if the parties tweak the rules in arbitration. In addition, it should be remembered that, unlike the court system, arbitration is not free to the parties: they have to pay

[119] Andrew Powell & Richard A. Bales, *Ethical Problems in Class Arbitration*, 2011 J. DISP. RESOL. 309, 310 (2011); *see also* Thomas A. Doyle, *Protecting Nonparty Class Members in Class Arbitrations*, 25 ABA J. LAB. & EMP. L. 25, 30 (2009) (discussing the same two potential conflicts of interest) ("Imagine an arbitrator facing a similar contest over who will be class counsel–after adding the complicating facts that one of the candidates for class counsel helped select the arbitrator and has advanced arbitrator fees for the proceeding. The situation is rife with potential conflicts of interest.").

[120] *AT&T*, 563 U.S. at 350–51 ("The AAA rules do authorize judicial review of certification decisions, but this review is unlikely to have much effect . . . . ").

[121] Christopher R. Drahozal & Stephen J. Ware, *Why Do Businesses Use (or Not Use) Arbitration Clauses?*, 25 OHIO ST. J. ON DISP. RESOL. 433, 450 (2010); *see also Concepcion*, 563 U.S. at 351 ("We find it hard to believe that defendants would bet the company with no effective means of review . . . . ").

[122] The Arbitration and Conciliation Act, No. 26 of 1996, India Code (1993).

[123] A. Ayyasamy v. A. Paramasivam and Others (2016).

the arbitrator by the hour in the United States. We think this will make it especially unlikely sclerosis will set it.

Nor are we concerned about the lack of confidentiality in class arbitration; there is probably too much confidentiality to begin with in arbitration; it is good that class members and the public can see what is going on in class arbitration.

Finally, if the lack of judicial review in the United States is deemed a problem, then the solution in India is simply not to adopt the constrained judicial review of the Federal Arbitration Act. But we think India should be careful here: much of the gain of using arbitration to avoid the Indian court system will be lost if India reintroduces the court system on appeal. Thus, whatever judicial review is allowed, it should be something less than the ordinary review of the Indian court system. As we noted above in Section 23.2.3, some appeals take six years to resolve in that court system.

Our bigger concern is that Indian companies will have no reason to agree to class arbitration because the Indian court system is so slow that it deters shareholders from filing securities fraud class actions at all; why would companies wish to facilitate securities fraud actions against them by agreeing to arbitration? They probably won't, which means that India may have to enact legislation that gives *either side* of a securities dispute the right to invoke arbitration. If the parties know that either side can invoke arbitration, this will give both of them the incentive to specify the terms of any arbitration beforehand. In this regard, we are recommending a different path from the one taken in the United States where both sides must agree to arbitration. Nonetheless, we think the difference will be necessary to bring corporations along.

And that is not the only difference we recommend. Unlike the United States, India may not wish to give the parties complete carte blanche in fashioning procedural rules. In the United States, companies used this carte blanche to insulate themselves from class actions altogether; it would obviously defeat the purpose of this entire line of inquiry if Indian companies could do the same. Thus, Indian legislation may need to require that any arbitration for securities fraud violations includes access to the class action device specified in the 2013 Act.

23.5 CONCLUSION

Although, as we have explained, India has now enacted one of the most robust private enforcement devices for shareholder-management disputes in the world, commentators are very pessimistic that it will do much good because the Indian court system is notoriously unhurried. Indeed, very few shareholder class actions have been filed in the years since the Companies Act of 2013 has become law. We believe the solution to this problem is not to try to reform the Indian court system but to send the actions to private arbitration. Indeed, until our Supreme Court allowed companies to evade class actions altogether through arbitration clauses, the United States had a great deal of experience resolving class disputes through arbitration. We believe that, with some tweaks, this experience points a way forward in India toward fertile use of Section 245 of the Companies Act.

PART V

Middle East and Africa

24

Class Actions in South Africa

A Need for Certainty

Theo Broodryk

24.1 INTRODUCTION

Class actions were first recognized in South Africa more than twenty-five years ago in the Interim Constitution of the Republic of South Africa, 1993 ("Interim Constitution").[1] However, it is nevertheless an area of South African law that continues to remain largely unregulated by statute or court rules. Legislative inaction has compelled the judiciary to step in and, through case law, to develop a structure for the adjudication of class actions. South African superior courts should be commended for developing the existing framework within which class actions operate and for giving substance to what could otherwise conceivably have been perceived as an illusory dispute resolution mechanism. The role that our courts have played in this regard is important, especially in view of the increase in recent times in the incidence of class actions.

A recent empirical study[2] conducted in respect of class actions in South Africa, demonstrates that there have only been fifteen cases – less than one case per year over the course of more than nineteen years – where a South African superior court made a definitive pronouncement on whether a matter could proceed as a class action and where it is clear from the judgment or order that the applicant(s) intended to frame the matter as a class action.[3] Only seven class actions have been certified. Although there have only been a limited number of certification judgments delivered to date, there has been rapid growth in the number of certification judgments delivered in the past five years. Most of these judgments are aimed at providing access to justice for poor and marginalised individuals. The data demonstrates that there were only three cases between 2000 and 2012 during which courts pronounced on whether class actions could proceed as such. However, there were twelve such cases between 2013 and 2019. There was accordingly a significant (300 percent) increase in the incidence of class actions from the first thirteen-year period to the next seven-year period.

South African superior courts have been required to develop the appropriate class action procedural rules using their inherent jurisdiction as entrenched in section 173 of the Constitution of the Republic of South Africa, 1996. This was done in *Trustees for the time being of the Children's Resource Centre Trust* v. *Pioneer Food (Pty) Ltd (Legal Resources Centre as*

[1] Section 7(4)(b)(iv).

[2] See T. Broodryk, "An empirical analysis of class actions in South Africa" (2020) *Law, Democracy and Development*. This is the first and, to date, only empirical study conducted in respect of class actions in South Africa.

[3] The study considers cases in which a certification judgment was handed down after October 27, 2000 but before November 15, 2019. The judgment in *Ngxuza* v. *Permanent Secretary, Department of Welfare, Eastern Cape* 2001 (2) SA 609 (E) was handed down on October 27, 2000 and in this case the court first introduced certification as a requirement.

amicus curiae),[4] which effectively details key aspects of the law relating to class actions in South Africa. The case of *Mukaddam* v. *Pioneer Foods (Pty) Ltd*[5] (*Mukaddam* CC) also created important judicial precedent regarding the South African class action mechanism.

Nevertheless, South Africa's class action law is currently in a state of flux. It is trying to shape and position itself within the civil justice system. As part of this developmental process, South African courts have not been able to address all the problems, contradictions and uncertainties associated with the introduction and development of its class action mechanism. For example, it remains unclear when a class action compared to joinder is the appropriate procedural device to be utilised for the adjudication of a claim. Neither the courts nor the legislature has provided definitive guidance on the test that should be applied to determine the appropriateness of class proceedings.

At present, the framework within which class actions operate is mainly based on case law. It might seem fitting that South African courts are currently responsible for developing a class action framework because of their atypical role in managing class actions. However, courts appear to be developing the procedural framework regulating class actions, and addressing problems that arise in class proceedings, on an ad hoc, case-by-case, basis. Such an approach, although it has been necessitated by legislative inaction, is neither preferable nor desirable. It does not lend itself to creating legal certainty or judicial consistency and uniformity.[6]

The chapter will commence by considering the historical development of the South African class action mechanism. Thereafter, the chapter will contain an exposition of the existing South African framework for the adjudication of class actions. This will entail detailing the class action procedure and requirements, and it will involve identifying certain problems, contradictions and uncertainties regarding the South African class action mechanism with a view to making certain suggestions for possible reform.

24.2 HISTORICAL OVERVIEW

South African civil procedural law is largely based on English common law.[7] The origin of the class action in common law systems can be traced to the "bill of peace" that originated in seventeenth-century English Chancery Courts.[8] The English Chancery Courts developed the "bill of peace" as a procedural device to enable representative parties to petition the courts to

4 2013 1 All SA 648 (SCA).

5 2013 10 BCLR 1135 (CC). The decision of the Supreme Court of Appeal is reported as follows: *Mukaddam* v. *Pioneer Foods (Pty) Ltd* 2013 2 SA 254 (SCA).

6 See, for example, the different conclusions reached in the *Mukaddam* Supreme Court of Appeal and Constitutional Court judgments regarding whether the existence of exceptional circumstances is indeed a requirement before the opt-in class action mechanism may be utilized. The author also wishes to draw attention to his PHD study at the University of Stellenbosch, the title of which is "Developing a structure for the adjudication of class actions in South Africa." The thesis was passed in 2017.

7 W. de Vos, "Is a class action a 'classy act' to implement outside the ambit of the constitution?" (2012) 4 *T.S.A.R.* 737.

8 G. C. Lilly "Modeling Class Actions: The Representative Suit as an Analytic Tool" (2014) 81 *Neb. L. Rev.* 1008, 1013. See also Z. Chafee, *Some Problems of Equity* (1950) 157–64; De Vos (2012) 4 *T.S.A.R.* 737 738; E. Hurter, "Some Thoughts on Current Developments relating to Class Actions in South African Law as viewed against Leading Foreign Jurisdictions" (2006) 39(3) *CILSA* 485 fn. 5. According to Professor Yeazell, however, the origin of the class action can be traced to twelfth century "medieval group litigation." In this regard, see S. C. Yeazell, *From Medieval Group Litigation to the Modern Class Action* (1987). See also N. M. Pastor, "Equity and Settlement Class Actions: Can There Be Justice For All in Ortiz v. Fibreboard?" (2000) 49(3) *American University Law Review* 773, 781 where, referring to Yeazell, Pastor states "[m]anorial, royal and ecclesiastical courts used group litigation to meet varying social needs of the medieval culture that were primarily political or religious in nature and often involved multiple litigants. For example, courts used group litigation to address issues arising from social obligations or privileges accorded to different rural groups, parishes, and guilds within the hierarchical-structured medieval community."

aggregate multiple claims in a single equity proceeding, with the "class" being bound by the court's judgment.[9] The bill of peace was used when the parties to a dispute were so numerous that it would create manageability problems and when all the parties shared a common interest in the issues. This type of representative action was believed to be more efficient than trying each case individually, and more consistent with equity's goal of doing complete justice.[10] Initially, the bill of peace was available only in equity; however, in 1873 when law and equity in England combined, class actions for damages were permitted.[11] Pastor states the following regarding the bill of peace:

> The English Courts of Chancery, as courts of equity, used the "bill of peace" to permit representative parties of larger groups of litigants with a joint interest to aggregate their claims and bring a collective action before the court. The "bill of peace" served two primary and equitable goals: (1) to reduce multiple, and sometimes unnecessary, litigation, and (2) to enable individuals to litigate claims as a group that would be too difficult to litigate individually. Eventually, due process issues relating to group litigation emerged. This emergence paralleled the shift in society "from a rural, customary, agricultural world to one that is urban, *individualistic*, entrepreneurial-capitalistic." To address such concerns, Chancellors scrutinized the representation of a group of litigants more closely. In particular, they required litigants to tender an explanation for litigating jointly rather than separately. Despite these due process issues, Chancellors continued to grant permission for group litigation, often justifying the aggregation of claims because of its suitability and efficiency. Thus, the face of group litigation changed and evolved into the current form of the modern-day class action. Along with this evolution, however, came increasing concerns over adequate representation and notice that often conflicted with the goals of expediency and equity.[12]

Class actions were therefore adopted by equity courts to, essentially, avoid the technical requirements of the law courts that all persons who may be affected by a judgment be named as parties and be given notice.[13] In *Ortiz* v. *Fibreboard Corporation*,[14] the United States Supreme Court referred to the necessary parties rule in equity and stated the following regarding the origin of the class action and the development of rule 23 of the American Federal Rules of Civil Procedure ("Federal Rules"):

> Although representative suits have been recognized in various forms since the earliest days of English law, class actions as we recognize them today developed as an exception to the formal rigidity of the necessary parties rule in equity, as well as from the bill of peace, an equitable device for combining multiple suits. The necessary parties rule in equity mandated that "all persons materially interested, either as plaintiffs or defendants in the subject matter of the bill ought to be made parties to the suit, however numerous they may be" but because that rule would at times unfairly deny recovery to the party before the court, equity developed exceptions, among them one to cover situations "where the parties are very numerous, and the court perceives, that it would be almost impossible to bring them all before the court; or where the question is of general interest, and a few may sue for the benefit of the whole; or where the parties form a part of a voluntary association for public or private purposes, and may be fairly

9 M. D. Hausfeld, G. C. Rausser, G. J. Macartney, M. P. Lehmann and S. S. Gosselin, "Antitrust Class Proceedings – Then and Now" in J. Langenfeld (ed.), *The Law and Economics of Class Actions* (2014) 77, 80.

10 K. L. Hall, J. W. Ely and J. B. Grossman (eds.), *The Oxford Companion to the Supreme Court of the United States* 2nd ed. (2005) 182.

11 J. S. Allee, T. V. H. Mayer and R. W. Patryk, *Product Liability* (2005) §17.02.

12 Pastor (2000) *American University Law Review* 784–85.

13 L. J. Tornquist, "Roadmap to Illinois Class Actions" (1974) 5 *Loy. U. Chi. L. J.* 45, 45.

14 527 US 815 832 (1999).

supposed to represent the rights and interests of the whole . . ." From these roots, modern class action practice emerged . . .

The representative action of the common law was never received into South African law. This is because the distinction drawn in English law between "law" (administered in the common law courts) and "equity" (administered in the Chancery Courts),[15] was never accepted into South African law. Roman-Dutch substantive law did not suffer the same fate at the hands of the British reformers as procedural law and, accordingly, there was no need to incorporate this distinction or to establish a court of law and a court of equity, respectively.[16] Instead, a single court was established in the Cape, following the introduction of the First and Second Charters of Justice of 1827 and 1834 respectively.[17]

As stated earlier, the first time class actions were recognized in South African law was in the Interim Constitution. It enabled the utilization of a class action as a means to enforce rights entrenched in the Bill of Rights.[18] The Interim Constitution was followed, in 1995, by a Working Paper on class actions prepared by the South African Law Commission (SALC).[19] The Working Paper contained various recommendations, including the proposed introduction of a class action over the whole spectrum of civil litigation.[20] In 1998, with reference to the recommendations contained in the Working Paper, the SALC published its final report, which inter alia recommended that the principles underlying class actions should be introduced by an Act of Parliament and the necessary procedures by rules of court.[21]

24.3 CLASS ACTION PROCEDURAL FRAMEWORK

Section 38(c) of the Constitution of the Republic of South Africa, 1996 (Constitution) provides as follows:

> 38. Enforcement of rights – Anyone listed in this section has the right to approach a competent court, alleging that a right in the Bill of Rights has been infringed or threatened, and the court may grant appropriate relief, including a declaration of rights. The persons who may approach a court are- . . . (c) anyone acting as a member of, or in the interest of, a group or class of persons . . .;

Section 38(c) clearly makes provision for class actions within the confines of the Constitution.[22] This means that class action proceedings instituted in terms of section 38 may only be used to enforce rights entrenched in the Bill of Rights, even in the absence of legislation

15 S. C. Yeazell, "From Group Litigation to Class Action - Part II: Interest, Class, and Representation" (1980) 27 *UCLA Law Review* 1067.

16 H. J. Erasmus, "Historical foundations of the South African law of Civil Procedure" (1991) 108 *S.A.L.J.* 265, 269; See also H. J. Erasmus, "The Interaction of Substantive Law and Procedure" in R. Zimmermann and D. Visser (eds.), *Southern Cross: Civil Law and Common Law in South Africa* (1996) 141, 147.

17 De Vos (2012) *T.S.A.R.* 738.

18 Section 7(4) of the Interim Constitution became section 38 of the (final) Constitution of the Republic of South Africa, 1996.

19 South African Law Commission, *The Recognition of a Class Action in South African Law* Working Paper 57 Project 88 (1995). At the time it was known as the South African Law Commission. It became the South African Law Reform Commission in 2002.

20 In preparing the Working Paper, the SALC primarily used the American class action model as a guiding principle but also gave consideration inter alia to the class action model of Ontario.

21 The South African Law Commission, *The Recognition of Class Actions and Public Interest Actions in South African Law* Report Project 88 (1998) para. 5.6.5.

22 2001 4 SA 1184 (SCA). Unlike rule 23 of the Federal Rules, section 38 of the Constitution does not set out a procedural framework in terms of which a class action is to be conducted.

and court rules that regulate class actions in South Africa. The Supreme Court of Appeal in *Permanent Secretary, Department of Welfare, Eastern Cape* v. *Ngxuza*[23] (*Ngxuza*) confirmed that, notwithstanding the absence of class action legislation and court rules, it is possible to use class proceedings to enforce constitutional rights. There is conflicting case law regarding whether a preliminary certification requirement should apply to constitutional claims against the government in the same way it applies to other class actions. As the law currently stands, it appears that certification is required for all class actions in most South African superior courts. However, as a result of *Mshengu and others* v. *Msunduzi Local Municipality and others*,[24] where the court adopted the *obiter dicta* of the Constitutional Court in *Mukaddam CC*, the Kwazulu-Natal Division of the High Court of South Africa does not require certification in Bill of Rights class actions against organs of state.[25] This approach is not binding on the other divisions of the High Court of South Africa, although it may have persuasive value. Although the need to certify Bill of Rights class actions against private persons have been questioned,[26] at present certification for such class actions is also required.[27]

Section 38(c) cannot be utilized in the absence of an allegation that a right contained in the Bill of Rights has been threatened or infringed. However, South African law also allows class actions to enforce nonconstitutional rights. In other words, it is also possible to institute a class action to enforce rights not contained in the Constitution, such as a claim for damages where no constitutional right was infringed.[28] As De Vos indicates, the distinction between class actions to enforce constitutional rights and class actions to enforce nonconstitutional rights is not always clear. The cases often do not all fall neatly into either of these two categories simply because the plaintiffs sometimes rely on the infringement of both constitutional and non-constitutional rights.[29]

In *Children's Resource Centre Trust*[30] the Supreme Court of Appeal recognized a class action outside the ambit of the Constitution.[31] The court dealt with the circumstances when a class action may be instituted and the procedural requirements that must be satisfied before such proceedings may be instituted. In this regard, Wallis JA held that the first procedural step prior to the issuing of summons is to apply to court to certify the process as a class action.[32] In other words, in class action proceedings, a court must first be approached to grant leave for the matter to proceed as a class action.[33] Should leave be granted for the matter to proceed as a class action, the court, as the judicial manager of the proceedings, would issue appropriate directives as to how

23 2001 4 SA 1184 (SCA).

24 *Mshengu and others* v. *Msunduzi Local Municipality and others*, 2019 4 All SA 469 (KZP).

25 Although it is questionable to what extent the court was permitted to deviate from the decision in *Children's Resource Centre Trust*, the latter being a decision handed down by the South African Supreme Court of Appeal.

26 *Mukaddam* v. *Pioneer Foods (Pty) Ltd.*, 2013 10 BCLR 1135 (CC), para. 41.

27 T. Broodryk, "Class action certification and constitutional claims: the South African case" (2020) *Maastricht Journal of European and Comparative Law* (forthcoming).

28 W. de Vos, "Judicial Activism Gives Recognition to a General Class Action in South Africa" (2013) 2 *T.S.A.R.* 370, 372.

29 De Vos (2012) *T.S.A.R.* 747.

30 2013 1 All SA 648 (SCA).

31 Para. 21.

32 Paras. 23–25.

33 According to V. Morabito and J. Caruana, "Can Class Action Regimes Operate Satisfactorily without a Certification Device? Empirical Insights from the Federal Court of Australia" (2013) 61 *Am. J. Comp. L.* 579, 580–82, certification of class actions is an important part of those class action regimes that currently regulate class actions in American federal district courts and in ten Canadian jurisdictions. Australia, however, does not require court certification. According to the author, the only other contemporary class action regime that does not employ the certification device operates in Sweden. Sweden uses an opt-in regime. Australia, however, also employs opt-out devices like Ontario and the United States.

the class action will proceed. The class action trial then follows.[34] However, until a potential action is certified, it is not a class action.

The following definition of a "class action" was endorsed by the Supreme Court of Appeal in *Children's Resource Centre Trust*:[35]

> A class action is a legal procedure which enables the claims (or parts of the claims) of a number of persons against the same defendant to be determined in the one suit. In a class action, one or more persons ("representative plaintiff") may sue on his or her own behalf and on behalf of a number of other persons ("the class") who have a claim to a remedy for the same or a similar alleged wrong to that alleged by the representative plaintiff, and who have claims that share questions of law or fact in common with those of the representative plaintiff ("common issues"). Only the representative plaintiff is a party to the action. The class members are not usually identified as individual parties but are merely described. The class members are bound by the outcome of the litigation on the common issues, whether favourable or adverse to the class, although they do not, for the most part, take any active part in that litigation.[36]

Wallis JA laid down the following certification "requirements," which should guide a court in making its decision regarding the certification of a class action:

(1) There must be a class, identifiable by objective criteria.
(2) There must be a cause of action raising a triable issue.
(3) There must be issues of fact and/or law common to all the members of the class.
(4) The relief sought or damages claimed must flow from the cause of action and must be ascertainable and capable of determination.
(5) If the claim is for damages, there must be an appropriate procedure for allocating damages to the class members.
(6) The proposed representative must be suitable to be permitted to conduct the action and to represent the class.
(7) It must be shown that a class action is the most appropriate means of adjudicating the claims of the class members.[37]

According to Wallis JA, the above requirements may overlap. For instance, it is not possible to determine class composition without considering the nature of the claim. Wallis JA added that a class action may be appropriate where the class members share common issues, but that it is not necessarily the case. He further held that it is conceivable that a class action could be certified in respect of some issues, such as negligence in a mass personal injury claim, with the result that other issues, such as damages, would need to be resolved separately.[38]

In *Mukaddam CC*, Jafta J referred to section 173 of the Constitution and confirmed the power of our superior courts to protect and regulate their own processes and, where necessary, to develop the common law to give effect to the interests of justice. Jafta J held that the interests of

34 Hurter (2010) *T.S.A.R.* 409, 413.

35 2013 1 All SA 648 (SCA).

36 R. Mulheron, *The Class Action in Common Law Legal Systems: A Comparative Perspective* (2004) 3, quoted with approval in *Trustees for the time being of the Children's Resource Centre Trust* v. *Pioneer Food (Pty) Ltd (Legal Resources Centre as amicus curiae)* 2013 1 All SA 648 (SCA) para. 16. The South African Law Commission *The Recognition of Class Actions and Public Interest Actions in South African Law* Report Project 88 (1998) para. 5.2.7 proposes the following definition of a "class action": "an action instituted by a representative on behalf of a class of persons in respect of whom the relief claimed and the issues involved are substantially similar in respect of all members of the class, and which action is certified as a class action in terms of the Act."

37 Para. 26.

38 Para. 26.

justice should be our courts' guiding consideration when considering class action certification applications.[39]

Regarding the certification "requirements" mentioned in *Children's Resource Centre Trust*, Jafta J stated as follows:

> In Children's Resource Centre ... the Supreme Court of Appeal laid down requirements for certification. These requirements must serve as factors to be taken into account in determining where the interests of justice lie in a particular case. They must not be treated as conditions precedent or jurisdictional facts which must be present before an application for certification may succeed. The absence of one or another requirement must not oblige a court to refuse certification where the interests of justice demand otherwise.[40]

In other words, according to the Constitutional Court in *Mukaddam CC*, the certification "requirements" laid down in *Children's Resource Centre Trust* should be treated as a set of relevant "factors" that have to be taken into account when determining whether or not the class action should be certified. A court is also not limited to considering these factors and may consider other relevant factors not mentioned by Wallis JA.[41] Further, in examining the prevalence or absence of each or all of the abovementioned factors, the court's certification decision should be informed by the interests of justice.[42]

Accordingly, there is no South African statute or court rule that regulates class actions. Our courts have been required to develop appropriate class action procedural rules through their inherent jurisdiction embodied in section 173 of the Constitution.[43] Consequently, in *Mukaddam CC*, Froneman J stated the following in relation to the development of the common law by the Supreme Court of Appeal in *Children's Resource Centre Trust*:

> My understanding of the legal position flowing from this development is that courts are bound by the authoritative exposition of the development of the common law by the Supreme Court of Appeal – or by this Court, if it adds to or alters any feature of the development made by the Supreme Court of Appeal. Courts have no discretion under section 173 of the Constitution not to apply the common law as authoritatively articulated by the Supreme Court of Appeal or this Court. What they may do is to apply the developed law within the framework of their own process. Their decision not to allow certification may be set aside on appeal only if there was a material misdirection of fact or law. I see no reason to deviate from this approach here.[44]

It may be worthwhile to briefly explain the South African court structure. South Africa has a single national court system.[45] The different types of ordinary courts include the lower district and regional magistrate's courts, and the South African superior courts, including provincial divisions of the High Court of South Africa, the Supreme Court of Appeal and the Constitutional Court. The Constitutional Court is the highest court in the country, with its decision being

39 Paras. 33–34.

40 Para. 35.

41 *Mukaddam* v. *Pioneer Foods (Pty) Ltd* 2013 5 SA 89 (CC) para. 47. According to W. de Vos, "Opt-in Class Action for Damages Vindicated by Constitutional Court: Mukaddam v Pioneer Foods CCT 131/12" (2013) 4 *T.S.A.R.* 757, 765–66, relegating the requirements for a class action to mere "factors" under the umbrella of "the interests of justice" is questionable. He states that "[t]his flies in the face of the very nature of a class action and the position in the leading class action regimes. A class action is very different from an ordinary civil suit. For a class action to proceed as such certain essential requirements must be satisfied, otherwise it would be a travesty to call it a class action."

42 *Nkala* v. *Harmony Gold Mining Company Limited* 2016 3 All SA 233 (GJ) para. 32.

43 C. Plasket, "South Africa" in D. R. Hensler, C. Hodges and M. Tulibacka (eds.), *The Globalization of Class Actions* (2009) 256, 261.

44 Para. 67.

45 Section 166 of the Constitution.

binding on all other South African courts.[46] It is the final court of appeals for all matters[47] and it has the power to make the final decision on the constitutionality of an act of parliament or of a provincial legislature.[48] The Supreme Court of Appeal may decide appeals in any matter arising from the High Court of South Africa or a court of a status similar to the High Court of South Africa, except in respect of labor or competition matters to such extent as may be determined by an Act of Parliament.[49] The High Court and Supreme Court of Appeal may make an order declaring an act to be unconstitutional, but the order must be confirmed by the Constitutional Court.[50] The provincial divisions of the High Court of South Africa have general jurisdiction over their defined areas, including hearing appeals from the magistrates' courts within their area, and acting as a court of first instance for cases outside the jurisdiction of the magistrates' courts.[51] South Africa is also divided into numerous magisterial districts with each district being served by a district magistrate's court. They can hear civil cases where the value of the claim does not exceed R200,000. The magisterial districts are grouped into regions and each region has a regional court. Regional courts can hear civil cases where the value of the claim does not exceed R400,000.[52] Class actions in South Africa are primarily the domain of the High Court of South Africa and may also be adjudicated upon by the Supreme Court of Appeal and the Constitutional Court.

In South Africa, it is possible to finance class actions in various ways. It is possible fund class proceedings through legal aid centers and pro bono organizations. However, these centers and institutes usually function within a severely resource constrained environment and are often unable to fund large scale litigation. It is also possible to fund class actions by entering into contingency fees agreements[53] (i.e., no-win, no-fee agreements) and third-party litigation funding.

The certification factor that class representatives must have capacity to conduct the litigation, according to the Supreme Court of Appeal in *Children's Resource Centre Trust*, involves considering inter alia the manner in which the class action will be funded and the basis on which the lawyers are compensated. If the litigation is funded on a contingency fee basis, the representatives must disclose details of the funding arrangements to avoid a conflict of interest from arising between class counsel and class members.[54] Careful scrutiny of such arrangements also ensures that class counsel fees are reasonable and that they are not overcompensated.[55]

Further, any settlement agreement reached after certification would also need to be approved by the court. In this regard, in *Nkala*, the court held that: "it is in any event correct that any settlement agreement reached after certification of the class action should be subject to the approval of the court and that it should only be valid once approved by the court. This is to ensure that the settlement reached is fair, reasonable, adequate and that it protects the interests of the class."[56]

46 Section 167(3)(*a*) of the Constitution.
47 Section 167(3)(*b*) of the Constitution.
48 Section 167(5) of the Constitution.
49 Section 168(3)(*a*) of the Constitution.
50 Section 167(5) of the Constitution.
51 Section 169(1) of the Constitution.
52 Section 29 of the Magistrates' Courts Act 32 of 1994.
53 The Contingency Fees Act 66 of 1997 regulates contingency fees arrangements entered into throughout the South African civil litigation landscape.
54 Paras. 147–66.
55 D. Unterhalter and A. Coutsoudis, "The Certification of Class Actions" in M. du Plessis, J. Oxenham, I. Goodman, L. Kelly and S. Pudifin-Jones (eds.), *Class action litigation in South Africa* (2017) 31.
56 Para. 39. See also *De Bruyn* v. *Steinhoff International Holdings N.V. and Others* (29290/2018) (2020) ZAGPJHC 145 (26 June 2020).

A brief note on costs in South Africa may also be appropriate. South Africa subscribes to the two-way costs rule, which requires the unsuccessful party to pay the other party's costs, that is, costs follow the event. These costs can vary in scale between party and party, and attorney and client costs. Generally speaking, the court cannot order a person who is not a party before it to pay costs.[57] Applying this general rule to class action, it is apparent that class members, insofar as they are not parties to the dispute, will generally not be liable for costs. This rule does not apply in relation to the representative plaintiff who is indeed a party to the dispute and can accordingly be held liable for costs.

24.4 CHALLENGES AND OPPORTUNITIES FOR REFORM

As mentioned earlier, the absence of legislation and court rules regulating the South African class action procedural framework has compelled the judiciary to take ownership of this developmental process. Although the progress made by our courts to establish a framework for the adjudication of class actions in South Africa should be commended, the courts have not been able to address all the problems, contradictions and uncertainties associated with the mechanism. Some of these issues will be considered below, with a view to making certain recommendations regarding possible opportunities for reform.

24.4.1 *Appropriateness of Class Proceedings*

As mentioned earlier, the certification "requirements" stated by Wallis JA in *Children's Resource Centre Trust*[58] include that there must be a class, identifiable by objective criteria, and it must be shown that a class action is the most appropriate means of adjudicating the claims of the class members.[59] After he listed the certification requirements,[60] Wallis JA proceeded to deal selectively with some of the requirements in more detail. He did not consider separately the certification requirement that a class action must be shown to be the most appropriate means of determining class members' claims. Instead, he essentially dealt with this requirement in the context of the first certification requirement, namely that there must be a class, identifiable by objective criteria. In this regard, Wallis JA mentioned *obiter* that:

> In defining the class it is not necessary to identify all the members of the class. Indeed, if that were possible, there would be a question whether a class action was necessary, as joinder under Uniform Rule 10 would be permissible. It is, however, necessary that the class be defined with sufficient precision that a particular individual's membership can be objectively determined by examining their situation in the light of the class definition.[61]

It can be inferred from the above comments of Wallis JA that, where all the claimants are identifiable,[62] they may need to be joined as plaintiffs to the proceedings. A class action may therefore not be the appropriate procedural device to be utilized in such circumstances. Wallis

[57] A. C. Cilliers, C. Loots and C. Nel, *Herbstein and Van Winsen: The Civil Practice of the High Courts and the Supreme Court of Appeal of South Africa* 5th ed. (2009) 952. See, for example, *Lasersohn* v. *Olivier* 1962 1 All SA 338 (T) 340 where it was held that "it is logical that if a person is not before the court then you cannot make an order against such a person."

[58] 2013 1 All SA 648 (SCA).

[59] Para. 26.

[60] Para. 26.

[61] Para. 29.

[62] In the sense that the individual claimants can be named and specified.

JA does, however, clearly fall short of saying that a class action may never be used if the claimants are all personally identifiable. He mentions that there is a measure of overlap between the certification requirements[63] and he also refers to the circumstances when a class action may be instituted in South Africa,[64] such as where the class is large, where the class members are poor, and where the claims are not large enough for it to be pursued separately.[65]

Wallis JA thus stated that it is unnecessary to identify all the class members, otherwise the necessity of a class action would be questionable. It accordingly remains unclear when, if at all, the identifiability of class members will preclude the certification of a class action. Moreover, it is unclear what the test is our courts must apply and what factors they must consider to determine the appropriateness of a class action.

In *Mukaddam SCA*[66] the class action was framed in an opt-in manner. This meant that the class would have been confined to individuals who took the necessary steps to opt into the class action. Nugent JA held that a class action was not suitable in *casu*. He held that once the class is confined to claimants who choose positively to advance their claims and are required to come forward for that purpose, he can see no reason why they are not capable of doing so in their own names – they do not need a representative to do so on their behalf. He then stated that the court rules make specific provision for multiple plaintiffs to join in one action.[67] The court in *Mukkadam SCA* therefore found, at the expense of the opt-in class action regime, joinder to be the more appropriate procedural device. The court in *Mukaddam CC* did not deal with the comments of the Supreme Court of Appeal on joinder.

A potential problem evidenced by the approach of the court in *Mukaddam SCA* is that where, for example, the individual claimants are poor, uneducated and lack access to resources, or where the class is large, joinder may in fact be cumbersome and inappropriate, even though all the claimants are personally identifiable.[68] This potential problem is significant in that a court ordering joinder in such circumstances could potentially undermine the primary rationale underpinning the incorporation of the class action mechanism into South African law namely, access to justice.[69]

63 Para. 26.

64 Paras. 19–22.

65 Para. 19.

66 2013 2 SA 254 (SCA).

67 Para. 12. Rule 10(1) of the Rules Regulating the Conduct of the Proceedings of the Several Provincial and Local Divisions of the High Court of South Africa allows joinder of multiple plaintiffs in a single action and provides that:

> Any number of persons, each of whom has a claim, whether jointly, jointly and severally, separately or in the alternative, may join as plaintiffs in one action against the same defendant or defendants against whom any one or more of such persons proposing to join as plaintiffs would, if he brought a separate action, be entitled to bring such action, provided that the right to relief of the persons proposing to join as plaintiffs depends upon the determination of substantially the same question of law or fact which, if separate actions were instituted, would arise on each action, and provided that there may be a joinder conditionally upon the claim of any other plaintiff failing.

68 According to Erasmus and van Loggerenberg, *Erasmus: Superior Court Practice* A2-21, the traditional rules governing joinder may be impractical where the claimants comprise a large group and/or all the potential claimants have not yet been identified.

69 The South African Law Commission, *The Recognition of Class Actions and Public Interest Actions in South African Law Report* Project 88 (1998) paras. 1.3–1.4. See also the South African Law Commission, *The Recognition of a Class Action in South African Law* Working Paper 57 Project 88 (1995) para. 5.28 where it is stated that "[t]he whole purpose of class actions is to facilitate access to justice for the man on the street." See also *Permanent Secretary, Department of Welfare, Eastern Cape* v. *Ngxuza* 2001 4 SA 1184 (SCA) para. 1 where Cameron JA states that "[t]he law is a scarce resource in South Africa. This case shows that justice is even harder to come by. It concerns the ways in which the poorest in our country are to be permitted access to both." In *Mukaddam* v. *Pioneer Foods (Pty) Ltd* 2013 2 SA 254 (SCA) para. 11 it is stated that "[t]he justification for recognising class actions is that without that procedural device

The primary difficulties associated with joinder is that it is a cumbersome and costly process. An interested party is required to file an application[70] in terms of which the party's direct and substantial interest in the matter is set out and in terms of which the court is requested to join the party to the proceedings. Joinder is a costly procedure, since the interested party is generally required to make use of legal representation to bring the application.

The identifiability of class members appears to be the key consideration which the court in *Mukaddam SCA* took into account to determine whether a class action is the appropriate means for adjudicating class members' claims. Accordingly, where the individual class members are all identifiable, regardless of inter alia their financial means, the size of their individual claims and the size of the class, they may need to be joined as plaintiffs to the proceedings. A class action may therefore not be the appropriate procedural device to be utilized in such circumstances. However, where for example the individual class members are not in a financial position to vindicate their rights through ordinary litigation, where the class is numerous or where the individual claims of class members are small, joinder may be costly, cumbersome and inappropriate. Requiring joinder in such circumstances may deprive class members of their right to access to justice. In other words, the fact that class members are identifiable should not necessarily mean that a class action is not the appropriate mechanism to adjudicate class members' claims. There are other considerations that must be taken into account in making this determination.

The approaches of the foreign jurisdictions upon which the South African class action mechanism has largely been modeled have effectively been to assess the appropriateness of class actions with regard to the principal advantages of the class action.[71] It is submitted that our courts should adopt a similar approach. The approach of our courts in assessing appropriateness should, however, be tailored to meet the needs and demands of the South African society. Hurter suggests that for a class action to be successful in the South African context, it needs to be uniquely South African "and cannot be the product of selective and haphazard adaptations of foreign solutions. It should be borne in mind that such solutions evolved in response to practice specific needs and are therefore not necessarily applicable to our situation, or may come with undesirable baggage."[72]

It is accordingly suggested that, in making this assessment, our courts should attach significant weight to access to justice, due to the constitutional prominence of this principle,[73] as well as the

claimants will be denied access to the courts." In *Mukaddam* v. *Pioneer Foods (Pty) Ltd* 2013 5 SA 89 (CC) para. 29 Jafta J stated that "[a]ccess to courts is fundamentally important to our democratic order. It is not only a cornerstone of the democratic architecture but also a vehicle through which the protection of the Constitution itself may be achieved."

70 Notice of motion supported by affidavit(s).

71 In the United States, the court in *Safran* v. *United Steelworkers of America AFL-CIO* 132 FRD 397 (WD Pa 1989) 401 held that the "numerosity requirement reflects the general theory behind class action lawsuits which is to permit a large group of individuals whose interests are sufficiently related to bring one lawsuit, instead of many lawsuits, so as to conserve judicial resources and increase judicial access." In *Bright* v. *Femcare Limited* 2002 FCAFC 243; 195 ALR 574 para. 152 Finkelstein J for the Federal Court of Australia held that whether or not it is in the interests of justice to make an order that the representative proceeding be terminated requires consideration of the principal objects of the class action. Similarly, the court in *Hollick* v. *Toronto (City)* 2001 3 SCR 158 held that the class action objectives should constitute the lens through which the preferability inquiry should be conducted. In *Excalibur Special Opportunities LP* v. *Schwartz Levitsky Feldman LLP* 2007 ONCA 334, 85 OR (3d) 321 para. 217 Perell J concluded that, on the facts, joinder was the preferable procedure inter alia because it was not shown that a "class action is necessary to overcome any barriers to access to justice." In *AIC Limited* v. *Fischer* 2013 SCC 69 paras. 24–38 it was held that a court must consider whether there are barriers to access to justice in the given case.

72 Hurter (2008) *De Jure* 303–04.

73 Section 34 of the Constitution.

importance of responding to acute social needs. Specifically, our courts should consider possible barriers to access to justice to determine whether certification is necessary. Furthermore, our courts should consider whether certification is necessary to achieve judicial economy and behavior modification. They should also determine whether it would otherwise be inappropriate to allow the class proceedings to continue by considering inter alia the manageability of the class action; the importance of the common issues in relation to the claims as a whole; and whether the class members' claims are large enough to warrant being pursued separately. However, the access to justice consideration should, in a South African context and upon considering all the circumstances surrounding the case, be attributed more weight than those factors that form part of the aforementioned supplementary inquiry.[74]

24.4.2 *Opt-in Class Actions Compared to Opt-out Class Actions*

As mentioned, Nugent JA in *Mukaddam SCA* held that, once the class is confined to claimants who choose positively to advance their claims and are required to come forward for that purpose (i.e., who choose to "opt in"), he can see no reason why they are not capable of doing so in their own names through joinder – they do not need a representative to do so on their behalf.[75] By suggesting that joinder is the appropriate procedural device where all the claimants are identifiable, Nugent JA clearly questioned the viability of the opt-in regime of class action litigation. Nugent JA also held that the opt-in class action regime can only be utilized in exceptional circumstances.[76] As exceptional circumstances were not proved, he found that a class action was not the most appropriate way to pursue the claims.[77]

The court in *Mukaddam CC* held that the Supreme Court of Appeal in *Mukaddam SCA* was wrong to find that an applicant in an opt-in class action is required to show exceptional circumstances. Although the court did not provide reasons for its disagreement with the finding of the Supreme Court of Appeal in this regard, the fact of the matter is that, as our law stands at the moment, there is no need to prove exceptional circumstances to be able to utilize the opt-in procedure. It nevertheless remains unclear in what circumstances the opt-in mechanism may be utilized.

The SALC recommended that courts should have a discretion to make opt-in, opt-out or no notice orders.[78] The SALC proposed that legislation should be adopted to regulate class actions in South Africa and that the legislation should deal with the questions of when, by whom, to whom and how notice should be given. As a general rule, according to the SALC, notice to class members and prospective class members should always be given and the court should retain a discretion to make opt-in, opt-out or no-notice orders. The court should, in all cases, consider whether notice of the certification application should be given to all persons eligible to elect to join the class.[79] The approach of the court in *Mukaddam SCA* regarding the opt-in class action

74 For a comprehensive discussion, see T. Broodryk, "The South African Class Action vs Group Action as an Appropriate Procedural Device" 1 (2019)*Stell. L.R.* 6–32.

75 Para. 12.

76 If the effect of Nugent JA's comment that joinder is appropriate where all the class members are identifiable is to negate the need for a South African opt-in class action regime, then Nugent JA seemingly contradicts himself by requiring that exceptional circumstances must be proved before the opt-in procedure can be used.

77 Paras. 11, 14.

78 South African Law Commission, *The Recognition of Class Actions and Public Interest Actions in South African Law* Report Project 88 (1998) para. 5.10.24.

79 Vii.

regime, as mentioned above, contradicts these recommendations. It also complicates the issue of notice in class action proceedings.

In the Working Paper, the SALC stated that provision should be made for opt-in notice in limited situations because there may be circumstances where class members with substantial claims would be severely prejudiced if the class action fails because it was not effectively prosecuted. A judgment in such circumstances would render the individual claims *res judicata*, therefore preventing further litigation on the same issue. It is therefore important to ensure that class members know of the class action if they are to be bound by the outcome.[80] Therefore, according to the SALC, circumstances may indeed arise that justify use of the opt-in, rather than the opt-out, procedure.

According to the SALC, the advantage of opt-in notice is that there is certainty as to who the members of the class are and what the aggregate value of the claims is. The defendant is thus in a better position to make a well-reasoned judgment as to his or her liability in order to decide whether to make a settlement offer.[81] The fact that the opt-in procedure is nothing more than a permissive joinder device is not a problem. Litigation through joinder is made possible by our court rules; however, there is a point at which joinder becomes cumbersome. The SALC states that "it becomes cumbersome when there are more than four or five plaintiffs and extremely cumbersome when there are more than about ten."[82] Claimants who opt in will be in much the same position as plaintiffs who join in an action, except that the representative will conduct the action on their behalf. The actual management of the action is likely to be simpler and less cumbersome than where a large number of plaintiffs are joined.[83] The SALC accordingly found that there are circumstances where joinder, although possible, would not be appropriate and that, in such cases, the opt-in procedure may be the appropriate means of adjudicating class members' claims.

The SALC recommended that the courts may require that opt-in notice be given, but stated that it would be an exception rather than the rule. According to the SALC it is obvious why the opt-out procedure is preferable. The SALC attached significant weight to financial and social barriers, the existence of which may preclude participation in class proceedings by potential class members. The SALC considered the fact that a large portion of our society is poor, illiterate and uninformed because they have not been properly educated. It is therefore important to ensure that this portion of society benefits from class actions, probably more so than in certain other foreign jurisdictions. Accordingly, the SALC recommended that courts should only order that opt-in notice be given where there is a possibility that class members may be severely prejudiced. Prejudice in this context entails being bound by a judgment without having knowledge of the class action. The SALC uses the following example: an airplane crash where a large number of people suffer damage, and where the individual claims are sufficiently large to make it probable that the claimants would enforce their own claims. In such a scenario, according to the SALC, the claimants should not be bound by a judgment unless they have expressly consented to be bound.[84]

From the above example it can be inferred that the SALC appears to have envisaged that the opt-in procedure should be used in circumstances where the size of the class would be much more limited compared to where an opt-out procedure would typically be used, the individual

80 South African Law Commission *The Recognition of a Class Action in South African Law Working Paper* 57 Project 88 (1995) para. 5.32.
81 Para. 5.24.
82 Para. 5.24.
83 Para. 5.24.
84 Para. 5.25.

class members would be identifiable as, for example, with the survivors of an airplane accident and, importantly, each class member would have a substantial individual claim. De Vos states that the opt-in regime of class action litigation caters especially for those circumstances where the members of the class have substantial individual claims.[85] He argues that, since the judgment in a class action has *res judicata* effect on all the class members, except those who have been excluded, it is important that class members with such claims should be apprised of the action and given the option to associate themselves with it. Otherwise they could be severely prejudiced if a class action fails due to mismanagement.[86]

In *Mukaddam* SCA, Nugent JA held that the fact "[t]hat the plaintiffs might be numerous – in this case it is said that there might be 100, although there is no reason to think that all will join – is in itself no reason to preclude a joint action. Perhaps there will be more paper – though even that is not necessarily true – but that is no more than administrative inconvenience . . ."[87] The court footnoted this comment with the following statement: "In the United States a class action is not competent if all the claimants can be joined. Rule 23(a) of the Federal Rules of Civil Procedure require a party seeking certification to demonstrate, amongst other things, that 'the class is so numerous that joinder is impracticable'."[88]

The abovementioned comments of Nugent JA are problematic in various respects. It is not the case in the United States that, where joinder of all the claimants is possible, class proceedings are not appropriate. American class proceedings may be appropriate where joinder is possible but not necessarily feasible.[89] If joinder is possible but would needlessly complicate the litigation of the case, then class action proceedings may be appropriate.[90] Impracticability of joinder does not entail impossibility.[91] Accordingly, the identifiability of individual class members will form part of the assessment of the impracticability of joinder – it is not the only consideration in determining practicability of joinder compared to class proceedings.[92]

It further appears that Nugent JA did not give proper consideration to the judgment of Cameron JA in *Ngxuza* where he held that joinder presupposes that prospective plaintiffs will approach courts *en masse*, but that this often fails to materialize insofar as the "various parties who have the common interest are isolated, scattered and utter strangers to each other."[93] In such circumstances, the conditions for group action through joinder do not exist. According to Cameron JA, society cannot simply set up courts and wait for litigants to bring their complaints as barriers may exist that preclude their participation in litigious proceedings; hence, the need for class proceedings.[94] Simply stating that a numerous class consisting of approximately 100 claimants is insufficient to preclude litigation through joinder – or stated differently, that joinder is possible where the class consists of 100 claimants – does not take account of the practicalities associated with joinder or the benefits of a class action. Such an approach disregards the considerations that are relevant in determining the appropriateness of class proceedings as a means of adjudicating the claims of class members.

The purpose of affording to the court a discretion to choose between the type of class action procedure to be followed is inter alia to determine, with reference to the facts of the specific case,

85 De Vos (1996) 4 *T.S.A.R.* 647.
86 De Vos (1996) 4 *T.S.A.R.* 647–48.
87 Para. 13.
88 Para. 13.
89 B. Anderson and A. Trask, *Class Action Playbook* (2014) 26–27.
90 26–27.
91 See *Robidoux* v. *Celani* 987 F.2d 931, 935–36.
92 R. H. Klonoff, *Class Actions and Other Multi-party Litigation in a Nutshell* 4th ed. (2012) 40.
93 *Permanent Secretary, Department of Welfare, Eastern Cape* v. Ngxuza 2001 4 SA 1184 (SCA) paras. 4–5.
94 *Id.*, paras. 4–5.

whether ordering that the opt-in procedure be utilized would have the effect of potentially denying people a legal remedy simply because they may fail to comprehend the opt-in requirement, may be fearful of taking action, or may otherwise be precluded from opting into the class action. Therefore, when considering the potential utilization of the opt-in regime rather than the opt-out regime, this discretion should operate to protect those individuals who may be excluded from the class proceedings by virtue of the nature of opt-in proceedings.

The finding in *Mukaddam* SCA that joinder is appropriate where the class members are identifiable, effectively obviates the need for the opt-in class action regime. It appears that Nugent JA subscribed to the view that the opt-in procedure is nothing more than a permissive joinder device. This cannot be correct. As mentioned, there are circumstances where the class members are identifiable but where joinder is nonetheless cumbersome and unfeasible.[95] A preferable approach is accordingly one in terms of which our courts are afforded a discretion to choose, with regard to the circumstances of each case, whether to require opt-in, opt-out or no-notice at all. The primary advantage of providing the court with judicial discretion to choose between requiring opt-in, opt-out and no-notice orders, is that it enables the court to decide, with reference to the circumstances of the particular case, which procedure would be most suited to the overall disposition of the case.[96]

24.4.3 *Manageability of Class Actions*

The manageability of class proceedings is an important consideration during the certification stage. Various factors could influence the application of this consideration and hence influence the appropriateness of class proceedings. The manageability of a class action was not listed by Wallis JA in *Children's Resource Centre Trust*[97] as one of the factors that our courts should consider when deciding whether to grant a certification application.[98] Earlier it was contended that the manageability consideration should form part of the appropriateness inquiry; in other words, the manageability of class proceedings becomes relevant when a court needs to decide on the appropriateness of class proceedings as a means of adjudicating class members' claims.

The manageability consideration entails taking account of "the whole range of practical problems that may render the class action format inappropriate for a particular suit."[99] For instance, it entails considering whether the administrative costs incurred in managing the class action would consume the award made in favor of the plaintiff class.[100] A further factor to be considered in the context of manageability is the difficulty associated with notifying a significant percentage of the class – this may count against possible certification. Although certification generally should not be denied solely because class members would have to prove their damages on an individualized basis, potential difficulty in calculating damages may also be a factor in assessing manageability.

Because of the management difficulties generally encountered in class action litigation, effective judicial management is considered increasingly important for the efficient functioning

95 South African Law Commission, *The Recognition of a Class Action in South African Law Working Paper* 57 Project 88, para. 5.25.

96 Alberta Law Reform Institute *Class Actions* (2000) Final Report No. 85. For a comprehensive discussion, see T. Broodryk, "The South African Class Action Mechanism: Comparing the Opt-out regime to the Opt-in regime" (2019) 22 *P.E.L.J.* 5.

97 2013 1 All SA 648 (SCA).

98 However, Mojapelo DJP did consider the manageability of proceedings in *Nkala* v. *Harmony Gold Mining Company Limited* 2016 3 All SA 233 (GJ) paras. 51–52.

99 *Eisen* v. *Carlisle & Jacquelin*, 417 US 156, 164 (1974).

100 Anderson and Trask, *Class Action Playbook* (2014) 62.

of class actions.[101] As class action litigation is traditionally more complex than other kinds of litigation, it requires greater administration and management of the case.[102] The importance of managing class actions effectively is evidenced by the fact that manageability problems could, as is the case in for example Ontario and the United States, result in a court refusing to certify a class action or,[103] as is the case in for example Australia, in the termination of a class action.[104]

To enable effective managerial judging[105] of class actions, the foreign jurisdictions upon which the South African mechanism has been modelled, have conferred upon their trial judges extensive powers to manage these proceedings. For example, in the United States, rule 23 of the Federal Rules of Civil Procedure ("Federal Rules") contains various provisions governing the trial court's powers, obligations and discretion in managing class actions.[106] Rules 23(c), (d) and (e) confer upon courts managerial authority over class actions.[107] For example, judges play a role in certifying the class and approving the adequacy of the class representative and class counsel.[108] Judges are also required to approve proposed and final settlements and to review objections by class members.[109] Ontario's Class Proceedings Act, 1992 (Ontario Act), also affords to judges extensive managerial powers to manage class actions.[110] Courts use their powers in case management to prevent class proceedings from becoming too cumbersome and to protect the interests of class members.[111]

The increasing size and complexity of class action lawsuits necessitate a more hands-on management approach than in the case of ordinary civil litigation.[112] Class actions are inherently complex and they involve the interests of large numbers of people and, generally, significant

101 C. Piché, "Judging Fairness in Class Action Settlements" (2010) 28 *Windsor Y.B. Access. Just.* 111, 121. C. S. Diver, "The Judge as Political Powerbroker: Superintending Structural Changes in Public Institutions" (1979) 65 *VA L. Rev.* 43, 45 states that the "transformation in the character of litigation necessarily transforms the judge's role as well."

102 See P. G. Karlsgodt, "United States" in P. G. Karlsgodt (ed.), *World Class Actions – A Guide to Group and Representative Actions around the Globe* (2012) 44; Piché (2010) *Windsor Y.B. Access. Just.* 117.

103 In the United States, a class action will not be certified if there is proof that it would indeed be unmanageable (due to inter alia the size of the class, the giving of notice and the distribution of damages) since it will then not be superior to other methods of adjudication as required by rule 23(b)(3). For example, in *Eisen* v. *Carlisle and Jacquelin* 417 US 156 (1974) the enormity of the class and related issues such as notice to absent members and the distribution of an aggregate reward to class members caused serious doubt about the viability of the case. In the recent mass personal injury class action of *Nkala* v. *Harmony Gold Mining Company Limited* 2016 3 All SA 233 (GJ), the class consisted of between 17,000 and 500,000 class members. Mojapelo DJP (at para. 52) held that "[w]hat we have here is that the sizes of the two classes may be very large but that does not make the . . . class action trial unmanageable."

104 In Australia, once a representative proceeding has been instituted, it will continue unless the respondent applies to the court for an order terminating it. Thus, unlike the class action regimes of Ontario, South Africa and the United States, where the party bringing the action must show that certain requirements are met before certification is granted, it is up to the respondent to raise noncompliance with them. Of relevance in the context of manageability is section 33N of the Federal Court of Australia Act of 1976 (Cth) in terms of which a court may order the discontinuance of class proceedings if it is satisfied that it is in the interests of justice to do so for one or more of the reasons specified in section 33N(1)(a)–(d).

105 According to T. B. Wolff, "Managerial Judging and Substantive Law" (2013) 90 *Washington University Law Review* 1027, 1027, Professor Judith Resnik coined the term "managerial judging" thirty years ago to describe the expanded role of federal district judges under the American Federal Rules of Civil Procedure.

106 Karlsgodt, "United States" in *World Class Actions – A Guide to Group and Representative Actions around the Globe* 35.

107 Klonoff, *Class Actions and Other Multi-party Litigation in a Nutshell* (2012) 25.

108 Rule 23(c). See also J. Brewster, "A Kick in the Class: Giving Class Members a Voice in Class Action Settlements" (2013) 41 *W. St. U. L. Rev.* 1, 11.

109 Rule 23(e).

110 See, for example, section 12 of the Class Proceedings Act, 1992, S.O. 1992, c. 6. titled "Court may determine conduct of proceeding."

111 J. Kalajdzic, W. A. Bogart and I. Matthews, "Canada" in D. R. Hensler, C. Hodges and M. Tulibacka (eds.), *The Globalization of Class Actions* (2009) 46.

112 C. Piché, "The Cultural Analysis of Class Action Law" (2009) 2 *J. Civ. L. Stud.* 101, 128, 130.

amounts of money. They necessitate a more active management approach by the judges who are required to adjudicate over them. As Hurter states:

> It should be pointed out that since class action litigation is complex litigation, the procedural rules required to achieve proper management are fairly complex and to this end the usual procedural rules regulating ordinary litigation are inadequate. The potential volume of plaintiffs in a class action offers a logistical challenge to the plaintiff attorney, representative plaintiff, and the court, requiring innovative procedural rules to ensure proper management of the litigation. Proper and effective management of class actions is crucial to the success of class actions.[113]

Court management is aimed at facilitating the achievement of justice in a speedy and cost-effective manner. This aim is not facilitated by unfettered party control because the legal representatives generally act in the interests of their own clients. For example, in some cases it may be in a party's interests to delay the proceedings or to engage in procedural disputes. Further, unidentified parties' interests may not be properly considered without active court management.[114]

South Africa still has some way to go insofar as its approach to the effective management of class actions is concerned, especially when compared to the foreign jurisdictions referred to above, all of whom have adopted comprehensive legislation to regulate class actions. Their legislation encourages and mandates an active role by courts in managing class actions. South African courts have mostly relied on their inherent jurisdiction, as echoed in section 173 of the Constitution, to manage class actions.[115]

Rule 37A deals with judicial case management and was recently introduced into the Uniform Rules of Court.[116] Rule 37A(1) provides as follows:

> A judicial case management system shall apply, at any stage after a notice of intention to defend is filed-
>
> (a) to such categories of defended actions as the Judge President of any Division may determine in a Practice Note or Directive; and
> (b) to any other proceeding in which judicial case management is determined by the Judge President, of own accord, or upon the request of a party, to be appropriate.

Rule 37A(2) provides that case management through judicial intervention will "be used in the interests of justice to alleviate congested trial rolls and to address the problems which cause delays in the finalisation of cases."[117] The nature of extent to which case management in terms of the rule occurs must be completed by the relevant directives or practices of the Division in which the proceedings are pending.[118] The rule confirms that the primary responsibility to prepare properly, to comply with the rules of court and to act professionally in expediting the matter towards trial and adjudication, rests with the parties and their legal representatives.[119]

113 Hurter (2006) *CILSA* 489. See also J. C. Alexander, *An Introduction to Class Action Procedure in the United States* (2000) Paper Presented at Conference *Debates over Group Litigation in Comparative Perspective*, Geneva, Switzerland https://law.stanford.edu/publications/an-introduction-to-class-action-procedure-in-the-united-states/ (accessed 21/07/2019), regarding the courts' active role in managing class actions.

114 Morabito (2003) *Texas International Law Journal* 672.

115 Supplemented by the practice directives of the respective divisions of the High Court of South Africa. Section 173 provides that "[t]he Constitutional Court, Supreme Court of Appeal and High Courts have the inherent power to protect and regulate their own process, and to develop the common law, taking into account the interests of justice."

116 GG 999 (12-01-1965): Uniform Rules of Court: Rules Regulating the Conduct of the Proceedings of the Several Provincial and Local Divisions of the High Court of South Africa. Rule 37A was inserted by GNR.842 of May 31, 2019.

117 Rule 37(2)(a).

118 Rule 37(2)(b).

119 Rule 37(2)(c).

Although the introduction of a general case management rule is a step in the right direction, the absence of a uniform rule or legislation regulating judicial management of class actions specifically is potentially problematic for various reasons.

The South African class action system remains exposed to the inherent limitations of unregulated ad hoc managerial judging in class proceedings. As mentioned, class actions pose unique challenges due to its size and complexity. Ideally, judges should be expressly empowered by legislation to assume an active role to enable class actions to be managed efficiently and to ensure that the interests of absent class members are protected against unnecessary dismissal of class actions because of manageability problems. A broad discretionary management power is necessary, because it is impossible to anticipate all the circumstances arising in a class proceeding where the intervention of the court is appropriate or desirable. However, where such circumstances can be contemplated, it should be dealt with in legislation or court rules promulgated especially for this purpose. According to Hurter, "much of the success of this procedural device depends on how it is viewed by the judiciary: if negatively, then its growth (application field) is restricted and its value as an instrument to facilitate better access to justice is diminished."[120] She therefore states that the extended judicial role should not be left to the courts to develop.[121] The proposed adoption of a legislative framework to regulate class actions is also premised upon the approaches of prominent foreign jurisdictions in this regard. For example, Brunet refers to Resnik when he states as follows regarding the change in the American judiciary following upon the introduction of the Federal Rules:

> Professor Resnik first described the federal judge sitting in 1915 as a "solo player," noting that there were only 120 district judges at that time who sat "with few shared practices." The early twentieth century federal judge toiled in isolation. Resnik points out that the twentieth century growth of the American Bar Association led to procedural reforms such as passage of the Federal Rules of Civil Procedure. In the pre-Federal Rules period, the lack of uniform procedures undoubtedly contributed to a culture of judging that excluded pressures to settle rather than to try cases. Resnik sees the passage of the Federal Rules as part of a more significant trend toward unifying the federal judiciary.[122]

It is concerning that the approaches to case management of the different divisions of the High Court may vary, perhaps even significantly, depending on which division is seized of the dispute. This could arguably result in a differential impact on parties' fundamental rights in different divisions. For example, a strict exercise of case management powers may adversely impact on civil litigants' fundamental rights, whereas a more flexible approach could be more tolerant of such rights. Where a party is refused leave to amend a pleading or to call a witness, due to some procedural failure, it may adversely impact upon a litigant's right to be heard. And where a case management judge in a particular division directs parties to consider engaging in mediation it could effectively amount to a denial of their right to access to court to obtain a judicial determination on the merits of the case. This would be in violation of the right to access to justice entrenched in section 34 of the constitution.[123]

Rule 37A makes extensive provision for circumstances where there has been non-compliance with the case management process. Daya explains that "[t]he draft rules establish a system to facilitate the just and timely disposition of proceedings, with the minimum necessary commitment of resources by the court and litigants, by monitoring the progress of individual proceedings against

120 Hurter (2006) *CILSA* 489.

121 Ibid.

122 E. Brunet "Judicial Mediation and Signaling" (2002/2003) 3 *Nevada Law Journal* 232, 242.

123 See De Vos and Broodryk (2018) *T.S.A.R.* 34.

predetermined timelines, and intervening when a proceeding is not progressing satisfactorily."[124] Any failure by a party to adhere to the principles and requirements set out in rule 37A may result in that party being penalized by way of an adverse costs order.[125] Of particular concern is sub-rule 12(d) which provides that the case management judge may "strike the matter from the case management roll and direct that it be re-enrolled only after any non-compliance with the rules or case management directions has been purged." In other words, a procedural error could conceivably result in the imposition of a judicial sanction causing an arguable claim to fail. Substantive justice may therefore, as a result of a procedural error, not be achieved. Individual justice between the parties could thus be exiled in favor of a strict exercise of a court's case management powers, which could adversely impact upon a civil litigant's fundamental right to present his or her case to court. What about a party's right to present his or her case fully and obtain a judicial determination on the merits? Surely, rule compliance should not become an end in itself. It should instead be a means to an end, viz. to achieve justice on the merits in a given dispute between parties.

The explanatory memorandum that accompanied the proposed rule 37A states that the rule is "to be applied by the courts with the objective of avoiding undue delay, expense and technicality and facilitating the purpose of these rules."[126] It is regrettable that the rule seems to place little emphasis on achieving individual justice between the parties.[127]

24.4.4 *Other Challenges*

There are numerous challenges associated with the South African class action mechanism other than those referred to above, a comprehensive discussion of which falls outside the scope of this chapter. However, some of these challenges are briefly referred to below and relate to class action notice, empirical data regarding class actions and funding of class actions.

As mentioned, the SALC recommended that courts should have a discretion to make opt-in, opt-out or no notice orders.[128] The Supreme Court of Appeal in *Children's Resource Centre Trust*[129] provided guidelines regarding the certification process but, as the court refused to grant leave to the applicants to proceed with a class action, the court did not deal with other complex issues, such as notice to absent class members. Notice to class members was not discussed separately as a class action certification requirement. In the absence of statutory or court guidance regarding notice in class actions, it is unclear whether and in what circumstances

124 R. Daya, "Proposed amendments to certain uniform rules and new rules submitted by the judicial case flow management committee of the office of the chief justice" (https://lawpracticeassist.co.za/Pdfs/proposed_Case_%20Management_%20rule_amendments.pdf (22-12-2019)).

125 Rule 37A(16).

126 Daya, "Proposed amendments to certain uniform rules and new rules submitted by the judicial case flow management committee of the office of the chief justice" (https://lawpracticeassist.co.za/Pdfs/proposed_Case_%20Management_%20rule_amendments.pdf (22–12-2019)) and the attached "Explanatory memorandum of objectives and motivation underlying the draft rules" submitted by the judicial case flow management committee.

127 For a more comprehensive discussion regarding case management, see T. Broodryk and W. de Vos, "Managerial judging and alternative dispute resolution in Australia: an example for South Africa to emulate?" part 2 (2018) *T.S.A.R.* 18–35; T. Broodryk and W. de Vos, "Fundamental procedural rights of civil litigants in Australia and South Africa: is there cause for concern?" (part 2) (2019) 4 *T.S.A.R.* 627–39; T. Broodryk, "Strategic Considerations in Global Litigation: Comparing Judicial Case Management Approaches in South Africa with the United States" (2017) *Stell. L.R.* 2 379–401; and T. Broodryk, "Mediation as a tool to manage and resolve class actions" (2020) *Stell. L. R.* (forthcoming).

128 The South African Law Commission, *The Recognition of Class Actions and Public Interest Actions in South African Law Report* Project 88 (1998) para 5.10.24.

129 2013 1 All SA 648 (SCA).

notice to class members is required, what the form of the notice should be and what its nature, scope, ambit and contents should entail.[130]

A further challenge confronting the South African civil procedural landscape is that the available data is inadequate to give any insight into the real operation of South African civil courts and, consequently, any impact that a change in civil procedural law may have on the current system of civil litigation. In this regard, Erasmus states as follows:

> We do not, for example, know how many civil cases of a particular nature are instituted in a particular court in a given year; we do not know how many of such cases are determined at a trial and what the median time is for determination at a trial and what the median time is for determination at a trial; we do not know what percentage of cases are settled and at what stage of the proceedings they are settled. We have no figures which would enable us to draw the distinction between so-called "lawyers induced delay" and "court induced delay." We do not even know what the real cost of litigation in this country is – the only true indication of the real cost of litigation is the amount paid by the client to his own attorney and this has not been the subject of any comprehensive study. We do not know how we compare with other jurisdictions . . . Where do we stand? The little information we do have is insufficient.[131]

In the absence of comprehensive research and empirical evidence regarding the functioning of the South African civil justice system, it is unlikely that one will be in a position to evaluate the impact that the aforementioned civil procedural changes may have on the effective functioning of the class action mechanism.

In South Africa, as mentioned above in Section 24.3, it is also possible to fund class actions by entering into contingency fees agreements and third-party litigation funding. Champertous agreements were previously prohibited under South African law, with the exception that if the funding was provided in good faith to give "financial assistance to a poor suitor and thereby helped him to prosecute an action in return for a reasonable recompense or interest in the suit," it was permitted.[132] It would appear that third-party agreements are becoming increasingly acceptable.[133] In *Price Waterhouse Coopers Inc and Others* v. *National Potato Co-Operative Ltd*[134] the court emphasized the importance of the right of access to courts embodied in section 34 of the Constitution and held as follows:

> In my view, upholding agreements between a litigant and a third party who finances the litigation for reward is also consistent with the constitutional values underlining freedom of contract . . . Accordingly it must be held that an agreement in terms of which a stranger to a lawsuit advances funds to a litigant on condition that the remuneration, in case the litigation wins the action, is to be part of the proceeds of the suit, is not contrary to public policy.[135]

Nevertheless, there is a tension that remains between third-party funding agreements that promote access to justice and agreements which don't serve this purpose and only aim to enrich the funder, who may have no real interest in the litigation. In this regard, in *Price*

[130] Kirby, "South Africa" in *World Class Actions – A Guide to Group and Representative Actions around the Globe* 384. For a comprehensive discussion, see T. Broodryk, "Giving notice to members of opt-out class actions" (2017) 3*T.S.A. R.* 498–510.

[131] H. J. Erasmus, "Civil Procedural Reforms – Modern Trends" (1999) *Stell. L. R.* 18.

[132] *Thomas Hugo & Fred J Möller NO* v. *The Tvl Loan, Finance and Mortgage Co* (1894) 1 OR 336 at 340.

[133] See S. Pudifin-Jones, "Funding and costs in class actions" in M. du Plessis, J. Oxenham, I. Goodman, L. Kelly and S. Pudifin-Jones (eds.), *Class action litigation in South Africa* (2017) 121.

[134] 2004 (3) All SA 20 (SCA).

[135] Para. 46.

Waterhouse Coopers Inc v. *National Potato Co-operative Ltd and Another* Wallis JA held as follows:[136]

> It is one thing to enable an impecunious litigant to obtain legal relief to which that litigant is entitled. It is another matter altogether to have a situation where an outsider to a dispute, motivated solely by considerations of profit, may be the sole beneficiary of a judgment. That is something that may have to engage this court on another occasion. Litigation exists for the proper settlement of disputes in society in the interests of the parties to those disputes. It comes at a social cost. It is undesirable that outsiders driven purely by commercial motives should be able to take over these disputes for their own benefit. When that occurs it is difficult to see how the constitutional guarantee of access to courts is engaged. It may perhaps be necessary at some future date to consider the precise ambit of our earlier decision in this regard and to what extent is permits a departure from the previous law in relation to champerty.[137]

This author holds the view that third-party funding arrangements should be permitted only if the interests of the funded party would be advanced if the dispute was resolved in his or her favor and/or if the litigation funder is joined to the litigation. In South Africa, the general rule is that in ordinary cases costs should follow the event; the successful party is ordinarily entitled to costs against the unsuccessful party. It is possible to join a third-party funder to the litigation and to make an award of costs against it where the nonparty substantially controls the litigation or is to benefit from it. In other words, the common law has been developed to enabled that a litigation funder may be directly liable for costs and may be joined as a co-litigant to the funded litigation.[138]

24.5 CONCLUSION

At present, the development of the procedural framework within which the class action device operates depends entirely on our courts. It is difficult to explain why our legislature has failed to legislate this area of law without resorting to speculation. According to De Vos, "[p]erhaps fear of the harm that class actions might cause to the economic sector has been haunting policymakers since the publication of the commission's Report."[139] Our courts have also performed commendably to develop a framework for the adjudication of class actions in the absence of legislation regulating the mechanism, which may have contributed to continued legislative inaction. As mentioned, however, it is not ideal to develop class action procedure on an ad hoc, case-by-case basis. The introduction of comprehensive legislation regulating class actions in South Africa is accordingly desirable. A haphazard developmental approach to the regulation of class actions could potentially result in a lack of uniformity and consistency in the approach of the various divisions of the High Court of South Africa.[140] Further, according to Karlsgodt, who lists thirty-eight jurisdictions plus the European Union with some or other form of class action proceeding,

136 2015 2 All SA 403 (SCA).

137 Para. 12.

138 See *Gold Fields Limited and others* v. *Motley Rice LLC*; *In re: Nkala and others* v. *Harmony Gold Mining Company Limited and others* 2016 3 All SA 233 (GJ); *Price Waterhouse Coopers Inc and others* v. *IMF (Australia) Ltd and another* 2013 6 SA 216 (GNP); *EP Property Projects (Pty) Ltd* v. *Registrar of Deeds, Cape Town and another, and Four Related Applications* 2014 1 SA 141 (WCC); *Scholtz and another* v. *Merryweather and others* 2014 6 SA 90 (WCC).

139 De Vos (2012) 4 *T.S.A.R.* 742.

140 G. Saumier, "Competing Class Actions across Canada: Still at the Starting Gate After Canada Post V Lepine?" (2009) 48 *Can Bus LJ* 462, 463. For example, Ontario is one of the provinces that allows certification of resident and nonresident class on an opt-out basis. As the number of provinces allowing class actions increased, the risk of competing and potentially overlapping actions grew and eventually materialized. This has led to inconsistent results.

the majority of these regulate class actions by special legislation or by rules of court.[141] Locally, several scholars have called for the introduction of specific class action legislation in South Africa.[142] The introduction of comprehensive legislation and court rules regulating class action suits in South Africa could ensure that development of class action procedure is not at the behest of our courts and could enable South Africa to follow in the footsteps of other countries with specific class action legislation.[143] As Zimand states, "[a] legislative solution is preferable. At a minimum, legislature must provide procedural legislation to bring some predictability, control and efficiency to this arena. It should be tailored to meet the modern crisis."[144] *In Re Fibreboard Corporation*[145] it was further held that "[t]he arguments [for class certification] are compelling, but they are better addressed to the representative branches – Congress and the State Legislature." Wallis JA in *Children's Resource Centre Trust* expressed similar sentiments.[146]

However, although it is desirable, it is unlikely that the South African legislature will, in the near future, adopt legislation that regulates class actions in South Africa. Given the failure by the South African government to act on recommendations to this effect from various experts and bodies since the commencement of our constitutional democracy, it is conceivable, if not probable, that our government would similarly ignore the recommendations contained herein. Therefore, although it is not the preferred route, and in the absence of a comprehensive court rule regulating class actions, it is recommended that our courts take it upon themselves, where possible, to develop guidelines and/or to implement practice directives to address the issues raised in herein, and also possibly issues not covered herein. It is further submitted that such guidelines or practice directives would assist in promoting judicial consistency and uniformity. The implementation of practice directives can generally be supported, as they are binding and acquire legal force and effect; however, they would not override the Uniform Rules of Court. Although the directives would be binding upon the courts, they are nevertheless flexible and could be developed further as class action law continues to mature in South Africa. It should, however, be understood that, if our government does decide to act on the abovementioned recommendations, the legislature would be well advised to take cognizance of the content of such guidelines or directives, as the case may be.

141 Karlsgodt, "United States" in *World Class Actions: A guide to Group and Representative Actions around the Globe*.

142 See inter alia W. De Vos, *Verteenwoordiging van Groepsbelange in die Siviele Proses* LLM dissertation RAU (1985); W. De Vos, "'n Groepsgeding in Suid-Afrika" (1985) 3 *T.S.A.R.* 296; W. de Vos, "'m Groepsgeding ('class action') as Middel ter Beskerming van Verbruikersbelange" (1989) *De Rebus* 373; De Vos (1996) *T.S.A.R.* 639; E. Hurter, "Some thoughts on current developments relating to class actions in South African law as viewed against leading foreign jurisdictions" (2006) 39(3) *CILSA* 485; E. Hurter, "The class action in South Africa: Quo Vadis?" (2008) 41(2) *De Jure* 293; E. Gericke, "Can class actions be instituted for breach of contract?" (2009) (2) *T.H.R.H.R.* 304.

143 F. Cassim and O. S. Sibanda, "The Consumer Protection Act and the Introduction of Collective Consumer Redress through Class Actions" (2012) 75 *T.H.R.H.R.* 586, 587–88.

144 P. Zimand, "National Asbestos Litigation: Procedural Problems Must be Solved" (1991) 69 *Washington University Law Review* 899, 917.

145 893 F2d 706 712 (5th Cir 1990).

146 Para. 22.

25

Class Actions and the Regulatory State

Lessons from Israel

*Shay Lavie**

25.1 INTRODUCTION

Israel presents an illuminating case for the study of class actions. On its face, the Israeli class action is a story of success. The uptake of the class action mechanism to Israel is unprecedented: Israel has become the world leader in the number of per capita class actions just a few years after the introduction of the class action law. On the other hand, the wave of class litigation has also raised serious concerns. Unique to Israel is the complaint that cases have little quality – most class actions seem to generate little impact, and filings often target the nonenforcement of obsolete provisions, rather than tackling important legal and social problems. The procedural aspects of class actions are also insightful. A robust regulatory framework underlies many Israeli class actions, and accordingly the Israeli law developed distinct tools that facilitate the interaction between agencies and class litigation. The lessons from the Israeli case study can therefore be useful for policymakers who consider the implementation of the class action mechanism, particularly in heavily regulated jurisdictions.

Against this backdrop, the purpose of this chapter is twofold. First, it attempts to provide a comprehensive picture of the current class action legal framework, landscape, and jurisprudence in Israel. Second, it then focuses on the interplay between public and private enforcement, analyzing the unique arrangements that the Israeli law presents in this respect, and attempting to draw broader lessons.

Section 25.2 describes the Israeli law on class actions. By and large, the Israeli class action statute, enacted in 2006, resembles its American counterpart (though some important differences do exist).[1] Indeed, similarly to the USA, class actions proliferate in Israel. In fact, Israel features American class litigation on steroids – it has become the Shangri-La of class litigation,[2] surpassing the USA as a worldwide leader in the number of class actions per capita. I lay out the institutional factors for this phenomenon, for example, many lawyers, liberal judges, and regulatory under-enforcement.

* I am grateful to Brian Fitzpatrick, Jonathan Hasdai, Alon Klement, Alon Priver, Jennifer Shkabatur, Randall Thomas, Maayan Yohay, and participants of the International Class Actions Conference at Vanderbilt Law School for helpful discussions and comments. Alon Priver and Maayan Yohay also provided excellent research assistance.

[1] I focus in this chapter on Rule 23(b)(3), "classic" class actions, that is, where a victim represents absent class members, who are bound to the judgment unless they opt out of the proceedings.

[2] This is, of course, to paraphrase the wording of justice Scalia with regard to securities class actions in the USA. *See* Morrison v. Nat'l Australia Bank Ltd., 561 U.S. 247, 270 (2010).

Another parallel to the USA, I argue, is the rise-and-fall pattern of the class action mechanism. Following their introduction to Israel, class actions quickly attracted the attention of practitioners, and filings of new cases have grown at an exponential rate. Then, familiar concerns regarding abusive litigation of meritless cases, over-enforcement, and cheap settlements were raised. Finally, we now observe a backlash from courts and legislators, who attempt to rein-in class litigation. I conclude that, overall, class actions in Israel are a story of (at least mild) success. Despite the recent backlash, and the fact that most class actions in Israel appear to lack a substantial impact, this mechanism has settled deeply in the legal arena.

Section 25.3 attempts to draw broader lessons from Israel regarding the interaction between agencies' enforcement and class litigation. The literature has long debated the right mix between public enforcement, through regulatory agencies, and private enforcement, mainly via class litigation. Israel can be seen as a unique laboratory to handle the private-public enforcement intersection. On the one hand, in line with the continental tradition, Israel's regulators deeply influence its norms. Likewise, agencies are typically perceived as impartial, expert decision-makers. On the other hand, Israel seems to suffer from suboptimal public enforcement, for example, due to lack of resources, and the new class action statute encourages private attorneys to pursue and enforce previously unenforced regulatory standards.

The Israeli design choices that are aimed to resolve the tension between class actions and the regulatory state manifest themselves in several interesting ways. One example is the unique capacity of the state to fund class actions that it deems valuable. Other examples are courts' willingness to consider the regulator's general enforcement behavior and legal position as key parameters in their decision to certify class litigation. Finally, one of the unintended consequences of the class action regime is the enforcement of obsolete regulatory technicalities. However, instead of litigating as a class action, these cases are often resolved in Israel through a distinct, quick procedure that does not preclude the class.

Section 25.4 concludes those lessons. The Israeli case illustrates the irreversibility of the class action mechanism, as well as its unintended consequences. Most importantly, the discussion in this chapter can enrich the relevant discourse on the intersection between private and public enforcement, and in particular regarding the implementation of class litigation in jurisdictions that traditionally defer to their regulators.

25.2 CLASS ACTIONS IN ISRAEL

This section depicts the current class action landscape in Israel. First, it will briefly describe key characteristics of the Israeli legal system. Then, it will present a brief history of the class action mechanism in Israel. Finally, it will discuss the class action landscape, along several important dimensions – who can file; remedies; preclusion; fee-shifting; and settlements.

25.2.1 *The Israeli Legal System*

Before going into the details, it will be worthwhile to mention several key features of the Israeli legal system. These characteristics are relevant to understanding its class action jurisprudence.

First, Israel is, by and large, a common law country. Judges follow precedents, and there is a fertile legal discourse over those precedents, among academics and practitioners alike. Second, although it is a common law system, the Israeli system does not employ juries.[3] This, in turn, gives a wide latitude to presiding judges in individual cases, particularly in pretrial phases.[4] Third, more generally, the legal culture embraces judicial discretion. Judges often interpret statutes and precedents liberally, to fit them to the exigencies of the relevant case.[5] Fourth, the Supreme Court of Israel, the highest instance, is highly occupied with mundane, civil cases (where judges typically sit in three-judge panels).[6] This stems, in part, from odd subject-matter jurisdiction rules – these rules give to the intermediate instance unique jurisdiction on many cases.[7] Where the intermediate level has unique jurisdiction, litigants can appeal its final decisions to the Supreme Court, as of right.[8] The Israeli Supreme Court, then, serves as an appellate jurisdiction to many important cases – including virtually all class actions. This setting generates many, sometimes conflicting, Supreme Court decisions.[9] Finally, the Israeli legal culture is inspired by other legal systems, and in particular the American legal system. In class action decisions, for example, it is not uncommon to see several references to American cases and law journals.

25.2.2 *History and Background for the Israeli Class Action Act*

The Israeli Class Action Act (ICAA) is a relatively new addition, enacted in 2006. The roots of the class action mechanism, however, lie deeper in the past.[10] Since the late 1980s, the Israeli legislature added distinct class action provisions to various substantive statutes, for example, banking, securities, and environmental laws. Though the different class action provisions were not identical to each other, they, by and large, were modeled after the American, Rule 23's version. However, beyond limited enclaves, these pieces of legislation did not allow a general, trans-substantive class action mechanisms. Lawyers who wanted to file class actions in other areas had to look for a different route. Driven by their experience with class actions in the areas in which it was allowed (most notably securities), attorneys started to argue that the specific class action provisions should be read into a trans-substantive joinder provision in the Israeli Rules of Civil Procedure. In essence, Israeli lawyers attempted to convince courts that a general class

3 *See, e.g.*, Issachar Rosen-Zvi, *Constructing Professionalism: The Professional Project of the Israeli Judiciary*, 31 SETON HALL L. REV. 760, 824 (2001) ("The Israeli legal system is frequently identified as part of the common law world ... Growing out of the colonial British legal system, Israel preserved many characteristics of its justice administration").

4 For instance, judges can use their so-called "managerial" powers and push the parties to settle, before trial, by expressing their views on the prospective outcome on the merits.

5 The most famous champion of this approach is the former chief-justice of the Israeli Supreme Court, Aharon Barak. *See, e.g.*, Ariel L. Bendor & Zeev Segal, *The Judicial Discretion of Justice Aharon Barak*, 47 TULSA L. REV. 465 (2011).

6 Approximately 10,000 proceedings are initiated in the Supreme Court annually (although many of these cases are dismissed with minimal effort). *See* the State of Israel, The Judicial Authority, Supreme Court, https://supreme.court.gov.il/sites/en/Pages/Overview.aspx (last visited Sep. 17, 2019).

7 More specifically, for civil cases where the remedy sought is greater than 2.5 million NIS (approximately $720,000) the intermediate instance, the district court, serves as the first, trial instance. Below this threshold, cases start at the first instance, the magistrate court, where the first appeal is to the intermediate level. Courts Law (Consolidated Version), 5744–1984, 38 LSI 271 (1984) ch. 2, art. 3, § 40 (Isr.). The 2.5 million NIS threshold is sufficiently low to funnel most class actions (and many important civil cases) to the intermediate instance.

8 *See id.* Ch. 2, art. 2, § 41(a) (Isr.).

9 The Supreme Court also has discretion to adjudicate interlocutory appeals from intermediate courts. Theodore Eisenberg et al., *Israel's Supreme Court Appellate Jurisdiction: An Empirical Study*, 96 CORNELL L. REV. 693, 708 (2011). This characteristic adds to the inability to extract clear precedents, as the Supreme Court's decision to deny review also has, in and of itself, some precedential value. Interlocutory review is particularly important in the context of class actions, as Israeli defendants and plaintiffs often seek to achieve an immediate review of certification decisions.

10 For a more elaborate discussion see Alon Klement & Robert Klonoff, *Class Actions in the U.S. and Israel: A Comparative Approach*, 19 THEORETICAL INQUIRIES IN LAW 151, 171–73 (2018).

action law exists. Lower courts have held differently on this question, and finally the Supreme Court – backed by the government's opposition to class actions – refused in 2005 to extend class actions to other areas through judicial interpretation.[11] This holding notwithstanding, the Supreme Court's decision depicted class actions in a favorable light, and it forcefully urged the Israeli legislature to enact a general, comprehensive class action statute.

The Supreme Court's 2005 decision achieved its goal. In a short legislative process, the Israeli legislature has followed suit and enacted in 2006 the ICAA. Similarly to the previous, sporadic class action provisions, the ICAA again resembles Rule 23, its American counterpart. However, the government's distaste toward a comprehensive class action mechanism (manifested by its opposition in the previous legal proceedings) influenced the new law in several ways. First, the ICAA does not allow for several types of class actions. While its provisions appear to be a procedural, trans-substantive arrangement, the ICAA includes a closed list of specific areas in which one can file a class action.[12] This list covers most potential class actions against private defendants. However, some claims, notably, a claim in torts against the government, cannot serve as a basis for class action. Second, even when one can file a class action against the government, the ICAA includes several provisions that are designed to protect government bodies from aggressive class actions – for instance, government bodies can easily evade monetary remedies in class actions that are based on overcharges.[13]

25.2.3 *Key Characteristics of the Act*

The next paragraphs will discuss some of the key characteristics of the Act. As noted above, the ICAA is inspired by the American experience. Accordingly, the ICAA heavily uses legal standards, leaving judges wide discretion over its implementation. More specifically, as in the USA, the ICAA envisions a class action by one victim (the so-called named plaintiff), which binds absent class members who failed to opt out. To do so, the representatives, that is, the named plaintiff and her lawyer, have to "certify" their case as a class action by showing that certain requirements are met. Among other things, the named plaintiff and her counsel have to show at the certification stage, as in the USA, that there are questions common to all class members and that the representatives adequately represent the class. Further, in line with the American practice, the ICAA is explicit about the monetary incentives to the representatives in case of successful completion of the proceedings. These characteristics notwithstanding, the ICAA is significantly more detailed than the American Rule 23, and it brought several procedural innovations.

25.2.3.1 Who Can File

The right to file a class action in Israel is provided to three types of plaintiffs – class members, who have an individual claim against the defendant; organizations; and agencies. The first option, a lawsuit by individual victims, is by far the most frequent and important. The following briefly discusses these three options.

CLASS MEMBERS Similarly to its American counterpart, victims – class members – can file a class action on behalf of fellow victims, who are not in court.[14] Likewise, any victim can file,

[11] FH 5161/03 E.S.T. Mgmt. v. The State of Israel 60 PD 196 (2005) (Isr.).
[12] ICAA, s. 3(a) and Appendix B.
[13] *See* the discussion around *infra* notes 32–33 and accompanying text.
[14] ICAA, s. 4(a)(1).

regardless of the monetary size of her claim. The only personal restrictions on victims who wish to serve as named plaintiffs are embedded in the certification requirements – the named plaintiff (as well as her lawyer) shall meet the requirements of adequate representation and good faith.[15] The adequate representation requirement has proven to be a low threshold for class members to pass – that is, it is very rare to see a court that disqualifies a named plaintiff, for example, for lack of expertise (lawyers are more often disqualified for these reasons). The good faith requirement has raised more interesting debates in the Israeli courts. Examples include cases where the victim deliberately triggered the defendant's behavior in order to later file a class action;[16] or where the victim had ingenuine motives to file a suit, for instance a parallel, unrelated business dispute with the defendant.[17] Overall, though, in most cases any victim can proceed as the class's representative, and defendants accordingly refrain from challenging the named plaintiff's adequacy.[18]

NGOS AND AGENCIES More unique provisions allow class actions by nonvictims. First, under several conditions, a relevant organization can file a class action. Most importantly, the organization can represent the class if it convinces the court that there are "difficulties" in filing by class members.[19] Courts have had to interpret this vague provision. In one leading case, an Orthodox Jewish feminist organization filed a lawsuit against an Orthodox Jewish radio station, on behalf of Orthodox Jewish women, claiming that the radio station discriminates against women in its broadcasts. Given the unique circumstances, the Supreme Court allowed the organization to proceed as a named plaintiff, as it questioned the willingness of discriminated women in secluded, traditional communities to stand up for their rights.[20] Simultaneously, the Supreme Court cautioned against a liberal interpretation of "difficulties" in finding a victim who can serve as a plaintiff. It should be noted that in typical cases, finding a class member who is willing to file should not be a particular problem.

Another interesting provision allows an agency to use the class action mechanism, striking a unique balance between private and public enforcement.[21] Unlike a class action by an organization, an interested agency need not show "difficulties" in bringing class action by ordinary class members. This suggests that the regulator can perhaps override a class action already filed by class members. Class actions by agencies can mitigate the problem of abusive litigation by entrepreneurial lawyers; however, this option raises concerns regarding captured regulators.[22] Be that as it may, in practice class actions by agencies are largely irrelevant in Israel.

15 ICAA, s. 8(a)(3), 8(a)(4).

16 *See e.g.*, LCA 3698/11 Shlomo transportation (2007) Ltd. v. S.A.M.G.R Enforcement services Ltd. (Sep. 6, 2017), Nevo Legal Database (by subscription, in Hebrew) (Isr.). (the named plaintiffs rented a car and returned it with an empty fuel tank, in order to sue for the associate fees).

17 For an example along these lines see Tami Bar v. Ateret Industries 1996 Ltd. (Dec. 20, 2010), Nevo Legal Database (by subscription, in Hebrew) (Isr.) With that, the Supreme Court clarified that a pure monetary incentive does not infringe the "good-faith" requirement, see CA 8037/06 Shay Brazili v. Prinir (Hadas 1987) Ltd. (Sep. 4, 2014), Nevo Legal Database (by subscription, in Hebrew) (Isr.).

More generally, note that the "typicality" requirement, FED. R. CIV. PRO. 23(a)(3), does not formally exist under the ICAA. However, atypical plaintiffs can be disqualified through the application of the good faith provision.

18 Relatedly, a complementary provision explicitly enables the court, where it finds that the named plaintiff is inadequate, to add another named plaintiff or replace the incumbent plaintiff. ICAA, s. 8(c).

19 ICAA, s. 4(a)(3).

20 *See* LCA 6897/14 Kol Barama v. Kolech (Dec. 9, 2015), Nevo Legal Database (by subscription, in Hebrew) (Isr.). The organization presented a survey according to which only 2.4 percent of the Orthodox Jewish women are willing to take legal action in these matters (though a larger proportion felt discriminated).

21 ICAA, s. 4(a)(2).

22 I discuss this option in greater detail below, *see infra* subsection 25.3.2.4.

Appendix A to the ICAA limits the scope of relevant regulators who can bring class actions to only three agencies.[23] Even these agencies rarely use their capacity to file class actions.[24]

25.2.3.2 Cases and Remedies

TYPES OF CASES As mentioned above, the ICAA's provisions apply to a closed list of subject-matter areas (detailed in Appendix B to ICAA). This list is sufficiently broad to cover most potential class actions. In particular, item 1 to Appendix B allows class actions against a "trader" – essentially enabling all class actions that are related to private transactions.[25] However, as abovementioned, class actions against the government (which by and large does not fit the "trader" definition) are limited to certain subject-matter areas, most notably, overcharges by government authorities.[26]

REMEDIES In general, the remedies sought in class actions are not limited, and class members can and do often receive monetary compensation.[27] Furthermore, the ICAA, unlike its American counterpart, explicitly envisions innovative compensation avenues – a prominent example is cy pres relief, that is, donations to third parties where the distribution to class members is impossible due to the small amounts.[28] Likewise, issues of standing for remote injuries, that obstruct class litigation in the USA in several areas,[29] are largely irrelevant in Israel.

Things are more complicated where the government is the defendant. First, in class actions for governmental overcharges restitution is limited to two years.[30] In a similar vein, the ICAA explicitly authorizes the court in class actions against the government to decrease the damages awarded to the class.[31]

A more practically important limitation on remedies against the government enables government authorities to avoid class litigation altogether – at the outset and before certification – in overcharge cases. All the government needs to do is admit the overcharge – and commit to cease its wrongdoing. While these "ceasing" admissions do not preclude individual class members from vindicating their personal rights, given the small amounts the odds of individual lawsuits

23 The relevant regulators are: Commission for Equal Rights of Persons with Disabilities, Israel Nature and Parks Authority, and Commission for Equal Opportunities at work. Along similar lines, ICAA allows the Israel Consumers Council, a non-profit government corporation, to file class actions (s. 4(a)(3)).

24 Apparently, filing a class action is a costly option for these agencies.

25 The definition is "trader" is taken from the Israeli Consumer Protection Law, 5741-1981, § 1, SH 1023 p. 248 (Isr.) ("Any person who, in the course of its occupation, sells assets or provide services, including a producer"). While the interpretation of "trader" for these purposes is not typically disputed, on the margin there are cases in which defendants argue that they provided free service and hence they cannot be exposed to class actions under item 1 to Appendix B.

26 ICAA, item 11 to Appendix B.

27 Some remedies, though, can only be sought in individual suits, such as punitive and statutory damages (ICAA, s. 20(e)).

28 ICAA, s. 20(c). See also Klement & Klonoff, *supra* note 10, at 185–87. A legislative amendment from 2016 mandates that, in principle, the precise destinations of these donations should be determined by a special governmental committee, rather than the presiding judge. ICAA, s. 27A.

29 *Cf.*, Spokeo v. Robins, 136 S. Ct. 1540 (2016).

30 ICAA, s. 21. This is a significant restriction, as the general statute of limitations allows filing claims within seven years of their creation. Statute of Limitation, 5718-1958, SH No.251 p.112 (Isr). The ICAA's two-year limitation provision does not preclude class members from suing for their personal rights, that is, beyond the two years (and up to seven years). However, as the individual amounts are typically small, the odds of personal lawsuits that complement class litigation are slim.

31 ICAA, s. 20(d)(1). A similar provision enables the court to decrease the damages in class actions against private defendants, where the damages will risk the financial stability of the defendant and harm its clients. ICAA, s. 20(d)(2). Both provisions have rarely been used. Note that unlike s. 21 to ICAA (supra note 30), the provision in s. 20(d) precludes absent class members.

are low. This provision, then, enables government bodies, usually municipalities, to rely on private enforcement to identify and cease illegal charges without bearing extensive liability. It expresses the fears of the legislature from enormous liability for petty mistakes of government bodies,[32] and the general trust in the government's good faith.[33]

25.2.3.3 Preclusion and Class Members' Consent

The hallmark of class litigation is precluding class members' individual rights.[34] An implicit prerequisite to precluding absent class members' rights, though, is the assumption that class members are adequately notified and represented.[35] Indeed, in the American as well as the Israeli jurisprudence, the constitutive moment for preclusion is class certification – the lawsuit can only bind after the class was certified.[36] Likewise, in line with the American practice, the Israeli class action binds all class members – except those who actively requested to opt out upon certification.[37]

Given the fundamental principle that class members should be given the opportunity to opt out, the ICAA details the manner in which class members should be notified. As in Rule 23's opt-out class actions, ICAA does not mandate personal notifications – the extent of the notice depends on various factors that the ICAA lists, such as the size of the individual claims and the ability to contact each class member.[38] ICAA's detailed provisions notwithstanding, in practice the obligation to notify class members is quite thin – notices of certification and settlement are given through various media outlets or on the defendant's website, and personal notice is far from being the norm in most cases.[39] With that, it is rare to find examples of cases in which class members have challenged the binding force of a previous class action on the ground that it lacked proper notice and/or adequate representation.[40]

25.2.3.4 Fee-Shifting and Financing Mechanisms

The Israeli class action, as other mechanisms of private enforcement, is driven by monetary incentives. The following briefly discusses these incentives: the fees to class counsel and the incentive award to the named plaintiff.

32 Importantly, although no money is transferred to class members via the class action vehicle in these cases, the representatives – the named plaintiff and her lawyer – are entitled to monetary awards (paid by the government). Hence, the ceasing provision does not eliminate the incentives to bring class actions in overcharges cases.

33 I discussed these ceasing arrangements in greater details elsewhere. Shay Lavie, *Tiered Certification*, 19 Theoretical Inquiries in Law, 69, 98–102 (2018). I argue that these arrangements provide an intermediate procedure that can break the binarity of the current rules, which allow for either no-class action; or full-blown, expensive and long class litigation.

34 Accordingly, ICAA, s. 24, explicitly holds that class actions bind absent class members.

35 *Cf.*, Phillips Petroleum Co. v. Shutts, 472 U.S. 797 (1985).

36 Relatedly, in principle class action that was not certified does not preclude other certification attempts. *Cf.*, Smith v. Bayer, 131 S. Ct. 2368 (2011) and the short discussion of the Israeli law at this point, Lavie, *supra* note 33, at 85, 90.

37 ICAA s. 11. The ICAA explicitly allows for an opt-in class, that is, a class that is composed of class members who actively requested to join. ICAA, s. 12. However, opt-in class actions are extremely rare.

38 ICAA, s. 25(e). In principle, notice should be given both upon certification and when the parties request to approve class settlement. ICAA, s. 25(a).

39 Although the extent of the Israeli notice is quite loose relative to the American experience, it should be noted that the judiciary maintains a public, online registry of class actions, which can theoretically fulfill, at least partially, the rationale behind the notice requirement, see ICAA, s. 28(a). In practice, however, relevant stakeholders often complain that the public registry is not updated.

40 Such cases are also scarce in the American jurisprudence. For one successful example see Hecht v. United Collection Bureau, Inc., 691 F.3d 218 (2d Cir. 2012) (a single notice in USA Today was not sufficient to preclude individual lawsuits).

CLASS COUNSEL The legal framework regarding monetary incentives for class counsel is largely similar to the American practice. Upon a successful completion of the litigation – through a settlement or a judicial decision – class counsel are entitled to their fees. The ICAA lists several parameters for the court to consider, such as the fruits that the proceedings yielded to the class, the work the lawyer invested, and the public importance of the case.[41] In practice, judges indeed exercise considerable discretion, and the precise fee depends on the idiosyncrasies of each case (and judge). Typically, the fees for the lawyer are calculated as a percentage of the common fund, that is, the overall compensation for all class members. As a rough generalization, the relevant percentage is in the range of 15 percent to 20 percent.[42] Although these are nontrivial figures, class action lawyers seemingly face financing problems. That is, they lack the financial resources to take even good cases, with a large anticipated award, to a full trial.[43]

THE NAMED PLAINTIFF The case of the named plaintiff is more interesting. First, in successful class actions the named plaintiff is also entitled to monetary compensation – incentive award – for her services. As before, the ICAA lists several general considerations, which are by and large similar to those that are pertinent to setting the fees for the lawyer.[44] Interestingly, the incentive award is quite sizeable, at least from an American perspective – roughly, in the range of one-third to one-fourth of the attorneys' fees (or: ~5 percent to 10 percent of the common fund).[45]

The high incentive award that the named plaintiff receives should be seen in light of other features, unique to the Israeli legal system. First, in general Israeli courts implement the so-called British, loser-pays fee-shifting rule, that is, the loser pays the legal expenses of the winner.[46] These fee-shifting expenses fall on individual parties, rather than their lawyers – that is, the named plaintiff in our context. In class actions the legal expenses of both sides are typically high, as they often submit expert opinions early on. While courts sometimes refrain from setting fees against the named plaintiff, in some cases they do impose a large amount.[47] Hence, the loser-pays rule poses a risk of a disproportional financial burden on named plaintiffs, typically, individuals with limited wherewithal. Second, unlike the American ethics rule, the Israeli rule prohibits attorneys

41 ICAA, s. 23(b).

42 "The median class attorney fee in pre-certification settlements was twenty percent . . . The respective percentages and absolute amounts in post-certification [cases] were lower." Klement & Klonoff, *supra* note 10, at 194 (the empirical data covers the first years of the ICAA, from 2006 to 2012). *See also* CA 2046/10 Shemesh v. Raichert 60(2) PD 681 (2012) (Isr.) (Grunis, J.) (an important Supreme Court case that sets a rough standard of 15 percent to 25 percent of the fund).

43 Indeed, practitioners typically raise the financing problem as a reason to accept relatively low settlements. As Klement & Klonoff, *supra* note 10, at 201 explain, "In Israel . . . class actions are handled mainly by solo practitioners and small firms" who suffer from "lack of deep pockets" and thus cannot optimally invest in filing and litigating class actions. Lawyers could use third-party financing to bridge their financial constraints before the successful completion of the case, but third-party funding in Israel is highly limited (see *infra* notes 52–55 and accompanying text).

44 ICAA, s. 22. While the court again has wide discretion in setting the precise monetary award, relevant considerations are investment in litigating, the proceeds to class members, and the public importance of the case.

45 *See*, Klement & Klonoff, *supra* note 10, at 194 (indicating a median award of 6 percent).

46 Theodore Eisenberg et al., *When Courts Determine Fees in a System with a Loser Pays Norm: Fee Award Denials to Winning Plaintiffs and Defendants*, 60 UCLA L. REV. 1452, 1464 (2013).

47 According to one prominent empirical study, that collected all filed class actions between 2006 and 2012, the court ruled that the named plaintiff has to pay the defendant's fees in about two thirds of the cases in which the court denied certification. Alon Klement & Keren Weinshall-Margel, *Class Actions in Israel: An Empirical Perspective*, 45 MISHPATIM [HEBREWU U. L.J.] 709, 750–52 (2016). The median fee in those cases is quite modest, ~$8,000; but the average is significantly higher, ~$20,000. This reflects some high-profile cases in which defendants were awarded exorbitant fees. These details notwithstanding, it is conventionally thought that the fees fall short of compensating the defendants for their legal expenses.

from advancing costs, including the costs of expert opinions, to their clients.[48] This means that formally it is the client – the named plaintiff in our case – who has to bear the substantial legal expenses that are associated with filing and litigating class actions. Given the heavier financial burden and risks borne by named plaintiffs in Israel, relative to American named plaintiffs, a greater incentive award is justified.[49] In sum, the named plaintiff in the Israeli legal system is relatively more important than its American counterpart. With that, in both systems the driving force behind class actions remains, by and large, the lawyer.[50]

It should be noted that, although questionable from the perspective of the Israeli ethics rules, agreements between class counsel and the named plaintiff are common. These agreements can specify the internal allocation – between the lawyer and the named plaintiff – of the prospective monetary award and the legal expenses.

Finally, while agreements to finance class actions by third parties (in exchange for some of its future fruits) do exist on the margin,[51] their legal status is unclear.[52] Public funding by government entities is available, but its effectiveness seems limited.[53] More importantly, the relatively small size of the Israeli market and the modest compensation fund in typical Israeli cases[54] appear to hinder financiers from funding class actions. In any case, the practice of third-party funding in Israel in general is, at best, nascent.[55]

25.2.3.5 Settlements and Voluntary Dismissals

The ICAA includes a detailed arrangement as to settlements, with some procedural innovations. This arrangement is highly important in practice, as most class actions are not decided on the merits.[56]

SETTLEMENTS It is well-known that settlements present a core, perennial problem to policy-makers. Class action settlements are agreed upon after (or with) certification, and thus they bind absent class members.[57] At this stage both parties, the defendant and the class's representatives, no

48 See Israeli Bar Association, Professional Ethics Rules § 44 (1986). For the different rule in the U.S. see MODEL RULES OF PROF'L CONDUCT R. 1.8 (2003). Both ethics rule are general, and not unique to class actions. See also Klement & Klonoff, *supra* note 10, at 189.

49 See also the analysis in Klement & Klonoff, *id.*, at 188–89.

50 Even with the incentive award, the personal stakes of individuals are too low to justify filing a class action. By contrast, in Israel and the USA lawyers are those who typically have the means and expertise to look for violations of the law that fit the class action mechanism. Along these lines, in a potential conflict between class counsel and a named plaintiff regarding the management of the case, Israeli courts seem to side with the lawyer. *See, e.g.*, 4263-03-11 Eshel Hayeor Ltd. v. Partner Communications Company Ltd. (Apr. 5, 2012), Nevo Legal Database (by subscription, in Hebrew) (Isr.).

51 For one example, in a case that is still pending in its initial stages, see Efrat Neumann *"Outrageous Payment": The Restaurant that Sues Ten-Bis and Cibus in the Name of Thousands of Restaurants*, THEMARKER (Nov. 4, 2018), www.themarker.com/law/.premium-1.6616400 (Isr.) (a complicated antitrust class action which is supported by Libra Fund; the case is CA (TA) 3324-11-18 Rodriguez Grill Bar Ltd. v. Sodexo Pas Israel Ltd. (Dec. 13, 2018), Nevo Legal Database (by subscription, in Hebrew) (Isr.)).

52 For a discussion of third-party funding to plaintiffs see Ronen Avraham, *Third Party Litigation Funding*, 20 LAW & BUSINESS [IDC L.J.] 131, 148–53 (2017) (in Hebrew) (concluding that third-party funding of plaintiffs appears to be legal). A different set of ethics problems exists with regard to class action lawyers who desire to take outcome-dependent loans, as Israeli lawyers are not allowed to share profits with nonlawyers (Israeli Bar Association, 5721-1961 (1961) (Isr.), s. 58).

53 I discuss public funding in *infra* subsection 25.3.2.1.

54 Klement & Klonoff, *supra* note 10, at 153.

55 Avraham, *supra* note 52, at 147–48.

56 In a prominent empirical study on Israeli class actions it was found that ~72 percent of the cases were voluntarily dismissed or settled (mostly, voluntarily dismissed); by contrast, only in ~9 percent of the cases did the judges decide on the merits (mostly, denying certification). Klement & Weinshall-Margel, *supra* note 47, at 738.

57 In pre-certification settlements, the judge has to certify the class before approving the settlement. ICAA, s. 19(a). *Cf.*, the parallel practice of settlement-only class actions in the USA.

longer have adverse interests; both desire to end the proceedings at the expense of absent class members. In essence, then, we should expect both parties to strive to sell to the court a settlement that provides low compensation for the class in exchange for high attorneys' fees for its counsel.[58] While courts have to approve class action settlements,[59] given the lack of an adversary process and their informational inferiority it is difficult for judges to optimally monitor inappropriate settlements.

The Israeli law, similarly to the American practice, guides courts to approve a settlement only if they find, in a reasoned decision, that the settlement is adequate, fair, and reasonable in view of class members' claims.[60] In addition, before approval courts should inform class members and conduct a "fairness hearing" to assess the fairness of the settlement.[61] Beyond the fairness hearing, the Israeli legislature, who was familiar with the problems associated with class action settlements, attempted to install additional mechanisms that better enable judges to assess and monitor settlements. First, the ICAA mandates that a settlement shall be approved, in principle, only after it is reviewed by a neutral, expert examiner, who is appointed by the court.[62] In the majority of cases, however, courts do not appoint an independent expert to examine the settlement,[63] hence the efficacy of this provision is quite limited.[64]

Second, the ICAA sought to amplify the adversary process by broadening the scope of potential objectors to the class action settlement.[65] While class members can of course object (and request to opt out), the ICAA, which was amended at this point in 2016, also enables relevant organizations and nonclass members to object.[66] More importantly, since its enactment the ICAA requires courts to invite the Attorney General (AG) to intervene and object to inappropriate settlements.[67] The AG is perceived as an impartial organ, whose motivation to object is eliminating bad settlements (whereas other objectors may intervene in order to blackmail class counsel). In practice, although the AG refrains from objecting in many cases, when it acts its position seems to carry weight and influence courts.[68]

58 For the agency problem in class actions see generally Jonathan R. Macey & Geoffrey P. Miller, *The Plaintiffs' Attorney's Role in Class Action and Derivative Litigation: Economic Analysis and Recommendations for Reform*, 58 U. Chi. L. Rev. 1 (1991). In Israel, as in the USA, it is typically the lawyer, rather than the plaintiff, who in practice leads the class. *Cf.*, *supra* note 50 and accompanying text.

59 The parties, of course, cannot bind the court – they can only recommend the agreed fees. ICAA, s. 18(g)(2).

60 ICAA, s. 19.

61 ICAA, s. 18.

62 ICAA, s. 19(b). While no parallel obligation exists in the USA, some American courts do appoint an independent expert to examine the fairness of the settlement. Klement & Klonoff, *supra* note 10, at 178.

63 Mostly, judges seem to think that an external review is redundant, especially if the judge was involved in the settlement, and, where the questions relevant for review are legal ones. See, for instance, LCA 8479/02 Dr. Tamar Sabo v. Israel Airports Authority (Dec. 15, 2012), Nevo Legal Database (by subscription, in Hebrew) (Isr.).

64 Nonetheless, there have not been proposals by the legislature to amend the ICAA in this respect.

65 See generally ICAA, s. 18.

66 Class members typically prefer not to object, as the benefit is small and the costs are nontrivial. Hence, organizations and "professional" objectors could play an important role in monitoring settlements. Indeed, a prominent objector is the Class Action Clinic at Tel Aviv University, which is headed by Prof. Alon Klement. See Class Action Clinic at Tel Aviv University, https://en-law.tau.ac.il/clinics/Class_Action (last visited Sep. 16, 2019).

67 Technically, the court must notify the AG when a settlement is filed, and the AG can intervene per its discretion. ICAA, s. 18(c), 18(d).

68 *Cf.*, Eran Goren et al., *Access to Justice in Class Action Settlements: Empirical Insights on the Role of the Attorney General*, 8 Hukim [Hebrew U. L.J on Legislation] 249–85 (2016) (as a rough generalization, the AG provides opinion – either as a formal objection or not – in about half of the cases, and in most of these cases its opinion was accepted/partially accepted by the presiding judge). For the correlation between the AG's opinion and the court's decision see also Klement & Weinshall-Margel, *supra* note 47, at 755. The AG is a particularly important actor given the low rate of objections in general. *See* Goren et al., *id.*, at 272 (finding objections by class members and

VOLUNTARY DISMISSALS In addition to settlements the ICAA also specifies the rules for voluntary dismissals. The main difference between the two is their res judicata effect: a settlement binds absent class members (it is approved after/with certification) whereas voluntary dismissals do not. Accordingly, given their limited effect, the procedure to approve voluntary dismissals is less onerous than the procedure to approve settlements.[69]

A particularly interesting setting is paid dismissals – agreements in which the representatives dismiss the class action and in return the defendant pays them a monetary award. These agreements are commonly reached early in the proceedings, sometimes even before the defendant submitted its answer. Oftentimes, the defendant also commits in these agreements to change its behavior prospectively, for example, comply with the relevant regulation from now on. Courts have wide discretion in approving paid dismissals. Paid dismissals have thrived in Israel in the relevant era,[70] triggering a heated public debate (as well as important court decisions and legislative amendments).[71] The following describes these arrangements.[72]

What are the interests of the parties in agreeing on paid dismissals? The representatives' interest in these arrangements is clear. Although the agreed fees are typically modest (at best, in the range of dozens of thousands NIS),[73] class counsel and the named plaintiff can achieve quick resolution with minimal litigation expenses.[74]

The interest of the defendant is more subtle. As they lack res judicata effect, one may wonder why the defendant would agree to pay for voluntary dismissals. To illustrate the defendant's interests take a typical voluntary dismissal, for example, a lawsuit based on the claim that the defendant failed to comply with the relevant labeling regulation concerning the food it produces.[75] Suppose also that the defendant commits to comply, from now on, with the relevant regulation. In that case, early dismissal is beneficial for the defendant, as it saves potentially long litigation. Moreover, although the dismissal does not preclude class members' rights, the risk of prospective litigation is miniscule. The legal basis for damages in these cases – although the defendant did infringe the law – is tenuous. It will be hard to prove that consumers relied on the misrepresentation and suffered any real damages due to the regulatory violation.[76] Given that the claim for damages is remote in these cases, the

organizations in only ~10 percent of the settlements). *See also* Klement & Klonoff, *supra* note 10, at 183–85 (discussing objections and the important role of the AG). Interestingly, a somewhat similar arrangement exists in the USA under the Class Action Fairness Act, inviting government officials to object to settlements. In the USA, though, this provision is considered ineffective. *Id.*, at 167.

69 *See* ICAA, s. 16 (delineating the procedure to approve voluntary dismissals).

70 To capture the importance of paid dismissals, consider that in ~30 percent of voluntary dismissals the court approved a payment to the representatives. Klement & Weinshall-Margel, *supra* note 47, at 748–49. Recall that most of the cases in Israel in the relevant era were voluntarily dismissed. *Supra* note 56.

71 Interestingly, a parallel phenomenon, which also raises broad concerns, exists in merger litigation in the USA. In these "mootness fees" cases, the defendant agrees to supplemental disclosures and the plaintiff voluntarily dismisses the case in exchange for a fee. *E.g.*, Matthew D. Cain et al., *Mootness Fees*, 72 VAND. L. REV. 1777 (2019).

72 Below, *infra* subsection 25.3.2.5, I briefly discuss the desirability of these arrangements.

73 In 2006–12, in pre-certification voluntary dismissals the overall remuneration for the class' representatives (both the lawyers' fees and the incentive award to the named plaintiff) was ~50,000NIS, that is, ~$15,000 (Klement & Weinshall-Margel, *supra* note 47, at 747–49).

74 Moreover, the plaintiff and her lawyer can typically replicate the same claims cheaply, such that similar class actions are filed against multiple defendants in the relevant area.

75 CA 8114/14 Markit Efficiency Products Ltd. v. Sonol Israel Ltd. (Aug. 5, 2018), Nevo Legal Database (by subscription, in Hebrew) (Isr.).

76 In addition, as the parties agreed to a voluntary dismissal in the first case and the first judge approved the dismissal, the judge in the second case may well be inclined to think that the claim lacks merits.

defendant's commitment to comply with the relevant regulation neuters the gist of prospective class actions.[77]

Voluntary, paid dismissals of this sort have proliferated in many seemingly "petty" class actions in the last decade, most notably in cases of minor, technical infringements of food or labeling regulation.[78] The practice of voluntary dismissals have been attacked by various stakeholders, who assert that defendants are pressed to pay for dismissals in cases with no legal basis. This view suggests, then, that courts should refuse to approve paid dismissals in order to chill class actions of this type. Indeed, the legislature amended in 2016 the ICAA in order to make the requirements to approve paid dismissals more onerous.[79] The Supreme Court similarly guided lower courts not to easily approve paid dismissals.[80]

25.2.4 *Assessment and the Way Forward*

The ICAA was enacted in 2006. Can this timeframe allow us to judge its effects? Is it a story of success? It is highly complicated to gauge the precise outcomes, let alone success, of any piece of legislation. Instead, the following provides a brief snapshot of the general understanding of class actions in the Israeli discourse.

One can draw parallels between the Israeli and the American experience. It is common to think that the American class action has shown a rise-and-fall pattern.[81] Class actions in Israel likewise present a rise-and-fall story, albeit in an accelerated manner and through a shorter period. The introduction of the ICAA quickly flared the Israeli legal arena, attracting many lawyers and judges.[82] After a few years, though, the initial enthusiasm waned, and policymakers have become aware of the dangers of class actions – particularly, the fear of nuisance suits and over-deterrence of defendants. Indeed, in the last years one can identify a backlash movement, where the Supreme Court and the legislature attempt to rein in class litigation.[83] The following will briefly discuss these anti-collectivization decisions and legislative amendments. Overall, though, one can still view Israeli class actions as a success story, as the introduction of class actions has surely influenced the daily experience of lawyers, judges, defendants, and consumers. With that, a lingering concern appears to be the quality of the cases – as most class actions seem to have little impact and filings in important areas are less common.

The success of the class action tool in Israel is not a mere coincidence. Israel appears to be an ideal jurisdiction for class actions, for several reasons. First, legal formalism is unpopular. Judges are liberal – they are used to implement wide discretion and utilize open standards, and, by and

77 Note that that this arrangement resembles somewhat ceasing admissions in overcharge cases against the government. In both cases, the outcome is quick legal resolution and a change in the defendant's wrongful behavior, coupled with a modest monetary incentive to the representatives – without damages to class members. Both procedures allow an intermediate solution to intermediate cases – that lie somewhere between "no legal right for class action" and "a full class action is justified." I have elaborated on this issue elsewhere, Lavie, *supra* note 33, at 98–102.

78 For a short discussion, including empirical data on voluntary dismissals and the paid fees in these cases, see Klement & Klonoff, *supra* note 10, at 181–83.

79 In principle, judges now have to find, before approving paid dismissals, that (1) there is a *prima facie* claim; and (2) the dismissal is beneficial to the class. ICAA, s. 16(a).

80 See the Markit decision, *supra* note 75.

81 E.g., Stephen B. Burbank & Sean Farhang, *Class Actions and the Counterrevolution Against Federal Litigation*, 165 U. Pa. L. Rev. 1495 (2017).

82 For the stunning empirical data *see infra* notes 87–89 and accompanying text.

83 Unlike the USA, *cf.* Burbank & Farhang, *supra* note 81, the move to rein-in class actions in Israel is not attributed mainly to the judiciary; this characteristic stems from the ease with which rules and statutes can be amended in Israel, relative to the USA.

large, they welcome procedural innovations.[84] Second, there is a significant number of lawyers in Israel – in fact, more lawyers per capita than in any other country in the world.[85] This suggests a competitive market in which lawyers are more willing to explore new terrains. Likewise, given the vast number of lawyers aggrieved victims should find legal support relatively easily. Third, more generally, Israel is well-known for its entrepreneurial culture[86] – indeed, lawyers and active consumers were quick to move to the seemingly lucrative field of entrepreneurial litigation. Finally, Israel also appeared to suffer from under-enforcement at the time the ICAA was enacted. Israel's under-enforcement should be contrasted with heavy regulation "on the books" in many areas. This gap invites private enforcement.

The combination of these factors indeed lured lawyers to the ICAA. It took some time for lawyers and judges to handle the new tool, and class actions gained momentum two to three years after the ICAA's enactment,[87] reaching an "unprecedented" annual rate of filings of more than 1,200 lawsuits.[88] It is safe to say that Israel leads the world in the number of per capita class actions.[89]

However, dissatisfaction with class actions also grew in an exponential rate. Various stakeholders and policymakers have raised the familiar concerns that many class actions – petty at best and frivolous at worst – lack societal value and are served to blackmail defendants who are, by and large, law-abiding. The chilling reaction to the wave of class actions was quick, and it manifests itself by both legislative amendments and Supreme Court decisions.

On the legislative side one can identify at least two important amendments. First, in the past there were no filing fees on class actions,[90] but since mid-2018 fixed filing fees, in the range of $2,000–$4,000, are imposed. This is a nontrivial amount.[91] The new filing fees address concerns that the previous, no-filing fee regime encouraged non-meritorious class actions. Though it is still early to judge their effect, it appears that the new fees did change the behavior of class action lawyers, at least to some extent. Indeed, the rate of filing of new class actions dropped dramatically – a new report documents a decrease of ~70 percent in new cases.[92] Of course, the data is still incomplete, and this decrease might be temporary.[93] Likewise, it is hard to isolate the fees from the effect of restrictive Supreme Court decisions that were given at about the same time.[94] Note

84 *See supra* notes 4–5 and accompanying text.

85 Tomer Zarchin, "Israel First in World for Lawyers per Capita, Study Finds" HAARETZ (Aug. 3, 2011), www.haaretz.com/1.5039519.

86 *See, e.g.*, DAN SENOR & SAUL SINGER, START-UP NATION: THE STORY OF ISRAEL'S ECONOMIC MIRACLE (2009).

87 Christoph Engel et al., *Diffusion of Legal Innovations: The Case of Israeli Class Actions*, 15 JOURNAL OF EMPIRICAL LEGAL STUDIES 708 (2018), analyze empirical data on filings and conclude that "[o]nly 1,000 days after [the] introduction [of the ICAA] did its use become more frequent, culminating in an approximately exponential pattern of adoption." *Id.*, at 729.

88 *Id.*, at 717.

89 In the USA, for instance, 12,500 class actions are brought each year, out of which about 7,500 in federal courts (the remaining in state courts). See Klement & Klonoff, *supra* note 10, at 189–90.

90 Interestingly, in regular civil cases there is a non-trivial filing fee, equal to 2.5 percent of the financial value of the sought remedy. *See* Eisenberg et al., *supra* note 46, at 1463.

91 This amount should be compared to the monetary awards for the representatives, taking into account the risk of unsuccessful class action. Recall, for example, that the payment to the representatives in voluntary dismissals cases is in the range of 50,000NIS, that is, ~$15,000.

Note also that, following the previous discussion, it is the named plaintiff who should carry the filing costs, though in practice parties of course deviate from the relevant ethics rules.

92 Gali Aviv & Asaf Stein, "Empirical Data Regarding Fees Applied in Class Action", The Israeli Courts Research Division (May 2019), available at www.gov.il/he/Departnents/the_israeli_courts_research_division (last visited, Jan. 13, 2020). Currently, then, the annual rate of class actions is ~450 cases per year. *Id.*, at 4.

93 One can argue that lawyers, who were aware of the new fees, hastened to file class actions before the fees became operative, generating an artificial decrease in the rate of filings immediately after the fees took effect.

94 *See supra* notes 79–80 and accompanying text.

also that the new filing fees include a host of exemptions and discounts, thus inviting strategic filings by lawyers. Indeed, lawyers have apparently moved to file relatively more class actions that are exempt from filing fees (e.g., discrimination and human rights).[95]

Second, an important legislative amendment from 2016 treats, among other things, the problem of paid dismissals (recall that paid dismissals enable quick resolution with no liability for the defendant and modest awards for the representatives). As discussed earlier, the sentiment that paid dismissals fuel unimportant class actions have grown among policymakers and judges, and the 2016 amendment imposes a greater burden on the approval of these dismissals.[96]

One can similarly identify important Supreme Court decisions that "chill" class litigation. First, in a series of decisions, starting in the beginning of the 2010s, the Supreme Court clarified that it requires a fact-intensive process before certifying a class, including (typically) expert opinions, testimonies, and some discovery proceedings.[97] These decisions parallel the so-called "front-loading" trend in the USA, which is generally considered a serious obstacle for plaintiffs.[98]

Second, other decisions of the Supreme Court have raised the demands from named plaintiffs (and, by extension, their lawyers). For instance, according to recent case law, the "good faith" requirement of the named plaintiff can be infringed if she triggered the defendant's wrongdoing;[99] or where she filed other class actions with similar claims (against different defendants) in other venues, without notifying the presiding judges.[100] The sanctions in these cases range from disqualifying the named plaintiff to reducing the representatives' prospective award.[101]

Third, as abovementioned the Supreme Court has guided lower courts to harden their view towards paid dismissals.[102] Finally, the Supreme Court instructed lower courts to give weight to the regulator's position and enforcement activities,[103] most notably, as a reason to deny class certification where the regulator seemed to enforce the law.[104] I will elaborate on this issue below.[105]

Following a brief heyday, then, the pendulum has swung in the contrary direction. These changes notwithstanding, Israeli courts are still very open to class actions, especially compared to American courts, and lawyers are still filing many lawsuits. More generally, class actions have

95 Aviv & Stein, *supra* note 92.

96 For more details see *supra* note 79. In addition to paid dismissals, the important amendment of 2016 includes other relevant changes, e.g., some restrictions on cy pres awards and settlement-only class actions. See, respectively, ICAA, s. 20(c)(2) and s. 19(a).

97 Two important decisions in this respect are LCA 3489/09 Migdal Ins. Co. Ltd. v. Metal Co. Ltd. Emek Zevulun (Apr.11, 2013), Nevo Legal Database (by subscription, in Hebrew) (Isr.), and CA 5378/11 Frank v. Allsale (Sept.22, 2014), Nevo Legal Database (by subscription, in Hebrew) (Isr.).

98 *See, e.g.*, Lavie, *supra* note 33, at 74–76.

99 *See* the discussion on the S.A.M.G.R decision, *supra* note 16 and accompanying text.

100 *See* the S.A.M.G.R decision, *supra* note 16. The gist here is the fear of forum-shopping – presumably, the named plaintiff could strategically request to move all similar class actions to the venue in which the most favorable judge was appointed.

101 Along these lines, another relevant discussion concerns situations where the named plaintiff failed to inform the defendant of the alleged violations (and allow it to resolve the problem), prior to filing the lawsuit. AFH 5519/15 Yousef Ahmad Younis v. Galil's Water – The Regional Sewage and Water Corporation Ltd. (Dec. 17, 2019), Nevo Legal Database (by subscription, in Hebrew) (Isr.). The absence of such notice appears to negatively affect the future award.

102 See *supra* notes 79–80 and accompanying text.

103 E.g., concerning the interpretation of the law, *see* LCA 9778/16 Shulamit Zeligman v. Fenix Ins. Co. Ltd. (May. 31, 2018), Nevo Legal Database (by subscription, in Hebrew) (Isr.).

104 Kolech, *supra* note 20.

105 *See infra* subsections 25.3.2.2–25.3.2.3.

occupied an important part of the relevant discourse. The change in the legal landscape that class actions have been inducing seems irreversible.

In this sense, the introduction of class actions can be referred to as a (at least mild) success story. Currently, the most important issue for concern appears to be the quality and type of cases. According to one study, the vast majority of class actions at the relevant time – about three fourths – were consumer cases.[106] Lawsuits against the government in overcharge claims comprise the most popular type among the remaining cases.[107] This leaves few class actions in other important areas, such as securities, antitrust, discrimination, employment, and environment.[108] The distribution of cases masks a deeper problem – consumer cases are popular because they are simple; entrepreneurial lawyers avoid the complicated, fact-intensive class actions in the important areas of securities, antitrust, and discrimination.[109] More generally, the empirical findings show that the majority of class actions in Israel end in pre-certification, voluntary dismissals.[110] The societal value of those dismissals is questionable.[111] The focus on minor cases, in particular, technical violations of unenforced regulatory norms, is presumably an unintended consequences of the 2006 ICAA.

The picture has somewhat changed in the recent years. However, legislative and judicial attempts to change the landscape of class litigation seem to have a limited success. Accordingly, a recent study, that surveys cases from mid-2018 to mid-2019 (particularly, after the implementation of filing fees) suggest that consumer cases are still by far the most important category in Israel.[112] Likewise, most cases still end with a pre-certification, voluntary dismissal.[113]

In sum, class actions have been proliferating in Israel. The counterreaction of courts and legislators will surely be chilling some litigation, but, overall, class actions have settled deeply in the legal arena. They will remain an important legal tool. However, their quality seems questionable. The dominance of class actions with little merits on the one hand (reflected by voluntary dismissals), and the paucity of filings in important areas (reflected by the distribution of class actions by subject-matter) suggest that class actions do not fulfill their deterrent role and that they may not be justified from a cost-benefit perspective.[114] Spurring socially valuable class actions (at the expense of less valuable ones) is the real issue for concern, and the counter-reaction of courts and legislators has a limited effect. The market forces that push lawyers to take easy cases – for example, financing problems and under-enforcement of various regulations – seem to be sufficiently deep to persist in the future. I surmise, then, that the landscape of class actions will not change materially in the coming years.

106 Klement & Klonoff, *supra* note 10, at 190. In particular, many consumer cases, which tend to be simple, end in voluntary dismissals before certification. *See infra* note 110.

107 *Id.* Overcharge cases typically end by ceasing admissions quickly after filing, without compensation to class members. *Supra* notes 32–33 and accompanying text.

108 *Id.* This is in stark contrast to the USA, where securities, antitrust, and employment comprise an important share of the class action landscape.

109 *Id.* at 200–02. Klement and Klonoff suggest several explanations for this phenomenon, such as the smaller size of the Israeli market and the financial difficulties for lawyers and named plaintiffs in Israel.

110 Alon Klement & Keren Weinshall-Margel, *Cost-Benefit Analysis of Class Actions: An Israeli Perspective*, 172 Journal of Institutional and Theoretical Economics 75, 92 (2016).

111 For an elaborate discussion see *infra* subsection 25.3.2.5.

112 Aviv & Stein, *supra* note 92, at 6. The next category is again overcharge cases against the government. Together, they account for about half of the cases in the study. *Cf.*, *id.* (describing an increase in the share of discrimination cases following the new fees).

113 *Id.*, at 10 (~55 percent to 60 percent of the post-fees cases, that is, from mid-2018 to mid-2019, are terminated with a voluntary dismissal).

114 For a discussion along these lines see Klement & Weinshall-Margel, *supra* note 110.

25.3 CLASS LITIGATION AND THE REGULATORY STATE

This section draws more general lessons from the Israeli practice, regarding the interface between the regulatory state and the class action mechanism. I will first briefly survey the conflict between private and public enforcement; then, I will explain why this conflict is particularly conspicuous in Israel; finally, I will analyze Israeli practices that strike a unique balance between private and public enforcement and infer the broader lessons from these practices.

25.3.1 *Private versus Public Enforcement*

The law can be enforced by agencies – public enforcement. Alternatively, it can be enforced by private actors, through courts – private enforcement. Each enforcement avenue has its own advantages and disadvantages. Class actions, the most prominent manifestation of private enforcement, hone the conflict between private and public enforcement. The literature on this topic is particularly voluminous,[115] and the following will provide the gist of this debate.

Agencies are commonly assumed to have expertise in the relevant subject-matter.[116] Also, as public enforcers, they are expected to take the public view and represent its interests. However, public enforcement is vulnerable to many drawbacks. First, public enforcers typically suffer from lack of resources. Agencies are often under-staffed, and they cannot compete with the salaries that the market can offer. Especially, agencies lack information about regulatees' wrongdoing – this information typically resides with on-site actors, such as regulatees and the victims of their behavior. The agency, then, has to actively look for information concerning regulatees' wrongdoing.[117] Second, one may suspect that regulators do not fully express the public interest. They can be vulnerable to the so-called "regulatory capture," advancing the interests of powerful stakeholders and lobbyists. This seems evident in the presence of "revolving doors," that is, from regulatory positions to the relevant industry.[118]

The advantages and disadvantages of private enforcement mirror those of public enforcement. On the one hand, private actors have more information, particularly with regard to the wrongdoing that was committed against them. Likewise, actors in the market are presumably more efficient, and they better respond to monetary incentives. On the other hand, private enforcers prioritize their parochial (typically monetary) interest, rather than the public's one. They thus may well generate more or less enforcement than there should be.[119] Familiar concerns about class actions that went out of control, in both the USA and Israel, echo this perspective. The absence of class actions in fact-intensive, important areas in Israel (e.g., discrimination) likewise illustrates the problem – entrepreneurial lawyers simply seek to maximize their monetary gains, and they flow towards the easier, consumer cases.

115 *See, e.g.*, Richard Posner, *Regulation (Agencies) Versus Litigation (Courts): An Analytical Framework*, in REGULATION VERSUS LITIGATION: PERSPECTIVES FROM ECONOMICS AND LAW 11–22 (Daniel P. Kessler ed., 2011); Matthew Stephenson, *Public Regulation of Private Enforcement: The Case for Expanding the Role of Administrative Agencies*, 91 VA. L. REV. 93 (2005).

116 *See, e.g.*, Peter Huber, *Safety and the Second Best: The Hazards of Public Risk Management in the Courts*, 85 COLUM. L. REV. 277 (1985), who stresses this point.

117 See, *e.g.*, the analysis at Steven Shavell, *The Optimal Structure of Law Enforcement*, 36 J. L & ECON. 255 (1993), who emphasizes this issue.

118 Capture, however, can be more subtle, e.g., regulators can have the same background and education as their regulatees.

119 *Cf.*, Steven Shavell, *The Fundamental Divergence Between the Private and the Social Motive to Use the Legal System*, 26 J. LEGAL STUD. 575 (1997).

TABLE 25.1 *Mapping private versus public enforcement tradeoffs*

	Fear of agency's under-activity	*Fear of agency's biased activity*
Too aggressive private enforcement	**Problem A**: Agency does little to restrain class actions, of all kinds.	**Problem B**: Agency does intervene, but it eliminates class actions that harm its favorites.
Too little private enforcement	**Problem C**: Agency doesn't enforce, nor private individuals.	**Problem D**: Agency does not enforce against its favorites (nor private individuals).

These advantages and disadvantages permeate the "gatekeeping" question.[120] Should we allow agencies to control the scope of class litigation?[121] On the one hand, we would like to give agencies the power to restrain and chill class actions that are futile (from a societal perspective). In that way, we can optimize the use of private enforcement. On the other hand, regulatory intervention in class actions is risky. Captured regulators can eliminate socially valuable class actions in order to ease the burden on the industry. This tension arises on both a case-by-case basis and a more general level.

Table 25.1 can be useful to synthesize, albeit superficially, the different considerations where agencies can both control the scope of class litigation and independently enforce the law. It presents two modes of suboptimal private enforcement: under- and over-enforcement[122]; and two public enforcement maladies: under- and biased-activity.[123] These result in four different types of problems:

In the first square ("A"), the problem is too many class actions, beyond the socially desirable level. Ideally, the (benevolent) agency should have intervened to restrain over-enforcement, however, it lacks the resources to do so. In the second square ("B"), class actions are again overly-used, but the agency, which is captured by industry interests, focuses on eliminating litigation that harms its favorites. In the third ("C"), class actions are not a useful tool in practice to enforce the law (think of discrimination or environment in Israel). However, the agency (again, benevolent) lacks resources to enforce the law either. In the fourth ("D"), class actions are likewise ineffective, but a powerful and industry-biased agency enforces the law selectively, shielding its favorites.

Table 25.1, then, presents the tradeoffs between private and public enforcement. Could these tradeoffs be resolved? Which procedures maximize the benefits of regulatory intervention but minimize the risks? Against this backdrop, the next subsections present the Israeli experience. Israel can be seen as a unique laboratory, as the tension between public and private enforcement in Israel is particularly conspicuous, and Israeli courts and legislators rely on unique procedures to ease this tension.

120 David Freeman Engstrom, *Agencies as Litigation Gatekeepers*, 123 YALE L. J. 616 (2013).

121 In many senses, this is the continental approach to class actions. *See, e.g.*, Brigitte Haar, *Regulation Through Litigation – Collective Redress in Need of a New Balance Between Individual Rights and Regulatory Objectives in Europe*, 19 THEORETICAL INQUIRIES IN LAW, 203, 211–15 (2018) (discussing, among other things, the control agencies in Europe have in some settings over standing of associations to bring collective proceedings).

122 In addition to enforcement, regulators have another prominent function – standard setting. Similarly to their enforcement capacity, regulators can overly or insufficiently fulfill the standard-setting function. The discussion in Table 25.1 and the text, though, is focused on over- and under-enforcement.

123 I omitted the cases of a well-behaved agency/class action.

25.3.2 *Lessons from the ICAA*

Israel seems a particularly interesting jurisdiction to test the tradeoffs between public and private enforcement, and the optimal control of regulators on class actions.

First, in line with the continental tradition, Israeli agencies are perceived by and large as impartial, expert decision-makers.[124] Indeed, Israel features a developed bureaucracy, and regulators deeply influence its norms.[125] While enforcement by regulators is by no means perfect, regulators are key players in shaping and enforcing policy. Second, as elaborated above, since the enactment of the ICAA in 2006 class litigation thrives in Israel, and its success conflicts with the traditional, pervasive role of regulators. Third and relatedly, many old regulatory standards have remained unenforced in the pre-ICAA era. The introduction of the ICAA pushed lawyers to enforce seemingly obsolete regulatory norms. This point echoes one of the reasons for which class actions thrive in Israel – wide, heavy regulatory framework, with little public enforcement.[126] Fourth, the regulatory landscape has changed in the recent years. New laws, enacted in the last decade and after the ICAA, give prominent agencies substantial enforcement powers. This results in a mismatch between the weak enforcement that was the background to the ICAA in 2006 and the current enforcement framework.

Against this backdrop, the following discusses and analyzes unique procedures that Israeli policymakers – courts, legislators, and regulators – have used to balance private and public enforcement.

25.3.2.1 The Public Financing Funds

One example for the unique private/public-enforcement interplay that exists in Israel is the capacity of the state to fund class actions that it deems valuable. The ICAA sets a public fund which receives requests for funding and distributes an annual budget of ~$300,000 to support class actions in various ways – for example, financing expert opinions.[127] The public fund is subject to the supervision of the ministry of justice, but the members of its board – which decide whether to approve funding requests – represent various stakeholders, such as regulators, public interests, academia, etc. Formally, the fund should support class actions with "social and public importance."[128] These criteria are sufficiently vague to allow the fund considerable leeway.

While another paper in this volume elaborates on the Israeli fund and its importance,[129] the following will briefly discuss the perspective of public versus private enforcement. State funding

124 For instance, regulators are typically appointed based on merits rather than party lines, and accordingly the administration remains in office regardless of the political identity of the governing minister. *See, e.g.*, Adam Shinar, *The Private Market of Public Work*, 31 Law Studies [Bar Ilan U. L.J] 17–53 (2017) (discussing the contours of the Israeli administration). Nonetheless, others point to difficulties unique to the Israeli context, such as concentrated markets, to argue that Israel is actually vulnerable to wide regulatory capture. Guy Rolnik & Roy Shapira, "Regulatory Capture Dynamics – the Israeli Case Study," 49–58, Samuel Neaman Institute (Jan. 2019), available at www.neaman.org.il/EN/Regulatory-Capture-Dynamics-the-Israeli-Case-Study.

125 *Id.*

126 *Supra* notes 176–177 and accompanying text.

127 These budget constraints suggest that the effect of the public fund might be limited. To get a better sense, in 2018, for instance, the annual budget of the fund was divvied up to sixty-four cases (representing about half of the requests for funding). Summary of The Israeli Public Class Action Fund Work for 2018, available at www.gov.il/he/Departments/General/representative_actions_fund (Ministry of Justice). For a similar conclusion *see also* Elizabeth Chamblee Burch, *Publicly Funded Objectors*, 19 Theoretical Inquiries in Law, 47, 61 (2018).

128 ICAA, s. 27.

129 E.g., Eli Bukspan. *The Israeli Public Class Action Fund: New Path for Integrating Business and Social Responsibility*, *in* Cambridge International Handbook of Class Actions (Brian Fitzpatrick & Randall Thomas, eds.) (forthcoming 2020).

of class actions is valuable to remedy problem C in Table 25.1 (neither agency nor private actors enforce). In that case, the (benevolent) agency can boost private enforcement in the "right" areas – where class actions are important but rare (e.g., discrimination, environment). However, one suspects that public funding is ineffective in rectifying problem D. Where the agency is biased, allowing it to fund class litigation would not help to spur class actions against the agency's favorites.[130] This concern seems largely irrelevant in the context of the Israeli public fund, as it does not seem vulnerable to industry-biases. The public fund is headed by an academic and its board represents different perspectives. Likewise, it is controlled by the ministry of justice, rather than a regulator with deep industry ties.

One should contrast this description with a less-familiar Israeli public fund (with a smaller budget). Israel Securities Authority (ISA) maintains a separate public fund, to support securities and corporate governance class actions.[131] Unlike the general public fund, here the regulator has direct say on the destinations of the funding. Thus, to the extent we think the ISA may be industry-biased, we should be more suspicious toward public funding of this sort (or: we suspect that we moved from square C to square D in Table 25.1). In sum, public funding of class actions can be valuable to complement ineffective private enforcement where concerns of regulatory capture are weak.

A related issue is the ability of funders, in general, to affect the outcomes at trial. In our context, the mere fact that a public fund chose to accept the request for funding might signal to the court the importance of the case.[132] In one securities class action, for instance, the court denied dismissal and indicated that it assigned some weight to the decision of the ISA, the relevant regulator, to fund the case.[133] The more the public fund affects the outcome of the case, concerns regarding biased agencies become stronger.[134]

25.3.2.2 Considering the Agency's General Enforcement Behavior

Another example for the private/public-enforcement interplay is courts' willingness to consider, in several high-profile Israeli cases, the regulator's general enforcement behavior as a key parameter in their certification decision.[135] Most notably, the agency's enforcement behavior is used to deny class treatment where the agency seemingly enforces the law. Illustrative is a leading case in which a class action was filed against an Orthodox Jewish radio station, alleging

130 Though of course the money will still support class actions.

131 The securities fund indeed supports only three to four cases per year. *See* Participation in the Financing of Proper Class Actions and Derivative Actions, available at www.isa.gov.il/%D7%97%D7%A7%D7%99%D7%A7%D7%94%20%D7%95%D7%90%D7%9B%D7%99%D7%A4%D7%94/Enforcement/Private_Inforcment/Pages/Fundation_Decision.aspx (Israel Securities Authority) (last visited, Jan. 13, 2020). *See also* Elizabeth Chamblee Burch, *Publicly Funded Objectors*, 19 Theoretical Inquiries in Law, 47, 61 (2018) (comparing both funds and suggesting that, notwithstanding budget constraints, the ISA's fund seems more effective).

132 See generally Ronen Avraham and Abraham Wickelgren, *Third Party Litigation Funding—A Signaling Model*, 63 DePaul L. Rev. 233 (2014). *See also* Bukspan, *supra* note 129, at *9 (discussing the expressive effect of the Israeli fund). The presiding judges are aware of public financing of class actions.

133 CA (TA) 2484-09-12 Hatzlacha The Movement for the Promotion of a Fair Society v. David Cohen, 16 (Feb. 18, 2013), Nevo Legal Database (by subscription, in Hebrew) (Isr.).

134 One can view some parallels between the filing-fee exemptions in certain important areas, *supra* note 95 and accompanying text, and the public funding of class actions – both are aimed at encouraging socially valuable class actions. Unlike the fee exemptions, the public fund, of course, screens the individual cases.

135 Doctrinally, this result is typically achieved through the pre-certification requirement that class litigation should be the "fair and efficient" way to adjudicate the case. ICAA, s. 8(a)(2). The fair and efficient standard parallels, to a large extent, Rule 23's superiority requirement.

that it discriminated against women in its broadcasts, for example, hired only male broadcasters.[136] The discrimination started in 2009, but, importantly, the regulator started to intervene only from 2011.[137] The Supreme Court affirmed the decision to certify class litigation, but only for the period in which there was no regulatory intervention, that is, before 2011. The Supreme Court acknowledged that the post-2011 regulatory enforcement was imperfect. Indeed, there were several incidences of discrimination after 2011, for example, where the station did not comply with the regulator's guidance. However, the court deemed these violations to be appropriate for individual, rather than class litigation.[138]

The move to consider the regulator's general enforcement activity is desirable.[139] Class actions, and, eventually, a private enforcement mechanism, substituting for public enforcement. If public enforcers do their job, class actions are by and large redundant. Heeding the regulator's enforcement efforts is particularly important in light of possible changes in the regulatory landscape. To illustrate through the case of Israel, the ICAA was enacted in 2006, against a background of perceived under-enforcement. However, in the past years several agencies have received stronger enforcement powers. Particularly, recent legislative amendments boosted the capacity of two important agencies – the Consumer Protection and Fair Trade Authority and the Securities Authority – to levy administrative sanctions (whereas in the past the main enforcement avenue was criminal law).[140]

Considering the agency's enforcement efforts, however, might raise other concerns. In the Orthodox Jewish radio station case, the court essentially determined that for the post-2011 period, class litigation would produce too much private enforcement (as the regulator has generally enforced the law).[141] This, however, fails to account for biased regulators. An interested regulator can create a façade of enforcement in order to shield regulatees from class litigation. In that case, we are in square B in Table 25.1.

A more nuanced policy should distinguish between squares A and B in the top row of Table 25.1. This can be done, for example, by scrutinizing more deeply the motives and behavior of the relevant regulator, in order to distinguish between authentic and ungenuine regulatory enforcement. In that case, at the certification stage the court should ask questions relevant to the regulatory behavior. Why did the regulator fail to enforce the law in the past? Can it enforce the law more vigorously now, and in the future? Does the regulator authentically enforce the law? Or, did it create a façade of enforcement in order to shield certain firms? What are the more general risks of revolving doors/regulatory capture? Practically, the defendant, who has the incentives to avoid class litigation, could provide the relevant arguments along these lines.

136 For a discussion on other aspects of that case, Kolech, see *supra* note 20 and accompanying text.

137 The regulator essentially started a dialogue with the radio station, in which it pushed the station to gradually integrate female voices.

138 Kolech, *supra* note 20, s. 78–79. It should be noted that a direct class action against the regulator, for failing to monitor and enforce, would be impossible under the ICAA. *See* ICAA, s. 3(a) (explicitly exempting agencies from class actions for failure to enforce).

139 Indeed, American courts also take sometimes the agency's enforcement efforts into account as part of the superiority requirement. *E.g.*, Belfiore v. Procter & Gamble Co., 311 F.R.D. 29, 73 (E.D.N.Y. 2015) (finding that the class action "is not a superior method of adjudication" given the pending FTC inquiry, as the FTC "is better suited to protect consumers").

140 *See* Consumer Protection Law, 5741-1981, § 1, SH No. 2461 p. 622 (as amended in 2014, No. 39) (Isr.); Securities Law, 5728-1968, SH No. 2274 p. 206 (Isr.), (as amended in 2011, No. 45, by The Streamlining of Enforcement Procedures at the Israel Securities Authority (Legislative Amendments) Law 5771-2011, SH No. 2274 p. 206 (Isr.).

141 Or, in the terminology of Table 25.1, the case moved from the lower to the upper row after 2011.

25.3.2.3 Considering the Agency's Legal Position

A third example for the public/private-enforcement interplay is the weight Israeli courts give to the regulator's legal position, both at the pre-certification stage and as objectors to settlements.

PRE-CERTIFICATION It is very common for Israeli courts to invite the regulator to opine on the relevant legal issues before certification, and consider the regulator's position in the certification decision.[142] While there is no precise empirical data, it seems that courts do provide considerable weight to the regulator's position.[143] In one class action decision, the Supreme Court went further to hold that as a (rebuttable) presumption courts should accept the regulator's legal position.[144] The Supreme Court relied on the regulator's interpretation in that case to reverse the lower court's decision to certify class litigation against an insurance company.

Considering the regulator's position can be justified, as the regulator is deemed to possess relevant expertise. However, as the foregoing suggests, courts should be better aware of the potential bias among regulators (or, in the terminology of Table 25.1, distinguish between squares A and B).[145] Interested regulators may well interpret the law in a way that serves the interests of their regulatees. Note that, as regulators are assumed to be biased in the direction of the industry, rather than the victims, concerns for biased regulators are solely relevant where the regulator desires to eliminate class litigation (square B in Table 25.1).[146]

SETTLEMENTS As noted before, the ICAA invites the attorney general (AG) to comment on each settlement. It does so in order to enhance the adversary process, through a seemingly impartial third party.[147] Lawyers from the AG's office do intervene, and their objections often lead courts to strike down settlements because the common fund is too small and/or the recommended attorneys' fees are too large.[148]

The use of the AG to monitor settlements seems less problematic than considering the agency's position before certification. First, compared to area-specific regulators (say, in securities or antitrust) the AG seems less vulnerable to industry forces.[149] The AG of course reflects regulatory positions; however, it is ultimately subject to the minister of justice. Second, even if the AG is captured, objecting to settlements may not be an effective avenue to shield favorable industries. In case the objection is accepted and the court strikes down a settlement the parties

142 While this practice is not unique to Israel, it seems more frequent and influential in Israel than in the USA. Interestingly, the class action rules mandate notifying the relevant regulator upon filing. *See* Israeli Class Action Rules of Procedure, 5766-2006, § 3, 35 LSI 298 (2010) (Isr.). Technically, the intervention of the third-party regulator resembles the familiar practice of amicus curiae briefs.

143 Indeed, the Supreme Court guides lower courts to ask for the agency's opinion before certification. CA 7169/17 Pelephone Communications Ltd. v. Merav Firth, s. 10 (Feb. 03, 2019), Nevo Legal Database (by subscription, in Hebrew) (Isr.) (Baron, J.).

144 Zeligman, *supra* note 103. The scope of the case is unclear – in Zeligman the regulator was asked to interpret its own rules (rather than a statute). It should also be noted that this ruling is now revisited by the Supreme Court. Likewise, it has been qualified by other cases, see e.g., CA 9294/16 Oshrat Shimon v. I.D.I. Insurance Company Ltd. (Feb. 04, 2020), Nevo Legal Database (by subscription, in Hebrew) (Isr.).

145 Practically, again, the relevant arguments and evidence could come from the defendant, who has the incentives to avoid class litigation.

146 In other words, we can presume that a regulator who argues in court that class litigation should be certified is not biased and thus embodies the case in square C (benevolent but weak regulator assists under-utilized private enforcement).

147 *Supra* note 67 and accompanying text.

148 *See supra* notes 178–179 and accompanying text.

149 For instance, senior officers at the AG do not typically move to the "regulated" industry. This follows from the AG's lack of expertise in the regulated subject.

may indeed settle for lower sums; but they may also go to trial, in which the defendant is exposed to greater liability.[150] Objecting to settlements, then, may bring uncertain results, and this uncertainty limits the capacity of the AG to sway the level of enforcement through objections. For the foregoing reasons, it seems that the AG's objection to settlements is a valuable tool to provide the public perspective on settlements.[151]

More generally, the ICAA can teach us that considering the agency's legal position in class proceedings is valuable; however, it also entails difficulties. Moreover, regulatory involvement at the settlement stage raises considerably fewer concerns relative to pre-certification phases.

25.3.2.4 Class Actions by a Regulator

An interesting mechanism under the ICAA is class actions by a regulator – as a named plaintiff.[152] Although this option is rarely used,[153] it opens up interesting perspectives.

On the one hand, such a provision enables agencies to boost enforcement where the private market does not find it worthwhile to bring class actions. Indeed, class actions are typically a more effective enforcement mechanism than other relevant options that the agency has at its disposal. Agencies can therefore leverage their expertise through the class action mechanism to achieve more powerful outcomes. In this sense, the option to bring class actions by agencies – where class actions are not filed by the market – can fill the gap in square C in Table 25.1 (weak private and public enforcement).

However, as the foregoing discussion has demonstrated, agencies can be biased. First, a class action by a regulator can be driven by the desire to mask its failure to enforce the law from the outset. In that sense, a regulator that files a class action is suspect of conflicting interests. More generally, the leeway agencies have under the ICAA to bring a class action may be used to the detriment of private enforcement. A prominent example is a case in which both individual victims *and* the agency file a class action. In that case, the agency may ask the court to be the lead plaintiff and dismiss the class actions filed by "regular" victims.[154] The incentives of (benevolent) agencies to bring class litigation where there is none are clear. But what motivates the agency to join an existing class action, and ask to remove the current representatives? A biased agency can, of course, take over the class action in order to mitigate its effect on its favorites and/or mask the agency's failures (square B in Table 25.1). A benevolent agency, on the other hand, may be driven by the desire to strengthen enforcement, perhaps believing that it can better adjudicate the case (this fits square C). Alternatively, a benevolent agency may also be motivated by the desire to "chill" overaggressive enforcement that the current representatives advance (Square A). However, an agency that desires to "chill" the case may be driven by benevolent (square A) or

150 The outcome depends on various factors, including, for instance, the relative bargaining power of each side. Somewhat counterintuitively, if the defendant holds considerable bargaining power then we expect that its gains from settlements are greater and the relative losses from trial are accordingly larger.

151 In the abovementioned terminology, the AG's position can help rectifying the problems in squares A and C – that is, both too aggressive (e.g., objecting to settlements in meritless cases) and too little private enforcement (e.g., objecting to a meager settlement).

152 *See supra* note 21 and accompanying text.

153 The ICAA lists only three agencies that can bring class actions, *supra* note 23, and these agencies have thus far chosen, by and large, not to employ the class action mechanism.

154 This example is based on an actual Israeli case, CA (BS) 14066-07-17 Guy Hoss v. Rotem Amfert Negev Ltd. (May. 31, 2018), Nevo Legal Database (by subscription, in Hebrew) (Isr.). In general, where several named plaintiffs compete over a case, the ICAA gives some preference to the first to file. ICAA, s. 7. In many cases, though, the chronological gap is insignificant (e.g., a few days), and courts prefer the plaintiff whose complaint seems more comprehensive at that stage.

industry-biased (square B) motives. Where the agency requests to replace the current representatives, then, courts should again attempt to decipher its motives and the risk of industry-biased considerations.

In sum, allowing agencies to file class actions is an interesting option, which could strengthen private enforcement where the market does not properly work. However, courts and policymakers should be cautious regarding the agency's motives. Policymakers should be particularly suspicious where agencies join existing class actions (as opposed to filing class action that no class member found valuable to file). A skeptical attitude is particularly warranted as the agency has at its disposal various other tools, though less powerful, to restrain too aggressive private enforcement. A prominent example is intervening before certification as an amicus curiae (subsection 25.3.2.3). Practically, then, a court can place the burden on the relevant agency, to show that its request to lead the case and substitute the incumbent class counsel is necessary from a public perspective.

25.3.2.5 Breaking the Binarity of Class Litigation: Intermediate Resolutions

Israel presents heavy regulation, thriving class litigation, and liberal courts. This combination has invited a wave of class actions that are based on violations of various regulatory standards. These violations often relate to regulations that seem highly technical or even obsolete, carrying minimal, if any, actual harm to consumers. Indeed, the regulatory rules that underlie current class litigation were often promulgated in an era of under-enforcement, when the class action mechanism was not in the offing.

The enforcement of these rules through class actions generated a vivid debate. On the one hand, proponents stress that even where the harm to consumers is trifling the law should be enforced. Accordingly, some of the cases in this group led to the enforcement of rules that seem to have real public value. To illustrate, a law from 1986 requires business owners (e.g., supermarkets, banks) to install drinking fountains to the free benefit of their clients. The law – which was not enforced for decades – triggered a series of class actions against various service providers. These cases often end with the defendant's commitment to comply with the law and install drinking fountains on its premises.[155] Opponents emphasize the abusive nature of these cases, and the heavy burden on defendants given the widespread technical rules. These concerns are most prominent in the context of food manufacturing and labeling. To illustrate, in one case a plaintiff argued that a yogurt that was marketed as "nature yogurt" was artificially processed and thus violated the rule that defines "natural" products.[156] The court denied certification, concluding that no harm occurred to consumers.[157] Many other cases present harder policy questions – it appears clear that the defendant violated the regulatory standard; but it is hard to conceive of any real damage to the customers.

The normative desirability of these cases is questionable, and, as the forgoing suggests, it depends on the relevant regulatory rule.[158] There may well be technical regulatory standards whose enforcement entails social value, as the water fountains example demonstrates. But even in those cases, the class action mechanism seems too heavy a tool. Class litigation envisions, in

155 E.g., CA (Jer) 43515-06-14 Rula Tannous v. Israel Coop – Supermarkets Ltd. (Jun. 29, 2014), Nevo Legal Database (by subscription, in Hebrew) (Isr.). The obligation to provide water seems particularly important given the Israeli weather. It also has a possible monetary value, as without drinking fountains clients have to buy water.

156 CA (Hi) 25161-01-14 Yosef Shahar v. Tnuva Central Coop. for the MKTG. of AGR Prod in Israel Ltd. (Jul. 02, 2015), Nevo Legal Database (by subscription, in Hebrew) (Isr.).

157 *Id.* Accordingly, the court distinguished between "nature" and "natural."

158 A separate question, beyond the scope of the current paper, is the under-optimal incentives of regulators to amend outdated regulation.

essence, two termination options: litigating as a class action or dismissing beforehand. One may think that such a binary one-size-fits-all approach is not helpful, and an intermediate rule will better fit the case of technical regulatory violations.

Indeed, as abovementioned,[159] the ICAA features another, intermediate approach – paid dismissals. Instead of litigating as a full-fledged class action, regulatory violation cases are often resolved in Israel through a distinct, quick procedure that (1) brings to a change in the defendant's behavior, such that it complies from now on with the regulation; (2) modestly rewards the representatives, and (3) does not preclude the class. As class members are not likely to sue for small individual damages, the likely outcome is a change in the defendant's behavior and a modest incentive to the class's representatives. In the water fountain cases, such an outcome – a quick resolution, in which the defendant commits to install drinking fountains and the representative receive a modest reward – seems attractive. More broadly, this option apparently fits small, technical violations of regulatory standards, for which a comprehensive (and binding) class action is too heavy a tool.

More generally, to the extent one thinks that current regulations should be enforced, the intermediate procedures in the ICAA address the problems associated with regulatory regimes that move from under-enforcement (without class actions) to complete or even over-enforcement (with class action).[160] These lessons can be shared more broadly with jurisdictions that desire to adopt new class action statutes.[161]

25.3.2.6 Remapping the Tools

We can now turn back to the general tradeoffs of private and public enforcement, and map the main tools that the ICAA uses in this respect.

The ICAA, then, provides useful tools to better cope with the traditional difficulties of private and public enforcement. To the extent that the problem is un-monitored private enforcement (square A), for instance, courts should consider the enforcement activity of the relevant agency and invite it to intervene. However, where agencies are biased (square B), courts should be skeptical towards agency intervention. To the extent both private enforcers and agencies fail to enforce, courts could encourage them to do so, for example, through higher fees to plaintiff and class counsel (if agencies are not trusted, square D). Public funding can also help enforcement in these circumstances. Benevolent agencies could intervene, pre-certification, to support class litigation; and agencies who have the capacity to do so could file and fund class actions (square C).

The ICAA, then, provides several interesting tools to better combine private and public enforcement. Some of which, for example, allowing pre-certification intervention by regulators, require courts to distinguish between impartial and biased agencies (squares A and B). For this reason, it might be better for courts to inquire through appropriate evidence, in those cases, as to

[159] *See supra* notes 180–181 and accompanying text.

[160] Alternatively put, the quick class action procedures for these cases can be seen as fitting square A – that is, alleviating the burden on defendants from full-fledged class actions. This is, of course, a generalization, as in reality, the quick procedure can induce more filings, ex ante. To the extent the quick procedure – paid dismissals – encourages over-enforcement, courts can chill it, through, e.g., lower monetary rewards. *Cf.*, *supra* note 80 and accompanying text (toughening the requirements to approve paid dismissals).

[161] Of course, one can think of various other options to achieve this transition. Courts can refuse to certify class actions where the individual damages seem remote. More generally, legislators who would like to adopt new class action statutes can be more mindful of existing regulation – e.g., amending obsolete rules and/or shielding defendants from class litigation for violations of technical regulatory standards. Likewise, legislators can create regulatory avenues, in the spirit of more familiar whistleblower regimes in the USA, that induce individuals to report violations of regulatory rules.

TABLE 25.2 *Remapping private versus public enforcement tools*

	Fear of agency's under-activity	*Fear of agency's biased activity*
Too aggressive private enforcement	**Problem A**: Agency does little to restrain class actions, of all kinds. **Solutions:** Considering the agency's enforcement activity; inviting the agency to intervene; using quick resolutions of class actions.	**Problem B**: Agency does intervene, but it eliminates class actions that harm its favorites. **Solutions:** Being skeptical of agency's interventions in class actions.
Too little private enforcement	**Problem C**: Agency doesn't enforce, nor private individuals. **Solutions:** Agencies could intervene in favor of certification; agencies should be encouraged to file and fund class actions.	**Problem D**: Agency does not enforce against its favorites (nor private individuals). **Solution:** Encouraging class actions, e.g., public funding and higher attorneys' fees.

the agency's potential favoritism. Courts have not, up to date, attempted to seriously decipher the agency's motives. This might be a natural path to follow given the growing tension between regulatory and private enforcement.

25.4 CONCLUSION

This chapter started with an attempt to depict the class action landscape in Israel. The Israeli law on class actions resembles, by and large, the American class action. Class actions indeed proliferate in Israel, even more (at least in per capita terms) than in the USA, and the chapter has laid out the institutional reasons for this phenomenon.

Similarly to the American experience, the Israeli practice of class actions presents a rise-and-fall story as in recent years we observe a pushback from courts and legislators. Nonetheless, and although most class actions in Israel seem to have a limited monetary impact, the Israeli class action is, overall, a success story. Further, this chapter highlighted the interesting mechanisms that the Israeli law provides to balance between private and public enforcement, given the robust regulatory framework in Israel. Examples include public funding, deferring to agencies, and quick procedures to handle trivial regulatory violations.

What are, then, the lessons from Israel? First, the rise-and-fall story suggests that, by and large, class actions are irreversible. Though we see a backlash, once the class action mechanism was introduced it may be weakened but not eliminated. Second, the transition to a class action regime implicates unintended consequences. In the Israeli context, it is the over-enforcement of regulatory violations through paid dismissals. More generally, as the Israeli context teaches us, the transition to a class action regime resurrects obsolete regulatory standards, unenforced in the old regime. The foregoing suggests that policymakers should take caution with the class action mechanism.

Finally, and most importantly, the discussion on the foregoing design choices that balance private and public enforcement can enrich the relevant discourse on the intersection between class actions and regulators. Thus, the design of the Israeli Act can especially inspire the implementation of class litigation in jurisdictions that traditionally defer to their regulators.

26

The Israeli Public Class Action Fund

New Approach for Integrating Business and Social Responsibility

*Eli Bukspan**

26.1 INTRODUCTION

The Israeli Class Action Law, 2006[1] (hereinafter the Law or the Class Action Law) brought about dramatic changes in the adjudication of class action lawsuits in Israel. If the number of cases filed is a parameter of success, this law is clearly a phenomenal success: the number of plaintiffs requesting to certify a claim as a class action suit is on a continuous upward trend and far exceeds the general trend in civil lawsuits filed, which has remained relatively stable during the same time period. In 2007, one year after the law was enacted, 28 motions were filed to certify class action suits, in 2010 this number rose to 335, in 2012, 820,[2] and in 2018, 1,250.[3]

One of the major innovations in the Israeli Class Action Law is the establishment of Public Fund to Finance Class Action Lawsuits to assist representative plaintiffs finance the petitions for certification of class actions with public and social importance.[4] The fund is a rare phenomenon throughout the world,[5] and therefore can also be viewed as a "test case" for some of class actions' descriptive and normative issues in other legal systems as well.

While I discuss the Fund in greater detail further on, it is important to understand three issues at the onset: (1) the Fund's mandate is to assess the social and public significance of the class

* I am grateful for comments from Barak Atiram, Ronen Avraham, Daphne Barak-Erez, Alon Klement, Sharon Yadin, and participants in the International Conference on the Resolution of Consumer Mass Disputes, Collective Redress, Class Actions and ADR (Faculty of Law at the University of Haifa, European Institute in Florence and City University of Hong Kong, March 16–17, 2017), in the International Symposium on The Corporation in a Changing World (Shanghai University of Finance and Economics (SUFE), School of Law, December 8–9, 2018), in the ICON-S, Conference on Public Law in Times of Change (Pontificia Universidad Catolica de Chile, July 1–3, 2019) and in the International Class Actions Conference (Vanderbilt Law School, Vanderbilt Law and Business Program, August 23-24th, 2019). Thanks to Renen Baranovitz, Tomi Davidson, Dvir Uziel, and Michele Manspeizer for research and editing assistance.

1 Class Action Law, 5776–2016, SH No. 2054 p. 264 (Isr.). The opinions expressed in this article are my own.

2 Camille Cameron, Jasminika Kalajdzic and Alon Klemt, Economic Enablers, in CLASS ACTIONS IN CONTEXT – HOW CULTURE, ECONOMICS AND POLITICS SHAPE COLLECTIVE LITIGATION 137, 164 (Decorah R. Hensler, Christopher Hodges & Ianika Tzankova eds., 2016).

3 Assaf Fink, 2018 *Summary of Class Action Law Suits*, Ninth Conference on Class Action Lawsuits (Mar. 2, 2019), *available at* http://knowit.org.il/Uploads/Documents/sikum2018.pdf [in Hebrew].

4 Class Action Law, *supra* note 1, art. 27(a).

5 To my knowledge, only two other *public* funds worldwide were established by law: in Quebec and in Ontario, Canada. Presently, there is now a proposal to establish similar funds in Australia and Hong Kong. In addition, in Israel there is separate fund to finance *securities* class actions.

action law suit; (2) the class action lawsuit is not adjudicated before the Fund, and its protocols and decisions cannot be submitted as evidence in court; (3) the Fund does not oversee issues related to securities class actions, which has a unique and separate public fund within the Israel Securities Authority – which is much smaller with only a few inquiries per year.[6]

The chapter begins with a short discussion on class action lawsuits in Israel (Section 26.2); proceeds with the Public Fund to Finance Class Action Lawsuits (Section 26.3) and concludes with a normative discussion on the relationship between class action lawsuits, the Public Fund, social change, and corporate social responsibility (Section 26.4).

26.2 CLASS ACTIONS IN ISRAEL: PURPOSES AND TRENDS

At face value, class action lawsuits are a procedural mechanism that serves first and foremost to unify and manage multiple claims against a singular defendant, but clearly their role is not solely limited to this and also has the potential to advance other significant and more substantial interests.[7] Additionally, while it is true that monetary ambitions often spur the submission of class action lawsuits, this in and of itself does not negate the realization of important public interests. In this manner, the representative plaintiff serves as a procedural "Robin Hood" and catalyst, since without her petition an important public concern would not "see its day in court."

Section 1 of the Law lists its four main objectives: (1) increase access to court, including for those with limited access; (2) enforce the law and deter violation; (3) provide appropriate remedies to those whose rights have been violated; and (4) promote an efficient, fair, and comprehensive legal process to manage these type of claims. While the relative importance of these objectives was not determined in the Law, case law has repeatedly pointed to public interest as the most important.[8] One possible explanation for this is the continuing and increasing importance of public interests in the civil law discourse, particularly in light of the general legal trend to rein in the growing strength and influence of corporations, the largest number of defendants in class action lawsuits.[9]

The pro-public/social approach that stands at the foundation of class actions is prevalent in legal literature as well, and points out that the plaintiff's personal interests (i.e., remedies), which ostensibly are relevant to a group of plaintiffs as well, is not the main goal of the class action process.[10] This position is clearly articulated in the Law's provisions, specifically in Article 27 establishing the Fund to Finance Class Action Lawsuits, and which is the focus of this chapter.

6 Securities class action lawsuits are governed by the Israeli Company Law 5759–1999, 44 L.S.I. 119 (not the Class Action Law).

7 *See* the explanatory note to the Israeli bill: "Legal representation is not necessarily viewed as a process to manage multiple plaintiffs with similar claims but rather as a tool to promote public interests. A considerable part of the changes made in the proposed law reflect this view." (*See* Proposed Class Action Law, 5766–2006, 234).

8 CA 03/345 Dan Reichart v. the Heirs of Moshe Shemesh, the deceased, p. 83 Nevo database (given June 7, 2007); CA 8037/06 Brazelai v. Priner, p. 88, Nevo database (given Sept. 4, 2014); CA 10085/08 Tnuva v. Estate of Tofik Ravi, deceased (given Dec. 4, 2011).

9 *Compare:* Western Canadian Shopping Centers v. Dutton, (2001) 2 S.C.R. 534, ¶ 26 (emphasizing the role of class actions in the modern era: "The class action plays an important role in today's world. The rise of mass production, the diversification of corporate ownership, the advent of the mega-corporation, and the recognition of environmental wrongs have all contributed to its growth … The class action offers a means of efficiently resolving such disputes in a manner that is fair to all parties").

10 Kerry Barnett, *Equitable Trusts: An Effective Remedy in Consumer Class Actions*, 96 YALE L.J. 1591 (1987); John C. Coffee, *Class Wars: The Dilemma of the Mass Tort Class Action*, 95 COLUM. L. REV. 1355 (1995); and Myriam Gilles & Gary B. Friedman, *Exploding the Class Action Agency Costs Myth: The Social Utility of Entrepreneurial Lawyers*, 155 U. PA. L. REV. 103, 105–06 (2006) ("The most critical and controversial feature of this argument is that compensation is not really an important goal in small-claims class actions … We must also do the easy (or at least intuitive) work of showing that the deterrence of corporate wrongdoing is what we can and should expect from class actions.").

However, the Law includes other pro-public/social arrangements, such as Article 22(b)(3) that instructs that the "degree of the class action's public importance" will be a positive consideration when determining the plaintiffs' compensation and/or attorney fees in a successful suit. So is the case with the participation of public officials in the class action proceedings. Prior to the Law's legislation only a private individual could sue using the class action mechanism; however, since its legislation, Article 4 (a) (2) of the Law allows public authorities, in the area of their jurisdiction and on behalf of a group of individuals whose claim raises fundamental questions, to initiate a class action lawsuit. The new law also allows public officials to participate, with court's permission, in proceedings they did not initiate.[11] In this manner, public officials can participate in settlement agreements between plaintiffs and class action defendants to prevent the misuse of the proceedings at the determent of the group's best interests.[12]

The ingrained public interests in class action lawsuits are not exhausted by the examples above and are readily found in legislative and case law developments as we discuss below.

26.2.1 *Legislative Innovations*

Beyond the public aspects of the Law detailed above, it is important to mention the 2016 fund to manage and distribute monetary judgments of class action suits.[13] The purpose of this relatively new fund is, by definition, public – to distribute funds for public uses that have goals closely associated with the claim that had been adjudicated and to prevent potential biases in the distribution of the funds, inter alia, due to concerns about previous ties between the defendant and recipients of the funds.

An additional development relating to the public nature of class action suits is the 2018 regulation on class action court fees.[14] Architects of the regulations claimed that class action plaintiffs should not be exempt from paying court fees – as do plaintiffs in other legal proceedings. While the new regulations originally were opposed on the grounds that they weakened the institution of class actions, it is impossible to ignore the fact that this amendment also includes public justifications, for example, subsidizing a percentage of the costs of the class action processes that are usually long, complex, and require vast resources. Another public purpose attributed to this new policy assumes that court fees will reduce submissions of false claims and deter defendants from initiating unnecessary proceedings.

As expected, these regulations were not passed without detractors, although recently the Israeli Supreme Court, sitting as the High Court of Justice, overturned a petition to revoke the regulations.[15] One of the central claims against imposing court fees concerns redundancy of the Class Action Law objectives since the objectives clearly advocate increased access to court, and court fees could act as a deterrent.

[11] Class Action Law, *supra* note 1, art. 15.

[12] *Id.* art. 18.

[13] *Id.* art. 27a. (for the fund's site see: www.justice.gov.il/Units/ApotroposKlali/Departments/ApotroposKlali/giloi/Pages/ClassActionLaw.aspx) [in Hebrew].

[14] Court Regulations (Court Fees), 2007, Regulation 7a.

[15] *See* HCJ 3646/18 *Friends of Community Rights' Centers v. Minister of Justice* (handed down on Jan. 16, 2019). The framework of the final regulations imposes a 16,000 NIS filling fee in the district court, where most of the class actions are filed, and a 8,000 NIS filing fee in the magistrate court. Half of the fee is paid before submitting the suit and the other half after the judgment. *See* Constitution, Law, and Justice Committee, Outline of Class Action Lawsuit Fees, Framework Compromise 2017, *available at* http://m.knesset.gov.il/Activity/committees/huka/Pages/CommitteeMaterial.aspx?ItemID=2023754 [in Hebrew].

26.2.2 *Case Law Innovations*

Three important judgments, which were handed down by the Israeli Supreme Court in recent years, and which their original suits were also backed by the Fund to Finance Class Action Lawsuits, assisted in consolidating the perception of the social and public importance of class action suits in Israel: LCA 6897/14 *Radio Kol BaRamah Ltd. v. Kolech – Religious Women's Forum*,[16] which emphasized the class action lawsuit's ability to protect human rights, alongside two additional precedents LCA 8771/16 *Nobel Energy Mediterranean Limited v. Moshe Nazri*[17] and LCA 3456/13 *The Israeli Electric Company Ltd., v. Yonatan Shlider*,[18] both which confirmed the regulatory nature of the class action suit.

Radio Kol BaRamah Ltd. v. Kolech claimed that Kol BaRamah radio station discriminated against women. In this case, Kolech – The Religious Women's Forum, a religious feminist movement in Israel, sued the ultra-Orthodox radio station "A Voice in Ramah" on grounds that it prevented women from broadcasting on the station, following its stated policy between years 2009 and 2011. The Israeli Supreme Court allowed the petition to continue as a class action lawsuit on the grounds that the radio station's position constituted prohibitory discrimination.[19] Following this ruling, the district court ruled on the suit as a class action law suit and required "Voice in Ramah" to pay one million NIS to traditional, religious, and ultra-Orthodox women empowerment programs; 250,000 NIS for legal expenses; and to repeal its discriminatory policy and begin to play women on the radio station.

Nobel Energy Mediterranean Limited v. Moshe Nazri, the largest class action suit in Israel, claimed that the gas company had exploited its monopoly by charging the electric company excessive prices and which were ultimately passed on to Israeli consumers. *Israeli Electric Company Ltd., v. Yonatan Shlider* petitioned to approve a class action suit claiming that electricity prices had been unlawfully inflated, including within the inflated prices high salary payouts – which had been previously criticized by the Supervisor of Wages in the Ministry of Finance. While both of these judgments discussed price control, which is one of the main functions of economic regulation in Israel and therefore, ostensibly, lies within the traditional realm of public enforcement, the Israeli Supreme Court saw fit to broaden the judicial review of the alleged acts through the class action law suits as a private mechanism (though assisted by the public class action fund) that works hand-in-hand with direct public enforcement and acts as deterrent against corporations that use illegally payments made by the public.[20]

16 Given Dec. 9, 2015.

17 Given Sept. 28, 2017.

18 Given Aug. 29, 2017.

19 See also Class Action 8214-05-14 Ronen Meirav v. IDI Insurance Company Ltd. (given Aug. 30, 2016) (as an example of using class action lawsuits as a tool for social change in the field of human rights). This lawsuit addresses the question of whether a car insurance offer, which provides free tire replacement services to women but not men breaches the Prohibition of Discrimination in Products, Services and Entry into Places of Entertainment and Public Places Law, 2000, thereby violating the rights of insured men. Judge Grosskopf discussed the difference between a personal discrimination claim – appropriate for pinpoint violations of the principle of equality – and a class action on similar grounds, suitable in those cases in which discrimination is based on policy and not individual instances.

20 Until these rulings, the Attorney General's position, as well as the courts' position, prevented indirect attacks on tariffs. This approach, termed the "Filed Rate Doctrine" fits the US approach denying petitions with indirect claims against tariffs set by the regulator but at the same time faces much criticism; see Judge Meltzer's ruling in Electric Company v. Shlider, *supra* note 18. In addition, US regulation is created by independent, professional authorities on a legal-economic basis and not a governmental basis. With that, this approach is incompatible with the Israeli legal system.

26.3 THE PUBLIC CLASS ACTION FUND

Class actions have a multitude of objectives, some explicit, others implied: they create, inter alia, a more efficient system of enforcement by grouping together individual claims of lesser monetary value that may otherwise not be filed due to their lower monetary value; they also create an efficient mechanism to internalize the law and deter its violation. However, this chapter focuses on the objective usually downplayed in the mundane analysis of class actions, and that is their potential to promote greater social and public changes in the business sector through the Public Class Action Fund.

Class actions act to introduce social and legal norms into private law, especially within the commercial sector, while strengthening private enforcement and reducing the need for public enforcement. These themes are clearly resonant in the establishment of the Israeli Public Class Action Fund. Initially, the Fund was established for a period of seven years;[21] currently, legislation is being drafted to ensure its continuation after the conclusion of seven years.[22] As mentioned above, this type of fund is almost unknown in the world. A similar fund exists within the Israel Securities Authority to finance securities-related claims. Both of these funds are public, and as such highlight the private-public duality of their mechanism while supporting class action lawsuits (which are considered a private enforcement mechanism); and each receive a state budget to assist representative plaintiffs in financing requests for approval of class actions of public and social importance.

The Public Class Action Fund has more of a public, and less of a legal, value. As I note, it does not replace court, and its decisions cannot be used as evidence in court because the Fund does not focus on legal issues, nor on the claim's chance of receiving a positive verdict (as the corresponding securities fund is), *but rather solely on the claim's social and public merits*. In addition, as a public fund, the Class Action Fund, as well as its nine representatives from various regulatory positions and as appointed by the Minister of Justice,[23] reflect the recognition, support, and indirect cooperation of the regulator with the class action mechanism as a private enforcement tool. Indeed, the Fund's composition may also raise criticism about apparent conservatism in discretion of the majority of the fund's members as representatives of regulatory agencies that are responsible for the public enforcement of many issues brought before the fund. However, the high rate of financing by the Fund shows that the regulator representatives, the public representative, and the Fund's chairman serve as an unbiased, de facto public jury, which uses the fund's resources to strengthen the other and alternative public enforcement mechanisms. In other words, the Class Action Fund's pluralistic composition and its mandate to finance class actions of "public and social importance in their submission and clarification" clearly attests to the legislature's recognition and support of the use of class action lawsuits to promote issues of social and public importance. These aspects all support the concept that the Public Class Action Fund acts as a magnifying glass for those public purposes that are embedded in class actions and in its active assistance to issues of great social and public importance.[24]

The Class Action Fund annual budget is relatively low (around 1.5 million NIS – approximately less than half a million US dollars) and cannot be carried over into the next fiscal year.

[21] Class Action Law, *supra* note 1, art. 27.

[22] Class Action Law (11th amendment), 2020.

[23] The Fund is composed of nine representatives from a variety of regulatory agencies and the public: the Consumer Protection and Fair Trade Authority; Antitrust Authority; Bank of Israel Supervision Department; Pension Fund Commission; Ministry of Environment; Commission for Equal Rights for Persons with Disabilities; Office of the Attorney General; the public; and the Fund chairman, who is qualified to be a district court judge.

[24] Catherine Piche, *Public Financiers as Overseers of Class Proceedings*, 12 N.Y.U. J.L. & Bus. 779, 801 (2016).

The fund mainly finances expert opinion fees, reimburses court expenses for failed claims and, more recently, pays court fees.[25] Since its creation, the Fund has reviewed approximately 700 requests and has approved more than 45 percent of them – a remarkably high percentage, demonstrating the poignancy of the submissions.

The unofficial policy guiding funding is to provide partial funding to as many just claimants as possible on a diversified range of issues, rather than provide full funding to fewer claimants or for a centralized area of claims. That is to say, even those claimants that receive financing still have to fund most of the suit's costs.

However, in addition to receiving direct financial assistance, the Fund's endorsement of the suit may also have an informal expressive and signaling effect within, and outside, the judicial process.[26] The Fund meets once every quarter, and the upward trend in requests for funding indicates a constant increase in awareness and volume of its activity.[27] Since its enactment, the Fund has received requests on a wide range of claims. Most requests that are approved are for consumer related claims, similar to those class action suits filed annually. With that, antitrust, environmental protection, discrimination, insurance, rights and equality for people with disabilities, and the restitution of illegally collected monies by authorities are areas that the Fund regularly approves.[28]

Many of the class actions filed point to the Fund's ability to impose corporate responsibility, inter alia for violations of pollution standards and environmental harms. The Israeli Railways and large factories are frequent defendants in these cases, and claims are based on a combination of health hazards suffered by the general public living in proximity to these violations.[29] Another area of requests include claims against monopolistic and restrictive trade practices, in which large corporations use restrictive arrangements and

[25] Camille Cameron, Jasminika Kalajdzic, & Alon Klemt, *Economic Enablers*, in *Class Actions in Context – How Culture, Economics and Politics Shape Collective Litigation*, *supra* note 2, at 137, 166. Due to the Fund's small budget, the authors are critical of the Fund's ability to make a difference. I disagree, particularly in light of the number of requests approved by the Fund and the benefit that may be connected to the Fund's approval which may help court identify "good" and just class actions. For an interesting discussion, also about the Israeli experience, see Elizabeth Chamblee Burch, *Publicly Funded Objectors*, 19 THEORETICAL INQUIRIES L. 47, 61 (2018) (suggesting establishing public funds to assist funding "objectors" – those who object to the terms of a proposed settlement – in order to bring unbiased opinions to the courts in settlements proceedings).

[26] Ronen Avraham & Abraham Wickelgren, Third-Party Litigation Funding – A Signaling Model, 63 DePaul L. Rev. 223 (2014).

[27] Ministry of Justice, Situational Report: The Fund to Finance Class Action Lawsuits, May 2011 Meetings to October 2015, *available at* www.gov.il/BlobFolder/generalpage/representative_actions_fund/he/%D7%94%D7%A7%D7%A8%D7%9F%20%D7%9C%D7%9E%D7%99%D7%9E%D7%95%D7%9F%20%D7%AA%D7%95%D7%91%D7%A2%D7%A0%D7%95%D7%AA%20%D7%99%D7%99%D7%A6%D7%95%D7%92%D7%99%D7%95%D7%AA-%20%D7%AA%D7%9E%D7%95%D7%A0%D7%AA%20%D7%9E%D7%A6%D7%91.pdf [in Hebrew].

[28] In 2018, 35 percent of the class actions approved were consumer class actions; 4 percent antitrust class actions; 8 percent environmental protection; 6 percent insurance; 8 percent discrimination; 1 percent restitution of illegally collected monies by authorities; 2 percent banking; 24 percent equality for people with disabilities; 11 percent labour law; and 1 percent anti-spam. *See* the 2018 Annual Fund Activity Report [in Hebrew], www.gov.il/BlobFolder/generalpage/representative_actions_fund/he/2018.pdf.

[29] *See* ClassAct. 45641-09-15, Horowitz v. Volkswagen; ClassAct. (Ja.) 4373-01-15 Meir Godush v. Israeli Railroad Co. Ltd.; ClassAct. (TA) 20901-03-Ron Reighter v. Israeli Railroad Co. Ltd.; ClassAct. (TA) 45897-01-17 Vered Schahar v. Israeli Railroad Co. Ltd.; and ClassAct. (TA) 14412-04-17 Omer Avrham v. Israeli Railroad Co. Ltd.; (all claiming extreme levels of air pollution, all above the accepted standard and endangering the residents, in areas around train stations throughout Israel). In ClassAct. 34564-05-15 (|Central) CSO of Citizens for the Environment v. Compost Agricultural Cooperative Ltd. and ClassAct. (TA) 14087-06-15 Jehusuha Klein v. Nesher- Israeli Cement Factory Ltd. (claiming environmental harm and violations by these factories). In ClassAct. (44000-06-12 (TA)) Mazel Hadad v. Osem Investments Ltd., (claiming an individual nuisance caused by an ammonia leak from defendant's logistics center). In addition, a recent request from the CSO of Citizens for the Environment was approved to help finance a first class action of its kind – mass tort – in Israel, against major environmental offenders in the Haifa Bay for causing an increase of incidences of cancer in the region.

price setting, violating provisions of the Israeli Restrictive Trade Practices Law (Economic Competition Law) and harming the public good.[30] A third example arises from suits against foreign companies, mainly against giant international conglomerates, for cross-border infringement,[31] particularly when the regulatory authority is limited in its ability to enforce Israeli law on a foreign company.[32]

A fourth and different type of request demonstrates the role of class actions in promoting constitutional and public rights in the private sector.[33] Examples of such requests include claims for alleged violations of the Equal Rights for Persons with Disabilities Law, 5748–1988, either for denying access to public places for people with disabilities,[34] or the receipt of a public service,[35] or of a service required by law.[36] Other requests for funding fall within violations of the provision against Prohibition of Discrimination in Products, Services and Entry to Entertainment and Public Places Law, 5761–2000 for discrimination against different groups of people based on gender,[37] age,[38] and nationality.[39] Other requests that have been

30 ClassAct. (Center) 46010-07-11 Ofir Naor v. Tnuva Agricultural Marketing Cooperative Center in Israel Ltd. and ClassAct. 57534-02-14, 43206-10-14 Yaron Zlicha v. Tnuva Agricultural Marketing Cooperative Center in Israel Ltd. (claiming unfair price and monopolistic actions); ClassAct. 31011-08-15 Meir (Maor) Klein v. Holon Halls Ltd., (claiming violation of antitrust law by bakeries after agreeing on price fixing, raising bread prices, and preventing competition). Israeli Electric Company v. Shlider (*supra* note 18) was a class action suit against the "undue inflation" of electricity rates, including within the rates inflated salaries as previously criticized by the Supervisor of Wages in the Ministry of Finance. In Nobel Energy Mediterranean Limited v. Moshe Nazri (*supra* note 17) as well, the Electric Company's monopolist was claimed to abuse and excessive pricing, which was passed on to its customers.

31 *See, e.g.*, ClassAct 44244-02-16 Niv Lev v. Booking; ClassAct. 63423-10-17 Yaron Greenberg v. eBay; ClassAct. 41239-04-18 Stinkaritzer v. WhattsApp; ClassAct. 1393-01-17 RotemGel v.Facebook Ireland Ltd.; ClassAct. 66426-06-17 Liron Priminger v. Instagram LLC; CaseStud. Ori Cohen v. hotels.com; and LC 5860/16 Facebook Inc. v. Ben Hamo (given 31.5.2018).

32 *See, e.g.*, ClassAct. (9615-09-17 (Center)) Baruch Yaniv Azrideil v. Viagogo (examining a foreign company that scalped tickets via its website even though scalping is prohibited by Israeli law). The Fund financed the translation of court documents and their procedural serving out of the country. *See also* ClassAct. 44244-02-16 Niv Lev v. Booking (alleging that the respondent, operating abroad, prevents clients from receiving money after canceling a transaction).

33 *Radio Kol BaRamah, supra* note 16.

34 ClassAct. (TA) 16317-06-12 Lihi Tsubari v. The Municipality of Tel Aviv-Jaffa; ClassAct. (TA) 25559-03-10 Reuben Baron v. Israel Railways Ltd. and Tel. Hecht v. Renoir Fashion Manufacturing & Marketing (1993) Ltd. (claiming the defendants failed to uphold Israeli legislation ensuring accessibility to public buildings and businesses such as bus stations and clothing stores).

35 ClassAct. (TA) 29387-09-14 Oren Tal Debuskin v. Egged Public Transport Cooperative Association Ltd., ClassAct. (TA) 57824-06-15 Noam Gershom Reshef v. Hot-Communications Systems Ltd. and ClassAct. (TA) 28211-09-16 Anna Barak v. Chamber Theater Inc. claiming the defendants failed to install necessary mechanisms ensuring accessibility to people with hearing loss in various services such as television stations and theaters.

36 ClassAct. (Ja) 43232-05-12 Ploni v. Migdal Insurance Company Ltd., alleging that respondents refused to insure applicants who had listed their disabilities, without providing a written, individual, and reasoned explanation, contrary to the provisions of the Equal Rights Act for Persons with Disabilities; ClassAct. (TA) 7789-06-15 Uri Karmi v. Knot Rent a Car Ltd. (alleging that respondents breached their duty under the law as a car rental company to own and rent at least two wheelchair accessible vehicles as required by law).

37 *See Radio Kol BaRamah, supra* note 16 and Class Act. (Ja) 65819-02-19 Hana Katzman v. Libnay Tzfoni Ltd., (claiming that IKEA published a separate catalog with pictures of men only, which it distributed to ultra-orthodox Jew populations).

38 ClassAct. (TA) 19385-08-15 Rina Dayan v. Clal Insurance Company Ltd., (claiming discrimination against the elderly by raising the proof needed to attain nursing assistance).

39 ClassAct. (TA) 48927-08-15 Aviva in San v. Dacla – Insurance Company Ltd., Class Act (Ha) 39672-01-16 Maher and Achim v. Shufersal Ltd.; and AP 59462-01 16 Awad Abu Freih v. The First International Bank of Israel Ltd. (alleging discrimination against Arab-Israelis population based on lack of accessibility to basic services such as food and banking due to the lack of deliveries to these citizens or the opening of branches in Arab cities and villages). ClassAct (Nz.)19886-07-12 Iyad Abu Ashaq v. Israel Post Company Ltd., (alleging that respondents had discriminated against Arab Israeli citizens by terming them in internal documents as "cousins" and fixing prices of postal services to them higher than those offered to non-Arab Israeli citizens).

approved in this context, relate to infringement of customer privacy[40] and violation of employee rights.[41]

In sum, the Israeli Class Action Fund is a body established under the Ministry of Justice, although its discretion is completely autonomous from that of the Ministry's and its members are representatives of the various regulators. The Fund expresses the involvement and support of the State – albeit indirectly through its budget – in individual attempts to adjudicate class action lawsuits on matters of public and social importance and emphasizes the quasi-regulatory status of the mechanism. It is important to note that class action suits are filed in addition to or in lieu of direct regulatory intervention. Accordingly, class action suits, funded by the Fund, which are usually filed against corporations, assist in imbedding public and corporate responsibility, and transfer government responsibility (and money) to public and legal market forces, while potentially contributing to reducing the need for direct government enforcement.

26.4 THE RELATIONSHIP BETWEEN CLASS ACTIONS, THE PUBLIC CLASS ACTION FUND, SOCIAL CHANGE, AND CORPORATE SOCIAL RESPONSIBILITY

After reviewing the Israeli Public Class Action Fund and its activities, I turn to address the broader normative and theoretical applications of the social role of class action suits, in general, and of the public Class Action Fund, in particular, in the modern era.

In the current era, the growing influence and prolificacy of corporations have increased; this has prompted an updated approach to traditional divisions between public and private law, including the application of human rights law in private law.[42] This phenomenon, which reflects deep social changes that contribute on the one hand to the strengthening of nongovernmental bodies and on the other hand to the weakening of governmental bodies and government supervision, naturally changes the substantive law, but also the procedural law that is supposed to assist in establishing the former.[43] Indeed, some may argue that government and public enforcement ought to be stronger and private enforcement, including class action suits, weaker. This chapter takes the view that both can, and should, work together and that they are not mutually exclusive,[44] especially as both, broadly

40 ClassAct (Center) 22141-03-15 Pinchas Yosef Greenberg v. Cellcom Israel Ltd., (alleging the respondents violated customer privacy by monitoring their movements 24-7, which it documented on huge servers and sold this information to third parties).

41 ClassAct (Ja) 53030-05-16 Elad Daniel N. Fox – Wiesel Ltd., (claiming violations of the Right to Work While Sitting and Appropriate Conditions 2007's law, since the company did not provide its employees with an appropriate seat while working). For additional information on class action suits that were financed by the Fund, see 2018 Annual Fund Activity Report, *supra* note 28.

42 Eli Bukspan & Asa Kasher, *Human Rights in the Private Sphere: Corporations First*, 40(2) U. PA. J. INT'L L. 419 (2019); DANIEL FRIEDMANN & DAPHNE BARAK-EREZ, HUMAN RIGHTS IN PRIVATE LAW (2001).

43 For a discussion about the relationship between class actions, big corporations, and structural reform, see Owen M. Fiss, *The Supreme Court 1978 Term. Forward: The Forms of Justice*, 93 HARV. L. REV. 1, 2 (1979); OWEN FISS, THE LAW AS IT COULD BE 122–32 (2003); LEORA BILSKY, THE HOLOCAUST, CORPORATIONS, AND THE LAW 51–54 (2017).

44 For a review of different aspects related to the balance and reciprocity between public and private enforcement, see REGULATION VS. LITIGATION – PERSPECTIVES FROM ECONOMICS AND LAW (Daniel P. Kessler ed., University of Chicago Press, 2011) – *see especially* Richard A. Posner, *Regulation (Agencies) versus Litigation (Courts): An Analytical Framework*, at p. 11. *See* William B. Rubenstein, *On What a "Private Attorney General" Is—and Why It Matters*, 57 VAND. L. REV. 2129, 2151 (2004) (expanding the fact that private enforcement mechanisms, including the class action mechanism, intends to complement traditional law enforcement mechanisms used in public enforcement); Matthew C. Stephenson, *Public Regulation of Private Enforcement: The Case for Expanding the Role of Administrative Agencies*, 91 VA. L. REV. 93, 112 (claiming that public enforcement suffers from rigidity and ineffectiveness – in contrast to private enforcement, which is flexible); Richard B. Stewart & Cass R. Sunstein, *Public Programs and Private Rights*, 95 HARV. L. REV. 1193 (1982). On the other hand, there are those who claim that

speaking, share the definition and goals of regulation, in the current era of the "regulatory state."[45] This is particularly appropriate with respect to the class action process, which can be viewed as the "missing link" in the encounter between private and public law, particularly due to the nature of the defendants, and the substance of the matters currently being adjudicated. Article 3 of the Israeli Class Action Law prohibits the use of class action law suits against state authorities and regulators that fail to use their power to monitor, regulate, or enforce their authority. Thus, class action lawsuits not only serve as an additional and effective mechanism to protect the rights of a large number of victims – even when the government fails to do so – its most widespread use, at least in Israel, is against corporations.[46] This observation reflects corporations' growing public standing and their ability to impact upon socially significant rights. In other words, the increase of corporate status and influence in the modern era, which explains their expansive presence as defendants in class actions, invites an up-to-date discussion of the social and public aspects inherent in the class action procedure and its expressions in business law. This chapter, therefore, intends to substantiate the argument that in the current era, in which the business sector's public responsibilities are becoming solidified, including the protection of individual human rights, the Class Action Law and the Public Fund to Finance Class Action Lawsuits with Public and Social Importance, is an appropriate and efficient regulatory tool for the private enforcement of public, social, and economic interests and will assist in the battle against the significant challenges facing modern corporate law.

26.4.1 *Class Action Lawsuit: a Legal Tool for Implementing Social Change*

Although the class action lawsuit is rooted in the world of procedural law, its central purpose, as set out in Section 1 of the Law, is to act "to improve the protection of rights" and to bring about realization of significant social and legal norms. To illustrate this issue in a picturesque manner, imagine class action lawsuits as a legal "demonstration" in which the public's voice is heard and has the strength and the power of legal mechanism on its side. As such, the class action has potential to effect profound social change and processes as is notable in a variety of examples of uses of the Class Action Law in Israel, and from the American experience with its class action law, which served as an inspiration for the Israeli arrangement. Thus, the use of the class action lawsuit as a tool for social change is not a stranger to American law, even though there has been some pushback in recent years.[47] There are those who claim it was behind the 1966 sweeping amendment to Regulation 23 of

the increased use of private enforcement will flood court with unjustified suits. *See* Jonathan R. Macey & Geoffrey P. Miller, *The Plaintiffs' Attorney's Role in Class Action and Derivative Litigation: Economic Analysis and Recommendations for Reform*, 58 U. CHI. L. REV. 1 (1991). An additional claim preferring public enforcement over private enforcement, relates to those instances that the person breaking the law cannot be identified due to informative costs, *see, e.g.*, A. M. Polinski, S. Shavell, *The Economic Theory of Public Enforcement of Law* 38 JOURNAL OF ECONOMIC LITERATURE 45 (2000).

45 David Levi-Faur, *The Odyssey of the Regulatory State: From a 'Thin' Monomorphic Concept to a 'Thick' and Polymorphic Concept*, 35 L. & POL. 29 (2013). See THE OXFORD HANDBOOK OF REGULATION (Robert Baldwin, Martin Cave, & Martin Lodge eds., 2010) (discussing the regulatory state).

46 A study on the types of defendants based on analysis of 2,056 class action actions from April 2006 to August 2012 – according to the first named defendant in the case – found that in most cases the defendant was a corporation. In 55 percent of the cases the defendant was a private company that was not traded on the stock exchange and in 25 percent of the cases, the defendant was a public company that was traded on the stock exchange. *See* Alon Klement & Keren Weinshall-Margel, *Cost Benefit Analysis of Class Action: an Israeli Perspective*, 172 J. INST. & THEORETICAL ECONOMICS 75 (2016); David Rosenberg, *Decoupling Deterrence and Compensation Functions In Mass Tort Class Actions For Future Loss*, 88 VA. L. REV. 1871 (2002); Alexandra D. Lahav, *Two Views of the Class Action*, 79 FORDHAM L. REV. 1939 (2011).

47 Rule 23(b)(2) of the-Federal Rules of Civil Procedure enables a declaratory and injunction, remedies that also fit constitutional breaches: Alon Klement & Robert H. Klonoff, *Class Actions in the U.S. and Israel: A Comparative Approach*, 19(1) TIL 151 (2018).

the Federal Rules of Procedure; which was a result of the social changes that took place in the US, particularly the civil rights movement and the collective power of the group,[48] leading to the crystallization of procedural measures required for the effective enforcement of the rights of groups who previously could not exercise their rights in the US legal system as individuals.[49]

It is no wonder then, and as argued by Abram Chayes in his iconic article on public law litigation,[50] that the class action can serve as a clear example of the potential of civil litigation to promote public reform to influence social and group issues. This observation demonstrates the ability of the adversarial process to advance social reforms of the highest order,[51] acting to acuminate the practice of federal courts in the United States on central issues on the public agenda.

A clear example of the social potential inherent in this mechanism is *Brown v. the Board of Education*, which interestingly began as a class action lawsuit.[52] This memorable and important case reached by the Supreme Court in the United States and led to a dramatic constitutional change in the "separate but equal" segregation in public education policy in the 1950s, when the US Supreme Court ruled that this doctrine violates the right to equality under the 14th Amendment to the US Constitution.

Another example is significant US case law in the field of social class action lawsuits focused on reparation of Holocaust survivors and the petitions filed against the ban against abortion.[53] The first claims were discussed in Liora Bilski's book *The Holocaust, Corporations, and the Law*,[54] in which the author analyzes transnational Holocaust litigation – class action suits filed against Swiss banks and German companies to claim restitution from Nazi war crimes and which were brought in the 1990s in US federal courts and ultimately were settled for significant financial compensation without the defendants formally assuming legal responsibility. Even though these cases ended in unprecedented settlements, albeit without declaring the defendants' legal culpability, Bilski claims that the public, social, and historical importance of these claims cannot be overlooked. Both of these examples are interesting in the Israeli context, since class action lawsuits in Israel developed to a large extent using American law as a benchmark. Both examples also fit the social backdrop of Israeli Law as can be inferred from its provisions granting public organizations and state authorities the authority to initiate class action suits; the type of causes of action for which a request to approve a class action can be filed and that usually

48 Deborah R. Hensler et al., Class Action Dilemmas: Pursuing Public Goals for Private Gain 12 (2000); John P. Frank, Response to 1996 Circulation of Proposed Rule 23 on Class Actions: Memorandum to My Friends on the Civil Rules Committee (Dec. 20, 1996), in Administrative Office of the U.S. Courts, 2 Working Papers of the Advisory Committee on Civil Rules on Proposed Amendments to Rule 23 266 (1997).

49 Barak Atiram, *From Brown to Rule 23: The Rise and Fall of the Social Reform Class Action*, 37 Rev. Lit. 47 (2018), Barak Atiram, *Socially Driven Class Actions: The Legacy of Briggs*. 23 Tex. J. Civ. Liberties & Civil Rts. 1 (2017).

50 Abram Chayes *The Role of the Judge in Public Law Litigation*, 89 Harv. L. Rev. 1281, 1291 (1976) ("The class suit is a reflection of our growing awareness that a host of important public and private interactions – perhaps the most important in defining the conditions and opportunities of life for most people – are conducted on a routine or bureaucratized basis and can no longer be visualized as bilateral transactions between private individuals. From another angle, the class action responds to the proliferation of more or less well-organized groups in our society and the tendency to perceive interests as group interests, at least in very important aspects.").

51 Lesley K. McAllister, Revisiting a "Promising Institution": Public Law Litigation in the Civil Law World, 24 Ga. St. U. L. Rev. (2012) 694; Neal Milner, *The Dilemmas of Legal Mobilization: Ideologies and Strategies of Mental Patient Liberation Groups*, 8 L. & Pol'y 105 (1986); Bryant Garth, *Introduction: Toward a Sociology of the Class Action*, 57 Ind. L.J. 371 (1982); P. A. Paul-Shaheen & H. Perlstadt, *Class Action Suits and Social Change: The Organization and Impact of the Hill-Burton Cases*, 57 Ind. L.J. 385 (1982).

52 Brown v. Board of Education, 347 U.S. 483 (1954).

53 Roe v. Wade, 410 U.S. 113 (1973); Linda Greenhouse & Reva B. Siegel, *Before (and After) Roe v. Wade: New Questions About Backlash*, 120 Yale L.J. 2028 (2011).

54 Leora Bilsky, The Holocaust, Corporations, and the Law (2017).

represent corporate stakeholders' interests; and above all the public fund that helps finance submission and hearing of petitions for the approval of class actions of public and social importance.

Class action lawsuits are private proceedings, alongside the public proceedings submitted to administrative courts (and the High Court of Justice in Israel), that can disseminate, ingrain, and enforce important public norms, including norms that are designed to protect against the violation of individual human rights. Still, today as we witness the increasing harm to public norms by the business sector, which cannot be sued in public proceedings in the High Court of Justice or before the administrative courts, class action lawsuits have become more significant than ever and in some sense are returning to their historical roots – that is, the protection of important social rights. Accordingly, the public fund, which was created to assist class action lawsuits of public and social importance, emphasizes and accelerates this trend.

26.4.2 *Class Actions, Corporate Responsibility, and Human Rights in the Business Sector*

Over the past few decades, discourse on corporate social responsibility has increased, including corporations' commitment to individual human rights.[55] Today, corporate actions extend far beyond corporations themselves and raise the question of corporate responsibility and their pledge to broader public considerations – and not just profit.[56] Today, and certainly after 2011, the year of worldwide social protests (e.g., Occupy Wall Street), it is clearer than ever that the business sector's impact has become significantly stronger, sometimes no less than that of the government's. In this context, Professor Aharon Barak, former president of Israel's Supreme Court and then a justice, wrote, "in modern society, the corporation is the main basis of human activity. There are countries that have more corporations than people."[57] In light of this phenomenon, it appears that class action law suits, as a "legal protest," and the Public Class Action Fund, embody the commercial sector's increasing social and public responsibilities and bolster the enforcement of public and social norms on the business sector. This approach is also consistent with the growing discourse on the applicability of human rights to the private sphere and to nonstate entities, a subject that has gained increasing significance in domestic, comparative, and international law.

Accordingly, the social and legal potential inherent in class action lawsuits, which mainly reflects the interests of corporate stakeholders, is related to, and even appears to be derived from, the growing strength of the commercial sector, on the one hand, and to the decline in the dominance of the state's traditional social, economic, and legal framework on the other. A comparison of the economic power of large corporations with the economic strength of countries reveals that corporations now account for approximately two-thirds of world trade in goods and services; 51 of the world's 100 largest economic bodies are corporations; the world's 200 largest corporations produce 27.5 percent of the world's gross domestic product, and their

[55] Eric De Brabandere & Marys Hazelzet, Corporate Responsibility and Human Rights Navigating between International, Domestic and Self-Regulation 6 (2017).

[56] Bukspan & Kasher, *supra* note 42. For an update and modern expression of this evolvement, see the Business Roundtable principles on the role of a corporation from August 2019 see: https://opportunity.businessroundtable.org/ourcommitment/, and Alan Murray *America's CEOs Seek a New Purpose for the Corporation* Fortune Magazine (Sep., 2019) ("... On August 19, the BRT announced a new purpose for the corporation and tossed the old one into the dustbin. The New Statement is 300 words long, and shareholders aren't mentioned until word 250 ... Before that, the group refers to creating 'value for customers', 'investing in employees,' fostering 'diversity and inclusion,' 'dealing fairly and ethically with suppliers,' 'supporting the communities in which we work,' and 'protect[ing] the environment'"). See also: Ronald Cohen, Impact: Reshaping Capitalism to Drive Real Change (2020).

[57] *See* CrA 3027/90 Modi'im Construction and Development Company Ltd. v. State of Israel, P.D. 45 (4) 364, 384.

annual income is greater than that of 182 countries, in which 82 percent of the world's population lives.[58]

This economic power translates into considerable social, environmental, political, and cultural power, both internationally and at the state level. Moreover, corporations' diverse activities in a wide variety of fields have led to the conclusion that modern society's ability to flourish depends to a great extent on the commercial sphere surrounding. Today most human interactions are based on corporate activities. Accordingly, it is impossible to overstate the power and influence of the commercial sector on human rights, and as an extension, concern regarding corporate violations of human rights is as undeniable and significant today as was the violation by government authorities in the past. This applies not only to serious violations of "classic" human rights, such as slavery or deplorable work conditions, but also to issues such as privacy, mental and economic welfare, and gender equality in employment. This chapter proposes, therefore, that the class action procedure, and the public fund to finance class actions lawsuits with public and social importance, can provide an effective restraint against the increasing power of corporations all the while enforcing public norms in the private sector. This point is evident when we acknowledge that most class action defendants in Israel are corporations and are sued, inter alia, for violating consumer protection, insurance, banking, antitrust, environmental, and labor laws; as well as antidiscrimination, including workplace discrimination and discrimination against people with disabilities.[59] These issues relate to stakeholders, and less to stockholders, similar to the new declaration of the Business Roundtable,[60] and as such focus on protecting those interests identified with social responsibility and not just the commercial functioning of corporations.[61] For this reason, and as time passes, there are many more examples of the law's "interest" in corporations, including their obligation to respect human rights.[62] This interest, in turn, creates new economic considerations and market, as well as legal, forces that encourage promoting social issues, including upholding human rights in order to minimize legal and public exposure and indirectly contribute to a beneficial business strategy.[63] This approach, which legally subordinates the commercial sector to public norms and human rights in Israel, has developed alongside growing international discourse in the Western world. This discourse is evident in present initiatives by various international organizations that invest great means to develop ways to apply public law norms to the commercial sector, in particular initiatives such as Professor

58 Ronen Shamir, Private Market and Public Pressure: Designing the Corporate Social Responsibility Concept, *in* GENERATIONS, SPACES, IDENTITIES: CONTEMPORARY PERSPECTIVES ON ISRAELI SOCIETY AND CULTURE 237–39 (Hana Hertzogm Tali Kochavi & Shimsjon Zelinkor eds., 2007).

59 The Israeli law books contain many laws targeting social and environmental challenges that apply to daily corporate conduct.

60 *Supra* note 56.

61 Indeed, most of the class action suits are initiated because of the plaintiff's personal interests; however this and of itself is not sufficient to detract from the public's interests in the claim. The prosecutor of the class action acts as a type of catalyst that, without her initiative, the case would not be brought before court and the various public goals underlying this instrument would not be fulfilled. In order to counter balance the plaintiff's pure self-interest and self-enrichment, which may impair the nature of the proceedings, the mechanism imposes legal expenses on the party losing the case and imposes court fees to file the claim and which should deter the prosecutor's inappropriate and excessive use of the mechanism.

62 Bukspan & Kasher, *supra* note 42; Ofer Sitbon, *About People, Corporations, and What Is in Between – whether the Basic Law: Human Dignity and Liberty should Apply to Corporations*, 8 KIRYAT HAMISHPAT 107, 131–37 (2009) [in Hebrew]; John G. Ruggie & Nelson Tamaryn, *Human Rights and the OECD Guidelines for Multinational Enterprises: Normative Innovations and Implementation Challenges*, 66 *Corporate Social Responsibility Initiative Working Paper, Cambridge, MA: John F. Kennedy School of Government, Harvard University* 1, 2–6 (2015), *available at* www.hks.harvard.edu/sites/default/files/centers/mrcbg/programs/cri/files/workingpaper.66.oecd.pdf.

63 Eric De Brabandere & Marys Hazelzet, *Addressing Human Rights in Business – Executive Perspectives*, KPMG International Cooperative 6 n.9 (Dec. 2016), *available at* https://home.kpmg/content/dam/kpmg/xx/pdf/2016/11/addressing-human-rights-in-business.pdf.

Ruggie's "Protect, Respect, Remedy" which was adopted by the United Nations in 2011 in its groundbreaking guidelines, "Guiding Principles on Business and Human Rights."[64] This document includes three tenets: (1) states' obligations to protect human rights; (2) corporations' obligations to respect human rights; (3) states' and corporations' joint obligations to provide legal remedies for human rights' violations – an obligation that is relevant to all states and all corporations regardless if they are national or international; their size; the sector they operate in; their owner; or their type of incorporation. Furthermore, the UN Committee on Human Rights has adopted these guidelines, and in fact, this was the first time that a UN Committee has adopted principles without conducting negotiations with its member states.[65] More than that, the Committee established a working group on the issue of human rights and transnational corporations and other business enterprises; the main objective of the working group is to promote the guidelines.[66] Today these guidelines are recognized as the global standard for business and human rights,[67] and while there is no legal mechanism to enforce these standards against states or corporations, they bolster the states' expected response to the commercial sector due to the latter's public and social influence, and of the search for a new conceptual framework to implement existing legislation in this important area.

This chapter, while discussing class actions, is in line with the UN guidelines that call upon states to provide legal protection, particularly access to legal "remedies," against the business sector's violation of human rights. This article reasons that class action lawsuits – and the Public Class Actions Fund – not only assists states in protecting human rights violations by the business sector, it also mainly improves access to remedies when these violations occur, and indirectly pushes corporations to uphold and respect human rights.

In other words, the Guidelines focus on substantive, legal, and practical issues that impact upon the effectiveness of judicial mechanisms to achieve corporate accountability and the public's access to a remedy (the third pillar of the Guiding Principles) in business-related human rights abuses. According to this framework, the class action procedure and the Public Class Action Fund are especially consistent with this goal and with the United Nations High Commissioner for Human Rights mission that launched the "Accountability and Remedy Project," promoting a more effective implementation of the Guiding Principles on Business and Human Rights.

26.5 CONCLUSION

In sum, in the growing interwoven, complex commercial and social world – and which is continually undergoing substantive social, economic, and legal changes – class actions could be the most significant and effective legal instrument to "power the masses." Class action lawsuits enable individuals to claim corporate responsibility by cooperating with others who have similarly been wronged by the same offender and together collectivize their lesser potential into a much more powerful mass, and in this manner protect their rights without solely relying on the regulator.

64 United Nations Human Rights, Office of the High Commission, *Guiding Principles on Business and Human Rights: Implementing the United Nations "Protect, Respect and Remedy" Framework* (2011), *available at* www.ohchr.org/Documents/Publications/GuidingPrinciplesBusinessHR_EN.pdf.

65 Ruggie & Nelson, *supra* note 62.

66 Overview of the Working Group on the issue of human rights and transnational corporations and other business enterprises, *available at* www.ohchr.org/EN/Issues/Business/Pages/WGHRandtransnationalcorporationsandotherbusiness.aspx.

67 Ruggie & Nelson, *supra* note 62, at 5; *see also* John Ruggie, *Guiding Principles on Business and Human Rights: Implementing the United Nations "Protect, Respect and Remedy" Framework* (2011) (Report of the Special Representative of the Secretary-General on the issue of human rights and transnational corporations and other business enterprises), *available at* https://journals.sagepub.com/doi/abs/10.1177/016934411102900206.

This approach is consistent with the public approach to the class action mechanism,[68] according to which the main justification for the class action lies in its ability to effectively enforce the provisions of the law that are intended to promote social values and goals.

As long as the business sector – the most common defendant in class action lawsuits in Israel – is forced to answer claims, especially those that have been financed by the Public Fund, and the Public Fund continues to enjoy strong public support and recognition, it is likely that corporations will continue to respond favorably to this pressure and act more responsibly. In this sense, the Fund not only has financial significance, it also has deterrent powers. The more the state continues to support the Fund (by at least ensuring the existing budget, if not increasing it), it will continue to assist plaintiffs to access justice to assert their rights, without needing to turn to an external regulator. No doubt that this not only empowers an individual to protect her rights, it can also help reduce the need for direct intervention of market regulators in the business sector.

The recruiting of the class action for these purposes is consistent with modern in-depth changes in substantive and procedural private law, as well as with the social and public importance implicit in the class action lawsuit, and which in fact accompanied it in its early stages in the US. In this regard, and especially with the impact of social media, class actions can contribute to social reform even when they conclude without a judgment, for example through a settlement.

Insights laid out in this chapter are based on the US history of class action suits, but more than this on the modern innovative and almost precedential body of the Israeli Public Class Action Fund that distinguishes the Class Action Law in Israel from class action laws in other countries. This public fund serves as a hybrid mechanism that uses state budget and representatives of the various regulators who are responsible for areas that class actions are frequently filed, in order to assist private enforcement by financing applications for approval as class actions with "public and social importance in their submission and clarification." The chapter suggests that the Fund's mandate and objectives, composition, and decisions, make it a unique and innovative tool to treat social and legal transgressions in the modern corporate era. As such, it claims that the Israeli Public Fund could assist in creating a new discourse, which has international merit, on a new mechanism that can sophistically influence and regulate corporations' violations of rights, including human rights, and facilitates legal remedies for corporate wrongdoings as inspired by the 2011 UN Guiding Principles on Business and Human Rights.

On a personal level, after years of research and teaching in the fields of contract law, corporate law, and corporate social and ethical responsibility, a responsibility that challenges a whole range of substantive and procedural law, and after ten years of familiarity with the activities of the Israeli Public Class Action Fund, I believe that the Fund demonstrates an interesting example of the relationship between private and public law, as well as an innovative mechanism cooperating between and combining public enforcement and private enforcement,[69] one that can significantly improve the growing and challenging interrelationship between corporations and society. Coincidentally, in Hebrew, the word "company" ("חברה") and "society" ("חברה") is the same word. This linguistic coincidence may just say it all ...

68 Martin H. Redish & Clifford W. Berlow, *The Class Action As Political Theory*, 85 WASH. U. L. REV. 753, 797 (2007); John Bronsteen & Owen Fiss, *The Class Action Rule*, 78 NOTRE DAME L. REV. 1419 (2003); Owen Fiss, *The Political Theory of the Class Action*, in THE LAW AS IT COULD BE 122 (2003).

69 *See*, text to *supra* notes 44–46.

For EU product safety concerns, contact us at Calle de José Abascal, 56–1°,
28003 Madrid, Spain or eugpsr@cambridge.org.

www.ingramcontent.com/pod-product-compliance
Ingram Content Group UK Ltd.
Pitfield, Milton Keynes, MK11 3LW, UK
UKHW051118290926
15471UKWH00010B/1740

* 9 7 8 1 0 0 9 2 9 5 6 9 7 *